WOMEN WORLDWIDE

Transnational Feminist Perspectives on Women

JANET LEE   SUSAN M. SHAW
Oregon State University

ISBN: 978-0-07-351229-7
MHID: 0-07-351229-X

Vice President & Editor-in-Chief: *Mike Ryan*
VP SEM, EDP & Central Publishing Services: *Kimberly Meriwether David*
Senior Sponsoring Editor: *Gina Boedeker*
Marketing Manager: *Caroline McGillen*
Development Editor: *Kate Scheinman*
Project Manager: *Erin Melloy*
Design Coordinator: *Margarite Reynolds*
Photo Research: *Natalia Peschiera*
Cover Image Credits: *Insets, clockwise from top: © 2009 Jupiterimages CorporationRoyalty-Free/ CORBISBananaStock/JupiterImagesRoyalty-Free/CORBISComstock/PunchStock © Copyright 1997 IMS Communications Ltd/Capstone Design. All Rights Reserved.Tim Hall/Getty ImagesBackground image: Tim Hall/Getty Images*
Production Supervisor: *Nicole Baumgartner*
Compositor: *Laserwords Private Limited*
Typeface: *10/12 Minion Web*
Printer: *R. R. Donnelly*

Library of Congress Cataloging-in-Publication Data

Women worldwide: transnational feminist perspectives on women / Janet Lee, Susan Shaw.
   p. cm.
  ISBN 978-0-07-351229-7 (acid-free paper)
  1. Feminism. 2. Feminist theory. 3. Globalization. 4. Women—Social conditions. I. Lee, Janet, 1954–
  II. Shaw, Susan M. (Susan Maxine), 1960–HQ1155.W675 2010
  305.4–dc22   2009054282

www.mhhe.com

*Dedicated to all the women and men worldwide
who work every day for peace and social justice.
Let us acknowledge our struggles and celebrate
our achievements!*

Contents

Preface

For many years we have taught courses at Oregon State University that focus on women's issues in global perspective, and each year we find ourselves putting together a reading packet and wishing for a textbook that covers a breadth of issues, provides good resources for our students, and gives us a teachable format. More and more, our students are interested in the world beyond their own backyards; as they become global citizens; we want them to be prepared to develop fruitful relationships with others around the world and to understand the lives of women in each corner of the globe. We hope that through this textbook students will enjoy glimpses into the lives of a variety of women in a variety of places and that they will develop understanding and empathy for the challenges women face, the strengths they bring, and the differences they make in the world. We also hope that students will be encouraged to pay greater attention to world events and trends and to become active participants in social and political processes that improve the lives of women.

We have structured this book to allow for a wide range of women's voices in order to highlight the great diversity that situates women differently across race, ethnicity, social class, nation, sexual identity, age, ability, and religion. We asked well-known experts in their fields to write framework essays that introduce key concepts and theories for each chapter topic, and we are grateful to each writer who gave such time and effort to produce a scholarly, accessible textbook. In the framework essays, we provide information, tell stories, or highlight activists who exemplify the main ideas of each chapter. We also include learning activities that encourage students to go beyond the readings and the classroom to discover more about many of the topics covered in the book. Given most students' propensity toward technology, we also include Web sites and have developed a number of activities encouraging students to utilize the Internet to learn more about global issues. In many ways, the Internet allows students incredible access to the world at large through its immediate connectivity to people and events everywhere. Through technology, students can literally see events around the world as they unfold, and we hope students use this technology through learning activities that broaden their virtual reach into the world. We also include cartoons in each chapter because feminists do indeed have a sense of humor, and humor may allow us to see things in a different light.

In addition, each chapter contains a "Day in the Life" story. These fictional accounts provide students with a view into a single day in the life of a character who experiences some of the events and activities that would be typical for a woman in that place and situation. While these stories by no means represent women generically, they do provide some details about the lives of some women that can enrich student's understandings of the diversity of women's lives. Finally, we have provided readings in each chapter that offer various perspectives on the chapter theme. While all the readings are accessible, some are scholarly research articles, while others are first-person narratives, poetry, short stores, or news/magazine stories. Very few of these readings have been anthologized elsewhere, so this text represents a new body of works from which students can learn.

Of course, we also recognize that no one can teach everything in this textbook in a term or a semester. We have tried to provide options so instructors can use what works best in their particular settings and what best reflects the goals for their courses. The chapters do make reference to one another, but they are written as self-contained units and can be taught in any order. Chapters that are less useful to a given course can be omitted, or only portions of chapters can be used. We want this book to be as useful as possible to both instructors and students.

ACKNOWLEDGMENTS

We are extremely grateful to all the people who have been part of the production of this book. Our framework essay authors brought an incredible breadth and depth of experience and knowledge to this project. We thank Valentine M. Moghadam, Charmaine Pereira, Priya Kandaswamy, Penny Van Esterik, Katharine Sarikakis, Leslie Regan Shade, Patti Lou Watkins, Alicia Bublitz, Hoa Nguyen, Mehra Shirazi, Meg Wilkes Karraker, Patti Duncan, Juanita Elias, Melanie Hughes, Pamela Paxton, Ana Isla, Trina Filan, Mary Hawkesworth, and Sonia M. Kandathil.

We also thank our graduate teaching assistants who provided us with input throughout the planning and writing process—Emily Wingard, Amanda Littke, Liz McNeill, Tucker Readdy, Diane Turner, and Jennifer Jabson. Our office manager, Lisa Lawson, as usual, provided us with invaluable clerical support. We also thank the current and former graduate students who wrote the "Day in the Life" stories for each chapter—Trina Filan, Marcia Chambers, Meghan Barp, November Papaleo, Jennifer Jabson, Kryn Freehling-Burton, Mikhelle Gattone, Michelle Marie, Sriyanthi Gunewardena McCabe, Heather Ebbe Maib, Giovanna Muir, R. Tucker Readdy, and Amber Wilburn.

We also appreciate the work of our reviewers, who provided us with insightful comments and suggestions that have helped make this a better textbook: Bettina Aptheker, University of California, Santa Cruz; Carrie N. Baker, Berry College; Suzanne J. Cherrin, University of Delaware; Danielle Marie DeMuth, Grand Valley State University, Vivian Fowler, Columbia College; Asma M. Abdel Halim, University of Toledo; Elyce Rae Helford, Middle Tennessee State University; Kasi Jackson, West Virginia University; Mahruq F. Khan, University of Wisconsin–La Crosse; Kathryn Libal, University of Connecticut; Chrisy Moutsatsos, Iowa State University; Kathleen Butterly Nigro, University of Missouri–St. Louis; and Rachel Standish, University of Maryland University College. Finally, we thank Gina Boedeker and Kate Scheinman, our wonderful editors at McGraw-Hill, who have again provided support, encouragement, and empathy when we had to cut the length of the book.

Foreword

A TIME TO EDUCATE AND ADVOCATE

Ten years into the twenty-first century, people have accomplished things that would once have seemed impossible—satellites orbit the Earth, medical advances enhance the quality of our lives, knowlege and information are exchanged instantaneously through the Internet. Yet despite these amazing feats, half of the world's population—women—still strive for equality and empowerment.

The reality is that too many women face unacceptable threats in their daily lives. Worldwide, women still comprise the majority of the world's poor; violence against women in the public and private spheres remains prevalent; countless women continue to die in childbirth; and in many places girls are pulled out of school to fetch water and wood or are sold to human traffickers across borders.

What does this say about us as human beings? Have we each defined our community such that it limits our ability to care for others beyond our immediate circle of family and friends? As a child, I learned that underneath our very thin layer of skin, we are all the same. We all begin life and leave life the same way. We all breathe and eat the same way. We all laugh and cry for the same reasons. We carry many shared hopes and dreams in this world.

Because of these commonalities, we must educate and advocate on behalf of those who are the most vulnerable and marginalized—primarily women in the developing world. But we are at a crossroads. For decades, the women's movement has been effectively mobilizing around environmental, political, economic, and social issues. The result has been securing commitments to gender equality at many levels—global, national, and local—but many of these commitments remain unfulfilled. Women's experience, expertise, and innovations continue to be excluded from the planning and policy-making that impact our daily lives and have the potential to shape progressive environmental, developmental, and human rights outcomes. Collectively we must identify effective strategies, alliances, and institutions to promote a comprehensive social-justice agenda. Women want to move forward rather than merely struggle to hold the line on prior gains.

In light of the major forces shaping the world—climate change, economic and market-driven policies that exacerbate poverty and food insecurity, and overconsumption by the privileged few, to name just a few—this anthology explores the meaning of sisterhood and the ways women are challenging power in a new global context.

While debates on women's issues and their complexities are abundant, it is important to acknowledge our uniqueness, understand our different approaches, and, at the same time, honor each other as sisters for a common goal. We are interconnected and we cannot subsist alone. My safety depends on my neighbor's safety. My real happiness depends on my sister's happiness.

At the Women's Environment and Development Organization (WEDO), we know first-hand that women's empowerment and gender equality are key levers of change—when the status of women improves, the whole of society benefits. Women's perspectives, values, skills are necessary for real transformation—whether through equality in governance, through gender-sensitive climate change policy, or through improvements to food security.

Although the present global financial and economic crisis presents unprecedented challenges for women's movements, it is an opportunity for all of us—women of the world, old and young—to rally and become involved. The same forces that cause so much insecurity in the world also give rise to global and local movements seeking alternatives to the status quo.

We must speak in unity, not just for ourselves, but for future generations and the survival of Mother Earth. The world depends on our working together, women and men, in partnership for a healthy, just planet. As my father taught me, people can easily break one chopstick, but a bundle of chopsticks tied together is unbreakable.

Listen to your heart. Listen to your community. And let's move forward.

Thanh Xuan Nguyen
WEDO Executive Director

About the Authors

JANET LEE is professor of Women Studies at Oregon State University, USA, where she teaches a variety of courses on gender and feminism. She grew up in Yorkshire, in the north of England, UK. She earned an undergraduate degree in Sociology from the University of Stirling, Scotland, and an MA and PhD from Washington State University, USA. Research interests include women's history and biography, issues concerning gender and the body, and global perspectives on women and feminism. She is author of *War Girls: The First Aid Nursing Yeomanry (FANY) in the First World War* (Manchester University Press, 2005); *Comrades and Partners: The Shared Lives of Grace Hutchins and Anna Rochester* (Rowman and Littlefield, 2000); coauthor with Jennifer Sasser-Coen of *Blood Stories: Menarche and the Female Body in Contemporary U.S. Society* (Routledge, 1996); and coauthor with Susan Shaw of *Women's Voices, Feminist Visions: Classic and Contemporay Readings* (McGraw-Hill, 4th edition, 2009).

SUSAN M. SHAW is professor and director of Women Studies at Oregon State University, USA, where she also directs the Difference, Power, and Discrimination Program. She was born and raised in Rome, Georgia, where she received her undergraduate degree in English from Berry College. She also holds a master's degree and PhD from Southern Seminary in Louisville, Kentucky, and an MAIS from Oregon State University. She is author of *God Speaks to Us, Too: Southern Baptist Women on Church, Home, and Society* (University Press of Kentucky, 2008) and *Storytelling in Religious Education* (Religious Education Press, 1999) and coauthor of *Girls Rock! 50 Years of Women Making Music* with Mina Carson and Tisa Lewis (University Press of Kentucky, 2004) and *Women's Voices, Feminist Visions: Classic and Contemporary Readings* (McGraw-Hill, 4th edition, 2009) with Janet Lee. She is also coeditor with Jun Xing, Larry Roper, and Judith Li of *Teaching for Change: The Difference, Power, and Discrimination Model* (Lexington Books, 2007).

Introduction

Janet Lee

Okay, so there's good news and bad news God said,
Which do you want first?
Well, I wasn't sure I wanted either, the good or the bad,
since good news makes me nervous and bad news makes me cry,
and the fact that God is speaking to me, well that's crazy anyway.
But mama always said politeness is a girl's best friend, and besides,
I had a feeling this was important.

So, I said the bad please, I mean, I know God must be mad,
I would be, figuring how much we've messed up the world
what with wars and mamas tired and babies crying and papas shouting
and sad things happening to girls just like me in countries I don't know where.

And God said, oh, I wasn't thinking of that,
I wanted you to know you got a 'D' on that paper you thought you could write
in one evening.
But, now you mention it, maybe you do have a point about wars
and droughts and hunger. I mean, is it hot in here, or is it just me?
And I said, you should know about global warming, you're in charge,
and as for wars and droughts and hunger maybe you can fix it to help
mamas all over the world instead of wasting time worrying about my paper.
Now I've gone and done it: talked back to God.

And so you can see why I'd be so flummoxed I'd forget to ask for the good,
news, that is,
But I do know what the good news is and I think God knows too.
It's not the little stuff that looms so large,
It's not even the 'A' I deserve for this poem,
The good news is girls just like me in countries I don't know where
Being friends
Helping each other
Figuring out ways to help stop the mamas crying.
That's the good news and we all know it.

"Stop the Mamas Crying" by Mariah Lockwood.

In the spirit of Mariah Lockwood's poem, we begin *Women Worldwide* with both good and
bad news, and we will give you the bad news first. And it is quite bad. According to estimates from World Development Indicators, women work two-thirds of the world's working hours, produce half of the world's food, but earn only 10 percent of the world's income

and own less than one percent of the world's property. Among almost one-quarter of the global population that lives in extreme poverty (less than the equivalent of one U.S. dollar per day), 70 percent are women. Over the last decade the global gap between the rich and the poor is widening, and for many women this means a declining quality of life as a result of reduced access to both resources and opportunities.

The expansion of free market economies has caused economic transitions and crises jeopardizing government support for social programs and exacerbating the plight of poor women and children worldwide. In addition, the wars of the late twentieth century, and some that still continue today, take a particular toll on women in terms of physical and sexual violence, displacement, and the inevitable stresses as they struggle to maintain families in times of crisis and chaos. Such problems are contextualized in the face of environmental issues like global warming that threaten the planet. They adversely affect the livelihood of communities vulnerable to increased sea levels and hasten the extinction of nonhuman communities. As Lockwood laments, there are wars and droughts and hunger and "the mamas are crying." She implicates a Christian God in this poem, but it is important to note the ways other deities or notions of God worldwide support women's subordination. Of course, religious traditions may also help empower women through spiritual healing, providing opportunities for community with other women, through leadership positions within religious organizations, and through the involvement in activist projects for social justice endorsed by religious organizations.

But now the good news from a global perspective: despite the breadth of these problems, over the last several decades there have been important improvements in women's status in such key areas as education, literacy, health care, and voting rights; and key international treaties affirming women's rights as human rights. As Lockwood asserts in her poem, the good news is that women around the globe are coming together as friends and allies to figure out ways to help work for change. Efforts through the twentieth century that still continue today have addressed the subordination of women and other marginalized peoples in ways that both influence attitudes and change social policies. Although

there is still a long way to go in terms of equality for all people in many countries around the world, there is a growing recognition that the subordination of the majority of the world's population is intolerable. As a result, international conferences and declarations have advocated for social justice and provided strategies for change. Women in many regions of the world use these international platforms to advocate for change in their own countries. In addition, alongside the destructive forces of globalization have come technologies uniting women who share common interests in different regions, encouraging transnational coalitions for feminist advocacy. Feminism seeks to improve women's status and advocate women's liberation from systems of power that oppress and limit individuals in families, communities, and societies. In this sense, feminism means equality for all women and anticipates a future guaranteeing social justice for all people.

Women Worldwide follows this feminist rubric with chapters presenting the status of women globally and sharing examples of individual activism and social movements for change. This anthology focuses on women around the world by integrating theoretical perspectives on global politics with narratives of a broad range of women's issues. It follows a trend in Women's Studies (the academic field devoted to topics concerning women, gender, and feminism) by addressing issues of global justice and studying the differences and similarities among and across women that both divide and unite them. Indeed, this focus on women in global perspective was highlighted over 25 years ago with the publication of *Sisterhood Is Global*.

Edited by U.S. feminist Robin Morgan in 1984, *Sisterhood Is Global* was hailed as the anthology for the international women's movement; it was embraced by many in Women's Studies (although not without controversy, as discussed below) just as this discipline was starting to become institutionalized on college campuses, and universities were beginning to recognize the importance of global citizenship. Noting "only she who attempts the absurd can achieve the impossible" (p. ix), the collection was groundbreaking in its documentation of patriarchal injustices worldwide. Patriarchy refers to the role of adult men who have power and authority in communities and societies and who act as dominant figures in social, economic, and political life. Following the feminist pattern of both analyzing and advocating change, *Sisterhood Is Global* used local and global networks to include a wide range of women's voices and was inspiring in its recognition of the "vast resources of womanpower" (p. 3) that could transform the politics of the late-twentieth century.

Despite these lofty goals and achievements, the project was controversial on three counts that have served to inform contemporary studies of women in global perspective. These issues are central to our analyses in *Women Worldwide*: (1) that *Sisterhood Is Global* advocated a "universal sisterhood" that overstated women's shared interests and understated the power differences between women, especially the ways women around the world are different from one another as a result of varied identities like class, religion, and region; (2) that the anthology's reliance on Western politics ignored the processes of colonialism, imperialism, and globalization that structure women's lives; and (3) that the premise of the anthology presumed the relevance of Western feminism imposed on women worldwide.

In the sections below I focus on these three themes associated with the critique of *Sisterhood Is Global* (universal sisterhood; processes of colonialism, imperialism, and globalization; imposition of Western feminism), emphasizing that in the years since the publication of Morgan's project these concepts have informed dialogue about feminism and its relevance around the world, shaping knowledge about ways to advocate for alliances that improve women's status. These themes are central in *Women Worldwide* and their discussion here helps provide a framework for the book. An exploration of these concepts also allows for definition and exploration of key terms and issues that are discussed in the following chapters.

"UNIVERSAL SISTERHOOD" AND THE POLITICS OF LOCATION

A key issue in feminism, the political theory and social movement for equal rights for women, concerns this concept of "woman." Although this might seem rather obvious (the idea that we all know a woman when we see one), it is actually more complex. To use the concept "woman" is to imply there is something unique or similar about that concept that carries across all situations. In other words, to speak of "woman," we invoke characteristics that are recognizable in a variety of situations. The case can be made that women worldwide share the experience and material conditions of raising children, maintaining families, and being the victims of sexual violence. Again, although this might be true generally, it is not the reality for all women. What this exercise helps reveal are the differences across a category that tends to claim some degree of similarity. Such a claim becomes important when a social movement (defined as a sustained, collective campaign that arises as people with shared interests come together in support of a common goal) seeks to speak for all women, advocating their shared interests in the name of a universal notion of sisterhood. "Sisterhood" means the solidarity of women based on shared conditions, experiences, or concerns. A universal sisterhood implies the presence or occurrence of this solidarity everywhere or existing in all situations under all conditions. *Sisterhood Is Global* advocated such a "universal sisterhood" that overstated women's shared interests and understated the ways women around the world differ from one another.

Differences between women shape their/our lives and provide differential access to resources and opportunities, both through privilege and limitation or discrimination. Difference reflects multiple and intersecting identities based upon age; body shape, looks and size; caste or class (socioeconomic status that tends to involve questions of literacy and access to education and certain kinds of work); sexual identity (heterosexual, bisexual, lesbian, and/or "queer"); race (constructed by cultures as a difference based upon certain phenotypes like skin color, nose shape, or hair texture); and ability (marked by differences in physical and mental health). Differences between women also include ethnic and regional distinctions associated with religion, culture, and national origin that include histories of nationalism. Nationalism is an ideology and social movement that reflects how members of a nation care about their national identity and how they seek to achieve or maintain their self-determination as a nation. National pride often involves social customs and rituals that tend to support political elites. National identity customarily serves to separate members of one nation from another. In the United States, for example, we see demonstrations of nationalism on the fourth of July, Independence Day.

Important regional differences between women that shape individual lives also arise as a result of location in either the Global North or the Global South. This North–South divide is less a geographic division than a political and socioeconomic distinction between "developed" more wealthy nations in, for example, Europe and North America (North) and "developing" poorer nations that include vast regions of Africa, Central and Latin America, and most of Asia (South). As countries become more economically "developed," they tend to be included as members of the Global North regardless of geographic location. It is important to note that the Global North is currently home to four of the five permanent members of the United Nations Security Council (United States, Great Britain, France, and the Russian Federation, with China as the fifth member), so this distinction is related to power in a broad global sense.

Other terms that mark distinctions among women, reflecting access to opportunities and resources, are "First World," "Second World," and "Third World." Like the Global South and North, these terms divide the world based upon political and socioeconomic distinctions, although they arose during the Cold War (the period of tension between the United States and the former Soviet Union and their allies from the mid-1940s to the 1990s). Countries aligned with the United States and NATO's (North Atlantic Treaty Organization) military alliance were known as the "First World," the Soviet Union and its allies were termed the "Second World," and those poor countries that were mostly non-aligned with either were characterized as the "Third World." The latter term has customarily been used to describe the non-Western, nonindustrialized or "developing" countries of the world. Given the relative collapse of Cold War mentality and the arrogant hierarchical value of "First" versus "Third" that potentially disparages huge regions of the world, these terms are less used today. In fact, some writers from those regions suggest the term "Two-Thirds World" to remind us that the people who live in these areas are actually the world's majority.

The terms "developed" and "developing" must also be used carefully to recognize that what industrialized nations recognize as "undeveloped" is relative and reflects their ethnocentrism (believing one's ethnic group is the most important and/or that one's culture is superior to cultures of other groups). Many "Third World" regions are or were rich in agricultural and scientific accomplishments and may have had extensive democratic social and political systems. Of course, it is important not to romanticize indigenous societies since many also had cruel and repressive systems. The point here is that when "development" is used synonymously with "industrialization" or to mean capitalist expansion, this does not necessarily imply that human communities benefit. Indeed, "maldevelopment" might more accurately describe the ways traditional development policies have, for example, created or sustained wealthy elites rather than facilitating the distribution of wealth throughout communities; built luxury hotels and economic infrastructure rather than providing housing for ordinary people; or encouraged cash crops like coffee instead of encouraging agriculture to sustain local communities. In these ways, women's geographical locations are connected to political and socioeconomic power associated with the broader world order.

In this discussion of difference it is important to emphasize the ways that identities (e.g., age, race, national identity, etc.) claimed by women worldwide intersect or operate together. This means that women are simultaneously a jumble or confluence of identities that intersect and create multiple subjectivities (e.g., young, heterosexual, Dalit [formerly "Untouchable"], poor, Indian, and so forth). In addition, we must understand that it is the hierarchical ranking of identities that results in privilege for some and limitations or discriminations for others through the operation of "systems of inequality and privilege" such as sexism, racism, ageism, classism, caste systems, and so forth. This means that women of similar identities will experience identities associated with these "isms" differently depending upon their location in other identities. For example, women of similar age or class will experience the privileges and limitations of these identities differently depending upon social location associated with other identities like race, sexual identity, or national origin.

Such a discussion of the social organization of specific bodies in specific spaces/places reflects what U.S. scholar Adrienne Rich ([1986] 1994, p. 210) calls "the politics of location." This phrase means that power and resources (or their lack) associated with individuals' identities result in socioeconomic and political positionings that affect the ways women live their lives. Used to discuss the differences among U.S. women that troubled a women's movement based on the realities and needs of white, middle-class women, this phrase also highlights the shortcomings of the "universal sisterhood" model. Such differences associated with the politics of location that divide women from one another imply that women may have more in common with men in their life than with women from another class, region, or nation. In addition, these politics also mean that women can oppress and limit other women and may benefit from that oppression. Again this complicates notions of "unity" among women.

COLONIALISM, IMPERIALISM, AND GLOBALIZATION SHAPING WOMEN'S LIVES

Colonialism can be defined as practices of domination that involve subordination of one society by another through the building and maintaining of colonies in one region or territory by people from another region. Colonialism occurs in order to expand the power of the colonizers through access to resources (gold, spices, timber, coffee, minerals—even human labor) and/or for strategic purposes associated with militarism. Some colonizers have asserted aid to indigenous colonized populations by bringing "civilization" or religion, although in reality they tended to impose displacement and subjugation. Native populations in North America, for example, were colonized by Europeans. Although European countries such as Great Britain, France, Belgium, Germany, Spain, Russia, and the Netherlands were important colonizing nations during the fifteenth through twentieth centuries, imposing colonialism on much of the rest of the world (the Americas, Africa, Australia, and huge regions of Asia, for example), they were not the only colonizing nations. Japan and China, for example, have colonized the Korean peninsula, just as Japan also colonized northeast China, formerly known as Manchuria. Younger nations like the United States have colonized regions like Hawaii and the Philippines (also colonized by Japan and Spain).

The term "colonialism" is related to the concept of imperialism. Note that while colonialism involves the transfer of population to a new region (settlement) while maintaining political allegiance to the original colonizing nation, imperialism is the political or geographical domain that exercises power over others, whether through settlement (colonialism) or through such contemporary practices as military domination, economic policies, or the imposition of certain forms of knowledge. You might recall from your history classes how imperialism was found in the ancient histories of the Aztec, Roman, Assyrian, and Chinese empires and in the Greek, Ottoman, Persian, and Egyptian empires, as well as in the more modern imperial nations described above in the discussion of colonialism. It is important to note that the maintenance of empire almost always involves ideologies (sets of ideas and values) or what is often termed cultural supremacy. These ideologies justify imperialism through advocation of the moral superiority of the empire and its entitlements to dominate and "save" or "civilize" others who are characterized, for example, as lazy, naive, childlike, ignorant, or barbaric. Traditionally dominated nations have been seen as "backward" or "savage," or, in more recent times, the case is made for the ways they are benefited economically or socially. In this way, imperialism involves not only colonial, territorial policies, but also economic, military, and/or cultural dominance. Women are directly impacted from colonial and imperial processes as a result of these practices that transform and regulate their lives. As discussed in later chapters, women live these practices within colonized nations in their experiences of sexuality, marriage, family, work, health, and so forth.

Globalization refers to the transformation of local or regional phenomena into global ones and describes the unification of people around the world into a global community. As such it includes both economic and cultural forces. Economic globalization involves capitalist expansion and can be defined as the integration and rapid interaction of economies through production, trade, and financial transactions by banks and multinational corporations. Cultural globalization involves the transnational (across national borders) migration of people, information, and consumer cultures. Critics of globalization emphasize that contemporary globalization reflects capitalist imperialism in that expanding capitalist global networks maintain practices whereby powerful countries and regions (such as the United States, the European Union, and China, for example) exercise imperialist power or domination over vast regions of the world. In many cases these forms of imperialism involve military invasion and occupation.

Contemporary dialogues within feminism now recognize the importance of addressing women's issues in the context of processes that integrate economies toward a global marketplace or a single world market. The accompanying growth of transnational corporations and the complex global networks of production and consumption rely on cheap female labor and the commodification and exploitation of female bodies. There is no shortage of evidence to illustrate the ways globalization is transforming indigenous communities and creating environmental crises of immense proportions. We are also constantly confronted with the ways globalization fosters militarism and plays a role in many conflicts around the globe. However, it is important to understand how such forces capitalize on histories of imperialism and colonialism that have exploited the peoples and raw materials from colonized regions of the world over the last centuries. Contemporary globalization is framed by these histories of colonialism and imperialism and maintains the legacies through economic, cultural, and, in some cases, military practices.

An important contribution of *Sisterhood Is Global* involved the ways it illustrated the impossibility of creating a global feminist movement free of asymmetrical (unequal) power relations as a result of these histories of colonialism and imperialism that construct women's lives and separate women from each other. Such legacies have shaped feminism as well as international development and modernization projects outside academia. Knowledge of these legacies compels us to examine, for example, the differences between women experiencing the privileges of being citizens of the colonizing nation and those who live in the nation that was colonized. Can these women come together and form alliances as equals? Such relationships are often uneven, unequal, and complicated. New feminist approaches to women in a global perspective pay attention to these histories and the ways current imperialist practices continue to shape women's lives and feminist activism. Contemporary feminist scholars anticipate the ways alliances between women around the globe are never free from these forces, acknowledging power differences and working to create networks that subvert and critique the legacies themselves while encouraging women's empowerment.

THE IMPOSITION OF WESTERN FEMINISM AND THE POSSIBILITIES OF TRANSNATIONAL FEMINIST SOLIDARITY

The recognition of false unities associated with the *Sisterhood Is Global* anthology (with its claim to a unified global sisterhood ignoring histories and current realities of imperialism and globalization that separate women) raised questions about feminism as a political ideology and as a social movement able to represent the needs of women worldwide. You will recall that feminism advocates women's socioeconomic and political equality and endorses social justice for all people. It does this by addressing inequities in key areas that include health, reproduction, work, political representation, and so forth (similar to the chapter themes in this book). Many women in the Global North who have greater access to education and communication technologies and who generally have more opportunities for participation in social movements have a privileged voice in defining feminism. They have benefited from the increased status of their countries of origin in terms of the broader world order and tend to enjoy a higher standard of living, opportunities for travel, and increased participation and voice in world conferences. As a result of such privileges, these (mostly) Western feminists have been able to define key areas for feminism and establish priorities for social change, setting the agenda for a "global women's movement." Although this movement was designed to represent the needs of all women, it tended to reflect the priorities of white, middle-class feminists in the Global North with its focus on individual rights, bodily integrity, and sexual freedom. In addition, some women in the Global South have been unwilling to accept the term "feminism" given its association with "sexual liberation" that in some contexts has been understood as sexual promiscuity.

This does not mean that a Western focus was never useful for women elsewhere, only that women of the Global South (and some in the North too) were not equally able to set the agenda and participate in dialogue about where, when, and under what conditions women may act in their own interests. In other words, what are considered the most important "feminist" issues in Europe and North America, for example, may not necessarily be understood as priorities in other parts of the world. In particular, since women's movements in many parts of the Global South have emerged alongside struggles for independence, the focus on nation-building has necessarily been intertwined with feminist struggles. Ultimately, the association of feminism with the very countries recognized as imperialist by the Global South served as an obstacle to the acceptance of feminism. When it was published in the mid-1980s, *Sisterhood Is Global* highlighted tensions about the meaning of feminism and ultimately about what "sisterhood" might entail. These tensions continue today and are central in feminist dialogue and debate.

Scholar Chandra Talpade Mohanty has written about Western feminism and its history of claiming unity across women's broad differences in the haste to structure a movement in its own image. Her influential essay "Under Western Eyes: Feminist Scholarship and Colonial Discourses," published in 1986 and reprinted in chapter 1, critiques this tendency of Western feminism to construct "Third World woman" as a monolithic (undifferentiated or forming a single whole), universal category, especially in projects associated with gender and development that ignored historical and geographical specificity. Gender and development projects (GAD) critique both the traditional development policies of industrial nations that provide aid and support to other countries as they convert to capitalist market economies as well as the women in development projects (WID) that emphasized the inclusion of women in this process. WID paid attention to the needs of women in local communities as development projects were initiated, highlighting their productive labor in sustaining communities and nations. GAD went on to advocate for women's increased status and gender equality as a result of development initiatives, working to empower women to have control and autonomy rather than merely improving their welfare (the focus of WID). However, Mohanty's point was that none of the approaches (traditional development projects, WID, and GAD) critiqued development itself as a strategy of capitalist expansion or incorporated the problems with the term "development" as already discussed above. It was the alliance between Western feminism and development that was the center of Mohanty's critique in "Under Western Eyes."

A similar analysis was offered in Inderpal Grewal and Caren Kaplan's *Scattered Hegemonies* (1994) that explored the possibilities of doing feminist work across cultural divides, incorporating postcolonial theory into the history of feminism as a political theory. Postcolonial theory reacts to the cultural legacy of colonialism, especially the ways literatures of colonial and imperialist countries have distorted and justified the experiences and realities of those dominated. These theorists emphasize that colonized people also internalize the messages of this literature. Scholar and filmmaker Trinh T. Minh-Ha uses postcolonial theory in her focus on women, art, and cultural politics as discussed in her influential book *Woman, Native, Other*, published in 1989. Along with Mohanty's later book, *Feminism Without Borders* and her article "'Under Western Eyes' Revisited: Feminist Solidarity Through Anticapitalist Struggles" (2003), such analyses continued to address the role of Western feminism in ideologies that support the cultural supremacy of Western societies. Alongside this critique, however, they also encourage transnational (across borders) solidarity-building among women.

Out of the dialogues of the last couple of decades has arisen the concept of transnational feminism that is hopeful of feminism as a truly liberating phenomenon as well as mindful of its ties to racism, colonialism, and imperialism. While it resists a universal sisterhood, it attempts to create the foundation for more equitable relationships among women across cultures. The term "transnational" implies "across borders" and anticipates a shifting of borders that encourages dialogue across nation-states. While the term "international" perpetuates boundaries of race and nation, "transnational" advocates a questioning of those boundaries and encourages a destabilization of borders. In other words, "transnational" recognizes inequities arising out of women's differences that frame these border crossings, yet it is committed to activism that encourages dialogue for change. Just as transnational feminism avoids universalizing women in its rejection of a universal sisterhood, this movement also rejects a universal notion of patriarchy that affects all women the same. Different kinds of patriarchies grounded in different countries with diverse histories and complex interactions with religion, nation, sexualities, and so forth, affect women in disparate ways. Because of this complexity, claiming universality is at best useless and at worst dangerous in its recirculation of stereotypes (e.g., Muslim women are all oppressed; sex workers are always disempowered; women in the United States have more rights; capitalism is synonymous with democracy, and so on.). Rather, it is important to recognize particular, culturally specific issues and to recognize the intersections among gender, sexuality, class, and nationhood that frame such dialogues. *Women Worldwide: Transnational Feminist Perspectives on Women* is positioned to recognize these challenges at the same time that it renews the commitment of feminism for improving the lives of women around the globe.

Ultimately, no woman can speak for another woman, although she can listen and learn and engage in dialogue. Women in local communities have diverse needs and must be empowered to set their own agendas. Transnational feminism supports the necessity for a diversity of feminisms that is responsive to the different concerns and needs of women worldwide. In these ways, controversies surrounding Morgan's *Sisterhood Is Global* have been instructive in shaping the transnational feminist movement today. However, like many other strong feminist activists of this era, Robin Morgan and contributors to *Sisterhood Is Global* still support women's efforts to change the conditions of their lives. They went on to found the Sisterhood Is Global Institute that still continues to advocate for women's equality today (http://www.sigi.org/).

ORGANIZATION OF WOMEN WORLDWIDE

As discussed in the preface, *Women Worldwide* is organized into a series of themes or topics that are explored in the following chapters. Each chapter begins with an introductory framework essay written by key scholar activists that introduces and contextualizes topics associated with the theme of the chapter. We have accompanied these essays by sidebars and textboxes to enrich dialogue about chapter themes and provide suggestions for activities and further study. The framework essays also introduce readings that follow each essay. These readings include first-person narratives, traditional academic articles, and research reports, as well as magazine articles, poetry, and short prose. Each chapter includes a focus on activism and social movements through information on women's individual and collective struggles for change.

Women Worldwide begins with chapter 1 "Transnational Feminisms," written by Valentine M. Moghadam. She provides a more detailed focus on transnational movements for feminist activism that discusses the history of global feminisms and addresses political and socioeconomic factors contributing to the development of transnational feminist networks (TFNs). This chapter explores different kinds of TFNs and their role in the empowerment of women in local communities. Chapter 2 "World Media," by Katharine Sarikakis and Leslie Regan Shade, addresses the role of media in the era of globalization, focusing on changes in media and their consequences for women's lives. They discuss women's representations in media and their access to information and communication technologies. The chapter closes with examples of women's activism in regard to blogging, social networking, mobile (cell) phone use, and radio and independent film and video production.

"Global Politics of the Body" is the topic of chapter 3, written by Penny Van Esterik. She discusses how bodies are constructed and represented in various contexts and addresses cultural practices that give meaning to the female body. Van Esterik examines the ways women's bodies have been commodified (turned into objects for the pleasure of others) and explores women's strategies to take back control over their bodies. This focus on the body continues in chapter 4, "Sexualities Worldwide," coauthored by Charmaine Pereira and Priya Kandaswamy. This chapter focuses on women's sexualities in a global context and explores the ways colonialism, nationalism, and contemporary forms of globalization set the stage for conflicts over sexuality. It looks at the role of gender in social constructions of sexuality and discusses three areas of conflict that include pornography, sex trafficking, and sex tourism.

Chapter 5 also concerns the body in its focus on "Politics of Women's Health." Written by Mehra Shirazi, this chapter presents health as a human right and provides a framework that addresses globalization and its consequences for women's health. Shirazi discusses three key health issues affecting women today: birthing and maternal health; breastfeeding; and breast cancer. The chapter ends with a focus on the millennium development goals and presents "a way forward" to promote health for women worldwide. Intimately connected to women's health is the issue of "Reproductive Freedoms," the focus of chapter 6, written by Patti Lou Watkins, Alicia Bublitz, and Hoa Nguyen. They discuss the politics of reproductive freedom, emphasizing the ways reproductive issues are not simply personal concerns but connected to broader social issues about women's status in society. This chapter discusses reproductive technologies, including birth control, forced sterilization, abortion, and assisted reproduction, and addresses specific vulnerabilities of marginalized populations with respect to reproductive freedoms.

"Families in Global Context," by Meg Wilkes Karraker, is the topic of chapter 7. Wilkes Karraker discusses the diversity of families and explores son preference and its consequences for the well-being of girls and women. This chapter addresses power in families and raises broader social questions regarding patriarchy and male control over women in families and communities. Although families are sources of comfort and love for individuals, unfortunately they are also the place where abuse of women and children is most likely to occur. This focus on violence against women is the theme of chapter 8, written by Patti Duncan. Although "Violence Against Women Worldwide" addresses gender-based violence in the family, with a focus on physical and sexual violence, dowry-related violence, honor killings, acid violence, and female genital cutting, it also discusses sexual harassment and assault, hate crimes, sex trafficking and prostitution, as well as violence perpetuated or condoned by the state.

"Women's Work in the Global Economy" is the topic of chapter 9, authored by Juanita Elias. This chapter overviews the work of women in the global economy and explores patterns of female employment that include migration and women's labor in export-oriented economies. Elias addresses the gendering of women's work and discusses the ways workplaces are sites for the (re)construction of certain identities. She writes about reproductive labor and women's employment, emphasizing that it is necessary to address the unpaid labor of women in the family and household in order to understand the gendered nature of female employment. This is followed by chapter 10 on "Women and Environmental Politics." Coauthored by Ana Isla and Trina Filan, this chapter continues the focus on economic globalization raised in chapter 9 by exploring the impact of these forces on the environment. The chapter outlines women's relationship to the environment and their role in sustainable agriculture. It also addresses "sustainable development" and its implications for human and non-human communities worldwide through a focus on contemporary rainforest ecopolitics.

Chapter 11 discusses "Women and Political Systems Worldwide." Coauthored by Melanie Hughes and Pam Paxton, this chapter explores women's formal representation in politics, their challenges and obstacles, and paths to women's power in politics. Hughes and Paxton also address the role of women in informal politics and emphasize the broad efforts of women acting politically to organize and put pressure on established power systems. This focus on global politics is continued in chapter 12, "Women, War, and Peace," by Mary Hawkesworth. Hawkesworth contrasts dominant accounts of war developed by international relations scholars with feminist efforts to demonstrate gendered aspects and consequences of war. She examines women's roles in war making and how their lives are shaped directly and indirectly by militarization.

The Conclusion, "Integrating the Themes: HIV/AIDS in Women's Lives," integrates previous chapter themes through a focus on HIV/AIDS as a case study in gender inequality.

Written by Sonia Kandathil and me, this chapter begins with a discussion of the HIV/AIDS global pandemic. It continues with a focus on explanations for the feminization of the disease and with strategies for addressing the problem and empowering women. Kandathil and I illustrate the intersectionality of issues covered in the various chapters and encourage application of knowledge from these chapters. Indeed, as you study the book you will find that most chapter themes are interrelated such that, for example, the chapter on the body

A DAY IN THE LIFE: Learning About Women

"Oh no!" Carmen leapt out from under the covers. She had slept through her alarm and only had 15 minutes to get to her women's studies class. She knew she shouldn't have stayed out until 2 in the morning, but she had enjoyed seeing her friends again after semester break. At least she had done the reading for class before the party. Now she tried to recall the main themes; she remembered feeling a bit unnerved about some of the information the reading gave about women's lives around the world—all those statistics about poverty and war and other awful things that women had to endure. She was curious to see what her teacher would have to say, and she really hated to be late to class.

She slipped into her favorite jeans and T-shirt and pulled her long, dark hair back into a ponytail. She was the first person in her family to go to college, and she didn't want to let them down, especially her mother, who worked two jobs to help support Carmen. Carmen grabbed her backpack and started her dash across campus. Her coffee would have to wait.

Carmen made it to her desk just as the instructor was beginning to talk about last night's readings. It was only the second class session, and this was Carmen's first women's studies course. She was a little nervous about it. She didn't call herself a feminist, even though she believed that women and men are equal. She thought that perhaps feminists were a little too militant for her taste. Carmen was surprised the first day when the teacher asked students to raise their hands if they identified as feminist. A lot of the women in the class raised their hands, and so did a couple of the men. Carmen didn't even know men could be feminists. Most of these women didn't look particularly militant, although one was wearing a "This is what a feminist looks like" T-shirt and several sported a variety of political buttons on their backpacks.

Carmen felt that women in the United States were pretty much equal, although she had a sense that her mother's life was made more complicated by the fact that she was a woman, especially after Carmen's father left and stopped paying child support. Still, Carmen thought, as long as she worked hard she could succeed just as easily as her male classmates.

As the instructor began an overview of the conditions of women's lives around the world, Carmen was struck with the obstacles women face—poverty, violence, lack of political power, religious discrimination, and lack of access to clean water and healthcare. She felt a little guilty, and she found herself being grateful she was an American. About that time, one of the young women who had identified as a feminist on the first day raised her hand and asked the teacher if any of these things were true for women in the United States. Carmen was shocked by the teacher's answer.

"Yes, Lindsey, women in the U.S., like women around the world, struggle with many of these same things. The issues often look different depending upon the culture—rather than face genital cutting, for example, women in the U.S. often struggle with anorexia and bulimia or undergo cosmetic surgeries to shape their bodies to fit cultural norms—but women everywhere face the pressures and difficulties of living in a patriarchal world."

The more the instructor talked about the problems women face, the more Carmen began to despair that things could change or that she could play a part in bringing about change. Her teacher said that as the term progressed, they'd talk about ways women could get involved to change the conditions of their lives. Despite this, Carmen didn't feel hopeful. Maybe, she thought, she just needed a caffeine boost.

As soon as class was over, Carmen headed to the student union coffee shop and ordered the biggest cup of coffee they had. As she looked for a seat, she noticed another student from her class sitting alone at a table. She asked if she could join her, and they began to talk about the class.

The other student explained that she had taken other women's studies courses that had primarily focused on the United States and that she was excited for a course with a global focus. Carmen asked her if learning all of this information about women's inequality didn't depress her.

"Oh, no," her new friend, Leticia, responded. "It empowers me. I know it's hard to learn all of the horrible things women face, but we also learn how women resist their oppression and work to bring about social justice in the world."

Carmen thought about this for a while, and she wondered if she'd end up feeling empowered or just sad by the end of the course. They sat for a while longer drinking their coffee and making plans to form a study group for the first exam.

Carmen had another class that afternoon; then, after a quick bite in the cafeteria, she returned to her dorm room to work on her women's studies homework. She was supposed to do a Web search for Transnational Feminist Networks. As Carmen began to read about all of the work feminist organizations were doing to improve women's lives, she began to feel a little hopeful, but she still wondered what exactly she could do to make a difference. Several of the Web sites offered activist ideas, and she considered whether or not she might be willing to do some of them.

"I could write a letter to a corporation that's exploiting women workers in sweatshops," she thought, "but would it do any good?" Before getting ready for bed, she went back to her Facebook page on her laptop and posted her thoughts about what she was learning. She'd be interested to hear back from her friends and see what they thought.

Suddenly, she really wanted to talk to her mother. She waited impatiently as the phone rang until she heard her mother's voice, "Ah, *mija*, it's late. What's on your mind?"

After Carmen had talked about her day and inquired about her younger brother and sister, she asked the question that was really on her mind: "Tell me about your life, Mama, as a woman, I mean."

Carmen's mother was not used to this line of questioning and found herself thinking about the ways college had changed her eldest daughter. It was a treat to talk about family, though, and she found herself telling Carmen all about the strong women who came before her. "Your grandmother was part of a popular organization in El Salvador in the 1970s that was calling for democracy," explained Carmen's mother. "Just before Archbishop Romero was assassinated in 1980, your *abuela* decided it was not safe to stay there and raise her daughters. I was only twelve and your *tia* was nine." Thinking about her younger sister always made Carmen's mother smile. "And then we came to the United States," she added. "Once we arrived, your *abuela* continued to work for justice in El Salvador. She wrote many letters to U.S. officials asking them not to support the junta that was killing peasants, labor organizers, students, and priests."

"Was she successful?" Carmen asked.

"Well that depends on how you define success, *mija*. Of course, she didn't stop the war in El Salvador, but she did use her voice. So, yes, I do believe that she was successful. She spoke up for herself and others. She stood up against injustice."

"Wow, I never knew that. So, she really was an activist."

"Yes, you come from a long line of strong women."

"Thanks. I'd better get to sleep. I have a math class at 9 in the morning."

"Good night, then. *Te amo.*"

"I love you, too."

also addresses women in families, the chapter on the family also addresses sexual violence, the chapter on sexual violence also addresses war and militarization, and so forth. We hope this is useful in underscoring the interconnection of topics and hopefully instructive in reiterating the themes in ways that make them more intelligible and memorable.

With these themes in mind, *Women Worldwide* faces the daunting task of representing the diversity of women's lives around the globe. This "mess" of global problems seems so immense and complex that we often feel immobilized by its proportions. Those of us living in nations that benefit from the extraction of human and natural resources from other regions of the world often feel guilt about the situation and confusion about how to respond. However, education is a first step to transformation, followed by self-reflection about the ways we participate in, and may benefit from, both the practices of contemporary globalization as well as other systems of inequality in our local communities. Changing personal behaviors and joining others in social change efforts are steps to changing broader social problems. With this in mind we hope this anthology is both instructive and inspiring: instructive in documenting the breadth of issues that affect women worldwide and inspiring in sharing the stories of amazing women who not only survive despite the hardships in their lives, but become empowered to change their worlds and empower others in the process. This, we hope, encourages optimism. Although some of the poignant knowledge here might depress and sadden, we hope that with knowledge comes motivation for you to get interested, get involved, and make a difference in the lives of women around the globe. All the best on your personal journey with women worldwide!

REFERENCES

Grewal, I. and Kaplan, C. (1994). *Scattered hegemonies: Postmodernity and transnational feminist practices*. Minneapolis: University of Minnesota Press.

Lockwood, M. (2009). Stop the Mamas crying. Unpublished poem. Used with permission of author.

Trinh, M. (1989). *Woman, native, other. Writing postcoloniality and feminism*. Bloomington: Indiana University Press.

Mohanty, C. Talpade. (2003). *Feminism without borders: Decolonizing theory, practicing solidarity*. Durham, NC: Duke University Press.

Morgan, R. (1984). *Sisterhood is global: The international women's movement anthology*. New York: Anchor Press/Doubleday.

Rich, A. ([1986] 1994). *Blood, bread, and poetry: Selected prose, 1979–1985*. New York: W. W. Norton and Co.

Transnational Feminisms

Valentine M. Moghadam

Valentine M. Moghadam is Professor of Sociology and Women's Studies, and director of the Women's Studies Program, at Purdue University, USA. She was previously at UNESCO (Paris), Illinois State University, and the United Nations University's WIDER Institute (Helsinki). Born in Tehran, Iran, Dr. Moghadam is the author of *Modernizing Women: Gender and Social Change in the Middle East* (2003), *Globalizing Women: Transnational Feminist Networks* (2005), and *Globalization and Social Movements: Islamism, Feminism, and the Global Justice Movement* (2009), among other books, edited volumes, and journal articles. Her areas of research are globalization, transnational feminist networks, civil society and citizenship, and women's employment in the Middle East and North Africa. She has lectured and published widely and consulted with many international organizations.

> The mountain moving day is coming
> I say so yet others doubt it . . .
> All sleeping women now awake and move
> All sleeping women now awake and move.

Excerpt from "Mountain Moving Day" by Yosano Akiko

This chapter focuses on transnational feminism, that movement for the social, political, and economic equality of women across national boundaries. Such an approach underscores the powerful opportunities associated with the development of new forms of international alliances and networks for the emancipation of women worldwide and the empowering consequences that can occur when, as predicted in the poem above, "sleeping women now awake and move." It also, however, addresses the challenges to unity that arise from such forces as economic globalization, neocolonialism, and racism. Still, most agree that the "women's movement" in its myriad forms is a global phenomenon that advocates gender justice. Despite cultural differences and national priorities, women's rights activists not only network across national borders, demonstrating solidarity in their struggles, but exhibit similarities in the ways they frame their grievances and demands, form networks and organizations, and engage with state and intergovernmental institutions (Moghadam, 2005; Naples and Desai, 2002). As discussed in the short reading "Edge of the Earth" by Hafsat Abiola, there is a "cord that links us all" and which connects us "across distances, time zones, [and] worlds." This cord, however, also "connects the different aspects of who we are." It is this quest for unity out of distinct differences that poses one of the greatest challenges for transnational feminism.

Transnational feminist activism has evolved in response to the continuing discrimination and worldwide suffering of women. Despite ongoing efforts throughout the twentieth century to address this discrimination through, for example, the United Nation's (UN) four World Conferences on Women (see sidebar), the Convention on the Elimination of All Forms of Discrimination Against Women (CEDAW), and other campaigns for legal and policy reforms to ensure women's civil, political, and social rights, we still have a long way to go. As Cynthia Wagner writes in the reading, "Women Still Have a Long Way to Go," the latter have yet to achieve full legal, economic and cultural equality with men even

World Conferences on Women

The International Women's Year was 1975, and the first world conference on women convened in Mexico City to examine the problems of continuing inequality for women and to propose solutions. The next 10 years became the United Nations Decade for Women that focused on women's advancement and global dialogue about gender equality. That conference was followed by three other world conferences. The UN's most recent update in 2005 points to the ongoing need for nations to continue to work to improve women's lives. The four conferences are described below.

FIRST WORLD CONFERENCE ON WOMEN

Mexico City, 19 June–2 July 1975

At this meeting, the process was launched and three objectives were identified in relation to equality, peace, and development for the Decade:

- Full gender equality and the elimination of gender discrimination
- The integration and full participation of women in development
- An increased contribution by women toward strengthening world peace

The conference urged governments to formulate national strategies, targets, and priorities. It led to the establishment of the International Research and Training Institute for the Advancement of Women (INSTRAW) and the United Nations Development Fund for Women (UNIFEM), which serve as an institutional framework for research, training, and operational activities in the area of women and development. At this conference, held in Mexico City, women played a highly visible role. Of the 133 delegations from member states, 113 were headed by women. Women also organized the International Women's Year Tribune, which attracted some 4000 participants, and a parallel forum of nongovernmental organizations that signaled the opening up of the United Nations to nongovernmental organizations, enabling women's voices to be heard in the organization's policy-making process.

SECOND WORLD CONFERENCE ON WOMEN

Copenhagen, 14–30 July 1980

This conference recognized that there was a disparity between women's guaranteed rights and their capacity to exercise them. Participants identified three spheres in which measures for equality, development, and peace were needed:

- Equal access to education

- Equal access to employment opportunities
- Equal access to adequate health care services

THIRD WORLD CONFERENCE ON WOMEN

Nairobi, 15–26 June 1985

The data presented by the United Nations to the delegations of member states revealed that the improvements observed had benefited only a limited number of women. Thus, the Nairobi Conference was mandated to seek new ways of overcoming obstacles for achieving the objectives of the decade: equality, development, and peace.

Three basic categories were established to measure the progress achieved:

- Constitutional and legal measures
- Equality in social participation
- Equality in political participation and decision making

The Nairobi Conference recognized that gender equality was not an isolated issue, but encompassed all areas of human activity. It was necessary for women to participate in all spheres, not only in those relating to gender.

FOURTH WORLD CONFERENCE ON WOMEN

Beijing, 4–15 September 1995

The Beijing Declaration and Platform for Action were adopted at the Fourth World Conference on Women, by the representatives of 189 countries. The platform reflects the new international commitment to achieving the goals of equality, development, and peace for women throughout the world. It also strengthens the commitments made during the United Nations Decade for Women, 1976–1985, which culminated in the Nairobi Conference, as well as related commitments undertaken during the cycle of United Nations world conferences held in the 1990s.

The 12 critical areas of concern in the Platform for Action are as follows:

1. Women and poverty
2. Education and training of women
3. Women and health
4. Violence against women
5. Women and armed conflict
6. Women and the economy
7. Women in power and decision making
8. Institutional mechanisms for the advancement of women
9. Human rights of women
10. Women and the media
11. Women and the environment
12. The girl child

The Platform for Action sets out strategic objectives and explains the measures that should be adopted by governments, the international community, nongovernmental organizations, and the private sector.

Source: http://www.un.org/en/development/devagenda/gender.shtml

in some of the world's more advanced societies. An explanation for this is discussed in the reading by legal scholar Catharine A. Mackinnon who refers to the 1949 Universal Declaration of Human Rights. In noting that most of these human rights are still violated in the case of women some 50 years after the declaration, she asks the question "Are Women Human?" and makes the case for transnational feminist advocacy.

Although by definition transnational feminist action involves feminism across borders, it entails recognition of different contexts and priorities. In other words, while transnational feminist action might exhibit similarities in critiques, goals, strategies, and mobilizing structures, there are identifiable differences among those claiming and using this label. One difference pertains to disagreements over abortion and gay/lesbian rights. In some cases this is a principled position and in other cases a matter of strategic priority-setting within a movement, network, or coalition. Another difference is discursive (about language). As already discussed, where the term "feminism" is either synonymous with interests of the Global North or strategically inadvisable (when, for example, using the label would derail alliances or place activists in jeopardy with the state), advocates instead talk of "women's rights" or of "law reform." In some countries in the Middle East or in eastern Europe, for example, women's rights groups frame their struggle as one for "civil society" or "democracy," avoiding the feminist label in claiming "national development" that implicitly might include women's rights. As discussed below, in many parts of the world, Christians who advocate feminism may refrain from using the label. The term "feminist" is also generally not openly used in Jordan and Egypt, for instance, although Iranian women's rights activists often defiantly call themselves feminists or "secular" feminists even though this puts them at risk vis-à-vis the Islamic authorities. This is also true of the *Association Tunisienne des femmes démocrates* and of several Algerian women's groups.

In this chapter I address transnational feminist activism through a focus on what I call transnational feminist networks (TFNs): organized and sustained forms of collective

action for the emancipation of women worldwide (Moghadam, 2005, 2009). The first section discusses the history of global feminisms and addresses political and socioeconomic factors contributing to the development of TFNs, including their relation to international development projects. It also explores strategies employed by TFNs to achieve their goals. This section is followed by an examination of several types of TFNs: (1) networks that target the neoliberal economic policy agenda or those policies that endorse free markets and economic privatization; (2) those that focus on the dangers of fundamentalisms and insist on women's human rights; (3) women's peace groups that target conflict, war, and imperialism; and (4) feminist humanitarian networks that address women's practical needs as well as their strategic interests. Most of these TFNs emerged in the 1980s and all continue to be active in some form today.

Because global feminism has emerged within the context of the world-system and is linked to economic globalization, this chapter describes how these forces unite women across the globe around common grievances and goals. However, because the world-system is unequal and hierarchical, the chapter also emphasizes points of contention among transnational feminist activists that sometimes challenge their alliances with each other. A key aspect here involves opportunities and difficulties associated with the potential alliance between women of color in core or "First World" nations and indigenous women in "Third World" or peripheral countries. For example, the classic reading by Chandra Talpade Mohanty titled "Under Western Eyes" refers to the arrogance of First World feminism in defining the realities and setting the agendas for international feminist struggle.

A DAY IN THE LIFE   ## *"Afua Knows Her Goal"* by *Trina Filan*

Twelve-year-old Nana Korbia Afua Konadu[1] awoke at 4:30 a.m. to start her day. She slid from her mat, slipped into her dress, and stepped from the bedroom she shared with her older sister and her sister's two young children into the family compound. The various sleeping and living rooms surrounding the courtyard of the family's large, rectangular compound were still dark, but there was activity in the interior. Afua's mother and her mother's mother already were at the fire, disdaining the charcoal stove in the enclosed kitchen for the cool air outside, preparing *ampesi* for breakfast.

Afua began her usual morning chores: running to the standpipe—a quick 15-minute walk from the house—to get three buckets of water, sweeping the family compound, and making a fire to heat some hot water for bathing before leaving for school. She helped prepare *ampesi* and bread with marmalade. In the evening, she would help make *abɛnkwan* and *fufu* for supper. She already was adept at using the wooden pestle to pound the cassava and plantains for *fufu* and also at turning the dough in the mortar as another woman pounded. In Ghana, cooking well was a skill prized by women from the meekest to the most successful.

The roosters crowed at 5:30, and the men and boys stirred in their sleeping quarters. Electric lights clicked on as Afua's father, her *wofa*, and her older brother, Kwame, found their clothes. When Kwame emerged, she ran to him: "Brother, let's fetch water, so we can go to school!" Afua loved school and hurried through her chores every morning to arrive on time.

"All right, sister, all right! Let me wake up first!" Kwame protested, still sleepy.

"No, Kwame! We should hurry!" Afua knew she would not be scolded for being so bold with her brother; he doted on her and gave in quickly. They grabbed two large buckets each and headed out to the standpipe.

Fetching water was a huge daily chore. They had to get enough for washing, drinking, and cooking for the morning, and when they got home from school, they fetched more for the evening. It was not a bad job, though. Afua knew other children who traveled much, much further—sometimes two kilometers each way—with their heavy buckets. And most girls did not have kind brothers to help them; they had to go alone. With this and other chores and because of the expense, very often these girls could not go to school. As the youngest child and with her sister's children too young to lift the buckets and Kwame nearly ready to go away to Kumasi for school, Afua knew the task soon would be hers alone.

After fetching water, Afua cleaned the family bedrooms, then she and Kwame washed, ate their *ampesi*, and dressed in their school uniforms. They ran to Father for chop money and left for school, a three-kilometer walk. The men headed to their shop, where they made and sold beautiful crafts to locals and tourists who traveled outside of Kumasi. After the morning work was done, her mother and grandmother would print batik designs on cloth to sell in the shop and at the market.

Afua's town was about 20 kilometers outside of Kumasi, where her mother's oldest sister had moved many years ago and where Afua's future beckoned. Her auntie was a nurse married to a British doctor. Unable to have children, they had decided to sponsor Kwame's and Afua's education through university, no mean expense and an unbelievable break: no one else in town was so fortunate. As they hurried along the dirt road through town, Afua dreamed about her good fortune and her future.

Some months ago, the school headmaster told the girls a new club would be opening for them alone. This girls' club, run by a development agency, would train them in math and science to encourage them to stay in school and enter a good profession. The idea of their own club thrilled the girls.

The first day, they were introduced to a cartoon character called Sara.[2] Sara, a little older than Afua, was trying to make the right choices in her life, and although many obstacles kept coming into her path, she found a way every time through courage and ingenuity to overcome them. When a "sugar daddy" tried to seduce her to sleep with him, Sara escaped from him. When one of Sara's friends became pregnant, Sara learned from Tamala's mistake and told her friend, Musa, she didn't want to have sex with him.

Sara was remarkable to Afua: she was strong and not afraid, and most importantly, she knew her goal and did not stray from it. Sara inspired Afua to believe that she, too, could have a big goal and reach it, and soon Afua knew her goal: to become a nurse like her auntie.

With this aim in mind, and wisely using her good fortune, Afua studied harder than ever. When the girls' club received a computer from the government, Afua quickly took to it, pecking at the keys, recording her friends singing, and drawing with the mouse. Each day, she grew closer to her goal.

Today was like most others. School went from 8:30 to 2:00 with two short breaks. Afua learned her lessons and answered questions then went to the club and learned to operate something called a "Bunsen burner." It was fascinating.

At 4:00, Afua hurried home; Kwame already was away helping Father with evening work. Afua had many things to do before her day was over. She had to help Mother in her fields, tending crops and gathering food. She had to gather firewood, clean the compound, and cook. She had to do her homework. It would be dark long before she slept. But Afua was a good daughter, and she was a smart and lucky girl who was strong enough to know her goal.

---

[1] Ghana is home to about 100 ethnic groups characterized by cultural and linguistic differences. Afua is a member of the matrilineal Ashanti, a subset of the country's largest ethnic group, the Akan. Afua speaks Twi.
[2] The Sara Communication Initiative (SCI) originally was developed by the United Nations Children's Fund in conjunction with more than 60 African writers, researchers, and health specialists to improve African adolescent girls' capacity to prevent HIV, pregnancy, and sexual abuse through esteem- and efficacy-building. In 2000, the US Agency for International Development and the government of Ghana partnered to bring *Sara—"I Know My Goal"* to adolescent girls throughout Ghana.

THE DEVELOPMENT OF TRANSNATIONAL FEMINISMS

Women have worked together across borders for women's rights since at least the era of "first wave" feminism (the nineteenth-century movement for women's rights occurring mostly in the Global North that included suffrage and other social and economic demands). This struggle for political and social rights, as well as peace and antimilitarism, united many women around the world in the early and mid-twentieth century. After World War II ended in 1945, global women's movements began to diverge, grouping themselves within national boundaries or economic zones and aligning with various ideological currents that emphasized different politics and priorities. First, for example, the Cold War (the conflict between the United States and the former Soviet Union and their allies concerning capitalism versus communism or state socialism) cast a shadow on feminist solidarity in the form of the East–West divide from the late 1940s through the 1990s. Second, the "second wave" feminist movement of industrialized Western societies, that arose in the 1960s and 1970s in response to demands for the improvement of women's status in both public and private arenas, brought various feminist perspectives providing different explanations for women's condition and varying strategies for change. These perspectives included liberal, radical, Marxist, and socialist feminist perspectives as well as critiques by lesbians and women of color for inclusivity within these approaches. Third, another division took the form of North–South that often played out as First World versus Third World feminism. These different feminisms had disparate priorities: many activists from the Global North saw legal equality and reproductive rights as key feminist demands and goals while those in the Global South emphasized "development," colonialism, and imperialism as obstacles to women's advancement. Such disagreements came to the fore at the beginning of the UN Decade for Women that sought to address the low status of women worldwide, and especially at its first and second world conferences on women that took place in Mexico City in 1975 and in Copenhagen in 1980, respectively.

Disagreements were exacerbated by international development projects that focused on population control while ignoring the basic needs and aspirations of local women. For example, many development projects excluded local communities from development planning and did not take into account women's productive roles and their reproductive responsibilities and needs. In particular, when the global debt crisis emerged in the late 1970s and early 1980s, structural adjustment policies (SAPs) were introduced by international lending agencies such as the World Bank and the International Monetary Fund. SAPs are economic policies that countries need to follow in order to qualify for international loans. In other words, SAPs are imposed through international monetary organizations as a condition of international lending. They require indebted countries to reduce levels of public expenditure in order to assist the repayment of debt and/or readjust spending patterns in line with perceived needs of a globalizing world economy. As a result, they often require countries to simultaneously cut social services, reduce trade barriers, and encourage foreign investment, halting social development projects in order to repay loans to First World banks. Although many indigenous women and some involved in gender and development research critiqued such capitalist development, other feminists tended to ignore the unequal relations between Global North and South. For example, in the reading "The Messy Relationship Between Feminisms and Globalizations," Manisha Desai argues that although feminism seeks to further women's agency and empowerment worldwide, some feminist perspectives are too connected with the problems of economic and cultural globalization that have exacerbated women's inequality.

A shift in the nature and orientation of international feminism began to take place in the mid-1980s during preparations for the Third UN World Conference on Women held in Nairobi, Kenya, in 1985. The shift took the form of bridge-building and consensus-making across both regional and ideological divides, and resulted in the emergence of a new type of women's organization—the transnational feminist network—that brought together women around a common agenda and goals. Three critical economic and political developments within states and regions, and at the level of the world-system, facilitated this development:

- The transition from Keynesian economics (with its emphasis on government intervention for full employment and citizen welfare) to neoliberal economics (with its emphasis on free markets, privatization, and trade and financial liberalization), along with a new international division of labor that relied heavily on (cheap) female labor.
- The decline of the welfare state in much of the Global North and the poverty of many countries, especially in the Global South. Both of these factors placed a heavy burden on women's reproductive and domestic roles.
- The emergence of various forms of fundamentalist and right-wing religious movements that threatened women's autonomy and human rights.

The economic and political realities of these global changes led to a convergence of feminist perspectives: feminists in the richer, "developed" nations found themselves focused on economic issues at the same time that those from "developing" countries were directing their attention to women's legal status, autonomy, and political rights. This encouraged the formation of a number of alliances that brought women together in response to economic pressures and to movements limiting women's rights. Out of these alliances, transnational feminist networks (TFNs) were born. Such networks included Development Alternatives with Women for a New Era (DAWN), MADRE, Women in Development Europe (WIDE), the Women's Environment and Development Organization (WEDO), Women Living under Muslim Laws (WLUML), and the Sisterhood is Global Institute (SIGI). The latter is the institute founded by U.S. feminist Robin Morgan and others after the completion of the anthology by the same name discussed in the introduction to *Women Worldwide*. By the 1990s, TFNs were engaged in policy-oriented research, advocacy, and lobbying around issues pertaining to women and development and women's human rights. Many individuals who formed or joined TFNs were scholar-activists who had been, and in some cases, continue to be, involved in the gender and development research community.

Some scholars have distinguished between different kinds of transnational feminist groups such as professionalized women's lobbying groups (nongovernmental organizations [NGOs] or international nongovernmental organizations [INGOs]) and "grassroots" women's groups. The former are sometimes described as "top-down" or potentially elitist groups where those in charge are separate from the broad base of women, while the latter tend to be seen as more local, community-based, and more centered around feminist principles of collaboration and power-sharing. This may be an arbitrary distinction, however, because many of the professionalized TFNs are led and staffed by feminist activists with strong commitments to gender equality, women's empowerment, and social transformation at the local level. It is more useful to see the international women's movement as diffuse and diverse, with different types of mobilizing structures, discourses, and action repertoires. The overarching frame is that of achieving gender equality and human rights for women and girls. How that is achieved varies across the different forms of groups. Change may occur through direct action, grassroots organizing, research and analysis, lobbying efforts, coalition-building, or humanitarian action. The strategies of TFNs are discussed in more detail below.

What should be noted in the development of all TFNs is the impact of the new information and computer technologies of the 1990s, which helped individuals connect and share information, plan and coordinate activities more rapidly, and mobilize more extensively. As emphasized in the next chapter, these technologies are still invaluable to feminist organizing worldwide. Two feminist networks focusing on communications came to serve as

LEARNING ACTIVITY **Feminist Networking Across the Globe**

In the past two decades, new technologies have provided feminist activists with unprecedented opportunity to communicate and collaborate globally. Isis International began in 1974 to help women, particularly women in the Global South, connect and communicate in order to be more actively involved in development processes. Visit the NGO's web site at www.isiswomen.org. Listen to "Isis Journey." Then browse the Web site and answer these questions:

- What is the mission of Isis International?
- What programs does the organization offer? Why do you think these programs are important for transnational feminist activism?
- Look at the most recent issue of *Women in Action*. What is the theme of the issue? How do the articles examine the issue from transnational feminist perspectives?
- What are Isis International's current campaigns? Why are these issues important for women across the globe?
- How do you think Isis International furthers transnational feminist activism?

Now visit the Web site of the International Women's Tribune Center at www.iwtc.org.

- What are its mission and programs?
- Why is its work important for transnational feminist activism?

Check out the Web site of the Global Sisterhood Network at www.global-sisterhood-network.org. GSN is "an information resource centre via the monitoring of media and institutional reports which seek emerging developments in agriculture, economics, employment, environment, health, law, militarism, politics, technology, trade and science, and which either directly or indirectly impact on the realities of women's lives. To meet this goal, GSN's electronic list places considerable emphasis on issues that have attracted sparse attention and/or analysis from a feminist perspective."

What do transnational feminist networks that are focused on communications offer women? How are new technologies helping women form networks? How might issues of access be problematic for some women? How might these TFNs help bridge differences and bring women together to work for change?

New technologies have greatly increased opportunities for feminist cyberactivism. Check out the article, "Cyberfeminism: Networking on the Net" by Amy Richards and Marianne Schnall on feminist.com: http://www.feminist.com/resources/artspeech/genwom/cyberfeminism.html. Also, visit the Web site of Equality Now at www.equalitynow.org. How is this organization utilizing the Web to engage people in activism on behalf of women around the world?

conduits and clearinghouses as well as distributors of activist materials: the International Women's Tribune Center, based in New York, and ISIS International Women's Information and Communication Service established in Quezon City, Philippines, and in Santiago, Chile (see sidebar).

As TFNs proliferated in the 1990s, they helped bridge the North–South divide among women activists and they worked to transcend political and ideological differences through adoption of a broader feminist agenda that included a critique of neoliberalism with its free markets and privatization (discussed below), as well as an insistence on women's full citizenship, reproductive rights, bodily integrity, and autonomy. Eventually that common agenda took the form of the 1995 Beijing Declaration and Platform for Action that came out of the Fourth World Conference on Women held in Beijing. In addition to the UN World Conferences on women, however, other UN conferences provided a platform for issues pertaining to gender justice. These included the United Nations Conference on the Environment and Development (UNCED) held in Rio de Janeiro in 1992; the Human Rights Conference in Vienna in 1993; the International Conference on Population and Development (ICPD) that was held in Cairo in 1994; and the World Summit for Social Development (known as the Social Summit) that took place in Copenhagen in 1995. At these conferences participants declared that environmental issues were women's issues, that women's rights were human rights, that governments were expected to guarantee women's reproductive health and rights, and that women's access to productive employment and social protection needed to be expanded. Slowly, new themes emerged that resonated globally and came to be adopted by women's groups throughout the world: women's human rights; gender justice; gender equality; ending the feminization of poverty; and resisting violence against women. These themes are elaborated in the following chapters of *Women Worldwide*.

Strategies of TFNs Worldwide

What are some strategies employed by TFNs to achieve their goals? First, TFNs mobilize pressure against outside forces and institutions that seek to undermine women's status. Such an institution is the World Trade Organization (WTO): an international organization designed to supervise international trade in accordance with neoliberal economic policies. TFNs mobilizing against outside forces impact global policy via e-petitions, action alerts, and appeals, as well as through direct actions that may include public protest and acts of civil disobedience. Like other transnational social movements, they also create, activate, or join global networks or coalitions in their struggle for gender justice by mobilizing pressure against outside forces. Important coalitions in this regard include Jubilee 2000 (involving labor, religious, environmental, and human rights groups highly critical of corporate capitalism); the Coalition to End the Third World Debt; Women's International Coalition for Economic Justice; the Women and Trade Network; Women's Eyes on the Bank; and United for Peace and Justice. Since "the Battle of Seattle" in November 1999 (a conference in Seattle convened by the WTO that was marred by power brokering on the part of First World countries, disagreements over agendas, and large street protests [see sidebar]), women have become active players in advocating global social justice, taking part in the World Social Forum. The World Social Forum is an annual meeting held by members opposed to corporate forces of globalization where efforts are made to coordinate world campaigns, share and refine organizing strategies, and inform each other about movements worldwide (Dufour and Giraud, 2007).

The Battle of Seattle

The extent of the protests of the 1999 World Trade Organization conference was unexpected. Protestors delayed the opening of the meeting and forced downtown Seattle businesses to close. Police arrested more than 500 protestors, amidst allegations of police brutality. Go to the WTO History Project at www. wtohistory.org for more information from the protestors' point of view. Also, go to www.cityofseattle.net/ wtocommittee for the results of Seattle's WTO Accountability Review Committee.

Second, TFNs act and agitate within their own borders and across nation-states to enhance public awareness and encourage public participation. They work with labor and progressive religious groups, media, and human rights groups on social policy that include humanitarian, development, and militarization issues. They link with local partners, participate in local coalitions, and provoke or take part in public protests. Third, TFNs network with each other in a sustained process of inter-networking and Internet-working. In all these ways, their activism spans local, national, regional, and transnational terrains. The "gift" of the Internet has allowed them to transcend borders, boundaries, and barriers in their collective action against forces that seek to keep women oppressed.

Finally, TFNs participate at the multilateral and intergovernmental level. Here they observe and address UN departments such as the Economic and Social Council (ECOSOC) that facilitates international cooperation on standards-making and problem-solving in economic and social issues (and especially with its Commission on the Status of Women [CSW]) through lobbying of delegates to raise awareness and cultivate supporters. TFNs also consult with UN agencies and regional commissions and attend meetings with

Tools for a Populist Uprising *by Noah Grant and Layla Aslani*

What can you do to make a difference? The following suggestions can help you collaborate with others to create a movement for social change. Think about a pressing issue for women around the world that you'd like to address. How can these tips help you begin to organize to do something about that issue?

HOW TO CROSS THE DIVIDE[1]

Before you talk, listen. Attend community gatherings. Get to know the people you want to reach and listen to their hopes and fears.

Discuss things that connect you, like being a parent or dealing with high gas prices, to build trust before bringing up issues that might spark disagreement.

Highlight others' points of view. For example, talk about how an Afghani villager feels about us attacking their country.

Avoid attacks on politicians or others who hold different views and the United States.

Focus on why the issues matter to you. Speak from your heart and experience.

Avoid jargon-filled language. Ask yourself if you come across as friendly or as a know-it-all.

Avoid emphasizing problems. Suggest actions people can take, and talk about examples of success.

HOW TO GET MEDIA ATTENTION

Find a newsworthy angle on your event or cause. Human interest, controversy, civil disobedience, superlatives (first, biggest) help.

Create a short press release. Make it accessible and factual, with contact information.

Find journalists who cover issues related to your own.

Develop a 30-second pitch for your story. Don't lie or exaggerate—build a reputation for accuracy.

Highlight previous coverage of your issue when pitching your story.

Identify knowledgeable and articulate spokespeople. An unexpected spokesperson (a veteran for peace or a doctor for single-payer health care) can be especially interesting to a journalist.

Don't give up if journalists aren't interested. Correct them if they get the story wrong, and thank those who cover it well.

HOW TO BUILD A COALITION

Identify a goal that is widely shared, for example, increased support for education. Avoid taking positions on unrelated issues; learn to respectfully "agree to disagree" on topics not essential to your purpose.

Research potential allies who share your concerns, including religious, political, civic, and neighborhood groups.

Explore participants' interest and concerns about collaborating, and explore ways to address both.

Structure decision making so that power is shared among coalition members and timely action is possible.

Clarify your plan. Set short-term and long-term goals. Choose among strategy options: large, public campaigns, behind-the-scenes lobbying, popular education, etc.

Encourage coalition partners to reach out to their own network of friends and allies to widen support.

HOW TO BUILD TRUST[2]

Offer reciprocal liberty. Each of us relies on society's commitment to freedom to assure our own liberty. I'll respect your liberty if you'll respect mine.

Remember that diversity includes diversity you don't like. Treat your opposition with fairness and respect, as potential allies rather than as certain enemies.

Bust a few stereotypes, and start thinking about somebody else's problems. You'll make new friends and change others' view of you. Gays against pension cutbacks, women for drug reform, blacks for small business, whatever.

Use short-term, easier wins to build momentum for the difficult issues that may take years to get.

Describe a future worth fighting for. Optimism is deeply ingrained in American culture. We need to point out what's wrong without simultaneously casting a pall over others' vision of the future.

HOW TO TAKE DIRECT ACTION[3]

Direct action can bring people together while raising awareness. Here, for example, is a model developed by City Life/Vida Urbana for protesting foreclosures:

Seek advice from an organization that provides legal advice and support for those facing foreclosure.

Canvass the neighborhood to find support. Tell the story of the family involved, and explain how a foreclosure harms the community.

Warn the bank that a protest is planned. Send out press releases.

Gather neighbors, family, friends, faith groups, and organization members at the house for the scheduled foreclosure. Hold signs and use a megaphone to tell the story of the homeowner.

If successful in thwarting the foreclosure, use the extra time to negotiate with the lender.

HOW TO ORGANIZE ONLINE

E-Mail Lists

To keep members of your group informed, set up a Listserv (find them at riseup.net or Google). Listservs allow people to subscribe, unsubscribe, and share files easily.

Write Effective E-Mails

- Get the reader's attention with an interesting hook.
- Make the text straightforward, not wordy, and break it up with bullet points and short paragraphs.
- Include everything the reader needs to take action and ask recipients to forward the e-mail.
- Limit e-mails to once every couple of weeks, except during a campaign climax.

How to Blog

Post short, confident pieces on a single subject. Update frequently, and reference your e-mails, along with information on how to subscribe to your e-mail list. Free blogging sites include: www.blogger.com, www.wordpress.com, and www.sixapart.com/typepad.

Other Uses of New Media

Share photos on Flickr or videos on YouTube. You can link to these shared images from your website, blog, or e-mails.

[1] Source: article by Doug Orbaker
[2] Source: Sam Smith at prorev.com
[3] Source: City Life/Vida Urbana

International intergovernmental organizations (IGOs). By preparing background papers, briefing papers, and reports, and by submitting these documents to IGOs, TFNs increase their expertise and influence on a whole range of issues. Their purpose is to raise new issues (such as gender and trade, women's human rights, and violence against women in war zones) with a view toward influencing policy.

TYPES OF TRANSNATIONAL FEMINIST NETWORKS

In this section I identify four types of TFNs: (1) feminism against neoliberalism; (2) feminism against fundamentalism; (3) feminism against imperialism and war; and (4) feminist humanitarianism. These networks combine a variety of the strategies discussed above.

Feminism Against Neoliberalism

In the latter part of the 1990s, alarmed by the global reach of neoliberalism, feminist scholar-activists began addressing issues of globalization and the new global trade agenda. You will recall that neoliberal economic policies emphasize free markets, privatization, and trade and financial liberalization, an international division of labor and cheap, feminized, labor forces. Numerous workshops were organized and publications produced to increase knowledge about the technical details of trade liberalization and its gender dynamics. Of particular concern was that neoliberal policies with their flexible labor markets, privatization of public goods, commercialization of all manner of services, and "free trade" threatened the economic security of workers, small producers, and local industries. Policies such as SAPs placed a heavy burden on women and children, increasing their poverty and vulnerability. As already mentioned, SAPs, with their prescribed measures of privatization, denationalization, and trade liberalization, paved the way for the global spread of neoliberalism, especially after the collapse of communism in the early 1990s (Moghadam, 2009).

TFNs such as DAWN, WIDE, WEDO, and others participated in the critique of neo-liberalism, arguing that new rules of global free trade undermined existing national laws protecting workers and the environment. They also argued that WTO intellectual property provisions allowed large corporations to appropriate (through patents) the knowledge and products of "developing" countries and their local communities. Additionally, transnational feminists argued that employment losses and dislocations brought about by new international trade agreements would be disproportionately borne by women and children (WIDE, 1998; Wichterich, 1999).

TFNs have been active in preparing documents and analyzing the policies and activities of multinational corporations, national governments, and global financial organizations like the World Bank, the International Monetary Fund, and the WTO. They emphasize the corporate bias of these financial institutions that initiates and supports policies undermining the well-being of workers and the poor, citing evidence that such institutions conduct deliberations in secret and are not subject to rules guaranteeing transparency and accountability. These and other transnational feminist groups have joined broad coalitions such as Jubilee 2000, mentioned above, and participate in what is known as the "global justice movement" dedicated to principles of **g**lobal justice for all; **r**espect for the earth; the knowledge that "**a**bundance and freedom are possible"; **c**reativity at work, or respect for all types of human labor; and **e**conomic democracy (GRACE principles) (http://www.globaljusticemovement.org/index.htm). It is important to note, however, that the global feminist agenda on neoliberalism preceded that of the global justice movement by about a decade.

Another example of transnational mobilizing around issues of neoliberalism is the World March of Women, initiated in 1998 by the *Fédération des Femmes du Québec* in Montreal, Canada. It culminated in 2000 in a series of coordinated marches and other actions held around the world to protest poverty and violence against women. Nearly 6,000 organizations from 159 countries and territories were represented in these rallies and marches. The initiative's "Advocacy Guide to Women's World Demands" emphasized the ways the world-system is governed by forces associated with neoliberal capitalism and patriarchy that cause poverty and violence against women. It proposed concrete measures that included an end to SAPs and their associated cutbacks in social budgets and public services. The "Advocacy Guide" also endorsed implementation of new taxes on international finance and such changes to global governance as a democratization of the UN (including the Security Council) and establishment of a World Council for Economic and Financial Security. These demands were presented to the president of the World Bank in 2000 (Moghadam, 2005).

Continuing its activities to this day, the World March of Women remains an important actor within international movements for social justice. In 2005, the World March of Women launched another global mobilization centered on the Women's Global Charter for Humanity. This action highlighted differences in feminist perspectives should unity, inclusion, and effective action be preserved. As a result, while the run-up to the 2005 mobilization entailed such compromises on the network's agenda as language pertaining to abortion and homosexuality, it had the effect of being more inclusive and avoided alienating groups such as those from Africa and India. While painful to some members, the compromise decision was important to the goal of building a global social movement with a collective identity (Dufour and Giraud, 2007).

TFNs Against Neoliberalism

Transnational Feminist Network	Web Site	Location
Development Alternatives with Women for a New Era (DAWN)	http://www.dawn.org.fj/	Fiji
Network Women in Development Europe (WIDE)	http://www.eurosur.org/wide/home.htm	Brussels, etc.
Women's Environment and Development Organization (WEDO)	http://www.wedo.org/	New York
Women's International Coalition for Economic Justice (WICEJ)	http://www.wicej.addr.com/	U.S.
International Women's Tribune Center (IWTC)	http://www.iwtc.org/	U.S.

Feminism Against Fundamentalisms

The 1980s saw not just the spread of neoliberalism and diminishment of Keynesian economics with its focus on government intervention and welfare policies, but also a rise and expansion of religious fundamentalist movements of various types, including Christian and Islamist movements. Fundamentalist religious movements, as Karen McCarthy Brown (1994) argues, construct their identities in opposition to an "external other" whose identity is perceived as different from, opposite to, and, importantly, less valuable than, their identity or identities. Fundamentalism requires an external other to create a sense of unity and maintain subcultural boundaries. This is because fundamentalists understand themselves in opposition to others who are not like them and who may pose a (perceived) threat to them. McCarthy Brown adds that fundamentalist men also pay great attention to controlling the "other" among them—women and children. Since controlling the external other is not actually possible, fundamentalist men may transfer their focus to the close and familiar "others" in their lives who can be controlled.

Christian fundamentalism utilizes a literal reading of the Bible to reinforce gender roles and hierarchies as God-ordained. It claims that male headship over women is part of the divine order of creation and that women's primary tasks include being wives and mothers. It also opposes women's leadership in the church, as well as the movements for gay and abortion rights and women's rights generally.

It was in the 1980s and 1990s that Christian fundamentalism in the United States increased dramatically. During these years of President Ronald Reagan's administration, Republican politics and the Christian Right became considerably more intertwined, with far-reaching implications for women's rights globally. For example, at the 1984 global population and development conference in Mexico City, Reagan announced a global "gag rule" for non-U.S. family planning NGOs. Under the gag order, NGOs receiving family planning funding from United States Agency for International Development (USAID) could not use even their own funds to provide or refer clients to abortion services, or offer counseling or medical advice on other issues if abortion was offered in the range of options available at the clinic or center. These policies were followed by other U.S. presidents, notably George W. Bush, who was influenced by Christian fundamentalism.

Also in the 1980s, fundamentalist Southern Baptists took over the Southern Baptist Convention, adopting increasingly restrictive statements about women's roles in family, church, and society. Southern Baptists are the largest Protestant denomination in the United States with nearly 16 million members and more than 5000 missionaries worldwide.

Another significant development among fundamentalist Christians within the past decade is the "quiverfull movement." Proponents of quiverfull theology suggest that married couples should not use birth control but should have as many children as God gives them. Some even suggest childlessness is a sinful act. Of course, requiring women to have as many children as possible controls them and limits their opportunities for education and employment. Finally, in early 2009, a small group of fundamentalist Christians in Singapore attempted to take over AWARE (Association of Women for Action and Research), a 25-year-old women's rights organization. They enlisted a large group of new members who joined at the last moment before showing up to vote in a new fundamentalist leadership that was also antigay. At the next general meeting, however, over 3000 people showed up and overwhelmingly passed a vote of "no confidence" in the new leadership and elected a new executive committee that was more diverse and representative of a wide range of races, faiths, and backgrounds.

While fundamentalist Christian movements have been predominant among evangelicals (the Protestant Christian movement with a high regard for Biblical authority and which believes in the need for personal conversion or being "born again"), the Catholic Church has been criticized for limiting women's rights, especially in its opposition to contraception and abortion rights—although it has played a very positive role in the expansion of girls' education. Feminists have challenged the church's position on contraception and on women's religious leadership. For example, Women Priests, an online organization for women in Catholic ministry, is a nonprofit organization based in the U.K. that advocates for the ordination of women in the Catholic Church. Catholics for Choice is a nonprofit organization formed in 1973 as a voice for Catholics who support women's rights to follow their conscience in matters of sexuality and health. The mission of Catholics for Choice is to shape and advance sexual and reproductive ethics based on justice, reflecting a commitment to women's well-being and respect, and affirming the capacity of women and men to make moral decisions about their lives.

Many Christian feminists organize their opposition to fundamentalism through women's organizations in their own denominations, such as Baptist Women in Ministry, or they join with international ecumenical women's organizations, such as Church Women United. While these organizations may not explicitly call themselves feminist, they can become a primary place for Christian feminists to organize and work with others toward equality and justice. Baptist Women in Ministry (www.bwim.info) was formed in 1983 in response to fundamentalist opposition to women in ministry within the Southern Baptist Convention. The group works to advocate for the ordination of women and to support women in ministry. Church Women United (www.churchwomen.org) engages women from 26 Christian denominations in social action and community building. Again, while the organization does not explicitly label itself feminist, many feminists find great affinity with the group and its work on behalf of women.

Responses to Christian fundamentalism through specifically transnational networks include the Evangelical and Ecumenical Women's Caucus that supports Christian feminists through educational and networking opportunities. The organization originated as a caucus of Evangelicals for Social Action in 1974, holding its first national conference in 1975. While located in the United States, the group is international and invites membership across all forms of difference, including sexual identity, and promotes itself as an inclusive organization. The group affirms gender justice or equality between women and men and advocates women's ordination in religious organizations. In addition, organizations like Women Advancing Freedom and Equality (WAFE) seek to eliminate religious fundamentalism in all faiths, believing religious extremism in all its forms serves as a key source of gender discrimination. They emphasize that the denial of women's rights in the name of God is a serious blasphemy, and they oppose the ways many political leaders call on God or placate their country's priests to justify women's subjugation.

The second form of fundamentalism addressed in this section is Islamic fundamentalism, which demands introduction and strict application, or reinforcement and strengthening, of existing Islamic norms and laws. Islamist movements—which began to spread first in the Middle East and then across the Muslim world in the 1980s—are religio-political in that they both adhere to a fundamentalist interpretation of the faith and insist that all national laws and policies be derived from Islamic law, or *Sharia*. In addition to the prohibition of alcohol and usury (the charging of unreasonable or relatively high rates of interest on loans), Islamic law in its orthodox application compels women to veil in public. Muslim family law—which regulates marriage, divorce, child custody, inheritance, and other aspects of family relations—puts women in a subordinate position. Dating from the Middle Ages and reflecting the four Sunni schools of jurisprudence that were classified in the modern period of state-building, Muslim family law place females under the authority of male kin, and wives under the control of husbands. Men have more rights and privileges than women, and Muslim citizens more than non-Muslim citizens.

Beginning in the 1980s, responses to these developments came from expatriate Iranian women in Europe and the United States and by South Asian feminists in the U.K. The Sisterhood Is Global Institute, for example, continued through the 1990s under the leadership of expatriate Iranian feminist Mahnaz Afkhami and emerged as a highly visible TFN dedicated to Muslim women's human rights. This institute has sponsored training workshops, conferences, policy dialogues, manuals, and publications to further their goals. In 2000, Afkhami formed the Women's Learning Partnership for Development, Peace, and Rights (WLP).

Another key example of feminism against fundamentalism is the international solidarity network Women Living Under Muslim Laws (WLUML) formed in July 1984 by nine women from eight different countries. Key figures such as Marieme Hélie-Lucas of Algeria and France, Salma Sobhan of Bangladesh, Ayesha Imam of Nigeria, and Khawar Mumtaz and Farida Shaheed of Pakistan were concerned about changes in family laws in their countries, the rise of fundamentalism and aggressive Islamist movements, and threats to the legal status and social positions of women in Muslim-majority societies. Tasks for the network included creation of international links between women in Muslim countries in order to exchange information on their situations, struggles, and strategies. The network also hoped to strengthen and reinforce women's initiatives and struggles through publications, exchanges, and an Alert for Action system (Hélie-Lucas, 1993).

Nawal El Saadawi

Nawal El Saadawi was born in a small village near Cairo in 1931 to parents who were a mix of both traditional and progressive. Like many young rural girls, El Saadawi was forced to undergo female genital cutting, an issue about which she would write passionately years later. Her parents also insisted on their children's education, and so El Saadawi eventually attended the University of Cairo and went on to practice psychiatry. She became Egypt's Director of Public Health Education and married another doctor, Sherif Hetata, who shared her left-leaning views. By the early 1970s she had begun to write both fiction and nonfiction. *Women and Sex* was considered so controversial among conservative political and religious leaders that in 1972 they forced the Ministry of Health to remove her from her post. She also lost her job as chief editor of the journal *Health*. In 1977 she published *The Hidden Face of Eve,* a feminist examination of women's status in Arab societies. In this work, she explored such issues as female genital mutilation, violence against women, virginity, sexual relationships, and marriage and divorce, situating her discussions in the social, political, and religious contexts of the Arab world. In 1981, she was arrested for "crimes against the state" after criticizing the rule of Egyptian president Anwar Sadat and spent two months in Qanatir Women's Prison. In 1982 she founded the Arab Women's Solidarity Association (www.awsa.net) to promote women's participation in political, social, religious, and cultural life. The Egyptian government closed the association's Cairo office in 1991 when the organization criticized the Gulf War. In 1983 she published her *Memoirs from the Women's Prison*. After her release from prison, her name appeared on fundamentalists' death lists, and eventually she moved to the United States for a few years to teach as a visiting professor. She returned to Egypt in 1996. In 2001, religious fundamentalists tried to force El Saadawi's divorce from Sherif Hetata on the grounds that her radical views put her outside the bounds of Islam, but the courts dismissed the case after international outcry. In 2004, she announced she would run for Egypt's presidency, but current president Hosni Mubarak manipulated

the electoral process to ensure he would win reelection, and El Sadaawi withdrew from the race early in 2005. El Saadawi has continued to write and advocate for women, and she continues to be a target for religious fundamentalists. In 2008, fundamentalists attempted to have her stripped of her Egyptian citizenship and to have all of her books banned from Egypt, but the court dismissed the case against her, arguing that the law does not allow removal of citizenship for holding controversial opinions. To find out more about Nawal El Saadawi, read her *Walking Through Fire: A Life of Nawal El Saadawi*. Her novels include *Woman at Point Zero* and *The Fall of the Imam*. She has won numerous literary awards and has received honorary doctorates from four institutions, including the University of Illinois at Chicago.

Read an interview with Nawal El Saadawi on *Women's E-News:* http://www.womensenews.org/article.cfm/dyn/aid/1726.
Read another interview with *Newsline* at: http://www.newsline.com.pk/NewsJul2006/interviewjul.htm.

Fiercely antifundamentalist since its inception, WLUML began to issue warnings as early as 1990 (at a conference on comparative fundamentalisms and women that I organized in Helsinki, Finland) about an "Islamist international" with the organizational, human, financial, and military means to threaten secularists, feminists, and democrats. In the 1990s, WLUML called for solidarity with women of Afghanistan under Mujahidin, and later Taliban, rule, and for the support of Algerian women during the wave of Islamist terror that same decade. In both cases, WLUML took a strong position against those responsible for violations of women's human rights, whether these were Afghan warlords or jihadists associated with Algeria's militant Islamist parties. WLUML has been especially critical of Western governments for their support of Islamists in the 1980s or for the granting of political asylum by European governments.

WLUML's central activity is its solidarity and support work. The network receives and responds to appeals as well as initiative campaigns pertaining to violations of women's human rights (Shaheed, 1994). In line with its focus on monitoring the human rights of women in Muslim countries, extending solidarity, and raising international awareness, WLUML has issued numerous Action Alerts and publicized the situation of Muslim women and their relationship to legal codes in various countries. WLUML also reports on the activities of women's organizations and has initiated petition drives in support of women under harsh regimes. Exemplifying the fluid and flexible nature of contemporary transnational social movements, such work is maintained through the activities of "networkers" who communicate largely via the Internet but who meet occasionally to agree on plans. The January 2006 meeting in Dakar that produced the most recent Plan of Action was attended by 50 networkers from 22 countries, but input was also received by affiliates via e-mail. This double strategy of real and virtual communication enabled the network to agree on four priority issues: (1) peace-building and resisting the impact of militarization; (2) preserving multiple identities and exposing fundamentalisms; (3) widening debate about women's bodily autonomy; and (4) promoting and protecting women's equality under laws.

Feminism Against War and Imperialism

Feminists and women's groups have long been involved in peace work in their focus on causes and consequences of conflict, methods of conflict resolution and peace building, and conditions necessary for human security (see, for example, Enloe, 2007; Moghadam,

Facts About Nations

To find out more about the demographics and status of women's human rights in individual countries, visit the Web sites listed below. There you can discover facts about each nation's sex ratio, birth rate, infant mortality rate, life expectancy, fertility rate, HIV/AIDS prevalence rates, ethnic groups, religions, languages, literacy, and suffrage. You can also learn about each country's laws on domestic violence, rape, trafficking, marriage, and inheritance. For each activist profile in the textbook, go to these sites to learn more about the countries where these activists work.

http://www.unifem.org/progress/2008/

https://www.cia.gov/library/publications/the-world-factbook/index.html

http://www.state.gov/g/drl/rls/hrrpt/2007/

http://www.infoplease.com/countries.html

http://travel.nationalgeographic.com/places/countries/index.html

TFNs Against Fundamentalism

Transnational Feminist Network	Web Site	Location
Evangelical and Ecumenical Women's Caucus	http://www.eewc.com	U.S.
Women Advancing Freedom and Equality (WAFE) (formerly Women Against Fundamentalism and for Equality)	http://wafe-women.org	U.K.
Association for Women's Rights in Development (AWID)	http://www.awid.org/	Canada
Equality Now	http://www.equalitynow.org/	U.S. & Kenya
Women's Human Rights Network (WHRNet)	http://www.whrnet.org/	N/A
Women's Caucus for Gender Justice	http://www.iccwomen.org/	U.S.
Sisterhood Is Global Institute (SIGI)	http://www.sigi.org/	Canada
Arab Women's Solidarity Association (AWSA)	http://www.awsa.net/	U.S.
Women Living Under Muslim Laws (WLUML)	http://www.wluml.org/	Nigeria, Pakistan, U.K.
Women's Learning Partnership (WLP)	http://www.learningpartnership.org	U.S.
Women for Women International	http://www.womenforwomen.org	U.S.

2007). One of the world's oldest peace organizations, and, indeed, one of the oldest TFNs, is the Women's International League for Peace and Freedom (WILPF), founded in 1915 by 1300 women activists from Europe and North America opposed to what became known as World War I (see sidebar). The activities of antimilitarist and human rights groups such as WILPF, Women Strike for Peace (U.S.), the Women of Greenham Common (U.K.), and the Mothers and Grandmothers of the Plaza de Mayo (Argentina) are well known, and their legacy lies in ongoing efforts to "feminize" or "engender" peace, nuclear disarmament, and human rights.

As discussed in later chapters, cultural and economic globalization has been accompanied by a new wave of conflicts in Afghanistan, Bosnia, Central Africa, and the Middle East that violated women's human rights. Women's groups have responded by underscoring the specific vulnerability of women and girls during wartime, the pervasive nature of sexual abuse, and the need to include women's voices in peace negotiations. They also formed a number of new women-led peace, human rights, and humanitarian organizations as well as more professionalized networks. These include Women in Black, Medica Mondiale, Women Waging Peace, and Women for Women International. Advocacy networks and scholar-activists produced research to show that women's groups had been effective in peace-building in Northern Ireland as well as in Bosnia and Central Africa.

In response to these efforts, the UN Security Council issued a resolution embraced by women's groups, if not governments themselves. In 2000 the UN Security Council in its Proclamation on International Women's Day (March 8) recognized gender equality as an integral component of peace. Later that year it convened a special session to consider the situation of women in armed conflict, and in October 2000, passed Resolution 1325 calling on governments (as well as the UN Security Council itself) to include women in negotiations and settlements with respect to conflict-resolution and peace-building. See below for key points of the resolution.

While Security Council Resolution 1325 was widely hailed as a historic achievement in a domain usually considered the preserve of men, its importance was diminished not long afterwards when new conflicts erupted postponing the resolution in the name of the "global war on terror." The aftermath of September 11, 2001, and the U.S. invasion of Iraq in 2003 galvanized women across the globe to support existing peace organizations or build new ones. Women participated in huge numbers in antiwar activities in India, Pakistan, Turkey, Tunisia, and South Africa. As discussed in chapter 12 on war and peace, in 2002 an important group to emerge from this context was the U.S.-based Code Pink: Women for Peace. The group's name is a play on the national security color codes established by President George W. Bush in the aftermath of September 11: "While Bush's color-coded alerts are based on fear, the Code Pink alert is based on compassion and is a feisty call for women and men to 'wage peace'" (http://www.codepink4peace.org). The organization identifies as "a women-initiated grassroots peace and social justice movement" working to end war and to redirect resources into healthcare, education and other "life-affirming" activities. Toward this end, Code Pink works with other feminist and social justice networks, including the National Organization for Women (NOW), United for Peace and Justice, the humanitarian women's human rights organization MADRE (discussed in more detail in the next section), Women in Black, and Women for Women International. Code Pink is also active in CARA, the Council for Assisting Refugee Academics. Together these coalitions engage in operational activities, information exchange, and solidarity work, as well as direct action to protest government policies or inaction. Indeed, cofounders Medea Benjamin, Jodie Evans,

LEARNING ACTIVITY   **Women's International League for Peace and Freedom**

In 1915, a group of women met in The Hague, Netherlands, to protest World War I. These women, also active in the suffrage movement, saw the connections between women's rights and peace. Out of the global gathering of women came the Women's International League for Peace and Freedom, one of the oldest peace organizations in the world.

Visit the WILPF's web site at www.wilpf.org.

The League's first president was Jane Addams. To learn more about her work, follow the link to Hull-House. Addams was the first U.S. woman to win the Nobel Peace Prize. To learn more about the prize, follow the link to the Nobel Foundation's site.

The vision and mission statements of the organization are as follows:

VISION STATEMENT

WILPF envisions a transformed world at peace, where there is racial, social, and economic justice for all people everywhere—a world in which:

- The needs of all people are met in a fair and equitable manner
- All people equally participate in making the decisions that affect them
- The interconnected web of life is acknowledged and celebrated in diverse ways and communities
- Human societies are designed and organized for sustainable existence

MISSION STATEMENT

WILPF members create the peaceful transformation they wish to see in the world by making connections that:

- Provide continuity with the past so that knowledge of historical events and patterns informs current activities for change
- Create analysis and action that reflect and reinforce each other
- Link and challenge root causes of oppression, especially racism, sexism, heterosexism, militarism, economic disparity, and political disempowerment
- Build and strengthen relationships and movements for justice, peace, and radical democracy

What are the organization's current issue priorities? What are the connections between these priorities and women's rights?

Check out the WILPF toolkit. What can you do to get involved?

and Gael Murphy already had considerable prior experience in activism and lobbying prior to initiating Code Pink. Benjamin helped establish Global Exchange in 1988; Evans had worked for former California Governor Jerry Brown; and Murphy was a long-time public health advisor in Africa and the Caribbean.

Innovation and creativity are key features of Code Pink activism. Protesters have been known to hand out "pink slips," for example, to politicians as forms of protest, parodying

Security Council Resolution 1325

- Increasing the representation of women at all decision-making levels

- Integrating a gender perspective into peacekeeping missions

- Appointing more women as special representatives and envoys of the Secretary-General

- Supporting women's grassroots organizations in their peace initiatives

- Involving women as participants in peace negotiations and agreements

- Ensuring protection of and respect for human rights of women and girls

- Protecting women and girls from gender-based violence

- Integrating a gender perspective into disarmament, demobilization, and reintegration of former combatants

the notices given to employees when their jobs are being terminated. In 2003 Code Pink activists staged a four-month vigil at the White House and a rally with over 10,000 women marching to honor International Women's Day. The next year they organized protests against George W. Bush's second presidential inauguration. Wearing pink costumes and engaging in daring acts of public protest, Code Pink activists have become known for infiltrating congressional meetings, unfurling antiwar banners, and shouting antiwar slogans and badgering members of Congress on their stand on the war, military spending, healthcare for veterans, and support for Iraqi civilians. In one bold act in 2007 that received much national and international coverage, a Code Pink activist, her hands painted red, approached then-secretary of state Condoleeza Rice on Capitol Hill when she was testifying before the House Foreign Relations Committee. The activist accused her of having the blood of the Iraqi people on her hands.

In addition to Code Pink, networks such as the Women's Initiatives for Gender Justice, Women in Conflict Zones Network, PeaceWomen, and Women Waging Peace engage in research, lobbying, and advocacy to ensure that war criminals are brought to justice and that local women's peace groups are recognized. They also advocate for the International Criminal Court (established in 1999 as the first international war crimes court) and for Security Council Resolution 1325 discussed above. In 2007, six women who were Nobel Peace Prize winners formed the Nobel Women's Initiative and organized its first international conference in Galway, Ireland, attended by about 75 women from across the globe. The conference focused on women, conflict, peace, and security in the Middle East (www.nobelwomensinitiative.org).

Feminist Humanitarianism

The final type of TFN described here is feminist humanitarianism and international solidarity. While almost all TFNs may be regarded as internationalist and solidaristic inasmuch as they are concerned about the plight of "sisters" across borders and boundaries

TFNs Against War and Imperialism

Transnational Feminist Network	Web Site	Location
Association of Women of the Mediterranean Region (AWMR)	http://digilander.libero.it/awmr/int/	U.S. & Cyprus
Women for Women International (WWI)	http://www.womenforwomen.org/	U.S.
Women in Black	http://balkansnet.org/wib/ http://www.womeninblack.net/	Various countries
Women's International League for Peace and Freedom (WILPF)	http://www.wilpf.org/	Switzerland & U.S.
Code Pink	http://www.codepink4peace.org/	U.S.
Grandmothers for Peace International	http://www.grandmothersfor-peace.org	U.S.
MADRE	http://www.madre.org	U.S.
Medica Mondiale	http://www.medicamondiale.org/_en/projekte/jugoslawien/	Germany

of nationality, religion, and class, not all engage in feminist humanitarianism as operational work. Feminist humanitarianism consists of moral support and material assistance for those in conflict zones or repressive states. Such actions to alleviate the suffering of women and children and efforts to meet their basic needs are informed by strategic goals for achieving women's human rights and gender equality. Such goals tend to be framed by a broad critique of international relations, including militarism and war. Note that this notion of "humanitarian" differs from the so-called humanitarian interventions conceptualized by nations to justify bombing Serbia or invading Iraq. Organizations that engage in feminist humanitarianism include MADRE, Medica Mondiale Kosovo, Women for Women International, and Code Pink. In addition to its strategy of direct action discussed in the previous section, Code Pink's action repertoire includes feminist humanitarianism and international solidarity, as evidenced by support for the Iraqi people and coordination of the historic "Families for Peace Delegation" with members of the antiwar group United for Peace and Justice and relatives of both U.S. military personnel killed in action and 9/11 victims. According to one report: "In an inspiring act of humanity and generosity, they brought with them US$650,000 in medical supplies and other aid for the Fallujah refugees who were forced from their homes when the Americans destroyed their city. Although the American press failed to cover this unprecedented visit, the mission garnered enormous attention from Al-Jazeera, Al-Arabiyya, and Dubai and Iranian television, who witnessed first hand the depths of American compassion" (Brim, 2003, pp. 10–12; Milazzo, 2005, p. 103).

The feminist humanitarian organization MADRE began its work in the early 1980s during the war in Nicaragua when the United States sponsored right-wing Contra rebels.

10 Policies for a Better America

In our increasingly globalized world, what happens in the United States has tremendous impact on the rest of the world, and vice versa. When we work for justice within the United States, we also work for justice in our relationships with the rest of the world. Often in our studies of other countries and cultures, we have a tendency to critique their problems without examining our own. But what would make the United States a better country? The following chart is the result of a poll by *Yes!* magazine about what Americans want in order to create a better nation.

ECONOMY

- Repair and rebuild neglected bridges, rail-roads, schools, and other infrastructure, designing for climate change and a post-petroleum world.
- Extend unemployment insurance benefits.
- Provide tax relief to middle- and low-income families, and reinstate fair taxes on high-wealth individuals and corporate profits.
- Adopt the Employee Free Choice Act to increase opportunities to unionize.

  67% Favor public works projects to create jobs.
  55% Favor expanding unemployment benefits.
  73% Say corporations don't pay a fair share of taxes.
  76% Support tax cuts for lower- and middle-income people.
  71% Say unions help their members; 53% say unions help the economy in general.

FAMILIES

- Make the minimum wage a "living wage" adequate to keep working families out of poverty.
- Provide everyone vacation and family leave.
- Provide gay and lesbian couples with the legal protections afforded to straight couples.
- Make bankruptcy and foreclosure laws protect families first, not predatory lenders.

  64% Are not confident that life for our children's generation will be better than it has been for us.
  80% Support increasing the federal minimum wage.
  59% Favor guaranteeing two weeks or more of paid vacation.
  65% Believe same-sex couples should be allowed to marry or form civil unions.
  75% Want to limit rate increases on adjustable-rate mortgages.

CONSTITUTION

- Fully restore habeas corpus for all people in U.S. custody.
- Protect our right to privacy and freedom from warrantless search and seizure.
- Keep the Internet free of corporate and government censorship and obstruction. Protect "net neutrality."
- Restore the balance of power between the executive, legislative, and judicial branches of government.

  70% Support restoring habeas corpus rights for detainees at Guantanamo.
  59% Would like the next president to do more to protect civil liberties.
  58% Believe a court warrant should be required to listen to the telephone calls of people in the U.S.
  68% Believe the president should not act alone to fight terrorism without the checks and balances of the courts or Congress.

ENERGY AND CLIMATE

- Take a leadership role in reducing our own greenhouse gas emissions.
- Maximize the conservation and efficient use of existing energy supplies.
- Launch and fund ambitious research and development programs, offer tax credits, invest in public works projects, and focus government procurement to jump-start renewable energy deployment.
- Invest in public transit and intercity rail.
- Tax carbon; use revenues for renewables and to help ratepayers.

   79% Favor mandatory controls on greenhouse gas emissions.
   76% Believe that oil is running out and a major effort is needed to replace it.
   90% Favor higher auto fuel efficiency standards.
   75% Favor clean electricity, even with higher rates.
   72% Support more funding for mass transit.

HEALTH CARE

- Offer all Americans the option of joining a single-payer national health insurance program, paid for with tax dollars.
- Break the drug companies' monopoly and lower drug prices by allowing Americans to buy prescription drugs abroad.

   73% Believe our health care system is in crisis or has "major problems."
   64% Believe the government should provide national health insurance coverage for all Americans, even if it would raise taxes.
   55% Favor one health insurance program covering all Americans, administered by the government, and paid for by taxpayers.
   69% Believe the government should make it easier to buy prescription drugs from other countries.

FOREIGN RELATIONS

- Lead global effort to abolish nuclear weapons.
- Rule out unilateral attacks, deploying weapons in space, and torture.
- Phase out U.S. role as global police, and instead work through the U.N. and other international agencies to develop and enforce international law.
- Work with other countries to improve global health and environment.

   73% Favor abolishing nuclear weapons, with verification. 80% favor banning weapons in space.
   81% Oppose torture and support following the Geneva Conventions.
   76% Say the U.S. should not play the role of global police.
   85% Say that the U.S. should not initiate military action without support from allies.
   79% Say the U.N. should be strengthened.

IRAQ AND IRAN

- Develop a timetable for a withdrawal of U.S. troops from Iraq.
- Build no long-term military bases in Iraq. Leave control of Iraq's oil in the hands of Iraqis.
- Fund an international effort to help restore the economy and infrastructure of Iraq.

- Abolish future uses of private mercenaries.
- Enter into negotiations with Iran about unclear issues and regional stability. End threats of attack and attempts to destabilize the Iranian government.

  63% Want U.S. forces home from Iraq within a year.
  57% Say going to war in Iraq was the wrong decision.
  47% Favor using diplomacy with Iran. 7% favor military action.
  69% Believe we should use diplomatic and economic means to fight terrorism, rather than the military.

ELECTIONS

- Provide public financing for elections campaigns.
- Bring back the Fairness Doctrine and get broadcasters to open the people's airwaves to free campaign information.
- Require voter-verified paper ballots that are audited and can be recounted.
- End partisan districting and voter-roll purges.
- Fully implement the Voting Rights Act and enforce existing laws against vote suppression.
- Restore voting rights to ex-felons who have served their sentences.

  86% Say big companies have too much power.
  74% Favor voluntary public financing of campaigns.
  66% Believe intentional acts are likely to cause significant voting machines errors.
  80% Say ex-felons should have their voting rights restored.

CRIMINAL JUSTICE

- Drop punitive sentences for drug possession and other nonviolent offenses in favor of substance-abuse treatment, fines, community service, and restitution.
- Offer training and counseling to prepare inmates for a crime-free life after release.
- Channel youth into schools and jobs, not jail.

  65% Believe attacking social problems is a better cure for crime than more law enforcement.
  87% Support rehabilitation rather than a "punishment-only" system.
  81% Say job training is "very important" for reintegrating people leaving prison. 79% say drug treatment is very important.

IMMIGRATION

- Implement trade policies that strengthen, not undermine, rural economies south of the border, reducing the poverty and displacement that spur migration. Start by ditching NAFTA.
- Increase minimum wage and worker protection for all, documented and undocumented.
- Provide a pathway to legal status and citizenship for immigrants already here.

  56% Believe NAFTA should be renegotiated.
  80% Favor allowing undocumented immigrants living in the U.S. to stay and apply for citizenship if they have a job and pay back taxes.
  64% Believe that on the whole, immigration is good for the country.

As a progressive women's organization, MADRE invariably champions feminist causes and pursues feminist humanitarianism, often in opposition to U.S. foreign policy. Partnering with sister organizations in Cuba, Nicaragua, El Salvador, Palestine, Sudan, and Haiti, among other countries, MADRE has consistently provided aid for women and children. For example, MADRE has worked in partnership to provide emergency aid to displaced women and families in Darfur, sending about a half-million U.S. dollars worth of clothing and bedding to small refugee camps in 2005 (http://madre.org/programs/index.html).

Key Features of Feminist Humanitarian Networks

Network	Core Goals and Activities	Country Projects	$ Disbursed
MADRE (1983) United States	Gender, economic and environmental justice; programs in peace building; women's health and freedom from violence; mobilizes resources for partner organizations to meet immediate needs of women and their families and develop long-term solutions to the crises they face. www.madre.org/	Sudan, Iraq, Nicaragua, Cuba, Haiti, Guatemala, Kenya, Peru, Colombia, Panama, Palestine	$22 million since 1983
Women for Women International (1993) United States	Addressing the needs of women in conflict and post-conflict environments; helping to effect transition from victims to active citizens; provides microcredits and business services. http://www.womenforwomen.org/	Afghanistan, Bosnia, Colombia, Iraq, Kosovo, Sudan, Nigeria, Rwanda, DR Congo.	$33 million as of 2006
Medica Mondiale (1999) Germany	Women's human rights and security; "We support traumatised women and girls in war and crisis zones"; medical assistance and counselling; safe houses http://www.medicamondiale.org/_en/projekte/jugoslawien/	Afghanistan, Albania, Bosnia, Cambodia, DR Congo, Aceh, Iraq, Kosovo, Liberia, Sudan, Uganda	Unknown
Code Pink (2003) United States	Against war, militarism; U.S. out of Iraq; solidarity with Iraqi people; support U.S. troops by bringing them home; provided medical supplies for Iraqis. www.codepink4peace.org/	Iraq	Unknown

MADRE's work in Iraq dates back to the 1991 Gulf War when it began collecting an assortment of needed supplies such as milk and medicines for Iraqi families. It continued this work throughout the 1990s, critiquing the detrimental effects of the sanctions regime on women and children. After the 2003 invasion and occupation of Iraq, MADRE partnered with UNICEF/Iraq and provided 25,000 citizens with supplies and emergency aid, including essential drugs and medical supplies to those in need (http://madre.org/programs/Iraq.htm). Working with local feminist partner the Organization of Women's Freedom in Iraq (OWFI), MADRE has helped to address the problem of "honor killings" (where, as discussed in other chapters, women are killed to avenge a notion of "family honor") that have spiked since the invasion began. MADRE has also worked to support the creation of women's shelters for victims of domestic and community violence in cities like Baghdad, Kirkuk, Erbil, and Nasariyeh. The campaign has given rise to a web of shelters and an escape route for Iraqi women (the Underground Railroad for Iraqi Women) run largely by OWFI volunteers (http://www.madre.org/articles/int/honorcrimes.html; personal interview with Yanar Mohammad, May, 2005).

CONCLUSION

Transnational feminism engages with issues of concern to women across national boundaries with the goal of increasing women's status worldwide. In particular, TFNs engage in research, advocacy, lobbying, public protests, and humanitarian assistance to advance women's strategic gender interests as well as to help meet women's practical or basic needs. A common feature of transnational feminism is international solidarity: the extension of support to "sisters" across borders. I close this essay with an ongoing example of transnational feminist activism: the One Million Signatures Campaign. It is a global campaign to support Iranian women's rights activists. (See if you can determine which kind of TFN is involved in this campaign.)

Feminism in Iran has a long and complicated history, but the postrevolutionary period of quietism came to an end at the start of the new millennium, when small networks began meeting and strategizing for change in the country's legal and policy frameworks, notably the family law that places women in a subordinate position within the family. The first public protests took place at the end of the liberal Khatemi presidency and just before the new and very conservative president Ahmadinejad took office in June 2005. Subsequent protests and rallies were broken up by police, and a number of activists arrested. The result of the state's repression was a decision to change the strategy from public protests to a petition drive, and the One Million Signatures Campaign was launched in September 2006. (It was adopted from the highly successful campaign of Moroccan feminists, initiated in the early 1990s: an example of how feminist ideas "travel," in this case from regions within the Global South.)

The Campaign is a grassroots, door-to-door initiative to obtain signatures for a change in family laws and other legal instruments unfavorable to women. The Campaign's activities include collecting signatures by approaching women in their homes. Activists also talk with women on the metro and in parks, shops, and classrooms. They run workshops and write articles in support of women's rights for the Campaign's Web site, Change for Equality (http://www.change4equality.com/english/). Despite its peaceful nature, however, the Campaign has been subject not only to harassment, but to prosecution. Campaign activists have been charged with security crimes, including acting against the state and spreading propaganda against the state. To date, more than 50 Campaign activists—the majority of whom are in their twenties, both men and women, living in Tehran and in the provinces—have been threatened, called into court, arrested, or forbidden to travel abroad. At this writing, two activists remain in prison. What is more, in January 2009, the authorities closed down a long-standing women's magazine, *Zanan*, which was an early exponent of "Islamic feminism."

Women's rights activists in Iran requested international solidarity (1) to support the campaign for law reform toward gender equality, and (2) to bring pressure to bear on the government for the release of feminist protestors. Expatriate Iranian feminists played an important role in helping to mobilize support from groups such as DAWN, WLUML, WLP, and Equality Now, as well as Amnesty International. Such transnational feminist organizing is an example of "cyberactivism" that includes the global circulation via Internet of action alerts and petitions, and the launching of a multilingual Web site, formed in Tehran, that provides extensive information on the campaign.

In these ways, transnational feminism is characterized by a critique of social and gender inequalities and a set of strategies to enhance women's rights within the family and society. These strategies involve networks engaged in research, lobbying, and advocacy for women's human rights and gender equality. They also include bold acts of direct action and acts of cross-border humanitarianism and solidarity. Many TFNs target discriminatory or oppressive laws, policies, and norms; and many take part in global campaigns to alleviate suffering and/or show solidarity with nationally based feminist action. Although many TFNs, along with other global social movements and networks, are based largely in the Global North (or are resourced, staffed, and funded largely from the North), it is important to note the ways such distribution of resources reflect the inequalities associated with the contemporary capitalist world system. While such discrepancies are unavoidable at present, they should not diminish the achievements of transnational feminist solidarity to reverse the logic of the present world-system and improve the lives of women worldwide.

Utilizing such strategies, TFNs are one of the principal organizational forms of a feminism aimed at uniting women worldwide. Central in this work is that of women learning to be allies with and for each other: coming together with conscious understandings of privilege and making commitments toward a politics of engagement that recognizes the difficulties of the struggle. These difficulties are illustrated in the short story reading "Comrades" by South African writer Nadine Gordimer. They are also underscored in Hafsat Abiola's reading, "Edge of the Earth." She makes the case for unity among women through an understanding and respect for our differences. She hopes we might "[bring] together what we have seen, who we have been, as we weave new patterns, streaking the land with our magic."

REFERENCES

Akiko, Y. (1997). Mountain moving day. In Y. Akiko and S. Hamill, S. (Eds.), *River of stars: Selected poems of Yosano Akiko* (p. 105). Boston: Shambhala Press.

Brim, S. (2003, March–April). Report from Baghdad. *Off our backs,* 10–12.

Brown, Karen McCarthy. (1994). *Fundamentalism and the control of women.* In John Stratton Hawley (Ed.), Fundamentalism and gender (pp. 175–201). New York: Oxford University Press.

Dufour, P. and Giraud, I. (2007). The continuity of transnational solidarities in the World March of Women, 2000 and 2005: A collective identity-building approach. *Mobilization,* 12(3), 307–322.

Enloe, C. (2007). *Globalization and militarism: Feminists make the link.* Lanham, MD: Rowman & Littlefield.

Hélie-Lucas, M. (1993). Women living under muslim laws. In J. Kerr (Ed.), *Ours by right: Women's rights as human rights* (pp. 52–65). London and Ottawa: Zed Books and the North-South Institute.

Milazzo, L. (2005). Code Pink: The 21st century mothers of invention. *Development, 48*(2), 100–104.

Moghadam, V. (2005). *Globalizing women: Transnational feminist networks.* Baltimore: The Johns Hopkins University Press.

Moghadam, V. (2007). Peace-building and reconstruction with women: Reflections on Afghanistan, Iraq, and Palestine. In V. Moghadam (Ed.), *From patriarchy to empowerment: Women's participation, movements, and rights in the Middle East, North Africa, and South Asia* (pp. 327–352). Syracuse, NY: Syracuse University Press.

Moghadam, V. (2009). *Globalization and social movements: Islamism, feminism, and the global justice movement.* Lanham, MD: Rowman & Littlefield.

Naples, N. and Desai, M. (Eds.). (2002). *Women's activism and globalization.* London and New York: Routledge.

Shaheed, F. (1994). Controlled or autonomous: Identity and the experience of the network Women Living Under Muslim Laws. WLUML Occasional Paper No. 5.

Wichterich, C. (1999). *The globalized woman: Notes from a future of inequality.* London: Zed Books.

WIDE. (1998) *Trade traps and gender gaps: Women unveiling the market.* Report on WIDE's Annual Conference (held at Jarvenpaa, Finland, 16–18 May 1997). Brussels: Women in Development Europe.

SUGGESTIONS FOR FURTHER READING

Antrobus, P. (2004). *The global women's movement: Issues and strategies for the new century.* London: Zed Books.

Feree, M. M. and Tripp, A. M. (2006). *Global feminism: Transnational women's activism, organizing, and human rights.* New York: New York University Press.

Moghadam, V. (2005). *Globalizing women: Transnational feminist networks.* Baltimore: Johns Hopkins University Press.

Mohanty, C. (2003). *Feminism without borders: Decolonizing theory, practicing solidarity.* Durham, NC: Duke University Press.

Naples, N. (2002). *Women's activism and globalization: Linking local struggles and transnational politics.* New York: Routledge.

Women Still Have a Long Way to Go

Cynthia G. Wagner (2008)

Despite the enactment of more laws and programs to eliminate discrimination, women have yet to achieve full legal, economic, and cultural equality with men even in some of the world's more advanced societies.

This is the conclusion of the UN Committee on the Elimination of Discrimination against Women, a body of the High Commissioner for Human Rights. Its most recent round of ongoing international reports examined the progress—or lack of it—of eight countries in their efforts toward meeting the obligations of the Convention on the Elimination of All Forms of Discrimination against Women (CEDAW). The countries studied were Bolivia, Burundi, Saudi Arabia, France, Lebanon, Luxembourg, Morocco, and Sweden.

The enactment of equality-promoting laws and programs, such as the Family and Domestic Violence Act, is an indicator of progress in Bolivia, but there remains a gap between increased legal protections for women and their ability to access those protections, according to the Committee. Women's access to justice is impeded by their high rates of illiteracy and their lack of information on rights and available legal assistance, particularly in rural areas.

In Burundi and Saudi Arabia, patriarchal attitudes and stereotypes regarding the roles and responsibilities of the sexes are reflected in family laws that continue to perpetuate women's subordination and disadvantage them economically.

The Committee describes as "distinctive" Saudi Arabia's understanding of the principle of equality, "which implied similar rights of women and men as well as complementarities and harmony between women and men, rather than equal rights of women and men." The Committee notes that "there was no contradiction in substance between the Convention and Islamic Sharia" and thus calls on Saudi Arabia "to confirm that international treaties had precedence over domestic laws."

But traditionally male-dominated societies are not the only ones where stereotypes impede women's progress toward equality. In France, for instance, persistent stereotypes are blamed for directing girls and women toward academic specialties that translate into a narrow range of employment options.

The Committee challenges the governments of Sweden, France, and Luxembourg to initiate campaigns encouraging women to bring up complaints of discriminatory treatment. And the mass media could do more to promote more diverse portrayals of women's roles, such as women as breadwinners and not just mothers, caregivers, or—notably in Sweden's case—sexual objects.

Eliminating stereotypes may not eliminate violence or discrimination, but proactive measures by governments to provide equal opportunities for women in the economy and a greater role in decision making would remove the principal obstacles "to women's enjoyment of their fundamental rights," the Committee concludes.

Source: United Nations, Office of the High Commissioner for Human Rights, Palais des Nations, CH-1211 Geneva 10, Switzerland. Web site www.ohchr.org.

Are Women Human?

Catharine A. MacKinnon (2006)

The Universal Declaration of Human Rights defines what a human being is.[1] In 1948, it told the world what a person, as a person, is entitled to. It has been fifty years. Are women human yet?

If women were human, would we be a cash crop shipped from Thailand in containers into New York's brothels?[2] Would we be sexual and reproductive slaves? Would we be bred, worked without pay our whole lives, burned when our dowry money wasn't enough or when men tired of us, starved as widows when our husbands died (if we survived his funeral pyre), sold for sex because we are not valued for anything else? Would we be sold into marriage to priests to atone for our family's sins or to improve our family's earthly prospects? Would we, when allowed to work for pay, be made to work at the most menial jobs and exploited at barely starvation level? Would our genitals be sliced out to "cleanse" us (our body parts are dirt?), to control us, to mark us and define our cultures? Would we be trafficked as things for sexual use and entertainment worldwide in whatever form current technology makes possible?[3] Would we be kept from learning to read and write?[4]

If women were human, would we have so little voice in public deliberations and in government in the countries where we live?[5] Would we be hidden behind veils and imprisoned in houses and stoned and shot for refusing? Would we be beaten nearly to death, and to death, by men with whom we are close? Would we be sexually molested in our families? Would we be raped in genocide to terrorize and eject and destroy our ethnic communities, and raped again in that undeclared war that goes on every day in every country in the world in what is called peacetime?[6] If women were human, would our violation be *enjoyed* by our violators? And, if we were human, when these things happened, would virtually nothing be done about it?

It takes a lot of imagination—and a determinedly blinkered focus on exceptions at the privileged margins—to see a real woman in the Universal Declaration's majestic guarantees of what "everyone is entitled to." After over half a century, just what part of "everyone" doesn't mean us?

The ringing language in Article 1 encourages us to "act towards one another in a spirit of brotherhood." Must we be men before its spirit includes us? Lest this be seen as too literal, if we were all enjoined to "act towards one another in a spirit of sisterhood," would men know it meant them, too? Article 23 encouragingly provides for just pay to "[e]veryone who works." It goes on to say that this ensures a life of human dignity for "himself and his family." Are women nowhere paid for the work we do in our own families because we are not "everyone," or because what we do there is not "work," or just because we are not "him"? Don't women have families, or is what women have not a family without a "himself"? If the someone who is not paid at all, far less the "just and favorable remuneration" guaranteed, is also the same someone who in real life is often responsible for her family's sustenance, when she is deprived of providing for her family "an existence worthy of human dignity," is she not human? And now that "everyone" has had a right "to take part in the government of his country" since the Universal Declaration was promulgated, why are most governments still run mostly by men? Are women silent in the halls of state because we do not have a human voice?

A document that could provide specifically for the formation of trade unions and "periodic holiday with pay" might have mustered the specificity to mention women sometime, other than through "motherhood," which is more bowed to than provided for. If women were human in this document, would domestic violence, sexual violation from birth to death, including in prostitution and pornography, and systematic sexual objectification and denigration of women and girls simply be left out of the explicit language?

Granted, sex discrimination is prohibited. But how can it have been prohibited for all this time, even aspirationally, and the end of all these conditions still not be concretely imagined as part of what a human being, as human, is entitled to? Why is women's entitlement to an end of these conditions still openly debated based on cultural rights, speech rights, religious rights, sexual freedom, free markets—as if women are social signifiers, pimps' speech, sacred or sexual fetishes, natural resources, chattel, everything but human beings?

The omissions in the Universal Declaration are not merely semantic. Being a woman is "not yet a name for a way of being human,"[7] not even in this most visionary of human rights documents. If we measure the reality of women's situation in all its variety against the guarantees of the Universal Declaration, not only do women not have the rights it guarantees—most of the world's men don't either—but it is hard to see, in its vision of humanity, a woman's face.

Women need full human status in social reality. For this, the Universal Declaration of Human Rights must see the ways women distinctively are deprived of human rights as a deprivation of humanity. For the glorious dream of the Universal Declaration to come true, for human rights to be universal, both the reality it challenges and the standard it sets need to change.

When will women be human? When?

NOTES

1. Universal Declaration of Human Rights, G. A. Res. 217, U.N. GAOR, 3d Sess., at 72–76, U.N. Doc. A/810 (1948). All quotations from the Universal Declaration in this essay can be found here.

2. For data supporting all statements on violence against women in this analysis, see Radhika Coomaraswamy, *Report Submitted by the Special Rapporteur on Violence Against Women, Its Causes and Consequences,* Commission on Human Rights, 50th Sess., Agenda Item 11(a), U.N. Doc. E/CN.4/1995/42 (1995); Radhika Coomaraswamy, *Report of the Special Rapporteur on Violence Against Women, Its Causes and Consequences,* U.N. ESCOR Hum. Rts. Comm'n, 52d Sess., Prov. Agenda Item 9(a), U.N. Doc. E/CN.4/1996/53 (1996); Radhika Coomaraswamy, Report, U.N. ESCOR Hum. Rts. Comm'n, 53d Sess., Prov. Agenda Item 9(a), U.N. Doc. E/CN.4/1997/47 (1997).

3. See Traffic in Women and Girls, Sub-Commission on Human Rights Resolution 2002/51 E/CN.4/RES/2002/51 (Apr. 23, 2002). The U.S. Department of State estimates that around 800,000 people are trafficked internationally annually, most of whom are women and children. *Trafficking in Persons Report* 7 (June 2003).

4. The majority of the world's illiterate people are women. See UNESCO, *Statistical Yearbook 1997* 2–6 tbl. 2–2 (estimating 28.8 percent of the world's women and 16.3 percent of the world's men are illiterate).

5. See Interparliamentary Union, *Women in Parliaments, 1945–1995: A World Statistical Study* (1995).

6. See "Women's September 11th: Rethinking the International Law of Conflict," below at No. 25 below for discussion of this concept.

7. Richard Rorty, "Feminism and Pragmatism," 30 *Michigan Quarterly Review* 231, 234 (Spring 1991) ("MacKinnon's central point, as I read her, is that 'a woman' is not yet the name for a way of being human").

The Messy Relationship Between Feminisms and Globalizations

Manisha Desai (2007)

For the past decade, I have been engaged both with transnational feminisms and with writing about gender and globalizations.[1] In the course of my engagement in these two fields, I have been intrigued by the interrelationship(s) between them. Yet, with some exceptions (e.g., Eisenstein 2005), feminist scholars have written about gender and globalizations or about transnational feminisms but have rarely examined the connections between the two. In this essay, I reflect on this relationship to highlight how they have shaped each other. I suggest that feminisms are important forces shaping globalizations. At the same time, the interrelationships are fraught and in some instances have furthered inequalities among women. But this does not preclude other possibilities, as is evident in the work of feminists around the world.

To begin with the issue of how the two have shaped each other, I draw on Hester Eisenstein's (2005) important, but not widely discussed, article: "A Dangerous Liaison? Feminism and Corporate Globalization." In it she argues that in the United States, global capitalism has used feminists' arguments for women's autonomy and need for economic independence to undermine welfare and the family wage and to send poor women into the workforce. Concurrently in the Third World, similar feminist ideologies have been used to feminize the workforce in the export processing zones and to discipline poor women, through micro credit, into becoming responsible economic agents.[2] Thus, like missionaries in the nineteenth century, feminisms in the twentieth act as "cultural solvent[s], as globalization erodes the traditions of patriarchy" (Eisenstein 2005, 487). Such a "legitimization of feminism masks the radical restructuring of the world economy, and the glitter of economic liberation disguises the intensification of poverty

for the vast majority of women" (Eisenstein 2005, 489–90). Eisenstein argues, then, that feminism has served unwittingly as the hand-maiden of corporate globalization.

While I agree with Eisenstein that actors of corporate globalization have used feminist ideologies for their own profit, this is only a partial account. The other story is how feminists have used globalizations to further women's agency and their political, economic, and cultural empowerment. To see these other stories, one needs to define globalizations in the plural and to understand feminists as both constitutive of, and important actors in, globalizations (Desai 2009b).

Here I will give a few examples of the ways in which feminists have shaped the spaces of global politics: by (1) providing theoretical frameworks, organizational structures, and strategies; (2) engaging economic globalizations to exploit both the opportunities provided by it and articulating alternatives to corporate globalization; and (3) creating new cultures of globalization.

The International Women's Decade, 1975–1985, brought together women's organizations from around the world. The feminist principles women from these organizations had developed across their respective local contexts facilitated the formation of a new transnational perspective for political action, new organizational structures, and new strategies. Primary among these was the commitment to an intersectional analysis and transversal politics. The contentious experiences of dealing with differences among women for those in women's movements in the North and South enabled the transnational women's gatherings to form solidarities across differences.

In addition to this transnational political perspective, transnational feminists were among the first to develop networks on the basis of nonhierarchical, informal structures and participatory processes, to share experiences and strategize for political actions at multiple levels. These networks were formed before information and communication technologies made such connections the norm in corporate and civil society. Finally, transnational feminists also pioneered strategies for articulating autonomous spaces—such as tribunals, caucuses, grassroots women's networks, partnerships with other movements and local authorities—exemplified in projects like the Feminist Dialogues. These strategies mobilize both a critique and an alternative to global politics today, especially those practiced in conjunction with the World Social Forum. Hence, contemporary global politics have to be recognized as feminist politics.

Even in the realm of economic globalization, feminists have made important contributions. From highlighting the ways global corporations have used gendered and racialized assumptions to feminize the labor force, to demonstrating how processes of economic globalizations are gendered, feminists have been at the forefront of challenging corporate globalizations. For example, feminists have demanded an end to what Acker (2006) calls corporate irresponsibility; they have proposed a "Maria tax" to acknowledge the reproductive labor of women; they have called for nongendered caring and provisioning as the basis of production and reproduction instead of profits (e.g., Beneria 2003); and they have crafted egalitarian institutions, organizations, families, and communities.

In addition to the feminist focus on waged work in corporate globalizations, in my own research I have shown how women cross-border traders[3] creatively use the openings provided by global trade to make better lives for themselves (Desai 2009b). Most women cross-border traders are able to build new houses, provide education for their children as public education becomes scarce, and expand their business. Cross-border trade has also enabled women to become independent and to develop local and regional networks and economies based on creative responses to the uncertainties created by the structural adjustment programs in the region.

Cross-border trading is not restricted to poor women. In many West African countries, middle- and upper-class women also engage in cross-border trade and bring in foreign consumer items for men and women in local markets. In southern Africa, cross-border trade was made possible by the new immigration policies of the postapartheid regime, which enabled other Africans to travel freely to South Africa, as well as by the structural adjustment programs that created the need for women to become traders. Women have engaged in this trade out of necessity as well as innovation. In the process, they have developed social networks and new collective identities that have empowered them as individuals and as members of communities.

In the cultural globalization realm, I have suggested that we move away from the homogenizing, hybridity, and clash of civilizations debates (e.g., Nederveen Pieterse 2004). Instead, I argue that we should focus on the nonconsumptive, interactive culture of globalization in which women weave their own traditions and practices along with other cultural and political traditions. In this sphere, women are using new technologies to create cultures of globalization that are both place and cyber based and that enable them to communicate with local, national, and transnational communities working for gender justice. These new cultures of globalization are invented and imagined based on traditions as well as modernities, combine new organizational structures with new forms of communication, circulate transnationally, and illuminate alternative cultural possibilities that blur the distinctions between the aesthetic and everyday sense of culture.

For example, in Guatemala, the Centro de Communicadoras is a Mayan site where Web surfers can sign up with women's cooperatives to learn how to make videos or access handicrafts produced by women's cooperatives in the rural areas. The sales are handled by women directly, thus, facilitating social economies outside the capitalist system. In Mexico, *Laneta* (slang for truth), which began promoting the use of the Internet for the women's movement in 1993, links women's organizations and networks in rural and urban Mexico for sharing information and strategizing for collective action. In Bolivia, Chasquinet has provided indigenous women access to computer training by opening telecenters, or cyber cafés. Women have used this training for opening Internet-based businesses as well as to address issues of violence against women in their communities. These new cultures of globalization embody hybridities of virtual and geographic communities, and of activists across movements and classes. In using technology for social change, activists develop a common culture based on social justice.

Despite these examples of the ways in which feminists and feminisms have shaped globalizations, these are uneven relationships. Although feminisms, in some organized fashion, are alive and well in more parts of the world today than at any other time, the lives of most women around the world are mired in poverty, ill-health, and injustice. Feminists have offered many explanations for this contradictory state, such as the new inequalities resulting from neoliberal globalization, the war on terror, religious fundamentalisms, the difficulties of transforming structures and institutions, and the lack of political will to redistribute resources. I would add to that list some of the strategies of transnational feminisms (Desai 2007; Pearson 2003; Simon-Kumar 2004).

For example, transnational feminisms have for the most part drawn on the expertise of educated, privileged women from the global North and the South who are well versed in a Euro- and U.S.-centric professional culture. To function as an activist in the global women's rights movement, one needs expertise—such as a familiarity with the UN system and its treaties and platforms, and the ability to raise funds for travel—that is, for the most part, available only among educated women from the North and the South. This is not to say that feminists have not made efforts to be more inclusive. But given the structural inequalities that exist, their efforts have been limited by the ability of women lacking formal education—and facility in English, in particular—to navigate global gatherings. This has led to inequalities among feminists who work in the global versus local arenas. Moreover, some of the spaces in which transnational feminists have operated, such as the UN, and even global meetings such as the World Social Forum, have ended up taking feminist insights and demands and transforming them into managerial solutions, such as gender mainstreaming, that

have not really addressed structural inequalities. This has led some feminists to advocate a move away from global spaces, where the victories are primarily symbolic and discursive, to local arenas where addressing issues of immediate relevance on a local scale is more likely to yield concrete improvement in people's lives.

The move to local and more concrete issues does not have to entail moving away from transnational perspectives, networks, or solidarities. Such networks and solidarities provide both support and resources. Rather, strategic uses of transnational connections for local actions are more useful as many women's groups have found.

But while transnational feminist strategies have played a part in the contradictory situation of women's continuing poverty and ill-health in the face of the rise of feminist power around the globe, the major reasons continue to be the greater power of other actors—new and old, global and local—in marginalizing and harming women around the world. And to deal with such entrenched power inequalities, we need to enact a dual politics of possibilities—a pragmatic politics of what is possible within the current conjuncture and a visionary politics of what can be possible—even as we recognize the power and complicity of some of us.

Feminists around the world have already been engaged in such a dual politics of possibilities. For example, in India, where religious differences are often so volatile, activists have used gender equality, to which the Indian state is committed, to gain rights for women while sidestepping religious debates (Desai 2009a). In fact, to some extent feminists have been doing this from the start. Since its inception, one of the strengths of feminisms has been their openness to self-critique and change. The plural, feminisms, in common usage now, is itself recognition of this regenerative process.

In conclusion, what the messy relationship between feminisms and globalizations suggests is the need to be aware of, and to critique, the complicity, unwitting though it may be, of some feminists and feminist ideologies with global capital. It also highlights the necessity of reinvigorating our alternative values of creating and living in societies where caring and provisioning are not gendered and racialized but rather are the framework that guides all of our actions. To achieve this, we need to remind ourselves of the dual politics of possibilities in our individual and collective lives.

NOTES

1. I define both as plural processes, the former reflecting the diversity of gendered realities around the world and the latter in terms of economic, political, and cultural processes. While both the multiple feminisms and globalizations are mutually constitutive, they are also distinct.
2. In addition to serving global capital through economic means, Eisenstein (2005) argues that the U.S. administration has used feminism for its imperial policies via the war on terror.
3. Cross-border traders are those who buy food and other consumer items in one country and sell it another. In some regions, women take goods from their home country to another and return with goods from the foreign country to their own. Such cross-border trade by women has been facilitated by the economic globalization that has opened borders between countries that previously did not allow such easy flow of people and goods across borders.

REFERENCES

Acker, Joan. 2006. *Class questions feminist answers. The gender lens.* Lanham, MD: Rowman & Littlefield.

Beneria, Lourdes. 2003. *Gender, development and globalization: Economics as if all people mattered.* New York: Routledge.

Desai, Manisha. 2007. The global women's rights movement and its discontents. *President's Message: SWS Network News* 24 (1): 2.

———. 2009a. From a uniform civil code to legal pluralism: The continuing debates in India. In *Gender, family, and law in the Middle East and South Asia*, edited by Ken Cuno and Manisha Desai. Syracuse, NY: Syracuse University Press.

———. 2009b. *Rethinking globalization: Gender and the politics of possibilities.* Lanhan, MD: Rowman & Littlefield.

Eisenstein, Hester. 2005. A dangerous liaison? Feminism and corporate globalization. *Science & Society* 69 (3): 487–518.

Nederveen Pieterse, Jan. 2004. *Globalization and culture: A cultural melange.* Lagham, MD: Rowman & Littlefield.

Pearson, Ruth. 2003. Feminist responses to economic globalization. In *Women reinventing globalization*, edited by Joanne Kerr and Caroline Sweetman. Oxford, UK: Oxfam.

Simon-Kumar, Rachel. 2004. Negotiating emancipation: Public sphere, Gender, and critiques of neo-liberalism. *International Feminist Journal of Politics* 6 (3): 485–506.

R E A D I N G 4

Under Western Eyes

Chandra Talpade Mohanty (1984)

What I wish to analyze is specifically the production of the "third world woman" as a singular monolithic subject in some recent (Western) feminist texts.

If one of the tasks of formulating and understanding the locus of "third world feminisms" is delineating the way in which it resists and *works against* what I am referring to as "Western feminist discourse," an analysis of the discursive construction of "third world women" in Western feminism is an important first step.

Clearly Western feminist discourse and political practice are neither singular nor homogeneous in their goals, interests or analyses. However, it is possible to trace a coherence of *effects* resulting from the implicit assumption of "the West" (in all its complexities and contradictions) as the primary referent in theory and praxis. My reference to "Western feminism" is by no means intended to imply that it is a monolith. Rather, I am attempting to draw attention to the similar effects of various textual strategies used by writers which codify Others as non-Western and hence themselves as (implicitly) Western. It is in this sense that I use that term *Western feminist*.

My critique is directed at three basic analytic principles which are present in (Western) feminist discourse on women in the third world.

The first analytic presupposition I focus on is involved in the strategic location of the category "women" *vis-à-vis* the context of analysis. The assumption of women as an already constituted, coherent group with identical interests and desires, regardless of class, ethnic or racial location, or contradictions, implies a notion of gender or sexual difference or even patriarchy which can be applied universally and cross-culturally. (The context of analysis can be anything from kinship structures and the organization of labour or media representations.) The second analytical presupposition is evident on the methodological level, in the uncritical way "proof" of universality and cross-cultural validity are provided. The third is a more specifically political presupposition underlying the methodologies and the analytic strategies, i.e., the model of power and struggle they imply and suggest. I argue that as a result of the two modes—or, rather, frames—of analysis described above, a homogeneous notion of the oppression of women as a group is assumed, which, in turn, produces the image of an "average third world woman." This woman leads an essentially truncated life based on her feminine gender (read: sexually constrained) and her being "third world" (read: ignorant, poor, uneducated, tradition-bound, domestic, family-oriented, victimized, etc.). This, I suggest, is in contrast to the (implicit) self-representation of Western women as educated, as modern, as having control over their own bodies and sexualities, and the freedom to make their own decisions.

"WOMEN" AS CATEGORY OF ANALYSIS, OR: WE ARE ALL SISTERS IN STRUGGLE

By women as a category of analysis, I am referring to the crucial assumption that all of us of the same gender, across classes and cultures, are somehow socially constituted as a homogeneous group identified prior to the process of analysis. This is an assumption which characterizes much feminist discourse. The homogeneity of women as a group is produced not on the basis of biological essentials but rather on the basis of secondary sociological and anthropological universals. Thus, for instance, in any given piece of feminist analysis, women are characterized as a singular group on the basis of a shared oppression. What binds women together is a sociological notion of the "sameness" of their oppression. It is at this point that an elision takes place between "women" as a discursively constructed group and "women" as material subjects of their own history.[1] Thus, the discursively consensual homogeneity of "women" as a group is mistaken for the historically specific material reality of groups of women. This results in an assumption of women as an always already constituted group, one which has been labeled "powerless," "exploited," "sexually harassed," etc., by feminist scientific, economic, legal and sociological discourses. (Notice that this is quite similar to sexist discourse labeling women weak, emotional, having math anxiety, etc.) This focus is not on uncovering the material and ideological specificities that constitute a particular group of women as "powerless" in a particular context. It is, rather, on finding a variety of cases of "powerless" groups of women to prove the general point that women as a group are powerless.

This mode of defining women primarily in terms of their *object status* (the way in which they are affected or not affected by certain institutions and systems) is what characterizes this particular form of the use of "women" as a category of analysis. In the context of Western women writing/studying women in the third world, such objectification (however benevolently motivated) needs to be both named and challenged. As Valerie Amos and Pratibha Parmar argue quite eloquently, "Feminist theories which examine our cultural practices as 'feudal residues' or label us 'traditional,' also portray us as politically immature women who need to be versed and schooled in the ethos of Western feminism. They need to be continually challenged . . . " (1984, 7).

WOMEN AND THE DEVELOPMENT PROCESS

The best examples of universalization on the basis of economic reductionism can be found in the liberal "Women in Development" literature. Proponents of this school seek to examine the effect of development on third world women, sometimes from self-designated feminist perspectives. At the very least, there is an evident interest in and commitment to improving the lives of women in "developing" countries.

For instance, Perdita Huston (1979) states that the purpose of her study is to describe the effect of the development process on the "family unit and its individual members" in Egypt, Kenya, Sudan, Tunisia, Sri Lanka and Mexico. She states that the "problems" and "needs" expressed by rural and urban women in these countries all center around education and training, work and wages, access to health and other services, political participation and legal rights. Huston relates all these "needs" to the lack of sensitive development policies which exclude women as a group or category. For her, the solution is simple: implement improved development policies which emphasize training for women fieldworkers, use women trainees, and women rural development officers, encourage women's cooperatives, etc. Here again, women are assumed to be a coherent group or category prior to their entry into "the development process." Huston assumes that all third world women have similar problems and needs. Thus, they must have similar interests and goals. However, the interests of urban, middle-class, educated Egyptian housewives, to take only one instance, could surely not be seen as being the same as those of their uneducated, poor maids? Development policies do not affect both groups of women in the same way. Practices which characterize women's status and roles vary according to class. Women are constituted as women through the complex interaction between class, culture, religion and other ideological institutions and frameworks. They are not "women"—a coherent group—solely on the basis of a particular economic system or policy. Such reductive cross-cultural comparisons result in the colonization of the specifics of daily existence and the complexities of political interests which women of different social classes and cultures represent and mobilize.

Thus, it is revealing that for Perdita Huston, women in the Third World countries she writes about have "needs" and "problems," but few if any have "choices" or the freedom to act. This is an interesting representation of women in the third world, one which is significant in suggesting a latent self-presentation of Western women which bears looking at. She writes: "What surprised and moved me most as I listened to women in such very different cultural settings was the striking commonality—whether they were educated or illiterate, urban or rural—of their most basic values: the importance they assign to family, dignity and service to others" (1979: 115). Would Huston consider such values unusual for women in the West?

What is problematical about this kind of use of "women" as a group, as a stable category of analysis, is that it assumes an ahistorical, universal unity between women based on a generalized notion of their subordination. Instead of analytically *demonstrating* the production of women as socio-economic political groups within particular local contexts, this analytical move limits the definition of the female subject to gender identity, completely bypassing social class and ethnic identities. What characterizes women as a group is their gender (sociologically, not necessarily biologically, defined) over and above everything else, indicating a monolithic notion of sexual difference. Because women are thus constituted as a coherent group, sexual difference becomes coterminous with female subordination, and power is automatically defined in binary terms: people who have it (read: men), and people who do not (read: women). Men exploit, women are exploited. Such simplistic formulations are historically reductive; they are also ineffectual in designing strategies to combat oppressions. All they do is reinforce binary divisions between men and women.

What would an analysis which did not do this look like? Maria Mies's work illustrates the strength of Western feminist work on women in the third world which does not fall into the traps discussed above, Mies's study of the lace makers of Narsapur, India (1982), attempts to analyze carefully a substantial household industry in which "housewives" produce lace doilies for consumption in the world market. Through a detailed analysis of the structure of the lace industry, production and reproduction relations, the sexual division of labor, profits and exploitation, and the overall consequences of defining women as "non-working housewives" and their work as "leisure-time activity," Mies demonstrates the levels of exploitation in this industry and the impact of this production system on the work and living conditions of the women involved. In addition, she is able to analyze the "ideology of the housewife," the notion of a woman sitting in the house, as providing the necessary subjective and sociocultural element for the creation and maintenance of a production system that contributes to the increasing pauperization of women, and keeps them totally atomized and disorganized as workers. Mies's analysis shows the effect of a certain historically and culturally specific mode of patriarchal organization, an organization constructed on the basis of the definition of the lace makers as "non-working housewives" at familial, local, regional, statewide and international levels. The intricacies and the effects of particular power networks are not only emphasized but form the basis of Mies's analysis of how this particular group of women is situated at the center of a hegemonic, exploitative world market.

This is a good example of what careful, politically focused, local analyses can accomplish. It illustrates how the category of women is constructed in a variety of political contexts that often exist simultaneously and are overlaid on top of one another. There is no easy generalization in the direction of "women" in India, or "women in the third world"; nor is there a reduction of the political construction of the exploitation of the lace makers to cultural explanations about the passivity or obedience that might characterize these women and their situation. Finally, this mode of local, political analysis which generates theoretical categories from within the situation and context being analyzed, also suggests corresponding effective strategies for organizing against the exploitation faced by the lace makers. Narsapur women are not mere victims of the production process, because they resist, challenge and subvert the process at various junctures. Here is one instance of how Mies delineates the connections between the housewife ideology, the self-consciousness of the lace makers, and their inter-relationships as

contributing to the latent resistances she perceives among the women.

> The persistence of the housewife ideology, the self-perception of the lace makers as petty commodity producers rather than as workers, is not only upheld by the structure of the industry as such but also by the deliberate propagation and reinforcement of reactionary patriarchal norms and institutions. Thus, most of the lace makers voiced the same opinion about the rules of *purdah* and seclusion in their communities which were also propagated by the lace exporters. In particular, the *Kapu* women said that they had never gone out of their houses, that women of their community could not do any work other than housework and lace work etc. but in spite of the fact that most of them still subscribed fully to the patriarchal norms of the *gosha* women, there were also contradictory elements in their consciousness. Thus, although they looked down with contempt upon women who were able to work outside the house—like untouchable *Mala* and *Madiga* women or women of other lower castes—they could not ignore the fact that these women were earning more money precisely because they were *not* respectable housewives but workers. At one discussion, they even admitted that it would be better if they could also go out and do coolie work. And when they were asked whether they would be ready to come out of their houses and work in one place in some sort of a factory, they said they would do that. This shows that the *purdah* and housewife ideology, although still fully internalized, already had some cracks, because it has been confronted with several contradictory realities. (p. 157)

It is only by understanding the *contradictions* inherent in women's location within various structures that effective political action and challenges can be devised. Mies's study goes a long way toward offering such analysis. While there are now an increasing number of Western feminist writings in this tradition,[3] there is also, unfortunately, a large block of writing which succumbs to the cultural reductionism discussed earlier.

As discussed earlier, a comparison between Western feminist self-presentation and Western feminist re-presentation of women in the third world yields significant results. Universal images of "the third world Woman" (the veiled woman, chaste virgin, etc.), images constructed from adding the "third world difference" to "sexual difference," are predicated upon (and hence obviously bring into sharper focus) assumptions about Western women as secular, liberated and having control over their own lives. This is not to suggest that Western women *are* secular, liberated and in control of their own lives. I am referring to a *discursive* self-presentation, not necessarily to material reality. If this were a material reality, there would be no need for political movements in the West. Similarly, only from the vantage point of the West is it possible to define the "third world" as underdeveloped and economically dependent. Without the overdetermined discourse that creates the *third* world, there would be no (singular and privileged) First World. Without the "third world woman," the particular self-presentation of Western women mentioned above would be problematical. I am suggesting, then, that the one enables and sustains the other.

NOTES

Terms such as *third* and *first world* are problematical both in suggesting over-simplified similarities between and among countries thus labeled, and in reinforcing implicitly existing economic, cultural and ideological hierarchies which are conjured up using such terminology. I use the term "*third world*" with full awareness of its problems, only because this is the terminology available to us at the moment.

1. Elsewhere I have discussed this particular point in detail in a critique of Robin Morgan's construction of "women's herstory" in her introduction to *Sisterhood Is Global: The International Women's Movement Anthology* (New York: Anchor Press/Doubleday, 1984). See my "Feminist Encounters: Locating the Politics of Experience," *Copyright* 1, "Fin de Siecle 2000," 30–44, especially 35–7.

2. These views can also be found in differing degrees in collections such as Wellesley Editorial Committee (ed.), *Women and National Development: The Complexities of Change* (Chicago: University of Chicago Press, 1977), and *Signs*, Special Issue, "Development and the Sexual Division of Labor," 7, no. 2 (Winter 1981). For an excellent introduction of WID issues, see ISIS, *Women in Development: A Resource Guide for Organization and Action* (Philadelphia: New Society Publishers, 1984). For a politically focused discussion of feminism and development and the stakes for poor Third World women, see Gita Sen and Caren Grown, *Development Crises and Alternative Visions: Third World Women's Perspectives* (New York: Monthly Review Press, 1987).

3. See essays by Vanessa Maher, Diane Elson and Ruth Pearson, and Maila Stevens in Kate Young, Carole Walkowitz, and Roslyn McCullagh (eds), *Of Marriage and the Market: Women's Subordination in International Perspective* (London: CSE Books, 1981); and essays by Vivian Mota and Michelle Mattelart in June Nash and Helen I. Safa (eds), *Sex and Class in Latin America: Women's Perspectives on Politics, Economics and the Family in the Third World* (South Hadley, Mass.: Bergin and Garvey, 1980). For examples of excellent, self-conscious work by feminists writing about women in their own historical and geographical locations, see Marnia Lazreg (1988) on Algerian women, Gayatri Chakravorty Spivak's "A Literary Representation of the Subaltern: A Woman's Text from the Third World," in her *In Other Worlds: Essays in Cultural Politics* (New York: Methuen, 1987), 241–68, and Lata Mani's essay "Contentious Traditions: The Debate on SATI in Colonial India," *Cultural Critique* 7 (Fall 1987), 119–56.

REFERENCES

Amos, Valerie, and Pratibha Parmar. 1984. "Challenging Imperial Feminism," *Feminist Review* 17: 3-19.

Huston, Perdita. 1979. *Third World Women Speak Out.* New York: Praeger.

Mies, Maria. 1982. *The Lacemakers of Narsapur: Indian Housewives Produce for the World Market.* London: Zed.

Comrades

Nadine Gordimer (South Africa, 1991)

As Mrs Hattie Telford pressed the electronic gadget that deactivates the alarm device in her car a group of youngsters came up behind her. Black. But no need to be afraid; this was not a city street. This was a non-racial enclave of learning, a place where tended flowerbeds and trees bearing botanical identification plates civilized the wild reminder of campus guards and dogs. The youngsters, like her, were part of the crowd loosening into dispersion after a university conference on People's Education. They were the people to be educated; she was one of the committee of white and black activists (convenient generic for revolutionaries, leftists secular and Christian, fellow-travelers and liberals) up on the platform.

—Comrade . . . —She was settling in the driver's seat when one so slight and slim he seemed a figure in profile came up to her window. He drew courage from the friendly lift of the woman's eyebrows above blue eyes, the tilt of her freckled white face:—Comrade, are you going to town?—

No, she was going in the opposite direction, home . . . but quickly, in the spirit of the hall where these young people had been somewhere, somehow present with her (ah no, she with them) stamping and singing Freedom songs, she would take them to the bus station their spokesman named.—Climb aboard!—

The others got in the back, the spokesman beside her. She saw the nervous white of his eyes as he glanced at and away from her. She searched for talk to set them at ease. Questions, of course. Older people always start with questioning young ones. Did they come from Soweto?

They came from Harrismith, Phoneng Location.

She made the calculation: about two hundred kilometers distant. How did they get here? Who told them about the conference?

—We are Youth Congress in Phoneng—

A delegation. They had come by bus; one of the groups and stragglers who kept arriving long after

the conference had started. They had missed, then, the free lunch?

At the back, no one seemed even to be breathing. The spokesman must have had some silent communication with them, some obligation to speak for them created by the journey or by other shared experience in the mysterious bonds of the young—these young.—We are hungry.—And from the back seats was drawn an assent like the suction of air in a compressing silence.

She was silent in response, for the beat of a breath or two. These large gatherings both excited and left her over-exposed, open and vulnerable to the rub and twitch of the mass shuffling across rows of seats and loping up the aisles, babies' fudge-brown soft legs waving as their napkins are changed on mothers' laps, little girls with plaited loops on their heads listening like old crones, heavy women swaying to chants, men with fierce, unreadably black faces breaking into harmony tender and deep as they sing to God for his protection of Umkhonto weSizwe, as people on both sides have always, everywhere, claimed divine protection for their soldiers, their wars. At the end of a day like this she wanted a drink, she wanted the depraved luxury of solitude and quiet in which she would be restored (enriched, oh yes! by the day) to the familiar limits of her own being.

Hungry. Not for iced whisky and feet up. It seemed she had scarcely hesitated:—Look, I live nearby, come back to my house and have something to eat. Then I'll run you into town.—

—That will be very nice. We can be glad for that.—And at the back the tight vacuum relaxed.

They followed her in through the gate, shrinking away from the dog—she assured them he was harmless but he was large, with a fancy collar by which she held him. She trooped them in through the kitchen because that was the way she always entered her house, something she would not have done if they had been adult, her black friends whose sophistication might lead them to believe the choice of entrance was an unthinking historical slight. As she was going to feed them, she took them not into her living-room with its sofas and flowers but into her dining-room, so that they could sit at table right away. It was a room in confident taste that could afford to be spare: bare floorboards, matching golden wooden ceiling, antique brass chandelier, reed blinds instead of stuffy curtains. An African wooden sculpture represented a lion marvelously released from its matrix in the grain of a Mukwa tree-trunk. She pulled up the chairs and left the four young men while she went back to the kitchen to make coffee and see what there was in the refrigerator for sandwiches. They had greeted the maid, in the language she and they shared, on their way through the kitchen, but when the maid and the lady of the house had finished preparing cold meat and bread, and the coffee was ready, she suddenly did not want them to see that the maid waited on her. She herself carried the heavy tray into the dining-room.

They are sitting round the table, silent, and there is no impression that they stopped an undertone exchange when they heard her approaching. She doles out plates, cups. They stare at the food but their eyes seem focused on something she can't see; something that overwhelms. She urges them—Just cold meat, I'm afraid, but there's chutney if you like it . . . Milk everybody? . . . Is the coffee too strong? I have a heavy hand, I know. Would anyone like to add some hot water?—

They eat. When she tries to talk to one of the others, he says *Ekskuus*? And she realizes he doesn't understand English, of the white man's languages knows perhaps only a little of that of the Afrikaners in the rural town he comes from. Another gives his name, as if in some delicate acknowledgement of the food.—I'm Shadrack Nsutsha.—She repeats the surname to get it right. But he does not speak again. There is an urgent exchange of eye-language, and the spokesman holds out the emptied sugar-bowl to her.—Please.—She hurries to the kitchen and brings it back refilled. They need carbohydrate, they are hungry, they are young, they need it, they burn it up. She is distressed at the inadequacy of the

meal and then notices the fruit bowl, her big copper fruit bowl, filled with apples and bananas and perhaps there is a peach or two under the grape leaves with which she likes to complete an edible still life.—Have some fruit. Help yourselves.—

They are stacking their plates and cups, not knowing what they are expected to do with them in this room which is a room where apparently people only eat, do not cook, do not sleep. While they finish the bananas and apples (Shadrack Nsutsha had seen the single peach and quickly got there first) she talks to the spokesman, whose name she has asked for: Dumile.—Are you still at school, Dumile?—Of course he is not at school—*they* are not at school; youngsters their age have not been at school for several years, they are the children growing into young men and women for whom school is a battleground, a place of boycotts and demonstrations, the literacy of political rhetoric, the education of revolt against having to live the life their parents live. They have pompous titles of responsibility beyond childhood: he is chairman of his branch of the Youth Congress, he was expelled two years ago—for leading a boycott? Throwing stones at the police? Maybe burning the school down? He calls it all—quietly, abstractly, doesn't know many ordinary, concrete words but knows these euphemisms—"political activity." No school for two years? No.—So what have you been able to do with yourself, all that time?—

She isn't giving him a chance to eat his apple. He swallows a large bite, shaking his head on its thin, little-boy neck.—I was inside. Detained from this June for six months.—

She looks round the others.—And you?—

Shadrack seems to nod slightly. The other two look at her. She should know, she should have known, it's a common enough answer from youths like them, their color. They're not going to be saying they've been selected for the First Eleven at cricket or that they're off on a student tour to Europe in the school holidays.

The spokesman, Dumile, tells her he wants to study by correspondence, "get his matric" that he was preparing for two years ago; two years ago when he was still a child, when he didn't have the hair that is now appearing on his face, making him a man, taking away the childhood. In the hesitations, the silences of the table, where there is nervously spilt coffee among plates of banana skins, there grows the certainty that he will never get the papers filled in for the correspondence college, he will never get the two years back. She looks at them all and cannot believe what she knows: that they, suddenly here in her house, will carry the AK-47s they only sing about, now, miming death as they sing. They will have a career of wiring explosives to the undersides of vehicles, they will go away and come back through the bush to dig holes not to plant trees to shade home, but to plant land-mines. She can see they have been terribly harmed but cannot believe they could harm. They are wiping their fruit-sticky hands furtively palm against palm.

She breaks the silence; says something, anything.

—How d'you like my lion? Isn't he beautiful? He's made by a Zimbabwean artist, I think the name's Dube.—

But the foolish interruption becomes revelation. Dumile, in his gaze—distant, lingering, speechless this time—reveals what has overwhelmed them. In this room, the space, the expensive antique chandelier, the consciously simple choice of reed blinds, the carved lion: all are on the same level of impact, phenomena undifferentiated, undecipherable. Only the food that fed their hunger was real.

R E A D I N G   **6**

Edge of the Earth

Hafsat Abiola (2006)

Some of us with the luck of the draw—born in the most auspicious place at the most auspicious time, and then fueled for any number of reasons—make that journey to the edge and poke our heads out into space. We look into territory previously uncharted by any in our sisterhood, gather courage as a cloak around our shoulders, trembling with fear or anticipation, and breathe deeply before taking the plunge.

Behind are others whose lives are still steeped in traditions and old ways of doing things. Others who adjust and adjust to changes that come and who yet believe that change is something that happens to them and not something that they can cause. For them, the immutability of things is its own good news.

And between those of us at the edge and those of us at the center is a cord that binds. A cord that we feel in both places. At the center, it is as an amorphous wondering: Might something else not be possible, or is this always all there is? And at the edge, it is a bittersweet realization: Life could have

been easier than this. If only we could have closed our eyes more, demanded less, accepted less, been less. Some say you can only be who you are, but in our hearts we recall, if vaguely, the choices that brought us onto roads less traveled, which for want of traffic become narrow paths, then trails, until all that remains is wilderness.

Far off in the distance, we hear a sound. It is only the wind. Or it might be a message from those who have ventured this far before. The wind might bear their wisdom to us. Except that we don't understand; there is no one among us who can interpret. Or if there are interpreters, we might not know of them.

At the edge there is little talking. Soon we realize that the edge is also harsh. It is a world with too many questions without answers; it entails living with the void that remains when all beliefs are taken away. Silence becomes an armor here. And our eyes focus on some distant place, or it may just be that we look there to avoid looking here, where the mess of uncertainty gathers at our feet.

At the center, our eyes are quiet and clear. They look warm and sweet. Here sisters hold hands, and during long walks to waters that move farther away, we sing. The sick find the small hollows of our hands, brimming with water, against their lips. Soon, their sickly forms full with our giving and our stories. With transitions, our keening connects the skies and the mother earth. Yet the center makes never-ending demands for our labor, so that from dawn to dusk we work, tending to everyone but ourselves.

At the edge, we begin to see that we ought to have brought our roots with us. But when we set off, baggage seemed tiresome and was left behind. So here we stand, perilously at the border, with the wind about our ears and our feet shaky on the ground.

What joy is the cord that links us all. The cord that connects our sisterhood across distances, time zones, worlds also connects the different aspects of who we are. So that even as each of us is an embodiment of contradictions, the center holds all the pieces together. We don't fall apart. Or if we do, it is possible to pick all the pieces up again. It is even possible to arrange them in a new design. This cord now brings us back to the lands we've known. From the edge, ours are the eyes filled with mystery. And from the center, ours are the feet rooted into the soil of time and place.

And now we come together.

Bringing together what we have seen, who we have been, as we weave new patterns, streaking the land with our magic.

CHAPTER **2**

World Media

Katharine Sarikakis and *Leslie Regan Shade*

Katharine Sarikakis, Ph.D., is the Director of the Centre for International Communications Research at the Institute of Communications Studies, University of Leeds, UK, and author of books and articles on media and cultural policy and international communication. She is editor (with Leslie Shade) of *Feminist Interventions in International Communication* (Rowman and Littlefield, 2008), coauthor of *Media Policy and Globalisation* (Edinburgh University Press/Palgrave 2006), and editor of the *International Journal of Media and Cultural Politics* (Intellect). Katharine is an honorary Research Fellow at Hainan University and the Chair of the Communication Law and Policy Section of the European Communication Research and Education Association.

Leslie Regan Shade is an Associate Professor at Concordia University, Montreal, in the Department of Communication Studies. Her research focuses on the social, policy, and ethical aspects of information and communication technologies, particularly issues of gender, globalization, and political economy. She is editor of *Mediascapes: New Patterns on Canadian Communication* (3rd edition, 2009); author of *Gender and Community in the Social Construction of the Internet* (Peter Lang, 2002); and coeditor with Katharine Sarikakis of *Feminist Interventions in International Communication* (Rowman and Littlefield, 2008).

I break into a lyrical freestyle
Grab the mic, look into the crowd and see smiles
Cause they see a woman standing up on her own two
Sloppy slouching is something I won't do
Some think that we can't flow (can't flow)
Stereotypes, they got to go (got to go)
I'm a mess around and flip the scene into reverse
(With what?) With a little touch of Ladies First
Who said the ladies couldn't make it, you must be blind
If you don't believe, well here, listen to this rhyme
Ladies first, there's no time to rehearse
I'm divine and my mind expands throughout the universe
A female rapper with the message to send the
Queen Latifah is a perfect specimen

Queen Latifah, excerpted lyrics from "Ladies First" from *All Hail the Queen*.

The study of women's status in communications spans over four decades. During the 1960s and 1970s, feminist scholars and activists posed questions about the position of women in media and culture. They began connecting mass media to education, economy, and politics, seeing it as part of a broader framework of culture in which women perform gender, negotiate stereotypes, and experience discriminatory practices. Although we generally think of media as forms of mass communication (television, radio, press, Internet, etc.), the media can be defined as technological processes that facilitate communication between the sender of a message and the receiver of that message. The terms "sender" and "receiver," however, are becoming increasingly contested, as traditional and established processes of "sending" and "receiving" information are changing due to advances in media technologies. "New media" and the digitalization of media have created possibilities for more flexible content and consumption. Information and communication technologies (ICTs) have thus brought about a range of possibilities for the production and sharing of information, unknown to previous generations.

This chapter addresses the role of media in the era of globalization, focusing on changes in media and their consequences for women's lives. We start this chapter with a focus on the emergence of global media and their relationship to neoliberal economic policies (free trade, deregulation, and privatization), exploring the political economy of world media and policy-making processes that tend to exclude women. This section is followed by a focus on the representation of women in media that includes a discussion of both women's under-representation in some forms of media genrés, such as print and broadcasting news, and their over-representations in others like pornography. Women's access to ICTs is the theme of the next section. We address explanations for women's unequal access to ICTs worldwide and explore policy initiatives to improve access. The chapter closes with a discussion of women's active role in media and ICT projects on gender and social justice with a focus on community radio, blogging, independent film and video production, mobile (cell) phones, and social networking sites.

A DAY IN THE LIFE **Telling the Truth** by *Marcia Chambers*

Gavriila tosses in bed one final time before deciding to rise for the day. She has been having trouble sleeping through the night since the recent assassination of yet another fellow journalist in Moscow, Russia. Too many determined and courageous colleagues have been victims of violence. It seems the choice to speak out against the atrocities and corruption once again comes with a high price. The optimism that set the tone for a new era of Russian journalism in the early '90's, through *glasnost* (openness) and *perestroika* (restructuring), a time that rallied in unprecedented tolerance for criticism of government and economic policies, is now vanishing due to the government's increasingly brutal efforts to silence all forms of opposition.

It is with this chilly thought in mind that Gavriila gets ready for the day, donning warm trousers and sweater before she joins her husband, Lyov, a fellow journalist. The forecast calls for more snow and the streets are icy. Their morning chai tea, with its cinnamon and spices, helps warm them, and the *oladi*, a scone-type pancake made with buttermilk, offers some nurturance as they steel up for the day.

They discuss their plans in the one-bedroom apartment they were able to purchase during the changes that took place during *perestroika* allowing citizens to buy their own homes. They are both fortunate to have parents who worked for key international posts in the government, enabling the passing of resources and opportunities. This makes living in Moscow possible, even on journalists' salaries, which can be equivalent to $200 U.S. per month. These ties also helped prepare Gavriila and Lyov for their journalism training at Moscow State University. It was here that they first met.

As they bundle up for the cold walk to the Metro station, Gavriila thinks about the hope that was generated during this time in 1991 when freedom of the press was written into Russian law. No longer were people forced to write material that was counter to their principles. Russian journalists studied investigative journalism; much different from the former model of reporting State-sanctioned news. Countries vied to provide favored journalism models to Russian training programs. They used to laugh at the proponents of "free press" models who were unable to see that the press, driven by commercial interests, could never truly be free.

As she prepares to depart on a different train than Lyov, she remembers how they had joined with their colleagues to form a cadre of passionate and committed journalists. They had left the university and entered in their various communities driven by the burning desire to help create a better society informed by truth.

Gavriila enters the subway train that will take her to her interview source as Lyov departs for his destination. She knows that any move to interact with someone from an oppositional side could mean the end for both of them. Yet, she sees the faces of fallen comrades and mentors, once fortified by their convictions before being brought down. She feels angry that these crimes are being ignored and covered up. She thinks about those who have escaped death and have had to seek asylum in other countries to continue writing commentary. She sees the faces of those around her, those who are in bondage to the current powers that be, enslaved by commercial and despotic interests, turning a helpless eye away from the heinous crimes around them as whole groups are purged from society, and corruption and bribery abound. What choice does she have? To become part of that would be to die. It is better this way.

Gavriila exits the train and walks a few blocks to the building she will enter. The street is busy with the bustle of commuters. She walks casually inside where she will be taken to a different place to meet her informant, who is also risking life and limb to speak openly today. Gavriila focuses on gender issues affecting the women in her country. She meets with the member of a rescue operation for Russian women exploited through the sex trafficking trade. She feels this trade has flourished unchecked in Russia because of the increasing influence of commercial priorities central to globalization which places profit over human life, the increased lawlessness and civil rights abuses that abound in the current political landscape which enables this corruption, and a change in national identity in which women and men are no longer linked as workers of equal value for the State. Women's unique issues have long been ignored here, but more women are being affected in the current environment. Gavriila thanks the informant for the valuable data offered and sneaks back into the flow of people outside.

She catches the train back to her office where she will meet Lyov, who has been probing into corruption involving a local business with possible ties to organized crime. They both work for the only independent newspaper left in existence in Russia today. All other media have been seized by big money moguls and government officials who work together to use these systems for their own ends. One press stands alone in its bid to bring knowledge to the people. It is located in Moscow and funded by a prominent and respected figure, whose support has kept this newspaper afloat. Gavriila and Lyov work with their fellow staff members to keep morale up in spite of their shrinking numbers and the grief they feel over the loss of their associates.

After an afternoon of typing up notes, writing articles, and calling on leads, Gavriila and Lyov catch the subway home to spend a quiet night together. They dine on *vareniki*, vegetable dumplings stuffed with cabbage and potato, and discuss the latest developments. Gavriila is grateful they are alive and have each other for support in spite of the dark atmosphere that clouds their world. She is not sure what will happen in the future except that the truth will still need to be told tomorrow.

EMERGENCE OF GLOBAL MEDIA MARKETS

For the past three decades, the map of the world's media has undergone dramatic transformations closely related to broader political, economic, and social changes associated with globalization. With the expansion of markets on local, national, and global scales, mass media corporations have grown bigger and stronger in their reach of international audiences and in their ability to organize production and distribution processes globally. Contrary to claims for a diversity of operations, a small number of giant corporations have established an oligopoly transnationally, dominating domestic markets, steering international ones, and influencing national governments. Intensified globalization has affected world media and shaped both women's representation in media and their use of those media. A key premise here is that new technology's interaction with preexisting cultural contexts shapes its social uses. This is demonstrated in the reading "Glamour and Honor: Going Online and Reading in West African Culture" by Wendy Griswold, Erin Metz McDonnell, and Terence Emmett McDonnell. This article discusses how new access to the Internet as a consequence of increasing globalization affects urban cultures and reading practices.

While expressions of media depend on the technologies available, degrees of technological diffusion, and levels of "literacy" required to use them, these advancements are not equitably shared, nor is there basic media literacy in some parts of the world. Inequalities, from the basic capability to read and write to accessing media and using advanced ICTs, derive from existing economic and social inequalities that create new forms of disadvantage. In the twenty-first century, media are central in the economies of the Global North, not only because ICTs are used for 24-hour financial and trade transactions, but also because of the cultural and economic power of media conglomerates. Therefore, the economies of less industrialized countries in the Global South are faced with the double-edged problem of lagging behind in technologies available in the North, yet depending on those technologies to break the cycle of poverty. And it is not surprising that women tend to have unequal access to media within those societies.

As discussed in more detail below, access is a key issue in global media markets. Where resources are scarce (such as among lower economic classes, less industrialized nations, and fund-stripped public service sectors), the gap between those with resources, access, know-how, and skills, and those without is growing. Hence, although women constitute a large percentage of the workers and the consumers in media, individually and as a social group, they are limited by material resources of social class that affect their capability to consume. They are also affected by limitations associated with skills and education. Despite women's unequal relationship to emerging communication industries in this time of expanding globalization, wealth associated with these industries is created in part from the labor of women in office and lower administrative jobs, in outsourced "call centers," as well as in factories in the developing world where media hardware like computer or mobile phone chips are mass produced. This global female labor force tends not to benefit from the profits of the new industries. Their jobs are precarious, intensive, and poorly paid, with little prospects for career development (McLaughlin, 2008). Indeed, media generally are male dominated and controlled with few women in positions of power and authority. The reading "Women Enter the World of Media" by Manal Ismail and Maysam Ali focuses on

Top 10 Global Media Corporations

Walt Disney Corporation (U.S.)
Diversified media and entertainment company
Market Value: 55B
CEO: Robert A. Iger
Web site: www.disney.go.com

Bertelsmann AG (Germany)
Transnational media
Transnational media company including
publishing and music
CEO: Hartmut Ostrowski
Consolidated revenues for 2007 €18.8B[1]
Web site: www.bertelsmann.com

Time Warner Inc. (U.S.)
Diversified media and entertainment company
Market Value: 43B
CEO: Jeffrey L. Bewkes
Web site: www.timewarner.com

News Corporation (U.S.)
Diversified media and entertainment company
Market value: 20B
CEO: Rupert Murdoch
Web site: www.newscorp.com

Viacom Inc. (U.S.)
Global entertainment content company
Market value: 13B
CEO: Sumner Redstone
Web site: www.viacom.com

Comcast (U.S.)
Cable company with entertainment and
communication products and services.
Market Value: 54B
CEO: Brian L. Roberts
Web site: www.comcast.com

Vivendi (France)
Media conglomerate from the merger of
Seagrams and Canal+
Market value: 27B
CEO: Jean-Bernard Lévy
Web site: www.vivendi.com

CBS (U.S.)
Media company with TV, radio, and publishing
Market value: 8B
CEO: Leslie Moonves
Web site: www.cbscorporation.com

DirecTV Group (U.S.)
Digital television entertainment provider in the
United States and Latin America
Market value: 27B
CEO: Chase Carey
Web site: www.directv.com

Thomson Reuters Corporation (Canada)
Diversified media, entertainment, publishing
and financial services company
Market value: 21B
CEO: Tom Gloser
Web site: www.thomsonreuters.com

Source: Adapted from Leslie Regan Shade and Michael Lithgow, The Cultures of Democracy: How Ownership and Public Participation Shape Canada's Media System, in *Mediascapes: New Patterns in Canadian Communication*, 3rd ed., Toronto: Nelson, forthcoming April 2009. Source: *Forbes Top 2000* List (2008), http://www.forbes.com/lists/2008/18/biz_2000global08_ The-Global-2000_IndName_14.html and *Columbia Journalism Review*, Who Owns What, http://www.cjr.org/resources.

[1] Press release: Bertelsmann Stabilizes Profitability for 2007 at a High Level, March 18, 2008, http://www.bertelsmann.com/ bertelsmann_corp/wms41/bm/index.php?language=2&ci=1

women in communication industries in Dubai, United Arab Emirates. The authors discuss the factors associated with women pursuing careers in this field.

Alongside the emergence of global media markets, and the integration of existing domestic ones, has come global oversight. Whereas in the past national policies alone would regulate national media, press, and broadcasting, now policies are initiated at the international level through, for example, the policies of the European Union or the North American Free Trade Agreement (NAFTA) and largely prescribed through the Group of Eight (G8) countries during their annual meetings. Civil society groups including women's organizations, farmers, students, media workers, and others that represent nonbusiness interests oppose the largely pro-market agenda and are demanding representation and accountability at various policy summits and forums. As media policy has shifted from national to international levels with global policies influencing national priorities, women's media activism is also shifting from the national to the global (although not without new problems).

REPRESENTATIONS OF WOMEN IN WORLD MEDIA

It is against this background of political and economic disparities, as well as diverse cultural contexts, that we focus on the representation of women as part of the complex relationship between women and media in the era of globalization. This section focuses on two main points: (1) presence or absence of stories about women in media; and (2) messages about gender (ideas about femininity and masculinity) within the programming itself. First, stories about women are often considered less newsworthy or are relegated to special features about family, looks, or romance, and women are less likely to be consulted as "experts" than men. Indeed, the 2005 Global Media Monitoring Project (GMMP), a global study of representations of women in news media in 76 countries (http://www.whomakesthenews .org/), reported that women are dramatically under-represented in the news: only one-fifth of news subjects (the topic of the news stories or those interviewed) are female. There was no single news topic in which women outnumbered men as newsmakers: political stories featured only 14 percent women, and business news 20 percent women. Women are dominant in the media as celebrities (42 percent), royalty (33 percent), or "ordinary" people. In terms of the professions, women are under-represented in law (18 percent), business (12 percent), and politics (12 percent), despite their increasingly strong presence in these occupations worldwide. Men dominate as expert opinion (83 percent) and as spokespersons (86 percent). Older women are almost invisible in the media, with nearly 75 percent of female newsmakers under the age of 50 years. Women are also presented more as victims (18 percent) than men (8 percent), and are more likely to be identified by their familial status (17 percent vs. 5 percent).

The reasons for this representation are twofold: (1) media are mostly owned and controlled by individuals who show bias about or lack of appreciation for women, or outright misogyny (woman hating); and (2) media largely treat women as the "other" (for example, in the word "mankind" maleness gets to stand in for humanness, but femaleness only ever represents itself, never humans generally). Programming often claims a lack of bias yet may report on the "human condition" that ignores women's experiences. The coverage of women's lives in recent wars is often belittled and random or overemphasized. For example, the recent "war on terror" coverage has portrayed women's suppression in Afghanistan and Iraq as justification for invasion (Jiwani, 2008). As discussed in chapter 12 on war and peace, Western media have helped construct this conflict as a process of "saving" women from totalitarian and repressive regimes. Indigenous women are rarely given a voice, dissenting opinions within and outside conflict zones are often minimized, and women's value is associated with their willingness to be "saved" by the West.

While general programming in Western societies often does not represent women's lives, still satellite and cable television are being used successfully to target female audiences. In the United States the 1990s witnessed an increase in specialized cable networks catering to a female audience with, for example, Lifetime, the Women's Entertainment Network, and

Oxygen Media creating popular prime-time television series featuring sexy, "empowered" women. *Ally McBeal*, *Buffy the Vampire Slayer*, and HBO's *Sex and the City* were among the most popular shows of this period. In Asia, too, women's lifestyle brands have burgeoned, with major media corporations creating country-specific channels and pay TV channels. Fox Life has expanded to Japan and Korea, the BBC Lifestyle and Sony Entertainment Television is found in Singapore, and new entrants include the Singaporian Mom-on-Demand video on demand channel (http://www.mom-on-demand.com/) and the South Korean Lotus Channel (Stein, 2008). In the Arab world, the Lebanese satellite broadcaster Heya (literally meaning "she") is the first pan-Arab station to target Arab women audiences through programs catering to diverse women (http://www.arabwomantv.com/). Established in 2002, the majority of Heya's staff and top management are women. Programming includes talk shows, cooking and sewing programs, soaps, and fashion and beauty programs. Despite this dominance of traditional "women's issues" content, Matar (2007) argues that Heya produces a feminist counter-public, particularly through its signature talk shows where gender and women's rights are debated. Its ability to discuss taboo topics like homosexuality, and its promotion of Arab women's voices in public, position Heya as a "grassroots women-generated medium aimed at fostering the right to communicate for various marginalized Arab societies" (p. 523). Finally, children's programming has also attempted to reach a wider audience. The children's show *Sesame Street* is the focus of the reading by Anthony Kaufman titled "Grover Goes Global." The essay discusses the controversial attempts of this U.S.-based public television show to reach a global audience.

Second, messages about gender in Western media and popular culture have been the object of critique among feminist media scholars for some time. Through most of the twentieth century, electronic and print media supported traditional notions of femininity. Women's main social and economic roles were considered to be that of homemaker, while men were expected to be the "breadwinner" despite the fact that women entered the professions (media included) in significant numbers since World War II and despite the fact that women's domestic labor has remained unpaid and unacknowledged for hundreds of years. Women were also associated with the body, while men with the brain: for example, advertisements for "hygiene" and household goods pictured women, whereas other nonhousehold technologies, such as cars or televisions, would be presented as the domain of men (often accompanied by the presence of half-naked females). Advertisements would show men or male voice-overs "advising" perplexed housewives what product would make their whites whiter or which vacuum cleaner would reach the toughest spots. Films and television series focused on women's roles as mothers and housewives and presented them happily servicing others. Broadcast and print media showed women in magazines, for example, preoccupied with "beauty" and romance. Even when women were portrayed in roles outside the domestic sphere, they were still shown in feminine, caring roles as nurses and social workers or limited to jobs such as receptionist or flight attendant where their looks were important and where they served the public (and especially males). Additionally, the representation of women in media was racialized through attributing certain roles and values to women according to their "whiteness" or by exoticizing women of color. Sexualization and objectification of women adhered to racialized models of representation through, for example, the complete absence of Black women in some contexts like the business world, as well as their predominance in other contexts as domestic workers, servants, and entertainers.

As the twentieth century progressed, these representations changed and women were found as central characters and increasingly portrayed as confident, worldly, and independent. The reading "Beautiful Betty" by Yeidy M. Rivero discusses the television show *Ugly Betty* and its origins in Latin American *telenovelas*. She argues that the show brings forth an assortment of issues about gender, class, and looks. However, although media representations of women are more diverse and favorable with more women in production roles, any time in front of a television, movie, or computer screen attests to the continuing sexualization and racialization of women and the way gender stereotypes still abound. Indeed, contemporary representations of women in media and popular culture are becoming increasingly more complex. Despite decades of global feminist activism, media are still resistant to embracing realistic and emancipatory portrayals of women. Feminist scholars continue to expose the problematic media misrepresentations about women in society, especially portrayals of violence against women. These representations often reflect the victim's "moral" character or degree of "alien-ness" in terms of their ethnic identity.

The Disney Corporation has been especially important in this regard in producing movies and merchandise supplying traditional notions of racialized gender. As demonstrated in the reading "Mirror, Mirror on the Wall," these images are internalized by children and affect the ways they think about themselves and others. In this reading author Tiya Miles shares her personal story watching Disney and discusses her work revising traditional fairy tales with a group of eight- and nine-year-old Puerto Rican and Haitian girls. Even though new Disney movies are much improved in terms of representations of women of color, they still show sexualized and exoticized characters.

As discussed in the next chapter, fixation with physical appearance and the body is overwhelmingly powerful in world media. Stories and images of female bodies occupy a vast volume of media coverage, across all types of media. Through the development of both body-altering technologies and computer-enhancement programs, the female body is continuously shaped to notions of "perfection." This quest for "beauty," commonly normalizes surgical and chemical procedures legitimizing them to female viewers/listeners/consumers through Western notions of "choice" and individualism. Media encourage women to understand these procedures of bodily modification and mutilation as opportunities for empowerment and personal

freedom. Advertisements for (liver damaging) skin-bleaching cosmetics promising white European skin for Asian women and Latinas can be found on billboards and magazines across the world. Popular culture media (fashion industries in particular) tend to portray the female body as something that needs "fixing" through intervention, thus promoting unrealistic, unhealthy, and often unachievable, portrayals of female bodies worldwide.

Obsession with the female body is also expressed in world media through expressions of physical or symbolic violence against the female or feminized body. In "regular" media (not understood as pornographic), women are often presented in passive poses with half-open mouths, backs arched, lying down, and/or with legs spread. Such portrayals involve women having things done *to* them. Men, on the other hand, are more likely to be presented as active and assertive. The hypersexualization of children and, in particular, the objectification of young girls is taking place in unprecedented force in magazines, music, and fashion; on the Internet; and in popular culture generally (APA, 2007; also see *Sexy Inc.*, a film produced by Sophie Bissonnette and the National Film Board of Canada: http://www3.nfb.ca/webextension/sexy-inc/). The female body remains a sexualized, fragmented, and mutilated body in the world of global advertising not only in the West but around the world. This mainstreaming of hypersexualized representations of femininity supports pornography and sex industries that until relatively recently have resided on the margins of society.

Today the pornography industry is by far the most prevalent of sexual exploitation on the Internet with profits exceeding the gross domestic product (GDP) of some small countries. A pioneer in adopting and promoting new technologies, the pornography industry was quick to utilize possibilities offered by the Internet for speedy and round-the-clock access to its products. Communications technologies, and, in particular, mobile communications, depend on pornographic content for their market expansion. Although questions concerning definitions and consequences of pornography have been broadly debated among feminist scholars for decades, studies of the industry as a global medium have been relatively limited. Currently, the industry is globally linked through networks of distributors, software, webmasters, and other intermediaries, as well as through new production networks across underprivileged regions like eastern Europe and the Philippines (Sarikakis and Shaukat, 2008). For pornography to create more markets and increase profits, content is becoming more violent and increasingly utilizing images of younger girls. Sex workers in pornography industries are from predominantly underprivileged backgrounds and regions of the world; are paid poorly, offered no job security, health or other benefits; and are exposed to various kinds of violence. In addition, as discussed in other chapters, this industry is linked to sex trafficking and tourism industries: multibillion-dollar endeavors that perpetrate prostitution and child abuse.

In order to dispel stereotypes and resist sexualization and objectification in favor of accurate and empowering representations of women, changes need to occur at all levels. Most agree that communication links need to remain open so that people are free and enabled to speak for themselves rather than being reduced to objects. Specific policy objectives included in the Declaration and Platform for Action coming out of the 1995 Beijing Fourth World Conference on Women suggest the following policy initiatives to improve the representation of women in world media: (1) promoting balanced and nonstereotyped portrayals of women and developing guidelines, codes of conduct, and self-regulation toward nonstereotyped images; (2) creating legislation against pornography and violence against women; (3) calling on governments, nongovernmental organizations (NGOs), the media, and private industry to develop specific programs, produce campaigns on women's

LEARNING ACTIVITY   **Global Women in the Movies**

Rent one or more of the following movies that focus on women around the world. How are women represented in these movies? Do their representations differ from the representations of global women in the blockbuster movies you'd typically see at an American multiplex? How is sexuality represented in these movies? Do these representations differ from a typical American blockbuster?

- Amelie (2000), France
- Babette's Feast (1987), Denmark
- Bend It Like Beckham (2002), UK
- Bhaji on the Beach (1993), UK
- Born into Brothels (2003), India
- Chaos (2001), France
- Chocolat (1988), France
- Crouching Tiger, Hidden Dragon (1999), China
- The Day I became a Woman (2000), Iran
- Fire (1996), UK
- Frida (2002), Mexico
- Lilja 4-ever (2003), Sweden
- Ma Vida Loca (1993), USA

- Ma Vie En Rose (1997), France
- The Magdalene Sisters (2002), Ireland
- Maria Full of Grace (2003), Colombia
- Missisippi Masala (1992), USA
- Persepolis (2008), France
- Rabbit Proof Fence (2002), Australia
- Rana's Wedding (2002), Palestine
- Saving Face (2004), USA
- Ten (2002), Iran
- Turtles Can Fly (2005), Iran
- Water (2005), India
- Whale Rider (2003), New Zealand
- XXY (2007), Argentina
- Yesterday (2004), South Africa

human rights and women in leadership, and support alternative media for women and women's groups; and (4) encouraging gender-sensitive programs for media professionals, including gender analysis in media training programs.

WOMEN'S ACCESS TO INFORMATION AND COMMUNICATION TECHNOLOGIES (ICTs)

Women's access to ICTs tends to involve both technological and social aspects. Technological infrastructure includes access to computers, hardware, software, Internet service providers, broadband connections, mobile (cell) phones, and wireless connections, while social infrastructure concerns knowledge about use of these technologies. Such knowledge involves possession of basic literacy and numeracy skills (including digital skills to navigate and search out relevant and timely information on the Internet for employment, education, and entertainment) and the ability to participate in interactive forums and produce and upload one's own digital content beyond passive receipt of content. Such access to ICTs is based on a variety of factors that include their cost, availability, and how easily they are accessed (e.g., at home through personal ownership of technologies, in the workplace, or at public access sites such as telecenters or public libraries). Access is also a function of "user" characteristics such as time constraints associated with family obligations as well as socioeconomic differences like income and education. Socioeconomic factors are shaped and complicated by race, ethnicity, being a member of a diasporic culture (movements or migration of populations sharing common ethnic identities) and physical or cognitive

PERCENT FEMALE INTERNET USERS IN RELATION TO OVERALL INTERNET PENETRATION, SELECTED COUNTRIES, 2005

Country	Internet Users Per 100 Inhabitants	% Female Internet Users
Norway	58.5	79.0
United States*	63.0	67.0
Thailand	11.0	51.9
Singapore	40.2	51.5
Syria	4.4	50.0
Sudan	8.0	49.9
Malaysia	42.4	49.8
Brazil	17.2	49.5
Hong Kong	50.1	49.3
Taiwan, China	58.0	49.0
Switzerland	50.9	48.9
Costa Rica	21.3	48.0
Czech Republic*	25.2	47.5
Lithuania	35.7	47.3
Slovak Republic	35.3	47.0
Republic of Korea*	65.7	45.5
Kyrgyzstan*	5.2	45.0
St Vincent & Grenadines	8.4	43.0
Egypt	6.8	42.0
Morocco	15.2	42.0
Netherlands*	61.6	41.0
China	8.6	40.4
Eritrea	1.8	40.0
Zimbabwe	10.1	40.0
Burkina Faso*	0.4	35.0
Azerbaijan	8.1	29.8
Nigeria	3.8	24.0
Ghana	1.8	23.9

Source: ITU, World Telecommunications Indicators, 2006 and adapted from Huyer and Hafkin, 2007, p. 38, Table 2.1
* 2004 data

differences. Cultural differences come into play as some cultures encourage young women's exploration of the Internet and some do not.

Digital literacy is a key area associated with social inequities. Sciadas (2005, p. 154), for example, reported that in European Union countries women score lower than men on digital literacy in four areas: (1) communication via e-mail; (2) downloading or obtaining software on a computer; (3) verifying the accuracy and reliability of online information and content; and (4) using search engines to find accurate and timely information. However, policy makers are starting to recognize that women need to be able to equally participate and benefit from the design, development, and diffusion of ICTs. Benefits include career enhancement and opportunities for participation in public spheres formerly restricted to men.

Access to ICTs varies widely between countries, and it cannot be assumed that country-wide increases in ICT use generally will correspond to greater use by women (Huyer and Hafkin, 2007). Digital divides vary widely between countries, with the gender divides often persisting in countries with high Internet access. Some countries experience low female access (Guinea has less than 10 percent; Nepal, less than 20 percent; and India, less than 32 percent) while in other countries with little Internet access such as Mongolia, Philippines, and Thailand, actually more women use the Internet. In some countries like Iran, South Africa, and Latvia, there is almost gender parity (see sidebar for country scores). Explanations for these differences include literacy and education levels, differences in employment in the ICT sector, financial autonomy within family structures, and age.

Policy Initiatives to Improve Women's Access to ICTs

Several global policy initiatives in the mid-1990s to improve women's access to ICTs were developed by supranational organizations such as the UN family, the International Telecommunication Union, the World Bank, and many NGOs concerned with developing programs under the rubric of ICT4D (information and communication technologies for development). These include first, more initiatives from the Declaration and Platform for Action of the 1995 Beijing Fourth World Conference on Women (discussed above) that emphasized the need to enhance women's skills, knowledge, and access to information technology. Second, the World Summit on the Information Society (WSIS) brought together "most developed," "developing," and "least developed" countries with private industry and civil society groups to develop an action plan for a global information society. It took place in two phases beginning with a 2003 Geneva Summit aimed at developing a Declaration of Principles and a Plan of Action for coordinated global development, and culminating in a 2005 Tunis Summit focusing on refinement of development themes, assessment of progress, and Internet governance.

In addition a WSIS Gender Caucus was formed during the African regional preparatory conference in 2002 as "a multi-stakeholder group consisting of women and men from national governments, civil society organizations, non-governmental organizations, the private sector and the United Nations system" (http://www.wsis.org). The strategic objective of the WSIS-Gender Caucus was to ensure that gender equality and women's rights were fully integrated into WSIS process and objectives. The caucus made six key recommendations for action. These included:

1. Gender as a fundamental principle for action
2. Equitable participation in decisions shaping the information society

3. **N**ew and old ICTs in a multimodal approach
4. **D**esigning ICTs to serve people
5. **E**mpowerment for full participation
6. **R**esearch analysis and evaluation to guide action (http://www.genderwsis.org)

Alongside the Gender Caucus, other groups like the Association for Progressive Communications (APC), a global network of civil society organizations whose mission is to empower individuals and groups through the use of ICTs (http://www.apc.org/), and their Women's Networking Support Group (concerned with gender and ICT advocacy and policy) also expressed concerns that WSIS initiatives have failed to reflect a critical awareness of gender and called for an intersectional approach to account for women in different socioeconomic, geographical, racial, and ethnic contexts. They hoped for a broader consensual platform that respected diversity, placed human rights and women's human rights as central principles in development, recognized the role of ICTs for peace and human development, and supported local solutions to ICT development, including use of open source (Association for Progressive Communications, 2003). Of concern to many was that despite its claims to represent many stakeholders, the WSIS process itself was bureaucratic, favoring industry groups and governments, and posing restrictions on the nature and involvement of civil society groups. Some feared that little attention was paid to educating women about ICTs or that women were positioned as a "special needs" group (McLaughlin and Pickard, 2005; Sreberny, 2005).

Finally, in 2008 (three years after the second WSIS summit), a retrospective focusing on the summit's impact on gender advocacy was convened in the Philippines. It emphasized a key difference in perceptions of gender and ICTs between local, grassroots women's groups, and broad regional and international networks and incorporated a study of the role of ICTs in women's everyday lives. It concluded that traditional media forms such as radio, film, and theater were the most effective and empowering tools for grassroots women's groups, with oral communication an efficient mediator between individual women and these groups. Technological infrastructure costs and access rendered the Internet and mobile (cell) phones the least accessible tool. The study emphasized the need to allow women to choose communication technologies that are most appropriate to their everyday needs (ISIS International–Manila, 2008).

WOMEN'S ICT PROJECTS FOR SOCIAL JUSTICE

Despite challenges to women worldwide in terms of their representations in, and access to, ICTs, women have been able to create independent and alternative media projects such as small press book and newspaper publishing, women's video collectives, and film distribution outlets (such as Women Make Movies, http://www.wmm.com).

Community Radio

For many women in developing countries, radio is the most democratic medium due to its affordability, portability, and opportunities for integrating local voices and language. Widely used as an instrument of popular mobilization and education, community radio is usually not controlled by corporate or government interests. As Mavic Cabrera-Balleza of the Women's International Network of the World Association of Community Radio Broadcasters (AMARC WIN) explains, community radio "transcends literacy barriers" and allows primary access by large numbers of women (2008, p. 16). Similarly, Rebone Molefe (2008, p. 49), a station manager of Tshwane University of Technology Community Radio in South Africa, argues that community radio gives voice to those who are marginalized by mainstream media. As such, it is the "perfect tool" for empowering grassroots women. When women gain radio production skills, they can educate others and increase their participation in community media organizations, labor unions, and political bodies. Such knowledge and skills can also liberate them from male dominance and abuse. Commenting on the introduction of community radio to groups in the hills of Uttaranchal, India, one researcher noted how disempowered community women in Chaani felt until their experiential knowledge of environmental issues was legitimized through radio programming (Negi, 2006).

Two feminist community radio distribution venues include WINGS and FIRE. In 1986 in Austin, Texas, Frieda Werden created WINGS, the Women's International News Gathering Service, "an all-woman independent radio-production company that produces and distributes news and current affairs programs by and about women around the world" (see http://www.wings.org/). Werden relocated to Vancouver, Canada, in 2002, and WINGS now broadcasts in over 150 community stations internationally. The Feminist International Radio Endeavour (FIRE) transmits live and archived radio programs via the Internet in English and Spanish on topics related to women's human rights, particularly for women in the Global South. FIRE originated in Costa Rica in 1998 with a mission to give voice to the voiceless, to promote nonsexist communication, and to strengthen local, regional, and global networks of feminist communication (http://www.fire.or.cr). FIRE is run by a staff of Latin American and Caribbean women with support from volunteers and other organizations. Funding comes from various divisions of the UN, international cooperative agencies, and philanthropic sources. Recent initiatives have focused on broadcasting women's experiences of war in conflict zones, strengthening their peace and security initiatives as an alternative to armed conflict.

Independent Film and Video Production

U.S. scholar activist Martha Lauzen (2007) reports on women working behind the scenes in Hollywood and the independent film industry in her annual "Celluloid Ceiling" studies. Here she provides ample evidence of the paucity of women as directors, executive producers, writers, cinematographers, and editors. In 2007, women represented 15 percent in all of those categories. Suggestions to counter this continued absence of women working in the film and television industries, and to encourage young women to enter the profession behind the camera, include first, the development of inclusive feminist activist media. Chica Luna (http://www.chicaluna.com), for example, is a U.S. New York-based nonprofit organization that works and supports women of color to use popular media to support social justice themes. Founded in 2001, Chica Luna has several projects, including The F-Word, a multimedia justice project for young women of color who learn filmmaking, organizing/advocacy skills, and self-healing. The goal is to train girls and women to be creators of media through direct involvement with the various technologies. Another organization is the Seattle-based "Reel Girls" that teaches girls to create their own videos and films (http://www.reelgrrls .org). YouTube, established in 2005 as a video-sharing Web site where users can view and share video clips, has provided opportunities for immediate uploading of videos. Although the content on YouTube is quite diverse and its goals are corporate, it does offer the poten-tial for the creation and sharing of feminist videos. A documentary on media consolidation and its impact on youth was produced by teenagers Sami Muilenburg and Brooke Noel after they heard about local Federal Communication Commission (FCC) hearings on proposed media policy legislation (http://www.archive.org/details/AGenerationOfConsolidation). Filmed presenting their views at the hearing, the video discusses the poignant challenges of creating feminist media in commercialized media policy environments.

Both Chica Luna and Reel Girls are involved in the second strategy: media literacy train-ing for young women that allows the latter to become critics of mainstream media images. Chica Luna's "Popular Media Justice Toolkit," for example, provides pedagogy, methodol-ogy, and strategies for analyzing race, class, and gender issues in the media (Sweeney, 2008). Third, it is suggested that documentary films about women's filmmaking be more readily shared. Kelly Hankin (2007), for example, describes several documentary films about inter-national women filmmakers such as Lesli Klainberg and Viriginia Riticker's *In the Company of Women* (distributed by Jericho, NY Independent Film Channel, 2004); Gerry Roger's film *Kathleen Shannon: On Film, Feminism, and Other Dreams* about Shannon's work with the Canadian National Film Board's women-run Studio D: (Montreal NFB, 1997); and Beti Ellerson's *Sisters of the Screen* (distributed by NYL Women Make Movies, 2002).

Social Media: Blogs and Web 2.0

Web 2.0. is the designator given to the participative Internet that includes social network sites (SNS) such as the popular MySpace, Facebook, and Twitter; blogging software; and video-sharing sites such as YouTube. These are the focus of much feminist activity, creating what Zacharias and Arthurs (2008) call "new architectures of intimacy." SNS activities are popular forms of com-munication used for socialization, entertainment, and, increasingly, social activism, especially among youth. A Pew Internet & American Life Project survey of teen use of social network sites highlights that more young women (the "super communicators") than young men use these sites to make interpersonal contacts and reinforce friendships (Lenhart & Madden, 2007).

Many women and women's groups are also using blogs to write about their personal experiences, politics, and culture. Popular U.S. blogs include BlogHer (http://www.blogher .com/), which aggregates personal blogs on a range of topics from parenting to fashion and entertainment, health, politics, and social issues. Its recent partnership with iVillage (BravoTV.com and Oxygen.com) will inevitably further commercialize the site. BlogHer has received much attention for its popularizing "Mommy Blogs" that allow monitory of content in advertising. Feministing (http://www.feministing.com/) is a forum for young feminists to blog on topical political, media, and pop culture issues. Founder Jessica Valenti started this forum after her disillusionment with the ways both mainstream media and traditional feminist organizations ignore young women's voices. Other examples of this include Jennifer Pozner's Women in Media and News (WIMN), a women's media analysis, advocacy, and education group supporting broad blogging activities on a diverse range of international issues (http://www.wimnonline.org/WIMNsVoicesBlog/), and the U.S.-based Cyberquilting Experiment. The Cyberquilting experiment brings together women of color to create a "cyber-communal training" space for social justice activism (http:// cyberquilt.wordpress.com/what-is-cyberquilting/). Other feminist blog sites include Western-focused "The Carnival of Feminists" (http://feministcarnival.blogspot.com/), a bimonthly themed collection of feminist blog postings, and the Muslimah Media Watch

Social Networking Goes Global

Score (NASDAQ: SCOR), a leader in measuring the digital world, today released the results of a study on the expansion of social networking across the globe, revealing that several major social networking sites have experienced dramatic growth during the past year.

Social networking behemoth MySpace.com attracted more than 114 million global visitors age 15 and older in June 2007, representing a 72 percent increase compared to the previous year. Facebook.com experienced even stronger growth during that same time frame, jumping 270 percent to 52.2 million visitors. Bebo.com (up 127 percent to 18.2 million visitors) and Tagged.com (up 774 percent to 13.2 million visitors) also increased by orders of magnitude.

WORLDWIDE GROWTH OF SELECTED* SOCIAL NETWORKING SITES
JUNE 2007 VS. JUNE 2006
TOTAL WORLDWIDE HOME/WORK LOCATIONS AMONG INTERNET
USERS AGE 15+

Social Networking Site	Total Unique Visitors		
	Jun-06	Jun-07	% Change
MySpace	66,401	114,147	72
Facebook	14,083	52,167	270
Hi5	18,098	28,174	56
Friendster	14,917	24,675	65
Orkut	13,588	24,120	78
Bebo	6,694	18,200	172
Tagged	1,506	13,167	774

* Sites selected from among those with at least 10 million visitors wordwide, 50 percent growth during the past year, and of particular significance to the North American region; future studies will focus on sites that are popular in other worldwide regions; the sites included do not constitute a ranking of the top social networking sites.
Source: comScore World Metrix

"During the past year, social networking has really taken off globally," said Bob Ivins, executive vice president of international markets. "Literally hundreds of millions of people around the world are visiting social networking sites each month and many are doing so on a daily basis. It would appear that social networking is not a fad but rather an activity that is being woven into the very fabric of the global Internet."

MySpace, Facebook Strong in North America; Bebo Grabs Hold in Europe
While attracting global users, specific social networks have a tendency to skew in popularity in different regions. For example, both MySpace.com (62 percent) and Facebook.com (68 percent) attract approximately two-thirds of their respective audiences from North America. That said, each has already amassed a large international visitor base and both appear poised to continue their global expansion. Bebo.com has a particularly strong grasp on Europe, attracting nearly 63 percent of its visitors from that region, while Orkut is firmly entrenched in Latin America (49 percent) and Asia-Pacific (43 percent). Friendster also attracts a significant proportion of its visitors (89 percent) from the Asia-Pacific region. Both Hi5.com and Tagged.

WORLDWIDE DAILY VISITATION OF SELECTED SOCIAL NETWORKING SITES JUNE 2007 VS. JUNE 2006
TOTAL WORLDWIDE HOME/WORK LOCATIONS AMONG INTERNET USERS AGE 15+

Social Networking Site	Average Daily Visitors		
	Jun-06	Jun-07	% Change
MySpace	16,764	28,786	72
Facebook	3,742	14,917	299
Hi5	2,873	4,727	65
Friendster	3,037	5,966	96
Orkut	5,488	9,628	75
Bebo	1,188	4,833	307
Tagged	202	983	386

Source: comScore World Metrix

VISITATION TO SELECTED SOCIAL NETWORKING SITES BY WORLDWIDE REGION JUNE 2007
TOTAL WORLDWIDE HOME/WORK LOCATIONS AMONG INTERNET USERS AGE 15+

Social Networking Site	Share (%) of Unique Visitors					
	Worldwide	North America	Latin America	Europe	Middle East-Africa	Asia Pacific
MySpace	100.0%	62.1%	3.8%	24.7%	1.3%	8.1%
Facebook	100.0%	68.4%	2.0%	16.8%	5.7%	7.1%
Hi5	100.0%	15.3%	24.1%	31.0%	8.7%	20.8%
Friendster	100.0%	7.7%	0.4%	2.5%	0.8%	88.7%
Orkut	100.0%	2.9%	48.9%	4.6%	0.6%	43.0%
Bebo	100.0%	21.8%	0.5%	62.5%	1.3%	13.9%
Tagged	100.0%	22.7%	14.6%	23.4%	10.0%	29.2%

Source: comScore World Metrix

com exhibit more balance in their respective visitor bases, drawing at least 8 percent from each of the five worldwide regions.

"A fundamental aspect of the success of social networking sites is cultural relevance," continued Mr. Ivins. "Those doing well in certain regions are likely doing an effective job of communicating appropriately with those regions' specific populations. As social networking continues to evolve, it will be exciting to see if networks are able to cross cultural barriers and bring people from different corners of the globe together in fulfilling the truest ideals of social networking."

ACTIVIST PROFILE   **RAWA**

The Revolutionary Association of the Women of Afghanistan began in 1977 to fight for human rights and social justice. While RAWA's activities initially focused only on women's human rights, the organization became actively involved in resistance to the 1979 Soviet occupation of Afghanistan. Unlike many of the religious fundamentalists who resisted the occupation, RAWA advocated for democracy and secularism. Additionally, RAWA became involved in assisting refugee women who had fled to Pakistan, establishing a hospital and schools, along with nursing, literacy, and vocational training courses for women. One of RAWA's founders, Meena, was assassinated in 1987 by the Afghan branch of the KGB while she was in Pakistan.

Following the overthrow of Soviet rule, RAWA struggled against fundamentalist control of Afghanistan, particularly the Taliban's antiwoman policies and laws. While the U.S. invasion of Afghanistan in 2001 removed the Taliban from governmental power, religious fundamentalists continue to control women's lives in many ways. Many of the warlords supported by the current government are themselves violent and misogynistic. Nonetheless, RAWA continues to provide education, healthcare, and financial support for the women of Afghanistan and to oppose the antiwoman laws and policies that remain in effect. RAWA has effectively used the Internet to reach out to women across the world to assist them in their struggle against misogyny and violence. Visit their Web site at www.rawa.org.

Meena's words, in this excerpt from the poem, "I'll Never Return," remain descriptive of the resolve of the Revolutionary Association of the Women of Afghanistan:

I'm the woman who has awoken
I've arisen and become a tempest through the ashes of my burnt children
I've arisen from the rivulets of my brother's blood
My nation's wrath has empowered me

My ruined and burnt villages fill me with hatred against the enemy
Oh compatriot, no longer regard me weak and incapable,
My voice has mingled with thousands of arisen women
My fists are clenched with fists of thousands of compatriots
To break all these sufferings all these fetters of slavery.
I'm the woman who has awoken,
I've found my path and will never return.

www.rawa.org/rawa.html
www.rawa.org/meena.html

(http://muslimahmediawatch.org/), a blog focusing on global media representations of Muslim women. The latter function in a precarious position in a volatile political climate (Khiabany and Sreberney, 2007). Oreoluwa Somolu, a founder of Blogs for African Women (BAWo), reiterates many of the same motivations for African women bloggers as women working in community radio. Focusing on Nigerian women, BAWo helps women connect with each other and strategize and map out ways to improve their lives. In the reading 'Telling Our Own Stories': African Women Blogging for Social Change," Somolu describes the ways African women have embraced the blogging phenomenon. She examines how African women are using blogs and also discusses obstacles to their use.

Mobile Phones

Scholarship on mobile (cell) phone culture has increased in the last decade with a focus on its uses in Scandinavia and South-East Asia where uptake and technological innovations have been swift. In Japan, *keitai* culture (a Japanese expression for a mobile phone and its uses) has been the purview of youth culture, and particularly young women, who have personalized and created a distinct phone culture in their everyday lives (Ito, Okabe, and Matsuda, 2005). Lee (2005, n.p.) also describes how young South Korean women have appropriated the camera phone for cultural production and sociability, despite the prevalence of commercials that show men snapping pictures of women: "these women are not the mere owners of camera phones, but performers who create various cultural meanings. They develop a more intimate relationship with technology,

LEARNING ACTIVITY   **Phone Home**

Do a quick survey of your classmates. How many have cell phones with them in class today? In what ways have they personalized their phones (covers, ringtones, photos)? Do you see any gendered patterns in cell phone personalization? Have them list in order from most important to least important their uses of their phones (calling friends, calling family, texting, taking photos, listening to music, surfing the Web, etc.). Again, do you see any gendered patterns in cell phone use?

Visit the Web site http://hollabacknyc.blogspot.com. Hollaback is a Web site to combat street harassment by using cell phones to snap photos of harassers and post them on the Web along with stories and comments. What other ways might activists utilize cell phones for organizing and activism?

challenge the conventions of gaze, give meaning to what is taken, and circulate their own expressions."

The case of the Village Phone project in rural Bangladesh funded by the Grameen Bank has become almost emblematic of the success stories of ICTD (Information and Communications Technology for Development, or, applying computer technology in ways that are beneficial for society). In this project, "phone ladies" own Village Phone Businesses acquired through microcredit loans and then rent phones to community members (most of whom are men) on a per-call basis http://www.grameenfoundation.org/what_we_do/technology_programs/village_phone/).

Mobile phone technology and SMS (or Short Message Service: a communications protocol allowing interchange of short text messages between mobile telephone devices) is also increasingly being used in citizen media to educate, inform, and bring people together. For example, uses include education about such issues as sexuality and HIV/AIDS, information for refugees about humanitarian aid, videos that expose police abuses, and knowledge about political processes and elections. Phone technologies can be used to gather and report on political news, to provide real-time election results, to aid in community economic development, to fight poverty and help workers find employment, and to aid women in keeping track of small loans for micro-enterprises (http://www.Mobile.Active.org). In the 2007 Kenyan election, mobiles were given to Community Information Volunteers who made short videos to promote electoral participation. One woman used it to probe why women were not running for political office and what Kenyans thought about women as political leaders (Verclas and Mechael, 2008). Fahamu, an African NGO, has also documented the use of mobiles and SMS for social justice advocacy and awareness. In one instance, Fahamu collaborated with the Solidarity with African Women's Rights coalition to mobilize citizens to register their support for the African Union's Protocol on the Rights of Women in Africa campaign. Fahamu is also working with the Rural Women's Movement in South Africa to teach women how to use SMS to report on land rights and violence against women (http://www.fahamu.org/advocacy/article/mobile_phones_for_social_justice/).

CONCLUSION

This chapter presents a brief overview of the current global mediascape, emphasizing the ways women are positioned in terms of status and representation. Structural inequalities combined with various expressions of patriarchal cultures across societies infiltrate women's efforts for social change, whether through policy making, representation in the media, or access and use of communication technologies. Moreover, old stereotypes persist in new forms dressed in the language of "choice" and "empowerment": terms utilized and introduced by the feminist movements around the world, but deployed today to perpetuate the myths of beauty and sexuality advocated by pornographic products in popular culture.

Despite structural realities of commercial media that tend to obscure and delimit women's positive contributions and representation, women are active agents of their own lives and are involved with new forms of media to educate, share information, and actively work toward social change. The active take-up of different media by many women, both as individuals and in social organizations, plus their interest in contributing to media policy at local and global levels, is cause for optimism. The creative and participatory nature of many of these projects, whether they are positioned within community radio, blogs, or mobile phones, points to an emergence of citizens' media that strengthens women's voices and counters corporate concentration of mainstream media.

REFERENCES

American Psychological Association. (2007). *Report of the APA task force on the sexualization of girls.* URL: http://www.apa.org/pi/wpo/sexualization.html.

Association for Progressive Communications. (2003). APC Women's Programme critiques the draft Declaration and Action Plan prepared for the UN World Summit on the Information Society (March 21, 2003). URL: http://www.apc.org/english/news/index.shtml?x=12233. social life. In D. Buckingham (Ed.), *Youth, identity and digital media* (pp. 119–142). Cambridge: MIT Press.

Cabrera-Balleza, M. (2008). Community radio as an instrument in promoting women's participation in governance. In M. Solervicens (Ed.), *Women's empowerment and good governance through community radio: Best experiences for an action research process* (pp. 13–16). Montreal: AMARC International Secretariat.

Hankin, K. (2007, Spring). And introducing. . . The female director: Documentaries about women filmmakers as feminist activism. *NWSA Journal, 19*(1), 59–88.

Huyer, S. and Hafkin, N. (2007). *Engendering the knowledge society: Measuring women's participation.* Montreal: Orbicom.

ISIS International–Manila. (2008). *People's communication for development: How intermediary groups use communication tools for grassroots women's empowerment.* Manila: Isis International. URL: http://www.isiswomen.org/index.php?option=com_content&task=view&id=832&Itemid=202.

Ito, M., Okabe, D. and Matsuda, M. (Eds.), (2005). *Personal, portable, pedestrian: Mobile phones in Japanese life.* Cambridge: MIT Press.

Jiwani, Y. (2008). Mediations of domination: Gendered violence within and across borders. In K. Sarikakis and L. Regan Shade (Eds.), *Feminist interventions in international communication: Minding the gap* (pp. 129–145). Lanham, MD: Rowman and Littlefield.

Khiabany, G. and Sreberny, A. (2007). The politics of/in blogging in Iran. *Comparative Studies of South Asia, Africa and the Middle East, 27*(3), 563–579.

Lauzen, M. (2007). *The celluloid ceiling: Behind-the-scenes employment of women in the top 250 films of 2007.* Center for the Study of Women in Television & Film, San Diego State University. URL: http://womenintvfilm.sdsu.edu/research.html.

Lee, D. (2005). Women's creation of camera phone culture. *FibreCulture,* Issue 6: Mobility, new social intensities and the coordinates of digital culture. URL: http://journal.fibreculture.org/issue6/issue6_donghoo.html.

Lenhart, A. and Madden, M. (2007). *Social networking websites and teens: An overview.* Pew Internet and American Life Project. URL: http://www.pewinternet.org/PPF/r/198/report_display.asp.

Matar, D. (2007). Heya TV: A feminist counterpublic for Arab women? *Comparative Studies of South Asia, Africa and the Middle East, 27*(3), 513–524.

McLaughlin, L. (2008). Women, information work, and the corporatization of development. In K. Sarikakis and L. Regan Shade (Eds.), *Feminist interventions in international communication: Minding the gap* (pp. 224–240). Lanham. MD: Rowman and Littlefield.

McLaughlin, L. and Pickard, V. (2005). What is bottom-up about global internet governance? *Global Media and Communication, 1*(3), 357–373.

Molefe, R. (2008). South Africa: Measures for ensuring women's participation and challenges that hamper the rapid empowerment of women. In Marcelo Solervicens (Ed.), *Women's empowerment and good governance through community radio: Best experiences for an action research process* (pp. 47–50). Montreal: AMARC International Secretariat.

Negi, R. (2006). Community radio and emerging information networks. *International Journal of Education and Development Using Information and Communication Technologies, 2*(2), 6–68.

Queen Latifah. (2000). *Ladies first: Revelations of a strong woman.* NY: Harper Paperbacks.

Sarikakis, K. and Shauket, Z. (2008). The global structures and cultures of pornography: The global brothel. In K. Sarikakis and L. Regan Shade (Eds.), *Feminist interventions in international communication: Minding the gap* (pp. 106–126). Lanham. MD: Rowman and Littlefield.

Sciadas, G. (Ed.) (2005). *From the digital divide to digital opportunities: Measuring infostates for development.* Montreal: Orbicom. URL: http://www.itu.int/ITU-D/ict/publications/dd/summary.html.

Sreberny, A. (2005). Gender, empowerment, and communication: Looking backwards and forwards. *International Social Science Journal, 57*(184), 285–296.

Stein, J. (2008, February 14). Women in focus as Asian cable booms. Reuters. URL: http://www.reuters.com/article/industryNews/idUSN1450056420080215.

Sweeny, K. (2008). *Maiden USA: Girl icons come of age.* NY: Peter Lang Publishing. URL: http://www.video-text.com/.

Verclas, K. and Mechael, P. (2008, November). *A mobile voice: The use of mobile phones in citizen media.* MobileActive.org. URL: http://mobileactive.org/mobile-voice-use-mobile-phones-citizen-media.

Zacharias, U. and Arthurs, J. (2008). Introduction: The new architectures of intimacy? Social Networking Sites and Genders. *Feminist Media Studies, 8*(2), 197–223.

SUGGESTIONS FOR FURTHER READING

Cuklanz, L. M. and Moorti, S. (Eds.). (2009). *Local violence, global media: Feminist analyses of gendered representations.* New York: Peter Lang Publishing.

De Jong, W., Shaw, M. and Stammers, N. (Eds.). (2005). *Global activism, global media.* London: Pluto Press.

Marciniak, K., Imre, A., and O'Healy, A. (2007). *Transnational feminism in film and media: Visibility, representation, and sexual differences.* Hampshire, U.K.: Palgrave Macmillan.

Markula, P. and Bruce, T. (Eds.). (2009). *Olympic women and the media: International perspectives.* Hampshire, U.K.: Palgrave Macmillan.

Oliver, K. (2007). *Women as weapons of war: Iraq, sex, and the media.* New York: Columbia University Press.

Glamour and Honor: Going Online and Reading in West African Culture

Wendy Griswold, Erin Metz McDonnell, and Terence Emmett McDonnell (2006)

When West Africans go online, what are the cultural consequences? This article investigates how public access to the Internet is affecting Nigerian and Ghanaian urban culture in general and reading in particular.

Research assessing the Internet's impact on sub-Saharan Africa has concentrated on the two faces of the digital divide: (1) will the Internet exacerbate, or reduce, the technological gap between the developing world and advanced industrial societies? and (2) what effect will the Internet have on internal patterns of social and political stratification? We are addressing a related but specifically cultural question: how are West Africans using the Internet, and how are their practices affecting other media, in particular print?

Although most research on the Internet's impact on book production and on reading practices comes from Western Europe and North America, Nigeria and Ghana offer intriguing grounds for addressing similar questions. Both have large populations of literate people, well-developed literary institutions, and internationally eminent writers. Nevertheless, their reading cultures may be fragile, for they involve a small fraction of the population and they operate in a cultural context that rewards socializing more than individual pastimes. As new entrants into the wired world, Nigeria and Ghana are living laboratories for investigating cultural responses to technological change.

Some working definitions are in order. Whereas *literacy* refers to the ability to decode written texts, *reading* is the actual practice of doing so. We further restrict *reading* (as do virtually all studies of reading) to refer to the leisure-time engagement with print. This excludes the reading required for job performance or for school, and it excludes reading online. Our informants define it the same way. *Readers* are

not people who *can* read, or who *do* read for work but those who *choose to read* in their spare time. The definition includes magazines and newspapers, although some of our respondents did associate "reading" with "books." We use the terms *using the Internet* and *going online* as equivalents, for the people we studied do not distinguish between the two. *West Africa* is shorthand for the places studied, urban Ghana and Nigeria. Despite many differences, West African countries share similar patterns of sharp North/South and rural/urban divides, ubiquitous cybercafés in cities, and ambitious youth who see education and global connections as their ticket to a brighter future; they differ from East and South Africa in lacking a (European) settler population and being less developed in terms of indicators like literacy rates.

Our methods were exploratory and opportunistic. One of the authors has studied Nigerian readers for many years (Griswold 2000). As she was completing a book on the Nigerian literary complex, Internet access became widely available in urban West Africa. The same people that constituted the Nigerian readers—the young, the educated, the well-off, the urban—were also the early adopters of such practices as sending e-mails, playing online video games, and surfing the Net for entertainment and information. So the substantive question arose: what impact would this development have on the literary culture that she had just finished mapping? Through this case one may consider more general questions about how electronic culture engages print culture: Do they compete? Do they support each other? Do they not engage at all?

Griswold observed Internet cafés and interviewed users in Lagos during August 2002 and January 2004. McDonnell and McDonnell carried out comparable interviewing and observation during the summer of

2003 in Accra. In March 2005 Griswold conducted focus group interviews on reading and Internet use at three secondary schools in Nigeria: Queen's College—Yaba; Igbobi College; and Federal Government Girls' College, Sagamu. Students at these elite schools do not represent Nigerians and Ghanaians as a whole. They do represent (1) the next generation of the reading class and (2) the first generation of youth who take Internet access for granted.

THE READING CLASS IN WEST AFRICA

People who routinely read in their leisure time constitute a social formation that we call the "reading class" (Griswold et al. 2005). Historically the reading class has been an elite group associated with religious hierarchies (the Church in the European Middle Ages) or regime hierarchies (the Chinese bureaucrats—literati—during the Qing dynasty). It was not until late the eighteenth-century that northwestern Europe and North America developed a reading culture, one wherein commercial, governmental, entertainment, and religious-ideological institutions presumed the widespread ability to read (Rose 2001). Other parts of the world caught up gradually. Africa lags the rest of the world in literacy, and West Africa lags the rest of Africa.[1] UNESCO reported that in 2000, 28.4% of adult Ghanaians were illiterate (19.7% of the men and 36.8% of the women); Nigeria was even worse, with adult illiteracy at 36.0% (27.8% male, 43.9% female) (UNESCO Institute for Statistics 2002).

West African readers—not those who are literate but those who read for pleasure—share some of the characteristics of readers everywhere. First and foremost, they are highly educated; education is invariably the strongest predictor of reading (Griswold et al. 2005). They are affluent and they are urban, standard characteristics associated with both literacy and reading as a practice. More specific to the African context, Ghanaian and Nigerian readers are disproportionately likely to be Christian. Islam as interpreted by West African mullahs tends to discourage secular reading; moreover, the literacy rates for Muslims, especially women, have historically been much lower than for non-Muslims (Griswold

2000).[2] In contrast, much colonial literacy was a product of Christian missionary schools, and the Christian churches have continued to involve themselves in education and book publication. Reading is prestigious, even for youth, and books are fairly hard to come by, so reading a book—any book—confers status (Griswold 2000; Newell 2000). One way in which African reading may be different from Western reading involves gender. In the West women read more than men; the difference, while not large, is very stable (Griswold et al. 2005). In Africa, however, because males lead females in literacy and because Africans have large families so even educated women have little leisure time, women's usual gender advantage may not apply.[3]

Although the West African transition to print culture is not complete, people there assume that it will happen. During interviews for a book on the social complex underlying Nigerian fiction, the editors, authors, readers, and booksellers repeatedly said something along the lines of, "Nigeria does not have a large reading culture yet, but when it does . . ."—for example, we'll sell more books, I'll live off my writing, it will be easier for me to get hold of books, the quality of our literature will improve, kids will be better off, and so forth (Griswold 2000). The Nigerian and Ghanaian reading class sees itself as a vanguard for this reading culture, small, beleaguered, but on the winning side of history.

The onset of electronic media and the Internet raises questions about this assumption. Contrary to the expectations of their writers, publishers, and readers, Nigeria and Ghana might never attain (or need) a larger "reading culture" than they already have; indeed, the reading culture might shrink. One way this could occur is that, heretofore, African popular literature has served as an entry point (the "rich compost of prior creativity," as Lindfors put it) into reading for youth and/or the newly literate, with some readers and writers then moving on to more challenging material (Lindfors 1996; Newell 2000). If the easy entertainment of lightweight reading (Macmillan's Pacesetters, romance magazines, Onitsha market literature, *soyayya* love stories) gives way to the easy entertainment of video games and the Internet, this would derail the expected move from less demanding to more demanding reading.

Defenders of print culture have worried about competition from electronic media since the early days of television. Dana Gioia, chairman of the NEA, argues that "reading a book requires a degree of active attention and engagement. . . . By contrast, most electronic media such as television, recordings, and radio make fewer demands on their audiences, and indeed often require no more than passive participation. Even interactive electronic media, such as video games and the Internet, foster shorter attention spans and accelerated gratification." The results of reading being displaced by other media would be disastrous. "[P]rint culture affords irreplaceable forms of focused attention and contemplation that make complex communications and insights possible. To lose such intellectual capability—and the many sorts of human continuity it allows—would constitute a vast cultural impoverishment" (NEA 2004, vii). This is the view held, without exception, by the adult Ghanaians and Nigerians with whom we spoke, even those who enthusiastically embrace the advantages of going online. West African educators, editors, authors, and middle-class parents fear the Internet could have a catastrophic effect on the fragile reading culture.

THE INTERNET IN WEST AFRICA

Three kinds of billboards assault the visitor coming into Lagos from the Murtala Mohammed Airport: ones involving HIV-AIDS, ones promoting religious revivals, and ones touting Internet services. Ads for dot.coms, cybercafés, and Internet service providers are ubiquitous. Accra offers the same visual landscape: ads for Busy Internet (the city's largest cybercafé) are everywhere. Service providers and dot.coms advertise widely, whereas cybercafés usually restrict their signs to their immediate neighborhoods.

West Africans' embrace of the Internet is not simply due to technological enthusiasm. Although e-mail has many advantages everywhere, it has one extra one in Nigeria and Ghana: it helps free West Africans from their abysmal local telephone service. Government-run Nitel and Ghana Telecom are notorious. Calls don't get through, phones go dead for hours, people wait years to get connected. (Ghanaians and Nigerians similarly love mobile phones because they circumvent

the national phone companies.) Most Africans don't use e-mail to contact people in the same city—an e-mail message won't be received until the recipient goes to the cybercafé—but e-mail is far more effective and less expensive than phones for keeping in touch with relatives in other towns or abroad.

All of the larger newspapers in Accra and Lagos have their own Web sites, and some—*This Day, Tell*—are quite sophisticated. In our observation of Internet use in both countries, however, we *never* observed anyone looking at a local paper's Web site, nor did anyone ever mention doing so. People do go online to look up sports scores or news information, but not from local newspapers. A newspaper Web site is to impress and thereby to encourage the sale of more print copies of the paper, though a secondary but much-appreciated function is to enable expatriate Africans keep up with local news. The same is true of all business Web sites: West Africans don't shop online anyway, and few spend much time in cybercafés checking on what Avery's engineers have been up to lately. These Web sites are for prestige, not utility. All businesses want to appear up-to-date, so the point is to have a Web site and e-mail address, not to have customers actually be able to use them.

Does all this mean Nigeria and Ghana are "wired"? Does this suggest West Africans routinely use the Internet? No, for we know this is not the case.[4] What it does suggest is that there is glamour associated with the popular IT complex—URLs, e-mail addresses, Internet use—even though people face obstacles in actually taking advantage of the new technologies. Part of the glamour comes from being on the cutting edge, but in countries such as Ghana and Nigeria additional panache comes from being connected to the outside world, being seen as and seeing oneself as a global player. Whereas West African youth can try to capitalize on this, for example by obtaining visitors' e-mail addresses and then contacting them for help getting into foreign universities, merely to have the connections is satisfying. In societies where dispensing patronage—being a "big man"—is an important cultural role, both businesses and individuals benefit from a reputation of being wired into external contacts. Promotion and advertising capitalizes on this cultural fact by generating anxiety, the fear of missing out by not being online. This is one reason why entrepreneur-ial West Africans have been so determined to go around their local infrastructures in order to reach cyberspace (Zachery 2002; Goldstein 2004).

Cybercafés

For the average Nigerian or Ghanaian, the road to cyberspace goes through an Internet café. Lagos seems to have a cybercafé on every block. Even if you miss the sign, the tall red-and-white towers sprout-ing everywhere pinpoint their locations. In Accra, although the towers are not always red and white, the cafés are everywhere.

Lagos cafés are pleasant places: air conditioned, clean, and—by West African standards—quiet. They may be crowded, with each actual user surrounded by a cloud of friends. The connection charge is modest, typically 60 naira (roughly 40 cents) for a half-hour or 100 naira per hour. This is not exor-bitant, and the middle class is well able to afford it. Cybercafés range from business-like operations with training programs and an adult, work-oriented cli-entele, to local hangouts with posters on the wall, loud music, snacks, and young customers. Because they are neighborhood based, most cafés serve both types of clients, but the feeling in each is distinct (cf. Miller & Slater 2000).

Accra likewise has two levels of cybercafé. High-end operations, which feature newer computers and operating software, are clean, air-conditioned, and relatively quiet and orderly. Busy Internet's red walls are covered with popular Adinkra symbols; Conect [*sic*] Café has locally made batik cloth for the wait-ing area couches and draperies. Such Cafés offer beverages and "small chops"—that is, home-baked biscuits and other snacks. They tend to have more terminals than the more humble operations, and they are more likely to offer auxiliary services such as long-distance calling, printing, computer software classes, and computer assistance. Low-end cafés are poorly lit, small-scale, and offer older computers and software. A single employee is on site and is often not able to help users much, though some such cafés charge extra for staff assistance. These low-end cafés tend to be located off the main traffic areas, and they serve a neighborhood, often working-class, clientele.

High-end cafés draw a mix of middle-class Ghana-ians, students, expatriates, and visitors.[5]

During the day most cybercafé customers are adults, either young men and women in their twen-ties or middle-aged adult men. When schools let out in mid-afternoon, youth take over the cafés and continue to dominate all evening (very young teens earlier, older ones later). Some adults show up after work, and some students show up during the day (and, of course, on weekends), but the general pat-tern seems to be adults earlier, youth mid-afternoon and later. Youth often go online in groups, with one paying customer accompanied by friends.

One demographic group rarely appears: women beyond their early twenties. Pressed for time, mature women seldom go to cybercafés; if they need Inter-net information, they usually send their children to the café to get it.[6] Women as a whole are under-represented, especially in Nigeria, and most cyber-café owners and virtually all computer technicians are men. The picture in Ghana is only slightly more balanced. The owner of the largest café in Cape Coast (one of the three main cities) is a woman, and one of her assistants is female, though she is not as involved with the hardware assistance as with soft-ware usage. In Accra, however, all owners are men. Although development organizations like the World Bank work "with missionary-like zeal" at putting IT in the hands of African women, social and economic patterns on the ground have reproduced gendered inequality so far (Robins 2002).

West African Internet users may be even more youthful than elsewhere because the schools introduce youth to computer skills and because high fertility rates mean that young people constitute an enormous portion of the population.[7] Certainly the cybercafés are largely domains of the young. Older people may be going online at their workplaces, but, if they are, their activities are likely to be limited. Because our focus is on leisure time, Internet use compared to leisure reading, and because the Internet penetration into the home is minimal, the cafés constitute a good register of who is going online in their spare time.

Café managers recognize the youthfulness of their clientele but underestimate the gender gap. For example, the Conect Café in the Osu neighborhood of Accra was observed five times from May to late

July 2003. Overall, there were thirty-six young male customers, one young woman, five middle-aged men, and one middle-aged woman. At Cyberlink Café in the Yaba neighborhood of Lagos, at 3:00 in the afternoon of January 2004, there were twelve males and one female at the terminals (all young). There were also three young men sitting and talking; it was not clear if they were waiting for someone or not, but they were not waiting for terminals, as several were free. The front desk personnel, two young women and one man, obscured how masculine the space actually was.

Going Online

Cybercafé managers report that adult customers go online to e-mail, look up sports and entertainment news, and search for jobs or educational opportunities—schools, test requirements, scholarships. Customers also troll for pornography; some managers actively discourage this while others shrug. One thing West Africans do not do online is make purchases. With both Nigeria and Ghana being cash economies, the credit card transactions essential to e-commerce are impossible for most people.

Youth go online primarily for social reasons. By far the most popular activity is e-mail.[8] They chat with people from around the world. They read about their favorite sports teams. They visit entertainment sites. They are seldom required to do schoolwork online, though some students do research (not easy in cybercafés because printing is expensive and the meter is always running).

Patricia, a fourteen-year-old Nigerian girl whose online activities we observe during a session at Cyberlink, exemplifies youth practices. After she pays her 60 naira, Cyberlink staff give her a username and password. She first checks e-mail via Yahoo messenger. Her e-mails are from school friends, from her brother who is studying medicine in Atlanta, and from people she has met online. She knows girls who meet dates online, though she would not do this herself.

She then begins surfing by going to Lyrics.com to check out some Eminem lyrics; Patricia is a huge Eminem fan. (Looking up music celebrities is popular in Ghana as well; Busy Internet has a menu devoted entirely to Tupac.) Patricia also look

at tickle.com, which has personality questionnaires and horoscopes. She participates in several chat groups, including a favorite for Christian teens. She doesn't download music or games because, if she saved them, she would have to get the same terminal next time; because of virus concerns, Cyberlink customers can't bring in diskettes or CDs.

Although Patricia's Internet access is very local, a half-block from her house, her online activities are global. For example, if she wants to check up on some Nigerian story or entertainer, she just Googles them. (A portal called onlinenigeria.com exists, but she doesn't bother with it.) She chats to a friend in India regularly, and exchanges e-mails with her brother and other relatives in the United States and United Kingdom. In many ways it is easier for her to navigate globally than locally. Information from places outside West Africa is more readily available than information from within; in Lagos and Accra, online services like locating addresses via MapQuest.com or online residential telephone directories simply don't exist.

In West Africa, like everywhere else, young people are confident Internet users whereas their elders tend to be diffident. Older users have a sense that, although everything can be found on the Internet, they do not know how to do it. One Ghanaian entrepreneur, who owned a rental housing complex and a restaurant, wanted to get into fish farming and asked the authors to search for information online; despite his successful enterprises, he assumed his own Internet incompetence. Younger people are savvier at finding things online. Friends particularly share information about free e-mail sites, and the average teenager knows a dozen or so. The time factor at cybercafés encourages extraordinary dexterity among the youth, who juggle a half dozen different online activities, fingers flying as they e-mail, participate in a couple of chat rooms, check out a singer's Web page. Multitasking is second nature to kids such as Patricia, and monitoring three Beyoncé Web sites while e-mailing your brother presents no problem.

YOUTH READING, YOUTH ONLINE

Looking at the practices of youth is essential for understanding cultural change or stability. How young, educationally advantaged, urban West Africans read and how they use the Internet matter because (1) these youth are the future West African reading class, if there is to be one, and (2) they are the demographic and socio-economic group most likely to be experiencing the satisfactions of going online.

We held focus group discussions at three secondary schools in or near Lagos: Queen's College–Yaba (girls), Igbobi College (boys), and Federal Government Girls' College, Sagamu (girls). These elite schools admit students through competitive examinations. Queen's and Igbobi are unity schools, supported by the federal government; Igbobi is a mission school, supported by the Anglican and Methodist churches. Queen's and Igbobi have boarding and day students; FGGC Sagamu girls are all boarders. The students at these schools are not representative of Nigerian youth as a whole. They are academic stars, and they are likely to come from educationally advantaged, middle-class backgrounds; both characteristics make them budding members of the reading class, and indeed they do read a great deal. Their considerable cultural capital makes them appropriate for a study of the cultural practices of the first West African generation to grow up with the Internet.

Our discussions, which took place in an assembly hall (Queen's), a library (Igbobi), and a classroom (FGGC Sagamu), began with the question of when and where the teenagers read for pleasure. Most read in the nighttime or anytime "I'm bored." One girl said she reads at times when she's feeling sleepy, often taking a break from studies to pick up a newspaper, but she also reads at night, especially if she's *not* sleepy. Another gave the typical response: she reads afternoons, nights, and on Saturdays, which is a "free day" for all the students. Boys and girls said they read during their leisure time—that is, on weekends, after school, and at night. A few girls, but no boys, read in the early mornings—one reported that she slept in the day and woke up around 3:00 AM to read until 6:00—because it was quiet then. Another said she liked to read "in the middle of the night" for the same reason: "I like very quiet places."

No one reported reading in any other place except "in my room" or in the school library. Day students say they read mostly at home, in their rooms, and

they are usually alone when they read. Boarders find it more difficult to be alone (the dormitory rooms house fifteen or so) but they lie on their beds and manage to lose themselves in a book. At Igbobi one boarder said it is never hard to find quiet places to read around the school, and he also reads late in his room at night: "I just keep turning the pages."

When asked where they got their books, most said they bought or borrowed them—"I get them from my cousins" was a common response—though a few mentioned their school library as well. Several mentioned home libraries. Books are valued family possessions, and old paperback novels or schoolbooks do not get discarded.

Both girls and boys cited "thrillers" as their favorite leisure reading. They repeatedly brought up crime and adventure writers such as James Hadley Chase, Tom Clancy, and Sidney Sheldon as well as romance writer Danielle Steel, the Harry Potter books, and local youth-oriented fiction series such as Pacesetters and Lantern Books. (Patricia, whose online activities we looked at earlier, had similar tastes, telling us, "I like to read suspense novels, mainly bestsellers like John Grisham, Jeffrey Deaver, Sidney Sheldon, etc. I also read autobiographies, or biographies. . . . I read a wide range of books, but suspense novels are my favorite.")

Not everyone reads fiction. One boy said he likes history, both African and non-African. Another loves basketball magazines and books. Another likes to read the newspapers at night. Several girls mentioned reading magazines. One girl reads the *Watchtower,* the magazine put out by Jehovah's Witnesses. Several girls at Queen's College reported that they didn't like to read at all and did so only for their schoolwork. Because their English teachers were present, this response seemed to indicate the girls' frankness, and indeed the teachers later commented approvingly that Queen's College girls are encouraged to "speak their minds."

One boy who hopes to be a writer himself some day was working on a copy of Isadore Okpewho's *The Last Duty;* he mentioned that he has a reading room/ library at home and that his family does a lot of reading. This prompted me to ask the group if anyone came from a family that did *not* do much reading, but no one said they did. These are children of the reading class, and they take for granted that reading wins parental approval as well as social honor.

Most of these same students go online regularly. They do it from cybercafés; only a handful, usually with a parent working in the IT sector, have Internet access at home. Sagamu did not have Internet access from the school, and while Queens and Igbobi did, going online was restricted to school-work (although there were a few knowing smiles on this point). Some youth go to the cafés after school, but most go on Saturdays. One typical boy said he goes on weekends because that is his only leisure time; after school he does assignments. The cybercafés aren't open on Sundays, so he goes on Saturday evenings, observing "the atmosphere is cool at that time." He often goes with his friends or meets them there, since they go to the same cyber-café because "we all like it." Girls also reported going with cousins, siblings, or friends or meeting them there, though both girls and boys go alone as well. Girls did not go at night because they didn't go out at night at all. Most seemed to think cyber-cafés themselves were safe places, though one girl, who can go online from her home, felt uncomfort-able with the mix— "all sorts of people"—there.

Going online fulfills social and informational functions. As we observed at the cybercafés, chatting and e-mail are key, and some youth cheerfully admit-ted that chatting was "the most interesting thing to do." Many talked about staying in touch with friends and relatives abroad, and some mentioned online friends all over the world. Entertainment and sports sites were also popular. One girl who reported that she goes to the cybercafé with her cousin proceeded to give a detailed account about what "the cousin" did there: "First of all check the top ten songs, top ten mov-ies, and that sort of thing . . . the latest cameras . . . she wants to go on with the crowd on everything, so she just goes and checks what the latest things are."

A number of students reported that they go online "for information." Few need to go online for school assignments—this would be impossible for Sagamu girls and difficult for boarders at the other two schools—but some use the Internet to supple-ment what they learn in school or church. Science students say that the books available are outdated, so they go online for the latest information on a topic, secure in their belief that the online informa-tion is "always updated." When asked about reliabil-ity of online sources, no one worried, claiming that the Web sites always cited their sources.

One girl discussed in detail how she seeks answers to religious questions. She said she might hear something from her pastor and then go to a religious chat group to discuss and check what she has learned. Several others students were familiar with religious chat groups (recall Patricia's Christian teen group) and used them "to find out if it's true or not." Many of these students are actively religious and use the Internet to bypass what they regard as more dogmatic religious instruction they receive in their churches or at home.

Overwhelmingly the students claimed that going online had no impact on their reading. Three rea-sons came up over and over: time and space separa-tion, time management, and the different functions reading and going online have in their lives. A theme that came up in discussing all three was the honored position that reading holds in West African culture.

When asked to describe their practices, the youth pointed out that their reading and Internet use took place at different times. They read at night or during the very early morning and went online on Saturday afternoons. Moreover, the activities took place at dif-ferent places: reading was done in relatively private spaces—home, school libraries, dorm rooms—and going online took place in the public space of the cybercafé. Such time and space separation meant that the two did not directly compete. The students said that their Saturday afternoons, if not spent at the cybercafés, would be spent hanging out with friends; their nights, if they were not reading, would be spent watching television.

A number of the students stressed their effective time management: by scheduling their time well, they had plenty of time for both reading and going online. (The implication was that other young peo-ple might not handle their time so well.) One said, "Actually, it depends on the person. If you know the time you are going to use the Internet and the time you are going to read, it won't really affect you. But if you are using your reading time for Internet things, then it will affect you and you read less." Another girl said, "[Internet use] doesn't affect my reading, because I have a timetable, a time to read and a time to browse and other things, so it doesn't affect me." I asked her about television, and she said she didn't watch it much. Another emphasized there was no problem because you can "plan your time well."

The third common response emphasized that the Internet served a different function—getting information and staying in touch—whereas reading was for pleasure and improvement. Many said, "I don't browse that much." They depicted their Internet time as communication (chat, e-mail) and getting information they wanted (schoolwork, leisure interests). Because their time online was metered, they could not indulge in long browsing sessions or online games.

Although a few students said going online might affect their reading, the reasons they gave were not that the two activities competed for their free time. Several said that, because they didn't like to read anyway, they welcomed anything that filled their leisure hours. These youth probably would not have read any more even if they didn't have the Internet; one girl who didn't like reading said she didn't patronize cybercafés much either, for she preferred to socialize with friends. Another girl said the Internet definitely reduced her reading because, if she were assigned a book for her literature class, she could just go online, learn about the book, and then write a paper on it without having actually read it. But when asked about her reading for pleasure, she said, "Oh, the Internet doesn't affect *that*." One of her classmates quickly added: "It's much more interesting reading a book in front of you than going to the Net to find out about a book. So like me, I only go to the Net when I need something, when I want to find out about something. So I only go there to do important things, not to browse, not to download music, not to do anything else."

THE INTERNET AND READING: CONCLUSIONS

West African Internet users of all ages seemed surprised when asked whether their online time affected their reading, They almost uniformly insisted that the Internet has no impact on reading, unless it was to support it by providing access to information about authors and books. They did think that their Internet use competed for time with a number of things—they mentioned phone calls, hanging out with friends, watching television after school, writing letters—but not with reading. In West Africa, to a far greater extent than in the West, *reading and going online occupy different physical, temporal, social, and cultural spaces from each other*. In Nigeria and Ghana

- People read for pleasure in their homes, in private vehicles for those lucky enough to ride in them, or—for students—in the school library. They go online in cybercafés.
- People read after their evening meal or in the early morning. They also read at work, more or less surreptitiously, and on their way to work if the vehicle is not too crowded. Adults, especially job seekers, use the Internet in the day-time (unemployed adults), and students—the most frequent users—go online in the mid-afternoon and early evening.
- West Africans view reading as a private activity. People read individually, even when surrounded by other people in a crowded room or vehicle. They regard going online, by contrast, as a social activity. Internet use takes place in public and often in groups. Moreover, going online is inherently social, maintaining ties to distant friends, relatives, and strangers (even scams are social).
- Middle-class women are a significant portion of the reading class but a negligible portion of the Internet class.
- Going online—new, trendy, associated with youth and with globalization—had the attractions of glamour. Reading—established, institutionally encouraged, associated with elite practices and with wisdom—has the attractions of honor. The two activities occupy different cultural positions.

Reading and Internet use do not compete in West African culture. Nigerians and Ghanaians read for information, for study, for self-improvement, for entertainment, and to enact and demonstrate their social status. They go online to maintain or initiate social connections, for fun, for school and job searches, and to demonstrate their cosmopolitanism.

The functions of the two activities overlap but are by no means congruent. West Africans regard reading as more serious, the mark of a refined person, someone of substance and gravity, whereas using the Internet is fun, practical, and the mark of the young and the trendy.

NOTES

1. A regional comparison shows that sub-Saharan Africa and South Asia have the lowest adult literacy, each a bit below 60%, with Arab states just a bit higher. These lagging regions also have the most extreme gender difference. Latin America and East Asia have roughly 90% literacy, and Europe and North America have near universal literacy (UNESCO Institute for Statistics 2005a).

2. Girls' educational disadvantage, made notorious by the case of Afghanistan under the Taliban, is by no means characteristic of all Islamic societies. While Pakistan and Egypt have vast differences in the literacy rates of men and women, Malaysia and Iran do not (UNESCO Institute for Statistics 2005b). In West Africa the general inequality between the sexes, polygamy, and female marriage at a very young age support an interpretation of Islam that downplays the importance of girls' education.

3. There are no reliable survey data on this point, beyond the difference in literacy. Both Ghanaians and Nigerians report that young people regardless of sex read "everything," including, for example, romance novels. Adult men are likely to read for career advancement (motivational books are popular) and women for pleasure (Griswold 2000; Newell 2000).

4. The overall picture of Internet access in sub-Saharan Africa in general and Nigeria and Ghana in particular is dismal. In 2001 the world average was one Internet user per 15 people; in North America and Europe it was one user per 2 people; in Africa it was one user per 190 people. Of the larger African countries, South Africa has best Internet density, 1.69 dial-up subscriptions per 100 people. Nigeria has a density of 0.44, and Ghana has 0.08. (Sonaike 2004, table 1, p. 47). All such figures must be taken with a grain of salt, but there is no doubt that Africa, along with South Asia, lags most other places in ICT. Ghana and Nigeria are by no means the worst off among African countries; this distinction probably goes to the Democratic Republic of Congo, with Liberia, Ethiopia, Central African Republic, Niger, Burundi, Sierra Leone, Chad, Somalia, and Sudan also trailing the rest of the continent (Sonaike 2004, table 3, p. 48; Baumgartner 2004: 24).

5. The portrait of the African Internet user as urban, educated, upper class, and male (e.g., Kenny 2000; Darley 2003; Robins 2002) obscures the participation of poorer people, who are online, especially if they are urban. Even small boys who beg outside of tourist sites have e-mail addresses that they press upon potential "pen pals"; they save all week to go together to one of the inexpensive cybercafés to check e-mail.

6. Virtually all West African women work, and they bear the entire burden of managing households and caring for their typically large families.

7. Ghana has a birthrate of 31/1,000 and 42% of its population is under 15. Nigeria is even higher, with a birthrate of 42/1,000 and 44% of the population under 15. These figures are typical of sub-Saharan Africa, which has far-and-away the highest birthrate and largest ratio of children to adults of any region. By comparison, other developing areas have less skewed populations: Latin America has a birthrate of 21 per 1,000 and 31% under 15; the Middle East and North Africa are roughly the same. Europe has only 16% of its population under 15, Japan even less (14%), and the United States has 21% (World Bank Group 2005, table 2.1 "Population Dynamics").

8. This is true everywhere; cf. Baym et al. (2004).

REFERENCES

Baumgartner, P. (2004). "Africa's poor connection." *World Press Review* (February) *51*(2).

Baym, N. K., Zhang, Y. B., and Lin, M.-C. (2004). "Social interactions across media: Interpersonal communication on the Internet, telephone and face-to-face." *New Media and Society 6*, 299–318.

Darley, W. K. (2003). "Public policy challenges and implications of the Internet and the emerging ecommerce for sub-Saharan Africa: A business perspective." *Information Technology for Development 10*, 1–12.

Goldstein, H. (2004). Surf Africa: Africa lit a shiny new fiber-optic cable almost two years ago—so why are so few Africans using it? *IEEE Spectrum.* Dow Jones Reuters Business Interactive. February 1.

Griswold, W. (2000). *Bearing witness: Readers, writers, and the novel in Nigeria.* Princeton, N.J.: Princeton University Press.

Griswold, W., & Wright, N. (2004). Wired and well read. In P. N. Howard & S. Jones (Eds.), *Society online: The Internet in context* (pp. 203–222). Thousand Oaks, Calif.: Sage.

Griswold, W., Wright, N., & McDonnell, T. (2005). Reading and the reading class in the twenty-first century. *Annual Review of Sociology 31*, 127–141.

Kenny, C. J. 2000. Expanding Internet access to the rural poor in Africa. *Information Technology for Development 9,* 25–31.

Lindfors, B. (1996). *Loaded vehicles: Studies in African literary media.* Trenton, N.J.: Africa World Press.

Miller, D., & Slater, D. (2002). *The Internet: An ethnographic approach.* Oxford: Berg.

National Endowment for the Arts. (2004). *Reading at risk: A survey of literary reading in America.* Research Division Report #46. Washington, D.C.: National Endowment for the Arts.

Newell, S. (2002). *Ghanaian popular fiction: "Thrilling discoveries in conjugal life" & other tales.* Oxford: J. Currey; Athens, Ohio: Ohio University Press.

Robins, M. B. (2002). Are African women online just ICT consumers? *Gazette: The International Journal for Communication Studies 64,* 235–249.

Rose, J. (2001). *The intellectual life of the British working classes.* New Haven, Conn.: Yale University Press.

Sonaike, S. A. (2004). The Internet and the dilemma of Africa's development. *Gazette: The International Journal for Communication Studies 66,* 41–61.

UNESCO Institute for Statistics: Literacy and Non Formal Education Section. (2002). Estimates and projections of adult illiteracy for population aged 15 years and above, by country and by gender 1970–2015. Retrieved from www.uis.unesco.org/en/stats/statistic/literacy2000. htm

UNESCO Institute for Statistics: Literacy and Non Formal Education Section. (2005a). "Regional youth and adult literacy rates and illiterate population by gender for 2000–2004." August 2005. Retrieved from www.uis.unesco.org/ev.php? URL_ID?5204& URL_DO?DO_TOPIC&URL_ SECTION?201

UNESCO Institute for Statistics: Literacy and Non Formal Education Section. (2005b). Youth (15–24) and adult (15?) literacy rates by country and by gender for 2000–2004. Retrieved from www.uis.unesco.org/ev.php?ID?6267_201&ID2? DO_TOPIC

World Bank Group. (2005). *05 World development indicators.* Section 2: People. Retrieved from www.worldbank.org/data/wdi2005/wditext/Section2.htm

Zachary, G. P. (2002). Technology review: Ghana's digital dilemma. *MIT's Technology Review* July 31.

R E A D I N G   **8**

Women Enter the World of Media

Manal Ismail and Maysam Ali (2008)

Standing before a camera, speaking to the public, having to constantly be on the move and expose oneself to different kinds of people and personalities—this would be the job description of anyone choosing to work in the media.

However, all these actions were also considered inappropriate for a woman in the Gulf states, and in many cases the stigma remains. So many challenges exist for a woman who wants to pursue her ambitions in the world of media, both in terms of family and society.

However, times are changing. Women are standing up for their rights. They are questioning the claims as to why one gender can pursue a career, a dream, and the other cannot. The number of female students pursuing the different fields of the communication industry is on the rise, and many factors help explain this development.

FAMILY SUPPORT

Perhaps the number one factor is family acceptance.

"Students love their parents and wouldn't want to do anything that upsets them," said Shammi Samano, media publication faculty at Dubai Women's College (DWC) in the United Arab Emirates (UAE). "So their support works like the backbone to their success."

For the applied communications program at DWC, students must have their parents sign a permission slip that states that they are permitted to pursue this field. Shammi said, however, that a continuum exists as to the level of conservation among parents. While some parents won't even consider the matter, others are ready to support their daughters in becoming successful in the media industry.

"In most cases, the issue lies in the image of a woman," said Eman Al Owais, applied communications student at DWC. "To not be shy and appear on the screen and mix with a lot of people. However, thankfully, I've always had my parents' support in my decision to pursue communications."

Shammi highlighted the importance of family support. "Families should encourage and provide their daughters with supportive dialogue and conversation," Shammi said. "I have found that students with supportive families develop better creatively once they enter the professional field. They are more confident and open about what they do."

Ahlam Mohammad Al Bannai, also applied communications first-year student at DWC, said that she is excited about her major of study and future opportunities. "I didn't study for nothing. I have skills and talents and thankfully support from my parents," she said. "Our projects require long hours outside the house and fortunately, my parents understand that. Some people think it is wrong for women to be in the field of journalism, but this doesn't scare me because I know that women are needed in this field in our society and I feel it is my duty and desire to do it."

Al Anoud Al Juneidy, an applied communications major who dreams of making it big in the media industry, also described the impact of family support. "Convincing one is better than convincing five," said Al Anoud. "When you get married all you have to do is convince one person of what you want to do."

SOCIETAL ACCEPTANCE

The effect of family and societal perception plays an integral role in the performance of these young women.

"When girls go out to shoot their videos, the perceptions of people have a huge impact on them by shaking their confidence," Shammi said. "It's not only just the matter of being in front of the camera, it's carrying the equipment—it's just looked at as not a feminine thing to do."

Despite society's perceptions, however, some girls are driven to accomplish their dreams.

"One girl had the courage to climb and stand on top of a vehicle, with her abayyah, to get the angle she wanted for the film she was shooting," Shammi said. "She was determined to shoot her movie the way she imagined it and make it a success."

"The stigma is always there," said Shahrazad Al Jazir, applied communications student at DWC. "We're just proving ourselves as equal citizens in society and moving towards success."

Shahrazad recently made a controversial documentary with the help of her colleagues Ameenah Eisa and Aisha Bin Zayed titled *A Silent Prayer of the Mind*. The movie discusses the issue of domestic violence in the UAE. Shahrazad said that institutes such as the Dubai Foundation for Women and Children and the City of Hope have opened to provide shelter and safety to victims of trafficking and domestic violence.

"The main purpose of the movie is to raise awareness and portray the government's role in supporting these victims," Shahrazad said. "What many people don't know is that there is support available, and this is one step forward to creating that awareness.

Ahlam found her inspiration in the world of media through the career paths of video-clip director Fatima Mohammad and journalist Maysaa Ghudayer. "I noticed that there are few women in the field of journalism, and since I have that kind of personality, I decided to pursue it," she said. "I would like to cover stories and deal with important issues that affect society."

She said that she is confident about doing an excellent job in this field and, unlike other students who disagreed, said that there is a nurturing and positive working environment for women. "We have equal opportunities; we just have to work for what we want," she said.

CHANGE IS HAPPENING

Arab society has greatly progressed in terms of accepting the media industry as a field for a woman to pursue.

"I definitely think that society is moving in the right direction," Shammi Samano said. "And this change needs to be in a way that respects the culture and values of the community and should not just imitate some Western model."

Eman Al Owais shared the same view. "The woman today is different than before," she said. "She can pursue any field she wants whether it's media, politics, business or science. Today, the role of the woman has changed."

Female students even feel freer about discussing their desires to pursue their careers. Al Anoud Al Juneidy has big ambitions for her future. "I want to travel to the University of Southern California and study directing," she said. Al Anoud, who cannot hide her enthusiasm, said that she has an urge to make something unique and will overcome all the obstacles she faces, including her mother's insistence that she get married.

"To me, a movie is better than a man right now," she says jokingly. "I want to work right now, and when I find the person who understands me, my ambitions and passion, I'll think about that then. But now I have ambitions and I want to make something that will show in Hollywood. Movie-making and directing here are not that exciting; I want to travel and learn more."

WORKING AGAINST THE ODDS

Aisha Bin Zayed is a 19-year-old applied communications student who is the editor of Dubai Women's College's student newsletter, MSAGE, and of a student magazine, *Desert Dawn*. She is also active in making movies and is working on producing a documentary, with her colleagues' collaboration, on domestic violence in the UAE.

As editor of the publication *Desert Dawn*, Aisha says that there are many responsibilities to be completed, as well as many ideas to be produced every day. "We are always trying to find new ideas and create projects. We are working in the new issue of the magazine on the topic of old Dubai. We are trying to highlight the authentic face of Dubai, to dig deep and find something important."

One of the documentaries that Aisha is working on is titled *A Silent Prayer of the Mind*. It is set to enter the Gulf Film Festival Competition in May. "I went to women's shelters and spent hours with them to better understand them and to connect with them before filming."

Aisha has difficulty balancing her extracurricular activities and passion on one side, and her parents' satisfaction on the other side. "It is certainly not fine with my family that I spend time at the shelters, that I come home late or that I chose this major at all," she said. "So I had to convince them."

"I decided to get into media because of my talent and interest in writing, photography and design," Aisha said. "My mother encouraged me but my father had his concerns. But in the end, he didn't mind because he himself had done the same major."

Aisha's friends are very fond of her and said very good things about her. Her colleague and friend Shahrazad Al Jazir said that Aisha is truly unique and extremely creative, but keeps her success very discrete.

Shahrazad said, "One day we all will be proud of her. There were times when she lost hope and started to do her tasks carelessly, but she is really creative. She inspires me by her love of education."

Despite the odds, Aisha's resilience continues. "It's a struggle being in this major every day. I have to fight for it."

Asked what she would like to wish her colleagues and other women on Women's International Day, Aisha said, "I'd encourage them to do whatever makes them happy. They have to do what they want because you never know who might be the next Einstein or Picasso."

She added, "This country has been giving opportunities to women, so women should use them. "So I encourage Emirati women to be creative and do things that they believe in, and would like to do."

Beautiful Betty

Yeidy M. Rivero (2007)

Since the 1970s, television critics have debated the "feminist" and "nonfeminist" credentials of prime-time fictional characters. Mary (Tyler Moore) Richards, Roseanne Conner and Murphy Brown received particularly high marks, setting standards for more recent women protagonists such as Ally McBeal, Buffy (the Vampire Slayer) Summers and Carrie (*Sex and the City*) Bradshaw. In truth, however, only white middle- and upper-class women—with the exception of working-class Roseanne—were included in the rankings. Why, for instance, are the strong, vivacious African American women of *Living Single* excluded from these conversations?

Now, along comes ABC's *Ugly Betty*, one of the most-watched shows of the new television season, and its immediate success stimulates, once again, a discussion of feminist credentials. For example, a colleague recently asked me to compare *Ugly Betty's* leading character, Betty Suárez, to Ally McBeal. "Well, they probably both have vaginas," I replied. Gender is about the *only* identity that Betty shares with previous and contemporary women television characters. How many working-class, Mexican American, clumsy, allegedly "ugly," intelligent women with an illegal-immigrant father have been portrayed on U.S. television? Until Betty's arrival, none.

In *Ugly Betty*, a first-generation, college-educated woman (played by America Ferrara of *Real Women Have Curves* and *The Sisterhood of the Traveling Pants* fame) lives with her father, sister and nephew in working-class and ethnically diverse Queens. Contrary to the *Sex and the City* troupe, Betty and her single-mother sister can't enjoy the wonders of New York City's nightlife, as they are the family's primary financial providers and have to worry about their father's health plan and the legal expenses related to his illegal status.

As an assistant for fashion magazine *Mode*, Betty has been labeled ugly, fat and classless, and suffers numerous humiliations from co-workers. But while Betty has apparently internalized the pain of being categorized as ugly, she does not seem concerned about her weight. She is more than her body, even though her body symbolically carries some of her social struggles. As an intelligent and ambitious woman, Betty wants to succeed at her job, yet her distance from upper-crust culture has thus far been an obstacle at class- and image-conscious *Mode*.

The uniqueness of *Betty* is partly related to the origins of the show's concept. The idea came from a *telenovela* (soap opera) developed by scriptwriter Fernando Gaitán for Colombia's RCN Televisión network. Produced between 1999 and 2001, *Yo soy Betty la fea* (I am Betty, the Ugly One) narrated the story of a single, physically awkward, working-class, brilliant and hard-working woman in her late 20s who was employed as a secretary at high-fashion company EcoModa. Following the conventions of Latin American *telenovelas*, which typically portray the complexities of an almost impossible love between two people from different social classes, Betty fell in love with Armando, the company's president. After a series of misunderstandings and much suffering, Betty and Armando married—a thematic resolution that defines the genre.

Yet, *Yo Soy Betty la fea* was more than a highly improbable match between a poor, "ugly" woman and a rich man. Although the narrative revolved around social norms regarding women's beauty or ugliness, this aesthetic division was more closely tied to class than physical attributes. Upper-class codes of conduct and appearance—related to one's carriage, dress and style, as well as to manners, elegance and "correct" use of the language—usually defined who was considered ugly or beautiful within the narrative. Therefore, the central message in the Colombian version was that women's beauty is defined by those who possess economic power.

Before Salma Hayek began producing *Ugly Betty* for ABC, many U.S. audiences were already familiar with *Yo soy Betty la fea*, as the *telenovela* was broadcast on Spanish-language network Telemundo. The show captivated audiences in major cities and briefly challenged the dominance of another network, Univision, in the U.S. Spanish-language television market.

Yo soy Betty la fea's success then transcended Colombia and the U.S., as it became a global phenomenon. The *telenovela* was an instant hit across Latin America and, according to a *Variety* report, either the original Colombian version or the concept alone have been sold to more than 70 countries. India, Germany, Mexico, Russia, Spain and others have each produced versions of *Yo soy Betty la fea*.

I am an avid *Ugly Betty* viewer, but initially I was partial to the *telenovela*. *Yo soy Betty la fea* has a harsher, more direct approach to women's self-esteem issues, and I appreciated the inclusion of Betty's six "ugly" girlfriends—a support network, who loved her and admired her deeply. Through Betty and the *cuartel de las feas* (the cartel of ugly women), the narrative created a space for gender and working-class solidarity. *Ugly Betty*'s cutesiness, evidenced by the presence of a boyfriend for Betty

(the original Betty was a virgin in her late 20s) and a parade of cartoonish characters masquerading cruelty, was not part of the Colombian version.

That said, *Ugly Betty* is an important and timely show. It brings forth a complex assortment of U.S. women's issues, interconnecting gender, ethnicity, race, class and, of course, dominant beauty norms. Significantly, the show also addresses the thorny migration question, indirectly confronting the anti-Mexican sentiment that prevails in the U.S.

So, where do we situate Betty within the discussion of television's feminist characters? Is she enduring some of the struggles faced by many real-life U.S. women? Yes. But that does not mean we should burden Betty with comparisons to Ally McBeal and company. Instead we should accept Betty and her ethnically diverse fans on their own cultural, ethnic, class, fictional and real-life terms. For my part, I will continue to welcome Betty into my home as long as the show's creators keep pushing the envelope regarding what constitutes ugliness in contemporary U.S. society. Am I expecting too much from a network television show? Maybe so, but I will dream on.

CITATION

Tarpley, Natasha. *Testimony: Young African-Americans on Self-discovery and Black Identity*. Boston: Beacon Press, 1995.

R E A D I N G **10**

Mirror, Mirror on the Wall

Tiya Miles (1995)

The black comedienne "Moms" Mabley once told this story: "There lived a little girl. . . . You'all call her Cinderella. . . . She had long black hair, pretty brown eyes, pretty brown skin. Well, let's face it—she was colored. Cindy-Ella turns to the mirror and says, 'Mirror, mirror on the wall, who's the fairest of them all?' The mirror replies, 'Snow White—and don't you forget it'" (Porter, 26).

Walt Disney released *The Little Mermaid*, a new version of the fairy tale about a mermaid princess who rebels against her father's wishes and falls in love with a human. When I saw the film I was pleasantly surprised that the heroine did not have blond hair. I was impressed that she was thinking independently of her father. I took notice when the little mermaid argued during a discussion with her father that he should not prejudge all non-mer-people/humans negative because they are different. After noticing these details, I had hopes that the film would revise past stereotypes and the exclusion of people of color, as well as the portrayal of traditional roles, in many of Disney's other films.

As I watched more of the movie, however, my expectations fell. Although the little mermaid does not have the typical fairy tale blond hair, she is white. The man she falls in love with is white. Every random mer-person and human in the film is white. The only characters who are of color are animals. The little mermaid's guardian is a crab who speaks with a Caribbean accent. A "black fish" in the film sings briefly in what sounds like a black woman's voice.

In addition to these black characters being sea creatures rather than humans or mer-people, they are stereotypically portrayed. The crab's lips are exaggerated in size. Like the black cops in the ubiquitous white-black duo action adventures, he is subservient to the white king and is at the center of comic moments. When the "black fish" is allowed her three seconds of attention, she sings gospel music.

Although the little mermaid is able to think independently of her father, she contemplates the same old, tired thing that all fairy tale princesses contemplate—marrying the prince. The little mermaid falls in love with the prince after seeing him only once. In a familiar portrayal of catty, jealous women, she and the evil female octopus fight to gain the prince's affections. The octopus steals the mermaid's voice, and, once again, a princess must be saved by a prince's kiss. The little mermaid will regain her voice only if the prince kisses her within three days. The prince's character is also defined by gender stereotypes. Like the typical prince of fairy tales, he quickly falls in love with a woman because he is attracted to one of her physical attributes. In this case, it is the little mermaid's voice. The prince is so focused on this single characteristic that his common sense fails him. He spends three fun-filled days with the little mermaid while she has lost her voice. Despite the fact that he has a wonderful time with her, he is holding out for the woman with the beautiful voice that he once heard. When the evil octopus disguises herself and sings to the prince with the little mermaid's stolen voice, the prince immediately falls for her.

The Little Mermaid was a big hit among little girls. I'm sure that many Black, Hispanic, Asian, and Native American girls saw the film and loved it. Unfortunately, when these girls left the theater, the love that they had for the film may have chipped away at the love that they had for themselves.

Even before a child reaches five years of age, she notices the variety in people's appearances (Porter, 13). Once a child can separate people into groups based on these differences in appearance, she learns to assign meaning to the differences according to the attitudes her family members, peers, and the media express (Porter, 13). In this way a child begins to distinguish between racial and gender categories and to determine which groups are considered superior and inferior in society. Children then fold what they learn into their developing identities: "Group membership is one aspect of the self-concept of young children. The child will value himself as he values the group to which he belongs" (Trager and Yarrow, 115, 117). In American society, this development process is likely to lead to a lack of self-worth in children who are neither white nor male. Many children's fairy tales, which are now cultural icons, contribute to the creation and reinforcement of these notions.

Last summer I worked with a group of little girls and saw my own theories and these psychological findings come to life. The group consisted of eight- and nine-year-old Puerto Rican and Haitian girls who lived in a Cambridge housing development. One of our projects was to identify and break down stereotypical ideas of race and gender.

The girls had all seen and loved several Disney fairy tales, so we worked with what they already knew. We began with a general discussion about fairy tales. I asked them to name as many as they could—*Cinderella, Little Red Riding Hood, Rapunzel, The Little Mermaid, Snow White*, and *Sleeping Beauty* were what they listed. I then asked them to think about things that those fairy tales had in common. The princess is always beautiful and blond, said Alisa. The princess is always white with long hair, said Jahyra. The princess always falls in love with a handsome prince, said Mary. The princess always kisses the prince, said Mimi. The princess always gets married and there is a happy ending, said Jahyra.

The next step in our project was to watch or read one of the fairy tales on the list and try to identify the characteristics that they had listed. We began by watching Disney's *Cinderella*. In this film we found the things on our list and more—all white characters, instant love, the conflict between the beautiful and the unattractive woman, the evil, ugly older woman (in this case, the stepmother, in other cases, the witch, the bad fairy, the female octopus), and the idealization of daintiness (Cinderella's small feet that could fit into the slipper).

After pinpointing these characteristics, we planned to revise what we disliked about the fairy tales. The *Cinderella* assignment was to alter her appearance and have her do something in life besides marry the prince. It is important to note that all of the girls described and drew pictures of Cinderellas who looked like them. When the girls wrote about Cinderella doing something, they wrote about things that were within their frames of reference. In one story, Cinderella married the prince and worked in a store. In another, she ditched the prince altogether and went to college.

We revised several fairy tales in this manner. Throughout the ongoing project, though, I recognized to my dismay that the children resisted changing the stories. When they had the power, they made the heroines look like them, but they knew from storybooks, movies, and television that their descriptions and pictures were not "right." They believed that the white princess was the authentic princess, and they wanted to identify with her. At the same time, they knew that they were not pale and blond, that they were unlikely to move into a prince's castle. Negative feelings about themselves born of this conflict between the traditional stories and their realities became evident in our discussions.

We watched and read three versions of Cinderella: Disney's version, a cartoon about a Native American Cinderella, and a story about a Cinderella with brown hair who is happy when she completes a book report for school. When I asked the children

which version they preferred and why, the majority chose Disney's *Cinderella*. Mimi, one of the Puerto Rican girls, said she liked Disney Cinderella's hair and wished that she also had blond hair. The Haitian girl, Paule, quickly responded that she thought Mimi's hair was prettier than her own.

As the end of the summer approached, we chose one of the revisions, "A Puerto Rican Cinderella," to perform as a play. When two older Black and Puerto Rican girls in the neighborhood heard of our plans, they asked me who would be Cinderella. They said that they hoped I would not choose Paule, the Haitian girl in the group. They wanted Cinderella to be played by Marybeth: "It just wouldn't be right to have Paule as Cinderella," they explained, "and Mary is so pretty." In the eyes of these adolescent girls with years of societal training about who is worthy of princess status, Marybeth was right for the part. Mary is a delightful, outgoing girl, but she was also the only girl in my group who most closely met traditional American beauty standards. One of the girls was Black; two were chubby; most had dark hair and eyes; the only child with blue eyes had already volunteered to be the director. Marybeth, on the other hand, has reddish-brown hair, hazel eyes, and a white, blond-haired mother.

When I asked the girls to choose the parts they wanted, Mary was the only one who volunteered to be Cinderella. Paule said she wanted to play the wicked stepmother. At only eight years old, they knew their roles well.

Perhaps this would change if those who create and perpetuate pervasive cultural narratives would write and legitimize new scripts.

WORKS CITED

Porter, Kidith D. R., *Black Child, White Child*. Cambridge, MA: Harvard University Press, 1971.

Trager, Helen G., and Yarrow, Marian Radke. *They Learn What They Live*. New York: Harper and Brothers Publishers, 1952, pp. 118–84.

Grover Goes Global

Anthony Kaufman (2007)

Getting to Sesame Street, it turns out, isn't always just a walk in the park. Ever since the children's television show phenomenon began in 1969, with its urban location, multiethnic cast, and mission to educate preschool children of all economic levels, Big Bird, Grover, and the gang have encountered a minefield of social and political entanglements.

"In 1969, a lot of public television stations refused to air *Sesame Street* because it had an integrated cast," says Linda Costigan, co-director with Linda Knowlton of *The World According to Sesame Street*, a documentary about the show's international reach. "Every country, including the United States, has thresholds it has to overcome."

It's these political underpinnings that drew Costigan and Knowlton to explore the 20 versions of *Sesame Street* that are co-produced around the globe, from Israel to Palestine, Kosovo to Russia, Germany to Mexico.

"When we started to learn about the strong political characters they had around the world, such as the HIV-positive Muppet in South Africa, and dealing with mutual understanding in the Israeli-Jordanian co-production, that's what got us interested," explains Knowlton. "They're dealing with these incredible issues for 3- to 5-year-olds."

In war-torn areas like El Salvador and Kosovo, *Sesame Street* becomes a symbol, far more significant than just a TV show. When the filmmakers attended a UNICEF conference in Kosovo to discuss the possible creation of a single *Sesame Street* for all of the countries in the former Yugoslavia, for example, "emotions were high," recalls Costigan. "People were getting very upset." The idea of a regional *Sesame Street* became a political issue: Could these countries rally behind a single production? "It boiled down to the fact that these people were not ready," says Costigan.

With the future of their children at stake, governments, broadcasters, and local producers see *Sesame Street* as treading upon delicate territory. "Education is political," acknowledges Sesame Workshop international co-producer Nadine Zylstra, who has helped plant *Sesame Street* signs in South Africa, India, and Bangladesh. "But even if you're talking about equal opportunity"—Egyptian and Palestinian productions, for example, feature empowered girl Muppets—"when you boil that down to what that means to a 2- or 3-year-old, it's really about saying, 'Dream and ask questions,' and everyone can rally around that."

Not everybody, exactly. Every time *Sesame Street* journeys into new territory, questions of American cultural imperialism inevitably arise. "*Sesame Street* has to re-prove itself in every country where it goes," says Costigan. "Here is an American organization coming in and wanting to teach their children. That's alarm-bell city."

Sesame Street goes out of its way to integrate local customs and culture into every show it co-produces overseas. While the documentary filmmakers were initially skeptical of Cookie Monster's transnational nature, the reality proved, as Knowlton says, that "it's not about them coming in and shoving their agenda down someone else's throats."

Close-knit collaboration with indigenous producers is simply a matter of effective education, according to Zylstra, who spent nine months with Bangladeshi educators, academics, and producers just on the development phase of *Sisimpur*, the country's version of *Sesame Street*. "The most important thing is that children learn best when the reality they see represented reflects their own," she says. "That's why we do it."

Zylstra recalls a meeting at which the locals asked why the Muppets all have the same eyes. "I was floored by that, and I thought, 'That's a bloody good point,'" she says. She discovered that Sesame Workshop prefers the round orb and big black pupil to make a point of connection with viewers. "But the deeper issue is that we, as an American company, were replacing their puppets and puppet history with our own puppets," she says. In *Sisimpur*, the production came up with a compromise that integrated both Sesame Workshop Muppets and Bangladeshi puppets and song into the show.

Filmmakers Costigan and Knowlton have become champions of Sesame Workshop, even though they maintain their objectivity. "Here is the real truth of the matter," says Costigan: "They're doing good work."

"When this is the only preschool education available to kids, whether they're in Bangladesh or Indonesia or Egypt, it's hard to argue with that," adds Knowlton. "Can a TV show that's on for half an hour create peace in the Middle East? No. However, if you look at what kids in Israel or the Palestinian territories have to watch on TV, here is an opportunity to see people behaving in a different way. Here is another option to see how we can behave and care for each other."

R E A D I N G **12**

"Telling Our Own Stories": African Women Blogging for Social Change

Oreoluwa Somolu (2007)

The Internet and other information and communication technologies (ICTs) have the potential to support the economic, political, and social empowerment of women and the promotion of gender equality. Examples include e-commerce initiatives that link women artisans to global markets through the Internet; e-governance programs, initiated by some governments, which use ICTs to make government services more accessible to citizens by providing them electronically; and health programs, where educators have used radio to communicate information related to women's sexual and reproductive health (Gurumurthy 2004). However, in the African context, this potential of ICTs is limited by poverty, illiteracy, lack of computer literacy, and language barriers—obstacles that are felt more keenly by women (Radloff, Primo, and Munyua 2004). For instance, in Africa only 3.6 per cent of people have access to the Internet (Internet World Stats 2007), and it is very difficult to know how many of these are women (Hafkin and Taggart 2001).

Despite these obstacles, there are many organizations implementing projects that use ICTs as a tool to improve African women's social, economic, educational, and political circumstances. Nigeria's Fantsuam Foundation, for instance, supported the Bayanloco Community Learning Centre, which set up community-based, community-sustained computer centers targeted at rural women in northern Nigeria.[1] The Women of Uganda Network supports and promotes the use of ICTs among its member organizations: activities have included ICT and entrepreneurship training.[2] Nigeria's KnowledgeHouse-Africa's Gender Team has organized several free and open source software training events.[3] Fahamu, a pan-African human-rights and social justice organization, set up the UmNyango Project, where SMS technology[4] is used to access information and report incidences of violence against women and children in rural areas of South Africa.[5] As part of the project, women produced their own radio programs, which were made available to local radio stations, as well as being distributed over the Internet as "podcasts."[6]

One new ICT tool that African women are gradually embracing is the "weblog" or "blog", as it is commonly known.

Blogs are widely heralded as an alternative to mainstream media, as they provide a forum for "ordinary" people to share their own perspective and experiences with other Internet users. Blogs and other Internet social networking facilities afford individuals, networks, and organizations the opportunity to communicate with each other quickly, share information and other resources, and collaborate to pool their collective knowledge. In particular, blogs provide arenas for discussion, dissent, and debate, which can translate into knowledge, and a feeling of empowerment that is critical for social transformation and development (Radloff, Primo, and Munyua 2004).

That said, while ICTs can contribute to socioeconomic and political development, they "are not a panacea to social ills and they can and do easily reinforce social inequity" (Radloff, Primo, and Munyua 2004, 5). Gender inequality may be reinforced due to the fact that women have less access to, and hence lack skills in using, ICTs. So, as with any technology, when assessing the value of blogs, it is critical to examine their impact and use by both women and men. With these considerations in mind, this article looks at African women's access to and use of blogging, and how blogs can be used as a tool to contribute toward gender equality and women's empowerment.

This article will focus predominantly on African women bloggers who live within the African continent. While it is acknowledged that there are many blogs by African women living outside Africa, as well as blogs by non-Africans writing on issues of gender equality and women's empowerment, these groups of bloggers might not share the unique challenges which women on the continent face. These include poor and slow Internet access, lack of access to information, lack of access to and control over ICTs, stereotyped portrayals of men as the typical ICT user, and patriarchal culture that discourages women from using ICTs. My analysis of African women bloggers will be based on a review of blogs by African women living in Africa, as well as a survey, which was completed by women whose blogs dealt with gender equality and/or women's empowerment issues.

What Are African Woman Blogging About?

From my sample of 92 blogs by African women resident in Africa, blogs were grouped into one or more of the following categories.

- Arts blogs included posts about books, music, paintings and drawings, sculptures, television, and film.
- Career/education blogs talked about working life, starting and building a career, and education.
- Current affairs blogs focused predominantly on politics within a national or regional context.
- Blogs in the faith category featured posts on religion, spirituality, and issues related to nurturing a relationship with God or a higher being.
- Fashion blogs explored fashion trends, fabrics, designers, and sewing techniques.
- Food/health blogs focused on well-being, mental and physical fitness, food choices and preparation.
- Parenting blogs included topics on pregnancy, bringing up children, and family life.
- Personal journals focused predominantly on the writer's day-to-day experiences. These were also characterized by a diary-style expression of thoughts, fears, and hopes.
- Relationships/sex blogs focused on developing relationships—these included with friends, family and romantic partners. These blogs also included discussions on sex.
- Sports blogs talked about sports, especially organized sports.
- Technology blogs predominantly featured discussions on the development, usage, and effects of tools and crafts, which could include ICTs, health technologies, agricultural technologies, science, and engineering.
- Women's issues/feminist blogs focused mainly on issues affecting women, such as gender inequity and discrimination, within a theoretical and practical context. This category also included blogs that discussed feminism.

While some bloggers explicitly stated the subject of their blog, some did not have a specific focus, although reading through the blog revealed certain dominant topics. In cases where the blogs did not focus on specific topics, and where the majority of the posts featured the blogger's personal experiences, they were classified as personal journals.

As I started to review and categorize the blogs, it became obvious that, due to the fluid nature of many women's writing styles, most blogs tended not to focus exclusively on one topic. Rather they encompassed a set of major subjects around which the blogger wrote. Most (65 per cent) were personal journals, although some of these focused on other topics as well. The review showed bloggers drawing extensively from personal experiences, so that even when writing on a specific topic, like politics or feminism, they would link to related experiences or examples from their lives.

It became apparent that within the genre of "personal journals," in describing everyday experiences, the bloggers were writing from their perspectives as women living in Africa. Some of the frustrations they experienced and wrote about were clearly shared by many other women (for example, cultural expectations of women's roles in life, sexual harassment from men, pressure on women to look attractive, societal pressure on women to marry before the age of 30), as these posts tended to generate many responses and much discussion, particularly from other women. It was rare for a blog to focus solely on a single subject and not include references to personal experiences and reflections: only one blog focused predominantly on feminism; one on food/health; one on parenting; three on arts; and three on relationships/sex. It was rarer to find blogs that focused on subjects like technology or current affairs: ten blogs focused on current affairs, while just one focused mainly on technology.

THE SURVEY

The purpose of the survey was to learn about the motivations of African women who blog about and/or for gender equality and women's empowerment; this could include talking about gender-based inequities and discrimination, proposing solutions, or organizing action to address these issues.

While the survey was open to African women bloggers from all over the world, my intent when analyzing the responses was to pay more attention to those responses from bloggers within the continent. However, due to the low response rate, I used all responses. Interestingly, and perhaps unsurprisingly, I found the motivations to be very similar.

A total of 21 bloggers responded, ranging in age from 21 to 47 years. The bloggers were, on average, very highly educated. Altogether, 19 respondents had an undergraduate or postgraduate qualification, and of the remaining two, one had a high school certificate, and the other was still studying at university. Nine lived outside Africa, 11 were based in Africa, and one split her time between the UK and Nigeria. The bloggers' career backgrounds tended to be professional and white-collar (e.g., journalist, consultant, financial analyst, lawyer, health researcher, NGO director). Their high level of education correlates with research findings relating to other developing countries, which indicate that most women Internet users in almost all developing countries are not representative of women in the country as a whole, but rather are part of a small, urban-educated elite (Hafkin and Taggart 2001; Thas, Ramilo, and Cinco 2007).

It would appear from the survey responses that many of the bloggers (nine) saw their blogs as a means to empower other women (although an almost equal number—eight—declared that they were indifferent in this regard). However, it is interesting to note that a high number (16) identified themselves as feminist and were using their blogs in ways that would speak meaningfully to women. Twelve were using their blogs to share perspectives on issues that affect women, four to reveal injustices perpetrated against women, four to foster discussion between themselves and their readers, and one to write positive stories about Africa and Africans. It was also particularly important to one of the respondents that she used her blog to mobilize people for specific social action.

Why Are African Women Blogging?

"Empowerment implies enabling people towards self-determination and for women, this emphasises the importance of increasing their power and taking control over decisions and issues that shape their lives" (Thas, Ramilo, and Cinco 2007, 14). It appears that the power of the blog as a tool for empowering women lies in its ability to provide an avenue for women to express themselves and connect with other women. The ability to write anonymously is regarded as an important factor in enabling women to share their experiences and opinions honestly and openly. Since, as one blogger puts it, women can be "very truthful and open about things we wouldn't dare talk about in public," women can be encouraged by and learn from each other. Many women capitalize on the ability of blogs to be "a powerful conversational tool with the potential to reach a wide audience" and to "empower by giving a voice to the unheard." Through "story sharing, encouragement, education, and words," women "promote strong positive images." This is especially important given the low numbers of women working in the mainstream media. A 2001 report by the International Federation of Journalists found that only 38 per cent of all journalists are women, with women accounting for only 0.6 per cent of editors, heads of departments, or media owners (Peters 2001). As a result, it is no surprise that "women's lives are still the untold story in today's media" (Peters 2001, 14). It is possible that dissatisfaction with how they are represented in most mainstream media has led women to turn to blogging as a way of portraying the real stories of their lives.

About half the bloggers felt that it is important to shed light on how African women live. One blogger felt that this could be best done "through reporting and writing commentary on all aspects of women's lives and providing a feminist and gender perspective on issues." This could include subjects as diverse as "African women's art, literature, and music, political involvement, and activism." Since these are issues that many women can relate to, for the most part, they tend to participate actively in blogs that talk about these topics. However, while it is important to welcome and encourage participation from women, discussions must explore women's lives through a gender-conscious lens and challenge traditional and patriarchal ways of thinking, if blogs are to be a truly empowering tool. Although it might appear that the responsibility for this would rest on the shoulders of feminist bloggers, all women—including those who do not identify themselves as feminists—have experiences to share with other women.

One wonders, though, how effective or popular a blog would be, if it were to present itself as largely focused on feminism or women's empowerment. Many young African women do not appear to identify with feminist ideology, often seeing it as a western import, or a way of life that is totally incongruent with the reality of their lives as women in largely traditional African society. One blogger concurred that it would be a challenge getting readership for such blogs.

Perhaps their effectiveness would lie in how they conveyed their message. One blogger commented "aside from content that discusses issues of gender equality, I feel that bloggers whose language and general content fosters an environment that welcomes women and encourages other women to join the blogosphere are in essence using their blogs to promote women's equality and empowerment." Openness to diverse ways of thinking is also essential in nurturing honest discussions, as well as the recognition that African women are not a monolithic group with the same experiences or ideals. This sentiment was articulated by another blogger: "We need to first identify that as a group of African women, we are diverse and with this comes a whole set of diverse opinions and these may not necessarily reflect our own views but these are the views of a lot of other women."

One challenge that women using or attempting to adopt technology face is that their input is often overlooked. To encourage more women to blog and use blogs constructively, it is important that "women's knowledge, culture, and tacit and uncodified skills are respected and enhanced" through the use of blogs—and ICTs in general—"enabling a better preservation and transference of traditional knowledge, wisdom and skills" (Thas, Ramon, and Cimon 2007, 10). When women blog—irrespective of the topic—they are sharing their life experiences and perspectives, documenting and passing on knowledge, reaching out to other women (and men), and giving women a voice. This ensures that the information needed by specific communities is generated and available (Thas, Ramon, and Cimon 2007).

These bloggers felt that blogs that actively sought to promote gender equality were in the minority in the African female blogosphere, with the more common topics being personal life, relationships, health, education, and music, with some commentary on current affairs and politics. While one blogger felt that "most blogs by African women do not discuss serious matters, or even the arts, but rather tend to talk about fashion, men, parties and stories about their lives," another blogger saw these types of blogs as being "just as important because they are about African women being out there and contributing to the conversation in a stream of consciousness sort of way." With the blogs that respondents felt addressed issues relevant to women and sought to promote gender equality, their appeal lay in the simple yet assertive language they used, communicating their message in a direct way. Respondents also liked the fact that these bloggers were honest about their lives, and freely shared their life experiences. Their style was considered welcoming and encouraging. Some of these bloggers were considered to have a good sense of what is happening in different parts of the continent. Some respondents liked the fact that some of these blogs spoke from a feminist perspective and covered a wide range of issues around women, gender issues, and social justice.

Ultimately, all respondents felt that there was a need for more blogs by African women that address issues of gender equality, feminism, and social development—especially as they pertain to women, although one blogger acknowledged that "the presence of women bloggers is in itself a positive step towards addressing issues of gender equality." Despite this, another blogger felt that more women would be represented in the African blogosphere if they had the requisite ICT skills.

OBSTACLES TO BLOGGING AND STRATEGIES TO ADDRESS THEM

Going through the survey responses, I was able to start identifying factors that contributed to the fairly small numbers of African women blogging. These can be grouped into three broad areas: technology factors, economic factors, and social factors.

Technology Factors

In many African countries, the telecommunication infrastructure that is necessary for people to have access to the Internet is usually concentrated in the cities, leaving the vast majority of women who live in rural and remote areas underserved (Radloff, Primo, and Munyua 2004). Where connectivity exists, prevailing low bandwidths mean that downloading web pages is a slow process, and this can limit the types of information—for example, multimedia content—that women can access or create. While some initiatives have been set up to provide Internet connectivity to specific rural areas, these efforts need to be more widespread. Across the continent, mobile phone companies are looking at newer technologies—for example, "3G" or third generation—which can deliver broadband Internet connection to a mobile phone (Heavens 2007). Since mobile phone use is rising rapidly throughout Africa, this opens up the opportunity for women to "mob-blog"; that is, to blog using their mobile phones.

A second challenge is that many blog tools are in English, and require the blogger to be able to read English at least, in order to set up their blog. After this, they have the choice to blog in their local language, provided the alphabet symbols are available for their keyboard. This puts the African woman who does not speak English at a disadvantage, and indicates the need to explore the development of blog tools in indigenous African languages, to open up the technology to women who do not understand English.

Economic Factors

The cost of accessing the Internet in Africa remains high, due to a host of factors, including the limited supply of national and international connectivity, limited and expensive satellite links, and poor internal telecommunications infrastructure (Radloff, Primo, and Munyua 2004). To compound the effect of these high costs, lower education levels and gender stereotyping in the employment market typically meant that women earn less than men, and so are less able to afford Internet access fees. The good news is that increasing competition between service providers is pushing costs downwards. Government policy is increasingly providing an enabling environment for this competition to grow, by putting in place favorable telecommunications regulations, as well as the necessary infrastructure.

Social Factors

Social factors, such as gender stereotyping, can be more pervasive obstacles to blogging than technology and economic factors, because they strongly influence women's desire to use blogs and other ICTs. One such stereotype is that technology is a male preserve. This, coupled with the technical jargon that surrounds ICTs, could discourage many women from blogging. Fear of censure is another factor. The freedom that encourages people to express themselves frankly and often anonymously in the blogosphere also allows for vigorous and sometimes hurtful dissent from readers, which could discourage some women from blogging about issues which might be considered contentious, or even discourage them from blogging altogether (Ekine 2006). Another challenge for many women is the time investment required to nurture their blog, and develop a community of readers. This is an investment which women are frequently unable to make, given their multiple roles as homemakers, mothers, wives, and career women. If a blogger is not able to build a community of readers, she may think that no one finds any value in what she has to say, and so may stop blogging. These feelings of inadequacy could be compounded by the patriarchal culture of many African countries, that makes many women feel that their contributions are less valued than those of their male counterparts. A fourth obstacle to women's blogging is the overall lower education and literacy levels of African girls and women. This puts them at a disadvantage in adopting the technology, because, while blogging does not involve a steep technical learning curve, it does require good writing and reading skills.

Encouraging more women to blog requires a multi-pronged approach. On one level, it requires a long-term and persistent campaign against patriarchy, with greater appreciation for women's contributions economically and socially. On a more practical level, it requires de-mystifying technology and being more aware of the language we use to talk about technology, so that it is more inviting to women. ICT skill-building programs can help women develop the capacity and confidence to use technologies, while mentoring programs can provide a safe space for women to start to express themselves openly and honestly with each other.

CONCLUSION

The blogging movement is still in its early stages in Africa, and as yet it is hard to see any concrete outcomes from women speaking out through blogs. However, blogs are providing an avenue for, and encouraging debate between, individual bloggers. For wide-reaching impact, individual efforts must ultimately become part of a bigger movement that involves networks of bloggers and organizations. Government support of blogging initiatives would lend credibility to the role that blogs can play in pushing for social change; however, bureaucracy and the inability to adapt quickly to changing situations and technology are real challenges for such initiatives.

The ability to implement blog-facilitated gender equality and women's empowerment strategies is likely to be more successful in smaller organizations, or in organizations with a vested interest in the issue of empowering women. Already, online spaces like the African women's blogs' aggregator, "reBlog," feature blog postings by African women only. And although many of the blogs featured are not overtly pushing for women's empowerment and gender equality, the fact that women are able to write about issues of interest to them is an important first step in giving them a sense of psychological empowerment.

It is also important that individual bloggers help build a community of people pushing for social change. Some bloggers in Africa are already doing this, by linking into campaigns on women's rights and gender equality issues. For instance, several African women bloggers participated in the Take Back the Tech initiative, a campaign against ICT-mediated violence against women organized by the Association for Progressive Communications, Women's Networking Support Programme, by speaking out against violence against women in their blogs.

The power of blogs for empowering women does not lie in alerting a western audience to gender-based injustices happening in Africa, and telling our stories to the west. Its true potency lies in its ability to give a voice to the previously unheard, and provide them with the tools to connect with others who share the same concerns, while reaching out to people who might have been unaware of these issues, and providing them with a platform on which they can map a strategy for raising the quality of women's lives in Africa. In real terms, this means African women connecting with each other as they tell their stories, support each other, and identify strategies for improving the quality of their lives.

NOTES

1. www.fantsuam.org. See also www.apc.org/english/hafkin/2001/haf_winner.shtml (last accessed June 2007) for details of the Bayanloco Community Learning Centre.
2. www.wougnet.org.
3. www.knowledgehouseafrica.org.
4. SMS or Short Message Service enables people send text messages from one mobile phone to another. This service is supported by most digital mobile phones and personal digital assistants (PDAs).
5. www.fahamu.org.
6. A podcast is a digital media file—this could include audio or video—that is distributed over the Internet for playback on portable media players and personal computers.

REFERENCES

Ekine, S. (2006) "Freedom to Abuse: Choices in the African Blogosphere," *Pambazuka News,* www.pambazuka.org/en/category/comment/32742 (last checked by the author April 2007)

Gurumurthy, A. (2004) *Gender and ICTs: Overview Report,* Bridge, Sussex, UK: Institute of Development Studies (IDS)

Hafkin, N. and N. Taggart (2001) *Gender, Information Technology and Developing Countries: An Analytic Study,* Washington, DC: United States Agency for International Development

Heavens, A. (2007) "The 3g Generation," *BBC Focus on Africa,* April-June: 11–12

Internet World Stats: Usage and Population Statistics "Internet Usage Statistics for Africa," www.internetworldstats.com/stats1.htm (last checked by the author April 2007)

Peters, B. (2001), "International Federation of Journalists, Equality and Quality: Setting Standards for Women in Journalism—IFJ Survey on the Status of Women Journalists," Brussels: International Federation of Journalists, www.ifj.org/pdfs/ws.pdf (last checked by the author May 2007)

Radloff, J., N. Primo and A. Munyua (2004) *The Role of Information and Communication Technologies in the Development of African Women,* Melville, South Africa: Association for Progressive Communications (APC)

Thas, A., C. Ramilo, and C. Cinco (2007) *Gender and ICT,* United Nations Development Programme Asia-Pacific Development Information Programme (UNDP-APDIP), New Delhi, India: Elsevier

Global Politics of the Body

Penny Van Esterik

Penny Van Esterik is Professor of Anthropology at York University, Toronto, Canada, where she teaches nutritional anthropology, advocacy anthropology, and feminist theory. Books include *Beyond the Breast–Bottle Controversy* (on infant feeding in developing countries), *Materializing Thailand* (on cultural interpretations of gender in Thailand), *Taking Refuge: Lao Buddhists in North America* (on the reintroduction of Buddhism by Lao refugees to North America), and *Food and Culture: A Reader*, edited with Carole Counihan. She is a founding member of WABA (World Alliance for Breastfeeding Action) and has been active in developing articles and advocacy materials on breastfeeding and women's work, breastfeeding and feminism, and contemporary challenges to infant feeding such as environmental contaminants and HIV/AIDS. In 2007, she received the Weaver–Tremblay award from the Canadian Anthropology Society (CASCA) for contributions to applied anthropology in Canada.

> The women over fifty
> Are convex from collarbone to crotch,
> Scarred armor nobly curved.
> . . . .Sometimes when they touch each other's arms
> They weep for a moment

Excerpt from "At the Party" by Ursula Le Guin

Bodies provide the foundation for many of the arguments developed in the other chapters of this book since bodies are significant in stories about sexual identities, reproductive freedoms, women's health, and gendered violence, to name a few. Bodies and the ways the body is interpreted are contextualized in cultural meanings informed by ideas about gender and other identities. As the excerpt from Ursula Le Guin's poem illustrates, age and meanings about aging bodies—and especially aging female bodies—are shaped by a variety of cultural messages specific to various communities. Bodies are at once local and global: the locus of both pain and pleasure and source of both objectification and empowerment. And, while bodies are the most personal and intimate parts of self, they are inscribed and shaped by a global hand, often guided by the interests of national and international politics. Take the example of an Inuit mother who has never left the Arctic, yet is told that her breast milk contains high levels of contaminants that traveled north on prevailing winds from industrial cities of North America and Europe. This one fact entangles the woman, her infant and family, and her local community, with both the politics of late capitalist industrial societies and UN efforts to regulate persistent organic pollutants.

Women's bodies are of particular concern to feminists, and, while most of the literature on the body applies to all human bodies (Tuana et al., 2002), there are topics that are of particular importance to women (such as pregnancy, lactation, menstruation, and menopause). When comparisons are made between women and men's bodies, we are likely to find that the former are more often judged by their surface appearance and are likely considered more "natural" or closer to nature, in spite of all we know about how bodies are culturally constituted. For example, we know that very unnatural processes such as foot binding, wearing tight corsets, and female genital cutting (FGC) have shaped women's bodies. These bodily practices have been interpreted as sources of oppression and evidence of women's subjugation. But bodies—particularly women's bodies—are exploited for a number of complex reasons. The short answers to understanding oppression include patriarchy and misogyny, male aggression, capitalism, and globalization. By grounding these broad processes in the experiences of real women's material bodies, we make these complex processes easier to understand. That is what makes bodies so interesting to scholars. Unlike philosophical and psychological questions, the evidence for questions about bodies is always and literally at hand.

Bodies and their representation in popular culture provide accessible material and symbolic evidence about gender politics in societies. The evidence encoded on our own bodies and those around us include scarification; piercing of ears, noses, and other body parts; tattoos; face painting; cosmetic surgeries; fashion clothing; hair styles; make-up; dieting; veiling; tooth filing; and dental decorations among others. From Thai topknots to Rastafarian dreadlocks, hair communicates messages about a person's identity and status. Life choice and chance are both made visible on bodies, either permanently or temporarily. Processes such as body manipulation and massage, body mapping, and eating disorders cannot be understood apart from theories of the body. Analyses of bodies also provide opportunities to raise important theoretical questions about gender, the nature of embodiment, and the relation between material conditions and practices and the symbolic meanings associated with them.

I begin this essay by reviewing theoretical work on the body and asking a series of questions about how bodies are constructed and represented in various contexts. The next section explores female bodies in time and space, including cultural practices that give meaning to women's bodies worldwide. Third, I examine the ways women's bodies have been commodified, or turned into objects for the pleasure of others, as well as some responses to that commodification through artistic re-presentation. Finally, consideration of the politics of the body draws us to "praxis" (the integration of theory and action) and to practical action. What have women done and what strategies might they employ to take back control over their bodies?

UNDERSTANDING THE BODY

Although questions of theory are often perceived as too difficult, too abstract, or too far removed from everyday life, theories are simply ways of asking "how" and "why" questions about the world: being what Cynthia Enloe (2004) calls the curious feminist. Advocacy and social change require grappling with theory and its relation to practical action. Bodies provide ways to understand and make visible processes that are hard to understand discursively (in words). Using one's own body as a "study guide," for example, can bring clarity to debates about structure and agency, embodiment, and the cultural construction of the body that includes racialization (how racial bodies are constructed). Paying attention to the body can be eye-opening since the body is one of the most basic and productive metaphors available

LEARNING ACTIVITY   **Hair, Long Beautiful Hair**

Reprinted with permission of David Sipress.

As women's studies professor and sociologist Rose Weitz notes, our hair is one of the first things people notice about us, and, for women the world over, hair plays an important role in their lives. The reasons, Weitz says, are numerous: "It is personal, growing directly out of our bodies. It is public, on view for all to see. And it is malleable, allowing us to change it more or less at whim," she says. "As a result, it's not surprising that we use our hair to project our identity and that others see our hair as a reflection of our identity."[1]

Interview a diverse group of women about their hair. How do they feel about their hair? What do they want to express with the way they wear their hair? What connections do they see between their hair and their gender? What influences how they wear their hair? How do they feel on "bad hair days"? What makes a "bad hair day" for them? Think about their answers and then write a brief essay theorizing about women's relationship to their hair.

For more information, read: Rose Weitz. *Rapunzel's Daughters: What Women's Hair Tells Us About Women's Lives.* New York: Farrar, Straus, and Giroux, 2005.

[1] http://researchmag.asu.edu/stories/hair.html

to humans to describe their experiences. This is because people use the body and its parts as a "root metaphor" (an underlying worldview that shapes an individual's understanding of a situation) to condense important symbolic messages. In some societies, for example, menstruation is seen as negative, contaminating, or shameful, and menstruating women have learned to hide evidence of menstrual blood. Think how much symbolic information is involved in your understandings of the heart, head, feet, and left or right hands, as well as in your society's interpretation of menstrual blood. Indeed, the most pervasive metaphor of the body in Western contexts is the body as a machine that breaks down and needs to be tuned up or repaired. This metaphor has practical results in the process of medicalization, or the process by which certain behaviors come to be defined and treated as medical issues. The reading by Anne E. Figert titled "Premenstrual Syndrome (PMS) as Scientific and Cultural Artifact" is a case in point. She addresses the question "Is PMS real?" and contextualizes her answer in medical, cultural, and economic forces, emphasizing that it is real if only because people in different situations define it as real. The following theoretical questions similarly help us contextualize the body, allowing us to understand its role in women's everyday lives. They also have political implications for action:

(1) *Are bodies material or symbolic?* Bodies are never just material (real, concrete) or symbolic (discursive or about language and words). Like many subjects within women's studies, this is a matter of both/and, not either/or. Bodies are both material and symbolic even though there may be a disjunction between real bodies and how they are imagined, talked about, and expected to behave. Research on the body requires using a combination of multi- and interdisciplinary perspectives since bodies are at once biological, social, cultural, and historical. The materiality of the body is always at hand as we eat, defecate, copulate,

LEARNING ACTIVITY   **Ideal Beauty**

Beauty is defined differently in various cultures around the world. Each of these photos represents an ideal of beauty. What do these photos suggest to you about the role of beauty culturally? How are social constructions of beauty and gender related? What do beauty ideals mean for women around the world?

and die: these are all real, concrete material processes that can be understood as separate from the words or symbolic representations that are used to think about or describe these practices. Sometimes these representations (like the fiction that "real women" don't sweat, pass gas, or defecate) are at odds with material realities of the body. Since every society has one or more symbolic idealized body images for women (see sidebar "Ideal Beauty"), it is often difficult for women to see themselves represented publicly in accurate ways. When real women fail to conform to these images, they may resort to cosmetic surgery, use of skin lighteners, and dieting to come closer to society's ideal body type or ideal symbolic representation.

(2) *How is analysis of the body linked to binary oppositions and oppositional thinking?* Many theorists argue that challenges in interpreting bodies are the result of theories of dualism. Dualism is a concept deeply rooted in ancient Greek thought that implies a split between the body and the soul. It encourages binary oppositions such as male/female and feminine/masculine that are not always helpful for clear thinking about social issues. Body/mind opposition ignores the extent to which the mind and body are one. Yet this false division, as well as related oppositions such as nature/culture, public/private, purity/pollution, inside/outside, self/other, and subjective/objective, pervade our thinking about the body. East/West (or "the West and the rest") is another dichotomy providing ways of thinking about others that hampers global organization around common concerns. Oppositions or

binaries within femininity like sexual/playmate and nurturing/mother, for example, break down in consideration of the breastfeeding body.

(3) *Does biology determine behavior?* Another difficult challenge in thinking about the body is creating biocultural understandings of the body that take biology into account while avoiding biological determinism (the notion that biological factors such as genes determine how an organism behaves, implying that biology is destiny). Biological determinism ignores social, cultural, and environmental factors. In efforts to avoid a biological essentialism that reduces women to their reproductive processes, some theorists avoid discussing the material body altogether. In reality, biology influences, but does not determine, behavior. A more useful framework than binary oppositions or biological essentialism is the "mindful body," a framework developed by Nancy Scheper-Hughes and Margaret Lock in 1987. Three approaches in this perspective include (1) the experienced, individualized body/self; (2) the real, material social body that relates to others; and (3) the body politic: the body as a product of social and political control. This framework allows us to consider how individual bodies are linked to the societies in which they reside and to national and international bodies. Consider research on HIV/AIDS as illustration. Analysts must consider (1) the vulnerable individual bodies who live with HIV as well as (2) how social stigma affects the ways infected bodies are perceived and how this shapes relationships with others. An additional level of analysis is needed to (3) consider the politics of HIV/AIDS that determines what programs are funded and who receives treatment.

(4) *Are individual bodies bounded?* Bodies give the appearance of bounded individuality or having clear boundaries, when, in fact, bodies are connected to each other. Women's bodies in particular are connected to other bodies. The maternal body engaged in sexual relations, childbirth, and breastfeeding provides some of the clearest evidence that the apparent "boundedness" of bodies is a cultural fiction. Is the fetus a separate body or part of a woman's body? The ethical and political questions raised by different approaches to the maternal body have policy implications for abortion rights. In addition, bodies are permeable: lives (and bodies) leak. As already mentioned, leaking menstrual blood is especially charged symbolically, and cultural interpretations have led to women's seclusion from daily activities of others. Discourses of the bleeding female body as polluting illustrate dangers associated with maintenance of bodily margins as fluids that transcend the body take on particular significance (Douglas, 1966). Ultimately, notions of pollution and uncleanliness are statements about exclusion and power relations. Repugnance associated with being close to polluting bodily fluids emerges as a powerful indicator of social relations of dominance and subordination. At the same time, however, menstruation has also been interpreted as magical and powerful, and women may be secluded to protect themselves and others from powers associated with leaking bodily fluids. In this example, seclusions originated in the magical and respected power of menstrual blood and women's reproductive capabilities. As such, while this example still reflects issues of power, these relations have different consequences for women's status in societies.

(5) *How does power actually impact bodies?* Michel Foucault (a French philosopher who, among other things, wrote a history of sexuality), focuses on the effects of power on bodies with attention to how cultures socialize bodies. He emphasized that while power works through the body, it can be productive and not just repressive. Veiling, a subject discussed

below, is a good example of a bodily practice that has been interpreted as both repressing and empowering women. Foucault (1980) stressed that bodies are constructed through discourses like language and material everyday practices and that these contribute to controlling the body, externally and internally. Social institutions often create "docile" female bodies through what is termed "disciplinary practices." These are practices that women are encouraged to perform that might include certain manners and hygienic practices to sculpt the body in ways that make them culturally "acceptable" (such as odorless or hairless) or ways to make the body "beautiful." (Note that what we consider to be "beautiful" is socially constructed and a relative concept.) Central in this notion of disciplinary practices is the concept of self-surveillance where women internalize standards and practices and monitor themselves. These "technologies of the self" refer to techniques of bodily management that people use to transform themselves in order to obtain what they consider to be the perfect body. Self-surveillance and bodily management encourage the body-based obsession reflected in extremes of dieting and fitness. External surveillance (imposed on people) also occurs as shown in cultural practices like fat jokes or other gestures that keep women in line, as well as the monitoring of women by women. This surveillance also includes the ways the body is objectified or turned into an object for the viewing pleasure of others. The "male gaze" refers to the practices of objectification that describe how men view women. As discussed in the previous chapter, these Western standards are exported through world media and fashion and have important consequences for women worldwide.

(6) *How does food link to bodies?* Food as a feminist issue relating to the body is underdeveloped theoretically, especially in terms of broad questions about how women nurture self and others through food and eating. Worldwide, however, pregnant women's bodies produce the first food for infants in the womb and through breast milk, and women's labor is most often employed in the daily task of feeding dependent children and family members. Exploring links between women and food is a valuable route to confirm there is no universal natural body untouched by culture; infants experience the world recognizing flavors of household food, first experienced through the taste of their own amniotic fluid, and, after birth, through the unique flavors of their mother's milk.

There is considerable scholarship on eating disorders, especially in the West, which links food with understandings of gender. Contemporary eating disorders are compulsive disorders that include a variety of behaviors: anorexia nervosa (self-starvation), bulimia nervosa (binge eating with self-induced vomiting and/or laxative use), compulsive eating (uncontrolled eating or binge eating), and muscle dysmorphia (fear of being inadequately muscled). In addition, there are general eating-disordered behaviors that include occasional binge eating and/or fasting, overly compulsive food habits, and compulsive dieting and/or exercising (sometimes called anorexia athletica). As the short story reading by Lesléa Newman, "Perfectly Normal," suggests, there are many forces in Western societies that encourage women to desire thinness and to associate this with "normality" and ultimately happiness. Although Western scholarship on eating disorders that stresses women's preoccupation with body image and beauty does not always translate well cross-culturally where there are a range of images of feminine beauty not all linked to slender bodies (O'Connor and Van Esterik, 2008), there is evidence that eating disorders are increasing worldwide as a result of cultural and economic globalization. A response to this and other problems associated with fashion and media is demonstrated in the reading "Spain Bans Skinny Mannequins."

Barbie at 50

Tiffany Hsu and Don Lee

Barbie turns 50, and to shake off a midlife crisis she's getting tattooed and opening the doors to her first megastore in China.

The developments are causing a stir on two continents, not bad for a plaything whose global cachet has been sagging of late.

We begin in Southern California, where, just in time for spring, Mattel Inc. has released "Totally Stylin' Tattoos Barbie." The doll comes with a set of more than 40 tiny tattoo stickers that can be placed on her body. Also included is a faux tattoo gun with wash-off tattoos that kids can use to ink themselves.

A spokeswoman for the El Segundo toy maker said it was a great way for youngsters to be creative with their pint-sized gal pal. But some parents are horrified by this body-art Barbie, labeling her the "tramp stamp" queen of play time.

On her parenting blog, Telling It Like It Is, Texas mother Lin Burress sarcastically predicted that "Totally Pierced Barbie" would be the next to roll off the assembly line. Readers commenting on the blog chimed in with their own fictional "Divorce Barbie," who would take possession of Ken's accessories.

Burress, a 46-year-old mother of six, said she was fed up with companies pushing racy fare to kids to make a profit.

"It's just one more thing being added to the pile of junk, like push-up bras and Bratz dolls, being marketed to these ridiculously young kids," she said. "These so-called toys just create a sense of rebellion."

This isn't the first time Barbie has had some eyebrow-raising accessories. The Butterfly Art Barbie from 1999 had a permanent tattoo on her stomach. In 2002, Mattel released a pregnant doll—not Barbie but her friend, Midge—replete with an infant that could be removed from her midsection. Consumer outcry chased the product off shelves.

Mattel said the new tattooed Barbie, priced online at around $20 and up, was selling better than expected. There are no plans to discontinue the doll.

Meanwhile, Mattel this weekend will unveil the House of Barbie in Shanghai, China.

The six-story retail emporium is the brand's first stand-alone store in China. It's a multimillion-dollar bet that its 11½-inch plastic toy will appeal to Shanghai's material girls, even in this horrible economy.

"There's no reason why in five to 10 years, China shouldn't be the biggest market in the world for us," said Richard Dickson, Barbie's general manager, sitting on a lattice boudoir bench on the store's fourth floor, where girls can design their own dolls.

The store also contains a salon where moms and daughters can get facials and manicures. There's a restaurant and bar. Naturally it offers thousands of Barbie products, from branded chocolate bars that cost a dollar or two to an adult-sized Vera Wang–designed wedding dress for $10,000.

Mattel is one of many Western retailers flocking to China to tap its growing middle class. Apple Inc. and Adidas opened their China superstores in Beijing. Walt Disney Co., Warner Bros., and others have beefed up their investments, even as piracy and tougher local competition have cut into their business.

At the moment, Asia accounts for less than 5 percent of Barbie's global sales. The doll has been showing its age in recent years; Barbie sales worldwide were off 9 percent in 2008, hurt by the recession and competition from rivals.

Whether China can give Barbie new life remains to be seen. Mattel's recently opened store in Buenos Aires, Argentina, has been drawing crowds. But there are plenty of doubters who point out that you only need to go into a Chinese home. You won't find many girls playing with dolls, let alone dolls with blond hair and blue eyes.

Dickson acknowledges that China's slowing economy will be a challenge, but to appeal to local sensibilities, Mattel has come up with a Shanghai Barbie—with bigger eyes, a rounder face, and a softer complexion. The price: about $36. The doll has no tattoos.

Another important aspect of the relationship between bodies and food is the gendered distribution of food where women and girl children in some patriarchal societies are less well-nourished than boys and men. Intrafamily food distribution refers to the distribution of food within families. Women eat least and last in many parts of the world. Such unequal food distribution patterns favoring males often produce differences in the body sizes of males and females. When this bias begins at birth, it results in differential mortality for infant girls compared to boys as well as unequal growth patterns in childhood. The subject is complicated by the ideology of the self-sacrificing mother who "voluntarily" reduces her food intake so that her children have more food.

BODIES IN TIME AND SPACE

Practices of colonialism, nationalism, and globalization shape female bodies from seemingly innocuous practices like the favoring of Western styles of dress to such institutions as slavery, prostitution, domestic service, child labor, and sex trafficking (Sharp, 2000). In particular, women's bodies take on special currency during times of war and civil unrest. As discussed in other chapters, the politics of gender in militarized conflict zones include the control of women's reproductive potential as well as the use of rape as a weapon of war. The extraction of resources such as diamonds (with which women in other parts of the world are encouraged to adorn their bodies as key aspects in the culture of romance), as well as other minerals, like oil, timber, etc., underlies many of these practices and is in itself a significant cause of war and ethnonationalist violence.

The politics of women's bodies in relation to practices of power over women is most clearly illustrated by extreme examples such as foot binding. This practice inflicted intense pain on young girls of the leisured upper classes in late imperial China. The pain was considered a preparation for childbirth, and "lotus feet" were considered the epitome of erotic beauty to Chinese men (Blake, 2000). Although foot binding in China was outlawed as long ago as the seventeenth century, it was practiced well into the twentieth. A more contemporary example is female genital cutting (FGC). Like foot binding, this practice developed in strongly patriarchal societies, and it is an example of discipline mothers impose on daughters. Both examples require historical and cultural information to explain their meanings and have been misunderstood by Western feminists taking them out of context and overgeneralizing them as evidence of male control over women's bodies without understanding the nuanced nature of the practices.

FGC, also known as female genital mutilation (FGM), is a contemporary issue of great complexity. It is framed as a problem of gender-based violence and is prominent on the international human rights agenda. Like foot binding in imperial China, the practice is initiated and promoted by mothers who want their daughters to be prepared for marriage. This is a problem in Somalia and Sudan and other regions of North Africa and the Middle East where these practices are incorporated into initiations of womanhood as highly valued cultural practices ensuring a girl's marriageability. The cutting varies from ritually "nicking" the clitoris to full infibulation in which external genitalia are cut away and the labia are stitched together. Advocates for the eradication of FGC argue that there are short- and long-term health consequences, particularly related to childbirth, and emphasize that it is important to distinguish between children who are unable to give informed consent and adult women who claim agency in carrying out a culturally valued practice.

It is important to note that physical modifications of genitalia as gendered practices also occur in the West. Some scholars compare FGC to the growing popularity in Europe and North America of female genital cosmetic surgery such as labia remodeling, vaginal "tucks," and other efforts to create "designer vaginas" (Shell-Duncan, 2008). Vaginal cosmetic surgeries include labiaplasty (resculpting the labia majora, and/or the labia minora, the folds of skin surrounding the structures of the vulva) and vaginoplasty (usually described as "rejuvenation" or tightening of the vagina). In addition, Western medical practitioners frequently assign intersex children as female or male at birth with or without the consent of parents and surgically modify infants' genitalia to conform to their own standards of what male and female bodies should look like (Van Lenning, 2004). Intersex individuals are children born with physiological characteristics (such as hormones, chromosomes, or reproductive organs) that are either a combination of, or different from, those conventionally associated with males or females. Although many intersex people prefer to have an identity that is neither male nor female (Monro, 2005), social acceptance of sexual ambiguity occurs in only a few cultures throughout the world (see sidebar on intersexuality).

Cosmetics and cosmetic surgery provide the means for some women to create the appearance of the "perfect" body, according to local ideal standards. Skin lighteners, Asian eyelid surgery, and practices to reshape the Jewish or Indian nose are all evidence that the processes of racialization operate to assign a value to particular body parts with the preferred value being the white European norm. When the fit between social ideals and real bodies becomes too distorted, some women resort to cosmetic surgery to improve the fit. This is illustrated in the reading "Changing Faces" by Lisa Takeuchi Cullen about the popularity of cosmetic surgeries in Japan, Thailand, Korea, Taiwan, and China. Although this essay does not focus on leg elongation as another form of cosmetic surgery among both women and men, it is important to mention this painful practice as an example of the relationship between social ideals and real bodies. Leg lengthening surgery breaks the bone and inserts lengthening rods to make people taller. Indeed, if one ever doubted the role of culture in sculpting the body, consider the case of cosmetic breast surgery in the neighboring countries of Brazil and Argentina. Breast reduction surgery has been commonplace among upper-middle-class women in Brazil as a popular "sweet sixteen" birthday present. In neighboring Argentina, young women request breast enlargement surgery to meet erotic beauty standards, with the result that Argentinean women have one of the world's highest ratios of silicone gel implants per person. In each country, women strive to meet standards of beauty formed through centuries of contact with other cultures: breast reduction surgery reflects the desire to avoid the stigma of large breasts associated with Black

Intersexuality Is a Human Rights Issue

The umbrella term *intersexuality* refers to all those situations in which an individual's bioanatomy varies from the male bodily *standard* and the female bodily *standard*. The most common intersex variations include chromosomal mosaics (XXY, XXO, etc.), certain gonadic tissue configurations and localizations (ovotestes, testicles that had not descended, etc.) as well as certain genital configurations (penises shorter than 1 cm, clitorises longer than 5 cm, urinary orifices located on the side or the base of the penis, lack of vagina, etc.).

Since the mid-1950s, all over the West those people who had been classified as *intersex* at the time of birth or in their early infancy by health professionals have been and are subjected to a variety of socio-medical procedures aimed at cosmetically "correcting" and "normalizing" the "ambiguous" appearance of their genitals. Such procedures include, for instance, surgical reconstruction of "normal" female genitals through systematic and compulsive clitoridectomies, cosmetic surgeries performed on labia majora and minora, vaginoplasties, and other related procedures, like periodical neovaginal dilatations. In the decades since this model for care was established, a very high number of intersex infants have been subjected to these "corrective" and "normalizing" practices, without having the opportunity to provide or deny their consent and, in may cases, without having access to their clinical records even when they reach adulthood.

Applying these procedures can cause a lack of or partial loss of genital sensitivity; total loss of reproductive capacity; temporary or permanent postsurgical trauma that in many cases can be compared to the experience of repeated rape or castration; and internalized inadequacy, shame, and fear.

WHY IS *INTERSEXUALITY* A HUMAN RIGHTS ISSUE?

- Because it creates inadmissible differences among human beings on the basis of their bodily appearance, distinguishing among those who will be able to enjoy their masculinity, their femininity, their reproductive capacities, and their sexuality, and those who will have to suffer mutilations in their bodies and personal histories in order to be considered men and women, human beings, and "normal" people
- Because sociomedical procedures currently in place that are applied in cases of intersexuality subject intersex children to cruel and inhuman practices whose consequences are irreversible
- Because the medical-legal arguments invoked in cases of intersexuality blatantly ignore the right of children to make informed decisions about their own bodies
- Because hiding and/or distorting intersex patients' clinical records violates their right to identity and to personal history
- Because identifying intersex corporal variations as pathologies, aberrations, or "exceptions of Nature" deeply damages intersex people's and their families' self-esteem and welfare
- Because surgical procedures for body "normalization" drastically reduce intersex people's possibility to fully enjoy their sexual rights and their reproductive rights
- Because the bodily, gender, and sexuality ideals underlying these procedures reproduce and reinforce sexism and homophobia
- Because reducing the diversity of bodies to a human bodily *standard*—female or male—violates the right to freedom of expression, that includes as a basic component the right to freely express one's gender in different ways, including one's body
- Because this reduction severely limits our own cultural capacity to live with diversity, to value, respect, and defend it

- Because justifying nonconsented, invasive, and mutilating "normalization" procedures, and concealment and distortion of personal identity as socially and medically accepted ways of dealing with *intersexuality* provides institutional status and reinforcement to discrimination, exclusion, and violence, evils that threaten all human beings equally

slavery in Brazil, while Argentinean women risk their health with breast implants to fulfill the erotic Spanish fantasy of large-breasted women. In both cases, industries are ready to meet or exploit these needs.

If bodies are culturally constructed, the ideal body in any society is unlikely to be the natural body. Bodies are differentiated, marked on the surface with signs of "feminine" beauty. The Padaung women of Burma, a subgroup of the Karen, lengthen their necks with brass rings, in addition to rings on their arms and legs, to meet local standards of beauty. Plates stretch under or over the lip of several ethnic groups in Kenya and Tanzania (see sidebar on ideal beauty). For groups such as the Mende of Sierra Leone, all members of the society constantly comment on the beauty of girls' and women's features. Most important is that all features must "fit together" harmoniously: large round eyes, thick separate eyebrows, luxuriant hair, copper or very black skin. And a beautiful girl must be a "good girl." Aboriginal women from Central Australia paint on their bodies with particular emphasis on the breasts. These bodily imprints are corporeal traces of the presence of their ancestors: embodied traces that write the social onto the body in the form of what we might judge to be beautifully painted designs—lines, circles, and dots—accentuating fertility. Here the fallen, sagging breast that can shake and quiver is valued and privileged (Biddle, 2007).

In these ways, expectations for "ideal" body shape and clothing preferences change through time and vary across cultures, with the forces of economic and cultural globalization exporting Western notions of "beauty" that become modified in new cultural contexts. Definitions of beauty, as well as understandings associated with cultural meanings of "fat" and "thin," are linked to ethnicity, class, and age, and are shaped by myriad

LEARNING ACTIVITY   **Cosmetic Vacations**

Sand, surf, and surgery . . . one of the newest trends in cosmetic surgery is having the procedure(s) done in an exotic location like Rio de Janeiro as part of a vacation package. Some airlines are even offering surgery/tour packages. For a few thousand dollars, people unhappy with their bodies can have breast augmentation, liposuction, or a tummy tuck and then recover sipping a margarita by the pool and taking guided tours of the local area.

Go to a search engine such as dogpile.com or google and type in "cosmetic vacation." Check out a few of these sites. Where are these vacations offered? What services do they provide? Who do you think are the targets of these vacation offers? How do these businesses rely on women's unhappiness with their bodies? Do you think these businesses foster this unhappiness in the ways they construct women's bodies on their Web sites?

What are the implications of wealthy Americans, Europeans, and Japanese traveling to the developing world for such surgeries? How might feminists evaluate cosmetic vacations?

local and transnational social forces from health institutions to media and diet industries. As demonstrated in the reading "Mi Estomago (My Belly)," a poem by Marjorie Agosin, claiming and celebrating the body allow women to feel empowered and encourage agency over the body in ways that may go against cultural expectations of how women's bodies "should" look.

Fashions change through time as specific items of apparel like high-heeled shoes, corsets, and bras have altered the appearance of women's bodies and, in some cases, also changed the material body. Skeletons from the Victorian period of Western societies, for example, show patterns of compressed ribs and internal organs from tightly boned corsets that attempted to produce the hourglass figure with tiny waist. In the 1930s, anthropologists measured fashion changes across time in the United States, measuring hem length, waist placement, and neckline. They found that changes in women's dress fashion were not simply random expressions of personal or entrepreneurial creativity, but were also part of long-term trends linked to economic and political stability. Wars, for example, triggered disturbances in the stability of fashions. Long-term trends in stylistic patterns are no longer of concern to most social scientists, but they are a reminder that styles in fashions and body image change for very complex reasons. It will be interesting to see if hems go up or down in North America as a response to economic downturns.

Women all around the world wear clothes for warmth and cooling and for the practical value associated with their work. Clothing combines messages about gender, ethnicity, age, and race in complex symbolic codes. For example, while teenagers might decide to wear certain types of shoes to express certain styles and because their friends are wearing them, perhaps they still pay attention to the color of shoelaces with green, for instance, implying environmentalism. Such color coding has absolutely no meaning unless the audience shares the same knowledge of the symbolic meaning coded in the shoelace color. In

A DAY IN THE LIFE   **Balance** *by Meghan Barp*

Kiri Mokai welcomes the cool early morning air on her skin from the open window next to her bed. It is 5:57 a.m.—she knows that her alarm is about to ring, indicating the start to another long day. The sun is just starting to peek through the slatted wood shutters covering the windows of the bedroom that she shares with her four-year-old daughter, Lini. As Kiri stretches awake, she can faintly hear the radio in the kitchen. She slides out of bed, allowing Lini to sleep for another half hour before she will wake her for school.

Kiri, 23, lives in a three-bedroom brick house in Rāpaki, a sleepy village overlooking the Bay of Rāpaki in the South Island region of Canterbury, New Zealand. Surrounded by dry brown foothills, Rāpaki was once a thriving fishing village, located 17 km south of Christchurch—the largest city in the South Island. There has been a recent prioritization of cultural regeneration in the region, one that has been welcomed by the nearly 80,000 Maori residents in the South Island, including Kiri's family. Their *iwi* (tribe) has struggled to maintain a sense of Maori heritage and pride after New Zealand was settled by Europeans in the early eighteenth century.

Kiri has been living with her parents, brother, and grandmother for the last six months, leaving a small flat in Christchurch that she shared with her former boyfriend, Lini's father, who is *Pakeha*, a New Zealander of European descent. Kiri feels fortunate to be surrounded by her *whanau* (family), especially for Lini. Even though the drive to Christchurch is not a long one, her family rarely made the visit, not approving of her relationship with her former boyfriend. By returning home, she now has a built-in support system to help raise her daughter with the Maori traditions that are so important to her and her family.

With the support of her parents and grandmother, Kiri continues to commute daily to Christchurch with her younger brother who attends high school there. During the day she works full time as an administrative assistant in a small law firm and takes evening classes two nights a week at the university to finish her degree in early childhood education. In the future, she hopes to work with Rāpaki community members and local government agencies to reopen the elementary school that has been closed for some time.

In the kitchen, Kiri finds her grandmother already on her second cup of tea. She affectionately presses her nose into her grandmother's and lights the gas stove to reheat the water that had cooled. Lately her grandmother's health has been deteriorating due to diabetes, so she often finds her grandmother awake, patiently waiting for early morning company. Kiri relishes the precious few moments that she has alone with her grandmother in the hours before the rest of the house is in full chaotic swing—it is an opportunity for the two women to speak candidly.

Her grandmother still longs for the days of the untamed wilderness, isolation, and clean living, and embraces the Maori tradition of *karakia*, herbal treatments, for her ailments. While Kiri respects her choices, she uses this quiet time to urge her grandmother to seek conventional medicine as supplemental care. Kiri finishes her cup of tea, refills her grandmother's, and quickly returns to her room to prepare Lini for school.

Kiri often feels the pull of her Maori roots as she carves out a new life for herself and her daughter. At the insistence of her grandmother, Lini attends the Kohanga reo, a newly established Maori immersion school for girls started by the Maori Women's League in Rāpaki. With funding from the regional government, the school is able to focus on teaching in a traditional Maori format that utilizes oral histories and with an emphasis on language and culture. Kiri has agreed that the school is a good idea; she wants her daughter to have a strong sense of Maori heritage similar to her upbringing, balanced with the economic opportunities that will await her upon completion of her degree.

Kiri's father, Haki, walks Lini to school every morning and picks her up in time for an early afternoon nap, enjoying quality time with his *mokapuna* (grandchild). Kiri kisses her daughter goodbye and heads to the car that she shares with her brother. As they curve through the winding, hilly roads on the way to Christchurch, Kiri coordinates her schedule with her brother's. He studies at the local library after school until Kiri finishes class in the evening, and they journey back to Rāpaki together around 8 p.m. While she is not able to see Lini off to bed twice per week, she knows that this small sacrifice will eventually allow them to have a better life.

Kiri slides into her chair at work just before 9 a.m. Her day is filled with answering the phone, typing memos, and scheduling meetings for the three attorneys who work at the firm. While the work pays for her education, affords her small necessities, and allows her to contribute to the household, Kiri is anxious to finish her degree to focus on being more rooted in social change in her community. She enjoys having social interaction during the day, which makes the time pass quickly. At 5 p.m., she gathers her belongings and starts the 20-minute walk to campus for her 5:30 p.m. class.

Finally, at 8 p.m., she meets her brother for the half-hour journey home. They share bits of their day, but most of the ride is silent. As they park the car, they enter the kitchen through the back door of the house. They can smell the remnants of tonight's dinner; their mother has left the wrapped leftovers on the kitchen table. Before eating, Kiri checks in on the sleeping Lini, gently kissing her on the forehead. Returning to the kitchen, Kiri ends her day with the comfort of a home-cooked meal before she slides into bed, falling asleep almost instantly to the sound of the bay waters.

industrialized countries with exuberant market economies, brand-name clothing may act in subtle and not so subtle ways to mark class differences. In addition, clothes not only reflect a person's individuality in establishing and maintaining personal identities and social relationships but are also markers of ethnicity and regional identity. Sometimes these are personal choices and other times they are enforced by husbands, fathers, and/or the state. Many diasporic (meaning the movement or migration of populations sharing common ethnic identities) South-Asian women, for instance, describe how their choice to wear a sari changed both their self-perception and the way others treated them since it allowed them more freedom in public. Similarly, new immigrants may choose to continue to wear traditional ethnic or national dress or are pressured to adopt the clothing of the majority in the country of resettlement (Purkayastha, 2002). In this way, gendered displays of fashion are expressive of individuals, controlled by others, and shaped by social and economic practices.

A woman's body often derives its meaning from the extent to which it is revealed or concealed by clothing, including head coverings. The surfaces of women's bodies may be exposed, displayed, or hidden for a variety of reasons. Widows and brides (and by extension, nuns) wear veils for ritual or religious reasons. Some Muslim groups require women to wear head coverings and gowns that cover the hair or face and entire body to hide the sexually charged aspects of the body. As part of the politics of Islamic self-identity, veiling often symbolizes the "otherness" of Islam to the West. But in Islamic societies, veiled women are markers of modesty and morality; to some women, this public invisibility gives them the freedom to move about publicly. The recent popularity of veiling in Egypt, Turkey, and Malaysia, for example, is a practice that carries political, religious, and gendered meanings that differ from the meanings associated with the traditional use of headscarves by older women to mark their ethnic and national origin. Observing a veiled woman provides no information about her motivation for wearing the veil. Veiling could signal patriarchal control, intensified religiosity, an act of political defiance, or fashion experimentation. Recently, France invoked its long-standing preference for the removal of all religious symbols in public spaces to defend the expulsion of veiled Muslim girls from their schools (Benhabib, 2002). The reading "Unveiled Sentiments" by Jasmin Zine examines the politics of veiling in a Canadian Islamic school and discusses the ways gendered religious identities are constructed in the schooling experiences of these girls.

Cultural rules about bodily deportment orient such everyday activities as walking down the street, eating a meal, wearing clothes, or greeting others. The Thai greeting with hands folded in prayer position (*wai*) reflects relations between beauty, femininity, or masculinity, and knowledge of power relations between people in the greeting as reflected in the height of the hands and the depth of the bow (Van Esterik, 1995). When Europeans first encountered Thai people, they complained they were unable to tell men from women. When both had shaved heads or brush cuts, and similar unfitted clothing, dress did not significantly distinguish between adults with similar body proportions. This inability to immediately anticipate and assign gender to people can cause anxiety among individuals used to making gender distinctions based upon the body. Such anxieties also occur in response to "trans" bodies that are not immediately recognizable as masculine or feminine, or if they are understood as gendered, the observer cannot decipher whether the trans individual is a "she" or a "he." The concept of transgendered involves resisting the social construction of gender into two distinct categories (femininity and masculinity) and works to break down these polarized categories. The reading "Transgender Identity in Japan" by Hiroko Tabuchi focuses on female-to-male transgendering and illustrates the ways individuals may seek sex reassignment surgeries and practices to change the sex characteristics of the body. Such individuals identify as transsexuals. In other words, transsexuals are considered transgendered individuals who have completed chemical or surgical altering of the body.

Time also shapes individual bodies throughout the life cycle. Maternal bodies produce infants whose bodies rapidly change in shape and size to become toddlers and children. Adolescents, transformed by hormonal and other changes, gradually acquire more sexualized bodies with the potential to reproduce. Some Western women seek to deny the effects of aging or actively seek ways to appear younger by regaining a youthful body ("age pass") since the aging or aged body has less prestige and is seen as less sexually attractive in their societies. This point is illustrated in the excerpt at the beginning of this essay from Ursula Le Guin's poem "At the Party" that described the experiences of old women. Aging bodies in these societies are often represented as pathological and sometimes treated as a condition to be cured with the use of "age-defying" makeup or accessories. In comparison, some Thai Buddhist elders withdraw from active participation in productive activities and spend more time meditating, fasting, and following a more ascetic lifestyle in active preparation for death (Van Esterik, 2000). Although bodies around the world experience similar biological processes like puberty and aging, societies define and name these life stages differently and impose different expectations on women's behavior.

COMMODIFICATION OF THE BODY

A commodity is a thing produced for commerce or trade for private profit. We do not usually think of bodies or body parts as commodities or things. Rather, bodies are totalities, holistic and integrated repositories of organs and complex meanings. But in modern industrial societies, bodies and body parts are increasingly being treated as things. Under the process of commodification, the integrity of the body is easily lost. For political, historical, and economic reasons, bodies have been fragmented and divided into their component parts: hearts, breasts, eyes, hair, lips, penises, and vaginas. Fragmented, dehumanized bodies are more easily commodified, and, hence, more easily transformed. Transforming bodies usually involves buying products and supporting consumer societies. Commodification of bodies also encourages the measurement of bodies as in 34AA, finger printing, body mass index, and new biometric technology including retinal scans and digital facial recognition. How will these new means of technological surveillance influence the future categorization of bodies and the subsequent treatment of people identified by particular body parts?

As discussed in other chapters, pornography is an example of the extreme commodification of the body. Most feminists decry the antifemale tone of pornography and its intentional degradation of women; they believe that it promotes the subordination of women to men, encouraging men to behave in harmful ways. They seek legal means to eliminate or control it, pointing out that pornography is violence against women in that it is not about sex as much as it is about power. Others have argued that pornography can be sexually empowering for women and should be freely accessible if it does not hurt anyone. There is general agreement, however, that child pornography should be banned because there is clear evidence of harm.

The fragmentation of the body is apparent in contemporary biomedicine as technologies such as dialysis machines, iron lungs, pacemakers, MRIs, and fetal monitors make it easier to blur the boundaries between body parts and machines. Medicalization of the body turns the suffering person, for example, into "the liver in bed four," and encourages the continued use of the body as machine metaphor: the heart as pump, the kidney as filter. Organ donation is implicated in this way of thinking, as the commercialization of the body raises ethical questions about organ donation, including the nature of the donation process, the definition of the end of life, and whether the poor and disenfranchised are more likely sources of corpses for medical dissection and of scarce organs such as kidneys. New studies of the body must consider who owns our body parts, including our DNA, our stem cells, and future products of biotechnology. In recognition of potential human rights abuses, most countries prohibit the sale of organs. The World Health Organization (WHO) also condemns the trade of human organs (Patel and Rushefsky, 2002).

Women's bodies are easily commodified and particularly prone to interpretation as objects because of their role in reproduction. Even the WHO and some maternal health projects have been accused of treating women as "wombs and breasts on legs." While male bodies may also be exploited in the military and in sports, for example, history reveals that women's special capacities lend themselves to particularly complex relationships with the products of their bodies. From wet-nursing to surrogate motherhood, the products of wombs and breasts may be freely shared as some of the greatest human gifts, or expropriated for the advantage of others. Breast milk, for example, is intended to nurture one's own child even though many women produce surplus milk. Wet nursing (breastfeeding an infant other than one's own by birth) kept millions of infants alive before a relatively safe substitute for breast milk was found. Wet nursing is always surrounded by complex rules affecting anyone who took on this work. If a woman is paid for this service, it makes sense to think of breast milk as a commodity. But in the case of slave women coerced into breastfeeding their masters' children, it was the woman herself who became the commodity. Recently, milk banks have been established to make breast milk available even though it is difficult to assign a monetary value to such a product. Some groups have estimated the cost of banked breast milk at around US$50 per liter. While putting a price on breast milk may seem offensive, ignoring its value may also be problematic since its production costs mothers in time and nutrients.

Performance artists, like dancers, use their bodies as a medium of expression that entertains and enlightens through a critique of the ways bodies are objectified and commodified. Feminist performance artists may use their bodies in ways that link to larger political movements with the aim of transforming the position and condition of women. Canadian performance artist Jess Dobkin, for example, has presented her art in ways that encourage women to see their breasts and breast milk in new ways. In a 2003 performance, "Presenting 2 boobs in 'Hangin Out,'" she used her breasts that were painted with faces as characters in a puppet show. In "The Lactation Station Breast Milk Bar," performed in 2006, she treated breast milk, a product of women's bodies and often hidden or reviled in Hollywood movies, as a product to be savored as at a vintage wine-tasting bar (Van Esterik, 2008). These performances address the commodification of the body by attempting to transform the negative, embarrassing, or hidden aspects of women's bodies and instead explicitly celebrate them as natural and wonderful human functions. In a similar vein, Orlan, a French performance artist, had herself filmed undergoing cosmetic surgery to transform herself into a new being. Since 1987, she has had liposuction, chin and face implants, and other procedures, all filmed and performed for audiences. She uses her body transformation to argue that art must disrupt thoughts, take risks,

ACTIVIST PROFILE   **Somaly Mam**

Somaly Mam was born in 1970 in the Mondulkiri province of Cambodia to an impoverished ethnic minority family. As a young child, she was sold into sexual slavery by a man who posed as her grandfather and forced her to work in a brothel along with many other young girls. When she finally saw a friend murdered by a pimp, she made her plans to escape. Once free, she turned attention to helping others like her and combating sex trafficking of young girls.

In a country where five- and six-year-old girls are often sold into sexual slavery by their families for as little as $100, Somaly Mam works to rescue girls and women from brothels and pimps and to try to change corrupt government practices that allow sex trafficking to continue. In 1996, she cofounded *Agir Pour les Femmes en Situation Précaire* (AFESIP), Acting for Women in Distressing Circumstances, to work with trafficked women. Since its founding, the organization has rescued thousands of girls, provided them with medical care, and helped them find work. Sex traffickers, however, have not taken Somaly's interference in their money-making lightly. A man who ran a brothel once put a gun to Somaly's head for talking to the girls who worked for him. Afterward, she had him arrested.

Through the years, Somaly has been honored with numerous awards for her work. She was one of eight women honored in the opening ceremony of the 2006 winter Olympics. In 2006, she was also named *Glamour* magazine's Woman of the Year. In 2008, *Time* magazine named her one of its "People Who Matter."

Somaly says, "I've committed my life to fighting this horrible scourge on humanity. Seeing innocent young women and children whose lives have been forever scarred leaves no doubt that they need a champion who is willing to invest all their time and energy towards eradicating the shameful practice of human trafficking. I cannot wage this fight alone and call upon anyone who cares about the innocent victims to donate their time, money and advocacy to this important cause."

To learn more about Somaly Mam, read her memoir, *The Road of Lost Innocence: The True Story of a Cambodian Heroine*. New York: Random House, 2008.

http://www.somaly.org
http://www.timesonline.co.uk/tol/life_and_style/article596932.ece

and be deviant. She also encourages us to consider the cultural meanings associated with cosmetic surgeries.

Philip Roth's book, *The Breast* (1972), describes the experiences of a man who wakes to find himself transformed into a 155-pound breast. Transformed into his own object of desire (a woman's breast), he imagines what the breast would feel and suggests to his readers the power of the sexualized body to shape our sense of self. While the book might be read as a writer's individual act of self-expression, like other examples of artistic performance, it also draws attention to the politics of the body or expressions of power associated with the body. Another performance that underscores the politics of the body, and especially the issue of gendered violence against the female body, is the play "Vagina Monologues" performed all over North America. Its creator, Eve Ensler, hopes to help women understand the ways the female body is a source of both oppression and empowerment. Such performances challenge silences about the body in ways that academics seldom can.

In these ways, art has the potential to bridge the concepts of commodification and political protest and provide more examples of "both/and" stories about bodies. "Body mapping" projects in South Africa, where women trace the outlines of their bodies and decorate them communally, illustrate the power of bringing together HIV positive support groups, factual knowledge about women's health, narrative and artistic therapy, treatment activism, resistance, and body-based performances. The traced and decorated outline of the body becomes a starting point for discussing life histories and experiences of being HIV positive, bringing together biomedical and local knowledge of the body. As one South African woman wrote about her body map: "In my picture, the HIV looks like fire because I felt that it was like something burning inside. . . . I had lots of pains in my body. But now I cannot feel it because now I'm healthy" (Wienand, 2006, p.23).

LOCAL AND GLOBAL ADVOCACY

As the body mapping project discussed above shows, bodies are sites of resistance against racism and sexism as well as the subject of resistance. The act of baring one's breast or going on a hunger strike draws attention to bodies themselves as sites of political protest. Bodies are used in these ways as loci of resistance both outside of and within social movements, either spontaneously or as part of very organized campaigns. A passivist Russian Christian group called Doukhobors, who settled in western Canada in the early 1900s, used mass nudity as a form of protest against the Canadian government. The immolation of Buddhist monks who protested the war in Vietnam by lying down in front of army tanks is another body-based form of protest, as is the resistance on the West Bank of Gaza where violence between Israelis and Palestinians is a routine occurrence and occupants of houses to be bull-dozed lie down in front of the machines. Individual women have used their bodies to block roads to stop clear-cut logging in the last North American temperate rain forest in Clayquot Sound, British Columbia, and in old-growth forests in other regions of the continent. Women have also used their bodies in imaginative acts of civil disobedience to protest war, and nuclear war in particular. At the Greenham Common Women's Peace Camp, located at an air base near London, in the 1980s and later, at the Women's Encampment for a Future of Peace and Security at Seneca, New York, women literally put their bodies on the line in attempts to secure peace. Similar antiwar organizations such as the Women in Black (as mentioned in other chapters) have protested and publicized rape as a weapon of war. As a result of the efforts of these groups and others, rape has been formally recognized as a weapon of war in the United Nations Resolution 1325 addressing gender, peace, and security.

Women have resisted external control over their bodies for as long as others have exerted control over them. However, only in the last few centuries has the growth of transnational feminist networks, with the help of new communication technologies, permitted more coordinated actions to link women's concerns in different parts of the world. Individuals and governments have come together to protest such issues as sex trafficking of women, the sale of human organs, violence against women, child pornography, prostitution, FGC, beauty contests, exploitive advertising, cruelty to animals in the cosmetics industry, child labor, unethical promotion of infant formula: all issues having direct or indirect impact on women's bodies. Still, not all national women's groups would define priority issues in the same way, nor even support global campaigns. While individual women, for example, may choose not to consume beauty products like make-up or refuse to follow fashions, such decisions have more impact when they are part of coalitions in integrated transnational approaches. Recognition of connections between issues and the need for advocates to work together is important. For example, sexual and reproductive rights for women seldom include breastfeeding; breastfeeding mothers' support groups might not be sensitive to the needs of lesbian mothers; lesbian mothers might not understand the needs of disabled mothers; and so on. Sex workers may stress their right to safe working environments, free from harassment, and fail to identify with campaigns to criminalize sex trafficking of children. To take body-based protests to the level of political advocacy, individual women need to come together to create pressure groups to influence larger numbers of people, and, particularly, to convince a wider public or those with authority to recognize the importance of their issues.

The United Nations is one transnational institution ready to take on international advocacy work on behalf of women through agencies such as the United Nations Development Fund for Women (UNIFEM) and regulatory initiatives such as CEDAW (Convention on the Elimination of All Forms of Discrimination against Women), where body integrity is

LEARNING ACTIVITY   **Real Beauty**

Dove, the beauty products company, commissioned a global study of the impact of beauty ideals on women's self-esteem. Not surprisingly, the study found that most women are unhappy with some part of their bodies. Surveying more than 3,200 women, aged 18–64, in 10 countries, the study revealed that 9 out of 10 women want to change some aspect of themselves, beginning with weight and body shape. Only 2% of women around the world describe themselves as beautiful. In Australia, the study found that 2/3 of women avoid certain activities because of the way they look. Only 6% of the Australian women said they were "very satisfied" with their looks.

In 2004, Dove launched the "Campaign for Real Beauty" to try to begin to change perceptions about beauty. Go to Dove's film sites (http://www.dove.us/#/features/videos/videogallery.aspx/) and watch *Onslaught* and *Evolution*. What do these short films suggest about beauty ideals? Take a look at the rest of Dove's Web site. How would you evaluate the company's efforts to challenge beauty ideals?

Dove's parent corporation is Unilever, the company that also makes Axe products for men. Go to www.youtube.com and search for "Axe." Watch some of the commercials for this product. How would you evaluate these commercials? What are their messages about women, men, and beauty?

How would you compare and contrast the Dove and Axe films? What do you think about the fact that Unilever produces both the Dove Campaign for Real Beauty and the Axe commercials?

Source: www.campaignforrealbeauty.com

understood as a basic human right. However, all initiatives, policies, and regulations require translating international instruments into the local vernacular so that they make sense to women in local communities. Even violence against women, what might be considered a universally recognized violation of women's bodies, requires negotiating local and cultural definitions of human rights (Merry, 2006). Addressing the violation of women's bodies, from such problems as domestic abuse and the sexual abuse of children to sex trafficking and war crimes, requires attending to what local and national women's groups consider the most pressing problems and what they understand as the priority of national governments. Multiple feminisms and a diversity of issues relating to women's bodies require the development of alliances that are inclusive and respect differences. Women's studies as a discipline assumes that the "personal is political" (or that personal issues have structural causes and consequences) and that there should always be a relation between theory and praxis, or practical action. This is particularly clear when we consider how our bodies connect us to one another and to the global environment we share.

REFERENCES

Benhabib, S. (2002). *The claims of culture*. Princeton: Princeton University Press.

Biddle, J. (2007). *Breasts, bodies, canvas*. Sydney: NSW Press.

Blake, F. (2000). Foot-binding in neo-Confucian China and the appropriation of female labor. In L. Schiebinger (Ed.), *Feminism and the body* (pp. 429–464). Oxford: Oxford University Press.

Douglas, M. (1966). *Purity and danger*. Harmondsworth, UK: Penguin.

Enloe, C. (2004). *The curious feminist*. Berkeley: University of California Press.

Foucault, M. (1980). *History of sexuality, vol.1. Introduction*. New York: Vintage.

Le Guin, U. (1986). At the party. In J. Alexander, B. Berrow, L. Domitrovich, M. Donnelly, and C. McLean (Eds.), *Women and aging: An anthology by women* (p. 85). Corvallis, OR: Calyx.

Merry, S. (2006). *Human rights and gender violence*. Chicago: University of Chicago Press.

Monro, S. (2005). *Gender politics: Citizenship, activism and sexual diversity*. London: Pluto Press.

O'Connor, R. and Van Esterik, P. (2008). De-medicalizing anorexia. *Anthropology Today*, 4(5), 6–8.

Patel, K. and Rushefsky, M. E. (2002). *Health care policy in an age of new technologies*. Amonk, NY: M.E. Sharpe.

Purkayastha, B. (2002). Contesting multiple margins: Asian Indian community activism in the early and late twentieth century. In N. Baples and M. Dasai (Eds.), *Women's activism and globalization* (pp. 99–117). New York: Routledge.

Roth, P. (1972). *The breast*. London: J. Cape.

Schepher-Hughes, N. and Lock, M. (1987). The mindful body. *Medical Anthropology Quarterly, 1*, 6–41.

Sharp, L. (2000). The commodification of the body and its parts. *Annual Review of Anthropology, 29*, 287–328.

Shell-Duncan, B. (2008). From health to human rights: Female genital cutting and the politics of intervention. *American Anthropologist, 110* (2), 225–226.

Tuana, N., Cowling, W., Harrington, M., Johnson, G., and MacMullin, T. (2002). *Revealing male bodies.* Bloomington: Indiana University Press.

Van Esterik, P. (1995). The politics of beauty in Thailand. In C. Ballero Cohen, R. Wilk, and B. Stoelje (Eds.), *Beauty queens on the global stage* (pp. 203–216). New York: Routledge.

Van Esterik, P. (2000). *Materializing Thailand.* Oxford: Berg Press.

Van Esterik, P. (2008). Vintage breastmilk: Exploring the discursive limits of breast milk. *Canadian Theatre Review, 137*, 20–23.

Van Lenning, A. (2004). The body as crowbar: Transcending or stretching sex? *Feminist Theory, 5*(1), 25–47.

Wienand, A. (2006). *An evaluation of body mapping as a potential HIV/AIDS education tool.* Capetown: Centre for Social Science Research, University of Cape Town.

SUGGESTIONS FOR FURTHER READING

Dewey, S. (2005). *Making Miss India Miss World: Constructing gender, power, and the nation in postliberalization India.* Syracuse: Syracuse University Press.

Jeffreys, S. (2005). *Beauty and misogyny: Harmful cultural practices in the West.* New York: Psychology Press.

Jeffreys, S. (2008). *The industrial vagina: The political economy of the global sex trade.* New York: Routledge.

King-O'Riain, R. C. (2006). *Pure beauty: Judging race in Japanese beauty pageants.* Minneapolis: University of Minnesota Press.

Nnaemeka, O. (Ed.). (2005). *Female circumcision and the politics of knowledge: African women in imperialist discourses.* Westport, CT: Praeger Paperback.

Transgender Identity in Japan

Hiroko Tabuchi (2006)

To most Japanese, Takafumi Fujio with cropped hair, thick arms and deep voice is a typical, middle-aged salaryman. But until four years ago, when the food company worker started on a range of hormonal treatments, he was a woman, a housewife and mother of two.

Fujio is one of an estimated 7,000 to 10,000 Japanese who believe they were born the wrong sex, a sexual minority that has been largely hidden from view in Japan. But that is quickly changing.

Japan's first sex-change operation was performed in 1998, and its first transsexual and gay politicians were elected to public office in 2003. A groundbreaking legal reform allowing some transsexuals to change their officially registered sex took effect the following year.

These advances, the result of long years of work behind the scenes, have given Japan's sexual minorities rising self-confidence and a greater willingness to come out of the closet despite the country's long-prized conformity and disdain for displays of individuality.

"These changes have been way overdue," Fujio said at a recent interview in Tokyo. "I think the law got people thinking, 'If the country has recognized these people, they must be acceptable after all.'"

Greater visibility and legal change are part of a general trend in Japan toward more personal freedom. Technology and tradition have also played a role. The Internet has spread information about alternative lifestyles to people who in previous generations would have been isolated. Meanwhile, Japan's lack of deeply rooted moral or religious censure of sexual minorities had made the transition easier. The rising visibility is a sharp turnaround for those like Fujio, who grew up in an era in postwar Japan where talk of transsexual lifestyles was rare.

"The transsexual community had a great dilemma. If we spoke out, we risked our jobs, our livelihoods. But by staying silent, nothing would change," said Aya Kamikawa, Japan's first and only transsexual politician.

Since 2003, Kamikawa, a male to female transgender, has played a key role in lobbying for changes at both the national and local levels, including the sex-change law. She has also successfully lobbied to eliminate unnecessary mentions of gender in public documents.

Still, obstacles to full acceptance remain. Under the 2004 law, for instance, only unmarried, childless applicants can change their official gender. Applicants also must have had a sex-change operation and been diagnosed by two doctors as having gender-identity disorder. A mere 151 people in Japan officially changed their sex between July 2004, when the law went into force, and the end of March 2005, according to the Justice Ministry. Fujio himself isn't eligible to change his official sex because he has children.

The stigma of transsexuality is also still high in Japan. Transsexuals say they are reluctant to seek work or even go to the dentist for fear their original gender will be revealed by documents such as health insurance cards. Moreover, transsexuals experience even more restrictions because some of them are also gay or lesbian. Same-sex marriages are forbidden in Japan, hospital visits by gay partners can be blocked and it's impossible for homosexual couples to jointly purchase a home or for a survivor to inherit the assets of a gay partner.

"We have no legal protection or assurances whatsoever, and that brings many worries," said Aki Nomiya, who was born male but now lives as a woman with a female partner, though she has not had a full sex-change operation. Japan first needs to allow for a partnership system like that of France, whose 1999 Civil Solidarity Pact gives some legal rights to unmarried couples, Nomiya says. But officials say Japan isn't yet ready for such changes.

"This is a very complicated and divisive problem that needs to be treated with caution" said Kunio Koide, councilor of the Civil Affairs Bureau of the Justice Ministry. "I don't see widespread support for reforms at the moment."

Still, Japan's sexual minorities as a whole have claimed some victories. Kanako Otsuji, Japan's first openly gay politician, successfully lobbied for a change in local regulations to allow non-married couples to apply for public housing including gays and transsexuals.

"My generation has been the first to speak out about sexual minority rights in any meaningful way," Otsuji, 31, said in Osaka prefecture, where she has held an assembly seat since 2003.

In the meantime, Japan's transsexuals are enjoying their increasing freedom while chafing against the enduring restrictions. As a young woman, Fujio says he suppressed his desire to live as a man and married a male coworker "mainly out of feelings of obligation," giving birth to two girls. Nine years later in 2002, Fujio made the decision to divorce and live as a man. The move, however, has had painful consequences. His ex-husband's family has allowed him to see his children only once since the divorce four years ago.

"Of course it's tough. We have to first get the public to think, "'It's OK to live that way of life,'" he said. "Then, maybe I'll get to see my kids maybe in 10 years."

R E A D I N G   **14**

Premenstrual Syndrome as Scientific and Cultural Artifact

Anne E. Figert (2005)

Is Premenstrual Syndrome (PMS) "real"? If the American Psychiatric Association's *Diagnostic and Statistical Manual of Mental Disorders* (DSM) includes a PMS-related diagnosis, then are all or most premenstrual women mentally ill? These are questions that I am often asked. I am not always sure how to reply. I think that most people who ask these questions (usually women) want a medical opinion or validation that I am not comfortable (or qualified) to give. In my mind, any answers to these questions are political answers. My usual answers are yes, PMS is real; and no, all menstruating women are not mentally ill. The longer version of my answer implies that there are many variations and versions of what and how something is "real." An old axiom in sociology (paraphrased and based upon work by W.I. and Dorothy Swaine Thomas) suggests that if people define things as real, then they are real in their consequences (1928:572).

In this essay, I show how PMS is real because various people in different situations choose to define

it as such. For example, when I first started investigating this topic in 1989, I clipped a three-sentence news item from the local newspaper, the Bloomington (IN) *Herald-Telephone*. The headline read: "School may change its PMS initials," and the item began: "Officials are considering changing the name of Pendelton Middle School or at least removing its initials from athletic uniforms to avoid embarrassment for its girls' teams." When and why did the initials PMS become such a source of embarrassment that people would actually consider changing a school's name or buying new uniforms? Who was more embarrassed? School officials or the girl's athletic teams? I never found out, but I knew that I had to understand the history and cultural meanings attached to PMS in my attempt to understand why late luteal phase dysphoric disorder (LLPDD) was so controversial. So, my question was, how is PMS "real" and why?

In this essay I explore the various definitions: PMS as a medical condition, as a social scientific and feminist issue, as an explanation for women's behavior and moods in the popular culture, and, finally, as something bought or sold in a market. The first answer to these questions takes us into the realm of science and medicine and how PMS came to be a twentieth-century (and particularly) western notion of a treatable disease. A second set of explanations comes mostly from academic studies of how menstruation and PMS are firmly rooted in cultural notions and ideas about women and their role in society. A third way to explain PMS explores how its shape and image construct women's bodies and minds in western popular culture. Part of the force behind this cultural portrayal of women and PMS comes from a fourth way in which PMS obtains definition—the PMS industry, which has tried to shape and explain PMS in a certain way (as something that makes women "crazy" and uncomfortable) to sell products.

What does this discussion have to do with whether or not premenstrual women are mentally ill? The image of women and how PMS is defined sets the stage for the discussion of how and why the American Psychiatric Association (APA) began to consider the inclusion of a PMS-related diagnosis in the DSM. Each of the ways that defines PMS as real helped to define the debate and controversy over whether PMS (as defined in LLPDD) is a psychiatric disorder.

THE SCIENCE OF PMS

The primary way in which new ideas or diseases achieve legitimacy or recognition in modern society is for scientists or physicians to call them real. Scientists and physicians have the "cognitive authority" in society to "define, describe or explain bounded realms of reality" (Gieryn and Figert, 1986). When M.D.s or Ph.D.s in chemistry or biology believe something is real, people usually go along with them. This is what happened to PMS in its various forms and incarnations in the twentieth century: PMS became real as a medical diagnosis and condition.

American gynecologist Robert Frank (1931) was the first to publish scientific studies about a condition he called "premenstrual tension." Frank identified excess estrogen as the cause of observed symptoms of this "medical" condition, which he described as hormonal in origin:

> These patients complain of unrest, irritability, 'like jumping out of their skin' and a desire to find relief by foolish and ill considered actions. Their personal suffering is intense and manifests itself in many reckless and sometimes reprehensible actions. Not only do they realize their own suffering, but they feel conscience-stricken toward their husbands and families, knowing well that they are unbearable in their attitude and reactions. Within an hour or two after the onset of the menstrual flow complete relief from both physical and mental tension occurs (1931:1054).

What is more interesting in this article are his published comments about particular case studies. Under a list of patient complaints, Frank's notations include "husband to be pitied," "psychoneurotic," "suicidal desire," and "sexual tension" (Frank, 1931:1055). Frank's prescription for severe cases of premenstrual tension was either complete removal of or radiation therapy ("X-ray 'toning'") upon the ovaries to decrease estrogen production in the body and thus to restore order in both the home and the workplace.

Between 1931 and 1980 there were steady references to premenstrual issues in the medical literature. In her review of the PMS literature, Rittenhouse states: "[a]uthors generally constructed PMS as a medical phenomenon requiring management and treatment by a physician or a psychiatrist/psychologist. However, PMS was not seen as a major problem for the majority of women" (Rittenhouse, 1991:416). Nor was PMS seen as a *major* research problem for most scientists.

PMS as a medical disorder received steady but relatively little attention until an English doctor, Katharina Dalton, began to investigate it. In 1953, Dalton co-authored an important article on PMS in the *British Medical Journal* (Greene and Dalton, 1953). This article first introduced the term "Premenstrual Syndrome," emphasizing that women need not accept the physical and emotional discomfort of PMS every month, and that modern medicine could help them.

Dalton has conducted research and written articles and books on PMS for over 40 years. She defines PMS as "any symptoms or complaints that regularly come just before or during early menstruation but are absent at other times of the cycle. It is the absence of symptoms after menstruation which is so important in this definition" (1983:12). According to Dalton's research, PMS is responsible for decreased worker productivity (in both the sufferer and "her husband"), increased divorce rates, and even murder. Dalton presents cases for her theory using vignettes of PMS sufferers and displays of medical/biological charts of women's hormonal cycles. She continues to argue for the medical control of women's hormones through progesterone therapy, prescribed by general practitioners and assisted by psychiatrists and gynecologists (1983:191).[1]

Dalton's own popularity, notoriety, and authority as a PMS "expert" heightened when she served as the chief defense medical expert in a 1981 murder trial in London, in which she successfully argued that the defendant was not responsible for murdering her lover because she suffered from a severe form of PMS (see Laws et al., 1985 for an account of this trial). The publicity generated from this trial and Dalton's claims of successful progesterone treatments found many different audiences in the United States and brought publicity to PMS.

Due in part to the publicity generated by these trials, PMS and related diagnoses have been called the "disease of the 1980s." As one science writer stated, PMS had "arrived." A disease that thousands of women had been told did not exist suddenly became a media event (Heneson, 1984:67). More importantly, Heneson points out that PMS acquired medical legitimacy: "After years of telling women their problems were 'all in the head,' the proportion of doctors who accepted PMS as a real disease reached critical mass" (1984:67).

bodies out of their own hands (Laws et al., 1985:17). The use of the word "syndrome" instead of "symptoms" itself suggests that there is an underlying disease process in women's bodies (Ussher, 1989:73).

Ironically, it was feminist researchers (especially in nursing and psychology) who were responsible for conducting a significant portion of the scientific research done on PMS during the 1970s and 1980s. Since the 1970s, feminist scientists have actively worked within the field of science to study PMS and to make sure that the research was conducted. Feminist critics of menstrual and premenstrual studies have long argued for different and better scientific methodologies, more appropriate research designs, and nonstigmatizing labels and assumptions (Koeske, 1983). So, feminist scientists took responsibility for the majority of scientific research on menstruation in the 1970s and 1980s because they believed otherwise it would not be conducted (Parlee, 1992; Tavris, 1992).

In the eyes of many early feminist researchers, PMS was initially a "woman's topic" and, therefore, not considered an important area of research for mainstream scientists and medical researchers. Psychiatrist Jean Hamilton (who was actively involved in fighting the inclusion of LLPDD) believes that another reason why PMS research was done primarily by women was that male researchers did not take seriously studies of menstruation and menstrual disorders.

So, what scientifically constitutes PMS—and how PMS research should be legitimately carried out—were questions raised by feminists within the scientific profession in the 1970s and 1980s. The aim (and possibly its result as well) of feminist scientific work on menstruation was to refute negative images of PMS using the tools and rhetoric of science. These feminists believed that changes in public perception and attitudes about the previously understudied topic of menstruation and PMS were achievable from within science.

PMS AS A FEMINIST SCIENTIFIC ARTIFACT

Feminist writers are quick to assert that the very use of the term "premenstrual syndrome" is an attempt by scientists to make premenstrual "tension" a more scientific term, and takes the control of women's

SCHOLARLY AND SOCIAL SCIENCE EXPLANATIONS OF PMS AND MENSTRUATION

While physicians and scientists studied and tried to define PMS and other menstrual disorders in terms of biology, mainly feminist anthropologists, sociologists, and other scholars tried to place and account for PMS in its social and cultural context. The second wave of feminism in the 1960s and 1970s was the impetus not only for studying PMS scientifically, but also for studying how PMS was portrayed as debilitating to women's bodies and minds. Studies of the history of menstruation in human society point out that menstrually related disorders are often associated with the practice of labeling women and their behaviors crazy (dating back to ancient Greek writings) (see Delaney et al., 1988; Martin, 1987; Olesen and Woods, 1986). Scholars have linked PMS to ancient descriptions of hysteria and other modern characteristics (lethargy, moodiness, and depression) previously attached to menstruation itself (Gottlieb, 1988; Rodin, 1992).

For example, in some cultures, menstruation has been portrayed as an evil spirit that invades women of childbearing age once a month (for reviews of this historical association see Weideger, 1976; Delaney et al., 1988; and Fausto-Sterling, 1985). Cultural taboos and negative stereotypes—such as not touching a menstruating woman and physically separating her have also existed. For example, in their book, *The Curse,* Delaney et al. (1988:10-11) point out that some cultures believe,

> contact with a menstruating woman can lead to bad luck in hunting; the contamination takes the form of an invisible vapor which attaches itself to the hunter so that he is more visible to game and therefore unable to catch it. Among the Habbe of the western Sudan, a man whose wife is menstruating does not undertake any hunting. Bukka women may not go into the sea to bathe for fear of spoiling the fishing.

The ancient Greeks believed that "the wanderings of the uterus in women's bodies were thought to cause all sorts of unusual behaviors—behaviors that bear a striking resemblance to those attributed to PMS today" (Rodin, 1992:50).

Other authors have tried to combat negative stereotypes of madness and PMS by tracing the diagnosis (as a cultural and political artifact) to capitalist patriarchal society. Martin (1987) argues that PMS is historically located within the stresses of modern capitalism in western culture. For Martin, PMS is a natural site for rebellion by women due to their oppressed situation, but that science and

industry have colluded in subverting menstruation and generating the need for artificial hormone and psychiatric treatment of women. Martin (1987: 114) asks how is it that "a clear majority of all women are afflicted with a physically abnormal hormonal cycle?" Her answer is that it is no accident that the initial interest in what is now called PMS emerged during the 1930s: "It strikes me as exceedingly significant that Frank was writing immediately after the Depression, at a time when the gains women had made in the paid labor market because of World War I were slipping away. Pressure was placed on women from many sides to give up waged work and allow men to take the jobs" (1987:118).

Katharina Dalton's and other post–World War II studies that emerged in the 1950s also appear to fit into this pattern of medical claims to diagnose and treat problems in the home and workplace. These medical studies have a distinct focus on the effect of a woman's PMS on her social roles of wife, mother, and worker. As Bell (1987) points out, this early scientific work on PMS stressed how disruptive it is in the home, factory, and social order. By focusing on this "disruption," Bell is able to show how the medical community has attempted to claim ownership over PMS and to medicalize women's bodies.

Another author identifies the specifically male composition of the medical profession as the source of control and power over women's bodies and PMS. In the introduction to *Seeing Red: The Politics of Pre-Menstrual Tension*, Jackson writes that women need to "suspect that the possibility of diagnosing PMT [PMS] increases the power of the medical profession over our minds and bodies, enabling them to redefine real conflicts and tensions in our lives as sickness, and put pressure on us to conform" (as quoted in Laws et al. 1985:7).

Sociologists and anthropologists have suggested that in fact PMS is a "culture bound syndrome." Johnson (1987:347) states that it

> involves bizarre behavior which is recognized, defined, and treated as a specific syndrome only by biomedical healers in Western, industrial cultures, and can be only understood in this specific cultural context.

Johnson argues that in western culture PMS serves as a symbolic mechanism for both the structural maintenance of society and for its social change due to the role conflict in which women find themselves. In this role conflict, women are expected to be productive (have a job/career outside the home) and to be reproductive (to have a family/children). Thus, PMS simultaneously and symbolically denies the possibility of each because "in menstruating, one is potentially fertile but obviously nonpregnant; in having incapacitating symptomatology one is exempted from normal work role expectations. With PMS, women can be seen as 'victims' who did not 'choose' to be sick" (Johnson, 1987:349).

This theme of role strain/conflict among western women is echoed by Pugliesi (1992:132), who proposes that "what is labeled as PMS is actually deviation from normative expectations regarding emotion". The pressure on a woman to "have it all" (career and family) gets symbolically released once a month in her PMS. Rodin (1992:50) explains how the PMS category and its explanation are consistent with western cultural themes about women's reproductive systems, "abnormal behaviors," and the gendered roles of wife and mother. Gottlieb (1988) takes "as a given" that PMS fits into late industrial society in the ways described above. Yet, she believes that women's subversion of "normally expected" gendered traits during the premenstrual time (and calling this PMS) is ultimately harmful because it allows people (including the woman herself) to trivialize and dismiss these feelings and anger.

The social, scientific, and feminist analyses in this section suggest that the diversity of meanings assigned to PMS in contemporary western culture (e.g., bitchy, moody, not responsible for behaviors, and uncontrolled emotional states) is related to the societies in which they are developed and is also indicative of the movement in modern society to assign a medical label or explanation for human behaviors.

POPULAR IMAGES OF WOMEN, MENSTRUATION, AND PMS

PMS also has a very real image in the popular culture of something that drives women crazy once a month. Both women and men have tried to explain women's unusual behaviors or bad moods as the result of the impending occurrence of the "monthly visitor." How PMS is portrayed and used in everyday life is yet another aspect of how PMS is real. I have a collection of PMS "artifacts" that I have been accumulating over the years. Friends and colleagues have provided me with a wide range of PMS jokes, anecdotes, shirts, buttons, and coffee cups. If (as the section above argues) PMS is firmly ensconced in modern, western industrialized society and its values, what exactly does this image consist of?

I looked to my PMS archive to see how women and PMS fit together and tried to find some common themes. These themes are at the same time shocking and funny or not shocking and not funny. What did I find? A wide variety of images of women as subject to their raging hormones, engaging in "abnormal" behaviors, and jokes that portray women as "bitchy," "mean," and "illogical." On the other hand, I also found images of women that were powerful and that try to "harness the energy" of PMS.

The most commonly cited example of cultural attitudes about PMS is the "Woman in Authority with Raging Hormones scenarios." We can probably trace the "raging hormones" idea to a public statement by Edgar Berman, Hubert Humphrey's physician, during the 1968 Presidential campaign. Berman stated that he did not want a woman in a position of power because she would be subject to "raging hormonal influences" each month (as cited in Corea, 1985; Fausto-Sterling, 1985). Berman clarified his views on the subject in a 1976 interview with journalist Gena Corea: "'Menstruation may very well affect the ability of these women to hold certain jobs,' he told me. 'Take a woman surgeon. If she had premenstrual tension—and people with this frequently wind up in a psychiatrist's office— I wouldn't want her operating on me'" (as quoted in Corea, 1985: 106–107).

Even Hollywood romances are not safe from PMS attacks. *People* magazine reported in 1994 that when Melanie Griffith filed for divorce from Don Johnson (and then withdrew the petition a day later) that it was "an impulsive act that occurred during a moment of frustration and anger" and attributed to Griffith's PMS. According to the article, Griffith "told an interviewer, 'I have terrible PMS, so I just went a little crazy'" (March 28, 1994:43).

Griffith later divorced Johnson (for reasons presumably other than PMS), but the PMS-made-me-crazy excuse offered a convenient account for what was seen at the time as an "impulsive" or "crazy" action. This negative image of women is also evident in the jokes, greeting cards, television shows, and even the advertisements for over-the-counter medications for PMS (Chrisler and Levy, 1990; Pugliesi, 1992).

The most common site for this attribution of "women subject to their raging hormones" is PMS humor. PMS jokes or humor themes have become common on television and in movies, often used as interpretations of women's "abnormal" or "deviant" behavior. A couple of years ago, an episode of the popular show *Roseanne* depicted a day in the life of the entire family affected by Roseanne's (the wife and mother) rapid mood swings, emotional outbursts, and unpredictable behaviors. Even an American icon of womanhood is not immune to PMS. Patricia Kadel's "PMS Barbi" is tragically transformed and warns the reader "Don't toy with me!"

Some jokes about PMS have been particularly vicious. The following joke appeared in the 1980s during the time in which pit bulls became popular as attack dogs and there were numerous public reports of these animals mauling young children: "What is the difference between a pit bull and a woman with PMS?" The answer to this question is that "A pit bull doesn't wear lipstick." Another joke appeared during the Gulf War crisis in 1989–1990: "Did you hear that they pulled 15,000 soldiers out of Saudi Arabia? They replaced them with 5,000 women with PMS because they're three times meaner and they retain water better." PMS also has its own "screw in a light bulb" joke contained in the following greeting card: Why does it take three women with PMS to change a light bulb? Answer: It just does!! I have two different versions of greeting cards to send people with this joke: What is the difference between a woman with PMS and a terrorist? Answer: You can negotiate with a terrorist.

I also have a button that warns the reader: "I've got PMS. Stay the Hell Away!" On the other hand, my coffee cup queries: "I've got PMS. What's Your Excuse?" This suggestion that somehow women might be excused from their normal roles and sanity during the premenstrual phase is taken even further

in a humor book about PMS called *Raging Hormones: The Unofficial PMS Survival Guide.* The authors define a "hormone hostage" as "Any Woman who for Two to Fourteen Days Each Month Becomes a Prisoner of Her Own 'Raging Hormones' and Plummets Her Life and the Lives of Those around Her into an Unholy Premenstrual Netherworld" (Williamson and Sheets, 1989:10). This book goes on to describe and portray various ways in which "hormone hostages" act and are affected by PMS such as "Do's and Don'ts of the Premenstrual Workplace," "How to Tell PMS From Your Own Stupid Character Flaws Quiz," and "The PMS–Elvis Connection."

PMS humor has also gone "high tech." I found a PMS Cartoon Gallery on the Internet at a World Wide Web site on women's health created by a physician. Mark Perloe states:

> PMS is a serious problem that can be debilitating for those suffering from its effects. The loss of control, mood swings and depression often impairs one's function within the family and at work. The cartoons displayed here are not meant to offend, or belittle the seriousness of the problems PMS sufferers have to face. Humor can often serve as an introduction to discuss a sensitive subject. That is the sole purpose wherein this material is provided (1995:http://www.mindspring.com/-mperloe).

Perloe's introduction to his PMS gallery suggests an important point with which I found myself struggling. At what point does PMS humor belittle or harm women with PMS and at what point is something "funny"? This is something that I became aware of as I analyzed my PMS artifact collection. The images and humor are contradictory and ambivalent. Granted some of the jokes (e.g., the pit bull joke) are in bad taste and do promote an extremely negative image of women. On the other hand, "PMS Barbi" seems like a perfect and ironic inversion of the stereotype of the perfect American woman.

Laws makes a similar point in her study of British men's attitudes toward menstruation. As schoolboys, their use of humor to talk about menstruation was different than the way in which schoolgirls used slang and made jokes about their periods. While growing up, boys' humor was more derogatory, and usually contained sexual references and a way to "get at girls." But, Laws (1990:72) points out the dilemma: "I certainly do not want to imply that taking an entirely solemn attitude to periods would do girls any good. Laughing at one's own bodily functions and the inconveniences they bring with them is a healthy sign and is quite different from the 'them and us' joking of the boys."

Humor and other popular images of women and PMS that appear on the surface to promote a negative image of women might instead also be suggesting alternative (and even positive) images for women. For example, an alternative rock band from Austin, Texas, called "Girls in the Nose" have a song called "Menstrual Hut" on their album. This song starts out with the following words:

> I'm bleeding down below
> I'm bleeding from my brain
> My hormones kick in
> They're driving me insane.
> (Words by K. Turner, Copyright 1987 by
> Peterson/Turner)
> Band: Girls in the Nose. (Reprinted with permission)

However, this song goes on to explain that modern science and medicine will not in help in women's experiences with the menstrual cycle. What is really needed is the return to a menstrual hut (used in other cultures) and its monthly release from traditional women's roles of cooking, cleaning, and family duties. This thought is echoed in a cartoon that I saw that portrayed an obviously worn out woman holding a screaming child and telling her husband (sitting in a lounge chair and reading the paper) that "this is stress, not PMS."

Other attempts to subvert the dominant thinking and image of women in PMS is contained in a favorite button and expression around my house: "PMS—Harness the Energy." Another expression found on a t-shirt defines PMS as: Putting Up with Men's Shit! Dena Taylor wrote *Red Flower: Rethinking Menstruation* (1988) as a response to women's negative comments about menstruation and as a vehicle to elicit more positive associations among women. The book contains poetry, stories, and other positive expressions about PMS and the menstrual cycle. That author states: "My goal is to show that women do celebrate and honor menstruation. I want to help dispel the idea that menstruation is shameful, that it should be kept hidden. We need to recognize this part of our cycle—to be aware of its subtle and powerful effects on us, and to see these in a way that enriches our lives" (Taylor, 1988:1).

How does this conflicting image of women and PMS (as both negative and positive) in the popular culture address the question of whether or not PMS is real? I think that it does more to solidify the image of women being ruled by their hormones. For better or worse, women's actions, moods, and feelings are being portrayed (by men and ourselves) as subject to influence of their menstrual cycle. This cycle "makes" them "go crazy," "be bitchy," and "be irresponsible." Furthermore, this excuse is seen as "legitimate" because it is based upon scientific and medical research. Since PMS seems to change women's moods and mental state, one next logical step would be to legitimate PMS as a psychiatric disorder.

THE PMS INDUSTRY

The discussion of PMS humor and artifacts brings us to the important consideration that in one very significant way PMS is "real": PMS is an industry. The PMS industry consists of what I call the 3 P's (products, pills, and prescriptions). Most of the PMS humor and artifacts are found as products that are bought and sold in the economic marketplace. The postcards, greeting cards, calendars, cartoon and humor books, and songs all come with a price tag attached. Greeting cards currently cost anywhere from $1.25 to $3.00; books, calendars, and t-shirts run in the $10 to $15 range. PMS products will be available as long as people are buying these and other PMS-related products.

Another set of PMS products are pills. In her examination of the creation and proliferation of PMS as a disorder, Eagan (1983) argues that there is a strong connection to the drug companies and treatment options. The drive for profits by drug companies exploits women.

Over-the-counter remedies for PMS symptoms are available at local drugstores or through the mail for those times when you cannot "control the witch in you" (Heneson, 1984). For those women that can afford it, more sophisticated hormone and antibiotic treatments are available at specialized PMS clinics or from your family physician to "tame the shrew in you" (Lehrman, 1988; Payer and Gross, 1989; Sneed and McIlhaney, 1989).

In the early 1980s, the pharmaceutical industry began to offer specific over-the-counter PMS drugs and more PMS-related products (Willis, 1983).

A marketing consultant attributed this surge in PMS over-the-counter products both to manufacturers' marketing of new products and to increased media attention of PMS. He stated that "[b]oth have raised women's awareness of the need to take a PMS product in addition to taking a product during menstruation" (as quoted in Ehrlich 1985:45)

The market for over-the-counter PMS products was so great that the Food and Drug Administration (FDA) came up with its own definition of PMS in 1982. Its Advisory Review Panel on Miscellaneous Over the Counter Internal Drug Products defined PMS as

> A recurrent symptom complex that begins during the week prior to menstruation and usually disappears soon after the onset of the menstrual flow. This symptom complex consists predominantly of edema, lower abdominal pain (including cramps), breast tenderness, headache, abdominal bloating, fatigue, and the feelings of depression, irritability, tension and anxiety (as quoted in Golub, 1992:182).

In 1983, this Advisory Review Panel released a review of over-the-counter PMS products. The panel recommended that various combinations of analgesics, diuretics, and antihistamines be considered effective PMS products (see Willis 1983 for a full report). They maintained that analgesics provide relief for pain, cramping, and headaches; diuretics give relief of water retention and bloating; and antihistamines relieve a variety of symptoms such as depression, irritability, weight gain, swelling, and backache. These over-the-counter treatments are considered safe and effective for mild to moderate symptoms of PMS.

But over-the-counter PMS pharmaceuticals were not the only product benefiting from increased attention to PMS in the early 1980s. A third part of the PMS industry is the prescriptive part. PMS treatment centers using progesterone therapy (that Katharina Dalton advocates) also became popular during the early 1980s:

> Progesterone's first big boost in America as a treatment for PMS came with the establishment in 1981 of the National Center for Premenstrual Syndrome and Menstrual Distress. Despite the imposing name, the 'national center' was actually established as a privately owned, profit-making clinic. The Manhattan office (there was also one in Boston) charged $165 for three visits, plus another $50 to $100 for lab costs (Heneson, 1984:68).

One gynecologist worried that such clinics would attract women who are desperate for help—ones who "can be easily ripped off. They're paying $5 for a 50-cent product [progesterone suppositories]. They're being told they're crazy, so they'll do anything" (as quoted in Heneson, 1984:69). According to this doctor, science and "legitimately" approved pharmaceuticals—not "rip-off" progesterone clinics—provided better, safer, and cheaper treatments for women with PMS.

Another important piece of the PMS industry is the PMS self-help books. Most of these books are soft cover, relatively inexpensive ($3–7), have been written since 1980, and are found in mainstream bookstores. Most of these books are written (solely or in joint authorship) by physicians or therapists associated with PMS or Women's Health clinics (e.g., Lark, 1984; Norris and Sullivan, 1983; Nazzaro and Lombard, 1985). They usually include short histories about PMS, and medical, nutritional, and exercise advice to overcome its symptoms.

So, according to the pharmaceutical industry, government officials, women with PMS, or authors of books, the key to defining PMS was as something that can be helped with pills, diets, and other products offered in the PMS industry. Thus, PMS is very real—complete with price tag attached to it.

WHAT'S AT STAKE IN THE CONSTRUCTION OF PMS?

For some women, the publicity and legitimization of PMS and its symptoms as real, a natural part of their body and its processes, have led to a positive sense of control over this phenomenon. However, a more negative image of PMS as something that controls women once a month, that makes them "crazy" and subject to their hormones, is much more pervasive in our contemporary western culture. This image has allowed women to use PMS as an excuse to express their emotions or to account for their otherwise "strange" behaviors. Other people (husbands, children, doctors, lawyers, judges, juries, co-workers) have also used PMS to explain women's behavior often within a scientific or medical framework that then gives physicians and scientists "expert" legitimacy over women's bodies and minds. PMS has been tried as a legal "insanity" defense in cases involving women accused of murder or other crimes in the United States, but with little success.[2] There are cases in which the threat of using PMS in child custody cases kept women in abusive relationships.

How PMS is defined—and who controls or owns the diagnoses related to it—has been and continues to be a matter of social, political, and economic concern. The degree to which "PMS" has become a major issue is best understood in light of current estimates that anywhere between 20% and 90% of all women would qualify as having some of the more than 150 recognized symptoms of PMS (Olesen and Woods, 1986). According to the American College of Obstetricians and Gynecologists, it is normal for women to experience some premenstrual symptoms. This organization more conservatively estimates that some 20% to 40% of all menstruating women do experience some symptoms of PMS. These changes include physical symptoms such as weight gain, bloating, and aches of all kinds, as well as emotional symptoms such as irritability, mood changes, and even positive symptoms such as vivid dream cycles.

As I have shown, PMS has been defined in a variety of ways (scientific, feminist, cultural, and economic) over the years, but there is no consistent or agreed upon definition. If the estimates given above are indeed true, and if almost all menstruating women do have at least some of these symptoms, then the "stability" of women's moods and behaviors can be called into question by scientists, doctors, politicians, bosses, and lawyers. This directly links to the issue of the inclusion of a PMS-related diagnosis in the DSM. What is considered "normal" for women itself is at the heart of the debate in the PMS/LLPDD controversy.

NOTES

1. The FDA does not approve of progesterone for the treatment of PMS, and there have been no scientifically proven studies documenting the efficacy of progesterone treatments.
2. The so-called PMS defense is most successfully used in England and in France. It has not had such success in American courts.

BIBLIOGRAPHY

American Psychiatric Association. 1987. Diagnostic and Statistical Manual of Mental Disorders, Third Edition, Revised. Washington, D.C.: The American Psychiatric Association.

Bell, Susan. 1987. "Changing Ideas: The Medicalization of Menopause." *Social Science and Medicine* 24:535–42.

Chrisler, Joan and Karen Levy. 1990. "The Media Construct a Menstrual Monster: A Content Analysis of PMS Articles in the Popular Press." *Women & Health* 16 (2): 89–104.

Corea, Gena. [1975] 1985. The Hidden Malpractice: How American Medicine Mistreats Women, Updated Edition. New York: Harper Colophon Books.

Dalton, Katharina. [1979] 1983. Once A Month. Claremont, CA: Hunter House, Inc.

Delaney, Janice, Mary Lupton and Emily Toth. 1988. The Curse: A Cultural History of Menstruation. Chicago: University of Illinois Press.

Eagan, Andrea. 1983. "The Selling of Premenstrual Syndrome: Who Profits from Making PMS 'The Disease of the 80s'?" *Ms.* October:26–31.

Ehrlich, Frederick. 1985. "OTCs: All Eyes on Ibuprofen While PMS Product Sales Soar." *Drug Topics* 129 (July 1): 45–55.

Fausto-Sterling, Anne. 1985. Myths of Gender: Biological Theories about Women and Men. New York: Basic Books.

Frank, Robert. 1931. "The Hormonal Causes of Premenstrual Tension." *Archives of Neurology and Psychiatry* 26: 1053–57.

Gieryn, Thomas and Anne Figert. 1986. "Scientists Protect Their Cognitive Authority: The Status Degradation Ceremony of Sir Cyril Burt." In The Sociology of the Sciences Yearbook (The Knowledge Society), Volume X, edited by G. Bohme and N. Stehr, Dordecht: D. Reidel.

Golub, Sharon. 1992. Periods: From Menarche to Menopause. Newbury Park, London and New Delhi: Sage Publications.

Gottlieb, Alma. 1988. "American Premenstrual Syndrome" *Anthropology Today* 4(6): 10–13.

Greene, Raymond and Katharina Dalton. 1953. "The Premenstrual Syndrome." *British Medical Journal* 1: 1007–1014.

Heneson, Nancy (with Celia Strain). 1984. "The Selling of P.M.S." *Science'84* 5 (May):6671.

Johnson, Thomas. 1987. "Premenstrual Syndrome as a Western Culture Specific Disorder" *Culture, Medicine and Psychiatry* 11: 337–356.

Koeske, Randi. 1983. "Lifting the Curse of Menstruation: Toward a Feminist Perspective on the Menstrual Cycle" *Women & Health* 8 (2/3): 1–16.

Lark, Susan. 1984. Premenstrual Syndrome Self Help Book: A Woman's Guide to Feeling Good All Month. Berkeley: Celestial Arts.

Laws, Sophie. 1990. Issues of Blood: The Politics of Menstruation. London: The Macmillan Press Ltd.

Laws, Sophie, Valerie Hey and Andrea Egan. 1985. Seeing Red: The Politics of Premenstrual Tension. London: Hutchinson.

Lehrman, Karen. 1988. "What is PMS?" *Consumers' Research* (February):20–22.

Martin, Emily. 1987. The Woman in the Body: A Cultural Analysis of Reproduction. Boston: Beacon Press.

Nazzaro, Ann and Donald Lombard. 1985. The PMS Solution. United States: Winston Press.

Norris, Ronald and Colleen Sullivan. 1983. Premenstrual Syndrome: A Doctor's Proven Program

on How to Recognize and Treat PMS. New York: Berkeley Books.

Olesen, Virginia and Nancy F. Woods. 1986. Culture, Society and Menstruation. Washington: Hemisphere Publishing Corporation.

Parlee, Mary Brown. 1992. "On PMS and Psychiatric Abnormality." *Feminism & Psychology* 2(1): 105–19.

Payer, Lynn with Ken Gross. 1989. "Hell Week." *Ms.* 17 (March): 28–31.

Pugliesi, Karen. 1992. "Premenstrual Syndrome: The Medicalization of Emotion Related to Conflict and Chronic Role Strain. "*Humbolt Journal of Social Relations* 18 (2): 131–165.

Rittenhouse, Amanda. 1991. "The Emergence of Premenstrual Syndrome as a Social Problem." *Social Problems* 38 (3): 412–25.

Rodin, Mari. 1992. "The Social Construction of Premenstrual Syndrome." Social Science and Medicine 35 (1): 49–56.

Sneed, Sharon and Joe McIlhaney. 1989. "How to Manage PMS." *Focus on the Family* July: 14–16.

Tavris, Carol. 1992. The Mismeasure of Women. New York: Simon & Schuster.

Taylor, Dena. 1988. Red Flower: Rethinking Menstruation. Freedom, CA: The Crossing Press.

Thomas, William I. and Dorothy S. Thomas. 1928. The Child in America. New York: Knopf.

Ussher, Jane. 1989. The Psychology of the Female Body. London and New York: Routledge.

Weideger, Paula. 1976. Menstruation and Menopause: The Physiology and Psychology, the Myth and the Reality. New York: Knopf.

Williamson, Martha and Robin Sheets. 1989. Raging Hormones: The Unofficial PMS Survival Guide. New York: Doubleday.

Willis, Judith. 1983. "Doing Something About 'The Curse.'" *FDA Consumer* 17:11–14.

Perfectly Normal

Lesléa Newman (1990)

Lesbians appear to make up a smaller percentage of women with eating disorders than of women in general. Most of the women with eating disorders who are described in the literature are either clearly defined as heterosexual, or their sexual orientation has not been a focus of inquiry. My personal communication with researchers in the areas of eating disorders has also yielded some consensus that lesbians are highly under-represented among bulimic women presenting for treatment or research studies. In the lesbian community, the question has been raised regarding the appropriateness of defining obesity as pathology; consequently, fat lesbians may experience some social or political support (or pressure) for defining their body size and eating styles as normative variations rather than disordered eating styles. Lesbians appear to be over-represented among fat activists, that is, people who define fatness as a normative variation and the stigmatization of fat people as political oppression.

—*Laura S. Brown, "Lesbians, Weight, and Eating: New Analyses and Perspectives"*

Nice to meet you, Dr. Polansky. My name is Harriet. Oh, you know that already, of course. I wasn't expecting a woman doctor. Well, life is full of surprises, isn't it? Yes, everything is fine, my room is just lovely. I love the light blue walls—robin's egg blue, they call it. It's the same color as our bedroom at home; isn't that a funny coincidence? Steve and I just painted it ourselves. See that tree outside my window? Just a minute before you came, a bird was singing in the branches—a robin, I think; maybe she thought my walls were her eggs. Just a joke.

I bet you weren't expecting to find someone so cheerful and healthy, were you, Doctor? There's nothing wrong with me; I'm fine really. I'm perfectly normal in every way, as you can see. It wasn't my idea to come here, you know. It was Steve's. He wants me to put on a little weight. I don't think I really need to,

but you know husbands—you've got to please them. Anyway, I could use a little rest—who couldn't?

Tell you about my weight? I'm five foot, seven inches and I weigh ninety-seven pounds. I've weighed ninety-seven pounds for three years now, ever since we got married. Was I thin before we got married? Of course—why do you think Steve married me in the first place? Steve would never date a fat girl. Never.

I wasn't always this thin. Before we got married I weighed one hundred and fifteen pounds, and then, once we set the date, I went on a diet so I'd look good for our wedding day. A girl only gets married once in her life—hopefully anyway, you never know these days—so of course I wanted to look my best. I got down to one hundred and seven pounds, and I wore a size three/four wedding dress. It was a beautiful dress—white lace sleeves, a low neckline, little pearl buttons going all the way down the front. Everyone said I looked just like a little doll. I'd wanted to get down to one hundred and five pounds, but somehow I couldn't get rid of those last two pounds.

When I was younger, dieting was easier somehow. I don't know, maybe your metabolism changes as you get older; it's much harder now for me to take off the weight. If it's like this at twenty-seven, imagine what it'll be like when I'm fifty! That's why I work so hard to stay thin. See this roll of flab around my stomach? It used to be much bigger. I know my stomach isn't as flat as it should be. I can't get rid of this roll for love or money. I do three hundred sit-ups every night and I still don't have a flat tummy. I keep trying, though. Never give up; the Lord hates a quitter. That's what I always say.

My relationship with Steve? Oh, he's wonderful. Really. I couldn't ask for a better husband. He lets me do whatever I want, and as long as the house is clean and his dinner's on the table, he doesn't complain. I like cooking for him—he's a real meat and potatoes man. When he comes home from work I sit and watch him eat. Do you know that man can consume a thousand calories in one sitting? Really. A hunk of steak, a baked potato with butter, salad and ice cream for dessert. Men have it so much easier than women. Steve never has to think about his weight, and I can gain five pounds just watching him eat dinner! I never eat with him. Usually I just drink black coffee or diet soda. I don't eat much for supper. A hard boiled egg and a raw carrot sometimes, or steamed spinach with half a cup of cottage cheese. I never eat breakfast or lunch. There's just no time. There's so much to do—I have to clean the house, do the laundry, shop for food and go to my aerobics class, of course. Steve says it's good for me to get out. He's afraid I'll get lonely in the house by myself all day, so I go to aerobics every afternoon. I usually do two or three classes. I know how important it is to stay fit.

Oh, those kind of relations. Well, Steve and I really don't have sex all that much. We did in the beginning of course—everyone does—but I don't know, I don't really think about it. I can't remember the last time Steve and I had sex. I think Steve's afraid he'll crush me or something. Sometimes in the night I'll roll over to hug him, and his hipbones will clank against mine, and it hurts. I think maybe that's why he wanted me to come here, so I'd gain weight and we could have sex again. Eventually we want children, of course, everybody does. I haven't told Steve this, but I haven't got my period in a long time. I don't know why. Maybe you can run some tests, as long as I'm in here anyway.

Sometimes I think Steve goes to a prostitute once in a while. I wouldn't blame him if he did—it's different for men, you know. They have needs, not like women. I just don't care that much about it. Steve would never have an affair or anything, he simply adores me to pieces, but he might go to a prostitute every now and then, you know, to satisfy himself. I don't really mind. It's perfectly normal, that's what those places are for.

He reads *Playboy* and *Penthouse*, you know, men's magazines. He keeps them in the bottom drawer of his dresser. Sometimes when he's at work, I look at them. Pages and pages of gorgeous women, I'd give anything in the world to look like. I still have a lot of

potential, you know. I'm not that old, and I have nice features, don't I? My eyes are pretty, everyone says so. You know, I would start eating a little more if you could guarantee that I'd gain weight in all the right places. I know everything would just go right to my stomach, and if there's one thing I cannot stand, it's a flabby belly. Ugh. I wouldn't mind a little padding on my derriere. That's why I'm sitting on this pillow—my bones hurt when I have to sit on a hard chair like this. At home I just sit on the couch or on the bed.

Siblings? Oh yes, I have a sister. Boy, do I have a sister! She's a real problem in our family. I don't talk about her all that much. She lives all the way across the country in San Francisco, so we don't see her very much, which is fine with me. You see, well, I don't tell many people this, but well, you're a doctor, I suppose it's all right to tell you our family secrets. Well, my sister is a lesbian. I know, it's a real tragedy, isn't it? At first I thought about it a lot; I mean, she is my baby sister. We grew up in the same house, and why one of us should turn out perfectly normal and the other one so sick is beyond me.

I think I know what happened, though. I think it's because she's fat. She always was a chubby kid, and then she was pretty big as a teenager, but now she's fat. And I mean fat. She's really let herself go the last couple of years, and I wouldn't be surprised if she weighed close to a hundred fifty pounds by now. She's only five foot three, she takes after my mother's side of the family, so you can just imagine.

Maybe she's slimmed down recently. I doubt it, but you never know. I haven't seen her in three years, not since our wedding. She left home when she was seventeen, and moved to San Francisco. I was twenty at the time, so that was . . . oh, seven years ago. She never came to visit—she said the air fare was too expensive—so I didn't get to see her for four years, not until the night before our wedding.

To tell you the truth, I really didn't want to invite her. I know that's a horrible thing to say about your own sister, but anyone would feel the same way. I mean, how was I going to explain her to Steve's relatives? I had hardly even mentioned her to Steve, but how long could I keep my baby sister a secret? Steve was great about it though. I didn't want to tell him, but finally I got all my courage up, and told him my little sister was gay. And you know what he said? He said,

"Oh, that's why you never talk about her," and then he changed the subject. He's so good that way—he never dwells on the bad things in life. He has a real positive attitude—that's one of the things I like about him."

He did look kind of shocked when he finally met my sister though. I guess I should have told him she was fat, but it was hard enough to tell him that she was queer. I was hoping that she'd slimmed down some, but I should have known better. She sends my mother pictures every year—my sister's really into photography. For the past few years, she's sent pictures of herself and a woman named Bev, who's her *friend*, if you know what I mean. And get this—Bev is even fatter than my sister is. Thank God the two of them found each other, that's what I say. I mean, who else would have them? Still, I know, it's very sad.

Oh, I tried to help her lose weight when we were growing up, but she never could stay on a diet. I taught her how to add up the calories of her food, how to use smaller plates so her meals would look bigger, how to drink a diet soda before she ate so she would be full before she started—you know, just basic common sense, things that everybody knows. But it never worked. So then I tried to teach her how to dress so at least she could look thinner than she was, even if she couldn't be thinner—you know, dark colors, no horizontal stripes, a necklace or a pretty scarf to draw the eyes away from her hips and up to her face. She really does have a pretty face—it's a shame, a crime really, that she's let herself go like that. She just doesn't seem to care.

I had so much to do before the wedding. I just didn't think about my sister coming until it was time to pick her up at the airport. I volunteered Steve and me to go because I don't really trust my sister—she's not too bright, and she doesn't know when to keep her mouth shut. Steve's brother said he would go, but what if she told him she was gay? I would just die. When she called to tell me she was coming, she said she was sorry but Bev couldn't make it—they couldn't afford two airfares. Thank God for that! Imagine having to explain the two of them.

Anyway, there we were, waiting at the United terminal, and out walks my sister, big as life. I could see all my years of fashion advice had been a complete waste, in one ear and out the other. My sister was wearing—get this—purple pants and a white, button-down blouse with these big purple irises splashed all over it. And, if that wasn't bad enough, she had her blouse tucked in! I could have died. Really, I couldn't believe it. I know Steve was in shock, because, like I said, I didn't warn him, and everyone else in my family is nice and thin, of course. And she had done something really awful to her hair, cut it very short in the front, almost like a boy's and left one piece hanging long in the back and part of it had been bleached. Oh, I tell you, she was a sight. I wanted to get her out of there as quickly as possible—I'm sure people were staring—but she took her own sweet time. She had to introduce us to some girl she had met on the plane and then we had to wait while they exchanged phone numbers and hugged and kissed goodbye like they had known each other for years.

One thing that's strange about my sister is she makes friends wherever she goes. I've never understood it. I think people just feel sorry for her. Women mostly. She doesn't have any men friends, of course—you know why. I don't like women all that much myself. Oh, nothing personal, Doctor. It's just that men are, you know, more interesting. I have one or two girlfriends I go shopping with, but mostly I like being with Steve. When he goes out with the boys, I stay home alone. He goes out, not that much, oh, I don't know, maybe three times a week.

To tell you the truth, I'd rather watch a good TV program and improve my mind than hang out with a bunch of women. Mostly they sit around and gossip, and I'll tell you a little secret—some of them are very jealous of me. I mean Steve's a very handsome guy and we're pretty well off, and I'm about the only one on the block who's kept my figure. All the girls want to know how I stay so thin. It's very easy. Willpower, I tell them, that's all. When you see something you want, you just don't have it. You feel much better about yourself that way. Also, I tell them, try and lose a few extra pounds—that's so you can have a little leeway. I'd like to weigh ninety-five, so I'd have five pounds to play with. That way, if I let myself go, for some reason and gained a pound or two, God forbid! I still wouldn't weigh over a hundred pounds. But it doesn't work that way for everyone, I guess. It seems too simple—I don't know why. I used to think it depended on your type of genes or something, but then how would you explain my sister?

When Steve dropped us off at my parent's house that night, my sister went inside, and I stayed in the car to kiss him goodnight. He took me in his arms and—I'll never forget this—he said, "Promise me one thing." "What?" I asked. "Promise me you'll never get as fat as your sister." I was shocked. "You know I wouldn't," I said to him. "I'd rather die."

After Steve left I went into my old room, the room I shared with my sister when we were growing up. This would be the last night I'd ever sleep in it—the last night I'd sleep anywhere without Steve. Oh, I was so happy! Of course, we'd slept together already; we even had our apartment by then, but we decided to be old-fashioned and not see each other until our wedding day. I think Steve went out with the boys to a strip joint or something. I don't mind. That's just the way men are.

My sister stayed downstairs to talk to my parents for a while and then she came upstairs to go to sleep. I didn't know what to say to her. When we were little we'd talk all night long—brush each other's hair, tell each other stories. She always wanted to be a famous photographer and travel all around the world taking pictures of everything. I wanted to be a ballerina. I took ballet lessons for a while—I still have my pink toeshoes with the satin laces—but then I stopped. I just got too fat. Ballerinas have to be really thin, much thinner than I'll ever be. I always have at least five extra pounds to lose, mostly around my belly, no matter how many sit-ups I do. It's a problem I've had all my life.

My sister still takes pictures though. It's not such a big deal. I mean she doesn't work for *Time* or *Newsweek* or anything. She works on a newspaper for people like her; I forget the name of it. Sometimes she sends pictures home to my mother. She's had some on the front page even, but I don't know, I don't think they're very good.

So there we are in our old bedroom, and my sister just got undressed, like she had nothing to be ashamed of. I couldn't believe it. I tried not to stare at her, but my God, I couldn't exactly ignore her; she took up half the room. And, I have to admit, I wanted to look. Morbid curiosity, I guess. I won't go into the gory details, but take my word for it, Doctor, if you ever get a chance to look at a fat, naked woman, do yourself a favor. One look, and I guarantee, you'll never go off your diet again.

I'll never forget the sight of her as long as I live. Especially her breasts—they were positively vulgar, hanging down from her like, like . . . I don't know, eggplants or something. And her belly was so soft and round—if I didn't know better, I'd have sworn she was pregnant. She looked like she could bounce, she was so soft, like the Pillsbury Dough Boy, for God's sake. Really. You couldn't see a bone anywhere in her entire body.

I felt so bad for my sister, but she didn't seem to mind. She's used to it, I guess. She . . . you'll never believe this, but she sat down on her bed, stark naked, for half an hour, polishing her fingernails and toenails bright red. "Where'd you get the polish?" I asked her. "From Mama," she said. "I'm getting all dressed up for tomorrow." I felt so awful then, I didn't know what to do. I mean, I never dreamed she cared about her appearance at all—you certainly wouldn't know it by looking at her—so, to see her painting her nails as if that would make a difference was just absolutely pathetic.

I wanted to say something to her, you know, to help her. I thought Steve and I could offer to pay for some kind of operation. She could get her stomach stapled or her jaw wired shut or they could take out part of her intestines. Really, there are so many options these days, there's no excuse for anyone to be fat. But I was scared she'd take it the wrong way—you know how sensitive fat people are. So I just kept my mouth shut.

I was dying to ask her how much she weighed, but I couldn't figure out how to fit it into the conversation. I mean you can't just ask someone a thing like that, especially a fat person. It's like asking a woman her age. Some things are too private to talk about, even between sisters.

Later, though, when she went to the bathroom, I did look at the labels in her clothes to see what size they were. She'd folded her pants and her blouse neatly and put them on top of her suitcase. Her shirt was an extra large, can you imagine? And her pants were a fifteen/sixteen. I felt horrible when I saw that. The least she could do was rip out the labels so she wouldn't have to be embarrassed.

Finally I asked her what she was going to wear to the wedding. I should have known not to ask. White pants and a red silk blouse that matched my mother's nail polish. I didn't know what to say. First of all, everyone knows fat people shouldn't wear white. I must have told her that at least a million times. And I could see right away she was planning on tucking her blouse in, which would be a disaster with her stomach and everything. But what could I do? We certainly couldn't take her shopping at eleven o'clock at night. I told her her outfit was very nice with my fingers crossed behind my back. One thing I've learned is that a little white lie to someone who's less fortunate than you isn't such a bad thing if it makes that person feel better.

While she was waiting for the second coat on her nails to dry, I opened the window. To get some fresh air, I told her, but really I was hoping the room would get drafty so she would cover herself up. A person can only take so much. Then I started hoping she would catch a cold and then she wouldn't be able to come to the wedding. I mean, how was I ever going to explain her to Steve's relatives? I know you're thinking that's a horrible thing to say about your own sister, but Doctor, I had spent months getting ready for my wedding. Months. Everything matched perfectly—the flowers, the bridesmaid's dresses, the ushers' tuxedos, and then my sister has to come along and ruin everything. Thank God I had sense enough not to ask her to be a bridesmaid. I mean, can you imagine with her punk hairdo and everything? My mother really wanted me to, but I just put my foot down.

I was hoping the photographer would have enough sense not to get her in any of the pictures, but no such luck. There she is, big as life, smiling all over the place. My sister is not shy, that's for sure. And she does have a beautiful smile—I'll give her that much. I used to be jealous of her smile, but now, well, there's nothing to be jealous of. Sure she seems happy, but everyone knows fat people are always jolly on the outside.

So finally she put on a long T-shirt, thank God. And then she asked me if I wanted to see some of her pictures. I said sure. What the hell, I mean, she probably doesn't have anyone else to show them to and, after all, she is my sister.

Well, first she showed me pictures from the newspaper she works on. They were pretty boring. A lot of them were from some kind of parade for people like her, and none of them knew anything about how to dress, believe me. Then she showed me about a million pictures of her and Bev, her friend, remember? My sister and Bev in their apartment, down at Fisherman's Wharf, on top of some mountain they'd climbed, cross country skiing, paddling a canoe, flying a kite, you name it, they've done it. There was even a picture of them at the beach. In bathing suits yet. They were lying side by side on a big purple towel, leaning up on their elbows, and all I could think about was whales. They looked like two beached whales.

Well, thank God they've found each other, that's all I can say. I mean, who else would have them, and anything is better than being alone. One thing bothered me though. My sister kept referring to Bev as her lover. I don't know why she just couldn't say friend. You see what I mean about not letting her around Steve's relatives. You never know what she's going to say next. What if she started talking about her lover to Steve's mother? I mean, can you imagine? And can you imagine two women having sex together? Two fat women? Ugh.

I asked Steve about it, and he told me they use dildos. He showed me a picture in *Playboy*. One of them straps it on and then climbs on top of the other one. I can't imagine my sister doing that. I used to look at that issue of *Playboy* a lot when Steve wasn't home. On the page after the dildos, they showed two women doing sixty-nine. Really, I know you think I'm making this up, but I can show you. It's so disgusting, I just couldn't get over it. Steve has never put his thing in my mouth. Never. He puts it, you know, right down there where it belongs. And he's never put his mouth down there either. Ugh. We have perfectly normal sex, at least we used to, and I'm sure we will again.

My sister had pictures of other women, too. Her friends. They were all like her, you know, I could just tell, but, thank God, not all of them were fat. There's still hope. She showed me pictures of her last birthday party—there must have been about fifty people there. All women of course. No man would be caught dead near her I'm sure. She says she doesn't like men, that she and Bev are really happy together, but I know she's just saying that. I know she'd give anything to be normal like me. Anyone would.

She asked me if I had any pictures, but all I had was one of Steve that I carry in my wallet. I never let anyone take my picture, everyone knows that a camera adds at least ten pounds. And I certainly would never let anyone take a picture of me in a bathing suit. I haven't worn a bathing suit since junior high. Of course I had to let the photographer take pictures of me at the wedding. I learned a trick though, from a woman who went to modeling school. You lift your hands over your head like this, see, and you automatically look five pounds thinner. See how my stomach flattens and my ribs stick out? So that's what I did every time the photographer came near me, I just lifted my hands and pretended I was adjusting my veil.

After we finished looking at the pictures, my sister got kind of sappy. She took my hand and said, "Harriet, are you sure you'll be all right?" I could tell she wanted to have one of those heart-to-heart talks with me—she's very emotional, my sister. I told her of course I was all right. She just kept looking at me kind of funny, and then she said, "But Harriet, are you happy?"

"Of course I'm happy," I told her. Who wouldn't be happy the night before their own wedding?

"I'm worried about you," she said. "You've gotten so thin, you've lost so much weight. Have you been sick?"

Well, then, I realized that she was just jealous. I wanted to tell her I was worried about her, she'd *gained* so much weight, but I didn't want to make her feel bad. So I just patted her hand and told her I was perfectly fine, just a little tired.

"You look tired," she said, putting her other hand on top of mine. "Are you sure you're taking care of yourself? Is there anything you want to tell me?"

"Of course I look tired," I told her. "Who wouldn't be tired with all the running around I've been doing lately? A wedding doesn't just happen all by itself. Let's go to bed," I said to her, "tomorrow's going to be a big day." She didn't say anything, but all of a sudden two big tears welled up in her eyes, and I just turned away. If there's one thing I can't stand, it's seeing a fat person cry. As soon as she fell asleep, I got down on the floor and did an extra three hundred sit-ups. I vowed that very night to get thin and to stay thin once and for all.

I didn't see my sister much the next day. Of course we had breakfast together with my parents. I had my usual black coffee and my sister had a piece

of toast, an egg, and some orange juice. Funny, I thought she'd eat a lot more, but I guess she's too embarrassed to really eat in front of anyone. I know I would be if I looked like that. I didn't even get a chance to say goodbye to her. There were so many people at the wedding, and of course Steve and I left right afterwards for our honeymoon.

I did catch sight of my sister out of the corner of my eye a few times though. She'd brought along her camera, even though I'd told her not to—we'd hired a professional photographer—but she really seemed to want to, so I said okay. She probably knew no one would talk to her, so at least with her camera she'd have something to do.

She sent me some copies of the pictures she took, but they weren't very good. I wasn't even smiling in any of them. It's almost like she was just lurking around, waiting to catch me at my very worst, and then she'd snap her camera. It's just because she's jealous, that's all. The pictures the photographer took are a hundred times better.

Do I want my sister to come visit me here? You've got to be kidding. Unless you mean to be a patient. Now that I could understand. She could really use a place like this to help her lose weight. Wouldn't that be funny—she'd lose weight and I'd gain. Though I only want to gain a pound or two at the most, and she could stand to lose a good fifty. Maybe if she got thin she could find some man to marry her. I'm sure that Bev would understand. I mean, I wish my sister could just be happy like me and Steve. I know I have a few problems—who doesn't—but at least I'm normal. I really do pity my sister.

Lunch time already? Oh, I never eat lunch. Just black coffee will be fine. I haven't had lunch in years. One thing I did want to ask you though—do you think I could get a VCR for my room? I brought my Jane Fonda workout tape along—I don't want to get flabby while I'm in here. If it's not possible, don't worry, I'll manage. I brought her workout book too, just in case. I put my membership at the aerobics club on hold. I can renew it as soon as I go home.

So I guess I'll get some rest now. It was nice meeting you, Doctor, I'm sure we'll speak again. I hope I didn't talk your ear off, I can be a real chatterbox. But as you can see, there's nothing at all the matter with me. I'll probably stay here a week, ten days at the most. I'm sure Steve misses me already. Of course I miss him terribly, but it's nice to just relax and not have to worry about things for a change.

Will you close the door on your way out, Doctor? I'm just going to do a few exercises, since I won't be going to aerobics this afternoon. I don't like to miss a day—before you know it, one day turns into two, then three, then four, and then it's all downhill from

there. I don't want to wind up fat like my sister. Can you imagine me, dressed in horizontal stripes or bright purple pants, like I didn't care about anything, smiling right in front of the camera for all the world to see? Laughing on the outside and crying on the inside? Not me. I've been very lucky. I've got Steve, I've got my health, my looks. I've got . . . well, that's enough, isn't it? I mean, what more could any woman possibly want?

R E A D I N G 16

Spain Bans Skinny Mannequins

Associated Press (2007)

Vanesa Lopez looked at the mannequin in the store window and burst out laughing. It was mostly leg, impossibly long and thin, with shorts hugging a tiny waist and a frilly top on delicate shoulders. "That's out of my league," said Lopez, a 30-year-old interior decorator with a medium build. "You see it and say, 'Wow, I'd like to look like that.'"

Such skeletal fashion dummies, symbols of a culture blamed for fueling a preoccupation with weight, are now doomed in Spain under a ground-breaking accord between the Health Ministry and major retailers like Zara and Mango. Also targeted for extinction is the dilemma of a size fitting just right in one store but being too tight at another—just one more way to make a woman feel fat.

The program is aimed at changing the perception that super-skinny women are fashionable—an image some believe contributes to eating disorders. Madrid and Milan banned ultra-thin models from their fashion week runways late last year, and this year the Council of Fashion Designers of America announced guidelines designed to help models eat and live more healthfully.

SPAIN TAKES AIM

The offensive might seem odd coming from Spain, a nation that to the casual eye is neither fat nor thin,

nor readily associated with anorexia, bulimia or obesity. The country prides itself on a Mediterranean diet rich in fruit, vegetables and heart-healthy foods like olive oil and fish. But just as Spain has quickly caught up with its European neighbors economically and culturally in the generation since it shed a right-wing dictatorship in the last 1970s, so has it matched them in the more dangerous trappings of an affluent, go-go consumer society. And today's Socialist government, vigorously assertive on a bevy of social issues ranging from gay marriage to gender violence, is now taking aim at the fashion world as a source of risky thought and behavior. "We are aiming for a model of healthy beauty," said Angeles Heras, director of consumer affairs at the Health Ministry. "There is a lot pressure, not just from the fashion world but society in general, for women to seek models of beauty that are unreal and even unhealthy."

NOTHING SMALLER THAN A SIZE 6

So two major changes, announced in January, are in the works: Stores run by four big names will start replacing window-display mannequins so that none is smaller than size 38 (size 6 in the U.S.). And designers will standardize women's apparel so a given size will fit the same way no matter who sells it.

To get a better idea of the shapes of Spanish women's bodies, the government is employing some heavy technology. Using laser-fitted booths that can take 130 measurements of a body in 30 seconds, the Health Ministry is fanning out across the country to assess the sizes of Spanish women. The program will study 8,500 women ages 12 to 70, and pass the data onto clothing designers who account for 80 percent of the production in the Spanish fashion industry. The manufacturers' garments will then reflect the dimensions of real women, not catwalk waifs. The standardization is to be phased in after the study is completed this year. Other designers have asked to join the program, and Italy sent a letter asking about it, Heras said. "It seems we are pioneers," she said.

GROWING ECONOMY, GROWING EATING DISORDERS

An estimated one in five Spanish women ages 13 to 22 suffers from an eating disorder, placing Spain on par with its European neighbors, said Gonzalo Morande, a physician who runs the eating disorders department at Madrid's Nino Jesus Hospital.

Such conditions became prevalent about 20 years ago elsewhere in Europe. Spain got a later start, but caught up quickly, Morande said.

"One of the peculiar things about Spain is that when processes happen, they happen very quickly," he said. Morande welcomed the standardization of women's clothing sizes, saying Spanish women are taller and bigger than they were a generation ago because of changes in eating habits. But Enrique Berbel, a psychologist who also works with eating disorder patients, said fashion and the beautiful people of pop culture are only part of the problem in Spain. Another major factor that is not being addressed is Spain's newfound wealth, he said. He said the mechanism works like this: The economy—poor under past dictatorships but now the world's eighth largest—has spawned a consumption-crazed society that creates artificial needs and fuels dissatisfaction. Teenagers have cell phones but they want BMWs. And they often take out their frustrations on themselves. "'I can't get the things I want. I can't lead the lifestyle I want. I can't be like I want, but I can control my body.' There are people who think this way," Berbel said.

Source: URL: http://www.msnbc.msn.com/id/17596139/

R E A D I N G **17**

Changing Faces

Lisa Takeuchi Cullen (2002)

At 18, Saeko Kimura was a shy, sleepy-eyed university student. Until she discovered a secret weapon. If she applied a strip of glue to her eyelids, her eyes became wider, rounder, prettier. "Men noticed me," she says. "I became outgoing. Suddenly, I had a life." Her new looks also landed her part-time work as a hostess in an upmarket bar, where she gets top dollar on a pay scale determined by beauty.

But Kimura lived in fear of discovery, rushing off to the bathroom several times a day to reapply the glue and never daring to visit the beach. And so, at 21, she finds herself in a doctor's office in a Tokyo high-rise, lying on an operating table with her fists nervously clenched. Plastic surgeon Katsuya Takasu breezes in wielding a cartoonishly enormous needle. "This will hurt a little," he says cheerfully. Once the anesthetic is administered, Takasu brandishes another, hooked needle and threads it through Kimura's upper eyelids, creating a permanent crease. He then injects a filler fluid called 'hyaluronic acid into her nose and chin and pinches them into shape. Takasu inspects his handiwork. "The swelling will go down in a few days," he says. "But even if you went out tonight in Roppongi, you'd be a hit." A nurse hands Kimura a mirror. Though red and puffy, she now has the face she's always dreamed of: big, round eyes, a tall nose, defined chin. The entire procedure took less than 10 minutes. But Kimura collapses with an ice pack on her face and moans, "Oh, the pain."

What we won't do for beauty. Around Asia, women—and increasingly, men—are nipping and tucking, sucking and suturing, injecting and implanting, all in the quest for better looks. In the past, Asia had lagged behind the West in catching the plastic surgery wave, held back by cultural hang-ups, arrested medical skills and a poorer consumer base. But cosmetic surgery is now booming throughout Asia like never before. In Taiwan, a million procedures were performed last year, double the number from five years ago. In Korea, surgeons estimate that at least one in 10 adults has received some form of surgical upgrade and even tots have their eyelids done. The government of Thailand has taken to hawking plastic surgery tours. In Japan, noninvasive procedures dubbed "petite surgery" have set off such a rage that top clinics are raking in $100 million a year.

Elsewhere in Asia, this explosion of personal re-engineering is harder to document, because for every skilled and legitimate surgeon there seethes a swarm of shady pretenders. Indonesia, for instance, boasts only 43 licensed plastic surgeons for a population of about 230 million; yet an estimated 400 illicit procedures are performed each week in the capital alone. In Shenzhen, the Chinese boomtown, thousands of unlicensed "beauty-science centers" lure hordes of upwardly mobile patients, looking to buy a new pair of eyes or a new nose as the perfect accessory to their new cars and new clothes.

The results are often disastrous. In China alone, over 200,000 lawsuits were filed in the past decade against cosmetic surgery practitioners, according to the *China Quality Daily*, an official consumer protection newspaper. The dangers are greatest in places like Shenzhen that specialize in cut-price procedures. "Any Tom, Dick or Harry with a piece of paper—genuine or not—can practice over there," says Dr. Philip Hsieh, a Hong Kong–based plastic surgeon. "They use things that have not been approved, just for a quick buck. And people in China don't know that they're subjecting themselves to this kind of risk."

Of course, Asians have always suffered for beauty. Consider the ancient practice of foot binding in China, or the stacked, brass coils used to distend the necks of Karen women. In fact, some of the earliest records of reconstructive plastic surgery come from sixth century India: the Hindu medical chronicle *Susruta Samhita* describes how noses were recreated after being chopped off as punishment for adultery.

The culturally loaded issue today is the number of Asians looking to remake themselves to look more Caucasian. It's a charge many deny, although few would argue that under the relentless bombardment of Hollywood, satellite TV, and Madison Avenue, Asia's aesthetic ideal had changed drastically. "Beauty, after all, is evolutionary," says Harvard psychology professor Nancy Etcoff, who is the author of *Survival of the Prettiest: The Science of Beauty*—not coincidentally a best seller in Japan, Korea, Hong Kong and China. Asians are increasingly asking their surgeons for wider eyes, longer noses and fuller breasts—features not typical of the race. To accommodate such demands, surgeons in the region have had to invent unique techniques. The No. 1 procedure by far in Asia is a form of blepharoplasty, in which a crease is created above the eye by scalpel or by needle and thread; in the U.S., blepharoplasty also ranks near the top, but involves removing bags and fat around the eyes. Likewise, Westerners use botox, or botulinum toxin, to diminish wrinkles—while in Korea, Japan and Taiwan, botox is injected into wide cheeks so the muscle will atrophy and the cheeks will shrink. Just as Asian faces require unique procedures, their bodies demand innovative operations to achieve the leggy, skinny, busty Western ideal that has become increasingly universal. Dr. Suh In Seock, a surgeon in Seoul, has struggled to find the best way to fix an affliction the Koreans call *muu-dari* and the Japanese call *daikon-ashi*: radish-shaped calves. Liposuction, so effective on the legs of plump Westerners, doesn't work on Asians since muscle, not fat, accounts for the bulk. Suh says earlier attempts to carve the muscle were painful and made walking difficult. "Finally, I discovered that by severing a nerve behind the knee, the muscle would atrophy," says Suh, "thereby reducing its size up to 40%." Suh has performed over 600 of the operations since 1996. He disappears for a minute and returns with a bottle of fluid containing what looks like chopped up bits of ramen noodles. He has preserved his patients' excised nerves in alcohol. "And that's just since November," he says proudly.

The cultural quirks of the plastic surgery business in Asia also extend to sexuality. In China, Korea and Indonesia, where virginity is highly prized, young women go in for hymen reconstruction in time for their wedding night. In Japan, Indonesia and Korea, men ask for penis-enlargement procedures, in part to avoid shame when bathing en masse. In Thailand, with its sizable population of so-called "lady boys," a thriving industry has sprung up to provide male-to-female sex-change operations.

Traditionally, most Asians going under the scalpel were women. But a mutant strain of male vanity has turned into a virtual epidemic. "Men are uptight about seeming too vain," says Dr. Takasu after completing the procedure on Kimura. "But it's true that when you look old, you're treated that way." He clicks his computer mouse and a close-up of a saggy-faced, dour man appears on a flat, wall-mounted monitor. "That's me four years ago," he says with a satisfied chortle. "Lifts," he explains, batting his eyes and stroking his jaw. "Chemical peel," he says, sweeping a hand across his face. "Plugs," he adds, tilting his brown-dyed hair forward. "I had a colleague insert a golden wire in my chin to prevent sagging." Takasu, who looks a decade younger than his 57 years, uses his own face as an advertisement prop for his trade, and it glows like a large peach.

Today, all beauty requires is cash—and Asians are blowing it on surgery at an unprecedented rate. "People want to look more beautiful as a way to show off their newfound wealth," explains Dr. He Xiaoming of the Peking Medical Union College's Plastic Surgery Hospital. Dr. Jean Lin, a plastic surgeon in Taipei, adds: "When the market goes up, I get more patients. When it drops, so do my appointments." On the other hand, a tight labor market also forces workers to compete by trying to look more attractive. In Japan, salarymen buzz about "recruit seikei"—cosmetic surgery for the sake of landing a job. The owner of a "beauty center" in Shenzen's Jiulong City Mall observes, "China has too many people. How do you make yourself stand out from 1.3 billion? Imagine your boss sees two people of similar ability.

He will definitely pick the person with the better appearance."

In China, surgically enhanced beauty is both a way to display wealth and a tool with which to attain it. Audis of the rich and well connected cram the parking lot of the high-tech Shenzhen Fuhua Plastic & Aesthetic Hospital, where the operating rooms look like a Star Trek set. The surgery center at Northwest University in Xi'an, a city in western China, targets a different demographic, handing out promotional flyers that offer procedures including hymen reconstruction at a 50% discount for students—"in order to make you tops in both your academic achievements and your looks!"

In recession-plagued Thailand, even the government has recognized the money-making potential of plastic surgery. The Tourism Authority of Thailand helps promote institutions like the Bumrungrad Hospital to foreigners, who make up one-third of its patients. "We're a hot commodity," says Ruben Toral, the hospital's director of international programs. Located on a traffic-clogged street in Bangkok, the 12-story, $90 million hospital is like a five-star, round-the-clock plastic surgery factory. There's a Starbucks in the lobby, high-speed Internet connection for the patients and room service offering halal and kosher meals.

In the mid-'70s, Thailand had only 10 plastic surgeons, so locals tended to go abroad to Japan or Singapore for cosmetic help. Today, the tide has reversed, and Thailand has become a surgical hub. "No country can compete with Thailand," says Dr. Preecha Tiewtranon, a surgeon specializing in sex reassignment at Bangkok's Preecha Aesthetic Institute, where 80% of the clientele is foreign. Much of the appeal is price: Preecha, who performed 300 operations last year, charges only $6,000 for a sex change, compared to $25,000 in the West. Price, too, is what attracts foreign patients—mainly from Japan, Taiwan and Hong Kong—To Apkujong, a section of Seoul with over 400 surgery clinics. Here, on a busy avenue nicknamed "Plastic Surgery Street," Park Chan Hoon pulls up in his sedan and leads three female passengers into a softly lit lobby decked out in black leather and chrome. A few years ago, the 38-year-old engineering Ph.D. quit a research job to start a travel agency offering plastic surgery tours for the Japanese. Packages include airfare, hotel, sight-seeing and, say, a boob job—all for the cost of the procedure alone back home.

Park jokes in fluent Japanese with Satsuki Takemoto, who has traveled to Seoul for shopping and liposuction. The 34-year-old homemaker from Hiroshima pulls out a snapshot of a stunning woman in a red kimono. "That's me 10 years ago," she says. She once weighed 40 kilos; today, after having two children, she's 75 kilos. "My husband says he doesn't care," rasps Takemoto, exhaling cigarette smoke, "but when the kids are mad at me they'll sometimes yell, '*buta*'"—pig. Over the years, Takemoto has tried prescription diets, spa treatments, specially-designed slimming underwear—all of which were expensive and none of which worked. Surgery, especially at a decent price, seemed the smart solution. "We told the kids, 'Mommy's in Korea getting her fat sucked out because we don't want her to drop dead from heart failure,'" she says. She takes another drag on her cigarette. "Yeah, they're a little scared."

Kawinna Suwanpradeep, an actress known throughout Thailand for her roles in TV soap operas, wasn't scared. Plastic surgery is no big deal in her line of work, and Suwanpradeep, 32, was less concerned about medical risks than the risk of losing work due to her hefty thighs. When Yanhee Hospital, a Bangkok plastic surgery center, offered her free liposuction in return for a public endorsement, she jumped at the chance. "I figured the doctors were internationally trained, and a lot of stars went there," she says. "I hadn't heard that a lot of things had gone wrong."

She was told she would be able to go home the same day as the operation, "but I had to stay three days," says Suwanpradeep. "I couldn't walk because of the pain and weakness." After the bandages were removed, she noticed wavy patches and scars. The doctor told her they would disappear in a few months, but when they still hadn't healed a year later, she demanded an explanation. "Then his whole tone changed and he said it wouldn't heal—that I would have to have another operation."

Instead, Suwanpradeep went to court: "I can't wear swimsuits. I can't do fashion shoots. And I can't play any sexy characters on television, because at some point they might have to show their legs." The hospital denies responsibility (and declined to comment for this article, citing the pending court case). Disgusted with her courthouse experience, Suwanpradeep is studying for a law degree. "Now," she says, "I'm the poster girl for plastic surgery disaster."

That's a poster that should be plastered around countless back lanes offering cut-rate beauty—especially in Thailand, Indonesia and China, where outdated laws offer scant protection against crooks and incompetents. In Indonesia, a thriving underground of beauty parlors and door-to-door salesmen cash in on perhaps the most rampant and dangerous procedure available in Asia: silicone injections, which are strictly regulated in the U.S. In Asia, silicone is still hawked to plump up noses, breasts and even sex organs like the labia or penis. It works at first, but liquid silicone can't escape the laws of gravity, resulting eventually in an unsightly droop. It can also cause swelling, tissue decay and—if it enters the bloodstream—death. Transsexuals are often both perpetrators and victims. Two year ago, a transsexual in East Java died after injecting silicone into her breasts. What's more, the injectable silicone typically used among transsexuals is industrial grade—much cheaper and more toxic than medical-grade silicone. "To make even more money," adds Dede Oetomo, a Surabaya-based anthropologist and gay activist, "they heat the substance and mix it with cod-liver oil, lard or frying oil."

Saleha, now 33, received her first silicone injection in 1995 from a fellow transsexual who owned a beauty parlor in Surabaya. Tall, slender and dressed in a tight, white top and matching miniskirt, Saleha would be attractive if not for her ruined nose and chin. After her first cosmetic injection, she wound up with a nose "Like Bozo the clown's," she says. So she visited another beautician who pinched and tweaked her nose into shape, then treated her with more injections than Saleha can now count. "I was totally broke after a while," says Saleha, who at the time sold noodles and moonlighted as a prostitute. Gradually, as the silicone shifted, her whole face began to sag and her chin withered. When she speaks, her large hands flutter constantly to her face to perform a furtive, futile massage. Part of the problem is that it's much harder to exact legal retribution in Asia than in the West, where medical malpractice suits often yield enormous settlements. Most Asian lawyers avoid malpractice cases, since so few result in victory and financial payoff. Above all, though, it's the bargain-hunting instinct that leads patients astray, tempting them to use unqualified cosmetic practitioners. "At the end of the day, the government will have to make a decision on whether to restrict surgery to specialists," says Dr. Woffles Wu, a plastic surgeon at the Camden Medical Center in Singapore. "This is a time bomb waiting to go off."

It may seem reckless to undergo medically unnecessary operations that could disfigure or even kill you. But who's to say that good looks aren't worth the risk? "The Japanese have a saying: 'It's not the face, it's the heart,'" says television producer Koji Kaneda. "But when I asked around, everyone acknowledged appearances count—often more than anything." With that in mind, Kaneda dreamed up a show called *Beauty Colosseum* that launched last fall. Each week, women pour forth tales of woe, and a panel of beauty experts offers makeover advice. The most desperate cases are referred to the show's "miracle doctor of beauty," Toshiya Handa, a surgeon at the Otsuka Academy of Cosmetic & Plastic Surgery, a chain of 13 clinics across Japan. The regular appearance of tanned, telegenic Handa on *Beauty Colosseum* has inspired a flood of young TV viewers to sign up for surgery at Otsuka. In 2001, 64% of the patients there were in their teens or 20s.

One of the program's most memorable guests was Yumi Sakaguchi, a 26-year-old from Osaka. Even today, her lips tremble as she recounts her life. Born with droopy eyes, a receding chin and prominent buckteeth, Sakaguchi endured merciless teasing in her youth. Classmates even drew caricatures of her on the chalkboard. "I always walked with my face to the ground," she says. After high school, when her diabetic father racked up big medical bills, Sakaguchi sought work as a bar hostess to pay off the family debt. "They turned me away flat, saying, 'You'd make the customers sick,'" she recalls. "It was then I realized I had only my body to sell." Sakaguchi found work at a brothel, but many customers rejected her because of her looks. "I was at rock bottom," she says, softly. "I kept thinking something will work out, somehow. My life depended on it."

Last October, Sakaguchi appeared on *Beauty Colosseum* and won free dental, eye and chin surgery that would otherwise have cost over $30,000.

She quit the skin trade, landed a high-paying hostess job, and plans to study psychology. But nearly a year after her surgical windfall, Sakaguchi sounds circumspect, as if the enormity of the change has come to weigh on her. Though open about her surgery and her past, she was hurt when a recent boyfriend told her he would not have dated her before her surgical alteration. "I always wanted to believe people were ultimately judged by what was inside," she muses, her gaze hesitant and sad. "But I knew from my personal experience that this wasn't true. It's always the pretty girls who win the good things in life."

Alvin Goh, a slight, impeccably dressed stylist and creative director of a soon-to-be launched lifestyle magazine in Singapore, understands better than most our tendency to judge a book by its cover. So, a year and a half ago, Goh, now 24, decided to get an eye job. "We live in a cruel society where everything is based on first impressions," he says. "If you look in the mirror and don't feel good about what you see, it won't help you in your life, in your work or in your relationships."

Much more so than women, men cite their careers as the driving reason to go under the knife. Taiwanese comedian Tsai Tou was once known as the ugliest man in show business. While his face helped win him laughs, he felt it limited his chances of hosting a talk show: so he too had surgery two years ago, adding folds to his eyelids, getting his eye bags removed, having his nose heightened and his wrinkles flattened with botox. A face free of bags and wrinkles, Tsai explains, captures the "trustworthy" look that TV viewers prefer. Dr. Kenneth Hui, a plastic surgeon in Hong Kong, remarks: "It can be a matter of necessity, not vanity."

Necessity drove Ching Wei to plastic surgery. Desperate for work, the struggling Taiwanese entertainer took a TV role in 1997 that required him to escape chains and a wooden box as it was set on fire. Instead, he found himself trapped. Covered with third-degree burns, Ching saw his career evaporate and attempted suicide. Five years and $60,000 worth of surgery later, Ching, now 37, is an award-winning media personality and owner of his own communications company. "It's a miracle," he says. "Everything you see about me is the work of plastic surgery—my facial skin, implanted hair, and restored retina."

Some people find tragedy in the plastic surgery clinic. Others, like Sakaguchi and Ching, are reborn. Most are somehow looking to achieve that most elusive of goals: to halt the march of time. "All of Asia is ruled by a youth culture," says Hiromi Yamamoto, a Tokyo hair and makeup artist who has written extensively about plastic surgery. "We may respect the old, but it's the young who play the lead roles. So it's no surprise that the old want to look young, and the young want to look fabulous."

In a plush cabaret in the Akasaka entertainment district of Tokyo, a slender woman in a slinky, red dress croons *Amazing Grace*. Despite her rich voice and charming stage presence, Teri Hirayama is, at 36, pushing the upper limits of the business. So, over the course of six months, she has had her baggy eyelids lifted, her nose and chin shaped, and her wrinkles smoothed away. Now the politicians and foreign executives who frequent the joint ply Hirayama with requests.

"I'm the one who urged her to get it done," boasts cabaret owner Kirisa Matsui, herself a gorgeous specimen of 60. "I don't hire homely girls. These are difficult times, you know, and I've got a business to run."

Whether for vanity, ego or cold hard cash, we all want to look better, younger, more fabulous. Think of all the clichès about beauty: that it is in the eye of the beholder, that it slayed the beast and, of course, that it is only skin deep. Teri Hirayama and millions more throughout the region seem to be buying into that last conceit as they go under the knife in the quest for an aesthetic beauty as malleable as silicone in a surgeon's hand.

R E A D I N G **18**

Mi Estomago (My Belly)

Marjorie Agosin (1986)

Naked and as if in silence
I approach my belly
it has gone on changing like summer
withdrawing from the sea
or like a dress that expands with the hours
My belly
is more than round
because when I sit down
it spreads like a brush fire
then,
I touch it to recall
all the things inside it:
salt and merriment
the fried eggs of winter breakfasts
the milk that strangled me in my youth
the coca-cola that stained my teeth
the nostalgia for the glass of wine
we discovered in La Isla
or french fries and olive oil
And as I remember
I feel it growing

and bowing down more and more ceremoniously to the
ground
until it caresses my feet, my toes
that never could belong to a princess,
I rejoice
that my belly is as wide as Chepi's old sombrero—
Chepi was my grandmother—
and I pamper it no end
when it complains or has bad dreams
from eating too much.

Midsummer, at seventy years of age,
this Sunday the seventh
my belly is still with me
and proudly goes parading along the shore
some say I am already old and ugly
that my breasts are entangled with my guts
but my belly is here at my side a good companion
and don't say it's made of fat
rather tender morsels of meat toasting in the sun.

Translated by *Cola Franzen*

Unveiled Sentiments: Gendered Islamophobia and Experiences of Veiling Among Muslim Girls in a Canadian Islamic School

Jasmin Zine (2006)

This discussion critically explores ethno-religious oppression encountered by Muslim girls in Toronto, Canada. Focusing on the experiences of Muslim girls attending a gender segregated Islamic school, the article critically explores how these young women reside at the nexus of dual oppressions, confronting racism and Islamophobia in society at large and at the same time contending with patriarchal forms of religious oppression in their communities. Islamophobia can be defined as "a fear or hatred of Islam and its adherents that translates into individual, ideological and systemic forms of oppression and discrimination" (Zine, 2003). For girls who adhere to Islamic dress codes, such as the hijab or headscarf, that visibly mark them as Muslims, issues of ethno-religious oppression in the form of Islamophobia are particularly salient. These Muslim girls construct their identities in opposition to the stereotypes they encounter in the media and in their public school experiences that portray them as "oppressed," "backward," and uneducated (McDonough, 2003; Zine, 2000, 2002; Zine & Bullock, 2002).

This discussion allows a deeper understanding of how gendered identities are constructed in the schooling experiences of young Muslim women, and examines how the multiple identities that they inhabit as social actors based on race, ethnicity, religion, and gender position them in marginalized sites within the racialized borders of diaspora and nation. This discussion situates the contested notion of veiling and gender identity in Islam and provides an examination of emerging discourses of identity among these young women that both affirm and begin to challenge traditional notions.

FRAMING THE RESEARCH: BRIEF OVERVIEW OF METHODS

This paper is drawn from a broader ethnographic study of Islamic schooling that focused on four Islamic schools in the Greater Toronto Area. The study was based on interviews of 49 participants, including students, teachers, school administrators, and parents, as well as 18 months of fieldwork including classroom observations and action research conducted while teaching in an Islamic girls' high school. This paper focuses on the data gathered among Muslim girls in a gender-segregated high school.

Several themes emerged that help frame the experiences of these girls, both inside and outside of school. These are discussed through a narrative analysis of ten female students who attended the Al Rajab[1] high school. They ranged in age from 16–19 and were from South Asian, Arab, and Somali backgrounds.

As a Muslim scholar and feminist who wore the hijab or headscarf for 15 years as a form of marking my faith and identity, the issues explored have both personal and political significance. The discussion that follows examines the politics of veiling from a historical and discursive purview and then examines some of the lived experiences of veiling among the young women in this study.

CONTEXT OF ISLAMIC SCHOOLS IN ONTARIO

The school featured in this discussion was one of over 20 full-time Islamic schools in the Greater Toronto Area and accommodated students from K-12.

The school was gender-segregated from grade four, and the high school had separate sections of the building designated for girls and boys. Gender segregation and the construction of gendered spaces within Islamic schools, such as separate lunchrooms, classrooms, and prayer areas, is common in Islamic school settings after children reach the age of puberty when religious codes for modesty in dress, manner, and social distance between members of the opposite sex become instituted. In addition to the physical barriers that separate boys and girls socially at this time, the Islamic dress code for girls, which also becomes operative by the age of puberty becomes another means of segregation and marking the shift to womanhood with greater emphasis on the seclusion of their bodies.

GENDERING ISLAMOPHOBIA

Central to the analysis of Muslim women and girls in Western diasporas is the notion I refer to as "gendered Islamophobia." This can be understood as specific forms of ethno-religious and racialized discrimination leveled at Muslim women that proceed from historically contextualized negative stereotypes that inform individual and systemic forms of oppression. Various forms of oppression, for example, racism, sexism, and classism, are rooted within specific ideological/discursive processes and supported through both individual and systemic actions. In the case of gendered Islamophobia, the discursive roots are historically entrenched within Orientalist representations that cast colonial Muslim women as backward, oppressed victims of misogynist societies (Hoodfar, 1993; Said, 1979). Such representations served to justify and rationalize imperial domination over colonized Muslims through the emancipatory effect that European hegemony was expected to garner for Muslim women. These stereotypical constructs have maintained currency over time and have served to mark the borders between the binary spaces of the West (read: progress, modernity) and the East (read: illiberal, pre-modern) as irreconcilable halves of a world living renewed relations of conquest and subjugation.

Beyond representational politics the epistemic violence behind these constructs bears material consequences for Muslim girls and women. Studies that highlight the impact of gendered Islamophobia have shown that Muslim women who wear hijab suffer discrimination in the workplace (Parker-Jenkins, 1999). For example, a recent study in Toronto identified significant barriers to veiled Muslim women accessing jobs (Keung, 2002; Smith, 2002). This study reported that 29 of the 32 Muslim women surveyed indicated that they had an employer make a reference to their hijab while applying for jobs in the manufacturing, sales, and service sector. Twenty one of the participants were asked if they could remove their head covers, and one third had been told at least once that they had to remove their veils if they wanted a job. Two sets of women were sent "undercover" to apply for the same job, bearing relatively identical resumes, age, and ethnic backgrounds, the only difference being that one of the women wore hijab. While 62.5% of the women without a head cover were asked to fill out a job application, only 12.5% of the women wearing hijab were given the same opportunities. These examples show the nature of gendered Islamophobia as it operates socially, politically, and discursively to deny material advantages to Muslim women.

BANNING HIJAB IN PUBLIC SCHOOLS: CASE STUDIES FROM FRANCE AND QUEBEC

In another example of gendered Islamophobia and mounting fears of religious fundamentalism infiltrating secular institutions, Muslim girls in France, Turkey, and Quebec have been exiled from public schools on account of their hijabs (a phenomenon the media dubbed "hijabophobia"). The hijab was viewed as an assault on dominant civic values of female liberty and a denial of the dominant national identity (Misbahuddin, 1996). These debates emphasize that balancing multicultural pluralism and religious freedom is a fragile act. A case in point is the French controversy known as *L'affair du foulard* or "affair of the scarf." The situation first became prominent in 1989 when three Muslim adolescent girls were denied access to public school because they wore the hijab or headscarf, an act that defies a 1937 French law prohibiting the wearing of conspicuous religious symbols in government-run schools. The *L'affair du foulard* ignited debates over nationalism and the perceived threat of growing ethno-racial and religious diversity. Against this political backdrop, right wing French politician Le Pen continued to urge the repatriation of all immigrants who had arrived in France since 1974. Such xenophobic sentiments were echoed in the conservative newspaper *Le Point* where a provocative headline read: "Should We Let Islam Colonize Our Schools?" (Gutmann, 1996, p. 161).

The debate over secularism and religious freedom that ensued over this issue divided even the Left in France where some socialists allied themselves with conservatives who were defending the 1937 law. Those on the Left who defended the law did so on the grounds that "the veil is a sign of imprisonment that considers women to be sub-humans under the law of Islam" (cited in Gutmann, 1996, p. 161). Many feminist responses also did not challenge this assertion, and instead supported the notion that the hijab is a symbol of gender inequality, and therefore incompatible with the ethos and values of French society (El Habti, 2004). However, such stereotypes deny the agency of Muslim women who wear the veil, and reduce the multiple meanings associated with the veil to a single negative referent. Therefore in the public debates that took place, the *L'affair du foulard* evoked troubling discourses of fear, aversion, otherness, and even sub-humanness in relation to Muslim girls and the veil that overshadowed the fundamental issue of religious freedom as a human right.

Within the Canadian context, the case of Emilie Ouimet captured national attention in 1994 when 12-year-old Emilie (a French Canadian convert to Islam) was expelled from her school for not complying with a request to remove her hijab. The largest teacher federation in Quebec supported this move by voting in favor of keeping the hijab out of French schools. The principal at Emilie's school justified his decision by saying that the wearing of a distinctive sign like the hijab or neo-Nazi insignias could polarize the aggressiveness of students, thereby equating the hijab with fascism and invoking a discourse of

fear and repression. The social, cultural, and political context in which the hijab ban erupted was critical in understanding these debates. In 1977, the passing of Bill 101 decreed that all immigrant children in Quebec had to attend French language schools. This law effectively changed the homogenous character of French schools and rapidly ushered in a new multicultural dynamic to these schools (Lenk, 2000). Therefore the backlash to integration and ethno-racial diversity underscores the contestations over religious dress in secular public schools.

Emilie's case also unfolded amidst a growing French nationalism in Canada and the veil came to epitomize the challenge of defining a distinctive Quebecois national identity in a changing social and cultural environment. The French and English media were polarized in their representation of the issue and used the forum to further the broader contestations over the nature of French society and hegemony in Quebec (Lenk, 2000; Todd, 1999). The English language newspapers became the champion of Emilie's cause citing the need to value individual and human rights. Representing the Anglophone minority in Quebec who also were subject to Francophone hegemony, the English language press capitalized on Emilie's plight as a way to further their own political critique of French society and the failure of Quebec nationalism to conform to the laws of English Canada's discourse (Lenk, 2000). So in this political context, the hijab was not only a way of constructing the Islamic other as a threat to liberal civic values but it also polarized French nationalism with Anglophone federalism.

Lenk (2000) reminds us that an important racialized dimension to the debate was the fact that Emile was a white convert to Islam. She argues that Emilie's Islamization was viewed as racial transgression, making her less sympathetic to the French nationalist constituency. As a result, she became racialized through her refusal to conform to the normative cultural standards and perform the dominant identity. It was seen as a disavowal of her dominant Francophone Quebecois identity and thus a threat to the French nationalist goal of developing a "distinct society" with a French character.

Lenk (2000) further points out the critical fact that news media widely excluded the point of view of

Emilie herself and failed to include the voices of other Muslim women in the debates. Therefore the fact that Emilie's control over her body, dress, and ultimately her schooling career were compromised by the ban became almost incidental to the broader social and political issues that framed the debates. This unequal representation also was evidenced by the fact that while Muslim women's views were silenced from the media and public discourse, a white female reporter received much attention when she decided to put on the hijab and write about her "experience" (Lenk, 2000). Throughout the media representation, political analysts and even the school principal who initiated the ban provided the dominant narratives on this issue to the exclusion and appropriation of Muslim women's experiences. In the end, however, Emilie was able to recuperate her agency and her religious rights by appealing to Quebec's Human Rights Commission, which ruled that public schools cannot forbid the wearing of religious headscarves (Khan, 2003). These landmark human rights cases represent gendered Islamophobia at play in the negotiation of gendered religious identities in secular educational sites.

THE POLITICS OF VEILING

The politics of gender can be mapped upon the bodies of women in various ways. For example, Muslim women's dress in one modality that provides a salient form of culturally and religiously encrypting the female body. For example, El Guindi (1999) notes that as a form of religious dress, the Muslim veil, the hijab, is located at the intersection of dress, body, and culture (p. xvi). Through the medium of the veil therefore, Muslim women's bodies are gender-coded and form a "cultural text" for the expression of social, political, and religious meanings.

Corporeal Inscriptions: Multiple Meanings of Veiling

As a form of social communication and bearer of cultural and gendered norms, the Muslim veil is one of the most provocative forms of dress, eliciting as many diverse and conflicting reactions as there are

reasons ascribed to its adoption as a distinctive dress code for women.

Despite the often static representations of veiling, there are multiple meanings associated with the veil that vary historically, culturally, and politically (Bullock, 2002; Hoodfar, 1993; Zine, 2002). Although women's practices of veiling predate the Islamic context, this symbol has entered into the popular imagination in Western societies as the quintessential marker of the Muslim world and as a practice synonymous with religious fundamentalism and extremism. In this conception, the bodies of veiled women operate as cultural signifiers of social difference and social threat and represent fidelity to a patriarchal order, which is a danger to women's autonomy (Bullock, 2002; Read & Bartkowski, 2000). These notions can be traced back to their Orientalist origins where depictions of veiled Muslim women in the colonial imaginary ranged from oppressed and subjugated women, to the highly sexualized and erotic imagery of the sensual, yet inaccessible, harem girl (Bullock, 2000, 2002; Hoodfar, 1993; Said, 1979; Zine, 2002). Therefore, historically, the veiled Muslim woman has been simultaneously constructed as an object of fear and desire. Muslim women's identities are negotiated within the nexus of these ambivalent constructs that mediate between the desire and disavowal of their social, racialized and gendered difference (Zine, 2002).

In some contemporary Muslim societies, the veil has been used as a form of political protest and class-based signification (Bullock, 2002; Hoodfar, 2003). In its symbolic and practical form, the veil also is regarded as a means of maintaining the body as a space of "sacred privacy" or being hidden from public view in accordance with religious prescriptions (El Guindi, 1999).

The Veil in Religious Paradigms: The Hermeneutics of Dress

In a scriptural sense, the veil has been interpreted as a Divine injunction based on specific verses from the Qur'an and supported by some hadith[2] literature that provide a historical documentation of the words and deeds of the Prophet Muhammed. For example, in the following Qur'anic verses addressing women's clothing, it is stated:

> And say to the believing women that they should avert their gaze and guard their modesty, and they should not display their adornment except what is apparent thereof, and they should throw their veils over their bosoms, and not display their adornment except to their husbands or fathers. (Holy Qur'an 24:31)
>
> O Prophet, tell your wives and the women of the believers that they should bring some of their cloaks closer/nearer to themselves, that is a minimum [measure] so that they would be recognized as such and hence not molested. (Holy Qur'an 33:59)

During the 7th century in Arabia when these verses were revealed, the customary pre-Islamic practice of women was to wear a long headscarf (khimar) that flowed loosely around their shoulders and left their breasts exposed. Some scholars view the verses related here as a corrective to this practice and as a means to signify Muslim identity (Abou El Fadl, 2001; Hajjaji-Jarrah, 2003). Significantly, there are no sanctions in the Qur'an for not covering, and only one report in the canonical collections clearly refers to the requirements of women's covering. In this tradition, it is related that the Prophet Muhammed stated that at the age of puberty, women should cover all but their hands and face. However, this hadith is found only in a singular collection and that this is not considered a strong account since the isnad or chain of transmission between various historical narrators had been broken and therefore the account cannot claim an unqualified validity.

Given the complexities of interpretation and the divergence between scholars who invoke literal versus historically contextualized readings, there is no juristic consensus among scholars as to the areas of the body to be covered (Roald, 2001). These range from the extreme of covering the entire face according to some of the early Islamic legal schools, to covering everything but the hands and face. Still other interpretations note that since the Qur'an does not explicitly state the mandate of covering the hair (rather it refers to drawing the veil over the bosom),

that this is not a requirement and that maintaining a dress code that is in accordance with the contemporary social and cultural norms of modesty is all that is required (Hajjaji-Jarrah, 2003).

Both the Qur'anic verses and references within the hadith narratives have been subject to rigorous reexamination by contemporary scholars who have presented alternative contextualized readings. Some argue that the hijab is a historically specific form of dress that was used during the 7th century as a means to visibly mark Muslim women so that they could be identified as being under the protection of the Muslim clan and therefore avoid being molested or harassed (Abou El Fadl, 2001; Hajjaji-Jarrah, 2003; Roald, 2001). The veil also was the marker of a free woman versus a slave or concubine and set certain social and sexual parameters for the engagement of men with these different social and class based categories of women (Hajjaji-Jarrah, 2003). These interpretations offset other religious views that situate the hijab as a static symbol of religious practice and as a means for the social and legal demarcation of women's bodies as being part of private, non-public space. This has concerned feminist scholars who rightly see this understanding as contrary and detrimental to the Islamic ethos of equality and justice, and as a sociological and ideological factor that has arrested the development of true gender equity among Muslim populations (Ahmed, 1992; Mernissi, 1987, 1991).

VEILING AS FEMINIST PROTEST OR FUNDAMENTALIST DOGMA?

As an Islamic feminist construct, the veil represents a means of resisting and subverting dominant Euro-centric norms of femininity and the objectification of the female body and as a means of protection from the male gaze (Bullock, 2000, 2002; Read & Bartkowski, 2000). As a sexually politicized referent, the veil has been identified as a symbol of the rejection of "profane, immodest and consumerist cultural customs of the West," making it an anti-imperialist statement marking alternative gendered norms (Read & Bartkowski,

2000, p. 398). These notions construct the practice of veiling as a part of an oppositional political discourse that counters the "tyranny of beauty" that objectifies and commodifies women for the edification of patriarchal capitalist desires. In this way, wearing the veil is viewed by some of its proponents as an empowering move that represents a feminist stance for resisting the hegemony of sexualized representations of the female body. Halstead (1991), for example, notes that such rationales have contributed to the saliency of the veil in the British Muslim diaspora:

> The Qur'anic requirements of modesty and decency in dress (Qur'an 24:30–31; 33:59) may be seen not so much as an exemplar of patriarchal domination as a practical attempt to defeat sexual exploitation and harassment, and as such it continues to be upheld by many second generation British Muslim women. (p. 274)

However, this notion places the burden of responsibility for avoiding sexual harassment upon women, who are expected to regulate their bodies to avoid eliciting the negative sexual attention of men, rather than placing the onus on men to regulate their behavior toward women.[3]

Therefore, in very reductive ways, narrations of Islamic womanhood, both inside and outside of Muslim ideological and ontological conceptions, have been intrinsically connected to religious attire. On the one hand, conservative Islamic discourses view the veil as a primary determinant of religiosity for women and unequivocally reject other articulations of female identification that do not include the veil as a legitimate constituent of Islamic womanhood. Many secular feminist readings of the veil also use equally reductive paradigms to essentialize the veil as the universal marker of women's oppression, negating veiled women's alternative constructions that locate the practice within spaces of social, sexual, and political empowerment (Lazreg, 1994; Mohanty, 1991). Muslim women must therefore navigate between these reductionist and essentialized paradigms to claim their own representation over the discursive practices that determine the way their bodies are narrated, defined, and regulated.

VEILING PRACTICES IN PUBLIC SCHOOLS AND ISLAMIC SCHOOLS

For Muslim women and girls who adopt Islamic dress codes, such as the hijab and niqab (face-veil) and wear abayas (long overcoats), these markers of Islamic identification often lead to social ridicule and ostracism in Western societies (Hamdani, 2004). Negative stereotypes and discrimination relating to Islamic dress codes were among the most salient concerns the girls interviewed had in their day-to-day secular experiences. Yet Muslim girls also must contend with how their dress codes are regulated within the Muslim community. Case studies of Muslim girls attending North American public schools and Islamic schools find similar tensions with respect to their veiling practices. In an ethnographic study of hijabat[4] Yemeni school girls in Dearborn, Michigan, Sarroub (2005) describes the complex ways in which they negotiate the liminal "in-between" spaces between home and community and the dominant mainstream culture in school as "sojourners" between two worlds. Navigating between the conservative orientations of their community and the challenges of secular public schooling Sarroub, using data from 1997–1998, documents the cultural interface within one school as these Yemeni students seek accommodations for their dress codes in physical education classes and attempt to maintain their traditions of gender-based social distance among members of the opposite sex by avoiding physical contact, such as shaking hands, or otherwise "mixing" with boys.

My earlier research examining Muslim students in secular public schools in Canada also examined similar issues of accommodation and negotiation relating to Islamic dress and lifestyle and the resistance strategies employed by students to achieve inclusion (Zine, 2001). The issue of racism and discrimination also were noted in the schooling experiences of these Muslim high school students. In particular Muslim girls wearing hijab described how their interactions with teachers were often framed by negative Orientalist assumptions that they were oppressed at home and that Islam did not value education for women (Zine, 2001). Such notions were often communicated through the hidden curriculum and through low teacher expectations and streaming practices where some Muslim girls noted that they were encouraged to avoid academic subjects and stick to lower non-academic streams.[5]

While Islamic dress was a site of negative attention and challenge in public schools and in Canadian society at large, within Islamic schools hijab was mandatory. The dress codes at the Islamic school involved in this study included a compulsory hijab and burgundy colored abayas or overcoats worn over street clothes. These dress codes were considered to be the school uniform for the girls and were enforced by school authorities. Boys also attended this gender-segregated school but occupied separate areas in the school building. They wore gray pants and white shirts as a school uniform. Male religious head covers in the form of a cap or toque, known as kufis, were optional. The compulsory nature of the hijab for girls was due to religious prescription as a matter of modesty, whereas for boys, the cap was a sign of Islamic identity and encouraged, though not mandated.

Outside of school, the girls were free to dress as they chose or in accordance with family expectations. For many of the girls, wearing hijab was a choice that they made as part of their expression of Islamic identity and modesty and as an act of worship. These girls wore hijab outside of school as well. Some also wore abayas over their clothes outside of school, although many wore their hijab with other clothes, such as the South Asian style shalwar kameez[6] or western-style clothes that conformed to traditional Islamic dress requirements and were loose fitting and opaque. None of the girls reported being forced to wear hijab outside of school by their families and took it up out of their own religious conviction, yet many girls in the school chose not to maintain these dress codes outside of school.

In addition to the regulatory practices within the school where their dress codes were subject to surveillance by the school authorities, the girls also were confronted with pressures outside the Muslim community where the veil has come to represent a marker of backwardness, oppression, and even terrorism (see Zine, 2001). This form of discrimination, Islamophobia, punctuates the experiences of many Muslim girls and women within Canadian mainstream society. The following section

draws on ethnographic data to explore Muslim girls' experiences of "gendered Islamophobia" and then continues to examine the experiences of Muslim girls who contend with the dual oppressions of sexism within their communities, and racism and Islamophobia outside.

UNVEILED SENTIMENTS: GENDERED ISLAMOPHOBIA AND LIVED EXPERIENCES OF VEILING

The Muslim girls in this study had to contend with the negative stereotypes regarding hijab outside school and the regulation of their dress within the school. Each situation became a challenge to agency and identity. The following narratives explore the experiences of Muslim school girls with respect to instances of gendered Islamophobia outside of school and the politics of veiling both outside their schooling experiences as well as within the discursive parameters of religious identification enforced within the school.

Aliyah, Nusaybah, Zarqa, and Imrana were grade 11 students at the Al Rajab Islamic school. All are 16 years old and of Pakistani descent except Aliyah who is Afghani. The topic of Islamic dress entered the conversations often, particularly when we spoke of their experiences outside of school and of why they liked being within an Islamic school environment. During one conversation where we talked about who wore their abayas home and who took them off, experiences of racism, xenophobia, and gendered Islamophobia were revealed as the girls explained the situations they encountered journeying to and from school. Most of the high school girls regularly used the public transit system and it was there that their encounters with people were often negatively punctuated by racist, xenophobic, and Islamophobic attitudes. In the following exchange these issues are revealed as the young women speak poignantly about how this discrimination impacted their sense of self and identity:

Aliyah: Truly, I don't wear my abaya home. Honestly I take it off.
Nusaybah: And I go home with mine on.

Aliyah: Because the thing is, you take your car. I take the TTC,[7] see, and people look at me and they see me, and sometimes I'm treated rudely, seriously. Just with the hijab, sometimes I'm treated rudely.

Jasmin: By whom? The passengers or the bus drivers?

Aliyah: The passengers *and* the bus drivers. Okay, like once this man, a passenger on the subway, called me an illegal immigrant. I think he was drunk. And I told him, "I'm here legally! I didn't come here illegally! I came here legally!" Another time, I was wearing the hijab and I was standing right in front of the bus door, like I made it to the door but the guy [the driver] still shut the door on me and he drove off! And if I hadn't been wearing hijab I think he would have stopped.

Researcher: Do you notice a difference when you go out without the abaya?

Everyone: [talking at once] "Very much, yeah. *Very* much!"

Zarqa: Okay, I was going on the bus one day in Ramadan and I was wearing my hijab and my abaya. I was going to take off my abaya, but then I didn't. And we were going past 5th St. and there was this lady on the bus right, and there was a little girl and she was really, really cute and I love children, and I was like, "Oh hi, she's so cute!" and her mom, she, like, looked at me and she turns the daughter away from me, and the girl just started crying. It makes you feel so bad!

Aliyah: It makes you feel like, "Oh if I hadn't been wearing this!"

Zarqa: That's exactly what I thought! The minute I saw that, it was in my mind—I should have taken it off! Like, I know I shouldn't, but at the time it made me feel that if I took it off it'd be different. It'd be like—the girl wouldn't be crying.

Aliyah: It's true. So many people do that. Like, if you look at their kid and you'd be, like, smiling at them, they'll just give you the dirtiest look, like: "Don't look at my kid!" But then when some white lady looks at their kid, they're, like, smiling back at the lady.

As the girls exchanged their stories of the lived experience of racism and Islamophobia, it became clear that these were patterns that they had all encountered as the result of having their bodies marked as Muslims through the practice of veiling. The veil located them as "foreigners" who did not belong to the Canadian social fabric, and the xenophobia they encountered cast them as "illegal immigrants," a tantamount denial of their citizenry. Being subject to this open hostility created a fragile narrative of "Canadianness" and belonging for these girls that was easily ruptured by the lack of social acceptance they encountered in mainstream society. These were also experiences of social rejection, of being excluded from the simple banal exchange of smiling at a child, and being treated as "persona non grata" simply because of their religious identity and the negative meanings imposed on the veil. Within these encounters, a specific discourse of "foreignness" and Otherness emerged and framed the way in which they came to see their identities as Muslims being socially evaluated and ultimately rejected. This positioning wove its way into their narratives of identity and implicated how they located themselves within the racially bordered spaces of nation.

CONFRONTING STEREOTYPES

The girls felt they had to represent Islam everywhere they went and that they needed to be careful of what they said or did since their behavior would be essentialized to represent all Muslims. These issues emerged in my interviews with Safia, Sahar, and Umbreen. Both Safia and Umbreen were South Asian of Pakistani and Indian descent and Sahar was a Palestinian Arab. The following discussion shows the scrutiny and surveillance that were placed upon them as young Muslim women and how they negotiated the burden of representation and negative essentialism.

Safia: There's so much pressure, especially for the female Muslims, because if we make one little mistake, the littlest mistake, they'll keep that as a stereotype about us and they'll make us look bad about that. Yet if another girl did it that, didn't wear hijab, or wasn't Muslim, it wouldn't be a bad thing for her. Yet for us we're, uh . . .

Sahar: Looked at greatly—

Safia: From every single point.

Sahar: Exactly.

Safia: So that's why we have more pressure on us outside in public to act modest and respectfully with everyone. Even if, say a stranger came up to us and started acting rude right? If we responded back rudely to them, they would say, "Oh look she's so rude!" this-and-that, but they wouldn't remember that they started it. So that's why even if someone's rude on the street or whatever, I'll still give them respect just so they can't say, "Oh, Muslims are this-and-that."

Umbreen: Yeah, but if one Muslim does something, they'll think all Muslims are like that. Everyone is like that. They'll be like, "Oh look at these Muslim people. They don't have any shame, blah blah blah." But then when they do it, it's an everyday thing. It's like, "Oh who cares?" Yeah, like if a white man goes and kills someone they don't go and say *all* white men killed someone. They don't say "Oh my God *all* white men kill people!"

Sahar: Exactly.

Safia: But if it was ever on the news that a Muslim man killed someone—

Samia: They'd spend years on it!

Safia: It'd be on the news forever.

Umbreen: And then Muslim people feel like more uncomfortable on the streets.

Safia: And you think everyone's looking at you and they're thinking, "Oh my God, this person's going to kill me!"

Sahar: "Oh God, terrorists!"

Jasmin: It's sort of more of a burden because you know your entire community is going to be judged.

Sahar: But here [in Islamic school] you come and they know it's not like that, so you feel more comfortable and more relaxed and freer and more open.

NEGOTIATING THE DISCURSIVE NORMS OF DRESS

Muslim girls entering the discursive spaces of Islamic schools are socialized to conform to the prevailing religious orientation within the school and must, therefore, accommodate to the social and institutional norms that impact on the construction of their gendered subjectivities. Therefore, while Muslim girls resist the way they are positioned within popular culture and Islamophobic representations, they accommodate to the prevailing discourse of "hijab-equals-piety" within the school and mosque community thereby exchanging one form of discursive representation and control (i.e., Orientalist) for another (i.e., religious/patriarchal).

Without a doubt, some young women did contest the policing of their dress in Islamic school, but recognized that it was being upheld as the standard school uniform as well as being seen as religious injunction. However, as these young women develop greater political maturity and knowledge and gain the ability to act and engage within the space of Islamic discourse—where such issues are the subject of debate—they may just as legitimately choose to re-define their notions of Islamic identity and identification in alternative ways. As spiritually-centered young women, the majority of those interviewed chose to express their faith within the acceptable norms determined within their Islamic school environment, although these boundaries were often challenged. Nevertheless, their notions of Islamic identity, were largely constructed within the prevailing discourse produced by the school and local religious authorities. Among the young Muslim women in this study, these discursively and physically regulated aspects of identity were either validated and upheld or openly contested.

Freedom, Sisterhood, and Articulations of Identity

Interestingly, although these girls attended a gender-segregated Islamic school, they actually reported feeling more "segregated" in public school since the lack of acceptance of their faith-centered lifestyle and religious dress meant they were set apart and more socially isolated from other students. Being in an Islamic school gave them a stronger feeling of freedom in expressing their religious identities without fear or ridicule or social exclusion.

Not having to conform to standards of dress that are dictated by MTV and the popular styles of youth culture allowed these girls to feel freer to express their identity in a more modest fashion that was in accordance with their faith-centered orientation. While Islamic school also mandates conformity with a particular form of Islamic dress, this was more congruent with the kind of sensibilities these girls had already inculcated based on their religious convictions and the way they articulated Islamically-appropriate styles of dress. Without the peer pressure to conform to more popular and less modest forms of clothing, they felt a greater sense of "fitting in" to the school environment. Girls reported that in public school there was a great deal of social pressure to take off their hijab and be like everyone else. Iman, an OAC student of Somali descent, discussed the peer pressure she and her friends encountered while wearing hijab in public school:

> I was wearing hijab and you know people ask too many questions. They'll be like, "Why do you wear that on your head? Aren't you hot?" You'll feel kind of bad. You'll answer them and they'll be like "take it off" and stuff like that . . . because, they want to look like their friends. They don't want to be different. They don't show pride in themselves and the faith that they have.

For Iman then, hijab represented pride in her faith and identity as a Muslim woman. She had started wearing hijab in middle school and because she did not have many Muslim friends, she felt pressured to take it off. Some friends, she reported respected the fact that she chose to wear hijab and when she later transferred to a school where there were a higher percentage of Muslims in the school wearing hijab, she felt more comfortable, and safe in expressing and living her Islamic identity.

Competing Constructions of Femininity

Deviating from the dominant discourses of sexualized femininity by wearing hijab and observing more modest dress codes meant situating oneself outside the socially accepted norms of behavior and dress for girls within mainstream public schools. For the Muslim girls interviewed, this was an act of resistance and non-conformity that often resulted in exclusion and social isolation. Yet this type of peer pressure is another powerful form of social control that levels sanctions against transgressing the socially constructed norms and expressions of feminine identity. Girls who did not subscribe to the latest fashions and did not wear revealing clothes to attract male attention were operating outside of the dominant discourse that regulated the representation of the female body.

In Islamic schools, Muslim girls confront a more conflicting set of standards for femininity and womanhood than those they encounter in public school. The normative standards of hegemonic religious views on gender, faith, and identity circumscribed their choices for expressing their sense of self and womanhood in radically different ways than did the secular, though also powerful, discourses of femininity in public schools. However, many girls found the Islamic constructions more conducive with the way they articulated their own sense of religious identity and gender, than the prevailing discourses of femininity they encountered in public schools. For example, from a feminist standpoint, they were opposed to the sexualization of women in popular culture and media and felt that this objectification of women detracted from being taken seriously for their intellect or spirituality. They embraced the veil as a marker of identity and act of worship, but also appreciated the way in which it gave them control over the male gaze.

From this standpoint, Muslim women take ownership of the veil as a means of regulating visual access to their bodies and limiting unwanted male sexual attention that they feel detracts from other aspects of their identity and selfhood. On the contrary however, it can be argued that the emphasis placed on covering the female form in effect limits the construction of women's bodies to a singular sexualized referent. In other words, the act of covering the body as a means of protection from the male gaze, also constructs women's bodies as solely sexual objects that need to be guarded and hidden so as not to attract sexual interest or attention.

The extent to which some girls attached their identities so intrinsically to the practice of veiling was disturbing. For example, Zarqa's reaction to my question regarding what it meant to be a Muslim was an immediate reference to veiling:

> I think it [being a Muslim] means to cover yourself. The main thing is to cover yourself, because um—where did I read it? A woman is a jewel. And when I hear Islam I think it's the most religious culture . . . I never used to see ladies wearing niqab and abayas and hijab and scarves. And now I see them so much. Like, I see them everywhere, like, on buses. And when I see that person, I see "that lady's Muslim." But you can never tell if you're not wearing hijab.

Zarqa highlights the visibility of the hijab as a marker of Islamic identity and applying the rationale often heard in lectures in the mosques about women and hijab, that a woman is like a precious jewel that one conceals because it is so valuable. This notion is further emphasized in the following remark by a Muslim woman participating in a recent study of Muslim veiling in North America.

> A woman is not a commodity or an object, but she is like [a] precious pearl. The oyster is the hijab that covers and protects it from the dangers of the sea. The pearl remains pure and untouched by any corruption. But it is the brutal nature of mankind that strips this treasured gem from its covering and places it for display or sells it for a price. (McDonough, 2003, p. 110)

Arguing powerfully against the commodification of women's bodies in society, this speaker nevertheless seems oblivious to the fact that she may be trading one discourse of subjugation for another, as her view is rationalized by a similar attempt to regulate women's bodies and sexuality to suit a different set of patriarchal norms and expectations. Whether the intent is to exhibit women's bodies in order to satiate the male gaze or to cover women's bodies in order to inhibit male desires, both realities force women to cater to specific patriarchal demands.

CHALLENGING GENDERED ISLAMOPHOBIA

Muslim girls were consciously and actively challenging some of the stereotypes that governed the way their identities were represented. In my own schooling experience as an undergraduate university student, I recall an anthropology professor who, after I had spoken out forcefully on a particular issue being discussed in class, remarked that he was "surprised" that I spoke so strongly since he expected me to be very "shy and demure." It was obvious that his assumption was based on the way that he read my body at the time as a veiled Muslim woman and the negative meanings and connotations with which my body had become discursively inscribed. Muslim women were not "supposed" to be intelligent, forthright, and outspoken, and therefore my speech created a dissonance in the mind of this professor who saw me from the perspective of dominant stereotypes that rendered me as "oppressed" and without voice or agency.

Some Muslim girls in the Al-Rajab school also were challenging these negatively essentialized constructions. In particular, when I was teaching in the Al Rajab Islamic school, I had arranged for some of my students to make oral presentations to the rest of the school in an assembly. We were examining women and migrancy and the sexual violence and harassment that many female refugees often face when they flee their homelands. Rehana, a 19-year-old student of Pakistani descent, delivered a powerful speech that addressed issues of rape and gendered violence. As she was preparing, I asked her if she felt comfortable speaking about these issues since the assembly would include male students and teachers. Rehana reassured me that she did not feel it was problematic for her to raise these issues since she felt strongly that they needed to be addressed and we could not afford to be shy about it. She reported that her mother had some concerns over the content of her speech, which she argued was necessary for her to make, since as a "niqabi"[8] it was always necessary for her to engage in ways that would challenge people's preconceptions of her:

> My mom said "Why do you have to talk about this?" And I'm like, no, you have to be open about what you want to say, or else you are just like the stereotype: quiet, you just see two eyes, you don't see anything else. But you have to go against the stereotype!

The type of gendered Islamophobia that Muslim women encounter, therefore structures particular counter-responses that openly challenge these constructions.

Muslim girls, therefore, face multiple challenges within the constructions of their gendered identities, being subject to patriarchal forms of regulation relating to their body and dress within the Muslim community, on the one hand, and negative stereotypes and gendered Islamophobia within mainstream society, on the other. Within the competing paradigms that dogmatically attempt to structure their identities, these young women struggle to determine a sense of agency, spirituality, and belonging within the discursive parameters of faith, community, and nation. These young women consistently located their strength and resistance within a framework of faith. Creating an alternate space for the articulation of Muslim female identity that resists both patriarchal fundamentalism and secular Islamophobia is a contemporary challenge for Muslim women negotiating the complex epistemological and ontological terrain of race, ethnicity, religion, and gender. By centering the voices and struggle of these young Muslim women, we can begin to see them as actors who at times reinforce traditional norms and at other times act in ways that begin to redefine the terrain of gender, faith, and identity.

NOTES

1. All school names and participant names are identified using pseudonyms to protect the anonymity of participants.
2. Hadith refer to the sayings of the Prophet Muhammed and, next to the Qur'an, form the primary corpus of Islamic knowledge providing guidance for daily life as well as the moral and ethical basis for Islamic legal codes.
3. The idea of the "dangerous feminine" is evoked in some Islamic discourses that regard women's bodies as sites of temptation that are in need of containment. Mernissi (1987) describes this as the result of a belief in the passive nature of female sexuality versus the active notion of male sexuality, placing the burden upon women to avoid provocation by employing restrictive dress codes and seclusion.
4. Hijabat is a plural feminine noun denoting the cohort of girls in one study who all wore the hijab or headscarf.
5. Academic "streams" in the Canadian context are the same as "tracks" in American schools.
6. A shalwar Kameez is a traditional South Asian form of dress which consists of a long tunic worn over baggy trousers.
7. The term "TTC" is used as an acronym by Torontonians to refer to the public transit system of buses, subways, and streetcars known as the Toronto Transit Commission.
8. The term niqabi is used among Muslim women to refer to women who adopt the niqab or face veil.

REFERENCES

Abou El Fadl, K. (2001). *Speaking in God's name: Islamic law, authority and women.* Oxford, UK: Oneworld.

Ahmed, L. (1992). *Women and gender in Islam.* New Haven, CT: Yale University Press.

Bullock, K.H. (2000). The gaze and colonial plans for the unveiling of Muslim women. *Studies in Contemporary Islam, 2*(2), 1–20.

Bullock, K. H. (2002). *Rethinking Muslim women and the veil: Challenging historical & modern stereotypes.* Herndon, VA: International Institute of Islamic Thought.

El Guindi, F. (1999). *Veil: Modesty, privacy and resistance.* London: Berg.

El Habti, R. (2004). Laicite, women's rights and the headscarf issue in France. Retrieved December 23, 2005, from: http://www.karamah.org/docs/veil_paper.pdf

Gutmann, A. (1996). Challenges of multiculturalism in democratic education. In R. K. Fullwider (Ed.), *Public education in a multicultural society: Policy, theory, critique* (pp. 156–179). Cambridge: Cambridge University Press.

Hajjaji-Jarrah, S. (2003). Women's modesty in Qur'anic commentaries: The founding discourse. In S. S. Alvi, H. Hoodfar, & S. McDonough (Eds.), *The Muslim veil in North America: Issues and debates* (pp. 145–180). Toronto: Women's Press.

Halstead, M. (1991). Radical feminism, Islam and the single sex school debate. *Gender and Education, 3*(3), 263–278.

Hamdani, D. (2004). *Triple jeopardy: Muslim women's experiences of discrimination.* Retrieved October 2, 2005, from: http://www.ccmw.com/publications/Reports/Triple_Jeopardy.pdf

Hoodfar, H. (1993). The veil in their minds and on our heads: The persistence of colonial images of Muslim women. *Resources for Feminist Research*, 22(Fall/Winter), 5–18.

Hoodfar, H. (2003). More than clothing: Veiling as an adaptive strategy. In S. S. Alvi, H. Hoodfar, & S. McDonough (Eds.), *Muslim veil in North America: Issues and debates* (pp. 3–40). Toronto: Women's Press.

Keung, N. (2002). The hijab and the job hunt. *Toronto Star*, p. A-27.

Khan, S. (2003, September 26). Why does a headscarf have us tied up in knots? *Globe and Mail*, Op Ed.

Lazreg, M. (1994). *The eloquence of silence: Algerian women in question.* New York: Routledge.

Lenk, H. M. (2000). The case of Emile Ouimet: News discourse on hijab and the construction of Quebecois national identity. In G. J. Sefa Dei & A. Calliste (Eds.), *Antiracist feminism*. Halifax: Fernwood Press.

McDonough, S. (2003). Perceptions of hijab in Canada. In S. S. Alvi, H. Hoodfar, & S. McDonough (Eds.), *The Muslim veil in North America: Issues and debates* (pp. 121–142). Toronto: Women's Press.

Mernissi, F. (1987). *Beyond the veil: Male-female relationships in modern Muslim society.* Bloomington: Indiana State University Press.

Mernissi, F. (1991). *The veil and the male elite: A feminist interpretation of women's rights in Islam* (M-J. Lakeland, trans.). Reading, MA: Addison-Wesley.

Misbahuddin, K. (1996). The lingering hijab question. *The Message*, 21(3), 29.

Mohanty, C. T. (1991). Under Western eyes: Feminist scholarship and colonial discourses. In C. T. Mohanty & A. Russo (Eds.), *Third would women and the politics of feminism* (pp. 51–74). Indianapolis: University of Indiana Press.

Parker-Jenkins, M. (1999). Islam, Gender and Discrimination in the Workplace. Paper presented to the Nationalism, Identity and Minority Rights: Sociological and Political Perspective Conference, University of Bristol, United Kingdom.

Read, J. G., & Bartkowski, J. P. (2000). To veil or not to veil?: A case study of identity negotiation among Muslim women in Austin, Texas. *Gender and Society*, 14(3), 395–417.

Roald, A. S. (2001). *Women in Islam: The Western experience.* London: Routledge.

Said, E. W. (1979). *Orientalism*. New York: Vintage Books.

Sarroub, L. K. (2005). *All American Yemeni girls: Being Muslim in a public school.* Philadelphia: University of Pennsylvania Press.

Smith, G. (2002). Muslim garb a liability in job market, study finds. *Globe and Mail*, p. A-10.

Todd, S. (1999). Veiling the "Other," unveiling ourselves: Reading media images of the hijab psychoanalytically to move beyond tolerance. *Canadian Journal of Education*, 23(4), 438–451.

Zine, J. (2000). Redefining resistance: Toward an Islamic subculture in schools. *Race, Ethnicity and Education*, 31(2), 293–316.

Zine, J. (2001). Muslim youth in Canadian schools: Education and the politics of religious identity. *Anthropology and Education Quarterly*, 32(4) 399–423.

Zine, J. (2002). Muslim women and the politics of representation. *American Journal of Islamic Social Sciences*, 19(4), 1–22.

Zine, J. (2003). Dealing with September 12: Integrative antiracism and the challenge of anti-Islamophobia education. *Orbit*, 33(3), 39–41.

Zine J., & Bullock, K. H. (2002). Editorial. *American Journal of Islamic Social Sciences*, 19(4), i–iii.

Sexualities Worldwide

Charmaine Pereira and *Priya Kandaswamy*

Charmaine Pereira is a feminist scholar-activist whose research and writing spans issues of sexuality, feminist thought and practice, gender and university education, and civil society and the state. Based in Abuja, she coordinates the Initiative for Women's Studies in Nigeria (IWSN), which strengthens capacity for teaching and research in gender and women's studies. As IWSN national coordinator, she oversees action research programs on the politics of sexual harassment and sexual violence in universities, gender justice and women's citizenship, and women's empowerment. She is the author of *Gender in the Making of the Nigerian University System* (James Currey/Partnership for Higher Education in Africa, 2007).

Priya Kandaswamy is an assistant professor of women's studies at Portland State University, USA. Her research and teaching interests examine articulations of race, gender, sexuality, and class in such contemporary issues as globalization, immigration, the welfare system, the criminal justice system, and violence against women. Her published work examines the racial politics of same-sex marriage recognition, the relationship between domestic violence and state violence, and approaches to antiracist pedagogy in U.S. universities. She is currently working on a book that is a comparative historical analysis of the U.S. welfare state's efforts to regulate women of color's labor and sexuality.

> Speak earth and bless me with what is richest
> make sky flow honey out of my hips
> rigid as mountains
> spread over a valley
> carved out by the mouth of rain.

Excerpt from "Love Poem" by Audre Lorde

This excerpt from Audre Lorde's "Love Poem" describes the pleasure, freedom, and power many women find in their sexualities. Written in the early 1970s, Lorde's publisher originally refused to publish the poem because of its lesbian erotic content. However, as a black, lesbian, feminist activist, and artist in the United States, Lorde refused to isolate sexuality from other issues of social justice and insisted that true freedom must include sexual freedom. Her work reflects the ways that sexuality is embedded in and shaped by multiple kinds of difference such as race, class, gender, age, and ability.

This chapter focuses on women's sexualities in a global context. While often thought of as an individual concern, an array of structural forces such as law, cultural norms, media, economic conditions, religion, and family organization shape women's sexual identities and practices in historically and geographically specific ways. Rather than being confined to the private sphere, ideas about sexuality permeate many different aspects of women's lives ranging from the work they do to the kinds of intimate relationships they have. For women, sexuality is a site of pleasure and personal expression as well as a site of intense regulation and social control. Often, whether or not a woman is seen as a "good" woman hinges upon perceptions of her sexuality, and most cultures hold men and women to very different standards when it comes to sexual behavior. Moreover, religious, nationalist, and imperialist interests often assert control over women's sexuality. For example, religious fundamentalist movements from the Christian Right in the United States to the Taliban in Afghanistan advocate limiting women's sexual freedom. Similarly, controlling women's sexuality is often seen as important to national interests, often by casting women as mothers of the nation or as sexual possessions to be protected. Colonial and neocolonial forces frequently justify occupation on the basis that imperialism (and the supposed "modernization" associated with it) brings greater sexual freedom for women. One example of this is the way that the George W. Bush administration framed the U.S. invasion of Afghanistan as an effort to liberate Afghani women. Ironically, this same administration simultaneously advocated for sexually conservative policies within the United States such as limiting access to abortion and sex education. These examples illustrate that questions, as wide ranging as how "beauty" is defined, what women should wear, with whom they can sleep, and what kinds of birth control are available to them, have tremendous political significance. The fact that controlling women's sexuality has so much symbolic value in global politics makes the expression of sexual identity more complex for individual women around the world. This suggests that the struggle for sexual freedom must be situated within a larger struggle for social justice.

The following sections address key concepts and themes in sexual politics worldwide. The chapter begins by exploring how colonialism, nationalism, and new forms of globalization set the stage for contemporary conflicts over sexuality. The next section explores the role of gender in social constructions of sexuality and focuses on sexual identities worldwide. The third section addresses three specific political conflicts over sexuality and globalization: (1) pornography; (2) sex trafficking; and (3) sex tourism. The chapter closes by looking at activist strategies for promoting sexual freedom at local, national, and international levels such as using sexuality education as a tool to empower girls and framing sexual rights as a human rights issue.

COLONIALISM, NATIONALISM, AND GLOBALIZATION

Colonialism, nationalism, and globalization have played significant roles in shaping sexual politics and curtailing women's sexual freedom. As already discussed, although colonialism is not a unified process but rather varies greatly over time and space, it can generally be understood as a system of rule in which one nation occupies and controls land that belongs to a different group of people. Under colonialism, colonized people are denied political, economic, and cultural autonomy. They are not allowed to participate fully in their own governance; their economic resources and labor are exploited for the profits of the colonizing group; and their indigenous cultures are devalued and often destroyed. European colonialism dramatically transformed the world, and the idea that Europeans were bringing civilization to "backward" parts of the world and that it was the "white man's burden" to educate and reform the "uncivilized" natives often rationalized colonial violence. While colonialism is usually thought of as an economic, political, and cultural system, it is also a system of organizing sexual power. Colonialism is an assault on the sexual autonomy of colonized people, and the sexual norms and beliefs associated with colonialism continue to shape global sexual politics and women's sexual lives today.

Colonization as a process requires the construction of a fundamental difference between the colonizers and the colonized. Ideas about sexuality play an important role in the construction of this dichotomy. Precolonial societies had diverse sexual norms and varied a great deal in the social meanings they ascribed to sexuality. When European explorers and colonists encountered this diversity, they understood it not on its own terms but rather saw these societies as both "exotic" and "backwards" in relation to European sexual norms. A key concept in the rationalization of colonialism was the idea that colonization and European influence would "civilize" colonized people. In this framework, one of the markers of civilization was conformity to heteropatriarchal gender norms (with "hetero" implying sexual relations between women and men and "patriarchal" concerning male power over women). In other words, the level of "progress" of a society was measured by how well people conformed to European ideas of masculinity and femininity and the extent to which societies enforced compulsory heterosexuality and sexual restraint. This linking of sexual difference and colonial difference normalized European ideas of sexuality as the most progressive and civilized and at the same time reinforced the depiction of colonized peoples as backwards and racially inferior. In the reading "Toward a Vision of Sexual and Economic Justice," Kamala Kempadoo discusses the long histories of colonialism in the Caribbean and makes the case that these histories have important consequences for sexual-economic relations.

As Andrea Smith (2005) has argued in the context of the colonization of the Americas, sexual violence and the depiction of colonized peoples as sexually depraved and sinful is fundamental to colonial projects. Noting parallels between the colonization of the land and the colonization of women's bodies, Smith argues that colonialism fundamentally relies upon the denial of native people's bodily integrity. Smith's work also points to the ways that colonialism required a reorganization of sexual relationships within Native American communities. Colonizers forced gendered and sexual hierarchies onto Native American communities as a way of naturalizing the hierarchies inherent in colonialism. For example, by sending Native American children to boarding schools where they were taught to perform heteronormative gender roles and subjected to intense forms of sexual violence, colonizers devalued sexual relationships that were not organized around heteropatriarchy and promoted sexual violence within Native American communities.

In response to colonial rule, nationalist movements that asserted the rights of colonized people to independence proliferated in Africa, Asia, and the Caribbean in the post–World War II era. While most of these movements were eventually successful in securing formal political independence, nationalist movements within particular countries did not necessarily secure greater sexual autonomy for women. Rather, because women are often seen as the "mothers of the nation" and bearers of future citizens, controlling women's sexuality and reproduction is viewed as vital to maintaining the purity and sanctity of the nation. In addition, women are often symbolically associated with national culture, adding more weight to the claim that controlling women's sexual morality is a question of national concern. In her work on the Bahamas and Trinidad and Tobago, M. Jacqui Alexander (1997) notes nationalism has been defined by the assertion of a black masculinity that seeks to control black female sexuality. Alexander points out that officials of the newly independent state have responded to colonial representations of colonized people as sexually depraved by asserting their own sexual respectability rather than critiquing the racist ways sexual respectability has been defined by colonial powers. This mimicry of colonial sexual norms has led to the criminalization of gays and lesbians. Ironically, the governments of the Bahamas and Trinidad and Tobago have simultaneously been willing to adopt policies that facilitate sex tourism because of the economic benefits associated with it. This illustrates the contradictory ways that nation-states selectively police sexual morality in relation to other interests.

Despite significant efforts at decolonization, the global inequalities engendered by colonialism persist. Multinational corporations and countries in the Global North profit greatly from the uneven capitalist development that is a legacy of colonialism, and many see global economic restructuring as simply an extension of colonial power. In particular, massive "Third World" debt and structural adjustment programs (SAPs) that require countries to simultaneously cut social services, reduce trade barriers, and encourage foreign investment have had devastating effects on women. While these effects are most frequently discussed in economic terms, globalization also significantly impacts women's sexual lives as sexuality is inseparable from the larger contexts in which women live. Militarism is another enduring legacy of the colonial era. Particularly, countries like the United States continue to maintain a strong military presence around the world, and U.S. military bases remain some of the most pronounced sites of racialized sexual exploitation of women (Enloe, 1989).

Globalization shapes sexuality in a number of different ways, many of which are discussed in more detail later in this chapter. First, globalization influences the kinds of sexual identities that people adopt and craft. While identities are often thought of as stable, fixed, and historical entities that people have, they are in fact dynamic, fluid, and historically and geographically specific constructs that people perform. In particular, the power relations experienced by individuals affect the ways they perform these identities. And, although globalization is often seen as producing cultural homogenization (sameness) or a one-way movement of culture from the West to the non-West, the reality is much more complicated. Globalization constrains people's sexual expression and practices by normalizing particular sexual identities, delegitimizing and sometimes eradicating local culture, and commodifying sexuality. However, globalization also produces various forms of resistance and enables new kinds of identities to circulate that people may adopt and employ in inventive ways. Second, the economic transformations engendered by globalization have led to the increasing demand for women's sexual labor. As discussed later in the chapter, globalization has produced growth both in sex tourism and in the migration of women to places where the sex industry thrives. Third, globalization has meant the more rapid circulation of cultural representations of sexuality, especially as media have become more global in their reach. As racialized and gendered representations of sexuality circulate more widely, they spark conflicts over standards of beauty, the commodification of women's sexuality, and the objectification of women.

Fourth, nationalist and fundamentalist leaders often mobilize the social anxieties produced by the rapid changes and mounting inequalities in the global economy into campaigns to control women's sexuality. In particular, because women are often thought of as the bearers of national or religious traditions, they are often highly visible targets when conflicts become framed simplistically as struggles between modernity and tradition. An example of this can be seen in the adoption of laws that mandate that women wear the veil in countries like Saudi Arabia and Iran. As Marie Aimée Hélie-Lucas (2003) notes, states are often quick to concede laws seeking to control women's sexuality to Islamic fundamentalist movements opposing the Western influence globalization is seen as bringing. However, these same states may simultaneously embrace the capitalist economic policies engendered by such globalization, illustrating how easily women's sexual autonomy is sacrificed. Conversely, in the West, the case of France's 2004 law that bans girls from wearing veils to school demonstrates again how women's bodies become the terrain on which struggles to define national identity are worked out. In this case (as in the reading in the previous chapter), French secular identity is being asserted in the face of increasing numbers of migrants from North Africa. The French law reframes a complicated social question into a reductive conflict between "modern" French identity and "traditional" Muslim identity that centers on what women and girls wear. Both Islamic fundamentalist and French secularist governments are inattentive to the multiple and complex meanings veiling has for Muslim women and ignore how veiling might function as an expression of women's agency.

Finally, globalization facilitates the possibility of the formation of new kinds of transnational coalitions around sexual politics and sexual identities. All of these ways that globalization shapes sexual politics suggest that sexuality is inseparable from the other dimensions of women's lives and that any discussion of sexuality must take into account how power relations are organized in the different historical and geographical contexts in which different women live.

SEXUAL EXPRESSIONS

Sexual practices are shaped by social norms, values, guidelines, rules, and customs, which act as "sexual scripts" presenting culturally available patterns of sexual activity. There are multiple sexual scripts—hence "sexualities" in the plural. Sexual scripts vary across cultures worldwide and reflect various organizations of power in societies. Women's position in particular societies and the specific gendered expectations placed on them shape, and often constrain, how women express their sexualities. One aspect of gendered sexual politics concerns the practices of reproduction. As discussed in later chapters, the control of women's reproductive abilities occurs in families, in communities, and at the state level, as well as at international levels associated with population policies. The short story reading by Alifa Rifaat, "Distant View of a Minaret" also illustrates ideas about women's sexuality that affect and regulate their lives.

A final example of the effects of gendered power relations is illustrated in the example of female genital cutting (FGC), also discussed in other chapters. This practice is entwined with cultural constructions of sexuality in local communities as well as structural conditions like poverty (see sidebar). As discussed in the previous chapter, the physical modification of genitalia is a gendered practice that also occurs in the West.

A key aspect of how we define sexuality is sexual identity or orientation: whether an individual is attracted to the "opposite" sex (heterosexual) or "same" sex (homosexual) or both (bisexual). The term "lesbianism" refers to women's experience of, or desire for, sexual relations with other women. Men who desire sexual relations with other men often refer to themselves as "gay," although this is often treated as a generic term that may be used to describe women too. It is important to recognize that not all people who have same-sex relations overtly identify as "lesbian" or "gay" and that these terms emerged from the West to describe a particular historical set of experiences. In some parts of the world, people who refuse stable identity categories like homosexual, lesbian, and gay use the term "queer." Queer reclaims the pejorative meaning of the word in celebration of an alternative nonheterosexual identity. The term provides opportunities for greater sexual diversity and expression by challenging the belief in a fixed relationship between gender and sexuality. Individuals who take up queer identities do so to challenge the normalization inherent in the identity categories themselves. Cathy Cohen (1997) argues

Berhane Ras-Work

For more than 25 years, Ethiopian native Berhane Ras-Work has labored to end traditional practices that are harmful to women and girls, especially female genital cutting (FGC) or female genital mutilation (FGM). The World Health Organization defines FGM as including "all procedures involving partial or total removal of the female external genitalia or other injury to the female genital organs for non-medical reasons."[1]

In 1984, Berhane helped to organize the Intra-African Committee on Traditional Practices Affecting the Health of Women and Children (IAC) that she now heads. Under her leadership, the organization has worked with 14 African countries to adopt legislation against FGC and other harmful traditional practices. The IAC also provides education to women about the harmful effects of FGC

According to Berhane, more than 130 million girls and women have undergone FGC, and another two million are at risk each year. The practice continues, she explains, because it is an unquestioned tradition. She adds, "The underlying factor is of course the economic vulnerability of women, the subordinate status attributed to women, ignorance about their bodies, the functions of their bodies, and ignorance of their rights. So they have accepted this. It is the subordination of women and their unequal power relations with men. That is the underlying factor. FGM is a manifestation of the unequal relationships whereby women have to sacrifice a part of themselves in order to be marriageable, in order to be accepted."[2]

Prevalence of FGM/C Among Younger and Older Women

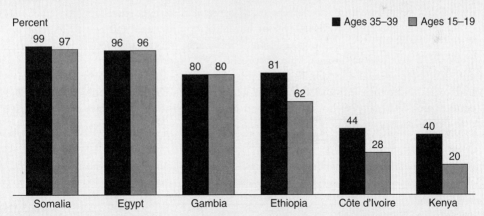

Source: Population Reference Bureau, *Female Genital Mutilation/Cutting: Data and Trends* (2008). http://www.prb.org/Articles/2009/fgmc.aspx

In 1995, the UN awarded Berhane its population award for her work with the IAC, and in 2005 she was a top 10 nominee for the Perdita Huston Human Rights Award.

To learn more about FGC, visit the World Health Organization's web site at http://www.who.int/ reproductive-health/fgm/. Also read the reports on the Sexual Violence Research Initiative's site at http://www.svri.org/female.htm.

[1] Source: http://www.who.int/reproductive-health/fgm/
[2] Source: http://www.plusnews.org/report.aspx?reportid=36590

that the radical potential of queer politics is often undermined by the construction of a rigid dichotomy between heterosexual and queer people. Cohen points out that failure to take into consideration other differences such as race and class has led to the centering of white, economically privileged experiences within queer activism in the United States and the marginalization of working class queers and queer people of color. Taken in a global context, Cohen's argument also suggests the importance of considering national and cultural differences. In particular, categories developed in the West cannot simply be extrapolated to describe the experiences of people in other parts of the world.

Heterosexuality is the dominant norm in most contemporary societies. The normalization and naturalization of heterosexuality are referred to as heteronormativity. Heteronormativity shapes women's experiences of sexuality (whether they are heterosexual or not) in that it is underpinned by patriarchy and linked to the objectification of women, the policing of female sexuality, and violence against women in many regions of the world. As discussed earlier, race also plays a large role in shaping how women experience their sexuality. For example, African and Afro-Caribbean women's sexuality has been constructed as licentious and promiscuous. Similarly, representations of Asian women are also often highly sexualized, frequently depicting them either as sexually submissive and passive or as conniving and threatening "dragon ladies." In other words, the power relations that shape compulsory heterosexuality cannot be understood without recognizing how racialized ideas about gender are implicated in the social construction of sexuality.

The term homophobia means fear or hatred of homosexuals and is used to refer to the violence and bigotry facing gays, lesbians, bisexuals, queers, and people who do not conform to heterosexual norms. Marc Epprecht (1996) questions the role of the state in enforcing heterosexual masculinity and highlights the relationship between homophobia and male dominance. Around the world, heads of state have made public statements condemning and vilifying homosexuals and homosexuality. In 2007, laws criminalizing non-penile-vaginal sexual acts were still found to exist in over 85 countries; most of these laws were remnants of European colonial rule. Punishments range, for example, from the

UNICEF Fact Sheet: Female Genital Mutilation/Cutting

Female genital mutilation/cutting (FGM/C) refers to all procedures involving partial or total removal of the external genitalia or other injuries to the female genital organs for cultural or other reasons that are not medical necessities. FGM/C reinforces the inequality suffered by girls and women and is a violation of universally recognized human rights—including the rights to bodily integrity and to the highest attainable standard of physical and mental health. While health consequences vary, they commonly include failure to heal, inflammatory diseases, and urinary infections. Gynecological complications that result from female genital mutilation/cutting can become particularly serious during and after childbirth, and include fistula. Increased susceptibility to HIV infection is a concern. The pain of the procedure is known to cause shock and long-lasting trauma, and severe bleeding and infection can lead to death.

The reasons for FGM/C are many and complex, but the most significant seems to be the belief that a girl who has not undergone the procedure will not be considered suitable for marriage. Traditionally, FGM/C is performed by local practitioners, most of whom are women. In some countries, efforts have been made to "medicalize" the procedure by having medical staff perform it in or outside of hospitals. This does not, however, make it less a violation of human rights, and communities should be helped to abandon the practice.

FACTS AND FIGURES

- FGM/C occurs mainly in countries along a belt stretching from Senegal in West Africa to Somalia in East Africa and to Yemen in the Middle East, but it is also practiced in some parts of southeast Asia. Reports from Europe, North America, and Australia indicate that it is practiced among immigrant communities as well.[1]
- It is estimated that more than 130 million women and girls alive today have been subjected to female genital mutilation/cutting.

- FGM/C is generally carried out on girls between the ages of 4 and 14; it is also performed on infants, women who are about to get married, and, sometimes, women who are pregant with their first child or who have just given birth.
- Most recent Demographic Health Survey data for Egypt indicate that the prevalence rate among ever-married women aged 15–49 has shown a slight decline from 97 percent to 96 percent.[2]

HUMAN RIGHTS

There are many international treaties and conventions that condemn harmful practices. They include the Convention on the Rights of the Child (1989), the Convention on the Elimination of All Forms of Discrimination against Women (1979), the African Charter on the Rights and Welfare of the Child (1990). A specific focus on female genital mutilation/cutting is found in UN General Assembly Resolution 56/128 on Traditional or Customary Practices Affecting the Health of Women and Girls (2001) and in the Protocol on the Rights of Women in Africa, or Maputo Protocol (2003).

MILLENNIUM DEVELOPMENT GOALS

FGM/C is a violation of the physical and psychosexual integrity of girls and inherently contradicts gender equality (MDG 3). One of the many negative health implications is an increased chance of death during childbirth, thus impeding efforts to reduce maternal mortality (MDG 5). Some studies also show a higher vulnerability to HIV/AIDS among girls who have been subjected to FGM/C, meaning that the practice hampers efforts to halt and reverse the spread of AIDS (MDG 6).

Notes

1. Unless otherwise indicated, data are from United Nations Children's Fund, *Female Genital Mutilation/Cutting: A statistical exploration 2005*, UNICEF, New York, 2005.
2. UNICEF, <http://www.childinfo.org/areas/fgmc/profiles.php>. Data from preliminary report.

death penalty in Afghanistan, to being sent to labor camps in Angola and Mozambique, to imprisonment for ten to fifteen years for offenses involving sexual acts between women in Trinidad and Tobago. Even in countries that do not enforce these laws, their continued existence creates a climate of state-sanctioned bigotry and violence.

Responses to homophobia have been varied. In 1996, for example, when President Sam Nujoma of Namibia condemned gays and lesbians in his address to the Women's Council Congress of the South West Africa People's Organization (SWAPO), he was challenged. While they did not identify as lesbians themselves, the SWAPO Women's Council Congress illustrates the diverse grounds for solidarity between heterosexual women and gays and lesbians. Elsewhere in Africa, organized action against homophobia spurred the adoption of the 2004 Johannesburg Statement on Sexual Orientation, Gender Identity and Human Rights. This statement was formulated and adopted by a meeting of African lesbian, gay, bisexual, and transgender organizations from sixteen African countries across the continent. In May 2008, Cuban lesbian and gay rights activists launched a campaign against homophobia chaired by the director of the Cuban Centre for Sexual Education, Mariela Castro, daughter of President Raul Castro. Cuba's parliament is working on proposals to legalize same-sex marriage and give gay couples the same rights as heterosexual couples. In South Korea, the advent of a new ultraconservative head of state, President Lee, has led to increased strategizing by lesbian, gay, bisexual, transgender, and queer (LGBTQ) activists on the government's antidiscrimination bill. The bill removes seven categories protected by the country's National Human Rights Commission Act, including sexual orientation.

LEARNING ACTIVITY **Queer Rights Activism Around the World**

Around the world, various organizations are advocating for human rights for lesbian, gay, bisexual, transgender, intersex, and queer people. Check out the organizations below.

- What is the organization's mission?
- What does the organization identify as problems faced by LGBTQI people around the world?
- What actions does the organization suggest you can take to advocate for human rights for LGBTQI people?

International Gay and Lesbian Human Rights Commission www.iglhrc.org
The Human Rights Campaign www.hrc.org
The International Lesbian and Gay Association www.ilga.org
The National Gay and Lesbian Task force www.thetaskforce.org
Gay Straight Alliance Network International www.gsani.org
The Lesbian and Gay Equality Project www.equality.org.za
Parents, Families, and Friends of Lesbians and Gays www.pflag.org
Rainbow Alliance of the Bahamas www.bahamianglad.tripod.com
Allied Rainbow Communities International www.arc-international.net
Society Against Sexual Orientation Discrimination www.sasod.org.gy
Gender/Sexuality Rights Association Taiwan www.gsrat.net
Australian Coalition for Equality www.coalitionforequality.org.au
The Swedish Federation for Lesbian, Gay, Bisexual, and Transgender Rights www.rfsl.se
The Pink Cross www.pinkcross.ch

LGBTQ activists formed the Alliance Against Homophobia and Discrimination Against Sexual Minorities, which is currently working with human rights lawyers to propose a new antidiscrimination bill.

In some countries, homophobic violence has most recently been categorized as a hate crime: a crime motivated by a deep prejudice, hatred, and/or hostility by perpetrators toward a particular social group identity. The Gay British Crime Survey has shown that one in five lesbians and gay men has been a victim of one or more homophobic hate crimes or incidents in the last three years. Seventy-five percent of these victims did not report the incidents to the police because they believed the police would not take homophobic hate crimes seriously. Incidents ranged from regular insults on the street and bullying at work to serious physical and sexual assaults. Although gay men were over two and a half times more likely to be a victim of a physical assault than lesbians, the latter were more likely than gay men to experience a hate crime committed by someone they knew, either someone living locally or a work colleague. Large numbers of lesbians and gays experience incidents that involve homophobic abuse, vandalism, and other acts designed to intimidate and scare them. Homophobic hate crimes can occur anywhere, including in the home and around locations identified with lesbians and gays such as bars and restaurants. Many homophobic hate incidents involve sexual assaults or other forms of unwanted sexual contact. Twice as many black and ethnic minority lesbians and gays experienced a physical assault as a homophobic hate incident than was the case for the sample overall (Dick, 2008).

SEXUAL POLITICS

As discussed in other chapters, the rapidly unfolding processes of change associated with economic and cultural globalization have had complex and contradictory effects worldwide. Globalization has resulted in increased exploitation of women at the same time that it has facilitated a strengthening of social movements and coalitions for global change. This section addresses the ways the forces of globalization influence the politics of sexuality, or relations of power associated with sexuality. It focuses specifically on the issues of pornography, sex trafficking, and sex tourism.

Pornography

Defining pornography is complex. At its broadest, pornography involves explicit representations of sex that objectify performers (usually women) and that are generally produced with the aim of sexually arousing its users, the majority of whom are male. Many feminists believe the production, distribution, and consumption of pornography perpetuate violence against women and maintain their sexual subordination (Mason-Grant, 2007). Such analyses tend to assume a homogeneous category of women, ignoring the ways sexualized representations of women vary greatly in relation to race. Pornographic images of white women, for example, do not invoke the same racialized power structures that pornographic images of black women invoke. As Patricia Hill Collins (1997) notes, black women tend to be represented as primitive and animalistic within pornography, and these representations resonate very strongly with the racist images of black women that proliferated during colonialism and slavery.

Pornography is an approximately US$60 billion global capitalist industry that trades in representations of female bodies through cable channels, Internet service providers, and

LEARNING ACTIVITY   ## Case Study—"Radical Feminism in Political Action: The Minneapolis Pornography Ordinance"

Go to the University of Minnesota's Center on Women and Public Policy to find a case study by Emily Warren on the Minneapolis pornography ordinance: http://www.hhh.umn.edu/centers/wpp/case_studies.html#ew. After reading the case and its epilogue, go to the teaching note and answer the questions about the case.

"In the city of Minneapolis, in the early 1980s, a series of events occurred that would throw this progressive city into the national spotlight. The mayor of Minneapolis, Don Fraser, had to decide whether or not to veto a proposed ordinance that contained a novel approach to the problem of pornography. Frustrated by the increasing number of adult entertainment businesses in Minneapolis, local feminists and community activists decided to fight back. Members of the community felt that the increased visibility of pornography in Minneapolis was a threat to women and caused neighborhood devaluation and decay. They enlisted the help of radical feminists Catharine MacKinnon and Andrea Dworkin, who were living in Minneapolis while teaching at the University of Minnesota. MacKinnon and Dworkin wrote a controversial ordinance for the city that defined pornography as sex discrimination in violation of a woman's civil rights. The ordinance included a broad new definition of pornography that some thought impinged upon the constitutional right to free expression. This case study looks at the contents of the ordinance, and the events in Minneapolis that led to the ordinance's creation. It also examines the relationship between First Amendment rights and the rights of women to be safe from sexual violence."

magazine and print distributors (Sarikakis and Shaukat, 2007). Like other forms of production, the production of pornography is shifting toward countries with low labor costs and little state regulation because these economic conditions favor producers. Currently, the most popular site for the production of pornographic materials is the Philippines. Sarikakis and Shaukat point to the increased interlinking of pornography, prostitution, and trafficking that creates a complex system of exploitation feeding the global sex industry. For women in these industries, the boundaries between violence, pornography, and prostitution are often blurred, and forced sexual performances and rape are becoming more normalized in the mainstream as well as in the more marginalized parts of the pornography industry. Women (at increasingly younger ages) face considerable pressure to give ever more graphic performances. These coercive conditions are at odds with the notion that pornography merely represents the fantasies of consumers and the free choice of women involved. Much attention has been focused on the question of whether pornography causes rape— a question that is impossible to answer. However, many scholars agree that pornography is implicated in sexual violence against women and children, while reinforcing a larger system of misogyny, or woman-hating.

Governments have predominantly responded to pornography in terms of legislation focusing either on questions of (a) decency and obscenity, and (b) harm to minors. The first type of legislation attempts to deal with what constitutes indecent or obscene material and is targeted at the censorship of pornographic products on the basis of morality. Ironically, laws such as these have been used to target erotic material aimed at lesbians and gays, and in Canada and Ireland, such laws have been used to censor material on abortion and women's reproduction. The second type of legislation is concerned with minors' access to pornographic material and is rooted in both the belief that exposure to pornography corrupts young people and that minors are abused in the production of pornography. Underlying both kinds of legislative response is the debate about free speech and censorship. Some who oppose pornography support censorship laws on the basis that violence inherent in pornography is damaging to women and society as a whole. Others oppose the use of censorship laws to regulate pornography since these laws are used against women and sexual minorities and may stifle public debate about sexuality. Indeed, neither censorship nor free speech provides an adequate framework to deal with the complex and multiple issues arising from the production, consumption, and culture of pornography. Importantly, they argue that poverty and inequality across the globe facilitate women's exploitation in pornography. As a result, they emphasize that legislation must focus on the context in which pornography is produced, including such factors as why and how women become involved, and the conditions of their employment. The voices of women working in the pornography industry globally are currently a significant absence in debates about the issue. These perspectives should be at the center of any political action taken around pornography.

Sex Trafficking

The United Nations Protocol to Prevent, Suppress and Punish Trafficking in Persons adopted in 2001 defines human trafficking as follows:

> "Trafficking in persons" shall mean the recruitment, the transportation, transfer, harboring or receipt of persons, by means of threat or use of force or other forms of coercion, of abduction, of fraud, of deception, of the abuse of power or of a position of vulnerability or of the giving or receiving of payments or benefits to achieve the consent of a person having control over another person, for the purpose of exploitation. Exploitation shall include, at a minimum, the exploitation of the prostitution of others or other forms of sexual exploitation, forced labor or services, slavery or practices similar to slavery, servitude or the removal of organs (Raymond, 2002, p. 495).

Although not all human trafficking involves sexual labor, the concept of sex trafficking has received particularly heightened attention in recent years. Many speculate that this is not necessarily because sex trafficking is more prevalent or more violent than other forms of trafficking, but rather because of the way accounts sensationalize "Third world women" as helpless victims in need of saving (Doezema, 2001). In addition, much of the dominant discourse about trafficking is not grounded in solid empirical research that addresses the specificity of trafficked women's experiences, but instead simply reproduces already existing assumptions about its nature (Kempadoo, 2005; Sanghera, 2005). This is partly because of the difficulty of collecting accurate data about trafficked persons and partly because sex trafficking has become such an emotionally charged issued (UNESCO, 2008).

Because human trafficking is a clandestine activity, it is difficult to know exactly how many women and girls are trafficked. Estimates from different nongovernmental, governmental, and UN organizations cite the number of trafficking victims as anywhere between half to four million persons a year (UNESCO, 2008). This broad range indicates the paucity of accurate empirical knowledge about trafficking. One of the most comprehensive efforts to collect statistics has come from the U.S. State Department in conjunction with the passage of the Trafficking Victims Protection Act (TVPA) of 2000, which reported approximately 80 percent of trafficked persons are women and girls, and up to 50 percent are minors (U.S. State Department, 2005). These data, however, do not include the large number of individuals trafficked within national borders. In addition, while the report suggests the majority of women and girls trafficked are forced into sexual labor, the statistics lump together all forms of human trafficking.

While the structural causes of sex trafficking are complex and vary across regions, the dislocations caused by (1) globalization and poverty, and (2) war generally play a large role in shaping trafficking and migration patterns. First, global economic restructuring has undermined local economies by granting multinational corporations increased access to both local markets and local sources of labor that exacerbate poverty. These changes have also led to decreased opportunities for male employment and an increasing reliance on women as low wage workers within the global economy. As a result, women, particularly women of color, are increasingly expected to bear the social costs of globalization by working harder and surviving on less. Global economic changes associated with poverty shape trafficking patterns in the following ways. In response to globalization, many women decide to migrate to sell their labor. However, because of the many barriers to legal migration, women may consent to be trafficked into another country where they hope their earning possibilities might be increased. In addition, globalization has produced an increasing demand for highly exploitable workers in the industries into which women are most frequently trafficked. For example, the growth of sex tourism (discussed below) and the increasing reliance on immigrant women as domestic workers in "First World" countries has meant there is a high demand for trafficked workers in many regions. While antitrafficking discourse frequently focuses on the difficult conditions in a woman's place of origin, it is important to emphasize that trafficking is largely driven by this demand for vulnerable workers (Sanghera, 2005).

Second, countries that have been wracked by military conflict have also become sources of trafficked women, either because women are abducted in the conflict or because poverty and danger force them to search for work elsewhere. That armed conflict and trafficking in women are connected is becoming increasingly evident as criminal networks involved in the trade of arms and drugs expand to include trafficking in people. State agents are often complicit with networks of organized crime, and state corruption is an element that contributes to human trafficking. Trafficking has become "big business," constituting the third-largest source of profits for organized crime (after drugs and guns) with annual profits worldwide at between five and seven billion US dollars (Rehn and Johnson Sirleaf, 2002). However, it is important to note that trafficking is not exclusively (and given the lack of accurate data on trafficking, perhaps not even primarily) perpetrated by large-scale organized crime rings. Much trafficking occurs at a smaller scale, with recruiters drawing upon personal and familial relationships to facilitate the process. The reading "Cambodian Sex Workers" by Karoline Kemp discusses the ways the increase in numbers of Cambodian women involved in sex work and those who have been trafficked into the sex industry is related to both poverty and legacies of war and genocide. Kemp focuses on the Cambodian Women's Crisis Center that works to advocate for women who request help as a result of sexual mistreatment.

Recently, sex trafficking has received a great deal of attention in the Western media and among Western feminists. In this context, sex trafficking often becomes enmeshed with complex feminist debates about prostitution and sex work. For example, the Coalition Against Trafficking in Women (CATW) emerged as a key advocate for legislative action in the United States, the European Union, and at the United Nations to end trafficking in women. CATW's analysis draws heavily on feminist critiques of prostitution, particularly the idea that prostitution is a form of sexual violence against women whether or not a woman "consents" to it. CATW and other antitrafficking groups have been critiqued on the grounds that they use sensationalized representations of "Third World" women as helpless

Sex Trafficking—The Facts

Trafficking for sexual exploitation has become an epidemic in the past decade.

What is it?
The UN defines human trafficking as:

'The recruitment, transportation, transfer, harbouring or receipt of persons, by means of the threat or use of force or other forms of coercion, of abduction, of fraud, of deception, of the abuse of power or of a position of vulnerability or of the giving or receiving of payments or benefits for the purpose of exploitation.'

UN Convention Against Transnational Organized Crime

1. HOW WIDESPREAD IS IT?

Human trafficking affects virtually every region of the world. People from 127 countries are exploited in 137 countries.[1]

An estimated 2.4 million people are currently in forced labor—including sexual exploitation—as a result of trafficking. This is around a fifth of the total number of people in forced labor worldwide.[2]

Some experts estimate that sex trafficking accounts for 80% of all trafficking.[1] Other estimates put it at around 40%—on the basis that other forms of slavery are even less reported.[2]

Trafficked forced labor by form[2]
According to the International Labour Organization

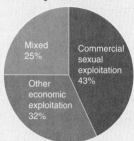

- Mixed 25%
- Commercial sexual exploitation 43%
- Other economic exploitation 32%

In Europe most trafficking is for sexual exploitation

2. WHO GETS TRAFFICKED?

The link between trafficking and poverty[2]

European country of origin	Identified victims of trafficking (2000–2003)	Population living on under $2 day
Albania	2,241	11.8%
Moldova	1,131	63.7%
Romania	778	20.5%
Bulgaria	352	16.2%
Ukraine	293	45.7%
Croatia	3	up to 2%
Czech Rep	2	up to 2%
Poland	1	up to 2%

Impacts[3]
A medical study of women and girls entering care after having been trafficked found that:
95% reported physical and/or sexual violence.
56% suffered post-traumatic stress disorder.
57% had 12–23 concurrent physical health problems.
60% suffered pelvic pain, vaginal discharge and gynecological infection.
38% had suicidal thoughts, **95%** depression—most showing little reduction after 90 days in care.

GENDER
Women and girls are more vulnerable to trafficking of all kinds—but especially that involving sex—than men and boys.[2]

Forced commercial sexual exploitation by sex[2]

- Women and girls 98%
- Men and boys 2%

POVERTY
Trafficking victims tend to be the poorest and most vulnerable people coming from poor countries.

Forced economic exploitation by sex[2]

- Women and girls 56%
- Men and boys 44%

3. WHERE FROM? WHERE THROUGH? WHERE TO?

The U.S. government estimates that between 600,000–800,000 people are trafficked across international borders each year.[1]

Countries of ORIGIN   There are some 127 countries that people are trafficked from.

VERY HIGH LEVELS:	Countries with HIGH levels include: Bangladesh, India, Nepal, Pakistan,
Belarus, Moldova, Russia, Ukraine, Albania, Bulgaria, Lithuania, Romania, China, Thailand, and Nigeria.	Latvia, Burma, Cambodia, Morocco, Colombia, Mexico, Brazil, Vietnam.

Countries of TRANSIT

VERY HIGH LEVELS:	Countries that rank HIGH as transit routes include: Bosnia-Herzegovina,
Albania, Bulgaria, Hungary, Poland, Italy, Thailand.	Czech Republic, Kosovo, FR Yugoslavia and Macedonia, Romania, Serbia and Montenegro, Slovakia, Ukraine, Burma, Turkey, Belgium, France, Germany, Greece.

Countries of DESTINATION

VERY HIGH LEVELS:	Countries that rank HIGH as destination include: Britain, Australia,
Belgium, Germany, Greece, Italy, the Netherlands, Israel, Turkey, Japan, Thailand, United States.	Canada, India, Pakistan, Saudi Arabia, Kosovo, Poland, China, Taiwan, UAE, France, Spain, Switzerland, Bosnia-Herzegovina, Austria, Denmark, Czech Republic, Cambodia.

4. WHO PROFITS

The profits from trafficked forced labor are estimated at $32 billion a year. Of this about $10 billion is derived from the initial 'sale' of individuals with the remainder representing the estimated profits from their exploitation.[2]

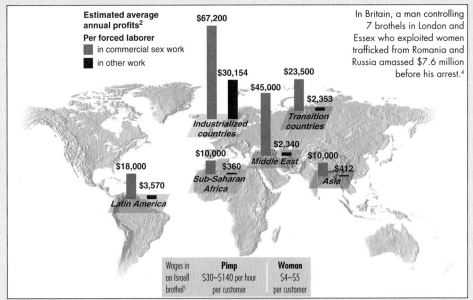

Estimated average annual profits[2]
Per forced laborer
— in commercial sex work
— in other work

$67,200
$30,154
$45,000
$23,500
$2,353

In Britain, a man controlling 7 brothels in London and Essex who exploited women trafficked from Romania and Russia amassed $7.6 million before his arrest.[4]

Industrialized countries
Transition countries
$2,340
Middle East
$10,000
$360
Sub-Saharan Africa
$10,000
$412
Asia
$18,000
$3,570
Latin America

Wages in an Israeli brothel[5]	Pimp $30–$140 per hour per customer	Woman $4–$5 per customer

Trafficked women often end up earning nothing at all due to the repayment of 'debts' and 'fines' imposed by traffickers, pimps, and brothel owners.[5]

5. WHO CREATES THE DEMAND?

Generally the people who buy sex are male and married or in long-term partnerships. They cross all social and economic boundaries.

Percentage of men who buy sex[6]

11%	UK
13%	Sweden
15.6%	Australia
39%	Spain
73%	Thailand

To what extent is demand being met by trafficking?

The case of Britain:

Estimated number of sex workers:
80,000[7]

Estimated number of people trafficked for sexual exploitation:
4,000[8]

Estimated number of commercial sex acts in Britain per year:
64 million[7]

So in Britain the ratio of regular sex workers to those who have been trafficked into sexual exploitation is probably around 20:1

6. INTERNATIONAL INITIATIVES TO COMBAT TRAFFICKING

- **Council of Europe Convention on Action Against Trafficking in Human Beings** adopted on 16 May 2005. The aim of the convention is to prevent and combat the trafficking in human beings. Of the 46 members of the Council of Europe, 36 have signed the convention and 7 have ratified it.

- **The United Nations Convention against Transnational Organized Crime** came into force in December 2003. It is supplemented by the UN Protocol to Prevent, Suppress and Punish Trafficking in Persons, Especially Women and Children. By 2004, it had been signed by 117 countries.

- **The UN Global Programme against Trafficking in Human Beings (GPAT)** was designed by the UN Office on Drugs and Crime (UNODC) in collaboration with the United Nations Interregional Crime and Justice Research Institute (UNICRI) and launched in March 1999.

[1] UN Office on Drugs and Crime, *Trafficking In Persons, Global Patterns*, 2006.
[2] UN International Labour Organization, *A Global Alliance Against Forced Labour*, 2005.
[3] Cathy Zimmerman, *Stolen Smiles: a summary report on the physical and psychological health consequences of women and adolescents trafficked in Europe*, London School of Hygiene and Tropical Medicine, 2006.
[4] Donna M Hughes, *Sex Trafficking Supply and Demand*, Carolina Women's Center, 2006.
[5] Rita Chaikin, Isha L'Isha, in *Trafficking and the Global Sex Industry*, ed Karen Beeks and Delia Amir, Lexington Books, 2006.
[6] Dr Teela Sanders, University of Leeds, 2006, except for the UK figure which is from UK Network of Sex Workers Project, 2004.
[7] Françoise Legros, *A literature review of the sexual health needs of commercial sex workers and their clients*, DHIVERSE, 2005.
[8] UK Home Office, 2003.

victims needing to be rescued (Doezema, 2001). Such critiques are grounded in the ways antitrafficking groups tend to conflate prostitution and trafficking. Many feminists in the Global South have argued for a more nuanced understanding of prostitution and sex work. For example, women who work in the sex industry and see themselves as workers rather than victims have challenged the assumption that prostitution is necessarily a form of violence against women. These women use the terminology sex work rather than prostitution to highlight that they choose to use their bodies to make a living in the context of the economic opportunities available to them in the same way that other workers do. Sex workers have focused on collective organizing, securing labor rights for women in the sex industry, and decriminalizing sex work. Many sex workers rights organizations point out that the conflation of prostitution and trafficking by organizations like CATW undermines sex workers organizations and their efforts to protect themselves (Kempadoo, 2005). In addition, CATW's strong emphasis on prostitution and sexual violence as the defining feature of women's oppression often obscures other factors that may be equally or more important in the lives of trafficked women. For example, to the extent that trafficking patterns are shaped by changes in the global economy, a singular emphasis on sexual violence may in fact do little to curb trafficking.

The voices of trafficked women themselves are often absent from debates about sex trafficking. In her ethnographic study of trafficked women in Spain, Laura Agustín (2005) argues that contemporary debates about sex trafficking frequently fail to capture the complexity with which trafficked women understand their own experiences. Many of her subjects revealed they chose to be trafficked out of a sense of responsibility for the economic well-being of their families, belying the representation of trafficked women as simply victims. They reported ambivalent feelings about sex work, citing both its benefits (more flexible work schedule and higher pay) and its drawbacks (shame, stigma, and fear that families might find out). Agustín notes that many of the women in her study engaged in multiple kinds of labor, making it difficult to distinguish women who were trafficked for sexual labor from those trafficked into other service industries. She also reported that a significant obstacle to their well-being was their undocumented nature that prevented rights in the destination country. This fact suggests that policies that decriminalize undocumented migrants would significantly reduce the harms trafficked women face.

Ultimately, how activists choose to frame sex trafficking as a political issue informs the kinds of actions that are taken against sex trafficking, and whether these actions benefit or inflict further harm on migrant women. For example, U.S. policy has tended to lump all forms of commercialized sex work with sex trafficking, emphasizing prosecution and policing while denying health and other social services to trafficked women. Such an approach has become part of the language and enforcement policies of the U.S. Trafficking Victims Protection Act and the U.S. government's Global AIDS Act of 2003 that prohibit the transfer of funds to groups without a policy opposing prostitution. Feminist organizations that support the legalization or decriminalization of prostitution as ways to provide better health and legal support for sex workers have been detrimentally affected by these policies. An alternative approach is to aim for more fundamental change that addresses the conditions of economic inequality and the demand for highly exploitable workers, which render women vulnerable to trafficking in the first place. Changing these conditions requires long-term strategies aimed at furthering social and economic justice across the globe (Correa, Petchesky, and Parker, 2008).

A DAY IN THE LIFE: **A Temporary Job** by *November Papaleo*

As the sun filters through the bamboo shades, Tola rolls over to avoid the brightness. She gets to sleep for at least another hour before the camera starts rolling. Dressed in a simple cotton shift with a delicate detailing of ribbon under the bust, Tola buries her head under a pillow and drops back into half-sleep. The other girls are up and moving about the apartment cooking, laughing, and poking fun at each other. Tola has three roommates, a large improvement over the dormitory she lived in last year. Three girls are much easier to deal with than eight. Not that she didn't like the other girls, there were just so many of them, and she couldn't have her own room. They lived in an apartment, billed as a low-rise, but it was really just some rooms over the laundry area no one else would rent. Surrendering to the sunshine, the warm temperature, and her roommates' noise, Tola swings her legs out from the bed. She stays there for a few minutes letting the sun hit her legs and her toes (which are always cold). The closet is just a few feet away, but she considers going to work naked rather than getting dressed and then going to work and getting naked. Or getting into lingerie. Or into a costume. Tola works two jobs so she can contribute to her family's income. Her extra wages have helped her father's business, a stand that sells handmade bamboo furniture at the market close to the Cambodian border in Aranyaprathet. Her mother teaches primary school but only works half-time to take care of the children. Tola takes pride that her merit is increasing as her family's position improves. The merit makes up for her job; she knows helping the family will help her in future lives. Although her family owns their own tract of land in eastern Thailand, the money from their second daughter's work supports them through slow seasons and emergencies. Her family suspects that Tola is a *pâet-yaa*, but they would rather believe she is a waitress at a tourist bar. Tola isn't a prostitute; she has resolved that question in her mind. She doesn't get paid to have sex with men. She gets paid to be photographed and to dance for men. Sometimes she accepts money for having sex with one she doesn't mind. She often laughs with the other girls about a recent encounter she had with a *farang*. They fumble with buttons, nervous, even though they are paying well and she is a sure thing.

While she has to split the money with the lady of the house, Tola still takes home enough money to send her family $300 American dollars a month. Her needs are relatively few: lingerie, shoes, and food are her daily expenses. Even the shoes can be swapped with the other girls to save money. At 16, Tola is well endowed compared to her house sisters who are one to two years younger. Their tops simply won't fit her and she avoids sharing bottoms. There are bad things out there that girls can get from men and from each other if they aren't careful. She is lucky to be in a caring house. Some girls are treated poorly and don't make much money. Then again, there are others who made lots more…but they'll do things Tola isn't sure she'd want to do or would do even if she did want to do them. The other girls are cute and soft, so spending time with them for the camera isn't bad; they know each other. Prime camera time begins at 1:00 P.M. since Americans are nine hours ahead and they spend lots of money on live web cam shows. Tola wiggles into her corset, ties in her pigtails, and tucks into bobby socks. Today she'll wear the bottoms with ruffles on the gôn.

Tola is one of several girls that works for the lady of the house as both a live cam girl during the day and a bar girl during the night, dancing for tips. Her shifts at the bar are short and the web cams are exciting; she earns money without even meeting with men. Usually she'll just lay in bed reading until someone comes into her room online. Hastily she'll drop the book out of the camera's view and seductively cat crawl across the bed to the computer. Almost half the men she "talks" to in a Web session actually want to talk—and they pay for it! Sometimes the girls pair up and spend their off time talking about dates or friends; then when the computer dings it is all sex and sexy. Tola works alone today and meditates until someone wants to see her perform.

The live camera shows are filmed in one of three back rooms in the club. Each has a theme, and they change often. After a slow afternoon Tola gets back into her street clothing and goes home for dinner. It is a short walk from the dance club to her apartment. Every day one of the girls has the day off and uses this time to prepare meals and clean the house. Mali was off for today and spent every second barefoot and in loose clothing: a change from the usual getup. Her soups are amazing, but she usually skimps on the meat, eating most of it as she cooks. Tola and the other girls eat dinner and laugh about Mali's no-meat soup.

The girls help Tola get ready for dancing, doing her hair and her make-up first. Tola hates doing her own face but loves to help the other girls learn how to make cat-eyes or disco lips. They finish dressing and walk in a loose pack to the club, shaking and swiveling the whole way. The stage is one place Tola feels alone and calm. When she dances and men throw her money, she feels free. It is like meditating but people watch her do it and pay her for it. One man who has been giving her big tips motions for her to be with him in a booth. She meets him in the back where he suddenly lunges at her. He is all drunk and sweaty. She chatters at him angrily and he wobbles back to the bench in the middle of the room. Tola finishes her dance, repaying him with some extra special attention. She expectes a nice tip, and he is generous, guilty for acting badly. It is only a few more hours until she can go home, wash, and get in her simple shift with the ribbon at the bust. It is only a few more years until she can go home, see her family, and make one of her own. It is only a job, and it is temporary.

Sex Tourism

Tourism is one of the few ways in which countries in the Global South, particularly small island nations, can compete in the global economy. In the Caribbean, for example, governments have adopted tourism as a way of diversifying their economies, overcoming economic crises and acquiring foreign currency. Tourism here rests on the exploitation of several of the region's resources, including the sun, beaches, music, cuisine, and culture. Although not overtly advertised, sex is another critical resource in this scenario. Sex tourism implies travel to a country with the intent to engage in sexual activity with others. The reading "Sex Tourism Booming" from the Integrated Regional Information Networks (IRIN), a humanitarian news analysis service of the UN Office of the Coordination of Humanitarian Affairs, discusses sex tourism on the Caribbean coast of Colombia. It focuses on child sex workers and projects like *Fundación Renacer*, a nongovernmental organization working to prevent the sexual exploitation of children.

Racialized "exoticism" plays an important role in sex tourism. As already discussed, exoticism implies "the charm of the unfamiliar" and involves the representation of one culture for consumption by another. As such it is implicated in colonial and imperial

Child Sex Tourism FAQs

WHAT IS THE PROBLEM?

An estimated 2 million children worldwide—some as young as 5 years old—are enslaved in the global commerical sex trade. Many are forced, coerced, or tricked into prostitution. "Child sex tourism," the practice of traveling to another country for the purpose of having sex with children, exacerbates the commercial sex trade. Some sex tourists are pedophiles, specifically seeking underage boys and girls. Others may be traveling for legitimate reasons, but decide to "experiment" with the sex trade. Health concerns, such as AIDS, create an increased demand for younger victims.

WHO ARE THE MOST VULNERABLE CHILDREN?

Although children from all social and economic backgrounds are at risk of sexual abuse, those most vulnerable live in economically depressed situations.

Street children are particularly vulnerable, as they have very few resources and networks to turn to for protection. Children in poverty-stricken countries can be more vulnerable if their families are desperate for income.

WHERE IS CHILD SEX TOURISM MOST PREVALENT?

Economically marginalized children are at highest risk of being lured into the sex trade, and developing countries have increasing sex tourism problems. Countries such as Cambodia, Thailand, Mexico, Costa Rica, Brazil, and the Dominican Republic are popular destinations for sexual predators because of the volume of sex tourism venues in operation and the large pool of potential victims who can be easily lured or forced into the sex trade. Additionally, in some countries, local law enforcement tends to be inadequately funded and/or corrupt.

ARE AMERICANS INVOLVED IN CHILD SEX TOURISM?

It is estimated that U.S. citizens account for 25 percent of child sex tourists worldwide, and as high as 80 percent in Latin America. Essentially, these predators are taking advantage of victims whose only "crime" is being poor and vulnerable.

HOW IS THE U.S. GOVERNMENT HELPING TO COMBAT THE PROBLEM?

Since 1994, federal law has prohibited U.S. citizens from having sex with minors abroad. The 2003 U.S. PROTECT Act has greatly assisted law enforcement agencies in prosecuting Americans who sexually abuse children overseas by the following measures:

- Increases imprisonment penalties to 30 years for convicted sex tourists
- Criminalizes persons or organizations that assist or organize sex tours
- Better enables federal prosecutors to convict offenders by modifying burden of proof requirements
- Establishes parallel penalty enhancements that apply to the production of child pornography overseas

U.S. ICE actively enforces this law by arresting U.S. citizens, both in the United States and abroad. The Department of Justice has prosecuted numerous offenders. The U.S. State Department also pushes governments around the world to tackle this problem. Since the PROTECT Act of 2003 was passed, 25 Americans have been arrested for sexually abusing children in Latin America, Asia, Africa, and Russia. All cases that have gone to court to date have resulted in convictions.

WHAT CAN YOU DO TO HELP STOP CHILD SEX TOURISTS?

- Raise awareness about this issue in your community, school, place of worship, or workplace.
- Advocate for increased resources to prosecute U.S. citizens who sexually exploit children overseas.
- Report an American sex tourist, if you have information regarding a person who has sexually exploited a child.

I'm not a tourist attraction.
It's a crime to make me one.

World Vision
Building a better world for children

Stop child sex tourism.

U.S. Immigration and Customs Enforcement

Copyright © 2005 World Vision, Inc. All rights reserved. All contents of this material may not be reproduced or used outside the context of which it was intended without the written permission of World Vision. 40579_0605   Paid for, in part, by the U.S. Department of State projects that combine romanticizing racial, ethnic, or cultural "Others" with their exploitation (Said, 1979). Cultural differences are viewed in sexual terms, and expressions of exoticism continue to permeate new forms of economic and cultural imperialism in contemporary tourist industries. The reading by Kempadoo on sexual-economic relations also makes this point.

However, despite the exploitative contexts they navigate that involve power inequalities between clients and workers, women who work in sex tourism are not simply victims. For example, since the early 1990s, Sosua, a small town on the north coast of the Dominican Republic, has been a popular destination for European sex tourists. Low-income women migrate from across the country to work in Sosua's sex trade where they hope to meet and marry foreign men who will cover the costs of their migration to Europe. They tend not to be coerced into this work, but find their way there through networks of female family members and friends. For most, work in a tourist town with European clients is not simply a rational survival strategy for impoverished women, but an advancement strategy with the goal of marriage and migration from the island (Brennan, 2002). Even if these goals are not met, transnational relationships can be sustained with the hope of financial support. The relatively assertive stance of these sex workers underscores debates over whether or not sex work is always exploitive of women. Moralizing media portrayals of sex workers in sex tourist destinations as passive victims easily seduced by the lure of consumer goods tend to be overly simplistic and deny low-income women the capability of making their own labor choices.

STRATEGIES FOR PROMOTING SEXUAL FREEDOM

All of the examples discussed thus far illustrate the importance of grounding struggles for sexual freedom in the larger context of women's particular political, economic, and social status and demonstrate the need for multifaceted approaches that take seriously differences of race, ethnicity, class, religion, disability, and age. This section takes a more sustained look at two strategies that activists have employed to promote sexual freedom at the local, national, and global scales: (1) the development of sexuality education programs to empower young women; and (2) efforts to include sexual rights in human rights frameworks for social justice.

Sexuality Education and Sexual Empowerment

For young women in many parts of the world, pregnancies at a young age and high rates of HIV and other sexually transmitted infections (STIs) are serious issues that contribute to high dropout rates for girls in school. STIs and pregnancy can be the result of consensual sexual activity, coerced sexual activity, or explicit sexual violence. Attempts to address these problems at the local level include programs in sex education or family-life education, and health and life-skills education. These trainings aim to educate about sexuality and the consequences of sexual activity by addressing issues such as sex, bodily changes during puberty, reproduction, STIs, the dangers of early pregnancy, and the importance of family planning. However, these programs tend to rest on the assumption that behavioral change occurs as an automatic consequence of new knowledge and attitudes, and that knowledge created by adults will be useful for, and acceptable to, adolescents (Burns, 2002).

*In the U.K. an "E" is the lowest passing grade a student can receive. © John Ditchburn. Reprinted with permission.

It is now clear that the most effective sexuality education is that which relates to young people's lived experience. One example of a project using this philosophy is a unique form of sexuality education aimed at preventing unwanted and early pregnancy, STIs, and gender violence in Brazil. Here young people form their own peer groups to educate about sexual and reproductive health issues using music, drama, and art. For example, a group of young mothers produced a "photo novel" (telling a story through photos) titled "Love Is Blind" on the theme of two adolescent girls who have unprotected sex with their boyfriends and become pregnant. After viewing the photo novel, boys and girls from a school in a low-income community were critical of how some of the issues were presented, particularly the happy ending, and decided to create their own photo novel in response. The students' new story, "With Love and Condoms," focused on their concerns and how they dealt with them. The success of the project stems not simply from the production of good materials that engage with issues of sexuality in a lively manner, but also from the overall philosophy of the work. Attention is paid to the formation of groups, their dynamics, diverse audiences, and the culturally grounded character of each message and its medium (Hassen, 2002).

Another study in eastern Uganda found that traditional sex education was limited because it did not address gendered expectations that play a huge role in girls' sexual attitudes and behaviors (Burns, 2002). For example, double standards and paradoxes often operate with regard to sexuality because parents are strict with girls but give boys freedom to have sexual relationships with girls. The latter are also taught to be submissive rather than assertive, leaving them unprepared to deal with these contradictory sexual demands. Teachers, administrators, and students often respond to this contradiction by advocating girls' isolation from boys, abstinence from sex, and avoidance of all forms of romantic love. Two detrimental consequences of such behaviors include: (1) girls are expected to know how to keep themselves from getting pregnant, even when such information is deliberately withheld from them; and (2) girls are blamed when they become sexually active or pregnant even though active expressions of sexuality are encouraged in boys and men.

In addition, sexuality education curricula tend not to address topics concerning sexual coercion, harassment, and violence (Panos Institute, 2003). Katharine Wood and Rachel Jewkes' (1998) study of the microdynamics of violence in young people's sexual relationships in Umtata in the Eastern Cape Province of South Africa, for example, highlights the importance of addressing questions of gender violence in sexuality education. Although they had originally set out to examine contraceptive use, bodily knowledge, and pregnancy in adolescent relationships, Wood and Jewkes found the predominance of male violence against women and girls suggested the need for different kinds of education. They emphasize the importance of not isolating sexuality education within the school curriculum, but instead integrating its content in as many school subjects as possible. They also encourage supplementation by community groups including police, welfare, and legal services, as a way of promoting awareness of community resources. Similarly, the Girls' Power Initiative (GPI) based in Nigeria recognizes the unnecessary risks and restricted opportunities that adolescent girls face due to gender-based violence. GPI promotes comprehensive sexuality education for adolescents and teachers that includes topics like personal empowerment, interpersonal relationships, human sexuality and sexual health, gendered violence, legal protection, and youth activism (GPI, 1999).

Sexual Rights as Human Rights

On the national and international levels, women's social movements organizing around themes of sexual education, reproductive rights, and maternal and infant health have emerged around the world since the 1980s. In countries such as Brazil, the Philippines, and Mexico where the Catholic Church is powerful, women's rights and gay and lesbian rights activists have struggled to legalize abortion, reduce maternal mortality, and educate people about safer sex and condom use. Women's organizations in Bangladesh have spoken out against brutal attacks on women accused by Islamic religious tribunals of going against sexual norms, and groups campaigning against FGC have stressed the resulting suppression of women's sexual pleasure and the severe risks to their health. Organizations of women of color in the United States and women's groups in India have strongly opposed coercive sterilization and the coercive promotion of long-acting contraceptives by family planning programs. These struggles situate key issues associated with sexuality like abortion, contraception, and childbearing in a framework concerned with furthering women's social and economic rights. This means replacing old notions of population control and family planning with a broad understanding of reproductive and sexual health issues linking sexual and reproductive freedom with women's rights. At the core of all of these struggles is the principle that women's human rights to self-determination and equality include the intimate spheres of family, reproductive, and sexual life. This was a controversial claim in most countries and political systems during the 1980s and early 1990s that still remains unaccepted in many countries today.

Mobilization for sexual freedom strengthened women's coalitions at the World Conference on Human Rights in Vienna (1993), the International Conference on Population and Development (ICPD) in Cairo (1994), and the Fourth World Conference on Women in Beijing (1995). As discussed in the chapter on reproductive freedom, the ICPD Programme of Action and the Beijing Declaration and Platform for Action define "reproductive rights" as "[resting] on the recognition of the basic right of all couples and individuals to decide freely and responsibly the number, spacing, and timing of their children and to have the information and means to do so, and the right to attain the highest standard of sexual and reproductive health. It also includes their right to make decisions concerning reproduction free of discrimination, coercion, and violence, as expressed in human rights documents" (Petchesky, 1998, p. 28). In Cairo, feminists lobbied official delegations for the inclusion of "sexual rights" in the definition of reproductive rights, but this was not achieved (Correa, 1997). However, the ICPD Programme of Action was able to establish the need for governments to provide adolescents with a full range of sexual and reproductive health services and education, including advocating male responsibility and condom use. In addition, one of the most controversial aspects of the Programme for Action was its reference to "various forms of the family" (family forms in the plural rather than the more conservative singular form ["the family"] preferred by the Vatican and some Muslim countries). This particular inclusion was considered a victory, since it meant that family forms different from the traditional nuclear family invoked by mainstream policy were included. For the first time in UN discourse, women were acknowledged as sexual as well as reproductive beings, with the right to decide freely about their sexuality without this right being qualified by age, marital status, or sexual orientation.

Despite these gains, most references to sexuality in the Cairo document tend to be located within the frame of heterosexuality, disease or violence, and stress protection and responsibility rather than pleasure or freedom. In addition, although the original draft referred to "the sexual rights of women," by the time it came to the final draft, specific language about sexual rights had disappeared (Girard, 2007). To date, the only UN document to refer explicitly to "sexual rights" is the report produced by the Special Rapporteur on the Right to Health, Paul Hunt, in 2004. In it, Hunt states that "sexuality is a characteristic of all human beings. It is a fundamental aspect of an individual's identity. It helps to define who a person is." This meant that fundamental human rights principles and norms must include a "recognition of sexual rights as human rights," including "the right of all persons to express their sexual orientation, with due regard for the wellbeing and rights of others, without fear of persecution, denial of liberty or social interference" (Hunt 2004, cited in Correa et al., 2008, p. 164). This reference to sexual rights is in part an effect of the HIV epidemic and the pressure on governments to recognize the realities of sexual relations in everyday life. Beyond this, the recent emergence of sexual rights discourse reflects the ongoing process of negotiation in the context of the UN conferences of the 1990s and their follow-up meetings from 1999 to 2006. It is in these forums that transnational feminists, LGBTQ (lesbian, gay, bisexual, transgender, queer) activists, youth groups, and AIDS activists have worked for sexual rights. Such activism is discussed in the reading "Lesbian, Gay, Bisexual, and Transgender Rights and the Religious Relativism of Human Rights" by D.Ø. Endsjø. Endsjø makes the case that, from a human rights perspective, the most serious consequence is not only the ways many religions support discrimination against the LGBT communities, but also the exclusion of LGBT rights from the greater context of human rights.

The meanings attributed to sexual rights vary considerably. In the African context, the lack of sexual rights is understood as a consequence of economic as well as gender inequality, particularly in sexual relationships. Although "sexual rights" is a relatively new concept, Correa et al. (2008) point out that such rights embrace longstanding human rights already enshrined in national laws, international human rights documents, and other similar consensus documents developed in processes coordinated by the UN and its diverse agencies. In 2006 a group of human rights specialists and LGBTQ activists used this approach to

LEARNING ACTIVITY   **The Yogyakarta Principles**

In 2006, a group of human rights experts developed a set of principles to apply human rights to sexual identity. The Yogyakarta Principles address the need for a binding set of universal standards with which all nations must comply. To see the principles, go to http://www.yogyakartaprinciples.org/ principles_en.htm. What arguments do the authors make for the necessity of the principles? Choose one of the principles and research its application in your home state. What laws does your state currently have about the issue at hand? Have there been recent incidences in your state related to the issue? Now research a particular country to see current laws and events related to the issue. How would you describe the need for this principle based on your research?

develop the Yogyakarta Principles for the Application of International Human Rights Law in relation to Sexual Orientation and Gender Identity (see sidebar) (Yogyakarta Principles, 2006). Sexual orientation or identity has been a critical dimension of sexual rights provoking major contestation in intergovernmental negotiations since the mid-1990s. For activists pursuing this route, the full realization of sexual rights depends not only on rights that are protected by the state, but on all people in society having the right to pursue a satisfying, safe, and pleasurable sexual life.

Social movements of feminists, lesbians, gays, bisexuals, transgender, and intersex people continue as major forces in bringing about changes in international human rights laws. How to create meaningful and politically viable connections across a wide range of identity-based groups without erasing the social differences among them, or falling back on abstract notions of humanity, remains a challenge. Recognizing the complexity and the plurality of sexualities across the world is a good starting point.

REFERENCES

Agustin, L. (2005). Migrants in the mistress's house: Other voices in the "trafficking" debate. *Social Politics, 12*(1), 96–117.

Alexander, M. J. (1997). Erotic autonomy as a politics of decolonization: An anatomy of feminist and state practice in the Bahamas tourist economy. In C. Mohanty and M. J. Alexander (Eds.), *Feminist Genealogies, Colonial Legacies, Democratic Futures* (pp. 63–100). New York: Routledge.

Brennan, D. (2002). Selling sex for visas: Sex tourism as a stepping stone to international migration. In B. Ehrenreich and A. Hochschild (Eds.), *Global woman: Nannies, maids and sex workers in the new economy* (pp. 154–168). London: Granta Books.

Burns, K. (2002). Sexuality education in a girls' school in eastern Uganda. *Agenda, 53,* 81–88.

Cohen, C. (1997). Punks, bulldaggers, and welfare queens: The radical potential of queer politics? *GLQ, 3,* 437–465.

Collins, P. H. (1997). Pornography and black women's bodies. In L. O'Toole and J. Schiffman (Eds.), *Gender violence: Interdisciplinary perspectives* (pp. 395–399). New York: New York University Press.

Correa, S. (1997). From reproductive health to sexual rights: Achievements and future challenges. *Reproductive Health Matters, 10,* 107–116.

Correa, S., Petchesky, R. and Parker, R. (2008). *Sexuality, health and human rights.* London: Routledge.

Dick, S. (2008). *Homophobic hate crime: The gay British crime survey 2008.* Stonewall http://www.stonewall.org.uk.

Doezema, J. (2001). Ouch! Western feminists' 'wounded attachment' to the 'Third World prostitute.' *Feminist Review, 67,* 16–38.

Enloe, C. (1989). *Bananas, beaches and bases: Making feminist sense of international politics.* Berkeley: University of California.

Epprecht, M. (1996). Culture, history and homophobia. *Southern Review, 9*(6), 33–38.

Girard, F. (2007). Negotiating sexual rights and sexual orientation at the UN. In R. Parker, R. Petchesky, and R. Sember (Eds.), *Sex Politics from the frontlines.* Retrieved 15 October, 2008 from http://www.sexpolitics.org/frontlines/home/index.php.

GPI. (1999). *Girls' power initiative: GPI Nigeria training manual on adolescent sexuality, sexual and reproductive rights and health, and GPI's experiences with women's empowerment programme.* Calabar: Girls' Power Initiative.

Hassen, M. (2002). Making sense of sexuality and reproduction: A participatory approach to materials development with young people in Brazil. In A. Cornwall and A. Welbourn (Eds.), *Realizing rights: Transforming approaches to sexual and reproductive well-being* (pp. 169–180). London: Zed.

Hélie-Lucas, M.A. (2003). The preferential symbol for Islamic identity: Women in Muslim personal laws. In C. McCaan and S. Kim (Eds.). *Feminist theory reader: Local and global perspectives* (pp. 188–196). New York: Routledge.

Kempadoo, K. (2005). Sex workers' rights organizations and anti-trafficking campaigns. In K. Kempadoo (Ed.), *Trafficking and prostitution reconsidered: New perspectives on migration, sex work, and human rights* (pp. 149–155). Boulder: Paradigm.

Lorde, A. (1997). Love poem. In A. Lorde (Ed.), *The collected poems of Audre Lorde* (p. 127). New York: Norton.

Mason-Grant, J. (2007). Pornography as embodied practice. In A. Soble and N. Power (Eds.), *The philosophy of sex: Contemporary readings* (pp. 401–418). Lanham, MD: Rowman and Littlefield.

Panos Institute, (2003). *Beyond victims and villains: Addressing sexual violence in the education sector.* Report, 47. London: Panos Institute.

Petchesky, R. (1998). Introduction. In R. Petchesky and K. Judd (Eds.), *Negotiating reproductive rights: Women's perspectives across countries and cultures* (pp. 1–30). London: Zed Books.

Raymond, J. (2002). The new UN trafficking protocol. *Women's Studies International Forum, 25*(5), 491–502.

Rehn, E. and Johnson Sirleaf, E. (2002). *Women, war, peace: The independent experts' assessment on the impact of armed conflict on women and women's role in peacebuilding.* New York: United Nations Development Fund for Women (UNIFEM).

Said, E. (1979). *Orientalism*. New York: Vintage Books.

Sanghera, J. (2005). Unpacking the trafficking discourse. In K. Kempadoo (Ed.), *Trafficking and prostitution reconsidered: New perspectives on migration, sex work, and human rights* (pp. 3–24). Boulder: Paradigm.

Sarikakis, K. and Shaukat, Z. (2007). The global structures and cultures of pornography: The global brothel. In K. Sarikakis and L.R. Shade (Eds.), *Feminist interventions in international communication: Minding the gap* (pp. 106–126). Lanham, MD: Rowman and Littlefield.

Smith, A. (2005) *Conquest: Sexual violence and American Indian genocide*. Boston: South End.

UNESCO. (2008). Data comparison sheet #1: Worldwide trafficking estimates by organization. http://www.unescobkk.org/culture/trafficking/.

U.S. State Department. (2005). Trafficking in persons report. http://www.state.gov/g/tip/rls/tiprpt/2005/.

Wood, K. and Jewkes, R. (1998). *"Love is a dangerous thing": Micro-dynamics of violence in sexual relationships of young people in Mtata*. Pretoria: Medical Research Council of South Africa.

Yogyakarta Principles (2006). Yogyakarta principles on the application of international human rights law in relation to sexual orientation and gender identity. http://www.yogyakartaprinciples.org/index.php?item=25.

SUGGESTIONS FOR FURTHER READING

Ebbe, O. and Das, D. K. (Eds.). (2007). *Global trafficking in women and children*. Boca Raton, FL: CRC.

Fields, J. (2007). *An intimate affair: Women, lingerie, and sexuality*. Berkeley: University of California Press.

Kawakami, S. (2007). *Goodbye Madame Butterfly: Stories of sex, marriage and the modern Japanese woman* (Y. Enomoto, Trans.). Tokyo: Chim Music Press.

Mezey, S. G. (2007). *Queers in court: Gay rights law and public policy*. Lanham, MD: Rowman and Littlefield.

Parrot, A. and Cummings, N. (2008). *Sexual enslavement of girls and women worldwide*. Santa Barbara, CA: Praeger.

Wardlow, H. (2006). *Wayward women: Sexuality and agency in a New Guinea society*. Berkeley: University of California Press.

Toward a Vision of Sexual and Economic Justice

Kamala Kempadoo (2007)

ON SEXUAL-ECONOMIC RELATIONS

The most pressing concern for me as an academic/activist is the liberation of sexual-economic relations in the "Third World"—especially the Caribbean—from oppressive laws and policies, conservative moralities, negative beliefs, stigma, prejudice, and violence. In other words, of concern is to unearth these relations from their current criminalized and stigmatized status and to have them recognized and accepted in dominant discourse as a part of everyday social life. By sexual-economic relations I refer not just to sex work, but especially to that which is defined in the Caribbean and African countries as "transactional sex"—activities that involve a deliberate exchange of sex, often by young women, for some form of "betterment"—material goods, clothes/fashion, education/school fees, accommodation, meals, social status. The urgency here is that sexual-economic relations have long histories in regions such as the Caribbean, seem to be widespread and on the rise, have important consequences for social and economic relations as well as for public health, yet are ignored or discriminated against in political, academic and activist discourses.

In order to do justice to sexual-economic relations, I propose that we need a fundamental transformation of understandings of sexuality. Important to such work is the interrogation of underlying assumptions and cultural meanings of sexuality. For example, in light of the pervasiveness of transactional sex in Caribbean societies, we can ask whether a notion of sexuality as separate from the ways in which we feed, clothe and house ourselves, is useful for apprehending contemporary social relations and identities. Or should we be open to the idea that sexuality is, in some instances, always-and-already "contaminated" by economic needs, wants and conditions?

If sexuality is an unstable category, and we allow that sexuality may at times be saturated with the economic, sexual praxis that involves economic dimensions need not signify degradation or alienation but can instead be viewed as part of a range of expressions of sexuality. Sexual relationships inspired by economic interests might then be considered equal to those that are inspired by physical desires or ideas of love, and conceptualized as equally valid and legitimate. In other words, I am suggesting that we need a close examination of the ways in which contemporary forms of sexual-economic praxis produce alternative conceptions of sexuality, and an engagement with the ways in which this discourse challenges and changes existing notions of sexuality. And if we are to follow this line of reasoning, some struggles for sexual justice would appear as struggles for economic justice.

Moreover, thinking through struggles of sexual-economic justice in this intersectional way may mean attending to other matters that may not appear immediately as "sexuality" issues. One clear example of this lies in the phenomenon of "the Caribbean beach boy" or "Rental" who sexually and otherwise services female and male tourists, and whose relationships with the tourists, while gendered and economic, are overdetermined by racialized constructions, fantasies and desires. We are forced then to engage with processes of racialized globalization, (neo)colonialisms and new imperialisms that continue to position "black" and "brown" peoples and the "Third World" as sites for western or EuroAmerican political and cultural domination, maldevelopment and hyperexploitation. The challenge, then, is not just to ask questions about how race, gender, sexuality and economics are linked or inscribed in the social but, rather, to develop conceptual tools for capturing complex sexual expressions, and to build struggles with these new conceptualizations.

Obstacles to responding effectively to the notion of sexual economic justice are ideological, political, legal, academic, social—and complicated!

One major obstacle is that there are a number of double-standards in operation. For example: prostitution and other types of sexual-economic relationships are on the one hand quite widely accepted as something poor women in the Caribbean engage in "to make do": as a survival strategy under patriarchal capitalism. On the other hand, this behavior is coded in most laws and policies as illegal, and women are heavily policed, judged and discriminated against if seen to be engaged in sexual-economic relationships. With regards to racialized sexual-economic relationships, we find on the one hand that the (white) global north and global metropoles are held up as the epitome of development, their populations welcomed to poorer areas of the world as tourists for the economic benefits they bring, and that race is strategically deployed to lure tourists to the countries. On the other hand, young black and brown men and women who engage in sexual-economic relations with tourists are disparaged—as "low-lifes" "traitors" to the community or ethnic group or "whores" etc,—and believed to sully the national and regional reputation.

A second obstacle surrounds the subject of sexuality itself, both at social and academic levels. On the social, it is often shrouded in double-entendre, secrecy and shame. In many families it is still taboo to talk about sex with girls, and the idea of sexual-economic relations evokes a social response about impropriety that is heavily influenced by conservative or fundamentalist religious beliefs. This obstacle easily wends its way from the social into academic work and research, politics, or HIV/AIDS and social activism. At the academic, level, sexuality theories draw strength primarily from GLBT social identity movements and studies in the global north from the second half of the twentieth century. "Sexuality studies" then has traditionally paid little attention to the economic, other than occasionally as an issue of class location of sexual identity groups. Sex work and other forms of sexual-economic practices have barely been taken up or recognized within this field, leaving huge gaps and silences in the academy that are replicated in political and activist domains.

A third major obstacle is the uneven global economic development that sustains racial and gendered imbalances of power, and ultimately supports the gross exploitation of sexual-economic relationships through industries such as tourism.

Initiatives that could be invoked/supported in the struggles for sexual-economic justice could involve:

i. campaigns to remove laws that criminalize and oppress sexual-economic expressions, including laws against prostitution and homosexuality;

ii. the production of academic and cultural work that exposes the double-standards, development of more knowledge about transactional sex, and support for the appreciation of the messy connections between sexuality and the economy;

iii. the creation of safe, sustainable income-generating alternatives for poor young women and men to participate in the global economy that may include, but does not place a premium on sexuality;

iv. opposition to limited or conservative views of sexuality that may be articulated through the Church, schools, the media, and the academy.

In such areas of the world as the Caribbean and Africa, HIV/AIDS activism is one of the main areas for developing this agenda, as it is through the lens of the epidemic that sexual praxis is made visible. And it is here that we are seeing some of the greatest strides in addressing sexual-economic relations (i.e., through sex worker rights health campaigns). There are several constraints and complications here, which require attention (and would need to be taken up in another paper).

For such a struggle to be effective we would need to start from the local, taking a "bottom-up approach," starting at the level of community in the global south with women's, sex worker, and "all-sexuals" organizations, drawing upon knowledge and actions of feminist academic communities and labor unions, and building upwards to influence national politics and agendas as well as regional and transnational policies (with and through UN agencies and feminist INGOs). Building resistance to sexual-economic injustice in the present context requires much patience, and involves small-steps. We need to continue to collaborate with people outside of the academy, particularly through involvements with communities and individuals at the local level, building good communication strategies and using appropriate technology and media (i.e., not everyone is internet connected). Global sexual-economic justice ultimately needs a redistribution of wealth, so that people are not economically pressured or forced into relationships with others—for sexual, racial, or gendered reasons—as well as alternative systems of production and consumption, the decriminalization and destigmatization of prostitution and homosexuality, an acceptance of sexual labor as a legitimate form of work, and greater appreciation of sexual difference and diversity.

R E A D I N G **21**

Distant View of a Minaret
Alifa Rifaat (1983)

Alifa Rifaat has spent most of her adult life in the Egyptian countryside, and it is from there that she draws the material for many of her short stories. She is the widow of a police officer and now lives in Cairo with her three children.

Through half-closed eyes she looked at her husband. Lying on his right side, his body was intertwined with hers and his head bent over her right shoulder. As usual at such times she felt that he inhabited a world utterly different from hers, a world from which she had been excluded. Only half-aware of the movements of his body, she turned her head to one side and stared up at the ceiling, where she noticed a spider's web. She told herself she'd have to get out the long broom and brush it down.

When they were first married she had tried to will her husband into sensing the desire that burned within her and so continuing the act longer; she had been too shy and conscious of the conventions to express such wishes openly. Later on, feeling herself sometimes to be on the brink of the experience some of her married women friends talked of in hushed terms, she had found the courage to be explicit about what she wanted. At such moments it had seemed to her that all she needed was just one more movement and her body and soul would be quenched, that once achieved they would between them know how to repeat the experience. But on each occasion, when breathlessly imploring him to continue, he would—as though purposely to deprive her—quicken his movements and bring the act to an abrupt end. Sometimes she had tried in vain to maintain the rhythmic movements a little longer, but always he would stop her. The last time she had made such an attempt, so desperate was she at this critical moment, that she had dug her fingernails into his back, compelling him to remain inside her. He had given a shout as he pushed her away and slipped from her:

"Are you mad, woman? Do you want to kill me?"

It was as though he had made an indelible tattoo mark of shame deep inside her, so that whenever she thought of the incident she felt a flush coming to her face. Thenceforth she had submitted to her passive role, sometimes asking herself: "Perhaps it's me who's at fault. Perhaps I'm unreasonable in my demands and don't know how to react to him properly."

There had been occasions when he had indicated that he had had relationships with other women, and sometimes she had suspicions that maybe he still had affairs, and she was surprised that the idea no longer upset her.

She was suddenly aroused from her thoughts by his more urgent movements. She turned to him and watched him struggling in the world he occupied on his own. His eyes were tight closed, his lips drawn down in an ugly contortion, and the veins in his neck stood out. She felt his hand on her leg, seizing it above the knee and thrusting it sideways as his movements became more frenzied. She stared up at her foot that now pointed toward the spiders's web and noted her toenails needed cutting.

As often happened at this moment she heard the call to afternoon prayers filtering through the shutters of the closed window and bringing her back to reality. With a groan he let go of her thigh and immediately withdrew. He took a small towel from under the pillow, wrapped it round himself, turned his back to her and went to sleep.

She rose and hobbled to the bathroom where she seated herself on the bidet and washed herself. No longer did she feel any desire to complete the act with herself as she used to do in the first years of marriage. Under the shower she gave her right side to the warm water, then her left, repeating the formula of faith as the water coursed down her body. She wrapped her soaking hair in a towel and wound a large second one under her armpits. Returning to the bedroom, she put on a long house-gown, then took up the prayer carpet from on top of the wardrobe and shut the door behind her.

As she passed through the living-room, the sounds of pop music came to her from the room of her son Mahmoud. She smiled as she imagined him stretched out on his bed, a school book held in front of him; she was amazed at his ability to concentrate in the face of such noise. She closed the living-room door, spread the rug and began her prayers. When she had performed the four *rak'as* she seated herself on the edge of the prayer carpet and counted off her glorifications of the almighty, three at a time on the joints of each finger. It was late autumn and the time for the sunset prayer would soon come and she enjoyed the thought that she would soon be praying again. Her five daily prayers were like punctuation marks that divided up and gave meaning to her life. Each prayer had for her a distinct quality, just as different foods had their own flavors. She folded up the carpet and went out on to the small balcony.

Dusting off the cane chair that stood there, she seated herself and looked down at the street from the sixth floor. She was assailed by the din of buses, the hooting of cars, the cries of street vendors and the raucous noise of competing radios from nearby flats. Clouds of smoke rose up from the outpourings of car exhausts veiling the view of the tall solitary minaret that could be seen between two towering blocks of flats. This single minaret, one of the twin minarets of the Mosque of Sultan Hasan, with above it a thin slice of the Citadel, was all that was now left of the panoramic view she had once had of old Cairo, with its countless mosques and minarets against a background of the Mokattam Hills and Mohamed Ali's Citadel.

Before marriage she had dreamed of having a house with a small garden in a quiet suburb such as Maadi or Helwan. On finding that it would be a long journey for her husband to his work in the center of the city, she had settled for this flat because of its views. But with the passing of the years, buildings had risen on all sides, gradually narrowing the view. In time this single minaret would also be obscured by some new building.

Aware of the approach of the call to sunset prayers, she left the balcony and went to the kitchen to prepare her husband's coffee. She filled the brass *kanaka* with water and added a spoonful of coffee and a spoonful of sugar. Just as it was about to boil over she removed it from the stove and placed it on the tray with the coffee cup, for he liked to have the coffee poured out in front of him. She expected to find him sitting up in bed smoking a cigarette. The strange way his body was twisted immediately told her that something was wrong. She approached the bed and looked into the eyes that stared into space and suddenly she was aware of the odor of death in the room. She left and placed the tray in the living-room before passing through to her son's room. He looked up as she entered and immediately switched off the radio and stood up:

"What's wrong, mother?"

"It's your father ..."

"He's had another attack?"

She nodded. "Go downstairs to the neighbors and ring Dr Ramzi. Ask him to come right away."

She returned to the living room and poured out the coffee for herself. She was surprised at how calm she was.

Cambodian Sex Workers

Karoline Kemp (2007)

In 1997, Chanthol Oung realized that women emerging from the effects of genocide, family violence, rape and sex trafficking had no services to assist them. Her response was to create the Cambodian Women's Crisis Center.

Ten years later, the center is providing reintegration programs and advocates on behalf of survivors, working closely with police and government to create laws and improve the enforcement of existing ones.

A small, soft-spoken woman, Oung's determination is strong. "You have to be brave enough to protect the victim. When we see what has been done to the women, we feel angry and have to confront those perpetrators," she explains.

A legacy of war and the effects of poverty, including a lack of education and economic opportunities, have all contributed to Cambodia's emergence as one of Southeast Asia's largest sex-tourism destinations. However, most of the men who buy sex are not foreigners; over 90 percent are Cambodian. Oung believes sex trafficking has weakened the social infrastructure of her country and destroyed the lives of tens of thousands of Cambodian girls and women.

"In 2000, I was married and was living in Phnom Penh," explains Mara, 23. "Prior to this, I had been living with my mother and stepfather, but he tried to rape me, and instead of staying with them I married a man I didn't love." Mara's story is similar to others who have escaped one violent or threatening situation only to find themselves in another one.

"After I told him I didn't love him, he told me we would go on a trip to see his mother, but instead we stopped in Battambang, and he sold me to a brothel for $250. I was forced to receive clients and was ill, but wasn't treated as badly as some of the other women there, who were shocked with electricity if they resisted."

Many of the women sold into Cambodia's sex industry are tricked, coerced or simply sold by relatives. With few viable economic options—over 80 percent of the country's population relies on the agricultural industry, which rarely generates enough income for a family's survival—some people are willing to go to great lengths to ensure their survival. Most of the girls and women who end up working in the sex industry come from rural areas.

"I was locked in my room when I wasn't working, and often wasn't fed enough. I was given drugs, and could not force the clients to use condoms," Mara says. She worked in the brothels of red light districts, karaoke bars and restaurants where sex is sold.

Exact figures are not known. However, some sources estimate that one out of every 10 girls in Cambodia between 15 and 25 has been trafficked. Other reports say that as many as 50,000 girls and women work in the sex industry in Cambodia; 35 percent are estimated to be under 18. Over 50 percent of these women are thought to have been trafficked, with the other half "voluntarily" choosing the work. HIV/AIDS is a growing problem in Cambodia. Its rate of 2.2 percent of the population is the highest in Southeast Asia, where as many as 40 percent of sex workers are infected.

Mara tried to run away several times, but each time she was caught. "The fourth time, I got away," she says. "I can't return to my family because I have HIV."

One of the most devastating effects of trafficking in Cambodia has been the breakdown of family and community structures. This story is echoed in Thyda's experience. A 13-year-old survivor of trafficking, she was sold by her mother at the age of 12.

"My mother took me to a woman's house, who took me into a room and told me to take off my clothes. She then checked if I was a virgin. The next day, I was brought back and given a haircut and some makeup." The woman sold her to a high-ranking official who paid $800 for Thyda. When she resisted, the woman who made the arrangements called her mother. "She told me that I had to—that my grandfather was sick and they needed the money—that he would die otherwise." The official paid more money and Thyda's mother received part of it. He returned the following week after Thyda's mother implored her to prostitute herself, this time telling her that her aunt was sick.

"One day I managed to find a phone and call my aunt to ask if she was sick, but she wasn't. I told her what happened, and she called a human rights organization. They called the police, who came to get me."

Thyda, who expresses shock over the fact that her mother sold her, doesn't know what she wants to do now. "I don't have any friends, and am afraid that I will be sold again if I leave this place."

The crisis center operates shelters in three provinces, where food and housing, as well as literacy education, training, counseling and legal services, are provided to women escaping violence. Women can also receive help finding jobs. Others receive start-up grants for small businesses such as restaurants and small shops, while many return to their families and communities.

Oung and others are committed to fighting a system where corruption runs rampant—from the level of police officers right up to court clerks and judges. She believes only a clear political commitment by government will make lasting change, and cites a need for judiciary reform.

What a decade of genocide and years of poverty have created will take time to undo. The women at the crisis center and the survivors of trafficking have hope, which has given way to strength and resolve.

R E A D I N G **23**

Sex Tourism Booming

IRIN (2008)

On the surface, the historic northern city of Cartagena on Colombia's Caribbean coast is an up-market tourist destination, with cruise boat passengers strolling through the old, walled city's maze of narrow streets as sight-seers duck into air-conditioned boutiques and cafés to escape the tropical heat.

But there is a seedier side to this travel-brochure charm. The backpacker hostels that line a picturesque street just outside the old city are in a notorious red-light district and many of the men dozing on benches in a nearby park are not having a siesta, but waiting to pick up sex workers.

According to Mayerlin Verqara Perez, a program coordinator at Fundación Renacer, a nongovernmental organization working to prevent the sexual exploitation of children and adolescents, almost every other person on Cartagena's streets after a certain hour at night is connected in some way to the sex trade.

The man in the sleeveless black t-shirt, smoking a cigarette, is a well-known pimp, she says, and the girl in the tight, yellow dress with the European-looking man in shorts are almost certainly a sex worker and her client. Even the group of over-dressed teenagers loitering near the entrance to the old city, are probably selling sex.

"It's become a lot worse in the last 10 years," said Perez. "There are more children doing sex work and they're starting younger."

CHILDREN DRAFTED INTO SEX WORK

Colombia's Caribbean coast has attracted a growing number of international visitors over the last decade as the country's security situation has improved. But beyond the walled city and the main hotel strip, Cartagena's inhabitants are still mostly poor, especially those displaced here from other parts of the country by the armed conflict between leftist rebel groups and right-wing paramilitary groups.

The combination of wealthy visitors and desperate locals has given rise to an alarming growth in sex tourism. "Cartagena is recognized as somewhere you can easily access sex with adults and children," Fabian Cardenas, regional director of Fundación Renacer, told IRIN/PlusNews.

"The authorities are doing a lot of surveillance, but the simple fact of looking like a tourist means you're likely to be offered these things by people working in the informal tourism industry."

Cardenas said it was common for male tourists to be approached by waiters, bellhops and taxi drivers offering introductions to sex workers and escort services. Even the drivers of the horse-drawn carriages that ferry tourists around the old city earn a commission for delivering clients to sex clubs.

Fundación Renacer estimates that some 650 children are working in the sex trade, many of them coerced into it by their parents or relatives. Every year, the organization convinces about 400 of them to participate in a psycho-social assistance program that includes testing and treatment for sexually transmitted infections (STIs), counseling, skills training and education about sexual and reproductive health and rights.

The organization used field workers like Perez to identify and gain the trust of the children and teenagers before inviting them to join the program, but pimps and abusers have started making use of new technologies to make them less visible. "Ten years ago we'd find the kids in the parks and in the night clubs, but the use of cell phones and Internet makes them harder to identify," she said.

Children who agree to participate in the program don't necessarily stay off the streets. "We try to convince them of the need for change and show them all the ways they're being maltreated, but it's hard because they have a strong link with the streets and they often don't think of themselves as victims," said Cardenas.

Many of the children are also hooked on drugs or alcohol, given to them by pimps to keep them in the sex trade. Our night tour of Cartagena takes us past a bar in the red-light district, where Perez recognizes two girls loitering near the entrance. They are drop-outs from Fundación Renacer's program, who have returned to the streets because of drug addiction.

HIV RISK

The prevalence of HIV among Colombia's general population has remained under one percent, with concentrated epidemics mainly affecting men who have sex with men.

The Caribbean region, however, has seen an increase in heterosexual infections in recent years. Whereas nationally only one out of every four people living with HIV is a woman, on the Caribbean coast the ratio is one in three.

According to Ricardo Garcia, UNAIDS country director, the region's macho culture, which makes it socially acceptable for men to have multiple partners, is probably one explanation for the trend, but the impact of sex tourism may be another.

Many of the young people who come to Fundación Renacer's centers are diagnosed with STIs. So far, the organization has only identified three with HIV, but Cardenas said many are afraid to be tested.

"Most don't take any protective measures and they're surrounded by myths," he said. "They think you can tell by looking at someone if they're sick with any of these diseases, and that washing the genitals with Cocoa-Cola after sex will protect them."

Condoms are also not always easy for child sex workers to come by. Some pimps provide them, and Fundación Renacer hands them out at clubs as a way of making contact with potential recruits to their program, but Cardenas said most under-age sex workers have low levels of knowledge about HIV and tend to comply with clients' preferences when it comes to condom use.

Clients also often harbor the illusion that child sex workers are free of STIs and that condoms aren't necessary, said Cardenas. "People come here from other countries or cities to have [unprotected] sex with children because they think it's safe."

Lesbian, Gay, Bisexual, and Transgender Rights and the Religious Relativism of Human Rights

D. Ø. Endsjø (2005)

Lesbian, gay, bisexual, and transgender (LGBT) rights are human rights. That LGBT people are not mentioned specifically in any international human rights convention does not mean that their fundamental rights are excluded from the protection offered by these conventions. As Eric Heinze argues in the monograph, *Sexual Orientation: A Human Right: An Essay on International Human Rights Law,* "those rights of sexual orientation which can be called fundamental human rights do not qualitatively differ from extant human rights in general. . . . It is for this reason that we need not 'create' rights of sexual orientation, and then 'add' them to the extant corpus of rights, but rather can derive them from that corpus, as implicit within it, and necessary for its fuller its fuller realization" (Heinze, 1995: 75).

Looking at the International Convention on Civil and Political Rights or ICCPR, one finds that there are three articles that are particularly relevant. The first of these is article 17 stating

No one shall be subjected to arbitrary or unlawful interference with his privacy, family, home or correspondence, nor to unlawful attacks on his honour and reputation.

This is not just a question of *laissez-faire*, as the article also requires the state to see to that "everyone has the right to the protection of the law against such interference or attacks." Another germane article is article 26, maintaining

All persons are equal before the law and are entitled without any discrimination to the equal protection of the law. In this respect, the law shall prohibit any discrimination and guarantee to all persons equal and effective protection against discrimination on *any* ground (my emphasis).

. . . . A similar prohibition against discrimination in general is found in article 2(1).

1. Each State Party to the present Covenant undertakes to respect and to ensure to all individuals within its territory and subject to its jurisdiction the rights recognized in the present Covenant, without distinction of *any kind* (my emphasis).

This is followed by article 2(2) requiring that "[w]here not already provided for by existing legislative or other measures, each State Party to the present Covenant undertakes to take the necessary steps."

However, when the human rights were first established, probably none of the parties considered LGBT rights to be included. Behaving in serious ways contrary to culturally established gender roles was at this time generally defined as criminal by most countries. The early decisions in the European Human Rights Commission also supported this. As Robert Wintemute points out in his book, *Sexual Orientation and Human Rights: The United States Constitution, the European Convention, and the Canadian Charter,* in a series of nine decisions dealing with applications with men being imprisoned for consensual sexual acts with other men "the Commission found all these applications inadmissible as 'manifestly ill-founded'" (Wintemute, 1995: 92).

The basic logic of the universal principle of human rights nevertheless meant that such a reading could not endure. This has been demonstrated in a number of cases in both the international and regional human rights systems in the last few years.

The way gays and lesbians, as a social group not specifically mentioned in any of the international conventions, nevertheless are included within the general prohibition against discrimination means that also other social groups like trasgenderists and the physically handicapped must be considered to be covered by the same rights. Although no cases involving transgenderists have been deliberated within the UN human rights regime, the European human rights regime has consequently clearly defined transsexuals as protected in a similar way as gays and lesbians.

A human rights article that relates to the rights of LGBT people is article 5(a) in the Convention on the Elimination of all Forms of Discrimination against Women (CEDAW), a convention ratified by most of the world's countries with certain exceptions like the United States, Iran and the Holy See.[1] Here it is declared that

> States Parties shall take all appropriate measures: (a) To modify the social and cultural patterns of conduct of men and women, with a view to achieving the elimination of prejudices and customary and all other practices which are based on the idea of the inferiority or the superiority of either of the sexes or on *stereotyped roles* for men and women (my emphasis).

This is truly relevant, as fighting for the acceptance for leading an existence beyond the "stereotyped roles for men and women" lies at the very core of the LGBT human rights struggle.

Looking at the various religious attitudes toward LGBT rights and human rights, we find that there are three different approaches

- There is the acceptance of LGBT rights as part of a general acceptance of the human rights.
- There is a general refusal to accept the human rights as in any way relevant. Although this represents an interesting case, looking here at the attitude toward any *particular* group protected by the human rights does not raise any principal questions.
- And, finally, there are those religious groups that embrace human rights, while denying that this is applying to LGBT rights.

As I have argued previously, most governments also relativize human rights in order to retain various discriminatory measures against LGBT people

(Endsjø, 2001). This attitude is however often connected with various religious traditions, either historically or directly. As reported by Amnesty International in 2001:

> Torture and other cruel, inhuman or degrading treatment are prohibited under international human rights law in all circumstances. But while some governments deny that such torture takes place, others openly justify torture and ill-treatment of LGBT people in the name of *morality, religion,* or ideology (my emphasis).[2]

Though most religions have problems with reconciling their own beliefs with the basic principles of human rights, a number of Christian churches stand prominent in what they claim to be an adamant support of human rights, while at the same time working against them.

The problem is not primarily the virulent animosity of certain churches against LGBT people. The right of religious freedom leaves any religious community at liberty to deliver whatever hateful message they may choose as long as this is theologically based. It is the embrace of human rights while simultaneously attacking the basic human rights of LGBT people in an attempt to make an effect on society at large that represents the most serious pattern. These churches use their own theological stand in order to redefine a legal term that originally has nothing to do with any religious tradition. This attempt to enforce one's beliefs through the means of civic law, even on people outside one's religious community, goes beyond any right to freedom of religion and infringes on the freedom of observance and practice, and consequently the freedom of conscience, of non-believers.

If we, for example, turn to the way the World Council of Churches, the umbrella organization representing most churches but the Catholic Church, expresses its support of the human rights in their 1998 Declaration of the Eighth Assembly, we find a number of peculiar statements which very clearly redefine human rights in order to exclude LGBT rights.

In the preamble to this Declaration, the exercise of full human rights is connected to how "All human beings are created in the image of God, equal, and infinitely precious in God's sight and ours." In this way people who may be said to distort the way they are created in the image of God, thus, it can be argued, act in a manner that is not protected by human rights. If one is not *created* as a LGBT person, *living* as a LGBT person is no human right the argument goes.

Many churches nevertheless claim that one is created as a LGBT person, but insist that the gender and sexual restrictions defined through heterosexual marriage still apply. As the World Council of Churches Declaration preamble argues that "the world has been corrupted by sin, which results in the destruction of human relationships," the way people are allowed to live out their desires, may thus be considered a result of sin.

According to the Catholic Church, the rights of lesbians, gays, and bisexuals clearly fall beyond the scope of human rights, as their very sexuality is defined as not *human*: In the official document of the Congregation for the Doctrine of the Faith of 3 June 2003, *Considerations Regarding Proposals to Give Legal Recognition to Unions between Homosexual Persons*, the Church makes clear that "[s]exual relations are *human when and insofar* as they express and promote the mutual assistance of the sexes in marriage and are open to the transmission of new life" (my emphasis). The Catholic Church as a religious community is in its right to define homosexuality as "evil," but the problem arises when the Church makes this the basis for instructing Catholic politicians, for example, to oppose any legal recognition of same sex couples, regardless of these couples being Catholic or not.

From a human rights perspective, the most serious consequence is not the way many churches support the rampant discrimination and attacks against LGBT people. The exclusion of LGBT rights from the greater context of human rights where they rightly belong means a relativism of the very concept of human rights. Once it is accepted that there are certain groups that due to certain religious or cultural prejudices do not qualify to be protected by human rights, one cannot keep others from excluding the rights of other groups because of bias found in other religions and cultures.

According to United Nations Special Rapporteur on Violence against Women, Radhika Coomaraswamy,

"the greatest challenge to international rights comes from cultural relativism and religious extremism" (Coomaraswamy, 1999: 79). The case of LGBT rights gives this claim an interesting perspective. In their effort to redefine human rights so that LGBT rights are excluded, most Christian churches insist that their own cultural relativistic perspective has a universal bearing. Extremist or not, this religious effort to reinterpret human rights based in certain religious dogma clearly fails in its universal pretension. Its insistence that historical Western values somehow are above what rights may be derived from the extant human rights corpus nourishes the cultural relativistic opposition on international rights.

The religious campaign for a relativistic understanding of human rights in order to exclude LGBT people is therefore not only something that concerns LGBT people themselves. As rights of a traditionally discriminated group in traditionally Christian societies, LGBT rights consequently stand prominent in the very defense of the universal principle of human rights. Indeed, the rights of LGBT people represent a touchstone in the Western attitude toward human rights at large. If human rights are understood in a way that makes it possible to exclude the basic rights of certain groups only because of religious and cultural prejudices traditionally found in the Christian West, we find that the principle of universality is taken right out of human rights, and human rights are transformed to a set of rules only reflecting historically Western values.

NOTES

1. With the ratification of San Marino on December 10, 2003, the number of states being party to the CEDAW is 175.
2. Amnesty International Report "Torture and ill-treatment based on sexual identity" (ACT 40/016/2001). See also Donnelly 2003:230–31.

REFERENCES

Congregation for the Doctrine of the Faith. 2003. "Considerations Regarding Proposals to Give Legal Recognition to Unions between Homosexual Persons," 3 June.

Coomaraswamy, Radhika. 1999. "Different but Free: Cultural Relativism and Women's Rights as

Human Rights" in Courtney W. Howland (ed.) *Religious Fundamentalisms and the Human Rights of Women*. New York & Houndmills: Palgrave 2001:79–90.

Endsjø, D. Ø. 2001. "I kjønnets grenseland. Vestens relative menneskerettighetsbegrep" in *Mennesker og rettigheter. Nordic Journal for Human Rights* 4: 81–90.

Heinze, Eric 1995. *Sexual Orientation: A Human Right: An Essay on International Human Rights Law*. Dordrecht, Boston & London: Martinus Nijhoff.

Wintemute, Robert 1995. *Sexual Orientation and Human Rights: The United States Constitution, the European Convention, and the Canadian Charter*. Oxford: Clarendon Press.

CHAPTER **5**

Politics of Women's Health

Mehra Shirazi

Mehra Shirazi completed her Ph.D. in Public Health Promotion and Education with a minor in Women Studies at Oregon State University, USA, where she also received her master's degree in Environmental Health Management. Her areas of research interest include immigrant women's health, international health, and transnational feminist studies. Her dissertation examined sociocultural barriers and attitudes of Iranian immigrant women with respect to breast care and access to breast health services in the United States. Dr. Shirazi teaches transnational feminist issues in Women Studies at Oregon State University and is currently a postdoctoral fellow at the School of Public Health at the University of California, Berkeley. By using a Community-Based Participatory Research (CBPR) approach, her research employs local knowledge in the understanding of health problems in order to determine whether religious, cultural impediments and their interaction, along with other psychosocial factors, preclude immigrant Muslim women from learning about their breast health care and from utilizing existing services.

Far from sweet dreams
how small is my world!
See, come near to me
so you may know the truths
of body torn with pungent
shame, leaking, weeping, and my baby
sleeping sweetly with love's hope.

"Far from sweet dreams" (anonymous).

The World Health Organization (WHO) makes the case for health as a human right, defining it as "a state of complete physical, mental and social well-being and not merely the absence of diseases and infirmity" (WHO, 1948). Central in this definition is the point that health involves not merely a right to be healthy or to access health care, but also includes a holistic notion of "well-being" grounded in a wide range of social, cultural, and economic factors that promote conditions in which people can lead a healthy life. As the poem "Far from sweet dreams" suggests, health problems diminish women's worlds and may bring shame and poverty rather than hope. This poem addresses the condition of obstetric fistula where an opening or tear between the vagina and bladder and/or rectum as a result of complications of pregnancy and childbirth causes leaking of urine and feces. Although easily preventable and treatable, an estimated 2 million women suffer from fistula worldwide.

This chapter focuses on women's health in a global context. It presents health as a human right and discusses the ways in which the politics of gender, or the ways in which power and resources are distributed according to gender, help construct health outcomes.

10 Facts About Women's Health from the World Health Organization

1. Smoking rates among men tend to be 10 times higher than for women. However, due to recent aggressive tobacco marketing campaigns aimed at women, tobacco use among younger females in developing countries is rising rapidly. Women generally have less success in quitting the habit and have more relapses than men, and nicotine replacement therapy may be less effective among women.
2. Of all adults living with HIV in sub-Saharan Africa, 61 percent are women. In the Caribbean, the proportion of women living with the virus is 43 percent. Though lower, the numbers of women living with HIV in Latin America, Asia, and eastern Europe are also growing.
3. Between 15 percent and 71 percent of women around the world have suffered physical or sexual violence committed by an intimate male partner at some point in their lives. The abuse cuts across all social and economic backgrounds. This has serious consequences for women's health.
4. Some studies show that up to one in five women reports being sexually abused before the age of 15.
5. Even though early marriage is on the decline, an estimated 100 million girls will marry before their 18th birthday over the next 10 years. This is one-third of the adolescent girls in developing countries (excluding China). Young married girls often lack knowledge about sex and the risks of sexually transmitted infections and HIV/AIDS.
6. About 14 million adolescent girls become mothers every year. More than 90 percent of these very young mothers live in developing countries.
7. Every day, 1,600 women and more than 10,000 newborns die from preventable complications during pregnancy and childbirth. Almost 99 percent of maternal and 90 percent of neonatal mortalities occur in the developing world.
8. Insecticide-treated nets (ITNs) reduce malaria cases in pregnant women and their children. When women earn an income, they are more likely than men to buy the nets for their households. However, use of the nets is often linked to sleeping patterns that sometimes preclude actual use by women.
9. In most countries women tend to be in charge of cooking. When they cook over open fires or traditional stoves, they breathe in a mix of hundreds of pollutants on a daily basis. This indoor smoke is responsible for half a million of the 1.3 million annual deaths due to chronic obstructive pulmonary disease (COPD) among women worldwide. In comparison, only about 12 percent of COPD deaths among men each year are related to indoor smoke. During pregnancy, exposure of the developing embryo to such harmful pollutants may cause low birth weight or even stillbirth.
10. Across the world and at all ages, women have a significantly higher risk of becoming visually impaired than men. Even so, women do not have equal access to health care to treat eye diseases often due to their inability to travel unaccompanied to health facilities, and cultural differences in the perceived value of surgery or treatment for women.

Source: http://www.who.int/features/factfiles/women/en/index.html

The first section provides a framework for analyzing women's health by addressing globalization and its consequences for women. This is followed by a section that discusses three key health issues affecting women today: birthing and maternal health, breastfeeding, and breast cancer. The chapter ends with a focus on the millennium development goals to promote health for women worldwide.

Human rights relating to health are embedded in international rights instruments as well as national constitutions all over the world. More than 40 years ago in 1966, for example, the International Covenant on Economic, Social and Cultural Rights (ICESCR) declared "the right of everyone to the enjoyment of the highest attainable standard of physical and mental health" and specifically called for the reduction of infant mortality and the maintenance of child health; the improvement of environmental and industrial conditions to ensure good health; and the prevention, treatment, and control of common diseases that occur at a constant but relatively low rate (endemic) and those that involve new cases in ways that exceed what might be expected (epidemic) (UNHCHR, 1966).

In 2000, the UN Committee on Economic, Social and Cultural Rights clarified the right to health to include: (1) availability of functioning public health and health care facilities, goods, and services, as well as programs in sufficient quantity; (2) accessibility of health facilities and goods and services for everyone. Accessibility implies that no one should be denied access as a result of discrimination, physical disability, lack of economic resources, or lack of access to information; (3) acceptability of health services and facilities in terms of medical ethics that include cultural and gender sensitivity; and (4) ample quality of health services that meet scientific and medical standards.

Also emphasized was the need for timely and appropriate primary health care; access to safe and potable water and adequate sanitation; an adequate supply of safe food, nutrition, and housing; healthy occupational and environmental conditions; and access to health-related education and information, including information on sexual and reproductive health. A final aspect required nations to create national public health plans of action that address the health concerns of the entire population (UNHCHR, 2000). In this way, the right to health is not to be interpreted as only a right to have health services, but embraces a wide range of socioeconomic factors for healthy living (Gruskin and Tarantola, 2005).

Although health has been constituted as a human right, it must also be understood in the context of gender relations and other differences among women. The reading by Anne Firth Murray titled "Aging in a Man's World" emphasizes that health is more than a

LEARNING ACTIVITY   **Women's Health in Your Community**

Research women's health issues in your own community.

- What state laws govern midwifery in your community?
- What are the maternal mortality rates in your community?
- Do local insurance providers cover contraception?
- Do women in your community have easy access to emergency contraception, condoms, and abortion services?
- What is the breast cancer rate in your community?
- What are the largest employers in your community? Do they offer health insurance? Do their practices create health risks?
- How do issues of race/ethnicity and social class intersect with gender in women's access to healthcare in your community?
- Are there many women war veterans in your community? What health services can they access?
- What resources does your community provide for women who experience gender-based violence?
- What are the hunger rates in your community?
- What services for women does your student health center provide? Are there services that are lacking?

Invite a local physician specializing in women's health to speak on your campus. Work with your classmates to develop informational posters and brochures about local issues and resources for women's health and distribute them on campus and in your community.

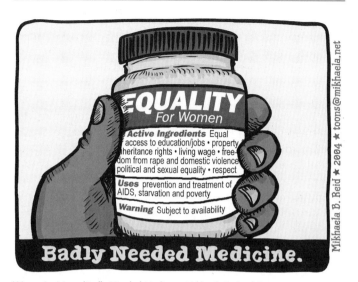

EQUALITY
For Women

Active Ingredients Equal access to education/jobs • property inheritance rights • living wage • freedom from rape and domestic violence • political and sexual equality • respect

Uses prevention and treatment of AIDS, starvation and poverty

Warning Subject to availability

Mikhaela B. Reid ★ 2004 ★ toons@mikhaela.net

Badly Needed Medicine.

Women's eNews/Badly Needed Medicine, Mikhaela B. Reid Commentoon.

medical issue and must be understood in a cultural, political, and economic context that pays attention to social justice. She writes that old women are one of the world's fastest growing populations and one of the most vulnerable. A framework giving significance to gender and other differences like age and class recognizes injustices and emphasizes the particular situations of women worldwide vis-à-vis health requirements. In terms of access, for example, women have unequal access to, and use of, basic health resources, including primary health services for the prevention and treatment of diseases. They also have different and unequal opportunities for the protection, promotion and maintenance of their health. Today, the subordinate position of women in society is globally recognized as a breach of human rights and a barrier to development. It is also now recognized that women's subordination in society has been institutionalized through structures that organize social life in ways that marginalize women. Many women and girls face serious obstacles in recognition of their human right to health, including unequal access to health care, food, and nutrition, and traditional practices detrimental to their health and well-being. All inequalities relating to health and practices are harmful to women and violate their fundamental human rights. Such inequalities precipitate high neonatal, infant, and maternal mortality rates worldwide. The reading "Using Human Rights to Improve Maternal and Neonatal Health" by Sofia Gruskin and colleagues addresses the ways mortality rates in the developing world came to be understood as a public health and human rights concern. It presents a program using a human rights framework to reduce these mortality rates.

GLOBALIZATION AND WOMEN'S HEALTH

As discussed in other chapters, globalization includes economic, technological, political, and cultural aspects whereby the forces of market economies expand beyond powers of the nation. This section focuses on six health consequences of contemporary globalization: (1) the transformation of traditional medicine and healing practices; (2) the consequences of structural adjustment policies (SAPs) on health status; (3) the health effects of women's work in transnational factories and in intensive agriculture; (4) women's health in the context of war; (5) health and environmental change and disasters; and (6) the feminization of poverty.

First, economic globalization is accompanied by cultural aspects of globalization or the transnational mobilization of information, people, and consumer cultures. A central aspect of this trend toward a fully integrated world is the loss of traditional healing practices in some traditional communities and the imposition of Western medicine. For example, traditional Aboriginal midwives in Canada were fundamental to the process of childbirth within their traditional communities. They were influential members of the tribe and had a prominent role in shaping cultural knowledge and identity from one generation to the next. Today the decline of Aboriginal midwifery and loss of traditional knowledge of maternity care and delivery have reached a point where only a few midwife elders currently exist in rural and northern communities (Benoit and Dena, 2001). The reading "Midwifery's Renaissance" by Marsden Wagner discusses the history and present status of midwifery in the United States, exploring the reasons for its low status and illustrating the rebirth of this practice as a legitimate health profession that reduces infant mortality rates.

Second, structural adjustment policies, or SAPs, are imposed through international monetary organizations such as the International Monetary Fund (IMF) and the World Bank as a condition of international lending. As already discussed, SAPs require indebted countries to reduce levels of public expenditure in order to assist the repayment of international debt and/or readjust spending patterns in line with perceived needs of a globalizing world economy. These policies directly influence health outcomes as a result of what is sometimes called a "hollowing out" of individual states that reduces the provision of health care and other services (Van der Gaag and Barham, 1998). While these practices may increase gross national product (GNP), measures in these countries destroy national infrastructure and bring hardship to individual citizens and especially women as caregivers in families. No such conditions are ever imposed on wealthy industrial countries. By expanding markets for transnational corporations, economic globalization tends to drive out rural production in industrializing countries and instead provides work with low pay and little job security, shelter, or benefits, and which poses health hazards and problems. The end result has been loss of livelihood, ancestral farms, and increased health problems.

Third, economic globalization has created transnational factory production as a result of the relocation of labor-intensive factories (such as garment-making and some electronics manufacturing) to lower-wage areas in Asia and Latin America. In these zones, companies are often exempt from health, safety, and environmental regulations that affect the health and well-being of workers. Very often young women are sought as cheap, easily controlled labor, and treated as disposable with no or few concerns about long-term health consequences. For example, since the passage of the North American Free Trade Agreement (NAFTA) in 1994, Mexico is home to over 3,000 maquiladoras (assembly sweatshops producing for export), employing over 1.3 million, mostly female, Mexican workers. They are paid an average of 50 cents an hour, have no job security or benefits, and are often subject to sexual harassment and unsafe working conditions (Moffat, 2006). In addition, as discussed in chapter 10, globalization has precipitated

ACTIVIST PROFILE   **Vjosa Dobruna and Flora Brovina**

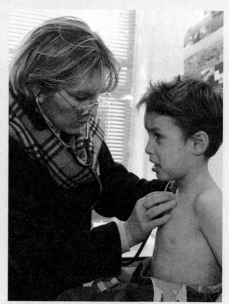

Flora Brovina

Vjosa Dobruna

Vjosa Dobruna and Flora Brovina are pediatricians in Kosovo who have dedicated themselves to advocating for the rights of women and children in their war-torn nation. Dr. Brovina is the founder and director of the League of Albanian Women, and Dr. Dobruna is the head of the Center for Protection of Women and Children.

Longstanding conflicts between Serbs and Albanians led to war in Kosovo in the late 1990s. Yugoslavian president Slobodan Milošević had consolidated power in the region in the hands of Serbians, withdrawing autonomy from the various republics that constituted Yugoslavia and beginning a systematic campaign of repression and ethnic cleansing. In Kosovo, Albanians resisted Milošević's rule, hoping the world community would recognize their plight and assist them. When this did not happen, the Kosovo Liberation Army began to fight the Serbs, and the Serbs retaliated, destroying villages and killing civilians. NATO at last intervened and attempted to broker a peace treaty, but those efforts failed, and Milošević saturated Kosovo with troops. Finally, NATO launched missiles against Serb military targets. Milošević's troops responded by attempting an ethnic cleansing of Albanians from Kosovo. The war ended a few months later when Milošević agreed to NATO's terms. Eventually, Milošević was arrested to be tried for war crimes and genocide, but he died in the UN detention center at The Hague before a verdict was reached.

During the war, Dr. Brovina founded the Center for the Rehabilitation of Women and Children, that increasingly cared for women and children fleeing the war. Unlike many other health care providers, she refused to leave Kosovo, explaining that she could not abandon her mothers and children. She also helped organize a number of peaceful protests against the violence in Kosovo. In April 1999, Serbian soldiers kidnapped Dr. Brovina and imprisoned her, subjecting her to more than 200 hours of interrogation across 18 day-long sessions. Serbs claimed the wool the women in her center were knitting was used in sweaters for the Kosovo Liberation Army. Brovina was tried for terrorist activities and sentenced to 12 years in prison. Following the war, tremendous international pressure led to her release on November 1, 2000. Just before she was arrested, *Marie Claire* magazine had named her one of the top three most influential women in the world. Following her release, she received numerous accolades, including the Henrich Boll award for civic courage, UNIFEM's Millennium Peace Prize for Women, and the Jonathan Mann Award for Health and Human Rights.

Receiving the Mann Award with Dr. Brovina was her friend and colleague Dr. Vjosa Dobruna. Dr. Dobruna was locked out of the hospital where she worked because she was Albanian. This event led to her involvement in civil disobedience as she helped wounded people and sent out reports of human rights violations. She was arrested by Serb Special Police in 1999 and sent to a refugee camp in Macedonia, where she opened a women's center. Following the war, she became Kosovo's minister in charge of democratization, good governance, and media. Throughout her participation she emphasized the necessity of women's involvement in the reconstruction of Kosovo. She left the ministry, however, because she felt that there was not an authentic partnership between Kosovars and the international community and that women were being prevented from participating in the reconstruction.

http://www.huntalternatives.org/pages/398_vjosa_dobruna.cfm
http://www.friendsofbosnia.org/kosovo/14.htm
http://www.globalhealth.org/conference/view_top.php3?id=526
http://www.albanianliterature.com/authors_modern2/brovina.html

environmental degradation and has endangered the health of agricultural workers and families living in these communities through exposures to toxic herbicides and pesticides. In the reading "Canadian Petrochemical Plants and Gender Imbalances," author Paul Webster discusses the health problems among the North American Chippewa on Canada's Aamjiwnaang Reserve where petrochemical plants pollute the environment. Chippewa complaints were ignored until a recent study found a significant reduction of male births caused by the toxins.

Fourth, as discussed in other chapters, economic globalization has facilitated wars worldwide that affect women's health. Of the more than 30 million refugees and internally displaced persons as a result of armed conflict or natural disasters, 80 percent are women and children. Wars often limit access to clean drinking water, food, adequate shelter, sanitary facilities, and health services, resulting in a higher risk of epidemics and nutritional problems. Armed conflict threatens women's rights, including reproductive rights and health, and can exacerbate culturally-rooted gender inequalities. Women refugees also often face unwanted, unplanned, and poorly spaced pregnancies due to a lack of access to contraceptive services and supplies (ICRC, 2008). The lack of sanitary supplies for menstruation can impede the mobility of women and girls and may cause them to experience discomfort, shame, and isolation for several days each month. Pregnant women and nursing mothers may also find that there is limited care available. While fleeing or during early settlement, women may have to give birth in conditions hazardous both to them and to their children (ICRC, 2008). Such conditions often result in higher maternal mortality rates. A study of Afghan refugees, for example, showed that 41 percent of women's deaths were due to maternal causes, exceeding any other cause (Bartlett, 2002). Rape, sexual exploitation, and sex for survival during war leads to early pregnancies and puts women at greater risk of HIV/AIDS, sexually transmitted infections (STIs), an increase in (often

Women and girls are most at risk of violence from men they know, particularly in the family.

Rape and sexual torture are used as weapons of war.

Violence against women has serious mental, physical and sexual health consequences.

Violence against women is a public health problem. It can be prevented.

World Health Organization

unsafe) abortions, psychological harm, and immediate and serious physical injuries, such as infertility, obstetric fistulas, and vaginal bleeding.

Fifth, in terms of environmental changes, the health consequences (including death, of course) of tsunamis, hurricanes, and tornadoes are tremendous for all involved. However, women face disproportionate harms in disaster situations. According to a UNIFEM report of the 2010 earthquake, Haiti's most vulnerable members were hardest hit. Similarly, an Oxfam report of the 2004 Indonesian tsunami emphasized that in four villages in Indonesia's North Aceh district, females accounted for over three-quarters of the deaths and in Cuddalore, India, almost three times as many women were killed as men. In fact, in one entire village, the only people to die were women (Oxfam International, 2005). From the time disaster strikes, women become more susceptible to violence that compromises their physical and emotional health. For example, after the Indian Ocean tsunami, some women who were pulled out of the water alive were assaulted as "payment" for being saved. In Nicaragua 27 percent of female survivors of Hurricane Mitch reported increased violence within the family. Similar trends were reported in the Philippines after the eruption of Mt. Pinatubo, and, following the Loma Prieta earthquake in California, reported sexual assault rose by 300 percent (Women's Edge Coalition, 2005). These statistics are representative of the greater trend of disproportionate harm to women during disasters.

In terms of both wars and natural disasters, alongside the health hazards of living as refugees in crowded conditions without adequate sanitation levels and with very limited resources, gendered cultural practices (such as serving a greater portion of nutritious foods to males and avoiding medical attention for women exhibiting signs of malnutrition) can also result in women's decreased immunity and increased susceptibility to disease. In Sri Lanka, for instance, where civil war rages, internally displaced women in refugee camps without any male relatives are particularly vulnerable to increased sexual violence (WHO, 2006). Female children, both inside and outside of refugee camps, who have lost one or both parents in disasters, may be forced into child marriage and trafficking for economic and cultural reasons. In post-tsunami Indonesia women were sexually harassed in camps, as well as forced or rushed into marrying much older men (WHO, 2006). All these situations take a toll on women's health status.

Sixth, economic globalization has led to a widened gap between the rich and poor around the world, placing an increased burden on women and children (Center for Concern, 2003). Although extreme poverty creates hardships for all people, especially as this number has been increasing worldwide (today 1.3 billion people are living on less than one U.S. dollar a day [UNDP, 2008]), it is especially women and children who are affected. During the past two decades, for example, despite several decades of "development," poverty levels for rural women in 41 developing countries have increased by almost a fifth (Antrobus, 2004). Female poverty affects women's roles in maintaining food security for families and households and therefore affects community health (World's Women, 2005). As already mentioned, women and girls receive fewer household resources like food leading to higher malnutrition and mortality rates. Because of their lower social and economic status, as well as their physiological needs (such as childbirth and lactation), women are often more vulnerable to nutritional problems. As the price of food has increased around the world, women face higher risks of malnutrition because they usually eat last, and less, after providing for their children and family. Since households in developing countries spend an average of 70 percent of their incomes on food (compared to the 15 to 18 percent spent in industrialized countries), increases in food prices cause them to sink further into poverty. For example it is estimated that 3.6 million people in Niger have been affected by the current food crisis. Pregnant and lactating mothers are among the groups considered most at risk, with more than 261,000 women in need of emergency care (UN Department of Public Information, 2008).

Poor female nutrition early in life reduces learning potential, increases reproductive and maternal health risks, and lowers productivity. Frequent pregnancies and heavy workloads, combined with poor diets and frequent infections can severely weaken a woman's health. In South and Southeast Asia, 45 to 60% of reproductive-age women are underweight, and up to 80 percent of pregnant women are iron deficient. All these factors contribute to women's diminished ability to gain access to other assets later in life and undermine attempts to eliminate gender inequalities (FAO, 2008). In addition, malnutrition is perpetuated from one generation to the next as up to 17 million children are born annually with low birth weight as a result of maternal malnourishment. Low-birth-weight babies are four times more likely to die in the first week of life from infections such as diarrhea and face a tenfold higher risk of dying during the first month of life. Those who survive are more likely to remain malnourished throughout childhood and face cognitive difficulties that impair their ability to learn (FAO, 2008). In these ways, investment in women's nutrition not only improves household nutrition generally, but overall human capacity given women's key roles in maintaining family welfare. The following sections provide specific examples of the consequences of female poverty and disempowerment for women's health through a focus on birthing, breast-feeding, and breast cancer. The conclusion to *Women Worldwide* also discusses a key aspect of women's health: HIV/AIDS. It uses the AIDS pandemic as a case study and integrates poverty and other socio-economic and cultural factors associated with chapter themes to help understand women's lives worldwide.

Women and Food Security: Access to Resources

Despite their role as the backbone of food production and provision for family consumption in developing countries, women remain limited in their access to critical resources and services. While in most developing countries, both men and women farmers do not have access to adequate resources, women's access is even more limited due to cultural, traditional, and sociological factors. Accurate information about men's and women's relative access to, and control over, resources is crucial in the development of food security strategies.

Access to land. Not even 2 percent of land is owned by women, while the proportion of female heads of household continues to grow. Land reform programs together with the break-up of communal landholdings have led to the transfer of exclusive land rights to males as heads of households, which ignores both the existence of female-headed households and the rights of married women to a joint share.

Access to credit. For the countries where information is available, only 10 percent of credit allowances are extended to women, mainly because national legislation and customary law do not allow them to share land property rights along with their husbands or because female heads of household are excluded from land entitlement schemes and consequently cannot provide the collateral required by lending institutions.

Access to agricultural inputs. Women's access to technological inputs such as improved seeds, fertilizers, and pesticides is limited as they are frequently not reached by extension services and are rarely members of cooperatives, which often distribute government-subsidized inputs to small farmers. In addition, they often lack the cash income needed to purchase inputs even when they are subsidized.

Access to education, training, and extension services. Two-thirds of the one billion illiterate in the world are women and girls. Available figures show that only 5 percent of extension services have been addressed to rural women, while no more than 15 percent of the world's extension agents are women. In addition, most of the extension services are focused on cash crops rather than food and subsistence crops, which are the primary concern of women farmers and the key to food security.

Access to decision-making. Given the traditionally limited role of women in decision-making processes at the household, village, and national levels in most cultures, their needs, interests, and constraints are often not reflected in policy-making processes and laws, which are important for poverty reduction, food security, and environmental sustainability. The causes of women's exclusion from decision-making processes are closely linked to their additional reproductive roles and their household workload, which account for an important share of their time.

Access to research and appropriate technology. Women have little access to the benefits of research and innovation, especially in the domain of food crops, which in spite of ensuring food security at the household and community levels, have a low priority in crop improvement research. In addition, women farmers' roles and needs are often ignored when devising technology that may cause labor displacement or increased workload.

Source: Food and Agriculture Organization of the U.N.

WOMEN'S RIGHT TO LIFE

No Woman Should Die Giving Life

Complications related to pregnancy and childbirth are among the leading causes of death for women of reproductive age in many parts of the developing world. The maternal mortality ratio (MMR), or number of maternal deaths per 100,000 live births, is an approximation of the risk of death of women for reasons related to pregnancy and childbirth. Every minute one woman dies during pregnancy or birth because she did not receive adequate care and prompt treatment, with estimated mortality rates at over half a million worldwide. Death is not the only tragic consequence of complications associated with reproductive health, since nonfatal complications can also have serious effects. Ten to 20 million women annually are estimated to suffer severe health problems related to pregnancy, including obstetric fistula, discussed earlier, that have painful and long-lasting effects on a woman's quality of life.

These high maternal mortality rates draw attention to the vast disparities in reproductive health status as a result of poverty and unequal access to maternal health care services. For example, sub-Saharan Africa and Asia account for 96 percent of maternal deaths worldwide. The lifetime risk of maternal death is as high as one in seven for women in some African and Asian countries such as Afghanistan and Sierra Leone, compared with 1 in 17,400 in the most developed countries like Sweden (UNICEF, 2008). The causes of maternal death are very consistent around the world. Some 80 percent are due to direct obstetric complications: hemorrhage, sepsis, complications of abortion, pre-eclampsia and eclampsia, and prolonged/obstructed labor. About one-fifth of deaths have indirect causes: generally existing medical conditions that are aggravated by pregnancy or delivery. These include anemia, malaria, hepatitis, and HIV/AIDS (UNICEF, 2008).

While there are differences between rich and poor countries in terms of access to maternal health resources, there are also great disparities within countries such as between the poorest and the wealthiest families and between rural and urban populations. Skilled care by trained health workers during births, in addition to basic interventions before, during, and after pregnancy, is one of the keys to maternal health. In Africa, just 46.5 percent of women have skilled birth attendants; in Asia, 65.4 percent; and in Latin America and the Caribbean, 88.5 percent. In sub-Saharan Africa, South Asia, and Southeast Asia, the proportion of women giving birth with the assistance of a skilled birth attendant is more than twice as high among the wealthy than among poorer women in the same region (UNFPA, 2008).

Maternal deaths related to pregnancy and childbirth are important causes of mortality for girls aged 15–19 worldwide, accounting for about 70,000 deaths each year. The younger a girl is when she becomes pregnant, the greater the health risks. Girls who give birth before the age of 15 are five times more likely to die in childbirth than women in their twenties. In addition, infants born to mothers under the age of 18 years have a 60 percent higher risk of dying in their first year of life than those born to older mothers. Even if the child survives, s/he is more likely to suffer from low birth weight, be under-nourished, and exhibit late physical and cognitive development (UNICEF, 2008). The lowest percentages (less than 10 percent) of early childbearing (defined as having a child before age 18 years) occur in industrialized countries such as Germany, Poland, France, Great Britain, and the United States. Japan, for example, has rates as low as 1 percent. This low rate is in part due to social and cultural attitudes toward teenage

Estimates of MMR, number of maternal deaths, lifetime risk, range of uncertainty by United Nations MDG regions

Region	MMR (maternal deaths per 100,000 live births)*	Number of maternal deaths*	Lifetime risk of maternal death*: 1 in:
WORLD TOTAL	400	536,000	92
Developed regions**	9	960	7, 300
Countries of the Commonwealth of Independent States (CIS)***	51	1,800	1,200
Developing regions	450	533,000	75
Africa	820	276,000	26
Northern Africa****	160	5,700	210
Sub-Saharan Africa	900	270,000	22
Asia	330	241,000	120
Eastern Asia	50	9,200	1,200
South Asia	490	188,000	61
Southeast Asia	300	35,000	130
Western Asia	160	8,300	170
Latin America and the Caribbean	130	15,000	290
Oceania	430	890	62

* The MMR and lifetime risk have been rounded according to the following scheme: <100, no rounding; 100–999, rounded to nearest 10; and >1,000, rounded to nearest 100. The numbers of maternal deaths have been rounded as follows: <1,000, rounded to nearest 10, 1,000–9,999, rounded to nearest 100; and >10,000, rounded to nearest 1,000.

** Includes Albania, Australia, Austria, Belgium, Bosnia and Herzegovina, Bulgaria, Canada, Croatia, Czech Republic, Denmark, Estonia, Finland, France, Germany, Greece, Hungary, Iceland, Ireland, Italy, Japan, Latvia, Lithuania, Luxembourg, Malta, Netherlands, New Zealand, Norway, Poland, Portugal, Romania, Serbia and Montenegro (Serbia and Montenegro became separate independent entities in 2006), Slovakia, Slovenia, Spain, Sweden, Switzerland, The former Yugoslav Republic of Macedonia, the United Kingdom, the United States of America.

*** The CIS countries are Armenia, Azerbaijan, Belarus, Georgia, Kazakhstan, Kyrgyzstan, Tajikistan, Turkmenistan, Uzbekistan, the Republic of Moldova, the Russian Federation, and Ukraine.

**** Excludes Sudan, which is included in sub-Saharan Africa.

pregnancy. Countries with the highest percentage age of early child bearing include Bangladesh, Cameroon, Mali, Liberia, Côte d'Ivoire (Ivory Coast), Uganda, the Central African Republic, Malawi, and Nigeria, where over a third of women have children before the age of 18 years (UNICEF, 2008).

As discussed in chapter 7, early marriage is prevalent in poor rural areas and is closely related to poverty. While reasons for child marriage vary, conservative traditional practices and strong social pressures, widespread illiteracy, and poverty are the underlying reasons. In these cultures parents may consent to child marriage because of economic necessity or because they believe that marriage will protect their daughters by providing male guardianship, prevent pregnancy outside marriage and exposure to HIV/AIDS, extend their childbearing years, and ensure obedience to the husband's household (UNICEF, 2005a). Socially, early childbearing contributes to factors that keep young women in a cycle of poverty (UNICEF, 2008). Early marriage and pregnancy are also associated with higher illiteracy rates and higher incidences of domestic violence (World's Women, 2005). For example, India has the highest levels of domestic violence (67 percent) among women married before age 18 years.

So why is the progress in reducing maternal mortality so slow? Although campaigns by the international community to improve maternal health have been widely accepted and motherhood as an institution has been praised for centuries as a noble goal, resources to ensure healthy mothers are denied to most women worldwide. In many countries, progress is inadequate and in some the situation has actually deteriorated as a result of increasing poverty, HIV/AIDS, malaria, and tuberculosis. Sub-Saharan Africa shows the least progress with an annual decline of maternal mortality rates by only 0.1 percent. Countries affected by humanitarian emergencies lack even the basic reproductive health services. According to the United Nations Population Fund (UNFPA, 2006), the answer is the lack of "political will" as well as the "inadequacy of resources" complicated by other competing social issues. Fathalla (2007), an Egyptian physician, discusses the tragedy of maternal mortality in developing countries, noting the gravity of the situation is underestimated since the majority of maternal deaths go unrecorded or the cause of death is not specified. Fathalla explains that health services tend to be oriented toward children rather than mothers, but emphasizes sexism as the main reason why maternal mortality is neglected: "[in these regions] women do not enjoy a high social status. It is a question of how much mothers are worth" (p. 251). There are, however, some improvements. In China, for example, as well as in Cuba, Egypt, Honduras, Jamaica, Malaysia, Sri Lanka, Thailand, and Tunisia, there have been significant declines in maternal mortality as more women gain access to primary health care that includes family planning and skilled birth attendance, backed up by emergency obstetric care including postabortion care. Many of these countries have been able to reduce their maternal mortality rates by half within a decade.

Breastfeeding Is a Child's and a Woman's Right

The importance of breastfeeding has been well documented, and several studies have indicated that early breastfeeding is associated with (1) increased survival, particularly decreased sepsis, diarrhea, pneumonia, sudden infant death syndrome (SIDS), and other physical problems; (2) reduced low birth weights and reduced growth stunting; (3) reduced obesity and other factors related to heart disease; and (4) reduced infectious and chronic illness. It is estimated that about 5 to 6 million babies are saved annually who would otherwise die from common infectious disease, and an additional 1.3 million lives could be saved if women breastfed exclusively for six months or longer. In other words, approximately 3,500 unnecessary child deaths occur every day due to lack of support for exclusive breastfeeding, contributing to a total of almost 6,000 deaths occurring daily for lack of optimal infant and young child feeding generally (Labbok, 2006). Breastfeeding is also beneficial to a mother's health. Women who breastfeed have better postpartum recovery; less iron loss; lowered incidence of breast, ovarian, and uterine cancers; and better bone status in older age. Breastfeeding also increases the duration of birth intervals, reducing maternal risks of too closely spaced pregnancies. Frequent pregnancies take a toll on the body and may result in nutritional depletions. At the same time, however, optimal breastfeeding requires adequate maternal nutrition.

Despite the proven risks in formulas and the benefits of mother's milk, few of the 136 million babies born each year receive optimal breastfeeding, and some are not breastfed at all. Early cessation of breastfeeding in favor of commercial breast milk substitute is far too common (Black, 2008). For example, breastfeeding patterns in Malaysia suggest that in recent years, only two in seven infants in Malaysia are exclusively breastfed for the first four months of life, two months short of the six months recommended by WHO and UNICEF. In the Philippines, the rate of exclusive breastfeeding at four to five months fell from 20 percent in 1998 to 16 percent in 2003. It is estimated that 16,000 deaths of children under five in the Philippines are caused by inappropriate feeding practices, including the use of infant formula (UNICEF, 2005b). Low rates in infant breastfeeding have been attributed to several factors such as aggressive marketing strategies of the infant formula industry, ineffective or unenforced code measures, insufficient policies to protect breastfeeding practices in the workplace and public spaces, and inappropriate advice and care by some maternity facilities. Such factors, coupled with the absence of encouragement and support from family members, make breastfeeding a difficult choice for mothers to make and sustain (UNICEF, 2008).

Two international conventions, the Convention on the Rights of the Child and the Convention on the Elimination of All Forms of Discrimination against Women (CEDAW), have framed and supported breastfeeding as a right for both the child and the mother. Both conventions place considerable responsibility on the state to provide accommodations to encourage women to breastfeed. Throughout the world, women's autonomy has often been limited in the name of ensuring children's well-being, subordinating women's rights to children's rights. However, by framing the issue as a woman's right to choose and succeed with breastfeeding, these campaigns have made the support of these rights an obligation for the family, society, and workplace (UNICEF, 2005b).

Women Should Be Able to Live Without Fear of Breast Cancer

Breast cancer is the most common cause of cancer-related death among women around the globe. According to the American Cancer Society (ACS) statistics from 2007, annually about 1.3 million women are diagnosed with breast cancer with an estimated 465,000 deaths. Breast cancer incidence and rates vary considerably by world region. Rates are highest in the high-income countries of North America, Australia, and northern and western Europe and lowest in the low- and middle-income countries of Asia and Africa. Intermediate levels are reported in eastern Europe (ACS, 2007).

While age is an important factor affecting breast cancer risk, biological risk is also increased by inheritance of two genetic mutations (BRCA1 and BRCA2), a personal or family history of breast cancer, high breast tissue density (a mammographic measure of the amount of glandular tissue relative to fatty tissue in the breast), and high-dose radiation to the chest as a result of medical procedures. However, there are other specific factors contributing to the considerable differences in incidence rates between industrialized and nonindustrialized countries. These involve differences in reproductive and hormonal histories that increase risk, including (1) extended exposure to estrogen over the life cycle (a long menstrual history or menstrual periods that start early and/or include late onset of menopause); (2) prolonged use of oral contraceptives; (3) use of postmenopausal hormone therapy (especially combined estrogen and progestin therapy); (4) never having children; (5) never having breastfed; and (6) having children after age 30. In addition, (7) women in high-rate countries consume more fat in their diet, are more likely to be overweight

FACING HEALTH CARE BARRIERS   **Maria's Story: Fighting Breast Cancer**

Maria Saloniki can hardly remember how many times she went to the local traditional healer; how many doctors she consulted; how many words she used to describe her pain. But one thing she clearly remembers is that each time, she returned home without receiving the right kind of treatment and care.

Today, Maria—a livestock keeper and mother of 10 children—is fighting for her life at the Ocean Road Cancer Institute in Dar es Salaam, United Republic of Tanzania.

It took her more than three years to discover the words that would describe her pain—breast cancer— and to receive the chemotherapy she desperately needed.

"It all started with a swollen armpit and a bad fever," the 60-year-old recalls. "The traditional healer prescribed herb ointments and doctors initially prescribed antibiotics. Some even told me that nothing could be done to help ease the pain."

It wasn't until later, in Dar es Salaam, that a biopsy revealed her disease.

Maria's husband works day and night to pay for her medicines and feed their children. His tribe has also lent him money to cover the full treatment costs, but he still can't afford the bus fares to visit his wife. The family has one year to pay back the loan.

Maria's story is common among the people she sees in the understaffed and poorly equipped hospital ward.

For thousands of women, poor access to quality health care often means that cancer is not detected until it is too late.

Around half a million women die from breast cancer each year. Seventy percent of these deaths are in low- and middle-income countries.

http://www.who.int/features/cancer/en/index.html

or obese after menopause, are less physically active, and consume one or more alcoholic beverages per day (ACS, 2007). Finally, (8) women in many high-rate industrialized countries have higher exposures to toxins such as xenoestrogens (human-made compounds that mimic the effect of naturally occurring estrogen) in the environment and in growth hormones used in beef, chicken, and dairy production.

In high-resource countries, guidelines outlining best approaches to early detection, diagnosis, and treatment of breast cancer have resulted in increased cancer survival rates. However, minority women in the United States are more likely to be diagnosed at an advanced stage of the disease and have higher death rates than do white women as a result of their lower socioeconomic status and reduced access to care. When white and black women are presented with cancer at a similar stage of disease and receive similar treatment, they have similar outcomes.

Breast cancer survival rates for women in low- and middle-income countries average 57 percent (and are as low as 46 percent in India and 32 percent in sub-Saharan Africa), mostly as a result of late-stage diagnosis that leads to particularly higher death rates when accompanied by limited treatment capacities. Many low- and middle-income countries have less than 5 percent of the resources required for adequate cancer control, and more than 80 percent of their cancer patients will be incurable at the time of diagnosis. Alongside insufficient resources, barriers to improving cancer care arise from lack of public knowledge and awareness, social and cultural barriers, and challenges in organizing health-care facilities. According to the International Atomic Energy Agency (2003), 85 percent of the world's population lives in developing countries, but is served by only 30 percent of the world's radiotherapy facilities. On the other hand, developed countries, with 15 percent of the world's population, have 70 percent of these facilities. Nearly 15 countries in Africa and several countries in Asia do not have even one radiation therapy machine.

With limited financial resources, these countries also face difficult choices in terms of the distribution of funds between such priority areas as prevention, screening, early detection, treatment, and pain management. Problems are also complicated by the fact that guidelines for optimal cancer care from high income countries are not always easily transferable to low income countries, and, as a result, are often unworkable. The reading "A Shared Journey in Breast Cancer Advocacy" by Kathleen M. Errico and Diana Rowden discusses common themes associated with breast cancer survivor-advocates that are transferable across cultures and which may help constitute an action agenda for support and advocacy. In addition, the first Global Summit Consensus Conference on International Breast Healthcare held in 2002 in Seattle, Washington, developed guidelines to address early detection, diagnosis, and treatment of breast cancer in countries with limited healthcare resources.

A WAY FORWARD

Throughout the world, women are addressing inequalities that deny their human rights, endanger their health, hinder them from productive opportunities, and threaten them with violence. This happens in various settings: within the family, in schools, and in commercial and political institutions. In the case of health, women's social, economic, and political status undermines their ability to protect and promote their own physical, emotional, and mental health, including their effective use of health information and services. Women deserve better. The "way forward" is grounded in practices that place improving women's health at the center of global efforts. Indeed, in September 2000 health issues were at the core of the Millennium Development Goals (MDGs). These include eight priority goals adopted by all UN member states with a 2015 realization date. Health is implicit in all MDGs, being explicitly mentioned in three goals and key to the realization of all eight. The eight MDGs are as follows:

- Eradicate extreme poverty and hunger
- Achieve universal primary education
- Promote gender equality and women's empowerment
- Reduce child mortality
- Improve maternal health
- Combat HIV/AIDS, malaria, and other diseases
- Ensure environmental sustainability
- Develop a global partnership for development

Despite these promises, many women and gender rights advocates believe that MDGs do not represent the comprehensive vision of gender equality, poverty eradication, and women's empowerment imagined in key human rights instruments. These advocates point out that in most developing countries gender inequality is a major obstacle to meeting the

MDG targets. In fact, achieving the goals will be impossible without addressing inequalities in terms of access to resources and opportunities, and vulnerability to violence and conflict. They argue that in MDGs women are often perceived as helpless victims, mere beneficiaries of policies determined by others, rather than women as agents of change. Speaking on behalf of many feminists and social justice activists, Peggy Antrobus (2003) considers the MDGs as strategic entry point[s] for raising issues that are important to women with people who pay no attention to women otherwise.

Equality between women and men is vital for realizing the world's goals to reduce poverty, eliminate hunger, fight disease, and promote education. Gender equality is a goal in its own right and central for the attainment of social policies in a wide range of areas, including the improvement of health (WEDO, 2008). As this chapter emphasizes, it is necessary to address discrimination on the basis of gender in healthcare practices and to ensure that interventions in health involve benefit to those who have least resources. Changes are occurring, but these changes are not fast enough. A woman dies in pregnancy or childbirth every minute. One in three women experiences gender-based violence in her lifetime. Almost two million girls are at risk of being harmed by female genital cutting each year. HIV infection rates among women are rapidly rising. Of the 115 million children who are not in school, 62 million are girls. Three out of four fatalities of war are women and children. And, too

A DAY IN THE LIFE   **Providing Care** by *Jennifer Jabson*

Aleksandra wakes before dawn to the sound of church bells ringing at 4 a.m. Aleksandra lives in the Podil district, the oldest district or neighborhood in Kyiv, with her aging parents. Podil is not only the oldest of the districts in Kyiv; since the "euro-renovation" movement began some years ago after the fall of Soviet rule, Podil has also become one of the few remaining affordable districts in Kyiv. The newly renovated houses and apartment homes are increasingly modern with many of the contemporary comforts of the Western world; however, they are also accompanied by much higher rents. Yet in Podil it is still possible to find a small and affordable (about $350 U.S.), albeit unrenovated, apartment residence.
The apartment that Aleksandra shares with her parents is modest and does not have any of the amenities of the more costly dwellings such as a dishwasher, washer/dryer, or garbage disposal. Despite the absence of such expensive amenities their apartment home is comfortable and suits Aleksandra's family's needs perfectly.

The old wood floor of the modest apartment is cold when Aleksandra slides out of bed and takes the few short steps to the room her parents share. Before Aleksandra prepares for her daily commute to the small hospice clinic where she works as a nurse, she must tend to her parents' growing needs.

Sasha, Aleksandra's ailing father, was diagnosed with Alzheimer disease 10 years ago while Aleksandra was completing her nursing degree at a nearby university. Instead of migrating away from Ukraine like her peers, Aleksandra stayed to provide the long-term care and financial support needed by her parents. She had not expected the degree of emotional support that her mother Iona would also require, as her husband of 60 years became increasingly debilitated.

Before making the short walk to the metro station where she rides the subway across Kyiv to the hospice clinic downtown, Aleksandra prepares the day's meals for her parents, administers Sasha's medications, takes and records his blood pressure, bathes and dresses him, and shares a cup of strong, hot coffee with Iona. During this morning ritual Aleksandra details the daily instructions for meals and midday medications for Iona who cares for Sasha while Aleksandra works during the day. Today there are no doctor's visits or trips to the district clinic for either Sasha or Iona, so the daily instructions are brief and straightforward.

After finishing their morning coffee Aleksandra packs her lunch and dresses for the day. By 6:30 a.m. she is bundled with gloves, hat, muffler, and a heavy coat to protect against the bitter cold as she walks to the metro stop. The metro is the fastest and most inexpensive route across Kyiv to the hospice clinic located downtown. Aleksandra purchases a monthly metro pass that allows her to ride the metro twice daily for less than 20 U.S. cents a day. The ride across the city always teems with commuters and yet it is one of Aleksandra's favorite times of day. The commute is her solitude. When she is on the metro no one needs tending, caretaking, or her time, and, even though she nearly always stands on the crowded metro train, she uses the time to read books she otherwise cannot enjoy.

Aleksandra arrives at the hospice clinic downtown by 7:15 a.m. She has worked here since she completed her internship on-site during her university education. This hospice is unique because it provides both home-based care and in-patient care for people who are terminally ill with cancer, AIDS, and various forms of dementia. Ukraine's overwhelming aging population leads most hospice clinics and long-term care facilities to specialize in treating patients with diseases that are common among the aging population such as dementia, Alzheimer disease, Parkinson disease, and some chronic illnesses such as cancer. In recent years there has been a growing prevalence of HIV/AIDS patients in the hospice clinics. Many have attributed this change to the influence of Western culture since the fall of Soviet rule.

Aleksandra spends her day caring for her patients by administering medications, recording vital signs, updating medical charts, communicating with doctors, and doing her best to manage her patients' pain. Aleksandra specializes in working with the "in-patient" patients and she starts her 10-hour shift at 7:30 a.m. by reviewing patient's charts.

Long-term care facilities in Ukraine differ from hospice facilities in that patients at hospices are within six months or less of the end of life, whereas patients in long-term care facilities have longer life expectancies. The main similarity between patients living in these settings is that they do not have family who are able to care for them at home. Aleksandra finds working at the hospice with the in-patient patients rewarding because she frequently becomes a surrogate family member and provides patients with the care necessary for a compassionate and peaceful transition toward the end of life. This intimate relationship with her patients is also met by great sorrow that she attributes to the loss that naturally accompanies her job.

At 6:00 p.m. after one last assessment of her patients' charts, Aleksandra leaves the hospice clinic for the day. On her way to the metro station she stops at the district's best bakery for a loaf of Iona's favorite braided bread, *kalach*. Ukraine is known as the "breadbasket" of eastern Europe, and Kyiv takes this designation seriously, producing some of the finest breads in the country.

With the loaf of *kalach* under her arm Aleksandra enters the train at 6:15 p.m. with a surge of commuters returning to their districts after a day of work in downtown Kyiv. As the train lurches forward, she is temporarily released from the weight of the day's work and the tasks that await her at home.

Iona greets Aleksandra warmly when she enters the small apartment, but her expression visibly brightens when she sees that Aleksandra has remembered her favorite bread. The last *shift* of the day begins with a dinner of borscht, a Ukrainian beet-based soup, and the *kalach* Aleksandra brings from downtown. The rest of the evening includes administering medications to Sasha, changing him into his night garments, cleaning the evening meal dishes, and taking a final cup of coffee with Iona. While they sip their coffee, discussion of Aleksandra's day at the clinic weaves with Iona's daily report of Sasha's symptoms and stories from the days before he became ill. The day comes to a close at 10:00 p.m. when Aleksandra kisses Sasha and Iona goodnight, turns out the lights, and crawls into bed.

many women are not receiving the benefits of their productive labor. Women want a better future.

Change must take place at the local as well as at the international policy levels. In other words, it is imperative to realize the importance of community-based approaches to health issues that are inclusive of marginalized women's voices. These efforts require collaborative action by a wide range of actors outside the government and development agencies, such as people's organizations, community-based organizations, women's groups at the local and national level, the media, and all others concerned with building a fair and just society. Such collective action creates pressure for accountability and puts social change onto the political agenda. Antrobus (2004, p. 25) identifies the "common difference" that "links us all in a political struggle for recognition and redistributive justice." She explains that its difference from other social movements "lies not only in the absence of homogeneity . . . but in the value it places on diversity, its commitment to solidarity with women everywhere, its feminist politics, and its method of organizing."

These health promotion programs must ensure that all research, policies and programs/ projects are designed from a gender perspective and that this is accomplished in a systematic and sustainable manner. Such goals cannot be achieved through isolated actions by any one group of society, no matter how committed. The fact remains that these health, gender, and development challenges as articulated throughout this chapter cannot be addressed merely through technical or managerial interventions, but instead require political will. Progress requires more than technical recognitions of harm to women's health. The causes of these problems must be identified and a feminist, human rights perspective employed to understand health in the context of wider social, cultural, and economic issues. Such a perspective recognizes that women are agents of social change who will be actively involved in reformulating both development thinking and development practice, influencing the implementation of MDGs as international human rights' obligations. Adopting a framework that is inclusive of gender, development, and human rights within a feminist agenda will lead to the design and implementation of programs that address not just the symptoms of a problem, but its underlying causes. By using equality and social justice as guiding principles, and participation and empowerment of women at grass roots levels as models for implementation, women's health advocates can work toward improving women's health worldwide.

REFERENCES

American Cancer Society. (2007). *Breast cancer facts and figures.*

Anonymous. (2009). Far from sweet dreams. Unpublished poem.

Antrobus, P. (2003). Proceedings from 2003 UNDP Caribbean Conference: *Presentation to working group on the MDGs and gender equality.* UNDP Caribbean Regional Millennium Development. Barbados.

Antrobus, P. (2004). *The global women's movement: Origins, issues, and strategies.* London: Zed Books.

Bartlett, L. (2002). Maternal mortality among Afghan refugees in Pakistan, 1999–2000. *Lancet, 359*(9307), 643–649.

Benoit, C. and Dena, C. (2001). Aboriginal midwifery in Canada: Blending traditional and modern forms. *Network Magazine of the Canadian Women's Health Network, 4*(3), 6–7.

Black, R. E. (2008). Maternal and child under nutrition: Global and regional exposures and health consequences. *Lancet, 371*(9608), 243–260.

Center of Concern. (2003). *IMF-World Bank-WTO close ranks around flawed economic policies.* International Gender and Trade Network and Institute for Agriculture and Trade Policy. Retrieved, February, 19, 2009, from http://www.coc.org/node/5025.

Fathalla, M. (2007). *Issues in women's health: International and Egyptian perspectives.* Assiut, Egypt: University Press.

Food and Agriculture Organization of the United Nations. (FAO).(2008). W*omen and the right to food; International law and state practice.* FAO Publishing: Rome.

Gruskin, S. and Tarantola, D. (2005). Health and human rights. In S. Gruskin, M. A, Grodin, G. J. Annas, and S. P. Marks (Eds.), *Perspectives on health and human rights* (pp. 3–58). New York: Routledge.

International Atomic Energy Agency. (2003). *Millions of cancer victims in developing countries lack access to life-saving radiotherapy.* Retrieved on September 20, 2008, from http://www.iaea.org/NewsCenter/PressReleases/2003/ prn200311.html.

International Committee of the Red Cross (ICRC). (2008). *Women and war.* Retrieved on February 10, 2009 from http://www.icrc.org/Web/Eng/siteeng0.nsf/htmlall/p0944/ $File/ICRC_002_0944.PDF.

Labbok, M. (2006). Breastfeeding: A woman's reproductive rights. *International Journal of Gynecology and Obstetrics, 94,* 277–286.

Moffat, A. (2006). Murder, mystery and mistreatment in Mexican maquiladoras. *Women and Environments International Magazines, 66,* 19–20.

OXFAM International.(2005). *The Tsunami's impact on women.* OXFAM Briefing Note. Retrieved on January 10, 2009, from http://www.oxfam.org/eng/pdfs/bn050326_ tsunami_women.pdf.

United Nations Children's Fund (UNICEF). (2005a). *Early marriage: A harmful traditional practice.* New York: United Nations. Retrieved on November 28, 2008, from http: //www.unicef.org/publications/files/Early_Marriage_12.lo.pdf.

United Nations Children's Fund (UNICEF). (2005b). *Celebrating the innocenti declaration on the protection, promotion and support of breastfeeding: Past achievements, present challenges, and the way forward for infant and young child feeding.* Innocenti Research Centre, Florence, Italy.

United Nations Children's Fund (UNICEF). (2008). *State of the world's children.* Biennial report. New York. Retrieved on November 28, 2008, from http://www.unicef.org/ sowc08/docs/sowc08.pdf.

United Nations Department of Public Information (UNDPI). (2008). *Press conference by world food program executive director on food price crisis.* New York. Retrieved on November 10, 2008, from http://www.un.org/News/briefings/docs/2008/080424_WFP. doc.htm.

United Nations Development Fund for women (UNIFEM).(2008). *Progress of the world's women: Who answers to women?* Retrieved on February 10, 2009, from http://www.unifem.org/progress/2008/media/POWW08_Report_Full_Text.pdf.

United Nations Development Program (UNDP). (2008). *United Nations Development Program annual report.* United Nations: World Resource Institute. Retrieved on November 10, 2008, from http://www.undp.org/publications/annualreport2008/pdf/IAR2008_ENG_low.pdf.

United Nations High Commissioner for Human Rights (UNHCHR). (1966). *International Covenant on Economic, Social and Cultural Rights.* Retrieved December 5, 2008, from http://www.unhchr.ch/html/menu3/b/a_cescr.htm.

United Nations High Commissioner for Human Rights (UNHCHR) (2000). Committee on Economic, Social, and Cultural Rights. *The right to the highest attainable standard of health (Article 12 of the International Covenant on Economic, Social, and Cultural Rights).* Retrieved December 5, 2008, from, http://www.ohchr.org/english/bodies/cescr/comments.htm.

United Nations Population Fund (UNFPA). (2006). *United Nations Population Fund annual report.* New York: United Nations. Retrieved on November 10, 2008, from http://www.unfpa.org/upload/lib_pub_file/692_filename_ar06_eng.pdf.

United Nations Population Fund (UNFPA). (2008). *State of world population 2008. Reaching common ground: Culture, gender and human rights.* New York: United Nations. Retrieved on November 28, 2008, from http://www.unfpa.org/swp/2008/presskit/docs/en-swop08-report.pdf.

Van der Gaag, J. and Barham, T.(1998). Health and health expenditures in adjusting and non-adjusting Countries. *Social Science and Medicine, 46*(8), 995–1009.

Women's Environment and Development Organization(WEDO). (2008). *Information and action guide women's empowerment: Gender equality and the millennium development goals.* New York. Retrieved on February 12, 2009, from http://www.wedo.org/wpcontent/uploads/mdgtoolkit_eng.pdf.

Women's Edge Coalition. (2005). *Fact sheet: Women, natural disaster, and reconstruction.* Retrieved on February 20, 2009, from http://www.womensedge.org//index.php?option=com_kb&Itemid=91&page=articles&articleid=5.

World Health Organization (WHO). (1948). Proceedings from the International Health Conference, 1948: *Preamble to the constitution of the World Health Organization as adopted by the International Health Conference.* Geneva: WHO Press.

World Health Organization (WHO). (2006). *Sexual and gender based violence in emergencies.* Retrieved February 12, 2009, from http://www.who.int/hac/techguidance/pht.SGBV/en.

World Health Organization (WHO). (2007). *Call for resource mobilization and engagement opportunities.* Retrieved December 12, 2008, from http://www.who.int/nmh/donorinfo/chronicdiseases/chp_intensifying_action_against_cancer.pdf.

World's Women.(2005). *Progress in statistics.* New York: Department of Economic and Social Affairs, Statistics Division, United Nations.

SUGGESTIONS FOR FURTHER READING

Bird, C. E. and Rieker, P. P. (2008). *Gender and health: The effects of constrained choices and social policies.* New York: Cambridge University Press.

Mahowald, M. B. (2006). *Bioethics and women: Across the life span.* New York: Oxford University Press.

Murray, A. F. (2008). *From outrage to courage: Women taking action for health and justice.* Monroe, ME: Common Courage Press.

Turshen, M. (2007). *Women's health movements: A global force for change.* New York: Palgrave Macmillan.

Van der Kwaak, A. and Wegelin-Schuringa, M. (Eds.). (2006). *Gender and health: A global sourcebook.* Oxfam.

Aging in a Man's World

Anne Firth Murray (2008)

Doña Eulogia has lived her sixty-five years in Esquencachi, an indigenous community in Bolivia. "I live on my own apart from two grandchildren, Lucia, eleven and Dania, six. I have four children—three girls and a boy. The girls have married and moved to other areas. My son's house is here, but he's working away. I look after my grandchildren who are orphans of one of my daughters. Their father abandoned them so I have to feed us all." Increasingly, young adults move to the cities to try to make a better living but, given Bolivia's recession, most earn only enough to keep themselves alive, and cannot afford to send money home for their children and parents.

The burden of feeding and educating the children falls on grandparents like Doña Eulogia. "We eat potatoes and wheat. It's not much. This year we don't have so many potatoes; we had a bad crop. I grow all our food myself and I keep animals. If there's no school, the girls help me with the llamas." Doña Eulogia is weary, but there is no rest in sight. "The work is the hardest thing, but how can I stop? We would have nothing to live on."[1]

Doña Eulogia's story exemplifies many challenges faced by older women throughout the world. Doña Eulogia is poor. She is tired. She lives in a rural community while her children have migrated to the city. She depends upon her own labor for her survival. Yet she also supports her grandchildren, serving as their primary care provider since their mother died.

Though she is marginalized in her own country, Doña Eulogia is a member of one of the world's fastest-growing population groups: older women. Coping with aging while struggling to survive is a challenge that eventually befalls all impoverished women (and men) who survive long enough. As with so many aspects of life, women bear a special burden. We know this because of stories and a few studies. In general, data and research on elderly women in resource-poor countries are minimal, though no doubt as this group grows in number, more information will become available. Statistics that are available paint a rather grim picture.

DEMOGRAPHICS AND THE FEMINIZATION OF AGING

The world has never had so many old people, and the pace of growth of the world's older population has accelerated. According to the Population Reference Bureau, the global population of people aged sixty-five or older was estimated at 461 million in 2004, an increase of 10.3 million since 2003.[2] The majority of the elderly are women, because on average women live longer than men (globally sixty-nine years versus sixty-five).[3] More than half of the world's women aged sixty years and over are living in developing regions, numbering 198 million compared with 135 million in the developed regions.[4] In some countries, notably Japan, a woman's longevity reaches over eighty years on average. This is a full 25% longer than the global average and approaching or exceeding 50% longer than the average for women in the poorest countries. In some countries in Africa (Botswana, Kenya, Lesotho, and Namibia, for example), life expectancy of women and men has dropped to between thirty-five and forty years, primarily because of the HIV/AIDS pandemic.

Nevertheless, this demographic group—women over sixty years of age—will only continue to grow as many poorer countries experience the increase in life expectancy already evident in richer countries. In twenty years, more than one billion people over the age of sixty will inhabit the world, with 70% found in poorer countries, more than half of them women.[5] In about seventy-five developing countries, there is a 150% projected growth rate for older women in the next thirty years.[6] Worldwide, women make up 54% of people aged sixty and over and 62% of elderly aged eighty and over. Experts call this growing percentage of females among the elderly the "feminization of aging."[7]

Longer life expectancy is no doubt a sign of progress, of increasing wealth and access to medical care among all people, and it is tempting to think that the problem of women in poverty is gradually ebbing. But, as discussed below, the situation is more complicated, and not nearly as rosy.

Not only are the old likely to be women, but they are also likely to be poor. Todd Peterson, chief executive of HelpAge International, explains that "the developing world faces the harsh reality that it is growing old before it is growing rich, with potentially traumatic consequences for old people, their families, and their societies."[8] The consequences of aging and poverty are not merely traumatic; they violate the human rights of the elderly. Article 22 of the Universal Declaration of Human Rights proclaims: "Everyone, as a member of society, has the right to social security and is entitled to the realization, through national effort and international cooperation . . . of the economic, social and cultural rights indispensable for his [/her] dignity and the free development of his [/her] personality." Put simply, poverty among older people, combined with social exclusion and discriminatory attitudes, is a violation of human rights.

Poverty, social exclusion, and discriminatory attitudes are generally more acute for older women than they are for older men. Women's disadvantaged status in childhood and adulthood is intensified in older age. Aging is a women's issue not only because the majority of older people are women but also because aging is a gendered experience. Throughout life "and in all societies," writes Clara Pratt, whose work is referenced in a 1999 UN International Institute on Ageing publication, "males and females play different roles, receive different rewards, and experience differing realities. . . . Many have suffered throughout their lives from poor health care, malnutrition, illiteracy and low social status simply because they were born female."[9]

These gendered experiences come together and may be magnified at the end of a woman's life.[10] The UN International Research and Training Institute for the Advancement of Women (INSTRAW) observes that "Examination of the myths and stereotypes that surround older women shows how gender bias and discrimination intensify in old age everywhere, although cultural forms may differ."[11]

WHAT DOES IT MEAN TO BE ELDERLY?

What does it mean to be "elderly" or "aging"? Women in West Africa live an average of fifty-two years; in South Asia the average is sixty-two. In New Zealand and in the United States women can expect to live at least to eighty.[12] In some countries, women over fifty or even younger may be considered "old." They are easily grandmothers, having been married in their teens and given birth soon after. Thus, it is common to find grandmothers who are in their forties, considering that half of girls aged nineteen worldwide are already married and many of them are mothers. Women in Africa, Asia, and the Caribbean who present themselves and are treated as "old" may be in their fifties or even their forties. Ill health, hard work, and multiple births have tired them out, and they look (and, in fact, are) old. Most international statistics on aging, when they refer to "older people" and "older populations," are describing people age sixty-five or older, sometimes describing people age eighty or older as the "oldest old." For the purpose of this discussion, however, we are focusing on women who are considered or consider themselves "older."

Do the words "older" or "elderly" bring to mind someone who is no longer productive? Or someone who is living a life of leisure, enjoying the "golden years"? Does the word imply an "elder," a person who over the years has accumulated and can now share wisdom? Or does the word describe who is bent over, sick, and disabled, a person who is dependent on others? The "elderly" and "aging" in our world are all of these people.

A LIFETIME OF WORK

Even in wealthy countries, older women's productive contributions are seldom formally recognized.

Many perceptions of older women as unproductive stem from the belief that women's productive role is limited to their reproductive capacity. Women's value is believed to lie in their ability to bear children, and particularly sons. Once women pass the age of reproductive potential, they are seen as useless. It is assumed that they will no longer contribute to society and will instead become burdens, dependent upon support from their children and possibly their national government. Margaret Lock, who writes on menopause among women in Japan, explains this as "the thinly disguised assumption … that reproduction of the species is what female life is all about, and that the situation [in which] we now find ourselves in 'advanced' societies [i.e., that older women may be relevant irrespective of their reproductive role], is not only an anomaly but a costly superfluity."[13]

Many more people around the world are living longer lives, thanks to medical advances. In richer countries, however, cancers, heart attacks, strokes, and other illnesses in which diet and lack of exercise are often believed to play a part are on the rise. So, too, in poorer countries, where lifestyles are changing and people are living longer. They are living longer but paying the price of living with chronic diseases.

Improved maternal care has added years to the lives of many women around the world, but for the 600,000 women each year whose lack of access results in their dying as a result of pregnancy and childbirth-related injuries and illnesses, this is not so. Ninety-five percent of deaths relating to maternity occur in developing countries. Nevertheless, given population growth rates, more and more women are surviving into old age. As more women are living longer, menopause has become a subject of interest and even a major issue of women's health, particularly in more developed countries. Locke notes that in the 1990s the great interest in menopause can likely be attributed to "the sheer number of women, baby boomers, soon to become old, and hence a burden to society."[14]

Increased longevity conjures up images of better diet and exercise, reduced smoking, greater financial security, and access to sophisticated medical interventions to fight cancer and heart disease and other ailments that chiefly afflict people in their later years in rich countries. All of these are signs of an increase in wealth. But as noted, these are not necessarily the forces driving the increase in women's longevity. For most women, increased longevity is the result of simple medical interventions at birth (which applies to men too) and at the point of giving birth. In industrialized countries, these can be complex and expensive interventions. But the interventions that have the biggest impact are inexpensive. Ensuring healthy infants (reducing infant mortality) involves the health of the mother and access to prenatal care and nutrition. In the case of maternal mortality, the critical factors are women's access to nutrition during pregnancy and access to medical assistance and possibly emergency care during childbirth. Ensuring healthy childbirth need not take a lot of money or fancy hospitals, but it does take the will to provide education to women and to trust community-based people to deliver basic care. Such critical interventions, which should be available to all, are not in themselves signs of the end of poverty. The fact that women are living longer does not mean they are leaving poverty.

The perceptions of older women as "unproductive" and "dependent" are ingrained in government polices that fail to compensate women for their labor and focus on the elderly solely receiving goods through social security and welfare programs.[15] Faced with the prospect of discrimination and lack of financial support in their later years, many women must attempt to find paid employment throughout their lives. Retirement for the vast majority of people in the world is a luxury. According to the United Nations Development Programme (UNDP), only a fifth of people over sixty worldwide have income security, and this group is likely to be predominantly male.[16] Since men are more likely to work in the formal economy and to serve in pensioned jobs like the military, and since they die sooner, they have greater financial security as they age than do women. The work that women perform, including care of children and other relatives, as well as labor in the informal sector, is under-compensated or not compensated at all. As noted earlier, women earn only 10% of the world's income but contribute about 60% of the work. In the developing world, only 53% of females are in the formal paid workforce, versus 84% of males. This discrepancy is a result of lack of education, sex discrimination in the work place, and women's household duties.[17] According to demographers Ronald Lee and John Haaga, failure to fairly compensate women's labor applies even in the case of systems such as Social Security in the United States.[18]

For many women in poorer countries, retirement or the end of labor is out of the question. A study in Botswana, for example, revealed that women over sixty continued to spend 16% of their time on work outside the home and one quarter of their time on household work, in addition to time spent providing care for themselves and others.[19] The UN International Institute on Ageing has reported that 41% of all women over the age of fifteen are involved in the formal economy while another 10% to 20% work in the informal economy and remain part of the informal economy well into their older years.[20]

OLDER WOMEN AS CAREGIVERS

The perception that older women are useless or unproductive means that their contributions often go unrecognized. However, contributions from older women are critically important to the functioning and maintenance of society. In most societies in the world, older women are with us at our most significant transitions: the moment of birth and the moment of death. Care giving and nurturing are seen as the stereotypical female roles. When we consider the lives of older women, we see how significant and important these roles can be, even as they continue to be undervalued by society in general. [21]

Although the transitions of birth and death are beginning to be medicalized and institutionalized in many societies, it is still true that for the vast majority of people in the world, the first and the last person that we see in our lives is a woman. Tish Sommers, the founder of the Older Women's League, connects the birth and death experiences by noting that at the time of dying, a person is likely to be tended by a woman: "the nurse's aide (significantly one of the least paid and least valued workers in our society). . . . These are, in a sense, the midwives of death."[22]

Women's care-giving activities are of course not limited to the moments of life and death. As they have for generations, women also tend the young, the sick, and the very old. The UN International Institute on Ageing observes that "Women at midlife and older years play a key role in both economic development and family stability in the Latin American and Caribbean region, far beyond that which would be anticipated by their numbers. This is true to such an extent that, if their productive resources and care-giving roles were suddenly withdrawn and abandoned, the effects on the region's economy and social structure would be devastating."[23] In fact, elderly women as caregivers for the young, the ill, and the even older provide more health care than the health care system. The elderly receive 80% of their care informally, from family, friends, and neighbors, the majority of whom are female caregivers.[24] Most of us would agree that such care from family and friends can be a very good thing. But for the caregiver—often uncompensated and unrelieved—such work can be both debilitating and impoverishing.

The Special Case of HIV/AIDS

In the face of HIV/AIDS in particular, many women are becoming essential parts of social service systems as they become sole caretakers of their grandchildren and of the sick and dying. The important role of grandmothers as caregivers extends around the world, but it is particularly vital in Africa, where AIDS is destroying a generation of younger adults. Elders, especially older women, are pressed into service, caring for young adults dying of AIDS and for their surviving grandchildren.[25] Over 60% of orphaned children currently live in grandparent-headed households in Namibia, South Africa, and Zimbabwe, and over 50% do in Botswana, Malawi, and Tanzania.[26]

HEATH CONSEQUENCES OF A LIFETIME OF WORK

The economic, social, and political inequalities that women face throughout their lifetime are magnified in old age, and many older women in poorer countries live in chronic ill health, according to the World Health Organization (WHO). For example, poverty at older ages often reflects poor economic status earlier in life and is a determinant of health at all stages of life. Countries that have data on poverty by age and sex (mostly the developed countries) show that older women are more likely to be poor than older men.[27]

The WHO reports that poverty is also linked to inadequate access to food and nutrition, and the health of older women often reflects the cumulative impact of poor diets.[28] Years of child bearing, heavy physical labor, and sacrificing her own nutrition to that of her family leaves the older woman with chronic anemia and general malnutrition.[29]

The gendered division of domestic tasks further contributes to older women's poor health. Women often procure and carry water, exposing themselves to malaria and the waterborne diseases of hookworm and schistosomiasis. Additionally, the water may be polluted with agricultural pesticides. Long-term exposure to pesticides has been linked to development of certain cancers and nervous-system impairment.[30] In most societies, women are in charge of cooking. Women in many developing countries spend between three and seven hours each day near an indoor stove, preparing food.[31] Of all deaths attributable to indoor air pollution, 59% are primarily due to chronic obstructive pulmonary disease and lung cancer, with the vast majority of these being of women.[32]

These factors, almost all derived from WHO sources, emphasize that although women may lead longer lives than men, a longer life does not translate into a healthier life. WHO studies in forty-five countries conclude that women can generally expect to spend more years of their lives with some functional limitations than men.[33] Men are more likely to die—from diseases such as heart failure, stroke, or cancer—whereas women live longer but suffer declining health because of such diseases as arthritis, osteoporosis, and diabetes—as well as cancer, stroke, and heart disease. Although with modern medical care the balance may shift, it is still true that, on a global scale, "men die from their diseases, women live with them."[34]

SOCIAL EXCLUSION AND LOSS

Discrimination often affects women past reproductive age particularly severely, directly because of ageism compounded with sexism, and indirectly because of the lifelong denial of opportunities that women experience. Older women face isolation, abandonment, social exclusion, and deprivation of choices, status, finances, and property. Whether with a partner or alone, women have less access than do men to assets like land and savings, and, if widowed, they may face cultural barriers that limit their activity and independence[35] or strip them of their homes. In parts of Kenya and Zimbabwe, for example, when a woman is widowed, she and her possessions become the property of her husband's family, usually a brother. Although this practice is slowly changing, to challenge it means further isolation for the widow.[36]

Women are likely to face old age without a husband because of the combination of shorter male lifetimes and the practice of older husbands taking younger wives. In Indonesia, 58% of older women are widowed. Among older men, only 11% are.[37] In sub-Saharan Africa, 90% of older men are married, compared with only 25% to 50% of older women. Men not only find younger spouses more easily than do women, but they also have a greater incentive to marry because of gender roles. Men who remarry gain in a woman her traditional role of companion and nurse for their old age.[38] Thus to be married in later years confers real advantage and at least a modicum of security.

In contrast, widows, who have spent time and energy caring for their dying spouses, are often stigmatized. In India, women may be blamed for their husbands' deaths, evicted from their property, and viewed as "socially dead." This a not a past practice now eliminated in thriving India but one that continues today, as Susannah Froman and Patrick May reported in 2006.[39] In many parts of Africa, a woman cannot inherit land, and upon the death of her husband, a woman's land is passed on to her son or to her husband's family.[40]

Accusations of witchcraft are often directed at older women. In Mozambique, accusations lead to attacks on older women and sometimes to killings. In Tanzania, an estimated 500 women are murdered every year as a result of witchcraft accusations. Older women receive the majority of witchcraft allegations because they embody certain characteristics (grey hair, wrinkled skin, red eyes, living alone) associated with witches. This issue became so serious that it was made the theme for International Women's Day in Tanzania in 1999.[41]

Not only can cultural attitudes of widow's rights and appropriate roles lead to social exclusion, but growing urbanization also leaves older women increasingly isolated, as we saw in Doña Eulogia's story. Rural women in poorer countries are often left behind by younger family members migrating to cities in search of jobs. These women continue to perform the labor of subsistence farming for themselves and children. Women cultivate 80% of the food but own only 1% of the land in sub-Saharan Africa.[42] In Ghana, 65% of food farmers are middle-aged and elderly women, many enduring lifelong poverty.[43] As Doña Eulogia explained at the beginning of this chapter, "The work is the hardest thing, but how can I stop? We would have nothing to live on." Rural life for elderly women is harsh, since it results in their being isolated, cut off from health and other services, and unable to access opportunities of training or paid employment.

Older women living in cities confront a different set of challenges, but like their rural counterparts, they face exclusion and isolation. Both Kenya and Brazil report the practice of abandoning older family members in health care facilities. Families drop off elders and never return to pick them up. In Kenya, 15-30% of elderly patients are abandoned in hospitals.[44]

Feelings of social exclusion, disintegration of rural communities, poor nutrition, physical exertion, poor living conditions, lack of employment opportunities, and grieving for the loss of loved ones strain women's mental health. It is not surprising, therefore, that older women experience much higher rates of mental illness and depression.[45] Unfortunately, there is a dearth of information on the mental health of older women in developing countries. What has been written focuses on the experience of growing older but can be used to analyze mental health. For example, an older woman in Kyrgyzstan eloquently voices the role of emotional health in aging: "I thought washing the crockery was the main thing for older people, but it seems that feelings are more important. . . . When we become old we are all the same; we are all alone. When you look back, take off your hat; when you look forward, be ready to work hard."[46]

CHARACTERISTICS OF OLDER WOMEN IN POORER COUNTRIES

Older women in poorer countries are particularly hard to discuss because so little has been written about them. Although there have been studies of menopause and aging among women in richer countries, even the UN International Research and Training for the Advancement of Women (INSTRAW) agrees that little is known about older women in poorer countries because so few formal studies have been published.[47] Organizations addressing the needs of older women in poorer countries are nearly as scarce as scholarship on the topic. Nevertheless, there are many ways to learn, and it is often through anecdotes, experience, reports from women's groups, and stories that the characteristics of older women in poorer countries can be revealed. It is known that older women in poorer countries share many of the following characteristics:

- Most are poor.
- Most suffer ill health.
- Most lack access to health care, food, and paid employment.
- Most are illiterate.
- Most are alone, unless they are caregivers for others.
- Many suffer violence.
- Most live in rural areas.
- Most are invisible, their lives not having been studied or written about.
- Most are assumed to have no value in society.
- Many are important as care givers of the young, the sick, and the older old.
- Many are the custodians of cultural traditions.[48]

Earlier in this article it was noted that virtually all problems of older women seem to be an outgrowth of problems in earlier life. Young women who are literate and able to earn money will fare better in later years than their less educated and poorer counterparts—because they hold onto those assets and the strength that comes with them. There are no doubt disadvantages for them compared to wealthy older males, but these are not as dire as for poor women. Thus, to create a population of secure, powerful elderly women, it is vital to empower and provide opportunities to girls and young women. In doing so, it sets the stage for their later years to turn out differently. Lifting young women out of poverty, educating them, and giving them access to services and opportunities are prerequisites to solving the problems of destitute older women.

HOPEFUL SIGNS

Desperation and practical necessity are beginning to change the lives of some older women. In many countries, the vital roles of older women as caretakers and nurturers are beginning to be appreciated, particularly among populations devastated by HIV/AIDS. Although there is little evidence that these important caretakers are being sought out and paid, there is beginning to be some recognition, particularly by non-governmental organizations that are encouraging older people to come together to share their concerns.

In the last twenty years, there has been a rapid growth of women's groups around the world and this is a hopeful sign for all women. The work of groups focusing on the well-being of women who are already older is desperately needed, and more and more older women are coming together around the world to offer connection and support to each other. Older peoples' clubs, like those formed in Thai Nguyen, Thailand[49] and Chisinau, Moldova, offer older caregivers a place where they can discus their problems and receive support from peers.[50] Some older people's clubs organize and mobilize for political action in their communities and abroad.

The assumption that older people, particularly older women, are unproductive has led to the exclusion of the elderly from many discourses on development. Yet evidence indicates that older women play a pivotal role in the health and survival of their families and communities. As the population of older women grows, they should be viewed as contributors to, not just beneficiaries of, development.

To do anything less violates elderly women's rights to independence, health, self-fulfillment, dignity, and participation.[51]

NOTES

1. HelpAge International, 2006a.
2. Population Reference Bureau, 2005.
3. Population Reference Bureau, 2003a.
4. World Health Organization, 2000b.
5. World health Organization, 1998.
6. Population Reference Bureau, 1999.
7. Ibid.
8. HelpAge International, 2000.
9. The UN International Institute on Ageing, 1991b.
10. Clara Pratt, quoted in the United Nations International Research and Training Institute for the Advancement of Women, 1999, p.v.
11. Ibid.
12. Population Reference Bureau, 2003a.
13. Locke, Margaret, 1994, p.xx.
14. Ibid, p.xviii.
15. The UN International Institute on Ageing, 1991b.
16. Cited in Women's Health Collection, 1999b.
17. The Population Resource Center, 2001.
18. Lee and Haaga, 2002.
19. Zeilinger, 1999.
20. The UN International Institute on Ageing, 1991d.
21. Paul and Paul, 1995.
22. Sommers, 1994.
23. The UN International Institute on Ageing, 1991d.
24. The UN International Institute on Ageing, 1991c.
25. World Health Organization, 2002b.
26. HelpAge International, 2006b
27. World Health Organization, 2000b.
28. Ibid.
29. Ibid.
30. World Health Organization, 2006.
31. World Health Organization, 2005a.
32. Ibid.
33. World Health Organization, 2000b.
34. That women live longer than men is explained in part by the balance of two forces, according to Thomas Perls, a geriatrician at Harvard Medical school: "One is the evolutionary drive to pass on her genes, the other is the need to stay healthy enough to rear as many children as possible. . . . Menopause . . . protects older women from the risks of bearing children late in life, and lets them live long enough to take care of their children and grandchildren." It appears that life spans are correlated with the length of time the offspring remain dependent on adults; in humans

this is a longer period than for most other animals. Another perspective on women's longevity is behavioral: between the ages of fifteen and twenty four, men are four to five times more likely to die than females, and most of the fatalities are due to reckless behavior or violence. A lot of these differences in behavior can be attributed to hormones. Male testosterone seems to promote aggressive behavior and increases levels of low-density lipoprotein, raising a male's risk of heart disease. In contrast, estrogen in women lowers levels of low-density lipoprotein and raises high-density lipoprotein, or good cholesterol, which lowers risk of heart disease. At other ages, the difference in mortality narrows until later in life, in the fifties and sixties, when more men than women die, mostly because of heart disease. "Why Women Live Longer than Men," by Thomas T. Perls and Ruth C. Fretts. *Scientific American Presents: Women's Health: A Lifelong Guide*, 1998. Other insights about women living longer than men include the belief that the reason for this inequality is that males engage in more risky behavior than females do. But new research published in *Science*, September 2002, reports on a study by Sarah L. Moore and Kenneth Wilson of the University of Stirling that may suggest that males are more likely than females to succumb to parasites: "With their generally larger size, males may just make more attractive targets." Ian P.F. Owens of Imperial College London notes that "In the United States, United Kingdom and Japan, men are approximately twice as vulnerable as women to parasite-induced death. . . . In countries with a higher overall incidence of deaths due to parasites, such as Kazakhstan and Azerbaijan, men are four times as vulnerable as women are. Still others (for example, Ronald Lee, a demographer at the University of California, Berkeley) posit that nurturing children into old age may result in people living longer.

35. The World Bank, 2001.
36. Personal observations in East Africa, 2004.
37. Population Reference Bureau, 1999.
38. United Nations International Research and Training Institute for the Advancement of Women, 1999, p. 6.
39. Frohman, Susanna and Patrick May, "Journey into the 'City of Widows.'" *San Jose Mercury News,* April 2, 2006.
40. HelpAge International, 2002a.
41. HelpAge International, 2000.
42. "Africa's Homeless Widows." *New York Times*, June 16, 2004.
43. The UN International Institute on Ageing, 1991a.
44. WHO/INPEA, 2002.
45. Carreño, 2001.
46. Participant in roundtable discussion, "Establishing inter-sector cooperation to improve the situation of vulnerable older people in Kyrgyzstan." Held November 16, 2004. Quoted in *Kyrgyzstan Newsletter* February 2005, Issue 3.
47. The United Nations International Research and Training Institute for the Advancement of Women, 1999.
48. Ibid.
49. HelpAge International/International HIV/AIDS Alliance, 2003.
50. "Reintegration of Older People into Moldovan Society: Good Practice Manual." Pontos: Chisinau, 2004. Manual accessed at http://www.helpage.org/Resources/Manuals#1118082365-0-10
51. HelpAge International, 2000.

Using Human Rights to Improve Maternal and Neonatal Health

Sofia Gruskin, Jane Cottingham, Adriane Martin Hilber, Eszter Kismodi, Ornella Lincetto, and Mindy Jane Roseman (2008)

INTRODUCTION

Maternal and neonatal mortality have barely declined in the past two decades. The most recent estimates indicating that about 536,000 women die every year from pregnancy-related causes demonstrate that, at the global level, maternal mortality has decreased at less than 1% annually between 1990 and 2005.[1] This is far below the 5.5% annual decline necessary to achieve the Millennium Development Goal (MDG) of improving women's health by reducing maternal mortality. Ninety-nine percent of these deaths occur in developing countries. Likewise, even as the under-five and infant mortality rates have dropped considerably in many developing countries, the rates for neonates (infants in the first 4 weeks of life) and, in particular, early neonatal mortality (infants in the first week of life) have declined much more slowly and in some regions have remained static.[2] An estimated 4 million babies die during their first 4 weeks, of which 3 million die in the first week.[3] Maternal and neonatal health are central for the MDGs, the global roadmap for eradicating poverty and improving human well-being by the year 2015.[4]

While the right of parents to determine freely and responsibly the number and spacing of their children was first articulated on the 1968 UN International Conference on Human Rights, the right of women to go through pregnancy and childbirth safely was first made explicit only in 1994 as part of the Programme of Action of the UN International Conference on Population and Development (ICPD). The definition of reproductive health included "the right of access to appropriate health-care services that will enable women to go safely through pregnancy and childbirth and provide couples with the best chance of having a healthy infant."[5] Subsequently, three organizations—WHO, United Nations Children's Fund (UNICEF) and United Nations Population Fund (UNFPA) declared that:

> *The right to life is a fundamental human right, implying not only the right to protection against arbitrary execution by the state but also the obligations of governments to foster the conditions essential for life and survival. Human rights are universal and must be applied without discrimination on any grounds whatsoever, including sex. For women, human rights include access to services that will ensure safe pregnancy and childbirth.*[6]

These commitments were built upon a foundation laid by authoritative sources. For example, the UN Human Rights Committee, which monitors implementation of the International Covenant on Civil and Political Rights, had previously confirmed that, in international law, the right to life not only applies to ensuring that capital punishment is not imposed in an arbitrary way but also requires that States adopt positive measures to ensure survival and development.[7] In 2000, the Committee elaborated its General Comment 28 on the equality of rights between men and women which, among other things, requires States to report their progress and to provide data on birth rates and on pregnancy and childbirth-related deaths of women.[8]

Human rights are used by international organizations, governments, nongovernmental organizations, civil society groups, and individuals in their work with respect to health in many different ways. These can broadly be categorized as: advocacy, application of legal standards, and programming, including service delivery. Some use one approach while others apply a combination in their work.[9–12]

To understand the historical context which shaped the rationale and approach of linking health and human rights to improving maternal and neonatal health, we summarize how maternal mortality in the developing world came to be seen as a public-health concern, a human rights concern, and ultimately as both, leading to the development of approaches using human rights concepts and methods.

HISTORICAL TRENDS

For most women living in industrialized countries, the experience of death and/or severe injury during childbirth is remote, both statistically and historically. Early declines in maternal and neonatal mortality were achieved in Sweden during the 19th century and in most other countries of western Europe and North America in the first half of the 20th century.[13] War, nationalism, industrialization, urbanization, and the attendant social dislocations and miseries all played a role in government attention to the mortality and morbidity of women living within these countries in the context of pregnancy and childbirth.[1]

A similar downward trend in maternal and neonatal mortality did not occur in countries of the developing world. Women in resource-poor countries still face a 1 in 16 risk of dying of pregnancy-related causes during their lifetime, in contrast to women in well-resourced countries where the risk is about 1 in 4800.[14] In sub-Saharan Africa, the infant and under-five mortality rates are 101 per 1000 live births respectively, as compared with 4 per 1000 live births and 6 per 1000 live births for industrialized countries.[15]

A Public-Health Concern

At a global level, maternal mortality was not recognized as a public-health concern until late in the 20th century.[2] Though there were occasional references in international fora, it was only in 1985, due in no small measure to a provocative article with the title "Where is the 'M' in MCH?"[16] that starkly presented the inherent neglect of women in maternal and child health (MCH) programs, that international attention started to focus on the health of pregnant women. Even then, those programs that focused

on maternal and child health were mostly driven by concerns about infant and child health. Interventions for children such as universal immunization, nutritional supplementation, oral rehydration therapy and growth monitoring showed increasing success in bringing down the rates of infant and child death and disease. Interventions for pregnant women lagged far behind with little to no attention to women suffering injury or dying in childbirth and/or from pregnancy-related causes. It is no coincidence that neonatal deaths account for 40% of the under-five mortality rate, since newborn survival is so closely linked to the health and survival of mothers.

The International Conference on Safe Motherhood, held in Nairobi, Kenya, in February 1987, issued a Call to Action urging the Member States of the UN to improve health conditions for women in general and to reduce maternal mortality in particular. In the same year, international agencies, governments, and a few international non-governmental organizations, launched the Safe Motherhood Initiative.[17] The purpose of this effort was to highlight the persistence of maternal ill-health and to devise solutions for maternal mortality and morbidity. It was only after its creation that the first global and regional estimates of maternal mortality were calculated[18] revealing the most dramatic of all public-health gaps between resource-rich and resource-poor countries. Within the public-health community, the Safe Motherhood Initiative framed the approach to addressing maternal and child health for the years to come. Consequently, it is only in recent years that the burden of neonatal mortality and stillbirths has been estimated,[19] and the importance of the continuum of care in maternal and child health programs recognized.[13]

Women's Health and Human Rights Movements

Concurrent with, and slightly ahead of, these efforts to address maternal mortality within the public-health community, international feminism—especially women's activism around health and rights, both within countries and globally—was also growing.[20] The early demands of the women's movement, particularly in western Europe and North America, focused on two key demands: equal pay for work of equal value, and the rights of women to have control over their bodies and to have access to contraception and abortion.[21] By the early 1980s, the health streams of the international women's movement had begun to come together through the "International Women and Health" meetings which, for the first time, brought together women from all over the world.[20] Among the key concerns which connected the efforts of women from very different contexts and regions were the need for safe and affordable contraceptives and access to antenatal care and safe childbirth services. Closely linked to this was the demand to abolish population control measures (including coercive sterilization) which at the time were being imposed by several governments.[22]

This global activism by nongovernmental organizations had a direct impact on the UN Decade for Women (1976–1985), which heightened attention by governments and the international community more broadly to the health of women, especially in developing countries. Sceptical, however, of whether the UN and its partners were really committed to acting, the women's health movement launched an International Day of Action for Women's Health in 1987, focusing initially on "Preventing Maternal Mortality."[23] Women's lack of autonomy to make decisions about their lives, including childbearing, was a central focus of these efforts.

Concurrent with these changes and the growth of the women's health movement, human rights organizations started to demonstrate how human rights could work for women in the so-called "private sphere," including in relation to sexuality and reproduction.[24] Throughout the 1990s, this activism and research contributed to a growing global awareness that women's health needed to be understood and addressed within the economic, social and cultural context of individual women's lives. Consequently, work on women's health broadened to include efforts at the household and community levels, as well as on the broader social structures, such as health, education, laws, and policies such as spousal authorization, that pose barriers to women accessing health services for themselves and their children.

Convergence of Efforts, Recognition of Human Rights

The women's health and human rights movements in many ways can be credited with a major contribution to the development of the 1994 International Conference on Population and Development (Cairo) and the 1995 Fourth World Conference on Women (Beijing). Despite being politically negotiated by governments, the Cairo and Beijing outcome documents were explicit about the need to promote and protect women's rights, particularly in matters relating to reproduction and sexuality to improve women's health. Both documents also drew attention to the need for women to have access to information and services to got through pregnancy safely.[25,26]

Two years after these ground-breaking international agreements on women's health and rights, an international consultation was held in Sri Lanka to evaluate the achievements of 10 years of the Safe Motherhood Initiative. Its self-examination was severe:

> *Despite the recognition achieved by the Safe Motherhood Initiative over the past decade, by 1997 public health specialists and women's health advocates were increasingly challenged by one incontestable fact: maternal death rates were not declining in most of the developing world. In fact, improvements in the collection and analysis of maternal health data, brought about in Large part by the Initiative itself, have led in some cases to higher estimates of maternal mortality.[27]*

Beyond the improvement in data collection and analysis, the 10-year review of the Safe Motherhood Initiative showed resoundingly modest results. Interventions that were assumed to be effective, such a risk screening during antenatal care, were found to have made little difference to maternal morbidity and mortality outcomes.[27] The 10-year review confirmed what the international health community already generally knew: death and injury due to pregnancy and childbirth was not inevitable; nearly all of it could be prevented. Despite the resonance of children's health issues within the international community, it is noteworthy that in neither the initial meeting nor the

10-year review was the health of the *newborn* identified as a priority issue. One can hypothesize several contradictory reasons for this, ranging from the fact that newborn care was perceived as expensive and complicated, to the fact that attention was finally being paid to women and those attending those events wanted to ensure this new spotlight on women was not lost.

The Safe Motherhood Initiative review produced several action messages intended to revamp and streamline global and national approaches to reducing maternal mortality. The components of high quality maternal health services were defined to include: care by skilled health personnel before, during and after childbirth; emergency care for life-threatening obstetric complications; services to prevent and manage the complications of unsafe abortion; family planning to enable women to plan their pregnancies and prevent unwanted pregnancies; health education and services for adolescents; and community education for women, their families and decision-makers. Perhaps most strikingly, and reflecting the developments which had occurred in the previous decade, safe motherhood was defined as a woman's human right. The review concluded that a major reason women were continuing to die from pregnancy-related causes was that they were discriminated against as women and that the severe neglect of women's health was a violation of their human rights.[27]

This explicit framing by the public-health community of death due to pregnancy-related causes in human rights terms meant that, from that time on, even as this was limited with respect to neonates, attention to the intrinsic value of human rights to maternal mortality reduction efforts was publicly accepted, at least in the rhetoric. This was explicitly demonstrated in the interagency statement on maternal mortality published in 1999.[6]

As life-saving and injury-preventing treatment existed, and many women did not have access to it, framing the issue in human rights terms highlighted the responsibility of those who either prevented women from obtaining such access or did nothing to foster access. The statement and the work that followed also highlighted the need for changes in legislation and policy, affirming that "a supportive social, economic and legislative environment allows women to overcome the various obstacles that limit access to health care, such as distance from their home to appropriate health facilities, lack of transport and, more critically, financial and social barriers."[6] The efforts of this period drew attention to the fact that governments are ultimately accountable for ensuring a functional health-care system and for creating an appropriate legal and policy environment in which health services can effectively operate.

The casting of maternal mortality and morbidity in human rights terms has shed light on a previously untargeted area for intervention, one that examines the positive and negative effects of the legal and policy environment in which health systems operate, nationally and locally. This in turn can lead to an analysis of government action and inaction and to the design of interventions grounded in an understanding and a concern for both health and human rights.[28]

Developing a New Approach

It is against this background that WHO's Department of Reproductive Health and Research, with the Program on International Health and Human Rights at Harvard School of Public Health, took up the challenge of "operationalizing" the use of human rights to improve maternal and neonatal health. Given the work of the past decade, we hypothesized that despite the considerable efforts that a country may have made to reduce maternal and newborn mortality and achieve improvements in maternal and newborn health services; legal, policy and other barriers might nonetheless exist both within and outside the health sector. Overcoming such barriers requires their identification, careful analysis and their subsequent modification—through laws, policies and regulations that are consonant with human rights—with the ultimate aim of improving women's access to needed services through the promotion and protection of their rights. We developed a process which aims to assist countries to conduct a self-assessment of their national laws, policies and practices that affect maternal and neonatal morbidity and mortality, using a human rights framework, and engaging stakeholders from different ministries, professional associations, nongovernmental organizations and academics.

CONCLUSION

While early decline in maternal and neonatal mortality were achieved in most countries in western Europe and North America in the first half of the 20th century, a similar downward trend in maternal and neonatal mortality did not occur in countries of the developing world. It was not until the late 20th century that maternal mortality started to be recognized as a public-health concern. The International Safe Motherhood Initiative, launched in 1987, gave a huge impetus to programme interventions and advocacy aimed at reducing maternal mortality worldwide. However, 10 years later, little or no progress had been made towards such a reduction.

During the same period, international feminism gathered force and, together with the human rights movements, contributed to a growing global awareness that women's health needed to be understood and addressed within the economic, social and cultural context of individual women's lives. Women's lack of autonomy to make decisions about their lives, including whether to bear children—their inability to enjoy their human rights infact—was a central focus of these efforts which in turn inspired the direction of the Cairo and Beijing international consensus documents.

The concerns of activists, governments, donors and the international community at large converged in the mid-1990s around the articulation of the centrality of women's human rights to achieve health and well-being, including the right not to die from preventable, pregnancy-related causes. The casting of maternal mortality and morbidity in human rights terms created a new arena for intervention, one that provides an approach for systematic examination of the legal and policy environment in which health systems operate, nationally and locally. This has been the focus of an initiative developed by WHO and Harvard, to provide countries with a way of analysing the impact of their laws and policies grounded in an understanding of both health and human rights.

REFERENCES

1. *Maternal mortality in 2005. Estimates developed by WHO, UNICEF, UNFPA and the world Bank.* Geneva: WHO; 2007.

2. The world health report 2005: make every mother and child count. Geneva: WHO:2005.

3. *Neonatal and perinatal mortality Country, regional and global estimates.* Geneva: WHO; 2006.

4. *Millennium Development Goals and targets,* United Nations. Available from: http://www.un.org/millenniumgoals [accessed on 2 June 2008].

5. *Programme of action of the International conference on Population and Development;* paragraph 7.3. New York: United Nations; 1994.

6. *Reduction of maternal mortality: a joint WHO/UNICEF/UNFPA/World Bank statement. Geneva: WHO; 1999.* http://www.unfpa.org/upload/lib_pub_file/236_filename_e_rmm.pdf [accessed on 2 June 2008].

7. *CCPR General Comment No. 6: The right to life (article 6).* United Nations office of the High Commissioner for Human Rights; 1982. Available from: http://www.unhchr.ch/tbs/doc.nsf/0/84ab9690ccd81fc7c12563ed0046fae3 [accessed on 9 June 2008.]

8. *CCPR General Comment No. 28: Equality of rights between men and women (article 3).* CCPR/C/21/Rev. 1/Add. 10. United Nations International covenant on Civil and Political Rights; 2000, Available from: http://www.unhchr.ch/tbs/ doc. nsf/0/13b02776122d4838802568b900360e80 [accessed on 9 June 2008].

9. Gruskin S, Mills EJ, Tarantola D. History, principles and practice of health and human rights. *Lancet* 2007;370;449–55 PMID:17679022 doi:10.1016/S0140-6736(07) 61200-8

10. Hogerzeil HV. Essential medicines and human rights: what can they lean from each other? *Bull World Health Organ* 2006;84:371–5. PMID:16710546 doi:10.2471/BLT.06.031153

11. Lewin E.*Programming for the realization of children's rights: lesson learned from Brazil, Costa Rica and Venezuela.* New York; UNICEF: 2000.

12. *Adopting a human rights approach to programming: the UNICEF Tanzania Case.* Dar-es-Salaam: UNICEF: 2002.

13. Van Lerberghe W, De Brouwere V. Of blind alleys and things that have worked: history's lessons on reducing maternal mortality. In: De Brouwere V, Van Lerberge W, eds. Safe motherhood strategies: a review of the evidence. *Studies in health organisation and policy,* 17:7-33. Antwerp: ITG Press: 2001.

14. Sen G, Cottingham J, Govender V. *Maternal and neontal health: surviving the roller-coaster of international policy.* Paper prepared for the WHO project on maternal—newborn health and poverty. 2005.

15. *State of the world's children 2007*. New York: UNICEF; 2006.
16. Rosenfield A, Maine D. Maternal mortality: a neglected tragedy. Where is the "M" in MCH? *Lancet* 1985;2:83-5 PMID:2861534 doi:10.1016/S0140-6736(85) 90188-6.
17. *Safe Motherhood links*, RHO Archives; 2005. Available from: http://www.rho.org/html/sm_links.htm#SMinitilative [accessed on 9 June 2008].
18. AbouZahr C, Royston E. *Maternal mortality: a global factbook*. Geneva: WHO; 1991. (WHO/MCH/MSM/91-3.)
19. *Neonatal and perinatal mortality: country, regional and global estimates*. Geneva, WHO; 2006.
20. Garcia-Moreno C, Claro A. Challenge from the women's health movement: women's rights versus population control. In: Sen G, Germain A and Chen LC, eds, *Population policies reconsidered; health, empowerment and rights*. Cambridge. MA: Harvard University Press: 1994, pp. 47–61.
21. Doyal L. *What makes women sick: gender and the political economy of health*. Basingstoke; MacMillan Press; 1995.
22. *Isis and the Dispensaire des Femmes* [Report]. Third International Women and Health Meeting: Geneva; 1981.
23. Berer M. Sundari RTK, Preventing maternal mortality: evidence, resources, leadership, action. *Report Health Matters* 1999;3
24. Sullivan D. The public/private distinction in international human rights law. In: Peters J, Wolper A, eds. *Women's rights—human rights: international feminist perspectives*. New York: Routledge; 1995 pp. 126–34.
25. *Programme of Action of the International Conference on Population and Development, Cairo, 1994*. New York: United Nations; 1995; paragraph 7.2.
26. *Platform for Action of the Fourth World Conference on Women, Beijing, 1995*. New York: United Nations; 1995; paragraph 96.
27. Inter-Agency Group for Safe Motherhood. *The safe motherhood action agenda: priorities for the next decade*. Report on the safe motherhood technical consultation, 18-23 October 1997, Colombo, Sri Lanka. New York: Family Care International; 1998.
28. Cook R. Dickens B. *Advancing safe motherhood through human rights*. Geneva: WHO: 2000.

R E A D I N G *27*

Midwifery's Renaissance

Marsden Wagner (2007)

Because the midwives feared God, they did not do as commanded by the king.

—*Exodus 1:17*

A midwife is lectured at by committees, scolded by matrons, sworn at by surgeons, bullied by a surgical dressers, talked flippantly to if middle aged and good humored, seduced if young.

—*London Times, 1857*

After working as a practicing physician for several years I became a perinatologist and perinatal scientist, as well as a full-time faculty member at the Schools of Medicine and Public Health at UCLA. Then I became a director of maternal and child health for the California state health department. In that capacity I learned that in the rural town of Madera, California, doctors had decided that they no longer wanted to attend births in the Madera County Hospital. They complained that it took too much of their time and didn't pay enough. So in 1968 the county recruited two midwives to fill the gap. After two years, the rate of babies dying around the time of birth in the hospital was cut in half. Alarmed that their style of maternity care was being made to look bad, the doctors in town agreed that they would once again attend births in the hospital if the two midwives were fired. The hospital fired the midwives, the doctors returned, and soon the rate of babies dying around birth rose to its earlier higher levels.

This natural experiment comparing the safety of doctors and midwives left me confused and full of questions, because, in spite of my years of experience as a physician, I had no real knowledge of midwifery. What are these midwives? How are they trained? Could it be that, as seen in Madera County, they are generally safer birth attendants than doctors? Through no fault of their own, Americans, including obstetricians, have little understanding of midwifery. In the early years of the 20th century, a witch hunt against midwives in the United States and Canada eliminated midwifery as a legitimate health profession. The profession has gained ground in the past two decades, but most people today have no personal experience with midwives and have been exposed to considerable misinformation about midwifery.

From California I left for Europe, where I joined the staff of the World Health Organization. There I was exposed to the essential role midwives play in maternity care in other highly industrialized countries and in developing countries.

Throughout history, there have always been women in the community to whom other women can turn for support with concerns—not just about reproductive health care but also issues such as spousal abuse. The word *midwife* is early English for "with woman." The French term for midwife, *sage femme* (wise woman), goes back thousands of years, as do the words in Danish, *jordmor* (earth mother), and in Icelandic, *ljosmodir* (mother of light).

In the fifth century B.C. Hippocrates formalized a midwifery training program in Greece. Phaenarete, the mother of Socrates, was a midwife. In the Bible, the Book of Exodus recognized the strength and independence of midwives who defied the pharaoh's command that they kill all sons born to Hebrew women. The first law to regulate midwifery in Europe was passed in Germany in 1452 and required that a midwife attend all births. Since then, every little girl in Europe has grown up with the understanding that if she has a baby, a midwife will assist her.

When Europeans migrated to the New World, midwives were among them. Midwives were a valued part of the developing health care system in colonial times, and by the mid-1880s they were teaching medical students in at least one university.

As the number of physicians increased in the United States, medical doctors attempted to monopolize health care through state medical practice acts that defined health care parameters, including who can practice. By the end of the 19th century, it was common for midwives to be accused of witchcraft and tried in court, and midwifery practice began to disappear. The case of Hanna Porn was one of the most famous and had far-reaching consequences. In Gardner, Massachusetts, in 1909, a judge sentenced Porn to three months in prison. Her crime? She was a practicing midwife. Fewer than half as many of the babies whose births she attended died as babies whose births were attended by local physicians. But the Massachusetts Supreme Judicial Court used her case to rule that midwifery was illegal in Massachusetts, based on the testimony of physicians who said that midwives were incompetent. Other states followed suit and made midwifery illegal, and it remained illegal in nearly all states for more than 50 years, until nurse-midwifery began to be legalized.

Despite this attempt to dismantle the profession in the United States and Canada, midwifery continued to thrive in Europe and other parts of the world. And while the profession was severely hampered in the United States for decades, it was not stamped out. Throughout history, every attempt at ending the practice has failed. It seems that there will always be women who want to be midwives and women who want midwives to attend them when they give birth.

When officially-sanctioned midwifery was attacked in the United States, midwives went underground. Women who became known as "granny midwives" (because they tended to be older) continued to practice, especially in poor communities. In the 1920s Mary Breckinridge, a public health nurse and midwife, formed the Frontier Nursing Service to provide maternity care to families in rural areas of Appalachia. Some of the staff members formed an organization that later became the American Association of Nurse-Midwives, as well as the Frontier School of Midwifery and Family Nursing, which trained hundreds of women in what became a new profession in America, nurse-midwifery.

The number of nurse-midwives grew, and by 1977 the profession was licensed in every state. After nursing school, a nurse can elect to go on to midwifery school for about two years and become a nurse-midwife. This is not the same as becoming a labor and delivery nurse, a nursing specialization that has no training requirement and usually involves about six weeks of on-the-job training.

Women can also train as "direct-entry" midwives, going directly to midwifery school without training first in nursing. Direct-entry midwives have grown steadily in numbers and recognition. In 2006 direct-entry midwifery was legal in 24 states, "alegal" (allowed without legal interference) in 17 states, and explicitly illegal in only nine states. In the past decade, more and more states have been legalizing direct-entry midwifery. The U.S. government recognizes the training for both nurse-midwives and direct-entry midwives and has authorized the Midwifery Education Accreditation Council to accredit midwifery schools and programs.

Despite the current resurgence of midwifery in the United States, the fact that midwives were harshly persecuted for more than a century has left the profession with a legacy of public reticence and confusion that must be overcome. Many myths surround midwives, myths that are often reinforced by obstetricians who view them as competition. One is that midwives are not trained but are "hippy-dippy" lay women who attend only home births. Another is that midwives are religious zealots or witches who use magical potions. That nurse-midwives attend births only in hospitals is a common misconception, as is the idea that a midwife is a second-class doctor for women who can't afford a real obstetrician. None of these ideas is remotely true. Science has proven that for attending low-risk births (that is, births without complications), midwives are not second-class obstetricians, but rather obstetricians are second-class midwives.

Generally speaking, a fundamental difference between midwifery care and physician care at birth has to do with control. Childbirth is a complicated physiological process regulated by the woman's nervous system. Childbirth is not under the conscious control of the woman giving birth, but rather is directed by hormones and the parasympathetic portion of the autonomic nervous system. Anything that causes fear or alarm shuts down the parasympathetic system and fires up the sympathetic nervous system (adrenaline). Any intervention that increases

a laboring woman's fear or anxiety will interfere with, slow down, or even stop the birth processes. A wise birth assistant, be it midwife, nurse, or doctor, knows how to facilitate these autonomic responses and not interfere with them. The key elements in the midwifery model of birth are normality, facilitation of natural processes (with minimal intervention), and the empowerment of the birthing woman.

Taking on the role of facilitator, midwives typically will reassure, calm, and encourage birthing women. Obstetricians, on the other hand, typically try to get the birth under their own control by overriding the natural processes with drugs and medical procedures and giving orders. The medical model and the midwifery model are essentially different ways of looking at women and birth. Doctors "deliver" babies and believe that having a baby is something that *happens* to a woman. Midwives assist at birth and believe that giving birth is something that a woman *does*.

Midwives tend to believe that a woman giving birth needs to be the one making decisions about her birth experience. The woman giving birth needs to believe in her own body and feel responsible for her body, while at the same time letting go of the need to control what is happening, since she cannot.

Another fundamental difference between midwives and doctors is how they view pregnancy and birth. Midwives understand that pregnancy is not an illness. They typically call the women in their care "clients," not "patients," since they are not sick and are not getting medical treatment. Though midwives know what can go wrong during pregnancy and birth and know how to identify problems early and to cooperate with doctors in managing complications, their focus is on birth as a life-enhancing experience. Although they believe it is essential to have medical assistance available when it is needed, they are trained to go beyond medical care and empower women to achieve their goals for themselves and their babies. Midwives trust in women's bodies and their capacity to give birth successfully with little or no intervention in most cases.

Obstetricians, on the other hand, tend to focus on what can go wrong during pregnancy and birth. All doctors have been trained to look for trouble (diagnose a problem) and decide what to do about it: decide on a treatment, and that is what comes naturally to obstetricians. In prenatal care they take the same approach, focusing on what can go wrong.

Another important difference between midwife-attended low-risk birth and obstetrician-attended low-risk birth is the quality of the experience for the woman. Many surveys have shown that women who have midwives as their attendants have far higher levels of satisfaction with their birth experience than women who have obstetricians attending their births. This is not hard to understand. Midwives give great attention to building close relationships with their clients and their clients' families.

Generally speaking, midwives are direct, open, and honest in their dealings with clients and take an egalitarian, intimate, woman-to-woman approach. Midwives do not guarantee a good outcome, and their honesty about their role and its limitations contributes to the level of satisfaction women feel with their services. On the other hand, in a doctor-patient relationship, there is no egalitarian tradition. Rather, the doctor's superior knowledge and status are for the most part unquestioned and there is a belief (or hope) that the doctor can perform miracles.

Midwives, like doctors, are human. They have bad days and they make mistakes. Science now tells us, however, that overall, midwives are safer than doctors for low-risk births. If a woman is among the 80 to 90 percent of all women who have normal pregnancies, the safest attendant for her hospital birth is not a doctor but a midwife.

In the past two decades we've seen a renaissance of midwifery in the United States. Each year, the number of births attended by midwives increases.

The more the practice of midwifery grows and succeeds, the more threatening midwives are to the obstetric monopoly, so, predictably, there has been an obstetric backlash. Now, a hundred years after Hanna Porn was persecuted, we have another American witch hunt against midwives. In many states, doctors are reporting midwives to various authorities as dangerous.

In many cases, these attacks are simply attempts by doctors to eliminate the competition. Cases against midwives are, with very rare exceptions, not initiated by the families the midwives serve, as is typical of litigation against obstetricians. Instead, they are initiated by physicians. In the past several years in many states, including Illinois, Utah, California, Vermont, Virginia, Nevada, Oregon, Indiana, and Ohio, police have arrested direct-entry midwives for practicing nursing or medicine without a license.

Maternity care in the United States is changing, and one of the most important changes still in progress involves who will catch the 3.5 million babies a year whose mothers have had normal pregnancies. That is, who will be the primary birth attendant for low-risk births? In the past decade, the percentage of births attended by midwives has gone from 5 percent to 10 percent, and there are a few places where it is closer to 25 percent. HMOs are hiring more and more midwives. Kaiser Permanente, one of the largest HMOs in the country, has many midwives on its staff. There are several reasons for the growth of midwifery in the United States, and a big one is money.

Midwifery is far cheaper than obstetrics for two reasons. On average, obstetricians take home a *net* income in the neighborhood of $200,000 a year, whereas midwives earn about one-quarter of that. Equally important, the cost of the obstetric interventions, such as induction and C-section, performed *unnecessarily,* can easily be cut in half by having midwives, rather than obstetricians, assist at normal births. Health care in the United States is very much driven by the bottom line, and slowly but surely the insurance companies, managed health care organizations, HMOs, and even state and federal government agencies, are realizing that the obstetric monopoly is wasting enormous amounts of money. The day that truth fully sinks in will be the day the obstetric monopoly is on its way out.

As midwifery becomes better established in the United States, it becomes more difficult for the obstetric establishment to perpetuate the myth that midwives are not as safe as doctors. Pushing the "safety" issue has backfired as a way for obstetricians to protect their territory. As more state legislatures look carefully at the data and realize that they have been denying families a safe maternity care option, momentum will grow and laws that support and protect midwives will spread to other states.

Another reason midwifery is going to grow: Americans believe in a free market economy with open competition. Obstetricians and midwives both offer primary maternity care.

Finally, midwifery will continue to grow as more women come to appreciate that maternity care is not primarily a health issue but a women's issue. Midwifery plays an important role in strengthening women's control over their own bodies and reproductive systems.

Canadian Petrochemical Plants and Gender Imbalances

Paul Webster (2006)

"You get strange smells here," Ada Lockridge says as she climbs out of her jeep and heads for her great grandfather's grave in the Aamjiwnaang cemetery, a once-quiet hillock now surrounded by humming oil and chemical plants. Facing a line of fire-spitting refinery smokestacks, Lockridge gives the air a slightly theatrical sniff. "Maybe it's naphtha today," she pronounces.

Lockridge is a volunteer environmental monitor on the Aamjiwnaang native reserve, once part of the Chippewa's central North American empire. The reserve, which is on the Canadian side of the Canada–USA border about an hour's drive from Detroit, directly faces Canada's largest concentration of petrochemical plants. About 40% of Canada's synthetic rubber, polyvinyl chloride and plastics is produced here. The area is also home to one of Canada's largest hazardous-waste dumps. Few tourists care to stop in this now-blighted place. In recent months, however, health researchers and news reporters from across Canada, the USA, and Europe have streamed into Aamjiwnaang.

The spotlight settled here last October, when the US journal *Environmental Health Perspectives* published a study indicating significantly fewer males than females were born over the last decade among the 850 aboriginals living on the reserve, where people have long complained about exposure to toxic pollutants.

Lockridge, who co-authored the article, says she's had little peace since the results were released: "The reporters and professors all want to take my 'toxic tour,'" she says with a slightly mischievous smile. "It's just ruined all my normal routines."

Lockridge's tour reveals a Dickensian juxtaposition of massive petrochemical facilities and rows of modest aboriginal family homes. After a stop at the Leaky Tank Truck Stop, there's a hike through an abandoned, unsecured open-air chemical dump, and a visit to a recently closed kindergarten located just a stone's throw from a massive chemical plant. The new kindergarten seems better situated, although the omnipresent chemical complexes still tower nearby.

Along the route, Lockridge flips open a diary recording a monthly average of five-to-ten local chemical release "incidents." Most of these remain unexplained by plant managers, Lockridge complains. Government regulators have issued many warnings and imposed numerous stiff penalties in recent years, but the troubles at the plants continue.

"Every few months we smell something really nauseating, black clouds fill the sky, the sirens go off, and we're all ordered indoors," Lockridge says.

The oil refineries and chemical plants date back more than a century to when oil was discovered near the Aamjiwnaang traditional lands, which border the St Clair river connecting the Upper and Lower Great Lakes to form the world's largest freshwater repository. By the 1960s, the small Ontario city of Sarnia had sprouted on land bargained-off by Lockridge's ancestors, and the area around the reserve had come to be known as Canada's "Chemical Valley." These days, numerous multinational oil and chemical giants operate massive refineries along the edges of the reserve.

Serious health concerns first surfaced in the 1970s, when investigators called attention to asbestos exposures among oil workers in the region. In 1985, chemicals dumped into the St Clair River coagulated into a massive underwater slick. The "Sarnia Blob," as it was dubbed, was found to contain arsenic, copper, cadmium, chromium, iron, lead, mercury, nickel, zinc, polychlorinated biphenyls (PCBs), hexachlorobenzene, phosphorus, chromium, iron, lead, mercury, and manganese, oil, grease and a cocktail of at least 30 toxic compounds known as polyaromatic hydrocarbons.

Although water quality in the region is notoriously dubious, it's the refineries' atmospheric emissions that attract most attention these days. A 2004 study noted extremely high male hospitalization for cerebral palsy, possibly associated with mercury exposures in the area. And a review by Toronto's *Globe and Mail* newspaper of census data gathered in 2001 found that communities downwind from the refineries have a skewed birthrate, though not as pronounced as on the reserve.

But despite the history of health worries and massive pollution, no broad-based epidemiological study has ever been commissioned to examine possible toxicological impacts on the 130,000 people living in the area.

The decision by Lockridge and colleagues to investigate gender skewing on the reserve resulted from a chance encounter. When someone mentioned that girls' baseball teams outnumber boys' teams on the reserve during a discussion at the Ontario government's Occupational Health Clinic for Ontario Workers, Constanze MacKenzie, a fourth year University of Ottawa medical intern, took note.

As a biology graduate, MacKenzie had spent years studying the gender-bending impacts of phenols and other chemicals on Ontario turtles and fish. She was well aware that studies of fish, birds and reptiles in the area around the reserve showed striking evidence of reproductive abnormalities including numerous intersex births, hormone production interference, thyroid function disruption, birth rate reduction, penis length reduction, and embryonic mortality. She also knew that many researchers consider these findings in wildlife highly relevant to humans. "When we have so much evidence from so many species

showing reproductive disorders you have to ask, are humans really so different?", says MacKenzie.

Working with Lockridge and Margaret Keith, a research coordinator at the Occupational Health and Safety Clinic, as well as with external help from Theo Colborne, a leading Washington, DC–based endocrine disruption investigator, Mackenzie set out to check whether concerns on the reserve about gender showing were simply a misperception. A review of the reserve's birth records between 1984 and 1993 showed no aberration. But between 1994 and 1998 the number of male births dipped noticeably. And during 1999–2003 they dropped even more. Of 132 births in that period, only 46 were males. Normally about 105 boys are born for every 100 girls. "We have to approach these findings with caution because the sample size is small," Mackenzie stresses. "Even so, there's only a 1% chance the trend we found is a fluke."

But the link between pollutants and reproductive effects remains speculative. Although researchers have established reproductive problems in people exposed to very high doses of gender-bending toxins—such as the Italian city of Seveso, where a dioxin-producing pesticide plant exploded in 1996—no study has firmly linked these outcomes to routine environmental exposures.

Arnold Schecter, a University of Texas environmental toxicologist who has investigated human exposure to several environmental toxins, praises the Aamjiwnaang study as a "well thought out" investigation. But the study hasn't persuaded him that the case for human gender-bending from environmental exposures to endocrine disrupters is growing.

Jake Ryan, a senior researcher at Health Canada, Canada's federal health agency, agrees. He has probed gender-skewing among pesticide workers in Russia and says the Aamjiwnaang study requires follow-up: "I would like to see whether these results can be repeated in the non-native population living near the reserve," says Ryan.

At least for the reserve communities, things seem to be improving. Scott Munro, manager of the Sarnia-Lambton Environmental Association, an environmental group funded by several chemical companies, has monitored local air emissions for decades. "People talk about pollution conditions that made them cry in the 1950s," says Munro. "It's much cleaner than it was." Even so, Munro acknowledges there are plenty of "fugitive emissions" from the plants. Many of these may not be recorded, nor their health effects well understood, he admits.

A full-scale health study of the sort recommended by Lockridge and Mackenzie is needed, he agrees. The only trouble with doing such a study, says Munro, is finding someone to pay for it.

Ada Lockridge says she's not holding her breath waiting for action. The Ontario and Canadian governments are still studying whether to even study the matter.

R E A D I N G   29

A Shared Journey in Breast Cancer Advocacy

Kathleen M. Errico and Diana Rowden (2006)

The women's health advocacy movement began in many countries during the second half of the 20th century. However, organizations by and for patients with breast cancer that provide support and information for patients have been active since the 1950s. In 1952, the American Cancer Society started the Reach to Recovery program. This was a group of women helping women: survivors of breast cancer helping women with newly diagnosed disease. Members of Reach to Recovery, all of whom had had mastectomies, provided a support group for women who had mastectomies. This organization continues today as an international organization supporting women throughout the world (1).

The politics of breast cancer accelerated in the United States in the 1970s and 1980s, when well-known women such as Betty Ford, Nancy Reagan, Happy Rockefeller, and Shirley Temple Black began to speak out about their experiences with the disease (2,3). As survivor-advocates, these American women helped raise public awareness about breast cancer and the need for early detection programs. Women increasingly identified themselves publicly as survivors. Breast cancer advocacy further developed as dedicated breast cancer advocacy organizations such as YME, the Susan G. Komen Breast Cancer Foundation, the National Alliance of Breast Cancer Organizations, and the National Breast Cancer Coalition added a political dimension to the provision of breast cancer information and support (3). Today, breast cancer advocacy movements are generally well established in North America and western Europe. The movement in the United States, one of the most successful worldwide, provides a good example of the development of a breast cancer advocacy movement and its power to improve breast health care.

During the 1980s and 1990s, organizations that advocate on behalf of breast cancer championed the Mammography Quality Standards Act, the establishment of a special fund in the U.S. Department of the Army for breast cancer research, the establishment and expansion of the Centers for Disease Control and Prevention's Breast and Cervical Cancer Early Detection Program, and extensive increases in federal funding for the National Cancer Institute. For example, during the 1990s, federal government funding for breast cancer research increased from $81 million to more than $400 million (4,5).

Internationally breast cancer advocates have faced the challenges of dealing with many languages, cultures, countries, and health systems. In particular, in many cultures it is difficult to transcend ethnic and religious differences to break the silence and profound stigma that still surround breast cancer. Because of these many differences, the model of breast cancer advocacy generally endorsed in the United States is not always appropriate or reproducible in other cultures, suggesting the need for alternative models. In addition, the experiences of breast cancer survivor-advocates and advocates in countries with limited resources differ significantly from those in developed countries. Although there is an emerging sense of global breast cancer advocacy, the growth of the advocacy movement in countries with limited resources is somewhat hindered by the difficulty of translating the ethos of advocacy into many languages and cultures. Furthermore, resource-constrained countries have differing financial needs, resource limitations, social barriers, and competing illnesses that frame how breast cancer advocacy can be implemented.

To identify commonalities and differences in the experiences of breast cancer and in the development of breast cancer advocacy movements in limited-resource settings, we undertook a qualitative analysis of statements and comments provided by breast cancer survivor-advocates and advocates at a recent international summit.

METHODS

The second biennial Global Summit Consensus Conference on International Breast Health Care (hereafter referred to as the 2005 Global Summit), sponsored by the Fred Hutchinson Cancer Research Center, co-sponsored by the Susan G. Komen Breast Cancer Foundation, and hosted by the Office of International Affairs, National Cancer Institute, provided a forum for the voice of breast cancer survivor-advocates and advocates from countries with limited resources. (For the purposes of this article, survivor-advocates are defined as breast cancer survivors who work in partnership with a community-based group or organization of survivors.)

Each of four sessions of the summit began with a 15-minute introductory statement by a breast cancer survivor-advocate or advocate from a country with limited resources in which she described her own experience or that of women from her country with breast cancer and advocacy. In addition, a 2-hour Advocates Roundtable Meeting provided an opportunity for survivor-advocates and other breast cancer advocates from around the world to discuss breast cancer advocacy from a global perspective. The meeting was facilitated by a representative of the Komen Foundation (D.R.) and was attended by 12 participants, each representing a different country (Belarus, Brazil, Canada, Chile, China, Ghana, Greece, India, Italy, Kenya, Malaysia, and the United States).

In an effort to understand the commonalities and differences in experiences of breast cancer survivor-advocates and advocates from countries with limited resources, we analyzed the introductory statements from the summit sessions and the transcripts from the roundtable discussion for themes. For analysis, we used a low-technology "long table" technique suggested by Krueger (6), which permits analysis of content to identify themes and categorize results.

RESULTS AND DISCUSSION

The introductory statements of the breast cancer survivor-advocates and advocates were a powerful addition to the proceedings of the 2005 Global Summit. The stories of these quietly eloquent women illuminated the connectedness of breast cancer survivors and their advocacy efforts around the world. Similarly, although participants in the roundtable meeting noted some differences between their countries in breast cancer experiences and advocacy movements, the commonalities were striking.

Overall, five major themes emerged from the analysis of the statements and the transcript that reflected common experiences of breast cancer survivor-advocates and of advocates worldwide:

- Common experiences and fears of breast cancer survivors
- Beliefs and taboos about breast cancer that hinder awareness programs and treatment
- The universal need for public education and breast cancer awareness programs in countries with limited resources
- The shared problems with language and difficulty translating the concept and ethos of advocacy into many languages
- Common experiences in establishing and maintaining advocacy groups to promote breast cancer awareness and to inform public policy

Experiences and Fears of Survivors

The experiences of breast cancer survivor-advocates from countries with limited resources were reflected in the statements and transcripts. Participants' comments indicated that the commonality of the experience of breast cancer survivors led to the development of support groups. Specifically, survivor-advocates and advocates recognized the need to provide emotional support and education for breast cancer survivors and to provide testimony "to the power of life." Certain issues are universal for all women with breast cancer, irrespective of age, ethnic group, nationality, or stage of disease, and this universality of the experience of breast cancer was reflected in the comments of survivor-advocates.

> I was thinking that breast cancer is the same disease for every woman all over the world, we were survivors. Maybe we felt the same way and we suffer the same, but one of the things I'm taking back home is that we are also different—each country, each culture has a different approach, even when you speak about countries of limited resources.

> I'm a breast cancer survivor, five years now, and I am also a breast health advocate. I'm with an organization called the Kenya Breast Health Program. This is basically the only advocacy group for breast health in my country, and I likely got involved with Kenya Breast Health Program at its formation, basically as a result of my experience with breast cancer.

Along with common concerns, experiences, and anxieties, each woman's journey with breast cancer has a unique set of circumstances. A frequent common experience and expression of survivor-advocates was that of fear. They described the personal fear that a woman experiences after receiving a diagnosis of breast cancer, as well as the societal fear manifested in the response by family members and neighbors:

> One of the greatest fears expressed by almost all newly diagnosed breast cancer patients is . . . am I going to die?

> Overcoming fear when alone is not easy . . . one feels no longer accepted. . . . The word cancer terrified me.

> A woman's journey in breast cancer in a developing country has a long way to go. For many years, people in developing countries have perceived breast cancer as a frightening disease surrounded by fear and myths.

> Avoiding awareness programs and information on this disease as a result of fear has worsened the plight of breast cancer patients in developing countries.

Survivor-advocates and advocates also identified common themes related to the changes in body image associated with mastectomy. In addition, they noted how women with breast cancer must assimilate into their lives the physical scars of treatment, emotional distress, and disruption in family relations. They identified the need for information about prostheses and the need for emotional support for breast cancer patients.

> The loss of a breast is a terrifying jolt to one's body image.

> Breast cancer creates an identity crisis with the initial loss of body image. Encouragement, hope, and emotional support from loved ones, family, friends, someone with a common experience, and health care professionals can help prevent social isolation and social discrimination, which can be devastating.

Beliefs and Taboos About Breast Cancer

Several survivor-advocates and advocates identified traditional societal beliefs and cultural taboos that affected women's access to information, early detection, and treatment. They noted how these beliefs may result in social isolation for women with breast cancer. In addition, their comments suggested that cultural attitudes and taboos, especially beliefs of fatalism, may deter breast cancer advocacy efforts:

> Traditional beliefs dominate the Asian lifestyle. Negative attitude of society toward cancer can be a greater killer than the disease itself. The woman is made to feel guilty that she has brought "bad genes" into the family. She keeps her disease under wraps just to avoid social rejection and social isolation. In some cases she is isolated from her family members, whereby her dining utensils are separated, fearing that she will "spread the disease to the rest of the family members."

> I will never give up to those who suggested that when you get close to a disease or have something to do with it, it will follow or it will affect your family.

> Cancer, if you talk about cancer, it comes into your house or if you go to the doctor to be examined for breast cancer, you end up with breast cancer. If you don't go, you won't get breast cancer.

Need for Public Education and Awareness Programs

Breast cancer survivor-advocates and advocates identified the need for culturally appropriate breast health awareness programs and problems with competing for scarce resources in the face of the burden of communicable diseases in countries with limited resources. Participants from such countries had a heightened awareness of disparities in access to diagnostic and treatment facilities that lead to late presentations of the disease.

> Most women in developing countries know very little about breast cancer and its warning signs, and as a result go to hospital for treatment when it is rather too late to get cured.

> We have a problem with awareness, we have stigmatization, we have all those and end up leading to late presentations, and we have lack of diagnostic facilities, lack of treatment facilities, financing constraints for the women, competition for resources. HIV/AIDS is a major problem, so you talk about breast cancer and say how many people are dying, and they say HIV, they're always quoting figures, 700 people per day, and they say, "Wow, this is the problem. Breast cancer, that's not a problem."

Difficulty in Translating the Concept of Advocacy

Advocacy in the English language is generally interpreted as the art of representing or promoting a cause or purpose on behalf of oneself or others. This may include increasing awareness, influencing policy, affecting legislation, and changing attitudes. Traditionally patient advocacy has involved pleading on behalf of patients' needs. Yet the word advocacy is not directly translatable in many languages (3,4). This difficulty with translation was a theme that emerged from the analysis of comments. Participants in the advocacy roundtable identified the need to develop an international word or language for advocacy that would reflect the broad range of activities and approaches generally interpreted as breast cancer advocacy. In addition, participants noted that in developing countries, women may not have open access to resources, information, or education that empowers them to implement change and promote advocacy.

> I must say that the word advocacy is absolutely new for me.

> What I'm trying to do is find what the word advocacy means exactly in Spanish. I know what it means, but I'm trying to find the exact meaning, not the exact word, but the exact meaning.

> We still don't have in Portuguese a word for advocacy, and it's a big problem because we cannot say "advogados"—or lawyers, it would mean—because we are not. We must find a word for this, outside English word, because we cannot say "advogados" or something like that. I don't know. We have to think as a group because I'm sure in Spanish and Italian, Latin countries have this problem of the word and we have to make it like an international word.

> We don't have a word for advocacy, it's exactly the same as what you say it may mean, that you are a lawyer or something like that, and you have to have that qualification to be one. So the word we use is networking and influencing.

> There were not rules that could regulate volunteer work, nobody was talking about social responsibility or advocacy was just out of question. It was a bunch of women that were shouting about something, just no credit whatsoever.

Experiences in Establishing and Developing Advocacy Groups

Although there was apparent difficulty with defining advocacy, breast cancer survivor-advocates and advocates identified common bonds, challenges, and steps that propelled their efforts forward. Their comments reflected the incremental nature of breast cancer advocacy and movement along a continuum from support and education, to developing social responsibility, and finally to influencing change. The burdens and hurdles on the road to breast cancer advocacy were reflected in their comments:

> So we decided that we have to work towards some other issues, not just giving support to the women themselves, and from there we started doing a little bit of advocacy work.

> We started with six people and this was '93 and things really moved fast, and we start after 2 years we became

official Brazilian kind of educational group, volunteer educational group, at that time volunteer work was not accepted in Brazil because we're intruders in hospitals.

So we came up with the idea that we need some form of guideline so that we make sure that everybody is trying to do something that is normal, or acceptable, so eventually we lobbied the ministry to set up what they call a breast cancer working group.

The message of breast cancer advocacy has been spreading throughout the world. In the early 1990s, EUROPA DONNA, the European Breast Cancer Coalition, was formed. The emergence of breast cancer advocacy throughout Europe can be traced through the development of EUROPA DONNA, a coalition of affiliated groups for countries across Europe (2). Similarly, Reach to Recovery has grown into an international network of survivor-advocates that includes 84 groups in 50 countries. While some are mature groups, the majority are new groups from Africa, Asia, eastern Europe, and Latin America that need help in establishing support services (1).

In the late 1990s, the Komen Foundation began to develop international affiliates in countries that were interested in implementing Komen activities, such as the Race for the Cure. Today the Komen Foundation has three international affiliates—in Germany, Italy, and Puerto Rico—that fund grants and carry out breast cancer education programs. In addition, the foundation has made grants to non-governmental organizations (NGOs) in more than 30 countries to support a range of breast cancer education, outreach, and support programs. Representatives from several of these organizations participated in the advocacy roundtable discussion and shared their experiences. They remarked that financial support from foundations and NGOs had been helpful in furthering their activities.

So you need some luck in life, and my lucky occasion came in 1998 when I had the privilege and fortune to cross roads with the Komen Foundation, very, very early when they were starting to become an international organization or at least to start some international efforts.

And we have had really the fortune to look at a wonderful model that in the United States has created, really

a switch in the way breast cancer is addressed and see how we could apply at least some part of this model in Italy, through innovation and new strategies, trying not to duplicate efforts that were already there, but creating new opportunities. And in 5 years, we have been able to become self-sufficient, we generate money that allows [us] to fund, we have supported 50 programs of other breast cancer groups in Italy, in small possibly groups that would have good ideas but not have access to funding, so that at the local level, the community level, this is helping women with breast cancer to have something more to face this disease better.

CONCLUSIONS

The last decade has been marked by rapid growth in the breast cancer advocacy movement around the world. There has been a shift in the activities of survivor-advocates and advocates as breast cancer advocacy campaigns have increased in intensity in regions with limited resources including Africa, Asia, eastern Europe, and Latin America. The practice of breast cancer advocacy has increasingly become international, with sustained, effective collaboration among groups. The goals and methods of these campaigns may vary with the social, economic, and cultural circumstances of the countries and women involved. Despite this diversity, survivor-advocates and advocates at the 2005 Global Summit voiced a set of common themes in international breast cancer advocacy that reflected their shared journey with breast cancer.

By virtue of their personal life experiences, breast cancer survivor-advocates possess unique insights regarding the complex sociocultural issues that may hinder the implementation of breast health awareness and early detection programs in countries with limited resources. Survivor-advocates and advocates at the summit expressed common themes pertaining to the experience of breast cancer, including societal fear of the disease, cultural taboos and myths, and a lack of adequate educational resources. Their statements indicated that these factors can be major barriers to breast health awareness and early detection programs in countries with limited resources. Their experiences are consistent with the findings of several studies that have documented that fear, perceptions, and lack of knowledge are obstacles to breast cancer screening (7–9). To successfully recruit women to breast health awareness and early detection programs, such programs must take into consideration women's perceptions and cultural beliefs about breast cancer. Participants' comments indicated that these perceptions and beliefs vary among countries and population groups, necessitating a tailored approach to program design. The impact of effective programs is potentially large, as participants' comments expressed confidence that such programs could contribute to improved survivorship for women with breast cancer.

Although the word *advocacy* is not directly translatable in many languages, the role of breast cancer survivor-advocates and advocates appears to be universal. Participants in the Advocacy Roundtable strongly believed that with the assistance of governmental and NGOs, breast cancer advocacy groups can continue to create change. In partnership with organizations such as Reach to Recovery International, the Komen Foundation, and the medical community, survivor-advocates and advocates may be instrumental in establishing effective breast health awareness programs as well as breast cancer research programs that cross social, economic, and cultural boundaries in countries with limited resources (9).

Breast cancer advocacy can have a marked positive influence on societal awareness of and attitudes toward the disease, on breast health care services, and on funding for research (3). However, establishing and expanding advocacy groups in countries with limited resources may be especially challenging. Resource-constrained countries have limitations in financial support, social barriers, and competing illnesses that frame how breast cancer advocacy can be implemented. Comments made by survivor-advocates and advocates at the summit indicated that they have a deep understanding of the barriers to developing breast cancer advocacy in such countries. These individuals are nonetheless motivated to integrate their insights and experiences to support and maintain advocacy groups. Given the potential of advocacy movements to improve breast health outcomes, the founding and growth of advocacy groups should be fostered in countries with limited resources.

Taken together, the five themes we identified constitute an action agenda for breast cancer advocacy groups in countries with limited resources. In particular, the survivor-advocates' and advocates' comments revealed barriers and challenges to breast health care and breast cancer advocacy, but at the same time suggested potential strategies for overcoming them. The themes also provide invaluable insight to policymakers, program planners, and others undertaking efforts to improve breast cancer outcomes in such settings.

REFERENCES
1. Reach for Recovery International 2005. Available at http://www.uicc.org; accessed March 28, 2005.
2. Buchanan M, Kyriakides S, Fernandez-Marcos A, *et al*. Breast cancer advocacy across Europe through the work and development of EUROPA DONNA, the European Breast Cancer Coalition. *Eur J Cancer* 2004;40:1111–16.
3. Braun S. The history of breast cancer advocacy. *Breast J* 2003;9(suppl. 2):S101–3.
4. Davis C, Salo L, Redman S. Evaluating the effectiveness of advocacy training for breast cancer advocates in Australia. *Eur J Cancer Care* 2001;10:82–86.
5. Houn F, Elliott ML, McCrohan JL. The Mammography Quality Standards Act of 1992. History and philosophy. *Radiol Clin North Am* 1995;33:1059–65.
6. Krueger RA. *Analyzing and Reporting Focus Group Results*. Thousand Oaks, CA: Sage, 1998.
7. Buki L, Borrayo E, Feigal B, Carrillo I. Are all Latinas the same? Perceived breast cancer screening barriers and facilitative conditions. *Psychol Women Q* 2004;28:400–411.
8. Lythcott N, Green B, Brown Z. The perspective of African America breast cancer survivor-advocates. *Cancer* 2003;97(suppl. 1):324–28.
9. Bener A, Honein G, Carter AO, *et al*. The determinants of breast cancer screening behavior: a focus group study of women in the United Arab Emirates. *Oncol Nurs Forum* 2002;29:E91–98.

Reproductive Freedoms

Patti Lou Watkins, Alicia Bublitz, and *Hoa Nguyen*

Patti Lou Watkins is associate professor of Women Studies at Oregon State University, USA, and a member of the National Women's Studies Association, Society of Behavioral Medicine, and Association for Behavioral and Cognitive Therapies. She obtained her doctoral degree in clinical psychology from Virginia Tech. Dr. Watkins's research focuses on women, especially issues surrounding weight, body image, and physical activity. She is an editor of *Handbook of Self-Help Therapies* (Routledge, 2008) and author of "Bon Bon Fatty Girl: A Qualitative Exploration of Weight Bias in Singapore" in the *Fat Studies Reader* and "Gender Role Stressors and Women's Health" in the *Handbook of Gender, Culture, and Health*. Her classes include "Women, Weight, and Eating Disorders"; "Self-Esteem and Personal Power"; and "Violence Against Women."

Alicia Bublitz is a graduate student in Women Studies and Peace Studies at Oregon State University, USA, focusing on global feminism and its applicability in international relations. Her research interests focus on feminist transnational partnerships as well as the role of international governance in women's lives. Her work includes program development, policy analysis, and blogging. Outside the academy she is a community activist, a Girl Scout leader, and a feminist advocate.

Hoa Nguyen is a graduate student at the University of Minnesota's School of Social Work, USA, where she researches immigrant and refugee populations. Prior to coming to the United States, she earned an undergraduate degree in English from Hanoi University and worked at the Institute of Policy and Strategies for Agriculture and Rural Development on various foreign aid projects. She also worked as an interpreter for an HIV/AIDS project associated with the United Nations Development Program. Her interests include immigrant and international social development issues.

> *Zdravo Marijo, milosti puna,*
> Hail Mary, full of grace,
> The Lord is with thee, may be,
> is not, or else who would
> allow such pain?
> In my kitchen, on this earth,
> where angels fear to tread.
>
> *Zdravo Marijo, Majko Bozja,*
> Hail Mary, Mother of God,
> Don't you remember
> small breath clouds on frosted panes,
> sharp cries sobbed in midnight deep?
> To save this love, I disobey.
> No more babies bless this home.
>
> K.L. Kunavic.

Reproductive freedom involves rights related to reproduction and reproductive health, including the ability to have children as well as to prevent having them, and to control the number and spacing of offspring. The World Health Organization (WHO) explains that reproductive rights rest on "the recognition of the basic right of all couples and individuals to decide freely and responsibly the number, spacing and timing of their children and to have the information and means to do so, and the right to attain the highest standard of sexual and reproductive health." "Freely and responsibly" implies freedom from "discrimination, coercion and violence" (http://who.int/reproductive-health/gender/index.html). As K. L. Kunavic's poem suggests, there are serious religious and cultural constraints on reproductive freedom, even in societies where legally women's "choice" is protected. In this case of Croatia, the government has been under pressure from the Catholic Church to enact pronatalist policies that encourage childbearing. Kunavic makes the point that pressure from the Church to increase family size jeopardizes children's well-being in families where resources are scarce. Women desire to control fertility in order to safeguard their lives and the welfare of existing children as they balance limited resources. The arrival of one more mouth to feed can disrupt and jeopardize the food security of the whole family. Certainly women experience complex economic, social, and psychological factors associated with continuous motherhood. The notion of "voluntary motherhood" underscores the ways women's reproductive control impacts other aspects of their lives that include education and career advancement as well as personal autonomy in relationships.

Although laws, policies, and governmental decrees specifically impact reproductive freedoms, so may less tangible social mores, norms (accepted social values), and customs that influence whether, how, when, and where a woman might conceive and give birth. For example, powerful cultural norms asserting that women should produce children ("compulsory motherhood") influence their choices. Reproductive rights encompass the right to choose *not* to reproduce at all, although this decision may provoke strong reactions in many parts of the world. Women without children are often seen as personally unfulfilled or deficient in some way. Women who choose not to have children, or who have them after establishing a career, may be accused of selfishness, deviance, and immaturity (Gillespie, 2000). Viewing reproductive rights as a personal matter ignores the reality that such social norms, practices, beliefs, and conditions shape women's options and behaviors surrounding conception, pregnancy, and birth. Most nations have legislation addressing age of marriage, guardianship policies, informed consent, and availability of abortion or other reproductive health services (Bahar, 2000). These laws both protect and can present challenges to women's reproductive freedom. A comprehensive discussion of reproductive rights must therefore address the broader political and sociocultural expectations exerted on women's bodies. The following sections highlight the influence of these pressures.

This chapter addresses the politics of reproductive freedom, beginning with a section on reproductive rights as human rights. As also emphasized in the previous chapter on health, this discussion addresses the ways reproductive freedom is not only a personal concern for women, but connected to broader social issues about their status in society. The next focus is on reproductive technologies with discussions about birth control, forced sterilization, abortion, and assisted reproduction. This is followed by a section that addresses specific vulnerabilities of marginalized populations with respect to reproductive rights and that explores these issues as they affect disabled, incarcerated, and migrant populations. The chapter closes with a call for activism to improve women's reproductive freedoms worldwide.

A DAY IN THE LIFE   *Partera Tradicional* by Kryn Freehling-Burton

Estela's four-year-old daughter stirred next to her as a banging on the door woke them just as the sky began to show the first color of dawn. A few minutes later, Estela kissed the little girl on the forehead and hurried out the front door of her mother's three room house covered with brown stucco made from the earth in the village she has called home her whole life. Her midwife bag slung over her arm, Estela hurried to the one bus stop in their little village in the hills of Oaxaca, Mexico, with her midwife mentor, Lupe. The sky lightened from rose-grey to yellow as the sun rose from behind the hills covered in avocado groves. The bus lumbered up the zigzagged road to the next village.

Lupe reviewed the plan for the day as Estela checked the supplies in her bag: rebozo shawl for massage and turning the baby before birth if necessary, various herbs and salves to ease pain and assist the mother's relaxation, scissors, suture needle and thread, disinfectant, ointment for the baby's eyes, clamp for the umbilical cord, gloves, a doptone for listening to the baby's heartbeat, and tea. Estela would assist the mother-in-labor while Lupe visited the other expectant mothers in the village for prenatal care visits. Lupe stretched her fingers gnarled with arthritis while reviewing last minute instructions with Estela, "Watch her face. A good *partera* remembers that the mother's body knows what to do. Listen to her." Estela laughed, "I know, *maestra*!" She caught Lupe's hands to massage them while they traveled.

Lupe remembered the day Estela showed up on her doorstep, seventeen, pregnant, and scared. The months of prenatal care led to a long, quiet birth with the baby's father leaving two months later to work at a factory in the United States. Estela hadn't seen him since, but he sends money each month to help her and her mother. He hopes she'll join him someday, but Estela didn't want to leave her mother after the baby was born, and when she became the midwife's apprentice, she promised to stay through her training and take over Lupe's practice.

"I'm so glad you came to me! I wondered what these mothers would do when I am gone," Lupe lamented. "Even my own daughter wanted nothing to do with the *partera tradicional* ways." She smiled at Estela and took out an avocado and a towel wrapped around corn tortillas. They sliced the creamy fruit and ate it tucked inside the cold tortillas. When the bus rolled to a stop by the stone fountain left from the days of Cortes's conquest, the women paid the driver and climbed down to the dirt road. Lupe rang the bell at the largest house in the center of the village while Estela walked down a side road to a small cottage where the laboring woman's mother opened the heavy wooden door. "We thought you'd never arrive!" Estela smiled and asked her to start heating water to make some tea. This *abuela* needed to feel helpful but stay busy while Maria labored. Hoping to make it back in time for the baby's arrival, Maria's husband, Sal, had left to work in the corn fields while it was still dark.

Estela examined Maria by moving her hands gently but firmly over and around the baby's fullness. "The baby is in a good position; let's hear the heartbeat." Placing the small round wand on Maria's belly, Estela turned the knob on the receiver of the doptone and moved the wand until the "goosh, goosh" of a fast beat could be heard. Maria's small son giggled as he recognized the sound, and when the uterus began to harden, Maria closed her eyes and breathed deeply as the tightening took all her focus. Her contractions were hard but remained far apart so Estela helped her into a loose cotton dress embroidered with brightly-colored flowers. Then they walked to help stimulate more consistent contractions. To pass the time, they met Lupe who laughed at Estela's use of fancy, new equipment, "See, I send her to that workshop in the city and they convince her machines will make things better!"

"*Abuelita*, it only gives us more information. And besides, it helps the doctors understand that we're not so backwards that we don't know when intervention is necessary. It's not invasive and besides, the kids love it!" Maria grimaced as another contraction began and Lupe hurried to see her last client so she could observe her assistant's first delivery as a lead midwife. Estela's preparations for this day were three years in the making. She had attended more than 400 births as Lupe's apprentice, conducted countless prenatal and family planning appointments, and spent three months at a new midwifery training school learning how contemporary midwifery can complement the traditional ways Lupe practiced. She brought back contacts to purchase the precious oxytocin that could save a mother's life if she began to hemorrhage. She also brought back the knowledge that she was connected to a tradition that stretched thousands of years into the past and thousands of miles around the globe.

Maria's husband joined them for the midday meal of stewed black beans and rice that the family shared with the midwives. Afterwards, Lupe sang an ancient *Nahuatl* lullaby as Sal danced with his wife, easing her pain and coaxing the baby down the birth canal. As the time came for Maria to begin pushing, Estela massaged Maria's perineum so she would open gently, and Sal cradled her between his legs so she was supported as she squatted over a soft blanket woven by the women in the village.

"There's the baby's head, Maria, reach down and help your baby out," Estela said softly as she slipped her finger under the cord that was draped around the baby's neck. Estela's hand cradled the head as Maria grasped the baby under the arms. As she pushed one last time, Maria brought her newborn onto her chest. The big brother exclaimed, "It's a boy! I have a brother!" Sal and Estela helped Maria onto the couch and the new midwife checked the baby's heartbeat and breathing. Lupe gave the new mother a cup of lemon juice to help the contractions, and, as Maria began to nurse the baby, the placenta was delivered.

After washing Maria and swaddling the baby, Estela and Lupe shared another meal with the family, then bid them farewell. Estela would return the following day to check on the mom and her baby. She was paid a small amount of money, but each time she returns to the village, Sal and Maria will send her home with eggs and corn. After returning to Lupe's home, the midwives saw two more pregnant women for prenatal care. Another baby is due to be born any day. The sun was slipping behind the western mountain when Estela opened her own door. Her daughter ran and jumped into her arms, "Mama, mama! Tell me about the baby-born!"

REPRODUCTIVE RIGHTS AS HUMAN RIGHTS

Although the UN adopted its first declaration of human rights in 1948, it was not until the 1968 International Human Rights Conference in Tehran that reproductive rights were recognized. Since that time the 1994 International Conference on Population and Development in Cairo, the 1995 Fourth World Conference on Women in Beijing, the 1995 World Summit for Social Development in Copenhagen, and the 1996 World Conference on Human Settlements in Istanbul, reinforced the immediacy of addressing reproductive rights on an international scale. More recently, at its 2005 World Summit, the UN Population Fund (UNFPA) defined reproductive rights as "valuable ends in themselves, and essential to the enjoyment of other fundamental rights," including the following:

- Reproductive health as a component of overall health, throughout the life cycle, for both men and women
- Reproductive decision making, including voluntary choice in marriage, family formation, and determination of the number, timing, and spacing of one's children and the right to have access to the information and means needed to exercise voluntary choice

- Equality and equity for men and women, to enable individuals to make free and informed choices in all spheres of life, free from discrimination based on gender
- Sexual and reproductive security, including freedom from sexual violence and coercion, and the right to privacy (UNFPA n.d., para. 3)

However, despite increasing international focus, the implementation of reproductive rights remains unevenly enforced across countries. This gap is particularly apparent between the Global North and the Global South, particularly those in South America, sub-Saharan Africa and South East Asia. Poverty is a key factor here. As the reading "Investing in Reproductive Health and Rights" by Thoraya Ahmed Obaid emphasizes, it is important to address the links between poverty and reproductive freedom. She writes of the significant social consequences of investing in reproductive health and rights for both the empowerment of women and the livelihood of communities.

This focus on reproductive rights as human rights emphasizes that a woman's desire and ability to control her fertility is not simply a personal concern grounded in the realities of her everyday life, but intimately connected to broader social issues about her place in society. This means that any movement for reproductive freedom must acknowledge that reproductive decisions are made within a social context that includes wealth and power. In this sense, reproductive liberties are matters of social justice, not individual choice. High birth rates, for example, are linked to poverty, low educational levels, and reduced access to security, opportunity, and other resources necessary for women if they are to have control over their lives and support themselves and their families (Lappé, Collins, Rosset, and Esparza, 1998). However, while poor women may produce more children due to lack of information about, and access to, contraception, the reasons for large families are complex. In many developing countries, especially agriculturally based nations,

Used with permission of Ann Telnaes and the Cartoonist Group. All rights reserved.

LEARNING ACTIVITY   **Organizations Working for Reproductive Rights**

Around the world, many organizations are working to ensure women's reproductive rights. In different countries, or in different areas of the same country, women often face social, cultural, political, legal, and economic barriers to access to reproductive knowledge, contraception, abortion, and reproductive healthcare. Visit the Web sites of the following organizations to learn more about what they are doing to enhance reproductive rights for women.

- Center for Reproductive Rights www.reproductiverights.org
- International Planned Parenthood Federation www.ippf.org/en
- National Abortion Federation www.prochoice.org
- Women's Global Network for Reproductive Rights www.wgnrr.org
- Religious Coalition for Reproductive Choice www.rcrc.org
- United Nations Population Fund www.unpfa.org
- Reproductive Choice Australia www.reproductivechoiceaustralia.org.au/
- Abortion Rights Coalition of Canada www.arcc-cdac.ca/home.html
- Alliance for Reproductive Health Rights www.arhr.org
- International Women's Health Coalition www.iwhc.org

women may produce more children to increase the family's labor power or to offset high rates of infant mortality. Such is the case in the African nation of Rwanda, which has one of the highest birth rates in the world (six live births per woman) as well as one of the highest mortality rates for children below five years of age (UN Development Programme [UNDP], 2008).

Governmental control or involvement in reproduction varies depending on the country, sociopolitical climate, and national population. Governments of countries with large populations like India and China have introduced "antinatalist" policies to reduce population growth in the face of poverty, environmental degradation, and the burden of maintaining services and infrastructure for so many citizens. A stringent antinatalist program is China's "one child policy" that has included incentives and disincentives (housing, health subsidies, cash stipends, fines, etc.) varying by region. A different problem faces developed countries with aging populations facing labor and military shortages as well as burdensome pension and healthcare systems (Grant et al., 2004). These countries have begun to adopt "pronatalist" policies to boost populations via incentive programs such as family tax benefits, child care benefits, flexible work schedules, legislated parental leave, and state funded childcare. Israel, as well as many European Union countries, provides allowances to families with multiple children, while Japan has issued patriotic appeals for women to have more children (McCurry, 2007; Winckler, 2008).

REPRODUCTIVE TECHNOLOGIES

There is slippage between the terms "birth control" and "contraception," although the latter is concerned specifically with preventing conception (fertilization of the egg by sperm, which then grows into a developing fetus) rather than preventing birth after fertilization has occurred. Individuals across time and place have attempted to control reproduction through such methods as nonvaginal intercourse, *coitus interruptus* (withdrawal of penis from the vagina prior to ejaculation), lactational amenorrhea (cessation of menstrual cycle as a result of breast feeding), emmenagogues and abortifacients (herbs and substances that provoke menstruation and induce abortion, respectively), and various barrier methods aimed at preventing sperm from reaching and fertilizing the eggs. For instance, women in Southeast Asia used oiled paper as a cervical cap while women in Europe used citrus fruit peel or beeswax for this same purpose (Davis, 2002). The "rhythm method" (avoiding sexual intercourse during fertile periods) is another practice that is widely used, although this requires physiological knowledge as well as the ability to control the timing and conditions of sexual relations.

In the twenty-first century there is now an outstanding array of technologies for preventing and facilitating pregnancy from hormone-based birth control (including "the pill," Depo-Provera, Nuva-Ring, Norplant, etc.) to in vitro fertilization (a process by which the egg is fertilized by sperm outside the uterus and implanted later). Despite their availability, access to these technologies worldwide is inequitable. Such inequity is in part a result in part of religious and ethical concerns, sociocultural stigma, and government legislation surrounding various reproductive practices. Ethical questions about when life begins and which parties should be privy to reproductive decisions are key issues shaping debate and policy. Religion influences both individual beliefs (such as a woman's decision whether to use contraception) and institutional practices and social policies (such as the right of a Catholic hospital to refuse a medically-necessary abortion). Ethicists continue to debate the rights of medical practitioners to deny services based on personal religious belief, while religious-affiliated agencies negotiate religious law and secular ethics boards (Grazi

Contraceptives Save Lives: Women Are Dying Every Day

In industrialized countries, where most women have access to contraception, skilled care, and emergency obstetric care, deaths owing to pregnancy and childbirth are rare. However, every minute, somewhere in the world, a woman dies in pregnancy or childbirth, and 20 more suffer disability.

We know what it takes to save women's lives. Universal access to contraception to avoid unintended pregnancies is key. So is access to skilled care during delivery and rapid access to quality emergency obstetric care when needed.

One in three of all deaths related to pregnancy and childbirth could be avoided if women who wanted effective contraception had access to it.

If maternal health is to be improved and Millennium Development Goal 5 is to be met, the international community must reestablish voluntary family planning at the top of the development and funding agenda.

THE CURRENT SITUATION

- Every year, 536,000 women die from pregnancy-related causes—more than 10 million women per generation. Almost all—99 percent—are in developing countries.
- Another 10 million women suffer injury or disability, such as infection, infertility, depression, and obstetric fistula.

- When women suffer and die, children also suffer and die. Every year, more than 1 million children are left motherless.
- Children who have lost their mothers are up to 10 times more likely to die prematurely than those who haven't.
- In nine sub-Saharan African countries, over 30 percent of married women have an unmet need for contraceptives. In 15 more countries, the figure is 20 to 30 percent.
- The risk of a woman dying from pregnancy-related causes during her lifetime is about 1 in 7 in Niger, compared to about 1 in 4,800 in the United States and 1 in 17,400 in Sweden.

Contraception, Unsafe Abortions, and Complicated Pregnancies

- Some 200 million women of childbearing age want to delay or avoid pregnancy, but 137 million use no method of contraception at all, and 64 million use less-effective traditional methods.
- Every year, 190 million women become pregnant, at least a third of them unintentionally.
- Nearly 50 million women resort to abortion every year, and 19 million are performed under unsafe conditions. An estimated 68,000 women die each year as a result. Millions more suffer infections and other complications, such as inferitility.
- Family planning can prevent the serious health consequences of becoming pregnant within six months of an abortion (anemia, membrane rupture, low birth weight, preterm delivery).

Contraception and Reproductive Healthcare

- Prompt use of contraception after childbirth can help lengthen the interval between births, benefiting the health of both mother and children.
- An estimated 35 percent of pregnant women in developing countries have no contact with health personnel prior to giving birth.
- In sub-Saharan Africa, about 70 percent of women have no contact with health personnel after childbirth—even though this could provide them with the contraceptives they need to postpone future pregnancies.

BENEFITS OF ACTION

- No woman should die giving life. Ensuring access to voluntary family planning could reduce maternal deaths by a third, and child deaths by as much as 20 percent.
- It is estimated that the global cost of maternal and newborn deaths is US$15 billion per year in lost productivity. Tackling the problem of maternal death is a significant step toward poverty eradication.
- Ensuring access to family planning, skilled birth attendants, and emergency obstetric care requires a strong and well-functioning health system benefiting all.
- Family planning programs can prevent sexually transmitted infections, including HIV, by promoting condom use. By preventing unwanted pregnancies among HIV-positive women, mother-to-child transmission is averted.
- Access to family planning and the ability to decide when and how many children to have allows women to overcome traditional gender roles and increase their level of education, which most often leads to better health.

and Wolowesky, 2006). Such issues are discussed in the reading "The 'Morning After' Pill: Debates and Conflicts in Ireland and the U.S.," which includes two essays by Katie Fairbank and Hélène Hofman. While Fairbank addresses the controversy in the United States over pharmacists who refuse to fill prescriptions for birth control because of moral and religious grounds, Hofman explores the case of Ireland where there is support among women for increasing accessibility of emergency contraception (EC; also known as the "morning-after" pill). At the international level of policy, ethical and religious issues are highlighted in actions by the Vatican to form alliances with fundamentalist Islamic states to oppose proposals advocating women's reproductive freedom. Similarly, church officials have also called on the governments of predominantly Catholic countries in Latin America and fundamentalist members of the church to infiltrate the women's movement internationally and at home (Stein, 2001).

Such ethical debates also play out in the international arena when aid to nations is circumscribed by certain religious and moral beliefs, as evidenced by the "global gag rule" associated with the U.S. presidencies of Reagan, G.H.W. Bush, and G.W. Bush that limited the reproductive rights of women worldwide. It stated that organizations receiving USAID funds could not provide abortions—except to save the life of the mother or in case of rape or incest—nor could they provide counseling or referral to abortion services or lobby to make abortion services legal or more available in their county. By limiting the actions of foreign clinics receiving funds from the United States, these policies imposed their particular view of morality on the rights of women's bodies worldwide. Countries not agreeing to the rule lost access to all U.S.-donated contraceptives, including condoms. As such, this policy has also hindered organizations working to prevent the spread of HIV/AIDS. Although U.S. President Barack Obama overruled the global gag rule in 2009, it can be reinstated at any time.

Balancing reproductive autonomy with religious belief is also complicated by the social, cultural, and economic realities within nations. It can be difficult to separate religious, secular, and cultural values, particularly in theocratic states where government heads are also religious leaders. The access of Muslim women to reproductive technologies has no religious obstacles, although cultural interpretations may create them (Schenker, 2000). In some areas, most notably Afghanistan under the Taliban, women are unable to receive reproductive and sexual healthcare because of so-called decency restrictions that prohibit women from seeing male doctors, while also prohibiting women to practice as physicians. These restrictions are not based on religion per se, but represent the complex interaction of religion with sociopolitical influences, in this case, a government's desire to control women's lives. Similar restrictions requiring chaperones during medical visits in Iraq, Venezuela, and Ukraine are argued to protect women's virtue, but can limit women's autonomy over their healthcare (Gawande, 2005). Similarly, religious values in the United States have been central to debates surrounding reproductive freedom as the power of the Christian Right with its rhetoric of "family values" works to deny reproductive services and sex education programs.

Below we focus on three specific technologies central to women's reproductive freedoms: (1) birth control; (2) abortion; and (3) assisted reproduction, emphasizing such issues as safety, health concerns, availability, affordability, and access.

Birth Control

Despite the availability of birth control (often in the form of herbal remedies and practices) in most countries for centuries, their use has become increasingly socially charged,

10 Facts on Sexually Transmitted Infections

- Sexually transmitted infections (STIs) are mostly spread from one infected person to another through sexual intercourse. Some infections may also be transmitted from mother to child during pregnancy and childbirth. Another way that infections are passed on is through the sharing of blood products or tissue transfers. Some diseases caused by STIs include syphilis, AIDS, and cervical cancer.
- STIs often exist without symptoms, particularly in women. Thus, men and women with sexual partners who have STI symptoms should seek care regardless of a lack of signs. Whenever an infection is diagnosed or suspected, effective treatment should be provided promptly to avoid complications.
- STIs disproportionately affect women and adolescent girls. Every year, one in 20 adolescent girls gets a bacterial infection through sexual contact, and the age at which infections are acquired is becoming younger and younger. Improving awareness and knowledge of STIs and how to prevent them among adolescents should be part of all sexual health education and services.
- Sexually transmitted infections are important causes of Fallopian tube damage that leads to infertility in women. Between 10 and 40 percent of women with untreated chlamydial infections develop symptomatic pelvic inflammatory disease. Postinfection damage of the Fallopian tubes is responsible for 30 to 40 percent of female infertility cases.
- In pregnancy, untreated early syphilis is responsible for one in four stillbirths and 14 percent of neonatal (newborn) deaths. About 4 to 15 percent of pregnant women in Africa test positive for syphilis. Interventions to more effectively screen pregnant women for syphilis and prevent mother-to-child transmission of the disease could prevent an estimated 492,000 stillbirths per year in Africa alone.
- One of the most deadly sexually transmitted infections is the human papilloma virus (HPV). Virtually all cervical cancer cases are linked to genital infection with the virus. Cancer of the cervix is the second most common cancer in women, with about 500,000 new cases and 250,000 deaths each year. The new vaccine that prevents the infection could reduce these cervical cancer–related deaths.
- When used properly and consistently, condoms are one of the most effective methods of protection against STIs, including HIV infection. Although the female condom is effective and safe, it is not as widely used in national programs because of its higher cost when compared to male condoms.
- The partner notification process, which is an integral part of STI care, informs sexual partners of patients about their exposure to infection so that they can seek disease screening and treatment. Partner notification can prevent reinfection and reduce the wider spread of infections.
- Social or economic conditions, and some sexual behaviors increase a person's vulnerability to STIs. Populations most-at-risk for sexually transmitted infections vary from setting to setting, depending on local culture and practices. Interventions to prevent and care for STIs should be intensified for such populations, while ensuring that services minimize potential stigmatization and discrimination.
- A global strategy to accelerate prevention and control of STIs was developed by WHO through broad consultation among Member States and partners, and then endorsed by the World Health Assembly in May 2006. To build momentum and effectiveness, the 10-year plan includes technical and advocacy components that can be adapted for use around the world.

Source: World Health Organization, http://www.who.int/features/factfiles/sexually_transmitted_diseases/en/index.html

garnering much political controversy. Currently approximately 200 million women worldwide are unable to access safe contraceptives and family planning information. As discussed, this situation is intimately connected to opposition from governments, multinational corporations, churches, communities, families, and/or male partners (UNFPA, 2007a). In addition, although many forms of birth control technologies are now available worldwide, safety remains controversial, and long-term health effects are only now being addressed. For example, reproductive rights advocates have challenged the use of Depo-Provera, a long-acting hormonal contraceptive administered in three monthly injections. Although widely used around the world, health risks include delayed fertility and decreased bone density. In 2002, activists in India successfully campaigned the government to remove Depo-Provera from the national health system due to potential health risks and misuse. Activists in the United States, Canada, India, and Great Britain have also campaigned against coerced use of Depo-Provera among poor and minority women (Committee on Women, Population and the Environment [CWPE], 2007).

The Intrauterine Device (IUD), a 3-inch "Y" or "T" shaped device of copper thread inserted in the uterus, is a popular contraceptive method due to its ease and effectiveness. Once inserted, it can prevent pregnancy for up to 10 years. However, the IUD can also have dangerous side effects that include heavy bleeding and increased risk of pelvic inflammatory disease and sterility, particularly if it is inserted in unsanitary conditions or if the woman contracts an STI (WHO, 2002). Thus, although women should be screened for STIs before receiving an IUD, in less developed countries where this method is widely used, few women are adequately screened (UNFPA, 2007a). U.S.-based aid programs remain a dangerous part of the puzzle, often sending expired or unsafe contraception (which cannot be sold in the United States) overseas. As Seager (2008, p. 35) explains, "[g]lobal pharmaceutical companies have aggressively marketed unsafe or experimental contraceptives to poor women. Women still face the dilemma that the safest contraceptives are not the most effective, while the most effective are not necessarily the safest."

Access to birth control is a key issue for women worldwide. As discussed in more detail in the following sections, various demographic factors such as social class influence their availability. Indeed, female sterilization remains the most common contraceptive method, reflecting the uneven nature of the availability of other forms of birth control around the world. Thirty-four percent of married or partnered women worldwide have been sterilized, whereas only 8 percent of men have undergone vasectomies (even though the latter is a considerably less-invasive procedure). In Brazil, Puerto Rico, and the Dominican Republic, the number of sterilized women tops 40 percent, while it is near 30 percent in India, China, and much of Central America (Seager, 2008). A key aspect of access is that medical practitioners may withhold or distort information about the birth control they provide to women, thus infringing upon reproductive rights. This is especially a problem in societies with low female literacy levels. Women may receive contraceptives without complete and impartial information about proper usage, benefits, and risks. Social and cultural stereotypes surrounding contraception may cloud accurate information, even if it is available. Although the Internet is a source of important information for women, it has also contributed to the spread of misinformation due to inadequate oversight. A substantial number of Web sites contain misinformation regarding the risks of IUDs, and sites such as "Crisis Pregnancy Centers" tend to be religious organizations that seek to deter women from accessing abortion services. In addition, as the reading by Fairbank and Hofman shows, women in the United States have been denied emergency contraception (EC) in part because of misinformation campaigns that equate it with abortion. In countries such as Mexico and Kenya that are concerned about high rates of unwanted pregnancy and unsafe abortions, EC is viewed as a viable and safe way for women to space births (Heimburger et al., 2002).

In these ways, the politics of birth control (or power surrounding development and distribution of these technologies and their accompanying economic and social practices) are complex. Abuses in terms of health, safety, and access are common, with governments and multinational corporations often heavily implicated. An example of such abuse is forced sterilization or surgically sterilizing women against their will. "Against their will" also includes targeting illiterate or uneducated women who may "agree" to these practices without full consent. Such practices reflect eugenic beliefs that some people have more right to reproduce than others. These beliefs have shaped population policies at national and international levels. In the reading "Hijacking Global Feminism," author Christina Ewig discusses the family planning program in Peru that sterilized primarily poor and indigenous women through the 1990s. She discusses how indigenous women were targeted for forced sterilization as a way to colonize and/or control populations, as well as destroy native populations (genocide). Forced sterilization of indigenous women is also well documented in Mexico, Norway, Australia, and the United States (Castro, 2004; Leinaweaver, 2005; Ralstin-Lewis, 2005). As a result, women may avoid seeking medical attention, fearing that they will be forcibly sterilized in the process. Governments have also engaged in policies to "breed out" undesirable native traits through rape and intermarriage, with children involuntarily removed from their families and communities and sent to boarding schools to learn their place in society as laborers and servants. Such practices were used against native populations in the United States as well as in Australia where Aboriginal children have been called the "lost generation" (Ralston-Lewis, 2005).

Infanticide and child abandonment have also been used to limit family size and control the economic and social consequences of unplanned pregnancies, especially female offspring who are valued less and seen as burdens jeopardizing family security in the context of poverty and scarce resources. Estimates from the UN's Children's Fund

(UNICEF) indicate that one million female babies a year are lost as a result of sex selective abortion (discussed below) and infanticide (Veneman, 2006). Over a generation this accounts for 60 million girls "missing" from the world population (Seager, 2008). Although sex-selective infanticide is illegal and not technically a form of "birth control," it is used to control family size and has resulted in higher infant mortality rates in Egypt, Pakistan, India, Bangladesh, and China, suggesting either intentional death or severe neglect and starvation (Seager, 2008). As the reading by Uma Girish, "For India's Daughters, a Dark Birth Day" reports, these practices contribute to growing skewed gender ratios. Girish focuses on the factors associated with both sex-selective abortion and infanticide, and discusses programs to protect girls. China's "one child policy" also encourages these practices because sons care for their elderly parents and carry on the family name. In the reading "Postpartum Depression in China," author S. Ramashwar describes the ways mothers are more likely to suffer such depression if they deliver a baby girl rather than a boy.

Abortion

The consequences of unplanned pregnancy can be extreme, including poverty and loss of livelihood, reduced family resources, and familial or social ostracism. The latter is particularly salient for girls and young women who lack the resources to raise a child in the absence of family and social support. Abortion (removal of a fetus) presents an alternative to these undesirable consequences. The Guttmacher Institute (2007) estimated that approximately 26 million legal abortions occur worldwide every year. Another 20 million illegal abortions occur, often resulting in maternal death and injury as a result of unsafe conditions. More than three-quarters of all abortions occur in developing countries. Abortion rates vary widely across countries in which legal abortion is generally available and have declined in many since the mid-1990s. Although there is opposition to abortion, most agree that women's legal access is imperative because abortions continue whether they are legal or not. That is, legal restrictions do not generally decrease the number of abortions performed. Restrictions do, however, compromise maternal health and lead to higher maternal mortality rates. Throughout Africa, for example, the abortion rate is 29 procedures per 1,000 women despite the fact that abortion is illegal in many circumstances in most countries on this continent. Comparatively, in Europe, where abortion is generally permitted on broad grounds, the abortion rate is strikingly similar: 28 procedures per 1,000 women (Guttmacher Institute, 2007).

Because abortion remains illegal in many countries, women risk illness, injury, and even death seeking unsanctioned, unsafe abortions. Grimes et al. (2006) found that 19 to 20 million abortions a year are performed by individuals without adequate skill or in environments lacking minimum levels of sterility. Most (97%) of these unsafe abortions are performed in developing countries. Ninety-five percent of abortions performed in Africa and Latin America are unsafe, as are approximately 60 percent of procedures in Asia, excluding Eastern Asia (Guttmacher Institute, 2007). Asia and Africa combined account for 96 percent of total deaths from unsafe abortions worldwide (Seager, 2008). Grimes et al. (2006) estimate that about 68,000 women die annually due to unsafe abortions, and millions more are injured, often permanently. Leading causes of death are hemorrhage, infection, and poisoning from substances including bleach, arsenic, and toxic plant oils ingested in hopes of inducing miscarriage. Thus, while legal sanctions against abortion do not deter women from seeking them, they do make it more difficult to access safe abortions. To improve women's reproductive health, legalization of abortion is necessary, but not sufficient. Even where abortion is legal, risks are still high if the procedure is performed in unsanitary conditions or without proper training. Researchers estimate that 92 percent of induced abortions in developed countries are safe, whereas more than half (52 percent) of abortions performed in developing nations pose a direct risk to the life and health of the mother (Guttmacher Institute, 2007).

Despite the essential role abortion plays in women's reproductive rights and freedoms, it remains an embattled right. Abortion remains illegal or severely restricted—allowed, for example, to save the life of the woman or in case of fetal impairment—throughout the Global South. In Central and South America abortion is legal on request (with gestational limits) only in Cuba, Puerto Rico, and Guyana. In Africa, abortion is legal only in South Africa and Tunisia. In 22 countries, including Nicaragua, Saudi Arabia, Mongolia, and South Korea, women are required to have their husband's permission to obtain an abortion (Seager, 2008). Even where abortions are legal, there is no guarantee that they are available. In 2005, 87 percent of counties in the United States had no abortion provider, while in rural areas that number rose to 97 percent (National Abortion Foundation [NAF], 2009). This number is likely to climb as current providers retire and new doctors are not being trained in the procedure. Less than half of OB-gyn residency programs in the United States include abortion as part of routine training (NAF, 2009).

The reasons women seek abortion are far more complicated than simply an immediate response to an unintended pregnancy. Women choose to end unwanted pregnancies for a variety of reasons, including wanting to postpone childbearing; having achieved optimal family size; financial concerns; concern about disrupting education or career; relationship problems, including abuse; being too young or old; and risks to maternal and fetal health. Each of these reasons is then further informed by social and cultural expectations of women. An extensive study found that in Asia, including Singapore, South Korea, and Sri Lanka, reasons for abortion centered on family planning issues. In sub-Saharan Africa including Kenya, Nigeria, and Zambia, women are especially concerned about completing education and developing careers. In Chile, Honduras, and Mexico, women are more concerned with relationships—including violence and lack of family support (Bankole, Singh, and Haas, 1998).

In areas with a decided son preference, particularly Asia, medical technology is being used to selectively abort female fetuses. Sex-selective abortion, much like female infanticide, is not about unplanned pregnancy, rather it is an attempt to control pregnancy outcome. As ultrasounds and abortions have become more affordable and available, birth rates in China, India, Korea, and Vietnam have shown increased use of sex-selective abortion to ensure boy babies. Natural birth rates indicate a ratio of 105 boys for every 100 girls born. However, rates in wealthier parts of China and India show 125–135 boys to 100 girls (Jacoby, 2008). Estimates suggest that approximately 10 million female fetuses have been aborted in India in the last 20 years, despite it being officially illegal for Indian doctors to disclose fetal sex after an ultrasound. This law, an attempt to reduce the rate of sex-selective abortion, is widely flaunted, with doctors giving coded information or offering pink or blue sweets to indicate the sex of the fetus (Gentleman, 2008, April 28). As the reading by Girish emphasizes, from a feminist perspective, sex-selective abortion represents a misuse of technology. It is not about giving women control over their bodies and reproduction, but rather is used as a tool to further oppress them.

ACTIVIST PROFILE　　**NARAL**

For more than 30 years, NARAL Pro-Choice America has been the leading national advocate for personal privacy and a woman's right to choose. Even before women won the right to safe, legal abortion—when some women died as the result of illegal, unsafe abortions—NARAL Pro-Choice America has championed reproductive freedom.

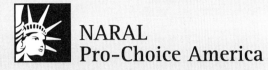

NARAL PRO-CHOICE AMERICA MISSION STATEMENT

NARAL Pro-Choice America's mission is to develop and sustain a constituency that uses the political process to guarantee every woman the right to make personal decisions regarding the full range of reproductive choices, including preventing unintended pregnancy, bearing healthy children, and choosing legal abortion.

Following are key moments in the history of NARAL Pro-Choice America and the pro-choice movement.

1969　　The National Association for the Repeal of Abortion Laws (NARAL) is founded.

1973　　On January 22, 1973, the U.S. Supreme Court hands down the landmark *Roe v. Wade* decision recognizing that the constitutional right to privacy encompasses the right to choose abortion.

　　　　NARAL changes its name to the National Abortion Rights Action League.

1975　　NARAL moves its offices to Washington, D.C., placing more emphasis on federal lobbying and policy.

1976　　Efforts by NARAL and other pro-choice organizations generate more pro-choice mail to Congress than ever before to oppose the Hyde amendment. The amendment passes and becomes law in 1977, banning federal Medicaid funding for abortion care for low-income women.

1979　　NARAL effectively continues to fight against resolutions in state legislatures calling for Congress to convene a Constitutional Convention to outlaw abortion.

1985　　NARAL launches the "Abortion Rights: Silent No More" campaign, using the slogan "We are Your Mothers, Your Daughters, Your Sisters, Your Friends, and Abortion is a Choice We Have Made."

1987　　NARAL and other pro-choice organizations are instrumental in defeating the nomination of anti-choice nominee Robert Bork to the U.S. Supreme Court.

1989　　In response to the Supreme Court's announcement that it will hear *Webster v. Reproductive Health Services*, a case threatening the protections of *Roe*, NARAL co-sponsors one of the largest pro-choice demonstrations ever held in the nation.

　　　　Following the *Webster* decision, which rendered the right to choose the most vulnerable it had been since 1973, NARAL develops its "Who Decides?" message.

1992   In *Planned Parenthood of Southeastern Pennsylvania v. Casey* the U.S. Supreme Court scales back the constitutional protections provided by *Roe v. Wade*. In response, NARAL holds Freedom of Choice Act (FOCA) hearings across the country and steps up its lobbying campaign to pass FOCA.

NARAL convenes the National Commission on America Without *Roe*, where national experts discuss and catalog the ramifications of losing the right to choose and recommend policies to save this important liberty.

1993   To more accurately reflect the organization's comprehensive approach to reproductive health policy, NARAL changes its name to the National Abortion and Reproductive Rights Action League. NARAL also launches the "Real Choices" campaign to highlight the goals of its expanded mission: to preserve access to abortion while working to enact policies to make abortion less necessary.

1994   NARAL and other pro-choice organizations work toward the passage and celebrate the enactment of the Freedom of Access to Clinic Entrances Act (FACE).

1995   NARAL representatives participate in the United Nations 4th World Conference on Women in Beijing.

1998   NARAL and other pro-choice organizations successfully work toward passage of equity in contraceptive coverage for federal employees and their families.

1999   After receiving its largest single grant in its history, the NARAL Foundation launches *Choice for America*, a multi-year marketing and mobilization campaign to reinforce the core principles and values underlying the pro-choice position.

2003   NARAL changes its name to NARAL Pro-Choice America, and launches the largest grassroots mobilization initiative in our history.

2004   NARAL Pro-Choice America cosponsors and helps organize the March for Women's Lives. With more than a million participants, the March is the largest demonstration of any kind in American history.

2005   To emphasize the fundamental American values of freedom and personal responsibility, NARAL Pro-Choice America issues its prevention challenge to President Bush and other anti-choice leaders.

NARAL Pro-Choice America President Nancy Keenan embarks on the "Heartland Tour," traveling to states like Texas, Minnesota, Oregon, and Washington to meet with affiliates, community leaders, stakeholders, and policy-makers to discuss proactive, pro-choice policies and messages.

NARAL Pro-Choice America launches the Choose Justice campaign to alert Americans to the threat posed to *Roe v. Wade* by a change in the composition in the federal judiciary, most notably two vacancies on the Supreme Court. The campaign attracts thousands of new member activists and engages a new generation in the fight to protect *Roe v. Wade*.

2006   In the historic midterm elections, Americans reaffirmed their commitment to the values of freedom, privacy, and personal responsibility by electing pro-choice candidates and defeating anti-choice ballot measures in races across the country, including the extreme abortion ban in South Dakota. NARAL Pro-Choice America capitalized on the public's call for change with a comprehensive $2.5 million political program, which included independent expenditures in congressional races, direct contributions to candidates, and contributions to the efforts to defeat anti-choice ballot measures.

Go to NARAL's Choice Action Center at http://www.prochoiceamerica.org/choice-action-center to learn what you can do to work for reproductive rights. To learn more about reproductive rights in your state, go to NARAL's In Your State site at http://www.prochoiceamerica.org/choice-action-center/in_your_state. There you can follow a link to learn about the status of reproductive rights in your state and to find out about pending reproductive rights legislation.

Assisted Reproduction

While efforts to decrease conception and births have existed for centuries, reproductive technologies have now been developed to facilitate conception. Assisted reproduction covers a variety of methods, including the use of medications (e.g., clomiphene, bromocriptine, or human chorionic gonadoptropin) that work with the body's hormones to induce ovulation and increase the chances of fertilization; artificial insemination; in vitro fertilization (IVF) (which can include external sex selection of embryos before implantation); in utero surgery; and the use of a surrogate uterus in the birth of a child. All of these technologies require medical and financial resources that are only available to economically-privileged individuals. Apart from access issues, assisted reproduction carries a host of social, moral, and ethical issues that cut across countries and cultures. These include the right to access the technologies and for what purpose; the rights of egg and sperm donors, surrogate mothers, and parents; and the use and misuse of the technologies to create "designer babies." While preimplantation genetic testing may be desirable in the case of disease prevention, it has the potential for parental selection of hair and eye color, body type, and personality traits (Steere, 2008).

Assisted reproduction must be viewed in the context of personal as well as global power structures. Access to all reproductive technologies is limited to wealthy people (currently IVF costs approximately $10,000 per attempt) and the medical care necessary for more complex procedures is only available in limited areas. As such, assisted reproduction remains more a luxury than a right. Additionally, global power imbalances have become a part of the debate as couples from wealthy nations begin to "outsource" surrogacy. In an attempt to avoid the costly legal arrangements necessary for surrogacy (including custody of the child as well as provisions for the surrogate's health, eating habits, and birthing options) couples from around the world have begun to use women in India as surrogates. The cost is about one-third of the price in Europe or the United States, and India's mix of skilled doctors, liberal laws, and poverty has made it the ideal place for such operations. The concerns that arise include the ease with which relatively economically-privileged Westerners can "rent" the body of a poor Indian woman, the lack of rights granted to the surrogate—her name will not even appear on the birth certificate—and the conduct of the agencies that arrange for the procedures (Gentleman, 2008, March 10).

Another contentious issue involving assisted reproductive technologies is the use of sex-selective implantation. Medically, couples who carry a sex-specific, life-threatening disease such as hemophilia (the inability of blood to clot resulting in uncontrollable bleeding) may seek to have a female child because only male children manifest the symptoms of this disorder. Unlike its medical counterpart, nonmedical sex-selective implantation is the subject of greater controversy and may present an infringement on women's reproductive choice. Like sex-selective abortion, nonmedical sex-selective implantation has become

LEARNING ACTIVITY   **Debating Choice**

Research the following reproductive choice topics. Make a list of arguments for and against each topic. Who supports these practices? Who opposes them? Give examples of how these practices have been beneficial for or have harmed women. Examine the role of religion in the arguments made for and against the topic. Examine the role of race, social class, age, ability, and sexual identity in each issue. How do various feminists assess each issue's impact on women?

- Abortion
- Contraception
- Emergency contraception
- Forced Sterilization
- The right to have children
- Assisted reproduction
- Sex education

popular in countries with strong cultural preferences for sons along with governmental control over the number of children that families are allowed.

Finally, rights of access to reproductive technologies for same-sex couples is another controversial issue, with debates in Denmark, Great Britain, Sweden, and the United States (Graham, 2004). Even when couples are able to access the initial technology currently necessary for producing a biological child, difficulties still remain in systems that deny adoption rights to both same-sex partners or that allow medical personnel to deny services to couples based on gender, sexual identity, or parenting choices (Darnovsky, 2008). Denmark, the Netherlands, and Sweden allow registered partners to adopt, but the rights of same-sex parents to access reproductive technologies has been restricted (Graham, 2004). Although the Ethics Committee of the American Society for Reproductive Medicine (2006, p. 1335) concluded that a physician's, "ethical duty to treat persons with equal respect requires that fertility programs treat single persons and gay and lesbian couples equally with married couples in determining which services to provide," the right to access assisted-reproduction services often remains an uphill battle for couples of diverse sexual identities in the United States. In the reading "Unusual Families," Susan Golombok writes about assisted reproduction and discusses lesbian motherhood and families headed by single heterosexual mothers, focusing on the well-being of children in these families. She concludes that it is the quality of family life that is important and emphasizes that problems faced by children in nontraditional families tend to result from outside prejudice rather than failures of parenting.

INTERSECTIONS: MARGINALIZED POPULATIONS, AND STRUGGLES FOR REPRODUCTIVE FREEDOM

For many women, intersecting systems of privilege and inequality further complicate access to reproductive rights, whether through overt violence or more covert means. This section examines the ways in which oppression based not solely on gender, but also on the intersection of gender with race, class, ability, and national origin further constrains women's reproductive freedom. It addresses (1) women with disabilities; (2) incarcerated women; and (3) migrants, refugees, and displaced women.

First, reproductive autonomy has often been denied the nearly 650 million people (approximately 10 percent of the global population) living with disabilities around the world. Despite persons with physical and/or mental disabilities being perceived as asexual or incapable of taking care of children, like persons without disabilities, they, too, want sexual relationships, children, and families. These stereotypes may lead health practitioners to withhold sufficient information about sexuality or to refrain from administering adequate sexual healthcare, including gynecological exams, Pap smears, and screening for STIs, which, if left untreated, can cause infertility. Furthermore, persons with disabilities may be denied access to birth control or access to reproductive technologies that facilitate conception (UNFPA, 2007b). Persons with disabilities are also more likely to be victims of physical or sexual abuse as well as forced sterilization, abortion, and marriage, further limiting their reproductive freedom. A final issue involves the rights of guardians to insist on birth control, abortion, or permanent sterilization. This is illustrated in the case in the United States where parents chose to permanently inhibit puberty in a severely disabled child in order to facilitate their ability to care for her. Doctors removed the child's reproductive organs and breast tissue and administered high doses of estrogen to close her growth plates. While the hospital ethics committee deemed that the procedures' benefits warranted their implementation, it conceded that such techniques can lead to a slippery slope regarding the bodily rights of individuals with disabilities (Gibbs, 2007).

Second, the rights of prisoners involve gray areas in many countries. As the population of incarcerated women worldwide grows, authorities debate their human rights, including rights surrounding reproduction. While international treaties specify that human rights are not lost during detention (Coyle, 2008), the realities of addressing reproductive rights in prison environments means that little work has been done in this regard. Reproductive concerns of women inmates range from a lack of reproductive healthcare to the ability to parent while imprisoned. Researchers highlight extreme medical neglect, particularly of obstetrical and gynecological care, that can lead to infertility and death among female prisoners (Pandit, 2005). Shackling prisoners during birth still occurs, despite the fact that the international community has banned this practice for both medical and humanitarian reasons. Shackling increases risks of falling and blood clotting. Furthermore, using restraints during delivery can pose life-threatening complications due to inability to position the legs or to move the laboring mother quickly should emergency medical intervention be necessary (Ehrlich and Paltrow, 2006). Another breach of reproductive freedom for incarcerated women comes from judges who order women, as part of their sentence, not to reproduce. Such legislation recently occurred in the United States where a woman was convicted of failure to protect and provide medical care for her 19-month-old daughter who had been beaten by her father. As a term of her 10-year probation, the mother was ordered to refrain from having more children (Kreytak, 2008).

Third, the reproductive rights of millions of women refugees and internally-displaced persons are at particular risk due to a relative lack of medical attention and the scarcity of health and reproductive services in settlements, as well as due to the loss of traditional healing traditions that accompanies migration and displacement. Women fleeing natural disasters and conflicts are often unable to seek medical attention, and when entire communities are forced to flee, the network of care providers is also scattered. Women are especially vulnerable at this time and often become victims of violence that, combined with a lack of care, may lead to permanent damage to a woman's body, including sterility, fistula (that causes incontinence due to damage to the urethra, rectum, or colon), and the contraction of STIs, including HIV/AIDS. In war-torn areas such as the Balkans, Afghanistan, and Sudan, available medical resources are often reserved for wounded male soldiers. When care is available, social stigma surrounding rape may prevent women from accessing it. Refugee women also face the uncertainty of services arising from an international situation with no clear governing body. Most refugee camps are run by the UN and international nongovernmental organizations (NGOs) that have no clear directive as to the rights of refugee women. Debate rages over the role of these organizations with regard to cultural practices such as forced marriage and when their interference might be justified. As organizations attempt to address immediate crises of food, water, and emergency medical care, long-term goals like reproductive health programming are often postponed. When such programs are not implemented at the initial establishment of a refugee camp, they can be difficult to institute later, with reproductive rights becoming eroded in the process (Palmer, Lush, and Zwi, 1999).

GRASSROOTS ACTIVISM

As with other social movements surrounding women's rights, much reproductive rights activism has taken place at the local, grassroots level. Because governmental response has been relatively lacking, women around the world have formed alliances, educated themselves, and opened clinics. The development of localized organizations is essential for changing the perception that the reproductive rights movement is only affiliated with wealthy Western women. Organizations such as DAWN (Development Alternatives with Women for a New Era), a coalition of grassroots organizations across the Global South, discussed in Chapter 1, argue that reproductive rights must be a part of comprehensive discussions of global disparities. Activism must also be socially and culturally informed. In Latin America, for example, activists have framed reproductive rights as part of democratization and citizen rights. In South Asia, activists highlighted poverty, sterilization, and sex trafficking as they impact reproductive rights. In Africa, activists have focused on survival, addressing high maternal and infant mortality, HIV/AIDS, and STIs (Petchesky, 2000).

Examples of transnational grassroots organizations include the organization Aahung, a Pakistani collective that advocates for sexual and reproductive health and includes online information for youth and healthcare providers (Aahung, 2004). The Urban Primary Health Care Project in Bangladesh, for example, combines the forces of local activists with its national government and international NGOs to create a network of urban healthcare centers. Such combinations of local activism with international NGOs create a positive relationship between locally oriented care and larger organizations with access to money and political influence. In addition, birth networks advocating for increased maternal rights and a "humanization of birth" exist in Brazil, Poland, Hungary, Israel, Uruguay, France, and Mexico (Goer, 2004). While many groups remain small, they are able to form coalitions and effectively use the Internet to expand their message.

Along with international mandates and government policy advocating reproductive rights, such projects and others worldwide are essential in improving the health and quality of life of both mothers and children. Reproductive rights are situated within cultural and political traditions, translated through patriarchal institutions such as family, medicine, religion, and government. Efforts to secure reproductive rights must address sexism inherent in these institutions as well as intersecting forms of oppression such as racism, classism, heterosexism, and ableism. Advocates must recognize that reproductive rights are strongly tied to global power imbalances. Finally, reproductive rights are, by definition, human rights. Factors that impinge upon reproductive rights affect not only women but entire communities. Thus, everyone benefits when women's reproductive freedom is secured.

REFERENCES

Aahung. (2004). Aahung: About Aahung. Retrieved February 12, 2009, from Aahung Web site: http://www.aahung.org/about/index.htm.

Bahar, S. (2000). Amnesty international and the family. In B. Smith (Ed.), *Global feminisms since 1945* (pp. 265–289). New York: Routledge.

Bankole, A., Singh, S., and Haas, T. (1998). Reasons why women have induced abortions: Evidence from 27 countries. *International Family Planning Perspectives, 24,* 117–127.

Castro, A. (2004). Contracepting at childbirth: The integration of reproductive health and population policies in Mexico. In A. Castro and M. Singer (Eds.) *Unhealthy health policy: A critical anthropological examination* (pp. 133–144). Altamira: Rowman.

Committee on Women, Population and the Environment. (2007, January 6). Depo-Provera fact sheet. Retrieved February 23, 2009, from *Committee on Women Population and the Environment* Web site: http://cwpe.org/node/185-15k.

Coyle, A. (2008). The treatment of prisoners: International standards and case law. *Legal and Criminological Psychology, 13,* 219–230.

Darnovsky, M. (2008). Homo genesis. *Bitch, 40* (Summer), 61–63.

Davis, S. (2002). Contested terrain: The historical struggle for fertility control. In I. Grewal and C. Kaplan (Eds.), *An introduction to women's studies: Gender in a transnational world* (pp. 106–110). Boston: McGraw-Hill.

Ehrlich, J. and Paltrow, L. (2006, September, 20). Jailing pregnant women raises health risks. *Women's eNews.* Retrieved from http://www.womensenews.org/article.cfm/dyn/aid/2894.

Ethics Committee of the American Society for Reproductive Medicine. (2006). Access to fertility treatment by gays, lesbians. *Fertility and Sterility, 86,* 1333–1335.

Gawande, A. (2005). Naked. *New England Journal of Medicine, 353,* 645–648.

Gentleman, A. India nurtures business of surrogate motherhood. (2008, March 10). *New York Times*, p. A9.

Gentleman, A. Sex selection by abortion is denounced in New Dehli. (2008, April 28). *New York Times*, p. A8.

Gibbs, N. Pillow angel ethics. (2007, January 7). *Time, 169*(4), 56–57.

Gillespie, R. (2000). When no means no: Disbelief, disregard and deviance as discourses of voluntary childlessness. *Women's Studies International Forum, 23,* 223–234.

Goer, H. (2004). Humanizing birth: A global grassroots movement. *Birth, 31*, 308–314.

Guttmacher Institute. (October, 2007). *Facts on induced abortion worldwide: Worldwide incidence and trends.* Retrieved April 25, 2008, from <http://www.guttmacher.org/pubs/fb_IAW.html>.

Graham, M. (2004). Gay marriage: Whither sex? Some thoughts from Europe. *Sexuality Research and Social Policy, 1,* 24–31.

Grant, J., Hoorens, S., Sivadasan, S., van het Loo, M., DaVanzo, J., Hale, L., Gibson, S., and Butz, W. (2004). *Low fertility and population ageing: Causes, consequences, and policy options.* Santa Monica, CA: RAND Corporation.

Grazi, R. V., and Wolowelsky, J. B. (2006). Addressing the idiosyncratic needs of Orthodox Jewish couples requesting sex selection by preimplantation genetic diagnosis (PGD). *Journal of Assisted Reproduction and Genetics, 23,* 421–425.

Grimes, D. A., Benson, J., Singh, S., Romero, M., Ganatra, B., and Okonofua, F. E. (2006). Unsafe abortion: The preventable pandemic. *Lancet, 368*(9550), 1908–1919.

Heimburger, A., Acevedo-Garcia, D., Sciavon, R., Langer, A., Mejia, G., Corona, G., del Castillo, E., and Ellertson, C. (2002). Emergency contraception in Mexico City: Knowledge, attitudes, and practices among providers and potential clients after a 3-year introduction effort. *Contraception, 66,* 321–329.

Jacoby, J. Choosing to eliminate unwanted daughters. (2008, April 6). *Boston Globe,* p. C9.

Kreytak, S. (2008, September 12). Travis judge tells woman to stop having kids: Constitutionality of order in child injury case is questioned by experts. *Austin American–Statesman.* Retrieved from http://www.statesman.com/news/content/news/stories/local/09/12/0912salazar.html.

Kunavic, K. L. (2009). Zdravo Marijo, Majko Božja (Hail Mary, Mother of God). Unpublished poem.

Lappé, F. M., Collins, J., Rosset, P., and Esparza, L. (1998). *World hunger: Twelve myths.* New York: Grove Press.

Leinaweaver, J. (2005). Mass sterilizations and child circulations in Peru. *Anthropology News, 46*(1), 13–18.

McCurry, J (2007, January 29). Japanese minister wants "birth-giving machines," aka women, to have more babies. *Guardian,* Retrieved from http://www.guardian.co.uk/world/2007/jan/29/japan.justinmccurry.

National Abortion Federation, (2009). Abortion facts: Access to abortion. Retrieved February 11, 2009, from National Abortion Federation Web site: http://www.prochoice.org/about_abortion/facts/access_abortion.html.

Palmer, C., Lush, L., and Zwi, A. (1999). The emerging international policy agenda for reproductive health services in conflict settings. *Social Science and Medicine, 49,* 1689–1703.

Pandit, E. (2005). Ten reasons why prisons are bad for reproductive freedom. *Different takes: A publication of the Population and Development Program at Hampshire College, 37,* 1–4.

Petchesky, R. B. (2000). *Reproductive and sexual rights: Charting the course of transnational women's NGOs.* Geneva, Switzerland: United Nations Research Institute for Social Development.

Ralstin-Lewis, D. M. (2005). The continuing struggle against genocide: Indigenous women's reproductive rights. *Wicazo Sa Review, 20*(1), 71–95.

Schenker, J. (2000). Women's reproductive health: Monotheistic religious perspectives. *International Journal of Gynecology and Obstetrics, 70*(1), 77–86.

Seager, J. (2008). *The Penguin atlas of women in the world* (4th ed.). New York: Penguin.

Steere, M. (2008, October 30). Designer babies: Creating the perfect child. *CNN*, Retrieved January 29, 2009, from http://www.cnn.com/2008/TECH/science/10/30/designer.babies/.

Stein, L.G. (2001). The politics of implementing women's rights in Catholic countries of Latin America. In J. Bayes and N. Tohidi (Eds.), *Globalization, gender, and religion: The politics of women's rights in Catholic and Muslim contexts* (pp. 127–156). New York: Palgrave.

United Nations Development Programme. (2008). *2007–2008 human development reports: Rwanda.* Geneva: Switzerland.

United Nations Population Fund (UNFPA). (n.d.). *Supporting the constellation of reproductive rights.* Retrieved April 29, 2008, from <http://www.unfpa.org/rights/rights.htm>.

United Nations Population Fund (UNFPA). (2007a). *Cairo to 2015: The road to success.* New York: United Nations Population Fund.

United Nations Population Fund (UNFPA). (2007b). *Sexual and reproductive health of persons with disabilities.* New York: United Nations Population Fund.

Veneman, A.M. (2006, March 8). Statement of UNICEF executive director Ann M. Veneman on international women's day. *UNICEF Press Center*, Retrieved January 23, 2009, from http://www.unicef.org/media/media_35134.html.

Winckler, O. (2008). The failure of pronatalism in developed states with cultural-ethnic hegemony: The Israeli lesson. *Population Space and Place, 14*(2), 119–134.

World Health Organization (2002). The intrauterine device (IUD)—worth singing about. *Progress in Reproductive Health Research, 60*, 1–6.

SUGGESTIONS FOR FURTHER READING

Ehrenreich, N. (2008). *The reproductive rights reader: Law, medicine, and the construction of motherhood.* New York: New York University Press.

Flavin, J. (2008). *Our bodies, our crimes: The policing of women's reproduction in America.* New York: New York University Press.

Haussman, M. (2009). *The morning-after pill: The battle over emergency contraception.* Westport, CT: Praeger Publishers.

Joachim, J. M. (2007). *Agenda setting, the UN, and NGOs: Gender violence and reproductive rights.* Washington, DC: Georgetown University Press.

Lopez, I. (2008). *Matters of choice: Puerto Rican women's struggle for reproductive freedom.* Piscataway, NJ: Rutgers University Press.

Mamo, L. (2007). *Queering reproduction: Achieving pregnancy in the age of technoscience.* Durham, NC: Duke University Press.

Investing in Reproductive Health and Rights

Thoraya Ahmed Obaid (2007)

A bold and ambitious agenda was set forth in the Millennium Development Goals to raise the quality of life of all individuals and promote human development. The MDGs represent our collective aspirations for a better life and provide a minimum road map on how to get there. However, they can only be achieved if governments, civil society and international agencies work together to address population issues as a development priority, in particular to secure the reproductive health and rights of people, especially the poor and particularly women. This vision is contained in the Programme of Action of the International Conference on Population and Development (ICPD), which was adopted by 179 Governments in 1979. The ICPD goal of universal access to reproductive health by 2015 is a target in the MDG monitoring framework, under MDG 5, to improve maternal health. Access to reproductive health can have a powerful impact on development, not only to improve maternal health but also to achieve all the MDGs.

Link among poverty, reproductive health and rights. Worldwide, illnesses and deaths from poor reproductive health account for one fifth of the global burden of diseases and nearly one third for all women. Every year, more than half a million women die during childbirth, with more than 95 per cent of them in Africa and Asia. Every minute, four people are newly infected with HIV and 2.1 million die of AIDS each year.

While devastating, these global statistics do not fully convey the true tragedy to a family when a mother dies during childbirth or when a child loses a family member to AIDS. This is a double tragedy because we know how to prevent these deaths. Effective interventions exist. Yet today, poor people have the least access to education and health care, including reproductive health, and this keeps them trapped in a vicious cycle of poverty and poor health, which

often runs from one generation to the next. It is this poverty trap that must be broken if we are to achieve the MDGs. Investments in sexual and reproductive health play a significant role.

Benefits of investing in reproductive health and rights. Good reproductive health enables couples and individuals to lead healthier, more productive lives, and, in turn, make greater contributions to their household incomes and to national savings. The health benefits of these investments are well known and documented. They are substantial. They include the prevention of deaths due to HIV/AIDS, cancer, complications of childbirth and unsafe abortion; the prevention or reduction of debilitating conditions, such as obstetric fistula and other sexual and reproductive illnesses; better nutritional status and decreased risk of anemia for women; and increased survival rates and better health for infants. It is estimated that ensuring access to voluntary family planning could reduce maternal deaths by 20 to 35 per cent, and child deaths by as much as 20 per cent. Moreover, the World Bank estimates that ensuring skilled care in delivery, particularly access to emergency obstetric care, would reduce maternal deaths by about 74 per cent.

These are significant benefits. But as striking as these numbers are, the personal, social and economic benefits of reproductive health may be even more important. They are extremely important for human welfare and economic development. They include improvement in women's status and greater equality between women and men, as well as benefits at the individual, household and societal levels. A study in Mexico found that for every peso the Mexican social security system spent on family planning services between 1972 and 1984, it saved nine pesos in expenses for treating complications of unsafe abortion and for providing maternal and infant care. In Thailand, every dollar invested in family planning programs saved the government more than $16. Even more dramatically, analysis in Egypt found that every dollar invested in family planning saved the government $31. This projection included government spending on education, food, health, housing and water and sewerage services.

Studies also show that the benefits go beyond government savings. Where mortality is high, parents are likely to have more children, but invest less in each child's health and education, impeding economic prospects. It is also known that chronic disease, poor health and low productivity discourage foreign direct investments in business and infrastructure. Furthermore, reproductive health investments, particularly in family planning, can produce what is called a demographic bonus. This is spurred by lower rates of fertility and mortality, and a larger healthy working population with relatively fewer dependents to support. If jobs are generated for the working population, this bonus results in higher productivity, greater savings and larger economic growth. In East Asia, where poverty has dropped dramatically, the demographic bonus is estimated to account for about one third of the region's unprecedented economic growth from 1965 to 1990. Given the world's largest youth generation in history, now is the time to focus investments on young people. The extent to which they enjoy education, health and job opportunities will determine our common future.

Investing in reproductive health works against HIV/ AIDS. There is also no doubt that investing in sexual and reproductive health is strategic for curbing the HIV/AIDS epidemic. With over 75 per cent of HIV cases due to sexual transmission, delivery and breast-feeding, it makes sense to link HIV/AIDS efforts with sexual and reproductive health, which would benefit particularly women and young people who suffer disproportionately from the disease.

Stronger linkages can result in more relevant and cost-effective programs with greater impact. By using the same services, the same health workers and the same infrastructure—with investment in training and upgrading—we can scale up responses that are so urgently needed to improve maternal health, decrease child mortality, prevent HIV infection and provide counseling, treatment and care. The countries that have significantly reduced HIV-infection rates have used reproductive health interventions. In Brazil, Thailand and Uganda, for example, community mobilization and behavior changes, including condom use, played a vital role.

Investing in reproductive health is investing in development. The final synthesis report of the Millennium Project, *Investing in Development*, stresses the importance of investing in sexual and reproductive health as part of overall development efforts, especially to strengthen health systems and improve public health. Expanding access to sexual and reproductive health services, including family planning, has been identified as one of the "quick wins" for the achievement of the MDGs. But these arguments are only words, unless bold and decisive action is taken. Strengthened political will, partnership and investment are needed to make reproductive health and rights a reality.

The "Morning After" Pill: Debates and Conflicts in Ireland and the U.S.

Essay 1

Pharmacists' Refusal to Fill Contraception Prescriptions a Question of (whose) Choice

Katie Fairbank (2005)

Steve Mosher's Medicine Shoppe pharmacy is inside a grocery store on one of the two main streets in this small town set amid West Texas scrub. It's the only place where residents can locally fill their prescriptions. Fabens may be miles from nowhere, but it is smack in the middle of the nation's decades-long fight over reproduction and contraception. Last year, Mosher decided he'd had enough. He joined the growing ranks of pharmacists refusing to dispense birth control because of moral objections.

"I'm a Christian, and I believe that abortion is taking the life of an innocent human being," said Mosher. Because birth control pills could keep a fertilized egg from implanting, he opposes them too.

"I look at that, that's the same thing as abortion. I know there are a lot of people that don't agree with me, but that's the way I see it," he said.

More than three decades after the Supreme Court held that it is a woman's constitutional right to have an abortion, the fight rages on. Now, it's moved into the local drugstore.

"This is absolutely a new way to keep women from having access to contraception," said Susan Hays, a Dallas lawyer who has represented minors seeking judicial approval of abortions. "I hear more of this idea from the right wing more and more. It stems out of their concept of when life begins."

On one side of this latest battle are pharmacists who refuse to fill prescriptions for birth control on ethical and religious grounds. They particularly oppose such medications as the "morning-after" pill, an emergency contraceptive that can prevent fertilization if taken within 72 hours of unprotected intercourse. An organization known as Pharmacists

for Life International, with 1,600 members, urges its members to refuse filling such prescriptions.

On the other side are reproductive-rights groups pushing for access to the drugs. And there are others concerned that pharmacists might refuse to dispense a wide range of prescribed medicine, not just birth control. Last year, a Dallas pharmacist refused to fill a child's prescription for Ritalin.

"There's a lot more to this than just a reproductive issue," said Julee Lacey, who was denied a birth control prescription by a North Richland Hills, Texas, pharmacist in March 2004. The month before, a Denton, Texas, pharmacist denied emergency contraceptive to a rape victim.

In that case, the pharmacist and two co-workers were fired for violating policies of the store (an Eckerds, which is now owned by another company). The incident has inspired bills in several states meant to shield pharmacists from losing their jobs if they refuse to prescribe emergency contraception.

Lacey, 33, a mother of two, was unaware of this growing national debate when she went to the CVS drugstore near her house where she regularly filled her birth control prescription.

"I pulled up to the drive-through and a pharmacist assistant took the prescription and said it would be 10 minutes. It was a Sunday, and I was getting ready for the work week," Lacey said. "A woman came to the window and said she couldn't fill the prescription."

At first, Lacey said, she thought something was wrong with the paperwork or that the store was out of the drug. Instead, the pharmacist told her that she didn't believe in birth control.

"She said I could go down the street and they could help me," Lacey said. "She didn't know my medical history. The pharmacist had no idea why I was even taking the birth control pill. I went home and talked to my husband, and he couldn't believe our doctor's prescription could be denied."

Lacey decided to call the company, which ultimately filled and delivered her prescription late the next day. But that hasn't ended the issue for her. Instead, she's gone public with her concerns.

"I'm not anyone's spokesperson or any organization's. I just think it's important for anyone to get a prescription from a licensed doctor," she said. "Most people have a prescription at a pharmacy and don't think twice about getting it filled. It's a much bigger issue than women's health. I put my trust in my doctor. It's a matter of the patient-doctor relationship. I don't think a pharmacist should be jumping in the middle."

CVS spokesman Mike DeAngelis said it is the company's policy to fill prescriptions for all legally prescribed medications. But, "if a pharmacist wanted an accommodation for a sincerely-held religious conviction, we would work to accommodate that pharmacist while ensuring that all customer needs are promptly and completely satisfied," he said in a statement.

That policy is in line with the American Pharmacists Association. The group, which has 50,000 members, says druggists can refuse to fill prescriptions on moral grounds, but they must make arrangements for a patient to get the medication.

But that's not always easy for small-town America. There are 6,093 licensed pharmacies in Texas and mail-order options, but it's a big state with 199 towns that have only one drug store. And those often have only one pharmacist.

"If somebody wants to get emergency contraception filled and they go to the one pharmacy and are refused, she then has to go 30 to 50 miles to the next town and just hope she can get the prescription filled in the time frame she has left," said Tony R. Thornton, president and chief executive of Planned Parenthood Association of Lubbock Inc. "Not everyone has transportation, you know."

The problem can be further exacerbated because many stores, including national chains, don't offer all forms of birth control. The morning-after pill is frequently not offered. National chains deciding against carrying a drug exacerbates the problem of accessibility for women who need it within a short time frame, said Hays.

"The pro-life movement has been very smart about pressuring corporations," she said. "If you pressure Wal-Mart out of the business and you take the money (away) from Planned Parenthood, many poor women will have no access to contraception, and they won't have access to emergency contraception."

Thornton isn't convinced politics has no role when companies decide not to carry contraceptives such as the morning-after pill. "It feels like it's against birth control and women's reproductive rights," he said. "I can almost guarantee you those same pharmacies wouldn't have an objection to Viagra."

Mosher, the Fabens pharmacist, bristles at that suggestion. "I don't see how that could possibly be related to the issue that we're talking about," he said. Mosher owns the store and said it was his personal decision to stop selling birth control, although he has discussed it with his wife, daughter and two sons.

"My wife is unsure, but that's her prerogative. My kids appreciate my taking a stand for my beliefs. I've had a lot of people who don't agree with my opinion, but they understand that I should be able to have the right to make a stand on a moral issue in my own business. I shouldn't be forced to dispense birth control pills if I choose not to," he said.

Few people in the town of 8,000 seem aware that his pharmacy doesn't sell birth control medications, emergency contraceptives and condoms.

"I think a lot of people don't know about it," said Jessica Porras, 20, who was shopping at the grocery store this week with her 18-month-old daughter, Audrey Ortiz. "Most of the people are Catholic, and they don't believe in birth control."

Those who do drive the 27 miles to El Paso to pick up their prescriptions. Or they head to nearby Mexico.

Eileen Lopez, 31, was shopping in the convenience store this week and said the whole subject is too touchy for such a small town to handle. "Nobody wants any trouble," said Lopez, a deputy for the El Paso County Sheriff's Department. "Everybody knows everybody from generation to generation. We don't talk about birth control with our Catholic upbringing."

Still, she believes a pharmacist's responsibilities is something that residents should talk about. "I think that a professional such as a pharmacist has to have a stake in his profession and separate it from his beliefs," she said. "It's really not up to them to decide what we need as far as medication is concerned."

Essay 2

The Accessibility of the "Morning-After" Pill in Ireland

Hélène Hofman (2006)

Many women in Ireland still have difficulty accessing the emergency contraceptive pill, according to groups offering advice on dealing with unplanned pregnancies.

The emergency contraceptive pill (ECP) or "morning-after" pill, Levonelle, is currently available only on prescription in Ireland.

The Crisis Pregnancy Agency and the Irish Family Planning Association (IFPA) say this means that a number of women, particularly those living in rural areas, may have problems obtaining it when they need it.

According to figures from the Crisis Pregnancy Agency, about 29 per cent of women have taken the ECP at some point in their lives. The Irish Study of Sexual Health and Relationships published last week also found that 90 per cent of people surveyed thought it should be available, with 52 per cent of men and 42 per cent of women saying it should be available to buy over the counter.

The IFPA operates a daily walk-in service for women who require emergency contraception. Since December 2004, its Dublin centers in Tallaght and on Cathal Brugha Street in the city center have opened on Sundays solely to accommodate women who need emergency contraception.

They now see about 15–25 women between the ages of 12 and 55 every Sunday.

"We've known for some time that there is a demand for an out-of-hours emergency contraception service, but we were taken aback when we opened our Dublin centers on Sundays," says IFPA chief executive Niall Behan.

"We thought the Tallaght center would attract women from Tallaght—we didn't realize that we would also get women from Carlow and Meath and all other parts of the country. It shows that for some women there is still a huge access problem."

The IFPA has been calling for the emergency pill to be made available to women over the counter in pharmacies. It argues that pharmacies may still be open when GPs are not available and that the drug is completely safe.

"There are no risks with this pill. It can even be given to breast-feeding mothers. The only side effect is the possibility of nausea," says IFPA medical director Dr Alyia Rahim.

"It works in three ways. First, it inhibits ovulation if it has not already occurred; two, it stops the sperm going up and fertilizing the egg and, three, it causes shedding of the womb," she says.

"We should not really call it the morning-after because really you can take it up to 72 hours after unprotected sex. But it is 80–90 per cent [reliable] if you take it within 24 hours and only 60–70 per cent within 48 hours," she adds.

"There is a stereotype out there surrounding going for emergency contraception," says Dr. Stephanie O'Keeffe, the Crisis Pregnancy Agency's director of research. "But women who go for it, know about it, know where to go for it and know that a risk has happened. They're doing the responsible thing. "Our research shows they're just as likely to have used contraception but that the method has failed, and no more likely to have consumed alcohol," she says. "It's protective behavior and it should be encouraged."

The Irish Study of Sexual Health and Relationships points out that in the 25 countries where the emergency contraceptive pill has already been made available over the counter, it has led to greater availability and use. However, there are also concerns that it has led to more sexual risk-taking, especially among young women, and argues they are less likely to use more effective barrier methods that would protect them from sexually transmitted infections at the same time. This is one reason why the Irish Medical Organisation (IMO) is opposed to making it available without prescription.

"In the UK, the NHS has gone down the route of making it available over the counter for the past five years and it has made no difference," says Dr Martin Daly, chairman of the IMO's GP committee. "We believe that the vast majority of women who seek it are in their late teens and early 20s and the opportunity should be taken to explain that emergency contraception is just that. It's a last resort. "It should not be the only form of contraception and we should take the chance to explain alternative methods of contraception and the implications of being sexually active and how to protect against sexually transmitted diseases," he says.

"Most of the country is covered by 24-hour GP services, which are far more available than out-of-hours pharmacies and a GP does not refuse to see someone if they are within the 72-hour time limit required to take the pill. If there was clear-cut advantage to making it available over the counter, I would consider it but so far there has been none," he says.

Health Minister Mary Harney, speaking last week following publication of the Irish Study of Sexual Health and Relationships, indicated that she was not currently in favor of making the morning-after pill available over the counter. "Clearly, it can only be done if it's medically safe to do so and until we get the advice of the regulatory body that has responsibility in this area, I wouldn't be in a position to make a decision," she says.

For Levonelle to be made available over the counter, an application must be made by its manufacturers, HE Glissmann & Schering, to the Irish Medicines Board. A spokesman for HE Glissmann & Schering say they cannot do this until the legislation banning evonorgestrel, which is found in Levonelle, from being sold over the counter is changed by the Department of Health.

Discussions on this are continuing.

R E A D I N G   **32**

Postpartum Depression in China

S. Ramashwar (2007)

Chinese women enrolled in a cohort study to identify factors associated with postpartum depression were more likely to suffer from the condition if they had given birth to a girl instead of a boy.[1] The risk of depression was also elevated among women older than 25, those who considered their living conditions dissatisfactory and those who had had at least four previous pregnancies.

The findings of the few studies that have examined the issue of fetal gender and postpartum depression have varied across cultures, with those in Asian societies finding an association and those in Western societies finding no evidence of a link. Because the Chinese literature lacks studies that go beyond descriptive data, the researchers conducted a cohort study among women who had recently given birth in Changsha, the capital of Hunan Province.

Women aged 18–40 were recruited when they visited the obstetric unit of any of four participating hospitals for a postpartum exam between September 2004 and January 2005. Women who had a psychological illness or a history of psychological illness, or who had had major pregnancy and obstetric complications were excluded from the sample, as these factors could be associated with postpartum depression. After collecting clinical and demographic information from the women, research nurses assessed them for postpartum depression using the Chinese version of the Edinburgh Postnatal Depression Scale.

The 300 women in the sample were, on average, 28 years old, and almost all (99%) were married. About two-thirds (61%) had given birth via cesarean section, and nearly one-fifth (17%) had postpartum depression. None knew the sex of their infant before birth. Women who had given birth to a boy and those who had delivered a girl were similar in age, marital status and education. Higher education, classified as 15 years or more, was slightly more common among women who had had a boy (24%) than among those who had had a girl (19%). Nine percent of women who had given birth to a girl reported having had three or fewer prenatal care visits, compared with only 1% of those whose baby was a boy. However, four in 10 women in each group reported nine or more prenatal care visits. More than 40% in each group reported very satisfactory living conditions, but only 6% of women who gave birth to a girl reported dissatisfactory living conditions, compared with 17% of women who gave birth to a boy.

This was the first pregnancy for about half of the women in both groups. The proportion of women who had a spontaneous vaginal delivery for this birth was twice as high among women who gave birth to a boy as among those who gave birth to a girl (40% vs. 23%). Sixteen percent of women who gave birth to a boy had had four or more pregnancies previously compared with 9% of those who gave birth to a girl. The majority of women had a cesarean section, but this mode of delivery was more common among women who gave birth to a girl than among those who gave birth to a boy (70% vs. 55%).

Women who gave birth to a girl tended to live in higher income households than those who gave birth to a boy. Some 55% of each group lived in middle-income households (with earnings of 1,000–2,000 yuan per month). However, 29% of women who delivered a girl and 11% of those who delivered a boy lived in households with higher income, while 16% of women who gave birth to a girl and 36% of those who gave birth to a boy lived in households with lower income.

Twenty-five percent of women who gave birth to a girl had postpartum depression, compared with 12% of women who gave birth to a boy. Among women who had had fewer than nine prenatal care visits, 21% were depressed, compared with 13% of those who had had nine or more visits. Nearly one-fifth (19%) of women older than 25 were depressed, while only 8% of women aged 25 or younger fell into this category. Depression was more common among women who had had at least four previous pregnancies than among those who had had three or fewer (24% vs. 15–18%). The proportion of women with postpartum depression did not differ between women who delivered via cesarean section and those who delivered vaginally (17–18%). About 38% of women who reported dissatisfactory living conditions had postpartum depression, compared with 14–15% of those who reported satisfactory or very satisfactory living conditions. Interestingly, the proportion of women with postpartum depression rose with the level of household income; 13–15% of women in households earning 2,000 yuan or less monthly were depressed, while 30% of women in the highest household income bracket had depression.

In a multivariate regression analysis, women who delivered a girl had significantly higher odds of postpartum depression than those who gave birth to a boy (odds ratio, 2.8). Compared with women for whom this was the first pregnancy, those who had had four or more previous pregnancies had a risk of postpartum depression almost three times as high (2.9). For women who reported dissatisfactory living conditions, the odds of postnatal depression were seven times as high as for those who reported very satisfactory living conditions (7.4).

The investigators acknowledge that their sample was too small for a stratified analysis and that a selection bias may have occurred if women who were very depressed or who had no feelings of postpartum depression decided not to participate. Another factor that could create bias, they note, is that the sample included only women who returned for a postpartum checkup rather than all women who gave birth in the four participating hospitals. Because prenatal factors do not appear to have been associated with the occurrence of postpartum depression, the investigators suggest that if a woman gives birth to a girl, a lack of familial support—stemming from a desire for sons to carry on the family name and provide economic support to their parents—may make her more vulnerable to postpartum depression.

NOTES

1. Xie R et al., Fetal gender and postpartum depression in a cohort of Chinese women, *Social Science & Medicine*, 2007, 65(4):680–684.

R E A D I N G **33**

For India's Daughters, a Dark Birth Day

Uma Girish (2005)

The oleander plant yields a bright, pleasant flower, but also a milky sap that, if ingested, can be a deadly poison. It's one of the methods families use to kill newborn girls in the Salem District of Tamil Nadu, a part of India notorious for female infanticide.

Though the government has battled the practice for decades, India's gender imbalance has worsened in recent years. Any progress toward halting infanticide, it seems, has been offset by a rise in sex-selective abortions. Too many couples—aided by medical technology, unethical doctors, and weak enforcement of laws banning abortion on the basis of gender—are electing to end a pregnancy if the fetus is female.

The consequence of female infanticide and, more recently, abortion is India's awkwardly skewed gender ratio, among the most imbalanced in the world. The ratio among children up to the age of 6 was 962 girls per 1,000 boys in 1981, but 20 years later the inequity was actually worse: 927 girls per 1,000 boys.

Infanticide is illegal in India (though never prosecuted), and laws are also in place to stop sex-selective abortions. But in some places, national rules don't hold enough sway to overcome local religious and social customs—which remain biased in favor of sons over daughters.

"Factors like dowry, imbalance in the employment sector whereby the male is seen as breadwinner, and societal pressure to abort female fetuses conspire to increase the antigirl bias," says Ajay K. Tripathi of the Advanced Studies in Public Health Programme, of the Institute of Health Systems in Hyderabad. Government and the medical profession, he says, need to put more resources—and more political will—into strengthening and enforcing the laws.

A case in point is legislation—introduced last year but now stalled—that would prohibit all genetic-counseling facilities, clinics, and labs from divulging the sex of the fetus. The hope is that if parents don't know "it's a girl" fewer will resort to abortion. But the proposal, which would amend a 1994 law, is opposed by medical groups. They argue that technology used to monitor fetal health—such as ultrasound scans and amniocentesis—cannot be put under such intense scrutiny.

Others, though, see another reason for the opposition: Abortion is a lucrative business that many doctors do not want to see curtailed. "Abortions are a low-risk, high-profit business. As a specialist in fetal medicine, I can tell you that no pregnant woman would suffer if the ultrasound test were banned," says Puneet Bedi, a gynecologist at Apollo Hospitals in New Delhi. "Right now, it is used to save 1 out of 20,000 fetuses and kill 20 out of every 100 because [it reveals that the baby] is the wrong gender."

India stipulates that only a government hospital, registered facility, or medical practitioner with appropriate qualifications may perform an abortion. The reality, however, is that only about 15 percent of all abortions take place under such circumstances, according to the Indian Medical Association. About 11.2 million illegal abortions are performed each year off the record. Such abortions are often "female feticide," experts say.

In Salem district, for instance, signs posted in towns reinforce the societal message: "Pay 500 rupees and save 50,000 rupees later," a suggestion that aborting a female fetus now could save a fortune in wedding expenses in the future.

Salem district, a mostly rural part of Tamil Nadu, has a longstanding reputation as a deathtrap for baby girls. The Vellala Gounder community, the dominant caste there, owns most of the land and is intent on retaining property rights within the family. Sons represent lineage; daughters marry and relocate to their husbands' homes. As a result, local women, like Lakshmi, who gave birth to a girl early last year, may refuse to nurse their newborns. They leave it to midwives or mothers-in-law to administer the oleander sap, say anti-infanticide activists.

Nearly 60 percent of girls born in Salem District are killed within three days of birth, according to the local social welfare department. That doesn't count the growing number of abortions there to ensure a girl baby won't be carried to term.

Amid such stubborn statistics, activists are at work to counter the forces of tradition. A focus of their work: improving the standing and self-image of women themselves.

Community Services Guild (CSG), a nongovernmental organization, works with rural women in particular to discourage female feticide. One of CSG's interventions targets women who already have at least one girl. Now 20 years old, the program sends workers to visit these mothers, teaching them and their daughters skills that contribute income to their families (such as basket-weaving or selling produce) and reeducating them about the value of girls to society.

"Educating the new-generation girl—and empowering her with the skills necessary for economic independence—is the only long-term solution," says G. Prasad, CSG deputy director. Though CSG works in a patriarchal culture where female inferiority is ingrained, the group encourages women to become decisionmakers.

In pockets of India where female infanticide persists, the practice is rooted in a complex mix of economic, social, and cultural factors. Parents' preference for a boy derives from the widespread belief that a son lighting his parents' funeral pyre will ensure that their souls ascend to heaven; that he will be a provider in their later years (India has no form of social security); and that he will preserve the family inheritance.

Conversely, a daughter is considered an economic burden. Pressure to conform can be intense in rural areas, and some families borrow heavily to pay for the rituals prescribed for a girl—the ear-piercing ceremony, wedding jewelry, dowry, and presents for the groom's family on every Hindu festival.

The Tamil Nadu government has started several programs to protect girls—with mixed results. One urged families to hand over their baby girls to local officials, who saw that they were adopted by childless couples. Between May 2001 and January 2003, officials received 361 baby girls. An informal survey by CSG, however, found that many women would abort rather than have a baby and give her up for adoption.

Tamil Nadu's "Girl Protection" program may be more practical. Here, the government opens a bank account in a girl's name at her birth, depositing between 15,000 and 22,000 rupees during her childhood, depending on the number of girls in the family.

"The only way to wipe out this evil is by an attitudinal shift," says CSG's Mr. Prasad. "Educate a girl beyond eighth grade and encourage her to find her voice."

Hijacking Global Feminism: Feminists, the Catholic Church, and the Family Planning Debacle in Peru

Christina Ewig (2006)

From 1996 through 1998, the state-run family planning program in Peru carried out mass sterilization campaigns that targeted women in poor, primarily indigenous, rural communities. The program prioritized sterilization over other forms of contraception, performed surgical contraception under low quality conditions that at times led to the death or serious injury of the patients, and often carried out the sterilizations without first obtaining voluntary informed consent. The sheer number of these sterilizations (217,446 from 1996 through 1998) was achieved in part through a system of quotas that provided little incentive for high quality care.[1] In late 1998, a feminist lawyer investigating abuses in state-run hospitals stumbled upon evidence of problems in the family planning program and began to disseminate her findings to the media. Her action initiated closer scrutiny and ultimately created demands for the program's reform.

Peru's problematic sterilization campaigns of the mid-1990s are in many ways an old story of the instrumental use of women by national planners and international organizations as a means of controlling population growth and promoting economic development. What is remarkable about Peru in 1996 is that these sterilization campaigns took place in strikingly new global and national contexts that appeared to favor women's reproductive rights. By the late 1990s, a new credo of reproductive rights dominated global population efforts, and Peru had seemingly absorbed this discourse. In 1982, Peru ratified all articles of the United Nations Convention on the Elimination of All Forms of Discrimination against Women (CEDAW), first adopted by the U.N.

General Assembly in 1979. The CEDAW promotes women's equality in political, social, and economic realms, and it is the only human rights convention that affirms women's reproductive rights. At the 1993 U.N. Conference on Human Rights, held in Vienna, and the 1995 World Summit for Social Development, held in Copenhagen, feminist activists were successful for the first time in placing women's rights on the international human rights agenda and women's poverty on the international development agenda. Women's movements were also influential at the 1994 International Conference on Population and Development (ICPD), held in Cairo, and the United Nations 1995 Fourth World Conference on Women, held in Beijing, conferences in which Peruvian feminists were active participants.

Peru's Family Planning Program was significantly reformed on the heels of the Cairo and Beijing conferences. Its guiding documents largely reflected the language and goals agreed upon at Cairo, including a commitment to reproductive healthcare, women's reproductive rights, and the promotion of gender equity. The program's focus on the poorest Peruvians had the potential to dramatically increase access to family planning methods in a country where previously the middle classes and the wealthy were the only ones privileged with access to contraception. In addition, feminists and the government had established a mechanism to monitor the implementation of the "Program of Action" agreed upon at Cairo: a corporative body called the *Mesa Tripartita de Seguimiento al Programa de Acción del Cairo* (Tripartite Board to Monitor the Cairo Program of Action), which included members from the state, civil society, and international institutions.

How, then, was it that abuses reminiscent of past sterilization campaigns, such as those in Puerto

Feminist Studies 32, no. 3 (Fall 2006). © 2006 by Feminist Studies, Inc.

Rico, India, and South Africa, could occur in the late 1990s when both international and national circumstances seemed specifically designed to prevent such abuses? In this article I will show how the Fujimori administration in Peru hijacked the global feminist language developed at Cairo and instrumentally used Peruvian feminists themselves to push a traditional Malthusian population policy that placed national economic development above women's human rights.

The difference between the Peruvian case and similar programs in other countries in the past is that national political actors not only used women to achieve their population goals, but also appropriated national and global feminist discourses to legitimize their actions. Peru's experience with family planning alerts us to the increasingly complex ways that global and national feminist agendas can be coopted for non- or even antifeminist goals. It also demonstrates the need for continual critical monitoring of state actions by feminists, even when these actions may on the surface appear to be positive for women.

INSTRUMENTAL USES OF WOMEN

The link between population control and economic development dates back to 1798 when English economist Thomas Malthus argued that population growth, if left unchecked, would outstrip agricultural capacity, leading to a general decline in world living standards. Drawing on the arguments of Malthus and of early-twentieth-century U.S. birth control advocates (including Margaret Sanger), U.S. policy, beginning in the 1960s, pushed population control efforts as intimately linked to economic development in the Third World and thus to U.S. security interests.[2] Even now, the United States continues to view Latin American population growth as a security threat, especially as Latin American immigrants to the United States have increased dramatically as a result of Central American wars and regional economic crises in the 1990s.[3] U.S. government funding of population control programs has helped to develop a worldwide "population establishment" of

diverse governmental and nongovernmental institutions dedicated to population issues. Although many of these international organizations argued for policies that were noncoercive, they still made instrumental arguments, for example, advocating the education of women as a means to reducing population growth.[4]

Malthusian population principles also had a strong regional presence in Latin America and a national presence in Peru, where many elites believed that indigenous, African descent, and other poor populations hampered national progress. In the 1920s and 1930s, the emerging Latin American state health systems promoted eugenics through such means as the requirement of prenuptial medical certifications, which barred the marriage of the physically or mentally "unfit." In the 1930s, eugenics also became part of state immigration policies, as countries sought to attract white, European immigrants. However, despite these policies and dramatic population growth in the 1940s through the 1960s, Peru did not yet have a well-defined population policy. This began to change in 1968 when the revolutionary military government of Juan Alvarado Velasco shaped a pronatalist population policy that coincided with Catholic tradition, while also reacting against what was perceived as imperialist interference by the United States, which was actively promoting control in Latin America. In 1976, however, the less militant government of General Francisco Morales Bermúdez reversed the pronatalist stance and outlined Peru's first official population control program. It included access to artificial contraception, considered procreation to be the decision of the couple, and advocated "responsible parenthood," a Catholic concept outlined in 1974 in which couples are encouraged to freely decide the size of their families. This first official policy also endorsed the Malthusian idea that population control was a prerequisite to sustained economic development.[5]

It was not until the mid-1980s, under President Alán Garcia of the Alianza Popular Revolucionaria Americana Party (APRA), that state-funded family planning was established, although still understood as a matter of economic development. In 1985, the Garcia government passed a national population law that emphasized the Catholic Church's position of responsible parenthood, but also established the right to a choice of contraceptive methods and individuals' rights to be free of manipulation or coercion in matters of family planning. In the debates over this law, the government accepted the church's position against abortion and sterilization. The government then developed the National Population Program 1987–1990, which outlined goals for reducing fertility rates and achieving contraception coverage and made some limited economic resources available for implementation. Subsequently, family planning programs were created in Peru's social security and state-run public health systems. Notably, the National Population Program was a component of the National Plan for Development.[6]

CO-OPTING FEMINIST RHETORIC

Anthropologist Ines Smyth has suggested that the definition of "reproductive rights" for the population establishment differs from feminist understandings. She explains that, whereas "the notion of self-determination in childbearing" became central to feminist definitions of reproductive rights by the late 1980s, the population establishment in the early 1990s equated reproductive rights with consumer choice in family planning options. In other words, she argues that the population establishment interpreted reproductive rights as a kind of free market rather than as a fundamental human right. Thus, feminist scholars expressed concern that fundamental concepts of international feminist discourse, such as reproductive rights, had been appropriated, manipulated, and used instrumentally by institutions and individuals for their own agendas.[7]

Family planning policy in Peru under the administration of President Alberto Fujimori illustrates this instrumental pattern. The Fujimori administration utilized international feminist discourses on reproductive health and rights, and alliances with Peruvian feminists themselves, to cloak a traditional population control agenda. During his second inauguration speech in 1995, Fujimori announced a major change in Peru's population policy. He proclaimed a concerted "struggle against poverty" and

promised family planning would play a critical role in this new initiative.

As the only male head of state to address the United Nations Fourth World Conference on Women in Beijing, and "as part of its policy on social development and the fight against poverty," Fujimori announced that his "government has decided to carry out an integral strategy of family planning that confronts openly, for the first time in the history of our country the serious lack of information and services available on the matter."[8] This announcement of expanded family planning was an attempt to win the favor of Peruvian feminists who had substantial national visibility in 1995 due to the conference and its preparatory meetings. Fujimori had arrived at the Beijing conference at a critical moment—when conservative actors like the Catholic Church were attempting to roll back some of the rights established in the Cairo accords. His announcement at the conference led to what some observers have called "an implicit alliance" between Fujimori and some feminists in civil society, although others remained wary of the Fujimori agenda, which, overall, was mixed on women's issues.[9]

The Beijing speech also garnered Fujimori badly needed kudos from the international community. His outspoken support of women's reproductive rights appeared to be a democratic gesture, assuaging those countries that had looked unfavorably upon Fujimori's earlier dismissal of Peru's congress. After his 1992 "self-coup," the U.S. Agency for International Development (USAID) had pulled funding for its two major health programs in Peru, one of which was for family planning.[10] Fujimori's new policy served to shore up international alliances and win tacit approval, if not financial backing, for its program from important bi- and multilateral agencies, such as USAID.

At Beijing, Fujimori, dressed in blue jeans and tennis shoes, not only shed the traditional formal attire of presidents and U.N. delegates, but also shed Peru's traditional governmental alliance with the Catholic hierarchy on issues of artificial contraception. This significant expansion of family planning services in Peru was made possible by a conflict between the Fujimori government and the Peruvian Catholic hierarchy dating to rifts during Fujimori's

1990 election campaign. Although the Catholic hierarchy is opposed to artificial contraception in general, it particularly opposes surgical forms of contraception, which it views as mutilation of the body. Surgical sterilization had been illegal in Peru, except in cases where pregnancy was considered a mortal risk. But just days before the Beijing Women's Conference in September 1995, after lively debate, the Fujimori-dominated congress passed legislation that legalized "voluntary surgical contraception," creating more dissent between the church and the government. Fujimori's Beijing announcement proceeded to take direct aim at the church, accusing "the Catholic hierarchy" of trying at all costs "to prevent the Peruvian State from carrying out a modern and rational policy of family planning" that would help "the poorest sectors of our population.[11]

This speech, portraying his government as modern and the church as irrational and backward, heightened tensions between the two and led the Peruvian bishops to proclaim the government family planning initiative as a "satanic" proposal that would turn "the entire country into a whorehouse."[12] Despite this vehement church opposition, the government proceeded to expand access to state-provided contraceptive services, including "voluntary" vasectomies and tubal ligations.

REPRODUCTIVE HEALTH OR MALTHUSIAN CONTROL?

Despite conflicts with the church, it is evident from Fujimori's placement of family planning within his broader "struggle against poverty" that he viewed family planning as a means to poverty reduction, rather than to women's rights. However, his use of international feminist forums such as Beijing and his citation of feminist-influenced development accords created the impression that the policy would balance poverty reduction objectives with reproductive rights, especially since Fujimori explicitly cited the Cairo accords in legal documents pertaining to population policy in Peru.

Peru's revised plan named gender equity as a goal to be achieved through equal rights for both sexes and "health services that will diminish the barriers that limit women's access to quality care." The plan attempted to ensure warm interactions between caregivers and clients, high quality attention, and respect for clients' self-determination within their cultural values. Finally, as already noted, for the first time, this family planning program included the option of sterilization as a contraceptive choice.[13]

In addition to the president's rhetoric about women's rights and the echo of the Cairo language, advertising for the family planning program appeared feminist in emphasizing the rights of women and couples to choose the number of their children. A newspaper ad for the program read: "There are those who still do not understand that Peruvian women, or the couples in Peru, have the right to choose."[14] These factors produced an image of a progressive government program that favored individual liberties and reproductive well-being for women and men.

However, other government documents reveal that the upper echelons of the Fujimori government—the presidency and the prime minister's office—viewed family planning principally as a tool for economic development, with little regard for the promotion of reproductive health or rights.

Clearly, the primary goals of the family planning program under Fujimori were economic growth and poverty reduction, not reproductive health and rights. The government logic was that a reduction in population would lead to an increase in GDP per capita. Thus, elite, primarily white, male policymakers sought control of women's bodies as a means of meeting their goals of economic growth.

These policy goals contributed to the record of mounting abuses. The president pressured family planning program staff to meet sterilization quotas, and the precarious working conditions of state health employees led to low quality care and human rights abuses. The state used the number of women sterilized as an indicator of successful poverty alleviation. According to former program staff members, the family planning advisor, Eduardo Yong Motta, appointed by the president, would contact the program weekly to set increased quotas for surgical sterilizations. Furthermore, the president or Yong Motta would attend the program's weekly meetings to monitor achievement of the quotas. Fujimori even met directly with subregional directors of the health system to promote local surgical sterilizations.[15]

Analysis of government propaganda reveals that it was not only *women's* bodies, but *poor and indigenous* women's bodies that were the object of these campaigns and of Peru's family planning program more generally. Unlike the feminist-inspired advertisements, this second strand of propaganda was not distributed to the general Peruvian populace. Instead, it targeted the low-income and poor clientele of state-run public health clinics, emphasizing that more children would cause greater poverty.

UNCOMFORTABLE ALLIES

In 1996 and 1997, Giulia Tamayo, a lawyer with the feminist human rights group, Latin American and Caribbean Committee for the Defense of Women's Rights (CLADEM), was the first to expose patient grievances with the government family planning program. Her report documents 243 cases of sterilization under questionable circumstances in nineteen department[16] and led Peru's *Defensoria del Pueblo* to launch a full investigation of the program that identified systematic deficiencies in gaining voluntary and informed consent for surgical sterilization. Of 157 cases investigated in 1999, forty-one had no consent procedure at all. Of the ninety cases that took place when a consent procedure was part of the program's policy, it was not used by staff in seventy-one. Finally of the nineteen cases where the consent form was used, it was filled out properly only eleven times.[17]

The *Defensoria* investigated twenty-four cases of death or serious injury as a result of surgical sterilization and found the majority due to low-quality care: a lack of sanitary conditions and thus infection, poor medical practices, including damage to other bodily organs during the procedure, or a lack of follow-up care, among other reasons. From 1996 to 1998, the *Defensoria* documented sixteen deaths as a result of female sterilizations, a rate of 7.35 deaths for every 100,000 operations.[18]

A few attempts were made to address the abuses in the family planning program, but members of the president's party or his ministers denied any wrongdoing. Thus, groups in civil society resorted primarily to outside means to demand change in the government family planning policy. An unusual alliance began to coalesce in opposition to the program: the Catholic hierarchy and Peruvian feminists. Indeed, in 1998–1999 few mechanisms of accountability existed in Peru because the Fujimori regime had grown increasingly authoritarian. For feminists, the task of responding to government abuses was made more complex by their implicit alliance with Fujimori since Beijing and their explicit engagement with the state and international population agencies through the *Mesa Tripartita*.

The hierarchy of the Catholic Church, which had opposed the family planning program from the start, took advantage of the newspaper reports of program abuses to launch its own campaign against government-provided family planning services. The church hierarchy ferreted out stories of abuses in the family planning program and provided these to the media. Cardinal Augusto Vargas Alzamora appeared on television news and made regular statements to the major newspapers denouncing the family planning program.[19] Vargas and his successor Cardinal Luis Cipriani also used Sunday masses to sway the public against the program and pressure the government. In addition, religiously conservative congressional members, such as Rafael Rey, a member of the conservative Catholic Opus Dei, demanded an investigation of the program on religious grounds.[20] Church agitation against the program led to the inclusion of "natural" family planning methods in the family planning program's array of contraceptive choices.

A number of factors compromised feminist responses to the abuses in the family planning program.[21] First, feminists faced the dilemma of speaking out against a program for whose expanded services they had advocated for decades. Criticizing the family planning program ran the risk of harming the cause of reproductive rights in the public eye and placed feminists in the unsavory position of apparent agreement with the Catholic hierarchy. Second, they faced the political problem of criticizing a very popular government. Third, feminists themselves were divided. Although some backed the regime, most did not; and among Fujimori's feminist opponents, some felt that problems in the family planning program were secondary to the larger fight against an authoritarian regime.[22]

Feminists' positions were further complicated by the involvement of Peru's three major feminist organizations—Manuela Ramos, Flora Tristán, and the Red Nacional de Promoción de la Mujer—in the *Mesa Tripartita*. These feminist organizations were caught in a web of political and financial relationships with the Peruvian state and the international population agencies. Their dependence both on good relations with the state and on financial support from international population agencies compromised their ability to speak out directly and quickly against abuses in the state family planning program.

The *Mesa Tripartita* was intended to represent the interests of the state, international institutions, and civil society in determining specific steps to carry forward the Cairo accords. The brainchild of the Latin American Women's Health Network, it was successfully implemented in Peru as a result of the combined efforts of the groups Flora Tristán and Manuela Ramos.[23] Its first steps, in 1997 and 1998, were to map out existing activities of the government, civil society, and international agencies in the field of reproductive health. The three sectors then prioritized which aspects of the Cairo agreements would be implemented immediately.[24] Finally, the Mesa developed indicators and mechanisms to monitor the implementation of the accords.

Some feminists felt that "the space decidedly allowed feminists to enter and present initiatives, or at least to promote debate and make proposals." Moreover, it was a means of holding the state accountable to the Cairo accords.[25] The *Mesa* was seen by these sectors as a means to influence an authoritarian regime otherwise closed to input from civil society. Other feminists outside the *Mesa* disagreed with its premise altogether, arguing that reproductive rights should not be negotiated.

Ultimately, CLADEM and a consortium of smaller Peruvian NGOs appealed to an international source of accountability, the United Nations. The U.N. Committee on Elimination of Discrimination against Women, which oversees signatories' adherence to CEDAW, called upon Peru to justify its family planning policy, after receiving a critical report on the policy prepared by CLADEM's Lima office, the Center for Reproductive Law and Policy in New York, and the Lima office of the Center for the Defense of Women's Rights (DEMUS).[23] The government sent representatives of the Women's Ministry to respond to the questioning. Although the U.N. action was effective in forcing the government to explain its actions publicly for the first time, this approach depended on Peru's voluntary agreement to abide by international accords and offered no guarantee for future compliance. The feminists who did speak out against the government did so in an increasingly authoritarian political context. By the late 1990s, the Fujimori government censored much of the media and denied its opponents basic civil and human rights. In 1998, Giulia Tamayo, the activist who first broke the story of abuses in the program and who was a central figure in bringing them to the attention of the CEDAW committee, was physically threatened, her home broken into, and videos of testimonials that she had been gathering as evidence of wrongdoing in the family planning program were stolen.

Curiously absent from the debates over family planning in the 1990s were the voices of the women most affected. Poor, rural, and indigenous women did not collectively organize to voice their opinions on family planning policy. Instead, their voices were primarily heard in the individual testimonials collected by Tamayo and the *Defensoria del Pueblo*. The collective response of indigenous and peasant women came much later, in 2001, from the "Mujeres de Anta"—twelve peasant and Quechua-speaking women of Anta in the department of Cuzco. Organized by the feminist organization, Movimiento Amplio de Mujeres, these rural women traveled from Cuzco to Lima to demand compensation for the sterilization abuses that they suffered at the hands of the family planning program.[24]

LEGACIES AND CONCLUSIONS

As a result of the efforts of feminist whistle-blowers, the proactive position of the *Defensoria del Pueblo*, as well as international agencies, Peru's family planning program was substantially overhauled in 1999. Moreover, demand for family planning options continued to be strong in post-Fujimori Peru. However, the Fujimori program's legacy of population control tactics did damage the cause of reproductive rights. In 2001, Peruvians elected Alejandro Toledo president of Peru by a very small margin, following President Fujimori's flight into exile due to a corruption scandal and following a brief transition under Valentin Paniagua. Due to his weak political support, Toledo sought allies among conservative Catholic politicians. Toledo's first two health ministers belonged to conservative sects; his first minister of health, Luis Solari de la Fuente, to the Sodalicio de Vida Cristiana, and his second, Fernando Carbone Campoverde, to Opus Dei. Both Solari and Carbone actively sought to reduce reproductive rights in Peru, in part by taking advantage of the family planning scandals of the 1990s. In his writings prior to becoming minister of health, Solari asserted that a "social alliance" bound "Northern nations" with feminists interested in controlling birth rates. In 2001, Solari introduced legislation, which never passed, that would have allowed healthcare providers "conscientious objection" to carrying out any medical act against their personal moral or ethical views. He also introduced successful legislation that made "The Day of the Unborn" an official national commemorative day.[25]

When Fernando Carbone became minister, he reopened the sterilization debate, claiming that under Fujimori there had been 300,000 cases of forced sterilization. His attempt to hold Fujimori accountable was based on questionable facts with an obvious underlying political agenda. Clearly Carbone sought to use the family planning scandal under Fujimori to severely weaken state family planning in Peru. Moreover, he did so by again invoking international rhetoric, this time of human rights. He labeled Fujimori's family planning actions as "genocide" and set up a "truth commission" to investigate them.[26] Under Solari and Carbone, many health ministry personnel, including those who worked in reproductive health, were replaced by religious conservatives. Minister Carbone banned the use of the word "gender" in any health ministry documents, reflecting the Catholic hierarchy's opposition to the term.

In its 2002 and 2005 investigative reports on family planning in Peru, the office of the *Defensoria del Pueblo* found that since 2001 there had been an increase in health establishments denying both access to surgical sterilization and full information on the range of contraceptive methods available. It also found that since 2001, stocks of contraception in state health establishments decreased, and patients were being charged for contraception, in violation of Peruvian law. Moreover, the *Defensoria* found that the ministry had refused to make the emergency contraception pill (legalized in 2001 before Toledo took office) available in public health establishments.[27] Carbone also argued that intrauterine devices were abortive and attempted to remove them from public health centers. A congressional commission in 2002 called for making voluntary surgical sterilization again illegal. In 2003, the Ministry of Health implemented a "Peru-Life Strategy" which emphasized the "rights" of the unborn.[28] The effects of these policies became apparent in national statistics on contraceptive use in 2003 and 2004. Peruvians' use of all artificial forms of contraception dropped by 26 percent between 2002 and 2004. The dramatic drop is likely due to instances of illegal fees, some doctors' refusals to provide contraception, and perhaps most importantly Solari and Carbone's refusals to restock state contraceptive supplies.[29]

In 2003, feminists and public health activists successfully lobbied Toledo to remove Carbone from the ministry. Again, rights language was invoked, this time to support sexual and reproductive rights. This second wave of battles over family planning again underlines how global human rights and feminist discourses were employed to shape national political agendas. The succeeding health minister, Pilar Mazetti, who was appointed in 2003, actively repaired the damage done by her predecessors to state family planning programs. That damage was extensive: religious conservatives gained direct power within the Ministry of Health and significantly weakened the state family planning program. Their influence on public and governmental attitudes outlasted the conservative ministers.

The family planning debacle in Peru raises theoretical questions in three areas: first, the relationship between feminists and the state and the viability of mixed state-civil society-international institutions like the *Mesa Tripartita*; second, the relationship between urban middle-class feminists and poor indigenous women; and third, the consequences of the instrumental use of global feminist language.

In terms of state-feminist relations, the family planning debacle demonstrates the need for multiple feminist locations. Although the Peruvian feminists who participated in the *Mesa* were constrained by their relationship with the state and international population agencies, the same relationships allowed them access to information on state policy and practices. In the increasingly authoritarian context of Peru in the late 1990s, the ties that feminists forged with the state were in fact some of the only bridges that existed between the state and Peruvian civil society. The *Mesa* was therefore a key point for information and negotiation that other groups, such as labor unions, lacked altogether. Yet, as this article has made clear, participation in the *Mesa* also limited the extent to which these feminists could be critical. On the other hand, feminists outside the *Mesa*, who were free of compromises with state and international agencies, were key in bringing international attention to the national problem of sterilization campaigns. In what Margaret Keck and Kathryn Sikkink call the "boomerang pattern," these feminists responded to an authoritarian national context by using international mechanisms to pressure the state.[30] I conclude, therefore, that both pragmatic feminist groups that are willing to interact with the state and autonomous radical feminist groups able to strongly criticize state actions are essential to the success of feminist policy positions.[31]

In Peru's family planning program, as I have shown, a hidden population control agenda was masked by the disingenuous use of feminist discourse. Recognition of this agenda was not obtained through administrative monitoring but through actual observations of the program in action in remote rural villages. Such efforts require state cooperation coupled with an autonomous base for investigation and contestation as well as a willingness to move beyond the urban centers to observe the effects of policies in remote areas. The fact that it took over a year for abuses in the family planning program to be discovered indicates a lack of connection between Peruvian feminist NGOs and the rural indigenous women they hoped to serve. Peruvian feminists are concentrated in Lima, and poor and indigenous women are poorly represented in the feminist movement; government cooptation of feminist discourse was facilitated by feminists' own relative privilege.

The events surrounding the family planning program in Peru demonstrate the complex ways in which conservative forces can appropriate feminist discourses disseminated in global (and national) arenas and even manipulate feminists themselves. The Peruvian case may be sobering, but we must keep in mind what Rosalind Petchesky aptly notes: although transnational activists often find their words and work appropriated, their work and words have also opened up "new strategic possibilities."[32] Advances in reproductive rights have been made in Peru, in large part due to the work of transnational and national activists. The fact that these gains have been tempered by opponents is the inescapable reality of politics. For feminists, appropriation of feminist discourse requires a continual effort to be precise about their own definitions, to critically observe the usage of these discourses, and to be willing to hold those who use these discourses accountable to their political intentions. Feminists must be on the leading edge of either defending or redefining particular concepts before others redefine them in undesirable ways.

NOTES

1. Defensoría del Pueblo, *La Applicación de la Anti-concepcion Quirúrgica y las Derechas Reproductives*, vol. 2, *Cases Investigados por la Defensoria del Pueblo. Informe Defensoral 27* (Lima: Defensoria del Puchlo, 1999), 289.

2. Betsy Hartmann. *Reproductive Rights and Wrongs: The Global Politics of Population Control*, rev. ed. (Boston: South End Press, 1995), chap. 6.

3. Susanne Joans. "Rethinking Immigration Policy and Citizenship in the Americas: A Regional Framework," *Social Justice* 23, no. 3 (1996): 68–85.

4. For a critique of the education/fertility connection, see Patricia Jeffery and Roger Jeffery, "Silver Bullet or Passing Fancy? Girls' Schooling and Population Policy," in *Feminist Visions of Development Gender*

Analysis and Policy, ed. Cecile Jackson and Ruth Pearson (London: Routledge, 1998), 239–58.

5. Alfredo Guzman, "Para Mejorar la Salud Reproductiva," in *La Salud Peruana en el Siglo XXI*, ed. Juan Arroyo (Lima: Consorcio de Investigación Económica y Social, U.K. Department for International Development, and AID's Policy Project, 2002), 190. The Peruvian church position on responsible parenthood was first outlined in the document *Familiar y Publición* published by the Episcopado Peruano, 19 Mar, 1974, cited in Alberto Varillas and Patricia Mostajo, *La Situación Poblacional Peruna Balance y Perspectivas* (Lima: Instituto Andino de lestudios en Población y Desarrollo, 1990), esp. 380.

6. Varillas and Mostajo, *La Situación Poblacional*, 322–23; Guzmán. "Para Mejorar la Salud Reproductiva": Varillas and Mostajo, *La Situación Poblacional*. 383.

7. Smyth, "Gender Analysis of Family Planning," 228–30; Hartmann, *Reproductive Rights*. 136–39.

8. From the original speech in Spanish delivered by President Fujimori to the United Nations Fourth Conference on Women, 15 Sept. 1995, Beijing, China. My thanks to U.N. staff for the fax of the original speech in Spanish and to Heather Roff for her assistance in obtaining it from the United Nations. English translations are by the author.

9. Rosa Maria Alfaro. *Agendas Publicas de Género Imcros de una Nueva Etopa Publica Entre Deficulrodes, Delemas y Avances* (Lima: Consultoría de Inserción e Impacto de las Contrapartes de la Fundacó Ford, 1996), cited in Maraja Barrig. "La Persistencia de la Memoria: Feminismo y Estado en d Peru de los 90" (Lima: Proyecto Socieded Civil y Gobernabilídad Democrática en los Andes y el Cono Sur. Fundacsón Ford, 1999)." I am indebted to Nancy Palomino for her insights into Peruvian feminists' reactions to Fujimori at the Beijing conference.

10. Interview with former official (Anonymous 6) of the Family Planning Program, 12 Aug. 1998, Lima. All interviews are with author.

11. President Fujimori to the U.N. Fourth Conference on Women.

12. Quotes by bishops in "Peru's Family Planning Fight Forgets the Poor," *National Catholic Reporter* 31 (October 6, 1995). 11.

13. Ibid., 30; 28–29.

14. Ads like this ran frequently in 1998. The line quoted is from a full-page ad that ran in *El Sol*. 21 Jan. 1998.

15. Anonymous 6, interview.

16. CIADEM. *Nada Personal Reporte de Derechos Humanos sobre la Aplicacion de la Anticoncepcion Quirúrgica en el Perú. 1996–1998* (Lima: CIADEM 1999).

17. The twenty-six remaining cases involved complaints about procedures that did not require consent (Defensoria del Pueblo, *La Aplicacion*, 2: 43–45).

18. Defensoría del Pueblo, *La Aplicacion*, 2: esp. 289. For comparison, the risk ratio of tubal ligation in the United States is 3.9 per 100,000 procedures. Vasectomies carry a much lower risk of 1 per 100,000. See Gregory L. Smith, George P. Taylor, and Kevin F. Smith. "Comparative Risks and Costs of Male and Female Sterilization." *American Journal of Public Health* 75. no. 4 (1985): 370–74.

19. Cardinal Vargas was interviewed on the show "Panorama" of Panamerican Television, 12 Apr. 1998. See also, "La ley divina está por encima de las leyes humanas." *El Comercia* 8 May 1998. On Cardinal Cipriani see, "La sociedad debe proteger la vida," *Cambio*, 5 Apr. 1999.

20. "Demandan que se parahcen campanas de esterilización," *El Comercie*, 26 Jan. 1998.

21. Interviews with Celeste Cambria, and Frescia Carrasco, 15 Apr. 1998, Lima, former representatives of Flora Tristan and Manuela Ramos, respectively, to the *Mesa Tripartita*. 16 Mar. 1998, Lima.

22. Interview with Ana Güezmes, 28 June 2005, Lima. This position was particularly strong among feminists in Flora Tristán.

23. CIADEM/CRLP/DEMUS, "Derechos Sexuales y Reproductivos de las Mujeres en el Perú," *Reporte Sombra, elaborade para lo Decuno Navena Sesion del Comte para la Elimination de Todas las Formas de Discrimation Contra la Mujer* (June 1998).

24. Maria Esther Mogollon, "Peruanas esterilizadas por la fuerza reclaman justicia." *Cimac Aetictas*, 2003, www.cimacnoticias.com/noticias/03mar/03030504.html. In response to the Mujeres de Anta, President Toledo granted women negatively affected by the sterilization campaigns free state health insurance under the *Seguro Integral de Salml* (Integral Health Insurance Plan).

25. Susana A. Chavez. "Cuando el Fundamentalismo Se Apudera de las Politicas Publicas: Politics de Salud Sexual y Reproductiva en el Perú en el Periudo Julio 2001–Juno 2003" (Lima: Flora Tristan, 2004), 33: 34: 36.

26. Ibid. 44

27. Defensoria del Pueblo, *La Aplication 3*, and *Superverson de los Servicos de Planification Famular*, vol. 4. *Cases Investigades por la Defensoria del Pueblo. Informe Defensonal 90* (Lima: Defensoría del Pueblo,

2005); Detensoria del Pueblo, *Anticonception Oral De Emergenca. Informe Defensoral 78* (Lima: Defensoria del Pueblo, 2004).

28. Chavez, "Cuando el Fundamentalismo." 42: 47: 37.

29. Defensoria del Pueblo, *Superversion de los Services*, 46–47. Percentage calculated from raw figures provided by the Defensoria: 1,411.646 in 2002 to 1,047,521 in 2004.

30. Margaret E. Keck and Kathryn Sikkink, *Activists beyond Borders. Advocacy Networks in International Politics* (Ithaca, N.Y.: Corneli University Press, 1998).

31. Geertje Lyeklama à Nijeholt. Joke Sweibel, and Virginia Vargas, "The Global Institutional Framework: The Long March to Beijing," in *Women's Movements and Public Policy in Europe. Latin America, and the Caribbean*, ed. Geortje Lycklama in Nijeholt, Virginia Vargas, and Saskia Wieringa (New York: Garland, 1998). 25–48: Dorothy McBride Stetson and Amy Mazur, eds. *Compatative State Feminism* (Thousand Oaks, Calif.: Sage, 1995).

32. Rosalind Pollack Petchesky, *Global Prescriptions Gendering Health and Human Rights* (New York: Zed Books, 2003), 27.

R E A D I N G **35**

Unusual Families

Susan Golombok (2005)

INTRODUCTION

When asked previously to give a talk on unusual families created by assisted reproduction, I have given the hypothetical example of a child with five parents: an egg donor (the genetic mother) a sperm donor (the genetic father), a surrogate mother who hosts the pregnancy, and the two social parents whom the child knows as mum and dad. This example is no longer hypothetical. Last month, the High Court granted an adoption order to the social parents of twins conceived using donated embryos and carried by their grandmother. Advances in assisted reproduction have led to a variety of unusual family forms, some more controversial than others. This presentation today concentrates on the issue of lesbian and single heterosexual women having access to assisted reproduction as a means of conceiving a child without the involvement of a male partner. These types of families are particularly relevant at the present time because of the ongoing review of the clause in the Human Fertilisation and Embryology (HFE) Act regarding the need of a child for a father.

LESBIAN MOTHERS

The first topic is lesbian mothers and this is followed by discussion about single-mother families. In the UK, widespread public awareness of lesbian mothers began in 1978 with a sensational piece of investigative journalism. It was reported in a London evening newspaper that lesbian women were attending a private clinic with the aim of conceiving a child by donor insemination. Headlines such as "Ban these Babies" and "Dr Strangelove" produced an outcry not just about the doctor helping lesbian women to have children but also about the fact that lesbian women were being allowed to raise children at all. One member of the British Parliament at the time, Rhodes Boyson, was quoted as saying, "This evil must stop for the sake of the potential children and society, which both have enough problems without the extension of this horrific practice. Children have a right to be born into a natural family with a father and a mother. Anything less will cause lifelong deprivation of the most acute kind for the child."

Around the same time, partly as a result of the growth in the women's movement and also the gay liberation movement, there was a rise in the number of lesbian women who were becoming involved in child custody disputes when they divorced. Although a great fuss was made in the media about lesbian women having children by donor insemination, almost all lesbian mothers at that time had had their children while married, and most of the children spent their early years in a heterosexual family before making the transition to a lesbian mother household. These women, almost without exception, lost custody of their children when they divorced on the grounds that it would not be in the children's best interests to remain with their lesbian mother.

The arguments against lesbian mothers seeking custody were the same then as they are today in relation to lesbian women seeking donor insemination. Those who were opposed to lesbian mothers argued that the children would be teased and rejected by their peers, and would develop emotional and behavioral problems as a result. It was also argued that they would show atypical gender development, i.e., that boys would be less masculine in their identity and behavior, and girls less feminine, than their counterparts from heterosexual homes.

At that time, no studies had been carried out on the psychological development of children in lesbian families, and nothing was known about what actually happened to children in these circumstances. The absence of such information meant that custody was almost always awarded to the more conventional parent, i.e., to the heterosexual father in preference to the lesbian mother. It was the lack of knowledge about these children and their parents that prompted the first systematic studies in the mid-1970s in the US and the UK. The UK study was conducted by Sir Michael Rutter, Anne Spencer and myself, and there were also American studies conducted by Richard Green, Martha Kirkpatrick and Beverly Hoeffer (Hoeffer, 1981; Kirkpatrick *et al.*, 1981; Golombok *et al.*, 1983; Kirkpatrick, 1987).

Regardless of the geographic or demographic characteristics of the samples studied, the findings of these early investigations were strikingly consistent. Firstly, in terms of the children's socio-emotional development, children from lesbian mother families did not show a higher incidence of psychological disorder, or of difficulties in peer relationships, than their counterparts from heterosexual homes, and for measures for which norms were available, they were found to be functioning within the normal range.

With respect to gender development, a distinction is usually made between gender identity, a person's concept of him or herself as male or female, and gender role behavior, i.e., the behaviors and attitudes that are considered to be appropriate for males and females in a particular culture. There was no evidence of gender identity confusion for any of the children studied; all of the boys identified as boys, all of the girls identified as girls. In terms of gender role behavior, no differences were found between children in lesbian and heterosexual families for either boys or girls, i.e., the daughters of lesbian mothers were no less feminine, and the sons no less masculine, in terms of their toy and activity preferences, than the daughters and sons of heterosexual mothers, and this was in spite of lesbian mothers' preference for less sex-typed toys and activities for their daughters and sons. It was concluded that children in lesbian families did not differ from other children as a result of their non-traditional family environment. These findings were replicated by other researchers over the years, culminating in a seminal review by Charlotte Patterson in 1992.

But that wasn't the end of the story. A number of criticisms were made about this body of research. Firstly, a limitation was that only school-age children had been studied. It was argued that "sleeper effects" may exist, such that children raised in lesbian households may experience difficulties in emotional wellbeing, and in intimate relationships, when they grow up. In order to address these questions, Fiona Tasker and I followed up the children from the UK study in 1991/1992, 14 years after they had first been seen, when their average age was 24 years old. It was possible to contact 25 young adults from lesbian families and 21 young adults from single heterosexual families, representing 62% of the original sample. Although the sample size was not large, the advantage of the study was that the majority of children were recruited before they had reached adolescence, and so the results were not confounded by the knowledge of their sexual orientation in adult life.

With respect to peer relationships, data were obtained on the proportion of young adults in each group who reported having been teased or bullied during adolescence. Young adults from lesbian families were no more likely to report teasing by peers in general, than those from heterosexual single parent homes. But with respect to teasing about their own sexuality, there was a tendency for those from lesbian families to be more likely to recall having been teased about being gay or lesbian themselves, although those from lesbian families may have been more likely to remember such incidents.

Interestingly, those who were most negative about their experiences of growing up in a lesbian family tended to come from poorer backgrounds and to live in a social environment that was generally hostile toward homosexuality. It seems, therefore, that the social context of the lesbian mother family is an important predictor of the experiences of the child. How the mother handled the situation also made a difference. It was important to the children that their mother was sensitive to their need for discretion, and that they themselves controlled who, and who not, to tell.

The findings relating to psychological wellbeing showed that children raised by lesbian mothers continued to function well in adulthood and did not experience long-term detrimental effects arising from their early upbringing. No differences between young adults from lesbian and heterosexual homes were found for anxiety or depression as assessed by standardized questionnaire measures, and their scores fell within the normal range. In addition, those from lesbian families were no more likely to have sought professional help for anxiety, depression or stress-related difficulties.

In terms of sexual orientation, the large majority of young adults with lesbian mothers identified as heterosexual. Only two young women from lesbian families identified as lesbian compared with none from heterosexual families. So the commonly held assumption that lesbian mothers will have lesbian daughters and gay sons was not supported by the findings of the study. The large majority of the children who grew up in lesbian families identified as heterosexual in adulthood.

Another criticism of research on lesbian mother families was that most of the children studied had spent their first years in a heterosexual home before

making the transition to a lesbian family. To the extent that early experience influences later development, knowledge about these children could not be generalized to children raised by a lesbian mother from birth. In recent years, however, controlled studies of lesbian families with a child conceived by donor insemination have begun to be reported: two from the US, one from Belgium and one from my own group in the UK. Unlike lesbian women who had their children while married, these couples planned their family together after coming out as lesbian and so the children that were raised in lesbian families would not have had a father present right from the start.

Although the children were studied when they were still quite young, around 6 years old on average, the evidence so far suggests that they do not differ from their peers in two-parent heterosexual donor-insemination families in terms of either emotional wellbeing or gender development, suggesting that the presence of a father, or of heterosexual models, is not necessary for the development of sex-typed behavior. In fact, the only clear difference to emerge from the studies was that comothers in donor-insemination lesbian families were more involved with their children than were fathers in heterosexual homes. The UK study followed up the children to early adolescence. The families were assessed again around the time of the child's 12th birthday and no major differences were found in the quality of parenting or child development between families headed by lesbian and single heterosexual mothers.

The Belgian study is particularly interesting as the children were asked about their attitudes toward their donor. Twenty-seven per cent of the children aged between 7 and 17 years said that they would like to know the identity of their donor, 19% wished to have non-identifying information about his appearance and personality, and the remaining 54% preferred not to have information about him at that point in their lives. In response to questioning about the reasons for wanting information about the donor, the overriding motivation appeared to be curiosity. There were no differences between children who wanted to know more about the donor and those who did not, with respect to their psychological wellbeing or the quality of their relationship with their parents. As the children were still of school age it is likely that a greater number will wish to know the identity of their donor in adulthood. To the extent that parallels may be drawn with adoption, it has been found that adopted adults who search for birth relatives begin to do so at age 30 years on average, and women are twice as likely to search as men. These demographic patterns may also be observed in relation to donor insemination. One striking difference between lesbian mothers of donor-insemination children and heterosexual mothers of donor-insemination children is that lesbian mothers are much more open with their children about the method of their conception. Almost all lesbian mothers tell their children about their donor conception, whereas the majority of heterosexual mothers currently do not.

FAMILIES HEADED BY SINGLE HETEROSEXUAL MOTHERS

Large-scale epidemiological studies of single-mother families consistently show that children raised by single mothers are more likely to show psychological problems, and are less likely to perform well at school, than their counterparts from two-parent homes. For example, an examination of four nationally representative samples in the US found that adolescents raised by single mothers during some period of their childhood were twice as likely to drop out of high school, twice as likely to have a baby before the age of 20, and one-and-a-half times more likely to be out of work in their late teens or early twenties than those from a similar background who grow up with two parents at home. In a recent UK study of 4 year olds, children from single-parent families showed higher levels of emotional and behavioral problems than their counterparts from two-parent homes.

So, why is it that children from single-mother families show poorer outcomes? Is it because of the absence of a father? Or are other factors involved? In examining this issue, researchers have found that factors such as financial hardship and the mother's lack of social support are largely responsible for children's difficulties. Another important contributing factor is exposure to conflict and hostility between parents before, during, and sometimes after, separation or divorce. The majority of single-parent families result from marital breakdown, and the negative effects of such conflict for children have been well documented.

Researchers have also looked at the impact of single parenthood for parenting itself, and have demonstrated that, on average, children in single-parent homes experience a poorer quality of parenting than children who live with two parents. In the UK study, single mothers were more likely than the mothers in two-parent families to endorse questionnaire items such as "This child gets on my nerves" and "I have frequent battles of will with this child," and these responses were associated with a higher rate of behavioral problems in children. Similarly, the US study reported that the single mothers exert less control over their children, in terms of supervision and establishing rules, than mothers in two-parent families. Not only do children in single-parent families experience less discipline and monitoring from their mother than children in two-parent families but also they receive no discipline from their father, an aspect of parenting that is often associated with the paternal role.

The poorer quality of parenting shown by single mothers is also explained by the higher rates of psychological problems, particularly depression, found among single mothers. Depression reduces the ability to be an effective parent, interfering with parents' emotional availability and sensitivity to their children, and also with their control and discipline of them. It has been demonstrated that depressed parents tend either to be very lenient with their children or very authoritarian, often switching between the two.

In recent years, a growing number of single women have chosen to have children by donor insemination. This had led to much controversy about whether single woman should have access to assisted reproduction. The concerns that have been expressed center around the effects on children of growing up in a fatherless family, and are based on the research that has just been described that shows negative outcomes in terms of cognitive, social and emotional development for children raised by single mothers following parental separation or divorce. However, these outcomes cannot necessarily be generalized to children born to single mothers following donor insemination since these children have not experienced parental separation and conflict, and generally are raised without financial hardship. It is possible, however, that other pressures on solo mothers, such as social stigma and lack of social support, may interfere with their parenting role and leave their children vulnerable to emotional and behavioral problems.

Little research has been carried out on single women who opt for donor insemination as a means of having a child. In the first controlled investigation, conducted by Clare Murray and myself (Golombok *et al.*, 1997), 27 solo mothers of 1-year-old children were compared with a matched sample of 50 married donor-insemination mothers with a 1-year-old child. The study was designed to assess the mothers' motivations, their psychological wellbeing and the quality of their relationship with their child. The main reason for embarking on solo motherhood was a growing sense that time was running out, and that there was no choice but to have a child in this way due to the lack of a partner. The average age at pregnancy of the solo mothers was 37 years. The primary reasons for attending a clinic were because they did not want to have casual sex, they did not want to deceive a man, and they wanted to avoid the risk of HIV and other sexually transmitted diseases. In terms of their financial situation, 96% were supporting themselves, and only 4% reported experiencing financial hardship. Contrary to popular assumption, the majority of solo mothers wished to have a relationship with a man in the future (87%). Solo donor-insemination mothers appeared to be more open to telling their child about the donor conception than were the married donor-insemination mothers; 93% of solo mothers reported that they planned to tell their child compared with 46% of the married donor-insemination mothers.

In terms of the mothers' psychological adjustment, there were no differences between the solo mothers and the married mothers in levels of anxiety, depression or stress associated with parenting. With respect to parent–child relationships,

solo donor-insemination mothers showed a similar degree of warmth and emotional involvement with their infants, and were just as likely to develop a strong bond with them as were married donor-insemination mothers. However, solo mothers did show a lower level of interaction with their babies and less sensitivity to their needs. A possible explanation for this finding is that the presence of a partner allowed married donor-insemination mothers more time with their child. These families were followed up again at the time of the child's second birthday using a standardized interview to assess the nature of the emotional bond between the mother and the child (Golombok *et al.*, 2005). The child's emotional and behavioral adjustment was also assessed, as well as cognitive development, at age 2 years. The results suggested that the solo donor-insemination mothers experienced greater feelings of joy and less anger regarding the child than married donor-insemination mothers. The children of solo mothers showed fewer emotional and behavioral problems but no difference in cognitive functioning. As far as is known, this is the first controlled study of the quality of parenting and the development of children in solo-mother donor-insemination families, and it is important to stress that the children were very young at the time of study and that very few such families are currently available for investigation. However, the findings indicate that solo-mother donor-insemination families are not experiencing marked difficulties in their child's early years. It will be some time before the children understand the nature of their conception. How these children will feel about the fact that they will never know the man who was their sperm donor remains to be seen.

CONCLUSION

These studies of both lesbian mother and single heterosexual mother families are of interest not just because of the implications for social policy making but also because they increase understanding of the processes involved in children's psychological development. It is no longer appropriate to assume that traditional families are good for children and that unusual families are bad. What matters for children's psychological wellbeing is not simply whether the mother is lesbian or heterosexual, single or married. Instead, what really matters is the same for all families—it is the quality of family life. The problems faced by children in non-traditional families are not problems in parenting but of prejudice from the outside world. But social attitudes are not fixed. They can, and do, change.

REFERENCES

Golombok, S., Spencer, A., and Rutter, M. 1983. Children in lesbian and single-parent households: psychosexual and psychiatric appraisal. *Journal of Child Psychology and Psychiatry and Allied Disciplines* 24, 551–572.

Golombok, S., Tasker, F. and Murray, C. 1997. Children raised in fatherless families from infancy: family relationships and the socioemotional development of children of lesbian and single heterosexual mothers. *Journal of Child Psychology and Psychiatry* 38, 783–791.

Golombok, S., Jadva, V., Lycett, E., Murray, C., and Maccallum, F. 2005. Families created by gamete donation: follow-up at age 2. *Human Reproduction*, in press.

Hoeffer, B. 1981. Children's acquisition of sex-role behavior in lesbian-mother families. *American Journal of Orthopsychiatry* 51, 536–544.

Kirkpatrick, M. 1987. Clinical implications of lesbian mother studies. *Journal of Homosexuality* 14, 201–211.

Kirkpatrick, M., Smith, C., and Roy, R. 1981. Lesbian mothers and their children: a comparative survey. *American Journal of Orthopsychiatry* 51, 545–551.

Patterson, C. J. 1992. Children of lesbian and gay parents. *Child Development* 63, 1025–1042.

CHAPTER 7

Families in Global Context

Meg Wilkes Karraker

Meg Wilkes Karraker, Professor of Sociology at the University of St. Thomas in St. Paul, Minnesota, USA, teaches courses on family, global gender, adolescence, and sociological theory. A recipient of her University's Aquinas Scholars Honors Program Teacher of the Year Award, Karraker is President of Alpha Kappa Delta, the international sociology honor society. She is author of *Global Families* (Allyn & Bacon, 2008) and coauthor of *Families with Futures: A Survey of Family Studies for the Twenty-First Century* (Lawrence A. Erlbaum, 2006). Karraker's interests in globalization and families are rooted in her experience growing up in a military family in Germany and traveling through Europe and the former Soviet Union. Her current research examines the social networks among Catholic women's religious congregations with ministries to migrant women and their children and families in the United States and Italy.

It is so still in the house . . .
And the dogs are rolled up with snouts under the tail.
My little boy is sleeping on the ledge,
On his back he lies, breathing through his open mouth.
His little stomach is bulging round—
Is it strange if I start to cry with joy?

Excerpt from "The Mother's Song," anonymous.
Translated from the Inuit by Peter Freuchen.

Perhaps no institution is in more flux worldwide than the family in its responses to changes in gender relationships. And, while the trend in families across the globe may appear to be one of increasing liberalization, in many communities the family continues to subordinate women, keeping them in relations of subservience. At the same time, however, as the excerpt from "The Mother's Song" above illustrates, relationships and practices in the family can be empowering and a source of comfort, support, and creativity. In this chapter I explore the intersection of family situations and women's gendered realities worldwide. In doing so, I present the family as an arena in which gender and women's status are increasingly contested.

One of my favorite family photographs is of my parents, Herbert and Mary, on their wedding day, December 22, 1952. My father is wearing the uniform and insignia of a sergeant in the U.S. Army. My mother is wearing a formal white wedding gown and veil, holding her prayer book and a bouquet of orchids. They stand in front of the altar at Shiloh Methodist Church, in Lumber City, Georgia. My handsome father, two years older and a head taller than his beautiful bride, looks lovingly into my mother's upturned and sweetly smiling face.

LEARNING ACTIVITY   **Build Your Own Genogram**

A genogram allows you to map family patterns across generations. It's like a family tree but with more detail that allows you more insight into yourself and your family's dynamics. To see basic genogram components, go to http://faculty-web.at.northwestern.edu/commstud/galvin/components.html. You can also use a genogram to map out family health issues to help you be aware of things you may want to pay attention to in your own health. As you construct your genogram, notice what has happened with the women on your family tree. What patterns emerge in your genogram? What do you learn about yourself and your family?

That nostalgic image offers a snapshot of the lives of many Americans who came of age, married, and formed new families in the last half of the twentieth century. That image also reflects several norms regarding families and gender practices in American society at the time. For example, many communities expected grooms to approach the bride's father to ask permission to marry his daughter. The story is told that my father expressed to my grandfather his intent to marry my mother and "take care of her," to which my grandfather replied of his rather independent daughter: "well, someone needs to [take care of her]!"

However, the early decades of the twentieth century saw both greater unsupervised dating and courtship and higher female employment. Thus women had the opportunity to develop relationships with future husbands away from intense parental scrutiny and supervision. This facilitated expectations among some women for more autonomy in marriage. Such a striving for greater autonomy is a central feature of women's relationship to family systems worldwide.

Since Herbert and Mary's marriage almost six decades ago, American families, like those in many parts of the world, have become more diverse. Higher educational and occupational achievements among women have been matched by dramatic changes in family structure. In developed countries in particular, women marry later (and some marry not at all). Marriages are less stable, although divorce rates began to stabilize and even showed slight signs of declining by the late 1980s. And the frequency of women raising children alone has increased (Population Reference Bureau, 2008).

Families worldwide are increasingly shaped by uniquely global forces. These forces include worldwide demographic shifts, transnational migration and employment across national and political borders, regional and international violence, and worldwide culture systems. In addition, families are increasingly sites of consumption that support economic systems relying on consumerism. Many families today are transnational, spanning national borders where "[their] members act, decide, feel, and express identities across social networks that traverse two (or more) societies, often simultaneously" (Karraker, 2008, p. 8). Many families can also be described as global. This means that families are simultaneously, and increasingly, shaped by not only economic and political realities of specific nation-states, but also by social and cultural systems on a global scale.

These changes in families worldwide remain profoundly gendered. For example, in developed societies, the dramatic shifts in gender attitudes and behaviors among women (and also among some men), represent the most significant transformation in families since industrialization. In many societies these developments set the wheels in motion for the education and employment of daughters and wives. Again, changes in education and employment have effectively reduced paternal scrutiny and control, hastening the erosion of familial patriarchy and transforming cultural systems (Hutton and Giddens, 2001).

This chapter is placed almost exactly in the middle of *Women Worldwide: Transnational Feminist Perspectives on Women*. In this location, the essay and readings complement the earlier chapters on world media, the body, sexuality, and reproductive and health issues, and anticipate the subsequent chapters on violence, work, politics, the environment, and war and peace. I begin with a section that focuses on families worldwide. It addresses definitions of family, explores systems of descent and inheritance, and discusses practices of son preference. It reflects on power and authority in families and the consequences for the well-being of girls and women. The next section explores gendered patterns of marriage and domestic relationships, including mate selection and marriage rituals. I examine how these patterns reflect cultural conceptions of women's autonomy. I also discuss the reasons for, and the consequences of, early marriage for girls. The chapter closes with a focus on local, transnational, and global strategies to improve the status of women in families.

FAMILIES WORLDWIDE

Definitions of "Family"

The conventional sociological definition of the term *family* runs something like "people related by marriage, blood, or adoption who share a common residence." But feminists and others charge that so narrowly defining family unjustly restricts individuals, relationships, and intimate units that do not conform to such a conservative vision.

Most anthropological and sociological definitions speak of nuclear families (parents and offspring) and extended families (families that include parents and offspring and other relatives or extended kin). Nuclear families arose with industrialization as the home became separated from work activities, including employment outside the home. Clearly, extended kin are a primary source of support for nuclear families. But even when extended families do not reside together, the nuclear family may rely on extended kin to assist with basic day-to-day activities such as child or elder care, and may rely emotionally and economically on family members outside the nuclear household. "In the Family," the reading that presents a short story by Cuban writer María Elena Llano, imagines extended relationships in novel ways. The story employs magical realism, a writing style where magical elements or illogical scenarios appear in otherwise realistic settings, to illustrate the bonds between generations (both living and deceased) who share the same family gatherings.

Generally social scientists specify four primary and culturally universal "social functions" served by the family. These functions include: (1) regulating sexuality; (2) bearing, rearing, and socializing children and providing care and comfort for adult members; (3) serving as a primary unit for the production and consumption of goods and services; and (4) providing a foundation for the social status of each individual in society. These functions reveal the links between women's reproductive and subsistence work in families. Women both bear and rear the next generation and contribute to the domestic and larger economy as workers. But around the world women work in the home and care for the physical and emotional needs of family members whether they also work outside the home or not.

Like many contemporary sociologists, especially the feminists among us, I prefer a definition that is more inclusive, if somewhat messier. I see the family as a collection of people related by blood, marriage, adoption, or other intimate bond, who often (but not always) share a common residence over a significant span of time. Certainly, legal, religious, and other definitions of marriage and family have critical effects on family and members' well-being (determining, for example, who can make medical decisions for another person in case the second person is unable to do so). But an important key to a socially meaningful definition of "family" is not limited to those legal, religious, or other formal definitions.

A DAY IN THE LIFE   **On Her Own** by *Mikhelle Gattone*

Glistening beads of sweat form on the dark skin of Chabela Aquino Argueta as she sleeps. In her dreams she revisits that moment in *her*/history when her grandmother and grandfather were massacred because of their ethnicity, and for their land. Fifty thousand Indian peasants were slaughtered during *la Matanza of 1932*. The government also sponsored "scorched earth" campaigns that destroyed traditional lands. *Being* Indian became outlawed in El Salvador. It is when the army dumps her grandmother's naked body into a ditch that Chabela sits straight up from the blanket on the earth floor. Chabela wipes away the sweat that covers her body. Looking left, then right, trying to focus she reaches to wake her daughters, Marianella, who will have to walk 40 minutes to reach the bus on her way to her manufacturing job in the city, and Dagoberta, who will need to prepare to sell homemade goods at the local market. Chabela had six children total; three are now dead. One son died in childbirth while she was living in a refugee camp in Honduras in 1982, and one of her daughters died at age three when she got sick from enteritis. The doctor told her that it was a waterborne disease. Between the disease and malnutrition, the child never had a chance of surviving. Through the pain she and her husband kept going and saved up to send their oldest son, Timoteo, to college. During his second year in college, Timoteo went with his father to locate an uncle who disappeared. They never came back, but Chabela found her son's body when searching the jails, morgues, and public body dumps on a Saturday five months ago. Chabela lets her youngest daughter, Toñita, sleep.

The five minutes it takes Chabela to brush her long, straight black hair, dress in her yellow *huipil* and long multicolored *corte* is the only time she has for herself. Chabela leaves the adobe home to gather the breakfast water from the stream. Getting water, grinding corn, and collecting firewood will fill up most of the day. Chabela's annual income of 4000.00 *colones* (about US$420) comes from farming, remittance from a niece who now lives in the United States, and her daughter's small wages. On the way back to the house from the stream, she stops at the communal pit latrine that her family shares with three other families. The four women each have 1.3 hectares of land where they grow corn, beans, sesame, and raise chickens. Chabela also has a plot where she cultivates tobacco, something her ancestors have always done. Chabela will use the tobacco for medicinal and spiritual purposes.

Chabela wakes her daughter, Toñita, for breakfast and then gets her dressed. The two of them feed the chickens and then Chabela takes her daughter to a teacher about two kilometers away who works with the local children for three hours a day. In return for her wisdom, Chabela offers food and other supplies, hoping to keep her in the rural areas. While Toñita learns to read and write, Chabela will head back home to *guaro* (distill and sell liquor) to make enough to buy some clothes for her daughters. She wishes she had the time to make the clothes like her mother did for her when she was a child.

Sangre, or Indian blood, runs through Chabela from her mother and father. Her missing husband's background is Chortí and Ladino. Chabela's mother was from the Nahua people and her father from the Lenca people. Chabela maintains some of the language of both Nahuatl and Ulua (Lenca). She learned a lot from her mother and misses her greatly. Her mother had made a living as a weaver, and Chabela remembers curling up at her feet and listening. Her other memories are in the fields with her father. Through him she studied the moon's path and how it affected planting and harvesting. She also gained knowledge about natural medicine, and also how to follow Catholicism. Her own children, like herself, speak both Spanish and their Native tongue, which helps them communicate with a variety of people.

In 1981 Chabela and her family fled for Mesa Grande Camp in Honduras where they stayed for four years. Her parents both passed away during these years. When leaving Chalatenango, they stayed a few nights in the El Hermitaño cave, a location where some of her mother's stories transpired. Chabela felt protected during the nights they spent in these caves. The only material item they took with them was a *molina* (corn grinder). In Honduras the children longed for the ritual of preparing and eating *pupusas* every Sunday after church. As a result, the family's first Sunday back in El Salvador in 1985 was marked by going to mass and then eating large amounts of tortillas, beans, chilies, and cheese. In 1994, two years after the end of conflicts in El Salvador, Chabela journeyed six hours to vote for the first time. Four years later Hurricane Mitch destroyed their home and meant they had to rebuild their hillside house for a second time in ten years.

One of her relatives tried to convince Chabela to head for the U.S. factories that had sprouted under the Central American Free Trade Agreement (*CAFTA*), but that was never really a possibility for her. Instead through the Environmental Program for El Salvador (*PAES*) she was able to secure a subsidy to improve her farm. Chabela is an *arrendatarios* (rents land) and she considers herself part of the *campesions* (organized peasantry). Clearing, fertilizing, working on the terrace, plowing the land, caring for the chickens and crops, and building fences are the typical daily routine. All of this combined with child-rearing and fighting for change are the focus of Chabela's daily work.

El Salvador's *Programa de Transferencia de Tierras* (*PTT*) has helped Chabela and her neighbors share their rented lands and practice cooperative agriculture. They work hard to use soil conservation practices in order to prevent land erosion. Each of these strong women will someday pass on this land and agricultural practices to their surviving children.

Marianella returns from her city job at 9 p.m. and cares for Toñita. Chabela continues to work the farm late into the evening. Soon Dagoberta, her second oldest daughter, returns from the market. Dagoberta made 3 *colones* from selling crops and homemade crafts. The money is divided between all of the women. Chabela returns to her modest home after collecting firewood and water for the evening meal of corn tortillas and beans. After dinner she puts Toñita to bed. The little girl always asks Chabela to read to her, but Chabela never learned to read. Instead she holds the worn book while she shows Toñita the pictures and makes up her own story. Tonight she tells a story that her mother told her when she was young: a story that her grandmother told her mother.

Finally, at 11p.m. Chabela places her own body on the earth. She looks forward to the five hours of sleep ahead of her. Sunrise will bring Saturday: a day when she wears a black (mourning) dress and white (seeking peace) scarf with other *CoMadres* (The Mothers and Relatives of Political, Disappeared, and Assassinated of El Salvador) to seek the truth about those who have disappeared during the political struggles. They also work to stop the *femicido* or rape that also leaves women dead, mutilated, and raising children alone because of the stigma that follows this violence. During these long days Chabela takes pictures to document what is really happening in Cuzcatlán (*El Salvador*). Maybe tomorrow will be the day she finds her husband.

LEARNING ACTIVITY **Gay and Lesbian Rights Around the World**

Visit Amnesty International's interactive map of LGBT rights around the world at http://www.amnestyusa. org/lgbt-human-rights/country-information/page.do?id=1106576. Select a country to find out the LGBT legal status in that country.

Did you know that while the United States allows heterosexual U.S. citizens and legal permanent residents to sponsor their spouses for immigration, gay and lesbian citizens and legal residents may not sponsor their partners for family-based immigration? Even if the American partner lives in a state that provides gay marriage and has married a partner in that state, the U.S. government does not recognize that relationship. Twenty-two countries recognize same-sex couples for immigration purposes: Australia, Belgium, Brazil, Canada, Denmark, Finland, France, Germany, Iceland, Israel, the Netherlands, New Zealand, Norway, Portugal, South Africa, Spain, Sweden, Switzerland, and the United Kingdom. To read stories of lesbian and gay couples affected by immigration policies, visit the Human Rights Campaign's Web site at http://www.hrc.org/issues/int_rights_immigration/int_rights_immigration_yourstory.asp.

We require a more inclusive definition: one that captures the myriad forms of family that exist across societies as well as within cultures. Such a definition takes into account the complexities of blended families and makes room for both cohabitation and marriage, single parents and their children. Such a definition also accommodates unions between gays, lesbians, bisexual, and transgender persons. This diversity is the topic of the reading by Carien Lubbe titled "Mothers, Fathers, or Parents: Same-gendered Families in South Africa." Addressing same-gendered families in South Africa, Lubbe discusses the ways the same-gendered couple as a family challenges the normative conceptions of the traditional model of a two-parent, heterosexual family. (Refer also to Susan Golombok's article on assisted reproduction among lesbian mothers, "Unusual Families," featured in chapter 6.) Lubbe makes the case that structural factors such as the gender composition of families and the division of parental labor matter less to families than the quality of relationships and care of children.

Increasingly, individuals and families cross geographic, cultural, and political borders. Contemporary definitions of family must also be informed by these transnational forces. Today, family members may migrate back and forth multiple times and in multiple waves across these borders.

Historically men have greatly outnumbered women migrating to a new country. Today, however, a "feminization" of international migration (Anthias and Lazaridis, 2000) is occurring as an increasing proportion of migrants worldwide are women. As discussed in chapter 9 on work and employment, the Philippines, Sri Lanka, and other areas now supply domestic and care workers to more affluent societies in increasing numbers. As a result, the number of women migrating across national borders now outnumbers the number of male migrants (Ehrenreich, Hochschild, and Russell, 2003). Obviously, this gender shift may have significant consequences for children left behind (Parrenas, 2005).

Economic globalization has resulted in more families living outside of their country of origin and living and working in new transfigurations. As a result, these families may face hardships and troubling issues of cultural identity associated with economic changes. They may also face political uncertainties in a rapidly globalizing world. New frontiers and

ACTIVIST PROFILE   **Shirin Ebadi**

Shirin Ebadi was born into a Muslim family of academics in Iran in 1947. She received a law degree in the late 1960s and became the first woman to serve as a judge in Iran. Following the Islamic Revolution in 1979, Ebadi and other women judges were removed from their posts because the new leadership believed that Islam does not allow women to be judges. She became a clerk in the court where she once presided. She and other women protested, and so the Justice Department promoted them to "expert" positions, but Ebadi could no longer tolerate the situation and so put in for an early retirement. Her initial application to practice law was turned down, and so she was housebound until she finally obtained her license and set up her own practice in 1992. During her time of unemployment, she wrote a number of books and articles, including *The Rights of the Child: A Study in the Legal Aspects of Children's Rights in Iran* and *History and Documentation of Human Rights in Iran*. Ebadi used her legal training to analyze Iranian domestic law and argue for human rights for women and children. In 1995, she cofounded the

Association for Support of Children's Rights. As a lawyer, she took on cases that challenged governmental violence and repression. She represented several journalists or their families who were accused in relation to freedom of expression. She also represented a mother who lost custody of her child as a result of Iran's child custody law. The child was found tortured to death. Her representation of the family of Ezzat Ebrahiminejad, a student who was killed in the 1999 protests at Tehran University, exposed links between vigilante groups and government officials and led to Ebadi's arrest in 2000. Over and over, Ebadi chose to represent vulnerable people in cases most lawyers feared to litigate. In 2001, she cofounded the Center for the Defense of Human Rights, and in 2002 she proposed a law to the Islamic Consultative Assembly to prohibit all forms of violence against children that was promptly ratified. In 2001, Ebadi was awarded the Rafto Human Rights Foundation Prize, and in 2003 she was named the winner of the Nobel Peace Prize. In 1999, she told the BBC, "Any person who pursues human rights in Iran must live with fear from birth to death, but I have learned to overcome my fear." The Nobel award committee cited Ebadi's focus on promoting human rights in Iran: "As a lawyer, judge, lecturer, writer, and activist, she has spoken out clearly and strongly in her country, Iran, and far beyond." While the Iranian government downplayed the honor, reformists in the country were elated. In 2006, she cofounded the Women's Nobel Initiative, along with other Nobel winners, Betty Williams, Mairead Corrigan Maguire, Wangari Maathai, Jody Williams, and Rigoberta Menchu Tum. The goal of the group is to strengthen the work being done around the world to further women's human rights.

www.nobelprize.org

www.bbc.co.uk/go/pr/fr/-/2/hi/middle_east/318992.stm

new global networks certainly strain the more conventional definitions of family roles and relationships (Bryceson and Vuorela, 2002).

Descent and Inheritance, Power and Authority

Systems of descent and inheritance legitimate the granting of power and authority to certain people in families. Descent and inheritance are grounded in complex cultural systems that include political-legal as well as economic, religious, and other institutional practices. Taken together, systems of descent and inheritance regulate not only the circumstances of marriage and family life, but also the basic order of society, from the family and neighborhood to the nation as a whole. In order to understand patterns of descent and inheritance, scholars must trace the political and cultural developments that construct male and female citizens with varying rights and responsibilities.

As anyone can attest who has tried to reconstruct a family tree or genogram (a pictorial display of a person's family relationships that visualizes hereditary patterns), patrilineage rules. Patrilineage—family descent and inheritance reckoned through the paternal or male line—is the most common pattern of descent across the world. Primogeniture, the practice of passing the lion's share of family assets to the firstborn son, is an example of patrilineage. As a result of these practices, women who marry and take the name of their husband's family often find their branch on the family tree sawed off behind them. Despite the fact that some women do keep the name of their family of origin and some choose other naming forms (such as adding the name of the husband's family, but retaining both names for herself, with or without a hyphen), most women take the name of their husband. These women might also find themselves invisible on the genogram. Very few husbands elect to either hyphenate or change a last name, and, even when a wife keeps her own name or uses some combination of her own and her husband's name, the children tend to receive the father's name.

An alternate form of reckoning descent and inheritance is matrilineage or through the maternal or female line. The far less common matrilineage is found most often in horticultural societies such as the Navajo of southwestern North America. However, often even matrilineal systems may reckon inheritance not mother to daughter, but rather through the mother's brother's line. Such a nominally matriarchal system thus perpetuates a patriarchal order, wherein adult men's power over women is preserved. Finally, bilateral systems involve recognizing descent and inheritance through both maternal and paternal lines. Industrialization encourages greater geographic mobility and smaller family size, deemphasizes extended family rights and responsibilities, and supports a tendency for bilateral systems. These are most likely found in Western, postindustrialized societies.

The mass migration of the Irish to North America in the late 1800s reveals the importance of patterns of descent and inheritance in shaping history. During that period Ireland (and much of the Western world) operated under systems of primogeniture. Under primogeniture, the oldest son inherited his father's property, leaving large numbers of widows and children destitute. Combined with repeated years of famine and political and economic oppression by colonial English authorities, primogeniture was a major catalyst for Irish immigration. Between 1856 and 1921 about half of the Irish immigrants to the United States were daughters. A large number of these immigrants were women whose families were unable to provide dowries for them. This reduced their ability to marry and jeopardized their livelihood (Miller, 1985). Likewise, the historical significance of wives as property or chattel to be bartered to enhance kin connections and sustain patriarchal power is illustrated in the case of the four daughters of the Count of Provençe (in today's southern France) in the thirteenth century. These sisters, Marguerite, Eleanor, Sanchia, and Beatrice, were married by their families to men who subsequently became kings of France, England, Germany, and Sicily. Those four queens, and other women throughout history, became major players in political, social, economic, and even religious contests, even while being embedded in deeply male-dominated societies (Goldstone, 2007).

Patterns of descent reflect the integration of gender into social systems of privilege. Norms about descent are not merely symbolic (as in "I take after my mother"), but are closely tied to patterns of inheritance: who gets what in terms of property, as well as who "counts" and enjoys autonomy and privilege. The most frequently observed system of inheritance is patriarchy (male domination). In patriarchal societies, oldest males, and especially fathers, are vested as heads of families and have power over women. Systems of matriarchy (female domination) where oldest females, and especially mothers, are vested with power over men as heads of families are, and have been, relatively rare. And even in those societies where women do have power over men in families, their authority tends not to extend across the full range of social institutions as is the norm in patriarchal families and societies where men control women in most facets of society. Western systems of family power and authority are best characterized as "modified patriarchy." In much of the Global North family power is slowly moving in the direction of egalitarianism, the sharing of power between women and men, in both families and society.

Descriptions of societies as patriarchal or matriarchal usually fail to capture the complexity of power relationships and distribution of resources within families. In most families throughout history and across the world, women's power in the family and in the broader society depends on their contributions to production, and explains why gender equity is more prevalent in pastoral and horticultural societies where women's role in production is strong. For example, the Ju/'hoansi (formerly known as the !Kung) people of Botswana and Namibia are a case where gender equity extends across a wide range of cultural institutions (Lee, 1984).

Traditionally, however, patrilineage operates in a symbiotic relationship with patriarchy as a defining organization of power in families and societies. Patrilineage and patriarchy interact as systems, one bolstering the other. In such systems, women exist primarily as social and legal property with little autonomy over their own lives. Contemporary societies where women's position in families leaves them vulnerable exist on every continent, from Indian girls sold into sexual slavery by fathers in order to earn dowries for younger sisters (documented by the United Nations Development Fund for Women, 2008), to a Saudi woman publicly executed following charges that she committed adultery. Her plight was portrayed in "Death of a Princess," what is perhaps the most sensational news story of the last quarter century (Frontline, 2008).

Global practices often disrupt traditional economic systems and facilitate the employment of women in transnational factories and other places that attract the cheap labor of women. Such practices often disrupt traditional families, as men are displaced as the chief economic providers. Although this disruption may in the short term give some women more power in families, in the long run such practices may destabilize communities and render those same communities—especially women and their children—more vulnerable in the global marketplace.

The Effect of the Food Crisis on Women and Their Families

Between March 2007 and March 2008, global food prices increased an average of 43 percent according to the IMF. During that period, wheat, soybean, corn and rice prices increased by 146 percent, 71 percent, 41 percent and 29 percent respectively.[1] World Bank also states in 9/09 food prices went up about 50 percent from a year ago. A spike in food prices can plunge households in developing countries even further into poverty, as families spend an average of 80 percent of their incomes on food, compared to the 15 to 18 percent that households spend in industrialized countries.[2]

Even before the food crisis hit, an estimated 7 out 10 of the world's hungry were women and girls.[3] Particularly vulnerable groups, such as young children and pregnant women, are now at risk of becoming permanently malnourished[4]—irreversibly impacting the next generation. Women are also more vulnerable to poverty, with less access to credit, property rights, education, training, good jobs, and farm inputs such as fertilizer and extension services, compared to men, making them one of the hardest hit groups in times of crisis. For example, women own less than 15% of land worldwide[5] and make up some 60% of the world's working poor, people who work but do not earn enough to lift themselves above the $1 per day poverty line.[6]

At the same time, investing in women is key to solving the food crisis. Rural women alone produce half of the world's food and 60% to 80% of the food in most developing countries, but receive less than 10% of credit provided to farmers.[7] Increasing women's access to the means of agricultural production, such as farming land or fertilizers, farm labor, credit and education, as well as decision-making authority within the household is crucial to guaranteeing food security and improving the nutritional status of children.[8] In some places, if women had the same access as men to land, seed, and fertilizer, agricultural productivity could increase by up to 20 percent. Further, decades of research and experience have shown that when women have extra income, they reinvest in their children's health and education, creating a positive cycle of growth for the entire family.

WOMEN AMONG THE HARDEST HIT BY THE FOOD CRISIS

As the majority of the working poor, informal workers, and farmers in developing countries, women who have already been living without secure food access and without social protections are among the hardest hit in the food crisis.

- In the Philippines, women make up the majority of those in the informal sector, some 27 million. "They have no social security, no protection and have to find small jobs that keep them afloat . . . workers in this sector are eating less and less these days."[9]
- 2.6 million people could face a food crisis in Niger in 2009, warned Association for Defense of Human Rights, and five of eight regions could expect to be affected. (Africanews: October 15, 2009). Pregnant and lactating mothers are among the groups considered most at risk, with more than 261,000 women in need of emergency care.[10] The increasingly poor nutritional status of pregnant and lactating women in Niger threatens to increase the already high rates of maternal and infant death and illness in regions hard-hit by the ongoing food crisis, according to reports from the Niger office of UNFPA.
- Female workers in Thailand, the world's largest rice exporter, are not immune from the hike in food prices either. "Women working in the informal sector are concerned about the rise in the cost of living. The cost of one meal with rice has almost doubled in some places."[11]
- In Malawi, as providers of food for their families, women are spending up to four nights at the state controlled grain marketing organization, the Agricultural Development and Marketing Corporation (ADMARC) in order to buy the mere 25 kgs of maize allowed per buyer, which has been rationed due to the food crisis. "This rationing is forcing women to spend most of their time making trips to ADMARC markets to buy maize as the 25 kgs is hopelessly inadequate for most families. . . . Women at the ADMARC market are at risk of attack as they often leave home at around 1 a.m. in the hope of making it to the queue in good time."[12]
- In extreme situations in Malawi, girls are being forced to drop out of school to help and some parents are reported to be forcing their daughters to be married in exchange for food. Sex work is also on the rise. "Desperate rural women and girls as young as 15, are indulging in commercial sex for survival thereby exposing themselves to HIV infection . . . Although sex work is illegal in Malawi, the sex workers said before the food crisis they used to charge K1000 (8 US dollars) for unprotected sex and K200 for sex with a condom. Due to the food crisis, worsening economic conditions, and competition for few clients their rates have plummeted to as low as K100 (81 US cents)."[13] "The crisis is having a devastating effect on maternal health in particular. Malnutrition renders pregnant women more susceptible to infection, miscarriage, and premature labor, and increases the likelihood that pregnant and lactating women who are HIV-positive will transmit the virus to their children."[14]

HOW WOMEN CAN BE PART OF THE SOLUTION TO THE FOOD CRISIS

In most places in developing countries, women produce the majority of the food and are responsible for feeding their families, and have done so with limited access to productive resources. Investing in women's ability to access these resources, meaningfully consulting with women in food aid and agricultural planning, and giving them voice in household decisions will be critical in stemming the current crisis and preventing another food emergency.

- "Women are often the guardians of traditional knowledge of seed varieties and crops that can be grown in less than ideal climatic conditions. More efforts should be made to learn from their specific knowledge and to build on it with information on new ways to achieve nutritional goals."[15]
- "Women's capacity to earn and control incomes is important in determining their ability to guarantee household food security."[16]
- "Not only are rural women among those most vulnerable to food shortages, but more importantly, they are the driving force behind African agriculture."[17]
- A recent FAO report indicates that "to stave off the worst effects of the global food crisis, it's important for all women—not just female farmers—to get better access to land, capital and technology. That's because an increasing number of households in developing countries are headed by women due to male emigration and HIV-AIDS."[18]
- "In comparative studies, households in which income was controlled by women demonstrated better levels of nutrition. Women tend to devote a greater share of their income to food and fuel as opposed to luxury items." [19]
- "The consequences of women's exclusion from household decisions can be as dire for children as they are for women themselves. According to a study conducted by the International Food Policy Research Institute, if men and women had equal influence in decision-making, the incidence of underweight children under three years old in South Asia would fall by up to 13 percentage points, resulting in 13.4 million fewer undernourished children in the region; in sub-Saharan Africa, an additional 1.7 million children would be adequately nourished."[20]

Source: Women Thrive Worldwide May 2008

[1.] USAID responds to global food crisis: May 2009.
[2.] "Rising Food Prices Hit Hungry and Poor People Hardest," Bread.org/learn/rising-food-prices, April 2008)
[3] UNIFEM and Women's Funding Network, "World Poverty Day 2007: Investing in Women—Solving the Poverty Puzzle." http://www.womenfightpoverty.org/docs/WorldPovertyDay2007_FactsAndFigures.pdf
[4] UN Department of Public Information, News and Media Division, New York. April 24 2008. "Press Conference by World Food Programme Executive Director on Food Price Crisis."
[5] ICRW. 2006. Reducing Women's and Girls' Vulnerability to HIV/AIDS by Strengthening Their Property and Inheritance Rights (Information bulletin).
[6] ILO, 2006 quoted by UNIFEM and Women's Funding Network in World Poverty Day 2007: Investing in Women—Solving the Poverty Puzzle, Facts & Figures.
[7] "Gender and food security: agriculture." FAO Web site brief. http://www.fao.org/gender/en/agri-e.htm as cited by: USAID. March 2003. Women's Property and Inheritance Rights: Improving Lives in Changing Times.
[8] IFPRI (International Food Policy Research Institute). 2002. Reaching sustainable food security for all by 2020. Getting the priorities and responsibilities right. Washington, D.C.: IFPRI
[9] Macan-Marker, Marwaan. "ASIA: Food Crisis Adds to Women's Burden." Inter Press Service (IPS) News Agency. April 29, 2008. http://ipsnews.net/news.asp?idnews=42162
[10] UNFPA. "Niger Food Crisis Especially Dangerous for Pregnant Women." Press Release. 24 August 2005. http://www.unfpa.org/news/news.cfm?ID=660
[11] Macan-Marker, Marwaan. "ASIA: Food Crisis Adds to Women's Burden." Inter Press Service (IPS) News Agency. April 29, 2008. http://ipsnews.net/news.asp?idnews=42162
[12] Phalula, Irene. "Malawi Food Crisis Hits Women Hardest." Genderlinks via AfricaFiles. 8 December 2005. http://www.africafiles.org/article.asp?ID=10378&ThisURL=./gender.asp&URLName=Gender
[13] Ibid.
[14] Del Vecchio, David, "Experts Plan Reproductive Health Response as HIV/AIDS Compounds Food Crisis in Southern Africa." UNFPA. 26 February 2003. http://www.unfpa.org/news/news.cfm?ID=185
[15] Hansen-Kuhn, Karen. "Women and Food Crises: How US Food Aid Policies Can Better Support Their Struggles—A Discussion Paper." Actionaid: Washington, DC. http://www.actionaidusa.org/assets/pdfs/food_rights/report_women_and_food_crisis_paper300.pdf
[16] Ibid.
[17] Ibid.
[18] Rossi, Andrea and Yianna Lambrou. "Gender and Equity Issues in Liquid Biofuels Production: Minimizing the Risks to Maximize the Opportunities." FAO: Rome, 21 April 2008. ftp://ftp.fao.org/docrep/fao/010/ai503e00.pdf as cited by: Ms. Magazine. "UN Official Says Women Hold Key to Solving Global Food Crisis." Feminist Majority Foundation: May 5, 2008.http://www.msmagazine.com/news/uswirestory.asp?id=10983
[19] Pan American Health Organization. "Fact Sheet: Women, Health, & Development Program." World Health Organization. http://www.paho.org/english/ad/ge/foodsecurity.PDF
[20] UNICEF. The State of the World's Children 2007. http://www.unicef.org/sowc07/. Pg.16.

Finally, as more women gain educations and earn their own incomes, they have less dependence on male breadwinners. A common belief is that households headed by women are poorer than those controlled by men. However, as the reading by Sylvia Chant, "Female Headship and the 'Feminization of Poverty'" suggests, a broader concept of poverty that focuses on social deprivation shows that women may often be better off without male partners. Chant hopes to debunk the myth of the close relationship between female headship and poverty.

Son Preference

Patrilineal systems that strive to keep wealth within families are most likely to express preference for sons. Daughters in these systems are expected to marry and their offspring is reckoned through the father's (her husband's) line with any inheritance following the father and not the mother. As a result, daughters in societies with patrilineage are more dispensable. These daughters may be seen as just another mouth to feed before they leave the family. Strong son preference ensures that daughters have a lower status in families and encourages early marriage. Families with strong daughter preference are exceedingly rare, although Western parents often desire daughters to balance the gender of siblings within families.

Societies with strong son preference range across the world and include parts of the Middle East, South Asia, and (most notably, due to the widespread publicity given its one-child policy) China. Although these preferences may involve not only desiring male offspring and providing better care for male children, as discussed in the previous chapter, they also extend to female infanticide, abandonment and neglect, and sex-selective abortion. In such societies boys receive better nutrition, physical, and social psychological care, and, ultimately, more wealth, power, and prestige in society (Sheng, 2004; Yi, 2002).

As discussed in chapter 3, baby boys are often nursed longer than their sisters and girl children receive less food as they grow, especially in societies with chronic food shortages. In many societies, men and boys eat first and women and girl children eat what remains. These practices result in dramatic gender disparities in the types and quantity of food and quality of nutrition available to women and their children. They leave women weaker, more lethargic, and disease prone, and they reduce their life expectancy. However, attitudes may be changing. For example, in South Korea one popular educational slogan reads: "One daughter raised well is worth 10 sons!" As economic transitions resulted in an industrial and then a postindustrial boom, aging parents in South Korea found their incomes rising, while families found sons more geographically mobile, and therefore less likely to remain close to the parental home. Most significantly, as employment opportunities for women improved, and as married daughters were less bound to care for their husbands' families and more available to care for their own parents, attitudes toward having daughters have shifted in directions more favorable to daughters (Sang-Hun, 2007).

MARRIAGE

Marriage is a contract in most cultures, defined by either tribal laws or the laws of modern nation-states and recognized by the public. A ritualistic signing of the contract in the presence of witnesses and/or religious or civil authorities is part of most wedding ceremonies. For example, in a temple wedding in India the officiating Brahman fills out the temple marriage register that has been signed by the groom and witnessed by at least one other important person, such as a village president. Norms and values associated with families worldwide are reinforced in a variety of marriage rituals (such as the "white wedding" or blood-stained sheets symbolizing the virginity of the bride, but not the groom, and the linguistic elaborations on female, but not male, virginity in Hindu texts). However, as cultures collide on a global scale, traditional practices may become out of step with laws in nation-states. For example, Hmong families settling in the Twin Cities of Minneapolis and St. Paul found themselves deviating from Minnesota laws that forbade early marriage and which give wives and daughters rights and autonomy within marriage. Marriage by the senior year in high school has not been uncommon among Hmong women whose families have settled in Minnesota or Wisconsin (Hutchinson and McNall, 1994). Sometimes, the collision of values results in modifications of traditional practices to conform to the dominant society. Such changes are illustrated in the reading "The Bride's Voice" by Irit Koren. In this article Koren shares her research with traditional Orthodox Jewish women living in Israel who oppose the traditional marriage ritual. She discusses the ways they utilize different strategies of interpretation that includes seeing the ritual act as merely symbolic and/or creating new meanings for the ritual, as well as making specific changes to the ritual itself.

Women and men are expected to marry in most societies around the world, as marriage substantially enhances both economic and social survival. As the reading "Old Maid," a poem by Philippine poet Vivian N. Limpin illustrates, expectations for marriage are normalized in traditional societies, and adult females who reach a certain age and are still unmarried are often pitied or regarded as cursed. Indeed, in patriarchal systems with patrilineage and a vested interest in keeping wealth within the male line, girls are married early to cement alliances and/or minimize their drain on resources. The consequences of early marriage mean that girls are effectively swallowed up by their husband's families. Their fate is often resigned to child bearing and producing heirs (in the case of the most advantaged families) or workers (in the case of the least advantaged families) and to providing domestic labor to the advantage of the husband or extended family.

As discussed in other chapters, girls' early marriage is associated with lower levels of education and literacy, as well as higher fertility rates and, in the case of girls who conceive at the youngest ages, higher maternal and infant mortality. Allison Ford discusses these issues in the reading on child brides in Yemen titled "Too Young to Marry" where poverty and the low status of girls support early marriage for girls. Many countries do have laws against child marriage, but in many regions of Africa and South Asia these laws have no accountability or are openly flaunted, or the marriages are traditional or religious marriages rather than registered legal unions. Although in patriarchal societies girls and women have few rights to dissolve the marriage and few prospects for survival if they were to refuse, this reading discusses a 10-year-old wife who was the first child bride to petition for divorce in Yemen.

Students in my family sociology classes are often surprised to learn that the marriage ring—that symbol of "never ending love" (or so the jewelry marketers tell us)—was, in fact originally a symbol of the transfer of authority over the woman from her father to her husband. Throughout much of history and across most societies, while couples may have developed deep feelings of attachment to one another, romantic love was never an acceptable guiding principal in mate selection. Rather, mates were most often selected by the elders of one's family or community in ways that would maximize the economic, political, and social assets of the family and kinship group as well as the community or society generally. In this way, Western expectations of love as the basis for marriage are culturally specific. In many parts of the world (including Western industrial societies in some situations), marriage is an economic transaction that binds individuals and kin in economic contracts.

In general, the more the extended family or community is vested in a marriage, the less control the individual members of the marriage have over their marital destinies. When divorce will strain or sever hard-won economic, political, or other ties between two families, clans, kingdoms, or other social groups, divorce is forbidden or strongly discouraged. Rates of divorce are highest in societies like the United States where couples marry "for love" and to pursue individual over familial collectivist interests, and when the respective families have little economic or other explicit investment in the marriage. Not surprisingly, divorce rates rise as a society becomes industrialized, particularly when women are employed (South, 2001).

Marriage may occur between one woman and one man (monogamy), but in some parts of the world marriage with more than one spouse (polygamy) is accepted and even desirable. However, more precisely, the marriage of one man to multiple wives (polygyny) is the most common form of polygamy. In some societies where polygyny is allowed, only well-to-do men can afford to have more than one wife, particularly if each wife requires maintenance of a separate household. In a practical sense, polygyny helps ensure the births of large numbers of children required for the survival of agrarian cultures with high infant mortality rates. Traditions in which a man inherits his brothers' wives (levirate marriage) may ensure that widows are taken care of in societies where women's status is low. Yenni Kwok focuses on polygyny in a changing world in the reading "Indonesian Feminists Confront Polygyny."

Throughout most of North Africa, polygyny is allowed and basically accepted, although, in actual practice, the frequency of polygyny varies (Schnier and Hintmann, 2001). Similarly, although the traditional form of Islam may permit as many as four wives, polygyny is frowned upon in more secularized states such as Syria, Egypt, Morocco, and Lebanon, and is illegal in Tunisia and Turkey. In Libya written permission is required of the first wife if her husband wishes to marry other wives (Khalidi, 1989). In North America, polygyny was officially discontinued by the Mormon Church of Jesus Christ of Latter-day Saints (LDS) in 1890, although it is still practiced (illegally) by some members of the Fundamentalist LDS church not recognized by the mainstream branch (White and White, 2005).

The marriage of one wife to multiple husbands (polyandry) is quite rare. Not only is women's status lower than men's in most societies, but polyandry limits population growth. A wife can only be pregnant once at a time, regardless of how many husbands are involved. But one man can impregnate multiple wives over the same period. Fraternal polyandry allows multiple brothers to marry the same wife. Just as primogeniture maintained family estates intact over generations by permitting only one heir (oldest son) per generation, fraternal polyandry also accomplishes this. Fraternal polyandry also keeps all the brothers together with just one wife, insuring only one set of heirs per generation. No known communities currently practice polyandry involving unrelated males, although that form was practiced in such regions as Tibet and sub-Saharan Africa.

Beyond general kinship patterns, age at marriage and subsequent subordination of brides to husbands clearly demonstrate the extent to which broader societal norms and values come to be reinforced and played out in everyday family life and domestic relationships. Dowry (in which a prospective bride comes to her new husband with land, livestock, or other material assets) and bride price (in which the prospective groom must extend material assets to the bride's family) are practices that underscore the transfer of property from one family to another (usually from the bride's father to her new husband).

Globalization is expanding the range of options and consequences for women and families through deeper and broader systems of mate selection. Often abetted by new computer-assisted technologies, highly profitable marriage brokerages have sprung up in places like Russia and parts of Southeast Asia. In those societies, the number of women desiring marriage far exceeds the number of men desirable for marriage. In the United States alone, over 250 marriage bureaus and catalogs annually advertise an estimated 150,000 women available for marriage across national borders (Seager, 2008). This number of international marriage brokers is exploding worldwide. During 1995, Germany reported only 1 in 25 marriages between a native-born German citizen and an *Ausländerinnen oder Ausländer betreiligt* (i.e., someone holding a foreign passport). By 1999, just four years later, that proportion had grown to 1 in 6. Among immigrants to the United States, one-fourth of men and almost half of all women enter the country as marriage migrants (Beck-Gernsheim, 2003).

In addition, as North American women increasingly decline to perform subservient roles, some men have turned to marriage brokers to secure a bride who meets their more traditional gender expectations. Although numbers of "mail order brides" are unknown and they make up a very small percentage of marriages, they reflect a troubling effect of globalization on marital and family practices. In such marriages, economic inequality, national inequality, and gender inequality confound the status and quality of life for women in these marriages. Such mail order brides are then at even greater risk for emotional, physical, and sexual violence.

LEARNING ACTIVITY **Mail Order Brides**

AT THE MAIL-ORDER BRIDE WAREHOUSE

Women's eNews/At the Mail-Order Bride Warehouse, Kirk Anderson Commentoon.

With the growth of the Internet, access to women as mail order brides has proliferated. Use a Web search engine and type in mail order brides. Visit some of the sites your search engine locates. What do you notice about these sites? How do they depict the women available for marriage by mail? Why do you think men find the idea of mail order brides appealing? How do you think these women might be especially vulnerable to exploitation and abuse by their husbands? Do you think marriage brokerage is a form of trafficking in women? Or do you see it as a legitimate way for men to find wives? Why or why not?

In 2006, the U.S. Congress passed a mail order bride law to protect women from abuse. The law requires extensive background checks for men wanting to use a mail order bride service. Some conservatives have argued that the law brands all American men as abusers. Other critics have argued that the law abridges free speech rights. Research this law, known as the International Marriage Broker Regulation Act of 2005. What do you think? Is this law good for women? Does it abridge men's rights? What do you think is the solution?

Indeed, violence within marriage and domestic partnerships is common, both in North America and worldwide. As a 2008 World Health Organization (WHO) study of almost 24,000 women in ten countries showed, women report suffering violence at the hands of spouses or intimate "partners" at a low of 15 percent in Yokohama, Japan, and a high of 71 percent in rural Ethiopia. Violence against women and girls occurring in families is a window to understanding women's low status in society. Such violence illustrates their vulnerability and has serious consequences for their physical, sexual, and emotional health. The next chapter focuses on this issue of gendered violence and explores the causes of male violence and its effects on women's lives.

In many patriarchal societies where violence against women by family members is rampant, any attempt of a woman to remove herself from a marriage that is dangerous, or even unfulfilling, is usually futile. Very often her family of origin does not want to (or cannot) reabsorb the burden of another person, and cultural and economic factors restrict her ability to secure an independent livelihood for herself and her children. Further, leaving a husband often has meant leaving one's children behind. In most societies throughout history, the presumptive parent with authority over children was/is the father, not the mother. Still today, in many parts of the world, the wife refusing to engage in sexual relations with an HIV-infected husband, or the wife seeking to leave a husband who abuses her or her children, has few or no options. Her residence and that of her children is often bound to her husband's family or village. In sum, a patriarchal society offers women little opportunity to control their own physical safety or future destiny, or even that of their children.

STRATEGIES TO IMPROVE WOMEN'S STATUS IN FAMILIES

Patterns of descent and inheritance, early marriage, and subordination across time and space have worked to reinforce women's low status in society generally. However, families worldwide are undergoing dramatic changes. Globalization and other transnational forces have disrupted families but provided opportunities for women's employment. In many places, particularly in the Global North, families are becoming more diverse in terms of structure, more flexible with respect to parenting and other roles, and more egalitarian with regard to gender roles (Silverstein and Auerbach, 2005). Mirroring the complex challenges faced by families worldwide where practices are embedded in disparate economic, as well as political, cultural, and other social factors, the responses to these challenges are also complex with strategies at both global and local levels. Coordinated efforts between these levels have the best chance for calling attention to injustices and inciting action to change the status of women and girls in families worldwide.

Throughout, *Women Worldwide: Transnational Feminist Perspectives on Women* describes social policies that shape the quality of life for women. Some of the most far reaching (and best funded) initiatives targeting women and their families are international efforts that continue to emphasize the needs of families in an increasingly transnational, global world. For example, in 2003 in recognition of the 10th anniversary of the 1994 declaration of the International Year of the Family, the United Nations (UN) affirmed six objectives targeting the well-being of families around the world. These objectives included the following: (1) increase awareness of family issues among governments and in the private sector; (2) strengthen abilities of national institutions to formulate, implement, and monitor family policies; (3) stimulate efforts to respond to problems both affecting and affected by families; (4) undertake reviews and assessments of the conditions and needs of families; (5) enhance effectiveness and generate new family programs at local, national, and regional levels; and (6) improve collaboration among national and international organizations that support families.

The UN Commission on the Status of Women monitors the status of women and their families worldwide, providing what one scholar has called "a free space of feminist activism"

Global Survey: Husbands Do Less Housework by *Jennifer Warner*

It may not come as a shock to most couples, but a new study shows that men, especially married men, do less housework than women.

Researchers surveyed 17,000 men and women in 27 countries, including the United States. The survey shows that men did an average of about nine and a half hours of housework per week compared with an average of more than 21 hours per week among women.

But even more noteworthy, researchers say, is that married men did significantly less housework than men who lived with their girlfriends but were not married.

Those results suggest that marriage as an institution may have an effect on how people behave in a relationship.

"Marriage as an institution seems to have a traditionalizing effect on couples—even couples who see men and women as equal," researcher Shannon Davis of George Mason University says in a news release.

MEN DON'T DO DISHES

In the study, published in the *Journal of Family Issues,* researchers compared the division of household labor among married and cohabiting (unmarried) couples.

The survey was conducted in Australia, Austria, Brazil, Bulgaria, Chile, Czech Republic, Denmark, Finland, France, Germany, Hungary, Ireland, Israel, Latvia, Mexico, the Netherlands, New Zealand, Norway, Poland, Portugal, Russia, Slovakia, Spain, Sweden, Switzerland, the United Kingdom, and the United States.

Overall, men reported performing 32 percent of total housework and women reported 74 percent. The results were based on how much housework each participant said they did, and only one member of each couple was questioned.

Men and women in Sweden, Norway, and Finland reported the most equitable division of housework, and these countries had the highest percentage of cohabiting couples in the study.

Researchers say couples with an egalitarian view of gender are more likely to share housework equally, but the results showed that even couples who viewed each other as equal partners did not share the housework equally.

Instead, the results suggest that marriage changes the division of household labor among couples.

"Our research suggests that couples across many countries are influenced by similar factors when deciding how to divide the housework," says Davis. "It's the way the society has defined what being married means, the institution itself, that affects behavior."

(Hawkesworth, 2006, p. 112). Other organizations, such as the Organization for Economic Co-operation and Development (OECD, 2002) and supranational government bodies like the European Commission of the European Union are advancing work-family balance. Efforts include family-friendly policies around child-related leave, childcare, and tax policies that can benefit not only child development and gender equity, but also family economics (European Commission, 2006). Across the world, pressure from international political bodies and transnational feminist networks at the national and local levels has had some effect.

To name but a few examples, Vietnam has banned practices such as polygyny and dowry. Chad has made sexual violence, including female genital cutting, a crime. Jordan has enacted laws allowing women to initiate divorce (Seager, 2008).

Despite these efforts, international organizations have mixed records with regard to advancing the well-being of women and their families. For example, the International Monetary Fund (IMF) and the World Bank have facilitated structural adjustment policies (SAPs) that, as discussed in other chapters, affect services to women and families. They have also endorsed aid and funding contingent on national policies that limit family allowances, maternity leaves, and childrearing assistance (Haney, 2003). Such requirements by the IMF, the World Bank, and other organizations force developing nations to choose between funds to advance macroeconomic development and programs that provide social safety nets and help empower women. As a result, developing nations are often faced with the need to conform to IMF and World Bank requirements, while placing families at greater risk.

As I argue in *Global Families* (Karraker, 2008, p. 173), "when it comes to social action, one size cannot fit all." Liu (2007) has similarly compared women's movements in China and India and found that effective movements build upon international (and, I would argue, national) agendas by taking into account the unique political and social context of each community through development of grassroots, local efforts. For example, *Forum Mulher* (Women's Forum) in Mozambique is an organization attempting to work at a more local level to improve the status of women and their families. Through Forum Mulher women network with other organizations, including academic, political groups, government representatives, NGOs, political groups, and trade unions to tackle issues like the collateral effects of war visited on women and children (Edelman, 2006). From the presence of Argentine women in the Plaza de Mayo (walking in vigil for their husbands and sons, sisters and daughters, and, eventually even some of their own who had been kidnapped by the military government) to women in Ahmedabad in western India organizing to improve the conditions of their self-employment by establishing fair credit (Ward and Edelstein, 2006), examples of women's activism to strengthen families abound.

Global forces such as immigration are changing the quality of gender relations in Bosnia (Al-Ali, 2002), Ghana (van Dijk, 2002), Somalia (Abdi, 2006, 2007), Turkey (Erel, 2002), and other societies. Although globalization often results in depreciated family status for women, it may provide opportunities for women's autonomy within families. Still,

LEARNING ACTIVITY   **The Universal Declaration of Human Rights and the Family**

Learn about the Universal Declaration of Human Rights at http://www.un.org/events/humanrights/ udhr60/declaration.shtml. Follow the link on this page to read the document in its entirety.

Then, visit the Web site Know Your Rights at http://www.knowyourrights2008.org. Click on the link to take the quiz to test your knowledge of human rights. Then click on the link to the Universal Human Rights Index. Under "Access to Annotations by Right," click on "Fundamental freedoms; right to private life; rights related to marriage and family." Then click on "Marriage and Family." Select various countries to learn more about marriage and family rights in those nations. Do you notice any patterns? How are issues of marriage and family rights gendered?

equality and justice have a long way to go. The future quality of life of women and girls in families will continue to be determined by consciousness of the impact of globalization on families and their members, coupled with effective social development at both transnational and local levels. Hence, an understanding of macrosociological forces at work on families—patrilineage and patriarchy, son preference and marriage patterns—is critical to any feminist agenda regarding female status in families.

REFERENCES

Abdi, C. M. (2006). Diasporic lives and threatened identities: Gender struggles of Somalis in America. Ph.D. dissertation, Department of Sociology, University of Sussex, Brighton, U.K.

Abdi, C. M. (2007). Convergence of civil war and the Religious Right: Re-imagining Somali women. *Signs: Journal of Women in Culture and Society, 32*(4), 83–207.

Al-Ali, N. (2002). Loss of status or new opportunities? Gender relations and transnational ties among Bosnia refugees. In D. F. Bryceson and U. Vuorela (Eds.), *The transnational family: New European frontiers and global networks* (pp. 83–102). Oxford, U.K.: Berg.

Anonymous. (1968). The mother's song [trans. Peter Freuchen]. In G. Summerfield (Ed.), *Voices: An anthology of poetry and pictures: the third book* (p. 12). Hosmondsworth, U.K.: Penguin.

Anthias, F. and Lazaridis, G. (2000). Introduction: Women on the move in Southern Europe. In F. Anthias and G. Lazaridis (Eds.), *Gender and migration in Southern Europe: Women on the move* (pp. 1–13). Oxford, U.K.: Berg.

Beck-Gernsheim, E. (2003). Household-migrant women and marriage-migrant women in a globalizing world. In E. Beck-Gernsheim, Butler, J., and Puigvert, L. (Eds.), *Women and social transformation* (pp. 61–80). New York: Peter Lang.

Bryceson, D. F. and Vuorela, U. (Eds.). (2002). Transnational families in the twenty-first century. In D. F. Bryceson and U. Vuorela (Eds.), *The transnational family: New European frontiers and global networks* (pp. 3–30). Oxford, U.K.: Berg.

Edelman, M. W. (2006). *The Global women's action network for children.* Child Watch™ Column. Retrieved December 26, 2006, from http://childrensdefense.org/site/News2?page-NewsArticle&id-7010.

Ehrenreich, B., Hochschild, A., and Russell, A. (2003) *Global woman: Nannies, maids, and sex workers in the new economy.* New York: Metropolitan.

Erel, U. (2002). Reconceptualizing motherhood: Experiences of migrant women from Turkey living in Germany. In D. F. Bryceson and U. Vuorela (Eds.), *The transnational family: New European frontiers and global networks* (pp. 127–146). Oxford, UK: Berg.

European Commission. (2006). *Gender equality.* Retrieved August 8, 2006, from http://ec.europa.eu/employment_soci/gender_equality/gender_mainstreaming/gender_ove.

Frontline. (2008). Death of a Princess. Retrieved November 10, 2008, from http://www. pbs.org/wgbh/pages/frontline/shows/princess/.

Goldstone, N. (2007). *Four queens: The Provençal sisters who ruled Europe.* New York: Viking.

Haney, L. (2003). Welfare reform with a familial face: Reconstituting state and domestic relations in post-socialist Eastern Europe. In L. Haney and L. Pollard (Eds.), *Families in a new world: Gender, politics and state development in a global context* (pp. 159–178). New York: Routledge.

Hawkesworth, M. E. (2006). *Globalization and feminist activism.* Lanham, MA: Rowman and Littlefield.

Hutchinson, R. and McNall, M. (1994). Early marriage in a Hmong cohort. *Journal of Marriage and the Family, 56*(1), 570–590.

Hutton, W. and Giddens, A. (Eds). (2001). *On the edge: Living with global capitalism.* London: Vintage.

Karraker, M. W. (2008). *Global families.* Boston: Allyn and Bacon.

Khalidi, M. S. (1989). Divorce in Libya. *Journal of Comparative Family Studies, 20*(1), 124.

Lee, R. (1984). *The Dobe !Kung of Nyae Nyae.* New York: Holt, Rinehart and Winston.

Liu, D. (2007). When do national movements adopt or reject international agenda? A comparative analysis of the Chinese and Indian women's movements. *American Sociological Review, 71*(6), 921–942.

Miller, K. A. (1985). *Emigrants and exiles: Ireland and the Irish exodus to North America.* New York: Oxford University Press.

Organization for Economic Co-operation and Development (OECD). (2002). *Babies and bosses: Reconciling work and family Life (vol. 1). Australia, Denmark and the Netherlands.* Paris: OECD.

Parrenas, R. S. (2005). *Children of the global migration: Transnational families and gendered woes.* Stanford: Stanford University Press.

Population Reference Bureau. (2008). Women. Retrieved November 10, 2008, from http: //www.prb.org/Educators/TeachersGuides/HumanPopulation/Women.aspx.

Sang-Hun, C. (2007). Where Boys Were Kings, a Shift Toward Baby Girls. *New York Times.* Retrieved December 23, 2007, from http://www.nytimes.com/2007/12/23/world/asia/ 23skorea.html?_r=1&oref=slogin.

Schnier, D. and Hintmann, B. (2001). An analysis of polygyny in Ghana: The perpetuation of gender-based inequality in Africa. *Georgetown Journal of Gender and the Law, 2*(3), 795–840.

Seager, J. (2008). *The Penguin atlas of women in the world.* New York: Penguin.

Sheng, X. (2004). Chinese families. In B. N. Adams and J. Trost (Eds.), *Handbook of world families,* (pp. 99–128). Thousand Oaks, CA: Sage.

Silverstein, L. B. and Auerbach, C. F. (2005). (Post)modern families. In J. L. Roopnarine and U. P. Gielen (Eds.), *Families in global perspectives* (p. 33–47). Boston: Allyn and Bacon.

South, S. J. (2001). Time-dependent effects of wives' employment on marital dissolution. *American Sociological Review, 66*(2), 226–243.

United Nations Development Fund for Women (UNIFEM). (2008). "UNIFEM and Trafficking." Retrieved November 10, 2008, from (http://www.unifem.org.in/Human%20Rights%20link%202.htm).

Van Dijk, R. (2002). Religion, reciprocity, and restructuring family responsibility in the Ghanaian pentecostal diaspora. In D. F. Bryceson and U. Vuorela (Eds.), *The transnational family: New European frontiers and global networks* (pp. 173–196). Oxford, UK: Berg.

Ward, M. and Edelstein, M. (2006). *A world full of women* (4th ed.). Boston: Allyn & Bacon.

White, O. K., Jr. and White. D. (2005). Polygamy and Mormon identity. *Journal of American Culture*, *28*(2), 165–177.

World Health Organization (WHO). (2008). *WHO multi-country study on women's health and domestic violence against women: Initial results on prevalence, health outcomes, and women's responses.* Geneva, Switzerland: World Health Organization. Retrieved March 3, 2008, from http://www.who.int/gender/violence/who_multicountry_study/en/

Yi, Z. (2002). A demographic analysis of family households in China, 1982–1995. *Journal of Comparative Family Studies, 33*(1), 1–71.

SUGGESTION FOR FURTHER READING

Covell, K. and Howe, R. B. (2008). *Children, families and violence: Challenges for children's rights.* New York: Jessica Kingsley Publishers.

Ling, H. (2007). *Voices of the heart: Asian American women in immigration, work, and family.* Kirksville, MO: Truman State University.

Maternowska, M. C. (2006). *Reproducing inequities: Poverty and the politics of population in Haiti.* Piscataway, NJ: Rutgers University Press.

Palriwala, R. and Uberoi, P. eds. (2008) *Marriage, migration, and gender.* Thousand Oaks, CA: Sage.

Polikoff, N. D. (2008). *Beyond (straight and gay) marriage: Valuing all families under the law.* Boston: Beacon Press.

Tucker, J. E. (2008). *Women, family, and gender in Islamic law.* New York: Cambridge University Press.

In the Family

María Elena Llano (1990)

When my mother found out that the large mirror in the living-room was inhabited, we all gradually went from disbelief to astonishment, and from this to a state to contemplation, ending up by accepting it as an everyday thing.

The fact that the old, spotted mirror reflected the dear departed in the family was not enough to upset our life style. Following the old saying of "Let the house burn as long as no one sees the smoke," we kept the secret to ourselves since, after all, it was nobody else's business.

At any rate, some time went by before each one of us would feel absolutely comfortable about sitting down in our favorite chair and learning that, in the mirror, that same chair was occupied by somebody else. For example, it could be Aurelia, my grandmother's sister (1939), and even if cousin Natalie would be on my side of the room, across from her would be the almost forgotten Uncle Nicholas (1927). As could have been expected, our departed reflected in the mirror presented the image of a family gathering almost identical to our own, since nothing, absolutely nothing in the living-room—the furniture and its arrangement, the light, etc.—was changed in the mirror. The only difference was that on the other side it was them instead of us.

I don't know about the others, but I sometimes felt that, more than a vision in the mirror, I was watching an old worn-out movie, already clouded. The deceaseds' efforts to copy our gestures were slower, restrained, as if the mirror were not truly showing a direct image but the reflection of some other reflection.

From the very beginning I knew that everything would get more complicated as soon as my cousin Clara got back from vacation. Because of her boldness and determination, Clara had long given me the impression that she had blundered into our family by mistake. This suspicion had been somewhat bolstered by her being one of the first women dentists in the country. However, the idea that she might have been with us by mistake went away as soon as my cousin hung up her diploma and started to embroider sheets beside my grandmother, aunts and other cousins, waiting for a suitor who actually did show up but was found lacking in one respect or another—nobody ever really found out why.

Once she graduated, Clara became the family oracle, even though she never practiced her profession. She would prescribe painkillers and was the arbiter of fashion; she would choose the theater shows and rule on whether the punch had the right amount of liquor at each social gathering. In view of all this, it was fitting that she take one month off every year to go to the beach.

That summer when Clara returned from her vacation and learned about my mother's discovery, she remained pensive for a while, as if weighing the symptoms before issuing a diagnosis. Afterwards, without batting an eye, she leaned over the mirror, saw for herself that it was true, and then tossed her head, seemingly accepting the situation. She immediately sat by the bookcase and craned her neck to see who was sitting in the chair on the other side. "Gosh, look at Gus" was all she said. There in the very same chair the mirror showed us Gus, some sort of godson of Dad, who after a flood in his home town came to live with us and had remained there in the somewhat ambiguous character of adoptive poor relation. Clara greeted him amiably with a wave of the hand, but he seemed busy, for the moment, with something like a radio tube and did not pay attention to her. Undoubtedly, the mirror people weren't going out of their way to be sociable. This must have wounded Clara's self-esteem, although she did not let on.

Naturally, the idea of moving the mirror to the dining-room was hers. And so was its sequel: to bring the mirror near the big table, so we could all sit together for meals.

In spite of my mother's fears that the mirror people would run away or get annoyed because of the fuss, everything went fine. I must admit it was comforting to sit every day at the table and see so many familiar faces, although some of those from the other side were distant relatives, and others, due to their lengthy—although unintentional—absence, were almost strangers. There were about twenty of us sitting at the table every day, and even if their gestures and movements seemed more remote than ours and their meals a little washed-out, we generally gave the impression of being a large family that got along well.

At the boundary between the real table and the other one, on this side, sat Clara and her brother Julius. On the other side was Eulalia (1949), the second wife of Uncle Daniel, aloof and indolent in life, and now the most distant of anyone on the other side. Across from her sat my godfather Sylvester (1952), who even though he was not a blood relative was always a soul relation. I was sad to see that Sylvester had lost his ruddiness, for he now looked like a faded mannequin, although his full face seemed to suggest perfect health. This pallor did not suit the robust Asturian, who undoubtedly felt a bit ridiculous in these circumstances.

For a while we ate all together, without further incidents or problems. We mustn't forget Clara, however, whom we had allowed to sit at the frontier between the two tables, the equator separating what was from what was not. Although we paid no attention to the situation, we should have. Compounding out regrettable oversight was the fact that lethargic Eulalia sat across from her so that one night, with the same cordiality with which she had addressed Gus, Clara asked Eulalia to pass the salad. Eulalia affected the haughty disdain of offended royalty as she passed the spectral salad bowl, filled with dull lettuce and greyish semi-transparent tomatoes which Clara gobbled up, smiling mischievously at the novelty of it all. She watched us with the same defiance in her eyes that she had on the day she enrolled in a man's subject. There was no time to act. We just watched her grow pale, then her smile faded away until finally Clara collapsed against the mirror.

Once the funeral business was over and we sat back down at the table again, we saw that Clara had taken a place on the other side. She was between cousin Baltazar (1940) and a great-uncle whom we simply called "Ito."

This *faux pas* dampened our conviviality somewhat. In a way, we felt betrayed; we felt that they had grievously abused our hospitality. However, we ended up divided over the question of who was really whose guest. It was also plain that our carelessness and Clara's irrepressible inquisitiveness had contributed to the mishap. In fact, a short time later we realized that there wasn't a great deal of difference between what Clara did before and what she was doing now, and so we decided to overlook the incident and get on with things. Nevertheless, each day we became less and less sure about which side was life and which its reflection, and as one bad step leads to another, I ended up taking Clara's empty place.

I am now much closer to them. I can almost hear the distant rustle of the folding and unfolding of napkins, the slight clinking of glasses and cutlery, the movement of chairs. The fact is that I can't tell if these sounds come from them or from us. I'm obviously not worried about clearing that up. What really troubles me, though, is that Clara doesn't seem to behave properly, with either the solemnity or with the opacity owed to her new position; I don't know how to put it. Even worse, the problem is that I—more than anybody else in the family—may become the target of Clara's machinations, since we were always joined by a very special affection, perhaps because we were the same age and had shared the same children's games and the first anxieties of adolescence . . .

As it happens, she is doing her best to get my attention, and ever since last Monday she has been waiting for me to slip up so she can pass me a pineapple this big, admittedly a little bleached-out, but just right for making juice and also a bit sour, just as she knows I like it.

Mothers, Fathers, or Parents: Same-Gendered Families in South Africa

Carien Lubbe (2007)

At the start of the twenty-first century, people are choosing to live their lives and rear their children in associations that only 50 years ago would not have been regarded as families. Societal factors such as working mothers, adoption, divorce, migrant fathers, and HIV/AIDS have all played a part in influencing the ways in which non-traditional family forms have developed. Advances and changes in globalized culture compel people to take cognizance of the wide variety of ways in which families are formed and in which children grow up. Such new family arrangements are forcing a redefinition of what is understood, meant, and implied by the concept 'family' (Dunne, 2000). One such non-traditional family form that has challenged society's traditional notion of what a family means is the same-gendered family (gay/lesbian family).[1]

Little is known about the ways in which same-gendered families operate and function in a predominantly heteronormative society [the assumption that heterosexuality is the norm in a society]. In addition, limited indigenous research is available, and researchers and practitioners often have to rely on international research. This article therefore highlights the most important research done in South Africa.

This article is based on the assumption that a person with a gay orientation or preference is a healthy, normal individual with essentially the same dreams, passions, hopes, fears, ambitions, aspirations, and the possibility of creating a spiritual richness in being alive as anyone else. However, because of historically negative constructions of homosexual people, living the life of a gay person is not always easy. I assume therefore that every person with a sexual orientation other than heterosexual needs to reconcile his or her sexual orientation somehow with the heteronormativity of society. In the same way that gay people need to do this, so the children of same-gendered parents need to engage in such a process of reconciliation and negotiation.

CHANGING TIMES, STAGNATING CONCEPTS, UNCHALLENGED VIEWPOINTS

Heteronormativity is evident in most societies. This is also true in South Africa, which is a strongly traditional and family-based society with a culture in which the traditional family is prominent, powerful, visual, and valued (Epstein, O'Flynn, & Telford, 2002; Johnson, 2004). The traditional nuclear family (which is widely accepted to mean a legally married, two-parent, heterosexual couple) has been the norm and benchmark against which all other kinds of couple or family arrangements have been measured and judged. Even when other dominant family structures such as the extended family are included (Ziehl, 2001), heteronormativity remains the norm.

In spite of a greater acceptance of sexual diversity in many quarters, the heterosexual couple remains enshrined as the normative form for adult sexual relationships. As Walters (2000) notes: 'It is hard to believe that the structures of exclusion and discrimination that surround gay life will not in some way impact gay family life' (p. 61). Significant societal biases remain evident in the media, for example in newspaper accounts of legal debates, television debates on moral and religious issues pertaining to the family, the portrayal of families in school textbooks, articles in popular magazines, and legal questions such as the debate that surrounds the sanctioning of marriage between same-gendered couples, and the use of the word "marriage" to portray such unions. However, descriptions of "societal attitudes" simply cannot capture the complex and content-specific aspects of everyday thought and practice, the practical reasoning and the gut reactions that inform everyday conduct (Jackson & Scott, 2004). A study carried out by OUT LGBT Well-being (the Gay, Lesbian, Bisexual, and Transgendered Organisation) in Pretoria, South Africa, revealed, for example, that 37 per cent of a sample of lesbian, gay or bisexual people ($n = 487$) had experienced verbal harassment or abuse because of their sexual orientation while 15 per cent had been asked to leave their faith or religious community because of their sexual orientation (Polders & Wells, 2004). Because the traditional family structure is widely accepted to mean a family with totally heterosexual parents, most researchers and investigators agree that same-gendered families are still stigmatized by society (Coyle & Kitzinger, 2002; Dunphy, 2000; Kershaw, 2000)

Children growing up in same-gendered families are aware of this discrimination and stigmatization. Jackson and Scott (2004) are of the opinion that the sexual world that children eventually learn about, and come to participate in, continues to be ordered by institutionalized heterosexuality. As children participate in the activities of their schools and churches, and as they watch television or surf the internet, they become aware of—and form their own perceptions of—what a family is or should be. Because of the heteronormativity of Western society, one of the major challenges for every child is the integration of her or his family experience with that of the wider society outside the home. Tasker and Golombok (1997) note that a major challenge for every child and his or her family is the integration of family experience with the expectations and values of the wider society outside their home. Although this is a universal dilemma, integration is more difficult to achieve when a family's divergence from prevailing norms within the wider social group is greater than average.

FOCUSING ON SOUTH AFRICA: BRIEF HISTORY AND CURRENT DISCOURSES

In South Africa, in addition to heteronormativity, the discourse on sexuality was also rigidly controlled by the apartheid system. While a blind eye was turned to the history of black male homosexuality in the mine compounds, incidents of white middle-class homosexual encounters were intensely scrutinized by the state (Elder, 1995; Gevisser & Cameron, 1994).

During the 1970s, the (mostly white) gay subculture of both men and women underwent an expansion, mostly because of increased urbanization, the effects of the women's liberation movement, the human rights movement, and greater post-World War II acceptance of a "single" lifestyle. Developments in media might also have improved communication and this meant that homosexuals of both genders were able to follow (to some extent) the ideological and political trends of the gay liberation movement in the United States and the United Kingdom. This was limited, however, in that censorship laws during the apartheid years prevented all but the most innocuous texts from entering the country.

Lesbian and gay voices are no longer silent in South Africa, and a relatively new (lesbian and gay) voice that is starting to speak out is that of the same-gendered family. Although they once lived on the margins of society, same-gendered families are also emerging as part of a "collective" gay community. In South Africa in particular, the terms of the new Constitution give gay people permission to advocate their right to establish life partnerships, become eligible to adopt children, keep custody of their own children in divorce proceedings, and, more recently, to be able to establish co-parenting. In spite of this, real-life attitudes toward gay and lesbian people are slow to change (Knoesen, 2004). Acceptance and understanding that are characterized neither by silence nor by open judgement and condemnation will naturally grow slowly after decades of bigotry, persecution, and discrimination because these negative attitudes are deeply embedded in the societal matrix. South African society still exhibits signs of a culture of discrimination and judgement.

Because of the legacy of South Africa's historically race-determined and neo-colonial system of capitalism in which "great men" dominated history textbooks, the points of view of workers, women, LGBT people, and people from lower socio-economic strata were seldom heard (Bozzoli, 1987, p. xiv).

From the beginning of the 1990s (and in tandem with the political changes in our country), reviews and commentaries that dealt with custody cases and the right to adoption began to appear in law journals (Bonthuys, 1994; Clark, 1998; Jordaan, 1998). This is similar to the international trend where the legal concerns for the welfare of the child with same-gendered parents prompted research into same-gendered families. As a result, some legal cases are breaking new ground for same-gendered parents and their children.

In 1993, even before the Equality Clause of the Constitution appeared, a court ruled that a divorced mother could not be denied access to her children because of her lesbian relationship (Isaack, 2003). In April 1998, a lesbian mother won custody of her child after the child had been removed by the Department of Social Services and placed in the care of its grandparents (Powers, 1998). In November 1998, a male gay couple was awarded custody of a child that they had fostered since birth (Oliver, 1998). In September 2002, the Child Care Act and Guardianship Act were formally changed after the groundbreaking case of De Vos and Du Toit, who jointly adopted two children. Another important judgement followed in November 2002 when a lesbian couple was together recognized as their twins' lawful parents (Cole, 2002). This case was also taken to the Constitutional Court, which declared the Children's Status Act to be unconstitutional. This act deals with the legitimation of children conceived by artificial insemination. Up to that point, it only made provision for "a woman" and "her husband" to be registered as the parents of their children (Ellis, 2003, p. 9). The judge who wrote the judgement for this case noted that changes in the legislation that regulates relationships between gays and lesbians were also necessary. Although gay people could now legally be parents, they still could not be legally married (Mphaki, 2003). In the reactions that followed these cases, the discriminatory attitudes of many

religious leaders were strongly apparent (Jackson, 2003; Mphaki, 2003), reinforcing the belief that a normative heterosexist culture still prevails in the minds of many South Africans.

At the end of 2004, an internationally groundbreaking court order ruled that the Constitution should be amended so that it would include marriages between two people of the same gender, although after a mere three weeks the Department of Home Affairs approached the Constitutional Court to appeal against this ruling (De Bruin, 2004; Jackson & Scott, 2004). The Supreme Court of Appeals declared the common law prohibition of same-gender marriages unconstitutional. However, the Marriage Act of 1961 remained unchanged until January 2006, when another court ruling ordered an amendment to this act as well, changing the "vows taken by husband and wife" to those of life partners.

The various reactions to the proposed changes to the Marriage Act reflect some of the discourses that inform arguments against same-gender marriages. Four main arguments against same-gender marriages can be identified, which impact directly on the status and recognition of same-gendered families (Knoesen, 2003). First, the discourse of procreation is used to assert that marriage is created for the purpose of procreation. This is no longer relevant because heterosexual people may marry even if one or both partners are unable to procreate. A change in the regulations of the Human Tissue Act recognizes the right of a single woman (irrespective of sexual orientation) to receive donor insemination for the purposes of having and raising children. This discourse on procreation is sometimes integrated with religious groups' objections to same-gender relationships and marriage. The second discourse that Knoesen (2003) mentions is the religious and moral one, which is probably the most deeply entrenched discourse that runs through our society, with views both for and against.

The other two discourses refer to the disintegration of the family and the alleged ill effects that same-gender parenting will have on children (Knoesen, 2003.) Families throughout history have taken different forms and they continue to develop. However, the *quality* of relationships in families is more important than the *form* or *structure* of the family. With the high divorce rate that prevails in traditional heterosexual marriages, this narrow definition of what a family entails is also under pressure. The argument that same-gendered parents will exert an injurious effect on their children was also used against the validity and the legality of inter-racial marriages (in South Africa), and it could also be logically extended to families of low socio-economic status. While it may be true that children from families of low socio-economic status may be materially and even emotionally disadvantaged, neither state nor society has the right to remove these children from their parents. These social changes challenge the view that the traditional nuclear family is the only safe and nurturing space in which to have and rear children.

NEW CONCEPTIONS OF THE "FAMILY"

The family is perhaps the most timeless, central, and enduring of all social institutions. Because of this, the concept *family* is often taken for granted and not subjected to the critical scrutiny that it requires. It should therefore be helpful to relay some of the views of feminist scholars who argue that the family is an *ideologically* based concept, experience, and institution. All the practical, material, and ideological premises that are used in defining the concept *family* depend on the cultural assumptions about families and gendered relations within families themselves (Dalton & Bielby, 2000; Gabb, 2001).

Same-gendered families present new challenges to the traditional nuclear family as well as to the extended family structure. Same-gendered families raise suspicions and engender skepticism in some quarters because any departure from the traditional family system and structure raises uncomfortable questions as to the exact nature of a parent, a family, a father, and a mother. Same-gendered families challenge dominant notions not only of gender but also of sexuality. The categories "lesbian mother" and "gay father" might seem to imply that a parent's *sexual* orientation is the most important factor in a gay person's parenting skills. King (2004) argues that people assume that to be gay means being

sexual. The very concept of lesbian mother or gay father means that any study of same-gendered families cannot be considered apart from sexuality. The same-gendered family is sexualized in the sense that the concept itself implicitly evokes the sexuality of the parents concerned as well as the dichotomy between homosexuality and heterosexuality. As Loutzenheiser and MacIntosh (2004) conclude, the queer family is "hyper-sexualized."

Bernstein and Reimann (2001) argue that it is in gay parenting that heteronormativity, and therefore the opposition of society, is most powerfully experienced. This happens because the modern Western social construction of sexuality masks a very real groundswell of opposition to the homo/hetero dichotomy and the maintenance of strict sexual borders that such a dichotomy requires. Although its opposition to any blurring of sexual boundaries is usually unspoken and ironically silent, heterosexuality remains the ever-present and influential subtext of modern sexual discourse.

Because most families convey strong heterosexual messages, they provide many opportunities for their children to received positive reinforcement, approval, and validation for their heterosexual orientation. Most parents encourage the dating of opposite-gendered individuals, marriage, and eventually children—particularly as adolescence and sexual maturity approach (Hunter & Mallon, 2000). Even the knowledge and values that are socially constructed in educational settings are constructed along heterosexual lines and are bound up with the organization and regulation of the heterosexual family. According to Epstein et al. (2002), myths of "happy heterosexuality" abound at every stage of childhood development—from the playhouse of the nursery school to the dating games of senior primary and secondary schools and universities. Children come to understand that hetero/homosexuality is a natural dichotomy that "proves" that heterosexuality is a normal and desirable end in itself. Heterosexual behavior and language are integrated and imposed to such a degree within the school culture that they have come to constitute a norm that reflects what is "natural" (p. 272).

Experience can be utilized to construct reality, and children growing up with same-gendered parents certainly have experiences that shape their reality. Johnson and O'Connor (2001) state that "parenting is universal. . . . But the day-to-day experiences that our family encounters can be unique. The homophobia that surrounds us affects our families in subtle and not so subtle ways" (p. 7). The scarcity of positive images and the abundance of negative stereotypes, as well as the invisibility of same-gendered families in the institutions outside the family, all combine to create a sense of difference, uniqueness, and secrecy (Bernstein & Reimann, 2001; Wright, 2001).

Queer and Postmodern Redefinitions of the Family

Scholars of queer theory contribute to the richness of understanding different families and the way in which individuals and society function. It is no longer possible to maintain one privileged view in the world of scholarship at least, and researchers, scientists, scholars, and psychologists should give an accurate account of the diversity and plurality that they encounter in ways in which people live their lives. In being confronted with the notion that sexualities are fluid and open, and the possibility of moving beyond the fixed fundamental categories of homo/hetero binaries, each of us is challenged to be self-reflexive and to actively shape and reshape our lives. It remains to be seen whether or not this is practically possible for everyone, but it certainly calls for a more flexible approach to parenting and the view that is taken of families.

The complexity that can be detected in understanding the concept of *family* is further evidence of postmodernist influences in the world. Absolute meaning has collapsed in many sectors of society because society itself offers more choice, fragmentation, and diversity (Kidd, 1999). Even though societies have always been ambiguous, variable, conflicted, and changing, conservative notions of "the family," of what it really means to be "a man," "a woman," and to know "the truth" about sexuality, are all ideas that have been seriously challenged in modern times. Whereas once it was possible to speak simply of "men and women," a postmodernist sensibility would speak of "masculinities, femininities and genders" (Plummer, 2003, p. 19).

Plummer (2003) argues that most people live simultaneously in traditional, modern, and postmodern worlds. Old stories endure side by with the new, because for every new story a rival one may be adduced from the past, and stories about new family configurations are countered by tales of family values and the inevitability of heteronormativity. There will always be opposition to whatever is new and non-traditional. There will always be "someone who is going to say 'No' to the queer, 'Don't touch me.' Don't touch me because you're sick and you'll contaminate me . . . ., or you'll contaminate Western civilisation" (Dinshaw, 1999, p. 173). Many prefer to cling to what they falsely idealize as a simpler and kinder past because they feel anxious and insecure. They try to preserve their distinctive identity as a person or group in contemporary societies that are changing with bewildering rapidity. Such nostalgic and authoritative voices can be heard emanating from religious fundamentalists of every kind, whether they are the fundamentalists of the religious right from the "Bible Belt" of the United States or religious fundamentalists from elsewhere. In Western countries, people fight what they regard as a threat to the alleged sanctity of the nuclear family by opposing the legalization of gay marriages (Kirkpatrick, 2004; Lacayo, 2004), and even in South Africa, homosexual identities have been condemned (McGill, 2002; Prins, 2003; Whisson, 2003).

Coontz (1992) argues that people often yearn for an idealized romantic past that never existed in the first place, or for the kind of happy and devoted family that was alleged to have existed in a world now lost. This kind of family is actually a sentimental delusion that forms part of the happily-ever-after mythology that people hark back to in contradiction of the record of what actually happened. Such pious hopes demonstrate how many of our "memories" of how families were in the past function primarily as mythical stories that are useful for morale building and family cohesiveness and exclusivity. "Families have always been in flux and often in crisis; they have never lived up to nostalgic notions about 'the way things used to be'" (p. 2).

No universally accepted definition of what is meant by "family" exists. Families are not "things" that are done to us, they are happenings, practices, and processes—we "do" the family through acting in life. Families are made or created through choices and actions in life. The postmodern approach to family is characterized by choice, freedom, diversity, ambivalence, and fluidity. Postmodern interpretations of the family argue that it is no longer possible to claim that any one type of family is "better," more "natural," or more "normal" than another. This latter kind of thinking is a residue of modernist and conservative thought in which social actors searched for fixed meanings about life and readymade truths according to which life could (and should) be lived (Kidd, 1999, p. 13). This kind of thinking negates a core issue, that family revolves around relationships, and relationships cannot be prescribed or structured and cannot be lived within fixed guidelines.

Gender, Reproduction, and Parenting

What lesbian families or their male counterparts succeed in achieving is to transfer the traditional focus away from *gender* in parenting and families. In addition, the development of reproductive technologies over the past few decades has challenged gender divisions by allowing potential parents to enjoy the advantages of *reproduction* without engaging in any sexual activity at all with a member of the opposite sex. This has given same-gendered couples opportunities to procreate within the bonds of same-gendered relationships (Bernstein & Reimann, 2001; Plummer, 2003). Because of this pioneering work, *parenting* has also been freed from the bonds of gender and sexual activity undertaken for purpose of procreation. The same-gendered couple as a family challenges the normative conceptions of the traditional model of the two-parent (hetero-gender) family because it is socially and legally constructed from a biological model of reproduction.

Same-gendered families offer a post-patriarchal vision of what families could be like if people were willing to abandon centuries of conditioning and accept a gender-neutral discourse that is sympathetic to the kind of feminist legal reform that discards the categories of "mother" and "father" and collapses them into the more generic concept of "parent" (Dunne, 2000, p. 12). The cultural change in the direction of a more egalitarian model of parenting is evident in same-gendered families as same-genered parental couples find solutions to problems such as how to make time for the children as well as time to earn a living. Same-gendered couples have to consciously negotiate agreed definitions of boundaries, meanings, and the attributes of parenthood that they wish to implement in their lives and families. Same-gendered parents and their children transgress the normative status of heterosexuality in relation to reproduction and the organization of parenting roles. Activities that are traditionally divided between mother and father are redefined or incorporated. These transgressive modalities offer more opportunities for cooperation and creativity, and in doing so they demonstrate the viability of non-heterosexual parenting models. It is indeed the absence of gender differences that permits a reconstruction of the cultural values of family and parenting (Dalton & Bielby, 2000; Walters, 2000). The probability that lesbians are more likely to share parenting equally and challenge traditional conservative gender arrangements seems to imply that gender is primarily a function of the division of labor (Dalton & Bielby, 2000; Malone & Cleary, 2002). This is not to deny that some same-gendered parents replicate heterosexual (male/female) role divisions—a practice that Dunne (2000) calls "theoretical heterosexism" (p. 134). Some same-gendered couples do indeed play out traditional roles of provider and nurturer/caregiver. However, that is a choice that has to be respected.

Parenting can be understood and analyzed culturally in terms of gender. The argument of Judith Butler (1990) is that if gender is a *performance* and connected within a heterosexual matrix, and if gender performances can be imitated in ways that are not necessarily linked to fixed gendered indentities grounded in nature, bodies, or heterosexuality, then *parenting can also be defined in terms of a performance*. The argument can be made that we "do" the family through performing various acts in life, just as we "do" or perform gender. And just as gender is constructed, so also are families constructed. I therefore argue that both *parenting* and *family* are constructed and performed. Gender and parenting should be regarded as fluid variables that shift and change to suit different contexts at different times. What are the implications of this for parenting? They offer people who want to be parents the possibility of choosing, forming, and performing their own individual identities as parents in a way that brings their unique abilities, strengths, skills, and talents into play. This challenges society to disregard the stigmas of the past. Is it inherently important if the mother of a family changes a light bulb or services the car? Or if the father cooks, minds the children, and takes care of the garden? Or indeed if all these functions are efficiently performed in a same-gendered family in which the children are loved, nurtured, cared for, and protected? What can be learned from this is that parental roles, duties, and functions can be performed in a wide variety of ways that are not linked to gender stereotypes. It also makes it clear that if people are willing to relinquish their traditional dogmas and stereotypes about gender and sexuality, structural variables, such as the gender composition of families and the division of parental performances, are less important than process variables such as the quality of relationships and the quality of care given to the children (Dunne, 2000; Malone & Cleary, 2002).

NOTE

1. "Same-gendered family" refers to a family constituted by two gay parents of the same gender (two females or two males), who are involved in an intimate and committed relationship. While "gender" in this sense refers to the biological sex of the parent, I acknowledge that "gender" is socially constructed. It is because of the effect of this construction that I refer to such families as "same-gendered" families and not "same-gender" families. Such families are also widely referred to as "lesbian" or "gay" families or "same-sex" families.

REFERENCES

Bernstein, M., & Reimann, R. (2001). Introduction. In M. Berstein & R. Reimann (Eds.), *Queer families, queer politics* (pp. 1–17). New York: Columbia University Press.

Bonthuys, E. (1994). Awarding access and custody to homosexual parents of minor children. *Stellenbosch Law Review, 5*(3), 298–313.

Butler, J. (1990). *Gender trouble: Feminism and the subversion of identity.* London: Routledge Falmer.

Clark, B. (1998). Competing custody rights. *Comparative and International Law Journal of Southern Africa, 31*(3), 288–306.

Cole, B. (2002, November 3). Egg-static! Court rules for lesbian parents. *Sunday Tribune*, p. 1.

Coontz, S. (1992). *The way we never were: American families and the nostalgia trip.* New York: Basic Books.

Coyle, A., & Kitzinger, C. (2002). *Lesbian & gay psychology.* London: Blackwell.

Dalton, S. E., & Bielby, D. D. (2000). That's our kind of constellation: Lesbian mothers negotiate institutionalised understandings of gender within the family. *Gender & Society, 14*(1), 36–61.

de Bruin, P. (2004, December 1.) Huwelikshek oop, skerp reaksie op hof se groen lig vir gays wat wil trou. *Beeld*, p. 1.

Dinshaw, C. (1999). *Getting medieval: Sexualities and communities, pre-and-post-modern.* Durham, NC: Duke University Press.

Dunne, G. A. (2000). Opting into motherhood: Lesbians blurring the boundaries and transforming the meaning of parenthood and kinship. *Gender & Society, 14*(1), 11–35.

Dunphy, R. (2000). *Sexual politic: An introduction.* Edinburgh: Edinburgh University Press.

Elder, G. (1995). Of moffies, kaffirs and perverts: Male homosexuality and the discourse of moral order in the apartheid state. In B. David & V. Gill (Eds.), *Sexuality* (pp. 56–65). London: Routledge Falmer.

Ellis, E. (2003, February 9). Same-sex parents can raise family, says court. *Star*, p. 3.

Epstein, D., O'Flynn, S., & Telford, D. (2002). Innocence and experience: Paradoxes in sexuality and education. In D. Richardson & S. Seidman (Eds.), *Handbook of lesbian and gay studies* (pp. 271–290). London: Sage.

Gabb, J. (2001). Querying the discourses of love. *The European Journal of Women's Studies, 8*(3), 313–328.

Gevisser, M., & Cameron, E. (Eds.). (1994). *Defiant desire.* Johannesburg: Ravan Press.

Hunter, J., & Mallon, G. P. (2000). Lesbian, gay and bisexual development: Dancing with your feet tied together. In B. Greene & G. L. Croom (Eds.), *Education, research and practice in lesbian, gay, bisexual and transgendered psychology* (pp. 226–243). Thousand Oaks, CA. Sage.

Isaack, W. (2003). *Equal in word of law: The rights of lesbian and gay people in South Africa.* Retrieved July 19, 2004, from http://www.equality.org.za/legal/articles/2003/equalworldlaw.php.

Jackson, N. (2003, August 27). 50%+ van sinodegangers meen gays sondig. *Beeld*, p. 4.

Jackson, S., & Scott, S. (2004). Sexual antinomies in late modernity. *Sexualities, 7*(2), 233–248.

Johnson, P. (2004). Haunting heterosexually: The homo/het binary and intimate love. *Sexualities, 7*(2), 183–2000.

Johnson, S. M., & O'Connor, E. (2001). *For lesbian parents: Your guide to helping your family grow up happy, healthy and proud.* New York: Guilford Press.

Jordaan, D. W. (1998). Homoseksuele ouerskap: 'n Grondwetlike analise. *De Jure ac Legibus, 31*(2), 302–321.

Kershaw, S. (2000). Living in a lesbian household: The effects on children. *Child and Family Social Work, 5*(4), 365–371.

Kidd, W. (1999). Family diversity in an uncertain future. *Sociology Review, 9*(1), 11–14.

King, J. R. (2004). The (Im)possibility of gay teachers for young children. *Theory into Practice, 43*(2), 22–127.

Kirkpatrick, D. D. (2004, February 28). Gay-marriage fight finds ambivalene from evangelicals. *New York Times.* Retrieved March 2, 2004, from http://nytimes.com.

Knoesen, E. (2004, March 3). Queering the vote. *Mail & Guardian*, p. 15.

Lacayo, R. (2004). For better or for worse? *Time Magazine, 163*(10), 18–25.

Loutzenheiser, L. W., & MacIntosh, L. B. (2004). Citizenships, sexualities and education. *Theory into Practice, 42*(2), 151–158.

Malone, K., & Cleary, R. (2002). (De)Sexing the family. *Feminist Theory, 3*(3), 271–293.

McGill, J. (2002, September 26). Ruling reflects moral problem. *The Herald*, p. 7.

Mphaki, A. (2003, April 20). Same-sex couples get equality and disapproval. *City Press*, p. 21.

Oliver, L. (1998, December 5). Tears as pair is given custody. *Saturday Argus*, p. 3.

Plummer, K. (2003). *Intimate citizenship: Private decisions and public dialogues.* Seattle, WA: University of Washington Press.

Polders, L., & Wells, H. (2004). Overall research findings on levels of empowerment among LGBT people in Gauteng, South Africa. Pretoria: OUT LGTB Well-being.

Powers, C. (1998, April 3). Lesbian mother wins custody of her child. *The Star*, p. 3.

Prins, J. (2003, November 11). Gays wat nie skrik, sal hel toe gaan, sê gospelsanger. *Beeld.* Retrieved November 11, 2003, from http://152.111.1.251/argief/berigte/beeld/2003/11/11/B3/03/05.html.

Tasker, F., & Golombok, S. (1997). *Growing up in a lesbian family: Effects on child development.* New York: Guilford Press.

Walters, S. D. (2000). Wedding bells and baby carriages: Heterosexuals imagine gay families, gay families imagine themselves. In M. Andrews, S. D. Sclater, C. Squire, & A. Treacher (Eds.), *Lines of narrative* (pp. 48–63). London: Routledge Falmer.

Whisson, M. (2003, May 5). Morals matter: Same Sex marriages. *Daily Dispatch*, p. 3.

Wright, J. M. (2001). Aside from one, little tiny detail, we are so incredibly normal: Perspectives of children in lesbian step families. In M. Bernstein & R. Reimann (Eds.), *Queer families, queer politics* (pp. 272–290). New York: Columbia University press.

Ziehl, S. C. (2001). Documenting changing family patterns in South Africa: Are census data of any value? *Africa Sociological Review, 5*(2), 36–62.

Female Headship and the "Feminization of Poverty"

Sylvia Chant (2004)

The term "Feminization of Poverty" has been much used, and arguably abused, in the development lexicon in recent years. It has become commonplace to hear that poverty increasingly has a "woman's face" given that females purportedly account for 70% of the world's 1.2 billion poor people.

Interestingly, the notion that women represent a disproportionate and rising share of the world's poor has been attributed, in large measure, to the growing incidence of female household headship. The alleged close link between household headship and the feminization of poverty is not surprising. It is not only invoked by the growing numbers of women who head families and are poor, but also by the widely held belief that they are among the "poorest of the poor."

This perception, in turn, rests upon the notion that poverty is a major catalyst for the formation of female-headed households—and, more particularly, an almost invariable consequence of it. Given that most societies are characterized by gender inequalities in access to resources, it is not unreasonable to suppose that these differences are exacerbated when poor women become responsible for household provisioning without male partners. The resultant privation not only affects these female heads but also is allegedly perpetuated across generations.

Female headship is now so firmly entrenched in the development discourse about gender and poverty that it has effectively become a proxy for women's poverty. This association has not been without its benefits insofar as concise slogans help secure resources to address the plight of poor women.

Development organizations may also find it appealing to have a female-only target group for policies as it spares them the need to intervene in the conflictive "private" domain of intra-household relations between two-parent famllies. Not surprisingly, such expediencies have flourished in a climate in which targeting has become an increasingly favored strategy in poverty-reduction efforts.

However, branding single-parent families headed by women as the "poorest of the poor" suggests that poverty is mainly determined by household characteristics, rather than the socio-economic context in which they are situated. Such labeling not only scapegoats female headship as a cause for poverty but also deflects attention from the wider structures of gender and socio-economic inequality that contribute to it. Placing excessive emphasis on the economic disadvantage of female heads misrepresents and devalues their enormous efforts to overcome gender obstacles. It also obliterates the personal significance that headship has for women.

This stereotyping also suggests that poverty among women is confined to cases where females head their families. There is no denying that households headed by women on low incomes stand to benefit from institutional support for parenting and provisioning. But one must acknowledge that women in male-headed households experience poverty too—and may even be worse off. This fact is obscured when one assumes that female-headed households are of necessity poorer than those controlled by men.

Prevailing methods of poverty research have undoubtedly played a role in popularizing the notion of a "feminization of poverty" and its linkage to female household headship. Despite mounting rhetoric about the need for qualitative, participatory tools to assess poverty, "money-metric" approaches continue to reign supreme. They prioritize questions of "physical deprivation" to the detriment of "social deprivation," which involves such dimensions as lack of power, agency or self-esteem. This concern has elevated the importance of the *level* of resources rather than focusing on who has *command* and *control* over them. By overlooking women's power to access household resources, standard "money-metric" approaches tend to over-emphasize the poverty of female heads relative to women who reside in male-headed units.

Moreover, the *household* rather than the *individual* persists as the dominant unit of measurement in poverty assessments. Consequently, households headed by women stand out in poverty statistics, even though they may not represent as large a proportion of poor people given their smaller size compared to dual parent households.

But even if one takes aggregate household incomes as the welfare measure of choice, there is precious little hard data that shows a systematic link across space or time between household headship and poverty. In Latin America, for example, the incidence of female headship in urban areas—where women-headed families are usually more common—rose in every single country for which data exist for 1990 and 1999. At the same time, the proportion of urban households in poverty declined across the region from 35% to 29.8%, while those below the extreme poverty line fell from 17.7% to 13.9%.

It appears, then, that the case for a greater share and depth of poverty among female household heads rests on rather tenuous grounds.

The lack of definitive links between female headship and poverty, as suggested by the "feminization of poverty" thesis, results in part from the *heterogeneity* of women-headed units. This heterogeneity can have important mediating effects on poverty depending on the social and cultural context.

It matters, for instance, whether a woman becomes head of a household by "choice" or involuntarily. Other sources of heterogeneity among female-headed units can be linked to household composition, the stage the woman is at in her lifecycle (e.g., age and relative dependency of offspring), the geographic location of the household (rural versus urban), and whether resources beyond the family unit are accessible.

It is not unusual for female heads to contend with discrimination, above-average work burdens and time constraints. But in order to offset the negative effects of gender bias, they often organize their households so as to optimize the resources at their disposal.

A common strategy is to invite co-residence by members of their extended kin networks.

Contributions from co-resident individuals as well as migrant family members can help compensate the personal disadvantage female heads face because of their gender. Those contributions increase a household's access to resources for productive and reproductive labor, thereby reducing its vulnerability while also bolstering its earning capacity.

Aside from intra-group diversity, two other factors help explain why female headship does not automatically translate into privation. The first relates to intra-household power relations and the attendant implications for resource allocation, while the second pertains to poverty's multi-dimensional and subjective nature. Analysis of these issues requires moving beyond the narrow focus of conventional money-metric poverty assessments and increasing scrutiny over what goes on inside households.

With respect to intra-household resource allocation, one must eschew the idealized notion that households are intrisincally cohesive and internally undifferentiated entities governed by "natural" proclivities to benevolence, consensus and joint welfare maximization. Indeed, a major contribution of feminist research has been to debunk the myth of households as unitary entities operating on altruistic principles. Rejecting orthodox Household Economics thinking, many authors have argued instead that households are "sites" of competing claims, rights, power, interests and resources, with domestic negotiations frequently shaped by a member's age, gender or position in the family hierarchy.

It is more difficult to shun idealized notions of "female altruism" and "male egoism." Findings from a remarkably large number of contexts confirm that women devote the bulk of their earnings to household expenditure, often with positive effects on other members' nutritional intake, health care and education. Men, on the other hand, are prone to retain more of their earnings for discretionary personal expenditure. In some instances, they even command a larger share of resources than they actually bring home.

This implies that even if sufficient assets exist in a male-headed household, its female members (women *and* girls) may not be able to access them—at least not in their own right. Along with reducing the resources available to other members, irregular financial contributions from male heads can lead to a situation of acute vulnerability and "secondary poverty" among spouses and children. Moreover, women in male-headed families all too often suffer from other extreme forms of dependence, including subjection to authority and violence.

Accordingly, lower incomes among female heads relative to their male counterparts may be countered by the extent to which income and assets are converted into consumption and investments for the benefit of the entire household. Seen in this light, the absence or loss of a male head may not necessarily precipitate destitution and may even enhance the economic security and well-being of other household members. Evidence from Mexico, Costa Rica and the Philippines reveals that many low-income women feel more secure financially without men, even when their own earnings are low or prone to fluctuations. They also claim to be better able to cope with hardship when they are not at the mercy of male *dictat* and thus freer to make decisions.

This evidence suggests that while the price of independence may be high for poor women, benefits in other dimensions of their lives may be adjudged to outweigh the costs. Many women seem willing to trade a lower income for a position of greater autonomy and self-reliance—a finding that fits well with "social deprivation" thinking about poverty. Even if women are poorer in terms of *income* as heads of their own household, they may *feel* better off and less vulnerable in the absence of male control. It is difficult to grasp the importance of these transactions unless one incorporates people's subjectivities into the conceptualization of poverty.

Indeed, viewing poverty as multidimensional helps explain why some low-income women make choices that, at face value, could seem prejudicial to their well-being. One such case is when female heads refuse offers of financial support from absent fathers in order to evade ongoing contact or sexual

encounters. Another instance is where women forfeit assets such as houses and neighborhood networks in order to exit abusive relations. While financial pressures may force some women to search for new partners following a conjugal breakdown, it is significant that others choose to remain alone rather than return to ex-partners or form new relationships. Those who live without a male partner often do so by choice, preferring to rely on sons or other family members rather than spouses.

In the end, the "feminization of poverty" thesis and its overriding preoccupation with both income and women household heads is dangerous for two reasons. First, it precludes an analytical consideration of the social dimensions of gender and poverty. Second, such preoccupation tends to translate into single-issue, single-group policy interventions with little power to destabilize the deeply embedded structures of gender inequality in the home, the labor market and other institutions.

Instead, explicit policies are required to redress the processes that make women poorer than men. The most important ones are *gender-aware* poverty interventions that do not just target women in isolation or focus mainly on those who head their own households.

We must recognize that, in most societies, women clearly lag behind men in terms of accessing the resources necessary for survival and self-determination. Yet in accepting the alleged "feminization" of privation, one also is implying that there is a counterpart process of "masculinization" of power, privilege and material accumulation.

If this is the case, then future research needs to explore how that process squares with the fact that, both collectively and individually, women appear to be forging new spaces in many countries. This is occurring not only in politics, the law and the labor market but even in their domestic environments, where women are arguably exerting more and more influence over their own lives.

Old Maid

Vivian N. Limpin (2006)

You keep asking me
why I still haven't married.
This time, I didn't find it funny.
I looked around to search for answers:
Perhaps they're written in my poems.
Perhaps they're sketched in my paintings.
Perhaps they're framed in my films.
I tried hard to remember
if this is what I chose:
the camera instead of the casserole,

the canvas instead of the cradle,
the metaphor instead of a mate.

You're still asking me
why I still don't have a companion.
Never did I consider
being single
a curse.
I won't look around for a while
even if you ask one more time.
The answer might still be long in coming.

Indonesian Feminists Confront Polygyny

Yenni Kwok (2007)

When Yayah Khisbiyah agreed to marry the love of her life, her friends were scandalized: The prospective groom, Abbas Ghozali, was already married.

"They talked of me betraying feminist and progressive Islamic agendas," says the 42-year-old Indonesian psychologist. Indeed, why *would* a highly educated, financially independent Muslim feminist agree to a polygynous union?

Khisbiyah and Ghozali had been college sweethearts 23 years earlier, but separated. She married another man, then later divorced. Ghozali was persuaded to marry another woman. When they met again, they realized they still felt strongly about each other. But Ghozali's wife didn't want a divorce, so they agreed a polygynous marriage would be the best alternative, and the first wife gave permission. Khisbiyah claims the decision was in the spirit of feminist solidarity. In a society where divorced women are often looked down on, she says, "I am not letting the other woman and children become disempowered or neglected." She insists her marriage is a personal choice analogous to same-sex unions.

The Indonesian language has a word for the "other wife": *madu*, literally "honey." Yet polygyny is not a matter of sweetness but a contentious issue in Indonesia, which has the world's largest Muslim population. Many religiously conservative Muslims justify polygyny and reject any efforts to restrict it. They claim the Prophet Muhammad had multiple wives and cite a Koranic verse permitting a man up to four wives— *if* he treats them equally.

One outspoken practitioner using this justification is Puspo Wardoyo, a restaurant entrepreneur

337

who boasts four wives and who initiated the "Polygamy Award." Another is actor Sitoresmi Prabuningrat, though she qualifies her defense of the practice: "Your wife needs to be *asked* whether she wants to enter the higher paradise or not," says Prabuningrat, the third wife of a musician.

But women's-rights activists are alarmed, seeing this as another sign that increasing Islamic radicalism is marginalizing women. The controversy reached new heights in late 2006, when popular Muslim preacher Abdullah Gymnastiar, better known as Aa Gym, admitted he had taken a second wife. Many women boycotted his talks thereafter.

Siti Musdah Mulia, author of *Islam Criticizes Polygamy*, argues that the religion in fact disapproves of polygyny: "During the Prophet's time, there was no limit to how many wives a man could have. Islam tried to eradicate this practice, beginning by limiting the number of wives and also stipulating the requirement to be fair." Furthermore, Muhammad was an advocate of monogamy: "For 28 years, the Prophet was married to one woman. Three years after his first wife died, he took other wives [only] to gain political alliances in his battles." She notes that Muhammad publicly refused to permit his son-in-law, Ali, to take a second wife, saying that whoever hurt his daughter hurt him.

Khisbiyah thinks polygamy should be heavily restricted, but not banned. But Nina Nurmila, lecturer at the State Institute for Islamic Studies in Bandung, agrees with Mulia that the government should be braver in outlawing polygyny outright, as in Tunisia and Turkey. "Some people may be outraged at first," says Nurmila, "but sooner or later they will accept it."

R E A D I N G **41**

Too Young to Marry

Allison Ford (2009)

In April of 2008, 10-year-old Nujood Ali walked into a court-house and demanded a divorce. Raised in poverty in Yemen, she had been forced into marriage with a stranger by her father. Although she claimed that her 30-year-old husband beat and sexually abused her, her family refused to intervene. "I asked and begged my mother, father and aunt to help me get divorced," Nujood told the *Yemen Times*. "They answered . . . 'If you want, you can go to court by yourself.' So this is what I have done."

Nujood was the first child in Yemen to petition for divorce on her own, but her tale of forced marriage is not uncommon in the developing world, where millions of girls are fated to become child brides. According to the Centers for Disease Control and Prevention (CDC), the practice is most common in Africa and South Asia, where, respectively, 42 percent and 48 percent of girls are married before age 18. In especially poor countries such as Yemen, it is not unusual for girls to wed even before reaching puberty.

Not only poverty but cultural biases against women are to blame.

"Girls are simply not valued as much as boys are," says Jennifer Wilen, assistant program officer of Francophone Africa for the International Women's Health Coalition (IWHC). Daughters are married off as early as possible so that families no longer need provide for them. Parents have little incentive to delay the marriages or keep children in school; they are exchanged for money or livestock, a windfall for the rest of the family. Child brides are transferred to the homes of their new husbands, where their educations and childhoods are halted and they begin lives of social isolation and forced labor.

It's difficult to estimate how many girls are affected by early marriage, since weddings in many countries are not registered legal unions but rather traditional or religious ceremonies. Although many countries have laws requiring that individuals consent to marriage, parents often arrange marriages without their daughters' knowledge or approval. "Laws prohibiting child marriage have been created, yet are openly flouted," says Dr. K.G. Santhya, senior program officer at the international nonprofit Population Council.

The practice has a disastrous impact on girls' health and development. Girls are pressured to prove their fertility by bearing children as soon as possible, although their still-developing bodies are not yet ready for pregnancy. "Young adolescents are more at risk of morbidity and mortality from pregnancy and childbirth," Santhya says. According to the CDC, girls 10 to 14 years old are five to seven times likelier to die in childbirth than women over age 20, and girls 15 to 19 twice as likely. Child brides typically suffer from obstructed labor, postpartum hemorrhaging, obstetric fistula and other debilitating complications, and have less access than older brides to health services that could prevent or treat many of these conditions. In addition, they are rarely able to decide for themselves when to seek help and must rely on husbands to make decisions about their medical care.

"Marriage itself has become a risk factor for HIV," according to Wilen. In sub-Saharan Africa, several studies have shown that married girls under age 20 have alarmingly high rates of HIV infection, partly due to the age difference between girls and their husbands. Older husbands are likely to have multiple sex partners and more likely to be infected with HIV or other diseases. Compounding the problem is the polygamy practiced in some parts of Africa and Asia, where younger girls are likely to be a third or fourth wife to a much older man. Because child wives are financially dependent on their husbands, they have no power to use birth control, abstain from sex or request HIV testing.

No matter how subservient a girl is in a traditional culture, there is also a risk that she will simply be abandoned. Girls who are infertile, suffer birth complications or contract HIV are often turned out into the street. "Even though their marriage is horrible, at least it's economically stable," Wilen says. "Once they leave or are kicked out, they often have no means of supporting themselves or their children."

Nujood was fortunate to plead before a sympathetic judge and was granted her divorce. But although her case garnered international headlines, it did little to help the millions of girls who still suffer forced early marriages every year. "We need to address the gatekeepers—parents, teachers, healthcare providers—to build awareness of the need to eliminate child marriage," says Santhya.

U.S. Rep. Betty McCollum (D-Minn.) has proposed the International Protecting Girls by Preventing Child Marriage Act, which would help fund groups that are trying to prevent child marriage by working to raise the value of girls in traditional societies, and by giving parents incentives to keep daughters in school. "The U.S. invests billions of dollars to improve the lives of people in poor countries," McCollum says. "Child marriage is a practice that undermines that investment. And it is a horrific violation of human rights."

For 20 years, the IWHC has supported local organizations in Western Africa that teach parents, communities and policy-makers that child marriage is not a harmless tradition but one that places their daughters in danger. These organizations spread the word that girls can become valuable members of their communities, able to earn money and support themselves and thereby reduce the burden on their families. "If you provide an education for your daughter, she will be able to get a job," Wilen says, "and educating and empowering women fortifies your whole country."

The Bride's Voice: Religious Women Challenge the Wedding Ritual[1]

Irit Koren (2005)

Halakhic marriage fixes the status of a woman as property. This status is, of course, not mutual and certainly not acceptable to me. . . . In general, I don't think it is healthy for a couple to live in consciousness of such power relations. . . . So it is completely unnecessary for a normal, healthy woman to submit herself to such nonsense. It is not respectful; it is not respectful of the institution, of the couple, of their relationship. (Tehila)

Tehila thus expressed her discomfort with her sense that the traditional Orthodox Jewish wedding ceremony amounts to a ritual of acquisition—a conviction she shares with a broader group of women. For my doctoral dissertation I chose to interview twenty-five women, each of whom sought to challenge, resist, and adapt her performance of the ritual by producing alternative interpretations and practices aimed at creating change in the religious system. This article begins by describing the different strategies of interpretation the women employed and then moves to the strategies of action they used to address their wedding rituals. It centers on the brides, but in order to place their actions in context, I shall also remark upon the responses of the rabbis with whom they negotiated regarding the actions they took.[2]

The women I studied comprise a fairly homogeneous group. All were in their mid-twenties to mid-thirties at the time of their marriage, and all of the marriages took place within the past decade; all are well educated and consciously identify as both religious and feminist; and all lived in Jerusalem while single, specifically in the neighborhoods of Rehavia, Katamon, and Baka.[3] Since they identify as religious, they feel constrained (to varying degrees) to abide by Jewish law (halakhah). Thus, they evinced a desire to have Orthodox weddings—either because they personally felt committed to religious Orthodoxy, or because their fiancés, parents, or communities were committed to Orthodoxy. They did not feel that they could take the path of some non-Orthodox women who opt for egalitarian ceremonies that are not acknowledged by the Orthodox rabbinate, the only body authorized to register Jewish marriages in Israel. Such marriages can be registered only by means of a civil ceremony performed outside the country—a route followed by many secular Israelis in order to avoid the religious ceremony altogether.[4]

Moreover, all but one of the marriages I studied received rabbinic certification. That is, the weddings were performed by rabbis certified by the Chief Rabbinate of Israel, which requires that they abide by its rules in performing wedding ceremonies—rules framed not only by halakhah but also by the policies and politics of the Rabbinate, as some of the rabbis pointed out. The rabbis allowed the women varying degrees of flexibility in modifying the ritual; indeed, they also varied in the degree to which they themselves identified with the Rabbinate. Notwithstanding these variations, they all located themselves on the liberal side of the religious spectrum. Some of them belong to a religious Zionist organization of rabbis called "Tzohar," which is known for its liberal attitude toward Orthodox marriage. Although the women I interviewed are still a local vanguard, I believe this phenomenon is expanding and increasing its influence on the wider Orthodox community and its discourse in Israel.

The transformative aims of the women's practices can be understood only in the context of the traditional wedding ritual as it is today performed in Israel (and throughout the Orthodox Jewish world). That ritual comprises the following steps: Before the wedding ceremony itself, the groom signs the *ketubah*, a contract delineating his financial obligations toward his wife. Then he is led to the bride, who has been sitting in a chair awaiting him. Upon reaching her, he covers her face with a veil. He turns and walks to the *hupah* (marriage canopy), accompanied by the wedding guests, and awaits the bride there. The bride, similarly, proceeds to the *hupah*, and upon reaching it, in the Ashkenazi (European Jewish) custom, she circles the groom seven times, accompanied by her mother and mother-in-law to be. Only now does the formal two-part ritual begin. The first part is the *kiddushin* (acquisition) ceremony, in which, following recitation of the betrothal blessing and the blessing over wine, the man fulfills the active role of acquiring the woman by addressing to her the Hebrew words *harei at mekudeshet li* ("you are hereby consecrated unto me") while giving her a ring. After this, the *ketubah* is read aloud, separating the two parts of the ritual. Now the second part begins—the *nisu'in* (marriage), in which the *sheva berakhot*, the traditional seven wedding blessings, are read by a man or several men. At the end of the ritual the groom shatters a glass by stamping on it.

Numerous feminist critiques have been leveled against the traditional wedding ritual, specifically targeting the *kiddushin* as an act of acquisition and therefore one of oppression.[5] Critiques have also been made of other ritual acts or elements associated with the wedding: The covering of the bride with the veil has been interpreted as symbolically rendering her invisible; the circling of the groom strikes many as indicating that he is at the center, while the bride is at the margins; and the seven blessings, recited by men only, do not give women a voice in this part of the ceremony.

The Jewish legal scholar Judith Wegner points out that the framers of the Mishnah view marriage first and foremost as the transfer of ownership of a woman's sexuality. In the mishnaic catalogue of various types of chattel and the legal procedures for acquiring them, wives head the list. Wegner suggests that

the Mishnah's framers listed the different types of property along with the wife so as to indicate both a formal and a substantive analogy between the acquisition of the woman's sexuality and the acquisition of chattel. Thus, the traditional text's view of the woman's sexuality (but not necessarily the woman herself) as chattel is further expressed in the unilateral ceremony of espousal, whereby the man recites a formula to the woman, who is forbidden to make any reply. Even if she were to speak, her words would have no effect.[6] In other words, it is specifically forbidden by halakhah for the woman to "acquire" her husband in a mutual act of acquisition.

There are some harsh implications of this legal arrangement, which is still valid in the rabbinical courts in Israel as well as in the rest of the Orthodox Jewish world. Most importantly, a Jewish woman wed by the laws of the Torah can be divorced only by her husband's act of giving her a traditional bill of divorce (*get*). Should her husband stubbornly refuse or otherwise be unable to release her in this way, she will remain a *mesurevet get* or an *agunah*, unable to remarry.[7] In this matter, Jewish law discriminates openly and explicitly between men and women. A *mesurevet get* or *agunah* who chooses to live with another man pays a heavy price. Her children by that man are considered *mamzerim* (bastards), and under religious law neither they nor their offspring for the next ten generations are allowed to marry Jews. Because all marriages between Jews in Israel are governed by Orthodox religious law, such children and their descendants are unable to marry in the State of Israel. In contrast, a married man can have children by another (unmarried) woman without legal sanction.[8]

1. STRATEGIES OF INTERPRETATION

The women in my study did not hold to a strict feminist interpretation of the Orthodox wedding ritual as an oppressive act. Rather, they chose to make their own interpretations of various of the ritual acts associated with the traditional wedding—such as the act of *kiddushin*, the lifting of the veil, the circling of the groom, the seven blessings—which they did not always classify as oppressive.[9] I found three main strategies of interpretation:

(a) viewing the ritual act as merely symbolic;
(b) imposing a personal and invented meaning upon the ritual act; and
(c) viewing the ritual act as oppressive.

I shall illustrate how these strategies were implemented with respect to the core ritual act of the wedding—*kiddushin*.[10]

(a) Viewing the Ritual Act as Merely Symbolic

The women who chose the first strategy emphasized the symbolic component of *kiddushin* and chose, to some extent, to ignore its legal ramifications as an act of acquisition. This approach is demonstrated in Rivki's view:

> It did not bother us at all, the issue of the acquisition, because it was clear to us that we have a relationship of equals. . . . It was clear that he wasn't acquiring me; it was also clear from the halakhah that this was not an act of acquisition. It is a symbolic act.

Rivki's understanding of *kiddushin* is linked to how she views her relationship with her husband, with whom she sees herself as being on an equal footing. This enables her to view the act as merely symbolic, softening the tension between her feminist consciousness and the act's traditional meaning.

(b) Imposing a Personal, Invented Meaning upon a Ritual Act

The women who chose the second strategy imposed various individual and invented meanings upon the act. Yael explained her interpretation thus:

> This concept [of acquisition] bothered me, but . . . I related more to the idea of the *kiddushin* in its meaning as distinction (*havdalah*), in that Udi differentiates me from the rest of the world and I differentiate Udi from the rest of the men. So it didn't depress me.

The women who chose this second strategy tried to interpret the act of *kiddushin* in a new way and to give the traditional halakhah a unique, personal meaning. They navigated between the public and the personal aspects of the act, conscious of the tension that exists between the traditional and generally accepted meaning and the personal meaning they chose to give it. Their personal interpretation is not expressed publicly but remains part of a dialogue they conduct internally, within themselves. The need of these women to reinvent the meaning of the ritual act recalls the writing of the feminist scholar Adrienne Rich, who formulated the notion of Re-vision and women's need to reinterpret canonical texts: "Re-vision—the act of looking back, of seeing with fresh eyes, of entering an old text from a new critical direction—is for women more than a chapter in cultural history: it is an act of survival."[11]

(c) Viewing a Ritual Act as Oppressive

In contrast to the women who chose the above strategies, by which they sought to minimize and reinterpret the act of *kiddushin*, most of the women I interviewed saw *kiddushin* as an act of acquisition and referred explicitly to its legal implications. They not only emphasized what they found problematic about the act itself but also pointed out the problematic social construct they felt it reflects and creates. Oshrat is one woman who expressed this feeling:

> I find *kiddushin* to be offensive. . . . It represents everything that I fight against with all my being. What was so difficult for me—I can still even cry about it when I think about it—was that here I was, at that moment that was going to be so important to me, and I was going to be standing publicly in front of everyone that I loved and cared about, and I was going to let halakhah treat me in a way that I never thought women should be treated. And I didn't know how I was going to do that. On the other hand, I thought, I wanted to be married according to halakhah, and this is a separate thing.

The women who chose the third strategy challenge and undermine this traditional act in the most direct and frontal way. To some extent, they chose to demystify, delegitimize and deconstruct the act of *kiddushin* and the hegemonic discourse. Unlike the other women, they chose not to separate the political from the personal, the symbol from the essence. They chose to acknowledge the power of tradition, patriarchy, visual performance, and the social construction that this act can be said to contain.

2. STRATEGIES OF ACTION

The women in my study confronted the wedding ritual not only via interpretation but also by trying to make various changes to the traditional wedding ritual. It would appear that the way one interprets a ritual act influences the strategy of action employed in performing that act. The women's interpretations were not necessarily consistent: A women could choose to view the act of *kiddushin* as symbolic while viewing the covering of her face with a veil as oppressive—and act accordingly. I discerned four distinct strategies of action among the women I interviewed:

(a) creating a parallel ritual act;
(b) introducing variations on the ritual act;
(c) avoiding a particular ritual act; and
(d) employing legal resistance.

(a) Creating a Parallel Act

The women who adopted the parallel strategy initiated ritual acts that attempted to mirror traditional male rites. By setting a female act opposite the male one, they endeavored to create a performance of equality without running afoul of halakhic prohibitions. Although this does not alter the legal status of *kiddushin* as an act of acquisition, it nevertheless carries important social significance. I shall present two examples of such parallel acts: a double *bedeken* and a double *kiddushin*.

A Double Bedeken

Yael created a counterpart to the traditional *bedeken* ("covering" in Yiddish), in which the groom walks up to the bride, who is sitting passively and quietly on her queenly throne, looks up at her face, and pulls her veil over it. The ritual recalls the story of Rebecca, who covered her face upon first seeing her future husband Isaac. Thus, "the *bedeken* ritual dramatically assimilates the body of the bride to a mythic national body."[12] The *bedeken* usually takes place in front of all the guests at the wedding. Yael proposed to mimic the male act by covering the face of her husband-to-be with his *tallit* (prayer shawl). Because she proposed to do this in tandem with the

traditional *bedeken*, however, she was compelled by the rabbi to perform the entire ritual off to the side. Only she and the two immediate families were present. Yael described the act as follows:

> My solution to these things was always . . . to double the act. . . . So we decided to do a double *bedeken*, but it did not happen in front of all of the guests. . . . I had a very long veil, which touched the floor. Udi covered me with the veil . . . and I covered Udi with his *tallit*, and Udi then did something sweet, he covered us both with his *tallit*, and that was really the most sentimental moment for me . . . because we were alone.

In this case, the woman's ritual innovation, while adding a new act for the woman to perform, reduced the visibility of the man's act. Yael's parallel act does not acquire the same value and meaning as the original act, which is considered obligatory and traditionally takes place in full public view. Nevertheless, Yael viewed the meaning of her act as far more significant than the traditional one. She emphasized its intimate and romantic meaning for her, in contrast to the subjection she said she would have experienced as a result of having her face covered. Yael expressed this feeling by referring to the veil throughout the interview as a *burka*.

A Double Kiddushin

Halakhah does not permit a woman to create a parallel act of *kiddushin*. The Talmud (BT *Kiddushin* 5b) explicitly emphasizes that even if the groom gives his bride the ring while she proclaims "I am hereby consecrated unto you," or if she gives him the ring while he proclaims the *kiddushin* formula, the *kiddushin* becomes invalid. Therefore, the woman cannot precisely mimic the groom in giving the ring, and she cannot recite a parallel statement to the *kiddushin* formula. Nevertheless, many of the women I interviewed sought to mimic the male act in some way. Michal was one such woman.

> Yonatan gave me the ring, and then the rabbi said, "And now Michal." It was right afterwards, although the rabbi said a few words in between, since according to halakhah you need to differentiate the two acts. And then the rabbi let me give Yonatan the ring, but I had to say to the rabbi beforehand that I wanted him to recite word

by word the verse I had chosen, because the woman always gives the ring, but no one notices that it has happened. So the rabbi read the verse "Simeni kahotam" ["place me as a seal (upon your heart)," Song of Songs 8:6] word by word out loud, and I repeated after him, word by word, and then I put the ring on Yonatan.

Michal demanded that the rabbi give her act the same prominence as that of her husband, by requiring him to recite her phrase aloud with her repeating after him. Thus, she subtly coaxed the rabbi not only into permitting and making room for her parallel act, but also into actually becoming an active participant in her act of resistance.

Many of the women who sought to mimic the male act of *kiddushin* encountered resistance from their parents, their fiancés, and mainly from the officiating rabbis, because of the halakhic problems such parallel acts aroused. Frequently they were compelled to compromise. Thus, a delicate game of semantics occurred in the negotiations between the rabbi and the woman or the couple. For example, a bride might be permitted to recite a phrase similar to the groom's *harei at mekudeshet li* but not to give a ring to the groom publicly; or she could recite a unique phrase that did not so explicitly mimic the male phrase and then be permitted to give him a ring publicly; and so on. There is also significance to the stage at which the rabbis allow the parallel act to occur. Some rabbis allowed the bride's parallel act to take place almost immediately after the groom's. Others insisted upon a longer interruption between the two acts and moved the female act to the end of the *hupah*. In both cases they emphasized that the bride's act is not to be considered *kiddushin*. The rabbis thus reasserted their control over the ceremony both by dictating the timing of the parallel female act and by imposing constraints on its content.

While the parallel acts formulated by the women are meant to demonstrate their potency and their active participation in the ritual by expressing mutuality, equal presence, and activity, the actions taken by the rabbis pulled in a different direction. While they were open to many of these expressions of mutuality and willing to make room for them, they nonetheless did not accept the proposed innovations without requiring that they be modified

in various ways. By insisting upon differentiation between the male act and the female act, the rabbis emphasize the different status of the innovative act rather than its mutuality. Ironically, then, the act of imitation, which is designed to express a diminution of the hegemonic, halakhic, and social power structure, may emphasize the women's exclusion and their limited equality.

(b) Variations on the Ritual Act

In this second strategy, the change is not an addition to the male act, but rather a variation on a traditional act such as circling the groom, the seven blessings under the *hupah*, the *bedeken*, or reading the *ketubah*. In this section I present two such variations. The first is Tehila's reinterpretation of the *bedeken*:

> I agreed with David that after he covered me . . . he would go to the *hupah*, and I would take off the veil. I would then approach the *hupah* without a veil and participate in the wedding ritual without a veil. . . . I learned this from my friend. . . . It was the first wedding in my life where I saw a bride whose face was not covered under the *hupah*. . . . She went to her *hupah* proudly, with joy and strength. I discovered that because she was not covered, she was more involved and was situated just as her husband was. When I saw a bride without a veil, I understood that a bride with a veil is merely a shadow; she doesn't really exist there. She is . . . extinguished—she is somehow transparent. . . . I have a need not to be an object and not to be annulled, so I project it all onto the veil.

Tehila and other women who performed similar variations on the *bedeken* felt that this ritual made them to some degree absent. For them, the *bedeken* symbolized their invisibility as women. Many of them described the veil in similar terms: shadow, transparency, covering, *burka*, object. These terms speak of invisibility in its deepest sense: They describe not only a physical absence, but an absence of the spirit—a reduced being. For these women, transforming their invisibility into an unconcealed presence effected a reparation. They created a discourse that connects physical visibility—revealing the face—with an essential spiritual visibility: as a subject, as a responsible being, equal in value and status, and, above all, present. They acted out an equal and powerful feminist identity.

Another ritual act that inspired variations was the *ketubah*. Notwithstanding the halakhic difficulty of making substantive changes to the required content of the contract, many women found creative ways to alter it. The changes included inserting their mothers' names alongside their fathers'; taking out certain expressions, such as the word "virgin" (describing the status of the bride); adding paragraphs declaring a mutual responsibility on the part of both spouses; reading the text in Hebrew instead of Aramaic; signing it themselves; and, finally, having it read aloud under the *hupah* by a woman.

It would appear that the women who choose to make variations on the *ketubah* do so in order to feel more comfortable with the legal contract insofar as it relates to the act of acquisition. By altering the *ketubah* ritual, they transform it from an alienating experience into one that has personal meaning. By using a woman's voice, altering the language, and emphasizing female presence and equality, they appropriate the act, in a way confiscating it from the male sphere. They thus perform not only their own identity but also that of the other women who become participants in the *ketubah* ritual.

(c) Avoiding the Ritual Act

I found only one ritual act with respect to which the strategy of avoidance was employed: the circling of the groom, which some women saw as a blatant manifestation of the patriarchal social order. Rivki described her reasons for not performing this act:

> I didn't want to circle him, although I learned about it and realized that one can interpret it in feminist ways. . . . The feeling, the experience of circling him, didn't seem to me appropriate.

Unlike the other ritual acts mentioned above, in which there is room for debate as to whether the ritual is only a custom or has more substantive halakhic status, circling the groom is clearly a custom, practiced only at Ashkenazi weddings. The interviewees told me that their negotiations with the rabbis regarding exemption from this act were usually

less contentious than those regarding other ritual acts. Nevertheless, their non-performance of this act reflected objection and protest. In this case, not performing the act is the performance itself.

(d) Legal Resistance

This fourth strategy differs from the other strategies in that it seeks directly to alter the acquisitional nature of the ritual. It typically does not involve a public performance under the *hupah*; rather, it has to do with drafting and signing documents in the presence of an attorney, with the intention of diminishing the legal status of *kiddushin* as an act of acquisition. The core legal document employed in this strategy is the prenuptial agreement,[13] which purports not to replace the *ketubah* but rather to supplement it by stipulating the exercise of economic pressure, in the form of increased alimony payments, in the case of a man refusing to give his wife her *get* (or of her refusing to receive it).[14] Many modern Orthodox rabbis agree that such an agreement is binding under Jewish law. The prenuptial agreement thus represents an attempt to balance the unequal power relations between the couple and to change the halakhic reality in which only a husband has the legal right to decide whether to grant a *get*.

All the women I interviewed dealt in one way or another with the issue of prenuptial agreements. Most of them emphasized that they wished to sign such an agreement, though not all of them actually did so. They gave many explanations to account for this gap between their intentions and their ultimate actions. Among them were their awareness that prenuptial agreements do not help in cases in which the husband disappears or becomes legally incompetent; the difficulties of dealing with divorce-related matters before marriage; the fear of hurting the fiancé's feelings; the belief that their future husband would never use the power granted him by halakhah in case of divorce; the ability of the rabbi to interfere and limit the power of the agreement; the superstitious belief in the "evil eye" which could result from addressing such an issue before marriage; and the general circumstances accompanying the signing. On this matter the women distinguished between the prenuptial agreement in its social context and what it meant to them personally. On the personal level, they felt secure enough with their future husbands that they did not feel the need for an agreement and did not bother to sign one, even though they were aware of the socio-political meaning and the ideological power of such an act.

Shira, an attorney, chose not only to sign a prenuptial agreement, but to do so in public. She had difficulties accepting the halakhic-legal status that the traditional ritual bestows upon the woman after her marriage.

> Obviously, the bottom line is, at least in my opinion, that the rituals reflect the whole distortion of women's status. The feeling that you are there but still rejected increased before my wedding. We had to decide how we wished to do the ritual and what we would do if, God forbid, something happens to Shachar after we are married . . . because the ritual is very, very problematic. The status (of the woman) is even more problematic than the ritual itself. . . . I told Shachar at that time: "Even if you want to be the most wonderful person in the world, if God forbid something happens to you and you can't exercise your volition [and grant a *get*], then I am stuck, and why should that be?" It has no apparent justification . . . so we signed a prenuptial agreement. . . . We signed it under the *hupah*, between the *kiddushin* and the *nisu'in*. Later, one of my brothers-in-law told me that he had heard someone saying that it seemed like I would be the one wearing the trousers at home. I said, "It's such a pity we wasted a plate on him."

Shira's act sought not only to express rebellion against the social order but also, in a way, to help initiate a revolution by changing the essential gender power difference that is expressed in and by the wedding ritual.[15] That this direction was apparent to others in attendance, at least to some degree, is indicated by the negative remark of Shira's male guest. The notion of signing a prenuptial agreement often makes both men and women feel uncomfortable, since it brings into the open gender-based power inequities that usually are veiled beneath a discourse that emphasizes romance, preservation of tradition, or divine sanction.

Assessing the Four Strategies

It is difficult to gauge which of the four strategies I have discussed is likely to prove the most significant, influential, or radical. It seems to me that the women are best differentiated from one another not by the strategy each of them chose, but rather by the ideology on which their strategy drew. Most of my interviewees, in the final analysis, hewed to a liberal feminist approach of striving to work within the male-dominated establishment to carve out legal, political, and economic rights and a life experience for women parallel to those available to men.[16] By and large, they sought not to attack the foundations of the system, but rather to make changes from within. Although their innovative practices lack immediate legal impact (except for the prenuptial agreement), they carry subversive meaning. The women I studied view their performance as a political and social act that places them at the center of the ritual, as independent religious actors: actors who are not only covered but also cover; who are not only acquired but also acquire; who are not only consecrated but also consecrate.

A smaller subgroup among my interviewees articulated an approach marked by elements of radical feminism, seeking, via the ritual, to create a new social order. According to Rosemarie Tong, radical feminism strives to undermine and challenge the most basic assumptions of existence and to examine in depth the social, psychological, and emotional constructs that characterize women and men.[17] Although the women in my study did ultimately take part in a hegemonic and patriarchal ritual, they expressed their protest by trying to create an alternative discourse that distinguishes itself from hegemonic power and halakhah and makes an essential break with the traditional language and content. The women who took the more radical path tended to be dissatisfied with the mere performance of equality, instead seeking out alternatives such as legal resistance.

As we have seen, invented acts that cannot be confused with the traditional parameters of the wedding ritual by and large are not perceived by the public and the rabbinic establishment as undermining the existing framework or boundaries of halakhah, in terms of how halakhah fixes gender roles. In contrast, the women who seek to undermine and invert ritualized gender roles, within the halakhic system and within the context of the traditional ritual (e.g., by giving a ring to the groom, allowing women to participate in the seven blessings under the canopy, removing the veil, and covering the groom), are seen as more threatening to society and the establishment. These women seek to relocate the delicate border lines of halakhah and maneuver between the permissible and the prohibited, thereby forcing the rabbis into complex negotiations, both in terms of halakhah and in terms of social politics.

CONCLUSION

I believe that the women in my study—whether or not they are aware of it—are driven in part by life politics. A politics of lifestyle emphasizing political issues that flow from processes of self-actualization and self-identity in post-traditional contexts. By acting on their interpretation of and their resistance to the traditional ritual, they create a performance in which they are able to unite their identities as religious women and as feminists. In so doing, they appropriate the wedding ritual and transform it from a formal one, repeated from one ceremony to the next, into a formulation and expression of their own values and ideals, thereby redefining themselves in the public sphere. Rivki said,

> To sum up, there isn't religiousness on the one hand and my life on the other hand.... My religiousness empowers the personal moment, and my personal moment expresses my religiousness.... Otherwise, it's just a mask.

Most of the women chose to deal with the inequalities of their wedding rituals by creating different ritual acts. They exploited performative opportunities to create balance in the ceremony, adding elements that they or other women could perform that would parallel the traditional men's performances. Most of them would not consider themselves "radicals"; they are not seeking outlets for free-floating creativity, nor do they wish to reject halakhah wholesale. They are essentially liberal feminists looking for some measure of equality and defining that equality, for the most part, in terms of women getting to do what men get to do—at least in terms of performative rituals.

Each of the different strategies the women chose has its own significance and force. Each deals in its own unique way with the different issues raised by the traditional ritual. The strategies ultimately influenced how the women see themselves—but they had a broader effect as well. Some of the women indicated that they themselves had been influenced by the actions of their female counterparts in public ceremonies they had attended. Many of them consciously and intentionally exploited the public event of the wedding to try and create a social declaration via their performances and thus to create social change in the religious system. These new performances thus become a form of "educating" the public toward a more feminist wedding ritual that emphasizes the alliance between two equal subjects. Based on my research, I argue that the combination of all these strategies can generate change on the public level and move these strategies and performances from the margins toward the center, where they can exert—and appear already to exert—significant influence.

Most of the women ultimately chose not to confront the core problem of the ritual as an act of acquisition. Their acts confront the traditional ritual without displacing the male hegemony and social order that sustain it. As feminism gains currency and more widespread acceptance in the culture, a more frontal confrontation with the essentially problematic nature of the woman's acquisition by her husband may be required, if the traditional ceremony is to retain its social relevance. The ritual that might result—lacking the component of acquisition but nevertheless based on traditional components and in dialogue with those elements—would have to draw on the interpretive and performative strategies of radical feminism. My interviews have revealed the budding of this approach; its future remains to be seen.

NOTES

1. This article is based on my ongoing dissertation research. I could not have written it without the dedicated help and advice of both my advisors, Prof. Susan Sered and Dr. Elisheva Baumgarten. I wish to thank them both. I also wish to thank Bar Ilan University and the Hadassah-Brandeis Institute for helping me fund this research. The article is based on a lecture I delivered at a conference hosted by Prof. Tova Cohen of the Gender Studies Department at Bar Ilan

University. Entitled "Harei at mehudeshet li" ("you are hereby renewed unto me"—a play on the traditional wedding formula *Harei at mekudeshet li*), the conference dealt with various interventions in the traditional wedding ritual. An earlier version of some of the ideas discussed herein appeared in my article, "Harei at mehudeshet li," *Eretz Acheret*, 22 (2004), pp. 69–73.

2. My dissertation addresses in detail the negotiations that took place with the grooms, the mothers, and the fathers. I will not enter here into a systematic discussion of the effect of those negotiations upon the actions of the brides.

3. These neighborhoods are the venue of several liberal Jewish study centers and of various types of social, religious, and spiritual activities. Their populations include a sufficient concentration of immigrants from English-speaking countries to constitute a reference group for the women I studied. Many of the religious Jews in these neighborhoods could fairly be characterized as liberal Orthodox, in that they seek to challenge some aspects of Orthodoxy while remaining within the halakhic framework. In this article, "halakhah" refers to Jewish law as interpreted by Orthodox rabbis, which is the halakhah that the women I studied had to challenge, resist, and adapt in order to formulate the type of wedding rituals they desired. All the rabbis I interviewed were Orthodox. The Conservative Movement has construed halakhah in ways that have allowed it to introduce significant changes in the traditional ritual.

4. There is no civil marriage in Israel, so that matrimony, for all sectors of the population, is governed by religious law (Orthodox Jewish, Moslem, or Christian). However, the state recognizes civil marriages performed outside its borders.

5. For feminist perspectives on the traditional wedding ritual, and specifically on the legal and cultural implications of *kiddushin* as an act of acquisition, see: Judith Wegner, *Chattel or Person? The Status of Women in the Mishnah* (New York: Oxford University Press, 1988); Orit Kamir, *Feminism, Rights, and Law* (Tel Aviv: Ministry of Defense Press, 2002), Chapter 9 (Hebrew); Susan Aranoff, "Two Views of Marriage—Two Views of Women: Reconsidering *Tav Lemetav Tan du Milemetav Armelu*," *Nashim: A Journal of Jewish Women's Studies and Gender Issues*, 3 (2000), pp. 199–227; Susan Okin, "Marriage, Divorce, and the Politics of Family Life," in Tova Cohen (ed.), *Marriage, Liberty and Equality: Shall the Three Walk Together?* (Ramat Gan: Bar-Ilan University, the Jewish Women's Research Center, 2000), pp. 7–26; Rachel Adler, *Engendering Judaism: An*

Inclusive Theology and Ethics (Philadelphia: Jewish Publication Society, 1998), Chapter 5; Susan Sered, Romi Kaplan, and Samuel Cooper, "Talking About Miqveh Parties, or: Discourses of Gender, Hierarchy and Social Control," in Rahel Wasserfall (ed.), *Women and Water: Menstruction in Jewish Life and Law* (Hanover, NH: University Press of New England, 1999), pp. 139–165.

6. Wegner, *Chattel or Person* (above, note 5), pp. 66–72. In Wegner's view, what is acquired is the woman's sexuality, not the woman herself. Even if the bride were to speak, her words would have no effect, since she is not legally capable of acquiring her groom's sexuality in the way that he is capable of acquiring hers.

7. An *agunah* is a woman whose husband has disappeared or is otherwise unable to give his wife a *get*. A *mesurevet get* is a woman whose husband abuses the power given to him by the halakhah and refuses to grant her a *get*. For more information on *agunot* and *mesuravot get* see www.agunot.org.

8. Kamir, *Feminism, Rights and Law* (above, noe 5), pp. 142–146.

9. What follows is a brief survey; I intend to elaborate further on the women's strategies of interpretation in my dissertation.

10. I treat *kiddushin* as the central act of the wedding ritual because halakhah regards it as the indispensable ritual element without which no marriage can be effectuated.

11. Adrienne Rich, "When We Dead Awaken: Writing as Re-Vision," in idem, *On Lies, Secrets and Silences: Selected Prose 1966–1978* (New York: W.W. Norton, 1979), p. 35.

12. Susan Sered, *What Makes Women Sick? Maternity, Modesty, and Militarism in Israeli Society* (Hanover, NH: Brandeis University Press, 2000), p. 117.

13. The Hebrew text of the prenuptial agreement worked out by Kolech: Religious Women's Forum for use in Israel can be found at: http://www.kolech.com/subcat1.php?main=1&&cat=48.

14. According to halakhah, for a Jewish couple to get divorced, the man must give the woman a *get* (writ of divorce) of his own free will, and she must accept it.

15. For the distinction between rites of rebellion and acts of revolution, see Max Gluckman, *Custom and Conflict in Africa* (Oxford: Basil Blackwell, 1970), pp. 122–123.

16. Rosemarie Tong, *Feminist Thought: A More Comprehensive Introduction* (second edition; Boulder CO: Westview Press, 1998), pp. 10–44.

17. *Ibid.*, pp. 45–93.

Violence Against Women Worldwide

Patti Duncan

Patti Duncan, Associate Professor of Women Studies at Oregon State University, USA, specializes in transnational feminist theories and movements, women of color, and Asian Pacific American women's writings and experiences. She is the author of *Tell This Silence: Asian American Women Writers and the Politics of Speech* (University of Iowa Press, 2004), and articles about women of color, feminist pedagogies, and transnational feminisms. She is co-producer/director of *Finding Face* (2009), a documentary film about acid violence as a gendered form of violence. Her current research focuses on the effects of militarism and war on women in Asia, and gendered forms of violence in global contexts.

> every 3 minutes a woman is beaten
> every five minutes a
> woman is raped/every ten minutes
> a lil girl is molested
> yet i rode the subway today
> i sat next to an old man who
> may have beaten his old wife
> 3 minutes ago or 3 days/30 years ago...

Excerpt from "With No Immediate Cause" by Ntozake Shange.

Gendered violence occurs within every continent, country, and cultural context, affects women of all racial, ethnic, cultural, religious, and socioeconomic groups, and is the most pervasive, yet least prosecuted, human rights violation worldwide. As Ntozake Shange suggests in her poem above, violence against women is normalized in its ordinariness, despite the magnitude of the crimes and their consequences in the lives of women and girls. The 1993 United Nations' Declaration on the Elimination of Violence Against Women (DEVAW) defines violence against women as "any act of gender-based violence that results in, or is likely to result in, physical, sexual, or psychological harm or suffering to women, including threats of such acts, coercion, or arbitrary deprivation of liberty, whether occurring in public or private life" (General Assembly resolution 48/104). Forms of gendered violence include domestic violence, sexual harassment, sexual abuse, rape, forced prostitution, trafficking, stalking, "honor" killings, dowry-associated violence, female genital cutting, and hate crimes directed at particular groups, including lesbian, bisexual, and transgender women, women of color and women of the Global South, and/or women of particular ethnic, religious, or cultural groups. Violence may range from sexist jokes in the workplace to mass rapes and even genocidal practices.

Many authors, activists, and organizations such as the United Nations (UN) and the World Health Organization (WHO) employ the terms "gendered violence," "gender-based violence," and "violence against women" to describe these crimes against women. While such terms are often used interchangeably in the literature, some authors suggest that "violence against women" is an important term because it stresses the fact that victims of domestic violence and intimate partner violence are usually women, and that these forms of violence, while they may be directed at all genders, are most likely to target women. Others attempt to highlight the ways in which "gendered violence," for example, may specifically target women—and men—who challenge or transgress local gender norms within their societies. In this chapter, I use these three terms somewhat interchangeably, specifying when I discuss particular forms of violence against women.

It is difficult to assess the incidence of gender-based violence because such violence is often accepted, seen as normal, natural, harmless, or even deserved. Also, domestic or family-based violence is often viewed as a private matter to be resolved between intimate partners or family members. Victims of gendered violence are also deeply stigmatized in most societies, and many survivors feel shame and humiliation, and may be reluctant to report the violence for fear of additional violence perpetrated by law enforcement officials. Indeed, WHO identifies violence against women as a major health problem and a human rights issue, citing the statistic that at least one in five of the world's female population has been subjected to physical or sexual abuse at some point in her lifetime. As in discussions of other themes in previous chapters, it is important to recognize that violence against women is not simply a private matter, or the acts of individual men against individual women. Rather, such violence forms a larger social, structural issue, created and perpetuated by social institutions worldwide, which serves as a means to maintain control over women.

The passing of the Declaration on the Elimination of Violence Against Women (DEVAW) by the United Nations General Assembly in 1993 represented a turning point in international discourse on violence against women. For the first time, the international community explicitly recognized gendered violence as not simply a private issue, but a human rights concern requiring state intervention. As a result, the Commission on Human Rights adopted Resolution 1994/45 in March 1994 and appointed Radhika Coomaraswamy as the first Special Rapporteur on violence against women. Coomaraswamy was charged with collecting and analyzing information on violence against women, particularly its causes and consequences, in order to recommend measures to eliminate such violence at national, regional, and international levels.

In her investigation, Coomaraswamy focused on three areas of concern in which women are particularly vulnerable: (1) the family, in which women and girls may experience domestic violence, sexual abuse, marital rape, and practices such as infanticide, female genital cutting, and dowry-related violence; (2) the general community, in which women may be subjected to rape and sexual assault, sexual harassment, labor exploitation, and trafficking; and (3) the state, in which women and girls may experience violence perpetrated or condoned by the government and other agencies, including violence associated with reproductive health, detention, and the criminal justice system. In considering these categories, it is important to emphasize the effects of the processes of economic and cultural globalization that include increasing militarism in many regions of the world, and to remember that these categories are interconnected and overlapping. Women and girls particularly vulnerable to violence include members of ethnic minority groups; indigenous, displaced, and refugee women and girls; migrant women, including migrant women workers; women and girls working in the sex industry; those living in poverty and/or on the street; women in detention; women and girls with disabilities; elderly women; and those in situations of armed conflict. Such an extensive list encompasses millions of people around the world!

Over the past few decades gendered forms of violence have received increasing international political attention. For example, the 1995 Beijing Platform for Action document, which emerged from the 1995 Fourth World Conference on Women, asserts that violence against women constitutes not only a human rights violation but also a direct obstacle to achieving equality, peace, and development. Ten years later, a 10-country study suggests that domestic violence remains just as prevalent, representing both a public policy and human rights issue that affects women and the children who experience and/or witness such abuse (WHO multi-country study, 2005). The reading "The Conservation of Energy," a poem by Chana Bloch, describes the effects of violence in children's lives.

Violence against women has profound and long-term consequences. For women and girls aged 15 to 44 years, violence is a major cause of death and disability. Forms of violence may lead to additional health problems, including a wide range of physical disorders (injuries, HIV infection, unintended pregnancy, trauma to the reproductive tract), as well as emotional distress, depression, post-traumatic stress disorder, substance abuse, and suicide attempts. Social costs associated with violence against women include limited ability to care for oneself or one's children, isolation, and lack of participation in regular activities, as well as stigma, and rejection by partners, husbands, families, and communities (WHO multi-country study, 2005; WHO, 2008). Unfortunately, many survivors of sexual violence are unable to report the assault because of shame, stigma, fear of rejection by one's family and/or community, and even the risk of further violence or even death. In some countries, legislation exists that allows a rapist to escape prosecution if he marries the victim. In these cases, women may be forced to marry their attackers, or they may be ostracized, beaten, or imprisoned for the crime of sex outside of marriage, or even killed by family members in the name of honor (UN, 2008). It is therefore likely that there are many more incidents of sexual violence than are currently reported. In addition, many scholars and activists note the fear and insecurity that results from threats of violence. Such fear severely limits women's movement and basic activities, as well as access to resources. Violence or the threat of violence creates barriers to women's and girls' full participation in society, and represents a serious obstacle to women's empowerment, gender equality, reproductive health, and human rights.

Ending Violence Against Women: From Words to Action

According to the Secretary-General's in-depth study on violence against women:

- There is compelling evidence that violence against women is severe and pervasive throughout the world. Surveys on violence against women conducted in at least 71 countries show that a significant proportion of women suffer physical, sexual, or psychological violence.

- The most common form of violence experienced by women globally is physical violence inflicted by an intimate partner. On average, at least one in three women is subjected to intimate partner violence in the course of her lifetime.
- Many women are subjected to sexual violence by an intimate partner. A WHO study in 11 countries found that the percentage of women who had been subjected to sexual violence by an intimate partner ranged between 6 percent in Japan and Serbia and Montenegro and 59 percent in Ethiopia.
- Psychological or emotional violence by intimate partners is also widespread. The proportion of women found to have suffered severe psychological violence ranged from 10 percent in Egypt to 51 percent in Chile. The first French national survey on violence against women found that 35 percent of women had experienced psychological pressure by an intimate partner over a 12-month period.
- Femicide—the murder of women—has different characteristics from murders of men and often involves sexual violence. Between 40 and 70 percent of female murder victims are killed by husbands or boyfriends in Australia, Canada, Israel, South Africa, and the United States. In Colombia, one woman is reportedly killed by her partner or former partner every six days. Hundreds of women were (and still are) abducted, raped, and murdered in and around Ciudad Juárez, Mexico, over a 10-year period.
- More than 130 million girls have been subjected to female genital mutilation/cutting. The practice, most prevalent in Africa and some countries in the Middle East, is also prevalent among immigrant communities in Europe, North America, and Australia.
- Women experience sexual harassment throughout their lives. Between 40 and 50 percent of women in the European Union reported some form of sexual harassment in the workplace. In Malawi, 50 percent of schoolgirls surveyed reported sexual harassment at school.
- The majority of the hundreds of thousands of people trafficked each year are women and children, and many are trafficked for purposes of sexual exploitation.
- Violence against women in armed conflict often includes sexual violence. Between 250,000 and 500,000 women were raped during the 1994 genocide in Rwanda; between 20,000 and 50,000 women were raped during the conflict in Bosnia in the early 1990s.
- Many women face multiple forms of discrimination and an increased risk of violence. Indigenous women in Canada are five times more likely than other women of the same age to die as the result of violence. In Europe, North America, and Australia, over half of women with disabilities have experienced physical abuse, compared to one-third of nondisabled women.
- Domestic violence and rape account for 5 percent of the total disease burden for women aged 15 to 44 in developing countries and 19 percent in developed countries. Violence places women at higher risk of poor physical and reproductive health outcomes, and abused women also show poorer mental health and social functioning.
- Women who have experienced violence are at higher risk of contracting HIV. Fear of violence also prevents women from accessing HIV/AIDS information and receiving treatment and counseling.
- Girls who are targeted for violence are less likely to complete their education. A study in Nicaragua found that children of female victims of violence left school an average of four years earlier than other children.
- The costs of violence against women—both direct and indirect—are extremely high. These costs include the direct costs of services to treat and support abused women and their children and to bring perpetrators to justice. The indirect costs include lost employment and productivity, and the costs in human pain and suffering.
- In Canada, a 1995 study estimated the annual direct costs of violence against women to be Can$684 million for the criminal justice system, Can$187 million for police, and Can$294 million for the cost of counseling and training, totaling more than Can$1 billion a year. A 2004 study in the United Kingdom estimated the total direct and indirect costs of domestic violence, including pain and suffering, to be £23 billion per year or £440 per person.

Source: http://www.un.org

Financial costs associated with violence against women are also considerable. Alongside inability to work and loss of wages on the part of individuals, gender-based violence severely impacts economic development for nations. A report by the Centers for Disease Control and Prevention in 2003 estimated the costs of intimate partner violence in the United States to exceed $5.8 billion each year, including over US$4 billion in medical and healthcare services and almost US$2 billion in productivity losses.

Of central importance in this discussion of gender-based violence is consideration of the ways Western paradigms shape discourse on violence against women, and, in particular, how they may produce stereotypes and misunderstandings about women in the Global South. For example, cultural relativism, the idea that individuals should be understood in the context of their particular society, is often used to suggest that "culture" can explain or rationalize violence against women. In her book *Dislocating Cultures,* Uma Narayan (1997) asks why "culture" is so often invoked as an explanation for violence against women in the Global South, but not in discussions about forms of violence that affect mainstream Western women. Narayan discusses stereotypes of women in India, for example, that facilitate statements like "Every day women are burned to death in India": a generalized assumption that Indian women (like other "Third World" women) suffer "death by culture" in their portrayal as perpetual victims of this culture. In this analysis Narayan questions "the 'effects' that national contexts have on the 'construction' of feminist issues and the ways in which understandings of issues are then affected by their 'border-crossings' across national boundaries" (p. 84). In the reading "Do Muslim Women Really Need Saving?" in chapter 12 Lila Abu Lughod similarly reminds us of the dangers associated with "cultural" explanations for violence against women.

The colonizing tendencies critiqued by Narayan, as well as by Chandra Talpade Mohanty (see introduction and chapter 1), include a critique of constructions of "Third World" women within a universal patriarchal framework. These constructions often result in women of the Global South being stereotyped, frozen in time, decontextualized, and seen as always already victimized by male violence, family, religion, and culture. It is this belief in the average, monolithic "Third World" woman who shares a common history, language, and set of experiences, that prevents acknowledgment of the distinct ways in which women negotiate their oppression and resistance. Forms of violence affecting women in the Global South such as dowry-related violence and acid throwing are no more "exotic" or "cultural" than the many ways in which women experience physical and systematic oppression within Western countries. It may be more a matter of context and expedience. Such an analysis compels us to examine intersectionality (intersections of gender with race, ethnicity, nationality, class, sexuality, religion, etc.) and understand the necessity to focus on social, historical, and political explanations and contexts that shape women's lives (in all our/their diversity). In other words, categories of violence often referred to as "traditional" should be understood in relation to shifting cultural, socioeconomic, and political processes.

This chapter explores the global reality of violence against women and is organized around the categories discussed above from the Commission on Human Rights. The first section addresses gender-based violence in the family and between intimate partners with a focus on the consequences of son preference; physical and sexual violence; dowry-related violence and honor killings; and female genital cutting. This is followed by a section on violence against girls and women in communities that explores sexual harassment and assault; acid violence; hate crimes; sex trafficking and prostitution; and militarism. The third section addresses violence perpetuated or condoned by the state and discusses violence against women and girls by law officials; health and reproductive issues; armed conflict; and globalization. The chapter concludes with a focus on social change efforts to address gender-based violence and promote the safety of women worldwide.

VIOLENCE IN FAMILIES AND BY INTIMATE PARTNERS

Son Preference

Violence affects women of all ages throughout the life cycle, and harm against women and girls in family contexts is all too common. As discussed in previous chapters, violence begins even before birth through a preference for sons, which may lead to sex-selective abortions. Sons are expected to take care of aging parents in many cultures, whereas daughters are seen as marrying into other families and therefore may be perceived as financial burdens to their parents. After birth, girls may also be vulnerable to neglect in terms of food, education, and basic health care, as well as multiple forms of physical, sexual, and emotional abuse that includes infanticide (Plan International, 2007). As discussed in the previous chapter, son preference may also lead to child marriage in many countries, particularly within sub-Saharan Africa, Asia, and parts of the Middle East. Children are often married early for economic reasons, and parents may justify the practice as a means of escaping poverty and securing a better future for their daughters and themselves. Also, in contexts of armed conflict, parents may marry their daughters off early to protect them from sexual violence or kidnapping. However, early forced marriages often result in young girls' increased risk for gender-based violence and exposure to HIV/AIDS, and limit their ability to obtain an education. Girls who marry early also tend to have less economic and household power, less mobility, less exposure to media, limited social networks, and greater reproductive health risks. It is estimated that more than 100 million girls under the age of 18 will be married over the next decade (Haberland et al., 2004).

Physical and Sexual Violence

By far the most common form of violence against women globally is domestic violence. In a 10-country study conducted by WHO, between 15 and 71 percent of women reported physical or sexual violence by a husband or partner. In the United States, domestic violence is defined as "a pattern of abusive behavior in any relationship that is used by one partner to gain or maintain power and control over another intimate partner" (U.S. Department of Justice). Globally, the term "domestic violence" is used interchangeably with "family violence," "intimate partner violence," and "wife abuse." Domestic violence includes physical violence, sexual violence, and psychological, emotional, and economic actions that influence another person in the home, within the family, or within an intimate relationship. It may include verbal or emotional abuse, threatening behavior, intimidation, insults and put-downs, shaming, humiliation, harassment, isolation, confinement, manipulation, coercion, and the control of physical, economic, and other resources. It may also include threats to take custody of children, or the use of a woman's racial, ethnic, cultural, religious, or sexual identity against her by threatening to withhold legal documents, for example. Given the fact that domestic violence is often underreported due to survivors' feelings of confusion, shame, and self-blame, as well as fear of public reprisals and the fact that domestic violence has long been considered a private matter, it is likely that incidence rates are actually much higher than reported. Additional studies indicate that women are more likely to be injured or killed by their own partners than by anyone else. Domestic violence or family violence may be so extreme that some researchers liken it to torture (Coomaraswamy, 2002).

Power Surge: Rural Women in South Africa Are Doing It for Themselves by *Heidi Bachram*

"I am rural. I am poor. I am black. And, of course, I am a woman," explains Sizani Ngubane, the founder of the Rural Women's Movement (RWM) in South Africa. "My mother was abused by my father and his male relatives. I grew up knowing I had to be part of the solution." Her conviction can be heard in the power of her words, but it's the twinkle in her eye and the warm smile that have the biggest impact. It feels like Sizani Ngubane can handle anything.

That same sense of power and confidence permeates RWM, an organization that has now grown to more than 500 community-based groups in Kwa-Zulu Natal.

RWM works from the principle that women need economic and political independence from male relatives and partners to guarantee their rights and survival. In theory, the South African constitution does recognize women's rights; in practice, it's been another matter, particularly in land ownership. Sizani elaborates: "In 1995 when the Government implemented the land reform program, the majority of people filing claims were men. This was because during apartheid land was seen as a 'men's issue' while health and childcare were seen as 'women's issues'." Exacerbating this problem is the continued observance of customary law which is biased toward male land ownership and inheritance rights. As a result women and girls could be forcibly evicted from family land if a marriage breaks down or a husband dies. To make matters worse these cases were often seen as "private family matters." Sizani realized there needed to be public debate on the issues. "As rural women we were voiceless in most situations. Women who spoke in public meetings were seen as 'unruly' and it was taboo."

In fact, women who did speak out were often beaten by their husbands for doing so and over 50 percent of RWM's membership faced domestic violence. The group's answer is to empower rural women to speak out in public and to run for local elections. They also take up legal cases for women who have been evicted and challenge discriminatory government policies.

"RWM speaks for itself—we do not need other people to speak on our behalf," Sizani states firmly. The network has racked up an impressive number of achievements—from supporting women to set up their own income-generating projects, helping members resist marriages with their brother-in-law after the death of their husband, to feeding into the drafting of legislation on land rights.

In fact RWM has been so successful that it has begun to connect with women's rights movements across Africa. At the World Social Forum in Nairobi over 40 women's organizations met to discuss tactics and share knowledge and information. Groups inspired each other to take on new campaigns where none existed before, fostering solidarity between African women's networks. Sizani's excitement is palpable. She clearly sees signs that times are finally changing.

"The very same men who used to beat up their partners when they found out that they had attended women's meetings are now taking care of the children while we're attending the World Social Forum."

It is important to highlight the fact that domestic violence cuts across national, geographic, socioeconomic, racial, ethnic, and cultural lines, and it occurs in both heterosexual and same-sex relationships, though the majority of victims of domestic violence are women and the perpetrators male. In the United States, for example, where a woman is beaten every 18 minutes, domestic violence is one of the leading causes of injury to women (U.S. Department of Justice; UN, 2008). Between 22 and 35 percent of U.S. women's emergency room visits result from domestic violence. In Pakistan, of 400 cases of domestic violence reported in 1993, nearly 50 percent resulted in the woman's death. In Peru, 70 percent of all reported crimes involve women beaten by their husbands (UN, 2008). Injuries associated with domestic violence include bruises, broken bones, cuts, burns, knife wounds, permanent injuries such as partial loss of vision or hearing, damage to joints, miscarriage, physical disfigurement, extreme trauma, and death (Kirk and Okazawa-Rey, 2004). While a growing number of countries are attempting to strengthen legislation against violence against women, in some parts of the world there are no laws or social sanctions against domestic violence. Even where laws do exist, there is a greater need for their implementation and enforcement. And, even in contexts where there are resources for survivors of domestic violence, members of marginalized communities, such as ethnic minorities, generally face additional barriers and a more difficult time accessing available resources. Because they often do not fit into mainstream strategies for addressing domestic violence, marginalized groups of women are often more reluctant to report such violence, as they are aware that they may face additional forms of violence, including state regulation and surveillance within their communities.

Rape and sexual violence are also widespread within families and between intimate partners. Sexual assault is defined as sexual contact or behavior that occurs without consent, whereas rape is forced sexual intercourse that may involve vaginal, anal, or oral penetration (U.S. Department of Justice). Rape is a form of sexual assault, although sexual assault can occur without incidence of rape. It is estimated that one in three women worldwide experiences sexual assault in her lifetime (UNIFEM; Marshall, 2006). Women everywhere face the risk of sexual assault from perpetrators who are more likely to be friends, family members, or acquaintances than strangers. Approximately one in four women experience sexual violence by an intimate partner and between one and two thirds of all victims are aged 15 years or less (Plan International, 2007; WHO multi-country study, 2005). In the United States, research indicates that a woman is raped every six minutes, with the majority of rapes committed against women by male acquaintances, dates, or partners (U.S. Department of

LEARNING ACTIVITY **Shopping for Shelters**

This project aims to benefit local domestic violence shelters. Work with your local shelter's volunteer coordinator to develop a list of items needed by the shelter that can be purchased at a local grocery store. Ask a local grocery store manager if she or he would be willing to have the store participate in a project to provide resources for the local domestic violence shelter. Then organize a group of people to staff a table outside the store. Copy the list of needed items and have volunteers give a copy of the list to each shopper who enters the store, asking the shoppers if they would be willing to purchase one or more of the requested items to donate to the shelter and drop it off at the table on their way out of the store. At the end of the project, volunteers should deliver the donated items to the shelter.

Justice; UN, 2008). Girls and young women may also experience forms of control, surveillance and stalking, threats, and intimidation from boyfriends, sometimes classified as dating or courtship violence (Kirk and Okazawa-Rey, 2004; Larkin and Popaleni, 1997). Jocelyn A. Lehrer and colleagues studied rape and sexual assault among college women in Chile and found a substantial proportion of young women reported experiences of rape, attempted rape, and other forms of forced sexual contact. The results of this study are reported in the reading "Prevalence of and Risk Factors for Sexual Victimization in College Women in Chile." Sexual assault may also specifically target children—both girls and boys—within families, and childhood sexual abuse is most commonly perpetrated by male family members. It is reported that worldwide as many as 1 in 5 women and 1 in 10 men experience sexual abuse as children (WHO, 2008).

While forced sex within marriage—marital rape—is considered a crime under international law as defined by the Declaration on the Elimination of Violence Against Women, it is still not taken seriously in many countries where men are seen as having a legal right to unlimited sexual access to their wives. Many countries in southern Africa, for example, have no explicit legal provisions criminalizing marital rape (Ali, 2008). In the United States, marital rape was legal until 1976 and is still considered a lesser crime in several states.

Dowry and Honor-Related Violence

Other forms of gender-based violence within the family and between intimate partners include dowry-related violence and honor killings. These are often considered to be rooted in traditional practices and are believed to be part of acceptable cultural practice because they have existed within particular societies for a long time. As already mentioned, while this may have some basis in specific contexts, it is also important to be critical of arguments that suggest certain forms of violence are somehow rooted in certain cultures or religions. Dowry-related violence is reported primarily within South Asia, where traditionally brides' families were expected to pay dowries to their husbands' families. So-called dowry-related harassment and dowry-murders involve women being harassed or killed by their husbands or in-laws, with an insufficient dowry cited as justification. In recent years, women have also been burned by husbands or in-laws with acid, or with kerosene in kitchen fires. In 2002, over six thousand women were killed in India in dowry-associated incidents. In Bangladesh, according to UNIFEM and the Acid Survivors Foundation, between 300 and 500 women were attacked with acid in 2002. Acid violence, while sometimes considered a form of dowry-related violence, also constitutes a form of violence within communities and will be discussed in more detail in the next section. The incidence rate of such practices seems to be increasing and must be adequately historicized and contextualized for a full understanding of the relationship to other forms of violence against women. For example, in sub-Saharan Africa, bridewealth consists of men giving gifts to new brides and their families and often results in women being seen as commodities and subsequently abused (Coomaraswamy, 2002). To fully understand the possible connections between dowry-related and brideweath-related forms of violence, it is necessary to analyze each practice within its social, historical, economic, and political context, and to examine variations across region, religion, culture, class, and caste, among other features.

Honor killings are another extreme form of gendered violence. As discussed in the Amnesty International reading "Killed in the Name of Honor," such violence is deeply rooted in societies in which women are devalued and seen as property. Honor killings refer to the premeditated murder of women and girls by male members of the immediate or extended family, usually as a reaction to some alleged act of sexual impropriety on the part of the victim. Reasons commonly cited for honor killings include women's or girls' suspected adultery, participation in premarital sex, or sexual assault or abuse for which the women victims are blamed. To restore the family's "honor," male family members execute the woman or girl. Each year approximately five thousand women worldwide are killed by family members in the name of honor (WHO, 2008). Honor killings are perpetrated in Pakistan, Turkey, Jordan, Syria, Egypt, Lebanon, Iran, Yemen, Morocco, and other Mediterranean and Gulf countries and have also been reported in Europe. According to Erturk, honor killings are "among the primary causes of unnatural deaths among women in the Kurdish region of northern Iraq" (UN News Centre). While honor killings are frequently associated with Islam and negatively stereotyped accordingly, Aysan Sev'er and Gokcecicek Yurdakul (2006) stress the fact that honor killings actually predate Islam and are not consistent with the Qur'an. Rather than invoke religion for an explanation of honor crimes, these authors suggest that we view this form of violence as one extreme in the worldwide patriarchal system of violence against women. In their analysis of honor killings in Turkey, for example, they highlight the context in which most women are economically dependent on male family members, and the fact that this dependence is legally entrenched. Furthermore, they suggest that the state is not benign in its response to honor killings; rather, male actors of the state, including police officers, judges, and representatives of the court system, often condone such violence and provide lighter senses for perpetrators of honor killings due to "provocation."

A DAY IN THE LIFE   **Duty** by *Michelle Marie*

Naked in her hospital bed, covered only by a sheet suspended a safe distance above her charred skin, Anjanamma wakes to the sounds of breakfast being served. She is in the burn ward of Bangalore's government-run Victoria Hospital, where poor women survivors of bride burnings are brought—and where three fourths of them eventually die. Nationwide, thousands of women are killed by husbands or in-laws each year because their parents fail to pay sufficient dowry after the marriage. Bangalore, in the southern Indian state of Karnataka, has one of the highest rates of dowry death in India. It is common practice for dowry demands, officially illegal in India, to continue throughout the marriage; when a husband wants to go back to school, when his sisters require dowries, or when children are born. When demands are not, or cannot be met, threats of beatings or murder are often carried out.

Generally, although love marriages do occur, Indian women do not choose their own husbands; application of the Hindu principle *dharma*, or the performance of one's duty according to the proper order of things, precludes even the possibility of refusing to marry. Anjanamma's husband Munish, a low-level employee in Bangalore's burgeoning technology industry, had seemed to her parents a husband worthy of the dowry his family demanded. Her parents had been rather relieved that a home theater system, air conditioner, and a suite of new kitchen appliances for his parents was sufficient dowry to secure a financially secure husband for their oldest daughter. Several months into the marriage, however, Munish and his parents began to demand additional cash payments, and threatened Anjanamma when her parents could not comply.

Soon, Munish was beating Anjanamma on a regular basis; when he was drunk, when she did not finish the many household tasks assigned to her, when she did not become pregnant, and when she became pregnant with a daughter. Indian husbands at all income and class levels often consider wife abuse to be an unremarkable fact of life and may beat their wives with minimal provocation. Wives, too, often expect cruelty and make their best effort to "adjust" to their husbands' families' expectations. Instead of acting to protect her daughter-in-law, Munish's mother Vilma joined in the abuse. Indian mothers-in-law may also be frequent agents of mental and physical abuse. Cruelly taunting her for her failure to conceive a son, she and Munish had coerced Anjanamma into agreeing to terminate the pregnancy. Sex-selective abortion, although illegal, is widespread because ultrasounds are a rich source of income for greedy, unethical doctors.

Each night since the abortion three months ago, Munish raped her in their marital bed, hoping to produce a valuable male heir. Schooled from birth to submit to men, Anjanamma did not protest; schooled from childhood that marriage is her sacred duty, she does not consider divorce to be an option. On her infrequent visits with her family, she conceals her bruises and feigns happiness in their choice of her husband to spare their feelings. Besides, her parents would not allow her to return to their home; the resulting stigma would disgrace the family and destroy her younger sister's marriage prospects. When brides do escape to their natal families and dare to display evidence of abuse, their parents often return them to their marital families, reasoning that they belong with their husbands. In extreme cases, such as those in the burn ward, this practice is essentially a death sentence.

Midmorning, as a nurse adjusts Anjanamma's IV medications, her mother-in-law's harsh voice rings in her memory. Coaching her on her cover story during their trip to the hospital the night before, she had admonished Anjanamma to report that her burns were the result of an accidental kitchen fire; that the edge of her sari, which was made of flammable synthetic cloth, had accidentally slipped into the open flame of the family's primus stove. Many such stove accidents are reported, particularly in lower-income urban residences, and there is no doubt that the stoves' poor design and construction constitute a true danger. These true accidents, however, serve to mask the prevalence of intentional wife burning, one of the most common methods of wife homicide and coerced suicide. The scent of kerosene clinging to the remains of Anjanamma's hair tells a different story. Over and over, she relives the moment when she realized that Vilma had splashed kerosene on her face and body. As her world burst into flame, her astonished brain registered that Munish was holding the box of matches.

After lunch, of which she can manage only a few bites, a doctor checks Anjanamma's wounds and assesses her condition. If she worsens to the point of near-death, a social worker will be summoned to record her final statement. In this dying declaration, Anjanamma will have a final opportunity to indict her mother-in-law—unless, of course, Vilma arrives to stand guard over her words. Because they have been married fewer than seven years, dowry death will be automatically suspected if Anjanamma dies. However, even if authorities investigate, the process may extend for several years, and fewer than 1 percent of cases ultimately result in conviction. Because even a coerced dying declaration is admissible evidence, Vilma will have a vested interest in ensuring that the burning is recorded as an accident.

Throughout the afternoon, as Anjanamma's burned skin is cleaned and bandaged, she contemplates her future. On their journey to Victoria Hospital, Munish had insisted that his family would accept her back into their home with a clean slate if only she would exonerate him and Vilma. Although her chances of survival are slim, with burns covering more than 80 percent of her body, Anjanamma is forced to accept his word at face value. Unless one of the women activists working to rescue women burn victims happens to stop by her hospital bed, she will have no choice but to return to her abusers—if she survives. As night falls and the ward transitions into stillness, Anjanamma drifts into a troubled sleep, not knowing if she will wake the following morning, and fearing what might happen if she does.

Female Genital Cutting

Female genital cutting, also commonly referred to as female circumcision or female genital mutilation (FGM), is considered a coming of age ritual for young girls in some parts of the world. As already discussed, it is associated with chastity and fertility and is often deemed necessary for a girl to marry. Affecting more than 130 million women and girls worldwide, the WHO indicates that at least two million more girls are at risk of this practice. Genital cutting may involve partial or total removal of the external female genitalia or female genital organs for non-therapeutic reasons. It is practiced in at least 28 countries in Africa and some Middle Eastern countries, and has also been reported among certain ethnic groups in India, Indonesia, Malaysia, and Sri Lanka, as well as among some indigenous groups in South and Central America, and within immigrant communities within North America, Europe, and Australia (UNIFEM; Abusharaf, 2006).

According to Rogaia Abusharaf (2006), the practice often involves the use of a knife, razor blade, or broken bottle, in unsanitary conditions and without anesthesia or adequate medical training on the part of the practitioner. Lack of sterilization may contribute to the spread of HIV infection as well as other infections, and the lack of anesthesia and medical training results in severe pain, hemorrhaging, shock, and sometimes death. Women who have experienced female genital cutting often suffer from long-term complications, including problems with fertility and childbirth. However, as Abusharaf suggests, female genital cutting is deeply embedded in local belief systems. Hence, when westerners attempt to intervene, local people may view this as an intrusion and another form of colonialism, thereby heightening the resistance to change. It is important to recognize local efforts to address female genital cutting and the fact that there are organizations in 23 African nations working to abolish the practice (Coomaraswamy, 2002). Also, it should be viewed in relation to other issues, such as poverty and lack of resources for local communities. Structural adjustment programs enforced by the World Bank, for example, have resulted in increased privatization and extreme poverty within many African countries. In a context in which women depend on marriage for economic survival (and female genital cutting is considered necessary to be eligible for marriage), it makes sense that this form of gendered violence continues. Furthermore, as already mentioned in chapter 3, some authors have likened the practices of female genital cutting in the Global South to vaginal cosmetic surgeries in the Global North and surgical procedures often performed on intersex babies for the purpose of "sex reassignment" (e.g., to "normalize" the genitals of infants and young children born with reproductive or sexual anatomy that cannot be easily categorized as male or female, and are thus perceived to be outside the traditional gender binary system). As Nancy Ehrenreich (2004) argues, some North American writers frame African practices of female genital cutting as harmful patriarchal rituals while justifying intersex surgeries as legitimate medical responses, thereby obscuring the ways in which both practices are actually rooted in specific cultural contexts and patriarchal systems.

VIOLENCE IN COMMUNITIES

Within their own communities women are also at risk for violence that includes physical violence, sexual harassment and assault, homophobic violence and bullying, hate violence targeting particular groups of women and girls, trafficking in women for forced labor or

LEARNING ACTIVITY **Violence Against Women in Your Community**

Violence against women happens all over the world, including in your own community and on your own campus. To find crime data for your campus for the past three years, visit the Office of Postsecondary Education's Campus Security Data Analysis Cutting Tool at http://ope.ed.gov/security/. You can find more data at the FBI's Uniform Crime Reports at http://www.fbi.gov/ucr/ucr.htm. Find out crime statistics for your state, country, and city, keeping in mind that many violent crimes against women go unreported.

Find out what resources your campus and area offer to support ending violence against women. Does your institution have a women's center? A sexual assault services counselor? Is there a domestic violence shelter in your community? Does your school offer violence prevention education?

Researchers at the University of New Hampshire developed an educational comprehensive bystander social marketing campaign that includes eight images that model bystander behaviors. The campaign images are displayed on posters, book marks, table tents, bus wraps, and computer screens to address issues of violence against women. The bystander campaign addresses students as potential bystanders who could intervene to disrupt violence. The development of the "Know Your Power" campaign has been a student-oriented and student-driven project. "We used feedback from about 500 students to develop the eight scenarios featured in the 'Know Your Power' campaign, which model safe ways to intervene in situations where sexual violence has the potential to occur, is occurring, or has occurred. The scenarios portray typical college scenes that explicitly model safe and appropriate bystander behaviors in the prevention and intervention of intimate partner and sexual violence and stalking," said Sharyn J. Potter, UNH Professor of Sociology and co-director of Prevention Innovations. You can find more information regarding the Know Your Power Social Marketing Campaign at http://www.know-your-power.org/.

sex, and forced prostitution. In each of these cases, violence is used as a tool of control and domination, and, in some contexts, is a tool of terror. Many forms of gendered violence that occur within communities are also initiated or regulated by the state and will be discussed in the next section.

Sexual Harassment and Assault

Sexual harassment consists of unwelcome sexual advances that occur in public spaces, in the workplace, and in educational settings. It includes any unwanted verbal or physical contact of a sexual nature, as well as intimidation and pressure for sexual favors. In the workplace, sexual harassment may involve a hostile work environment through an abuse of power by those in authority as well as by co-workers. Worldwide, women and girls in educational settings report high rates of sexual harassment that affect their ability to learn. In addition, sexual harassment may also be racialized. Asian American women, for example, are often negatively affected by converging racial and gender stereotypes that assume they will be receptive to sexual advances (Cho, 1997). This results in higher levels of sexual harassment from employers who may become increasingly violent when their advances are rebuffed. In the reading "No Longer Silent," author Megan Shank writes about working women in Shanghai, China, emphasizing how economic transformations from a socialist, planned economy to capitalism have resulted in new and increased forms of sexual harassment.

Although as already discussed, rape and sexual assault occur most often by men in intimate relationships with women, stranger assaults also occur. Street children may be particularly vulnerable to sexual violence by strangers. Lesbian girls experience homophobic bullying and violence within schools and in public spaces. Other vulnerable groups include girls who are members of indigenous groups, girls of racial and ethnic minority groups, girls with disabilities, girls held in detention, refugees, and girls living in conflict areas (Plan International, 2007). In India, Nepal, and other parts of Asia, Dalit girls and women (lower caste girls formerly known as "untouchables") face extreme rates of violence. According to a five-year study conducted in India, 23 percent of Dalit women and girls had been raped, 47 percent had endured sexual harassment, and 55 percent had survived physical assaults. Of all of these cases, less than 1 percent ever went to court, due to police obstruction or intervention by dominant caste members who express caste prejudice against Dalits (Plan International, 2007). In the United States, Native American women have experienced high rates of sexual violence. According to a recent study by the Bureau of Justice Statistics, Native American women are twice as likely to experience sexual assault as members of other groups, and one in three Native American women reports having been raped (U.S. Department of Justice). Andrea Smith argues that sexual violence has been used as a primary tool of genocide against indigenous peoples in the United States and elsewhere, with indigenous women seen as more "rapable" (Smith, 2005). These practices are often linked to colonialism and conquest, and result in a naturalization of the sexual violence against women and subsequent impunity for perpetrators.

Acid Violence

Acid violence is another form of violence that targets women and is often reported in Bangladesh, India, Pakistan, Vietnam, Cambodia, Afghanistan, Ethiopia, and Uganda, as well as other contexts. This involves the deliberate throwing of sulfuric or nitric acid into the face of another person, usually young women. Motives for the attacks include rejection or refusal of marriage proposals or sexual advances, family/marriage disputes and domestic violence, and disputes over land, property, or money. Often, acid attacks are said to target women who commit social transgressions or break gender norms, or whose male family members have had conflicts with others. Generally, such attacks are intended not to kill but to maim the victim, resulting in a lifelong experience of disfigurement, pain, and suffering. The Acid Survivors Foundation in Bangladesh reported almost 500 victims in 2002. Two assumptions help to explain this violence: (1) women are often considered property; and (2) a woman's appearance is often considered her most valuable asset (Chowdhury, 2005). Therefore, acid attacks are structured in part by attempts to ruin victims' marriage prospects, economic security, and social status. Such attacks generally have long-lasting physical, psychological, social, and economic consequences. Perpetrators are rarely prosecuted, and those who survive the attacks are often stigmatized as "fallen women," perceived to have brought the attacks onto themselves. Many victims are characterized as having

Finding Face

Finding Face (2009) is a feature-length documentary film by Skye Fitzgerald and Patti Duncan. It details the controversial case of Tat Marina, a young woman who was brutally attacked with acid in Cambodia in 1999. At the age of sixteen, when Marina was a rising star in Phnom Penh's karaoke music scene, she was coerced into an abusive relationship by Cambodia's Undersecretary of State, Svay Sitha. When his wife, Khoun Sophal, learned of the relationship, she retaliated by attacking Marina with acid in the middle of a crowded public market, with the help of several bodyguards. Despite the fact that hundreds of people witnessed the attack, which left Marina disfigured and deeply traumatized, no one has ever been prosecuted. The film also investigates the fracturing of Marina's family across national boundaries and documents her family members' disparate responses to the knowledge that none of Marina's attackers has ever been arrested despite widespread knowledge of their identities.

Finding Face contextualizes acid attacks in Cambodia by examining this form of violence as both a human rights violation and a gendered form of violence. In it, young women survivors and human rights workers discuss the many challenges faced by survivors of acid violence, and what they see as a culture of impunity surrounding violence against women. They also discuss the rise of acid violence following Marina's attack, a result of public knowledge that most perpetrators of acid attacks will not face any serious penalties. Marina, who was granted juvenile asylum to enter the United States, struggles to emerge from a shattered self-image and escape a constant state of fear. She breaks her long silence with the hope that she can gain some form of justice, if not in the State judicial system then at least in the court of public opinion. For more information, see www.findingface.org.

provoked the attacks themselves through what is considered outspoken, "unfeminine," or sexually promiscuous behavior.

Hate Crimes

Some forms of violence target specific groups of women in particular ways. In South Africa, for example, Black women have faced numerous forms of violence both during and after apartheid. "Curative rape"—sexual violence targeting lesbians for the purpose of "curing" them of their sexual identity—is often directed specifically at Black lesbians in townships. Often there are multiple perpetrators, and many women report multiple rapes. This situation, reflecting the ways sexism intersects with homophobia and heterosexism, as well as racism and classism, has become so critical that activists like Wendy Isaack have declared a state of emergency. They suggest that high rates of hate crimes against Black lesbians and transgender women in South Africa can be likened to torture as defined by international law, illustrating the ways they are systematically abused within the community and by the state (Gqola, 2006). Isaack discusses the ways state actors such as police and judges perpetrate a secondary victimization by not investigating these cases and by not recognizing the human rights of Black lesbian and transgender women.

Even in countries where violence against protected groups is considered hate violence and prosecuted accordingly, it is difficult to get many people to recognize that violence against women is also a hate crime. For example, in her discussion of hate violence against Asian and Asian American women in the United States, Helen Zia (1997) asks why it appears that most (documented) victims of anti-Asian violence are male. Even while violence against women is the most pervasive form of violence throughout society, gender was not added as a protected category or class in the United States until the 1994 Violence Against Women Act. Despite this addition, violence against women has not generally been classified as a hate crime. If it were, hate crime statistics would increase exponentially.

Sex-Trafficking and the Global Sex Industry

As discussed in chapter 4, it is estimated that annually half to four million people are trafficked across national borders worldwide (UNESCO, 2004). The large relative span in this number reflects the covert nature of the practices of trafficking and illustrates the difficulties associated with knowing how many people are actually transported against their will. Most reports, however, indicate that the majority of victims of trafficking are women, and many are trafficked into the informal economy to work as prostitutes, domestic workers, and/or in agriculture or garment industries. Victims of trafficking may be coerced or forced into the sex industry, where they may face violence from pimps, clients, and law enforcement officials. Some are reportedly forced into slave-like conditions, and there is often involvement by police and state officials. Due to the fact that trafficked women and girls generally lack legal documentation, they are vulnerable to multiple forms of violence. According to a 2006 UN global report, trafficking occurs in all regions of the world. One hundred and twenty-seven countries have been documented as countries of origin for trafficked persons that include central and southeastern Europe, the Commonwealth of Independent States (CIS), and Asia. Similarly, 137 countries have been documented as countries of destination that predominantly include countries within western Europe, Asia, and North America (General Assembly, 2006).

The UN Convention against Transnational Organized Crime, adopted by the General Assembly in 2000, is the main UN entity addressing issues of human trafficking, focusing primarily on the criminal justice element of trafficking. It is supplemented by three Protocols, including the Trafficking in Persons Protocol, adopted in 2003, which enables international cooperation including law enforcement cooperation and extradition between and among countries. At the nongovernmental level, the Global Alliance Against Traffic in Women (GAATW) comprises nongovernmental organizations from all over the world, including anti-trafficking organizations, survivors of trafficking, human rights and women's rights organizations, and self-organized groups of sex workers, migrant workers, and domestic workers. GAATW understands that trafficking in women and children is deeply embedded in processes of globalization and a globalized labor market, and therefore works for the human and labor rights of all migrant workers.

Four situations result in women's and girls' involvement in the global sex industry: (1) women are completely tricked or coerced into it; (2) women may be told half-truths by recruiters and are then forced to do work they did not expect to do; (3) women are aware of what they will be doing, but see no other viable options for survival; and (4) women are informed about the work they are to do and have no objections to it. The first three categories are examples of trafficking where women and girls may face debt bondage, confiscation of travel documents, and restricted movement. In all categories, women are subject to violence, particularly sexual violence; however, trafficked women are more likely to suffer violence and violation of their rights (Coomaraswamy, 2000). Women in the sex industry are also vulnerable to HIV infection, police harassment, and additional forms of discrimination and violence. Linked to prostitution, some activists and researchers suggest that the pornography industry also represents a form of violence against women in that it may glamorize forms of violence against women, and/or that women may be forced to participate against their will.

While the global sex industry is often framed in terms of trafficking and "sex slavery," authors like Kamala Kempadoo (2001, p. 28; see also chapter 4) suggest that "the global sex trade cannot be simply reduced to one monolithic explanation of violence to women." Rather, we must recognize the ways in which specific local histories and contexts, including colonialism, militarization, and globalization, shape women's experiences of the sex industry. Kempadoo urges readers to recognize the fact that globally, women of color are disproportionately represented in sex industries, particularly through prostitution around military bases, migrant labor, and sex tourism, often associated with the ways in which women of color are sexualized and racialized as exotic "others," and thereby objectified. It is problematic to view sex work within a "voluntary" versus "forced" dichotomy since this model often results in viewing women as either innocent victims or people responsible for their own potential victimization. Such a framework may simply become another method for denying sex workers their human rights (Doezema, 1998).

Sometimes women leave their homelands voluntarily as a result of processes associated with globalization and structural adjustment programs. For example, women in the Philippines face great pressure to migrate for employment opportunities at the same time that the Philippines' national economy depends on remittances sent home by migrant women workers. As domestic workers, women migrant laborers are vulnerable to exploitative working conditions, abuse from employers, sexual harassment, physical and sexual violence, and threats to withhold pay or important documents, including passports, as well as the fear of deportation. They often find their movement and mobility severely limited

(Parrenas, 2001). Similarly, some women migrate for the purposes of international marriage, often referred to as "mailorder brides." Vulnerable under the law and subject to the risk of deportation, these women may migrate for economic reasons, and often experience domestic violence, including marital rape, with few resources for legal protection. It is important to recognize that not all migrant women are victims of trafficking, and that sometimes women make strategic decisions to support their families or improve their economic situations. However, this fact does not mitigate the risks they face and should not lead us to believe that they are deserving of violence or abuse.

Militarism in Communities

Finally, violence targeting women in communities may also include forms of violence associated with militarism. As discussed in the next section, while women experience extremely high rates of violence in actual situations of armed conflict, they also suffer as a result of living and working in militarized communities and especially in communities with military bases (Enloe, 2007; Moon, 2007). Militarism, defined here as a system and process that often rely on objectification of others, should be distinguished from individuals in the military, who may or may not agree with a militarized worldview. However, militarism as an institution often encourages both violence and misogyny (woman hating) and results in increasing rates of sexual harassment and sexual assault committed against civilians by military personnel, including both local and foreign militaries. For example, U.S. military personnel in South Korea have committed over 100,000 criminal acts (about 2 per day) against members of the local population, often targeting women and children in the military camptowns surrounding U.S. bases (Moon, 2007). Violence against civilian women in this context also includes forced prostitution, trafficking, and murder. Many trafficking routes tend to appear in close proximity to military bases, and, in the mid-1990s, more than five thousand women were reportedly trafficked into South Korea for the purposes of prostitution in U.S. military camptowns (Marshall, 2006). Finally, incidences of violence within military families are also key problems.

The reality of high rates of violence in militarized communities exists despite the rhetoric of "security" linked to military presence and occupation. The U.S. bases in South Korea, Okinawa, and the Philippines, for example, have long been justified in the name of national security for these countries (Enloe, 2007; Fukumura and Matsuoka, 2002). Recently, groups such as the East Asia–U.S. Women's Network Against Militarism have challenged this premise, arguing that militarism does not provide security for local civilians, and that women in such environments become more vulnerable to violence. Others, like Anna Agathangelou (2004), suggest that globalization is actually constituted *through* militarization, with both processes resulting in increased poverty in the Global South, affecting women disproportionately and increasing rates of sexual violence against women.

VIOLENCE BY THE STATE

Physical, sexual, and psychological violence perpetrated or condoned by the state takes numerous forms that include violence against women and girls in detention; police harassment; violence perpetrated by the criminal justice system (such as by immigration officials and border police); and violence associated with reproductive health. Also, women

ACTIVIST PROFILE   **Esther Chávez Cano**

Esther Chavez holds the weeping girl in her arms and chants the words, as if to convince herself that they are true: "It's really wonderful, my dear girl. You are alive. You could've been one of them." Esther looks over the girl's shoulder toward the row of pink crosses placed on the edge of a ditch, where eight raped and mutilated bodies of young girls, the same age as Rosaisela, the girl in Esther's arms, were dumped by their killers in 2001.

Rosaisela Lascano is only 16. She was attacked and raped on December 30 by a man who left her for dead in the desert. But she survived. Now she is pregnant with the baby from the rape. There, in the middle of a rubbish dump, once a cotton field, where the last windowless boxes of the maquiladoras meet open desert, Rosaisela whispers her story. Like thousands of others, she came from the poverty of the south to look for a better life in Ciudad Juárez with its 380 maquilas (U.S. and European-owned plants, using Mexico's cheap labor and paying young women less than $5 a day) built along the U.S. border. Ciudad Juárez, a city of 1.3 million, lies just across the Rio Grande from El Paso, Texas.

The man dragged Rosaisela by her hair, while hitting her all over her body. Then he raped her and left her for dead among the old tires and broken bottles. She crawled home many hours later, fearful for her life, avoiding people and houses. Her parents took her to the police the next day. The police were barely interested. The only one who offered to help Rosaisela was Esther Chavez—a beautiful, ever energetic and always elegant 70-year-old woman who established Casa Amiga about 10 years ago as the first and only crisis center in Juárez to provide help to the victims of sexual abuse and domestic violence.*

—Mariana Katzarova, *The Nation*

In 1993, Esther Chávez Cano was a retired accounting executive in Ciudad Juárez, Mexico, just across the border from El Paso, Texas, when she began to notice story after story in the city's newspaper of young women who were being raped and murdered. She also noticed that the government seemed to be doing nothing. She and other women joined together to demand answers, but officials didn't seem interested. So these women protested, wrote newspaper columns, and encouraged women in government to support their cause. Finally, in 1998, the government set up a special unit to investigate these homicides.

Hoping to intervene in the violence, in 1999, Esther founded Casa Amiga, a rape crisis and violence prevention center, the first in her city. Visit their Web site at http://www.casa-amiga.org/english/portada.html.

Still the deaths continued, and the homicides remained unsolved. In more than a decade of killing, Amnesty International estimates, more than 400 women have been murdered in Juárez. Hundreds of others are still missing. Many of the victims were employed by the maqulidoras, sweatshops that export primarily to the United States.

* http://www.alternet.org/story/18145/

These women simply disappeared, and then days later their mutilated bodies turned up in the desert. Very few of these crimes have been solved, as local government has downplayed the violence and mishandled the investigations. Human rights leaders, like Esther Chávez Cano, have become targets of violence themselves as they have spoken out against the killings and the government's inability and unwillingness to address the crisis. One reporter offered this story as an example: The phone rang at Casa Amiga. A counselor answered it, and a man's voice asked for Esther Chavez. The counselor responded that Esther was busy and asked if the man would wait. "No," he replied, "just tell her to remember Digna Ochoa," and hung up. The counselor realized the man was referring to a Mexico City human-rights lawyer who was found shot to death.[†]

Undaunted, Esther has continued her work to support survivors and to prevent violence against women. The violence continues in Juárez, and the government has continued to ignore the magnitude of the problem.

In 1997, Esther received the "Woman Helps Woman" award from the International Optimist's Club and was recognized as a "Woman Pioneer" by the Feminist Majority in 1999. In 2008, she was awarded the Human Rights Prize in Mexico and the Lannan Foundation Cultural Freedom Award.

A film released in 2009, *Backyard*, tells the story of the femicides in Juárez. According to one film critic, the film's protagonist, who sets out to find the killers, uncannily resembles Esther Chávez Cano.[‡]

[†] http://www.ocregister.com/news/2004/juarez/part8.shtml
[‡] http://news.newamericamedia.org/news/view_article.html?article_id=910ba01693bec5c05fb4cd25a32d06fe

experience forms of violence associated with poverty, homophobia, racism, colonization, and war, among other features. As mentioned in the previous section, indigenous women are often subjected to extreme forms of violence, including sexual violence, often used as a tool of conquest and even genocide (Smith, 2005). In situations of armed conflict, women and girls are particularly vulnerable to violence as the political motives underlying war are also often used to justify sexual violence against women and girls. While the Declaration on the Elimination of Violence against Women asserts that states should condemn violence against women, it is clear that such violence continues.

Violence by Law-Enforcement and "Justice" Systems

Worldwide, women experience violence, including physical violence, sexual assault and abuse, and psychological and verbal abuse by members of law enforcement and criminal justice systems. In the United States, women of color, poor women, lesbians, and transgender women are at greater risk for police harassment and forms of violence by the criminal justice system. This situation influences their willingness to report the violence they experience. Globally, women in the sex industry and women migrant workers also experience high levels of police harassment and violence. For example, 70 percent of sex workers in India report being beaten by police, and more than 80 percent report being arrested without evidence (WHO, "violence against sex workers," 2005). In Bangladesh, between 52 percent and 60 percent of street-based sex workers reported being raped by men in uniform in the previous year. In many countries, police also use antiprostitution laws to harass, threaten, abuse, and sexually coerce or assault women in the sex industry.

Migrant women lacking legal documentation are also subject to police harassment and violence. For example, at the U.S.–Mexico border, women attempting to cross into the United States are regularly subjected to harassment, beatings, and assault, including sexual assault by both representatives of the state and members of racist vigilante groups (Falcón, 2006). Female migrant workers, usually domestic workers, are particularly vulnerable, and report suffering violence when seeking police protection (Amnesty International, 2001). Finally, there is widespread violence against women in custody. Women held in prisons or pretrial detention are at risk for physical and sexual assault. Amnesty International reports that women held in custody by police routinely endure rape and torture. In Lebanon, for example, women detainees have reported widespread abuses including rape and attempted rape, beatings, torture, forcible stripping, constant invasion of privacy by male guards, and lack of adequate facilities for pregnant women (Amnesty International, 2001). As women's presence in prisons increases worldwide, it becomes more and more important to examine the conditions for women in detention, as well as the reasons for women's imprisonment. In the United States, for example, poor women and women of color make up the greatest numbers of women in prisons, and their mass incarceration is often linked to structural forms of oppression as well as neoliberal economic policies (Reynolds, 2008). Women living in refugee camps or camps for internally displaced persons (IDP camps) also face higher incidence rates of violence and exploitation. Representing the majority of displaced people, women and children are subject to violence, including sexual violence, from military and immigration personnel as well as male refugees and rival ethnic groups.

Health and Reproductive Issues

As discussed in previous chapters another form of gender-based violence is associated with lack of health and reproductive justice worldwide. Women and girls experience state-inflicted violence through a lack of access to safe abortions, reproductive health care, family planning, and safe contraception. They may also experience forced sterilization and/or forced impregnation, as these two practices have been used as tools of eugenics, ethnic cleansing, colonialism, and genocide. Silliman, Fried, Ross, and Gutierrez (2004), for example, document the ways in which women of color have often resisted policies directed at controlling their fertility. Population control tactics were used during the colonization of the United States and during slavery, targeting Native American and African American women, and often justified by racist ideologies. More recently, women of color and women of the Global South have been targets of provider-controlled hormonal methods of contraception whose side effects and risks are not yet known, including Depo-Provera and Norplant. While white middle-class women have often experienced difficulties securing safe access to contraception and abortion, many poor women and women of color have been targets for coercive sterilization campaigns, linked to a population control model that suggests that poor women and women of color are to blame for the world's overpopulation and dwindling resources (Hartmann, 2002). This ideology can also be linked to specific economic policies. When people of color no longer function as simply "cheap labor," the fertility of women of color becomes problematic and is subject to state control.

Many countries report high mortality rates related to lack of access to safe abortions. Young women and girls in forced early marriages also face increased risk for complications associated with pregnancy, as well as a lack of medical resources and obstetric care in many countries. And women in poverty often face difficulty accessing prenatal care and medical care during childbirth. Approximately 536,000 women die each year due to maternal health complications, with 533,000 of these deaths occurring in the Global South (Alsop, 2007).

Finally, a collaborative report by the Joint United Nations Programme on HIV/AIDS (UNAIDS), the United Nations Population Fund (UNFPA), and the United Nations Development Fund for Women (UNIFEM) links gender-based violence to an increase in HIV/AIDS, with women who have experienced violence being at higher risk for HIV infection (UNAIDS, UNFPA, UNIFEM, 2004). Women and girls trafficked for sex work experience greater risk for infection (Erturk, 2005), and women in situations of armed conflict may be deliberately infected with HIV as a weapon of war. However, violence is also a consequence of HIV/AIDS because women may avoid treatment in fear of violence and abandonment that results from such disclosure.

Armed Conflict

Women and girls are particularly vulnerable within situations of armed conflict, during which gender-based violence often increases. This is poignantly demonstrated in the reading "War Against Women," essays by Peter Finn and CBS News producers for the U.S. television show *60 Minutes*. They discuss the rape of women and children in the Bosnian war of the 1990s and the present (as of this writing) conflict in the Congo. Worldwide, 70 percent of casualties during armed conflict are civilians, many of them women and children (UNIFEM). In such contexts, women may face physical and sexual assault, including mass rape, forced marriage, forced prostitution, military sexual slavery, increased domestic violence, and, within some contexts, a resurgence of female genital cutting as a means to reinforce cultural identity (WHO, 2008). As discussed in chapter 12, rape is consistently used as a weapon of war, but according to the UN, it is "the least condemned war crime" (Plan International, 2008). In some instances, mass rape is also used as an instrument of policy and a deliberate tool of genocide (Tetreault, 2001; WHO, 2008). Often young women and girls are targeted for rape, and many are victims of multiple rapes, including gang rapes. Victims of rape face increased risk for HIV infection, the possibility of pregnancy, and potential rejection by families and communities (Erturk, 2005).

Between 1992 and 1995 up to 60,000 Muslim and Croatian women and girls were raped by Serbian soldiers in Bosnia-Herzegovina; many were forcibly impregnated as part of a campaign for "ethnic cleansing." Similarly, during the 1994 genocide in Rwanda, approximately half a million women and girls experienced war-related sexual violence, and it is estimated that 67 percent contracted HIV (UNIFEM). Rehn and Sirleaf (2002) suggest that some women were purposely infected with HIV as a tool of war. In Sierra Leone, as many as 64,000 internally displaced women were raped between 1991 and 2001, and as many as 257,000 Sierra Leonean women and girls may have been subjected to sexual violence, perpetrated predominantly by rebel forces. A large proportion of these women were subsequently infected with HIV (Human Rights Watch, 2003). In Colombia, rape has been used not only by soldiers in government armed forces but also by guerillas and paramilitary forces. In Darfur, thousands of women and girls have been raped, with about 40 percent of victims under 18 years of age. In the Democratic Republic of Congo sexual violence has reached unprecedented levels and women and girls face violence perpetrated not only by armed combatants but also by UN peacekeepers. Violence against women during or immediately following armed conflict has also been reported in Afghanistan, Burundi, Cambodia, Chad, Columbia, *Côte d'Ivoire*, Liberia, Peru, Chechnya/Russian Federation, Darfur, northern Uganda, Mexico, Kuwait, Haiti, Iraq, and the former Yugoslavia (General Assembly 2006; UN, 2008; Erturk, 2005). In refugee camps, women may be abused or raped by military, immigration personnel, male refugees, and men of rival ethnic groups. They may also be forced into prostitution (UN, 2008). Other vulnerable groups include members of ethnic minorities, unaccompanied women and children, female heads of household, disabled women, and elderly women (WHO, 2008).

Systematic rape during armed conflict has been recognized as a human rights violation, yet it continues to occur. The UN identifies four categories of wartime rape: (1) genocidal rape, intended to destroy an entire ethnic, cultural, or political group. (2) opportunistic rape, in which crimes against women increase when male perpetrators take advantage of the breakdown in law and order; and (3) political rape, where women are punished for their association with men, as a means to subjugate men holding particular political perspectives. In such cases, women are often viewed as property, and sexual violence against them is used to subjugate and humiliate the men of their communities, including husbands, fathers, brothers, and sons (WHO, 2008). Finally, (4) forced concubinage, the forced sexual servitude of women, often in "rape camps" such as those established by the Japanese during World War II, is another category of wartime rape. Between 200,000 and 400,000 women were forced into a system of sexual slavery in which they were systematically raped in what were called "comfort" camps (Yoshiaki, 1995).

Although the Beijing "Platform for Action" from the 1995 World Conference on Women declared rape in armed conflict a war crime that can be classified as genocide in some cases, impunity for perpetrators is common. Until quite recently, no perpetrators of war rape had ever been prosecuted for crimes of war. However, in 1996, a UN tribunal indicted eight Bosnian Serb military and police officers in connection with their rape of Muslim women during the Bosnian war and more recently the Security Council adopted resolution 1820 (2008), which recognizes sexual violence in situations of armed conflict as a threat to national and international peace and security. In post-conflict periods, gender-based violence often continues. Reports associated with the recent war in Afghanistan show higher rates of rape, acid attacks, forced marriages, forced prostitution, and bombings of girls' schools (Marshall, 2006).

Globalization

Gendered violence can also be linked to processes of globalization associated with both state and non-state actors. As already discussed, hundreds of thousands of women worldwide are forced to migrate in search of work opportunities, often as a direct result of economic restructuring in their home countries. While it has been argued that gendered violence exists largely because of unequal gender relations and women's subjugated status in society, it should also be recognized that gender-based violence increases with processes of globalization that may actually heighten problems associated with these unequal gender relations. For example, violence against women in Juarez, Mexico, where hundreds of women have disappeared and have been found raped and murdered, must be understood in the context of globalization that contributes to the "cheapening" of women's labor and therefore their bodies. Such forces contribute to problems associated with organized crime, prostitution, drug trafficking, and police corruption (Livingston, 2004). We might ask what role the global economy plays in making women's bodies and labor expendable. Economic systems that devalue women and cheapen their labor also cheapen women's bodies and make it easier for state actors and legal and political systems to inflict violence upon them.

RESISTING GENDERED FORMS OF VIOLENCE

Violence against women is the least punished crime in the world and must be seen as a human rights violation. Violence against women both results from, and reinforces, gender inequality and women's subordination in society. It affects women in the family, the community, the workplace, and in society in general. It is a public health issue as well as an obstacle to peace and development.

Addressing gender-based violence must involve recognition of multiple levels of violence that include both individual experiences of victimization as well as the long-term structural or systemic violence that accompanies it, including the lack of prosecution of perpetrators, a general lack of resources for survivors, and the stigma associated with certain forms of violence. Ending gendered violence requires education, resources, support for survivors, political movement, and enforcement of laws. State support to end gendered violence is problematic, however, since states are also involved in the oppression of women (Kirk and Okazawa-Rey, 2004). As we have seen, states condone and legitimize violence against women through the legal system, police treatment, violence against women in detention, rape of women in prisons, violence against women by military personnel, and assaults against women at the national border by immigration officials.

As already discussed, in order to imagine a world free of gender-based violence and to strategize about ways to address the problem worldwide, it is important to question Western

Earthquake in Haiti Kills Women Activists

Three Haitian activists known for their work against gendered violence against women were among the thousands killed in the earthquake that devastated Haiti in January, 2010. Myriam Merlet was the chief of staff and a top adviser at Haiti's Ministry for Gender and the Rights of Women, established in 1995. She fled Haiti in the 1970s but returned in the mid-1980s to found *Enfofamn*, an organization that raises awareness about violence against women through media and story-telling. Merlet worked with Eve Ensler (author of the play "The Vagina Monologues" that is produced all over the world to educate about women's issues), bringing the play to Haiti, and helping establish safe houses to shelter survivors of violence in Port-au-Prince and Cap Haitien. Anne Marie Coriolan was also a top adviser in Haiti working with the women's rights ministry. She founded *Solidarite Fanm Ayisyen* (Solidarity with Haitian Women, or SOFA) that provides advocacy and services to women. Coriolan worked as a political organizer who helped bring the issue of rape to the forefront of Haitian courts. Magalie Marcelin, a lawyer and actress who appeared in films and performed on the stage, established *Kay Fanm*, a women's rights organization that addresses domestic violence, offers services and shelter to women, and makes microcredit loans available to women. These activists join the thousands of nameless others working to improve the lives of Haitians who died as a result of this tragedy.

assumptions that blame violence against women on "culture" while ignoring specific structures of power and inequality and the particular forms patriarchy may take in different contexts. In Cambodia, for example, acid violence should be addressed in relation to a long history of French colonialism, a recent history of war and genocide, and a UN peacekeeping mission that introduced new forms of sex tourism and trafficking to the region. Today, the current Cambodian government is notoriously corrupt: human rights violations proliferate and violence against women increases. The rift between the very rich and the extremely poor continues to widen as globalization and economic restructuring have taken hold. Women in Cambodia are not easily able to resist marriage, and marriage laws make it almost impossible to divorce. Acid violence is produced and interpreted and subsequently addressed through and alongside these institutions, institutional practices, and discourses.

Thus, it is important to move from a focus on "culture" or "tradition" to a more critical examination of the effects of institutional structures. Once tradition or culture is blamed, there is no reason to critically examine the role of institutions, local patriarchies, and gender dynamics. In these ways, while it is important to raise awareness about the myriad forms of gender-based violence, much of the focus relies on Western stereotypes about "Third World" women and girls and assumes a universal oppression of women of the Global South. Instead, programs for change must reference specific local contexts, institutions, and increasingly global practices that contribute to forms of violence against women.

Women's and human rights organizations continue to challenge gender-based violence around the world. Sister Namibia, a feminist organization in Namibia, operates to strengthen women's voices in an emerging democratic postcolonial society. With the publication of their magazine, *Sister Namibia,* the organization raises awareness about violence associated with sexism, racism, homophobia, and other forms of oppression. In Cambodia, the Cambodian Women's Crisis Center (CWCC) works to eliminate violence against women, particularly domestic violence, sexual abuse, and trafficking. The nongovernmental organization conducts research and provides crisis centers for women in need of protection from violence. In Afghanistan, the Revolutionary Association of the Women of Afghanistan (RAWA) fights for human rights and social justice, working to increase women's political power and access to education, health care, and employment. RAWA challenges violence associated with both the fundamentalist Taliban regime and the U.S. military occupation of Afghanistan. Resisting domestic violence is also the theme of Kirk Semple's article "Domestic Violence in Afghanistan." It focuses on the Afghan Women Skills Development Center in Kabul that provides shelter for survivors of domestic violence and seeks to empower women.

In South Africa, Sex Worker Education and Advocacy Taskforce (SWEAT), a nonprofit organization based in Capetown, works with sex workers on the issues of health, human rights, and labor rights, challenging stigma and violence against sex workers. On the Thai border, as the reading by Ingrid Drake ("Finding Dignity in Exile") explains, the Shan Women's Action Network (SWAN) works to support Burmese women displaced and victimized by the conflict in Burma. This group seeks empowerment for the Shan, an ethnic group from southeast Burma who, as of this writing, has not yet received refugee status from the Thai government. Finally, in the Philippines, *Gabriela* attempts to transform women into an organized political force, highlighting incidents of violence when they occur, and making critical connections between violence against women and forms of violence associated with colonialism and militarism. All of these examples highlight the ways in which individuals and communities around the world organize to challenge and eradicate violence against women. In each case it is important to consider the specific local histories and contexts of violence against women. Only then is it possible to develop methods and strategies of intervention that will be effective within each context. As noted earlier, it is also crucial to keep in mind that gendered forms of violence always exist alongside, and in fact are sustained by, structural inequalities, which must also be addressed.

REFERENCES

Abusharaf, R. (2006). Unmasking tradition. In I. Grewal and C. Kaplan (Eds.), *An introduction to women's studies: Gender in a transnational world* (2nd ed.) (pp. 91–98). New York: McGraw-Hill.

Agathangelou, A. M. (2004). Gender, race, militarization, and economic restructuring in the former Yugoslavia and at the U.S.–Mexico border. In D. D. Aguilar and A. E. Lacsamana (Eds.), *Women and globalization* (pp. 347–386). New York: Humanity Books.

Ali, N. (2008). The costs of marital rape in Southern Africa. Retrieved February 20, 2009, from Human Rights Watch. Website: http://www.hrw.org.

Alsop, Z. (2007). Kenya's maternal wards deliver abuse with babies. Women's eNews. Retrieved October 28, 2007, from http://www.womensenews.org/article.cfm?aid=3363.

Amnesty International. (2001). *Lebanon: Torture and ill-treatment of women in pre-trial detention: A culture of acquiescence.* Retrieved January 4, 2009, from www.peace women.org/resources/Lebanon/aitorture.pdf.

Centers for Disease Control and Prevention. (2003). *Costs of intimate partner violence against women in the United States.* Atlanta, GA.

Cho, S. K. (1997). Asian Pacific American women and racialized sexual harassment. In E. H. Kim, L. V. Villanueva, and Asian Women United of California (Eds.), *Making more waves: New writing by Asian American women* (pp. 164–173). Boston: Beacon Press.

Chowdhury, E. H. (2005). Feminist negotiations: Contesting narratives of the campaign against acid violence in Bangladesh. *Meridians: Feminism, Race, Transnationalism,* 6(1), 163–192.

Coomaraswamy, R. (2000). *Integration of the human rights of women and the gender perspective: Violence against women.* Report of the Special Rapporteur on violence against women, its causes and consequences. Trafficking in women, omen's migration and violence against women. E/CN.4/2000/68. 29 February 2000.

Coomaraswamy, R. (2002). *Integration of the human rights of women and the gender perspective: Violence against women.* Report of the Special Rapporteur on violence against women, its causes and consequences. Cultural practices in the family that are violent towards women. E/CN.4/2002/93. 31 January 2002.

Doezema, J. (1998). Forced to choose: Beyond the voluntary v. forced prostitution dichotomy. In K. Kempadoo and J. Doezema (Eds.), *Global sex workers: Rights resistance, and redefinition* (pp. 34–50). New York: Routledge.

Ehrenreich, N. (2004). The "not our problem" problem: Female circumcision, intersex surgery, and race privilege. Paper presented at the annual meeting of the Law and Society Association, Chicago Illinois. Retrieved February 19, 2009 from http://www.allacademic.com/meta/p116956_index.html.

Enloe, C. (2007). *Globalization and militarism: Feminists make the link.* Lanham: Rowman and Littlefield Publishers, Inc.

Erturk, Y. (2005). Integration of the human rights of women and the gender perspective: violence against women. Intersections of violence against women and HIV/AIDS Report of the Special Rapporteur on violence against women, its causes and consequences. E.CN.4/2005/72 17 January 2005.

Erturk, Y. (2008). Promotion and protection of all human rights, civil, political, economic, social and cultural, including the right to development. Report of the Special Rapporteur on violence against women, its causes and consequences. Mission to the Democratic Republic of Congo. A/HRC/7/6/Add.4. 28 February 2008.

Falcón, S. (2006). "National security" and the violation of women: Militarized border rape at the US–Mexico border. In Incite! Women of color against violence (Ed.), *Color of Violence: The Incite! Anthology* (pp. 119–129). Cambridge, MA: South End Press.

Fukumura, Y. and Matsuoka, M. (2002). Redefining security: Okinawa women's resistance to U.S. militarism. In N. A. Naples and M. Desai (Eds.), *Women's activism and globalization: Linking local struggles and transnational politics* (pp. 239–263). New York: Routledge.

General Assembly. (2006). *In-depth study on all forms of violence against women: Report of the Secretary General.* A/61/122/Add.1.6 July 2006.

Gqola, P. D. (2006). Pumla Dineo Gqola speaks with Wendy Isaack. *Feminist Africa 6: Subaltern sexualities.* Capetown: African Gender Institute, University of Capetown, South Africa, 91–100.

Haberland, N., Chong, E. L., and Bracken, H. J. (2004). A world apart: The disadvantage and social isolation of married adolescent girls. Brief based on background paper prepared for the WHO/UNFPA/Population Council Technical Consultation on Married Adolescents. New York: Population Council.

Hartmann, B. (2002). The changing face of population control. In J. Silliman and A. Bhattacharjee (Eds.), *Policing the national body: Race, gender, and criminalization* (pp. 259–289). Cambridge, MA: South End Press.

Human Rights Watch. (2003). *"We'll kill you if you cry": Sexual violence in the Sierra Leone conflict.* 15(1). New York: Human Rights Watch. Retrieved February 19, 2009, from http://www.hrw.org/en/reports/2003/01/15/well-kill-you-if-you-cry-0.

Kempadoo, K. (2001). Women of color and the global sex trade: Transnational feminist perspectives. *Meridians: Feminism, Race, Transnationalism, 1*(2), 28–51.

Kirk, G. and Okazawa-Rey, M. (Eds.) (2004). *Women's lives: Multicultural perspectives* (3rd ed.). New York: McGraw-Hill.

Larkin, J. and Popaleni, K. (1997). Heterosexual courtship violence and sexual harassment: The private and public control of young women. In M. Crawford and R. K. Unger (Eds.),

In our own words: Readings on the psychology of women and gender (pp. 313–326). New York: McGraw-Hill.

Livingston, J. (2004). Murder in Juarez: Gender, sexual violence, and the global assembly line. *Frontiers, 25*(1), 59–75.

Marshall, L. (2006). The connection between militarism and violence against women. In P. S. Rothenberg (Ed.), *Beyond borders: Thinking critically about global issues* (pp. 307–310). New York: Worth Publishers.

Moon, K. H. S. (2007). Resurrecting prostitutes and overturning treatises: Gender politics in the "anti-American" movement in South Korea. *Journal of Asian Studies, 66*(1), 129–157.

Narayan, U. (1997). *Dislocating cultures: Identities, traditions, and Third World feminism.* New York: Routledge.

Parrenas, R. S. (2001). *Servants of globalization: Women, migration, and domestic work.* Stanford: Stanford University Press.

Plan International. (2007). *Because I am a girl: The state of the world's girls 2007.* London: Plan U.K.

Plan International. (2008). *Because I am a girl: The state of the world's girls 2008. Special focus: In the shadow of war.* London: Plan U.K.

Rehn, E. and Sirleaf, E. J. (2002). *The independent experts' assessment on the impact of armed conflict on women and the role of women in peace-building, Progress of the world's women,* Vol. 1, UNIFEM.

Reynolds, M. (2008). The war on drugs, prison building, and globalization: Catalysts for the global incarceration of women. *NWSA Journal, 20*(2), 72–95.

Sev'er, A. and Yurdakul, G. (2006). Culture of honor, culture of change: A feminist analysis of honor killings in rural Turkey. In P. S. Rothenberg (Ed.), *Beyond borders: Thinking critically about global issues* (pp. 288–306). New York: Worth Publishers.

Shange, N. (1978; 1991). With no immediate cause. In *Nappy Edges* (p. 14). New York: St. Martin's Press.

Silliman, J., Fried, G. F., Ross, L., and Gutierrez, E. (Eds.) (2004). *Undivided rights: Women of color organize for reproductive justice.* Cambridge, MA: South End Press.

Smith, A. (2005). *Conquest: Sexual violence and American Indian genocide.* Cambridge, MA: South End Press.

Tetreault, M. A. (2001). Accountability or justice? Rape as a war crime. In L. Richardson, V. Taylor, and N. Whittier (Eds.), *Feminist frontiers* (5th ed.) (pp. 466–478). New York: McGraw-Hill.

United Nations, *Violence Against Women.* Retrieved December 27, 2008, from www.un.org/rights/dpi1772e.htm.

United Nations News Centre, Violence against women remains widespread and largely unpublished. Retrieved December 26, 2008, from www.un.org/apps/news/story.asp?NewsID=29066&Cr=UNIFEM&Cr1.

UNAIDS, UNFPA, and UNIFEM. (2004). The link between violence and HIV/AIDS. In *Women and HIV/AIDS: Confronting the crisis,* a joint report. Geneva and New York.

UNESCO Trafficking Statistics Project. (2004). Retrieved December 27, 2008, from http://www.unescobkk.org/fileadmin/user_upload/culture/Trafficking/project/Graph_Worldwide_Sept_2004.pdf.

UNIFEM United Nations Development Fund for Women. Ending violence against women. Retrieved December 28, 2008, from www.unifem.org/gender_issues/violence_against_women/.

U.S. Department of Justice. Documents on violence against women. Retrieved December 31, 2008, from www.ovw.usdoj.gov.

World Health Organization. (1997; revised 2008). Violence against women. Retrieved December 27, 2008, from http://www.who.int/mediacentre/factsheets/fs239/en/print.html. Reprinted (2006) in P. S. Rothenberg (Ed.), *Beyond borders: Thinking critically about global issues* (pp. 278–287). New York: Worth Publishers.

World Health Organization. (2005). *Violence against sex workers and HIV prevention.* Department of Gender, Women, and Health (GWH) and Family and Community Health (FCH). Information Bulletin Series, Number 3. Web site: http://www.who.int/gender.

World Health Organization. (2005). *WHO multi-country study on women's health and domestic violence against women: Initial results on prevalance, health outcomes, and women's responses.* Geneva: WHO Press, World Health Organization.

Yoshiaki, Y. (1995). *Comfort women: Sexual slavery in the Japanese military during World War II.* New York: Columbia University Press.

Zia, H. (1997). Violence in our communities: "Where are the Asian women?" In E. H. Kim, L. V. Villanueva, and Asian Women United of California (Eds.), *Making more waves: New writing By Asian American women* (pp. 207–214). Boston: Beacon Press.

SUGGESTIONS FOR FURTHER READING

Blanchfield, L., Margesson, R., and Seelke, C. R. (2009). *International violence against women.* Hauppauge, NY: Nova Science Publishers.

Das Dasgupta, S. (2007). *Body evidence: Intimate violence against Southasian women in America.* Piscataway, NJ: Rutgers University Press.

Johnson, H., Ollus, N., and Nevala, S. (2007). *Violence against women: An international perspective.* New York: Springer.

Ochoa, M. and Ige, B. K. (Eds.). (2008). *Shout out: Women of color respond to violence.* New York: Seal Press.

Rodriquez, T., and Montané, D. (2008). *The daughters of Juarez: A true story of serial murder south of the border.* New York: Atria Books.

Shalhoub-Kervorkian, N. (2009). *Militarization and violence against women in conflict zones in the Middle East: A Palestinian case study.* New York: Cambridge University Press.

The Conservation of Energy

Chana Bloch (1998)

Why was that locked? I want
the front door open when I get home,
and the lights on, the minute
you hear me honking. He slams
the door behind him, dashes
the porcelain bowl from the table.
Drips of oil shiver to the floor,
fork and knife, little wings

of frayed lettuce. A few
bleak words bitten off and I snap
at our son, who enters
laughing. And now
the child is pulling the cat's tail
with both hands. The cat
is storing up minus signs like a battery,
sharpening its claws.

Prevalence of and Risk Factors for Sexual Victimization in College Women in Chile

Jocelyn A. Lehrer, Vivian L. Lehrer, Evelyn L. Lehrer, and Pamela B. Oyarzún (2007)

Recent studies have documented a high level of gender-based violence in Chile and other Latin American countries.[1–4]Although there have been some exceptions,[5,6] most of the research to date has focused on violence against women within the context of cohabitation or marriage.[7] Substantially less is known about gender-based violence perpetrated against adolescent and young adult women. This is a concern, as previous research has shown that experiencing sexual victimization during late adolescence or young adulthood can have far-reaching consequences, including unwanted pregnancy and increased risk of psychological, sexual and reproductive health problems.[8–10] In addition, analyses conducted in developing countries have found that experiences of sexual violence can limit young women's ability to achieve their educational potential.[11]

The present study focused on college students. Approximately 46% of youth aged 20–24 in Chile

are enrolled in an institution of higher education.[12] No published quantitative studies have examined dating violence or sexual assault in this population, and campuses across the country lack systematized programs to prevent or respond to these problems.

To begin to address this gap in knowledge, we developed the 2005 Survey of Student Well-Being. Administered to male and female students at a large public university in Chile, the survey included questions on experiences with sexual victimization within or outside the context of dating relationships, and with physical and psychological dating violence. The survey also included questions on rape myth acceptance, childhood sexual abuse, witnessing of violence between parents, and socioeconomic and demographic characteristics. The purpose of the present study was to examine the prevalence of and risk factors for sexual victimization in the female sample, the extent of women's rape myth acceptance and the contexts of sexual assault.

In assessing risk factors, we considered two primary domains: childhood experiences with violence, and socioeconomic and demographic factors. There is some evidence that witnessing domestic violence during childhood may increase vulnerability to subsequent sexual victimization.[13] The evidence with regard to early experiences of sexual abuse is stronger: Both retrospective and prospective studies of U.S. college students have found a positive association between sexual abuse during childhood or adolescence and sexual revictimization later in life.[13,14] It has been suggested that this association partly reflects psychological sequelae [after-effects of injury or trauma] of childhood sexual abuse (e.g., negative self-image, depression, learned helplessness) and resulting behavioral manifestations (e.g., substance abuse, multiple sexual partners).[15,16]

Such abuse is by no means rare, although estimates of prevalence vary: A study of 19 countries around the world found that 7–36% of women reported having been sexually abused during childhood.[17] Although data for Latin America are scarce, a recent study in urban areas of Peru found a prevalence of sexual abuse by age 15 of 19–20% (depending on the reporting method used.)[18]

Our study also examined possible associations between sexual victimization and various socioeconomic and demographic factors. While research findings are mixed, several studies in the United States and Latin America suggest that youth who live in socioeconomically disadvantaged households are more likely than those in more privileged households to grow up with domestic violence.[1,2,19,20] In addition, low socioeconomic status has been linked to a higher prevalence of childhood sexual abuse, although this association may in part reflect the greater ease of detecting such abuse in lower-income groups.[19] To the extent that low socioeconomic status is associated with a heightened risk of early experiences with these forms of violence, there may be a resulting indirect link between low socioeconomic status and increased vulnerability to sexual victimization later in life.

Another factor that may be relevant to the risk of sexual victimization is religiosity. Young people raised with some participation in religious activities tend to engage in fewer risk behaviors, including use of alcohol and other drugs,[20,21] and are more likely to have friends who do not use substances,[22] compared with youth who grow up with no involvement in religious activities. These patterns may partly account for findings that link religious participation to a lower risk of physical dating violence victimization.[23,24] For similar reasons, religiosity may be associated with a reduced risk of sexual victimization.

Initiating sexual activity at a young age and having multiple sex partners have each been associated with a heightened risk of sexual victimization, results that have been interpreted within a situational vulnerability framework—i.e., these behaviors may increase exposure to potential aggressors.[25,26] Although youths' living arrangements have received little attention in the literature, they may also be associated with victimization risk; college students who live independently are likely to be more vulnerable than their counterparts who reside with their parents. Finally, place of residence (urban vs. rural) may affect exposure to risk, but results to date, based on studies of high school students, have been mixed.[27,28]

METHODOLOGY

Study Design

The survey instrument, a closed-ended questionnaire, was compiled in English by the lead author and translated into Spanish by the third author, a Chilean native. To ensure accuracy, the questionnaire was back-translated into English. Most of the items were adapted to the Chilean social context from scales validated in the U.S. and other countries, and were revised further based on comments from professors and students at the participating university regarding content, cultural appropriateness and wording. The second author conducted the fieldwork after the project was approved by the university Ethics Committee for Research on Human Subjects.

The university, which is located in Santiago, is one of the largest and most prestigious in Chile, and enrolls students from diverse socioeconomic backgrounds. University officials demonstrated strong interest in participating in this research project and allowed us to administer the survey to students in the 25 general education courses offered during the winter of 2005. We surveyed students in all of these courses, except for one that was affected by class cancellation. The resulting sample included male and female students enrolled in all of the university's educational programs. Total enrollment in the 24 courses was 2,451, although the number of individual students was somewhat smaller because some students were taking more than one course. At the time of survey administration, which took place over several weeks, 1,193 students were present in the 24 classes, consistent with typical attendance in general education courses at the university; 970 students returned completed surveys, reflecting an 81% response rate. Students who had already completed the questionnaire in another class were instructed not to do so again, accounting for some of the nonresponses.

Measures

We asked respondents about their unwanted sexual experiences, both those that had occurred in the past 12 months and those that had occurred since age 14. The first item, regarding attempted rape, read: "Someone tried to make me have sex by using threats, arguments or physical force, but this did not happen." (Sex was defined in the survey instructions as referring to vaginal, oral or anal sex.) The next three items addressed rape and asked whether the subject had ever been forced to have sex through physical force; through verbal pressure; or while being unable to resist because of the effects of alcohol or other drugs. The final item inquired if the subject had experienced any other type of unwanted sexual contact, such as touching or forced kisses.

For use in analyses of risk factors for victimization, we created a trichotomous dependent variable specifying the most severe type of unwanted sexual experience, if any, that the respondent had experienced since age 14. The mutually exclusive categories indicated that the subject reported having experienced attempted rape or rape; less severe forms of sexual victimization; or no unwanted sexual experience.

The independent variable included two measures of childhood experience with violence. Subjects were classified as having experienced childhood sexual abuse if they responded affirmatively to at least one of the following questions: "Before age 14, did anyone make you have sex against your will?" and "Before age 14, did you ever have any other form of unwanted sexual experience, such as forced kisses, touching, etc.?" They were considered to have witnessed domestic violence if they responded affirmatively to the question "Before age 14, did you at some point witness physical violence between your parents or other people who raised you (e.g., hitting, slapping)?"

We also included several dichotomous socioeconomic and demographic variables in our analyses. Parental education was categorized as low if the subject's parent or guardian with the highest level of education had had no more than a secondary school education, or had not completed advanced technical schooling. Religious participation was defined as having attended religious services at least several times per year at age 14. Additional variables indicated whether the subject had ever had voluntary sexual intercourse (vaginal or anal), whether the subject had resided in Santiago or another large urban area at age 14, and whether the subject's primary place of residence during the college years had been the parental home. The subject's age in years, coded as a continuous variable, was included in all analyses to control for length of exposure to the risk of victimization. Finally, the survey included items assessing rape myth beliefs.

RESULTS

Participants

Subjects ranged in age from 18 to 30 years, with a median of 19, reflecting students' tendency to take general education courses early in their studies. Thirty-one percent came from homes with low parental education; 79% reported living mainly with their parents during their college years, consistent with the norm for college students in Santiago (with the exception of students coming from other parts of the country).

Thirty-five percent of the young women reported having witnessed domestic violence before age 14, and 21% reported having experienced some form of sexual abuse before age 14. Subjects whose parents had low levels of education were more likely than those with better educated parents to have witnessed domestic violence (45% vs 31%) and to have been sexually abused (29% vs 17%) before age 14 ($p < .01$; not shown). The prevalence of childhood sexual abuse was 25% among subjects who had witnessed domestic violence and 19% among those who had not ($p = .11$).

Prevalence and Contexts of Sexual Victimization

Overall, 2% of subjects reported that they had been physically forced to have sex (on one or more occasions) since age 14, 4% had been verbally pressured into having sex, and 7% reported that someone had had sex with them while they were under the influence of alcohol or other drugs and unable to stop what was happening (Table 1). In addition, 11% of respondents reported an attempted rape, and 25% reported another type of forced sexual contact.

Subjects could report more than one type of sexual victimization, if applicable. When we classified subjects according to the most severe type of sexual victimization they reported having experienced since age 14, we found that rape was the most severe event for 9%, attempted rape for 6% and another form of unwanted sexual contact for 16%. In total, 31% of subjects reported having experienced at least one type of sexual victimization since age 14, and 17% reported having experienced at least one event in the past 12 months alone.

Other survey items explored the context of the most severe incident of sexual victimization subjects had experienced since age 14.* Both the victim and the perpetrator had used alcohol or other drugs in 56% of rapes or attempted rapes and 24% of other incidents of unwanted sexual contact (not shown); the victim, but not the perpetrator, had used alcohol or other drugs in 6% of rapes or attempted rapes and

2% of other incidents of unwanted sexual contact, and the perpetrator, but not the victim, had used alcohol or other drugs in 9% of rapes or attempted rapes and 18% of other incidents. Only 2% of rapes or attempted rapes, and none of the less severe sexual contacts, were reported to the police. The incidents most commonly occurred at the home of the subject or perpetrator (38%), or at parties at a home (31%). Most subjects identified the perpetrator of the most severe incident as someone they knew but who was not related: an acquaintance (28%), friend (9%), casual date (13%), or steady dating partner (27%). Seven percent of the cases involved a family member and the remaining 17% a stranger.

TABLE 1 Percentage of subjects who experienced various forms of sexual victimization, and percentage distribution of subjects by the most severe form experienced — both according to timing of event

Measure	Since age 14 (N = 455)	Past 12 months (N = 430)[†]
Experienced		
Rape		
Physical force	2.0	0.9
Verbal pressure	3.5	1.2
Alcohol/other drugs	6.8	4.2
Attempted rape	10.8	4.2
Other forced sexual contact	25.1	12.8
Most severe form experienced		
Rape	9.4	5.6
Attempted rape	6.2	2.1
Other forced sexual contact	15.6	9.5
None	68.8	82.8
Total	100.0	100.0

*Approximately one-fifth of subjects did not complete these survey items; these cases were excluded in calculating the descriptive statistics in this paragraph.

[†] Data on sexual victimization in the past 12 months were missing for 25 respondents.

Rape Myth Acceptance

For six of the ten rape myth items, the proportion of women who agreed or strongly agreed was less than 4% (Table 2). At the same time, substantial minorities of women subscribed to the other myths. For example, 28% of respondents agreed or strongly agreed that "the degree of resistance that a woman

presented should be the main factor in determining whether what happened was a rape," and 22% agreed or strongly agreed that "women often lie about having been raped." Ancillary analyses of the male sample (not shown) revealed that agreement with each rape myth was higher for men than for women; differences by sex were large and statistically significant.

TABLE 2   Percentage of subjects who agreed or strongly agreed with rape myths

Statement	%
In most cases, when a woman is raped, she was looking for it.	1.1
Women provoke rape by their appearance or behavior.	3.1
A man can control his behavior regardless of how sexually excited he is.[†]	86.4
The degree of resistance that a woman presented should be the main factor in determining whether what happened was a rape.	27.7
If someone makes a rape charge two weeks after it happened, it probably was not a rape.	3.7
Women often lie about having been raped.	21.5
If a woman goes to the home of her date, this means she is consenting to have sex.	2.0
If a woman fondles a man's genitals, this means she is consenting to have sex.	41.5
If a couple has had sex before, the man should be able to have sex when he wants to.	2.4
A man is justified in having sex if his partner agreed to but changed her mind at the last minute.	1.8

† Statement was reverse coded in analyses. *Notes:* Subjects were asked to indicate strong agreement, agreement, disagreement or strong disagreement with each statement. Surveys with responses missing on four or more statements were excluded. For surveys with responses missing on 1–3 statements, responses for the missing items were imputed using the mean of the subject's completed items, taking into account the reverse coding for the third item. Cronbach's alpha for the scale was 0.69.

DISCUSSION

Numerous studies conducted in the 1980s and 1990s revealed a high prevalence of sexual victimization among female college students in the United States, spurring initiatives to address this issue.[29] Sexual assault prevention and education programs were instituted in colleges across the country, in part due to a mandate that campuses receiving federal funding sponsor such programs.[30] Evidence from the present study suggests the importance of initiating similar efforts in Chile: Thirty-one percent of the female respondents reported that they had experienced some form of sexual victimization since age 14, and 17% had been victimized in the past 12 months alone.

Nine percent of female respondents reported having been raped since age 14, a proportion that is lower than the 15% prevalence for the same time frame reported for U.S. college women using a similar definition of rape.[31] A more recent national study of U.S. college students also found a rape prevalence of 15% since age 15 in female respondents.[32] However, it should be noted that our sample, unlike the U.S. samples, was disproportionately composed of students in their first or second academic year. Caution is also required in international comparisons, as findings may be affected by cultural differences in various factors, including the propensity to disclose sexual victimization incidents to researchers.[10] This propensity is likely to be comparatively low in a socially conservative country such as Chile.

Rape Myth Acceptance and Assault Context

The belief that men may demonstrate their love through violent behaviors is pervasive in Chilean society, creating an environment in which violence against women can thrive.[2,33] National laws in Chile have both reflected and reinforced social conservatism and traditional gender-role norms: Divorce remained illegal until 2004, and legislation against sexual harassment in the workplace was not passed until 2005. Although only a small proportion (<4%) of women in this study agreed with most of the rape myths that we presented to them, there was a relatively high level of acceptance of several myths, consistent with Chile's traditional gender norms; these findings may help inform education programs. In addition, ancillary analyses showed that rape myth acceptance was greater by large margins in male students. Although previous studies have yielded mixed findings regarding the relationship between women's rape myth acceptance and vulnerability to sexual victimization[14,34] acceptance of rape myths among men has been found to be a strong predictor of aggressive behavior.[35,36] Studies have shown that men's and women's rape myth acceptance can be reduced through prevention programs; however, thus far, favorable attitudinal changes have been short-lived.[37]

Consistent with findings for U.S. college students,[26] substance use by the victim, perpetrator or both was involved in more than half of the instances of rape or attempted rape, suggesting that it would be beneficial for sexual assault prevention and risk-reduction programs in Chile to focus on substance use awareness.[38] Our finding that the perpetrators of the most severe incident reported by respondents were mainly identified as acquaintances, dating partners or friends is also consistent with data on U.S. college students[26,39] as is our finding that rape is a highly underreported crime.[31]

Risk and Protective Factors

About one-fifth of respondents reported having experienced sexual abuse during childhood. This high prevalence points to a need for further public health attention to this issue in Chile, especially given the potentially serious immediate and long-term consequences of such abuse. Childhood sexual abuse

was the strongest predictor of sexual victimization since age 14 in this study: The odds of victimization among women who reported childhood sexual abuse were approximately five times the odds among women who did not report such abuse. Witnessing domestic violence before age 14 was a weaker predictor.

Consistent with study findings documenting an association between religiosity and a broad range of beneficial outcomes for youth,[20,21,23,24] we found reduced odds of sexual victimization among young women who had participated in religious activities to some degree at age 14. In addition, ancillary analyses (not shown) suggest a lower risk of sexual victimization among students who live primarily with their families while attending college. This may be due in part to higher levels of parental supervision and less opportunity for exposure to risk; there may also be unobserved differences in the characteristics and risk behaviors of students who live with versus without their parents. In either case, the findings suggest that it would be helpful to address safe living outside of the parental home in Chilean risk-reduction programs.

Conclusions

This study provides the first data on prevalence of and risk factors for sexual victimization among female college students in Chile. Our findings indicate a need for additional public health attention to sexual violence in Chilean college campuses, through further research on prevalence and on risk factors for victimization and perpetration, and through the development of theory-based programs to prevent and respond to this problem.

REFERENCES

1. Urzúa R et al., eds., *Detección y Análisis de la Prevalencia de la Violencia Intrafamiliar*, Santiago, Chile: Servicio Nacional de la Mujer, 2002.
2. Ceballo R et al., Domestic violence and women's mental health in Chile, *Psychology of Women Quarterly*, 2004, 28(4):298–308.
3. Rivera-Rivera L et al., Prevalence and determinants of male partner violence against Mexican women: a population-based study, *Salud Pública de México*, 2004, 46(2):113–121.

4. Flake DF, Individual, family and community risk markers for domestic violence in Peru, *Violence Against Women*, 2005, 11(3):353–373.

5. Krugman S, Mata L and Krugman R, Sexual abuse and corporal punishments during childhood: a pilot retrospective survey of university students in Costa Rica, *Pediatrics*, 1992, 90(1):157–161.

6. Olsson A et al., Sexual abuse during childhood and adolescence among Nicaraguan men and women: a population-based anonymous survey, *Child Abuse & Neglect*, 2000, 24(12):1579–1589.

7. Almeras D et al., Violencia contra la mujer en relación de pareja: América Latina y el Caribe, *Serie Mujer y Desarrollo*, Santiago, Chile: La Comisión Económica para América Latina, 2002, No. 40.

8. Rickert VI, Vaughan RD and Wiemann CM, Adolescent dating violence and date rape, *Current Opinion in Obstetrics and Gynecology*, 2002, 14(5):495–500.

9. Rickert VI, Vaughan RD and Wiemann CM, Violence against young women: implications for clinicians, *Contemporary OB/GYN*, 2003, 48(2):30–45.

10. Krug EG et al., eds., *World Report on Violence and Health*, Geneva: WHO, 2002.

11. Mirsky J, Beyond victims and villains: addressing sexual violence in the education sector, *Panos Report*, London: Panos Institute, 2003, No. 47.

12. International Institute for Higher Education in Latin America and the Caribbean (IESALC), *Informe Sobre la Educación Superior en América Latina y el Caribe 2000–2005*, Caracas, Venezuela: IESALC, 2006.

13. Koss MP and Dinero TE, Discriminant analysis of risk factors for sexual victimization among a national sample of college women, *Journal of Consulting and Clinical Psychology*, 1989, 57(2):242–250.

14. Himelein MJ, Risk factors for sexual victimization in dating: a longitudinal study of college women, *Psychology of Women Quarterly*, 1995, 19(1):31–48.

15. Browne A and Finkelhor D, Impact of child sexual abuse: a review of the research, *Psychological Bulletin*, 1986, 99(1):66–77.

16. Messman TL and Long PJ, Child sexual abuse and its relationship to revictimization in adult women: a review, *Clinical Psychology Review*, 1996, 16(5):397–420.

17. Finkelhor D. The international epidemiology of child sexual abuse, *Child Abuse & Neglect*, 1994, 18(5):409–417.

18. Garcia-Moreno et al., *WHO Multi-Country Study on Women's Health and Domestic Violence Against Women*, Geneva: World Health Organization (WHO), 2005.

19. Finkelhor D, Current information on the scope and nature of child sexual abuse, *The Future of Children*, 1994, 4(2):31–53.

20. Donahue MJ and Benson PL, Religion and the well-being of adolescents, *Journal of Social Issues*, 1995, 51(2):145–160.

21. Koenig HG, McCullough ME and Larson DB, *Handbook of Religion and Health*, New York: Oxford University Press, 2001.

22. Bahr JS et al., Family, religiosity, and the risk of adolescent drug use, *Journal of Marriage and the Family*, 1998, 60(4):979–992.

23. Howard D, Qiu Y and Boekeloo B, Personal and social contextual correlates of adolescent dating violence, *Journal of Adolescent Health*, 2003, 33(1):9–17.

24. Gover AR, Risky lifestyles and dating violence: a theoretical test of violent victimization, *Journal of Criminal Justice*, 2004, 32(2):171–180.

25. Wyatt GE, Newcomb MD and Riederle MH, *Sexual Abuse and Consensual Sex: Women's Developmental Patterns and Outcomes*, Newbury Park, CA, USA: Sage, 1993.

26. Abbey A et al., Alcohol and dating risk factors for sexual assault among college women, *Psychology of Women Quarterly*, 1996, 20(1):147–169.

27. Bergman L, Dating violence among high school students, *Social Work*, 1992, 37(1):21–27.

28. Spencer GA and Bryant SA, Dating violence: a comparison of rural, suburban, and urban teens, *Journal of Adolescent Health*, 2000, 27(5):302–305.

29. Rozee PD and Koss MP, Rape: a century of resistance, *Psychology of Women Quarterly*, 2001, 25(4):295–311.

30. National Association of Student Personnel Administrators (NASPA), *Complying with the Final Regulations: The Student Right-to-Know and Campus Security Act*, Washington, DC: NASPA, 1994.

31. Koss MP, Gidycz CA and Wisniewski N, The scope of rape: incidence and prevalence of sexual aggression and victimization in a national sample of higher education students, *Journal of Consulting and Clinical Psychology*, 1987, 55(2):162–170.

32. Brener ND et al., Forced sexual intercourse and associated health-risk behaviors among female college students in the United States, *Journal of Consulting and Clinical Psychology*, 1999, 67(2):252–259.

33. McWhirter PT, La violencia privada: domestic violence in Chile, *American Psychologist*, 1999, 54(1):37–40.

34. Muehlenhard CL and Linton MA, Date rape and sexual aggression in dating situations: incidence and risk factors, *Journal of Counseling Psychology*, 1987, 34(2):186–196.

35. Malamuth NM, Factors associated with rape as predictors of laboratory aggression against women, *Journal of Personality and Social Psychology*, 1983, 45(2):432–442.

36. Craig ME, Coercive sexuality in dating relationships: a situational model, *Clinical Psychology Review*, 1990, 10(4):395–423.

37. Breitenbecher KH, Sexual assault on college campuses: Is an ounce of prevention enough? *Applied and Preventive Psychology*, 2000, 9(1):23–52.

38. Ullman SE, A critical review of field studies on the link of alcohol and adult sexual assault in women, *Aggression and Violence Behavior*, 2003, 8(5):471–486.

39. Koss MP, Hidden rape: sexual aggression and victimization in a national sample of students in higher education, in: Odem ME and Clay-Warner J, eds., *Confronting Rape and Sexual Assault*, Wilmington, DE, USA: Scholarly Resources, 1998, pp. 51–70.

R E A D I N G **45**

Killed in the Name of Honor

Amnesty International (2005)

Ankara, Turkey—Ignoring the pleas of his 14-year old daughter to spare her life, Mehmet Halitogullari pulled on a wire wrapped around her neck and strangled her—supposedly to restore the family's honor after she was kidnapped and raped . . . "I decided to kill her because our honor was dirtied," the newspaper Sabah quoted the father as saying. "I didn't listen to her pleas, I wrapped the wire around her neck and pulled at it until she died" (The Associated Press).

Every year around the world an increasing number of women are killed in the name of "honor." Relatives, usually male, commit acts of violence against wives, sisters, daughters and mothers to reclaim their family honor from real or suspected actions that are perceived to have compromised it. Due to discriminatory societal beliefs and extremist views of gender, officials often condone or ignore the use of torture and brutality against women. As a result, the majority of so-called honor killings go unreported and perpetrators face little, if any, consequence.

Although "honor" killings are widely reported in regions throughout the Middle East and South Asia, the United Nations Special Rapporteur on Extrajudicial, Summary and Arbitrary Executions reported that these crimes against women occur in countries as varied as Bangladesh, Brazil, Ecuador, Egypt, India, Iran, Iraq, Israel, Italy, Jordan, Morocco, Pakistan, Sweden, Turkey, Uganda and the United Kingdom. In September 2000, the United Nations Population Fund (UNFPA) estimated that as many as 5,000 women and girls are murdered each year in so-called honor killings by members of their own families. In a recent study on the gender gap ratio among states by the World Economic Forum, Jordan scored exceptionally low as a country where gender discrimination incites violence. Jordan currently stands as one of the greatest practitioners of so-called honor killings.

The Concept of Honor

So-called honor killings are based on the belief, deeply rooted in some cultures, of women as objects and commodities, not as human beings endowed with dignity and rights equal to those of men. Women are considered the property of male relatives and are seen to embody the honor of the men to whom they "belong." Women's bodies are considered the repositories of family honor. The concepts of male status and family status are of particular importance in cultures where "honor" killings occur and where women are viewed as responsible for upholding a family's "honor." If a woman or girl is accused or suspected of engaging in behavior that could taint male and/or family status, she may face brutal retaliation from her relatives that often results in violent death. Even though such accusations are not based on factual or tangible evidence, any allegation of dishonor against a woman often suffices for family members to take matters into their own hands.

Convicted killers often speak with defiant pride and without regret about their actions. "We do not consider this murder," said Wafik Abu Abseh, a 22-year-old Jordanian woodcutter who committed a so-called honor killing, as his mother, brother and sisters nodded in agreement. "It was like cutting off a finger." Abdel Rahim, a convicted killer who was released after two months, also said he had no regrets. "Honor is more precious than my own flesh and blood" (New York Times).

INTERNATIONAL HUMAN RIGHTS FOUNDATIONS

- Article 1 of the UN Declaration on the Elimination of Violence Against Women proclaims "the term 'violence against women' means any act of gender-based violence that results in, or is likely to result in, physical, sexual or psychological harm or suffering to women, including threats of such acts, coercion of arbitrary deprivation of liberty, whether occurring in public or in private life."
- The Convention on the Elimination of Discrimination of All Forms Against Women (CEDAW) concludes that "… State Parties [should] take all appropriate measures […] to modify the social and cultural patterns of conduct of men and women, with a view to achieving the elimination of prejudices […] and all other practices which are based on the idea of inferiority or the superiority of either of the sexes or on stereotyped roles for men and women."
- CEDAW General Recommendation 19 clarifies that traditional public and private ideologies that regard women as "subordinate to men" and seek to "justify gender-based violence as a form of protection or control" deprive women of mental and bodily integrity.

- The Platform for Action on Women's Human Rights from the UN Fourth World Conference on Women calls upon states to "take urgent action to combat and eliminate violence against women, which is a human rights violation resulting from harmful traditional or customary practices, cultural prejudices and extremism."
- The International Covenant on Civil and Political Rights (ICCPR) asserts that "every human being has the inherent right to life" in addition to "the right to liberty and security of person."

What Can Precipitate an "Honor" Killing?

Women and girls can be killed for a variety of behaviors, which may include talking with an unrelated male, consensual sexual relations outside marriage, being a victim of rape, seeking a divorce, or refusing to marry the man chosen by one's family. Even the suspicion of a transgression may result in a killing. Amnesty International received a report of a man who killed his wife on the basis of a dream he had about her committing adultery. Women have been killed for ostensibly disrespecting their husbands. In one case, a woman was beaten to death for not performing her domestic duties quickly enough. Women may also be assaulted physically but not killed. When they attempt to seek help from law enforcement, they may be disbelieved or they may be discredited by officials who support the prevailing cultural expectations for women. Some countries have passed laws that allow lesser penalties for men who kill "in the name of family honor." In others, the police may be bribed by the family of the killer to ignore attempts to report the killing as a murder.

In 1999, twenty-nine year old Samia Sarwar was shot dead in her lawyer's office in Lahore. Her parents instigated the murder, feeling that Samia had brought shame on the family by seeking divorce after 10 years of marital abuse. Although the perpetrators can be easily identified, not one of them has been arrested. Instead, her lawyer, Hina Jilani, and her colleague, Asma Jahangir, have been publicly condemned and received death threats.

Religious, Social and Institutional Justifications for "Honor" Killings

So-called honor crimes occur in societies in which there is interplay between discriminatory tribal traditions of justice and statutory law. In some countries this is exacerbated by inclusion of Shari'a, or Islamic law, or the concept of *zina* (sex outside of marriage) as a crime within statutory law. Due to women's enforced seclusion, submission to men and second-class citizenship, women seldom know their rights under national or international law, and rarely have a chance to defend themselves in a court of law. Local law enforcement officials often turn a blind eye or fail to enforce significant punishments for the murder of women. In Pakistan, for example, a woman may be imprisoned if convicted of *zina*. In the parallel tribal justice systems of Pakistan, a woman may be killed for actual or suspected sex outside of marriage. Police and members of the public may help the killer's family cover up the murder by refusing to register it as a crime, or by delaying long enough to allow the killer to escape the vicinity. For example, under both Jordanian and Pakistani law, women are expected to meet impossible requirements for "corroborating evidence" in order to prove allegations of rape. Even if a woman meets these requirements, evidence of previous sexual activity may be admitted in proceedings and lead to her being charged with *zina*. In both Jordan and Pakistan, any form of perceived "immorality," whether adultery or rape, is considered a way of dishonoring the family and may lead to "honor" related violence.

Communal Aspect of "Honor" Killings

So-called honor killings are part of a community mentality. Large sections of society share traditional conceptions of family honor and approve of "honor" killings to preserve that honor. Even mothers whose daughters have been killed in the name of honor often condone such violent acts. Such complicity by other women in the family and the community strengthens the concept of women as property without personal worth. In addition, communal acceptance of "honor" killings furthers the claim that violence in the name of "honor" is a private issue and one to be avoided by law enforcement. Community acceptance of these killings stifles accurate reporting of the number of violent crimes against women in the name of "honor." As a result, the true extent of the prevalence of "honor" killings is still not fully known.

> It is an unholy alliance that works against women: the killers take pride in what they have done, the tribal leaders condone the act and protect the killers and the police connive the cover-up.
>
> (Nighat Taufeeq, Lahore, Pakistan).

The murder of women in the name of "honor" is a gender-specific form of discrimination and violence. In societies where so-called honor killings are allowed to occur, governments are failing in their responsibility to protect and ensure women their human rights. "Honor" killings should be regarded as part of a larger spectrum of violence against women, as well as a serious human rights violation. Amnesty International calls on you to help bring an end to "honor" killings, and to demand that governments take steps to ensure that women and men enjoy equal treatment under law.

For more information on women's human rights, visit AIUSA's Women's Human Rights Program website at www.amnestyusa.org/women.

No Longer Silent

Megan Shank (2009)

As working hours wound down in Sichuan, a southwestern Chinese province, 29-year-old human-resources manager Liu Lun invited recent college graduate and new hire Chen Dan into his office and asked her to be his girlfriend. When she refused, he grabbed her by the neck and forcefully kissed her. Colleagues overheard and called police. Chen escaped.

Across the country in Shanghai, 29-year-old Xiong Jie says she accompanied her foreign manager on a walk after a company dinner. "Suddenly, he kissed me," says Xiong. "I didn't have time to react, and there was no one around to witness it." When he apologized, Xiong says, she forgave him—until he did it again. She protested. He fired her.

Xiong searched for a new job. But Chen filed suit, using the 2005 amendment to the Law of the People's Republic of China on the Protection of Rights and Interests of Women, which recognizes women's right to arbitrate or litigate cases of sexual harassment and to seek legal or judicial aid in case of financial difficulty. In July 2008, Chen became the first to win a criminal case using the amendment. The court sentenced Liu to five months in jail.

Mao Zedong once famously declared, "Women hold up half the sky"; today, they also constitute half of China's formal workforce—330 million of the nation's 711.5 million employees, according to the All-China Women's Foundation. Scholars conservatively put the number of Chinese women who have suffered workplace sexual harassment at 25 to 30 percent, but surveys over the past decade report numbers as high as 80 percent, with the majority of incidents occurring on the job. Sociologists and legal experts say few women seek legal recourse.

"Our country still has a 'blame the victim' culture," says Wang Xingjuan, founding director of the Maple Women's Counseling Center, one of China's earliest women's-rights NGOs. Many victims won't come forward from the shame of having done something wrong, "saving face" rather than seeking justice.

Foreign and domestic firms have set policies for environmental, labor and corporate social-responsibility practices, but lag in providing sexual harassment polices and staff training, says Tang Can, a sociologist with the Chinese Academy of Social Sciences. Companies blame local governments for failing to define the national law in more concrete, applicable terms. Shanghai was the first municipality to do so, in 2007, two years after the women's rights amendment was enacted. Since than, 16 more of China's 31 provinces and special administrative regions have begun drafting local definitions. Meanwhile, with women facing pressure to adhere to the rule of the collective and also navigate a competitive job market, it's unclear how many women will step forward.

In 2001, China's first sexual harassment case was brought by a woman employee who refused a manager's advances at a state-owned company in Xi'an, Shaanxi. With no sexual harassment law yet in place, the case was brought under a law protecting "human dignity." Ultimately, the court ruled the evidence insufficient and questioned the connection between human dignity and sexual harassment. Still, "sexual harassment" entered Chinese consciousness.

"An Internet survey got conversation going and harassment became a very hot topic," says Edward Chan, a University of Hong Kong associate professor. In 2002, *Women No Longer Silent*, billed as the "first Chinese television program to take on sexual harassment and sexual abuse," tackled fictional power-abusing bosses and government cadres, along with victims' lack of legal recourse—but ended happily. Life mimicked art in 2003 when a woman in Wuhan became the first plaintiff to win a harassment case under the "right to good reputation" statute.

"No official body has recorded how many suits have been brought, and most aren't public record," says Li Ying, deputy director of the Center for Women's Law Studies & Legal Services of Peking University. Only Chen has won a criminal case; a few others have won civil settlements. But some women who have won such suits struggle to collect compensation, notes Jo Ling Kent, a Fulbright Scholar who studied sexual harassment cases in Beijing: "These verdicts are hailed as victories, but you have to go back and say, 'Judge? Company? City? Government? *Hello*—you need to deliver!'"

"[The amendment] was very clear, but it was only a few sentences," says Wang. And in China, making a law "doesn't mean you have the support of the entire system," adds Chan. "It's a top-down approach."

As Tang explains it, China's metamorphosis from a socialist, planned economy to a capitalist one has robbed it of the institutionalized morality of the old *danwei* (work unit) that managed all personal as well as professional issues, including marriage licenses, housing and schooling for workers' children. "Perhaps these strict *danwei* moral controls weren't humanistic, but they were effective in controlling workplace sexual harassment," says Tang. "Now, as companies turn towards marketization, the standardized evaluation is not based on moral rightness but monetary returns."

Untrained employees pardon sexual harassment as cultural misunderstanding. "I thought maybe that was just the way foreign men behaved," says

Xiong. Similarly, an American working for a Beijing governmental health organization thought the same thing when her Chinese boss returned from an HIV-AIDS conference in Thailand and regaled her with stories of his extracurricular activities in Bangkok's brothels. His behavior discomfited her, but she "chalked it up to cultural relativism."

"A respectful workplace is about more than compliance with the law," says Nicole Zhang, corporate marketing and public affairs manager of 3M China, which provides its 5,700 local employees with anonymous mechanisms to report abuse. "It is a working environment free of inappropriate behavior."

Trying to help companies develop antiharassment policies, the women's legal aid center at Peking University, which also represents sexual harassment victims in court, has cooperated with brand-name corporations to draw local companies into educational workshops. "[Chinese managers think it's a great thing] that General Electric puts such serious effort into this 'small matter,'" says Feng Jianmei, senior counsel of public policy for General Electric China, who presented the company's policy to two Chinese firms.

The legal aid center will soon release a new three-year plan to confront sexual harassment, and Tang and Wang plan to publish new research. Meanwhile, everyday 330 million Chinese women go to work—each, in some way, very much alone.

R E A D I N G **47**

War Against Women: Congo and Kosovo

Essay 1

The Use of Rape as a Weapon in Congo's Civil War

CBS News (2008)

Right now there's a war taking place in the heart of Africa, in the Democratic Republic of Congo, and more people have died there than in Iraq, Afghanistan, and Darfur combined.

You probably haven't heard much about it, but as CNN's Anderson Cooper first reported last January, it's the deadliest conflict since World War II. Within the last ten years, more than five million people have died and the numbers keep rising.

As Cooper and a *60 Minutes* team found when they went there a few months ago, the most frequent targets of this hidden war are women. It is, in fact, a war against women, and the weapon used to destroy them, their families and whole communities, is rape.

Dr. Denis Mukwege is the director of Panzi Hospital in eastern Congo. In this war against women, his hospital is the frontline. One of the latest victims he's treating is Sifa M'Kitambala. She was raped just two days before the team arrived by soldiers who raided her village.

"They just cut her at many places." Dr. Mukwege explains.

Sifa was pregnant, but that didn't stop her rapists. Armed with a machete, they even cut at her genitals.

In the last ten years in Congo, hundreds of thousands of women have been raped, most of them gang raped. Panzi Hospital is full of them.

"All these women have been raped?" Cooper asked Dr. Mukwege, standing near a very large group of women waiting.

All the women, the doctor says, have been patients of his.

Within a week, Dr. Mukwege says this room will be filled with new faces, new victims.

"You know, they're in deep pain. But it's not just physical pain. It's psychological pain that you can see. Here at the hospital, we've seen women who've stopped living," Dr. Mukwege explains.

And not all the people the hospital treats are adults. "There are children. I think the youngest was three years old," Mukwege says. "And the oldest was 75."

To understand what is happening here, you have to go back more than a decade, when the genocide that claimed nearly a million lives in neighboring Rwanda spilled over into Congo. Since then, the Congolese army, foreign-backed rebels, and home-grown militias have been fighting each other over power and this land, which has some of the world's biggest deposits of gold, copper, diamonds, and tin. The United Nations was called in and today their mission is the largest peacekeeping operation in history.

Since 2005, some 17,000 UN troops and personnel have cobbled together a fragile peace. Last year they oversaw the first democratic election in this country in 40 years. But now all they have accomplished is at risk. Fighting has broken out once again in eastern Congo and the region threatens to slip into all-out war.

Each new battle is followed by pillaging and rape; entire communities are terrorized. Forced to flee their homes, people take whatever they can, and walk for miles in the desperate hope of finding food and shelter. Over the last year, more than 500,000 people have been uprooted. A fraction of them make it to cramped camps, where they depend on UN aid to survive.

One camp Cooper visited sprang up just two months before. It was already overcrowded, but more people kept arriving. They would go there seeking refuge, a safe haven. However, the truth is that in Congo, for women, there's no such thing. Even in these supposedly protected camps, women are raped every single day.

"Has rape almost become the norm here?" Cooper asks Anneka Van Woudenberg, who is the senior Congo researcher at Human Rights Watch.

"I think because of the widespread nature of the war, because there has been so much violence, rape is now on a daily basis—rape is the norm," Van Woudenberg replies.

"Women get raped in wars all the time. How is it different here?" Cooper asks.

"I think what's different in Congo is the scale and the systematic nature of it, indeed, as well, the brutality. This is not rape because soldiers have got bored and have nothing to do. It is a way to ensure that communities accept the power and authority of that particular armed group. This is about showing terror. This is about using it as a weapon of war," she explains.

It's hard to imagine this war happening in the midst of such breathtaking natural beauty and abundance. But after decades of dictatorship and corruption, the country is broken. Most of the fighting and the raping takes place in remote areas difficult to get to.

Cooper and the team headed to an isolated village in the mountains in eastern Congo called Walungu. For years there have been armed groups fighting in this region; thousands of men emerge from the forest to terrorize villages and steal women. Congo's government seems unable or unwilling to stop them.

In the week before they arrived there were three attacks in which women were raped. The youngest victim was just six years old.

In some villages as many as 90 percent of the women have been raped; men in the villages are usually unarmed, and incapable of fighting back. In Walungu the team found 24-year-old Lucienne M'Maroyhi. She was at home one night with her two children and her younger brother, when six soldiers broke in. They tied her up and began to rape her, one by one.

"I was lying on the ground, and they gave a flashlight to my younger brother so that he could see them raping me," she recalls.

"They were telling your brother to hold the flashlight?" Cooper asks.

"Yes," she says. "They raped me like they were animals, one after another. When the first one finished, they washed me out with water, told me to stand up, so the next man could rape me."

She was convinced they'd kill her, just as soldiers had murdered her parents the year before. Instead, they turned to her brother. "They wanted him to rape me but he refused, and told them, 'I cannot do such a thing. I cannot rape my sister.' So they took out their knives and stabbed him to death in front of me," she recalls.

Lucienne was then dragged through the forest to the soldier's camp. She was forced to become their slave and was raped every day for eight months. All the while, she had no idea where her children were.

"Did you know if they were alive or dead?" Cooper asks.

"I was thinking that they had been killed. I didn't think I would find them alive," she replies.

Finally, Lucienne escaped. Back in her village, she found her two little girls were alive. But she also learned that she was pregnant. She was carrying the child of one of her rapists. Lucienne's husband abandoned her. That happens to rape survivors all over Congo.

"When a woman is raped, it's not just her that's raped. It's the entire community that's destroyed," says Judithe Registre, who is with an organization called "Women for Women." They run support groups for survivors of rape.

"When they take a woman to rape her, they'll line up the family, they'll line up other members of the communities to actually witness that," Registre says. "They make them watch. And so, what that means

for that particular woman when it's all over, is that total shame, personally, to have been witnessed by so many people as she's being violated."

Many of the women in Dr. Mukwege's hospital are not only blamed for what happened to them, they are shunned because of fears they've contracted HIV and shunned because their rapes were so violent they can no longer control their bodily functions.

Dr. Mukwege says he's doing about five surgeries a day.

His patients often have had objects inserted into their vaginas, like broken bottles, bayonets. Some women have even been shot between the legs by their rapists.

"Why would somebody do that? Why would somebody shoot a woman inside?" Cooper asks.

"In the beginning I was asking myself the same question. This is a show of force, of power, it's done to destroy the person," Dr. Mukwege says. "Sex is being used to commit evil. People flee. They become refugees. They can't get help, they become malnourished and it's disease which finishes them off."

Asked what he can tell a young girl about her future, Dr. Mukwege says, "The most difficult thing is when there is nothing I can do. When I see a 16-year-old, a pretty 16-year-old who's had everything destroyed, and I tell her that I have to give her a colostomy bag … that is difficult."

Despite those difficulties, more often than not, Dr. Mukwege is able to repair the damage to these women's bodies. They see him as a miracle worker, one of the only men they can trust.

While Dr. Mukwege gives Cooper a tour of the hospital wards, one of his patients gives him the thumbs up.

"And now she's very happy," he says, "Very happy."

That reaction not only gives him hope, he says, but also the strength to continue his work.

Strength is something that few women in Congo lack. They bear the burdens, farm the fields, and hold the families together, yet nothing it seems is being done to protect them.

The war is so widespread that rapes are increasingly being committed by civilians. A few washed out billboards tell men that rape is wrong, but there's little evidence Congolese officials take the problem seriously.

In the prosecutor's office, the complaints pile up. We were told a $10 bribe could get a rape accusation investigated, but few cases ever go to court.

We asked the prosecutor to show us the prison, to see how many rapists were actually behind bars, but when we got there, we were in for a surprise. The prison had no fences, and the guards had been kicked out. The inmates had taken over the asylum.

"The fact is the justice system is on its knees in Congo," says Van Woudenberg, the human rights investigator. "I can count on one hand the number of cases that we're aware of that have been brought to trial. Literally here people get away with rape, they get away with murder. The chances of being arrested are nil."

There may be no justice in Congo, but there are organizations trying to help rape survivors get back on their feet. "Women For Women" teaches survivors how to make soap, how to cook—skills they can use to earn money. They also learn how to read

and write. It is the first time many of these women have ever been in a classroom—it is their chance for a whole new life.

Remember Lucienne M'Maroyhi? She's jumped at that chance. She hopes to start her own business one day.

She is also now the mother of a little baby girl, born a year ago. The father is one of her rapists, one of the men who killed Lucienne's brother. She named the girl "Luck."

"I named her Luck because I went through many hardships," she explains. "I could have been killed in the forest. But I got my life back. I have hope."

Hope is not something you'd expect Congo's rape survivors to still cling to. But they do.

Each morning in Panzi hospital they gather to raise their voices, singing at a religious service. Our sufferings on earth, they sing, will be relieved in heaven.

Relief in Congo, it seems, is just too much to ask for.

Essay 2

Signs of Rape Scar Kosovo

Peter Finn (1999)

At 8:15 on the evening of June 9, three days before NATO troops arrived in this city, a drunken Serbian paramilitary waving a gun entered a house where 13 ethnic Albanians were sheltered. He corralled the frightened people in a single room, and started looking over the women.

There were three young women—a 25-year-old hairdresser; her sister, a 29-year-old schoolteacher; and a 24-year-old new mother, a neighbor of the sisters who held in her arms a 4-month-old daughter. The paramilitary settled his eyes on the hairdresser and said, "You, out."

In the hallway, he forced her to strip and threatened to kill her if she shouted, the woman recalled in graphic detail during an interview last week. "He put his finger inside me to see if I was a virgin," she said, and then he raped her. She was later returned bleeding to the room where the others, including her mother and father, sat helpless and horrified.

"I want fresh girls," the paramilitary, who was wearing a light green uniform, said in fluent Albanian.

The sexual assaults would continue for another hour before a Yugoslav soldier came upon the scene and, enraged by what he saw, beat and drove off the militiaman as he attempted to rape the new mother.

"Only when I'm sleeping is there silence in my heart," said the hairdresser as she sat in her home. Her parents remained outside during the interview because they cannot bear to hear her talk about what happened.

Ever since ethnic Albanian refugees began streaming out of the province in late March at the start of a Serb-led Yugoslav offensive and NATO bombing campaign, there have been allegations of systematic rape by Yugoslav and Serbian forces. During the war, the State Department reported evidence that two locations in Kosovo—a Yugoslav army camp in Djakovica in the southern part of the Serbian province and a hotel in the western city of Pec—were used as rape camps.

Reporting across Kosovo since the arrival of NATO troops has yielded no conclusive evidence to support the existence of such camps or the use of rape by Yugoslav forces as a systematic weapon of war, as it was during the conflict in Bosnia in 1992-95. Although there are indications that women, as well as other refugees, were held at facilities the State Department claimed could be rape camps, visits to the locations turned up no testimony or physical affirmation that rape occurred.

However, it is clear on the basis of interviews with women and evidence left at several sites by departing Yugoslav forces that sexual violence was common in Kosovo during the war. In some cases, private homes taken over by security forces after the expulsion of their ethnic Albanian owners and police stations occupied by Yugoslav forces were used to detain women and carry out assaults and sexual torture.

At a home in Orahovac, for example, refugees returned to find women's blood-stained clothing, restraints, used condoms and other signs that the basement and attic had been used for sexual assaults. A number of women who were detained by Yugoslav forces in Orahovac remain missing. Elsewhere, such as in the provincial capital, Pristina, war crimes investigators have found evidence of rape at police stations and are examining stains on mattresses.

Rape is a deeply sensitive subject in ethnic Albanian Kosovo, a Muslim and largely traditional society, where a sexual assault can permanently stigmatize a woman, shaming her family and ruining her marriage or prospects of marriage. Gathering first-hand accounts of rape has proved very difficult for war crimes investigators, and the scale of sexual assaults here may never be fully known.

"Women lie and say nothing happened," said Vjolca Kastratit, a nurse at the hospital in Djakovica. "It is very embarrassing for them and for their families."

Yet the anger that many ethnic Albanians feel over of the destruction of their lives is propelling some, like the women in Prizren, to speak to strangers about the most intimate of violations. Indeed, the two sisters who were interviewed said that if it were not for their father's anguish, they would gladly allow their names to be published. *The Washington Post* does not identify victims of sexual assault without their permission.

"I am proud to tell my story," said the older sister. "I would like to tell everybody I was raped so people will know what that Serb did. But my father doesn't allow it. . . . He is drinking all the time. It is very tough on him."

Across Kosovo, the extent of the horrors that occurred under Yugoslav repression is being revealed as refugees race home, and this has been the case with allegations of rape. In the yard of her mother's home in Orahovac, Labimote Shabani, 20, burned pornographic magazines, used condoms, bloody rugs and torn women's underwear. Shabani returned to her home from Albania, where she was a refugee, and discovered what appeared to be a sex dungeon in her mother's basement.

In a corner of the basement, a steel stake has been driven into the dirt floor and ropes formed into nooses are tied to the stake. Women's makeup, a sheer blouse and stockings litter the floor. A mattress has been thrown into the corner, and outside, a blood-soaked sheepskin rug lies on the ground. In the attic, Shabani found noosed ropes tied to the beams and chains. Pornographic pictures were tacked to the walls.

"This is my mother's home and we cannot live with this stink," she said, explaining why she was burning what might be evidence of crimes. "I can't stand to see this."

At least four women are missing from Orahovac, according to residents. In late April, Hajdije Spahiju, 33, a tall, gregarious woman, was picked up by security forces who arrived at her mother's house in a jeep. She was dragged away as family members screamed. Hajdije had no political affiliations, relatives said, although she may have dated a member of the Kosovo Liberation Army.

"Only Hajdije was taken that day," said Zejnepe Spahiju, her cousin. She has not been seen since.

If physical evidence of rapes existed at the sites identified by the State Department, it has been swept away. Farmers in Djakovica who live near a former shelter for Serbian refugees from Croatia that later became a military staging area said that women were held there and could be heard screaming. But a walk through the compound, which has been destroyed by NATO bombs, produced no physical evidence. The buildings were littered with the traditional clothing of ethnic Albanian women, children's toys and coloring books. Other army facilities in the area also lacked evidence of abuse.

The Kosovo Liberation Army, the ethnic Albanian guerrilla force, now occupies the Hotel Karagac in Pec—the other site named by the State Department—and fighters there said they had found pornographic magazines, condoms and women's clothing when they entered the hotel. But they said that [they] had discarded the evidence.

Shpesa Gashi, who lives down the street from the hotel, said that on the day before NATO troops arrived in Pec, two Yugoslav soldiers entered her house and hustled her and her 17-year-old sister, Shqipe, into a jeep. The soldiers, whom Gashi said were from Bosnia, told her family the women were being taken away for questioning.

The women said they were driven around for about an hour and the soldiers threatened that if they didn't agree to have sex with them, they would be taken to some majors who would rape them. The soldiers asked if the women had boyfriends and if the women were virgins.

The more senior soldier, Gashi said, was alternatively nervous, polite and threatening. The women said they begged him to let them go in the name of the cross he wore around his neck. After driving around Pec and its surrounding countryside, the women said, they were released untouched.

In Prizren, the rapes at the home where the two sisters and their neighbors were sheltered occurred in a neighborhood surrounded by Yugoslav forces during a nighttime operation. But the paramilitary who carried out the assaults appeared to be acting without the approval of his comrades.

When the Yugoslav soldier arrived, according to the women, he started to kick and punch the paramilitary and threw him out of the house. The soldier, whose name they recalled as Vladan, then started to cry, the women said.

"He said, 'I'm so sorry. I have sisters. I have a wife. I have children'" said the young mother, Lumturije, who said he kissed her hand and held her baby as he wept. "One was so bad, and one was so polite, like an angel. He saved us." Military police later took the women to the Prizren hospital where they said they received a perfunctory examination from a Serbian gynecologist.

The three women, who saw a German military doctor for their first full medical examination on Friday, have recently torn hymens and irritated vaginas, the physician said.

Other wounds were also evident. Their moods shifted suddenly between defiance and fear. They said they wanted to find journalists to tell their story, but they rarely leave the house because they think everyone on the street is looking at them. And the effect on their families is also profound. The father of the sisters is quiet and withdrawn; their mother holds visitors in a long, needy embrace, tears staining her cheeks.

"I would like to go and identify that man," said the younger sister. "If I find him, I will kill him. I am praying for that chance."

Domestic Violence in Afghanistan

Kirk Semple (2009)

Mariam was 11 in 2003 when her parents forced her to marry a blind, 41-year-old cleric. The bride price of $1,200 helped Mariam's father, a drug addict, pay off a debt.

Mariam was taken to live with her new husband and his mother, who, she says, treated her like a servant. They began to beat her when she failed to conceive a child. After two years of abuse, she fled and sought help at a police station in Kabul.

Until only a few years ago, the Afghan police would probably have rewarded Mariam for her courage by throwing her in jail—traditional mores forbid women to be alone on the street—or returning her to her husband.

Instead, the police delivered her to a plain, two-story building in a residential neighborhood: a women's shelter, something that was unknown here before 2003.

Since the overthrow of the Taliban in 2001, a more egalitarian notion of women's rights has begun to take hold, founded in the country's new Constitution and promoted by the newly created Ministry of Women's Affairs and a small community of women's advocates.

The problems they are confronting are deeply ingrained in a culture that has been mainly governed by tribal law. But they are changing the lives of young women like Mariam, now 17. Still wary of social stigma, she did not want her full name used.

"Simply put, this is a patriarchal society," said Manizha Naderi, director of Women for Afghan Women, one of four organizations that run shelters in Afghanistan. "Women are the property of men. This is tradition."

Women's shelters have been criticized as a foreign intrusion in Afghan society, where familial and community problems have traditionally been resolved through the mediation of tribal leaders and councils. But women's advocates insist that those outcomes almost always favor the men.

Forced marriages involving girls have been part of the social compacts between tribes and families for centuries, and they continue, though the legal marrying age is now 16 for women and 18 for men. Beating, torture and trafficking of women remain common and are broadly accepted, women's advocates say.

Until the advent of the shelters, a woman in an abusive marriage usually had nowhere to turn. If she tried to seek refuge with her own family, her brothers or father might return her to her husband, to protect the family's honor. Women who eloped might be cast out of the family altogether.

Many women resort to suicide, some by self-immolation, to escape their misery, according to Afghan and international human rights advocates.

"There is a culture of silence," said Mary Akrami, director of the Afghan Women Skills Development Center, which opened the first women's shelter in Afghanistan six years ago. The majority of abuse victims, she said, are too ashamed to report their problems.

As recently as 2005, some Afghan social organizations did not publicly acknowledge that they were working in support of women's rights, said Nabila Wafez, project manager in Afghanistan for the women's rights division of Medica Mondiale, a German non-governmental organization that supports women and children in conflict zones.

"Women's rights was a very new word for them," Ms. Wafez said. "But now we're openly saying it."

Women's advocates insist that they are trying not to split up families, but rather to keep them together through intervention, mediation and counseling.

"Out aim is not to put women in the shelter if it's not necessary," said Ms. Naderi, who was born in Afghanistan but grew up in New York City and graduated from Hunter College. "Only in cases where it's dangerous for the women to go back home, that's when we put them in the shelter."

If mediation fails, Ms. Naderi said, her organization's lawyers will pursue a divorce on behalf of their clients. Cases involving criminal allegations are referred to the attorney general's office.

Ms. Naderi's organization has even taken the bold step of helping several clients find new husbands, carefully vetted by the shelter's staff. The men could not afford the customary bride price, making them more accommodating of women who deviated from tradition.

When Mariam arrived at the Women for Afghan Women shelter in 2007, the group's lawyers took her case to family court. Her husband pleaded for her return, promising not to beat her again, Mariam consented. In a recent interview, Mariam, a waifish teenager with a meek voice, said she had feared that "no one would marry me again."

But soon after her return, the beatings resumed, she said. She fled again.

Mariam's case was moved to criminal court because she said her husband had threatened to kill her, said Mariam Ahadi, the legal supervisor for Women for Afghan Women and a former federal prosecutor in Afghanistan.

At the shelters, others told still more harrowing tales. For the same reason as Mariam, none wanted their full names used.

Nadia, 17, who has been living in Ms. Akrami's long-term shelter since 2007, recounted that to avenge a dispute he had with her father, her husband cut off her nose and an ear while she was sleeping. She has undergone six operations and needs more, Ms. Akrami said.

"I don't know anything about happiness," Nadia said.

At 8, another girl, Gulsum, was kidnapped by her father, who was estranged from her mother. She says she was forced to marry the son of her father's lover. Her husband and her new mother-in-law beat her and threatened to kill her, she said.

Now 13, Gulsum said that before eventually escaping, she tried to commit suicide by swallowing medicine and rodent poison.

Advocates say governmental response to the issue has significantly improved since the overthrow of the Taliban. Judges are ruling more equitably, advocates say, and the national police have created a special unit to focus on family issues. But women's advocates say that even so, protections for women remain mostly theoretical in much of the country, particularly in rural areas, where tradition runs deepest and women have limited access to advocacy services and courts.

Mariam said she felt fortunate to have found refuge. Asked what she hoped for the future, she replied, "I want my divorce, and then I want to study." She was pulled out of school in the fourth grade. Turning to Ms. Ahadi, she added, "I want to be a lawyer like her."

But for all of Mariam's suffering, her family apparently has not changed. Her younger sister was married off a year ago, at age 9, in exchange for a $400 bride price that helped cover another drug debt, Mariam said, and her youngest sister, who is 6, appears to be heading toward a similar fate.

R E A D I N G **49**

Finding Dignity in Exile

Ingrid Drake (2004)

Twenty-five women file into a room on the Thai side of the Thai-Burmese border to begin a five-day leadership workshop. Ranging in age from 16 to 60, the women, several of whom carry babies, wear traditional longhi, sarongs of woven cotton. At first, the women sit in rows by age, the eldest in front. This is how it is done among the Shan, an ethnic group from southeastern Burma. The women seem startled when Nang, the facilitator, tells them to sit in a circle. After they are resettled, Nang, a founding member of the Shan Women's Action Network (SWAN), says everyone will have an opportunity to speak about her experiences fleeing Burma. Nang realizes it is difficult, so she starts by sharing her own story.

In 1990, when she was 17, Nang's father, a farmer, was killed by the Burmese military. Across the Shan state, soldiers were forcing villagers to serve as porters or road-builders for no pay, not even food. To resist meant death. Groups of soldiers, often under the influence of drugs, would rape and kill women and young girls. Scared and not able to finish school, Nang left her mother and siblings to venture across the border for a future in Thailand. She traveled alone through the jungle, arriving in northern Thailand, where she worked at a construction site, a factory, and a night market. As an undocumented laborer, she put in long hours, earned low wages, and feared being returned to Burma by Thai authorities.

Many women in the circle, now wide-eyed or sobbing, hear in Nang's experience an echo of their own. A safe space has been created for them to tell their own stories, some speaking for the first time about their experiences with rape and prostitution. Through piecing together their stories, the women learn how the Burmese junta, with the Orwellian name of the State Peace and Development Council (SPDC), has especially targeted the Shan for repression because the Shan region, which was independent from Burma until 1962, has been a base for a number of opposition groups. But there is another reason why the military has relocated hundreds of thousands of people from more than 1,400 Shan villages since 1996, Nang tells the group. The SPDC has been seeking international investment to privatize natural resources in the Shan state.

By the last day of the workshop, participants have a much fuller understanding of the reasons behind their predicament—and they've learned some practical skills. They've learned how to counsel survivors of sexual violence and to teach others about HIV/AIDS, family planning, and Thai law. Nang calls the workshops a success when the women start discussing what role they can play to end 40 years of brutal military rule in Burma and when they ask her to return with more training. For many, this is the only formal education they have ever received.

Traditionally, in Shan villages, village headsmen had decision-making power, fathers assumed control in the household, and young people were expected to follow their elders. When the SPDC disrupted Shan society, forcing men from their farms to build roads for the military and leaving women as heads of households and targets for rape by the military, village headsmen could do little to protect their citizens. No longer safe in their homeland, more than 100,000 Shan made the dangerous trip across the border to Thailand. The young women who fled faced not only soldiers, but also human traffickers for the infamous Thai sex industry.

Once inside Thailand, women like Nang did not find a strong support system. Unlike other refugees fleeing Burma, the Shan have not received refugee status from the Thai government, which would entitle them to health and education services and freedom of movement. After being injured doing construction work in northern Thailand, Nang could not get medical care, nor be alone in her tent without unwanted sexual advances from her boss and other laborers. Instead, Nang rested in the shade at the construction site as a friend kept watch over her.

Like the women in the workshops she leads, Nang did not know how her experiences were connected to the larger political situation in Burma and to the global economy until she started talking with other refugees. When she began volunteering with the Burma Relief Center and the Migrant Assistance Program, civic groups that served Shan exiles, Nang met women who worked with groups like the Shan Herald Agency for News and Alt-ASEAN. Together, they talked about how Thailand benefits from the low-wage labor of Shan refugees working in pineapple plantations, massage parlors, or textile factories. Nang learned that Thailand is heralded by international financial institutions as a model of free enterprise and economic development, but has not signed the United Nations Refugee Convention or ceased its business dealings with Burma. In fact, Thailand is planning to purchase 500 megawatts of electricity from the damming of the Salween River, which runs through the Shan state.

Weaving a Safety Net

The women discussed what they could do for Shan people, especially women and children, and how to stop the SPDC. In 1999, Nang and 40 other women formed SWAN. The group met on weekends, so women who worked during the week could attend. Meetings made up of a circle of 10 to 25 women, with a bowl of steaming Shan-style rice noodles in the center. Together they would weave a safety net to support internally displaced women in the Shan state and those living as undocumented laborers inside Thailand. They offered late-night literacy classes for youth and adults, as well as medical and childcare, and an emergency hotline and safe house for those escaping prostitution.

They are collaborating with Thai-based women's groups to distribute posters and comic books written in the Shan language that break down the myth that women are to blame for rape and HIV infection. SWAN is now building an understanding in the Shan community that violence against women is not a woman's problem, but a human rights violation everyone must address. For example, they are working closely with a supportive headsman of a refugee village to create a women's crisis center staffed by local women who have attended SWAN workshops.

To raise funds for their programs, provide a livelihood for Shan refugees, and preserve cultural traditions, SWAN initiated a training program in which women prepared Shan food for catering events and sewed Shan clothes to be sold around the world. They conducted human-rights and gender-equality workshops on the border, networked with Shan, Thai, and Burmese organizations, and launched an ambitious internship program in which interns gain computer and facilitation skills, as well as language instruction in Shan, Thai, English, and Burmese.

As women on the border continued to report cases of sexual violence, SWAN realized it needed to get the story of the military's systematic rape of Shan women to the world. In 2002, SWAN and the Shan Human Rights Foundation published the report "License to Rape" in three languages, and distributed more than 12,000 copies to UN agencies, embassies, and human-rights and women's groups. The report succeeded in focusing international attention on the SPDC's activities. SWAN members testified before the United Nations, the U.S. Congress, and numerous other governmental bodies about the need to maintain sanctions against Burma's military government. It also awakened many in the Burmese opposition movement to the effectiveness of women's work.

Informed by their experiences laboring in sweatshops and watching massive projects like the proposed Salween Dam displace native people, SWAN members are joining the global movement for environmental and social justice. Several young Shan women have interned with groups such as the Bank Information Center to better understand the forces behind corporate globalization. SWAN members now have contacts at the UN and relationships with donors from places such as Australia and Norway.

Though groups like SWAN face increased surveillance by Thai authorities, the women continue to reach out to allies and other indigenous people's groups around the world. SWAN members who met women activists from Guatemala and South Africa discovered common experiences. "We share the same feeling … why do women have to face being more vulnerable to violence?" said 22-year-old member Charm Tong.

Building a Movement for Equality

In 1999, SWAN co-founded the Women's League of Burma (WLB) with 11 other ethnic women's organizations to advocate for greater women's influence in the Burmese resistance movement. Despite the fact that Burma's popularly elected president is a woman, Nobel Prize-winner Aung San Suu Kyi, it was still difficult for women, especially ethnic minority women, to find a seat at the table with exiled Burmese democracy activists. WLB is pushing for gender equality to be written into the new constitution. By working closely with other ethnic women's organizations and demonstrating how pluralism can thrive in Burma, SWAN countered the SPDC's claim that disputes between various ethnic groups make democracy impossible.

When the Shan women chose not to have an executive director govern their new organization back in 1999, onlookers said, "You'll be a ship without a sail, lost and looking for direction." Yet five years later, SWAN has grown to a membership of more than 100, touched the lives of thousands more, and not veered from a course of equality and peace for all.

Despite being refugees, without land, money, or security, SWAN challenges the Burmese military, which is well-funded from exploitation of natural resources and participation in the illicit narcotics trade, by building women's leadership capacity. The women opted for a collective leadership model where all members share decision-making power, because, as Charm Tong explains, "everyone has an important contribution to make."

Women's Work in the Global Economy

Juanita Elias

Juanita Elias is a senior lecturer in International Politics at the University of Adelaide, Australia. Her Ph.D. was awarded in 2002 from the University of Warwick and she has previously worked as a lecturer at the University of Manchester. Her book *Fashioning Inequality: The Multinational Corporation and Gendered Employment in a Globalizing World* was published in 2004. Her main research interests include gender and globalization, international political economy, women's human rights, and the political economy of Malaysia.

> A woman is a baobab, the tree that builds
> the village. She is the head of the household.
> She has the responsibility for the whole family and
> for work. She rises with the sun and doesn't sleep
> before the sun sets.

Artist's statement, Mariko Kadidiatou

Mariko Kadidiatou paints the stories of women's lives, graphically showing how women's work is never done. As she declares in her statement above, whether we are in Tessaoua, Niger, where Kadidiatou lives and works, or towns in the "heartland" of the United States, many women take responsibility for home and for providing economic resources to maintain families. This work in all its different facets as paid and unpaid labor, and its relationship to economic globalization, is the focus of this chapter. You will remember that economic globalization refers to processes integrating economies toward a global marketplace or a single world market, and it is illustrated by the rapid growth of transnational corporations (TNCs) and complex global networks of production and consumption. It is notable that studies of globalization often disregard the significance of women (or more broadly gender relations) even though the practices of economic globalization involve vast numbers of women traveling across state borders and serving as cheap labor (Griffin, 2007). In addition, analyses often ignore women's role in social relations of reproduction (care and domestic-related activities such as unpaid housework, the emotional care of family members, and the raising of children) by prioritizing their formal participation in paid employment. Such analyses of socially reproductive labor are often neglected and are rarely included in national statistics of a country's productivity such as GNP (gross national profit) or GDP (gross domestic profit).

The world's top 25 non-financial TNCs, ranked by foreign assets, 2006[a]

Ranking by:

Foreign assets	TNI[b]	I[c]	Corporation	Home economy	Industry[d]
1	71	54	General Electric	United States	Electrical & electronic equipment
2	14	68	British Petroleum Company Plc	United Kingdom	Petroleum expl./ref./distr.
3	87	93	Toyota Motor Corporation	Japan	Motor vehicles
4	34	79	Royal Dutch/Shell Group	United Kingdom, Netherlands	Petroleum expl./ref./distr.
5	40	35	Exxonmobil Corporation	United States	Petroleum expl./ref./distr.
6	78	64	Ford Motor Company	United States	Motor vehicles
7	7	99	Vodafone Group Plc	United Kingdom	Telecommunications
8	28	51	Total	France	Petroleum expl./ref./distr.
9	96	36	Electricite De France	France	Electricity, gas and water
10	92	18	Wal-Mart Stores	United States	Retail
11	37	34	Telefonica SA	Spain	Telecommunications
12	77	88	E.On	Germany	Electricity, gas and water
13	86	82	Deutsche Telekom AG	Germany	Telecommunications
14	58	65	Volkswagen Group	Germany	Motor vehicles
15	73	57	France Telecom	France	Telecommunications
16	90	63	Conoco Phillips	United States	Petroleum expl./ref./distr.
17	56	89	Chevron Corporation	United States	Petroleum expl./ref./distr.
18	11	75	Honda Motor Co Ltd	Japan	Motor vehicles
19	35	62	Suez	France	Electricity, gas and water
20	45	48	Siemens AG	Germany	Electrical & electronic equipment
21	10	11	Hutchison Whampos Limited	Hong Kong, China	Diversified
22	84	85	RWE Group	Germany	Electricity, gas and water
23	9	7	Nestlé SA	Switzerland	Food & beverages
24	62	38	BMW AG	Germany	Motor vehicles
25	51	33	Procter & Gamble	United States	Diversified

Source: UNCTAD/Erasmus University database.

[a] All data are based on the companies' annual reports unless otherwise stated. Data on affillates are based on Dun and Bradstreet's *Who owns Whom* database.

[b] TNI, the Transnationality index, is calculated as the average of the following three ratios: foreign assets to total assets, foreign sales to total sales and foreign employment to total employment.

[c] H, the Internationalization Index is calculated as the number of foreign affiliates divided by the number of all affillates (Note: Affillates counted in this table refer to only majority-owned affilliates).

[d] Industry classification for companies follows the United States Standard Industrial Classification as used by the United States Securities and Exchange Commission (SEC).

[e] Data are for activities outside Europe.

[f] Data are for activities outside North America.

[g] Foreign employment data are calculated by applying the share of foreign employment in total employment of the previous year to total employment of 2006.

(Millions of dollars and number of employees)

Assets		Sales		Employment		TNI[b] (Percent)	No. of affilliates		
Foreign	Total	Foreign	Total	Foreign	Total		Foreign	Total	I[k]
442,278	697,239	74,285	163,391	164,000	319,000	53	785	1,117	70
170,328	217,601	215,879	270,602	80,300	97,100	80	337	529	64
164,627	273,853	78,529	205,918	113,967	299,394	46	169	418	40
161,122[e]	235,276	182,538[e]	318,845	90,000	108,000	70	518	926	56
154,993	219,015	252,680	365,457	51,723	82,100	68	278	345	80
131,062	278,554	78,958	160,123	155,000[f]	283,000	50	162	247	56
126,180	144,386	32,641	39,021	53,138	53,384	85	30	130	23
120,645	138,579	146,672	192,952	57,239	95,070	74	429	598	72
111,916	235,857	33,879	73,933	17,185[g]	155,968	35	199	249	80
110,199	151,193	77,116	344,992	540,000	1,910,000	41	146	183	90
101,891	143,530	41,093	56,367	167,851	224,939	69	185	205	80
94,304	167,565	32,154	85,007	46,598	80,612	51	279	590	47
93,488	171,421	36,240	76,963	88,808	248,800	46	143	263	54
91,823	179,906	95,761	131,571	155,935	324,875	57	178	272	65
80,871	135,876	30,448	54,863	82,148	191,038	52	145	211	68
89,528	164,781	55,781	183,650	17,188[g]	38,400	43	118	179	66
85,735	132,628	111,608	204,892	33,700	62,500	58	87	226	43
76,264	101,190	77,605	95,333	148,544	167,231	82	141	243	58
75,151	96,714	42,002	55,563	76,943	139,814	69	686	884	66
74,585	119,812	74,858	109,553	314,000	475,000	66	919	1,224	75
70,679	87,146	28,619	34,428	182,149[g]	220,000	62	116	125	92
68,202	123,080	22,142	55,521	30,752	68,534	47	221	430	51
66,677[e]	83,426	57,234[e]	78,528	257,434[e,g]	265,000	83	487	502	93
66,053	104,118	48,172	61,472	26,575	106,575	56	138	174	79
84,487	138,014	44,530	76,476	101,220[h]	138,000	59	369	458	81

[h] Foreign employment data are calculated by applying the average of the shares of foreign employment in total employment of all companies in the same industry (omitting the extremes) to total employment.
[i] Data are for activities outside Asia.
[j] Data are for activities outside western Europe.
[k] Data are for activities outside Spain and Portugal.
[l] Data are for activities outside Other Europe.
[m] Data are for activities outside Other Americas.
[n] Foreign employment data are calculated by applying the share of both foreign sales in total sales and foreign sales in total sales to total employment.
[o] Total employment data are calculated by applying the annual percentage increase of nonconsolidated total employment data to the consolidated total employment data from the previous year.

Note: The list covers nonfinancial TNCs only. In some companies, foreign investors may hold a minority share of more than 10 percent.

Research on the impact of economic globalization on women's labor presents a mixed picture. On the one hand there are opportunities for some women as a result of employment opportunities in the rapidly expanding service economy, as well as in the highly globalized manufacturing sectors such as electronic component assembly and garment production. A familiar argument recognizes the ways these job opportunities have granted women, and particularly women in the Global South, access to greater levels of economic freedom as they move out of the household and into the global market economy. This perspective that stresses women's "empowerment" has underpinned much thinking within the neoliberal-oriented international development community in recent years (Elias & Ferguson, 2009). Such an approach endorses free markets and economic privatization, and sees economic growth as having a relatively positive impact on female workers, especially if states pursue policies of export-oriented growth that absorb high numbers of women into labor-intensive forms of work. However, this perspective overlooks the extent to which women ever enter the labor market on equal terms to men. Women's disadvantage stems from a number of different sources, including discriminatory attitudes within local communities and/or multinational corporations, as well as women's relationship within social relations of reproduction (birthing, child care, housework, etc. [Bakker and Silvey, 2008]). Indeed, this optimistic "empowerment" perspective is frequently countered by critics who suggest that women entering these globalized industries are overwhelmingly stratified into the lower rungs of the occupational hierarchy where the work is monotonous and low paid and there are limited opportunities for promotion.

Central in the discussion of women's work and employment worldwide is the point that their experience is dependent on numerous contextual factors that include race, class, and nationality. As Jan Jindy Pettman in *Worlding Women* (1996, p. 171) explains, "we cannot make sense of women's lives if we attend only to gender. For nationality, place of residence and work, class, age, marital status and membership of particular racialized and cultural groups all intersect to constitute the working lives of women." In other words, although women's working lives in both the Global North and South have undergone great changes due to the processes of economic restructuring associated with both globalization and neoliberalism, these processes are experienced very differently by different groups of women. This suggests there is no straightforward explanation of the role and position of (all) women in the global economy. As it will be argued in this chapter, the construction of women as a source of cheap, flexible, and efficient labor is frequently a deeply racialized process that draws upon ideas of "Third World" women as best suited to the monotonous working conditions found in some of the most globalized sectors of the world economy.

My goal in this chapter is to provide a general overview of the kind of work women are performing in the global economy and give commentary on the ways a focus on women's work enables us to recognize the centrality of gender relations and identities to the functioning of the global market economy. The first section explores patterns of female employment in the global economy, documenting their predominance in export-oriented economies. It also discusses women's migration and makes the case for the inclusion of women's stories in understanding the conditions of women's work in the global economy. The next section discusses the gendering of women's work and explores the ways workplaces are gendered and racialized sites for the reconstitution and performance of certain identities. The third section explores reproductive labor and women's employment, emphasizing that it is necessary to address the unpaid labor of women in the family and household in order to understand the gendered nature of female employment. The chapter concludes with an analysis of the challenges and opportunities facing women worldwide as they attempt to organize and resist the often highly exploitative and gendered practices of global capitalism.

WOMEN'S WORK

Where Are Women Working?

The first point to be made in considering women's employment worldwide is that most statistical data relate solely to women's employment in formal labor markets, or jobs recognized in official government data. As a result, much of the work done by women worldwide in informal markets or in the home is unaccounted for. For example, it is estimated that there is a large proportion of people around the world engaged in informal forms of employment (e.g., running a roadside food stall) and the majority of these are women. Such individuals are also frequently employed as home workers involved in activities like sewing or embroidery subcontracted from local factories or work in a home-based workshop. Again, these are the sort of workers who frequently go unaccounted for in government statistics. Furthermore, given the increased numbers of women engaged in undocumented labor migration across national boundaries, there may well be many more women working in both formal and informal labor market settings than the data indicate. Finally, as already mentioned, much unpaid reproductive labor in the home is not considered to be "work" at all (Hoskyns and Rai, 2007).

With these caveats in mind, as a recent International Labour Organization (ILO) survey has shown, there is no simple overall picture of women's employment in the global economy (ILO, 2007). For example, while the 1980s and 1990s did see an overall increase in the female labor force worldwide, in more recent years the share of working-age women who work or are seeking work (what is called the "female labor force participation rate") leveled out and, in some areas of the world, even went into decline. On the other hand, women constitute approximately 40 percent of the global labor force: a figure that is higher than ever before. In addition, more women than ever are unemployed (ILO, 2007).

Traditionally, agriculture is the sector in which women's labor force participation rate is highest, reflecting their central role in food production. Women's labor is vital to the nourishment of families and communities through production of staple food stuffs such as maize (corn), rice, and wheat. While it is estimated that women's agricultural production accounts for at least half of the world's food production, these three staple crops account for 60 to 80 percent of food intake in most developing countries (ILO, 2007). The production of these basic foodstuffs, however, is not especially profitable, and women's agricultural production is often linked to high levels of poverty in many parts of the world. In some regions agricultural markets have collapsed under pressure from neoliberal structural adjustment policies (SAPs), as discussed in previous chapters, which often removed subsidies and price guarantees available to farmers and compounded problems of rural poverty. Women's contribution to agricultural production thus provides a clear example of how the work many women do around the world is central to national and global economies yet drastically undervalued. The pressures on women's labor in the agricultural sector are therefore immense: women are working as farmers, performing household and childrearing work, and may also be taking on informal sector work in order to supplement the meager income that agricultural work provides.

As the reading by Megan Rowling titled "Women Farmers Toil to Expand Africa's Food Supply" emphasizes, women are the main food provider in families, growing up to 80 percent of crops for food production in Africa, despite the fact that they own very little of the land and work incessantly. If these producers had equal land rights and better incomes, this would improve the health and welfare of the whole community.

Despite their importance, in recent years agricultural sectors have ceased to be the main employers of women globally and are being replaced by the hiring power of the service and light-industrial sectors. The growth in these sectors reflects trade practices and economic policies called "export-oriented industrialization" (EOI) aimed at connecting countries to the global market through exportation of goods from that nation. Women's cheap labor is essential to these practices as shown in their presence in such industries as garment and electronics. Still, export-oriented development occurs in agricultural sectors because commercial agricultural production based on profitable cash crops (e.g., coffee, pineapples, or tobacco), rather than staple food staples, has long been an important source of export revenues. While many, though not all, sectors of the "plantation" (cash crop) economy remained male dominated (see, for example, studies of labor market feminization in the banana plantations of Central America [Frank, 2005]), an interesting development occurred in some aspects of horticultural work. As air travel became more accessible, some developing countries began exporting fresh agricultural products like strawberries, green beans, or cut flowers with limited shelf-lives (Hale & Opondo, 2005; Stephen, 2000). These horticultural sectors are more overtly feminized than such traditional cash crop sectors as palm oil or sugar (see sidebar "Where Have All the Flowers Come From?").

Although women are employed in high numbers in the service sector, they tend not to be in high-paying occupations. Compared to men, for example, women are grouped into

LEARNING ACTIVITY   **Where Have All the Flowers Come From?**

In recent years, growing demand for cut flowers in the United States, western Europe, and Japan has created new horticultural sectors in the globalized economy. Rooted primarily in places like Colombia, Ecuador, Kenya, Ethiopia, India, Israel, and the Netherlands, this market has produced employment opportunities, especially for women, who make up 65–80 percent of the laborers in cut flower production. Of the 350 million flowers imported to the United States each year, 90 percent are grown in Colombia.

These new employment opportunities, however, are not without drawbacks. The labor is intensive and not often well-paid. Many times women are hired as day laborers and therefore excluded from health benefits. The flower industry has not been as regulated as the food plant industry, and so workers are often exposed to toxins in pesticides. The flower industry also produces pollutants that contribute to environmental degradation. In response, workers within the cut flower industry are demanding better labor practices and codes of conduct for the industry.

To view the International Code of Conduct for the Production of Cut Flowers, go to http://www1.umn.edu/humanrts/links/flowerscode.html.

Visit your local grocer's cut flower section. Examine the product labels to see where the flowers were grown. Ask the store manager if the grower practices the behaviors outlined in the Code of Conduct. If the manager doesn't know, ask her/him to find out for you. If the grower does not follow the code, organize a letter-writing campaign or a protest to encourage your grocer to utilize growers that follow the code.

such low-paid work as shop assistants or domestic servants, while men tend to dominate in higher paying areas of the service economy such as real estate or financial services (ILO, 2007). Another key area for women's employment in the global service economy is the tourism sector where women account for 46 percent of wage employment and 90 percent of workers involved in catering and accommodation specifically. For many states in the developing world, tourism is seen as one of the easiest ways to attract foreign investment. As the reading "Women and Tourism" by Shaker Hussain explains, this industry is highly seasonal and feminized in requiring high numbers of flexible, low-wage workers who are required to interact with the public. Although men also work in the tourism industry, it is notable that the work women do is more likely to be seasonal, part-time, and low paid, and confined to such areas as cleaning and retail as well as sexualized positions in entertaining and hospitality.

Men significantly outnumber women in industrial sectors of the economy such as mining and manufacturing, although there are certain sectors of the global manufacturing economy like garment manufacture and electronic component assembly that employ extremely high numbers of women. These "light-manufacturing" industries require high numbers of workers in low-paid assembly line production. They reflect the kinds of industrial sectors that poorer countries are able to develop since they take advantage of relatively low-cost labor and involve participation in the global market economy. This highlights the ways women's labor is central to export-oriented industrialization, widely viewed as the main way for countries in the Global South to secure economic growth (Seguino, 2000).

Scholarship on women working in manufacturing industries has traced the ways the relocation of labor-intensive manufacturing from the Global North to the Global South was a distinctively feminized process (Nash and Fernandez-Kelly, 1983) with new employment opportunities for women in low-paid, labor-intensive, assembly line production. The motivation for these changes included not only lower labor costs on the part of transnational corporations, but also, as discussed, desire across the developed world to develop export-oriented industrialization or labor-intensive manufacturing industries producing goods for the export market. In particular, countries sought to establish "export processing zones" (also known as "free trade zones") that provided tax and other incentives to export industries. Export processing is characterized by the emergence of "world market factories" that emerged from the 1960s onwards in such countries as Mexico, Puerto Rica, Taiwan, and South Korea. These consisted of both multinational corporations that had relocated parts of their production process to countries with lower labor costs, as well as locally owned companies linked into global networks of subcontracted production and producing products primarily for markets in the Global North. As the reading, "Assembly Line," a poem by Shu Ting laments, such policies often encourage alienating work that may numb women working in these jobs and affect the rhythms of their everyday lives.

Work and Female Migration

Understanding female employment worldwide requires more than just a counting of the numbers of female bodies found in particular sectors of the global economy. It is also important to focus on patterns of labor migration across national borders and the role of women within these labor flows. In their study of globalization and international political economy, Rupert and Solomon (2006, p. 82) emphasize a trend that is frequently refered to as the feminization of migration—something that is widely understood as involving two processes: (1) the growth in absolute numbers of female migrants; and (2) the emergence

Occupational Hazards for Women: Abstracts from the World Health Organization

The World Health Organization has identified a number of occupational hazards faced primarily by women in occupations around the world. Because of the gendered nature of the workplace, women are more likely to occupy these positions, and, because of their relative economic powerlessness, they are unlikely to be able to challenge or change the workplace conditions that put them at risk.

PESTICIDE EXPOSURE IN THE CUT FLOWER INDUSTRY

Of the 350 million cut flowers imported every year into the United States, 90 percent are grown in Colombia. Although a relatively new industry, floriculture employs large numbers of Colombians. Floriculture workers risk exposure to 127 different kinds of pesticides. A study was undertaken among 8,867 employees of 58 companies who had worked for at least six months in the flower growing industry to ascertain the occurrence of certain reproductive events among a population occupationally exposed to a heterogeneous group of pesticides, and to assess the possible association between adverse reproductive events and such exposure.

EXPOSURE TO NEUROTOXINS IN THE MICROELECTRONICS INDUSTRY

Women are employed in the majority of production and assembly jobs in the microelectronics industry. Organic solvents are used in many of the industry's production and assembly processes. Neurotoxic effects of organic solvent exposure include abnormalities and impairments in the behavioral area, notably mood change, irritability, anxiety, fatigue, depression, defective impulse control, personality change, and development of psychosis. Emotional and personality changes are among the first symptoms reported by persons exposed to neurotoxins. In many cases, affective changes are present even when neuropsychological or neurologic effects cannot be detected.

PSYCHOLOGICAL AND ERGONOMIC STRESSORS IN GARMENT WORKERS

Women's jobs are often seen as low-risk in terms of severe work accidents and specific industrial diseases. Consequently, the health problems of women's work have not been adequately researched, with the exception of risks associated with pregnancy. However, adverse health effects are associated with female-dominated jobs, including those in the manufacturing and service industries, involving high time pressure. There are potential psychological and ergonomic stressors (such as repetitive strains associated with certain tasks) which can, over time, lead to adverse health effects.

HEALTH CONSEQUENCES OF MAQUILADORA WORK

Foreign-owned assembly plants in Mexico (maquiladoras) enable these industries to operate with low labor and operation costs, and to avoid stringent health and safety regulations enforced at home. The plants employ large numbers of predominantly young women (over 60 percent of the total maquiladora workforce). Adverse working conditions are frequently reported in the plants, including poor ventilation, few rest periods, excessive noise levels, unsafe machinery, long hours of microscopic assembly work, and exposure to toxic chemicals and carcinogens. The work requires high production quotas and repetitive tasks which, coupled with lack of decision-making capacity and often poor supervisory relations, add to stressful work conditions. However, empirical data concerning the health issues are scarce.

REPETITIVE STRAIN INJURY AND OCCUPATIONAL TASKS

Repetitive strain injury (RSI) is the term commonly used to describe a set of musculoskeletal symptoms affecting large numbers of people, often women, in many countries. It occurs in workers who perform repetitive tasks over a prolonged period, most commonly in the hands, wrists, and arms, although other areas may be affected depending on the type of work performed. RSI causes considerable pain and discomfort in the affected areas, including loss of grip strength in the hand. Over time, disability can become so severe that temporary or permanent cessation of employment results.

SILICOSIS IN SWEDISH WOMEN

Silicosis (a respiratory disease caused by inhaling silica dust) remains primarily a "male disease," and hence pneumoconiosis in women has received little attention in the literature. In Sweden, only about 1 percent of registered cases are women, employed mainly in potteries. Indeed, most silicosis in women, in Sweden and elsewhere, is contracted in the ceramic industry. Two earlier studies noted that the duration of exposure to pottery dust in the women studied was appreciably shorter than that of a comparable male group. Since the issue of greater sensitivity (or otherwise) of women to inhaled silica dust was not demonstrated in previous research, an analysis of silicotic women observed over a long period was considered useful in clarifying the incidence, course, and evidence of progression of this disease. The effects on this small group may be relevant to many women in other parts of the world who are engaged in pottery work or employed in the ceramics industry.

CASSAVA PROCESSING AND CYANIDE POISONING

Cassava is the third most important food crop in the tropical world, following rice and maize. Although it is low in protein, production is increasing because it grows well in poor soils and tolerates drought. But it has a major disadvantage in that its preparation as a food liberates hydrogen cyanide, a deadly poison. Careful preparation is therefore needed to initiate the various chemical interactions needed to eliminate this poison. Cassava is largely grown and processed by women.

http://www.who.int/occupational_health/publications/womanthology/en/index.html

of feminized migration sectors. First, despite difficulties of collecting statistics on global migratory flows, it should also be noted that alongside the increase in lone female migrant workers in recent decades, large numbers of women have always migrated as part of family groups. Women in these situations may go unreported in labor migration statistics even though many of them will take up work in their newly adopted countries (Kofman, 2004). Research into (nonfamily) female migration has focused largely on the movement of women from some of the poorer parts of the world to regions with more wealth in order to take up what is viewed as "unskilled" work. While often this is characterized in terms of the movement of women from the Global South to the Global North, this is an overly simplistic picture of labor migration. For example, in eastern and southeastern Asia there are numerous examples of "South–South" labor migration as women and men move from some of the countries with higher levels of poverty (Indonesia, Laos, Cambodia, Philippines) to countries experiencing rapid economic growth and labor shortages in unskilled and care-related sectors of the economy (Malaysia, Thailand, Korea) (Ehrenreich and Hochschild, 2002).

Second, Rupert and Soloman also emphasize that there has been an emergence of female "sectors" of migration such as domestic work and nursing and other forms of "care work" that helps explain these numbers. A rapidly expanding feminized sector is that of sex work as women migrate (both willingly and unwillingly) across national borders to take positions in the sex industries. Data on these women are frequently ignored in the labor migration literature because of the dominance of perspectives arguing that women crossing borders to engage in sex work are simply the victims of trafficking. As discussed in other chapters, this trafficking perspective has been challenged by writers such as Laura Agustin (2007) who emphasizes that while sex work is a highly exploitative form of employment, it should not be assumed that all women engaged in this form of work do so unwillingly or are victims of trafficking. Women who are well aware of the work they are moving into, as well as the dangers and risks associated with sex work, regard it as a viable strategy for earning an income. In this sense it is important to understand that, although women may be "willingly" employed in hazardous sex work industries, they may have little choice to do otherwise.

Studies of women's work and migration highlight tensions between women's agency as individual workers and broader patterns of patriarchal social relations and practices of global capitalist production that structure employment experiences. Indeed, a strength of much feminist scholarship on women's employment is its focus on women's experiences and an inclusion of stories about their working lives that are lacking in more economistic

LEARNING ACTIVITY   **What's in Your Closet?**

Every day, each of us uses products created by people from all over the world. Take a look at the labels on the clothes in your closet and list the countries where your clothes were made. Now, take a look at your electronics and list the countries where they were made. What about your food? Where does it come from? What about your towels? Your cosmetics? Your shoes?

Select a few of the companies that produced some of the goods in your home. See what you can find out about these companies' ethical and environmental practices. Do they have a statement of corporate ethics or social responsibility? What are their human rights and environmental records? Do they use their profits in the community where their products are created to better the community? How do they treat their employees?

Talk to your classmates about your findings. Then talk about your own ethical responsibilities as a consumer. Does it matter to you whether or not your clothes were made in a sweatshop? Is it important to you to buy from companies that have good environmental practices? How are you as a consumer in relationship with the people around the world who produced the goods you have and use? What is your obligation to them?

For more information, see Kelsey Timmerman's *Where Am I Wearing? A Global Tour to the Countries, Factories, and People That Make Our Clothes* (Hoboken, NJ: Wiley, 2009).

accounts of global industrial restructuring and migration. This is illustrated in Aihwa Ong's (1987) classic study of women employed in Malaysian electronics firms. The excerpt below, taken from an interview with a young Malay woman factory worker, exposes both the harshness of the factory environment and the agency of women workers as they sought to resist and challenge factory discipline.

> . . . sometimes . . . they want us to raise *production.* This is what we sometimes contest (*bantahlah*). The workers want just treatment (*keadilan*), as for instance, in relation to wages and other matters. We feel that in this situation there are many [issues] to dispute (*bertengkar*) over with the management—because we have to work three shifts and when the *midnight shift* arrives we feel sort of drowsy and yet have to use the *microscope,* and with our wages so low we feel as though we have been tricked or forced (*seolah macam dipaksa*) (p. 202).

Recognizing and celebrating women's employment narratives expose the contradictory processes at work when women enter the labor market. On the one hand, paid work may well present new economic opportunities for women, but on the other, workers may be subject to harsh working conditions (Briones, 2009). It is important that these contradictory processes are recognized and that women in the Global South are not simply constructed as the voiceless victims of global capitalism. At the same time, however, it is imperative that feminist scholarship provides a structural analysis of economic globalization and neoliberalism alongside this focus on individual women's voices. For example, feminist analyses must critique export expansion as the only viable economic development strategy for economic growth and address the deeply gendered practices associated with these strategies.

GENDERED WORK

It is often argued that export-orientation always leads to increases in low-wage female employment as a result of cheap and flexible female labor. Teri Caraway (2007), however, argues that the reality of the feminization of global labor markets is much more complicated than this. Caraway suggests that (1) not all export sector industries are feminized and those that are less labor-intensive tend to employ more men than women; (2) if an economy moves away from such labor-intensive manufacturing industries as garment production and toward more "high-tech" or capital-intensive sectors, then it is likely that women's labor force participation rate in the formal economy will decline; (3) the extent to which industries become feminized is dependent on certain local contextual factors. When there is a strong presence of trade union movements, for example, the entry of women into the formal labor market is slower. Since trade unions are often male dominated and provide obstacles to women's entry into formal employment, those countries pursuing repressive anti-union policies have witnessed more women in the industrial labor market; and (4) the preference for employing women workers in export sector work is often not simply a matter of the low cost of female labor. Although the jobs that women move into are low paid, there may well be groups of men within society who are equally willing to work for these wages. Women workers employed in multinational export-sector firms are often paid above-average wages and are not recruited simply because they provide a source of low-cost labor.

Instead Caraway suggests that it is the gendered nature of the work, or the ways certain occupations have become associated with particular feminized or masculinized gender identities, that is central in understanding women's employment in the global economy. For example, it is interesting to note that the share of female employment in the garment sector is considerably higher than that found in the electronics industries. While this difference might be explained in terms of the higher levels of capital intensity in the electronics sector that encourage male participation, we should also point to the fact that the garment sector, and sewing work in particular, is overwhelmingly seen as "women's work." Understanding production as gendered requires that we focus on how both gender relations and gender identities are fashioned and re-fashioned through engagement with the productive economy. This point is the focus of Michael Ross's work on oil production in the Middle East. In the reading "Oil, Islam, and Women," Ross makes the case that the masculine work associated with oil production reduces the number of women in the labor force, thus reducing their political influence. He emphasizes the role of the economic system over the influence of Islam in understanding gender inequalities.

Central in this discussion is the need to recognize the contradictory processes at work when women enter paid employment. A classic article by Diane Elson and Ruth Pearson (1981, p. 31) attempts to convey the ways in which gender relations undergo processes of "decomposition," "recomposition," and "intensification" as women enter formal employment. They emphasize the intersecting forms of gendered power relations in society with which women workers are confronted. For example, processes of "decomposition" can be observed as women entering formal paid work are increasingly able to contribute to household finances thereby raising their status within the household and unsettling traditional patriarchal family structures. However, it is frequently the case that certain groups of female export sector workers (especially young, unmarried women) are stigmatized by families and communities and their independence equated with sexual promiscuity or moral values out of sync with local communities (Ong, 1987). For Elson and Pearson this is understood as a "recomposition" or reassertion of patriarchal gender relations. Others, who do experience autonomy, may also (like the Bangladeshi garment sector worker cited in the first section of this chapter) experience new forms of patriarchal power relations within the workplace (an "intensification" of gender relations). In other words, local gender relations are being transformed and challenged in families and communities at the

A DAY IN THE LIFE   **Meeting the Production Goal** by *Sriyanthi Gunewardena McCabe*

Premavathi tosses and turns. It's hard for her to sleep in her small room (130 square feet) with seven other young women. The heat is stifling, but they are all afraid to sleep with the door open. Premavathi lives in the Katunayake Export Processing Zone (KEPZ) in Sri Lanka. She is fortunate that she found a boarding facility for $20 a month because now she doesn't face a commute. A commute would subject her to derogatory comments, or *juki kali* (a term referring to garment factory workers), men grabbing at her because they think she is morally loose, and mothers who don't want her riding the bus next to their children just because she works in the garment factory.

A relatively new worker, her monthly salary is $60 (U.S.).

She tries to sleep so that she'll be better able to do her job. She knows that workers who do not meet production targets are very expendable, and, like many 20-year-old women from the village, she is a primary income generator and needs this job to send home money to her family. Why else would she bear the aches in her arms and shoulders, fingers, back, feet, and neck? Why else would she bear the constant humiliation wherever she goes? Why else would she tolerate the comments from the supervisor, "You stupid idiot! You have ruined several garments! Pay attention!"

"I know they have their jobs to do and if they don't yell at us to help us be more competitive, then we will all lose our jobs or we will be like those other girls who get paid one week late or get laid off with no pay. I know, but why can't I have that nice supervisor who is gentle in her comments . . .?"

She sees the light of day and hears the clock tower chime 7 a.m. She grabs her dress from a nail where it hangs on the wall. She goes to the back of the dormitory to the well where she pulls up a bucket of water for her morning toilette. She shares a toilet with 30 others, so she must get up early. She pulls on her dress, still a bit stiff from drying in the sun a couple of days ago. She washes her feet and slips into some flip flops. She runs a plastic comb through her long black hair, parts it, and braids it at the nape of her neck. She figures she can manage until lunch time with a cup of tea and the company-provided breakfast.

"I am doing my share for my homeland? I work so hard. I don't want any handouts, but how is a person to manage with this salary? They told us this work would help pull us out of poverty, but after I pay for my lodging and though I try not to eat too much, I still can't send much home."

"I have to sew 120 pant legs each hour. They have to be perfect. I can't lose this job. It's 86 degrees in here, and I'm sweating, but I don't want the sweat to touch the material. It will get spoiled and I could get in trouble." She thinks of purchasing a headband from the little shop across the street . . .

"But I won't spend my money carelessly. I will be disciplined. I will only spend what I need to survive here. If only I had some time off to find a way to learn English." Like most of her coworkers, Premavathi is Sinhala Buddhist, and, though she was educated through two years of junior college and is very smart, she can't read most of the signs in the factory that are in English.

"I must focus. I am a hard worker. I am not afraid of work. Though my body is hurting, it is my sacrifice for Sri Lanka which needs our labor to earn foreign currency to fight the war; for my sisters so that they can afford more education and have a better life; for my mother because she has worked so hard her entire life to give me a better life. . . . If only I had done better in my exams . . . Perhaps I could be at university now. . . . For my brother who joined the army. Please spare his life. . . ."

Today she gets to take a lunch break. For 30 minutes she can talk and laugh as much as she wants. When working, she can talk sometimes if she continues to work fast, but her supervisors really don't like workers laughing loudly. They think the workers are not working as hard if they are laughing. Several of the young women brought in home-cooked meals. She buys one from the woman who sells lunch just outside the factory gates because last night she worked until 1 a.m. She and the other young women trade until they each have a sample of everything. They eat with their hands, using just the tips of their fingers to form little rice balls mixed with curry. The other young women eat on banana leaves. They talk about boyfriends and marriage, and she learns a lot from them. (Be careful of men who drink too much or who meet you only on payday). She drinks very little because she doesn't want to waste time using the bathroom. It's not very clean, and every minute counts.

She skips her 15 minute afternoon break because she needs to fulfill a certain amount of work. She stands for four more hours in a row sewing this one section of the pants over and over again. Sometimes she feels so hot and dizzy that she can't even see straight. Many of her coworkers have asthma and other respiratory illnesses.

Her work day ends at 10 p.m. because they had a deadline. Sometimes her work day ends at 7 p.m. when there isn't as much work. This time they met the production targets. Her limbs feel numb but she is proud of herself. She'll have a job for another day.

very same time that workers are exposed to new sets of gendered power relations within the factory.

Furthermore, processes of recomposition and intensification are often backed by the power of the state. This is shown for example in Seungsook Moon's study of gender relations in South Korea's emergence as a modern industrial economy. Moon (2005) observed the ways the secondary status of women workers was supported by both a militarized state in the form of repressive anti-labor policies in the feminized export sector and by state provisions for women's domestic training. These provisions reflected expectations that women workers would leave their employment on marriage. Cynthia Enloe's work (1990) also highlights the role that states have played (in collaboration with militaries and corporations) in keeping women's labor cheap and confined to certain sectors of the economy.

It is, of course, important that discussions of gendered employment relations in the global economy do not solely focus on the industrial sector. The employment of domestic workers is an illustrative case study of the gendered nature of work in the global economy as it demonstrates how the functioning of the global economy is just as dependent on women employed cleaning homes and caring for children as it is on those working in the factories, tourist resorts, and agricultural packing plants (even though the latter are more readily associated with the globalized economy). The migratory flows of domestic workers and other groups of workers in care-related professions through "global care chains" (a play on the phrase "global commodity chains": language frequently used in studies of economic globalization and transnational production [Hochschild, 2000]) are often overtly encouraged by governments who see female migrants as an important economic resource. In this way, women play a significant role in a country's economic development since they tend to return at least half of their earnings to families in their countries of origin. In the Phillippines, for example, a country that has actively pursued outward labor migration as both an economic development strategy and a solution to chronic unemployment, remittances from migrant workers constitute the country's largest source of foreign currency. However, as women struggle to send money home to families, they may find themselves locked in low-paid employment with difficult working conditions. The consequences of migratory domestic employment of care-workers also affect families and communities left behind as well as women workers themselves. In the Philippines where care workers (be they domestic workers, nurses, preschool teachers, or care assistants) are now one of the country's major exports, it is suggested that the country is experiencing its own "crisis of care." This is linked to the loss of women's unpaid caring labor as well as the mass departure of female workers who could have been employed in these capacities in their country of origin (Parreñas, 2002).

The migration of domestic workers also provides an example of the intersections between gender and race in the global political economy. Although these workers are often highly skilled and qualified as teachers or nurses, race and nationality (plus in some cases, unofficial employment status) mark "Third World" women as low-skilled and uneducated and thus deserving of significantly lower wages than "local" workers (Kofman, 2004).

REPRODUCTIVE LABOR

In order to understand the gendered nature of women's employment, it is necessary to address the reproductive labor usually performed within the private sphere of the family, household, and/or community. These everyday activities that include the care of household and children as well as the "kin-keeping" involved in the care and maintenance of contacts with family, friends, and extended kin, are overwhelmingly devalued within capitalist economies and not considered "productive" work, or in some cases, even "work" at all. Such physical and emotional labor is not only central for the reproduction of individuals and families, but also essential to national productive economies. If women, for example, were paid for the reproductive labor performed free in families, it would affect the economy in serious ways. The short story reading "Girl" by Jamaica Kincaid centers on the socialization of female children into this unpaid reproductive labor of women in the family.

While there has been a significant shift in social attitudes around the need for men and women to share domestic work equally, women's share of unpaid work is significantly higher than that performed by men. This burden of unpaid work has negative consequences for women. Career interruptions or greater likelihood to work part time leads to lower lifetime earnings and places women at greater risk of poverty (Bittman, 1999; Noonan, 2001).

What is interesting, however, is that in certain countries there has been a decline in the amount of unpaid domestic work in which women are engaged. An important reason for this is the ability of families to "outsource" domestic work. In part, this involves the employment of domestic workers—something that has increasingly taken on a transnational dimension as women from poorer parts of the world are employed within middle-class households (Anderson, 2007; Arat-Kroc, 2006). This "subcontracting" might also take the form of accessing laundry services and even eating out in restaurants/purchasing take-away food. Indeed, Bittman notes that, although there has been a considerable feminist-informed literature that focuses on the poor working conditions of women and immigrants employed as domestic workers, there is much less of a focus on the work of women and immigrants in the restaurant and fast food sectors that are themselves arenas of deeply exploitative employment. What is interesting, therefore, is the way in which reformulations of Western household gender relations often deemed "progressive" in gender terms are frequently dependent upon the availability of low wage feminized and racialized labor that provides services traditionally performed by female household members. This means, for example, that some white women are able to hire brown women to do their housework for them.

Cultural meanings associated with the practices of women's role in reproductive labor shape their experiences of productive labor outside the domestic sphere. First, women are expected to perform tasks in paid labor that are specifically performed in the household (such as sewing or cleaning). These tasks tend to be devalued and paid poorly. In the case of domestic workers, the boundaries between socially reproductive and productive labor are exceptionally blurred. Some of the major problems faced by migrant domestic workers stem from their position as employees who are working (and often living) in the home of their employers. Frequently this means that the work migrant domestics do is not officially recognized as "work," preventing the documentation of these workers as employees with the same kinds of rights available to other groups of workers. In addition, when domestic workers live in their workplace, they have fewer opportunities to leave or take days off work. The household context may also function as a site for the perpetuation of social fears over the intimate relationship between domestic workers and family members and lead to the view that domestic workers need to be tightly controlled. Christine Chin's (1998) research into female domestic workers employed in middle-class Malaysian households has charted employers' utilization of control and surveillance practices that serve to confine the worker

Used with permission of Ann Telnaes and Women's eNews in conjuction with the Cartoonist Group. All rights reserved

to the home and prevent her from interacting with outsiders. These practices contribute to a curtailment of access that prevents them from learning of their contractual rights (e.g., stipulations regarding rates of pay) and makes them especially vulnerable to abusive labor practices and other forms of violence.

A second related point is that gendered ideas about an essentialized women's "nature" encourages their hiring into certain kinds of "womanly" employment. Indeed, most studies of women's employment in the global manufacturing sector have noticed the widely held beliefs among managers that women are an important source of docile, diligent, and dexterous "nimble fingered" workers. They recruit them into assembly line work because they believe the repetitive and mundane (and often debilitating) aspect of the work suits their nature. Such discourses of "productive femininity" are a key mechanism for maintaining control and discipline over feminized groups of workers (Elias, 2005). Thus we see in Pun's study of Chinese export sector employment that managers enforced workplace discipline by explicitly identifying female bodies as "docile" labor (Pun, 2005, pp. 143–5). Managers often had very clear ideas about what constituted "feminine" employment and saw the importance of certain gendered characteristics in securing a productive and reliable workforce. In these ways, workplace control is not only enforced through these discursive mechanisms (words and language), but also through relatively high levels of control and surveillance. This surveillance (that may mimic the control of women by males in the home) is often part of the everyday experience of women workers on assembly lines who find their performance subject to constant observation by supervisors as they strive to meet production targets (Salzinger, 2003).

Third, employers often regard women's employment as "secondary" work. Factory work is frequently viewed as a short-term strategy that young women undertake prior to marriage (at which point it is assumed that they move into the realm of social reproduction as wives and mothers). In her work on female factory employees in Shenzen, China, Lee (1998, p. 128) notes the persistence of ideas held among managers concerning young female factory workers as "girls who worked while waiting to be married off" and thus not deserving of training, promotion or better rates of pay. By contrast, "men's plans for marriage and family meant that they would be dedicated to climb the company ladder because of their imminent family burdens." The reality, however, is that most women continue to combine paid work (in both the formal and informal sector) with unpaid household work. This notion of women's paid labor as secondary to their family work encourages the myth of female disposability whereby employers can avoid investing in training and developing female workers, paying higher wages to more senior employees, or providing health and safety practices since they assume women will leave the workplace upon marriage.

RESISTANCES, CHALLENGES, AND TRANSFORMATIONS

Having outlined the ways women workers are subject to harsh and often abusive workplace practices, social stigmatization and systems of intense workplace control, I now turn to consider the possibilities for resistance and change. Cultural meanings associated with gender and the ensuing identities performed by individuals "do more than merely sustain existing structures of power in global labor relations; these complex dimensions of gender also constitute a dynamic cultural terrain wherein forms of domination may be contested, reworked, and even potentially transformed" (Mills, 2003, p. 42).

Women's resistance to unfair or particularly harsh labor practices is threefold. First, resistance occurs at the local level when individual workers employ everyday resistance strategies (sometimes called "weapons of the weak" [Scott, 1985]). This might be as simple as challenging an employer's authority and/or drawing attention to similar class, cultural, and educational backgrounds that domestic workers frequently share with their employers.

In Aihwa Ong's study of Malaysian factory workers, we are introduced to another individual-level form of resistance strategy—so-called "spirit possession": incidents or acts of mass hysteria within the workplace. For Ong, such acts of resistance reflected how young rural women struggled to adapt to the rigors of capitalist control and discipline on the factory floor. However, Ong notes that "the enactment of 'ritualized rebellion' . . . did not directly confront the real cause of their distress" (1987, p. 210). Instead these acts of resistance act more like a "safety value." Although such behaviors grant workers a few hours away from the workplace during which time the workplace is ritually "cleansed," they enable employers to view female workers as essentially irrational and therefore unsuited to higher status or paid employment (see also Elias, 2005).

Workers might also engage in mundane everyday acts of resistance such as absenteeism or taking additional breaks during shifts. Sally Theobold (2002), for example, discusses the multiple forms of resistance among female Thai workers employed in electronics manufacturing. Some of these are culturally specific, localized forms of resistance and include things like making jokes at a manager's expense in a language or dialect that he or she cannot understand, or wearing consciously unfeminine clothing outside of the factory setting as a way of challenging the hyperfeminization of assembly line work (i.e., the association between a feminine identity and feminized forms of employment) found on the factory floor.

Second, the agency and resistance strategies of women workers are also often seen in more organized forms in, for example, women's cooperatives and organizations that provide economic and social support to women-owned enterprises. This is portrayed in the reading "Banking on Women": two essays by Sean Kelly and Somini Sengupta that discuss women's economic empowerment through microloans and women-owned banks in regions of Ghana and India. Microcredit has frequently helped women to take control of their economic futures by providing opportunities for them to start and succeed in enterprises in both the formal (a company, selling, for example, handcrafted goods overseas through fair trading practices) and informal (a road stand or booth selling food to local people) sectors. Third, alongside such practices, organized resistance also includes efforts to provide protective labor legislation and laws and policies to promote gender equity in employment. This may occur through nongovernmental activist organizations and lobbying efforts, as well as through the efforts of unions discussed in more detail below. Such strategies are illustrated in the reading "The 40-Percent Rule" by Martha Burk that discusses policies in Norway to require publicly funded firms to include a certain percentage of women on their corporate boards. As of this writing, France is also considering this policy.

Access to trade union activism is severely limited for some women workers. Migrant domestic workers, for example, are often prevented by government policies from joining trade unions. Even in states with more progressive labor relations policies, they may not be able to join unions when domestic work is categorized as short-term temporary employment. Within export sector industries there has also been limited unionization among female workers, in part because countries keen to attract much-needed foreign direct investment have sought to limit labor rights. However, another problem lies within the gendered politics of male-dominated trade union movements themselves. Male trade unionists may not take the specific concerns of women workers (such as child care provision or workplace sexual harassment) seriously or may have vested interests in ensuring that certain higher paying jobs remain male dominated. Furthermore, in some countries, unions are closely tied into state patronage networks thereby limiting the extent to which unions will act as effective champions of women workers' rights (for example, Chinese unions are part of the apparatus of the state and should not be understood as an independent force representing the interests of workers [Cooke, 2008]).

Women's labor organizing therefore has frequently not been undertaken through the auspices of large trade union movements; rather it has tended to take a more "grassroots" (bottom-up) form. A good example of this is Bickham Mendez's (2005) account of the Nicaraguan Working and Unemployed Women's Movement, María Elena Cuandra (MEC), a grassroots advocacy organization seeking to organize women in the country's free trade zones. The MEC was founded by women activists who were disillusioned by the failure of the official trade union movement to elect any female representatives. Brown and Chaytaweep (2008) note how similar events occurred in Thailand whereby frustrations with the male dominance and ineffectiveness of official trade union movements meant that female activists were at the forefront of labor activism taking place outside the official movement. This has led to the emergence of important coalitions of activism around the rights of women workers that involve labor-focused nongovernmental organizations, civil liberty groups, academics, and certain trade unions that take a more progressive approach to issues of gender equality (such as the Thai Federation of Textiles, Clothing and Leather Workers).

Organizing groups of workers such as migrant domestic workers, homeworkers, and sex workers is challenging because they may be confined to households in which they work

ACTIVIST PROFILE   ## Rigoberta Menchú Tum

Rigoberta Menchú Tum was born in Guatemala in 1959 to a Quiché family, a subgroup of Mayans, and grew up helping her family farm. As a teenager she became involved in the women's rights movement and other social reform activities.

As guerilla groups began to form around the country to challenge the Guatemalan government, crackdowns ensued, and unofficial government death squads emerged, targeting guerillas and Mayans. From 1966 to 1970 these army campaigns killed an estimated 10,000 Mayans. In 1978, the Committee of the Peasant Union (CUC) formed to advocate for peasant and Mayan rights. Rigoberta joined the CUC in 1979, the same year her brother was arrested, tortured, and killed by government forces. The next year her father was killed, and then her mother died after being arrested, tortured, and raped. Not surprisingly, Rigoberta became even more deeply involved with the CUC and played a large role in CUC-organized strikes and demonstrations. Eventually she joined the radical 31st of January Popular Front and helped educate other peasants in resistance to government oppression. In 1981 she was forced to flee to Mexico, where she began to organize opposition to Guatemala's oppression of peasants. She helped found the United Representation of the Guatemalan Opposition and later became a member of the National Coordinating Committee of the CUC.

While in Paris, Rigoberta told her story to Elizabeth Burgos Debray, who helped shape the resulting autobiography, *I, Rigoberta Menchú*. The book brought a great deal of attention to the plight of Mayans in Guatemala. The Guatemalan government labeled Rigoberta a communist and guerilla. She returned to Guatemala three times to plead the case of Mayan peasants, but each time death threats forced her to return to exile.

In 1992, she was awarded the Nobel Peace Prize "in recognition of her work for social justice and ethno-cultural reconciliation based on respect for the rights of indigenous peoples." Only 33 years old, Rigoberta was the youngest person ever to win the Prize and the first indigenous person. She used the prize money to establish the Rigoberta Menchú Tum foundation that works for indigenous rights around the world.

In 1998, the credibility of Rigoberta's book was called into question when investigators suggested that parts of the book were not factual. Rigoberta later explained that the book was not so much an autobiography as a testimony: "It tells my personal testimony, but it also has parts of the testimony of the collectiveness of Guatemala," she says. "For common people such as myself, there is no difference between testimony, biography, and autobiography. . . . What we do is tell what we have lived, not just alone."

In 2007, Rigoberta ran for the presidency of Guatemala, but came in 6th out of a field of 14 with only 3 percent of the vote. The campaign was filled with political violence, with at least 50 people killed, including two who were distributing leaflets for Rigoberta's campaign.

Rigoberta continues to work for the rights of indigenous people and women in Guatemala and around the world. In 2007, she joined with five other women Nobel laureates in sending a letter to the Burmese junta, which keeps Aung San Suu Kyi in detention, calling them to restore democracy in Burma.

For more information, read *I, Rigoberta Menchú: An Indian Woman in Guatemala*. Brooklyn, NY: Verso Books, 1984.

or they are undocumented migrants who would be unwilling (as well as unable) to become involved in union activities: a situation that is compounded for many groups of sex workers who are involved in illicit forms of employment. Trade unions are increasingly coming to recognize the need to become involved in organizing these groups of workers due to the highly exploitative nature of these forms of employment. In Malaysia for example, the national trade union movement has been involved in (ultimately unsuccessful) attempts to organize migrant domestic workers (Elias, 2008). Involvement in these nontraditional areas of union activity can also lead to nontraditional forms of trade unionism. For example, the U.K.-based General Workers union (the GMB) established an adult entertainment branch in order to organize workers in the sex industry. This reflects a new form of union emerging that is not based on high membership numbers, but on the needs of workers in individual workplaces. Rather, activist unions or collective self-organized groups emerge that sit somewhere in between activist pressure group/NGO and trade union (Gall, 2006). This is a very useful way of thinking about trade unions—especially in relation to some of the most unorganized and often deeply feminized sectors of the service economy. In other words, the (masculinist) norm of the formal sector permanent full-time worker as trade unionist cannot be applied to these sectors.

Finally, alongside individual strategies and efforts at local and global levels to organize women, are transnational efforts that challenge global gender inequalities, especially those related to the economic practices of neoliberalism with its emphasis on free markets, privatization, and trade and financial liberalization, international division of labor, and cheap, feminized labor forces. As discussed in chapter 1, beginning in the 1980s, transnational feminist networks such as Development Alternatives with Women for a New Era (DAWN) and Women in Development Europe (WIDE) organized against "free trade" with its privatization of public goods and commercialization of services that threatened the economic security of workers, arguing that women would disproportionately bear the burden of the employment losses and dislocations caused by international trade agreements. These transnational bodies analyzed the activities of multinational corporations and global financial organizations like the World Trade Organization, the World Bank, and the International Monetary Fund, lobbying for transparency and accountability and joining coalitions with environmental, labor, religious, and human rights groups to advocate for social justice.

Strategies have included campaigns (such as the one directed against Nike) addressing corporate codes of conduct that have forced companies to adopt a commitment to improving labor standards in their supply chains. Codes of conduct are statements of minimum standards, usually pertaining to labor, environmental, and human rights' issues. Although these campaigns may be progressive, few codes of conduct actually mention specific problems and issues that women workers face on a day-to-day basis. These problems include low wages and wage inequality; a lack of protection and respect for pregnant workers; inadequate occupational health, safety, and social security rights (especially for part-time workers); absence of freedom of association or the right to collective bargaining; and enforced overtime, over-long working days, and the intensity of work (Pearson & Seyfang, 2002). In addition, women workers are often unaware that such codes of conduct even exist. The high levels of subcontracting in industries such as garment production compound these problems and make it exceptionally difficult to trace when and where workers are covered by particular codes (Hensman, 2005). Nevertheless, codes of conduct are often presented as offering an opportunity for women's activism and positive change on a practical level. It is widely conceded that codes may eventually come to play an important role in the setting of labor standards that will benefit women workers. Ultimately it is important that codes are developed in cooperation with women workers themselves and that impacts of labor practices on female workers are a central priority (Prieto & Bendell, 2002).

In closing, it is important to emphasize that global forces constructing women as a pool of cheap and exploitable labor incorporate ideas of "productive" and "flexible" femininity that underpin global business practices. In the case of migrant domestic workers, for example, we see how discourses around the need to control workers, and definitions of work as unproductive, expose them to exploitative labor practices and underlines the racialized nature of the organization of care work in today's global economy. Simultaneously it is important to recognize these workers as having agency and avoid treating them as "victims" of global capital. Work can offer women opportunities and may break down traditional gender relations within families and households, serving as ways to avoid poverty and potentially bring a level of autonomy and independence not previously available. Our most important challenge, however, is to provide a strong critique of the broader structures of economic governance facilitating gendered systems of exploitation and to advocate strategies addressing these inequalities for the economic, social, and human rights of all women.

REFERENCES

Agustin, L. M. (2007). *Sex at the margins: Migration, labour markets and the rescue industry*. London: Zed Books.

Anderson, B. (2007). A very private business: Exploring the demand for migrant domestic workers. *European Journal of Women's Studies, 14*(3), 247–264.

Arat-Kroc, S. (2006). Whose social reproduction? Transnational motherhood and challenges to feminist political economy. In K. Bezanson and M. Luxton (Eds.), *Social reproduction: Feminist political economy challenges neoliberalism* (pp. 75–92). Montreal and Kingston: Magill-Queens University Press.

Bakker, I. and Silvey, R. (Eds.). (2008) *Beyond states and markets: The challenges of social reproduction.* London: Routledge.

Bickham Mendez, J. (2005). *From the revolution to the maquiladoras: Gender, labor and globalization in Nicaragua*. Durham: Duke University Press.

Bittman, M. (1999). Parenthood without penalty: Time use and public policy in Australia and Finland. *Feminist Economics, 5*(3), 27–42.

Briones, L. (2009). *Empowering migrant women: Why agency and rights are not enough.* Farnham: Ashgate.

Brown, A. and Chaytaweep, S. (2008). Thailand: Women and spaces for labour organizing. In K. Broadbent and M. Ford (Eds.), *Women and labour organizing in Asia: Diversity, authonomy and activism* (pp. 100–114). Abingdon: Routledge.

Caraway, T. L. (2007). *Assembling women: The feminization of global manufacturing.* Ithaca and London: ILR Press.

Chin, C. B. N. (1998). *In service and servitude: Foreign female domestic workers and the making of the Malaysian "modernity" project.* New York: Columbia University Press.

Cooke, F. L. (2008). China: Labour organizations representing women. In K. Broadbent and M. Ford (Eds.), *Women and labour organizing in Asia: Diversity, autonomy and activism* (pp. 34–49). Abingdon: Routledge.

Ehrenreich, B. and Hoschschild, A. R. (Eds.). (2002). *Global woman: Nannies, maids and sex workers in the new economy.* London: Granta.

Elias, J. (2005). The gendered political economy of control and resistance from the shopfloor of the multinational firm: A case study from Malaysia. *New Political Economy, 10*(2), 203–222.

Elias, J. (2008). Struggles over the rights of foreign domestic workers in Malaysia: The possibilities and limitations of 'rights talk'." *Economy and Society, 10*(4), 383–388.

Elias, J. and Ferguson, L. (2009). Production, reproduction and consumption. In L. Shephers (Ed.), *Gender matters in global politics.* London: Routledge.

Elson, D. and Pearson, R. 1981. The subordination of women and the internationalization of factory production. In K. Young, C. Wolkowitz, and R. McCullagh (Eds.), *Of marriage and the market: Women's subordination in international perspective* (pp. 18–40). London: CSE Books.

Enloe, C. (1990) *Bananas, beaches and bases: Making feminist sense of international relations.* London: Pandora Press.

Frank, D. (2005). *Bananeras: Women transforming the banana unions of Latin America.* London: South End Press.

Gall, G. (2006). *Sex worker union organizing: An international study.* Basingstoke: Palgrave MacMillan.

Griffin, P. (2007). Refashioning IPE: What and how gender analysis teaches international (global) political economy. *Review of International Political Economy, 14*(4), 719–736.

Hale, A. and Opondo, M. (2005). Humanising the cut flower chain: Confronting the realities of flower production for workers in Kenya. *Antipode: A Radical Journal of Geography, 37*(2), 301–323.

Hensman, R. (2005). Defending workers' rights in subcontracted workplaces. In A. Hale and J. Wills (Eds.), *Threads of labour: Garment industry supply chains from the workers' perspective* (pp. 189–209). Oxford: Blackwell.

Hochschild, A. R. (2000). Global care chains and emotional surplus value. In T. Giddens and W. Hutton (Eds.), *On the edge: Globalization and the new millennium* (pp. 130–146). London: Sage.

Hoskyns, C. and Rai, S. (2007). Recasting the global political economy: Counting women's unpaid work. *New Political Economy, 12*(3), 297–317.

ILO. (2007). *Global Employment Trends for Women Brief.* March, 2007. Geneva: International Labor Office.

Kadidiatou, M. K. (2006). Mariko Kadidiatou: Nigeria. In P. Goldman (Ed.), *Imagining ourselves: Global voices from a new generation of women* (pp. 92–3). Novato, CA: New World Library.

Kofman, E. (2004). Gendered global migrations: Diversity and stratification. *International Feminist Journal of Politics, 6*(4), 643–665.

Lee, C. K. (1998). *Gender and the South China miracle: Two worlds of factory women.* Berkley: University of California Press.

Mills, M. B. (2003). Gender inequality in the global labor force. *Annual Review of Anthropology, 32*, 41–62.

Moon, S. (2005). *Militarized modernity and gendered citizenship in South Korea.* Durham: Duke University Press.

Nash, J. and Fernandez-Kelly, M. P. (Eds.). (1983). *Women, men, and the international division of labor.* Albany: SUNY Press.

Noonan, M. C. (2001). The impact of domestic work on men's and women's wages. *Journal of Marriage and the Family, 63*(4), 1134–1145.

Ong, A. (1987). *Spirits of resistance and capitalist discipline: Factory women in Malaysia.* Albany: SUNY Press.

Parreñas, R. S. (2002). The care crisis in the Philippines: Children and transnational families in the new global economy. In B. Ehrenreich and A. R. Hochschild (Eds.), *Global woman: Nannies, maids and sex workers in the new global economy* (pp. 39–54). London: Granta.

Pearson, R. and Seyfang, G. (2002). "I'll tell you what I want . . .": Women workers and codes of conduct. In R. Jenkins, R. Pearson, and G. Seyfang (Eds.), *Corporate responsibility and labour rights: Codes of conduct in the global economy* (pp. 43–60). London: Earthscan.

Pettman, J. J. (1996). *Worlding women: A feminist international politics.* London: Routledge.

Prieto, M. and Bendell, J. (2002). *If you want to help then start listening to us! From factories and plantations in central America, women speak out about corporate responsibility.* Occasional Paper. Bath: New Academy of Business.

Pun, N. (2005). *Made in China: Women factory workers in a global workplace.* Durham and Hong Kong: Duke University Press & Hong Kong University Press.

Rupert, M. and Solomon, M. S. (2006). *Globalization and international political economy: The politics of alternative futures.* Lanham: Rowman and Littlefield.

Salzinger, L. (2003). *Genders in production: Making workers in Mexico's global factories.* Berkley: University of California Press.

Scott, J. (1985). *Weapons of the weak.* New Haven: Yale University Press.

Seguino, S. (2000). Gender inequality and economic growth: A cross country analysis. *World Development, 28*(7), 1211–1230.

Stephen, L. (2000). Sweet and sour grapes: The struggles of seasonal women workers in Chile. In A. Spring (Ed.), *Women farmers and commercial ventures: Increasing food security in developing countries* (pp. 363–382). Boulder: Lynne Rienner.

Theobald, S. (2002). Working for global factories: Thai women in electronics export companies in the Northern Regional Industrial Estate. In D. S. Gills and N. Piper (Eds.), *Women and work in globalizing Asia* (pp. 131–153). London: Routledge.

SUGGESTIONS FOR FURTHER READING

Barndt, D. (2007). *Tangled routes: Women, work and globalization on the Tomato Trail* (2nd ed.). New York: Rowman and Littlefield.

Harley, S. (Ed.). (2007). *Women's labor in the global economy: Speaking in multiple voices.* Piscataway, NJ: Rutgers University Press.

Lan, P. (2006). *Global Cinderellas: Migrant domestics and newly rich employers in Taiwan.* Raleigh, NC: Duke University Press.

Parrenas, R. (2005). *Children of global migration: Transnational families and gendered woes.* Palo Alto, CA: Stanford University Press.

Wright, M. W. (2006). *Disposable women and other myths of global capitalism.* New York: Routledge.

Women Farmers Toil to Expand Africa's Food Supply

Megan Rowling (2008)

Like many African women, Mazoe Gondwe is her family's main food provider. Lately, she has struggled to farm her plot in Malawi due to unpredictable rains that are making her hard life even tougher.

"Now we can't just depend on rain-fed agriculture, so we plant two crops—one watered with rain and one that needs irrigating," she explained. "But irrigation is back-breaking and can take four hours a day."

Gondwe, flown by development agency ActionAid to U.N. climate change talks in Poland, said she wanted access to technology that would cut the time it takes to water her crops and till her farm garden. She would also be glad of help to improve storage facilities and seed varieties.

"As a local farmer, I know what I need and I know what works. I grew up in the area and I know how the system is changing," Gondwe said.

This year, agricultural experts have renewed calls for policy makers to pay more attention to small-scale women farmers such as Gondwe, who grow up to 80 percent of crops for food consumption in Africa.

After decades in the political wilderness, farming became a hot topic this year when international food prices hit record highs in June, sharply boosting hunger around the world. The proportion of development aid spent on agriculture has dropped to just 4 percent from a peak of 17 percent in 1982.

Former U.N. Secretary-General Kofi Annan has called for women to be at the heart of a "policy revolution" to boost small-scale farming in Africa.

Women have traditionally shouldered the burden of household food production both there and in Asia, while men tend to focus on growing cash crops or migrate to cities to find paid work.

Yet women own a tiny percentage of the world's land—some experts say as little as 2 percent—and receive only around 5 percent of farming information services and training.

"Today the African farmer is the only farmer who takes all the risks herself: no capital, no insurance, no price supports, and little help—if any—from governments. These women are tough and daring and resilient, but they need help," Annan said.

A new toolkit explaining how to tackle gender issues in farming development projects, published by the U.N. Food and Agriculture Organization (FAO), highlights the potential returns of improving women's access to technology, land and finance.

In Ghana, for example, if women and men had equal land rights and security of tenure, women's use of fertilizer and profits per hectare would nearly double.

In Burkina Faso, Kenya and Tanzania, giving women entrepreneurs the same inputs and education as men would boost business revenue by up to 20 percent. And in Ivory Coast, raising women's income by $10 brings improvements in children's health and nutrition that would require a $110 increase in men's income.

"The knowledge is there, the know-how is there, but the world—and here I'm talking rich and poor—doesn't apply it as much as it could," said Marcela Villarreal, director of FAO's gender, equity and rural employment division.

EQUALITY

Many African governments have introduced formal laws making women and men equal, but have trouble enforcing them where they clash with customary laws giving property ownership rights to men, she said.

Often if a woman's husband dies, she has little choice but to marry one of his relatives so she can keep farming her plot and feeding her children, Villarreal said.

But if a widow is HIV positive, she might be chased off her land.

In Malawi, FAO is working with parliamentarians and village chiefs to let rural women know they are legally able to hold land titles. They are given wind-up radios so they can listen to farming shows in local languages and are taught how to write a will.

"People continue to think that doing things for women is part of a welfare program and doing things for men—big investments or credit—that is agriculture, that is GDP-related," Villarreal said.

"Women continue not to be seen as part of the productive potential of a country."

One powerful woman trying to change that is Agnes Kalibata, Rwanda's minister of state for agriculture. She said government land reform and credit program specifically target struggling women farmers—many of whom are bringing up children alone after their husbands were killed in the 1994 genocide.

This has helped raise their incomes, leading to better nutrition, health and education for their children, Kalibata said. Women are also getting microcredit loans, which they use to access markets and cooperatives or set up small businesses, such as producing specialty coffee for export.

"They are not like rocket scientists, they are women from the general population who finally feel empowered that they can come out and do some of these things," explained Kalibata.

In the private sector, the Bill and Melinda Gates Foundation has decided to put women at the center of its agricultural development program by attaching conditions to grants. It no longer finances projects that ignore gender issues, and it requires women to be involved in their design and implementation.

Catherine Bertini, a senior fellow at the foundation and professor of public administration at Syracuse University, said aid donors had not spent enough on support for women farmers.

"You can find the rhetoric but it's a limited number of people who actually walk the walk," she said.

Bertini, who headed the U.N. World Food Programme in the 1990s, said policy makers could best be persuaded to focus on women farmers by playing up the economic benefits rather than talking about gender equality.

"You convince people to do it because it's the most practical way to increase productivity and income to women," she said.

R E A D I N G **51**

Women and Tourism

Shaker Hussain (2007)

World Tourism Day 2007 was observed on September 27 with the theme "Tourism opens doors for women," to celebrate women's achievements in the tourism sector and encourage continuous action in support of the UN's Millennium Development Goal 3: "Promoting Gender Equality and Women Empowerment." This year's host country is Sri Lanka, an active UNWTO member for 30 years, which has a vibrant cultural heritage in which women have played a prominent role. The theme highlights an issue of fundamental importance for our future.

Bangladesh Parjatan Corporation has chalked out programs, which include rallies, telecasting of interviews of the tourism adviser as well as tourism secretary and chairman of the corporation, publication of special supplements in national dailies, and arranging seminars. But there has been no concrete step taken by the private tour operators to highlight or promote participation of women in this sector yet.

WOMEN'S EMPLOYMENT AND PARTICIPATION IN TOURISM

The tourism industry is a major employer of women, which offers various opportunities for independent income generating activities and, at the same time, affects women's lives in destination communities. The tourism sector provides various entry points for women's employment and opportunities for creating self-employment in small and medium sized income generating activities, thus helping in the elimination of poverty of women and local communities in developing countries. There has, consequently, been a rapid rise in job creation and development.

The general picture suggests that the tourism industry seems to be a particularly important sector for women (46% of the workforce are women), as the percentage of employment in most countries is higher than it is in the workforce in general (34–40% are women, ILO data).

The percentage of women in tourism varies greatly from country to country—from 2% to over 80%. There has been a broad increase in the participation of women in the tourism industry at a global level. This increase in female participation may have been driven by the growth of the industry in countries such as Puerto Rico, Chile and Turkey. For the industrially developed countries, there has been little change.

WOMEN'S OCCUPATIONS AND POSITIONS IN THE TOURISM INDUSTRY

Some facts about women's positioning in terms of hierarchical levels have been extracted from the very few sources giving such information. However, it seems very clear that the situation in the tourism industry resembles the one in the labor markets in general. As in many other sectors, there is a significant horizontal and vertical gender segregation of the labor market in tourism.

Horizontally, women and men are placed in different occupations—women are being employed as waitresses, chambermaids, cleaners, travel agency salespersons, flight attendants, etc., whereas men are being employed as barmen, gardeners, construction workers, drivers, pilots, etc.

Vertically, the typical "gender pyramid" is prevalent in the tourism sector—lower levels and occupations with few career development opportunities are dominated by women, and key managerial positions are dominated by men. The good news is that women now hold jobs across the employment spectrum, from artisans or guides to CEOs and Chairmen of boards in countries and companies of all sizes around the world.

Recent research shows that in some countries women occupied positions such as general manager of hotels, chairperson of Tourist Boards, airline director, conservation area manager and, by no means least, tourism minister.

WOMEN'S RIGHTS, STEREOTYPICAL IMAGES, SEXUAL OBJECTIFICATION

The United Nations Convention on the Elimination of all Forms of Discrimination Against Women (CEDAW, 1979) and the Universal Declaration of Human Rights (1948) must form the basis of addressing human rights and women's rights issues in tourism. Women can suffer specific discrimination within the tourism sector.

They are consistently denied positions of leadership and responsibility within the industry, they are concentrated in low skilled and low paid occupations, they are being objectified as part of the tourism "package," and they have their traditional roles perpetuated within an industry that feeds on uncomplicated images.

In less direct ways, too, women will be among those most adversely affected by tourism development. Tourism can violate women's rights, but it can also be used to challenge traditional roles and to empower women in economic, social, cultural and political terms. Women can find a voice and independence through getting involved in tourism activities—by becoming part of the decision-making process and carving out new roles in their families and homes, and within local power structures.

With sex tourism being the most negative and prominent example, there is a significant amount of sexual objectification of women working in the tourism industry. Studies have shown that women are expected to dress in an "attractive" manner, to look beautiful (i.e., slim, young, pretty), and to "play along" with sexual harassment by customers. Stereotypical images of women are, in many cases, part of the tourism product.

The portrayal is of friendly smiling women, fitting certain standards of attractiveness, who seem to be waiting to submissively serve the customer's every wish. Women working at destinations as well as indigenous women are being shown in a stereotypical way in tourism brochures and other material.

RECOMMENDATIONS FOR TOURISM INDUSTRY

- Governments, local governments, employers, trade unions and community groups should jointly create community-based institutions and services to help women and men to cope with the double burden of family and household work as well as work outside the home to generate income, such as child care facilities, which, in turn, can create jobs. The industry can look into opening child-care facilities in tourist resorts for the children of the employees.
- The support for women to become self-employed through tourism-related activities should be linked with micro-credit programs.
- Loans to women's initiatives should be included as a means of creating opportunities for the industry to buy and source locally, thus maximizing the benefits for local communities.
- Training should also be provided to promote activities that are indirectly linked to tourism, such as printing, dying and folk-arts. Special training for women might be needed in many cases.
- Development of the handicraft industry should form an important part of strategic planning for community participation in tourism, especially the participation of women.
- Employers should set up programs and schemes encouraging women to move into non-traditional occupations, invest in women's training, appoint them in managerial positions, and re-appoint them after years of less involvement due to family responsibilities.
- The tourism industry and tourism boards should abolish marketing strategies using women's stereotypical images as part of the product.

- Employers should review their standards and criteria for employing women and men, and their policies, to protect women from sexual objectification and sexual harassment by customers.

WHAT ROLE SHOULD WOMEN PLAY

The development of women's role not only gives a society balance, it also strengthens economic and social structures. The challenges now revolve around issues like ensuring income parity, raising employment quality, creating reasonable workplace conditions and penetrating glass ceilings—issues which are relevant generally to Millennium Development Goal 3 and gender equality.

Women, especially in rural communities, have a particularly important role to play in the development of responsible tourism. The employment of women can be a fundamental determinant of the development impacts of the tourism industry. The potential employment impact of the tourism industry on both men and women in rural areas will considerably improve family life. The urban drift among men who migrate to cities in search of employment has had a deleterious impact on rural women, who continue to suffer not only from hard labor in the rural fields, but also poor access to infrastructure and basic necessities such as water.

The special roles that women can play in the new tourism drive of Bangladesh are identified below:

- As teachers, mothers and mentors, to generate awareness of the potential of tourism to stimulate community growth and development.
- Actively assist in shaping a responsible tourism industry in Bangladesh, as policy-makers, entrepreneurs, entertainers, travel agents, tour guides, restaurateurs, workers, managers, guest house operators, and other leading roles in the tourism business environment.
- Ensure equality in the conditions of employment of women. Too often, women are seen as a "cheap" alternative to employing men, with no security of tenure, maternity leave, or investment in career development.

- Promote and, where possible, ensure respect for and dignity of women in the development, marketing, and promotion of tourism.
- Lobby for the support of developers and local authorities for the provision of services and infrastructure to enhance the position of women in communities.
- Secure the provision of craft training and other opportunities to expand the skills base of rural women.
- Give special attention to the needs of women tourists, with particular emphasis on safety and security.
- Supporting rural women's full participation in economic activities associated with the development of ecotourism through training in running micro-enterprises, tour guiding, home-stays and handicraft production.

PERSPECTIVE OF WOMEN IN BANGLADESH

Though women in Bangladesh have, since liberation, been encouraged to enter all kinds of professions alongside the men, their persistent social backwardness prevents them from having equal access to the top levels of administration in the governmental hierarchy. The government has been trying hard to involve and integrate women in the policy and decision making processes. Many steps are being undertaken to change the status and conditions of women through provisions of laws, executive orders, policy interventions, and building of institutions.

These steps and measures seem consistent with similar steps of the United Nations, e.g., the Declaration of International Women's Year in 1975, designation of UN Decade for Women (1975–85), and adoption of the Convention on the Elimination of All Forms of Discrimination Against Women (CEDAW). Indeed, all these measures seem to have influenced the government a great deal for adopting policies and programs to enhance women's status, roles and rights.

Bangladeshi women have a significant role to play in social and economic development, both nationally and globally. Women are associated with development activities, and an environment has to be created to make their participation possible. Women in Bangladesh often suffer from the traditional value system of a patriarchal society, and from gender discrimination. They do not have adequate access to, and are deprived of, many benefits from services in education, health, employment and governance.

The Constitution of Bangladesh recognizes equal rights of women, but the family laws and laws relating to religious rites put men and women on unequal platforms. Women emancipation movements and efforts in women empowerment open new avenues for their broader participation in economic activities, and also for recognition of women as agents for change and development.

R E A D I N G **52**

Assembly Line

Shu Ting, translated from the Chinese by Carolyn Kizer (1991)

In time's assembly line
Night presses against night.
We come off the factory night-shift
In line as we march towards home.
Over our heads in a row
The assembly line of stars

Stretches across the sky.
Beside us, little trees
Stand numb in assembly lines.
The stars must be exhausted
After thousands of years
Of journeys which never change.

The little trees are all sick,
Choked on smog and monotony,
Stripped of their color and shape.
It's not hard to feel for them;
We share the same tempo and rhythm.

Yes, I'm numb to my own existence
As if, like the trees and stars
—perhaps just out of habit
—perhaps just out of sorrow,
I'm unable to show concern
For my own manufactured fate.

R E A D I N G **53**

Oil, Islam, and Women

Michael L. Ross (2008)

In the Middle East, fewer women work outside the home, and fewer hold positions in government, than in any other region of the world. According to most observers, this troubling anomaly is due to the region's Islamic traditions (e.g., Sharabi 1988; World Bank 2004). Some even argue that the "clash of civilizations" between the Islamic world and the West has been caused, in part, by the poor treatment of Muslim women (Inglehart and Norris 2003a; Landes and Landes 2001).

This paper suggests that women in the Middle East are underrepresented in the workforce and in government because of oil—not Islam. Oil and mineral production can also explain the unusually low status of women in many countries outside the Middle East, including Azerbaijan, Botswana, Chile, Nigeria, and Russia.

Oil production affects gender relations by reducing the presence of women in the labor force. The failure of women to join the nonagricultural labor force has profound social consequences: it leads to higher fertility rates, less education for girls, and less female influence within the family. It also has far-reaching political consequences: when fewer women work outside the home, they are less likely to exchange information and overcome collective action problems; less likely to mobilize politically, and to lobby for expanded rights; and less likely to gain representation in government. This leaves oil-producing states with atypically strong patriarchal cultures and political institutions.[1]

This argument challenges a common belief about economic development: that growth promotes gender equality (e.g., Inglehart and Norris 2003b). Development institutions like the World Bank often echo this theme, and it is widely accepted among development experts (World Bank 2001). This paper instead suggests that different types of economic growth have different consequences for gender relations: when growth encourages women to join the formal labor market, it ultimately brings about greater gender equality; when growth is based on oil and mineral extraction, it discourages women from entering the labor force and tends to exaggerate gender inequalities.

It also casts new light on the "resource curse." Oil and mineral production has previously been tied to slow economic growth (Sachs and Warner 1995), authoritarian rule (Ross 2001a), and civil war (Collier and Hoeffler 2004). This paper suggests that oil extraction has even broader consequences than previously recognized: it not only affects a country's government and economy but also its core social structures.

Finally, it has important policy implications. The United States and Europe consume most of the world's oil exports, and hence have strong effects on the economies of oil-exporting states. One of these effects is to reduce economic opportunities for women; another is to reduce their political influence. A third effect may be to foster Islamic fundamentalism: a recent study of 18 countries found that when Muslim women had fewer economic opportunities, they were more likely to support fundamentalist Islam (Blaydes and Linzer 2006). Changes in Western energy policies could strongly affect these outcomes.

THE CONSEQUENCES OF FEMALE LABOR FORCE PARTICIPATION

Social theorists have long claimed that women can achieve social and political emancipation by working outside the home (e.g., Engels 1978 (1884)). Many recent studies support this claim. Female labor force participation helps raise female school enrollment and literacy: when families know that girls will be able to earn their own income—and contribute to house-hold income—they tend to invest more in their health and education (Michael 1985). Female labor force participation is also linked to lower fertility rates: when women earn their own incomes, they gain an incentive to delay the onset of parenthood, and hence bear fewer children over their lifetimes (Brewster and Rindfuss 2000).

Female labor force participation also affects gender relations more broadly—particularly when women work in factory jobs that bring them into contact with each other, allow them to share information, and lower the barriers to collective action. Studies of female garment workers in Bangladesh—who typically come from poor rural areas, and are hired when they are young and single—have found that factory work helps them gain self-confidence, develop social networks, learn to negotiate with men, and learn about health and contraception (Amin et al. 1998; Kabeer and Mahmud 2004). Other studies show that when women have an independent source of income, they tend to gain more influence within the family (Beegle, Frankenberg, and Thomas 2001; Iverson and Rosenbluth 2006). They also develop more egalitarian beliefs about gender relations (Thornton, Alwin, and Camburn 1983).

Finally, the entry of women into the labor force tends to boost female political influence. There seem to be many reasons for this effect. According to studies in the United States, when women enter the workforce they become more likely to engage in conversations that promote an interest in politics,

to join informal networks that facilitate collective action and help them develop their civic skills, and perversely, to experience gender discrimination in a manner that motivates them politically (Sapiro 1983; Schlozman, Burns, and Verba 1999).

Studies of female political participation in developing states are broadly consistent with these findings. Indian women are more likely to participate in politics and elect female representatives when they have established an identity outside the household, often through work (Chhibber 2003). In many countries where women work in low-wage manufacturing—including Guatemala, Taiwan, Hong Kong, India, Indonesia, Tunisia and Morocco—they have formed organizations to protect their interests; often these organizations lobby for broader reforms in women's rights (Moghadam 1999).

These and other studies imply that joining the labor force can boost female political influence through at least three channels: at an individual level, by affecting women's political views and identities; at a social level, by increasing the density of women in the labor force and hence the likelihood they will form politically salient networks; and at an economic level, by boosting their economic importance and hence forcing the government to take their interests into account.

THE CAUSES OF FEMALE LABOR FORCE PARTICIPATION

Women commonly face special barriers to entering the labor market. Labor markets are typically segregated by gender: men work in some occupations and women, in others, even when their qualifications are similar (Anker 1997). Occupational segregation tends to reduce both the number of jobs available to women, and their wages (Horton 1999).

In theory, women could gain greater access to labor markets by persuading governments to adopt and enforce laws that cause employers to end discrimination, to facilitate maternity leave, to allow women to own property, and to let them travel without the consent of a male relative. But in practice, when women are excluded from labor markets, they typically have little political influence—which leaves governments with little incentive to act on their behalf.

When labor markets are segregated by gender, and women have little political power, how can they enter the work force in large numbers? Since the early days of the industrial revolution, the answer has often come from the development of low-wage export-oriented industries, especially in textiles, garments, and processed agricultural goods. In 1890, women held over half of the jobs in the U.S. textiles industry (Smuts 1959). Today more than 80% of all textile and garment workers in the world are women (World Bank 2001).[2]

There are several reasons why these industries are conduits for new female workers:

- they do not need workers with great physical strength: men have no natural advantage in these jobs;
- the jobs require little training and few specialized skills, which makes it easier for women to intermittently leave their jobs to care for their families;
- and making cloth and clothing is often perceived as traditional women's work.

Factories are even more likely to employ women when they export their products. Several studies show that even within a single industry, export-oriented firms employ women at a higher rate than do similar firms that produce goods for domestic markets (Başlevent and Onaran 2004; Ozler 2000). This seems to occur because:

- Export-oriented industries can grow quickly since they are selling into a global market. Hence they can produce large numbers of new jobs, which also means women can be hired without displacing men.
- Factories that produce goods for export are more likely to be owned or managed by foreign companies that—for legal or cultural reasons—are less prone to discriminate against women in hiring;
- Export-oriented firms produce goods for highly-competitive global markets, and wages constitute a large fraction of their production costs; this places them under exceptional pressure to seek

out labor at the lowest cost. Since female wages are lower than male wages, export-oriented firms often target them for recruitment.

HOW OIL PRODUCTION CAN AFFECT FEMALE LABOR FORCE PARTICIPATION

When countries discover oil, their new wealth tends to produce an economic condition called the "Dutch Disease," which is characterized by a rise in the real exchange rate, and a transformation of the economy away from the "traded sector" (agriculture and manufacturing) and toward the "nontraded sector" (construction and services) (Corden and Neary 1982). Classic models of the Dutch Disease, however, do not consider whether these changes might affect men and women differently (Frederiksen 2007). Once we extend the model to better capture the conditions that women face in most low-income countries, we can see how a boom in oil production will squeeze women out of the labor force.

In the classic Dutch Disease model, a boom in oil production will crowd out the production of other traded goods, via two mechanisms.[3] First, the influx of foreign currency—that is, the new wealth generated by oil sales—will raise the real exchange rate, making it cheaper for locals to import tradable goods from other countries than to buy them from domestic producers. Second, the new wealth will increase the demand for non-tradable goods—things that cannot be imported, like construction and retail services—drawing labor away from the tradable goods sector and hence raising its production costs. The net result is that an oil boom causes a decline in the traded goods sector (agriculture and manufacturing) but an expansion in the non-traded sector (construction and retail).

How does this affect women? According to standard models of female labor supply, two key factors influence the number of women in the labor market (Mammen and Paxson 2000). One is the prevailing female wage: as it rises, women are more inclined to enter the market for wage labor and "substitute" work for leisure. The other is "female unearned income," which means the income that accrues to a woman's household, but that she does not earn directly: as her family's income rises, she becomes less inclined to join the labor market and provide a second income. A women's "reservation wage" is the wage at which she finds it worthwhile to join the labor force. If her unearned income is high—for example, if her husband has a sizable income—then her reservation wage will also be high, and only a well-paying job will lure her into the work force. If her unearned income is low, her reservation wage will also be low, meaning she will be willing to join the labor force even if the prevailing female wage is low.

In a classic Dutch Disease model, the impact of an oil boom on female labor force participation is ambiguous: it will increase the prevailing wage (which is assumed to be the same for men and women), and this in turn will increase a women's incentive to join the work force. But there is also a countervailing force: higher wages will boost household income, which will raise a woman's reservation wage and reduce her incentive to join the labor force. The classic model does not tell us which effect will prevail.

Now consider what happens if we modify the Dutch Disease model to reflect gender-based segregation in the labor force—that is, the fact that many kinds of jobs are closed to women. Dutch Disease models show that oil booms lead to a shift away from the traded sector to the nontraded sector. In many developing countries, women are largely employed in the traded sector, in low-wage jobs in export-oriented factories and agriculture; and they are excluded from many parts of the nontraded sector, such as construction and retail, since these jobs typically entail heavy labor, or contact with men outside the family (Anker 1997). If we assume that women can only work in the traded sector, and men in the nontraded sector, how will an oil boom affect female labor force participation?[4]

When there is gender segregation in the labor market, men and women have different wages. Since men in this model work in the non-traded sector, its expansion will boost the demand for male labor and cause male wages to rise; since women cannot enter the nontraded sector, male wages will rise even more than they would otherwise. Since women work in the traded sector, the sector's decline will reduce the demand for female labor, and hence, the prevailing female wage.

An oil boom should also reduce the supply of female labor by raising womens' unearned income, and hence, their reservation wage. This occurs through two mechanisms: through higher male wages (caused by the expansion of the non-traded sector, which employs only men), and through higher government transfers to households (caused by the effect of booming oil exports on government revenues).[5] The decline in the demand for female labor, plus the decline in the supply of female labor, will reduce the number of women in the workforce.

Now consider what occurs if we loosen some key assumptions. The model assumes an open economy. But sometimes oil-rich governments use tariffs and subsidies to protect their tradable sectors. Will this affect the results? Probably not: oil-rich governments tend to protect heavy industry, not light industry—and hence, male jobs instead of female jobs (Gelb and Associates, 1988). Even if an oil-rich government did protect light industries, once domestic firms received protection they would no longer have to compete with overseas firms—reducing their incentive to seek out low-wage labor, and hence, female workers.

The model also assumes that the number of working-age men and women is fixed. But many small, oil-rich countries import both male and female labor; how would this change the model? If we allow for immigrant male workers—in effect making the supply of male labor more elastic—then a boom in the nontraded sector might not raise male wages, eliminating one source of higher female unearned income. But a second source of female unearned income would remain: governments would still receive a boost in revenues, generating more transfers to households.

If we allow for female immigration, the prevailing female wage would drop. Since women withdraw from the labor market when the prevailing wage falls below their reservation wage, this would further discourage local women from entering the work force.

Both male and female immigration would also swell the overall size of the labor force. Hence even if there were no change in the number of working female citizens, the fraction of female citizens in the total labor force would fall.

FIGURE 1 How Oil Production May Reduce Female Political Influence

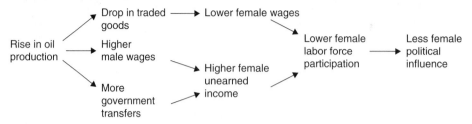

What if we partially ease the assumption of occupational segregation, by allowing both men and women to work in the traded sector? Again, there should be little change in the outcome: when the traded sector contracts, both men and women will lose their jobs. But although men can switch to jobs in the non-traded sector, women cannot because of occupational segregation. As a result, female wages will still fall, and unearned female income will still rise, since both male wages and government transfers will increase.

What if we further ease the assumption of occupational segregation and allow both men and women to work in the nontraded sector? Here there is a change in the results: the effects of an oil boom are now ambiguous. If more female jobs are lost in the traded sector than are gained in the nontraded sector, the demand for female workers will still drop; if more jobs are gained in the nontraded sector, the demand for female workers may increase.

If the demand for female workers rises enough, the increase in the prevailing female wage will exceed the increase in the reservation wage (which will still rise thanks to higher male wages and higher government transfers) and lead to a net increase in female labor force participation. This implies that oil may not harm the status of women if they are free to work in the nontraded sector. It may also explain why the booming oil markets of the 1970s reduced female labor force participation in countries with high levels of occupational segregation (like Algeria, Angola, Gabon, Nigeria, and Oman), but not in those with low levels of occupational segregation (like Colombia, Malaysia, Mexico, Norway, and Venezuela).

The main implication of the model is,

H_1: *A rise in the value of oil production will reduce female participation in the labor force.*

The earlier discussion suggests that female political influence is partly a function of female labor force participation: when the fraction of female citizens in the work force rises, it should enhance women's political influence through dynamics at an individual level (as their exposure to the work place affects their identities and perceptions), a social level (as their density in the labor force rises, so does the number of formal and informal female networks), and an economic level (as their growing role in the economy forces the government to take their interests into account). If an increase in oil production reduces the percentage of female citizens in the labor force, we can infer

H_2: *A rise in the value of oil production will reduce female political influence.*

CASE STUDY: ALGERIA, MOROCCO, AND TUNISIA

To explore the causal mechanisms that link oil to female status—while still controlling for Islam and regional culture—we can look more closely at a set of highly similar countries that have different petroleum endowments: Algeria, Morocco, and Tunisia. All three states were French colonies, all gained independence in the late 1950s or early 1960s, all granted suffrage to women soon after independence, and all are overwhelmingly Muslim.

Although they are otherwise similar, they have different levels of oil wealth: Algeria has been a major producer since the 1960s, whereas Morocco and Tunisia have relatively little. They also have different levels of female political representation: in oil-rich Algeria, women held 6.2% of the seats in parliament in 2002; in oil-poor Morocco and Tunisia, they held 10.8 and 22.8%, respectively. Differences in their oil wealth

Comparison of Algeria, Morocco, and Tunisia

	Algeria	Morocco	Tunisia
Population (million)	31.8	30.1	9.9
Muslim population (%)	97	98	99
Income per capita	$ 1915	$1278	$2214
Oil rents per capita	$ 937	$ 0	$ 61
Textile/clothing exports per capita	$ 0.09	$ 94	$ 287
Female labor force participation (%)	12 (est.)	33.5	N.A.
Female-held parliamentary seats (%)	6.2*	10.8*	22.8*
Fertility rate	2.72	2.66	1.99
Gender rights index	2.8	3.1	3.2

* 2002 figures.
Note: Figures are for 2003, except where indicated. Income, oil rents, and textile and clothing exports per capita are in constant 2000 dollars.

can help explain differences in the number of working women, which in turn helps account for differences in the number of women entering parliament.

With little or no oil, labor costs in Morocco and Tunisia are relatively low by international standards. Beginning around 1970, both countries took advantage of these low labor costs to develop export-oriented textile industries.

In both countries, these industries played a major role in drawing women into the work force. In Morocco, for example, the government began to promote textile and garment exports to Europe in 1969, hoping this would reduce the high unemployment rate for men. To the government's surprise, companies deliberately sought out and hired unmarried women, since they could be paid lower wages; by keeping their labor costs low, these firms were able to compete in the European market. By 1980, Morocco's textile work force was 75% female, even though men continued to outnumber women in textile factories that produced goods for the domestic market (Joekes 1982).

In the late 1970s, the Moroccan textile industry hit a slump when Europe closed its markets. But after the government carried structural reforms in the late 1980s and early 1990s, the industry once

again grew quickly: by 2004, it was Morocco's main source of exports. It also accounted for three-quarters of the growth in female employment in the 1990s (Assaad 2004).

The Tunisian textile industry has followed a largely similar path—expanding since about 1970 through exports, relying on low-wage female labor, and weathering changes in European trade policies (Baud 1977; White 2001). Morocco and Tunisia now have the two highest rates of female labor force participation in the Middle East.

The high rates of female labor participation in Morocco and Tunisia have contributed to each country's unusually large and vigorous gender rights movements. Unlike other Middle East countries, Morocco and Tunisia have women's organizations that focus on female labor issues, including the right to maternity leave, raising the minimum work age, sexual harassment, and gaining rights for domestic workers (Moghadam 1999).

In Tunisia, the women's movement began with an important advantage: shortly after independence, President Bourguiba adopted a national family law that gave women greater equality in marriage, and opened the door to major improvements in female education and employment. But Moroccan family laws were much more conservative, and women's groups had little success in reforming them in the 1960s, 1970s, and 1980s (Charrad 1990).

Although Morocco had a small number of women's organizations in the 1950s and 1960s, they were headed by men and focused on social and charitable work. Between 1970 and 1984, however, the number of women's organizations jumped from five to 32, and many began to focus on women's rights.

Between 1990 and 1992, a coalition of women's groups (including labor unions) gathered more than 1 million signatures on a petition calling for reform of the family laws to give women new rights in marriage, divorce, child custody, and inheritance. Conservative Islamists rallied their own supporters to block any new laws. Morocco's political parties—even secular opposition parties—declined to support the petition campaign. Still, the movement placed strong pressures on King Hassan II, and he eventually backed a more modest package of reforms (Brand 1998; Wuerth 2005).

In the late 1990s and early 2000s, the women's groups continued to face strong opposition, and even death threats. Yet their lobbying led to further reforms, including a new labor code that recognizes gender equality in the workplace and criminalizes sexual harassment; a more complete reform of the family laws; and an informal 20% female quota for political parties in parliament. These new measures, coupled with the grassroots strength of the women's movement, led to a tripling in the number of women running for local office from 1997 to 2002, and an increase in the fraction of parliamentary seats held by women from 0.6% in 1995 to 10.8% in 2003 (World Bank 2004).

In Tunisia, women's groups have been even more successful, raising the fraction of female-held parliamentary seats from 6.7% in 1995 to 22.8% in 2002—the highest in the Middle East, and higher than in Western countries like the United States, the United Kingdom, and Canada (Moghadam 1999; World Bank 2004).

Oil-rich Algeria provides a telling contrast to oil-poor Morocco. A naïve observer might expect Algeria to have *more* women in the labor force and in parliament than Morocco: Algerian incomes are considerably higher; Algeria has had a series of socialist governments, while Morocco has been ruled by monarchy with strong tribal roots; and Moroccans hold more conservative religious views than Algerians (Blaydes and Linzer 2006). Yet Algeria has fewer women in its nonagricultural labor force (about 12% vs. 33%), fewer women in its parliament (6.6% vs. 10.8%), and a higher fertility rate (2.72% vs. 2.66%) than Morocco.[6] According to the gender rights index, Algeria ranks lower than Morocco and Tunisia on "nondiscrimination and access to justice," "autonomy, security, and freedom," "economic rights and equal opportunities," and "social and cultural rights."

These differences in female status can be at least partly explained by Algeria's oil industry. The Algerian economy has long been based on the extraction of hydrocarbons: between 1970 and 2003, oil rents made up about 44% of its GDP. It has also long suffered from the Dutch Disease: since at least the early 1970s, its tradable sector (agriculture and manufacturing) has been unusually small, and its nontradable sector (construction and services) has been unusually large, for a country of Algeria's size and income. Despite reform efforts in the 1990s—pushed by the International Monetary Fund—Algeria failed to diversify its export sector, and its small manufacturing sector remained highly protected, capital-intensive, and oriented toward domestic needs (Auty 2003). Consequently, Algeria's manufacturing sector had little need for low-wage labor, and little reason to hire women.

If Morocco had a large oil sector like Algeria, it would not have become a major textiles exporter, since the Dutch Disease would have made its labor costs too high. Without a large, export-oriented manufacturing sector, Moroccan women would have been slower to enter the labor force, women's groups would have been smaller and less influential, and major reforms would have been less likely.

CONCLUSION

The extraction of oil and gas tends to reduce the role of women in the work force, and the likelihood they will accumulate political influence. Without large numbers of women participating in the economic and political life of a country, traditional patriarchal institutions will go unchallenged. In short, petroleum perpetuates patriarchy. This dynamic can help explain the surprisingly low influence of women in mineral-rich states in the Middle East (Saudi Arabia, Kuwait, Oman, Algeria, Libya), as well as in Latin America (Chile), sub-Saharan Africa (Botswana, Gabon, Mauritania, Nigeria), and the former Soviet Union (Azerbaijan, Russia).

This dynamic has implications for our understanding of both the Middle East and Islam. Many observers claim the unusually low status of women in the Middle East is due to the patriarchal culture of Islam, the Arab states, or perhaps the Middle East region. Some suggest that the treatment of women is the central issue that divides the Islamic and Western worlds, and hence drives the "clash of civilizations." Writing in *Foreign Policy*, Inglehart and Norris (2003b) argue,

> the real fault line between the West and Islam . . . concerns gender equality and sexual liberalization. In other words, the values separating the two cultures have much more to do with eros than demos. As younger generations in the West have gradually become more liberal on these issues, Muslim nations have remained the most traditional societies in the world.

Some observers also argue that gender inequalities in the Middle East are at the core of the region's failure to democratize, and are linked to a more general lack of tolerance (Fish 2002; Inglehart and Norris 2003a).

These criticisms are at least partly misplaced. The persistence of patriarchy in the Middle East has relatively little to do with Islam, but much to do with the region's oil-based economy. Economic growth that is based on export-oriented manufacturing and agriculture tends to benefit women; economic growth based on oil exports diminishes their role in the work force and the political sphere, and hence allows patriarchal norms, laws, and institutions to endure.

The link between oil and patriarchy also has ramifications for the way we think about economic development. Many scholars argue that in low- and middle-income countries, economic growth leads to social modernization, including greater gender equality (e.g., Inkeles and Smith 1974; Inglehart

and Norris 2003a). In his classic book *The Passing of Traditional Society*, Lerner (1958, 45) wrote that

> Whether from East or West, modernization poses the same basic challenge—the infusion of a 'rationalist and positivist spirit' against which, scholars seem agreed, "Islam is absolutely defenseless."

This study suggests that different types of economic growth can have different effects on gender relations. When economic growth is the result of industrialization—particularly the type of export-oriented manufacturing that draws women into the labor force—it should also bring about the changes in gender relations that we associate with modernization. But income that comes from oil extraction often fails to produce industrialization—and can even discourage industrialization by causing the Dutch Disease.

Of course, oil wealth does not *necessarily* harm the status of women. Seven countries have produced significant quantities of oil and gas, but still made faster progress on gender equality than we would expect based on their income: Norway, New Zealand, Australia, Uzbekistan, Turkmenistan, Syria, and Mexico. The first three countries are probably exceptions to the general pattern because of reasons implied by the model: since women already had a large presence in the nontraded sector (thanks to the size and diversification of these economies), rising oil exports did not crowd them out of the labor market. The two Central Asian states were strongly affected by many years of Soviet rule, which promoted the role of women through administrative fiat; this may have inoculated them against oil-induced patriarchy.

Perhaps the most interesting exceptions are Syria and Mexico: women in both states may have benefited from many years of rule by secular, left-of-center parties that showed an interest in women's rights. Mexico also gained from its proximity to the U.S. market, which allowed it to develop a large, low-wage export-oriented manufacturing sector along the border—which pulled women into the labor market despite the flow of oil rents. These cases show that both good fortune, and a committed government, can sometimes counteract the perverse effects of oil on the status of women.

NOTES

1. Here and elsewhere, "oil" refers to both oil and natural gas; and "work force" and "labor force" refer to men and women who work in non-agricultural jobs that are outside the home and inside the formal sector, and who are nationals of the specified country.
2. I use the term "textile" to refer to all types of yarns, fabrics, and garments.
3. Frederiksen (2007) develops a more complete and explicit Dutch Disease model with gender segregation and an elastic female labor supply. This simpler model draws on parts of the Frederiksen model.
4. A country does not need to export oil to be affected by the Dutch Disease. Even if it consumes all of the oil that it produces, a rise in oil production will still lead to a rise in the real exchange rate, since it will reduce the country's oil imports.
5. Transfers can take the form of welfare programs, but also tax cuts, food and energy subsidies, patronage jobs, and so forth.
6. Women comprised 6.6% of the nonagricultural work force in Algeria in 1980 and 9.0% in 1990. The estimate of 12% in 2000 is a projection based on changes between 1990 and 2000 in the fraction of women in the total work force.

REFERENCES

Amin, Sajeda, Ian Diamond, Ruchira T Naved, and Margaret Newby. 1998. Transition to Adulthood of Female Garment-factory Workers in Bangladesh. *Studies in Family Planning* 29 (June): 185–200.

Anker, Richard. 1997. Theories of occupational segregation by sex: An overview. *International Labour Review* 136 (Autumn): 315–39.

Assaad, Ragui. 2004. Why Did Economic Liberalization Lead to Feminization of the Labor Force in Morocco and De-feminization in Egypt? Working Paper, University of Minnesota.

Auty, Richard M. 2003. Third time lucky for Algeria? Integrating an industrializing oil-rich country into the global economy. *Resources Policy* 29 (March): 37–47.

Başlevent, Cem, and Ozlem Onaran. 2004. The Effect of Export-Oriented Growth on Female Labor Market Outcomes in Turkey. *World Development* 32 (August): 1375–93.

Baud, Isa. 1977. Jobs and Values: Social Effects of Export-Oriented Industrialization in Tunisia. In *Industrial re-adjustment and the international division of labour*. Tilburg (The Netherlands): Development Research Institute.

Beegle, Kathleen, Elizabeth Frankenberg, and Duncan Thomas. 2001. Bargaining Power within Couples and Use of Prenatal and Delivery Care in Indonesia. *Studies in Family Planning* 32 (June): 130–46.

Blaydes, Lisa, and Drew A Linzer. 2006. The Political Economy of Women's Support for Fundamentalist Islam. Working paper, Department of Political Science, University of California, Los Angeles.

Brand, Laurie A. 1998. *Women, the State, and Political Liberalization*. New York: Columbia University Press.

Brewster, Karin, and Ronald Rindfuss. 2000. Fertility and Women's Employment in Industrialized Nations. *Annual Review of Sociology* 26: 271–96.

Charrad, Mounira. 2001. *States and Women's Rights: The Making of Postcolonial Tunisia, Algeria, and Morocco*. Berkeley: University of California Press.

Chhibber, Pradeep. 2003. Why Are Some Women Politically Active? The Household, Public Space, and Political Participation in India. In *Islam, Gender, Culture, and Democracy*, R. Inglehart. Willowdale, ON: de Sitter.

Collier, Paul, and Anke Hoffler. 2004. Greed and Grievance in Civil War. *Oxford Economic Papers* 56 (October): 663–95.

Corden, W. M., and P. J. Neary. 1982. Booming Sector and Deindustrialization in a Small Open Economy. *The Economic Journal* 92 (December): 825–48.

Engels, Friedrich. 1978 (1884). The Origin of the Family, Private Property, and the State. In *The Marx-Engels Reader*, ed. R. C. Tucker. New York: Norton.

Fish, M. Stephen: 2002. Islam and Authoritarianism. *World Politics* 55 (October): 4–37.

Frederiksen, Elisabeth Hermann. 2007. Labor Moblility, Household Production, and the Dutch Disease. Working Paper, University of Copenhangen.

Gelb, Alan, and Associates. 1988. *Oil Windfalls Blessing or Curse?* New York: Oxford University Press.

Horton, Susan. 1999. Marginalization Revisited: Women's Market Work and Pay, and Economic Development. *World Development* 27 (3): 571–82.

Inglehart, Ronald, and Pippa Norris. 2003a. The True Clash of Civilizations. *Foreign Policy* 135: 62–70.

Inglehart, Ronald, and Pippa Norris. 2003b. *Rising Tide*. New York: Cambridge University Press.

Inkeles, Alex, and David H. Smith. 1974. *Becoming Modern*. Cambridge: Harvard University Press.

Iverson, Torben, and Frances Rosenbluth. 2006. The Political Economy of Gender: Explaining Cross-National Variation in the Gender Division of Labor and the Gender Voting Gap. *American Journal of Political Science* 50 (January): 1–19.

Joekes, Susan P. 1982. Female-led Industrialization: Women's jobs in Third World Export Manufacturing—the case of the Moroccan clothing industry. Sussex (UK): Institute for Development Studies.

Kabeer, Naila, and Simeen Mahmud. 2004. Globalization, Gender, and Poverty: Bangladeshi Women Workers in Export and Local Markets. *Journal of International Development* 16 (January): 93–109.

Landes, David S., and Richard A. Landes. 2001. Girl Power: Do Fundamentalists Fear Our Women? *New Republic*. October 8: 20–23.

Lerner, Daniel. 1958. *The Passing of Traditional Society*. New York: Free Press.

Mammen, Kristin, and Christina Paxson. 2000. Women's Work and Economic Development. *Journal of Economic Perspectives* 14 (Autumn): 141–64.

Michael, Robert T. 1985. Consequences of the Rise in Female Labor Force Participation Rates: Questions and Probes. *Journal of Labor Economics* 3 (January, part 2): S117–S146.

Moghadam, Valentine. 1999. Gender and Globalization: Female Labor and Women's Movements. *Journal of World-Systems Research* 5 (Summer): 367–88.

Ozler, Sule. 2000. Export Orientation and Female Share of Employment: Evidence from Turkey. *World Development* 28 (July): 1239–48.

Ross, Michael L. 2001a. Does Oil Hinder Democracy? *World Politics* 53 (April): 325–61.

Sachs, Jeffrey D., and Andrew M. Warner. 1995. Natural Resource Abundance and Economic Growth. In *Development Discussion Paper 517a*. Cambridge, MA: Harvard Institute for International Development.

Sapiro, Virginia. 1983. *The Political Integration of Women*. Urbana: University of Illinois Press.

Schlozman, Kay Lehman, Nancy Burns, and Sidney Verba. 1999. "What Happened at Work Today?": A Multistage Model of Gender, Employment, and Political Participation. *Journal of Politics* 61 (February): 29–53.

Sharabi, Hisham. 1988. *Neopatriarchy: A Theory of Distorted Change in Arab Society*. New York: Oxford University Press.

Smuts, Robert W. 1959. *Women and Work in America*. New York: Columbia University Press.

Thornton, Arland, Duane F. Alwin, and Donald Camburn. 1983. Causes and Consequences of Sex-Role Attitudes and Attitude Change. *American Sociological Review* 48 (April): 211–27.

White, Gregory. 2001. *A Comparative Political Economy of Tunisia and Morocco: On the Outside Looking In*. Albany: SUNY Press.

World Bank. 2001. *Engendering Development*. New York: Oxford University Press.

World Bank. 2004. *Gender and Development in the Middle East and North Africa*. Washington DC: World Bank.

Wuerth, Oriana. 2005. The Reform of the Moudawana: The Role of Women's Civil Society Organizations in Changing the Personal Status Code in Morocco. *Hawwa* 3 (December): 309–33.

R　E　A　D　I　N　G　**54**

Girl

Jamaica Kincaid (1983)

Wash the white clothes on Monday and put them on the stone heap; wash the color clothes on Tuesday and put them on the clothesline to dry; don't walk barehead in the hot sun; cook pumpkin fritters in very hot sweet oil; soak your little cloths right after you take them off; when buying cotton to make yourself a nice blouse, be sure that it doesn't have gum on it, because that way it won't hold up well after a wash; soak salt fish overnight before you cook it; is it true that you sing benna in Sunday school?; always eat your food in such a way that it won't turn someone else's stomach; on Sundays try to walk like a lady and not like the slut you are so bent on becoming; don't sing benna in Sunday school; you mustn't speak to wharf-rat boys, not even to give directions; don't eat fruits on the street—flies will follow you; *but I don't sing benna on Sundays at all and never in Sunday school*; this is how to sew on a button; this is how to make a button-hole for the button you have just sewed on; this is how to hem a dress when you see the hem coming down and so to prevent yourself from looking like the slut I know you are so bent on becoming; this is how you iron your father's khaki shirt so that it doesn't have a crease; this is how you iron your father's khaki pants so that they don't have a crease; this is how you grow okra—far from the house, because okra tree harbors red ants; when you are growing dasheen, make sure it gets plenty of water or else it makes your throat itch when you are eating it; this is how you sweep a corner; this is how you sweep a whole house; this is how you sweep a yard; this is how you smile to someone you don't like too much; this is how you smile to someone you don't like at all; this is how you smile to someone you like completely; this is how you set a table for tea; this is how you set a table for dinner; this is how you set a table for dinner with an important guest; this is how you set a table for lunch; this is how you set a table for breakfast; this is how to behave in the presence of men who don't know you very well, and this way they won't recognize immediately the slut I have warned you against becoming; be sure to wash every day, even if it is with your own spit; don't squat down to play marbles—you are not a boy, you know; don't pick people's flowers—you might catch something; don't throw stones at blackbirds, because it might not be a blackbird at all; this is how to make a bread pudding; this is how to make doukona; this is how to make pepper pot; this is how to make a good medicine for a cold; this is how to make a good medicine to throw away a child before it even becomes a child; this is how to catch a fish; this is how to throw back a fish you don't like, and that way something bad won't fall on you; this is how to bully a man; this is how a man bullies you; this is how to love a man, and if this doesn't work there are other ways, and if they don't work don't feel too bad about giving up; this is how to spit up in the air if you feel like it, and this is how to move quick so that it doesn't fall on you; this is how to make ends meet; always squeeze bread to make sure it's fresh; *but what if the baker won't let me feel the bread?*; you mean to say that after all you are really going to be the kind of woman who the baker won't let near the bread?

R E A D I N G   **55**

Banking on Women

Essay 1
Microcredit in Northern Ghana

Sean Kelly (2007)

Like every other day, Sheri Feyakoyo wakes up at 4 a.m. She wraps herself in the colorful head-scarf common to Muslim women in Northern Ghana, and sets off to search for water. As she walks under the pre-dawn sky, chain lightning jumps between clouds that have so far refused to release any rain.

The young woman fills two buckets from a not-so-nearby well that is in danger of going dry, returns to the family compound of huts surrounding a common courtyard, and cooks breakfast for her husband and children.

She sends the oldest kids off to school, straps her baby to her back, and helps her husband weed their fields of millet and maize before preparing lunch.

And then, Sheri gets to work.

"I also have my own business," says Sheri. "I buy raw rice, parboil it, dry it, and grind off the husks. People buy my rice because it takes less time to cook, and that means less time finding fuelwood."

This budding entrepreneur lives in Sanergo village, in a corner of rural West Africa that is rich in culture and tradition, but poor economically. Seven out of ten people in this region live in poverty, according to the official World Bank definition.

Most citizens here scratch out a subsistence living in soil that can be scorched or sodden, depending on the time of year. If the harvest is healthy, some of the staple crops can be sold on the open market, although yields are usually just enough to feed a family.

But because of her small business, Sheri earns the money she needs to pay for school fees, uniforms and supplies, so that all her children can get an education. "I now have the opportunity to pay for my children's schooling," says Sheri. "The business lets me contribute to the family, by buying food or fuel. I can also help solve problems in the household, like if someone is sick and needs medicine."

Sheri owns no land, and has few belongings. Her home is made with bricks of mud and straw, capped with a thatch-roof. Illiterate and with no collateral, she couldn't just walk into a bank and fill out a loan application, even if she only needed a few dollars to kickstart her business.

So Sheri and nine other women in her village formed a "lending circle" and received a collateral-free loan from the Amasachina Self-Help Association, a community development group based in Northern Ghana. That first advance of $100 was divided into 10 micro-loans of $10 each, one for each woman to start a very small business. Sheri used her share to buy a first batch of raw rice.

As a condition of their involvement, the Sanergo collective guarantees the repayment of each individual loan. This is a defining characteristic of microcredit; the women act as each other's collateral. "It's a group loan, but we each have our own business," says Sheri. "We select women who we know can make a business work. There's been no problem paying back the loans. We have to, or we can't get future loans."

It Takes the Women to Raise a Village

In the nearby village of Datoyili, 70 women are members of micro-business groups. Some women make food products for local consumption, while others travel the hour's drive to Tamale, the region's commercial center. That city's sprawling market is a chaotic choreography of people selling goods ranging from magnificent crafts to mundane essentials.

The Datoyili women all started their businesses with loans and training from another community group, Maata N Tudu, which translates as Women of the North. This is their third year in the program. Once one loan is re-paid, the group is eligible for another, usually larger, advance. Flera MaHumma is the president of the loan circles in the village, and says that there were no other options for women trying to improve their economic fortunes.

"We had been looking for a long time for money to start our businesses," says Flera. "We couldn't find anything until we met Maata N Tudu. We're happy to work with them, and we all started businesses because of the loans."

"Before I got my first loan, I was in distress. I used to rely on my husband, but there were times he could not provide for me or the children. Today, when my husband doesn't have money, I can help. Now that I am involved in the loan programs, I have seen a change in my family."

Like most microcredit organizations around the world, Amasachina and Maata N Tudu both target women, who are often the poorest in their communities. They are usually the caregivers of the family as well, so if you help the women, the thinking goes, you help the children. If that includes education for the children, you also help the entire village.

Blessing or Burden?

Back in Sanergo, her now sleeping baby still strapped to her back, Sheri Feyakoyo walks on a dusty path that leads from one family of round huts to another. In the center of a courtyard, rice in a huge cast iron pot slowly simmers over a charcoal fire. Sheri occasionally stirs the rice with a rough hewn wooden spoon.

So could the microcredit focus on women just add to an already heavy burden? Sheri admits it does, although you won't hear her complaining. "It takes more time but it's worth it because of the money and the satisfaction I get out of it," she says. "It's my own business. It's not too much of a burden."

"And a lot of the businesses like processing rice can be done right in the compound alongside other

What Is Microcredit?

Microcredit is a development tool that offers a hand-up, not a hand-out. It's a way to provide small business start-up capital—often $100 or less—to people who don't qualify for traditional bank loans because they have no collateral or credit history. An amount that small may not seem like a lot, but for many living in the Southern world, it's enough to kickstart a micro-business selling food or crafts or telephone calls to people without phone service. In most programs, groups of people form lending circles, and act as each other's collateral. If one fails, the collective carries the loss.

Without access to capital, it's difficult to start or expand a business, even the tiniest of operations. In the absence of alternative banking options, many people are forced to borrow from money-lenders who charge outrageous interest rates. The poor can get trapped deeper in the pit of poverty.

In most cases, microcredit participants can borrow additional money once earlier loans are re-paid. Like business people everywhere, the entrepreneurial poor often need access to credit for a number of years to accumulate enough assets and savings to become self-reliant.

Many people argue that microcredit is not a panacea to poverty. The scheme can't help everyone lift themselves up by their bootstraps. For some people, just getting those metaphorical boots is the struggle. Konlan Lambongang is the executive secretary of Maata N Tudu—a microcredit group in Ghana that boasts of 7,000 members—and he admits that it's a challenge to help the poorest of the poor.

"There are people who might need grants at first so they can just survive, so they can just eat and live. They need to get themselves healthy enough so that they can make use of the loans, and have the ability to pay them back. We are actually reaching the entrepreneurial poor."

Microcredit was popularized—but not created, as earlier initiatives can be traced to South America—by Nobel Peace Prize winner Dr. Muhammad Yunus and the Grameen Bank, which he founded in 1976. It all started when he lent a few dollars from his own pocket to a group of poor artisans struggling to make ends meet. They had no savings, and to buy the supplies needed for their wares, they had turned to a loan shark. At the end of the day, their hard work amounted to mere pennies.

But because of the professor's investment of about a buck-and-a-half each, the 42 enterprising street vendors dramatically increased their profit margins. And all the "micro" loans were re-paid. These artisans became the first borrowers of the Grameen Bank, which today has seven million clients, helping over 30 million family members.

Globally, microcredit is being bankrolled by non-governmental organizations, community groups, foreign aid agencies, multilateral development institutions, credit unions and progressive banks, and social investors. Many programs also include skills training, and some encompass community development initiatives including health and education.

Today, microcredit programs around the world are helping over 100 million people get credit where credit is due.

chores, so we can do the work on both at the same time."

The women involved in lending circles in Northern Ghana have gained respect in the household and the village because they are bringing in money through their efforts. The micro-loan method strengthens dignity and independence in a way a handout could not. That, advocates say, is one of the main non-monetary benefits of microcredit.

The women here do seem more confident and ready to assert themselves. And that's been difficult for some men to accept. When one husband is asked if the new business ventures are good for his family, he acknowledges that they do help feed the kids and pay for school. He then puts down his meal of rice and groundnut stew, and complains that the men have never received a single penny. He also thinks the husbands should have more say in how the profit is spent. The women strongly disagree, and they let him know.

No Panacea to Poverty

There are many ideas other than microcredit that could contribute to change. For example, most of the microcredit women earmark their earnings for school fees and uniforms, so lower-cost education is one obvious way to help families.

Flera MuHumma, of the Datoyili loan groups, offers her wish list. "Besides the loan, we need a mill. The women who make shea butter or husk rice have to transport it all the way to Tamale to have it milled, and that's too far away. We have to arrange a truck to take us and that costs money. But if we had a mill that we could walk to, our profits would go up."

"What would also help families in the village," she adds, "is water. We don't have clean water. The women have to spend many hours looking for water and walking far, and that is time we can't spend on our businesses. And electricity. If we had light, the children could study at night and do better at school. And I wouldn't have to spend money buying kerosene for light."

The loans have fronted the start-up costs of many micro-enterprises in Northern Ghana, and the women have earned much-needed cash. Yet microcredit can only take the poor so far down the path of development. For those hoping to sell their products beyond their regional borders, marketing and distribution support is needed to take the next step.

A lack of credit is not the only cause of hardship in the Southern World. Many factors contribute to under-development, and providing business loans may or may not be the best way to lift the poorest of the poor out of poverty. But while the debate goes on, Sheri and Flera say they can't wait. They are too busy trying to turn small change into a better economic future.

Essay 2
An Empire for Poor Working Women

Somini Sengupta (2009)

Thirty-five years ago in this once thriving textile town, Ela Bhatt fought for higher wages for women who ferried bolts of cloth on their heads. Next, she created India's first women's bank.

Since then, her Self-Employed Women's Association, or SEWA, has offered retirement accounts and health insurance to women who never had a safety net, lent working capital to entrepreneurs to open beauty salons in the slums, helped artisans sell their handiwork to new urban department stores and boldly trained its members to become gas station attendants—an unusual job for women on the bottom of India's social ladder.

Small, slight and usually dressed in a hand-spun cotton sari, Mrs. Bhatt is a Gandhian pragmatist for the New India.

At 76, she is a critic of some of India's embrace of market reforms, but nevertheless keen to see the poorest of Indian workers get a stake in the country's swelling and swiftly globalizing economy. She has built a formidable empire of women-run, Gandhian-style cooperatives—100 at last count—some providing child care for working mothers, others selling sesame seeds to Indian food-processing firms—all modeled after the Gandhian ideal of self-sufficiency but also advancing modern ambitions.

She calls it the quest for economic freedom in a democratic India.

Her own quest offers a glimpse into the changing desires of Indian mothers and daughters, along with their vulnerabilities. Tinsmiths or pickle makers, embroiderers or vendors of onions, SEWA's members are mostly employed in the informal sector. They get no regular paychecks, sick leave or holidays. Calamities are always just around the corner, whether traffic accidents or crippling droughts. Without SEWA, they would be hard pressed to have health benefits or access to credit.

SEWA's innovations bear lessons for the majority of workers in the new Indian economy. Since economic reforms kicked off in 1991, the share of Indians employed in the informal sector—where they are not covered by stringent, socialist-era labor laws from the time of the cold war—has grown steadily to more than 90 percent, according to a recent government-commissioned report.

Among them, the report found, nearly three-fourths lived on less than 20 cents a day and had virtually no safety net. "Why should there be a difference between worker and worker," Mrs. Bhatt wondered aloud, "whether they are working in a factory, or at home or on the footpath?"

With 500,000 members in western Gujarat State alone, the SEWA empire also includes two profit-making firms that stitch and embroider women's clothing. More than 100,000 women are enrolled in the organization's health and life insurance plans. Its bank has 350,000 depositors and, like most microfinance organizations, a repayment rate as high as 97 percent. Loans range from around $100 to $1,100, with a steep interest rate of 15 percent. "We don't have a liquidity problem," its manager, Jayshree Vyas, pointed out merrily. "Women save."

A SEWA loan of roughly $250 allowed Namrata Rajhari to start a beauty salon 15 years ago from her one-room shack in a working-class enclave called Behrampura. At first, the neighborhood women knew little about beauty treatments. They only wanted their hair trimmed.

Then Mrs. Rajhari began threading their eyebrows to resemble perfect halfmoons, waxing the hair off their forearms and offering facials. During the wedding season, business blossomed. Mrs. Rajhari, who only has a 10th-grade education, expanded to a small room in the next lane.

With money from her business, Mrs. Rajhari installed a toilet at home, added a loft and bought a washing machine. "Before, I felt blank. I didn't know anything about the world," she said the other day. "Now, with my earnings, my children are studying."

Mrs. Rajhari then motioned to an object of pride in the living room. "The computer is also from my parlor money," she beamed. A daughter, Srishti, is now enrolled in a private English school. She wants to be an astronomer.

Behrampura buzzed with work and hustle on this morning. Men disassembled old television sets and put together new sofas. A woman pushed a cart loaded with used suitcases. Another herded a half-dozen donkeys loaded with construction debris.

Nearby, in another slum, shortly after dawn, Naina Chauhan rode a motorized rickshaw across town to start her shift as a gas station attendant. Her mother, Hira, now 65, had spent a lifetime ferrying coal, cleaning hospitals and going house to house to collect old newspapers. Naina said she resolved never to slog as her mother had.

Today, she contributes about $1 a month to her own SEWA-run pension plan. A SEWA loan has allowed her to clear a debt from relatives. She easily makes three times what her mother made collecting newspapers and as she shyly admitted this afternoon, almost as much as her husband, a hospital cleaner. She just recently married, and plans to move into her husband's family home soon. She said she hoped he would let her manage at least some of her own money.

Mrs. Bhatt's Gandhian approach is most evident in the way she lives. Her two-bedroom bungalow is small and spare. The one bit of whimsy is a white swing that hangs from the ceiling in the center of the living room. She uses her bed as a desk chair. Her grandson has painted a child's pastoral mural on the bedroom wall. She is known for having no indulgences.

"Above all you should emphasize her simplicity," said Anil Gupta, a professor at the Indian Institute of Management here who has followed SEWA's work for over a decade, sometimes critically. "In her personal life, there is not the slightest tinge of hypocrisy."

Mrs. Bhatt is not without detractors. The chief minister of Gujarat, Narendra Modi, accused her group of financial irregularities three years ago in the management of a rehabilitation program for earthquake victims. SEWA denied the charges and pulled out of the government-run program. Mrs. Bhatt accused Mr. Modi of trying to discredit the organization. Their war of words has since cooled down.

Born to a privileged Brahmin family, Mrs. Bhatt charted an unusual path for a woman of her time. She earned a law degree and chose the man she would marry. She began her career as a lawyer for the city's main union for textile workers, the vast majority of them men, and broke away in 1981 to create a new kind of union for women.

Early on, she won higher rates for women porters, then a landmark legal victory that allowed women to sell fruits and vegetables on the street without harassment from the police. The fishmongers and quiltmakers who were SEWA Bank's earliest customers sometimes stashed their checkbooks in the bank's steel cabinets, she recalled, lest their husbands discover they had money of their own.

At first, the women's ambitions were limited, she said. They wanted toilets, hair shears or sewing machines for work and money to pay for their children's school fees. Slowly, she noticed, they began to dream big. Mothers now want their daughters to learn to ride a scooter and work on a computer.

"They didn't see the future at that time," she said. "Expectations have gone very high."

Not long ago, Mrs. Bhatt recalled, she asked SEWA members what "freedom" meant to them. Some said it was the ability to step out of the house. Others said it was having a door to the bathroom. Some said it meant having their own money, a cellphone, or "fresh clothes every day."

Then she told of her favorite. Freedom, one woman said, was "looking a policeman in the eye."

R E A D I N G **56**

The 40-Percent Rule

Martha Burk (2006)

In 2004, women occupied just 10.4 percent of the seats on corporate boards in the world's largest 200 companies, reported Corporate Women Directors International. Two years later, the government of Norway announced that it would no longer be party to that disappointing statistic: The country's publicly traded firms would have to meet a 40 percent requirement for female board membership by 2008 or be shut down.

Predictably, Norwegian business interests cried foul. This was a quota—a word that has become synonymous with something unfair, undemocratic and, in this country, un-American. Critics trotted out the same hackneyed arguments we hear over here: *What if we can't find enough qualified women? We need more time for women to fill the pipeline. We need the best talent.*

But Karita Bekkemellem, Norway's minister of children and equality, was unbending. "The government's decision is to see to it that women will have a place where the power is, where leadership takes place in this society," she said. "This is very forceful affirmative action. I do not want to wait another 20 or 30 years for men with enough intelligence to finally appoint women."

It's almost unimaginable that the U.S. government, the Securities and Exchange Commission (which regulates publicly traded companies) or state governments (where corporations are chartered) would ever put forth such a requirement. If a U.S. woman legislator proposed a law similar to Norway's, she'd surely be slapped down by male colleagues, called a "quota queen" and seriously challenged in her next election campaign.

So how did the women in Norway get away with it? The corporate board quota was actually enabled by a history of quotas in Norwegian politics. Since 1986, the country's political parties, both left and right, have maintained gender quotas in government appointments. Subsequently, the Cabinet has been composed of at least 40 percent women and currently has its highest-ever ratio of women: eight out of 17 Cabinet ministers. In the Storting, Norway's parliament, women hold 65 of the 165 seats, or 39 percent. There goes the "can't find enough women" argument.

Not surprisingly, Norway now ranks fourth in the world in female representation in parliament. That's critical mass: Women can wield real power when it comes to setting priorities and passing legislation. By contrast, the U.S. ranks 68th, with only 15.1 percent of congressional seats held by women—about the same ratio as women on Fortune 500 boards (14.7 percent).

"No parliament has gone to critical mass without some affirmative mechanism"—like Norway's quotas—says Laura Liswood, secretary general of the Council of Women World Leaders, an organization composed of the 30 female presidents and prime ministers worldwide. The question Liswood struggles with, in regard to corporate boards, is how we get any sort of numbers without quotas. Shareholder actions, social pressure and corporations swearing they'll do better have not worked. It is well-known in business that like chooses like, whether in hiring or in nominating board members.

Nell Minow, founder of the Corporate Library, a research and information service on corporate governance, agrees that boards are chosen by what she calls "the CEO buddy system." But she disagrees on the solution. "I would oppose a quota system for boards," she says. "We need to break the stranglehold that CEOs have on the nominating process. We need genuine independent oversight—shareholders should choose the board."

Minow and Liswood agree on one other thing: The tipping point for women to become changemakers is when they hold 25 to 30 percent of the seats, either in government or business. Without those numbers in the U.S. Congress or state legislatures, laws to mandate equal participation for women on corporate boards aren't even a remote possibility. But just because the U.S. lacks a law like Norway's doesn't mean that boards *can't* fill board seats with women. Gender-balanced company leadership, besides bringing a broader perspective to the business table, would undoubtedly create more loyalty from female customers and investors—and, incidentally, avoid more government regulation, something corporate America constantly complains about.

Experts on gender and power believe we need new quotas that work as well as the old quotas—you know, the ones that aren't written down but are quotas just the same. For example, Wal-Mart—where

60 percent of employees and 70 percent of customers are female—gives only 38 percent of its management slots to women. Saks, which markets almost exclusively to women, has no female corporate officers and only two female board members. If unspoken quotas were not in place, would this happen? Hidden quotas arise from the same culture that says, *Let's reserve the presidency for men; the majority of Cabinet positions for men; the leadership of our largest businesses, universities, charitable institutions, media organizations and government agencies for men; and let women in only on a token basis.*

This is not just about the few women who reach the top echelons of business, but about how those in charge of company policy and behavior view women up and down the line. It's hard to imagine a majority-female corporate board tolerating pay and promotion policies that shortchange such women as the clerks at Wal-Mart, who have filed the largest sex-discrimination suit in history. It's equally implausible that a female governing board would have sanctioned male brokers at Morgan Stanley who entertained clients at strip clubs, or paid out record sexual harassment claims at Citigroup while transferring the guilty men instead of firing them, or spent millions at CBS wining and dining program sponsors at venues such as the Augusta National Golf Club which proudly discriminate against women.

Women who are all alone in a male boardroom can't be agents of change because they will be ignored or marginalized as "pushing an agenda." Women must reach that critical mass of about 30 percent. But how do we get there?

Not surprisingly, the most progress in overturning old quotas in business is happening in women-headed companies—which, in the Fortune 500 average 25 percent female board membership. In smaller firms—those ranked 501 to 1,000 on Fortune's list—women have appointed even more of their sisters to the board (33 percent, on average).

The bad news is that those women-on-top companies number a measly 20 out of the whole Fortune 1,000. And according to Catalyst, a research organization that tracks female board memberships, it will take another 70 years at the current rate for women to fill half the seats. That's two work lifetimes.

So . . . quotas, anyone?

CHAPTER **10**

Women and
Environmental Politics

Ana Isla and *Trina Filan*

Ana Isla, associate professor at the Centre for Women's Studies and the Department of Sociology at Brock University, Canada, teaches courses in social, environmental, and feminist theories, as well as sexuality, class, race/ethnicity, and women and development. Her expertise is within the women and development field (especially gift and subsistence economies). Her work in progress includes *Accumulation by Dispossession or Sustainable Development: An Ecofeminist Perspective*. Some of her papers appearing in local and international media because of their relevance to broad social concerns and policy development include "Who pays for the Kyoto Protocol?"; "Conservation as enclosure: An eco-feminist perspective on sustainable development and biopiracy in Costa Rica"; and "A struggle for clean water and livelihood: Canadian mining in Costa Rica in the era of globalization." Dr. Isla serves as a board member for the journals *Canadian Woman Studies* and *Capitalism Nature Socialism*.

Trina Filan is a Ph.D. candidate in Geography at the University of California, Davis, USA. Her dissertation focuses on material feminist and feminist political ecological framings of the rise in women farm ownership and operation in California, even as farm ownership has decreased in the general population. She also is interested in the socio-natural constructions of the uses of water and other natural resources in the western United States, a feminist environmentalist rethinking of nature–culture interactions, and the creation and legitimization of entrepreneurial space by marginalized populations, such as the homeless.

The day was clear
The sun shone bright
Upon my island home
When all at once wailing, echoed from her shores.
And it came whirling, swirling, churning and sweeping
A monstrous twenty-foot wave
With a booming voice and mighty hurt
Destroying everything in its way . . . .
Oh Tsunami you hit us
Expecting us to fall.
But we will rise stronger,
Much better than before.

Excerpt from "Tsunami You Hit My Island Home" by Thrishana Pothupitiya.

In this excerpt from her poem "Tsunami You Hit My Island Home," 17-year-old Sri Lankan poet Thrishana Pothupitiya writes of the loss she and others experienced when the 2004 tsunami devastated her community. It is a poignant reminder of the effects of global warming that is projected to change the earth's climate, shift weather patterns, exacerbate extreme weather events such as droughts and floods, melt ice caps, raise sea levels, and fragment habitats (IPCC, 2007). These changes are endangering the planet as we know it and are beginning to cause havoc to human communities through such "natural" disasters. The 2010 earthquake in Haiti is case in point. Scientists believe earthquakes are part of a host of geological disasters unleashed as a consequence of global climate change. The tragedy in Haiti, however, was especially devastating because it affected a nation impoverished by a history of colonialism and domestic corruption as well as by global capitalist "development."

Global system alteration is driven, in large part, by the burning of fossil fuels like coal and oil and by large-scale, industrial agricultural techniques that are employed to support and perpetuate global cycles of production and consumption. As discussed in the previous chapter, these cycles are also shaped by economic and governmental policies at local, regional, and global levels. They are designed to deregulate markets, lower economic and environmental barriers to trade, and allow natural resource extraction to proceed unimpeded. The reading "Temperature Rising: Four Essays on a Theme" by Minu Hemmati and Ulrike Röhr, Myralyn O. A. Nartey, Sabrina Regmi, and Leigh Brownhill provides a gender analysis of climate change, exploring its consequences on the world's most vulnerable people. It discusses the ecological crisis driven by global climate changes and the millions of environmental refugees who will lose families, homes, and livelihoods.

Climate change and other environmental problems are not the only adverse consequences of global economic development agendas. As discussed in other chapters, development also results in the displacement of women from the land into cities and factories where their use as cheap labor is exploited. While these policies are destructive in general to both human and nonhuman systems, people who belong to marginalized sociocultural groups (women, indigenous people, people of color, the poor, the very young and the very old, and the infirm) disproportionately experience the environmental effects of globalization. This is because they possess little political or social power to bring about changes either to policy or to practice. However, despite this lack of power, many groups participate in political movements around environmental issues in order to highlight their own struggles and the consequences of unbridled development. They work to effect changes in policy and practice, rather than allowing themselves and nonhuman nature to become victims of circumstance.

Climate Change

Climate change is an established scientific fact. Humans contribute with our rising output of greenhouse gases such as carbon dioxide and other products of fossil fuel consumption. Policies to halt climate change must address human impacts as well as technical aspects of the problem if they are to succeed. Women are essential to the solutions.

U.S. INACTION IS HARMING PEOPLE AT HOME AND ABROAD

- The United States, with only 6 percent of the global population, has been the largest contributor to climate change, producing the most greenhouse gases per capita in the world.

- Hotter weather is raising U.S. death rates among the very old and the very young and for those with heart and lung conditions. The cost: $31 billion per year by 2100.[1]
- Warming seas are blamed for increasing the number and severity of tropical storms and hurricanes in the North Atlantic, and for changing patterns of droughts and floods worldwide.
- Food emergencies in Africa, often from drought or flood, have risen threefold every year since the mid-1980s.[2]

WOMEN ARE ESSENTIAL TO CLIMATE CHANGE SOLUTIONS

- Women produce 60 to 80 percent of the household food supply in most developing countries and have long experience in coping with environmental shifts.[3]
- Women carry water, gather wood for fuel, and manage household resources worldwide. They are also the chief caregivers for victims of weather-related and other natural disasters.
- Acknowledging gendered divisions of labor, especially in the agriculture and informal sectors, is essential in drafting policy, not only to support the most vulnerable populations but also to enlist their knowledge.

WORLDWIDE, WOMEN ARE DISPROPORTIONATELY AFFECTED BY CLIMATE CHANGE

- The world's poor suffer most from erratic weather and its disruptions because they live in substandard housing in marginal land subject to drought or flood, or in crowded urban areas lacking essential services—and women are the majority of the world's poor.
- Discrimination means women worldwide are the first to lose their homes and their jobs after weather-related disasters, and the last to receive credit, technical help, and education on energy and resource conservation.

THE U.S. CONGRESS CAN RESTORE U.S. LEADERSHIP AGAINST GLOBAL WARMING THROUGH COMPREHENSIVE LEGISLATION

- Legislation must reflect the particular impact of climate change on women and their role as key agents in the U.S. and global response.
- Gender-specific data should guide discussions on the impact of climate change, possible policy remedies, and their effects.
- Women, their advocates, and gender experts must take part in the debate, and their recommendations must be heeded.

Notes

[1] Deschenes, Olivier and Greenstone, Michael, "Climate Change, Mortality, and Adaptation: Evidence from Annual Fluctuations in Weather and Mortality," National Bureau of Economic Research, Inc. (NBER) Working Paper No.13178, NBER, Cambridge June 2007.
[2] New Economics Foundation (NEF) and Working Group on Climate Change and Development: "Up in Smoke 2," NEF, London 2005.
[3] FAO (Food and Agriculture Organization of the United Nations). "FAO Focus: Women and Food Security", http://www.fao.org/ focus/e/ women/Sustin-e.htm. Accessed 6/24/08.

Source: http://www.wedo.org.

The chapter begins with an overview of globalization and economic development practices, addressing the ways women and gender are incorporated into those practices. This section discusses "sustainable development" and its implications for human and non-human communities worldwide. It is followed by a section on rainforest ecopolitics that presents two case studies of the effects of development policies, and sustainable development in particular, on women's lives. The third section explores environmental activism and presents examples of struggles to prevent degradation of the environment and the human communities that rely upon it. The chapter closes with a discussion of knowledge fostering progress toward truly life-sustaining practices in a sustainable society.

GLOBAL DEVELOPMENT AND THE ECOLOGICAL CRISIS

Development and Its Consequences

There is consensus among scholars that the present organization of most human societies is unsustainable. They reject the belief of unlimited economic growth and emphasize the natural limits of the planet to industrialization and consumerism (Lechner and Boli, 2004). In addressing the problems associated with economic growth, we must begin by recognizing global development and its consequences as a crisis of society, rather than as a referendum on the inadequacies of nature to meet human desires (Wallerstein, 2004). This crisis is rooted in contemporary globalization, economic development, and the accompanying proliferation of technologies and their consumption. The reading "Waikīkī," a poem by Hawaiian scholar-activist Haunani-Kay Trask, speaks of the development of Hawaii by corporate interests and the spoiling of its natural beauty and social communities by colonization, consumer indulgence, crime, and the vagaries of modern industrial growth. The beaches of Hawaii are currently being contaminated by a huge mass of floating garbage (mostly plastic) that some have described as twice the size of Texas. This garbage patch in the Pacific Ocean makes up the world's largest landfill and presents numerous hazards to marine life, fishing, and tourism.

You will remember from other chapters that economic policies of neoliberalism include the privatization and deregulation of economies that allow "free markets" to expand and operate with few impediments. Core ("First World") nations have instigated global trade practices that result in peripheral ("Third World") nations paying higher prices for imports while receiving lower prices for exports. Over time this price differential has meant that peripheral countries have had to export more coffee, timber, cotton, and other resource-extractive crops in order to pay their debt and to maintain access to development assistance. These extractive practices are not only exploiting ecosystems but are transforming entire cultures, displacing people from their land, and destroying the environment upon which all life depends.

U.S. president Harry Truman opened the era of development as an economic growth program to "underdeveloped" areas after World War II despite emerging evidence of the consequences of unbridled industrial growth on ecological systems. The Green Revolution (GR) of the 1960s, for example, which focused on increasing food crop yields through intensive breeding and heavy input of fertilizers and pesticides/herbicides, offers a cautionary tale for the successes, excesses, and failures of early development efforts. While some countries in Asia and Latin America did see increased yields, others (especially in Africa) did not. Importantly, a heavy environmental and economic price was paid as the fertility of the soil was lost and poor farmers became dependent on these new agricultural practices (Barndt, 2008). Women benefited little from GR technologies since they focused on cash crops destined for export (an arena belonging to men) rather than on subsistence crops that might alleviate family poverty and hunger (traditionally women's arena) (Sachs, 1996).

Over time, economic development policies encouraging economic growth have become one of the single most important strategies for extending the political and cultural influence of the Global North, maintaining its economic dominance, and advancing industrialization. Such global economic development extends capitalist markets worldwide and involves the transformation of goods and resources previously held in common into commodities (Vaughan, 2007). Although expansion of global economies in the late twentieth century coincided with recognition of the impending global ecological crisis, the concept of "sustainable development" was invoked in 1987 as a way to reconcile these forces on a global scale. Sustainable development implies the need for continued economic development as a way to save the planet. Defined as "development that meets the needs of the present without compromising the ability of future generations to meet their own needs" (World Commission on Environment and Development, 1987, p. 8), sustainable development recognizes that environmental problems are global and emphasizes that it is in the common interest of all countries to establish development policies that are sustainable. While this recognition is important, unfortunately it suggests that equity and social justice, economic growth, and environmental maintenance are all possible to achieve at once; it also implies that each country is capable of achieving its full economic potential without depleting its resource base. Sustainable development was debated in 1992 at the United Nations Earth Summit in Rio de Janeiro, Brazil, and again in Johannesburg, South Africa, at the 2002 Earth Summit. Meanwhile, the focus on development and sustainable growth serves to disguise the fact that the higher standard of living enjoyed in the industrial world is a result of the extraction of resources from peripheral nations through debt and trade.

This discourse of sustainable development has witnessed the movement away from traditional, locally oriented, and/or subsistence production toward "modern," export-oriented, and/or cash-crop production. In this kind of production, growth is measured in terms of exchange for profit in the global marketplace, and profits are derived from crops that depend on the clearing of large swaths of land and on the use of chemical fertilizers, herbicides, and pesticides that adversely affect both human and nonhuman communities. Farmers today face new challenges in the form of crop enhancements like genetically engineered (GE) plant species (Ronald and Adamchak, 2008). For example, this issue has become a problem in the central region of Vidarbha, India, where the multinational corporation Monsanto advocates the benefits of genetically modified cotton seed, promising high yields to farmers (men and women alike) but requiring the use of the herbicide Roundup®. Unfortunately, the costs of seeds and herbicide require most farmers to take out loans, often beyond their means, and if production does not go as well as planned, they are unable to repay their loans. Since Monsanto owns the intellectual property associated with the seed, farmers are unable to reuse seeds without paying Monsanto and no longer have the buffers of traditional agricultural practices that allowed them to recycle seeds from one harvest to the next or swap seeds with neighbors. In the Vidarbha region, where cotton crop failure has reached high levels, farmers are finding themselves in debt, and many have chosen suicide as a way to protest their problem (Shiva, 1999). A 2007 U.S. Public Broadcasting television program called the "The Dying Fields" estimated that one farmer commits suicide in Vidarbha every 8 hours (Scola, 2007).

This example also illustrates the ways the biotechnology industry is securing patent (ownership) rights over plants, animals, and genetic material. Indeed, since 1994 the

Agreement on Trade-Related Aspects of Intellectual Property Rights (TRIPS), which is administered by the World Trade Organization (WTO), has allowed core nations like the United States to put pressure on indebted peripheral countries and to block access to its market if those countries are unwilling to share environmental resources or commercial interests of nature with transnational corporations. One of the consequences of TRIPS is the commodification of resources, such as genetic material, DNA sequences, and knowledge created and held by indigenous and poor people, which had previously existed outside of the market system.

In this way, the conflation of economic development with sustainability and the international ratification of these principles have led to serious cultural and environmental problems, even as select groups of people around the world, particularly in the Global North, have benefited (Momsen, 2004; Resurreccion and Elmhirst, 2004). In other words, global economic arrangements provide benefits for the wealthy nations yet tend to cause a drain of resources from less wealthy nations. It is estimated, for instance, that the United States makes up about 5 percent of the world's population but consumes about one-quarter of the world's resources. According to the Global Footprint Network (2008), the per-capita ecological footprint (the amount of land and water used per person to produce the resources they consume and to absorb the wastes they produce) for the United States is over eight times greater than the ecological footprint for Africans.

Women and Development

Until 1970, women's place in these development policies focused mostly on maintaining their roles as wives and mothers as defined by Western cultures (Momsen, 2004). Women and gender did not have a prominent place in development efforts until 1970 when Ester Boserup published *Women's Role in Economic Development*, highlighting the integral role women play in subsistence agriculture in Africa and addressing the impacts of colonization and agricultural modernization (that is, the move away from subsistence toward cash-crop production) on gender relationships. Boserup's assertions that neither process took place to the benefit of women, despite women's prominent economic and resource-management roles, set in motion a wave of subsequent studies and activism around women and development throughout the world.

Since this time, nation-states, nongovernmental organizations (NGOs), international banks, and other organizations involved with development have attempted, in various ways and with varying levels of success, to incorporate women and women's interests into development efforts (Momsen, 2004). These efforts began with a focus on creating income-generation projects for women so that they might benefit from broader economic development schemes. Such blossoming of women in development (WID) programs in NGOs throughout the world and the international recognition of the importance of women's social and economic equality can be viewed as testament that women's lives and work matter. However, the abundance of these programs and their failure to adequately address the problems of women, the environment, and sustainability is illustrative of the complexities and difficulties of dealing with gender and power inequities. For example, WID programs have sometimes lacked cultural sensitivity and, rather than empowering women, have made their lives more difficult (Doss, 2001; Jewitt, 2000; Paulson, 2005).

An interesting illustration of WID programs missing their mark comes from Richard Schroeder (1993) and Judith Carney (1993). These authors studied the repercussions of various development programs in the Gambia, a region of western Africa. The area in question suffered two decades of drought through the 1970s and 1980s that prompted competition between male farmers (who traditionally planted in the drier uplands, but who were seeking new sites to plant) and female farmers (who traditionally planted in the lowlands and wetlands). In addition, development schemes had encouraged women as primary breadwinners by giving them rights to farm vegetables for the export market. This situation had unbalanced gender dynamics in families and provoked conflict between women and men. Over time these vegetable gardens had become so successful that women were asked to expand the lands on which they grew gardens, edging out male landholders and inciting more male resentment. At this point, a separate development scheme was initiated involving tree planting to "stabilize" the local environment. Although trees were to be planted in the same gardens the women were using for growing their export vegetables in order for simultaneous irrigation of the vegetables and trees, there was a complicating factor. Trees in this particular culture belong to the person who plants them (in this case, the women gardeners), but the land on which the trees are planted belongs to men. The trees, therefore, had the potential to complicate the landownership situation and give women claim to the land. Alternatively, if the women cared for the trees and did not claim the land, in a matter of years their garden plots would be shaded out, destroying their vegetable cultivation as well as giving men ownership to the land, the trees, and the infrastructure associated with the trees. This example illuminates gendered relationships to power, labor, land, agricultural products, and other resources that complicate development projects. In this case, not only were the attempts to create new agricultural opportunities gendered (a quality sorely misunderstood by "helpful" development agencies), but also attempts to "stabilize" the ecosystem had gendered ramifications that brought about gender-based conflict.

Critiques of WID gave way to an understanding that women and men, because of their different social and cultural roles and relationships, are affected by development differently and, therefore, have different access to the empowerment that development is supposed to provide. This new approach, known as Gender and Development (GAD), also acknowledged that women's experiences are not uniform even within a culture, but shaped by ethnicity, class, age, marital status, and religion, among other factors. Finally another approach, Women and Development (WAD), was based on a critique by women from "developing" nations that development, as demonstrated in both WID and GAD projects, was seldom undertaken from the perspective of the target or peripheral countries in mind. It called for a critique of colonialism and a focus on poverty reduction alongside women's empowerment.

These and other approaches to incorporating women into development efforts are always evolving, being critiqued, and changing to include new understandings (Momsen, 2004). Rationales for encouraging women's participation in development have included (1) the efficiency argument that including women makes good economic sense; (2) the empowerment argument that women's lack of power might be redressed through development; (3) the gender and environment argument that women are closer to nature and therefore most affected by environmental degradation as well as best positioned to care for the environment; and (4) the gender mainstreaming argument that women's equality with men is a fundamental human right and a prerequisite for successful development efforts.

As women lose traditional relationships to the land, they are encouraged to work in newly emerging industries. Such challenges to traditional lifestyles expose women to unfamiliar ways of living that cause stress and unsettle families and communities (Barndt, 2008; Resurreccion and Elmhirst, 2004). For example, globalization and market imperatives have drastically changed the circumstances of the formerly nomadic Negev Bedouins (Israel), whose new settlements have created problems associated with solid waste disposal. Ilana Meallem and Yaakov Garb discuss this problem in the reading "Bedouin Women and Waste-Related Hazards," focusing on Bedouin women's exposure to toxic effects that have increased their vulnerability as already-marginalized Arabs in a Jewish state. As mentioned in the previous chapter, research on the health impacts of toxic environments also focuses on field workers who are exposed to toxins through their work in floriculture (flower growing). For example, the reading "An Ugly Picture for Flower Workers and Their Children" by David A. Taylor explores the fresh flower industry in Ecuador and discusses the exposure of women and children to toxic pesticides. Similarly, as Hanna-Andrea Rother explains in the reading "Poverty, Pests, and Pesticides," poor women in South Africa are also exposed to health risks from using street pesticides in their homes as well as selling them in their efforts to earn money.

RAINFOREST ECOPOLITICS

With economic development comes the transformation of nature's bounty into commodities of global economic value (Isla, 2005; Shiva, 1999). Not surprisingly, local communities are at a disadvantage to effectively contradict development efforts backed both by their own governments and by global economic and political forces. The following section provides two case studies of the specific effects of economic development (especially sustainable development) on women's lives through a focus on the rainforest ecosystems of Costa Rica and Peru. It asks the following questions: (1) How has "debt-for-nature" been used to take over the natural commons and subjugate women in the rainforest of Costa Rica? and (2) How are free trade agreements being used to dispossess the natural commons and deprive women in the rainforest of Peru?

Debt-for-Nature in the Rainforest of Costa Rica

As already discussed, sustainable development frameworks advocate an expanding market system to solve the twin problems of peripheral countries' poverty/indebtedness and their environmental problems. One specific practice is the use of "debt-for-nature swap funds" whereby indebted countries repay loans with natural resources. The indebted country's "obligation" is to organize conservation areas and create conditions for sustainable development projects (such as ecotourism, mining, selling carbon credits, biotechnology) in exchange for the reduction of some of their foreign debt. Debt-for-nature mechanisms are supported by the Global Environmental Facility program of the World Bank and assisted through U.S. Agency for International Development (USAID) funds. Debt-for-nature has become a central mechanism for the Kyoto Protocol (an international agreement on climate change that, as of this writing, has still not been signed by the United States) as witnessed by the sale of oxygen or carbon "credits" from the rainforest to act as a "carbon sink" to help remedy problems associated with greenhouse gases. In other words, the absorption of CO_2 by the forest is used to compensate for the high emissions of industrialized countries. What this means is that the rainforest takes on economic value through the securing of CO_2 strategies, and it paves the way for carbon emissions to be traded on the open market. Many citizens, activists, and academics object to this method of commodifying the earth's resources. It is, in effect, the application of economic policies of neoliberalism to nature itself (Kovel, 2002).

Costa Rica, an indebted peripheral country, was persuaded to participate in this scheme. As a result, environmental nongovernmental organizations (ENGOs) in Costa Rica that organize conservation, forest management, and reforestation began to sell environmental services in the form of carbon credits to Norway, Germany, Holland, Mexico, Canada, and Japan (*El Estado de la Nacion*, 1996). In addition, the Costa Rican government enthusiastically promoted converting its diverse forest ecosystems into cash-crop producing regions by planting homogeneous forests of just one plant species like melina, teak, and eucalyptus, despite the fact that these trees do not naturally form part of Costa Rica's rainforest. This choice was clearly dictated by lumber-related North American industries. Since economically productive homogeneous forestation requires the cutting of all native trees and vegetation, soil erosion occurs, facilitating the loss of nutrients and the productive capacity of the soil. It also requires the application of chemical fertilizers. All these practices have negative effects on soil fertility, water retention, and biological diversity. In the rainforest, biodiversity means a great number of different tree species with different sizes of leaves, which lessen the impact of the rainfall and prevent erosion.

While sustainable development has defined the forest as "natural capital," rural women become "human capital." As forests become commodities for selling oxygen/carbon sink provisions to the industrial world, the sexual division of labor and women's condition have changed. Evicted from a forest, peasant families migrate toward cities to look for employment. Rural women need to find resources to assure subsistence and emotional support for themselves and their dispossessed family members. In this context, women become increasingly vulnerable to economic and sexual exploitation (Isla, 2007).

Pressured by the International Monetary Fund and the World Bank, indebted Costa Rica has become the premier ecotourism and tourism destination since the early 1990s. As discussed in other chapters, both local men and privileged men from core countries (United States, Canada, Spain, and others) collude to profit from the commodification of women in racialized sex tourism (Pettman, 1997). Not surprisingly, Costa Rica is a popular destination for child-sex tourism and has been called "a paradise for pedophilia." Ecotourism promotion, therefore, has linked conservation areas with tourism and promises a world of leisure, freedom, taste, and safe risk, at the same time that it portrays an image of women and children as exotic and erotic (Vaughan, 2007).

A DAY IN THE LIFE   **Preparing for Guests** by *Heather Ebba Maib*

Entza wakes in the morning and dresses herself in a skirt and button-down shirt. She then takes a hollowed out pumpkin to fetch the *yumi* (water) her family will use that morning to make a breakfast of manioc stew for the children. Manioc is also known as cassava or yucca and is quite poisonous if eaten raw. Sweet manioc is a staple of the Ecuadorian Anchuar diet and can be prepared much like a potato. It can be fried, boiled, baked, and ground into flour. After the children are fed, she goes to work in the family's *chacra* (garden) for about two hours.

Every family in the village has their own *chacra*. The *chacra* is the responsibility of the *núwa* (woman). Though the space for the *chacra* is cleared by the *áishmag* (men) of the family, it is cultivated and tended by the wives. Entza's husband Naanch has two wives, Santamik and Entza. Santamik and Entza go to the *chacra* and gather some of the plants they will need for that evening's dinner. Today they gather *inchi* (sweet potatoes), *kenke* (yams), *mama* (sweet manioc), *sepui* (onions), *namau* (jicama), *nuse* (peanut), *kuish* (pineapple), *kai* (avocado), and *jirnia* (pepper). Though *sepui* and *kuish* are not used as frequently as *jirnia* or *mama*, Entza and Santamik are gathering them to prepare for the guests their husband will bring to their home tonight. Medicinal and cosmetic plants, narcotics, and fishing poisons, in addition to fruit and vegetables, are also grown in Entza's *chacra*. Their family also grows *uruch* (cotton), *tsaank* (tobacco), *thai* (red dye for the textiles and face paint), *ajej* (ginger), and a variety of fruits such as *tsapa*, *katsuint*, *chiiyumi*, *yuwi*, and *unkuship*, which are hollowed out and used as bowls, plates, and pitchers for transporting a variety of things such as water.

When Entza and Santamik leave the garden, they go back to their oval-shaped home and begin to clean. The women wash the dishes and clothes and then sweep the floor, which is made of packed dirt, to remove the excess debris. Normally, their husband, Naanch, would leave in the morning to spend his day either hunting for game or fishing in the river. This month he is working at a resort on another part of the Kapawi River called an ecolodge. The Kapawi is located at the basin on the Ecuadorian Amazon. The Anchuar are native to this area and have been able to maintain their land, even in the face of the logging and oil companies. Some believe the ecolodge is a way for the Anchuar to preserve their native lands as well as to provide an economic alternative to logging and oil.

The lodge is located near the village, but it takes several days for her husband to walk from the village to the resort. Entza's eldest son, Pinchu, also works at the lodge. Only men work at the ecolodge and perform duties traditionally done by women. Many men are not accustomed to doing the work normally done by women. Their jobs at the lodge include cooking, cleaning, and serving the guests at the ecolodge. Entza's husband and son work at the lodge for a month at a time and come home for about three weeks or so. When they come back to the village from the lodge, the men spend their time hunting, fishing, clearing land for the *chacra*, and working on their blow guns. When the *áishmag* are home they spend their days socializing with the children and wives, as well as doing less strenuous tasks such as gathering logs for the fire and repairing, if needed, the baskets they have made.

The *áishmag* of the village will go hunting or fishing every few days for several hours. They will spend one day focusing on the hunting and take very few breaks. The days after they hunt they will stay home resting and working on smaller tasks. To prepare for the guests the *áishmag* of the village spend additional time hunting for game and fishing. It is customary for the Anchuar people never to let a guest go without meat.

When Entza's husband is away, she and the other wife do not allow visitors into their home. The person who builds the home is the head of the household and it is the decision of the head of the house to allow visitors. However, when Naanch is home, they will often welcome visitors to their home.

Today, Naanch, who guides tours of the land, has brought people to visit the village. Yesterday, he and the visitors traveled by boat to the village. The boat ride lasts approximately six hours, which is much quicker than the several days it takes to get to the village on foot. The people he has brought have come to the resort to learn about the beautiful lands around the Kapawi. The Anchuar people are the most knowledgeable about the land in their part of Ecuador. They can name every animal, plant, tree, and insect and have been called living encyclopedias by the people who have studied them. Naanch is leading the group on a tour of the land around the village while Entza and Naanch's eldest son, Pinchu, fishes for the dinner they will serve to their guests.

For their guest tonight, Entza and Santamik will make another manioc stew and serve fish, *kuish, nuse,* and *apai* (wild mango) from the trees in the forest. Entza boils the water and adds the *mama, kenke, sepui, namau,* and *jirnia.* After the ingredients are added, she covers the pot with *wawa,* which are large leaves. When the dinner is finished being prepared, Entza and Santamik serve their guests the stew, fish, and fruits. Anchuar women rarely speak to their guests or look them in the eye. After dinner, the women serve the manioc beer. The guests politely accept, though they are hesitant to drink because the beer is made from Entza's and Santamik's saliva. Since manioc is a shrub that has dense, starchy roots, the ancient "chew-and-spit" recipe is the traditional way to make this drink.

After Entza and Santamik have finished cleaning up after their guests, and the children have gone to sleep, Entza goes to bed, lulled to sleep by the symphony of frogs in the night forest.

In these ways, the corporatization of nature and commodification of life have profound consequences for human communities as well as for nature. The Costa Rican rainforest is disappearing at the rate of approximately 20,000 acres of land annually to make way for cattle grazing to supply cheap beef to the global fast food industry, for banana plantations owned by Chiquita® Banana of the United States, and for coffee plantations whose development has been stimulated by export-oriented policies (Pendergrast, 2000). This systematic deforestation results in lost biodiversity and cultural diversity, compromises the global ecosystem by removing a portion of the world's "lungs" (a reference to the fact that the tropical rainforest "breathes" in carbon dioxide and "exhales" oxygen), and undermines human communities and their most vulnerable members.

Free-Trade Agreements in the Rainforest of Peru

Although negotiations began in the 1990s to expand the North American Free Trade Agreement (NAFTA) to all countries in Central and South America and the Caribbean under a Free Trade Area of the Americas (FTAA), opposition has resulted in the signing of bilateral free trade agreements on a country-by-country basis. The negotiation of the agreement between the United States and Peru has been controversial, since Peru is encouraged to privatize its rainforest. In order to comply with free trade rules encapsulated in this trade agreement, the current administration of Peru attempted to create new regulations with the intention of eliminating laws sustaining collective property rights among indigenous communities in the upper and lower rainforests. This occurred despite the fact that communal property is recognized by the Peruvian Constitution, by the International Labour Organization (ILO), and by the Declaration on the Rights of Indigenous Peoples, approved by the United Nations. The approval of such legislation would cause significant changes in indigenous ways of life that sustain the forest ecosystem and its human communities.

Top 10 Surprising Results of Global Warming

AGGRAVATED ALLERGIES

Have those sneeze attacks and itchy eyes that plague you every spring been worsening in recent years? If so, global warming may be partly to blame. Over the past few decades, more and more Americans have started suffering from seasonal allergies and asthma. Though lifestyle changes and pollution ultimately leave people more vulnerable to the airborne allergens they breathe in, research has shown that the higher carbon dioxide levels and warmer temperatures associated with global warming are also playing a role by prodding plants to bloom earlier and produce more pollen. With more allergens produced earlier, allergy season can last longer. Get those tissues ready.

HEADING FOR THE HILLS

Starting in the early 1900s, we've all had to look to slightly higher ground to spot our favorite chipmunks, mice, and squirrels. Researchers found that many of these animals have moved to greater elevations, possibly due to changes in their habitat caused by global warming. Similar changes to habitats are also threatening Arctic species like polar bears, as the sea ice they dwell on gradually melts away.

ARCTIC IN BLOOM

While melting in the Arctic might cause problems for plants and animals at lower latitudes, it's creating a downright sunny situation for Arctic biota. Arctic plants usually remain trapped in ice for most of the year. Nowadays, when the ice melts earlier in the spring, the plants seem to be eager to start growing. Research has found higher levels of the form of the photosynthesis product chlorophyll in modern soils than in ancient soils, showing a biological boom in the Arctic in recent decades.

PULLING THE PLUG

A whopping 125 lakes in the Arctic have disappeared in the past few decades, backing up the idea that global warming is working fiendishly fast nearest Earth's poles. Research into the whereabouts of the missing water points to the probability that permafrost underneath the lakes thawed out. When this normally permanently frozen ground thaws, the water in the lakes can seep through the soil, draining the lake; one researcher likened it to pulling the plug out of the bathtub. When the lakes disappear, the ecosystems they support also lose their home.

THE BIG THAW

Not only is the planet's rising temperature melting massive glaciers, but it also seems to be thawing out the layer of permanently frozen soil below the ground's surface. This thawing causes the ground to shrink and occurs unevenly, so it could lead to sink holes and damage to structures such as railroad tracks, highways, and houses. The destabilizing effects of melting permafrost at high altitudes, for example on mountains, could even cause rockslides and mudslides. Recent discoveries reveal the possibility that long-dormant diseases like smallpox could reemerge as the ancient dead, their corpses thawing along with the tundra, get discovered by modern people.

SURVIVAL OF THE FITTEST

As global warming brings an earlier start to spring, the early bird might not just get the worm. It might also get its genes passed on to the next generation. Because plants bloom earlier in the year, animals that wait until their usual time to migrate might miss out on all the food. Those who can reset their internal clocks and set out earlier stand a better chance at having offspring that survive and thus pass on their genetic information, thereby ultimately changing the genetic profile of their entire population.

SPEEDIER SATELLITES

A primary cause of a warmer planet's carbon dioxide emissions is having effects that reach into space with a bizarre twist. Air in the atmosphere's outermost layer is very thin, but air molecules still create drag that slows down satellites, requiring engineers to periodically boost them back into their proper orbits. But the amount of carbon dioxide up there is increasing. And while carbon dioxide molecules in the lower atmosphere release energy as heat when they collide, thereby warming the air, the sparser molecules in the upper atmosphere collide less frequently and tend to radiate their energy away, cooling the air around them. With more carbon dioxide up there, more cooling occurs, causing the air to settle. So the atmosphere is less dense and creates less drag.

REBOUNDING MOUNTAINS

Though the average hiker wouldn't notice, the Alps and other mountain ranges have experienced a gradual growth spurt over the past century or so thanks to the melting of the glaciers atop them. For thousands of years, the weight of these glaciers has pushed against the Earth's surface, causing it to depress. As the glaciers melt, this weight is lifting, and the surface slowly is springing back. Because global warming speeds up the melting of these glaciers, the mountains are rebounding faster.

RUINED RUINS

All over the globe, temples, ancient settlements, and other artifacts stand as monuments to civilizations past that until now have withstood the tests of time. But the immediate effects of global warming may finally do them in. Rising seas and more extreme weather have the potential to damage irreplaceable sites. Floods attributed to global warming have already damaged a 600-year-old site, Sukhothai, which was once the capital of a Thai kingdom.

FOREST FIRE FRENZY

While it's melting glaciers and creating more intense hurricanes, global warming also seems to be heating up forest fires in the United States. In western states over the past few decades, more wildfires have blazed across the countryside, burning more area for longer periods of time. Scientists have correlated the rampant blazes with warmer temperatures and earlier snowmelt. When spring arrives early and triggers an earlier snow-melt, forest areas become drier and stay so for longer, increasing the chance that they might ignite.

Source: http://www.livescience.com/environment/top10_global_warming_results-1.html

Other groups associated with privatization include nongovernmental organizations with carbon credit projects linked to the Kyoto Protocol, especially those involved with eco-tourism in Peru. For instance, protected areas are under *Intendencia de Áreas Naturales Prote-gidas* (INRENA), which, in "association" with Yanesha indigenous communities, has created the *Reserva Comunal Yanesha* where ecotourism and oil drilling "exist" jointly. Even though protected areas are under INRENA, international groups are becoming involved in rainfor-est management. For instance, land in *Reserva Comunal Cutivireni* is organized by Cool Earth, a British organization, to sell half an acre of rainforest for USD$50. Cool Earth has projects in Peru, Brazil, and Ecuador. Another international project is *Reserva Comunal El Sira*, organized by Parks Watch from Duke University's Center for Tropical Conservation, in Shipibo-Conibo, Asháninka and Yanesha's land. Parks Watch promotes reforestation using "valuable species" with "interesting potential" for markets such as oils, cosmetics, industrial supplies, and natural medicine. These organizations promote ecotourism.

Land privatization also implies a serious alteration of indigenous knowledge about soil and its proper management for food security. Such practices are dictated by oil prospecting and homogeneous plantations. For instance, after 38 years of oil drilling, Occidental Petro-leum Company and Pluspetrol-Korea-Yukong corporations have allowed the construction of labor camps, roads, and pipelines. Pollution and noise produced by bomb operations are modifying the land, contaminating rivers, and destroying ecosystems and wildlife on which indigenous communities depend (Earth Rights International et al., 2006). Privatiza-tion also facilitates the expansion of biofuels and the mono-cultivation of cash crops such as corn, sugarcane, African palm, and soy. In contrast, the traditional migrant agriculture of *roza-tumba-quema* is compatible with Amazonian ecology and the nature of its soil. Burning the slashed plot accelerates the decaying process to the advantage of certain food-producing plants, and the remaining ashes provide mineral energy utilized for cultivation. This kind of agriculture fosters wildlife, reduces external dependency, decreases climate-change risk, and removes vulnerabilities such as plagues and other problems and illnesses (Flores, 1998).

Amazonian people are endowed with one of the most diverse ecosystems on the planet. Antonio Brack (1997), current Minister of Environment in Peru, has estimated that indigenous communities know 890 medicinal plants, 557 wood species, 1500 ornamental plants, 102 dyes, and 44 types of oil. More than 65 indigenous and mixed communities derive their livelihood from the forest and its waters, an existence that has nurtured com-plex socioeconomic and cultural systems with distinct ways of describing and interacting with the world. Subsistence forest-dwelling households, despite the pressures of the market economy, have been able to create an "art of good life" with free access to natural resources and with the knowledge and means to use and transform them. The freedom of these for-est dwellers lies in the knowledge of, and access to, forest resources (Gasché et al., 2006). This knowledge does not separate people from nature. As described below, this is the "art of good life" in the Peruvian Amazon:

> For Amazonian people, rivers are alive. Rivers are at the centre of activities where men gather before sunrise to fish and hunt and women congregate to wash the clothes, collect water for cooking, take baths, and wash their young children. In each town, the river allows the women and men to grow food and raise cattle. Every household has a piece of land which they are responsible for ploughing, planting and collecting its fruits. Since the land is still common land, agriculture is practiced through the slash and burn technique which is a very sustainable system because it allows the forest to regenerate. During the afternoon, after school, girls and boys

gather at the river to swim, bathe, pick up shrimp, fish, collect drinking water, practice art with small stones, canoe, and participate in jumping competitions from the tree which is usually standing in the middle of the river during widening season. Medicinal plants which grow on the banks of the river are used in food and to cure illnesses. At night, the river provides the quiet needed for a good night's sleep. The river is always there waiting to be used. It produces food and drinks, medicine and entertainment; in effect giving rainforest inhabitants life and livelihoods. The river and its products belong to everyone who lives there and thanks to it, people grow up physically and mentally healthy. Now, this may seem to some of you as a despicable state of underdevelopment and some of you would refer to Peru as a non-resource nation, but rainforest people think of it as subsistence, you have what you need (Isla, 2005).

ENVIRONMENTAL ACTIVISM

Political activism against the degradation of both human and nonhuman environments has proliferated throughout the world as rural people, the poor, and indigenous people defend their lives, environments, cultures, and knowledge from destruction and/or appropriation by the free market. In the foregoing example of the rainforests, despite their hardships and the scope of the problem, indigenous people have organized resistance. In Costa Rica, for example, forest dwellers know their human rights have been violated by MINAE (the Costa Rican Ministry of the Environment and Energy responsible for the management of Costa Rica's national parks and other protected areas) and other organizations that call themselves "environmentalist." With the support of local municipalities, women are defending their rights to secure livelihoods. Similarly, in Peru in 2008, after several months of negotiation, indigenous women and men confronted the privatization laws and what they called a systematic violation of their human rights. People from 65 different ethnicities initiated a national mobilization by taking over and paralyzing the oil, gas, and electricity production of the entire country in order to oppose laws placing their communal land for sale. After nine days of tense negotiations in which the entire country participated (and where many were ready to die rather than submit to the alienation of land as property), the Peruvian parliament eventually voted to approve the elimination of all proposed legal instruments for privatization orchestrated by its president.

Two examples of local, grassroots environmental activism by women that have had global effects also include the Chipko Movement and the Green Belt Movement. The Chipko movement originated in the Garwhal Himalayas in India in the 1970s in resistance to economic development threatening their land and livelihood. The women used nonviolent resistance through tree hugging to keep trees from being felled for commercial forestry and mining efforts. Such practices were affecting women's abilities to gather wood for fuel and contributed to soil erosion that threatened farming and the raising of livestock. Although both men and women took part in the Chipko Movement, they did so for different reasons: men tended to want to preserve the forest for local commercial development, while the women sought to preserve their subsistence livelihoods and to prevent soil erosion; they were also the first to create organized resistance (Mellor, 1998). After the government placed a ten-year ban on logging, the women of the region began to develop new and less-resource-intensive ways of using the forest (FAO, no date). The Chipko Movement has inspired many other indigenous people to take political action against the exploitation of traditional resources.

ACTIVIST PROFILE **Wangari Maathai**

Wangari Maathai, born in Nyeri, Kenya, in 1940, was the first woman in East and Central Africa to earn a doctorate. She joined the faculty of the University of Nairobi, teaching veterinary anatomy. Soon she became the first woman to head a university department in Kenya.

In the late 1970s, she became active in and eventually chaired the National Council of Women in Kenya, where she introduced the idea of community-based tree planting to prevent soil erosion. Her idea eventually became the Green Belt Movement, and, through its work, Professor Maathai has helped African women plant more than 40 million trees. By making connections between women's rights and the environment, she soon became known as "The Tree Mother of Africa." She says, "I placed my faith in the rural women of Kenya from the very beginning, and they have been key to the success of the Green Belt Movement. Through this very hands-on method of growing and planting trees, women have seen that they have real choices about whether they are going to sustain and restore the environment or destroy it. In the process of education that takes place when someone joins the Green Belt Movement, women have become aware that planting trees or fighting to save forests from being chopped down is part of a larger mission to create a society that respects democracy, decency, adherence to the rule of law, human rights, and the rights of women. Women also take on leadership roles, running nurseries, working with foresters, planning and implementing community-based projects for water harvesting and food security. All of these experiences contribute to their developing more confidence in themselves and more power over the direction of their lives."[1]

As a political activist, Prof. Maathai advocated for multiparty elections and ending government corruption. As a result, she was imprisoned and attacked. In 2002, she was elected to parliament and then appointed Assistant Minister of Environment, Natural Resources, and Wildlife.

In 2004 she was awarded the Petra Kelly Prize for the Environment, the Sophie Prize for environment and sustainable development, and the Nobel Peace Prize. In 2005, *Time* magazine named her one of the 100 most influential people in the world, and *Forbes* magazine hailed her as one of the 100 most powerful women in the world. In 2006, she joined with other women Nobel laureates to form the Nobel Women's Initiative that advocates for peace and women's rights.

To learn more about Wangari Maathai, read her memoir, *Unbowed: A Memoir.* New York: Alfred A. Knopf, 2006, and visit the Greenbelt Movement's Web site at www.greenbeltmovement.org.

[1] http://greenbeltmovement.org/c.php?id=11

In Kenya, the Green Belt Movement (GBM) began in 1977 when Dr. Wangari Maathai started a rural tree-planting program (see sidebar) to address the lack of trees for fuel, the gathering of which was (and still is) women's work. The lack of nearby trees for fuel can add many hours of labor to a woman's day and expose her to dangers as she goes far from her village to find fuel. The tree-planting initiative was also supposed to prevent advancing desertification and soil erosion problems (Mellor, 1998). Hundreds of women's groups were set up, hundreds of tree nurseries began to employ thousands of women, and more than a million trees had been planted by 2000. In 2007, the GBM planted 4.9 million trees in Kenya alone (GBM, 2008). GBMs have been started in many other African countries, and the principles of the movement have been employed in greening projects in U.S. inner cities (Mellor, 1998). For her work, Maathai was awarded the Nobel Peace Prize in 2004. The Green Belt Movement is discussed in the reading "Temperatures Rising" and featured in the essay by Leigh Brownhill.

Other instances of women's activism at the grassroots level to resist the environmental and social consequences of development include the struggles of the Zapatistas of Chiapas (the poorest state in Mexico) who began their opposition to NAFTA in 1994. As Zapatistas faced increasing hostilities from government-armed forces and paramilitary groups, they organized four autonomous municipalities (*San Pedro de Michoacán, General Emiliano Zapata, Libertad de Los Pueblos Mayas,* and *Tierra y Libertad*), provided healthcare for communities, and built an herbalist laboratory and center for preserving foods. They also launched *La Otra Campaña* (The Other Campaign), designed to allow grassroots organization of political platforms and movements that embrace the needs and desires of indigenous people, the poor, and the disenfranchised (Barndt, 2008). In addition, indigenous women are now able to teach traditional knowledge in their villages and in their languages. These projects have encouraged the empowerment of women herbalists, bone healers, and midwives (Muñoz, 2008).

A final example of grassroots, local activism by individuals, groups, and coalitions includes activities against the widespread use and dumping of toxins. Such toxic disposal of pesticides, electronic waste, and industrial chemicals is an especially serious problem that has increased over the past few decades (especially in regard to the large amounts of electronic waste generated mostly by the Global North). Toxic dumping relies on the premise that (1) the lives of individuals in the poor nations are worth less than those of individuals in wealthy regions; (2) peripheral countries tend to be "under-polluted" compared with core nations; and (3) a clean environment is a luxury good to be pursued by people in rich countries with high life expectancies. However, this dumping has been challenged by indigenous Ecuadoreans, for example, who resist the dumping of billions of gallons of toxic oil wastes into the region's rivers and streams by the Chevron Corporation and its associates (Charman, 2008).

Political activism also takes place at the national and international levels as struggles against the corporate world have increased with knowledge of the relationship between globalization and environmental degradation. Radical political action was taken in Ecuador, for example, on behalf of nature by granting it constitutional rights and resisting the idea that nature is property to be exploited. Nature now "has the right to exist, persist, maintain and regenerate its vital cycles, structure, functions and its processes in evolution" (Revkin, 2008). Similarly, Brazilian education minister, Cristovo Buarque, has critiqued the arrogance of sustainable development by commenting that if the riches of the Amazon are to be understood as a global commons, then the riches of the West and such resources as oil reserves and financial capital should also be shared. "New York," he explained, "as the central location of the United Nations, must [also] be internationalized. At least Manhattan should belong to humanity. Also Paris, Venice, Rome, London, Rio de Janeiro, Brasilia, Recife. Every city of the world, with its specific beauty and history, should belong to humanity. If the U.S. wants to internationalize the Amazon, due to risks of leaving it in the hands of Brazilians, we have to internationalize the U.S. nuclear arsenal, because it has been provoking destruction a million times more than the regretful burnings done in the Amazon forest."

Talking Trash by *Martin Medina*[1]

The world throws away more than 2 billion tons of garbage every year. And though recycling rates are at historic highs, trash heaps are piling up in rapidly growing countries like China and India. So, how do we create a solution to the global garbage crisis that isn't a load of rubbish?

RICH REFUSE

Unsurprisingly, the wealthier the person, the more garbage he or she produces. The good news? As recycling rates increase, the amount of trash per person in rich countries is leveling off. But it's beginning to overflow everywhere else.

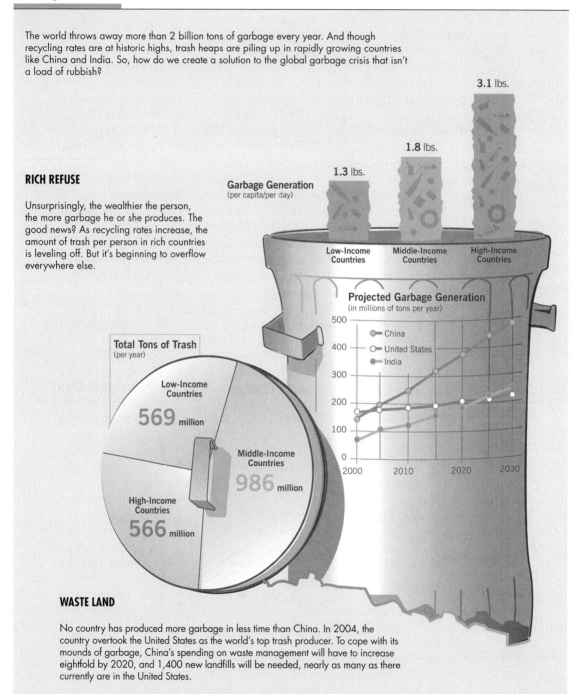

Garbage Generation
(per capita/per day)

1.3 lbs. — Low-Income Countries
1.8 lbs. — Middle-Income Countries
3.1 lbs. — High-Income Countries

Projected Garbage Generation
(in millions of tons per year)

- China
- United States
- India

Total Tons of Trash
(per year)

Low-Income Countries
569 million

Middle-Income Countries
986 million

High-Income Countries
566 million

WASTE LAND

No country has produced more garbage in less time than China. In 2004, the country overtook the United States as the world's top trash producer. To cope with its mounds of garbage, China's spending on waste management will have to increase eightfold by 2020, and 1,400 new landfills will be needed, nearly as many as there currently are in the United States.

IN THE DUMPS

Your trash says a lot about you. Open up a trash can in New York City, for example, and you will find evidence of its resident's wealth: There will be as much food packaging—paper, wrappers, or plastic—as leftover food, plus toys and electronics barely off the shelf. But in poorer cities such as Cairo, garbage piles are full of the inedible remains of fruits and vegetables.

Waste Composition

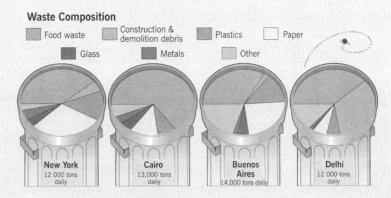

- Food waste
- Construction & demolition debris
- Plastics
- Paper
- Glass
- Metals
- Other

New York — 12 000 tons daily
Cairo — 13,000 tons daily
Buenos Aires — 14,000 tons daily
Delhi — 12 000 tons daily

BAG IT, BURN IT, OR BIN IT

How countries take out the trash varies enormously. Some countries, such as Turkey, rely on landfills; countries with space constraints, like Japan, send most garbage to incinerators. In the United States, where more than half of all trash heads to landfills, the number of dump sites has decreased significantly in recent years—from 6,300 in 1990 to fewer than 1,800 in 2006—but the average size of each site has grown dramatically.

Where Trash Goes:

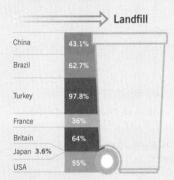

Landfill

China	43.1%
Brazil	62.7%
Turkey	97.8%
France	36%
Britain	64%
Japan	3.6%
USA	55%

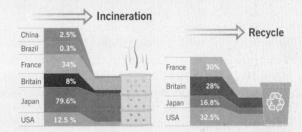

Incineration

China	2.5%
Brazil	0.3%
France	34%
Britain	8%
Japan	79.6%
USA	12.5 %

Recycle

France	30%
Britain	28%
Japan	16.8%
USA	32.5%

CHOOSING TO REUSE

Americans recycle twice as much trash as they did 20 years ago, mostly due to thousands of local recycling programs. In countries where such programs are rare, the poor often step in to fill the void. Worldwide, at least 15 million people make a living by recovering and recycling trash. Brazil boasts one of the world's highest aluminum recycling rates thanks largely to the 500,000 trash pickers who toil on the streets collecting refuse.

Recyclying Rates

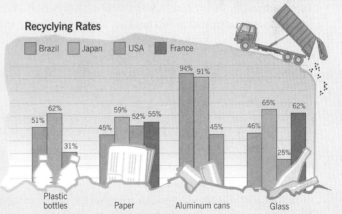

- Brazil
- Japan
- USA
- France

Plastic bottles: 51%, 62%, 31%
Paper: 45%, 59%, 52%, 55%
Aluminum cans: 94%, 91%, 45%
Glass: 46%, 65%, 25%, 62%

[1] Martin Medina is a waste management consultant for the World Bank and the United Nations and author of The World's Scavengers (Lanham: AltaMira Press, 2007).
Sources: NEW YORK CITY DEPARTMENT OF SANITATION LIVING FROM WASTE: LIVELIHOODS OF THE ACTORS INVOLVED IN DELHIS INFORMAL WASTE RECYCLING ECONOMIC, ASSOCIATION PARA EL ESTUDIO DE-LOS RESIOUS SOLIDOS; WORLD BANK; UNITED NATIONS: DEFRA, JAPANESE MINISTRY OF ENVIRONMENT: ENVIRONMENTAL PROTECTION AGENCY: OECO; COMPROISED EMPRESARIAL PARA RECICLAGEM

The international environmental justice movement also offers another powerful outlet for addressing toxic dumping and other forms of environmental degradation. It emphasizes the ways corporations affect already marginalized communities by seeking to operate in places where environmental and economic regulations are severely diminished or nonexistent (Schroeder et al., 2008; Sze and London, 2008). At the transnational level, individuals and groups with global environmental awareness, mostly in the Global North, have organized against development, imperialism, and its relationship to environmental degradation. Such efforts by Development and Environment Social Movements and NGOs facilitated the "alternative summit" of the 1992 Earth Summit. Also on the occasion of the 50th anniversary of the founding of the World Bank and the International Monetary Fund in 1995, a campaign for their dismantling was led by international NGOs, who cited evidence of widespread poverty, inequality, and suffering among the world's peoples and damage to the world's environment as a result of these international agencies.

Since 2001, the World Social Forum (WSF) has been the biggest antiglobalization gathering in which almost a quarter-million people meet annually to coordinate world campaigns, share and refine organizing strategies, and inform each other about movements from around the world and their issues. It usually meets in January when the "great capitalist rival," the World Economic Forum, is meeting in Davos, Switzerland. Initially convened in 2001 and 2002 in Porto Alegre, Brazil, by local civic organizations, the annual forum has taken place in peripheral nations around the world.

One of the most important networks organized through the WSF is the World March for Women (WMW), an international feminist action movement that focuses on identifying and eliminating the causes of poverty and violence against women worldwide. The WMW seeks to act through solidarity and collective political action by women and grassroots organizations around the world to create political, social, and economic change. The WMW is not alone, however, in uniting women in political action to seek redress for impingement upon, and destruction of, livelihoods, lifestyles, and environments. The Women's Environment and Development Organization (WEDO) was founded in 1989 to influence environmental policy-making around the world by bringing women's voices and environmental perspectives to the table (MacGregor, 2006). Finally, the Women's Environmental Network (WEN) was founded in 1988 to help "ordinary women" understand the links between gender, environment, and health, and to make healthier consumer and household choices for their families and the planet (WEN, 2004).

CONCLUSION: TOWARD SUSTAINABILITY FOR LIFE

This chapter has addressed environmental degradation as a crisis of production and consumption rather than a crisis of nature. The higher standard of living enjoyed in the industrial world is an outcome of unequal exchange relations between core and peripheral nations over the last centuries. Appropriation of the resources of poor nations has resulted in their underdevelopment at the same time that it causes severe environmental degradation. As illustrated by the ecopolitics of the rainforest of Costa Rica and Peru, the concept of "sustainable growth" encourages privatization and commodification and continues to be backed up by depredation, fraudulence, and violence against nature and indigenous peoples.

Two related approaches facilitate knowledge on ways to best understand and resist environmental degradation. First, feminist political ecology asserts that gender is crucial to understanding the ways various power relations influence people's interactions with, and struggles over, the environment and resources. It uses a feminist perspective to analyze women's knowledge, rights, access to, and control over, resources (Hovorka 2005; Sultana 2006; Rocheleau, 2008). Gender is expressed, in part, through rules dictating the ways men and women may interact with their natural and built environments and with one another. According to Hovorka (2005, p. 297), "men and women interact with the environment in different ways for different purposes, with differential rights of access to, control over, and use of productive resources, such as land and labor, because of their relative position and power within socio-structural hierarchies and the wider political economy." Feminist political ecology seeks to understand these differences and their consequences for people's everyday lives, especially in terms of their implication for environmental and natural resource management. This approach analyzes the gendered experiences associated with environmental change that brings with it changing landscapes, social relations, and livelihoods.

Ecofeminism is very similar in approach to feminist political ecology, although it is more often used to explore the relationship or intersectionality between the domination of nature and that related to class, race, sex, and species (assigning different values or rights to beings on the basis of their species membership). Ecofeminism challenges sustainable development and maintains the view that there exists a direct link between the oppression of women (gender justice) and the oppression of nature (ecological justice). This is a specific difference between ecofeminism and feminist political ecology. The latter avoids essentializing and universalizing "women" by equating the oppression of all women with the domination of the environment and instead examines gender's place in the environmental landscape, exploring gender as a factor in women's lives. In contrast, ecofeminists insist that women's and nature's liberation are a joint project (Merchant, 2005; Mies, 1986; Salleh, 2004, 2009; Warren, 2000) and they point out that concepts like growth, development, and progress are inextricably linked to the "masculinist" technology of warfare and conquest (von Werlhof, 2008).

Ecofeminists critique practices that reduce nature to inert resources and exploit women as free domestic labor, cheap wage labor, and fodder for the sex industries. They argue that nature is an exhaustible good that humans must learn to conserve by living

IDEA FOR ACTIVISM   **Sisters on the Planet Party Guide**

EVERYTHING YOU NEED TO KNOW TO HOST A SUCCESSFUL PARTY AND TAKE ACTION ON CLIMATE CHANGE

1. PLAN, PLAN, PLAN

Time and Place

Plan the party at a time when your group normally meets for meetings, i.e., after classes, work, and/or during evening hours of the week, when most people are in town and available to meet.

Perhaps, the group can meet in someone's home, apartment, dorm room, community center, church, or other venue that you can use for a few hours that is equipped with a television and DVD player.

Equipment Needed

Order your "Sisters on the Planet" DVD from Oxfam America's Web site or download the videos from WEDO's Web site at www.wedo.org.

—If you order the DVD:

Television and DVD player would be ideal to play the full "Sisters on the Planet" video.

—If you download from the Web site:

Laptop, a full Internet connection, a projector, speakers, screen, or wall for easy viewing.

2. GET YOUR INVITATIONS OUT

Send guests your Sisters on the Planet House Party invitations. Develop your guest list, and send your invitations! Be creative and show that fun and politics do mix. Be sure you're clear about the purpose and activities of your event. Title your invite something like this: "Support Global Sisterhood—help the women around the world lead climate change solutions and adapt to the climate crisis. Demand Congress to pass equitable climate change legislation now!" When you write your invitation, we suggest that you set the party duration between one and a half to two hours.

Follow up directly. By maintaining personal contact, you can make sure your friends and family read your invitation and reply.

WEDO recommends: *Instead of paper invitations create an invite using programs such as evite.com to easily send a creative invite to your guests. If you do use paper invitations send them on recycled or sustainably produced stationary. Calling is always a great way to invite people to parties as well as connect with them.*

3. DECIDE ON ONE OR MORE ACTIVITIES AND GATHER MATERIALS

Letter Writing

Collect email addresses or the local mailing addresses of your legislators at www.senate.gov and www.house.gov. Search for your local legislators to find their individual Web sites and contact information. Go to the "contact" tab on their sites to find the district office addresses. Note: It's important that you only mail to local district offices. Do not send mail to the Washington, DC, offices because delivery will be delayed.

If you are e-mailing the letters, have your guests type personalized letters about their experience with climate change in their communities and how they want their representatives to approach the issue.

If you are mailing letters gather enough envelopes, pens, and stamps for your guests; don't expect your guests to bring them. Have paper and pens available so that your guests can write their own, personal letters about women and climate change.

Review your RSVP list. Make sure you have enough copies of the materials you'll need to write the letters. Don't force people to share.

Write Letters to the Editor of Your Local Newspaper

Bring a woman's perspective to a story on climate or the environment that's reported in your local paper by writing a 300-word or less letter to the editor. You may want to use information from WEDO'S resources and fact sheets available in the 'Learn' section of our online toolkit. Sign the letter with your name. Send it to the editor in a timely fashion following the story about climate change in the newspaper.

WEDO recommends: *Emailing is the most environmentally sustainable way to send letters to your legislators. However, we recognize this is not the most effective. If you do plan to mail the letters use recycled and sustainably produced paper, envelopes, and pens. Buy stamps that support environmentally sustainable initiatives and/or women's rights.*

Create Your Own Addition to Sisters on the Planet

Are you already doing something in your community about climate change? Is there a woman or women in your organization/community/networks who are advocating for action on climate change? Want to show the U.S. why your community is demanding U.S. action on climate change? Add your story to the "Sisters on the Planet" video by creating your own! Here's how:

Have a video camera available to record why you want your senator or congress person to support mitigating or adapting to climate change.

Create a video about how your particular community is impacted by climate change or what you are doing to lessen your impact and help in preventing further climate change.

Send your video to WEDO and we will post it on our website!

WEDO notes: *Examples of what you are doing in your community to mitigate your impact include recycling, using LED light bulbs, driving a hybrid, eating less meat, shopping at local farmer's markets and buying sustainably grown food and/or sustainable products.*

4. PREPARE YOUR HOUSE

- Make sure there's enough seating.
- Make sure there are enough tables. You'll need them for food, materials, and writing.
- On the day of the party, make sure the venue is visibly marked. This is especially important if you live in an apartment complex.
- Make sure your DVD player and TV or Internet and projector are working.
- Select food that's easy to eat. You don't want messy food to get in the way of the task at hand. Don't forget the drinks!

WEDO recommends: *Get your food and drinks from a local farmer's market or buy food from your grocer that is sustainably or locally grown. Less meat is better.*

5. GATHER YOUR MATERIALS

Within three weeks after letting us know you want to have a "Sisters on the Planet House Party," you'll receive a packet of materials from Oxfam. These include handouts for your guests as well as information you can use to guide your house party discussion.

Make nametags! Some guests might not know each other.

WEDO recommends: *Use recycled materials to create your nametags. Be creative and reuse paper or other materials around your home to make your nametags; this will save money and the planet.*

6. PARTY, PARTY, PARTY—FOLLOW THE AGENDA

Give yourself at least one and a half to two hours to conduct your Sisters on the Planet House Party.

Guests arrive (all)—15 minutes. Have your guests add their names to your sign-up sheet, put on nametags, get food, and mingle.

Welcome (host)—five minutes. Introduce yourself, welcome your guests, and thank everyone for working to pass significant climate change legislation.

Guest introductions (all)—five minutes. Ask guests to quickly introduce themselves and share where they are from and why they came.

Watch the DVD (all)—30 minutes. Watch the DVD about how climate change affects women in various countries, including the U.S. The DVD will be part of the packet you receive from Oxfam America after registering.

Discussion (host)—25 minutes. After viewing the DVD, lead a brief talk about climate change.

Hand out pens, paper, envelopes, and other materials (host)—five minutes. Make resources on women and climate change available. Tell people to visit the resource section of WEDO's Web site to learn more about our campaign From Katrina to Copenhagen: Women Demand U.S. Action on Climate Change.

Letter-writing (all)—20 minutes. Make sure you have stamps on hand. Guests will use the materials you hand out to write their personalized letters to their Members of Congress. Collect the letters so that you can mail them after the party.

Wrap up (host)—5 minutes. Thank all the guests for coming.

7. FOLLOW UP

Mail your letters to Congress. First sort them into piles for each senator and representative, count each pile, and then mail them to the local addresses. Tell WEDO how things went!

We need your input in order to improve how we do our work. Let us know how many letters were written and to which legislators. You can email rachel@wedo.org.

Send in the sign-up sheet. Help us build a campaign support base. As part of WEDO's online action kit, you can download a sign-up sheet. This will allow your guests to opt into WEDO's online community and receive periodic updates on our work in the U.S. Return your sign-up sheets to the following address:

Women's Environment and Development Organization c/o Rachel Harris 355 Lexington Ave, 3rd Floor New York, NY 10017

To conserve paper you can e-mail your guests' information to rachel@wedo.org.

Thank your guests via email. Remind them to check out WEDO at www.wedo.org.

Source: http://www.wedo.org.

10 COMMUNITY CONSERVATION IDEAS **Build Stronger Communities and Protect the Environment Together** by *Sandra Williams*

1. Organize a litter clean up party and get participants to invite their friends in the neighborhood. It's a great way to get everyone together, get to know your neighbors and band together for a mutual cause.
2. Plan an organic community fruit and vegetable garden. First, give out a plant that has just started to sprout and follow up the next week so that everyone can plant their growing vegetables together. If possible, make it a raised bed garden so that it's more accessible and all can participate. Form a garden committee and decide who will take turns weeding and watering. Use organic gardening methods.
3. Organize an educational event about recycling. Your city may provide someone to come, speak, hand out literature, and even provide recycling bins. Some people want to recycle but don't know how to go about it.
4. Start a clothing swap and schedule where it will be held and when you will meet. Plenty of people have good clothes that their children have grown out of that they don't want to throw out.
5. Learn how to build a compost bin and/or rain barrel and teach others how to do the same. It's great for the environment and your garden. Children love to paint and decorate them.
6. If you live in the city, take a trip to the farmer's market and/or a farm. When people see where their food really comes from, they learn to appreciate nature and show more of an interest in protecting it.
7. Gather a group of interested crafters together and use recycled items to create new treasures. Some ideas:

   - Candle holders from baby food jars
   - Purses out of old jeans
   - Mini green houses out of CD cases
   - Totes from rice bags
   - Jewelry out of buttons and bottle caps
   - Rock people
   - Pinecone crafts
   - Bird feeders from old laundry and milk bottles

8. Organize a walkathon and donate the proceeds to an organization that helps protect the environment. Some suggestions and ideas are the Nature Conservancy, Audubon (bird conservation) Society, and the David Suzuki Foundation.
9. Have a giant annual community garage sale and invite as many neighbors as possible. It's a wonderful opportunity to get rid of things you don't need while providing them to someone who could use them.
10. Create a book swap and meet monthly to exchange books that you're finished with that others might like to read.

When we all get together we can have fun and learn from each other about ways to conserve while helping to strengthen and enhance the sense of community in our neighborhoods.

simply and recognizing "sufficiency" as a good life. A focus on subsistence recognizes "enoughness" rather than excess and critiques economic globalization that provides limitless satisfaction of people's needs. This form of subsistence embraces concepts like "moral economy": a new way of life that advocates joy in life, happiness, solidarity-bound societies (Shiva, 1989), and gift economies (Vaughan, 2004, 2007). Ecofeminism endorses the notion of "gift economies" as alternatives to market economies. These occur when valuable goods and services are regularly given without any explicit agreement for immediate or future reward. As discussed in the reading by Genevieve Vaughan titled "The World of the Gift Economy," socioeconomic systems based on the logic of market exchange degrade and dominate both gifts and their givers and destroy the remnants of traditional gift giving societies. For instance, women's free domestic labor is gift labor, and it has been estimated as adding some 40 percent or more to the Gross National Product in even the most industrialized economies. The goods and services provided by women to their families are qualitative gifts that create the material and psychological basis of community. These gifts pass through the family to the market, which could not survive without them.

Both feminist political ecology and ecofeminism emphasize that alongside these analyses of gender and attention to the subordination of women and the environment must follow a focus on the ways capitalism causes poverty and environmental degradation. Their focus is on understanding the ways women's environments and livelihood are impacted by economic and political developments. In this sense they both focus on gendered knowledge used in the creation and maintenance of healthy environments. Ultimately the decolonization of peripheral nations, the rescue of nature, and the liberation of women can only be accomplished by adhering to sound ecological principles contained in these approaches that support the earth and its inhabitants. Through exposing the problems of "sustainable development" and working in organizations and coalitions at all levels, women may work for an international system of cooperation that fosters life-centered political economies and supports a healthy planet.

REFERENCES

Barndt, D. (2008). *Tangled routes: Women, work, and globalization on the tomato trail* (2nd ed.). Lanham, MD : Rowman and Littlefield.

Boserup, E. (1970). *Women's role in economic development.* New York: St. Martin's Press.

Brack A. (1997). Conocimientos tradicionales. In GEF/PNUD/UNOPS, *Amazonia Peruana, comunidades indigenas, conocimientos y tierras tituladas.* Lima, Peru: Atlas y Base de Datos. Proyectos. RLA/92/G31, 32, 33.

Carney, J. (1993). Converting the wetlands, engendering the environment: The intersection of gender with agrarian change in the Gambia. *Economic Geography, 69*(4), 329–348.

Charman, K. (2008). Ecuador first to grant nature constitutional rights. *Capitalism Nature Socialism, 19*(4), 131–132.

Doss, C. R. (2001). Designing agricultural technology for African women farmers: Lessons from 25 years of experience. *World Development, 29*(12), 2075–2092.

El Estado de la Nacion en Desarrollo Humano Sostenible. (1996). San Jose, Costa Rica.

Earth Rights International, Racimos de Ungurahui, and Amazon Watch. (2006). A legacy of harm. Occidental petroleum in indigenous territory in the Peruvian Amazon. Retrieved October 2, 2008, from http://www.contaminacionpetrolera.com/pdf/a_legacy_of_harm.pdf.

Flores, S. (1998). Agroforesteria Amazonica: Una Alternativa a la Agricultura Migratoria. In R. Kalliola and S. Flores (Eds.), *Geoecología y Desarrollo Amazonico: Estudio Integrado en la Zona de Iquitos-Peru* (pp. 417–440). Annales Universitatis Turkuensis Ser. A II.

Food and Agriculture Organization, (FAO) United Nations. (no date). How women react: a global round-up. Retrieved July 11, 2009, from http://www.fao.org/DOCREP/006/S5500E/S5500E09.htm.

Gasché J., Vela Mendoza, N., Vela Mendoza, J. C., and Cáceres, E. B. (2006). Libertad, dependencia y constreñimiento en las sociedades bosquecinass amazonicas. ¿Que significa para los bosquesinos "autonomía", "ciudadanía" y "democracia"? Instituto de Investigaciones de la Amazonia Peruana—CONCYTEC. Unpublished final report.

Global Footprint Network. (2008, May 19). Footprint reports for countries and regions. Global Footprint Network: Advancing the Science of Sustainability. Retrieved July 9, 2009, from http://www.footprintnetwork.org/en/index.php/GFN/page/national_assessments/.

Green Belt Movement. (2008). Green Belt Movement International newsletter, July 2008. Retrieved July 11, 2009, from http://greenbeltmovement.org/w.php?id=63.

Hovorka, A. J. (2005). The (re)production of gendered positionality in Botswana's commercial urban agriculture sector. *Annals of the Association of American Geographers, 95*(2), 294–313.

Intergovernmental Panel on Climate Change (IPCC). (2007). *Climate change 2007: Synthesis report.* Contribution of Working Groups I, II and III to the Fourth Assessment Report of the Intergovernmental Panel on Climate Change [Core Writing Team: R.K. Pachauri and A. Reisinger (Eds.)]. IPCC, Geneva, Switzerland, 104 pp.

Isla, A. (2005). Conservation as enclosure: An eco-feminist perspective on sustainable development and biopiracy in Costa Rica. *Capitalism Nature Socialism, 16*(3), 49–61.

Isla, A. (2007). The tragedy of the enclosures: An ecofeminist perspective on selling oxygen and prostitution in Costa Rica. In G. Vaughan (Ed.), *Women and gift giving: A radically different world view is possible* (pp. 157–170). Toronto: Inanna.

Jewitt, S. (2000). Unequal knowledges in Jharkhand, India: De-romanticizing women's agroecological expertise. *Development and Change, 31*, 961–985.

Kovel, J. (2002). *The enemy of nature: The end of capitalism or the end of the world.* New York: Fernwood.

Lechner, F. J. and Boli, J. (Eds.). (2004) *The globalization reader* (2nd ed.). Oxford: Blackwell Publishing.

MacGregor, S. (2006). *Beyond mothering earth: Ecological citizenship and the politics of care.* Vancouver: UBC Press.

Mellor, M. (1998). *Feminism and ecology.* New York: New York University Press.

Merchant, C. (2005). *Radical ecology: The search for a livable world.* New York: Routledge.

Mies, M. (1986). *Patriarchy and accumulation on a world scale: Women in the international division of labour.* London: Zed Books Ltd.

Momsen, J. (2004). *Gender and development.* London and New York: Routledge.

Muñoz, G. (2008). Caracol #1: La Realidad. In Americas Program Special Report (Washington, DC: Center for International Policy). Retrieved December 12, 2008, from http://americas.irc-online.org/am/5742.

Paulson, S. (2005). Gendered practices and landscapes in the Andes. In S.Paulson and L.L. Gezon (Eds.), *Political ecology across spaces, scales, and social groups* (pp. 174–195). New Brunswick, N.J.: Rutgers University Press.

Pendergrast, M. (2000). *Uncommon grounds: The history of coffee and how it transformed our world.* New York: Basic Books.

Pettman, J. J. (1997). Body politics: International sex tourism. *Third World Quarterly, 18*(1), 93–108.

Pothupitiya, T. (2005). Tsunami you hit my island home. Retrieved September 30, 2009, from http://www.bbc.co.uk/wales/southwest/sites/poetry/pages/thrishana_pothupitiya.shtml.

Resurreccion, B. P. and Elmhirst, R. (2004). *Gender and natural resource management: Livelihoods, mobility and interventions.* London: Earthscan.

Revkin, A. C. (2008, September 29). Ecuador constitution grants rights to nature. Dot Earth: Nine Billion People. One Planet. New York Times Blog. Retrieved July 11, 2009, from http://dotearth.blogs.nytimes.com/2008/09/29/ecuador-constitution-grants-nature-rights/.

Rocheleau, D. (2008). Political ecology in the key of policy: From chains of explanation to webs of relation. *Geoforum, 39*(2), 716–727.

Ronald, P. C. and Adamchak, R. W. (2008). *Tomorrow's table: Organic farming, genetics, and the future of food.* Oxford: Oxford University Press.

Sachs, C. (1996). *Gendered fields: Rural women, agriculture, and the environment.* Boulder, CO: Westview Press, Inc.

Salleh, A. (2004). Global alternatives and the meta-industrial class. In R. Albritton, S. Bell, J. R. Bell, and R. Westra (Eds.), *New socialisms: Futures beyond globalization* (pp. 201–211). London and New York: Routledge.

Salleh, A. (2009). From eco-sufficiency to global justice. In A. Salleh (Ed.), *Eco-sufficiency and global justice: Women write political ecology* (pp. 297–312). New York: Pluto Press.

Schroeder, R. A. (1993). Shady practice: Gender and the political ecology of resource stabilization in the Gambian garden/orchards. *Economic Geography, 69* (4), 349–365.

Schroeder, R., St. Martin, K., Wilson, B., and Sen, D. (2008). Third world environmental justice. *Society and Natural Resources, 21*(7), 547–555.

Scola, N. (2007). Why Iraqi farmers might prefer death to Paul Bremer's Order 81. *Global Policy Forum.* Retrieved December 19, 2008, from http://www.globalpolicy.org/security/issues/iraq/attack/consequences/2007/0919iraqifarmers.htm.

Shiva, V. (1989). *Staying alive: Women, ecology and development.* London: Zed Books.

Shiva, V. (1999). *Biopiracy: The plunder of nature and knowledge.* Toronto: Between the Lines.

Sultana, F. (2006). Gendered waters, poisoned wells: Political ecology of the arsenic crisis in Bangladesh. In K. Lahiri-Dutt (Ed.), *Fluid bonds: Views on gender and water* (pp. 362–386). Kolkata: Stree Publishers.

Sze, J. and London, J. K. (2008). Environmental justice at the crossroads. *Sociology Compass, 2*(4): 1331–1354.

Vaughan, G. (2004). Gift giving and exchange: Genders are economic identities, and economies are based on gender. In G. Vaughan (Ed.), *The gift, il donno* (pp. 15–37). Rome: *Athanor*, XV (8).

Vaughan, G. (2007). Introduction. A radically different worldview is possible. In G. Vaughan (Ed.), *Women and the gift economy. A radically different worldview is possible* (pp. 1–38). Toronto: Inanna Publications and Education Inc.

von Werlhof, C. (2008). The globalization of neoliberalism, its consequences, and some of its basic alternatives. *Capitalism Nature Socialism, 19*(3), 94–117.

Warren, K. (2000). *Ecofeminist philosophy: A Western perspective on what it is and why it matters.* Lanham, MD: Rowman & Littlefield.

Wallerstein, I. (2004). *World-system analysis: An introduction.* Durham: Duke University Press.

Women's Environmental Network (WEN). (2004). History: The changing face of Women's Environmental Network. Retrieved July 15, 2009, from http://www.wen.org .uk/general_pages/history.htm.

World Commission on Environment and Development. (1987). *Our common future.* New York: Oxford University Press.

World March for Women. (2007). Who we are. Retrieved July 11, 2009, from http://www. marchemondiale.org/qui_nous_sommes/en/.

SUGGESTIONS FOR FURTHER READING

Gould, K. and Hosey, L. (2007). *Women in green: Voices of sustainable design.* Bainbridge Island, WA: Ecotone Publishing.

Kheel, M. (2007). *Nature ethics: An ecofeminist perspective.* New York: Rowman and Littlefield.

Moser, S. and Dilling, L. (Eds.) (2007). *Creating a climate for change: Communicating climate change and facilitating social change.* New York: Cambridge University Press.

Ress, M. J. (2006). *Ecofeminism from Latin America.* New York: Orbis.

Salleh, A. (2009). *Eco-sufficiency and global justice: Women write political ecology.* London: Pluto Press.

Shiva, V. (2008). *Soil not oil: Environmental justice in an age of climate crisis.* Boston: South End Press.

Temperatures Rising: Four Essays on a Theme: Women and Climate Change

Essay 1

A Huge Challenge and a Narrow Discourse

Minu Hemmati and Ulrike Röhr (2007)

WHY GENDER IN CLIMATE CHANGE POLICYMAKING?

Humanity faces a huge challenge limiting the consequences of our behavior and adapting to changing conditions of life: global warming and climate change signal more frequent and more severe droughts, storms, floods, and rising sea levels. While we know that women carry specific burdens of changed climates, we must recognize that women can make specific contributions to climate protection. However, there is virtually no discussion of gender consequences of climate change and little mobilization of women to inform the policy and practices. Most sectors carry on with "business as usual." International agreements on climate are sketchy. The goals and targets set are much lower than they would need to be. Countries that are among the biggest emitters of greenhouse gases are not playing their part in the global community to deal with climate change.

Integrating a gender analysis adds to the quality, effectiveness, legitimacy, and likelihood of implementation of climate protection policies. For example, if we know more about why women and men use different modes of transport, we can develop public transport systems that make it easier for everyone to meet their transport needs without using private cars. In the absence of a gender analysis of climate-related policymaking, climate protection measures may increase the inequities for women. For example, replacing fossil fuels with renewable sources of energy can raise energy prices and create an additional burden for poor people, the majority of whom

are women. Redistributive measures are needed to avoid further impoverishing the poor.

The international debate about climate protection has focused on digesting scientific facts, projections, and developing technologies—like renewable energies, energy efficiency, bio fuels, economic or market measures, allowing developed countries to "buy" emission reduction credits by spending money on "clean" energy technologies in developing countries, or creating a carbon market, has also been a focus. It is questionable that such a narrow approach would satisfy the need to realize a vision of sustainable development in the context of climate change. Rather, the current discourse—at international and national levels—needs to be broadened, based on sustainable development as the overarching goal and the principle of gendering human development, taking into view the environmental, social, and economic parts of the problem and of possible solutions.

There are differences between women and men in their respective access to and control over resources, their perception, attitudes and behavior. From a sustainable development and from a gender and justice perspective, the climate debate is striking in several ways. Little consideration has been given to:

- Poverty (South and North) and its negative impacts on the global climate: e.g. poor people, mostly women, without access to other energy sources cutting down forests for heating and cooking;
- Over-consumption of resources in industrialised countries and by global elites: e.g. avoidable

usage of energy for status purposes (luxury goods, housing and travel);

- Social implications of climate change outcomes and the threats these pose for poor women and men: e.g. farmers struggling with water shortages and changes in weather patterns;
- Strategies for adaptation: What can and should communities and nations in different parts of the world do to prepare for the future? How can we ensure that all groups in society are fully involved in planning and decision-making for adaptation?
- Questioning the dominant development paradigm that equates economic growth and well-being. While there are discussions about how to de-couple economic growth and increasing fossil fuel use, economic growth itself is still understood as equivalent to increasing human well-being.

While we are not saying that integrating gender into climate-related policy-making would rectify all these shortcomings, taking a gender perspective will bring these issues to the table.

WHAT ARE THE ISSUES? GENDER IN CLIMATE POLICYMAKING

Energy, mobility and transport, agriculture and forestry, water, biodiversity, disasters and extreme weather, land use and urban planning, building and housing, and health are among the range of issues, practices and events that affect and are affected by climate and its protection. The availability of gender-disaggregated data varies considerably, depending on which issues and which regions of the world we look at. Below are a few examples of the knowledge we have. While much more research is needed to build a comprehensive knowledge base for climate policy making, these findings are a starting point, and sufficient to show that gender is indeed an important aspect of climate protection.

Energy production and demand are particularly closely linked to climate protection. From a women's perspective in developing countries, we know of the lack of women's access to energy; the need for affordable energy supporting women's income generating activities; the high number of victims of indoor air pollution, particularly women and children, and the need to replace inefficient biomass stoves: the physical burden of collecting firewood and the impacts on women's time.

Private and public transport: For many industrialized countries, we know that women and men have access to different kinds of transport and that they use them for different purposes. For example, existing transport systems in many countries serve middle-aged, full-time working men well, but women more often depend on public transport, which does not meet their transport needs arising from paid work, household duties, and child and eldercare. Integrating a gender perspective would enable us to make transport systems both more user-friendly and more climate-friendly. If public transport routes and schedules were designed so that women can take their children to school and get to work in time, they would not need to use a private car.

Risk perception is gender specific. Women are generally more sensitive to risks and more averse to taking risks, including in relation to climate change. Fewer women than men believe that governments are doing enough to address the challenge. They are more sceptical about technological solutions to environmental problems and are also much more critical of nuclear energy than are men. They are more convinced that we have to change our lifestyles to protect the climate.

Women's participation in planning and decision-making is still dismally low. If it is true that women take smaller risks and would support either different or a wider range of solutions to climate problems, then it would be good if women were more influential in determining energy and climate policy, research and development, and investment. It would be interesting to find out if women would, if they had an effective voice in decision-making, invest more resources in climate protection, including motivating and enabling reduced energy consumption. Would women support investing in the wide-spread use of renewables instead of further supporting nuclear technologies?

Adaptation, which must be context-specific and participatory, requires that all members of affected communities be part of a climate change planning and governance process. If women are not fully involved in planning and decision-making—using gender analysis and appropriate mechanisms for participation—the quality of adaptive measures will be limited and successful implementation will remain doubtful.

Health issues have arisen in various contexts. For example, during the hot summers of recent years in Europe, mortality rates among women of all ages were higher than among men. Future projections indicate a higher incidence of serious illness in older people and urban poor—among them being more women than men. Also, since it is primarily women who care for family members affected by extreme weather conditions and air quality, their illnesses put an additional burden on women and impact their ability to work outside the home (see, for example, several articles in the Oxfam Journal 2002).

Poverty: It is widely acknowledged that climate change will likely hit the poorest people in the poorest countries hardest. Since women represent a disproportionate share of the poor, women are likely to be disproportionately vulnerable to the effects of climate change. Hence, all economic consequences of climate change and response measures need to be analyzed by gender to identify and effectively counter disproportionate disadvantages for women.

Drought and deforestation also impact women in particular. In many developing countries, women are responsible for fetching water and firewood. These tasks become more difficult and time-consuming in the face of widespread climate changes. It is girls, more often than boys, who will drop out of school to fulfil these tasks. In addition, women will be further limited in their opportunities to engage in work outside the home.

Conflicts are predicted to increase in the course of climate change as natural resources such as water and arable land become scarce. Integrating women and gender perspectives in conflict prevention and resolution processes has proven an effective success factor, and many traditional cultures indeed rely on women's skills to bring about harmony and collaborative problem-solving. A continued lack of women in power and decision-making is likely to hinder effective dealing with conflict.

Natural disasters particularly impact women's income, caring work, and safety. In traditional disaster research, women are mostly seen as victims. Gender analysis in disaster research, on the contrary, suggests an alternative to the dominant approach of technologically supported disaster management: preventing disasters through sustainable development based on the participation of all community members and the contribution of everybody's skills.

WHERE THEY MAKE CLIMATE POLICY: RELEVANT ORGANIZATIONS & PROCESSES

As climate science delivers more and more precise information about the changes occurring, the effects of climate change are becoming more visible and the projections more alarming. An increasing number of organizations and processes are becoming involved in the debate. We are focusing here on the key international ones, and add a few ideas on how women can get involved.

United Nations Framework Convention On Climate Change (UNFCCC)

The UNFCCC, an international legally binding instrument, is one of the environmental conventions that were agreed to at the Earth Summit in Rio in 1992. It is a framework convention, and specific agreements, i.e. protocols, have to be developed to create targets, policies and monitoring mechanisms. The Kyoto Protocol is the first protocol created under the Climate Convention. Conferences of the Parties to the Convention (COPs) are held every year. Several thousand people attend these: 20–30% of them are government delegates, others represent the recognized observer constituencies like environmental NGOs, researchers, business and media. Women are not among the officially recognized observer constituencies although some women's organizations have registered as environmental NGOs.

Women were active during the first COPs (from 1995). Then there was a period of low participation from women. Women's groups have picked up the strands again since 2002, holding side events, distributing statements, hosting an exhibition booth, discussing gender issues with delegations, and convening a Gender & Climate Caucus.

Intergovernmental Panel On Climate Change (IPCC)

This Panel is the main global scientific body that reviews, collates and publishes climate-related research. So far, IPCC has not paid any attention to gender issues in their assessment reports. Although seven 'cross-cutting' issues have been identified for future reports—including sustainable development, integration of mitigation and adaptation, and vulnerability—gender is not identified among them.

The IPCC, however, bases its reports on published, peer-reviewed research and, since there is little available in the area of gender and climate change, the absence of gender can only be resolved by conducting gender-sensitive research on climate change as well as bringing relevant knowledge and hypotheses to the attention of the panel.

United Nations Environment Programme (UNEP)

UNEP operates climate change related activities in several of its centers around the globe. After having championed work on gender and environment issues in the 1980s, UNEP was not as significantly engaged during the 1990s. They have picked up the agenda again though, and published an overview booklet on women and the environment, and convened "The Global Women's Assembly on the Environment" in 2004 (See www.unep.org/dpdl/cso/wave/Official.asp). Gender was also on the agenda of UNEPs 23rd Governing Council in February 2005, which laid out a gender mainstreaming plan for the whole organization and its work. It remains to be seen when and how this decision is being implemented. Women will continue to monitor UNEP's progress by observing the number of women in decision-making posts, staff development measures and project criteria. They will also continue to collaborate with UNEP on specific programmes focusing on UNEP's organizational development and gender mainstreaming in its work.

United Nations Commission On Sustainable Development Process (CSD)

The CSD was created after the Rio Earth Summit (1992) and is mandated to monitor the implementation of Agenda 21. It is now focusing on a new set of sectoral issues every biennial cycle, along with a permanent set of cross-cutting issues (including poverty eradication, consumption and production patterns, globalization, health, education, gender equality). Having been identified as one of the "Major Groups" in Agenda 21, women are participating actively in CSD sessions. However, there are few governments that support the attendance of women and gender experts financially. In addition, very few governments include gender experts in their delegations, while including NGOs has become a wide-spread practice.

WORK IN OTHER AGENCIES AND BODIES

The United Nations Food and Agriculture Organization (FAO) has published an overview paper on gender and climate change 2005 (Lambrou et al. 2005), and is supporting the first review of existing research on gender & climate change (to be published by the present authors & FAO in early 2007).

The World Health Organization (WHO) is working on climate change under its "Global Change and Health" program but has not paid much explicit attention to gender yet.

The G8, having focused on energy, energy security and climate issues in recent years, will continue this focus during its meetings in 2007. The G8 could, if it reversed its current practice of ignoring gender, set a very positive and influential example for others.

WHAT WE NEED TO DO

Bringing gender onto the climate change agenda needs investments in research, networking, and advocacy. And it will represent a much-needed innovation. In other words: it will be tough. Hence, we need a multi-pronged strategy, including the following components:

Closing knowledge gaps relating to gender and climate change: All climate protection measures and programs and all instruments for mitigating climate change or adapting to climate change must be subjected to a gender analysis. All climate change related data, scenarios, etc. need to be disaggregated by gender. Gender experts and climate researchers need to engage in the issues.

Raising women's voices: Women must become involved in climate negotiations at all levels. But representation by numbers is not enough. We need women represented, gender experts, and preferably gender and climate experts.

Advocacy for gender mainstreaming in policy-making, implementation, monitoring, and communication strategies and materials includes an array of practical steps:

- The Gender & Climate Caucus meets and advocates at UNFCCC meetings. These activities need to spread to regional and national levels as well as to other bodies and processes; women's organizations and networks that operate at these levels should take this up. These activities need to include bringing research and actions on gender and climate change to the attention of policy makers, and in particular the practices and campaigns of poor and of indigenous women, which should be sought, documented and given weight in negotiations.
- Mobilizing the international women's movement, including building on the considerable engagement of women in the anti-nuclear and peace movements. However, many women and women's organizations are not sufficiently informed about climate change and how it relates to women and gender. We need information tools and networking.
- Building networks & strategic alliances, for example, with the Global Women Environment Ministers Network, local government initiatives (e.g. Climate Alliance), trade unions, indigenous peoples' organizations, and environmental justice groups. Scientific bodies and conservation organizations that are traditionally are less inclined to include gender in their thinking. They should be urged to rethink this exclusion and should be kept informed about gender-related work.
- Prominent women's/environment advocates, environment ministers, leaders of regional groups, well-known scientists, business leaders,

or journalists could "champion" gender & climate issues over a longer period of time.
- Timing: In 2005, international discussions began on protocol points to be in place for 2012. For new issues and aspects to be included in international negotiations, they need to be raised very early on in the process, and persistently over time.

OUTLOOK

During recent international climate conferences, women have picked up the thread again and further developed their work around UNFCCC. An initial break-through was achieved at COP11 in Montreal (2005), where the first-ever statement on behalf of women was delivered to the closing plenary. A workshop held on the margins of COP11 helped to identify priority issues for future research. An exhibition booth and two "Climate Talk" events, one by the Ministers co-chairing the Global Women Environment Ministers Network, attracted a lot of attention.

General advocacy for women's rights and gender equity is crucial, but so is the ability to articulate in detail why and how gender should and can be in integrated into climate related policymaking. Such expertise is hardly available within the process right now, and the participation of gender and climate experts—from the governmental or observers' side—would help formulate policies that avoid putting women at a disadvantage but rather be gender neutral or help to further gender equity.

There is a range of established analytical and practical tools that can and should be used, such as gender analysis, gender impact assessment, gender budgeting, and the knowledge and practical experience gained in participatory community development that is particularly relevant for adaptation. Even if we don't have all the necessary data yet, there is no reason to delay getting involved. The importance of climate protection and climate justice cannot be overstated—we need it now, and we need it to include gender analysis in order to get it right!

Essay 2

Temperatures Rising

Myralyn O. A. Nartey (2007)

In many developing regions of the world where the balance of peace is barely maintained, imminent climate change events could eventually tip the scales and cause unprecedented social and political catastrophe. Climate change in its many forms threatens and destroys the viability of these traditional societies and their ways of life. Most societies still burden women with all or most care giving and domestic chores while all but excluding them from the economic and public realm and rendering them vulnerable and powerless in the face of such catastrophe. Yet, climate change has been overlooked as a catalyst in the present humanitarian crisis in Darfur, Sudan. As global atmospheric temperatures have been rising, Darfurians have been reaching their metaphorical boiling points. The severity of the situation in Darfur should compel each of us to attempt to understand the relationship between climate and conflict, and to anticipate what the consequences of global warming might be for women in vulnerable regions.

Global warming describes the increase in the atmospheric concentration of greenhouse gases (GHGs) that causes an elevation in global atmospheric temperatures and long- and short-term climate and weather patterns. The debate between scientists—and governments—from around the world has centered on the extent to which anthropogenic activity is impacting the rate of change. What we do know, with relative certainty, is that these changes are occurring at an exponential rate and that there is some correlation between human activity and the concentration of GHGs in the atmosphere.

Yet, even as climate scientists are making headway in convincing policy makers and the public of the realities of global warming, we have not succeeded at communicating how these major ecological changes will affect human societies. In regions of the world where there is little economic development, low Human Development Indices, tenuous infrastructure, and fragile socio-political conditions, the risks and consequences of micro- and macro-climate change events are much greater. Thus, it is imperative to understand what may be described as *socio-climatic* impacts of global warming. Socio-climate impacts are defined here as the relationship between human society and the climate. These are the dynamic results of interacting and correlating climatic and ecological factors and social factors impacting humans embedded within a specific cultural context.

As a result of continued global warming, climate change will cause more frequent and more extreme weather events, such as drought, flooding, tornados, hurricanes, and other hydro-meteorological disasters. These disasters have the potential to devastate human settlements and imperil human health on vast scales. Much of the infrastructure used for shelter, transportation and the supply of water, electricity and natural gas will likely be irreparably damaged in many places. Vector-borne diseases (human diseases that are transmitted by any animal vector) will proliferate, and more people will face ill health, famine and starvation.

Climate change will wreak havoc on human settlements and human health, but the greatest, although least-known, threat of climate change is to human relationships, including these between men and women. New ecological challenges and stresses on natural resources will disturb favorable or symbiotic human relationships, and lead to more episodes of intense conflict and violence in many places. Poverty-stricken parts of the world suffer especially, because the consequences of violence are so severe, particularly for disenfranchised women who typically suffer the most in times of war and devastation.

CONSIDER DARFUR

Situated adjacent to the Red Sea and bordering nine other countries, Sudan is like a small model of Africa. It replicates the enormous biodiversity, cultural diversity, tumultuous history, and corrugated terrain characteristic of the entire African continent. The country has a population of 39 million people, divided into over 130 different cultural groups. According to the UNDPS Human Development Index (a measurement index of human progress that combines indicators of real purchasing power, education, and health), Sudan is a Least Developed Country (LDC), ranking 139 in 2004.

BASIS FOR THE CURRENT CONFLICT

From the time when Sudan established its independence in the mid-1950s, the country has been continually devastated by violence and corruption. Since February 2003, the conflict has intensified between the Janjaweed, a Baggara militia group and the non-Baggara people (including the Fur, Zaghawa, and Massaleit ethnic groups) in the western state of Darfur. In this time span, more than 40,000 people have died as a result of the violent conflict, malnutrition, and disease. There is large-scale destruction throughout the villages in Darfur. Nearly 1.65 million people are internally displaced, and 200,000 Darfurians refugees are in Chad.

Women in Darfur have experienced the brunt of the brutality. Since 2003, tens of thousands of women have been displaced, raped, and killed. The violence against women has received international attention. According to Dr. William F. Schulz of Amnesty International, U.S.A.: "Government forces and allied groups in Darfur are waging war on women's bodies." The National Organization for Women (NOW) has reported that rape is being used as a weapon of terror and ethnic cleansing in Darfur.

Climate change has played a quiet, but critical role in creating this crisis. Several ecological devastations occurred within the life span of one generation. These micro- and macro-climate change include diminishing and erratic rainfall, seen in the floods and torrential rains of 1988 and accelerating desertification such as the practically continuous Sahel drought since 1967. These major ecological changes have only been accentuated by the near doubling of population in less than a quarter of a century (15.4 million in 1970 to 25.4 million in 1990), the displacement—both internal and external—of some six million people, the doubling of livestock numbers within 20 years, deforestation on a massive scale, renewed civil war in the South, and the aggressive expansion of legal and illegal rain-fed mechanized farming.

The hyper-arid, semi-arid and dry subhumid lands cover an area of 178 million hectares in Sudan, and all of this area is affected to various degrees by one or more of the desertification processes. Desertification has reduced the amount of land that is available for herding, grazing, and farming, replacing the once fertile land with arid desert and sand.

Within Darfur, the stratifications between cultural groups are emphasized by religion and, as the ecosystem has evolved, ethno-cultural divisions have reinforced the contests for resources. Today, intermarriage and socio-economic interaction have obscured the historical territorial boundaries in Darfur, but the significance of land to cultural and ethnoreligious identity remains.

About 7% of the Sudanese population is nomadic or semi-nomadic. These groups are also typically Arabic Muslims; whereas the sedentary agriculturalist populations in Darfur are Christians and non-Arabic Muslims, or they practice traditional animist religions.

Although the literature is unforthcoming about the roles of women in Sudanese society, it is estimated that women comprise nearly 27% of the total labor force. Most women are in the agriculture sector. In both the nomadic pastoralist and sedentary agriculturalist groups, women fulfill similar roles related to childcare, household management, some culture-specific activities, and animal care. While men are generally responsible for herd management, women are charged with milking animals and marketing dairy products. This is a result of gender-specific perceptions of milk. Women in the nomadic or semi-nomadic population are also typically responsible for building and rebuilding shelter as their communities relocate.

In Darfur, the nomadic tribes have historically passed through lands belonging to other tribes with fairly little disharmony. But as the Sahara has expanded (more rapidly throughout the 1970s and 1980s, a consequence of climate change and desertification, the grazable land has diminished. There has been less and less fertile area to share, and this has incited conflict between the two groups.

Nomadic cattle herders began to disrespect previously determined boundaries and began invading the settled peoples' land. As the climate changed, the farmer's tolerance for this invasion diminished and the conflict became violent.

Until the 1970s, the local tribal leadership handled disputes that could lead to major inter-tribal conflict (i.e.: land disputes, murders, or theft). Then, President Nimeieri abolished the tribal system, changed land laws, and attributed ownership to the state. The state began appointing the local administrators based on their loyalty to the political regime. This corrupted justice and impartiality at the local level. This corruption has continued until today. The Janjaweed militia (birthed from the Arabic nomadic tribal groups in Darfur), backed by the predominantly Arabic Sudanese government, is responsible for the indiscriminate attacks and widespread and systematic crimes against humanity, including killing, torture, rape and other forms of sexual violence against women, forced displacements and pillaging.

All of this violence and death has been brought about by the coinciding changes in the climate and the socio-political structure in Darfur. Despite what has been reported, the conflict in Darfur is not solely motivated by religious or ethnic intolerance. These are dangerous oversimplifications (as analyses of African societies often are). They disregard the possibility that the harsh socio-climatic impacts experienced in Darfur can also be experienced in other places.

Many countries throughout Africa, Asia, South America, the Middle East, and Eastern Europe, have all of the conditions that existed in Darfur before the conflict; low Human Development Indices, unstable agro-economics, fragile socio-political situations,

a history of violence, and corrupt governments. Women in these countries where patriarchy and gender inequality are so deeply embedded, are acutely vulnerable.

In general, natural disasters and epidemics, like those that climate change events may incite, uniquely affect women. For example, many Pakistani women were not saved in the recent earthquake due to the cultural views that prohibit male rescue workers from touching women who are not in their immediate family. Disease proliferation can also have a distinct impact on women related to cultural perceptions about women's health, accessibility to healthcare, and treatment-seeking behaviors.

Observations from Darfur and throughout history show that war, now also a recognized potential socio-climatic outcome of climate change, usually has especially dire consequences for women. During wartime, women are charged with supporting the household when their husbands are fighting or are killed or injured. This is universal, but is very challenging for women in undeveloped regions where there is little economic opportunity for men, much less women. Where social traditions have prevented women from taking part in the economic and public spheres, women tend to be victims of the violence during conflict and suffer rape, torture, abuse, displacement, or death. Desertification, as in Darfur, currently affects more than 70% of the earth's dry land. As other places also begin to experience these and other socio-climatic impacts of global warming and climate change, what will be the result for human societies and for women, in particular? Climate scientists are reporting that temperatures are rising. It is time we understand this metaphor, especially in terms of women.

Essay 3
Japanese Women's Roles in Climate Change Mitigation

Sabrina Regmi (2007)

The climate change debate led by agreements such as the Kyoto Protocol and United Nations Framework Convention on Climate Change (UNFCC) concentrates more on the scientific and technological

means to mitigate climate change. It is somehow heavily dominated by men and ignores or doesn't understand the domestic reality. Deforestation for wood to cook with, the over-use of appliances and heating which waste the electricity frequently produced by heavy green-house-gas (GHG) emitting processes, all contribute to global warming and climate change. It is important to address, support and value women's contribution to reducing global warming, provide education and encourage life style adjustments. Scientific and technological theories alone cannot ensure a sustainable environment.

The Japanese expression "*mottainai*" means "it is very wasteful when things are not utilized fully." *Mottainai* is often used for the 3R Initiative—reduce, reuse, and recycle. I conducted research in Japan where I interviewed and surveyed about 50 employed women. They belonged to different environmental, educational, and business organizations, and were located in Tokyo and Kanagawa. The purpose of my research was to understand women's roles in climate change mitigation from an industrialized country's perspective. While the women were employed they also performed their dual roles and duties at home as wives and mothers. The research found that the women respondents were using numerous strategies that helped reduce global warming and climate change impacts.

JAPANESE WOMEN'S DOMESTIC DECISION MAKING

A few years ago, Japanese men were still principally incharge of buying technical equipment from cars to stereo equipment. Nowadays it is increasingly women who are making such purchasing decisions. In their day to day household responsibilities of providing food for the family, shopping and maintaining the dwelling, women become more familiar with products and services. This awareness allows them to place greater value on health, climate change and environment related factors.

The study shows that women's decision making power and status at home has improved. About 44% women answered that they participate equally in decision making with their husbands while 54% women answered that they are the one making decisions regarding the consumption and management of domestic requirements including purchasing, investing and spending.

WOMEN'S AWARENESS OF AND RESPONSES TO GLOBAL WARMING

About 70% of women respondents were highly or very highly aware of global warming and climate change issues (Table 1). This high level of awareness has made women more conscious about developing and practicing environment friendly habits in their daily lives as well as travels. Although the great majority (about 85%) of respondents' households possessed cars, most of the women (about 92%), both with and without access to cars, preferred to walk or ride a bicycle to go to nearby places (Table 2). The situation is reversed when the women had to travel longer distances. Then, most of them preferred to use some sort of motorized transportation. Younger women (28% of the sample) used cars or taxis while older women (50% of the sample), preferred to ride public means of transportation such as trains and buses.

EFFICIENT USE OF ENERGY

Eighty four per cent of respondents are in the habit of turning off the electric appliances and lights when these are not in use both at home and at work (Table-3). About 46% use energy-efficient fluorescent lights to economize electricity. In Japan most heating is produced by both nuclear energy and burning of fossil fuels like gas and coal, which emit large amounts of GHGs. Over one third of the women are therefore minimizing the use of a heating system by using sweaters and blankets at home as much as possible. Moreover about 20% of them prefer to use fans during summer instead

TABLE 1	Level of Awareness of Climate Change		
SN	Type of Responses	Response, #	%
1	Very high	12	24
2	High	23	46
3	Medium	10	20
4	Low	5	10

TABLE 2 Means of Transportation While Going to Near-by and Far-off Places

		Nearby		Far Away	
SN	Means of Transportation	Response	%	Response	%
1	Walk	44	88	–	–
2	Walk or ride bicycle	2	4	–	–
3	Ride a car/taxi [young women]	4	8	14	28
	Ride a car/taxi [elderly women]	–	–	–	–
4	Ride public means of transportation [elderly women]	–	–	25	50
	Ride public means of transportation [younger women]	–	–	11	22

TABLE 3 Ways of Preserving Energy at the Household Level

SN	How energy is preserved	Response, #	%
1	Turn off electric appliances and lights when not using them	42	84
2	Use energy efficient fluorescent lights	23	46
3	Use sweaters/blankets in winter instead of heater	17	34
4	Use fan in summer instead of air conditioning	10	20
5	Wash dishes by hand instead of using dishwasher	19	38
6	Use already used bathwater for washing clothes and use water for multiple purposes such as boiling water for eggs as well as vegetables and then for washing oily dishes and pans	2	4
7	Use special table cap to switch off the standby electricity [This device is called energy saving electrical outlet. It is used for saving energy which is mostly consumed during the standby mode [ex TV, computers are often left at standby mode which consumes lots of energy and emits ghg].	1	2
8	Use no-iron clothing	3	6

of air-conditioning. Women reuse bathwater for washing clothing and other hot water from cooking, for washing oily dishes and pans, thus minimizing energy consumption at the household level.

WOMEN PRACTICE THE 3 R's

The study found that women place great importance on waste reduction. Over one third (36%) shop for less packaged food, slightly fewer (32%) buy fruits and vegetables which are not prepackaged, while almost half (48%) reuse the plastic bags for storing leftovers and other household items. Others buy eco-friendly products such as eco-friendly cars, use the waste recycling program in the community, and take cloth or paper bags for shopping instead of using plastic bags (Table-4). Some shopping centers of Japan have an eco-point card system, giving shoppers incentive points for not using plastic bags. This is popular mostly among young women (60%). Some older women, who were not aware of it before the survey, showed interest in using this system after they came to know about it.

TABLE 4 Ways of Reducing Waste and Recycling

SN	Waste Reduction and Recycling	Response, #	%
1	Use the waste recycling program in the community	30	60
2	Composting household waste for garden fertilizer	8	16
3	Reuse plastic bags or containers to store leftovers and household items	24	48
4	Shop for less packaged food	18	36
5	Buy fruits and vegetables which are not prepackaged	16	32
6	Using eco-point card system [bringing own cloth bag and not using new plastic bags in the supermarket, in return for incentive points]	30	60

WOMEN AS ROLE MODELS

As mothers, women can play an important role in teaching their children environmental ethics and influencing them to develop environmental conservation habits. A survey by the Japanese Ministry of Environment asked children what inspired them to participate in environmental conservation. The majority answered they were told by their mothers to do so or they saw their mothers doing it. Hence women proved to be role models for climate protection and the 3R's.

My study showed clearly that caring for the environment falls largely on women's shoulders—all while being employed as well as responsible for the home and care of their families. Women take the extra steps, thought and time to store and reuse, recycle, compost, travel by foot or transit rather than car, shop and cook to waste as little as possible to protect the environment and reduce GHG emissions that pose a serious threat to human lives and future generations. Meanwhile the men still debate whether or not to accept the Kyoto Protocol or if so, haggle about trading emission levels to appear in compliance with it while their GHG emissions keep rising.

Essay 4
Gendered Struggles for the Commons

Leigh Brownhill (2007)

The negative effect on the atmosphere of emissions produced by the burning of fossil fuels is well-known. Less well-known, however, is the detrimental impact of deforestation. According to the November 2006 *Stern Review*, emissions from deforestation are greater than the emissions produced by the entire global transport sector. Africa has the fastest rate of deforestation in the world. Commercial logging and subsistence farming are the main sources, according to the *Stern Review* and UNEP.

As women make up the majority of subsistence farmers in Africa, are they implicated in this widespread deforestation and resultant climate change? To answer this question we must find out what drives African subsistence farmers to cut down trees.

"Population growth" is the typical answer from neoliberal analysts whose interests lie mainly in protecting multinational corporations' profit-generating activities. They charge that African women have too many children. Family planning policies and income generation projects are proposed as ameliorative actions to combat poverty and ecological degradation. Some go so far as to suggest that more industrialization is necessary in Africa in order to remove subsistence farmers from the land. But a different answer and different solutions emerge when the gendered conflict between subsistence and commercial uses of land in Africa is taken into account.

Let us take the example of Kenya, where 75% of household energy needs are supplied by firewood.

Wangari Maathai, Kenya's former assistant Environment Minister and a 2004 Nobel Peace Prize winner, argues that a country needs to maintain at least ten per cent indigenous forest cover to achieve "sustainable development." She estimates that Kenya has less than two per cent of such forest cover remaining.

In 1992, Maathai spoke to an international audience at the Sierra Club about how she returned to Kenya in the 1970s after some years of education abroad to find that ancient fig trees were being felled throughout her home area. These trees were traditionally never cut down and even the twigs were not picked up from the ground or burned as kindling. Fig trees were sacred, in part because they acted as protectors of the vital water catchment areas. During the expansion of tea plantations in the 1960s and 1970s, the fig trees were sacrificed. Desiccation of the soil quickly followed.

Subsistence farmers in East Africa began to cut down the fig trees not because they no longer respected their age-old customs. Nor did they encroach on the forests because they were having too many children. They cut the trees because there was not enough food produced after coffee and tea began to be widely grown and exported from Kenyan farms both large and small. When world market prices for African export crops fell, many male "heads of household" put more land under coffee and tea to make up the shortfalls in income. When prices rose, these farmers had further incentives to expand cash crop production. In the process, women's food gardens were plowed under.

The World Bank and other international institutions touted commercial farming as Africans' way out of poverty. Beginning in 1980 the Bank encouraged the conversion of food farms to export cash crop plantations with development policies, programs, research, grants and loans. But the more farmers planted coffee, tea, sugar, cut flowers and cotton, the less land was available for food production. Starvation and malnutrition have become endemic, especially for people in East Africa's burgeoning city slums and in the arid and semi-arid regions where people's access to food and water is increasingly at risk. Anemia, stunted growth and vulnerability to disease affect millions, especially women and children.

Women have been at the forefront of resisting commercial policies and promoting a return to a food-centred political economy. To address deforestation, Wangari Maathai founded the Green Belt Movement in 1977 under the auspices of the National Council of Women of Kenya. The Movement sought to counter the decline in ecological resources and the loss of principles of stewardship. Maathai had observed these coinciding developments with the advance of commodity production in farming areas. With minimal funding and with self-help efforts, the Green Belt Movement established branches, first throughout Central Kenya and then throughout Africa.

The Green Belt Movement encouraged women's groups to plant trees. Seminars educated women in rural areas about how trees might be planted along boundaries and in different sites within the homestead. The women could choose trees for their fruit-bearing capacity, medicinal qualities, ritual purposes, firewood-producing capability, water catchment protection or for their decorative appeal. Women also began to plant trees on public land, including their children's school compounds, church yards, public squares, road verges and other common lands. Through advocacy and a massive educational campaign, the Green Belt Movement encouraged the return to indigenous seeds and cultivation techniques which raised soil fertility and slowed desertification.

When women planted trees, they also strengthened their claims to the land. Women's tree-planting activities were partially based in customary practices which devolved responsibility for food provision to women. While running tree nurseries and reforesting public areas may not have been "customary" practices, women did apply customary cooperation and indigenous environmental knowledge to the these activities. With this heritage, women contributed to the success of the Green Belt ventures and laid the groundwork for a new form of women's power: the power to heal the heavily damaged ecology, first in Central Kenya and later across the country and the continent.

The Green Belt Movement used tree-planting as an entry point into wider discussions and actions in five areas: food security, the negative impacts of petrochemical-based agricultural systems on health and environment, genetically modified seeds, civic education and voter registration. Tree planting and associated activities were adopted by hundreds of women's groups, many of which continued to engage in other types of activities such as merry-go-rounds, or collective savings groups, shared work on earth others' farms and collective care for common resources. By creatively combining several of the most pressing needs of Kenyan peasant women, the Green Belt Movement engaged hundreds of thousands of rural Kenyans in expanding and defending their rights to control and protect land on which, by the new millennium, they had planted some 20 million trees.

Although the Green Belt activities addressed soil erosion, food insecurity and income generation needs of the rural people, Maathai herself was vilified by President Moi in the 1980s. Why did the activities of this ecological movement raise the ire of businessmen and others in the government? The land on which women planted and defended their trees was clearly land not available for mechanized plantation style cash crop production. Women were becoming more and more adamant about the need to limit plantation agriculture and return land to indigenous uses. In addition, women are directly protecting forests and water catchment areas from real estate development, logging, plantation agriculture and mining. The subsistence uses of the land that peasant farm women pursued were, however, direct challenges to private interests who wished to buy forest land, clear it and either "develop" or subdivide and sell the land. For the land speculator or plantation owner, the Green Belt Movement was an impediment to trade.

Where industrial logging, mining, plantation agriculture, ranching, real estate development, manufacturing, and private "game parks" monopolize large areas of arable land, the land is no longer available for the production of food for local consumption. In Kenya, as in many other parts of Africa, those displaced by industrial and plantation development have to search elsewhere for land on which to secure a livelihood or fill the hopeless urban slums. Those looking for land clear forests to create space for food production. It is in this way that in Africa, like in Asia and South America, commercial logging and export oriented large-scale farming contribute to the destruction of the local environment and the earth's climate.

Rural and urban women's engagement in reforestation in Kenya is integrated into a larger subsistence-oriented farming system focused on self-provisioning and women-controlled trade. This indigenous approach to farming replicates what international social movements call "food sovereignty" or the right of farmers to choose what to grow, to feed themselves and their communities, and to be free from pressures to commercialize production to the exclusion of food security. With its food-centered land and water use practices, the Kenyan peasant women's "food sovereignty" movement builds upon their subsistence political economy. This political economy is remarkably free from petroleum product dependence. Food self-sufficiency also helps reduce the need for transportation and hence, petroleum products to move food from producer to consumer.

As Kenyan women engage in reforestation, they shift agricultural practice toward indigenous biodiverse and mixed farming systems. The overall implications of women's reforestation practices and subsistence food production include most prominently the realization of a post-climate destroying agriculture. This realization emanates from a communal culture that is in opposition to the postcolonial culture of international exploitation and environmental destruction.

With the dramatic increase in the price of petroleum products in 2005 and 2006, following the US military onslaughts in the Middle East, the practices of Kenyan rural women have been thrown into crisis. This follows from food growers' confrontations with small and large entrepreneurs who give priority to the production of charcoal from any available trees. This charcoal-intensive response to the high price of kerosene and other cooking and heating fuels directly counters women's prioritization of tree-planting and small-scale, biodiverse food production.

In Kenya and elsewhere in Africa, where rain-fed agriculture is the dominant economic activity, extractive industries such as commercial logging, mining and export-oriented agriculture are part of the climate change problem, leading to a downward cycle of deforestation, ecological decline, drought, conflict, famine and disease. African women's pursuit of "food sovereignty" through shifting land-use practices toward conservation, food production and other uses which mitigate climate change, can only make small gains unless an overall transformation takes place. This transformation requires an end to the commercializing policies and activities which strip Africa's environment and deny Africans' access to the necessities of life. This transformation also requires "energy sovereignty" via a strong emphasis on the localized development of solar, wind and water power, all of which have tremendous potential in Africa.

This article presents alternatives to the recommendations arising from mainstream climate change studies. The Stern Review and other reports suggest that a carbon trading world can provide solutions to climate change. Carbon trading relies heavily on the privatization of nature that exacerbates social inequality and allows industrialists to continue their rapacious activities. Within the carbon trade clauses of the Kyoto Protocol, women's collective tree-planting activities are not recognized as contributing to the reversal of climate change.

To return to the original question about African women's contribution to climate change via deforestation, it is pertinent to ask whether Africans should be expected to stop growing food so that African land can instead be allocated to the extraction of resources such as petroleum, hardwood, gold, diamonds, titanium and other minerals, and the production of exported agricultural products such as chocolate, coffee and tea? Or should Africans simply keep their food-producing activities out of large areas of forest which have been sold to northern industries as carbon sinks? The answers are clear enough if one is a stockholder or CEO in a mining venture. For the rest of us, the priority should be clear: African land is for African peoples, especially food producers geared toward the supply of local and regional markets. Herein lies a solution to deforestation and hunger on the continent.

In January 2006 Klaus Toepfer, the head of the United Nations Environment Programme (UNEP), warned that rainfall patterns in East Africa were at risk from climate change, deforestation and loss of forests, grasslands and other key ecosystems. He recommended that forests not only be maintained and conserved, "but that we invest in their restoration and expansion" (UNEP, 12 January 2006). This "restoration and expansion" is already underway in the "food sovereignty" movement. The Green Belt Movement is an outstanding example. Everyone agrees that global action is required to combat global climate change. Africa's women-led movements "from below" provide an alternative path out of the profit-centered, exclusionary, industrial cul-de-sac and toward a revitalization of the commons that serves the needs of all.

R E A D I N G **58**

Waikīkī

Haunani-Kay Trask (1994)

all those 5 gallon
toilets flushing
away tourist waste
into our waters

Waikīkī home
of *aliʻi*

sewer center
of Hawaiʻi

8 billion dollar
beach secret
rendezvous for
pimps

Hong Kong hoodlums
Japanese capitalists
haole punkers

condo units
of disease
drug traffic
child porn

AIDS herpes
old fashioned
syphilis
gangland murder

gifts of industrial
culture for primitive
island people
in need

of uplift discipline
complexity sense
of a larger world
beyond

their careful *taro*
gardens chiefly
politics, lowly
gods

Waikīkī: exemplar
of Western ingenuity
standing guard against

the sex life
of savages

the onslaught of barbarians

R E A D I N G **59**

Bedouin Women and Waste Related Hazards

Ilana Meallem and Yaakov Garb (2008)

Traditional semi-nomadic pastoralist Bedouin lifestyles generated little waste that was hazardous or non-organic. As Bedouin adopted more sedentary and westernized lifestyles, however, the nature of their consumption changed, generating volumes and kinds of waste that require organized disposal. Because of deep levels of deprivation and other social factors, however, the Negev Bedouin settlements lack the means to adequately dispose of these wastes, resulting in severe health and environmental hazards. Women—a marginalized segment within this already marginalized population—are hardest hit.

THE CONTEXT

The Bedouins of the Negev, Israel, are a minority population estimated at between 140,000 and 159,000 people, geographically and socio-culturally distinct from other Israeli Arabs and Jews. In many

Near Eastern and African countries, the relations between nomadic peoples and the state have grown increasingly tense over the course of the last century, with nomads becoming increasingly constrained spatially and politically. In Israel, this situation was intensified by the Israeli-Arab conflict. The Bedouin suffering massive out-migration following the 1948 war and establishment of the State of Israel, followed by years of military administration, loss of use of their traditional range lands, forced relocation, and, beginning in the late 60s, unilateral policies of urbanization that left them without traditional livelihoods on the one hand, and scarce possibilities for employment on the other.

After decades of these policies, currently about half of the Bedouin live in 7 planned settlements and the remainder in 46 unofficial settlements termed "unrecognized villages." Even in the former, conditions are very harsh; they rank lowest on Israel's socio-economic index and suffer from limited access to resources, sources of employment, and the inadequate provision of municipal services. The level of infrastructure and services in unrecognized villages is far worse; they lack formal infrastructure and services almost entirely. Electricity, running water, sewage and solid waste disposal, proper access roads, and the provision of decent health, educational and social services are mostly absent. This material "invisibility" from the state's perspective is reflected even at the symbolic level, as unrecognized settlements do not appear on official maps nor do they have road signs indicating their presence. Though some of these settlements predate the state of Israel, and are located on lands that traditionally had been Bedouin and were expropriated by the state, dwellings in these settlements are classified as "illegal" and subject to fines and demolition. Consequently, dwellings are mostly shacks and tents. Understandably, such conditions compromise the ability of these settlements to safely deal with the increased amounts of solid waste they produce.

THE CHANGING FACE OF WASTE: FROM RESOURCE TO BURDEN

Traditionally the pastoral seminomadic lifestyles of the Negev Bedouin revolved around raising livestock (camels, goats and sheep) and practicing rain-fed agriculture (wheat, barley, olives and figs). The traditional kinds of waste were organic (e.g. slaughter waste, manure, carcasses and food scraps) and were put to use, either as food for guard dogs or livestock, fertilizer for land, or sources of energy for heating and cooking. Old clothes were reused as rags for sanitation purposes, or as patches to repair clothes and tents. Hides from slaughtered animals were used to make bags, shoes and rugs. Wool or hair from livestock was used as stuffing for mattresses or pillows, to weave tents or make decorations.

In the past 25–30 years, government policies to fully sedenterize the Negev Bedouin and their increased engagement with modern lifestyles and western consumer culture has resulted in a shift from the traditional "closed cycle" and "waste free" lifestyles. Present day consumption levels are much higher and the kinds and amounts of solid waste

being produced and needing disposal in Bedouin settlements have changed dramatically. Home grown tomatoes that could be dried and salted to last all year were replaced by tins of tomatoes paste; fresh milk from herds has given way to shop bought sachets or powered products; breast milk replaced or supplemented by powdered milk formula—the list is endless. These "new" products almost all come in some form of packaging, whether tin, aluminum, plastic, glass, cardboard, or simply the plastic carrier bags used to bring home food. Residents in Bedouin settlements describe initially disposing of this "new waste" by simply throwing it out of the tent opening or windows. But over time it became obvious that this waste did not disappear, and, indeed, could be hazardous to children and livestock.

BACKYARD BURNING: A TOXIC SOLUTION

Despite the large volumes of new forms of waste, municipal waste disposal services are inadequate or entirely absent, especially in the unrecognized villages, and residents resort to informal waste disposal methods. In particular, waste burning has become a common practice in backyards, in or adjacent to ephemeral streams (that fill with water a few times a year after heavy rains), and in open areas. For example, in the village of Um Batin (pop. 4500), where a pilot study was conducted, over 70% of households surveyed reported using backyard burning in barrels or earthen pits as the primary mode of disposal.

Informal burning is highly hazardous since the types of solid waste generated by the Bedouin contain materials that are non-combustible (e.g. tin, glass, aluminum), explosive (e.g. pressurized canisters, closed bottles) or produce harmful chemicals when burned (plastics, polystyrene, chromated copper arsenate-CCA, pressure-treated wood, and bleached or colored papers). The lower incineration temperatures and poor combustion conditions in burning barrels or pits means fires tend to smolder and produce large amounts of harmful chemicals.

Dioxins and furans are the most problematic air pollutants emitted during waste burning—only a very small amount of chlorinated material (found in all plastics) needs to be present in waste for their release. The predominant pathway of exposure for humans is air-to-leaf, followed by bio-concentration (build up) in animal fat and consumption (especially animal fats and dairy products). For other pollutants, such as fine particulates, inhalation is the pathway of greatest concern. Also, the ash residue from backyard burning may contain toxic pollutants (mercury, lead, chromium, and arsenic), which can contaminate vegetables if scattered in gardens, or be ingested through hand to mouth contact.

As a result of the state's policies of restricting access to traditional grazing lands and the forced shift from seminomadic to sedentary lifestyles, only Bedouin with large herds (over 100 sheep, goats and camels) are able to migrate seasonally, while the majority cannot access grazing lands. The smaller unauthorized herds are kept out of the authorities' sight, inside pens or enclosures next to the owners' home, where they are fed fodder. This results in the exposure of these animals to pollutants from burning trash. In Bedouin settlements, waste burning sites were observed mere meters from livestock fodder stocks and on a number of occasions poultry was seen pecking at food waste left out for them on piles of burnt debris.

In addition to waste burning as an informal method of disposal, cooking and heating fires often use scavenged wood (which may be painted or pressure-treated), and plastic waste is often used as an ignition aid. Women and children were often seen sitting around these fires (making bread, cooking or keeping warm) and are at great risk of inhaling toxic fumes. Regular burning of waste or contaminated wood may increase the risk of health problems including chronic and acute toxicity, cancer, high blood pressure, brain damage, cardiovascular problems, birth defects, throat and skin irritation, headaches, loss of coordination, kidney and liver damage, nausea, fatigue, vomiting, and the worsening of existing respiratory and heart problems. A study by Cwikel and Barak on the health and welfare of Bedouin Arab women (aged 22–75) in the Negev, found high levels of hypertension (25%) and respiratory tract illnesses or asthma (13%). In Um Batin, the head doctor in the local health clinic and the head nurse at the Mother-Child clinic both saw respiratory illnesses as among the most common health problems. While their assumption has been that wood cooking fires are the major source of exposure to airborne pollutants and respiratory irritation, in fact, waste disposal practices may be a major factor.

BEDOUIN WOMEN: LESS SOCIAL POWER, GREATER EXPOSURE TO RISK

Exposure to informal waste disposal and its hazards is tied to the social conditions and power relations characterizing Bedouin settlements. An overwhelming factor is the extreme and systematic deprivation of the Bedouin settlements, especially the unrecognized ones, which lack almost all state infrastructures and services, including those for solid waste disposal. The impacts of this general incapacity fall most heavily on women, since, in Bedouin society the interaction of men with household waste is largely stigmatized, while women do most of the household work. Unless waste is dumped at a distance from the home (which requires transportation), the task of household waste disposal always falls largely or entirely on the women (from teen age upwards) who light household and waste fires, and are most likely to use plastic waste as an ignition aid or use contaminated wood in cooking or heating fires. Often, the movement of women is largely confined to the household compound where backyard burning occurs, and they are exposed to the air pollutants for prolonged periods of time (especially if they "guard" fires to keep children away or to stop it from spreading out of control). Thus, women are more at risk than men to injuries and diseases relating to waste disposal.

Further, in a patriarchal society, exposure to waste-related hazards correlates with a women's access to the assistance and goodwill of men. Even within the adjacent individual homes making up a single household compound in Um Batin, different methods of waste disposal—and thus impacts— were documented. Since women in unrecognized villages hardly ever have driving licenses or access to cars, they are dependent on men to help distance their waste. Women of lesser social power (who are not from the local tribe or are uneducated) are less able to demand that their husbands take part in the waste disposal process by removing the waste to a municipal container or to a distant dumpsite. When there is no man, they have no option but to backyard burn or dump household waste in close proximity to their homes. This is the case for single mothers who are separated from their husband or widowed, or for women who see their husbands infrequently, such as those in a polygamous marriage and not privileged to regular visits or whose husband is largely absent from the village grazing herds, imprisoned, or working in a distant factory.

DOUBLE HAZARD IN POORER HOUSEHOLDS

The gendered division of labor experienced by Bedouin women and their resultant exposure to toxins from waste disposal is compounded by poverty. Bedouin women from poorer households are at even greater risk of exposure to waste related hazards. They are more likely to use wood fires (rather than gas or electricity) for cooking and heating, and to live in exposed houses (such as tin shacks) which are very difficult to seal from the cold, pests and air pollution from waste burning. Additionally, poorer households are more likely to raise livestock for subsistence use (e.g. cows for milk, chickens for eggs) and be exposed to bioaccumulated toxins in the animal products they consume. Scavenging and storage of bulky waste in backyards for later reuse, a common practice among poorer residents, also increases a family's chances of exposure to the vermin or snakes sheltered by this waste.

WHEN TRADITION AGGRAVATES WASTE MANAGEMENT PRACTICES

Many practices in traditional Bedouin society are strongly based on blood relations, lineage and cooperative units. Scholars of Bedouin society, such as BenDavid, have seen this as an adaptation to the unpredictable and resource scarce environment of the desert, where being a member of a cooperative group requires loyalty and commitment, but ensures protection and increases the chances of survival. The structures found today are not timeless, however, as the Bedouin are themselves an amalgam of several groups, the constellation of tribal affiliations

and definitions changed under Turkish, British, and Israeli rule. In particular, as with other areas in Israel, tribal chiefs (Sheikhs) gained considerably in power under Israeli rule as intermediaries between the Arab population and the Israeli authorities.

Abu Lughod, Dinero, Hundt, Marteu and Nelson have illustrated various and shifting modalities of power that women have in Bedouin society. They were largely (and perhaps increasingly) excluded from political life under Israeli rule which is dominated by the strengthened position of sheikhs, intensification of tribal patronage relationships, and, most recently, the rise of party politics in the Bedouin sector. It has also been argued that the need of Bedouin men for domestic control has heightened corresponding to their subjugation and frustrations within the Jewish state and the loss of traditions and social continuity. In the last decade, however, new spaces and channels have opened up for Bedouin women to participate in or bypass male-dominated politics through the feminist stances of (and associated funding by) national and international NGOs, as well as new forms of organizing by the Islamic movement, educational opportunities for women, and the activities of non-profit associations working in health, domestic and educational spheres.

Our study found several ways in which tribal ties undermine the ability to protest harmful waste practices, and the organization of sounder arrangements. Bedouin tradition and limited access to land leads sons to build their homes in close proximity to their fathers' and men in polygamous marriages to locate the homes of their wives adjacent to each other in one compound so that dwellings and waste burning occur in dense quarters. And, though a consolidated burn location and time would make it possible to keep children away and reduce exposure, household waste piles are perceived as "personal" and not for open display. Conflicts between wives from polygamous marriages are common, also hindering co-operation. At the same time, respect for family members and caution in maintaining peaceful relations makes it very difficult to complain about the waste burning smoke of one's neighbors, who are often relatives. "We have reached a level of too much respect," said one Um Batin resident in frustration when this circumspection came at the expense of health and safety.

Similarly, in a second Bedouin village we studied that does have official state recognition and resources allocated for formal waste disposal, traditional tribal patronage relations undermined the allocation and governance of municipal capacities so that the situation of residents with respect to toxic waste exposures was not much better than in Um Batin.

TOWARD WASTE MANAGEMENT EDUCATION: WOMEN AS AGENTS OF CHANGE

While solid waste disposal is a major public health issue for Bedouin women and their families, awareness of waste handling options and hazards is low, with almost no educational efforts by the relevant authorities (e.g. Ministry of Health, Ministry of Education, and local health clinics). In the local clinics in the village of Um Batin, for example, there were educational displays on earthquake procedures and two educational events on nutrition and household hazards were organized for women, but no mention of the dangers of waste disposal. Indeed, the (non-Bedouin) Head Nurse in Um Batin's Mother-Child clinic had no idea how residents disposed of their waste, even though respiratory problems are among the most common complaints in the clinic. In a pilot survey among Um Batin residents, only a small minority considered plastics to be potentially hazardous if burnt, and about half were more concerned about the spread of diseases from mosquitoes than about inhaling air pollutants from burning waste piles. Over two-thirds of the houses who burn their household waste include empty insect spray canisters in the burn. One woman was scarred for life when one of these exploded in her face, as she watched over the waste fire.

In the longer term, a fundamental solution to these exposures must address the nested set of social forces discussed above. Equality in the eyes of the state and the provision of effective municipal infrastructures and services, sustainable livelihood options that allow reduction of the disposed waste stream, and more egalitarian household relations are key. But in the shorter term, the education of women regarding waste hazards and options for improved practices is an immediate means to begin mitigating the impacts of harmful informal waste disposal practices. Despite restrictions on the Bedouin women's movement, such information needs to reach women in their homes.

A model for such a program is provided by an innovative program conducted in 2001 by Ben Gurion University and the Centre for Women's Health Studies and Promotion that empowers Jewish and Bedouin women to work as Community Health Activists (CHA). This program, described by Hadjes and others, gives training in project implementation, leadership skills and knowledge in women's health to CHA's who were then able to educate women in their own communities by holding small group meetings in different households. A similar format could help educate women about waste related hazards and environmental health, modify the behavior of their families (especially their children) and help improve health conditions for the entire household. This awareness campaign needs to be coordinated with local health clinics; posters in Arabic with clear diagrams can be put up in waiting rooms and a waste disposal hazards section included in the existing "household safely" education program. It is also imperative that doctors and nurses be educated about the living conditions of their patients. Other actions would include separation of plastics and other hazardous materials from burn piles, organization into collectives to remove household waste to municipal bins in other settlements, and, possibly, the reuse of agricultural and organic waste to generate biogas, which can be a source of energy for cooking heating and lighting.

CONCLUSIONS: THE OVERLAID MARGINALIZATIONS OF BEDOUIN WOMEN

Exposure to toxic effects from solid waste is a major health threat, and also a metaphor for the toxic social situations of Bedouin woman in the Negev. Bedouin women are triply marginalized as Arabs in a Jewish state, residents of Israel's periphery, and females in a sharply patriarchal society. Also, solid waste is itself a "marginal" problem: diffuse, banal, less well known—and quite literally at the "disposal" and "waste" end of the cycle of production and consumption that so preoccupies society. These forms of marginalization interact with each other making it harder to develop adequate responses. But while women feel the impacts of improper waste disposal most severely, it is not only the waste handlers, but their neighbors, all the residents of the settlements, and also populations living well beyond the boundaries of the Bedouin settlements who suffer, as waste dumped in riverbeds is carried long distances. These overlapping forms of discrimination will need to be overcome in order for Bedouin women to obtain the status, resources and services afforded to other citizens of Israel.

R E A D I N G **60**

An Ugly Picture for Flower Workers and Their Children

David A. Taylor (2006)

Every year, Americans spend nearly $20 billion on fresh flowers, about 70% of which come from abroad, mainly from Latin America, according to the Society of American Florists. While this can represent an economic boon for some countries, overuse of pesticides and lack of protections for female workers can cause serious health effects for those women's children, according to a paper in the March 2006 issue of *Pediatrics*.

The study of female workers in Ecuador's flower industry and their children found that a mother's work exposure to pesticides during pregnancy was associated with neurological impairment, including a significant decrease in visuospatial performance. After accounting for other factors such as malnutrition, the researchers concluded that "prenatal pesticide exposure may adversely affect brain development."

The authors, led by Philippe Grandjean, an adjunct professor at the Harvard School of Public Health, also found that children whose mothers were exposed during pregnancy tended to have higher blood pressure than unexposed children, a finding with broader implications. "Increased blood pressure, when present in childhood, is a risk factor for cardiovascular disease in later life," the researchers noted.

The researchers looked at schoolchildren under the age of 10 in the Andean community of Tabacundo. Physical exams checked each child's blood pressure and certain neurobehavioral functions, such as motor coordination, dexterity, attention, short-term memory, balance, and spatial perception

and performance. Mothers were interviewed about their own exposure history and background as well as their children's medical history and health. The data analysis took into account each family's housing and nutritional situation, as well as maternal education. The researchers also measured current pesticide exposure among the children.

Of 72 children included in the analysis, 37 were considered to have been exposed prenatally—they were born to women who had worked in the floriculture industry while pregnant. All of these mothers reported following normal safety precautions, and none had worked as pesticide applicators. Nineteen of the exposed children's fathers and 16 of the unexposed children's fathers also had worked in floriculture during the pregnancy, while most other fathers worked in construction trades.

Prenatal exposure was associated with significantly higher systolic blood pressure and substantial deficits on spatial performance. In this regard, the researchers concluded that pesticide toxicity may add to the adverse influence of malnutrition. Also, the effects of prenatal pesticide exposure seemed to last longer than those known to be associated with pesticide exposures in adults. However, the investigators found no link between prenatal exposure and stunting.

Elizabeth Guillette, an anthropologist at the University of Florida who has studied the health effects of pesticides in Mexico, says Grandjean's study reinforces earlier findings. "Pesticide use is definitely impacting the offspring in terms of mental and neu-rophysical abilities," she says.

Such concerns motivated the founders of Organic Bouquet, which since January 2001 has marketed flowers produced with fewer toxic pesticides. It sells flowers online and in natural food stores such as Whole Foods, using only producers certified by one of three programs. VeriFlora, one of the three certi-fication programs, sets criteria for U.S.-sold flowers that include low pesticide residue and compliance with local labor laws.

As for traditional flower farms, Guillette says much better education is needed—not just on safe use at work, but also safe practices in the home, such as washing exposed clothes separately and minimiz-ing in-home pesticide use. Grandjean agrees that education would help, but only if industry and indi-viduals follow through with less extensive fumiga-tions at work, use of less-toxic chemicals at work and at home, and use of protective equipment.

"I'm optimistic we can do something and change," says Guillette, "but action needs to be taken now."

R E A D I N G   **61**

Poverty, Pests, and Pesticides

Hanna-Andrea Rother (2008)

Kagiso[1] awoke to the sound of whimpers, scratching at the small red welts covering her arms. Her gaze was captured not by her three children lying on mats on the floor, scratching and softly whining, but on the quick movement of the cockroaches descending the walls and scurrying under the wardrobe. Hun-ger, malnutrition, poor amenities, unemployment and security risks are the daily experience of poverty in South Africa (SA), but the bed bugs, cockroaches and rats that plague life in informal settlements/shanty towns were more than Kagiso could bear. Sardined in the taxi heading to the taxi rank market where she has a stand to sell the traditional drink of Mahewu to make a meager living, Kagiso counted the bed bugs' victories on her fellow passengers' arms. The solution to her insect woes greeted her on arrival at the taxi rank where numerous street sellers tout cheap pesticides, unlabeled in local con-tainers such as brandy nips and juice bottles. For R5 (approximately US$0.69), Kagiso slipped a used juice bottle with a clear substance (mostly likely the highly hazardous organophosphate, methamida-phos, commonly sold on SA streets) into her bag to spray that evening onto her and the children's beds, as well as apply everywhere in the house for

cockroaches. Placing the pesticide containing juice bottle behind her makeshift Mahewu stand, she left her son in charge in order to look for change for her morning's prospective customers. Kagiso could not foresee the life altering events that followed her good intentions of protecting herself and her family from pest-related disease and discomfort. Upon her return, Kagiso discovered that a regular customer, a local taxi driver, had diluted his Mahewu with the recently purchased pesticide, mistaking the bottle under the table to contain water. Within two hours, the taxi driver was dead and Kagiso was left with a funeral bill of R2000 (approximately US$285) and a furious community, forcing her to leave her home to relocate to an area where her anonymity would enable her to sell her product among people who would trust buying Mahewu from her without the fear of her poisoning them.

THE THREE P'S—POVERTY, PESTS AND PESTICIDES

Research on the health impact on women exposed to pesticides tends to focus on women engaged in agricultural practices. However, studies show that poverty, pests and pesticides are interlinked and while agricultural exposures are a serious issue, what must not be underestimated are the risks associated with urban domestic use of pesticides, particularly for poor women living in informal settlements/shanty towns. Poor South African women are particularly at risk of acute poisonings and chronic health effects resulting from the use of cheap and illegal pesticides commonly sold at taxi rank markets and on trains, that are known as "*street pesticides.*" The example of Kagiso's story highlights how street pesticides provide a "solution" to the intense poverty-related pest problems poor urban women in South Africa must live and deal with while increasing their exposures to unforeseen risks. In particular, her case shows that the use of street pesticides puts women at risk of inadvertently poisoning their own children and others. Women are not only exposed to health risks from using street pesticides in their homes, but from selling these in an effort to earn much needed income. The use and sale of street pesticides is a complex and silent public health problem. This is particularly a problem for women sellers and users for the following reasons: the mobility of sellers, the products sold are unlabeled and untraceable, the high exposure application and decanting procedures, the high toxicity of the pesticides, the potential for environmental contamination and the general lack of awareness of the associated risks. Perhaps one of the reasons this is a silent public health problem is because there is so little research on the problems women face with poverty-related pests, controlling these and the risks associated with using highly toxic street pesticides. My current research project is investigating the use of street pesticides in Cape Town, South Africa, with the aim of assisting poor South African women to reduce poverty-related pests while protecting themselves and their families from the risks linked to street pesticides. This article presents some of my current findings resulting from interviews with street sellers, reviewing child poisoning cases and documenting women's perceptions of pests and pesticides. Furthermore, what is highlighted is how women are caught up in, and often ill affected by, the poverty, pests and pesticides interlinked cycle.

POVERTY

Poverty plays a major role in women's exposure to street pesticides, especially in relation to unemployment and poor housing conditions. Between 45–50% of South Africans live in varying degrees of poverty with approximately 60% of SA's 45 million inhabitants living in urban areas (poverty statistics in SA are based on households, not gender). Urban poor women in SA face countless socio-economic problems as a result of poverty, such as high unemployment (approximately 37% for black South Africans; higher for black women with women earning 55% less than men). With high unemployment and the responsibility of caring for children predominately falling on women, selling pesticides in the informal market becomes a means to survive. Street pesticides are in high demand, based on my current research findings, and desirable to sell. Women predominately sell a variety of items (e.g., food, socks, razors) along with street pesticides. Housing shortages plague urban areas in SA, particularly in informal settlements (includes both formal and informal housings) where anywhere up to 25 people share a 50 square meter house or shack. In terms of amenities in informal settlements, up to 50 dwellings can be expected to share one water tap and one toilet. Poor urban living conditions including overcrowding, makeshift houses, poor sanitation and limited/no refuse collection create the breeding grounds for numerous pests.

PESTS

Pest populations are much higher in urban poor areas than elsewhere in the country, adding extra stresses to the plight of poor women. Each urban pest carries different diseases, discomfort levels or both. For example, rats expose women and children to disease. The current unofficial statistic in Cape Town is four rats per person living in the city. Another related pest are bed bugs, which suck the blood of urban inhabitants while they sleep (as illustrated in Kagiso's story). The problem of poverty-related pests is not viewed as a vital public health problem, and this burden falls predominately on women who attempt to manage these pests to protect their families. Women also carry the burden of looking after sick children from exposures to pests, as well as not being able to sell (earn an income) if they themselves are sick.

PESTICIDES

Women commonly use street pesticides to control urban pests because of the high cost of commercially sold pesticides and their lack of accessibility in urban townships. A 2001 study highlighted that 80% of inner city houses in SA controlled cockroaches and rats with pesticides. Street pesticides refer to pesticides sold in SA at local city train and taxi rank stations for uses not legally permitted, and predominately in small, unlabeled and inexpensive packages by street vendors.

One common street pesticide sold for rat control is the agricultural insecticide *aldicarb*. Aldicarb (also know as "two step" as the rat can only take two steps before dying) is a carbamate pesticide which acts as a nerve poison by disrupting nerve impulses, banned in 13 countries and according to the World Health Organization (WHO), ranks as one of the most acutely toxic pesticides still in use. Uniformed women purchase this cheap pesticide for about 20–50 cents (approximately US 3–8 cents). *Chlorpyrifos*, an organophosphate pesticide recently banned for domestic use in the USA because of the high related poisoning cases, has also been identified as being sold in unlabeled bottles to be sprayed in homes. Women often pour the liquid pesticide into empty cosmetic spray bottles for applying at home which means they handle these pesticides more than a commercial product and increase their risks. *Methamidophos* is a highly toxic agricultural insecticide, especially when taken orally (oral doses have resulted in the mortality of half of the laboratory test organisms). This was most likely the pesticide in the story above and is commonly the clear liquid sold in juice bottles (from Rand 5–10 per bottle; US 76 cents $1.50) and medicine containers (Rand 25;~US$4). *Methamidophos* is currently banned in 13 countries and it cannot be imported into 44 countries; however it is still registered for agricultural use in South Africa and sold on the streets of Cape Town for controlling pests in the home.

HEALTH COSTS

Both the diseases associated with urban pests (e.g., typhus and Eosinophilic Meningitis from rats), as well as the acute and chronic (i.e., long-term) health effects from street pesticides pose a threat to the health of urban poor women and their families. Thus the question arises as to whether the chronic health effects associated with street pesticide exposures are the inevitable price women have to pay for the daily toil of trying to survive the burdens of poverty? Many South African women living in poverty are not aware of the trade off that is being made between their survival and their families' health. Global research on pesticides has shown that pesticides are associated with causing multiple health effects such as asthma, birth defects, neurological effects, developmental effects, various cancers, and hormone disruptions (e.g., fertility problems, endometriosis, early on-set of puberty in girls). Furthermore, poverty-related malnutrition, common for poor South African women and children, has been shown to increase the effects of pesticide poisonings. Thus South African women have to bear the hidden costs (e.g., health care, unable to work or care for children) resulting from exposures to pesticides.

SOCIO-ECONOMIC COSTS

There are several hidden socio-economic costs for South African women associated with the use and sale of street pesticides. Kagiso's story illustrates some of these such as Kagiso having to pay for the funeral of the deceased taxi driver, being ostracized by the community she sold to, and having to uproot her family to a new location further away to rid herself of the new stigma attached to her.

CHILD POISONINGS AND HEALTH EFFECTS

Children in Cape Town are particularly vulnerable to poisonings from street pesticides for three main reasons: 1) street pesticides are often sold in old beverage bottles (e.g., brandy nips, popular juice bottles) and children mistakenly drink these; 2) street pesticides, particularly aldicarb granules, are mixed with food the family eats (e.g., a maize porridge staple) and put on the floor for pests to eat (e.g., rats) making these accessible to children; and 3) illiterate adults who accidentally administer a street pesticide to children assuming that the bottle, which resembles common medicines, is a cold remedy (the cause of death for three children admitted to Cape Town's Red Cross Children's Hospital [RXH] during 2004–2006). In the current study, 21% of children admitted to RXH for pesticide poisoning were under the age of one and 62% were three or younger. Women have to bear the various costs of their children's health being affected both by pesticides and pests—e.g., taking time off work to take a poisoned child to hospital, looking after a child that is impaired by pesticides and who can not contribute to the household.

SUICIDES

The high toxicity of street pesticides, their easy accessibility and low cost make them a viable option for South African women who want to commit suicide. Recently, two women in Cape Town have used street pesticides (i.e., aldicarb and methamidophos) to take their own and their child's life (i.e., one and eight months old). Although unsuccessful in their attempts, the women were aware that these products killed pests and therefore could be lethal to humans. Although not having access to street pesticides will not reduce suicide and homicide attempts, the hidden cost here is the potential health effects that will burden the already troubled woman/family as a result of consuming pesticides.

ENVIRONMENTAL CONTAMINATION COSTS

Contamination of the environment by street pesticides, particularly water bodies and soil, occurs through several means. For example, spillage and run off into water bodies (often used for drinking and washing) occurs when decanting, transporting, mixing and using street pesticides. Another means of

environmental contamination occurs from throwing used containers into rivers, urban canals, pit toilets, rubbish dumps and land fills. The implications for women is further and compounded exposures through contaminated water and plants (from uptake from contaminated soils). The hidden costs here are both in terms of environmental cleanup, as well as health costs to exposed women.

A NICHE MARKET

The high demand for street pesticides in South Africa is driving a viable supply market. Regulating the use of street pesticides in South Africa is complex and complicated. The current main pesticide Act is from 1947 and although more recent regulations include that the use of aldicarb other than as an insecticide is illegal, there are no other specific regulations regarding street pesticides. Controlling the illegal uses and sale of these highly toxic pesticides is extremely difficult given the lack of information on sources/distributors to street sellers (women sellers buy from mobile distributors who buy from others), trying to find sellers who are highly mobile, as well as South Africa not having the capacity to police street sellers when crime, drug abuse and violence directed at women are more pressing. The economic and social benefactors from using and selling street pesticides is wide spread from women having temporary relief from devastating and annoying pests, reduction in exposures to pest diseases, employment, street pesticide sellers distributors making a profit, to the transnational pesticide companies making profits beyond agricultural sales. Thus the demand for street pesticides for the benefits of killing pests and the resulting profit making from sales drives and sustains this niche market in poor urban communities.

CONCLUSION

Kagiso was an ordinary poor South African woman trying to make money to survive and using street pesticides to reduce the enormous discomforts and potential health affects associated with poverty-related urban pests. However, within a matter of a few minutes, the time it takes to drink a cup of Mahewu, Kagiso's life moved out of the ordinary into a brutal nightmare. Family and friends are trying to organize trauma counseling for her, but the damage is done. Her nightmare is shared by South African parents of deceased and poisoned children exposed to street pesticides, as well as by those women who have attempted suicide and homicide with street pesticides. The use and sale of street pesticides are an over-looked poverty related outcome. Too difficult to control and too difficult to monitor, women and children are vulnerable victims.

The use of street pesticides for controlling pests by the urban poor is not a problem confined to South Africa. Reports of the use and sale of street pesticide exist from Mozambique, Zambia, Zimbabwe, Tanzania, Kenya, Brazil and New York, to name a few. Thus a global effort needs to be made to remove toxic street pesticides from the global sale arena. Street pesticides fall through the legislative cracks both nationally and on the global chemical management arena. This is due to the fact that they are not monitored or easily traceable. How does one regulate a product that is unlabeled, comes from various sources and is made of varying inconsistent concentrations? Despite the obvious difficulties, international initiatives for managing and reducing the risks of chemicals need to address the intense use and sale of street pesticides (e.g., the Rotterdam Convention—Prior Informed Consent, the Strategic Approach to International Chemicals Management—SAICM). Currently chemical safety and pesticide regulation is often not a development priority, especially in

terms of poverty reduction. Further, public awareness raising interventions are needed (e.g., this current project has produced pamphlets highlighting street pesticide dangers and pesticide alternatives in some of the local South African languages to be distributed at hospitals and clinics). There is a need for interventions and policy support to make alternative approaches accessible, especially for women. This would aid current poverty reduction initiatives through promoting cheaper means for controlling pests and reduce potential costs of ill health.

As controlling street pesticides at point of sale is extremely difficult, a more viable strategy for South Africa and other countries where street pesticides are problematic, would be to outright ban these highly toxic street pesticides that cannot be controlled in order to protect women's health and livelihood. However, South Africa exports many agricultural goods and no doubt women are caught in an export and health of poor women trade off. The balancing act of economic gain and women's health leaves women the losers when it comes to street pesticides. Publicly voicing Kagiso's story and drawing attention (through research findings) to street pesticides' enormous detrimental effects on women (especially in developing countries) is the first step to addressing this silent and global public health problem.

NOTE
1. Names and events altered for protection purposes. Thanks go to Tembinkosi Qondela for researching this incident.

R E A D I N G **62**

The World of the Gift Economy

Genevieve Vaughan (2008)

Dear Distant Friend,
    As you know, in 2220 there will be the worldwide festival of the Goddess, which we are preparing for now. Some people from different regions will travel to the places marked by ley lines, others will travel to the historical memory places where humanity made

wrong choices, and they will pray there for the healing of the earth.
    I plan to stay at home, help to make the festival here and be part of the hospitality committee for our honored guests.

At the entrance to our town there is a huge statue of the many-breasted Artemis, the symbol of our economy and our society. We will decorate her with flowers, and there will be flowers throughout the town. The town Grandmothers Council made a list of necessary jobs, and I chose that one. I chose to do it because it is not too hard and because I love flowers and the Goddess. My fellow townspeople will bring me flowers from their gardens because they know I signed up for the job and will need them. My garden does not produce enough flowers to cover the base of the statue, much less the statue itself.

Let me tell you a little about our life here, since you will come to visit . . .

From my history classes I learned about poverty and how in the past with the market system, Patriarchy and Capitalism, most people did not even have enough to eat. That seems so strange to me. How could those people live? How could the ones they called "rich" live with themselves?

Many-breasted Artemis is the symbol of the gifts that come from everywhere, the way the Goddess Earth nurtures all of us abundantly. She is a symbol of our nurturing economy where we give freely to each other the way Earth gives to us.

Once we learned that the logic of gift giving and receiving (not the logic of exchange and the market) was the basis of our language and our positive human relations, we were able to derive a new psychology that allowed us to live in peace and to avoid constructing the kinds of pathological personalities that were functional to the market economy and Patriarchy. Gender in languages used to convince little "male" hums that they were not supposed to be nurturing like their mothers, so they used to hit people instead just to have some kind of relation with them. Poor things! That developed into all kinds of violence, and big groups people called "nations" tried to destroy each other through the terrible violence they called "war." Wars helped to create the scarcity that their market economy needed to keep control. People spent lots of that symbolic instrument they called "money" on them.

We have many new words now that avoid linguistic gender, and that helps all of us keep our identities with our mothers. Our gift economy maintains a continuity between mothers' care and the caregiving society at large.

I was brought up in a loving family group. My mother was my primary caregiver but I had many other people who loved me when I was a birl. People who choose to be mothers live in the center of our town, while those who only want to be mothers' helpers live in a circle around them. People who provide the sperm are allowed to live with the mothers if that is agreeable to both and can help in the mothering. Some hums do not choose to live in towns, so they live in the countryside, also usually in groups.

Little birls are a focal point in our society. We love to play with them and care for them and watch what they do so we can learn from them, and they can learn from us. They have collective play and storytimes where teachers help them learn about different ways and different gifts. They learn sports and songs and playing musical instruments, painting and drawing, storytelling and inventing poetry. They don't learn to read until they are about eight years old because it was found that early reading caused a leaning toward too much abstraction. But mentors teach them the ways of all the species as well as the history of humanity and the earth. Later in school they also do biology, geology, philosophy, psychology, spirituality, health, sentimental education and relationship training.

Birls learn all kinds of crafts. As teenagers they familiarize themselves with the ways of making the many different kinds of things that are necessary for living, from shoes and clothing to carpentry and plumbing. As adult hums then they can both do these things for themselves and/or specialize and do them for others.

Hums like to guess each other's needs, so it is not unusual if I need a new pair of shoes to find them on my doorstep without my even asking anyone. However, if I need something and no one has guessed it, I can ask. I go to the person who has specialized in plumbing, for example, and s/he willingly comes to my house. There are some jobs that nobody likes to do of course, but all of us are willing to satisfy real needs, especially community(ies) needs, so we do them.

Most of the birls living in the gift economy show signs of psychic ability, so there is also psycho/spiritual training. Some of our adult hums are learning to communicate psychically with animals and plants and we try to prepare the little birls for that possibility. If they are particularly open to their intuition, they can become part of the Grandmothers' Council youth auxiliary. It is in the Grandmothers' Council that important collective decisions are made. In the Council of All, though, anyone is allowed to speak, because the Goddesses can speak through anyone and all voices are important, even those of the oldest hums and the littlest birls.

Collective production such as factory work, road building and repair is done by young hums in their early twenties for a period of three years. This is sufficient for the purpose. After the age of 30, we begin to study the ancient texts so as to understand better the gift-giving human logic and its consequences, what we should emphasize and what we should avoid. Committees study needs and how they arise and diversify, and they help invent things for people to do. New art forms, both virtual and real, allow a flowering of creativity.

At 18, birls choose a sexual orientation as by that time it will probably have become clear to them the kinds of others they will love the most. There is a big ritual for this coming of age (actually we have lots of rituals marking all the stages of our lives). It is possible, however, to change sexuality later if that is desired. At that period potential mothers also begin to know if they want to have little hummies themselves. Some young adults enjoy promiscuity, so they live near the temple of Artemis and function as what would have been called in ancient times "temple prostitutes." However, since we have no money or exchange in our society, these relationships are very different from those of the past.

Living in abundance as we do, with birth control easily available, we have found that after the limitations of population, which were instituted two centuries ago, very few hums wanted to have large families. Since care of the little ones is shared by many adults, the family spirit includes the little birls of one's neighbors, and so families of more than two or three birls have become quite unusual. One hummie is most common. Birls call all the others in their age group their close kin. The fact that many of us decide not to have offspring contributes to the maintenance of relatively small living communities. Service to elders and the sick is highly valued in our society. Many of us find pleasure in healing and elder care, and the work is usually light because so many do it together.

There are large permaculture areas around our towns where food is grown with very little need for hard work. When work is necessary the Grandmother's Council decides upon days, times and allocations. We participate in numerous gifting circles at home and with hums from other towns near and far. Travelers bring gifts and are greeted with great hospitality. There are also circulations of cultural gifts and performances as hums from far places and different cultures visit us and communicate with us about their history, art and ways of doing things. All of this interconnection is arranged by internet and we also keep friendships on the internet with hums we have met through the gifting circles. Transportation is easy in our solar-powered vehicles, mostly light rail trains, but there are also some airplanes, which use solar power. For short distances many of us are using horses and light wagons again (and bicycles are still popular).

Hums are encouraged to love the local earth, as it was discovered that the urge for private property also satisfied Mother Earth's need to be loved in all Her particular places. Private property in part satisfied this need but it had so many negative aspects in the exchange economy that it had to be changed. Now we have property attributed to individuals and families to be conscious of and care for, as well as the commons we all share. This love of the earth keeps everyone sane and grounded and creates an individual and a collective consciousness focused on the Great Mother.

We call our way of life a Maternal Anarchy. When it was found that what was called "male gender" was a false historical psychological construction that was functional to the toxic Patriarchal Capitalist economy, all the hums of that time decided to give it up (or stop enabling it) and base all their identity constructions on gift giving. This was made easier because they also discovered that language was a kind of verbal gift giving, so they did not need to divide mothering from other aspects of life like thinking and decision making. They realized that everyone was already doing gift giving, practicing the logic of extended mothering, the logic of a better world, in language and communication. When they realized that exchange and the market were reinfecting everyone all the time, they organized the free distribution of goods directly to needs. The earlier failure of Patriarchal Communism had already demonstrated the need for maternal rather than patriarchal values. The leadership of mothers and grandmothers was what finally saved the species and the planet.

Giving rather than exchange is the way we transmit our goods. This puts us in alignment with language. We project the Mother onto Nature and so are always in a creative-receptive state. We live in community with Mother Nature and the spirits of nature. Computers help us know who has needs and who has supplies. Since Patriarchal domination no longer exists, and everyone is brought up to be equally nurturing, there is almost no tendency toward hierarchy, not even in the competition for reputation as the greatest giver, which was once a tendency not only in market societies but also in some indigenous societies and among early free software providers.

There is a lot of study on the logic of gift giving, and applying its principles. The other-interest and inclusiveness that are part of gift giving have brought an end to the ugly ancient practices of racism. The elimination of Patriarchy and exchange everywhere has defused the emphasis on categorization and belonging to superior categories that was part of racism, classism and sexism.

During the great transition that occurred two centuries ago, stimulated by the devastating environmental changes, it became clear that Patriarchal Capitalism was wasting all the wealth of humanity on wars and phallic symbols of power. The recognition of the logic of the gift paradigm as the basic human logic and therefore the redefinition of the species as homo donans instead of just homo sapiens caused a shift in everyone's thinking and values. They stopped spending money on violence and began refunding the wealth that the system had parasitically drained from the Global South and from the poor everywhere. The Great Give-Back marked the practical shift toward the gift economy and the Age of the Restoration of the Mother. Land was given to all those who wanted it, capital was returned to its places of origin. Exploitation stopped and abundance was allowed to accrue at the local level. There was no more competition for scarce resources but a situation of plenty allowed the circulation of gifts, the nurturing of positive human relations and the leisure for education and travel, which improved the lives of so many.

Experimental communities of several thousand hums each tried out different types of social organization and finally arrived at the one we have now. It is a global system, which avoids the possibility of the reassertion of patriarchal domination while still celebrating local traditions.

There is a healers' community near our town. Many diseases have disappeared and addictive or pathological personalities are very rare, given the positive human relations coming from the gift economy. Issues of what used to be called justice are now a branch of healing. Taking the cue from an indigenous practice, we have singled out some islands where hums who have done particularly grievous things can be isolated in Nature for a certain period, so they can come back into contact with themselves.

After the Great Give-Back, hums began to think about the symbolic aspects of Patriarchy and decided to eliminate all the symbols of patriarchal power, including skyscrapers. The destruction of these immense phallic symbols was cathartic for the collective unconscious and helped to eliminate patriarchal motivations of domination and greed. The gift economy functions best in nature, so most hums happily moved to the country. Some libraries and art museums are still maintained, however, to give us a sense of the past.

The fear of death is less strong now, not only because of the atmosphere of safety, positive relations and love in which we live but also because this atmosphere allows more communication across the boundaries between the worlds.

I guess the same must be true for you too since you have been making yourselves known to us through flying saucers and crop circles for so long but have only just recently contacted us in person. I am so glad you can meet us now without concern for our safety or for your own. As I give the offerings of flowers to the statue of Artemis for the festival, I will thank her for the blessing of your presence among us.

For an ever expanding community of the heart,
Igniviva Terrasbirl
11/21/2219

CHAPTER 11

Women and Political Systems Worldwide

Melanie Hughes and *Pamela Paxton*

Melanie M. Hughes is assistant professor of sociology at the University of Pittsburgh, USA. She has published articles on women in politics in such journals as *American Sociological Review*, *Politics & Gender*, *Social Problems*, *Annual Review of Sociology*, and the *International Journal of Sociology*, and has coauthored *Women, Politics, and Power: A Global Perspective* (Pine Forge, 2007) with Pamela Paxton. Her current research focuses on the intersection of gender and minority status in national legislatures around the world.

Pamela Paxton is associate professor of sociology and political science (by courtesy) at the Ohio State University, USA. Some of her previous research on politics and gender appears in the *American Sociological Review*, the *American Journal of Sociology* and *Social Forces*. She is coauthor of *Women, Politics, and Power: A Global Perspective* with Melanie M. Hughes (Pine Forge, 2007). Her current research considers women's political participation over time and connections between social capital and social networks.

> If I were to bleed realizing
> in these marbled halls only the blood of men
> gets spilled over treaties and laws
> pens poised, demanding;
> I say, let it flow, be my witness,
> Senator, King, and Lord.
>
> Let's talk real democracy;
> it's only once a month and comforting to be
> so regular; no sharp screams and cannon,
> gun and stick; sporadic blood
> is worse than monthlies
> even in your dreams.

"If I Were to Bleed," anonymous.

Formal politics, the realm of official state policy, is notoriously a masculine place where women's voices are diminished and men's words are paramount. As the poem "If I Were to Bleed" suggests, these "marbled halls" are spaces where men "talk democracy" and wrangle over treaties, wars, and laws. This is where men have traditionally ruled and where the presence of women is novel and almost alien. The poem makes the case for women's inclusion; it also hints at the potential transformation of these marbled halls were they to be inclusive of women's everyday realities. This chapter explores this formal notion of politics and explores women's representation in this arena; it also broadens the definition of politics to include women's informal political activity and addresses political movements at both local and transnational levels that seek to improve women's lives worldwide.

Politics is an important arena for feminist concern because it is where decisions occur that have serious consequences for women's everyday lives. The legitimate power of the state gives authority to certain people who hold official positions in government. This authority allows them to decide how to allocate scarce resources such as tax revenues and to make decisions that may help some people at the expense of others. Decisions by politicians impact individuals' choices by encouraging some behaviors and outlawing others. Public officials also have power to enforce their decisions, sometimes with force. The power of the state is thus central in shaping major social institutions like the family or education, and codifying particular beliefs and practices into law. Because women have traditionally been associated with the "private" feminized spheres of home and family, they have had to fight to gain entrance into the "public" masculinized world of politics. A Web search for the phrase "If women were to rule the world" produces a host of both serious and humorous suggestions of what the world might look like with more women in power. In considering such a scenario it is important to note differences between "women" and "feminism": even though the presence of women in politics generally has a positive influence in promoting legislation favorable to women and children (Swers, 2002), this is not always the case. Feminism is a political belief and strategy for change and is not owned by women.

This chapter begins with a discussion of women's formal representation in politics, exploring this representation worldwide and addressing paths to women's power in politics. The next sections focus on challenges and obstacles to women in politics, providing explanations for women's underrepresentation as well as national and international strategies for their participation in formal politics. The final section addresses the role of women in informal politics and emphasizes the broad efforts of women acting politically to organize and put pressure on established power systems.

WOMEN'S FORMAL REPRESENTATION IN POLITICS

The most basic formulation for political equality between women and men is formal representation, meaning that women have the legal right to participate in politics on an equal basis with men. Giving women formal representation means that women have the right to vote, run for political office, and participate in political life. Indeed, looking at the makeup of political figures or public officials in a country highlights who is allowed to make decisions for that society, and, sometimes, who is even considered a "citizen." The reading "Please Mind the Gap" by Alyssa McDonald attests to disparities in the political gender gap (the differences by gender of individuals' relationships to politics). Consider the following statistics and think about their implications for the women in those societies. Did you know, for example, that . . .

- The average percentage of women in national parliaments around the world is currently 18 percent?
- In almost three-quarters of national legislatures worldwide, women make up less than a fifth of political officials?

- In the almost 200 countries in the world, a woman is the head of government (president or prime minister) in only eight of these countries?
- Rwanda has had among the highest percentage of women in its legislature: surpassing 50 percent?
- Ten countries have no women in their national legislatures?
- Women only gained the right to vote nationally in Switzerland in 1971?
- In 2005, the United States ranked 61 of 185 countries in percent of women in the national legislature, falling behind countries such as Bosnia and Herzegovina, Ecuador, and Mozambique?

Perhaps this last bullet surprises you since the United States touts itself as a democracy supportive of equal rights. However, since Jeannette Rankin became the first woman elected to the U.S. Congress in 1917, women's representation in U.S. politics has grown rather slowly. It was not until 1981 that women held even 5 percent of seats in the House of Representatives, and there have been years with *no* women in the Senate as late as 1977. In 2010, the 111th Congress includes 17 elected female senators (17 percent) and 75 female congresswomen (17 percent). Seventeen percent is certainly an improvement from earlier levels, but it remains far below the percent of women (51 percent) in the U.S. population.

Women's representation in the United States mirrors that of many other countries. In fact, the United States is right at the world average in terms of its levels of female representation in politics. Although the United States does better than some countries, such as Micronesia or Saudi Arabia that have no women in parliament, it is far worse than others. Sweden and Rwanda have over 40 percent women in their national parliaments, while countries such as Spain, Argentina, and South Africa have more than 30 percent women in their national legislatures. Like in the United States, in many countries today, women's struggle for equal representation in politics proceeds slowly. And some populations and governments remain openly hostile to the notion of women in politics.

As Table 1 shows, it is clear that Scandinavian nations have surpassed all other regions in their levels of women's political representation through the last half century. In contrast, the Middle East has persistently had the lowest average levels of female representation. While women's representation in Latin America, Africa, and the West progressed

TABLE 1   Percent Women in National Legislatures: Historical Comparison of Regions

	1955	1965	1975	1985	1995	2005
Scandinavian	10.4	9.3	16.1	27.5	34.4	38.2
Western nations	3.6	4.0	5.5	8.6	12.8	22.7
Eastern Europe	17.0	18.4	24.7	27.0	8.4	15.7
Latin America	2.8	2.7	5.2	8.1	10.0	17.1
Africa	1.0	3.2	5.3	8.0	9.8	16.3
Asia	5.2	5.3	2.8	5.6	8.8	15.3
Middle East	1.2	1.2	2.9	3.5	3.9	8.1

The History of U.S. Women in Politics

1872	Susan B. Anthony becomes the first woman to register to vote. She is arrested and thrown in jail for her actions.
1872	Victoria Woodhull is the first woman to run for president of the United States, nominated by the Equal Rights Party.
1917	Jeannette Rankin of Montana is the first woman elected to the U.S. House of Representatives.
1922	Rebecca Latimer Felton, D-Ga., takes the oath of office for the U.S. Senate on November 21. She was appointed for 24 hours to fill a vacant seat, becoming the first female to serve as senator.
1925	Nellie Tayloe Ross is elected the first female governor of a state (Wyoming). She was elected in 1924 to succeed her husband, William Bradford Ross, upon his death.
1932	Hattie Caraway, D-Ark., appointed in 1931 to fill the seat vacated by the death of her husband, U.S. Senator Thaddeus Caraway, runs for Senate on her own and is the first woman elected to the Senate.
1933	Frances Perkins, the first U.S. female Cabinet member, is appointed secretary of labor.
1934	Florence Allen is appointed to the U.S. Circuit Court of Appeals for the Sixth Circuit, becoming the first woman to serve on a U.S. court of appeals.
1948	Margaret Chase Smith, R-Maine, is elected to the Senate, becoming the first woman to serve in both chambers of Congress.
1949	Burnita Shelton Matthews becomes the first woman to serve on a U.S. district court after Pres. Harry Truman issues her a recess appointment to the District of Columbia district court. The Senate later confirmed her nomination in 1950.
1964	Margaret Chase Smith becomes the first female nominated for the presidency by a major party.
1965	Patsy Takemoto Mink, D-Hawaii, become the first Asian-American woman elected to Congress.
1969	Shirley Chisholm, D-N.Y., becomes the first African-American woman elected to Congress.
1981	Sandra Day O'Connor is appointed the first female Supreme Court justice of the United States.
1984	Geraldine Ferraro, D-N,Y., becomes the first woman nominated for the vice presidency by either major party.
1991	Sharon Pratt Dixon, D-D.C., is elected mayor of Washington, D.C. She is the first black woman to be mayor of a major U.S. city.
1992	Dianne Feinstein and Barbara Boxer of California become the first pair of women senators from any state.
1992	Carol Moseley-Braun, D-Ill, becomes the first African-American woman elected to the U.S. Senate.
1997	Madeleine Albright becomes the first female secretary of state.
2005	Condoleezza Rice becomes the first African-American female secretary of state.
2007	Nancy Pelosi becomes the first female Speaker of the House following the Democratic sweep of the 2006 elections. This is the highest-ranking leadership position ever held by a woman, and the third highest-ranking position in the country behind the president and vice president.

Source: Campaigns & Elections, January 2007

Rwanda: Votes for Women

At last women will outnumber men in a national parliament. The landmark results came not in Sweden (where 47 percent of seats are held by women) or Cuba (43 percent) but in Rwanda, where the September 2008 election results gave 44 out of 80 seats—or 55 percent—to female candidates. The country's post-genocide constitution of 1994 already guaranteed 30 percent of parliamentary posts to women, and even before this election. Rwanda topped the standings with nearly 49 per cent female representation. The Rwandan electoral commission also announced that 55 percent of the 4.7 million registered voters are now women. Female voters are thought to be more likely to back candidates promoting education and health, and fighting discrimination against women, regardless of the party they represent.

Source: New Internationalist, November 2008

slowly until 1995, since that time these regions show substantial growth: almost doubling their percentages in the decade between 1995 and 2005. Explanations for these gains differ across region. For example, gender quotas (legislation or party rules that require a certain percentage of candidates or legislators be female) were instrumental to women's political gains in Latin America, while armed conflict spurred growth in Africa. Eastern Europe demonstrates that high levels of women's representation need not be permanent. As Marxist–Leninist countries transitioned to "democracy," women's levels of representation declined precipitously (Matland and Montgomery, 2003). In addition, it is also important to remember that women's legislative representation varies within regions. Indeed, Scandinavia aside, many of the countries that lead the world in women's parliamentary representation are in the Global South, including Argentina, Burundi, Costa Rica, Cuba, Guyana, Mozambique, Rwanda, South Africa, and Tanzania.

Women's paths to political office may include a traditional rise through the ranks from lower political office to higher political office. Examples include Golda Meir of Israel and Margaret Thatcher of the United Kingdom. Some political leaders like Benazir Bhutto, who became prime minister of Pakistan in 1988 and the first elected Muslim woman to lead a Muslim country, represented dissident voices. She was assassinated for her politics in 2007 when campaigning to become prime minister once again. Women have also gained office around the world by being viewed as a surrogate for a politically powerful male, typically a deceased husband or father. Examples of this latter path include Corozon Aquino of the Philippines or Indira Gandhi of India. Of course, family ties are one way that men obtain political power as well. After Indira Gandhi was assassinated in 1984, she was succeeded in the prime minister's office by her son, Rajiv Gandhi.

Female voting rights, known as women's *suffrage*, are an essential component of women's formal representation in politics. Although today many of us cannot imagine women lacking the ability to participate in the electoral process, just over a century ago, women in almost all countries lacked the basic right to vote. From what some consider the world's first democracy in ancient Greece through the mid-1800s, political thinkers excluded women from notions of citizenship, and, as discussed, politics was considered a man's domain. Thus, in many countries, suffrage victories followed long and trying national-level struggles. The struggle for suffrage is essential for women's citizenship and for their right to

Women's Suffrage: A Timeline

Unless otherwise indicated, the date signifies the year women were granted the right both to vote and to stand for election. The countries listed below currently have a parliament or have had one at some point in their history.

1788—United States of America (to stand for election)

1893—New Zealand (to vote)

1902—Australia*

1906—Finland

1907—Norway (to stand for election)*

1913—Norway**

1915—Denmark, Iceland

1917—Canada (to vote)*, Netherlands (to stand for election)

1918—Austria, Canada (to vote)*, Estonia, Georgia, Germany, Hungary, Ireland*, Kyrgyzstan, Latvia, Poland, Russian Federation, United Kingdom*

1919—Belarus, Belgium (to vote)*, Luxembourg, Netherlands (to vote), New Zealand (to stand for election), Sweden*, Ukraine

1920—Albania, Canada (to stand for election)*, Czech Republic, Slovakia, United States of America (to vote)

1921—Armenia, Azerbaijan, Belgium (to stand for election)*, Georgia, Lithuania, Sweden**

1924—Kazakhstan, Mongolia, Saint Lucia, Tajikistan

1927—Turkmenistan

1928—Ireland**, United Kingdom**

1929—Ecuador*, Romania*

1930—South Africa (Whites), Turkey (to vote)

1931—Chile*, Portugal*, Spain, Sri Lanka

1932—Maldives, Thailand, Uruguay

1934—Brazil, Cuba, Portugal*, Turkey (to stand for election)

1935—Myanmar (to vote)

1937—Phillippines

1938—Bolivia*, Uzbekistan

1939—El Salvador (to vote)

1941—Panama*

1942—Dominican Republic

1944—Bulgaria, France, Jamaica

1945—Croatia, Guyana (to stand for election), Indonesia, Italy, Japan, Senegal, Slovenia, Togo

1946—Cameroon, D.P.R. of Korea, Djibouti (to vote), Guatemala, Liberia, Myanmar (to stand for election), Panama**, Romania**, The F.Y.R. of Macedonia, Trinidad and Tobago, Venezuela, Vietnam, Yugoslavia

1947—Argentina, Japan, Malta, Mexico (to vote), Pakistan, Singapore

1948—Belgium**, Israel, Niger, Republic of Korea, Seychelles, Suriname

1949—Bosnia and Herzegovina, Chile**, China, Costa Rica, Syrian Arab Republic (to vote)*

1950—Barbados, Canada (to vote)**, Haiti, India

1951—Antigua and Barbuda, Dominica, Grenada, Nepal, Saint Kitts and Nevis, Saint Vincent and the Grenadines

1952—Bolivia**, Côte d'Ivoire, Greece, Lebanon

1953—Bhutan, Guyana (to vote), Mexico (to stand for election), Syrian Arab Republic**

1954—Belize, Colombia, Ghana

1955—Cambodia, Eritrea, Ethiopia, Honduras, Nicaragua, Peru

1956—Benin, Comoros, Egypt, Gabon, Mali, Mauritius, Somalia

1957—Malaysia, Zimbabwe (to vote)**

1958—Burkina Faso, Chad, Guinea, Lao P.D.R., Nigeria (South)

1959—Madagascar, San Marino (to vote), Tunisia, United Republic of Tanzania

1960—Canada (to stand for election)**, Cyprus, Gambia, Tonga

1961—Bahamas*, Burundi, El Salvador (to stand for election), Malawi, Mauritania, Paraguay, Rwanda, Sierra Leone

1962—Algeria, Australia**, Monaco, Uganda, Zambia

1963—Congo, Equatorial Guinea, Fiji, Iran (Islamic Republic of), Kenya, Morocco, Papua New Guinea (to stand for election)

1964—Bahamas**, Libyan Arab Jamahiriya, Papua New Guinea (to vote), Sudan

1965—Afghanistan, Botswana, Lesotho

1967—Democratic Republic of the Congo (to vote), Ecuador**, Kiribati, Tuvalu, Yemen (D.P.R.)

1968—Nauru, Swaziland

1970—Andorra (to vote), Democratic Republic of the Congo (to stand for election), Yemen (Arab Republic)

1971—Switzerland

1972—Bangladesh

1973—Andorra (to stand for election), Bahrain, San Marino (to stand for election)

1974—Jordan, Solomon Islands

1975—Angola, Cape Verde, Mozambique, Sao Tome and Principe, Vanuatu

1976—Portugal**

1977—Guinea Bissau

1978—Nigeria (North), Republic of Moldova, Zimbabwe (to stand for election)

1979—Marshall Islands, Micronesia (Fed. States), Palau

1980—Iraq, Vanuatu

1984—Liechtenstein, South Africa (Coloreds and Indians)

1986—Central African Republic, Djibouti (to stand for election)

1989—Namibia

1990—Samoa

1993—Kazakhstan, Republic of Moldova

1994—South Africa (Blacks)

2005—Kuwait

2006—United Arab Emirates***

In Saudi Arabia, men were granted the right to vote for the first time in 2005, but women were explicitly denied the right of suffrage.

Reference to several dates for one country reflects the stages in the granting of rights.
* Right subject to conditions or restrictions
** Restrictions or conditions lifted
*** UAE held their first elections for both men and women in Mid-December 2006. However, they may only vote for 20 seats in the UAE Federal National Council, which serves only an advisory purpose. No elected officials have actual political power. Ranking government officials are appointed.

Source: Data from the Inter-Parliamentary Union. http://www.iwdc.org

political participation. At this time, over 98 percent of countries in the world have granted women the formal right to vote and the formal right to stand for election.

Although women almost everywhere have the right to participate in politics, the degree to which women take advantage (or are allowed to take advantage) of those rights varies across countries. For instance, in countries like Guatemala and India, men continue to vote at significantly higher levels than women, while in countries like Barbados, women have voted more often than men in national elections by around 10 percent since the 1950s. In places like Malta, Sweden, Liberia, and the U.K., men and women vote at roughly similar rates (IDEA, 2008). In most countries women's participation as voters has clearly grown over time. In both the United States and Finland, for instance, men outpaced women as voters through the 1960s, matched rates in the 1980s, and today women now vote in higher numbers in national elections than men.

Although formal representation guarantees that women have the same chance to participate in politics as men, and despite increasing numbers of women voters in many countries, these changes may not necessarily result in women gaining positions of political power. The key here is the difference between "opportunity" and "outcome." Just because you have the opportunity to do something does not mean you can do it. Thus, even though

LEARNING ACTIVITY   **Your Elected Officials**

Who are your elected officials? Do some research and find out who holds these various offices in your area:

- Sheriff
- Judge(s)
- District attorney
- Mayor
- County commissioners
- City council members
- School board members

- State representative
- State senator
- Governor
- Lieutenant governor
- State attorney general
- U.S. congressperson
- U.S. senators

How many of these elected officials are women? What positions do these elected officials hold on women's issues? Have these officials accomplished changes that have improved the lives of women in your area?

most countries of the world grant women the right to vote and to participate in politics, as Table 1 clearly shows, women remain underrepresented as public officials almost everywhere. Few countries have more than 20 percent women in their legislative bodies. Women's presence is higher in local, less prestigious political offices but is still not equal to men's participation in public office.

The reading "Leading Women" by Emira Woods focuses on female leaders in Africa, including Ellen Johnson-Sirleaf, who is faced with the daunting task of leading a country ravaged by war and corruption.

OBSTACLES TO WOMEN'S PARTICIPATION IN POLITICS

When discussing opportunities and obstacles associated with women's attempts to gain political power, scholars often divide explanations into three groups that include supply-side, demand-side, and overarching cultural factors. First, *supply-side* explanations are those concerned with characteristics people bring to a situation. Researchers in this area are interested in understanding factors that increase the pool of women with the will and experience to compete against men for political office. Second, *demand-side* explanations focus on outside factors that bring women into politics such as characteristics of countries, electoral systems, or political parties. These factors affect the likelihood that women will be pulled into office from the supply of willing candidates. In other words, while supply-side centers on factors associated with individuals or that women bring in, demand-side addresses factors outside of individuals that instead bring women in. Third, the *cultural explanation* is an overarching perspective based on the premise that cultural beliefs and attitudes influence both the supply of, and demand for, female candidates.

Supply-Side Explanations

Supply-side explanations focus on the specific characteristics and "human capital" that people bring to situations that allow them to participate in certain activities. Supply-side arguments explain that the money and human capital needed to run for office can be acquired through education and employment. In the United States, law and other professional degrees provide an important path to political office, and having more women in such "pipeline occupations" leads to more female legislators. In other countries, other occupations or levels of education may be more relevant. For example, in Uganda seven years of education and English language skills are sufficient educational credentials for women to run for political office (Johnson, Kabucha, and Kayonga, 2003). As we might expect therefore, differences between men and women in terms of literacy (the ability to read and write) and education are important explanations for differences in political participation.

In terms of women and politics, supply-side approaches also seek to identify and enhance those characteristics that increase the participation of women in political life. For example, women gain skills to help them in politics from non-work activities such as volunteering or activism in social movements like labor unions or the women's movement. A number of studies in the United States have shown that women use the civic skills and networks gained from their voluntary associations to make the transition to politics. In addition, across a range of countries, women's participation in the women's movement and in grassroots activism provides them with both political experience and political ambition. Indeed, some Rwandans lament the loss of such engagement in community activism and complain that the best female volunteers are drawn into government or named to commissions or ministries (Longman, 2006). Voluntary associations, including churches, are also important ways that women may be drawn into participation.

Such organizations are also important in promoting literacy as a precursor to women's political participation. Literacy is an important aspect of personal and social agency, although it has been used as a tool of colonization when colonizers employ literacy education as a way to teach or impose the ideas and knowledge of imperial nations. Very often this has meant the denigration of traditional forms of knowledge (Burn, 2005). In the reading "Women's Words," author Aimee Dowl discusses the powerful connections between language and women's political rights. She highlights the work of Fatima Sadiqi, a Moroccan-Berber professor who found that Berber-speaking women lacked information and resources because they spoke a feminized language associated with the home. Dowl describes Sadiqi's work to promote the 2004 Moudawana (Family Law) in Morocco, which entitles women to a range of civil rights.

Since political participation requires personal characteristics such as interest, ambition, or knowledge, the supply of women available for political office is partly determined by gender socialization, or the ways individuals make sense of, and identify with, the social constructs of femininity and masculinity. These ideas about gender influence people's interest and ambition for politics. To understand the role that gender socialization may play in women's motivation to run for political office, consider the following study of political ambition. Richard Fox and Jennifer Lawless (2004) surveyed men and women who could run for political office. That is, they surveyed people in the four professions most likely to yield political candidates in the United States: law, business, education, and politics. Looking just at this group of women and men (who share the same professional credentials), women were much less likely to aspire to political office (43 percent of women compared to 59 percent of men). And even when they did aspire to political office, the women were less likely to actually run (15 percent of women compared to 20 percent of men). Part of the explanation Fox and Lawless found for this difference is that the women were less likely to view themselves as qualified to run. Women stated this belief even though a parameter of the study was that men and women were actually equally qualified to run for political office. This difference in women's perception of their own qualifications reflects the ways politics is constructed as a masculine endeavor. Having few role models for women also encourages women's lower levels of political ambition (Campbell and Wolbrecht, 2006).

A key problem with this focus on gender socialization, of course, is that women's motivations for political office are not only influenced by ideas about gender, but also by other supply-side characteristics such as personal resources associated with education, money, and time, as well as power and status that come from other identities like race and ethnicity. Interest or ambition aside, women have fewer of the necessary resources to participate in politics. In terms of time as a critical resource for participation in politics, women worldwide have less time than men since they perform the lion's share of domestic tasks such as cooking and cleaning and are the primary caregivers for children alongside their work for paid employment or their efforts outside the home in sustaining families. Responsibility for these tasks may deprive women of the free time required to participate in politics.

The supply-side approach can help us understand both women's lack of political power in general, and also differences among women in terms of who achieves political office. People's political aspirations are shaped by systems of inequality and privilege like racism, classism, and heterosexism that limit and entitle individuals based upon positions vis-à-vis these systems. What this means is that White women are privileged by racism, and these privileges provide resources that shape political activity. Economically privileged women are privileged by classism, and those who have few monetary resources are often unlikely to be able to afford to aspire to political office. And, heterosexuals are also privileged in heterosexist societies, making it significantly less likely that lesbians or bisexual, trangendered, or transsexual people will be able to gain high-level political office and be open with their constituents. There are, of course, exceptions. For instance, in 1999, Georgina Beyer became the world's first openly transsexual elected to parliament in New Zealand. See also the sidebar on the next page about the Oregon, U.S., town that elected a transgendered mayor in 2008. But examples like these are comparatively rare. In many countries, gays and lesbians face insurmountable legal obstacles to public office. In more than 70 countries in the world, being gay is against the law, and in several predominantly Muslim countries such as Saudi Arabia, Iran, Pakistan, and Sudan, gays and lesbians even face execution (Amnesty International, 2001, 2008). Overall, the interaction of social forces such as these creates opportunities for some and challenges for others, ultimately affecting their ability to participate in political life.

Demand-Side Explanations

What about the demand side of the equation? The demand side refers to the external systems, parties, and individuals that make gaining political office easier or more difficult for women. The "rules of the political game" are important because they influence whether women can attain, and how they attain, political power. In the United States, for example, high reelection rates for incumbents (those who already hold a political office and seek to

Transgender Mayor

Plenty of politicians reinvent themselves. But none quite like Mayor-elect Stu Rasmussen.

Rasmussen, 60, has been a fixture in Silverton, Oregon, politics for more than 20 years, and had twice before been the mayor of this small city 45 miles south of Portland. Those terms, however, were before the breast implants and before the once-discreet crossdresser started wearing dresses and 3-inch high heels in public.

In a week when America loudly chose its African-American president, Silverton quietly made Rasmussen the country's first openly transgender mayor, according to the Gay and Lesbian Victory Fund, a group that works to help openly lesbian, gay, bisexual, or transgender people win elected office.

Rasmussen unseated incumbent mayor Ken Hector, with whom he had long clashed—1,988 votes to 1,512. Because Rasmussen's appearance is no secret, it was policy issues that dominated the campaign.

"I've blackmail-proofed myself," said Rasmussen.

The story of Rasmussen's election was first reported by *JustOut*, a bimonthly publication for Portland's gay, lesbian, bisexual, and transgender communities.

"Stu never sought this recognition out," said Stephen Marc Beaudoin, the reporter who broke the story. "He's interested in doing a great job for the community that he loves. The gender identity thing is just a total backseat thing."

"I am a dude," Rasmussen said. "I am a heterosexual male who appears to be a female."

His longtime live-in girlfriend, Victoria Sage, told *The Oregonian* newspaper that she and Rasmussen have been an item for almost 35 years.

"I heard a quote, and I don't know who said it but I think it's fabulous, that Silverton is a place where Mennonites and transvestites can get along," she said.

The quote rang true when two cowboys came across the new mayor on a downtown sidewalk. "Good job, Stu," one of them said to the man wearing a leather skirt and maroon stockings.

"Congratulations, Mr. Mayor," called the other.

Source: http://www.komonews.com

be reelected) must be accounted for when predicting whether and where women can win elections. In other words, if a woman runs against a man who is already in that position, she will face a more difficult challenge. Ultimately, however, a wide range of political factors generate differences in the demand for women's political participation, including the electoral system and the presence and structure of gender quotas. Political parties and party leaders also pull women into, or push women out of, the political process in response to ideologies about women in leadership as well as perceptions of the "winnability" of women. At the individual level, voters may be more or less likely to support female candidates over their male counterparts.

Perhaps the most consistent and well-documented finding in international research on demand-side explanations for women in politics is the importance of a country's electoral system. Electoral systems determine how the votes cast in an election get translated into seats won by parties and candidates. A general and simplified distinction is between plurality-majority electoral systems and proportional representation systems. In plurality-majority

Illegal Homosexuality Around the Globe

HOMOSEXUAL ACTS ILLEGAL

Afghanistan	Ghana	Namibia	St Vincent & the Gren.
Algeria	Grenada	Nauru	Sudan
Angola	Guinea	Nepal	Swaziland
Antigua & Barbuda	Guinea-Bissau	Nigeria	Syria
Bahrain	Guyana	Niue (New Zealand associate)	Tanzania
Bangladesh	India		Togo
Barbados	Iran	Oman	Tokelau (New Zealand associate)
Belize	Jamaica	Pakistan	
Benin	Kenya	Palau	
Bhutan	Kiribati	Panama	Tonga
Botswana	Kuwait	Papua New Guinea	Trinidad & Tobago
Brunei	Lebanon	Qatar	Tunisia
Cameroon	Lesotho	São Tomé & Princ.	Turkish Republic of Northern Cyprus
Comoros	Liberia	Saudi-Arabia	
Cook Islands (New Zealand associate)	Libya	Senegal	Turkmenistan
	Malawi	Seychelles	Tuvalu
Djibouti	Malaysia	Sierra Leone	U. Arab Emirates
Dominica	Maldives	Singapore	Uganda
Eritrea	Mauritania	Solomon Islands	Uzbekistan
Ethiopia	Mauritius	Somalia	Western Samoa
Gambia	Morocco	Sri Lanka	Yemen
Gaza (Palestinian authority)	Mozambique	St Kitts & Nevis	Zambia
	Myanmar/Burma	St Lucia	Zimbabwe

HOMOSEXUAL ACTS PUNISHABLE WITH DEATH PENALTY

Iran	Nigeria	Sudan	United Arab Emirates
Mauritania	Saudi-Arabia	United Arab Emirates	Yemen

Source: http://www.ilga.org

systems the voters in an electoral district typically vote for only one person to represent them and the candidate with the most votes wins. Voters go into the voting booth and choose from a list of people, one for each party. This is the system in most states in the United States. In contrast, proportional representation systems typically ask voters to vote for a party with a designated list of candidates. Voters go into the voting booth and choose a party, each of which has published a list of candidates. Parties win legislative seats in proportion to the number of votes they receive. For example, if a party won 30 percent of legislative seats, the party would go down their list of candidates from the top and the first 30 percent would get seats in the legislature. Sweden and Argentina are examples of countries where a proportional representation system is in place.

It is well-documented that women do better in gaining political office in countries that use proportional representation electoral systems. For example, in New Zealand where both proportional representation and plurality-majority systems are in effect simultaneously, during the 2005 national election women were elected at higher rates under proportional representation systems (women won 43 percent of seats) than the plurality-majority system (women won only 20 percent of seats). Similarly, countries that switch to proportional representation systems may experience dramatic gains in women's representation. In 2007, for example, when Kyrgyzstan transitioned from a plurality-majority to a party-list proportional representation system, women's representation in the national legislature jumped from 0 percent to 26 percent. Women do better under these systems because they can get on a party's ballot without displacing a male. In a typical plurality-majority electoral district, getting on the ballot is a zero-sum process. If one person gets on the ballot, it means another person is not on the ballot. In plurality-majority contests, therefore, parties must make a choice between male and female candidates rather than being able to place both on the ticket. As relative newcomers to politics, when women candidates compete head-to-head against men they are disadvantaged. Men have been in politics longer, are entrenched in positions of power, and do not want to give up that power.

Further, as already mentioned, under plurality-majority systems if women are seen as worse candidates then men, perhaps due to longstanding cultural traditions against women in politics, it is not in the party's interest to run women. The party elite wants candidates whom they believe are electable. In contrast, proportional representation systems usually operate such that voters vote for parties with published lists of candidates. When a party needs to produce a list of candidates, it is under pressure to balance its ticket across interest groups in society. "Rather than having to look for a single candidate who can appeal to a broad range of voters, party gatekeepers think in terms of different candidates appealing to specific sub-sectors of voters" (Matland, 2002, p. 6). As a result, a political party in a proportional representation system will want to have some women on its list of candidates so it can attract female voters. In addition, if women in the party demand to be included as candidates, it is easier for a party operating in a proportional representation system to accommodate them. The "cost" is lower because men do not have to step aside in order to include women. Instead men and women can run side-by-side on the same party list.

Another factor associated with the demand side of politics is the presence of gender quotas that influence the demand for female candidates and legislators. Gender quotas are legislation or party rules that require a certain percentage of candidates or legislators to be female. In other words, gender quotas require political parties to field a certain number of female candidates or require a legislature to include a certain percentage of women.

In 1990, Argentina became the first country in the world to adopt a national electoral law quota, resulting in a 17 percent increase in women's representation in the Chamber of Deputies in the subsequent election. Similarly, efforts to implement quotas in Afghanistan and Iraq led to some of the largest jumps in women's representation ever seen. Over the past 15 years, more than 100 countries have adopted gender quotas at the national or party level. Indeed, more countries in the world today have gender quotas in politics than do not. Gender quotas are discussed in more detail in the next section.

Finally, an important demand-side characteristic includes the role of political parties themselves. Parties are gatekeepers: in order for an individual, man or woman, to run for political office, he or she must be selected and supported by a political party. The characteristics of political parties therefore matter for women. Parties that are politically "left" or "left wing" (more liberal) in their political leanings tend to espouse more egalitarian ideals and are more likely to promote traditionally underrepresented groups such as women. "Right-wing" parties are more conservative and are less likely to support women's rights to equality. In the United States, for example, women have been more successful achieving power in the more leftist Democratic Party than in the Republican Party. Historically, only 36 percent of women in the United States Congress have been Republicans (Paxton and Hughes, 2007).

Cultural Explanations

Culture influences both the supply of, and demand for, women. Cultural expectations about gender mean that even in countries where women have made gains in employment or education, they may face cultural barriers to participation in politics. As surveys of gender attitudes expand across the globe, scholars have increasing evidence that cultural

ACTIVIST PROFILE   **Unity Dow**

Judge Unity Dow has done just about everything a person can do in the judiciary system. She's been a public prosecutor, defense lawyer, human rights lawyer, litigant, researcher, and judge. "I hope the only thing I have not been is a criminal. I have enjoyed all sides of the law."[1] Judge Dow was the first Motswana (citizen of Botswana) woman appointed to be a judge on the nation's high court. Before that, she was the only woman in law school at the (then) University of Botswana and Swaziland, and she co-founded the first all-woman law firm in the country. She also co-founded the Baobab Primary School in Gaborone and founded the Metlhaetsile Women's Information Centre. She's also an accomplished novelist.

In 1991, Unity Dow was a human rights attorney. Her rise to fame came with a groundbreaking case that became known as the Citizenship Case. The 1984 Citizenship Act conferred citizenship on children born in Botswana only if the father was a citizen of Botswana or, in the case of a child born out of wedlock, the mother was a citizen. Dow, who had three Botswana-born children with her American husband, believed the law discriminated against women and violated Botswana's constitution, and so she determined to challenge it. The high court agreed with her, and, though it took years of fighting appeals, eventually the decision stood. While those years were difficult, Dow persisted. "At the end of four years, I had cried with sadness and laughed with triumph. I had felt both victimized and validated. I had felt both isolated and embraced. I had lost old friends and gained new ones. I had met opposition where I had expected support and received support from unexpected quarters. I survived. I continue to survive," she recalls in the foreword of her book, *The Citizen Case*.[2]

In 1998, she herself was named to the high court where she spent the next decade involved in a wide range of cases, including a contentious and costly case over the land rights of the Basarwa, an ethnic minority group in Botswana. Dow ruled that the case was ultimately about dignity and respect, and the court decided that the Basarwa were entitled to live and hunt on their ancestral lands in the Central Kalahari Game Reserve.

Dow's novels also explore issues of gender, tradition, and justice. Her first novel, *Far and Beyon'*, examines issues of AIDS, tradition, and the abuse of women. Her other novels are *The Screaming of the Innocent*, *Juggling Truths*, and *The Heavens May Fall*.

In 2003, Rutgers University awarded her the William Brennan Human Rights Award.

[1] http://allafrica.com/stories/200811170581.html
[2] Ibid.

beliefs about women not only vary worldwide, but also affect levels of women's activity in politics. For example, when asked whether men make better political leaders than women, the average answer in Nigeria is between "agree" and "strongly agree." In contrast, the average answer in Norway is between "disagree" and "strongly disagree" (Paxton and Kunovich, 2003). However, even in regions where women's place in politics is supposedly accepted, traditional ideas encourage assumptions that male politicians are better able to address foreign policy, defense issues and arms control, foreign trade, farm issues, and other issues associated with the economy, and female politicians are better able to deal with family and child-related policies, poverty, education, civil rights, and the environment (Kahn, 1996). This means that depending on the issue involved, women may have an edge in certain policy debates. Indeed, in the case of the United States, if voters think women are better advocates of an issue such as poverty, and they care about that issue, they are more likely to support female candidates (Kahn, 1996).

Women face prejudice as they try to become leaders because many people worldwide assume leadership is a masculine trait and politics is no place for women. Effective leadership has traditionally been associated with masculine traits of aggression, competitiveness, dominance, and decisiveness. Femininity is stereotyped as nurturing, helpful, likeable, gentle, and polite. The resulting "match" between gender and leadership has encouraged men to be seen as more appropriate and effective leaders. Once women do become leaders, however, they often face additional problems because they must serve two (often uncomplementary) sets of expectations associated with their role as a leader and as a woman This gendered double standard was illustrated in the ways the media associated with the 2008 U.S. national election represented then-senator Hillary Rodham Clinton and Alaskan governor Sarah Palin. No male politicians encountered the same high level of scrutiny associated with looks and body or their role as parent. This means that female leaders are often in a difficult position. Should they act the way people expect them to act as women? Should they be nurturing, supportive, and gentle or should they act the way people expect leaders to act with "masculine" behaviors such as aggressiveness and dominance? If female leaders choose the second path, research demonstrates that they will be negatively evaluated. Psychologists have found that people evaluate autocratic behavior by women more negatively than the same behavior by men. Women who act assertively violate the expectations of those around them and are subsequently penalized. Margaret Thatcher, for example, a very assertive British prime minister who served during the 1980s, was referred to as "Attila the Hen" and "the Iron Lady" (a name also given to President Ellen Johnson-Sirleaf of Liberia, discussed in the reading by Emira Woods). Such a situation puts female leaders in a real "Catch-22" since "conforming to their gender role can produce a failure to meet the requirements of their leader role, and conforming to the leader role can produce a failure to meet the requirements of their gender role" (Eagly and Johannesen-Schmidt, 2001, p. 86).

Religion is a key aspect of culture that influences women's participation in politics worldwide. Arguments about women's inferiority to men are present across all dominant religions, and religion has long been used to exclude women from aspects of social, political, or religious life around the world. But the major religions of the world are differentially conservative or patriarchal in their views about the place of women, both in the church hierarchy and in society. For example, some Protestant Christian traditions promote nonhierarchical religious practices and more readily accept women as religious leaders than Roman Catholicism and Orthodox Christianity (e.g., Greek Orthodox or Russian Orthodox). Similarly, Islamic law is typically interpreted in a manner that constrains the political activities of women (Ahmed, 1992). Researchers have demonstrated that countries with large numbers of Protestant adherents are more supportive of female legislators than countries with large numbers of Catholics, Orthodox Christians, or Muslims.

STRATEGIES FOR INCREASING WOMEN'S PARTICIPATION IN FORMAL POLITICS

Because "equal opportunity" in formal political representation does not appear to automatically produce large numbers of women in politics, feminist political theorists have argued that we need new strategies for equal representation. This implies that action must be taken beyond just giving women the right to vote and the right to participate in political life. The next sections explain notions of descriptive and substantive representation and discuss the role of transnational feminist movements in advocating for women in politics worldwide.

Descriptive and Substantive Representation

Attempts to address the inadequacies of formal representation point to the necessity of imposing *descriptive representation*: a descriptive similarity between representatives and the population they represent. If women make up 50 percent of the population, for example, then they should also make up roughly 50 percent of legislative and executive bodies. Arguments for descriptive representation hinge on the idea that racial, ethnic, and gender groups are uniquely suited to represent themselves in democracies. In the case of women, the argument is that women differ from men due to varying socialization and life experiences that facilitate different sets of beliefs, experiences, and expertise. Because women can best represent themselves, they need to be numerically represented in politics, not simply formally represented.

As already mentioned, gender quotas involve the requirement that political parties include a certain percentage of women candidates. Although quotas are helpful in increasing the numbers of women in politics, national gender quota laws do not always generate significant increases in women's representation. France, for instance, has a 50 percent gender quota but only 18 percent of their national legislature is female. To understand this, consider what might happen if a national law was passed in the United States requiring Democrats and Republicans to run 20 percent women for Congress. Parties might choose to run women in electoral contests they were sure to lose, and it would have no impact on the number of women in Congress. Similarly, if national laws tell parties that they must include 30 percent women on their party lists, those parties could choose to put women in the bottom 30 percent of the list (where they would be unlikely to be elected). To address these dynamics, quota research has examined why some quotas are more effective than others. Scholars often focus on particular features of quota legislation that may impact the law's effectiveness. Placement mandates, such as two women required among the top five candidates, may prevent parties from burying women at the bottom of party lists. Sanctions for noncompliance introduce accountability and set consequences if party leaders fail to comply with quota regulations. Such provisions are in place in countries such as Argentina, France, and Slovenia, and have had varying levels of success ensuring compliance with quota laws. Some countries understand the strategic advantage in adopting quotas. Across Latin America, for example, the adoption of quotas by male-dominated legislators happened in part because of the desire of political leaders to present their countries as modern.

Political theorists advocating descriptive representation do not assume that all women share an identity with the same interests and concerns, and they avoid essentialism (the view that for any specific entity, there is a set of characteristics or properties that any entity of that kind must possess). Instead they advocate that women have common interests because of their social position in societies. Women have shared experiences because their gender has been historically marginalized, because they are generally relegated to certain economic roles, and because they typically have primary responsibility for child and elder care. This implies that their shared experience or social position leads to similar interests allowing women to represent other women. Indeed, women in national legislatures have been shown to increase the amount of legislation favorable to women and children and their welfare, educational and health needs (Swers, 2002).

Still, because women do not always represent women in ways that improve their well-being, another type of representation has been presented: *substantive representation*. This form of representation works to ensure that women's interests are advocated in the political arena. Substantive representation requires politicians to speak for, and act to support, women's issues. The implicit criticism of descriptive representation is that increasing the numbers of women involved in politics is a necessary, but not sufficient, condition for women's interests to be served. For women's interests to be represented in politics, female politicians have to be willing and able to represent those interests. Some advocates of substantive gender representation point to the possibilities of transforming societies through broad-based notions of social justice. In the reading "Revenge," a poem by Kim Rogers, the reader is invited to imagine a scenario where different forms of justice occur. In this African village, Rogers recognized the responsibility given to victims and their families about the fate of perpetrators. This is very different from the ways judicial systems work in most industrialized countries.

Advocates of substantive representation argue that not only must the numbers of women in politics increase, but those women must also receive support when they attempt to act for women's interests. For example, women's caucuses can help achieve substantive representation by supporting women and providing them with resources. The bipartisan U.S. Congressional Caucus for Women's Issues is a case in point. It attempts to move women's issues forward in the U.S. Congress and links like-minded congressional women to each other and to outside groups. Some advocates of substantive representation argue that rather than simply electing women to political office, we should elect feminists, either women *or* men, who are more likely to be directly supportive of women's interests (Tremblay and Pelletier, 2000). Substantive representation is discussed in the reading "*Dal Dy Dir*/Stand Your Ground" that describes gender parity in the Welsh Assembly where there are equal numbers of men and women. This reading gives some background to Welsh politics, reviews the women's movement in Wales, and addresses future challenges for this small country that is a part of the United Kingdom.

However, just as the problem with descriptive representation was whether women can represent other women, so an issue with substantive representation concerns the politics associated with "pro-woman" or "women's interests." Who actually is "woman" and what are her interests given the competing interests across women as a group? In other words, given the diversity of women within societies in terms of such identities as race, ethnicity, national origin, religion, class, sexual identity, and linguistic group, whose interests are being served? Although women's unique relationship to reproduction and the family cuts across other social categories, women are not a monolithic group. This means that female politicians of a particular racial, ethnic, caste, or class may not desire to, or be able to, act for *all* women. Given that in most societies access to political office occurs in part as a result of class privilege, can an elite or upper-class woman represent the interests of her less-economically-privileged sisters? Indeed, as of 2008, all women in the legislatures of Albania, Bangladesh, Denmark, Israel, and Panama are from the dominant racial, ethnic, and/or religious groups in the societies. In this way, even when talking about substantive representation, we must also remember to ask whether female politicians, in their desire to address the interests of women actually represent all women, or whether they represent only rich, or white, or Western interests.

International Efforts for the Advancement of Women in Formal Politics

Transnational feminist movements are powerful contemporary forces attempting to promote women's involvement in politics worldwide. As transnational women's movements advocating for a broad array of women's rights have grown in size and strength through the twentieth century and into the twenty-first, they have worked to expand women's political rights through international organizations such as the League of Nations and the United Nations (Berkovitch, 1999). For example, as early as 1943, U.S. suffragist Alice Paul and her World Women's Party lobbied for inclusion of the phrase "the equal rights of men and women" in the preamble to the UN Charter. In the decades that followed, pressure on the UN by women's international organizations continued as feminists worked to keep women, and the political rights of women, on the agenda of the UN and its conferences.

As already discussed in other chapters, women's political rights and representation have also been a focal point of UN World Conferences on Women. For example, one resolution at the First World Conference in Mexico in 1975 called on governments to pay special attention to political rights of women (United Nations, 2000). At the outset of the second conference in Copenhagen, conference delegates suggested that one of the obstacles preventing attainment of goals set out in Mexico was that too few women held decision-making positions. And at the 1985 NGO forum in Nairobi, the most heavily attended workshop was "If Women Ruled the World," where 18 female parliamentarians from around the world discussed women's contributions as political leaders and the struggle to gain support for women's political representation (United Nations, 2000). By the 1990s feminists concerned about women in politics were calling for a "critical mass" of women in parliament of 25 or 30 percent. The "Platform for Action" coming out of the Fourth World Conference on Women held in Beijing, China, in 1995 clearly advocated for increased political representation of women. By 2000, several feminist organizations were calling for full equality: 50 percent of national seats. For example, in June 2000, the Women's Environment and Development Organization (WEDO) launched a 50/50 campaign to increase the percentage of women in local and national politics worldwide to 50 percent. Since its inception, the campaign has been adopted by more than 154 organizations in 45 countries.

International influence directly affecting women's formal representation in politics is most apparent in the two recent constitutional transitions in Iraq and Afghanistan. Arguably, neither of these countries had either a strong internal demand or supply of women for political office. But outside agents were central in the formation of their new, post-war constitutions that both include substantial gender quotas. Though Nordlund (2004) finds no evidence that the UN actively promoted the adoption of a gender quota in Afghanistan, it did strongly advocate increases in women's parliamentary representation. In fact, the UN actively worked to get the issue included on the agenda. Further, the international community pressured for women to be represented at the table during constitution building. Women's inclusion during this stage, and a lack of other options for increasing women's representation, may have been influential in the choice to adopt gender quotas (Dahlerup and Nordlund, 2004).

The influence of international organizations on women's political outcomes may also operate through financial channels. International bodies grant the loans and provide the foreign aid that poor countries so desperately need. Countries receiving international aid may be more likely to respond to external suggestions for change, including the adoption of quota laws. In Bangladesh, for example, a UN-funded governance program allegedly facilitated both the extension of lapsed quota legislation and an increase in the quota threshold from 7 percent of women political candidates to 30 percent (UNDP, 2000).

International bodies may also work directly to increase the supply of female candidates running for office. For example, the United Nations Development Programme (UNDP) provided training to female political candidates in Vietnam that in 2000 contributed to a rise in women's representation in Vietnam's national legislature from 18 percent to 26 percent (UNDP, 2000). More indirectly, the UN, the International Labor Organization, the World Bank, and a wide range of international nongovernmental organizations have provided money, personnel, and training to promote women's empowerment through employment training, education, and/or access to valuable resources. These programs may encourage women with the knowledge, skills, and interest to run for political office.

Further, alongside lobbying to increase the representation of women in formal politics, the international women's movements have also taught participants social movement tactics and encouraged resistance to enduring cultural beliefs that work against women's participation in politics. Women swap ideas to develop new strategies for action and unite with other women from their home countries to seek common goals. For example, activists from Namibia and Uganda have described how UN conferences on women encouraged domestic women's organizations in their countries to pressure their governments to adopt national gender policies (Bauer, 2006; Tripp, 2006). In this way, national and local women's organizations may also join with international forces to encourage women in politics. By taking advantage of links to international agencies and movements, local women's groups can gain leverage, information, money, and other resources that would otherwise be out of reach. Keck and Sikkink (1998) call this process of seeking international support pressuring governments to act the "boomerang effect." One active example of this process is under way in Namibia where women pressing for 50 percent women in parliament have linked to the WEDO's global 50/50 campaign, lending greater resources and legitimacy to their efforts (Bauer, 2006).

WOMEN'S EFFORTS IN INFORMAL POLITICS

It is important to emphasize that there is more to women's involvement in politics than their relationship to formal politics and the official governmental decision-making arena. Indeed, the relative absence of women in politics is in part caused by a tendency to define politics as official electoral activities and focus on women as "state actors." Such an approach underestimates their role in politics and ignores their political activity in community-based activism and national social movements. In addition, as the reading "The Public and Private Domain of the Everyday Politics of Water" by Juana Vera Delgado and Margreet Zwarteveen suggests, strategies for feminist action should not solely be aimed at formal laws and policies. In their ethnographic research in the Andes of Peru, Delgado and Zwarteveen describe the struggles of Peruvian women to gain access and control over water and land. Power over these resources resides in practices embedded in culture and manifested in norms and customs, occurring in social domains such as the household that are not usually associated with water management. The authors argue that a focus on nonformal water powers, or everyday water politics, reveals important sources of agency for women. Water is also an issue for women's organizations in the reading "The Post-Katrina, Semiseparate World of Gender Politics" by Pamela Tyler. This article discusses the activities of three women's organizations formed in 2005 to deal with the aftermath of the destruction and flooding associated with Hurricane Katrina in New Orleans, USA. It addresses how race and social class identities affected the work of these different organizations.

As Ruth Lister (2003) explains, a distinction should be made between the level of women's political representation and women's political activity. Even though in many countries women are absent as state actors in formal positions of power, they have been active in labor and union movements, peace activism, and environmental groups. They have also worked to challenge the political system through informal struggles to inherit property and control their wages, the right to divorce, the struggle for universal female education, and the right to be safe in their homes. For example, women used their roles as mothers to protest human rights abuses and advocate for democracy in Latin American countries. Perhaps the most famous example of women fighting for democratization is the "Mothers of the Plaza de Mayo," a group of mothers who protested the "disappearance" of their children by the Argentinean military. Beginning in 1977, mothers gathered on Thursdays on the Plaza de Mayo, wore distinctive white headscarves, and processed in front of the presidential palace carrying pictures of their kidnapped children. Over time, the number of women participating in the weekly demonstration grew, drawing international attention to human rights abuses in Argentina.

In conclusion, although women are grossly underrepresented in formal politics, making up less than 10 percent in many countries and reaching 50 percent in only one, women worldwide have made inroads into every area of political decision-making and are especially active in informal politics. While for centuries they lacked basic political rights, women today have won the right to vote in almost all countries and are active in the public sphere working in organizations and coalitions to improve the lives of women and their families. Many nations have observed steady and sometimes even dramatic growth in the numbers of women participating in local and national legislatures and witnessed women as leaders in informal organizations. Since 1950, over thirty women have led their nations as heads of government and countless more serve as grassroots activists,

A DAY IN THE LIFE   **Her Most Important Work** by *Giovanna Muir*

Before the sun rises a call to prayer (*adan*) rings out from the local mosque and the cry *Allah Akbar* is echoes throughout the city of Al Jamah. Miriam and her husband Ahmed get up to make their morning prayers. Ahmed will perform his ablutions and do his prayers at the mosque. Miriam does her prayers at home, as most women generally do. She begins her ablutions by washing her right wrist first and then the left wrist three times. She then rinses her mouth three times with water and then rinses her nose three times with water. After that she washes her face three times with water, then her right hand three times, and then her left hand three times from the wrist to the elbow. She then splashes water on her hair and her ears. Lastly, she washes her right foot three times and then her left foot. She puts on a light robe called an *abaya* and covers her head with a *hijab* or scarf to prepare for her prayers. She recites an *aya* or verse of her choice from the Holy Quran.

Upon finishing her prayers, she decides she will let the children sleep in a bit while she has some quiet time to herself this morning. She gets ready for work by picking out her outfit. She generally wears business casual to work. Today she decides to wear a pair of slacks, with a modest blouse and high heels. She picks out a stylish scarf to match her outfit and covers her hair with it.

She goes to wake the children and prepare them for school. She fixes a breakfast of fresh juice, eggs, cheese, olives, and bread. For herself, she prefers a Turkish coffee with no sugar. She gathers her son and daughter into their 1997 brown Honda Civic and then drops them off with her mother who will take them to school.

Miriam is Jordanian and works as an office assistant for a travel agency. She graduated from high school where she studied English, French, and Arabic. After high school she studied business administration for a year and a half at the University of Jordan. She works Saturday through Thursday from nine to six and earns a decent salary. Under Islam, Miriam is allowed to keep her income for herself. Her husband Ahmed is expected to provide financially for the family. However, she always uses her salary to buy groceries for the household and clothes and small gifts for the children.

At the office, she answers phones, files, and performs general clerical duties. On her one-hour lunch break she makes her ablutions once again and prays on a prayer rug in her office facing the holy city of Mecca. After her prayers she snacks on fresh fruit and nuts and peruses one of the travel catalogs while daydreaming of going to Turkey, Italy, or maybe Belgium, for a holiday.

After lunch she will attend her weekly staff meeting and then finish up some paperwork she did not get to the day before. Around four o'clock she takes a break to perform her ablutions and make her *Asar* prayers in her office. Although not all of her co-workers take time in the day to make their prayers, Miriam always makes it a priority. She enjoys her job immensely and it gives her a sense of pride. However, her ultimate pride comes from raising her family and instilling both religious and cultural values in them. Her most important job is within the home. It is this commitment that has prevented her from following one of her dreams: joining the handful of women deputies recently elected to the Jordanian parliament. Jordan has a parliamentary monarchy whereby the Prime Minister is head of government, although executive authority is vested in the King and his council of ministers. Miriam knows how difficult it is for women to be elected and was elated when she heard about the success of these women candidates. Now she just hopes they will vote in ways that will help women and children in her community.

After work Miriam goes to her mother's house to visit and pick up the children. She finds that one of her sisters stopped by to visit with their mother. Her mother fixes *marameeya* tea (sage tea) and serves homemade *baklava* with it. In a while they will all prepare for the *Mugrib* prayers. After prayers, they talk about their day and how the kids are, the latest gossip in the neighborhood, and especially the news of the neighbor girl's upcoming wedding. They discuss how they will do their hair, and Miriam's sister recommends one of the neighbor girls to do their makeup for the big *hefla* (party). Miriam enjoys coming to visit her mother every day after work. It is one of the highlights of her day. Family is an intrinsic part of her daily life. Her family influences the decisions she makes; they support her emotionally and spiritually, they mediate when there are problems in her marriage, and they hold her accountable for her behavior in both her private and public life. It would give Miriam great distress to displease or dishonor her family. It is extremely important for Miriam to uphold the family honor, and she does this by obeying her family, even when it might go against her liking, better judgment, or against aspirations like running for political office in her local community.

After a lengthy afternoon visit, Miriam and her two children, Omar and Sara, head home. Her husband arrives home shortly thereafter. Miriam prepares *Megloobah*, a traditional dinner of rice seasoned with aromatic spices, carrots, potatoes, eggplant, and lamb. She serves it with a fresh yogurt sauce and some *Kibbeh* for appetizers. Afterwards, she prepares mint tea and serves it with fresh fruit and nuts.

Ahmed, her husband, gets a call on his cell phone from his friend Fabel who wants to meet at a local coffee shop called Villa Café. While they are at the cafe smoking *hookah*, a fruit flavored tobacco, and drinking Turkish coffee until the wee hours in the morning, Miriam will put the children in the living room to watch television for the evening while she invites her two closest friends, Hamida and Nagia, over for tea and sweets.

Miriam met Nagia and Hamida at the Jordan Design and Trade Center. Miriam and her friends work at the center two weekends a month. The center teaches women traditional handicraft skills and offers them micro-loans to start their own businesses. Miriam has focused her skills on making traditional carpets and learning embroidery. The profits from the center go to support women and children in the community. Miriam has thought about taking out a micro-loan from the center that will allow her to quit her full time job and start up her own business. Miriam does not know any female business owners in her community, and she likes the idea of owning her own business, but her husband says that if she quits her office job then she has to stay home with the children.

When Nagia and Hamida arrive they greet Miriam by saying *Salam Alekum* (Peace be upon you). They give each other four kisses, two to each cheek, and extend more salutations. Miriam invites them into the ladies' sitting room (*majlis*) where she showers them with traditional Arabic hospitality. She offers them something to eat out of etiquette, and her friends politely decline. She extends the offer again several times and her friends decline again and again. Miriam brings out a tray with tea and Arabic sweets for them to enjoy nonetheless. The three of them talk as though they have not seen each other in ages, when in fact they just saw each other last week at a wedding. They talk about the wedding weekend, the bride's attire and makeup, the other women's clothes, and, of course, the food. Nagia proudly shows off a new piece of jewelry she has been working on at the Jordan Design and Trade center. Hamida and Miriam both offer their compliments on her skilled handicraft by saying "*ma shallah*." As it is getting late in the evening and all the women have to work tomorrow, they politely say their goodbyes, kissing each other on the cheek several times and promising to see each other later in the week for the special lecture on women's political participation at the University of Jordan. While women were granted the right to vote in Jordan in 1974, few women actually participate in local or national politics. Though Miriam and her friends are traditional Jordanian women in many ways, like many young women, they have become more interested in politics as recent efforts encourage more political participation by women. Hamida hopes that she will someday be elected to the parliament and spends most of her free time volunteering in various organizations and agencies.

After Nagia and Hamida leave, Miriam goes to check on the children and get them ready for bed. She dresses them in their pajamas and reads them a bedtime story. As she is walking through her house she can hear the *adan* (call to prayers) being called out by the *imam* "*Allah Akbar*," "*Allah Akbar*." Miriam ends her day by performing her last set of ablutions for the *Isha* prayers. She puts on her *abaya* and *hijab* and begins her prayers. Maybe her young friend Hamida will become the politician known for improving the lives of women and children. She really hopes so.

revolutionaries, and everyday voters participating in political activity in unprecedented numbers. Truly, despite how much work still needs to be done in this area, the increase in women's political participation over the last century is one of the success stories of the contemporary world.

REFERENCES

Ahmed, L. (1992). *Women and gender in Islam.* New Haven: Yale University Press.

Amnesty International. (2001). *Crimes of hate, conspiracy of silence: Torture and ill-treatment based on sexual identity.* Oxford, UK: Amnesty International Publications.

Amnesty International. (2008). LGBT legal status around the world. Available online at http://www.amnestyusa.org/lgbt-human-rights/country-information/page. do?id=1106576.

Anonymous. (2008). If I were to bleed. Unpublished poem.

Bauer, G. (2006). Namibia: Losing ground without mandatory quotas. In G. Bauer and H. Britton (Eds.), *Women in African parliaments* (pp. 85–110). London: Lynne Rienner Publishers.

Berkovitch, N. (1999). *From motherhood to citizenship: Women's rights and international organizations.* Baltimore: Johns Hopkins University Press.

Burn, S. B. (2005). *Women across cultures: A global perspective.* New York: McGraw-Hill.

Campbell, D. and Wolbrecht, C. (2006). See Jane run: Women politicians as role models for adolescents. *Journal of Politics, 68,* 233–247

Dahlerup, D. and Nordlund, A. T. (2004). Gender quotas: A key to equality? A case study of Iraq and Afghanistan. *European Political Science, 3,* 91–98.

Eagly, A. H. and Johannesen-Schmidt, M. C. (2001). The leadership styles of women and men. *Journal of Social Issues, 57,* 781–797.

Fox, R. L. and Lawless, J. L. (2004). Entering the Arena? Gender and the decision to run for office. *American Journal of Political Science, 48*(2), 264–280.

International Institute of Democracy and Electoral Assistance (IDEA). (2008). Voter turnout by gender. Available online at http://www.idea.int/gender/vt.cfm.

Johnson, D., Kabuchu, H., and Kayonga, S. V. (2003). Women in Ugandan local government: The impact of affirmative action. *Gender Development, 11*(3), 8–18

Kahn, K. F. (1996). *The political consequences of being a woman: How stereotypes influence the conduct and consequences of political campaigns.* New York: Columbia University Press.

Keck, M. E. and Sikkink, K. (1998). *Activists beyond borders: Advocacy networks in international politics.* Ithaca, NY: Cornell University Press.

Lister, R. (2003). *Citizenship: Feminist perspectives* (2nd. ed). Basingstroke, UK: Palgrave MacMillan.

Longman, T. (2006). Rwanda: Achieving equality or serving an authoritarian state? In G. Bauer and H. Britton (Eds.), *Women in African parliaments* (pp. 133–150). London: Lynne Rienner Publishers.

Matland, R. E. (2002). Enhancing women's political participation: Legislative recruitment and electoral systems. In International IDEA (Ed.), *Women in parliament: Beyond numbers* (chap. 3). Stockholm: IDEA.

Matland, R. E. and Montgomery, K. A. (Eds.). (2003). *Women's access to political power in post-Communist Europe.* Oxford: Oxford University Press.

Nordlund, A. T. (2004). Demands for electoral gender quotas in Afghanistan and Iraq. Working paper series, 2. The Research Program on Gender Quotas. Stockholm University.

Paxton, P. and Hughes, M. H. (2007). *Women, politics, and power: A global perspective.* Thousand Oaks: Pine Forge Press.

Paxton, P. and Kunovich, S. (2003). Women's political representation: The importance of ideology. *Social Forces, 81*(5), 87–114.

Swers, Michele L. (2002). *The difference women make: The policy impact of women in Congress.* Chicago: University of Chicago Press.

Tremblay, M. and Pelletier, R. (2000). More feminists or more women? Descriptive and substantive representations of women in the 1997 Canadian federal elections. *International Political Science Review, 21*(4), 381–405.

Tripp, A. M. (2006). Uganda: Agents of change for women's advancement? In G. Bauer and H. Britton (Eds.), *Women in African parliaments* (pp. 111–132). London: Lynne Rienner Publishers.

United Nations. (2000). *Women go global.* [CDROM]. New York: United Nations.

United Nations Development Programme (UNDP). (2000). *Women's political participation and good governance: 21st Century challenges.* New York: UNDP.

SUGGESTIONS FOR FURTHER READING

D'Costa, B. and Lee-Koo, K. (2008). *Gender and global politics in the Asia-Pacific.* New York: Palgrave Macmillan.

Edwards, L. (2007). *Gender, politics, and democracy: Women's suffrage in China.* Palo Alto, CA: Stanford University Press.

Hellsten, S., Holli, A. M., and Daskalov, K. (Eds.). (2006). *Women's citizenship and political rights.* New York: Palgrave Macmillan.

Logan, A. (2009) *Feminism and criminal justice: A historical perspective.* New York: Palgrave Macmillan.

Mackinnon, C. A. (2007). *A women's lives, men's laws.* Cambridge: Belknap Press.

Mezey, S. G. (2007). *Queers in court: Gay rights law and public policy.* New York: Rowman and Littlefield.

Sedghi, H. (2007). *Women and politics in Iran: Veiling, unveiling and reveiling.* New York: Cambridge University Press.

Revenge

Kim Rogers (2005)

Somewhere in a village
a murderer is given,
after one year, to the victim's family,
arms and legs bound with rope.

It happens near a river,
family gathered
at the bank. Above,
the sky is the spring blue
it has been for centuries.

They toss him in,
limbs still tied.
He moves downstream,
a branch beneath water.

Sun bright, water clear,
The family decides:
sink or swim,
avenge or forgive.

They dive in.

Revenge, they say,
is a lazy form of grief.
The tongue and hands sharp,
slashing about,

more dead
make only more dead,
pain does not cancel pain.

They take the bound man
with them to shore,
place him heaving
on the bank,
untie his hands and legs,

unable now to hate
that which they themselves have saved.

Please Mind the Gap

Alyssa McDonald (2007)

When it comes to inequality, it takes only a quick glance at the World Economic Forum's Gender Gap Index, published in 2007, to see that women are much worse off in political life than they are in any other area.

The index measures political representation as well as the difference between men's and women's salaries, health and access to education. And while the findings show women to be disadvantaged in every category to some degree, the political gender gap sticks out from the rest like a particularly swollen thumb. This disparity does not, however, receive anything like the press attention that the gap between men's and women's pay attracts.

To be fair, at 42 percent, the global gap in pay between the sexes reported in the study is pretty appalling. The UK figure is better—30 percent—but still not exactly impressive. Two other reports on pay disparity in the UK were published around the same time, returning similarly bad results, so it's not surprising that inequality in salaries has had the lion's share of the coverage. But this pales in comparison to the political power gap. Measured by the ratio of men to women in parliament and in ministerial jobs, the gap stands at a shocking 86 percent.

This global figure isn't a meaningless average: the political gender gap is significant across the board. Even in the Nordic countries which top the index—Sweden, Norway and Finland—the gap stands at about 50 percent, and the UK is lagging well behind.

With just one in five UK parliamentary seats filled by a woman, our gap stands at 70 percent. Even worse, the UK has lost two places in the overall rankings since 2006—we now rank 11th rather than ninth—as other countries have done more to close their gender gap. Thanks in part to the increasing numbers of women in the Spanish and Irish parliaments, both countries have overtaken the UK.

Despite these figures, the index's authors publicised the economic rather than the political findings. Although the index doesn't take into account overall development, the countries that score best tend to be the rich ones, ranking high in the WEF's *Global Competitiveness Report.* One of the authors of the index, Laura Tyson, suggests that this points to a general financial advantage conferred by equal rights. "Our work shows a strong correlation between competitiveness and the gender gap scores," she notes, suggesting that "countries that do not capitalise effectively on one-half of their human resources run the risk of undermining their competitive potential."

This makes sense, but it's a shame she didn't point out that there is also a strong correlation between a high rating for competitiveness and fair parliamentary representation. An unrepresentative parliament disadvantages everyone, as Katherine Rake, director of the Fawcett Society, which campaigns for equal rights, pointed out.

"It's not just that talented women face difficulties in breaking through the glass ceiling—a lack of diversity of perspective affects the whole populace." She estimates that it will take another 200 years to achieve parity unless efforts to redress the gender balance in UK politics are stepped up.

R E A D I N G **65**

Leading Women

Emira Woods (2006)

In many countries that have been mired in strife, women are now playing lead roles in demanding peace.

When I was a little girl growing up in Liberia, West Africa, my grandmother, a schoolteacher in Gedetarbo, Maryland County, was a leader in her church and a uniter in her community. She wielded power over her schoolhouse and, of course, over her nine children. My great-grandmother, a midwife, pediatrician and herbalist, used natural roots and herbs to groom and grow the small town in the shadows of Firestone's vast rubber plantation. My mother went through a difficult divorce and fought a male-dominated court system to gain custody of me in spite of my dad's position and influence as a beloved doctor.

All of the women around me were sources of strength and wisdom. But I don't think any of us ever imagined that in my lifetime Liberia would be celebrating a woman president.

Ellen Johnson Sirleaf, a grandmother and a Harvard-educated economist, was sworn in as the first democratically elected female head of state on the African continent in January 2006. Liberian women crossed class, ethnic and political lines to cast this historic vote. After two decades of war that destroyed families and livelihoods and systematically used sexual violence as a weapon, women throughout the country created momentum and demanded change. Their voices and their votes propelled Sirleaf into office.

Africa's first woman president has already responded by appointing women to the posts of finance minister and chief of police—rarities not only in Africa, but in the entire world. Steps have already been taken to change rape and inheritance laws in Liberia to protect the interests of women.

While Sirleaf is in the world's spotlight, she is only one example of African women's emerging political leadership.

Women, who have often borne the brunt of the violence in countries mired in strife, are now playing lead roles in demanding peace as well as an end to male dominance of their countries' political processes.

Rwanda, the site of one of the world's most brutal genocides, now ranks number 1 in the world in women's representation in parliament, with women making up close to 50 percent of members. South Africa and Mozambique are also high on the list, with women comprising more than 30 percent of Parliament, compared to only 15.7 percent of the U.S. Congress. Overall, in Africa, the number of women legislators rose from 1 percent in 1960 to 14.3 percent in 2003.

Of the five women prime ministers in the world, two are in Africa—Mozambique and Sao Tomé. African countries top the list of nations with the highest percentage of women in cabinet-level positions. In South Africa there are 12 women Cabinet members and 16 men, and in Rwanda there are 10 women and 19 men. This stands in stark contrast to the United States, where there are less women in political office.

According to Colleen Morna, a South African researcher investigating the impact of quotas on women's political participation in Africa, "the countries with the highest proportion of women in decision-making structures have either recently emerged from struggle or conflict situations or have had ruling parties with social democratic inclinations, or a combination of the two."

In Rwanda, as in many other post-conflict countries, women lobbied hard, helped draft new constitutions and developed a quota system with voting guidelines that guaranteed seats for female candidates. They were also able to expand even further women's role in political processes by pushing for the creation of a government ministry of women's affairs.

At the newly formed African Union, the Pan African Parliament also implemented affirmative action measures to ensure a minimum of 30 percent women's representation. In this parliament representing all 53 countries on the continent, all delegations must have at least one woman among their five representatives. Some countries, like South Africa, have three, or like Senegal, have two.

The real test for these new women leaders will be measured by their ability to govern. Will they have the courage to translate their leadership into a fresh agenda for peace, sustainable development, resource rights, debt cancellation and democracy in the region?

There is much at stake for Liberia and the rest of Africa. But as we push for a fresh agenda, let's take a moment to celebrate how far we've come. I think back to my grandmother and great-grand and can almost see them dancing with the angels as joy pours out from the hearts of Liberian women around the world. Our Liberia suddenly holds the promise that my twin 9-year-old daughters (or their brother) can one day envision for themselves, new paths to political leadership that-embolden them to contribute toward a better Liberia, a strengthened Africa and a safer world.

Women's Words

Aimee Dowl (2007)

Until 2007, Moroccan women who married foreigners could not pass citizenship to their children—who had to apply, year after year, for residence permits to live in their own country. Finally, after decades of feminist protest, parliament has guaranteed paternal *and* maternal equality in determining nationality.

The new citizenship law follows the 2004 Moudawana (Family Law), which entitles women to a range of civil rights. The minimum marriage age was raised from 15 to 18; women may now wed without the consent of a male *wali* (marital tutor); polygamy is restricted to cases in which wives, including the new bride, consent by written contracts approved by a judge; and men may no longer unilaterally "repudiate"—divorce—their wives without compensation.

One feminist responsible for such rights is Fatima Sadiqi, a Moroccan-Berber professor at the University of Fes and a linguist specializing in how women and men use language in Morocco. She found that Berber-speaking persons lack access to information and resources because they speak a "female language" associated with the home and hearth. In this country, where Arabic, French and English predominate, many more women and girls than men speak only Berber, don't attend school and are illiterate—approaching 90 percent in some rural areas.

Sadiqi has shown powerful connections between language and women's rights. "I see the official recognition of Berber as a recognition of Berber women," says Sadiqi, author of the first grammar textbook for this ancient language still spoken by millions. She has also struggled for the inclusion of women's voices in Moroccan education. "I wanted to help democratize our higher education by introducing gender studies," says Sadiqi, who also founded the first gender-studies program in North Africa when she realized the absence of women's texts in university syllabi.

"The Family Law has greatly democratized debate on women's issues and introduced the idea of equality between spouses. Of course, not everyone believes in this equality, but at least people discuss it," says Sadiqi. Networking with other Moroccan feminists and keenly aware of the power of words, she agitated for the Family Law by speaking on television and in the printed press, and organizing major international conferences on women, language and development. "The present king [Mohammed VI] made clear in his very first speech that he wanted to improve the lot of women," she says. "Symbolically, this was huge for the feminist movement, which had to constantly negotiate power with both the monarchy and the radical Islamists."

Even before the Family Law struggle, Sadiqi used her work on language and power to strengthen Moroccan feminism. Her studies have led to teaching invitations abroad (including this past year at Harvard), and to her establishment of the ISIS Center for Women and Development in Fes. She is also editor of the forthcoming *Women Writing Africa: The Northern Region* (Feminist Press, 2007), which includes oral and written works of numerous languages and cultures. But she says it all began in her Berber village, where few women read or wrote: "I owe this to my father, who took me to school and believed in me."

Dal Dy Dir/Stand Your Ground: International Lessons on Women's Equality from a Small Nation

Laura McAllister (2006)

In a nondescript office block overlooking Cardiff Bay, an extraordinary moment of political history was played out in 2006. It passed without any great fuss or fanfare in the wider world, but, in the long history of women's struggle for proper political representation, it was ground-breaking, earth-shattering, almost incredible . . . the Welsh Assembly, created in 1999 following devolution [the transfer of power from a central government to a subnational (e.g. state, regional, or local authority)], has became the first legislative body in the world to be made up of equal numbers of men and women. Did you catch that? In the 60-strong Welsh Assembly, there are 30 men and 30 women. Parity! And in Wales of all places, home of patriarchal old Labour, born out of the coal and steel industries, and steeped in male-dominated trade-union politics. Better than Sweden, which has long been a beacon for female political representation, whose parliament is 45.3 percent female. Better than Blair's Babes. Better than anywhere.[1]

People may think Wales is leading the way for women because of the number of female AMs we have in the National Assembly but . . . Wales is still not in the 21st century as far as its treatment of women in politics is concerned . . . The mines have gone in Wales and times have changed—but attitudes to women have not. We are still in the Dark Ages.[2]

These statements sum up the paradox of women's position in contemporary politics in Wales. Wales has seen a dramatic shift in the gender balance of its politicians. The first elections to the National Assembly for Wales (Assembly) in 1999 delivered a significant step-change with 40 percent political representation for women. Four years later in the second elections, women achieved their goal of equal representation in Wales, taking 50 percent of the seats at Cardiff Bay in 2003. Achieving high visibility as elected members, women also hold prominent positions of power in the Assembly and the Welsh Assembly Government (our executive) as ministers and as committee chairs. For most of the first Assembly, women were in the majority of the Cabinet and took around equal shares of subject and standing committee chair positions. The seeming "gender coup" delivered by devolution highlights a set of puzzles as to how such a breakthrough was achieved and its wider significance for political organization.

These achievements, an apparent world firsts,[3] focused international attention on Wales. However, formal equal gender representation in the Assembly was achieved in a historically unpromising climate, with powerful continuing legacies of marginalizing women in public and political life, and a largely unreconstructed overarching political culture entrenched within parties and existing political institutions. Until devolution, few women had been elected at any level in Wales. Historically, levels of representation have been yet lower than the dismal records of England and Scotland, themselves laggards in world tables. The high visibility of women in the Assembly stands in stark contrast to their continuing low profile in other branches of politics and positions of public and economic decision-making—for example, women hold fewer than one in five of the top jobs in public life, there are no female Chairs of Police Authorities, Chief Crown Prosecutors, University Vice Chancellors or political party leaders in Wales. Only 9 percent of local council Chief Executives and 14 percent of council leaders are women.[4] There has been no more than modest improvement in the proportion of women MPs representing Welsh constituencies (20 percent elected in 2005)[5]; and at local government level women now make up 23 percent of local councillors.

The under-representation of women in political and public life has become an issue of increasing political concern as governments, parties and other organizations have come under pressure from the women's movement for action, especially positive action. Apart from demonstrating "fair play," the presence of women in substantial numbers brings with it a set of theoretical expectations relating to the enhanced quality of deliberation, democratic workings of institutions and social legitimacy. More controversially, there are expectations that female politicians will act as agents for the *substantive* representation of women: in other words, that they will not only "stand for" women, but that they also will "act for and in the interests of women."

The achievement of exactly equal numbers of women and men in the second Assembly is a magnificent success for *descriptive representation* and brings with it the potential for further *substantive* equality gains. That said, there remain concerns with the *process* and *sustainability* by which women have achieved equal representation in the face of much opposition, especially from political "elites."

Uncovering some of the less publicized dynamics in our new Wales—positive and negative—will enable us to draw some lessons that *might* apply in some ways in Australia, just as our experiences in Wales and Scotland are being used by campaigners for equality in the UK and Europe. Essentially, our "gender coup" highlights a set of puzzles as to how the breakthrough was achieved and what its wider, international significance is for women as political actors, as civic activists and as citizens. My principal themes are *victory, vulnerability* and *vigilance*. Wales has achieved dramatic successes at some levels yet, if you scratch the surface, many of the gains are fragile. They are scarcely entrenched, they do not come with a lifetime guarantee and some might easily be unraveled.

THE BACKGROUND: CAMPAIGNS AND CONFLICTS

Following New Labour's victory in the 1997 election, the then Secretary of State for Wales, Ron Davies, described inclusiveness as the "foundation stone" of devolution and constitutional reform.[6] Prime Minister Blair had used notions of "inclusiveness" to advance the case for constitutional change, stating that: "a Welsh Assembly and a Scottish Parliament are good for Britain and good for Wales and Scotland. . . . It will bring government closer to the people, make our politics more inclusive and put power in the hands of the people where it belongs."[7]

This lexicon that accompanied devolution is important for two reasons: first, the very presence of this vocabulary was itself massively influenced by women and, second, its momentum offered opportunities for women to take part in the Welsh political stage in an unprecedented way.

Top Down but Influential: The Women's Movement in Wales

The connection between women's "movements," broadly defined, and political change is often underplayed, as influences can be subtle and indirect, as well as transparent and quantifiable. In Wales, the women's movement is long established and has won some notable successes, including gradually improving women's formal political representation, major concessions in policy development and more subtle changes in political operational styles. There developed a consensus inside women's organizations around devolution, even traditional bodies, that "it would be better for women if some of these decisions were being made in Wales . . . women's organizations felt their capacity to influence the national assembly would be much bigger than their capacity to influence the appropriate government departments." As one activist explained:

> In a devolved Wales you would have an opportunity . . . to get decision making based on [Welsh] political culture which would be about a more redistributive agenda, about more social justice and in the context of the women's movement a better chance to make the case for gender equality.

The devolution campaigns featured specific contributions by individual women and from the wider women's movement within this. Undoubtedly, immeasurable opportunities came from "being in at the start" of a new institution. Constitutional change and institutional restructuring can provide an important window or "moment" of openness and fluidity for different social groups to struggle and contest which values, norms, rights, rules of governance and identities should be reflected and entrenched in the reshaped polity. In an unprecedented manner, devolution established a more accessible stage for women to participate. It brought together civic, civil, social and political actors in a new democratic arena, giving unique opportunities for women to participate, represent and be represented. Women activists (within the women's movement broadly defined) and feminist ideas played a key role in influencing the "gendering" of constitutional change and the prioritizing of women's representation. Yet these developments were also consequences of an interplay of other factors.

Foremost, in terms of overall impact, was women (sometimes supported by male colleagues) in the Welsh Labour party (WLP) who, partly in reaction to similar developments in Scotland, secured in the early 1990s a commitment to equal representation for men and women in the new Assembly. As noted earlier, this was accompanied in May 1996 by a WLP undertaking to include an equality clause in the future devolution statute, requiring that the National Assembly promote equality. This was reinforced by the development of the referendum campaign group *Women Say Yes*. Subsequent lobbying and participation by women in the National Assembly Advisory Group ensured that the Standing Orders Commission codified a full range of mechanisms to promote equality in the Assembly's internal procedural law. The Assembly is subject to a statutory duty, set out in sections 48 and 120 of the Government of Wales Act 1998 and in its Standing Orders, to promote equality of opportunity relating to Assembly business and functions and with regard to all people. The statutory equality duty states that the Assembly "shall make appropriate arrangements with a view to securing that its functions are exercised with due regard to the principle that there should be equality of opportunity for all people." The duty has underpinned a raft of reforms aimed at promoting equality, including gender equality. Together this has resulted in a reprioritization of equality matters;

since 1997 unprecedented time, political will and resources have been invested in promoting reform to "mainstream" equality, including gender equality.

A critical role was played by so-called "strategic women," characterized by their shared feminist conviction, and membership of women's NGOs and other gender organizations in civil society. These women were well connected in key social and political networks and able to exert considerable political influence. Despite the generally top-down nature of women's constitutional activism in Wales, analysis of the process reveals a more complex set of developments in which women's movements reconfigured and influenced policy, but were driven by key women.

In a process that mirrored the top-down character of the general reform project in Wales, "strategic women" staked a claim for women and promoted measures for their improved descriptive and substantive representation. The shape of the eventual devolution settlement bore some of the hallmarks of internal lobbying by influential feminists, even if there was no sustained mobilization of grassroots women's organizations. However, in the absence of a broad-based, cross-party organization in Wales, there needed to be effective channels within traditional party structures and in the eventual internal architecture of the Assembly to ensure women took more prominent roles. As we shall see, this was to prove problematic.

Equality in the Building Blocks of the New Institution

Wider systemic factors were also in play. Periods of rapid political and institutional change (like devolution) often create opportunities for substantial progress with respect to the political representation of women, and for the prospects for the regendering of politics to make space for women, women's issues and women's perspectives.[8] However, important questions remain about sustainability. Evidence from Latin America post-democratization, for example, suggests vulnerability. The incorporation of equality "within the bricks" of the new institution was a major achievement but by no means brought guarantees about sustainability. Thus, it is a little early to judge *how* new the "new politics" in Wales actually is.[9]

Political change and state reconfigurations are identified in the literature on women's movements as providing important political opportunities for organized women to make claims for improved political representation, political voice and input into policy processes. The successful promotion of women's representation and policy interests can arise from a number of measures such as the operation of a "dual strategy," whereby women mobilize within parties and state institutions as "insiders" as well as bringing pressure to bear from outwith through autonomous women's organizations.[10] This can take the form of affiliated and autonomous women working separately but in parallel or through instances of groups of women having "dual" or "multiple militancy" in other words, where gender concerns are promoted by the same women through their multiple memberships of different organizations, both autonomous and mixed, and through the interaction of their different political identities.[11] "Dual goals" feature in a number of successful mobilizations, whereby women demand improved descriptive representation through increased numbers of female elected representatives and enhanced susbstantive representation through the institutionalization of women's "voices" and the creation of women's policy machinery. Other contributory factors include the strength of the women's movement or movements; the ability to form time-limited coalitions[12]; the existence of sympathetic and powerful allies or carrying agents that can promote women's demands; and the framing of women's demands within discourses and arguments that have mainstream legitimacy or congruence with party or state agendas.[13]

Clearly, in Wales, it is the presence of women as elected AMs that remains the most visible sign of change. So how did this come about? Easily the most significant initiative that boosted the dramatic increase in the number of women AMs was the procedures introduced by two of the main parties, Labour and Plaid Cymru, to select and prioritize candidates for the elections of 1999 and 2003. Both parties selected different "add-on" mechanisms to help ensure that women featured prominently within their successful Assembly groups. These positive action measures brought immediate and visible improvement in the representation of women in each case. Labour used "twinning," which created pairs from the forty Welsh constituencies represented in the Assembly and this resulted in 16 women and 12 men being elected in 1999, and 19 of its 29 after 2003. After some fraught discussions, Plaid Cymru rejected twinning and instead used a system of "top-up" prioritization on the party's regional lists, with women guaranteed first and third places on each of the five regional party lists. This meant it had six women AMs (from its party group of 17 in 1999) and six out of 12 since 2003.

Neither party had it easy. The challenges facing women activists during this period are summed up in this remark from a Welsh Labour Party candidate:

> It got quite nasty when we had the twinning debate . . . that would have been 1998; the Welsh Labour Party conference. It was *very* bitter and *very* nasty. They were extremely threatening, sort of "in your face." And these were your macho males and they were physically trying to intimidate women—or any male—(and, I would perhaps guess that it was slightly worse for the males that were standing with us). It was quite frightening . . . there were clearly women who were very, very upset. These men were sticking their heads and their chests forward saying "who do you think you are?" And you would even hear: "This isn't your place. *We've* been here a long time, *we* know what people want, *we* know how it works." And yet they couldn't see that outside [the party] people weren't voting for them. They couldn't put the two together.

Moreover, there have been significant tensions as to the ongoing application and development of the parties' equalities strategies. Plaid Cymru was criticized both for its low number of women candidates in the 2005 General Election and for consideration of "flexibility" for "favored sons" in its list "zipping" policy for the next Assembly elections, while Labour's all-women shortlist policy remained controversial, nowhere more so than in the southern valley's seat of Blaenau Gwent where a 19,000 Labour majority was overturned by an independent standing in protest at the "imposition" of a woman candidate—an outcome that eventually forced the Secretary of State for Wales to publicly apologize. —*vulnerability* and *vigilance* again.

In particular, there has been little acknowledgement that positive actions should not be time-limited to help prevent a boom and bust approach to equality. This is encapsulated in the claim made by one prominent woman Labour minister that it would not be necessary to use twinning again since the objective of equality had been achieved and its impact on the culture of the institution was likely to be permanent.[14] The mechanisms discussed here are essentially fragile and almost entirely dependent on good will, leadership and wider support from the membership for their continuance. This is in part due to their implementation as top down strategies, rather than organic, bottom up ones planned after prolonged and rational discussion, raising again questions of stamina.

Party Women

Once elected there is the question of the nature and focus of women politicians' activities. One Welsh Liberal Democrat AM highlighted the need for the adoption of a specific, conscious gender identity:

> to make a difference here in this Assembly, or indeed in any other institution, it does rely very heavily on them identifying themselves as *female* politicians and having a critical mass of female politicians around them to help them to pursue that particular agenda . . . now we are seeing a shift in emphasis in the agenda.

A Labour woman AM identified a role model function too: "I would certainly hope that women would see us as role models and especially for younger women, girls that are coming through school. Just that difference of 'Oh my God, women can do these jobs too, women *can* get there.'"

There remain apparent (although modest) differences in the attitudes, motivations and policy priorities of female and male parliamentarians but these are mediated—and sometimes trumped—by party loyalties. Women consistently report that they behave and experience political institutions in different ways, although these differences are difficult to quantify. Childs (2001, 2002)[15] sees the differences as gender, rather than sex based, meaning it is not fixed. Women politicians tend to recognize the connections between themselves and other women who aspire to office, or who want greater access to their government, or who

want to see policy changes. They are also more likely to consult a wider and more diverse range of opinion when considering policy options than are men. Substantive outcomes are most obvious in the Nordic countries where high levels of female representation over a sustained period have had a discernible impact on the shaping of welfare state policy, particularly around care issues.

The increase in descriptive representation "has not necessarily been associated with shifts in policy discourse, let alone increased expenditure."[16] International studies suggest that the overall proportion of female elected members may be less significant than the positional influence of sub-groups of women. Thus, it is argued that the proportion of women backbenchers belonging to the executive party or parties[17] or the proportion of women holding ministerial office[18] is of primary importance in influencing substantive change. Studlar and McAllister argue that, beyond numbers, women need to be representatives of parties that are sympathetic to women's substantive goals and require the strategic capacity to frame policy demands and exercise influence within their party groups.[19] In certain circumstances, an increase in numbers or an increased drive to improve numbers may coincide with a decrease in the capacity for substantive representation.[20] In the context of the UK and the operational styles of New Labour, this phenomenon has been described by McRobbie[21] as one of including "women without feminism." We have some of those in Wales too!

The "Re-Gendering" of Welsh Politics

> It is not that women do not have many issues about which we feel equally passionate, but that we have *different* priorities, *different* expectations and *different* aspirations. Policy and decision-making is not effective unless it take account of *all* of those considerations.[22]

Evidence from the Assembly's early years shows that descriptive representation has *begun* to translate into substantive representation. Strikingly, 47.7 percent of all plenary debates included discussion of "women's issues,"[23] and just over a half of all plenary debates included references to equality.[24] In terms of gender dynamics, data reveal that women AMs had a greater propensity than their male colleagues to both engage in, and initiate, political debate on "women's issues." Women AMs also drew more directly from gendered life experiences in order to inform debate.

Furthermore, they acted to promote women's interests across a broader range of policy areas than their male counterparts. Notwithstanding this, the propensity of some male AMs to engage in debate on equality issues underlines the need to conceptualize the substantive representation of women in terms of the gender dynamics of political debate rather than an outcome arising exclusively from the actions of women elected representatives. Overall, this lends support to theoretical assertions that women elected representatives can be more trusted to promote "women's interests"[25] and that they have different political priorities to male politicians.[26]

Yet, there is again evidence of fragility in some of the new practices. In terms of the gender dynamics of Assembly political debate, this is illustrated by women AMs' disproportionately high use and invocation of the National Assembly's statutory equality duties; a fact that likely reflects a lack of embeddedness of the equality agenda.

This interim assessment does require a caveat; since the Assembly is a young and developing institution, the continuance of gender-equal patterns of debate and representation may achieve protection and development. As one woman AM put it: "it is very important not to be complacent. Not to think that the fact that we got it right to begin with doesn't mean that we need to be vigilant."

The Future?

So there have been some major *victories* in Wales, of which we are rightly proud. The gender dynamics of the Assembly's first term show that descriptive representation has *begun* to translate into the substantive representation of women and duly initiated the regendering of policy-making. Gender equality policies in Wales are now underpinned by EC, UK and Welsh law; supported by an increasing range of institutional mechanisms and procedures in government and, monitored by a new and extensive state regulatory framework. Nevertheless, significant challenges remain before the government achieves its stated goal of a fully mainstreamed approach to engendering policy.

Where do our *vulnerabilities* lie? While applauding the major steps taken toward mainstreaming gender equality within the context of Welsh devolution, it is right to flag up some of its inherent instabilities. There remains work to be done—for example, in the fuller adoption of gender monitoring especially via budgeting in the spending plans of the Welsh Assembly Government (drawing on experiences in Australia) and further use of impact assessments; the development of more nuanced approach to gender equality in public policy that addresses simultaneous, *multiple* identities founded on gender as well as age, sexual orientation, language and so on (that is, gender cannot be the only index); fostering extensive, mature, well-informed media coverage of post-devolution politics that, in particular, engages girls and younger women (an area woefully inadequate at present); and, increasing the numbers of women in civil society able and willing to engage in, and shape, the devolved policy process.

Further tensions surely lie ahead within ongoing debates on how to promote women politicians, for the simple reason that power and access to it is a scarce resource. Also, as women begin to achieve critical mass, the base of the movement is likely to widen and new and diverse voices must be heard and incorporated. As one female Minister recently acknowledged: "Our big challenge now is to act to bring black and minority ethnic women into the process—out of the wings and onto the stage. Only then will we have made use of this once in a lifetime opportunity." In the absence of "bottom-up" political campaigns, women in Wales (and, in some cases, men) have been forced to construct temporary organizational infrastructures to achieve their objectives. This is an added *vulnerability*. Analysis of election study data points to the emergence of a new electoral politics characterized by subtle differences between the political behavior of the sexes. This arises from gendered responses to political factors such as party ideology, leadership style and public policy priorities. Parties face further challenges in the electoral arena; as the devolved system of governance matures, it is likely that the parties will increasingly appreciate that women may cast their votes in a manner informed by the extent to which their sex is marginalized or mainstreamed in the policy process.

Until now, women have acted as the principal agents of change, particularly with regard to pressure for substantive equality: clearly, this cannot be relied upon indefinitely. Notions of substantive representation assume female politicians will "act for" other women. As levels of women's descriptive representation increase, gender mainstreaming will improve, meaning women politicians have less direct involvement with promoting a new generation of female politicians. We have understood this in Wales with differing contributions with different levels of enthusiasm from existing women AMs to developing a sustainable structure for promoting other women.

Thus, I predict future struggles for equality in Wales will not follow a linear or straightforward path, rather history suggests the trajectory is likely to be faltering, with gains counterbalanced by a slowing momentum, drift or setback. Until the structures and opportunities for equality are fully entrenched and mainstreamed, questions as to their security and stability will remain. As such, despite our victories, there is a need for women politicians and activists—and their allies—to maintain momentum and stay vigilant in their struggle for a voice and a place in Welsh politics. The declaration of one of our foremost artists in Wales, Mary Lloyd Jones, that graces the front cover of a forthcoming book (and that I have also borrowed to title this article) serves as both current advice and a forewarning—*Dal dy Dir*: Hold Your Ground.

NOTES

1. Sally Weale, "At last! The new Welsh assembly is the first legislative body in the world made up of equal numbers of men and women." *Guardian* 9.05.2003.
2. Baroness Anita Gale, quoted by Nicola Porter, "Baroness Attacks Welsh Men," *The Mirror*, 29.06.2001
3. It should be acknowledged that there are differences between "national" and sub-state devolved legislatures, and that therefore an exact international comparison cannot be drawn. It is also the case that the National Assembly for Wales is relatively weak in terms of formal powers, even compared to other sub-state entities such as the Scottish Parliament and the Northern Ireland Assembly. Nevertheless it would be churlish not to concede the significance (in both symbolic and substantive terms) of achieving gender parity in a national political forum with a substantial

budget. In this context, the Welsh achievement is groundbreaking.
4. EOC/WWNC (2004) *Who Runs Wales?* http://www.eoc.org.uk/cseng/abouteoc/who%20runs%20wales.pdf
5. Eight women MPs were elected in the May 2005 General Election: Madeleine Moon (Bridgend), Jenny Willot (Cardiff Central), Julie Morgan (Cardiff North), Betty Williams (Conwy), Ann Clwyd (Cynon Valley), Nia Griffith (Llanelli), Jessica Morden (Newport East), Siân James (Swansea East).
6. R. Davies (1999). Devolution: A Process Not an Event, *Gregynog Papers* 2.2, Cardiff, Institute of Welsh Affairs, 6.
7. T. Blair, (1996). *Speech by the Rt. Hon. Tony Blair MP, leader of the Labour Party to the Wales Labour Party Conference*, Brangwyn Hall, Swansea, Friday 10 May 1996, 9.
8. Defining "women's issues" and "women's perspectives" is a tricky business, given our understandings of the heterogeneity of women and the complexities of identities. C. Cockburn (1996) "Strategies for gender democracy: strengthening the representation of trade union women in the European social dialogue," *European Journal of Women's Studies*, 3(1) and others argue that a plausible set of interests and concerns exist that relate to the gendered social location of women, which have been subject to articulation and negotiation, and that can be empirically investigated. While differently located women may have different preferences with respect to policy outcomes, they share a common interest in the articulation of such issues and their inclusion on the political agenda. For the purposes of simplicity, we follow Trimble and Arscott by defining women's issues as those "where policy consequences are likely to have a more immediate and direct impact on significantly larger numbers of women than on men" (L. Trimble and J. Arscott (2003) *Still Counting: Women in Politics Across Canada*. Peterborough, Ontario: Broadview Press, 185.). We define women's perspectives as "women's range of views as well as their approaches to all policy issues, not just those with an immediate and direct impact on women" (185). Lovenduski and Norris suggest women's issues refer to "all political issues where women and men may disagree . . . women's shared interests are those policies that increase their autonomy" thus "recognition of women's issues is a process of politicisation" where "the inequalities of power between the sexes are acknowledged" (2003: 88).
9. L. McAllister (2000), "The New Politics in Wales: Rhetoric or Reality?", *Parliamentary Affairs*, 53, 3, 591–604.

10. J. Lovenduski and P. Norris (eds), (1993) *Gender and Party Politics.* London: Sage; L. Wängnerud (2000) "Representing Women" in P. Esaiasson, and K. Heidar (eds) Beyond Westminster and Congress: The Nordic Experience. Columbus, Ohio: Ohio State University Press, 140–154.

11. K. Beckwith (2000) "Beyond Compare? Women's movements in comparative perspective," *European Journal of Political Research* 37:431–468; Beckwith, K. (2003) "The Gendering Ways of States: Women's representation and State Reconfiguration in France, Great Britain and the United States" in Banaszak et al. (eds) *Women's Movements Facing the Reconfigured State.*

12. H. Britton, (2002) "Coalition Building, Election Rules and Party Politics," *Africa Today* 49, (4), 33–67.

13. A. Dobrowolsky and V. Hart (eds) (2003) *Women Making Constitutions: New Politics and Comparative Perspectives*, Basingstoke: Palgrave; L.A. Banaszak, K. Beckwith and D. Rucht, (eds) (2003) *Women's Movements Facing the Reconfigured State*, Cambridge, Cambridge University Press.

14. *The Western Mail* supplement, 31.12.1999.

15. S. Childs (2001) In their own words: New Labour Women and the substantive representation of women. British Journal of Politics and International Relations 3:2, 173–190; Childs, S. (2002) Hitting the Target: Are Labour Women MPs Acting for Women? Parliamentary Affairs 55:1, 143–153.

16. M. Sawer (2002) "The Representation of Women in Australia: Meaning and Make Believe," in *Parliamentary Affairs* 55:1, 5–18.

17. S. Grey (2002), "Does Size Matter?", in K. Ross (ed) *Women, Politics and Change.* Oxford: Oxford University Press.

18. A. Karam (ed) (1997 and 2002) *Women in Parliament: Beyond Numbers*, at http://www.idea.int/gender/wip

19. D.T. Studlar and I. McAllister (2002) "Does Critical Mass Exist? A Comparative Analysis of Women's Legislative Representation Since 1950" *European Journal of Political Research*, 41, 233–253.

20. I.M. Young (2000) *Inclusion and Democracy*. Oxford: Oxford University Press; K. Beckwith (2000) "Beyond compare? Women's movements in comparative perspective," *European Journal of Political Research* 37:431–468; K. Beckwith (2003) "The Gendering Ways of States: Women's representation and State Reconfiguration in France, Great Britain and the United States" in Banaszak et al. (eds) *Women's Movements Facing the Reconfigured State.*; M. Sawer (2002) "The Representation of Women in Australia: Meaning and Make Believe," in *Parliamentary Affairs* 55:1, 5–18.

21. A. McRobbie (2000) "Feminism and the Third Way," *Feminist Review*, 64, 97–112.

22. Val Feld, Assembly Official Record, 8 March 2000.

23. 156 debates out of a total 327 or 47.7%.

24. 174 debates out of a total 327 or 53.2%.

25. See R. Gargarella, (1998). "Full representation, deliberation and impartiality," in J. Elster (ed.) (1998). *Deliberative Democracy*, Cambridge, Cambridge University Press.

26. M.M. Taylor Robinson and R.M. Heath (2003) "Do Women Legislators Have Different Policy Priorities Than Their Male Colleagues? A Critical Case Test," *Women and Politics*, 24, (4), 77–101.

R E A D I N G   **68**

The Public and Private Domain of the Everyday Politics of Water

Juana Vera Delgado and Margreet Zwarteveen (2007)

GENDER AND WATER: TRACING THE CONNECTIONS

Water constitutes one important area of feminist struggle: access and control over water and (irrigated) land are central in the livelihoods of rural households, and key to determining one's bargaining power in different social domains of interaction (NEDA 1997). Rather than focusing on changes at national and international policy levels (see Bennett *et al.* 2005; Vera 2005, 2006), in this essay we instead want to draw attention to the day-to-day struggles and strategies of female water users themselves in their attempts to access and control water and land. Our main point is that an understanding of the linkages between water, gender and power cannot be obtained by just looking at the "formal" powers and status of men and women, as reflected in policies and laws. Important water powers also reside in day-to-day water management and control practices that are embedded in culture and partly manifested in customary norms and laws, and that occur in social domains that are not normally associated with water management such as the household.

Like almost everywhere in the world, in the Andes "official" or "formal" rights to irrigation water, infrastructure and irrigated land tend to be predominantly vested in men. By "official," we mean registration as a member and right holder in the water users' organization. Both water users and personnel of state agencies dealing with water tend to limit this registration to men, in their capacity as heads of households.[1] In the not so recent past, the very activity of water management was often seen and labeled as a distinct masculine activity; it was not just something that only men did, but also something that culturally belonged to the male domain and that was associated with perceptions of masculinity. This is true even in those communities where irrigating is understood as a task of both women and men, or even is mainly the task of women (Vera 2005; Zwarteveen 2006). Participation in formal water users' associations is another activity that tends to be linked to masculinity and one that tends to be reserved for men. Women thus often do not have a formal voice in decision making and do not have the same possibilities for influencing choices about the mobilization of resources for maintenance or about water distribution as men do (see Lynch Deutch 1991; Boelens and Zwarteveen 2003). Even though the General Water Law of Perú (DL 17752) is gender neutral, the water bureaucrats and the water users themselves usually limit the registration of members of formal water associations to men as "heads" of the households (also see Kome 2002; Vera 2006).

Because of the rather strong connections between water management and masculinity, for women to gain water powers and rights means challenging not only existing divisions of land and water resources, but also values, beliefs and normative systems, and it involves a re-valorization and re-definition of female identity and work (Agarwal 1997; Arroyo and Boelens 1997; Boelens and Zwarteveen 2003). For women, water powers are not straightforwardly conveyed to them through institutions or laws, but need to be wielded and constructed through complex processes that may entail struggle, negotiation and compromises. Agency is an important concept to name what is at stake here: the capacity of social actors to process social experience and to devise ways of coping with life, even under the most extreme forms of coercion, and within the limits of information, uncertainty and other physical, normative and politico-economic constraints (Long 2001: 16; also see Villareal 1994).

WOMEN STRATEGIZE TO ACCESS AND CONTROL WATER AND LAND

In this section, we present two cases of women struggling to obtain or reinforce their control over land and water. These cases were studied[2] in Coporaque, an Andean community situated on the right bank of the famous Colca Valley in the Caylloma Province in the Arequipa Region, Perú. Coporaque has around 684 hectares of irrigated land and 320 water users are registered in the water user organization, of which around 30 percent are women. Water management in Coporaque is guided by two relatively distinct water authorities; one that has been established according the General Water Law (being in force since 1969) with the *Comisión de Regantes* (the irrigators' committee) as its most visible manifestation at the local level, and the other established according to customary local norms, with so-called *regidores* or water mayors as their visible representatives. The *Comisión de Regantes* is responsible, among other things, for charging water fees, for organizing the maintenance of irrigation infrastructure in cases of emergency and for maintaining contacts with other governmental and non-governmental organizations. The *Comisión de Regantes* is perceived as a male domain. Most of its office-bearers are men, with an occasional woman acting as treasurer.

The *regidores* are more directly in charge of water distribution, and also play a key role in organizing the main maintenance works. Probably their most important duty, at least according to the *Coporaqueños* (the people of Coporaque), is the organization of the yearly water feast, a significant social event in the village. Although water distribution tends to be seen as a man's task, most villagers would agree that a man cannot be a *regidor* without the active support of his wife. The role of women is most prominent and visible in the organization of the water feast (Vera 2004).

Lupe

Lupe is a married woman and mother of four children, who has already lived ten years separated (but not divorced) from her husband Leodan. Since she was young she has participated in different training courses, work exchanges and women's organizations. This is how she twice became the president of Caylloma's Peasant Women Federation (*Federación de Mujeres Campesinas de Caylloma*). Leodan did not approve of Lupe's leadership ambitions, and regularly mistreated her physically and psychologically. During the time of their cohabitation, he also began to drink, neglecting the work necessary to the running of their small farm.

At the beginning of their marriage, Lupe felt resigned to her fate, bearing the mistreatment and assuming responsibility for earning the family income; this placed a heavy burden both upon her and her children who necessarily did more work around the home. Most of the time, she also had to undertake the public tasks more commonly carried out by men, instead of Leodan, because Leodan was either too drunk to do so or not interested. She was often the one to assist in the communal meetings and works (*faenas*), she was also the one who would participate in the meetings of the water users' organization and assist in compulsory canal cleaning activities. Lupe's prominence in the public domain was not very well accepted by the rest of the *comuneros* (an officially registered member of the community who has the right to access and use community lands). She was questioned and sometimes even insulted, and people told her that "the husbands must come to the *faenas* and not the wives, the husbands are the official members, otherwise we will also send our wives to these works."

Lupe nevertheless continued and even assumed official functions in water management; she first served as a treasurer in the water *Comisión de Regantes* and later even assumed the central and very visible position of *regidor*.

In spite of all the evidence of Lupe's work and sacrifice, the communal authorities still supported Leodan when Lupe complained to them about how Leodan physically abused her. As she recalls: "They (authorities) used to say to me: you have a strong character and you want to command him, that is why there are problems in your house, you must try not to talk back to him when he is bossy or when he comes home drunk."

After seven years of mistreatment and in response to the pleas of her eldest children, Lupe decided to separate from her husband. She did not, however, want a formal divorce, because she feared it would result in the division of the matrimonial property, especially the land:

> I did not want to do the partition because I already knew that he would immediately sell all the land in order to buy his alcohol. And my children? What would we leave our children? Besides, I am the one who made most of the investments in these lands; we have them because of my sacrifices.

After the separation, Lupe devised strategies to take control of the most important conjugal properties: the land and water. A first and important step was to become an official member of the community (the institution that administers and manages the communal lands). To achieve this, she had to ask the communal authorities to register her name instead of that of her husband. She justified this by showing that she was assuming all the responsibilities of the household, as well as all the public activities. Getting the board's acceptance was not easy, because Leodan had been the president of the communal board some years before and still had some influence there. Lupe took advantage of the fact that one of her relatives was on the communal board. He mediated for Lupe, and supported her requests for membership.

A second step was to become an official and recognized member of the *Comisión de Regantes*. Lupe asked the water authorities to be registered as a member. For this to happen, the water users' organization had to remove the name of her husband from the register and replace it with hers. This proved difficult. Lupe had to get formal approval from the engineers of the provincial Technical Administration of Irrigation (ATDR), the government irrigation agency. To grant this approval, the ATDR engineers asked Lupe for proof of the fact the she was a landholder as well as the head of the household. Lupe succeeded in providing this proof, although it required quite some stamina and patience. It helped that she was already accepted by the community as a *comunera*. She asked, and received, an official declaration from the local judge stating that she was indeed physically separated from Leodan. In addition, she obtained written testimonies of the water users' organization showing Leodan's poor reputation in performing the duties and meeting the obligations of a user, due to his alcohol abuse. After a long process and a lot of paper work, and to the astonishment of the *Coporaqueños*, Lupe succeeded in having Leodan's name removed from the register of the water users' organization. She received the *tarjeta de control de riego*[3] in her name.

Most other water users did not support Lupe's struggles, but on the contrary often referred to her as a negative example for the other women of Coporaque. They called Lupe a *machista*[4] to indicate that she was not behaving as is expected of a proper woman, that she was trespassing symbolic and normative gender boundaries.

Illa

Illa is an illiterate woman and a mother of seven children, who has been separated (rather than divorced) from her husband Teodoro, for the last twelve years. She took the decision to separate after enduring twenty-five years of his continuous mistreatment and unfaithfulness. Teodoro has tried to share his life with three different women in the same village, but it is only with Illa that he has had children. When Illa married she did so without any land because she was considered an "illegal" daughter, even though her father had a considerable amount

of land, and according to the law she had rights to inherit a share of it.[5] In contrast, Teodoro had inherited his share of land from his family. When they were together Illa and Teodoro bought more land, but Teodoro sold most of it without Illa's agreement. During the time they lived together, Illa was in charge of cultivating their land and looking after the children, while Teodoro was busy with public functions or as a salaried employee. He hardly ever brought money home.

After Illa went to the local judge to demand a separation, Teodoro decided to let her and the children keep the few pieces of land that had not yet been sold. Once Illa had obtained the land, after the separation, she was able to register as a member in the water users' organization. She obtained the *tarjeta de control de riego* as an acknowledgment of her membership.

In the year 2000, and seven years after Illa and Teodoro were separated, two new irrigation systems were constructed that allowed more land to be irrigated. Coporaque's Community Assembly decided to distribute around 172 hectares of its communal land among 250 *comuneros* and *comuneras*. Teodoro was one of the members of the communal board that year. The requirements for accessing the land were, first, to be a *comunero* and, second, to contribute with a symbolic quota (150 *nuevos soles*, roughly $45). Illa, just like other separated women living in the community, as the head of her household tried to access these lands, and so did her husband.

At first the community allocated the land to her, but after a few days the Community Assembly noticed that both Illa and Teodoro had received land. This was not the case for the rest of the separated couples, where only the head of the household (mostly the woman) had got the land. Being on the communal board, Teodoro was in a position to influence decisions in his favor and this is how he succeeded in obtaining land in his name too. Rather than disputing his claim to land, the Community Assembly referred to the rule that the husband had to share the land with his wife. As they were not divorced, the Assembly put pressure on Illa to renounce the land that she had received. Teodoro convinced and promised her and his children that he would share his new one hectare of land with them, and Illa agreed to give up her land. However, and as was his custom, one of the first things he did was to pawn the land. As he did not have the money to redeem it, he later asked Illa to help him. Illa and her eldest children made all the effort to collect the required money and redeemed one-third (0.3 hectares) of the land that had been pawned.

Illa consequently registered this piece of land with the water users' organization and tried fulfilling all the tasks and requirements needed to get water rights for this land. However, after two growing seasons during which Illa had cultivated the land, Teodoro "illegally" sold the entire hectare, including the one-third that Illa considered hers, to another user without asking for permission from Illa or their eldest sons. She came to know about this transaction when the water users' organization gave her a copy of the document that showed that the owner of the land was another man who had registered as a water right holder of this land.

Illa tried to recover her water rights as well as her piece of land, asking for help from different lawyers and from the engineers of the ATDR. In spite of many journeys to their offices, she did not succeed in her appeals. The engineers told her that "water belongs to the land," and because the land had a new owner, water would also be given to the new owner.[6] Illa felt that the lawyers she approached behaved dubiously, because many of them turned out to be friends of the actual owner. At the time of writing, Illa and her eldest sons are still trying to recover this land.

CONCLUSIONS

This essay emphasizes three points that must be taken into account when looking at water policies and laws from a feminist perspective. First, in order to analyze water politics it is necessary to enter into the "private" domain and open the "black box" of the household. Gender ideologies, roles and identities—generally, but also in relation to access and control of resources like water and land particularly—are created and negotiated, first and foremost, in the sphere of the household among family members.

Second, it is important to understand how "water actors" are constructed in more public domains.

Formal recognition as a member of land and water committees is often linked to formal ownership of land and water, but that is not enough. In Coporaque, women can inherit land as men do, but they still lose the possibility of controlling the land—as well as the water—when they get married, because their husbands are the ones who tend to be registered with land and water committees.

Lastly, discourses and ideology play a fundamental role in the construction and legitimation of institutions and authorities, and in shaping the spaces for women's political actions. In the case of Coporaque, prevailing notions about what it means to be a woman and idealistic ideas about households as harmonious entities make it difficult for women to assume public tasks and be recognized beyond their roles as mothers and wives.

NOTES

1. The Civil Code of Perú and the Family Legislation do not use the term "head of the household" in any of their articles. Instead they state that the household can be represented by either partner in the couple, unless one of them gives to the other an official authorization to act on his/her behalf.
2. These data were collected by the first author, Juana Vera Delgado and form part of the material she collected for her PhD research on water security in Coporaque. The material was gathered between August 2005 and November 2006. The two cases discussed here are two women with whom Juana interacted closely during the entire period. The representation of their stories is based on frequent interviews with them, and with their neighbors, relatives and involved officials. The quotes are their own words, translated by the first author from Quechua and Spanish. The names of all interviewees and their family members have been changed to protect their identities.
3. The *tarjeta de control de riego* (TCR) or irrigation control card is the official membership card of the water users' organization.
4. People from Coporaque use the term *machista* to refer to women whose behavior and character deviate from what is considered acceptable and normal in women. It expresses the view that such women behave like men, *machistos*, and it is not meant as a compliment.
5. In Coporaque, as in the rest of the communities in the Colca Valley, daughters and sons inherit the land in the same proportion. Those who are considered

"illegal" (born outside of marriage) can also inherit, though not in the same proportion as legal children. In spite of the law, Illa's "legal" brothers and her stepmother denied her her rights to a part of the inheritance when her father suddenly died, arguing that she was an illegal daughter.

6. The Peruvian General Water Law 17752 (in force since 1968), as well as the complementary new decrees and regulations (D. Leg. No. 653–DS No. 0048-91-AG and the DS No. 057-2000-AG), do not specify that the "water belongs to the land" in these terms.

REFERENCES

Agarwal, B. 1997. "Environmental Action, Gender Equity and Women's Participation," *Development and Change* 28 (1): 1–44.

Arroyo, A. and Boelens, R. 1997. *Mujer Campesina e Intervención en el Riego Andino: Sistemas de Riego and Relaciones de Género, Caso Licto, Ecuador [Peasant Women and Intervention in Andean Irrigation: Irrigation Systems and Gender Relations, the Case of Licto, Ecuador]*. Ecuador: CAMAREN, Riego Comunitario Andino, CESA-SNV.

Bennett, V., Dávila, S. and Rico, M. N. (eds). 2005. *Opposing Currents: The Politics of Water and Gender in Latin America*. Pittsburgh, PA: University of Pittsburgh Press.

Boelens, R. and Zwarteveen, M. 2003. "Water, Gender and 'Andeanity': Conflicts or Harmony? Gender Dimensions of Water Rights in Diverging Regimes of Representation," in Salman, T. and Zoomers, A. (eds) *Imaging the Andes: Shifting Margins of a Marginal World*, pp. 145–65. Latin America Studies no. 91. Amsterdam: CEDLA.

Kome, A. 2002. "La Copropiedad de la Tierra, el Derecho de Uso de Agua and el Derecho de Asociación de las Organizaciones de Usuarios del Norte del Perú [Co-Ownership of Land, the Right to Use Water, and the Right to Membership of Water User Organizations in the North of Peru]," in Pulgar-Vidal, M., Zegarra, E. and Urrutia, J. (eds) *Perú: El Problema Agrario en Debate [Perú: The Agricultural Issue Debated]*, pp. 379–97. Lima: SEPIA IX.

Long, N. 2001. *Development Sociology: Actor Perspectives*. London & New York: Routledge.

Lynch Deutch, B. 1991. "Women and Irrigation in Highland Perú," *Society and Natural Resources* 4 (1): 37–52.

NEDA (Netherlands Development Assistance). 1997. *Rights of Women to the Natural Resources and Water*. Working Paper 2, Women and Development. The Hague: NEDA.

Vera, D. J. 2004. "'Cuánto Más Doy, Más Soy . . .': Discursos, Normas y Género: La Institucionalidad de las Organizaciones de Riego Tradicionales en los Andes del sur Peruano ["I Am as Much as I Give" . . . Discourses, Norms and Gender: The Institutionalization of Traditional Water Organizations in the South Andes of Perú]," in Peña, F. (ed.) *Los Pueblos Indígenas y el Agua: Desafíos del Siglo XXI [Indigenous people and Water: Challanges of the Twenty-First Century]*, pp. 17–35. San Luís Potosí: Colegio de San Luís, WALIR, SEMARNAT, IMTA.

Vera, D. J. 2005. "Irrigation Management, the Participatory Approach, and Equity in an Andean Community," in Bennett, V., Dávila, S. and Rico, M. N. (eds) *Opposing Currents. The Politics of Water and Gender in Latin America*. Pittsburgh: University of Pittsburgh Press (PITT).

Vera, D. J. 2006. "Derechos de Agua, Etnicidad y Sesgos de Género: Un Estudio Comparativo de las Legislaciones Hídricas de Tres Países Andinos [Water Rights, Ethnicity and Gender Divisions: A Comparative Study of Water Legislation in Three Andean Countries]," in Boelens, R. Getches, D. and Guevara, A. (eds) *Políticas Hídricas, Derechos Consuetudinarios e Identidades Locales [Water Policies, Customary Rights and Local Identities: Water Law and Indigenous Rights]*, pp. 385–405. Lima, Perú: Instituto de Estudios Peruanos (IEP).

Villareal, M. 1994. "Wielding and Yielding: Power, Subordination and Gender Identity in the Context of a Mexican Development Project," PhD dissertation, Wageningen Agricultural University.

Zwarteveen, M. 2006. "Wedlock or Deadlock? Feminists' Attempts to Engage Irrigation Engineers," PhD dissertation, Wageningen Agricultural University.

R E A D I N G   **69**

The Post-Katrina, Semiseparate World of Gender Politics

Pamela Tyler (2007)

When the *New York Times* reported "a wave of citizen activism" in New Orleans after Hurricane Katrina, it failed to mention that much of the wave was wearing lipstick and carrying a purse.[1] Mopping up is, and always has been, women's work, so it comes as no surprise that large numbers of local women were active in post-Katrina recovery efforts in New Orleans. While some worked singly, volunteering their help in countless ways, others chose the timeworn path of women's associations. This essay focuses on the activities of three organizations formed by women after the hurricane: Citizens for 1 Greater New Orleans, the Katrina Krewe, and Women of the Storm.

In the weeks after Katrina, educated, economically comfortable women in New Orleans passed through historically familiar stages that led from a growing awareness of unmet needs, to frustration over official ineptitude, to the formation of women's organizations, which flowered into full-blown women's activism. Indignation over the failure of government galvanized New Orleans women as it had women reformers of the Progressive Era, with whom they have much in common. As women have done for decades, they responded by joining with like-minded women and pursuing a course of activism to bring change.

The experiences of these New Orleans women activists reprise themes of Progressive Era women who battled along a broad front of issues, including the prevention of cruelty to animals, the care of the mentally disabled, consent laws for marriage, and better teacher salaries. These activist women in post-Katrina New Orleans exemplify the silk-stocking tradition of reformism, which has a long history in the Crescent City. In the 1890s, the Women's League for Sewerage and Drainage, led by the sisters Jean and

Kate Gordon, of later woman suffrage fame, advocated a modern sewerage and drainage system to curb the periodic epidemics and flooding caused by primitive waste disposal methods and entirely inadequate drainage, which the city had done nothing to improve. Their energetic work resulted in the passage of a property tax increase; the New Orleans press claimed that their small women's pressure group "probably did as much work for the special tax as all the men in this city put together." After 1920, enfranchised New Orleans women frequently participated in electoral campaigns under the banner of "good government" to oust individuals they labeled "corrupt." Their unpaid work of lobbying, canvassing, monitoring, and publicizing often bore fruit. Women pressed state and local governments to adopt measures to protect women and children in factories, to close saloons on election day, and to pay male and female school teachers equally. Elite women reformers became darlings of the local media, as press coverage typically lauded their efforts and praised their motives.[2]

New Orleans women reformers of those earlier eras made use of the southern lady mystique and the magic cloak of privilege as they worked toward their goals. Woven of manner, speech, and social connections, enhanced by the wardrobe and confidence that money can buy, that cloak guaranteed them entrée and helped shield them from criticism. In the wake of Katrina, New Orleans women of the economic elite, equipped with similar advantages, again donned that cloak and stepped forward to work for reforms that they found compelling.

Ruth Jones (Ruthie) Frierson, the founder of Citizens for 1 Greater New Orleans, enjoyed unassailable social position; her husband's status as a former Rex, king of Carnival, meant that the Friersons were a kind of local royalty. She had also earned a reputation as the city's top-selling agent for residential real estate. Concern and frustration over the stalled Katrina recovery motivated her to embark on a time-consuming, unpaid effort at reform. Like many New Orleanians, Frierson feared that negative perceptions about her hometown were retarding recovery. Investors clearly feared putting their money into New Orleans property without a guarantee that the Katrina catastrophe would not be repeated; residents and businesses hesitated to return, for the same reason. However, even if the U.S. Army Corps of Engineers upgraded and armored the levees, discredited local entities would still be responsible for their maintenance. Frierson's concern focused on the balkanized New Orleans area levee system, which was under the jurisdiction of no fewer than eight separate levee boards. Politicized levee board members had expanded their authority far beyond inspection and maintenance of floodwalls. Compared by a local political reporter to "Afghan war lords: inscrutable, immovable, and immutable," the multitasking Orleans Levee Board members managed casinos, developed real estate, owned a lakefront airport and two marinas, and patrolled the board's holdings with its own uniformed police force.[3]

Three months after the storm, a proposal to reorganize and professionalize the patronage-ridden levee system failed in the state legislature, where, despite strong backing from the region's business community, the bill never even made it out of committee in the House of Representatives. A conversation between a frustrated Frierson and her equally distressed neighbor Jay Lapeyre, chairman of the New Orleans Business Council, led her to mount a massive petition drive to force a reconsideration of the levees legislation. Just after Thanksgiving 2005, Frierson, who later commented that "people have gone from mourning to outrage," hosted a gathering of over one hundred indignant individuals in her home, in the affluent Audubon Park neighborhood. They formed a group called Citizens for 1 Greater New Orleans with Frierson as head. The group's goal was to end the crony-filled fiefdoms of the incompetent levee boards.[4]

Keenly aware of the warnings from Louisiana's congressional delegation that without reforms it would be difficult to convince Washington to allocate more relief, Citizens for 1 Greater New Orleans embarked on a campaign to bring deep systemic reform. Within the next few months, Frierson's group expanded its original mission to include a second and equally ambitious goal: to reform the byzantine system that employed seven city tax assessors, a vestige of late nineteenth-century machine politics. The entrenched New Orleans system for assessing real estate value was nothing more than whimsy fueled by personal relationships. People who cultivated assessors reaped the reward of low property taxes, the result of rampant underassessments. Frierson's group assumed the task of bringing transparency and formulaic regularity to property assessments in the city. Citizens for 1 Greater New Orleans argued that bringing competence and fairness to local government, especially regarding levees and taxes, would aid recovery by improving the city's national reputation.[5]

In a city whose storm-reduced population had not yet reached two hundred thousand, the group quickly collected fifty-three thousand signatures on a petition calling for levee board reform. They trained volunteers, then financed and carried out an expensive public education campaign to spur citizens to demand a levee board comprised of experts guided by principles, which conducted its business with transparency and without a hint of political patronage. Signs clamoring for action sprouted throughout the city like mold after the flood. The public uproar stimulated by Frierson's movement ultimately forced Governor Kathleen Blanco to call a special legislative session in February 2006. Clad in their trademark red jackets, Frierson and her associates lobbied relentlessly in Baton Rouge and became a notable presence during the twelve-day session.[6]

The outcome was nothing short of amazing. A majority in the legislature voted to present to the state electorate measures that would consolidate the levee boards and the tax assessor system. In September 2006, 80 percent of the voters statewide approved a constitutional amendment for levee board consolidation, while an enthusiastic 97 percent of Orleans Parish voters agreed. Two months later, an amendment to dismantle the assessor system also won overwhelming statewide approval, passing with 78 percent of the vote. Seizing the moment presented by Katrina, Frierson's movement helped sweep away the arcane, entrenched levee and assessor systems, clearing the way for reforms. The independent weekly newspaper *Gambit* ranked the stunning consolidations of the levee boards and assessor system as the number one story of 2006.[7]

Garbage was the catalyst for the New Orleanian Rebecca Curry (Becky) Zaheri.[8] After Katrina, the thirty-eight-year-old Zaheri rented an apartment in Baton Rouge so that her children could enroll in school there. Her husband soon returned to his medical practice in New Orleans, and Zaheri and their two children commuted to spend weekends with him. The blight of the sodden, violated cityscape assaulted her senses on every visit back to her city. She quickly realized that city sanitation services, insufficient in normal times and now depleted of workers displaced by the storm, were utterly inadequate to the task of collecting garbage and the moldy contents of gutted houses. Even with the assistance of Federal Emergency Management Agency (FEMA) contractors, mountains of uncollected refuse and debris festered at curbside for weeks. The garbage problem seemed to grow exponentially, begetting an unprecedented outbreak of blatant littering and largescale dumping. A frustrated Zaheri e-mailed friends to suggest a cleanup day; her first call brought fifteen women to pick up litter, clear sidewalks, and bag the unsightly mess on Thanksgiving weekend 2005. By Christmas, the group was staging two cleanups a week, and, at each, upwards of two hundred people turned out to participate.

Christening themselves the Katrina Krewe, Zaheri's group quickly harnessed a national desire to help. They set up committees, mastered the art of publicity, established a sophisticated Web site, and worked up a sweat twice a week, clearing block after city block. By early 2006, a phenomenal growth had occurred; volunteers were coming from around the country, and turnouts on cleanup days easily exceeded a thousand people. National broadcasters interviewed Zaheri repeatedly, boosting the Krewe's profile. Having started by spending over $2,000 herself on equipment, Zaheri soon tapped area businesses for bottled water, garbage bags, work gloves, and rakes; an auto dealer loaned vans for transporting and storing the supplies. The Katrina Krewe

filed for 501(c)3 status under the federal tax code, making donations to it tax exempt. During Mardi Gras and spring breaks, college students came to help; foreign tourists added their muscle, and locals continued to rally to the cause. Zaheri directed the project with the assistance of ten board members, all women, most of them like herself, mothers of young children.[9]

Ultimately, the success of the Katrina Krewe exhausted Zaheri and her board. Zaheri felt obligated to respond personally to the voluminous e-mails she received, often numbering three hundred daily. Successful, twice weekly cleanups required significant advance work. Zaheri scouted locations, driving slowly through unfamiliar parts of the city to identify appropriately large, littered chunks of New Orleans that could fully occupy the labors of a thousand volunteers for three hours at a time. She and her team coordinated the delivery of supplies to the location, tried to arrange for city garbage trucks to collect the bagged debris, and dealt with the sheriff's office to obtain traffic control in their work areas. The city sanitation director estimated that the Katrina Krewe collected two hundred fifty thousand tons of debris and refuse.[10] But Zaheri noticed a frustrating pattern: cleaned blocks blossomed with junked appliances, discarded carpet, and routine litter all over again. The reliability of Katrina Krewe volunteer sanitation workers seemed to confirm New Orleanians in their rampant dumping and littering.

In summer 2006, the Katrina Krewe reduced cleanups to one per month and discontinued them entirely in the fall. In place of the cleanups, the women instituted new initiatives focused on enlisting neighborhoods, businesses, and schools to police their own areas, advertising an antilitter campaign through their Web site and through brightly painted signage that they purchased for the city. In a major new push aimed at teaching good habits to children, they established the KAT (Kids Against Trash) Krewe. Working through schools, they distributed T-shirts, devised clever activities for building litter consciousness among young children, and hired members of Tulane University's drama department to write and perform antilitter skits for elementary school audiences. Like Citizens for 1 Greater New Orleans, the

Katrina Krewe revised their goal to aim higher; they hoped to inspire New Orleanians to take charge of keeping their city clean, and, in particular, they hoped to instill better habits in an impressionable younger generation.[11]

The third group, Women of the Storm, owes its genesis to Anne McDonald Milling, a sixty-five-year-old seasoned community activist widely respected for her extensive civic involvement. Four months after Katrina, with many lawmakers indicating strong reluctance to finance the rebuilding of New Orleans, Congress still bickered over allocating aid for hurricane recovery. Notably, Speaker of the House J. Dennis Hastert had opined right after the storm that "it looks like a lot of that place could be bulldozed." In January 2006 Milling convened six women to elicit their help with a mission: Because local officials were too dysfunctional to lobby effectively for the city's needs, Milling proposed that a group of confident, articulate women travel to Washington, D.C., to establish personal contact with every Congress member's office. Convinced that a firsthand look at the extensive devastation would move lawmakers to vote for aid more effectively than any amount of lobbying, Milling planned to have the women extend personal invitations to every member to visit New Orleans on an expense-paid tour. For those who accepted the hand-delivered invitation, the women would offer much more than an eyeful of misery and a general wish list; they planned a carefully mapped city tour and a concise, factual, illustrated seminar on the need for wetlands restoration, levee reconstruction, and financial aid for homeowners.[12]

On January 30, 2006, 130 Women of the Storm boarded a chartered flight from New Orleans to Washington. Milling had raised the cost of the flight, commenting in an aside that reveals the advantages of her elite status, "If I can't raise $80,000 in a couple of hours, I'm no kind of a fund-raiser at all." The original nucleus of Milling's group, six white women of like status, knew each other well from years of activity in civic affairs and nonprofit organizations. The final group of 130 was organized in concentric circles, with the inner group reaching out to add others, who then did the same, and so on until the group reached its intended size. The participation of Hispanic, African American, and Vietnamese women, as well as women from Gulf Coast areas beyond New Orleans, provided a modicum of diversity.[13]

The seventeen-hour whirlwind trip to Congress required massive coordination. The inner circle had assigned each woman a partner for the Washington visit, with each pair responsible for four predetermined congressional offices as they carried out a full-court press on the afternoon of their visit. Earlier information sessions made all of the women conversant with the subjects of coastal erosion, levee protection, the extent of the city's losses, and the importance of New Orleans to the nation and the world. Armed with their trademark blue tarp umbrellas and joined by Louisiana's senior senator, Mary Landrieu, the women held a press conference on the Capitol steps, which CNN carried live.[14]

Leaving nothing to chance, the steering committee also formulated a dress code. Avoiding voicing assumptions about who might wear what, but obviously fearing that some women might violate the cultural norms of their own upper-class taste, they simply mandated "no jewelry, no plunging necklines." To explain the policy, a board member stated, "We wanted to be perceived as very serious."[15] Milling relied on some familiar stereotypes about the South and its women to explain their approach. "It's a natural thing for Southerners to do, ask people to come and visit. . . . Why not ask [members of Congress] to come down?" she said. Describing the persistence of her group, she commented, "One of the things women do well is nag. We nagged and nagged the congressmen. . . . And we [did] it with Southern grace."[16] A colleague conceded that "we do play off the southern charm." She paused to clarify. "And then we hit them with the wealth of our knowledge."[17]

When Women of the Storm approached Congress in early 2006, only 5 percent of the House and 12 percent of the Senate had seen the post-Katrina wreckage of the Gulf South; the remaining 498 lawmakers had no plans to do so. Personal invitations, persistent lobbying, follow-up contacts, and a second visit to Washington by the women helped turn the tide and thaw the apathy. Through spring and summer of 2006, members of Congress flowed into New Orleans, putting Women of the Storm into a dual show-horse/ work-house role. In public, self-effacing charm ruled as they hosted dinners, accompanied visitors on devastation tours, worked with the press, and facilitated seminars for their guests. Behind the scenes, it was hard work, details, and deadlines. Members of Congress routinely arrived on short notice, necessitating a scramble to arrange the press exposure and logistics critical to a successful visit. Scheduling spokespersons for tours and booking busy civic leaders for the informational seminars presented challenges. A preexisting edgy relationship between Louisiana's senators, the Democrat Mary Landrieu and Republican David Vitter, sometimes complicated the women's efforts, necessitating patience and tact to avoid irking either office. The six Republicans and four Democrats of the group's executive committee worked smoothly with visitors from both parties and at strategy sessions frequently repeated their watchword, "nonpartisan." To harness the abilities and connections of other women nationally, they enlisted the cooperation of four major national women's organizations—the Links, Incorporated; the Association of Junior Leagues International; the National Council of Jewish Women; and the Women's Initiative of the United Way—each of which pledged to support the Women of the Storm's goal.[18]

As of August 2007, fifty-seven senators and 122 representatives had accepted the women's invitation to travel to New Orleans, totaling 57 percent of the Senate and 28 percent of the House, up from 12 and 5 percent, respectively. Particularly gratifying to the Women of the Storm was the response of the previously dubious Speaker Hastert, who stated, "I saw things here I never expected to see in my lifetime, in my country. You have to be here firsthand on the ground to grasp the extent of the damage." Similarly, an initially crusty and skeptical Senator John McCain, after his tour in March 2006, stated emphatically to the press, "It's necessary for every member of Congress to come down here. You can't appreciate the enormity of it until you come down here. We have an enormous long-term environmental challenge here. . . . I am for doing what is necessary." Hastert's and McCain's conversions were representative of the reaction of most visiting lawmakers. Across the aisle, Senator Joseph Biden

and Speaker Nancy Pelosi attested that Women of the Storm had had a significant impact in getting more attention for New Orleans. In June 2006, a previously reluctant Congress voted to appropriate an additional $4.2 billion for rebuilding Louisiana homes and businesses.[19]

As had elite women reformers in earlier eras, the women of Citizens for 1 Greater New Orleans, the Katrina Krewe, and Women of the Storm received accolades and much media attention. The major broadcast news programs, *USA Today, Fortune Magazine*, National Public Radio, *Ladies Home Journal*, the *New York Times*, the *Chicago Tribune*, and many Associated Press wire stories spotlighted the women and their work. President George W. Bush praised the Katrina Krewe in his speech on the first anniversary of Hurricane Katrina. Also meaningful to the women were the appreciative comments from local media and awards from many quarters.[20]

Unlike an earlier generation of New Orleans women, the elite women reformers after Katrina consciously attempted to avoid errors born of racism and elitism. Race and class undeniably generate important experiential differences among women, which often lead to differences in perception of needs. The historical record documents a series of troubled and suspicious alliances between white and black women suffragists, for example; and within the feminist movement, closer to our own times, the difficulties that middle-class white women, on the one hand, and working-class and black women, on the other, had in agreeing on a shared agenda also speak to differences in experience and perception.[21]

The white women of the inner circle of Women of the Storm intended to have African American women represented in their group. They invited two women of color, well educated and of comfortable economic status, to join the steering committee. Their contributions were welcomed; they apparently enjoyed a cordial working relationship with the group. By providing conditions for shared understanding, commonalities of gender and class seemingly mitigated any divide of racial difference that might have existed. Similarly, Citizens for 1 Greater New Orleans began with women of like background and expanded swiftly to become "metrowide, diverse, and irresistible."[22] The Katrina Krewe harnessed the volunteer work of literally thousands who represented all regions, races, and experiences.

Certainly, status influenced priorities and positions; it is axiomatic that "where you stand depends upon where you sit." Applying the seating metaphor to the women of Frierson's, Zaheri's, and Milling's groups shows them enjoying box seats, not bleachers. For the most part, the upper middle-class women in this essay educated their children at private schools, lived in neighborhoods patrolled by private security, and did not require government-provided social services; as they sought to assist in the recovery of New Orleans, they did not choose to address weak public schools, inadequate police, or absent social services. That their lives were such bastions of comfort and security allowed them the luxury of concentrating first on large systemic reforms, changes that might have seemed abstract to New Orleanians reeling from flood losses, seeking an affordable apartment or a reopened public school, and struggling with the intractable bureaucracy to rebuild in a depopulated post-Katrina neighborhood. These women's goals of achieving professional, streamlined levee boards, fair and professional tax assessments, clean neighborhoods, an enlightened coterie of New Orleans youth opposed to litter, and greater appropriations (for home and business owners, but, significantly, not for renters) from a converted Congress are worthy aims. The reforms they pursued have helped and undoubtedly will continue to help their stricken city, and the women who labored to accomplish them deserve high praise. Meanwhile, however, other deeply troubling problem areas—schools, crime, housing, public health—await champions of their own in New Orleans.[23]

NOTES

1. Adam Nossiter, "Bit by Bit Some Outlines Emerge for a Shaken New Orleans," *New York Times*, Aug. 27, 2006, sec. 1, p. 1.

2. *New Orleans Daily Picayune.* July 7, 1901, quoted in Carmen Lindig. *The Path from the Parlor: Louisiana Women, 1879–1920* (Lafayette, 1986), 116–17. On women's reform efforts in New Orleans, see Pamela Tyler, *Silk Stockings and Ballot Boxes: Women and Politics in New Orleans, 1920–1963* (Athens, Ga., 1996); Leslie Gale Parr, *A Will of Her Own: Sarah Towles Reed and the Pursuit of Democracy in Southern Public Education* (Athens, Ga., 1998); Kathryn Kemp, "Jean and Kate Gordon: New Orleans Social Reformers, 1898–1933." *Louisiana History*, 24 (Fall 1983), 389–401; and Lynn D. Gordon, *Gender and Higher Education in the Progressive Era* (New Haven, 1990).

3. On Ruthie Frierson, see Charles C. Mann, "The Long, Strange Resurrection of New Orleans," *Fortune*, Aug. 29, 2006, http://www.money.cnn.com/magazines/fortune/fortune_archive/2006/08/21/8383661. On the Orleans Levee Board, see Jeremy Alford, "Clamp Down," *Gambit Weekly*, Nov. 22, 2005, http://www.bestofneworleans.com/dispatch/2005-11-22/news_feat.php.

4. Senate Bill 95, the measure for levee board consolidation, passed the Senate unanimously. Late in the session, however, a controversial procedural vote in the House denied the measure a House committee hearing; thus, the proposal died without debate two days before the legislature adjourned. Robert Travis Scou, "Seven Legislators Change Levee Votes," *New Orleans Times-Picayune*, Dec. 1, 2005, http://www.nola.com/archives/t-p/index.ssl?/base/library-90/113344927147170.xml&coll=1. Within days of the legislature's failure to enact levee reform, national credit rating agencies Standard and Poor's and Moody's downgraded Louisiana's credit rating. A local politician explained bluntly that "Louisiana taxpayers will have to pay more money to rebuild because the state's levee boards are crooked." Audrey Hudson, "Legislature Takes Hit on Credit," *Washington Times*, Dec. 6, 2005, available at HighBeam Research, Angela Hill, "Activist Developing Petition for Politicians to Rethink Single Regional Levee Board," *WWLTV.com*, Dec. 2, 2005, http://www.wwltv.com/topstories/stories/wwl120205activists.2ed36750.html. Anne Rochell Konigsmark, "Residents Push to Rid N.O. Levee Boards of Politics," *USA Today*, Dec. 22, 2005, http://www.usatoday.com/news/nation/2005-12-22-levee-board_x.htm.

5. John Hill, "Lack of Levee Board Reform May Make Relief More Difficult". *Shreveport Times*. Feb. 14, 2006. http://www.la-par.org/PAR%20.News%20Files/Shreveport Times02142006.pdf. *The New Orleans Times-Picayune* investigated the system in 2004 and found a strong correlation between owners' campaign contributions to assessors and their undervalued property; properties owned by donors were more than three times as likely as other properties to be valued at 80% or less of their most recent sales price. Though observers scathingly criticized the system's deficiencies for years, little changed. For a three-part newspaper

report, see Gordon Russell, "Dubious Value," *New Orleans Times-Picayune*. April 4, 2004; Gordon Russell. "Getting a Break," ibid. April 5, 2004; Gordon Russell. "Resisting Change," ibid. April 6, 2004; or *nola.com*. http://www.nola.com/speced/dubiousvalue/.

6. Clancy DuBos. "Engaged and Enraged," Dec. 12, 2005, *Gambit Weekly*, http://www.bestofneworleans.com/dispatch/2005-12-13/politics.php. Ruthie Frierson interview by Pamela Tyler, June 16, 2007, audiotape (in Pamela Tyler's possession).

7. Frank Donze, "Voters Merge Levee Boards," *New Orleans Times-Picayune*. Oct. 1, 2006, http://www.la-par.org/PAR%20News%20Files/TimesPic10012006.pdf; Gordon Russell, "New Assessor System to Take Effect in 2010," *ibid*, Nov. 8, 2006, p.1; Clancy DuBos, "Top 10 Political Stories of 2006," *Gambit*, Dec. 26, 2006. http://www.bestofneworleans.com/dispatch/2006-12-26/politics.php.

8. For the account of the Katrina Krewe, I relied on Becky Zaheri interview by Tyler, June 16, 2006, audiotape (in Tyler's possession); and *Katrina Krewe*, http://www.cleanno.org/.

9. Zaheri interview; Deanna Hart, "Wasted No More," *Waste Age*, May 1, 2006, http://wastage.com/mag/waste_wasted_no/.

10. Ron Mott, "Cleaning Up New Orleans. One Piece at a Time." Aug, 25, 2006. *MSNBC.com*, http://www.msnbc.msn.com/id/14517716/.

11. Steve Ritea, "Katrina Krewe Calls It a Day," *New Orleans Time-Picayune*, Aug, 25, 2006, p. 1, http://www.nola.com/news/t-p/frontpage/index.ssf?/base/news-16/1156486170218950.xml&coll=1.

12. Charles Babington, "Hastert Tries Damage Control after Remarks Hit a Nerve." *Washington Post*, Sept. 3, 2005, p. A17, http://www.washingtonpost.com/wp-dyn/content/article/2005/09/02/AR2005090202156.html. Nancy Marsiglia interview by Tyler, March 16, 2006, audiotape (in Tyler's possession); Becky Currence interview by Tyler, March 14, 2006, audiotape, *ibid;* Pamela Bryan interview by Tyler, March 21, 2006, audiotape, *ibid.*; Diana Pinckley interview by Tyler, March 15, 2006, audiotape, *ibid.*

13. Bryan interview; Pinckley interview; Marsiglia interview.

14. "Women Who Inspire Us: Women of the Storm," *Woman's Day Magazine*, http://www.womansday.com/home/10848/women-of-the-storm.html; "International Women's Day New Orleans 2006 Podcast: Women of the Storm Panel Discussion," March 7, 2006, http://www.tulane.edu/-wc/iwd2006/womenofthestormtuwa030706.mp3.

15. Marsiglia interview.

16. April Capochino, "Stormers Not Ready to Stop Congress Push," June 12, 2006, *New Orleans CityBusiness*, http://www.neworleanscitybusiness.com/viewStory.cfm?recID=15811.

17. Marsiglia interview.

18. Tours were usually led by a National Guard brigadier general, Hunt Downer, with a concise seminar presented by three businessmen: Rod West, the head of the local utility company Entergy; Sean Reilly, an advertising executive who chairs Governor Kathleen Blanco's Louisiana Recovery Authority; and King Milling, the president of American's Wetland Foundation (and also president of the Whitney National Bank and Anne McDonald Milling's husband). Women of the Storm persuaded the Greater New Orleans Association to provide lodging gratis. Women of the Storm steering committee meetings, March 8, 13, 20, 2006, audiotapes (in Tyler's possession). "National Women's Groups Join Women of the Storm, Urge Congress to Visit New Orleans and South Louisiana," March 29, 2006, *The Association of Junior Leagues International*. http://www.ajli.org/?nd=women_of_the_storm. On the number of Congress members who had visited, see "About Women of the Storm: Plans, Progress, and Initiatives," *Women of the Storm*, http://womenofthestorm.net/about_det.php?wots_content_ID=60.

19. "Who's Visited," *Women of the Storm*, http://www.womenofthestorm.net/visited.php; Babington, "Hastert Tries Damage Control after Remark Hits a Nerve"; "What Congressional Leaders Are Saying When They See New Orleans," undated Women of the Storm leaflet (in Tyler's possession). John McCain quoted in Jeff Duncan, "Two Key Senators Go to Bat for N.O.." *New Orleans Times-Picayune*, March 11, 2006, http://www.americaswetland.com/article.cfm?id=359&cateid=3&pageid=3&cid=18. Terry O'Connor. "Women of the Storm Persist in Trying to Make a Difference," *New Orleans CityBusiness*, Sept. 25, 2006, http://www.neworleanscitybusiness.com/viewStory.cfm?recID=16825; Department of Housing and Urban Development, "Funding for Recovery in the Hurricanes' Wake Part II," *Research Works*, 3 (Nov. 2006), http://www.huduser.org/periodicals/ResearchWorks/nov_06/RW_vol3num10tl.html.

20. All three groups maintain Web sites with links to their coverage in print and broadcast media. See *Citizens for 1 Greater New Orleans*, http://www.citizensfor1greaterneworleans.com/; *Katrina Krewe*,

http://www.cleanno.org/Press.html; and *Women of the Storm*, http://www.womenofthestorm.net/news.php.

21. See Bonnie Thornton Dill, "Race, Class, and Gender: Prospects for an All-Inclusive Sisterhood," *Feminist Studies*, 9 (Spring 1983), 131–50; Rosalyn Terborg-Penn, "Discrimination against Afro-American Women in the Woman's Movement," in *The Afro-American Woman: Struggles and Images*, ed. Sharon Harley and Rosalyn Terborg-Penn (Port Washington, 1978), 17–27.

22. Clancy DuBos, "Da Winnas & Da Loozas," *Gambit Weekly*, Nov. 14, 2006, http://www.bestofneworleans.com/dispatch/2006-11-14/politics.php.

23. As this article goes to press, the three women's groups remain intact. Frierson's group has joined with civic and business organizations to demand more effective measures to combat violent crime in New Orleans, Becky Zaheri's group continues its effort of educating schoolchildren about litter, and Anne Milling's group is attempting to persuade the Commission on Presidential Debates to hold one debate among the 2008 presidential hopefuls in New Orleans as a way to focus more attention on the city's ongoing post-Katrina struggle. See "War on Career and Violent Criminals," *Citizens for 1 Greater New Orleans*, www.citizensfor1greaterneworleans.com/; "Kat Krewe; Kids Against Trash Krewe," *Katrina Krewe*, www.cleanno.org/Schools.html; and Bruce Eggler, "Group Seeks to Draw Presidential Debate," *New Orleans Times-Picayune*, March 21, 2007, http://www.nola.com/news/t-p/washington/index.ssf?base/news/1-1174455810102470.xml&coll=1. Rumor has it that some women activists may seek public office in the next election cycle, but confirmation was not forthcoming.

CHAPTER 12

Women, War, and Peace

Mary Hawkesworth

Mary Hawkesworth is professor and chair of Women's and Gender Studies and a member of the Graduate Faculty in Political Science at Rutgers University, USA. Her teaching and research interests include feminist theory, women and politics, contemporary political philosophy, philosophy of science, and social policy. Hawkesworth is the author of *Globalization and Feminist Activism* (Rowman and Littlefield, 2006); *Feminist Inquiry: From Political Conviction to Methodological Innovation* (Rutgers University Press, 2006); *Beyond Oppression: Feminist Theory and Political Strategy* (New York: Continuum Press, 1990); and *Theoretical Issues in Policy Analysis* (Albany: State University of New York Press, 1988); coauthor of *Women, Democracy and Globalization in North America* (Palgrave, 2006); editor of *War and Terror: Feminist Perspectives* (University of Chicago Press, 2008), *The Encyclopedia of Government and Politics* (London: Routledge, 1992; 2nd Revised Edition, 2004), and *Feminism and Public Policy (Policy Sciences* 27(2–3), 1994), and coeditor of *Gender, Globalization and Democratization* (Rowman and Littlefield, 2001). Her articles have appeared in leading journals including the *American Political Science Review, Political Theory, Signs, Hypatia, Women and Politics, Journal of Women's History, NWSA Journal, International Journal of Women's Studies, and the Women's Studies International Forum.* She has served on the editorial boards of *Signs: Journal of Women in Culture and Society, Women and Politics* and the *International Feminist Journal of Politics.* She is currently serving as the editor of *Signs: Journal of Women in Culture and Society.*

> One eagle after another
> vanished into darkness.
> One by one they were
> slain
> for having towered above the clouds.
> . . . . . Waterless we shall remain
> here at the mouth of this fountain
> till the day of their return
> with the ocean of dawns that they embraced:
> A vision that knows no death.
> A love that has no end.
>
> Excerpt from "Gone Are Those We Love" by
> Fadwa Tuqan.

War is often romanticized. Nations celebrate wars as essential to their founding and preservation. Revolutionaries celebrate war as a strategy of emancipation. Fiction and film depict war as a site of valor, where warriors deploy their strength to protect their homelands and families. Even poems that capture the profound loss of life in war may romanticize the patriotic cause—"a vision that knows no death"—and the heroism of those who sacrifice their lives for it ("[o]ne eagle after another" that "towered above the clouds").

©John Ditchburn. Reprinted with permission

As an instrument of mass death for combatants and noncombatants, however, war is far from a romantic affair. This chapter provides an overview of scholarship that illuminates dimensions of war seldom considered in popular culture or in traditional approaches to violent conflict. It begins by contrasting dominant accounts of war developed by international relations scholars with feminist efforts to demonstrate gendered aspects and consequences of war. It examines women's roles in war making and how their lives are shaped directly and indirectly by militarization. Tracing one feminist view of war as a mechanism of gendered power that perpetuates women's subordination within domestic, national, and international arenas, the chapter concludes with a discussion of women's peace activism in the twentieth and twenty-first centuries.

GENDERING WAR

Popular understandings and academic analyses of war tend to mask its gendered nature. When war is defined as "organized violence between groups of people" (Osterud, 2004, p. 1028), those dimensions of war that affect men and women differently disappear. The inclusive term, "people," for example, hides skewed gender ratios among those who declare war (disproportionately men), those who fight in wars (disproportionately men), and those who are casualties of war (disproportionately women). Academic explanations of the causes of war similarly ignore gendered and racial components of organized violence. Within international relations theory, for example, a "war of all against all" has been described as the natural human condition (Hobbes, [1651] 1971). Following this logic, some theorists, who call themselves "realists," link conflict in the international system to the absence of a sovereign force with sufficient power to establish world order. In such a condition of violent anarchy, nations fight to promote their own interests, to secure a balance of power, or indeed to achieve a balance of terror. Other theorists emphasize domestic roots of war, suggesting that dictatorships and authoritarian regimes are particularly prone to the instigation of violence as a means of mobilizing their populations against a common enemy while aggrandizing their power. Yet other analysts argue that war stems from exploitive economic systems, which are a hallmark of capitalism, colonialism, imperialism, and globalization. Nationalists often construe war as a mechanism of nation building and a means to consolidate the people's loyalty. Historians emphasize specific causes of particular conflicts, such as boundary disputes, ethnic and tribal divisions, religious clashes, competing factions in civil wars, or aggression by rogue states. None of these frameworks note that militaries have been by design almost exclusively male institutions or that gender may play a role in warfare.

Recent research by feminist scholars has challenged mainstream constructions of war as a gender-neutral phenomenon. By asking the question, "where are the women?" Cynthia Enloe (1988, 1990, 1993, 2000, 2007) opened new lines of investigation into the multiple roles that women play in war (as mothers, lovers, soldiers, insurgents, munitions makers, caretakers, nurses, cooks, sex workers) and the consequences of such gendered divisions of labor for women's citizenship. Over the past two decades, feminist scholars have examined the complex dimensions of gender in war, documenting disparate direct and indirect effects of war on women. Contrary to stereotypes about war deaths that focus on male combatants, women are the majority of direct casualties in war since they constitute the vast majority of civilian casualties (Turpin, 1998). Over the past seventy years, the majority of war dead have been civilians, rising from 50 percent of the casualties in World War II to 90 percent of all war casualties by the new millenium.

In addition, women comprise 80 percent of the refugees displaced by war. They also experience increasing levels of domestic violence and sexual violence in war time. Women's lives and livelihoods are irrevocably affected by displacement and environmental devastation caused by war, even as women assume increasing responsibilities for subsistence provision during war time. As military expenditures divert much-needed revenue from domestic programs, including health, education, and social welfare provision, women are often expected to fill the gaps created by cutbacks in state provision. Women are also directly involved in war making as revolutionaries, militants, soldiers, spies, and participants in the military-industrial complex, just as they are actively engaged in war protesting, peace activism, and war resistance. Moreover, within nationalist symbol systems, particular representations of women circulate as the embodiment of nation that men seek to protect and defend (Lorentzen and Turpin, 1998; Yuval-Davis, 1997), while racialized representations of certain groups help constitute both internal and external boundaries of the nation. Consider, for example, how African Americans who fought in the Revolutionary War and the Civil War were denied full benefits of citizenship; or how whites in Great Britain have struggled to accept British of Indian and Pakistani heritage as "real" British citizens; or how racial profiling in the aftermath of the September 11 bombings of the World Trade Towers and the Pentagon has undermined Constitutional rights of Muslim citizens of the United States.

Carol Pateman (1998, p. 248) has demonstrated how nations have used mandatory male military service, conscription, and militia duty as means to construct heterosexual men as "bearers of arms," while "unilaterally disarming women," barring them from military service and from combat duty. Similarly, Shane Phelan (2001) and Gary Lehring (2003) have traced the exclusion of gays and lesbians from military service as means to privilege particular modes of citizenship that maintain homophobia and support heterosexism as a system of privilege and inequality. By assigning heterosexual men responsibility for the protection of women and children and deploying them in armed combat, states produce the military and citizenship as heteromasculine institutions.

Militaries are perceived as masculine institutions not only because they are populated mostly with men, but also because they constitute a major arena for the construction of masculine identities, which are then given privileged access to social benefits and leadership opportunities afforded by the state. These processes help maintain patriarchal social systems. Exploring these dynamics in the state of Israel, Orna Sasson-Levy and Sarit Amram-Katz (2007) examined an attempt by the Israeli government to alter the gender composition of the military officer corps in order to transcend masculine privilege in the military and in Israeli citizenship. In attempting to disrupt masculine hegemony, Israel heeded the arguments of liberal feminist egalitarian militarists who suggest that because the military is a *sine qua non* of citizenship, women have a right to serve at all levels in the armed forces. Indeed, proponents of this version of egalitarianism insist that women's exclusion from combat duty is discriminatory; it treats women as an inferior category of citizens, limits jobs available to them, and denies them access to educational benefits and routes to power and political leadership. Despite the state's intention to degender the officer training program by abolishing gender-segregated leadership programs, however, Sasson-Levy and Amram-Katz demonstrate the enormous difficulty of changing the national gender order. Paradoxically, incorporating men and women in the same leadership training program created the conditions for even greater gendering than had existed when trainees were gender segregated as gender stereotypes were resurrected and circulated to re-create advantages for men. Introducing objective, performance-based measures of ability were insufficient to trump gender stereotypes or the assumption that men perform better than women, regardless of task. Contrary to the hopes of feminist egalitarian militarists, gender integration did not generate gender equality. Nor did the presence of women generate gender-neutral modes of military operation. Instead, gender integration reproduced and strengthened the combat model as a universal military norm, entrenching male gender power within the military and within Israeli social and political life.

Women's Participation in Armed Conflict and Political Violence

Although the military has been and remains a male-dominant institution, women have been active participants in armed conflict across the ages. In the words of historian Linda Grant De Pauw (1998, p. xiii): "Women have always and everywhere been inextricably involved in war, [but] hidden from history. . . . During wars, women are ubiquitous and highly visible; when wars are over and the war songs are sung, women disappear." In the American Revolution, for example, women provided labor essential to the success of the boycott of British goods, the central economic weapon used by the American revolutionaries against the Crown. To ensure the success of the boycott, women had to change their purchasing practices and expand their production of essential goods to meet market demand. They produced sufficient homespun clothes to accommodate civilian populations and to supply revolutionary troops. They produced food, blankets, and medicines to provision the troops. They removed lead weights from their windows and melted them down to make bullets. Some 12,000 "women of the army" fed the armies on the march, provided laundry and sexual services, and nursed the wounded. British and American war records

LEARNING ACTIVITY   **Rosie the Riveter**

Rosie the Riveter was the name given to the primary character in a media campaign to encourage women to take factory and other jobs vacated by men fighting in World War II. Her slogan was "We can do it!" Eager to take on new responsibilities and support the war effort, women learned to operate machinery, work in mills, and build munitions. By the end of the war, women's participation in the workforce had doubled, though they made only about two thirds of what their male counterparts had made in the same jobs. Of course, as soon as soldiers began to return from the war, women were forced to leave these jobs so men could have them again. While many women would have preferred to keep their jobs, few were given that opportunity, even though their contributions had been essential.

To see more Rosie images, go to the Library of Congress site for Rosie pictures at http://www.loc.gov/rr/print/list/126_rosi.html.

Watch a webcast about Rosie at http://www.loc.gov/rr/program/journey/rosie.html.

Listen to stories of real Rosies at the Veterans History Project:

Marcella Balbach, Indiana shipyards, http://lcweb2.loc.gov/diglib/vhp/story/loc.natlib.afc2001001.10343/

Meda Brendall, Baltimore, Bethlehem-Fairfield Shipyards, http://lcweb2.loc.gov/diglib/vhp/story/loc.natlib.afc2001001.04951/

Dora Janet Au Mahoney, munitions/TNT plant, http://lcweb2.loc.gov/diglib/vhp/story/loc.natlib.afc2001001.05919/

indicate one woman "camp supporter" for every 10 members of a British regiment and for every 15 revolutionary soldiers. Because they could move more freely across enemy lines, women were recruited to serve as spies for both sides in the revolutionary conflict. Women who supported the American troops also launched fundraising efforts to cover the costs of the revolutionary effort. Women in Philadelphia, for example, raised $300,000 in one campaign to support Washington's forces (Evans, 1997). Women served as auxiliaries (nurses, ambulance drivers, and cooks) in both World War I (1914–1918) and World War

II (1939–1945), supporting the soldiers at the same time that they were also exposed to the dangers of war. The reading "The City in the Desert" written in 1929 by U.S. nurse Mary Borden poignantly describes the experience of working behind the front lines in the First World War and dealing with the carnage of war. Russian women also served as soldiers in the Soviet military during World War II; 70 percent of these women soldiers participated in front line action. Drawing evidence from nationalist struggles in various regions of the world over the past two centuries, feminist scholars have demonstrated that women have been actively involved in long and dangerous struggles for national independence, organizing against oppressive regimes, mobilizing as citizens, demanding the transformation of the political system, standing publicly against colonial and imperial rule, and participating in revolutionary violence. Although some societies have refused to allow women to fight for their countries, others have relied heavily on women's service to win wars.

Women are recruited to serve in the military in most countries in the twenty-first century, but only two countries, Eritrea (an African nation north of Ethiopia) and Israel require mandatory military service for women; and only a few nations allow women to serve in combat roles. Although Australia, Belgium, Britain, Canada, Denmark, Eritrea, France, Israel, Japan, the Netherlands, Norway, Portugal, Russia, South Africa, Spain, Sri Lanka, Taiwan, and the United States permit women in certain combat roles, no nation offers women the same panoply of military roles accorded to men (for a full discussion, see Goldstein, 2001, chapter 2). Women currently comprise 15 percent of the United States military; and one in seven soldiers serving in Iraq is a woman.

In contrast to wars fought by nationstates that depend upon and reproduce race and gender hierarchies, Frantz Fanon suggested that people's wars—revolutionary struggles to overthrow colonial domination—could reverse racial and gender inferiority complexes created by colonization. By asserting their humanity through a violent confrontation with their oppressors, the colonized could achieve not only national independence but also recognition of their humanity, which had been denied by their colonizers. Fanon broke new ground in suggesting that revolutionary violence held transformative potential for women as well as for men. He claimed that Algerian women's participation in the armed struggle altered their "feminine" colonized identities and family relationships in positive ways that challenged feudal, patriarchal traditions (Fanon, 1967, pp. 99–120).

Aaronette White (2007) has investigated whether anticolonial violence has the psychological effects predicted by Fanon, whether the debilitating effects of colonized identity are transformed through revolutionary violence, and whether participation in revolutionary violence has the same effects for men and women. Drawing upon the testimonies of women revolutionaries in Algeria, Angola, Cape Verde, Guinea, Mozambique, Namibia, Zimbabwe, and South Africa, White suggests that there are many reasons that participation in revolution may fall short of Fanon's emancipatory hopes for men and women. Patriarchal mentalities may be shored up by military systems of command. The authoritarianism deemed essential to military organization may foster hierarchies and systems of command that are inimical to democratic practices. Soldiers trained to obey unquestioningly may lose the autonomy requisite to equal recognition and equal citizenship. Notions of combat as the ultimate test of manliness may generate modes of masculinity in newly independent states that are incompatible with sexual equality.

White argues that gendered dimensions of revolutionary violence produce differing effects for men and women militants. Through an examination of the experiences of women revolutionaries in several African nations, White suggests that gendering in the context of revolutionary war constructs modes of femininity and masculinity that empower men while disempowering women revolutionaries. The sexual division of labor within revolutionary struggles, for example, typically assigns secondary roles—as clerks, couriers, porters, nurses, laundry workers, cooks, child-care providers—to women combatants. Although revolutionary rhetoric suggests that every role in the revolution is valued, every role is not valued equally. Nor is every person, particularly if she is a woman, equally recognized for the role she plays.

In addition to sexual divisions of labor that structure gender inequities, revolutionary cadres captured during armed conflict are often subjected to torture. Some torture techniques—sleep deprivation, physical beatings, and electric shocks to genitals—were used against men and women. Other torture techniques specifically targeted women's sexuality. White notes that most women combatants are ashamed to speak about these incidents, so first-person accounts are few; however, confidential psychological reports suggest that these forms of violence traumatize rather than affirm women cadres, leaving enduring emotional scars that national independence does not erase.

This is especially the case since testimonies by women revolutionaries indicate that sexual torture and abuse were not confined to the activities of enemy forces. Revolutionary armies also engaged in horrific human rights abuses including rape, torture, and brutal abductions. Among their own comrades, women combatants were subjected to sexual duty, forced marriage, and sexual politics that could require marriage to a commanding officer to rise through the ranks. Regardless of their training and status as fighters, women were expected to care for, serve, comfort, and sexually satisfy men. Women cadres who resisted these impositions could be judged disloyal to the cause, a fate with dire consequences of imprisonment or death. Speaking about the horrific treatment they endured at the hands of their comrades was also viewed as a form of disloyalty, and the women themselves often chose to remain silent rather than to be accused of betraying their brothers in arms and the cause for which they fought. Their silence often coexists with their erasure as nationalist myth making celebrates the founding fathers of the new nation.

Meg Samuelson (2007) demonstrates the powerful social pressures women militants face to erase their revolutionary valor and conform to fantasies of domesticity during periods of demobilization. Using testimony given at the South African Truth and Reconciliation Commission (TRC) hearings, she depicts the paradoxical position of the female African National Congress (ANC) guerrilla commander during the postapartheid period of demilitarization and redomestication. Samuelson offers an alternative explanation of the silence of women militants who refuse to testify about their wartime experiences, suggesting that a woman's concealment of a painful history of sexual exploitation or indeed sexual torture during her military service may be "a repudiation of a certain kind of femininity" (p. 849), a refusal to be reduced to a victim, a resistance against sexualization, and a rejection of pressures to abandon her revolutionary subject position. Yet, Samuelson points out that even such a tactical deployment of silence was insufficient to avoid sexualization in postapartheid South Africa. "As the TRC became increasingly anxious about its failure to capture both the story of women and the story of sexual violence, it began to conflate the two: 'woman's' story was reduced to one of sexual violence, and sexual violence was identified as a defining female experience. While only 40 percent of the TRC's cases of sexual abuse, where the victim's sex was specified, concerned women, 'Sexual Abuse' is a central category in the chapter dedicated to the Special Hearings on Women in the *Final Report*" (p. 845).

As White and Samuelson point out, demobilization in the aftermath of armed conflict is profoundly gendered. In newly independent states, women combatants may not be celebrated as revolutionary heroes, but rather asked to put down their weapons, abjure their active military service, maintain silence about abuses suffered at the hands of their comrades, and return to the domestic sphere. Male nostalgia for "the normal" may mandate wifehood and motherhood for women revolutionaries. Those who resist this mandate may not fare well. Rather than restoring their dignity through war, participation in violence may subject women combatants to shaming practices that challenge their integrity. Participation in armed struggle may restore male combatants' dignity precisely because it

Fact Sheet: Adolescent Girls Affected by Violent Conflict

WHY LOOK SPECIFICALLY AT ADOLESCENT GIRLS?

Adolescent girls, many of them mothers and heads of households, are an overlooked group within conflict-affected populations. They are crucial actors in post-conflict reconstruction and in the rebuilding of peaceful communities. There are many age, development, and social position-related differences among girls, women, and adolescent girls. At the same time, it is important to recognize that there is no universal line between girlhood and womanhood; it differs greatly from context to context. Often, "adolescence" is not a phase in the life-cycle of girls who marry and/or become mothers immediately, these girls go directly from "childhood" to "womanhood."

WHAT DO ADOLESCENT GIRLS EXPERIENCE IN ARMED CONFLICTS?

Gender-Based Violence (GBV)

In conflicts, adolescent girls are particularly vulnerable to gender-based violence—rape, sexual slavery, mutilation, trafficking, forced prostitution, forced marriage, and forced impregnation. Gender-based violence experienced during the formative adolescent years can have different lifelong impacts than violence experienced by women.

Displacement

Being forced to flee violent conflicts can increase the vulnerability of adolescent girls to sexual abuse and exploitation. For example, the traditional responsibility of some adolescent girls in collecting firewood may become riskier in refugee camps due to longer distances between the camp and the collection site. Displacement also tends to alter social structures and support mechanisms by separating family members, and by loss of livelihood, which can increase the risk of abuse and exploitation for adolescent girls.

HIV/AIDS

Adolescent girls may face increased exposure to HIV/AIDS transmission when they are targeted for gender-based violence. A high rate of HIV/AIDS prevalence in communities may also mean they are responsible for caring for infected family members in addition to coping with the loss of family members from both war and disease. In some situations, adolescent girls may have less access to preventive information and to treatment.

Girls in Fighting Forces

Adolescent girls can be vulnerable to forced recruitment into fighting forces as combatants, cooks, porters, spies, "wives," and sex slaves. The experiences and unique needs of adolescent girls who have been armed fighters are often ignored in post-conflict reconstruction, especially in Disarmament, Demobilization and Reintegration (DDR) processes.

Early Marriage and Forced Marriage

Poverty is a key factor in war. Adolescent girls may be forced into early marriage or "taken as wives" in situations of armed conflict. Adolescent girls from poorer families may be more vulnerable to forced marriage. Families sometimes marry off daughters at younger ages, to reduce the number of people depending on food, and to try to enhance security. Marriage usually means the end to education.

Forced Impregnation and Early Childbirth

Adolescent girls can be at risk of forced impregnation as a strategy of ethnic cleansing which seeks to forcibly change the ethnic make-up of a population. Forced impregnation and rape increase the likelihood of early childbirth, with its high risk of potential death or disability for the young mother and her infant.

Household Workload

The effects of HIV/AIDS, displacement, and deaths of family members during conflict increase the already heavy workload of adolescent girls—cooking, collecting water, gathering firewood, and minding children. Adolescent girls may also be heads of households or single mothers.

Lack of Education

These experiences often result in reduced opportunities for primary and secondary education, or informal education/livelihood development opportunities. The lack of education opportunities can leave adolescent girls even more at risk of abuse, violence, poverty, disease, and exploitation.

WHAT CAN WE DO?

The responsibility to protect adolescent girls threatened by violent conflict is a responsibility shared by adolescent girls themselves, their communities, governments, international organizations—and ourselves. Resolution 1325 on Women, Peace and Security provides a common moral and legal platform through which individuals, organizations, governments, and international institutions can advocate for the inclusion of adolescent girls in conflict prevention, peace-building, and reconstruction.

What Can We Do?

Recognize adolescent girls affected by armed conflict as having distinctive needs which may not be the same as those of women, children, or adolescent boys. The distinctive needs of adolescent girls require distinctive responses—which should be a priority for program developers and policy-makers. Write a letter or email to your elected representatives urging them to prioritize women's rights and gender equality throughout international policy sectors, and to emphasize the special needs of adolescent girls.

What Can Governments Do?

Increase human and financial resources toward women's rights monitoring and implementation with special attention to the needs and aspirations of adolescent girls. Standards set out in Resolution 1326, the Convention on the Elimination of Discrimination Against Women (CEDAW), the Convention on the Rights of the Child (CRC), the Beijing Platform for Action and the Protocol to the African Charter on Human and Peoples' Rights on the Rights of Women in Africa all provide a strong footing for national governments to ensure adolescent girls are protected from violence and are empowered as peacebuilders.

Specific Areas for Government Action:

- Provide HIV/AIDS and sexual and reproductive health education to adolescent girls and boys.
- Increase protection for refugee and internally displaced adolescent girls.
- Support gender-based violence prevention programs, survivor support, clinical care, and confidential reporting procedures.
- Provide girl-friendly primary and secondary education including early childhood education (ECE) and parallel formal and non-formal programs.
- Include the unique needs of adolescent girls involved in fighting forces in peace agreements and Disarmament, Demobilization and Reintegration (DDR) programs.

What Can International Organizations Do?

International organizations including the United Nations should ensure their policies, programs, and practices are sensitive and responsive to the needs and aspirations of adolescent girls.

Specific Areas for International Action:

- Enforce zero-tolerance sexual abuse and sexual exploitation policies by peacekeeping forces and humanitarian officials working in conflict situations and in refugee/IDP camps.
- Ensure international criminal justice mechanisms such as the ICC or other tribunals are responsive to adolescent girls through sensitive reporting, investigation, witness support, and reparations.
- Develop gender and youth sensitive early response strategies to identify how adolescent girls may be affected by armed conflict.
- Support the participation of adolescent girls in conflict prevention, peacebuilding, and reconstruction processes.

reinscribes dominant conceptions of masculinity. By contrast, the valor of women combatants may violate traditional gender norms (real or imagined), generating public condemnation for loss of femininity and respectability, while posing serious challenges to the dignity and psychological well-being of women combatants. Lying about their war experiences and becoming respectable wives and mothers may be required of demobilized women combatants as an alternative to being ostracized permanently (Lyons, 2004). With few exceptions, women revolutionary "creators of history," to borrow Fanon's terms, have been pressured to disappear from history.

Gendered patterns of exploitation in war have surfaced among younger and younger populations. During Sierra Leone's decade-long civil war, which began in 1991, girls were abducted by warring factions (mainly rebel forces) and forced to assume the roles of combatants, commanders, wives, and slave laborers—often in combination. Girls were assigned an array of domestic and supportive tasks including cooking, washing, taking care of young children, and carrying heavy loads of ammunition, supplies, and arms and subjected to dire forms of punishment including brutal physical assaults, starvation, and even death for failing to carry out their duties. They were also subjected to severe physical abuse at the hands of those who commanded them—sexual violence, forced marriages, coerced childbearing and child rearing. They witnessed brutal forms of violence against men, women, and children—combatants and civilians. Worldwide thousands of children are still being used as soldiers in conflict regions. The reading "Children of War" by Wray Herbert documents the experiences of former child soldiers in Mozambique's civil war in southeast Africa and discusses programs to support them and promote healing.

This extreme violence was designed to ensure compliance with a fairly traditional gendered division of labor, but it also produced girl soldiers who perpetrated severe acts of violence as a means of negotiating their survival. As Myriam Denov and Christine Gervais (2007) have pointed out, girls made conscious attempts to protect themselves by developing skill in the use of small arms. Within the ranks of the Revolutionary United Front of Sierra Leone (RUF), for example, girls became increasingly aware that carrying guns afforded them a measure of protection and decreased their chances of victimization. Seeing armament as a way to increase their safety and security, girls became eager to possess their own weapons. In the words of one former girl soldier, "The gun became my bodyguard and protector. The gun was power, and that's why I was anxious to have one" (Denov and Gervais, 2007, p. 895).

The girls also realized that the more aggressive they were seen to be and the more they destroyed and looted, the more valuable were within the ranks of the RUF. The more violent they were, the safer they became within the armed group. Engaging in extreme forms of violence brought privileges within the RUF, such as better access to food and looted goods, and, in some cases, led to promotion within the ranks. In these dire circumstances girl soldiers moved from sustained sexual exploitation to a strategic mode of consenting deemed essential to their long-term survival. The girls manifested their agency by cultivating their capacity to kill. Far from being the "natural disposition of all mankind" described by Hobbes in the *Leviathan*, the equal capacity to kill emerged as one effect of the brutal militarization of girls within war.

Complex Gendered Effects of War

Women and girls who avoid combat roles in war-torn regions are far from immune to the indirect effects of war. The technologies of war have changed dramatically over the past two centuries, and guerilla warfare, urban warfare, and counterinsurgency have gradually eroded the distinction between combatant and noncombatant. As the notion of a "front line" of battle grows increasingly murky, women have become the chief casualties of war. Not only do they incur the highest number of civilian deaths, they are subjected to increasing levels of sexual violence and domestic violence, and they are at risk of being displaced internally and across national borders as refugees. Women constitute 80 percent of 11.4 million refugees in camps organized by the Office of the UN High Commissioner for Refugees, and a comparable percentage of the 26 million people displaced by conflict but remaining in their home countries. Despite the efforts of international aid organizations, life for refugees and the internally displaced is bleak. Inadequate food, clothing, shelter, education, and employment are exacerbated by the prevalence of disease, exploitation, sexual violence, and the profound anxieties of a wholly uncertain future. As the reading by Elizabeth Ferris, "Abuse of Power: Sexual Exploitation of Refugee Women and Girls" explains, girls and women are especially vulnerable as victims of sexual exploitation in these camps.

The collapse of governance in Somalia provides a powerful example of the complex gendered effects of war on women. Since the collapse of the Mohamed Siad Barre regime in Somalia in 1991, millions of Somalis have been displaced to Ethiopia, Kenya, Yemen, Europe, and North America. More than half a million sought refuge in camps in Kenya, where their precarious struggle for existence was exacerbated by sexual assault by roving bandits and humanitarian aid workers. Cawo Mohamed Abdi (2007) has investigated how pervasive physical insecurity and the opportunistic interventions of certain Islamist organizations colluded in the reinvention of "tradition" that imposes new constraints on women. Women's heightened vulnerability in conflict and post-conflict situations provided a rationale for changing dress codes and behaviors associated with conservative Islam. Responding to the danger of sexual assault in a world where protective family networks and state police services, as well as traditional mores, have been destroyed by warfare, women turned to the *jalaabiib or jilbaab*: long, heavy flowing dresses accompanied by a veil as a form of self-protection. Indeed, women in Somalia and in adjacent refugee camps in Kenya reported that they began wearing trousers for protection in defense from violence. Although neither trousers nor *jilbaab* were traditional modes of dress in Somalia, women adopted this attire for complex reasons. Some believed that extra layers of clothing might create a barrier to rape by delaying the assault and providing time for someone to come to their aid. Some suggested that the veil lowered their visibility and heightened their respectability, enabling them to be in public spaces and thereby facilitating their economic efforts to sustain their families. Others adopted conservative forms of dress as an expression of religion, which helped them cope with the hardships and dangers created by war.

The dress choices available to women were also affected by fundamentalist versions of Islam that Saudi Arabia and Sudan began exporting to war-torn Somalia during the 1990s. These patriarchal Islamists actively politicized gender, interpreting the war as divine punishment for women's deviation from the "authentic" rules of Islam. Women were told that they must repent, and the adoption of the veil was one visible mark of repentance. Although this mode of dress differed markedly from that traditionally worn by Muslim women in Somalia, those who refused to conform were subjected to street harassment including physical assaults such as stoning. Women's attempts to reduce their vulnerability then involved efforts to avoid such street harassment and physical assault as well as sexual assault (Abdi, 2007).

This reinvention of "tradition" encompassed new modes of education as well as attire. The new Islamist society also introduced gender segregation in schools (madrassas) funded by Saudi Arabia and Sudan. Girls have been increasingly excluded from educational opportunities in Somali refugee camps—now comprising only 10 percent of high school students. Far from being a return to traditional practice, new modes of dress, and new gendered divisions of labor and knowledge, are effects of war, enforced through a potent combination of charity and violence as mechanisms of social control. Somali women operate under new constraints and are subjected to new sanctions as they attempt to preserve their precarious existence.

That women may actively embrace more conservative modes of dress in regions plagued with war makes sense when considered in the context of the heightened sexualization of women associated with war and militarization. As Cynthia Enloe documented, many types of violence against women are exacerbated by militarism, including sexual assault, sexual trafficking, prostitution, and domestic violence. From the violent conscription of 100,000 to 200,000 *Karayuki-san* or "comfort women" from 14 nations by the Japanese Army during World War II to the organization of brothels in Hawaii for American soldiers on "R&R" (rest and relaxation leave), provision of sexual services to soldiers has been a continuing concern of the military. From 1941 to 1944, close to 250,000 men a month paid three dollars for three minutes of sexual contact in Honolulu (Enloe, 1993, p. 145). While the proliferation of brothels around military bases is sometimes a result of private entrepreneurialism, it often stems from government to government agreements that require prostitutes to register, carry photo ID, undergo weekly medical examinations, and use condoms with military customers (Enloe, 1993, pp. 147–148). The scale of these mobilizations of sexual services is daunting. Prior to U.S. base closings in the Philippines in 1992, for example, 100,000 women worked in the "entertainment business" around Clark Air Force Base and Subic Naval Base as Filipino officials collaborated with U.S. military

WEAPON OF MASS DESTRUCTION

Used with permission of Ann Telnaes and Women's eNews in conjunction with the Cartoonist Group. All rights reserved.

officials on policing, public health, and commercial zoning to regulate the brothels, bars, and discos servicing U.S. military personnel.

State-sanctioned prostitution to provide "sexual release" for military personnel has not succeeded in eliminating sexual violence against women soldiers and civilians in proximity to military installations. Thirty percent of women treated at U.S. Veterans Affairs clinics in recent years report that they experienced sexual assault while serving in the military. The vast preponderance of these were acquaintance rapes: women soldiers were assaulted by men with whom they worked closely on active duty.

Sexual assault of civilian women by military personnel often involves gang rape and sexual slavery. Rather than spontaneous acts by individual soldiers, rape on a large scale has been orchestrated as a means of ethnic cleansing with increasing frequency over the past 50 years. As discussed in chapter 8, women and children in conflicts around the world have been systematically raped on orders from military officials as part of campaigns designed to demoralize the population and destroy particular ethnic communities. The reading "War Against Women Rape in Darfur" by Femke van Zeijl tells of the brutal rapes of women and children in the ethnic conflicts in Darfur, Western Sudan. She discusses the violence occurring on a massive scale in this region where rape is a taboo subject.

War as a Mechanism of Social Transformation

War has been and continues to be a powerful mechanism for social transformation at the national and international levels, but the direction of change is not necessarily women-friendly. Writing in the newsletter of the International Woman Suffrage Association (IWSA), *Jus Suffragii*, during World War I, Mary Sargent Florence and C.K. Ogden, two British anti-war suffragists, noted that "In war time, only men matter" (Offen, 2000, p. 252). Taking the argument one step further, Irish feminist Francis Sheehy Skeffington insisted that "war is necessarily bound up with the destruction of feminism" (Offen, 2000, p. 260), pointing out that World War I triggered an impressive counter-offensive by conservative forces to undermine and erase feminist transformative efforts. Women were forced out of the lucrative jobs to which they had been recruited as part of the war effort. Pro-natalist legislation encouraging women to be mothers was passed to enlist women in a new effort to fight the "depopulation" caused by war. Family allowances and mothers' pensions were introduced in a number of European states as an incentive for women to bear more children. Abortion and birth control were criminalized to restrict the options for those uninspired by the pro-natalist incentives. Then—as now—war, armed conflict, and terrorism play crucial roles in disrupting old racial and gender orders, while establishing and maintaining new racial and gender regimes. War alters existing sexual divisions of labor but not necessarily in degendering ways. Organized violence may produce militant women, but it may also increase the vulnerabilities and sense of defenselessness of certain nations, "feminizing" them. Armed conflict may also contribute to significant regendering, as masculinist models are validated through manifestations of physical brutality or as men's longing for a return to "normal life" generates forms of redomestication, a pattern of post-conflict restructuring that resurrects male dominance.

The "war on terror" brings these dynamics into stark relief. Launched by the G.W. Bush administration in the aftermath of the September 11, 2001, bombings, the "war against terror/terrorism," is not a war between states, but a war that pits a coalition of Western military forces operating under executive order against a non-state actor, the Al Qaeda

LEARNING ACTIVITY   **The War on Terror in the Media**

Browse through newspapers and popular magazines (such as *Time* or *Newsweek*) published after September 11, 2001, and search for articles on the "war on terror." Look closely at the language used to describe this "war." What words are used? Or not used? What images? How are various groups of people depicted? What role does religion play in the rhetoric about the "war on terror"? How is opposition to the "war on terror" depicted? Where are women in these stories and images? What do you think are the effects of the language and images used in these articles?

Now take a look at articles about peaceful protests against the "war on terror." What language is used to describe the protests and protestors? What images? How are various groups of people depicted? Where are women in these stories and images? What do you think are the effects of the language and images used in these articles?

How do you think rhetoric and media images shape our understandings of war, violence, and protest? What role do you think gender plays in our interpretation of events, articles, and images?

network, which moves clandestinely within and across national boundaries of some 60 states. As one justification for its initial invasion of Afghanistan, the Bush administration cited the importance of "saving Afghan women" from the Taliban. Lila Abu-Lughod's essay, "Do Muslim Women Really Need Saving?" explores the ethics of the "War on Terrorism" and the ways the U.S. invasion of Afghanistan has been justified in terms of liberating poor, downtrodden Afghan women. She suggests such actions reify cultural stereotypes and considers the limits of cultural relativism through a focus on the burqa and the many meanings of veiling in the Muslim world. Abu-Lughod emphasizes the need to develop a sincere respect of differences among women in the world and practices to help support, rather than "save" them.

Expanding its field of operations, the Bush administration launched an equally unconventional war against Iraq, breaking with international law and its own conventions for the deployment of military force. The United States unilaterally launched a preemptive war against the regime of Saddam Hussein, which quickly extended into an exercise in occupation/peace-keeping/nation-building/insurrection quelling. According to Iraq Body Count, by the end of 2008, deaths in Iraq totaled 4538 military participating in the U.S. Coalition and 98,521 civilians. Although there are no official figures of civilian deaths caused by the U.S. invasion of Afghanistan, Human Rights Watch and the UN Mission in Afghanistan estimate direct and indirect deaths range from 9,269 to 27,607 since 2001. As of this writing, U.S. and allied military deaths continue to rise.

The war on terror has had profound effects at home as well as abroad, giving rise to and legitimating a gendered logic of "the national security state" (Young, 2003), which promises protection of the "homeland" in return for citizens' obedience. As thousands of vigilantes converge on ranches spanning the Mexican border, pledging their guns and their lives to protect the United States from "security threats" lurking south of the border, the state withdraws constitutional rights and protections. The "USA PATRIOT Act" authorizes securitization measures that suspend the right of *habeas corpus,* as well as Fourth Amendment guarantees against unwarranted searches and seizures. According to the logic

A DAY IN THE LIFE **She Wonders** by *R. Tucker Readdy*

As the sun rises an intense red over the Marshall Islands, she wonders if she will ever start a day without recalling the blast. For her, the burning color is a permanent reminder of the horrific legacy created when the United States conducted a series of 21 thermonuclear tests on the islands between 1954 and 1957. The most dreadful was Bravo, equivalent to 15 megatons of TNT or 1,000 times the intensity of the atomic bomb that was dropped on Hiroshima. The recurrent breezes that ruffle the fronds of the palm trees and keep the islands' 80 degree temperatures tolerable are also a bitter messenger; according to the U.S. government, it was "unexpected winds" that caused radioactive fallout to be showered on the residents of her tiny country. The single room residence she lies in feels as small as the islands themselves, which total only 3.4 square miles but are scattered over 357,000 square miles of ocean. The pain and fatigue from her end-stage cancer keep her in bed most of the day; when not asleep, she often lies looking west toward Honolulu, Hawaii, and the government that ultimately shortened her life. It had been entrusted to help the people of the Marshall Islands by being granted United Nations trusteeship in 1947.

Fifty years removed from the incident and unable to read to pass the time, she often spends a majority of her day wondering whether the restitution provided by the U.S. could ever begin to compensate for the disruption—personal, economic, political—that she and the people of the Marshall Islands have endured. Is $100,000 for a mastectomy coupled with $125,000 for ovarian cancer really equitable, especially since she is now dying from her third bout with cancer? She shakes her head silently as she realizes that the $2.5 billion that has been distributed by the Nuclear Claims Tribunal isn't enough; there can never be adequate compensation for the anxiety, depression, and countless other cancer side-effects that other islanders like her have had to endure. She also questions whether the money is worth the resentment from those Marshallese that are not entitled to restitution, and whether her people have been trapped by a mentality of victimization. Will the people of the Marshall Islands look past their historic illnesses to face the current diabetes, alcohol, and sexually transmitted infection epidemics that touch the lives of the younger generations?

Even her small house, located on Kili island where many residents of Bikini island were relocated, is a vibrant memento of her history. While a few have since returned to the land they once inhabited to reclaim their land-ownership rights that are the primary asset and source of social power for the Marshallese, most are reluctant to go back, fearing further poisoning from the nuclear fallout. She is lucky that her eldest daughter, on the way to and from her job as maker of fine handbags and hats, is willing to ride her bike over to help; her daughter always brings water to help conquer her constant thirst, and often shares a meal of pig or chicken. On Sundays, they use her wheelchair to attend the Protestant church and then return home to enjoy each other's company, conversing in English about anything that comes to mind. Sometimes they look at the framed picture of Amata Kabua, the first president of the Marshall Islands, and they are secretly thankful for the assistance the U.S. government continues to provide. Other times, however, they cast their eyes on the 1997 special edition of the Health Physics Journal, *Consequences of Nuclear Testing*, the first complete compilation of medical and environmental research about the consequences of the testing . . . how could any compensation be enough?

The family tie is very strong; her eldest daughter will inherit all she has because the matrilineal line, historically the method for distribution of status and land-use rights, is still intact. She wonders whether her younger daughter will return from Hawaii, where she moved for a better education and employment. Since all citizens of the Marshall Islands are provided the right to work in the United States as non-immigrant residents, the youngest left. She missed the *kemem*, or first birthday celebration of her granddaughter, and she knows that her granddaughter will never know the native Marshallese tongue, hear the ancient chants (*roro*) sung by the fishing parties that sailed in the *proa*, or listen to the folktales told by the storytellers (*Ri-bwebwenato*). But by being born in Honolulu, her granddaughter will not have to worry about the cancer that has consumed the lives of many Marshallese.

Late in the evening when she snacks on *copra*, the succulent meat of the coconut that is the only cash crop of the Marshall Islands, she ponders whether the new tourism economy is something that can sustain her small country. While visitors to the islands pay money to be taken to shipwrecks from World War II or to see the amazing coral reefs that surround the islands, she is thankful to no longer be of working age. Unemployment is a serious problem for the younger generation of Marshallese, and there is little foreign investment to stimulate economic growth. Coupled with low revenue from income tax, these problems result in a social service climate where she can only see a dentist if a tooth extraction is required.

When the day closes with the same red hue with which it began, she wonders why she has been cursed to live past the 71 years that Marshallese women are expected to live. Removing her shirt, she reveals her wrinkled skin that distorts the shape of the traditional tattoo that adorns her back. Her elongated ears remain also, relics of days past. While she knows some may see long life as a benefit, she closes her eyes lost on the verge of transition; from awake to asleep, from survivor to victim, from traditional to contemporary . . . the sunrise of tomorrow and countless hours to continue wondering loom ahead.

of the national security state, the provision of protection necessitates critical trade-offs: civil liberties are eroded; racial and ethnic profiling are legitimated; surveillance is heightened; detention absent due process of law is routinized; foreign nationals passing through American airports are "rendered" to Egypt, Poland, Romania, or Syria for torture and confinement; and the citizenry is reduced to a subordinate position of dependence and obedience. Rather than enacting their democratic rights through protests against such constitutional violations, citizens of the national security state are expected to be grateful for the protection provided.

WOMEN AND PEACE-MAKING

Emphasizing men's disproportionate role in war making, some feminists suggested that men are inherently drawn toward violence—necrophilia—while women as life-givers are drawn toward peace (Daly, 1978). Other feminists suggested that women's affinity to peacemaking grew from their roles as mothers and nurturers (Ruddick, 1989). As those who gave birth to children and struggled to feed and clothe them, mothers were not only more reluctant to sacrifice their children in war but were uniquely concerned to protect the earth from the devastations of war. Although some feminist peace activists and ecofeminists found this logic compelling, others pointed out that rigid constructions of men as war makers/women as peacemakers fell into a form of gender essentialism at odds with the complexity of lived experience. Such a simplistic binary masks pacifism among men and belligerence among women, replicating damaging cultural stereotypes, and failing to consider the intricate social and political factors that influence individual decisions to support or oppose war. Moreover, such a stark opposition between men and women is not needed to account for women's peace activism, which has a long and distinguished history. In the reading "Building Cultures of Peace," Riane Eisler discusses the four cornerstones for peace and the necessity for a shift from domination to partnership worldwide.

A History of Women Peace-Makers

In understanding war as a dehumanizing process that rests upon and reinscribes male power, some feminists have focused their energies on peace-making. In February 1915, in the midst of the First World War, International Women's Suffrage Association activists from the Netherlands, Belgium, Britain, and Germany met in Amsterdam to organize an International Congress of Women to be held in The Hague at the end of April. Issuing a "Call to the Women of All Nations," these feminist activists invited women's organizations in all parts of the world to send delegates to the Congress to consider two major resolutions. The first stipulated that international disputes should be settled by peaceful means; the second called for the enfranchisement of all women. Against the explicit opposition of their governments, feminist activists from neutral and belligerent nations, including Austria, Belgium, Britain, Canada, Denmark, Germany, Hungary, Italy, the Netherlands, Norway, Sweden, and the United States traveled across war-torn Europe to participate in The Hague Conference (Rupp, 1996, pp. 27–28). Denied voting rights in their home nations and excluded from institutions of national governance, 1500 women's rights activists nonetheless tried to insert themselves into the male-controlled world of war and international relations. While their governments pursued a deadly war in which 20 percent of the casualties were female (Turpin, 1998), women peace activists devised a plan to end the war, producing a plan with many similarities to the Fourteen Points developed by U.S. president Woodrow Wilson two years later. In particular, they urged the end of war-making and the creation of an international organization, "a conference of neutral nations," which would remain in permanent session to mediate conflicts and resolve disputes peacefully. Advancing a profound critique of militarism and imperialism, these feminist peace activists opposed conscription and urged the creation of mechanisms to provide practical assistance for victims of war, including the provision of war relief work for refugees and internees. Although these transnational feminist peace activists did not achieve all their objectives, they did succeed in injecting feminist issues into the international arena; they challenged the male monopoly of the international sphere; they established the precedent that sex discrimination should not be tolerated in international institutions; and they demonstrated complex linkages between gender inequality within nations and gendered hierarchies in the international order.

Renaming themselves the Women's International League for Peace and Freedom (WILPF), these early feminist peace activists created headquarters in Geneva, Switzerland, and continued to work for world disarmament, full rights for women, racial and economic justice, and an end to all forms of violence. For their path-breaking efforts in peacemaking, two WILPF presidents, Jane Addams and Emily Greene Balch, won Nobel Peace Prizes in 1931 and 1946, respectively. Where WILPF chose to lobby governments and UN agencies to press the cause of peace, more recent women peace activists have chosen symbolic politics and direct action.

Women Peace Activists in the Contemporary Era

Over the course of the twentieth- and early twenty-first centuries, women have continued to work as peace activists, founding new organizations and developing innovative tactics to protest organized violence. For example, the Mothers of the Plaza de Mayo became human rights activists in Argentina to fight for knowledge of their abducted children and family members. They wore white head scarves with their children's names embroidered and

ACTIVIST PROFILE   **Women in Black**

In 1987, Palestinians began a series of uprisings (the intifada), ranging from protests and strikes to violent clashes, against Israel's occupation of the West Bank and Gaza. Israel responded with force, and tensions escalated. One month after the first uprising, a small group of Israeli women initiated a protest of the conflict. Once a week, at the same time, at a busy traffic intersection, they met, dressed in black, and raised a hand-shaped black sign with white lettering that read "Stop the Occupation." As word spread, other women began their own vigils, which eventually numbered around 40 throughout Israel. Soon women in other countries began to organize vigils in support of the women in Israel. A group of women from Italy who had formed a "Women Visiting Difficult Places" project went to Israel and Palestine in 1988 to give support to the women there. They returned home and founded their own Women in Black, *Donne in Nero*. As wars have broken out elsewhere in the world, women have responded by creating new Women in Black groups. For example, *Zene U Crnom* was founded in Belgrade in 1991 in response to the war between the former Yugoslav republics, and *Femmes en Noir* in Brussels and *Vrouwen in het Zwart* in Leuven formed in support of *Zene U Crnom*. In 1995, Women in Black of India collaborated with the Asian Women's Human Rights Council to stage a massive protest in Beijing during the UN World Conference on Women, calling for a world "safer for women" and an end to wars and armed conflict. Following the attacks of September 11, 2001, Women in Black issued a statement urging the US to forgo vengeance and reject war as an option for response. Instead, they encouraged US leaders to develop strategies for justice and equality. In 2001, Women in Black were awarded the Millennium Peace Prize for Women by the United Nations Development Fund for Women (UNIFEM).

If you'd like to start your own vigil, Women in Black suggest the following:

To start a Women in Black vigil, all you need is a commitment to a cause that falls into the category of "against war and for justice." That's the main thing. Below is a description of how many vigils work, but you can establish any formats or rules you like. Remember: every vigil is autonomous. You don't have to ask permission about anything from anybody, other than your own group.

Here are some general guidelines.

(1) What's a vigil?

A vigil, as Women in Black use the term, generally means a nonviolent demonstration of one or more people in which we hold signs in a public location to express our political views. It's not a march, but Women in Black around the world have sometimes also held marches.

A vigil can be one woman (yes!) or a small group or even a large group.

A vigil is good to do at a busy intersection or a public location (e.g., in front of a government building or embassy), if that has any symbolic importance. It's good to always meet in the same location, just so women know where they can find you, even if they don't come regularly.

(2) Most vigils are composed of women.

However, men have joined in a great many vigils throughout the world.

(3) Most vigils meet on a regular basis.

Some meet once a week, others once a month, others just "upon occasion." Some last for one hour at a time, others for longer.

(4) At vigils, we hold signs that declare our political beliefs.

The variety of slogans is amazing. Some address international issues, such as the war against Iraq, while others address local issues, such as the rise of neo-Nazism in some countries.

Israeli Women in Black vigils hold signs that say "End the Occupation." Internationally, many signs read "End the Israeli Occupation."

In some countries, signs read, "End War" or "End All Oppression" or "Stop the Cycle of Violence" or simply "Peace."

(5) Are vigils silent?

Some vigils are silent—women stand with their signs. Others are not, and allow participants to talk to each other (or to bystanders). Some designate one woman to be the spokesperson to onlookers or the media.

Most vigils do not have chanting of slogans, but some do.

Most times, participants just begin holding a vigil, and discover over time what is right for them.

At some vigils, Women in Black pass out flyers to passersby; some don't. Those who pass out flyers often speak to those they meet.

In short:
There's a great deal of flexibility, and every vigil gets to decide for itself.

Source: www.womeninblack.org/start.html

protested every Thursday afternoon at the Plaza de Mayo in central Buenos Aries, Argentina, until 2006. The protests began in 1977 in response to the violence by government forces during what has come to be known as the "Dirty War" (1976–1983). After the fall of the military regime, a civilian government commission put the number of disappeared at close to 11,000. The reading "Plaza de Mayo," a poem by Dacia Maraini, is written from the perspective of one of the Mothers of the Plaza.

Women in Black (WIB) is a women's group for peace activism that draws upon the rich symbolism of the color black—a color of mourning in certain cultures, tragedy in others, a color of married women's attire in some cultures, the hijab, chador, or veil in others—to mobilize women in silent protest against war, militarism, and other forms of violence and injustice. Insistent that they are not an organization, but a means of mobilization and a formula for action, WIB grew out of a sustained silent protest organized by Israeli and Palestinian women in 1988 in an effort to stop the Israeli occupation of the West Bank and Gaza. Committed to non-violence, some Israeli and Palestinian women chose to stand together at the same hour each week at a major intersection bearing signs to "stop the occupation." Standing together against the official policies of their governments, these activists sought to demonstrate the possibility of peaceful coexistence and cooperation. Holding a weekly silent vigil, they sought to enter the consciousness of their compatriots as a powerful reminder that "bridges can be built across differences and borders," but not through war. By advocating new forms of "solidarity within our own differences," WIB conceptualized non-violent silent protest as a political act of resistance and feminist solidarity (Einhorn and Sever, 2003).

As discussed in chapter 1, WIB has evolved into a worldwide feminist network committed to peace with justice and actively opposed to injustice, war, militarism and other forms of violence, operating in hundreds of cities in 25 nations. In addition to the silent vigils conducted by WIB groups in specific locations, WIB is a virtual community, sharing information and action alerts through the Internet. The action alerts mobilize groups across the globe in support of particular actions. For example, when WIB in Israel/Palestine called for vigils in June 2001 against the occupation of Palestinian lands, 150 WIB groups across the world responded by organizing vigils. More than 10,000 women in Australia, Austria, Azerbaijan, Belgium, Canada, Denmark, France, Germany, India, Israel, Italy, Japan, Maldive Islands, Mexico, Netherlands, Northern Ireland, Spain, Sweden, Switzerland, Turkey, the United Kingdom, and the United States participated in silent protests. In the aftermath of the bombings of the World Trade Towers and the Pentagon on September 11, 2001, WIB launched a virtual drafting session over email to generate a statement, issued on behalf of its international network, appealing for "justice not vengeance." In 2003, tens of thousands of WIB joined millions of anti-war demonstrators across the world in a series of protests against the U.S. invasion of Iraq. Mobilizations against the U.S. "war on terror" continue.

The Iraq War mobilized a new generation of transnational peace activism that drew upon the Internet to organize mass protests at multiple sites. Code Pink: Women for Peace is an anti-war group that devised innovative tactics to capture media attention for their war protests. They choose the name "Code Pink" in response to a color-coded alert system created by the U.S. Department of Homeland Security that used "Code Orange" and "Code Red" to signify the highest levels of danger. Dressed in flamboyant pink, a color often associated with hyperfemininity, Code Pink activists organized a four-month vigil outside the White House to protest the proposed U.S. invasion of Iraq. From October 2,

2002 to March 8, 2003, they became a visible symbol of conscientious objection to war. They concluded this direct action campaign on International Women's Day with a massive march on Washington, D.C., that attracted 10,000 participants. As a grassroots peace and social justice movement that seeks to end the war in Iraq, stop new wars, and redirect resources into healthcare, education, and other life-affirming activities, Code Pink has organized trips to Iraq to document the devastation of war and they have organized speaking tours of Iraqi women who provide detailed testimony of the human costs of the war. Since their first public demonstration, Code Pink has launched 250 chapters worldwide, which mobilize men and women against war. They have also conducted fundraising campaigns to aid the victims of U.S. military action. In cooperation with other groups, they donated over $600,000 in humanitarian aid to refugees of Fallujah, Iraq, in 2004.

Expanding the Framework of Peace Activism

Understanding war as a mechanism of gendered power that perpetuates women's subordination within domestic, national, and international arenas, transnational feminist activists have identified various strategies to limit war and its disparate gendered effects. Mobilizing at the 1995 World Summit for Social Development in Copenhagen, for example, the Women's Caucus to the Copenhagen Declaration and Program of Action proposed a cap of 1 percent gross domestic product (GDP) on military spending of nation-states. Until that cap becomes effective, they urged annual reductions in military spending equivalent to 5 percent of GDP and they recommended that the funds reclaimed from military uses be dedicated to programs designed to meet pressing social needs (Petchesky, 2003, pp. 55–56). Others worked through the United Nations to secure passage of UN Security Council Resolution 1325 (discussed in chapter 1) which requires that women and women's concerns play an integral role in every new security institution and at every decision-making stage in peacekeeping and national reconstruction in the aftermath of armed conflict. Women in conflict and post-conflict situations across the world, including Afghanistan and Iraq, are currently appealing to Resolution 1325 in their efforts to ensure women's participation in public life as fully autonomous and effective citizens. By empowering women, they hope to undercut the gender hierarchies produced and sustained through war.

Some transnational feminist activists have also tried to address the evils of war by creating international mechanisms of accountability. They have sought to create mechanisms to hold individuals, partisan groups, and governments to account for egregious crimes against women in conflict and post-conflict situations. Feminist mobilization around the creation of the International Criminal Court (ICC), for example, succeeded in expanding the conceptualization of sexual violence in war to include rape, sexual slavery, enforced prostitution, forced pregnancy, and enforced sterilization, including the complex forms of gendered violence as war crimes and crimes against humanity for which individuals, regardless of their official position or status, can be held accountable. To help ensure that the ICC would take sexual violence seriously, feminist activists lobbied for equitable gender representation on the Court and the inclusion of judges with expertise in areas of violence against women and violence against children. Seven of the eighteen judges elected to the ICC in February 2003 are women. By comparison, only one woman has ever served on the 15-member International Court of Justice (Spees, 2003).

To break away from narrow understandings of war associated with dominant institutions, another group of feminist activists launched a new global project in 2003, the "1000 Women

Taking Strategic Action: What Can Women Peacebuilders Do?

1. Use existing networks of women's groups to raise awareness about conflict prevention issues; consult with them regularly to learn about conflict trends at the community level, their impact on women and potential roles in mitigating violence.

2. Identify and invite NGOs to a workshop on conflict analysis and mapping of actors.
   - Identify a range of indicators including gender-based indicators that highlight trends in society.
   - Develop a common strategy to address root causes of conflict.

3. Seek to work with other groups with a potential for involvement in conflict prevention, including religious institutions and the business community and mobilize their resources and expertise to promote non-violence.
   - Organize dialogues within communities, or among different sectors of the population (e.g., youth) on issues of concern and possible solutions.
   - Identify traditional conflict resolution mechanisms and explore ways of using them to de-escalate tensions.
   - Commission surveys in conflict-affected communities to identify demands for nonviolence.

4. Identify and consult with key international actors, to gain awareness of their concerns and strategies for conflict prevention.
   - Advocate for wider interaction and support of women's groups and use of gender-based indicators.
   - Using international networks and interaction with the UN and national diplomats, call for a UN fact-finding mission—and lobby for the presence of gender experts.
   - Publicize Security Council Resolutions 1325 and 1366, which advocate for the inclusion of civil society in conflict prevention efforts.

5. Reach out to educators to promote conflict resolution training and peace education in schools and colleges.

6. Develop ties with local media and international services (e.g., the BBC's World Service) to publicize stories of non-violent conflict resolution in society.

7. Work with local journalists to promote objectivity and moderation in reporting.

8. Reach out to key stakeholders most susceptible to resorting to violence and encourage civic engagement and non-violence.

9. Identify key actors that can be a moderating force, including trade union leaders, media personalities and journalists, and religious leaders, and mobilize their support against violence.

10. Reach out to the government and military to withhold the use of force and encourage nonviolence.

Source: Inclusive Security, Sustainable Peace: A Toolkit for Advocacy and Action, http://www.huntalternatives.org/pages/87_inclusive_security_toolkit.cfm

for the Nobel Peace Prize 2005," also known as the "PeaceWomen Across the Globe" Project. This project seeks to illuminate women's invisible labor to sustain communities against the systemic violence that accrues not only from warfare but from physical violence (ranging from domestic violence to bombings), structural violence (including damage done to the environment, sustainable livelihoods, health and safety by predatory economic policies), and cultural violence (discrimination, prejudice, systems of advantage and disadvantage).

Although organizers of the PeaceWomen Project did indeed nominate 1,000 women from 150 nations for a shared Nobel Prize in 2005, their larger goal is to demonstrate that the causes of war extend well beyond governments' calculations of national interest and that strategies for peace require far more than the cessation of war (Association of 1000 Women for the Nobel Prize, 2005). By examining women's peacemaking in everyday life, the PeaceWomen Project explores modes of social and cultural transformation that resist the pervasive individualism and competition of capitalist globalization and maps the contours of mutuality and reciprocity critical for alternative modes of sustainable development. Within this larger frame, cooperative endeavors, collective work, social redistribution, subversion of unequal power relations, preservation of indigenous rights, cultural diversity, and alternative ethical practices that foster sustainable environments are crucial dimensions of peacemaking.

CONCLUSION

Feminist scholarship expands the framework of analysis to make race, ethnicity, class, gender, and sexuality central categories of analysis. Refusing to grant that war is the unique preserve of official institutions of the nation-state or international organizations, feminists challenge many received views about war and peace. Investigating armed conflict as a product of culture and society that changes over time, feminist scholarship demonstrates how war disrupts old racial and gender orders, but peacemaking may reestablish regimes that replicate inequitable hierarchies. By mapping the complex operations of gender and racial power in warmaking and peacemaking, feminist scholarship shows why feminist activism that engages all aspects of physical, structural, and cultural violence remains a pressing priority.

REFERENCES

Abdi, C. M. (2007). Reimagining Somali women: Collusion of civil war and the Religious Right. *Signs: Journal of Women in Culture and Society, 33*(1), 183–207.

Association of 1000 Women for the Nobel Prize. (2005). *1000 peacewomen across the globe.* Zurick: Scalo.

Daly, M. (1978). *GYN/Ecology.* Boston: Beacon.

Denov, M. and Gervais, C. (2007). Negotiating (in)security: Agency, resistance, and resourcefulness among girls formerly associated with Sierra Leone's Revolutionary United Front. *Signs: Journal of Women in Culture and Society, 32*(4), 885–910.

De Pauw, L. G. (1998). *Battlecries and lullabies: Women in war from prehistory to the present.* Norman: University of Oklahoma Press.

Einhorn, B. and Sever, C. (2003). Gender and civil society in East Central Europe. *International Feminist Journal of Politics, 5*(2), 163–190.

Enloe, C. (1988). *Does khaki become you? The militarization of women's lives.* London: Pandora Press/HarperCollins.

———. (1990). *Bananas, beaches, and bases: Making feminist sense of international politics.* Berkeley: University of California Press.

———. (1993). *The morning after: Sexual politics at the end of the Cold War.* Berkeley: University of California Press.

———. (2000). *Maneuvers: The international politics of militarizing women's lives.* Berkeley: University of California Press.

———. (2007). *Globalization and militarism: Feminists make the link.* Lanham, MD: Rowman and Littlefield.

Evans, S. (1997). *Born for liberty: A history of women in America.* New York: Free Press.

Fanon, F. (1967). *A dying colonialism.* Trans. H. Chevalier. New York: Grove.

Goldstein, J. (2001). *War and gender.* Cambridge: Cambridge University Press.

Hobbes, T. ([1651] 1971). *Leviathan.* Harmondsworth: Penquin Books.

Lehring, G. (2003). *Officially gay.* Philadelphia: Temple University Press.

Lorentzen, L. A. and Turpin, J. (Eds.) (1998). *The women and war reader.* New York: New York University Press.

Lyons, T. (2004). *Guns and guerilla girls: Women in the Zimbabwean liberation struggle.* Trenton, NJ: Africa World Press.

Offen, K. (2000). *European feminisms, 1700–1950.* Stanford: Stanford University Press.

Osterud, O. (2004). War. In M. Hawkesworth and M. Kogan (Eds.), *Encyclopedia of government and politics* (pp. 1028–1038). London: Routledge.

Pateman, C. (1998). The patriarchal welfare state. In J. Landes (Ed.), *Feminism, the public and the private* (pp. 241–274). New York: Oxford University Press.

Petchesky, R. (2003). *Global prescriptions: Gendering health and human rights.* London and New York: Zed Books.

Phelan, S. (2001). *Sexual strangers: Gays, lesbians, and dilemmas of citizenship.* Philadelphia: Temple University Press.

Ruddick, S. (1989). *Maternal thinking: Toward a politics of peace.* Boston: Beacon Press.

Rupp, L. (1996). Challenging imperialism in international women's organizations, 1888–1945. *NWSA Journal, 8*(1), 8–27.

Samuelson, M. (2007). The disfigured body of the female guerilla: (De)militarization, sexual violence, and redomestication in Zoe Wiccomb's *David's story. Signs: Journal of Women in Culture and Society, 32*(4), 833–856.

Sasson-Levy, O. and Amram-Katz, S. (2007). Gender integration in Israeli officer training: Degendering and regendering the military. *Signs: Journal of Women in Culture and Society, 33*(1), 105–134.

Spees, P. (2003). Women's advocacy in the creation of the international criminal court: Changing the landscapes of justice and power. *Signs: Journal of Women in Culture and Society, 28*(4), 1233–1254.

Tuqan, F. (2002). Gone are those we love. In M. Arnold, B. Ballif-Spanvill, and K. Tracy (Eds.), *A chorus of peace* (pp. 36–7). Iowa City: University of Iowa Press.

Turpin, J. (1998). Many faces: Women confronting war. In L. Lorentzen and J. Turpin (Eds.), *The women and war reader* (pp. 3–18). New York: New York University Press.

White, A. (2007). All the men are fighting for freedom, all the women are mourning their men, but some of us carried guns: A raced-gendered analysis of Fanon's psychological perspectives on war. *Signs: Journal of Women in Culture and Society, 32*(4), 857–884.

Young, I. M. (2003). The logic of masculinist protection: Reflections on the current security state. *Signs: Journal of Women in Culture and Society, 29*(1), 1–25.

Yuval-Davis, N. (1997). *Gender and nation.* London: Sage.

SUGGESTIONS FOR FURTHER READING

Homstedt, K. (2008). *Band of sisters: American women at war in Iraq.* Mechanicsburg, PA: Stackpole.

Hunt, S. (2004). *This was not our war: Bosnian women reclaiming the peace.* Durham, NC: Duke University Press.

Oliver, K. (2007). *Weapons of war: Iraq, sex, and the media.* New York: Columbia University Press.

Umutesi, M. B. (2004). *Surviving the slaughter: The ordeal of a Rwandan refugee in Zaire.* Madison: University of Wisconsin Press.

Weatherford, D. (2008). *American women and World War II.* Secaucas, NJ: Castle Books.

Zangana, H. (2009). *City of widows: An Iraqi woman's account of war and resistance.* New York: Seven Stories Press.

The City in the Desert

Mary Borden (1929)

What is this city that sprawls in the shallow valley between the chalk hills? Why are its buildings all alike, gaunt wooden sheds with iron roofs? Why are there no trees, no gardens, no pleasant places? The sheds are placed on top of the muddy ground like boxes, row after row of them, with iron rails down the center where the main street of the town should be. But there are no streets. There are only tracks in the mud and wooden walks laid across the mud from one shed to the other, and a railway line.

I see no children playing anywhere. The wind brings no sound of laughter from the place, or splendid shouting, no sound of any kind. Silent men in couples are carrying heavy bundles between them from one shed to the other, heads down to the wind. The small white figure of a solitary woman is crossing a wide open space. She is slipping in the mud. Her white dress is fluttering. The place is immense and empty, new and still and desolate. But the naked wet hills are throbbing. There's a noise of distant booming as if the sea were breaking against their sides.

You tell me there is no sea over there. But the roar? Surely there are waves breaking, and this desert is wet as if a great wave had just receded, leaving the muddy bottom of the earth uncovered. A bare sea bottom, strewn with bits of iron, coils of wire, stones. No sign of life, no fish fossils, or rotting seaweed, no plant of any kind, not a blade of green; a dead sea must have lain here.

Whoever built this city on this slippery waste, built it quick, at ebb tide, between tides, to serve some queer purpose between low and high tide. They put up these sheds in a hurry, covered them with sheets of corrugated iron, pinned them to the mud somehow, anyhow, knowing that a roaring surge would rise again, come rolling back over the hills to carry them away again. Then all these new buildings, all this timber and these sheets of iron will be broken up, and will rush down in a torrent.

Down where? How do I know. I'm lost. I've lost my way. The road was slippery. There were no landmarks. The village I used to know at the cross-roads was gone. Everything was sliding in the mud and all the villages that I knew here once on a time had slipped clean out of sight, and now all the men and horses in the world with wagons and motor lorries seem to be pouring after them into a gulf. The earth is a greased slide, tilted up and shaking. And the men who built this place knew evidently that there was danger of the face of the earth itself slipping—for look over there on that hill-side and that one— they've tied the earth down with wire. You see those intersecting bands of wire, looking like a field of tangled iron weeds and iron thistles? That is evidently to keep the mud from slipping away.

Queer, isn't it? This new city where there once was a snug town huddled round a church with cafés, little tables under the trees, schoolboys in black pinafores playing on the church steps. The inn, I remember, was famous for its cuisine. What has become of the fat landlord who watched the plump succulent fowls turning on a spit and dripping? Now, there's this place that looks like a mining town or a lumber camp, only it can't be. There's not a tree to be seen, north, south, east, or west, nothing but mud glistening. It's very queer, I say. That flimsy gate there with a banner across it as if for a celebration, with H.O.E. 32 on it in big black letters, and a flag flying, and those red crosses painted on the iron roofs of the buildings. H.O.E. 32 must be the name of the place; but why such a name? What does it mean?

Perhaps there has been a new flood, since Noah, and you and I slept through it. Perhaps a new race of men has been hatched out of the mud, hatched like newts, slugs, larvae of water beetles. But slugs who know horribly, acutely, that they have only a moment to live in between flood tides and so built this place quickly, a silly shelter against the wrath of God, and gave it a magic hieroglyphic name, and put the name on a banner and hoisted a flag, and then put those red crosses up there, tipped skywards. Everything showy in the place points skywards, is designed to catch an eye in the sky, a great angry eye.

Otherwise it seems a secret place, vast, spread out, bare but secret; and some strange industry, some dreadful trade is evidently being carried on here in the wet desert, where a flood has passed and another flood will come.

The workers have a curious apprehensive look with their big secretive bundles. They may be smugglers. Certainly some shameful merchandise is being smuggled in here from the shore that you say is not the shore of the sea. If the booming noise beyond the hills were the roar of waves breaking, one would say that these old men were gangs of beach-combers, bringing up bundles of wreckage; that they go out across the mud under cover of the night to hunt in the backwash. You can see from the way they move that the stuff is valuable and breakable. They come out of the sheds cautiously and go carefully along the narrow board walks, two by two, with the heavy brown bundles swinging between them. They are as careful as they can be. They seem to be old men. They stagger under the weight that swings from their arms and their old shoulders cower as if under the lash of an invisible whip; but they go up and down the long rows of sheds, patiently, carefully, gently, taking small careful steps.

You say that these bundles are the citizens of the town? What do you mean? Those heavy brown packages that are carried back and forth, up and down, from shed to shed, those inert lumps cannot be men. They are delivered to this place in closed vans and are unloaded like sacks and are laid out in rows on the ground and are sorted out by the labels pinned to their covers. They lie perfectly still while they are carried back and forth, up and down, shoved into sheds and pulled out again. What do you mean by telling me that they are men?

Why, if they are men, don't they walk? Why don't they talk? Why don't they protest? They lie perfectly still. They make no sound, They are covered up. You do not expect me to believe that inside that roll there is a man, and in that one, and in that one?

Ah, dear God, it's true! Look! Look through the window. The old men are undoing the bundles inside this shed. Look, there's a face and there's an arm hanging down crooked, and there I see a pair of boots sticking out at one end of a bundle.

But how queer they are! How strangely they lie there. They are not the usual shape. They only remind one of men. Some, to be sure, are wearing coats, and some have on iron hats, but all of them seem to be broken and tied together with white rags. And how dirty they are! The mud is crusted on them. Their boots are lumps of mud. Their faces are grey and wet as if modelled of pale mud. But what are those red, rusty stains on their dirty white rags? They have gone rusty lying out there in the mud, in the backwash. Ah, what a pity. Here is one without an arm, and another and another, and there, dear God, is one without a face! Oh! Oh! What are the old men doing to them? They are pulling off their clothes, uncovering the dreadful holes in their sides. Come away, come away from the window. I know now. There is no need to sneak up and stare at them.

They are lost men, wrecked men, survivors from that other world that was here before the flood passed this way, washed up against the shore of this world again by the great backwash. They thought that they had done with it, thought it was over and done with, thought they had left it for ever. But they've been brought here, brought back again to this city of refuge called H.O.E. 32, that sprawls under the angry Eye of God. Bundled into vans they were, all mangled and broken, carried back over the sliding mud through that flimsy gate where the flag is flapping, to be saved. To be hauled about and man-handled, to have their broken, bleeding nakedness uncovered, to have their bodies cut again with knives and their deep wounds probed with pincers, and to have the breath choked back in their sobbing lungs again, so that they may be saved for this world.

How strange it must look to them when they open their eyes! There are no trees anywhere. There is no shelter, except under the iron roofs. The place is new and still and desolate. But the wind is howling over the wet desert, and the old men who go carefully up and down with their heavy oblong bundles, stop and listen to the booming sound beyond the hills as if they heard the flood rising.

Children of War

Wray Herbert (2004)

The former child soldiers of Mozambique's civil war offer insights into morality and human resiliency Alfredo Betuel Macamo and Joaquim Fernando Quive live only a couple of hundred yards from each other, and they share a lot of history and culture. These two 23-year-old men grew up in the same primitive village near Malehice in the rural Mozambican province of Gaza (southeast Africa), and both still live there today. It's a poor place, and neither Macamo nor Quive is doing that great financially. Macamo is struggling to raise three kids—6, 3, and a 4-month-old—by harvesting reeds on a riverbank. Quive does odd jobs when he can find them, though these days he doesn't work much at all. They both live in small reed huts with dirt floors and no running water.

Despite all they have in common, Macamo and Quive are worlds apart psychologically and socially. When I visited Macamo recently, I was greeted not only by him but by 12 members of his extended family, all decked out in traditional African garb. We sat around in plastic chairs, the kind you buy at Kmart, or on mats under the mafureira tree that is the center of their yard, and talked about Macamo's life, past and present. It was celebratory.

Quive's home is a lonelier place. It has two huts, but the larger of the two—his father's—sits empty. His father has been expelled from the village for stealing a radio. Quive occupies the smaller hut in a grim, empty yard. He doesn't have any chairs, but he borrows a couple of the Kmart chairs from a neighbor and lays out a reed mat for a visitor. Quive has also dressed up, in a silky white shirt. But there's no family here, just Quive.

I'm talking to Macamo and Quive, and other young men in a few villages nearby, because of something they all have in common. During the 16-year civil war that devastated this sprawling coastal nation in southeastern Africa, Macamo, Quive, and their neighbors were all child soldiers, abducted from their villages as kids and taken to distant camps run by the rebel forces trying to topple the government at the time. All, eventually, escaped and through circuitous routes ended up in the Lhanguene orphanage in Maputo, the capital city to the south. All the boys were eventually reunited with their families in their natal villages, and that's where most live today. And there the commonalities end.

U.S. News first reported on these child soldiers in 1989, when the war was still raging. The purpose of my trip to this beautiful but primitive region of Africa was to revisit the child soldiers 15 years later, to see how they are doing now that the civil war is over and they have resumed something like a normal life. Most, like Macamo and Quive, are men now. Some, like Macamo, are raising kids of their own. All suffer to some degree from their abductions and their experience of war as children. Some are doing better than others.

Soldiers and spies. Mozambique has not known much other than war since the mid-1960s; until the 1990s, many Mozambicans grew up not knowing what peace looked like. First, there was the 10-year revolutionary war to oust the Portuguese, who had colonized the country in the 1500s and ruled it for more than four centuries. The Portuguese were finally challenged by the Mozambique Liberation Front, or Frelimo, the Marxist insurgency that ousted the colonizers in 1975. But as soon as Frelimo prevailed and the Portuguese fled, the new Frelimo government faced an insurgency of its own, financed mostly by what was then the neighboring nation of Rhodesia and later by South Africa. The guerrillas, known as the Mozambique National Resistance, or Renamo, were based mostly in the rural north. They had no particular ideology, other than their desire to oust Frelimo.

That's where the child soldiers came in. The Renamo leaders began recruiting from rural villages, and if they couldn't recruit able-bodied young boys, they simply kidnapped them. Most of the recruits were 12, 13, 14 years old, but some were as young as 6. The youngest boys often served as porters and servants to Renamo officers, or as spies, but most were systematically trained to be soldiers. They were exposed to the noise of rifle blasts, to desensitize them. They were ordered to kill cattle; then, when they got used to that, to kill other humans, often those who ignored orders or tried to escape. The perimeters of the rebels' camps were often littered with the skulls of those who had tried to escape but failed.

It is remarkable, given all of the terrorist indoctrination, that Renamo converted so few of the kids it captured. Perhaps because Renamo stood for nothing, perhaps because its soldiers were so brutal, it appears that most of the child soldiers in its ragtag ranks never stopped thinking of themselves as captives or victims. Some certainly "went Renamo" out of self-preservation, and some even liked their newfound power as warriors, but most kept their minds focused on finding a chance to escape.

Inevitably, given Renamo's obvious lack of soldierly deportment and order, the opportunities eventually presented themselves. Rafael Vicente Saveca's chance came when his camp was switching locations. Rafael was sent by Renamo officers to fetch water. He seized the chance to flee, hiding in huts in friendly villages before finally returning to his village, near Chibuto. To avoid recapture, or worse, Rafael disappeared, wandering for months, until Frelimo soldiers finally detained him in a prisoner-of-war camp.

A lot of Mozambican boys like Rafael had similar experiences. The Renamo camps were heavily policed, but the boys managed to escape during battles or while on missions to gather wood or hunt for food. Then, often, they would vanish into the bush, moving from village to village at night, resting and hiding during the day. The stretch of bush between Maputo and Gaza is pretty desolate even today. Back in the late 1980s it was salted with land mines, almost constantly policed by government and guerrilla troops.

Like Rafael, many of Renamo's child soldiers ended up in Frelimo jails before they were transferred to the Lhanguene orphanage in Maputo. Orphanage, actually, is something of a misnomer. The kids at Lhanguene came from such tightly knit, extended families that their language hardly distinguished between father and uncle, sibling or cousin. With such large families, and such tight bonds among members, the true orphan at Lhanguene was rare. But calling Lhanguene an orphanage had public-relations value for the Frelimo government, because it was a visible reminder of Renamo's brutality toward Mozambique's children. Whatever its significance to the larger world, Lhanguene was a safe haven for the kids lucky enough to find their way there—and the first step on their uncertain journey of healing.

Power of soccer. There were thousands of boys abducted by Renamo and forced to train as soldiers. Some were with the rebel forces just months, others for as long as three years. The person who has treated and studied these kids most intensely is psychologist Neil Boothby. Now a professor of public health at Columbia University, Boothby at the time worked for Save the Children, the international aid organization that works to assist kids around the globe whose lives have been disrupted by war, including the deslocados who ended up at the Lhanguene orphanage.

The interventions at Lhanguene were deceptively simple. Indeed, when I asked the men about their time at Lhanguene, without exception the first thing they mentioned was playing soccer. At first I just noted this and dismissed it as a childish memory, but when it came up again and again I began to realize that soccer wasn't trivial to these child soldiers' psychological recovery. What they wanted more than anything—and Boothby's later research with many other child soldiers documented this—was to once again be "like everyone else." Playing soccer did a lot of things—it re-established rules and sense of fair play—but perhaps most important, it made them feel "normal" in their own minds. In psychological jargon, they were moving from a survival mentality, which they had adopted of necessity, to a security mentality normal for their age. In other words, they were learning to become kids again.

Other interventions more directly involved resolving the wartime traumas of these children. They were encouraged, for example, to draw pictures, and when they did their drawings included typical childhood things like houses and family—but they also included, often tucked off in a corner, an automatic weapon, a slain body. Such drawings provided an opening for discussion about the horrific experiences they were reluctant to bring up themselves. So did the use of psychodramas, which were explicit opportunities for the kids to act out, and denounce, the hateful acts of Renamo, and in addition to celebrate the virtues of nation, community, and family.

I asked Boothby at one point if there was a clear greatest success story among the kids with whom he worked to heal and reconnect with their homes and families. He explained that there are three dimensions that define success and failure for these young men: financial success, marital stability, and the classical measures of mental health, like clear thinking and emotional steadiness.

If you're talking about traditional western ideals of career and financial success, almost none of these former child soldiers could be called successful. One, Angelo Jose Macouvele, went on to become a professional photographer, working both in Mozambique and in the much more affluent South Africa. But he is the exception. Most are subsistence farmers, raising maize and beans to feed their own families, then looking for real currency income where they can find it.

Take the case of Israel Armando Massingue, who was abducted by Renamo in 1987, when he was 14 years old; he's in his early 30s today. He dresses in western clothes, including an "America on the Rise" T-shirt. He is handsome and fit, like a college running back, with an engaging smile. He is the president of the local equivalent of the PTA. His wife, Saugina Salvador Sitoe, attests that he is a good husband: He doesn't drink and he isn't rough with me, she says.

Yet Massingue cannot find work. He raises his food crops right now, but he is more ambitious than that and feels he just needs a leg up to start some sort of small business. He dreams of getting a small piece of property where he could build a furnace, and produce concrete blocks for construction, or

perhaps have a small chicken farm. But such dreams are a long shot.

Massingue is representative of how these young men were often financially crippled by their abductions and forced servitude in the Renamo forces. Typically, teenagers from rural Mozambique will venture away from home for a few years, often to South Africa to work in the mines, and earn enough money to return home with a financial stake. They use their savings to attract a bride, they marry, and raise families. These young men never got to South Africa and lost those prime earning years.

They also lost their chances for a decent education. Basic education is not an entitlement in Mozambique; the cost of textbooks alone makes schooling prohibitively expensive for many, especially those in rural areas. Yet most of the boys from Lhanguene, who were all offered stipends to resume their education once they were back home, turned them down. They wanted to make up for lost time, to get on with the lives that had been interrupted. So Macamo, who had gotten only to fourth grade, never resumed his schooling. Massingue did try to go back to school, but then he was drafted into the Frelimo Army and lost even more time. Now in his 30s, he sees education as a luxury he can't afford to indulge.

Yet despite their poor financial fortunes, many are married and raising families. By that measure, Boothby notes, most would be considered successes, though raising families in such abject poverty is tough. Massingue and Sitoe's infant daughter had died just days before I visited, the second of their two children to die. The cause of death isn't known. Macamo has also lost one child. Losing children is not uncommon in rural Mozambique.

Despite such losses and the accompanying grief, Massingue and Macamo would have to be considered successes in terms of social functioning. Certainly compared with Firinice Nharalae. Firinice was only 6 when he was abducted by Renamo and witnessed the brutal murder of family members who were Frelimo supporters. When he ended up at Lhanguene, he was mute, and although he later regained his voice, he was by all reports never completely healthy again. He was delusional much of the time, and in his early 20s he was still living in the care of his mother. That is where I was supposed to meet him, but I never got the chance. Ten days before I arrived in Mozambique, Nharala drowned in a nearby lake while fishing.

Quive is another who never really recovered from his wartime experience. He has never married, and his prospects aren't very good. The fact is he doesn't have much to offer. His teeth are rotten, and he has no income. Indeed, he represents the walking wounded of the children's civil war. He spent two years in a Renamo base camp, working as a colonel's bodyguard. In that role, he would have both witnessed and committed some brutal acts. He says he still has nightmares and flashbacks about his time with Renamo, sometimes so disabling that they keep him from doing even the simplest work. One day, while cutting wood with a machete, he had flashbacks so severe that he nearly severed his arm, and he hasn't worked much since. If he were in America, he would most likely be diagnosed with post-traumatic stress disorder, or PTSD, and treated with psychotherapeutic techniques and perhaps psychiatric medications.

Stress and culture. Diagnosis and healing in Mozambique are very different from western practices, but there are interesting commonalities as well. I spent some time talking to traditional healers, known locally as curandeiros: Rosalina Mondlane and Teresa Xitlango live and work in the same Malehice village as Macamo and Quive. Beatriz Armando Massingue lives in Israel's village; she's his sister. These women are highly regarded in their communities. They have all apprenticed to other healers for three to five years, and although the specifics of their healing practices appear to vary a bit, they all share some general beliefs about mental health and psychotherapy.

They wouldn't use those words, of course, though when pushed they do come up with words for conditions that are roughly translatable to our psychiatric diagnoses. For example, the Shangana word kuxukuvala is a close equivalent of what we would call clinical depression. Kuxukuvala is characterized by abnormal sadness and emotional paralysis. Similarly, Quive and others are thought to suffer from npfuka, which corresponds pretty well to what American psychiatrists would label PTSD. It has the

symptoms of nightmares and flashbacks to specific experiences of trauma and violence.

But the Mozambican healers' theories about the causes of such stress disorders are quite different. They believe, for example, that when a soldier murders someone, the spirit of the dead takes up residence in the killer—even if the murder has been coerced, as with the child soldiers. For the sake of mental stability, the spirit of the victim must be driven out.

To that end, the healers might heat a concoction of local herbs and have the returning soldiers breathe it in to accomplish spiritual cleansing. Or they might kill a chicken or a goat, mix the blood with water, then use this potion to "vaccinate" them through pinpricks in the arm. If the healers sense the need for a stronger treatment, they might take the child down to the riverside, because certain spirits are known to reside in the water or in the riverbanks and exposure to these spirits can be tonic. All of this must be done before the emotionally traumatized child is allowed to re-enter the household, to prevent contamination of the home. The healers appear to have an innate sense of what American mental health practitioners call psychiatric prevention; they assume that such trauma and stress will take a toll even if it hasn't already, so they intervene immediately to ward off illness by realigning the spirits.

It's impossible to know which specific elements of these healing practices helped the returning child soldiers, but it's clear that the cleansing rituals were essential to the kids' transitions back to community and family life. When the civil war come to an end, there was a widespread fear that the boys who had served under Renamo would be socially tainted and unwelcome back in their villages because of their "treason" and the hideousness of their war crimes. Indeed, this idea was perpetuated by the Frelimo government, which saw PR value in the idea that Renamo had ruined these kids' lives. But the rejections never happened. Most of the kids were welcomed back with compassion, even joy, and the healers' belief in recovery certainly helped communities embrace their victimized sons.

Back home. So why have some done so much better after the war than others? Put another way, why aren't all of the former child soldiers psychological wrecks given what they were put through? The answer is no doubt complex, but at least two factors appear important to the survivors' resilience. The first is the amount of time the child spent with Renamo. Some, like Macamo and Rafael Saveca, escaped after just a couple of months, while others, like Quive, were in Renamo camps for two years or more. According to Boothby's analysis, there is an emotional "threshold" somewhere between months and years. Once passed, it's much harder to repair the psychological damage.

Then there is family. All of these kids got basically the same psychological help at Lhanguene, and almost all went through some kind of cleansing ritual upon returning to their villages. But Macamo and Massingue came home to large, exuberant families. Quive, by contrast, came home to a disintegrating household. His parents had split up while he was gone, and when he sided with his mother, his father disowned him. The village healers, Mondlane and Xitlango, say Quive's mother is unstable; they use a Shangana word that roughly translates as "she sleeps around." Indeed, she and her latest boyfriend left the village soon after Quive returned.

So Quive has not had much emotional support at home. But consider that he is one of the lucky child soldiers. He at least ended up at Lhanguene, where he benefited from Save the Children's model therapy program. When the civil war ended in 1992, both Frelimo and Renamo denied ever enlisting children in their war efforts, so about 25,000 kids were left to reintegrate themselves into their communities without any help whatsoever. Those young men's life stories are not known.

R E A D I N G *72*

Abuse of Power: Sexual Exploitation of Refugee Women and Girls

Elizabeth G. Ferris (2007)

The fact that refugee and displaced women and children are particularly vulnerable to violence has been widely acknowledged by the international community over the past twenty years. Sexual violence is frequently used as a tool of war; thus, women flee their communities because of sexual and gender-based violence. Too often, they encounter violence and exploitation in their flight to safety—at the hands of warlords, soldiers, armed gangs, and border guards. In refugee and displaced persons camps, they are vulnerable to violence when they search for firewood and food. With the breakdown in social norms, they are at increased risk of domestic and community violence. When humanitarian relief in the form of food and other necessities is insufficient for their families, they sometimes turn to prostitution. But in the past few years, there has been growing awareness of sexual exploitation

by a different group of perpetrators: humanitarian workers who are charged with protecting and assisting refugees and the displaced.

> You people should have taken care of me. Instead you abandoned me.
>
> —Refugee child (UNHCR and Save the Children UK 2002, 2)[1]

In February 2002, the United Nations High Commissioner for Refugees (UNHCR) and Save the Children UK released a report entitled "Sexual Violence and Exploitation: The Experience of Refugee Children in Liberia, Guinea, and Sierra Leone." Written by staff from both organizations, the report was intended to investigate sexual violence and exploitation in the region, including its extent, causes, and consequences, and to make recommendations for future action. The study was based on interviews with and focus groups of refugee and displaced children, as well as adult refugees, community leaders, and humanitarian workers, in these three countries. A total of 1,500 people were interviewed by the researchers, mostly in groups.

The researchers found that not only was sexual exploitation widespread, it was also perpetrated by aid workers, peacekeepers, and community leaders. Humanitarian workers traded food and relief items for sexual favors. Teachers in schools in the camps exploited children in exchange for passing grades. Medical care and medicines were given in return for sex. Some forty-two agencies and sixty-seven individuals were implicated in this behavior.[2] Parents pressured their children to enter sexually exploitative relationships in order to secure relief items for the family.

> If your family does not have a girl, your family is in crisis.
>
> —Mother, camp for internationally displaced persons in Sierra Leone (UNHCR and Save the Children UK 2002, 34).

The researchers found that although sexual exploitation affected boys and girls from the age of five, the most frequently exploited were girls ages 13–18. Girls living in single-parent households, separated and unaccompanied children, children from child-headed households, and girls who were street traders were particularly vulnerable. The exchange rate for sexual transactions was very low, with payment most often in kind (a few biscuits, a bar of soap, a plastic sheet, pencils, etc.) rather than cash. The girls usually received very little money; for example, in Liberia, the girls were reported to receive the equivalent of ten cents (U.S.), with which they could buy a couple of pieces of fruit or a handful of peanuts but not a full meal.

> If you see a young girl walking away with a tarpaulin on her head you know how she got it.
>
> —Refugee leader, Guinea (UNHCR and Save the Children UK 2002, 37)

Finally, the report found that sexual exploitation occurred with impunity. No staff member of an agency lost his or her job for exploiting children.

The costs of reporting such cases are high for vulnerable refugee and displaced women—particularly when complaints would have to be lodged with people who themselves are perpetrators of sexual exploitation.

> If I tell you the name of the NGO worker I have to have sex with, he will get fired, and then how will I feed my child and myself?
>
> —Girl-mother, Guinea (UNHCR and Save the Children UK 2002, 44)

WHY SO MUCH SEXUAL EXPLOITATION?

> It's difficult to escape the trap of those (NGO) people; they use the food as bait to get you to [have] sex with them.
>
> —Adolescent, Liberia (UNHCR and Save the Children UK 2002, 36)

The authors of the study highlighted poverty and abuse of power as the main reasons for the sexual exploitation of children. The fact is that aid in these situations is inadequate. Humanitarian agencies have not been able to raise the necessary resources to allow people in low-profile emergency situations to live in dignity and security. As the authors of the study poignantly argue, the inequities in power relationships create opportunities for exploitation:

> The pattern of humanitarian assistance has led to overwhelming dependency by the refugee population. The size of the plastic sheet determines the size of the house. The food ration is for thirty days but it is calculated on kilocalories and not quantity. It finishes within ten days, but there is not enough land to grow food. The non-food items given are not replaced as often but there are not enough income-generating jobs for the refugees to earn money to buy their own. Education is free but all the other related expenses are left for the parents to provide, like books, pencils, uniforms and shoes. The parents have no income and the girl has to fend for herself. It's like their bodies are the only currency they have left. At the same time, surrounding the refugee population and controlling so much of their lives, is a moneyed elite—UN and NGO workers, peacekeepers, etc,—whose resources are

10 ×, 100 ×, 1000 × more than what the refugees have. They can afford to exploit this extreme disparity and pay for sex when they want and with whom they want. (UNHCR and Save the Children UK 2002, 45)

Inequities of power are evident on different levels. Gender roles often change in refugee camps. In this study the researchers found, for example, that fathers felt that they could not prevent their daughters from entering into exploitative relationships because their own traditional role as family provider was no longer possible. At the same time, refugee men may be more apt to assert their power as men because the social mechanisms that held that power in place are weakened. For example, men may push women and children aside in order to get food. Most of the nongovernmental organization (NGO) and UN humanitarian workers who were named by the children as abusers were national rather than expatriate staff. The relationship between national and international staff has its own power dynamic, as the international staff of an organization tends to be perceived as having higher status and more power. In both UN agencies and international NGOs, decisions about programs and staffing are usually made by the expatriate staff in a given country. The study also found a tendency for male humanitarian workers to protect one another when confronted with evidence of sexual exploitation. Female humanitarian workers may find it difficult to protest, particularly when those in charge of the camps are male, which is usually the case.

The report, with its many quotations from children, is difficult to read. The fact that humanitarian workers from the United Nations and NGOs were found to have sexually exploited refugee and displaced children sent shock waves through the international community. The circulation of the report led some to attack its methodology, to question the integrity of the researchers, and to take steps to limit the damages. It also led to a great deal of soul-searching in the humanitarian community. There was a widespread sense that the international community had failed these children and a realization that the problem extended far beyond the West African countries where the research was done. Many UN and NGO missions were sent to the region to investigate the charges, and many launched further studies of sexual exploitation and took a serious look at their own policies and procedures.

THE UNITED NATIONS RESPONSE

All the UN agencies and international NGOs named in the report carried out investigations of their staff and procedures in the region. Almost all also developed or revised guidelines or codes of conduct for their staff.

The UN Inter-Agency Standing Committee (IASC) is made up of all UN agencies involved in humanitarian responses as well as NGO networks and other intergovernmental bodies. The IASC formed a Task Force on Protection from Sexual Exploitation in Humanitarian Crises in March 2002. In June 2002, the IASC released a document called "Report of the Inter-Agency Standing Committee Task Force on Protection from Sexual Exploitation and Abuse in Humanitarian Crises," which included a "Plan of Action" and "Core Principles of a Code of Conduct on Protection from Sexual Abuse and Exploitation in Humanitarian Crises" (IASC 2002, 8). The core principles for humanitarian agency codes of conduct include prohibition of sexual relations with child beneficiaries, mandatory reporting of suspected exploitation, and managerial responsibility for the enforcement of the code. Many other agencies within and beyond the United Nations adapted the core principles into codes of conduct for their humanitarian workers. In February 2005, the U.S. Congress passed the Humanitarian Assistance Code of Conduct Act of 2005, which declared that U.S. funds may only go to those humanitarian refugee agencies that have adopted codes of conduct consistent with six specific IASC core principles.[3]

The UN Secretary-General issued a bulletin on "Special Measurers for Protection from Sexual Exploitation and Sexual Abuse," defining sexual abuse as "the actual or threatened physical intrusion of a sexual nature, whether by force or under unequal or coercive conditions" (Annan 2003). Sexual exploitation was defined as "any actual or attempted abuse of a position of vulnerability, differential power, or trust, for sexual purposes, including, but not limited to, profiting monetarily, socially or politically from the sexual exploitation of another" (Annan 2003).

In September 2005, the IASC issued "Guidelines for Gender-Based Violence Interventions in Humanitarian Settings" (IASC 2005), which includes a matrix of recommended actions in three phases: emergency preparedness, minimum prevention and response (to be conducted even in the midst of emergency), and comprehensive prevention and response (stabilized phase).[4] The rest of the IASC plan of action has received less attention among humanitarian agencies. Its recommendations relating to staff gender balance, staff training, beneficiary and host-community awareness, empowerment of women and children, and self-reliance all have substantial roles to play in preventing sexual exploitation but are harder to implement than codes of conduct.

BEYOND CODES OF CONDUCT

While there are many new codes of conduct intended to ensure that humanitarian workers do not sexually exploit beneficiaries, codes of conduct are not enough. Two large international NGO consortia have gone further than codes of conduct. The Steering Committee for Humanitarian Response, which is made up of nine of the largest humanitarian NGOs, initiated a peer review process in which its members reviewed one another's policies and procedures for preventing and responding to sexual exploitation of beneficiaries. This was an intensive process, using interviews with headquarters and field staff to look at the culture of the organization, accountability, compliance with and enforcement of codes of conduct, training, and mechanisms for addressing suspected sexual exploitation. Those participating in the peer review found it to be a rigorous and useful process and are reporting back on concrete actions taken to implement the findings of the peer review.

The International Council of Voluntary Agencies (ICVA) took a different approach with its members. Recognizing that many NGOs lacked procedures for dealing with cases of suspected sexual exploitation, ICVA initiated a project called "Building Safer Organizations," which aims to train senior management in the implications of codes of conduct and to train designated managers in the investigation

of complaints of sexual exploitation.[5] Investigating sexual exploitation is not an easy task, and the training workshops in the field provide specific tools to participants to enable them to conduct investigations if it becomes necessary.

Although these are all good initiatives and may well reduce the incidence of sexual exploitation in refugee and displaced persons camps, they do not address the fundamental disparity of power and the inadequacy of relief assistance that lead women and children to exchange sex for things that they need to survive. As long as refugees do not have sufficient food or medical care, they will be vulnerable to sexual exploitation. As long as humanitarian workers control access to the necessities of life, they will be in a position where the abuse of their power is not only possible but likely. As long as the international humanitarian community is not able to mobilize sufficient resources for the people entrusted to its care, young girls will trade sex for a handful of peanuts.

NOTES

1. All quotations are taken from the UNHCR and Save the Children UK (2002). This report was of a UNHCR and Save the Children UK assessment mission carried out from October 22 to November 30, 2001. It is impossible to capture the full impact of the eighty-four-page study in this short article.
2. Security and military forces, including UN peacekeepers, were also identified as being involved in sexual exploitation of children, as were local businessmen.
3. Humanitarian Assistance Code of Conduct Act, HR 912, 109th Congress, first session, 2005.
4. Note that the guidelines contain a comprehensive listing of available resources to support taking concrete actions to address sexual exploitation.
5. See the International Council of Voluntary Agencies Web site (http://www.icva.ch) for a fuller description of the Building Safer Organizations project. More information is available at http://www.icva.ch/cgi-bin/browse.pl?doc=doc00001249.

REFERENCES

Annan, Kofi A. 2003. "Secretary-General's Bulletin: Special Measures for Protection from Sexual Exploitation and Sexual Abuse." United Nations Secretariat, New York, October 9. http://ochaonline.un.org/DocView.asp?DocID=1083.

IASC (Inter-Agency Standing Committee, Geneva). 2002. "Report of the Inter-Agency Standing Committee Task Force on Protection from Sexual Exploitation and Abuse in Humanitarian Crises." Inter-Agency Standing Committee, Geneva. http//www. humanitarianinfo.org/iasc/content/products/docs/IASC%20english%20POA%20and%20report.pdf.

___. 2005. "Guidelines for Gender-Based Violence Interventions in Humanitarian Settings: Focusing on Prevention of and Response to Sexual Violence in Emergencies."

Inter-Agency Standing Committee, Geneva. http://www.humanitarianinfo.org/iasc/content/ products/docs/tfgender_GBVGuidelines2005.pdf.

UNHCR (UN High Commissioner for Refugees) and Save the Children UK. 2002. "Sexual Violence and Exploitation: The Experience of Refugee Children in Liberia, Guinea, and Sierra Leone." WomenWarPeace.org (UNIFEM—a Portal on Women, Peace, and Security), New York. http://www.womenwarpeace.org/sierra_leone/docs/savereport.doc.

R E A D I N G **73**

Rape in Darfur

Femke van Zeijl (2007)

Nura sits quietly in her family's recently built hut. She leans against the bamboo fence and stays silent. Newly arrived in Duma, a small town in the middle of the barren plains of South Darfur, the 15-year-old girl has refused to come out for two days now.

Her older brother does the talking: "The day before yesterday we returned to our village together." He points at the horizon in the direction of the mountains. "When we had to flee last week, we didn't have time to dig up the money box buried in the yard. So we went back for it."

On the journey they encountered the feared men with machine guns. The Arabs on horseback—he daren't utter the word *Janjaweed*—forced the two to an abandoned village nearby, where they battered him with their gun barrels. His sister was next. "They dragged her to another house. I could not see what happened, but I heard her screaming and couldn't do anything. The whole way back, Nura cried."

The father of the siblings arrives at the hut, and tells the story to me once more. He is especially keen that the correct amount of money that was stolen from him gets put down on paper. He painstakingly dictates the exact number of Sudanese dinars and adds that he was also robbed of a strong mule. He doesn't say a single word about the fact his 15-year-old daughter was raped by four men.

Sexual violence against women is occurring on a massive scale in Darfur. Amnesty International calls these mass rapes a weapon of war. After years of pressure from women's organizations around the world, a 1998 landmark United Nations decision confirmed the concept of rape as a war crime, one that has increased during recent years. Darfur fits the pattern of Cambodia, Liberia, Peru, Bosnia, Sierra Leone, Rwanda, Somalia and Uganda, with violence against women being systematically used by warring parties.

DESTROYING THE FUTURE

Mariam is a midwife at a hospital in South Darfur. She's been in the profession for decades, but when I met her, she told me the last few years have been incredible.

A girl she had seen that very morning had been raped by five Arabs. The sixth cut her vagina with a knife. She was in hospital for months and now is going back to her family—in a refugee camp. "She is afraid of what her parents might say. I am going with her for a conversation with her family. Step by step we tell them what has happened, that it wasn't her fault. I try to prevent her repudiation," the midwife explains.

Rape is an enormous taboo in Sudan. Survivors mostly keep the experience to themselves, though they frequently say they "know somebody who has been abused"; only after long talks might a survivor admit that she herself was the victim.

Women impregnated from rape are in even worse circumstances. According to a popular myth, you cannot *get* pregnant from rape. So there have been cases where pregnant rape survivors have been imprisoned for "adultery." Mariam says: "A lot of abused girls do not want a baby from the enemy and ask for a pill to make it go away." But she cannot help; abortion is legal only to save the life of the woman. "I tell the girl it won't matter any more whether her baby is Arab once the war is over. I go with her to her family to talk about this."

In Darfur, the Arab militia and military make a point of abusing women in front of their families or entire village. Raping a woman is such an effective weapon because it affects an entire community, for decades. French anthropologist Véronique Nahoum-Grappe calls it "destroying the future." Children who witness the crime are traumatized, men flee from their partners out of shame, and women become "damaged goods," sometimes literally, if they can no longer have children because of the violence. Through raping wives and daughters, Nahoum-Grappe explains, the attackers actually target the "real enemy": the men behind them. Having to have your enemy's baby goes one step further and turns this sexual violence into a tool for "ethnic cleansing."

STRUGGLE TO SURVIVE

Meanwhile, the rape victims in Darfur struggle to survive. A report by the Dutch branch of Médecins San Frontières, issued two years ago, noted that their organization alone had treated almost 500 rapes in a four-and-a-half-month period. Because comprehensive research is made impossible by the lack of humanitarian access to much of Darfur, it is hard to state exact numbers. But it is safe to say that there are many thousands of women who have been raped.

Hawa, 18 years old, is one of them. She now lives alone in a tiny cabin. In the midst of a teeming Darfur refugee camp where most families must share huts, this seems a luxury. But for Hawa it's terrible, especially at night, when gunshots sound throughout the camp. "I hide under my bed till it's over," Hawa tells me. "Those moments remind me of that last night in my village."

One Friday night, gunshots woke her. She saw other villagers running from attackers: men with Kalashnikov rifles riding horses and camels. "Janjaweed, I started running, but . . ." Two men caught her and another girl. "They tied our hands together and raped us."

Hawa fled to Camp Kalma, South Darfur, near the capital Nyala. I met her three months later, but she was still being reminded of the rape every day, not only because she suffers pain in her stomach and cannot sit for long, but because the rapes are why she now lives alone in her hut built of sticks and plastic bags. The uncle and aunt who raised her ignore her: a raped woman isn't worth much in Darfur. Hawa asks plaintively: "Who will marry me now?"

With impunity for rapists still the rule, it is not easy to help women and girls such as Hawa. Relief workers in Sudan face difficult circumstances. The Sudanese Government is displeased with foreign witnesses of the violence in Darfur, especially when they focus on helping abused women. The regime dismisses stories of systematic rapes as "concoctions," and they respond to reports about it by arresting or threatening the aid workers or journalists responsible.

"Educating women about health and hygiene is just about possible," sighs an aid worker in Darfur who wants to remain anonymous. "But psychosocial help to rape victims is a very sensitive issue." Her organization has started training local women, two of each tribe, to recognize victims of gender-based violence. It would not work to start a center specifically for rape victims, she says: "Much too stigmatizing, nobody would dare go there." So aid workers try to integrate this help with their other activities. Such cumbersomeness can be terribly frustrating: "The number of women in Darfur that have faced horrible traumas is unimaginable. Yet we can only help a fraction—if we're lucky."

GRUESOME INJUSTICE

Rape of women in times of war is not a new phenomenon. The Old Testament repeatedly speaks of attackers aiming to kill a man, but instead raping "his concubine." The soldiers in the Second World War were no better. The "comfort girls" forced into prostitution by the Japanese are a well-known example—and a fact of history which Japan still struggles to recognize. That victorious Allied Forces also forced themselves on the German women they conquered is less commonly known.

In recent years the war in former Yugoslavia and the Rwandan genocide were the stage for a horrendous amount of rapes. In eastern Democratic Republic of Congo one out of three women has been raped during the last decade by militia, government soldiers or both. And the gang rape of a 14-year-old girl by US soldiers in Iraq confirms how pervasive this terrible practice is.

Rape, used as a weapon of war, can be construed as a gruesome enlargement of societies' unequal attitude toward women in peacetime. Women in many parts of the world are still seen as the property of men, rather than their own person. In Sudan, rape within marriage is not seen as a crime—and beating your wife when she "misbehaves" is widely condoned.

In this context it is useful to look into the evidence against Ali Kushayb, one of the two men whom the International Criminal Court (ICC) has named as suspected of war crimes in Darfur. The prosecutor accuses this Janjaweed leader of targeting not rebel troops, but civilians. "This strategy became the justification for the mass murder, summary execution and mass rape of civilians," the prosecutor states.

Kushayb is said to have encouraged his men to consider Darfur people as their "loot." Which translates culturally as: kill the men, rape the women. He might never have said exactly that, but in this context the meaning was clear. And, according to the ICC, the Janjaweed leader went further than that. The prosecutor's evidence puts him in Arawalla, West Darfur, in 2003. During an attack on that village he was seen personally inspecting a group of naked women tied to trees before they were raped by men in soldiers' uniforms.

Feminists like Susan Brownmiller and Robin Morgan argue that rape is inherent in the nature of war: it is never about sex, but about power and the military culture of violence. With gender equality far from reality, it is imperative that those involved in rape are punished.

In this respect national and international justice failed terribly for years. It was not until the last decade of the 20th century that rape was taken seriously as a war crime. Male-dominated international institutions, male judges, prosecutors and researchers preferred to concentrate on "serious crimes" like murder. In its initial stages the Rwanda Tribunal, for example, did not even mention rape in any of the charges. It only came up coincidentally when a witness referred to it in her testimony.

For the mass raping of women in wartime to come to an end, there has to be an end to impunity for rapists, and those who incite them. Until the perpetrators can be sure that they will be held legally accountable for their actions, they will not change.

R E A D I N G **74**

Building Cultures of Peace: Four Cornerstones

Riane Eisler (2008)

How can we end the cycles of violence that cause so much suffering? When we envision a world of peace, what does it really look like? And what can we do to help build the foundations on which this better world can rest?

My research over two decades has focused on these questions. They are questions deeply rooted in my own life experience, in my flight as a small child from the Nazis after Crystal Night, the first official night of terrorism against Jews in Germany and my native Austria.

One result of my research has been a new set of social categories: the partnership system and the domination system. Another result has been a new perspective on modern history, showing that underlying seemingly random events lies the tension between organized challenges to traditions of domination—from the "divinely-ordained" right of despotic kings to rule their "subjects" to the "divinely-ordained" right to men to rule the women and children in the "castles" of their homes to the "divinely-ordained" right of one race or nation to rule over another—and enormous dominator resistance and periodic regressions.

This research also shows something of pivotal importance that is still ignored in conventional analyses. This is that to build cultures of peace we have to pay particular attention to how a culture structures the most fundamental human relations: the relations between the female and male halves of humanity and between them and their daughters and sons.

The reason, simply put, is that it is in these primary human relations that people first learn either respect for human rights or to accept human rights violations as only normal and even moral.

Indeed, if we look at history from this larger perspective, we see something else ignored in conventional analyses. This is that those who would push us back to more autocratic, violent and unjust times uniformly work to maintain or impose rigid rankings of domination in gender and parent-child relations.

A top priority for the Nazis was getting women back into their "traditional" place in a "traditional" family—code words for a top-down, male-dominated, authoritarian family. This was also a top priority for Khomeini in Iran and Stalin in the former Soviet Union. And it still is for so-called religious fundamentalists today—whether Eastern or Western—people who also believe in "holy wars" and authoritarian rule in the state or tribe.

But ironically, for many progressives, women's rights and children's rights are still "just" women's and children's issues. This is again why we need a new language: social categories that show that the cultural construction of gender and childhood relations is key to whether cultures are peaceful or violent, equitable or inequitable, sustainable or unsustainable.

TWO NEW SOCIAL CATEGORIES

As Einstein said, the same thinking that created our problems cannot solve them. Building foundations for a more peaceful and equitable world requires thinking that goes beyond conventional categories such as capitalist vs. socialist, East vs. West, religious vs. secular, technologically developed vs. undeveloped and so forth. None of these categories tell us what kinds of cultures support peace.

Underlying the many differences in societies, both cross-culturally and through history, are two basic cultural configurations: the domination system and the partnership system.

Societies adhering closely to the domination system have the following configuration:

- top-down authoritarianism in both the family and state or tribe
- the subordination of the female half of humanity to the male half
- a high degree of institutionalized or built-in violence, whether in the form of wife and child beating or in the form of warfare and terrorism, as violence ultimately backs up rankings of domination
- beliefs that present rigid rankings of domination—beginning with the ranking of male and "masculine" over female and "feminine"—as divinely or naturally ordained.

Moving toward the partnership side of the spectrum—and it is always a matter of degree—we see a different configuration:

- a more democratic organization in both the family and state or tribe
- both halves of humanity are equally valued, and stereotypically feminine values such as caring and nonviolence (which are considered "unmanly" in the domination system) are highly regarded, whether they are embodied in women or men
- a less violent way of living, since violence is not needed to maintain rigid rankings of domination, whether in families or the family of nations
- beliefs that value women as well as stereotypically "feminine" feminine traits and activities—such as caring, nonviolence, and caregiving—whether they are embodied in women or men.

Unlike conventional categories, the partnership and domination systems take into full account the most foundational human relations without which none of us would be here: the relations between the female and male halves of humanity and between them and their daughters and sons. They fully recognize that these relations shape how people think and feel, how they vote and how they govern, what they think is normal or abnormal, moral or immoral, possible or impossible.

These categories also make it possible to identify key interventions with a cascade of systemic effects: interventions that are unfortunately still viewed as secondary to more "important" matters by many people who consider themselves progressive.

THE FIRST CORNERSTONE FOR PEACE AND PARTNERSHIP: CHILDHOOD RELATIONS

The physical structure of the brain—including the neural pathways that will determine not only intelligence, but creativity, predisposition to violent or nonviolent behaviors, empathy or insensitivity, venturesomeness or overconformity, as well as other critical behavioral developments—are not set at birth. They are largely determined during the childhood years. Coercive, inequitable and violent childrearing—dominator childrearing—is foundational to the imposition and maintenance of a coercive, inequitable and chronically violent social and cultural organization.

Through our intimate relations we learn habits of feeling, thinking and behavior in all human relations, whether personal or political. If these relations are violent, children learn early on that violence from those who are more powerful toward those who are less powerful is acceptable as a means of dealing with conflicts and/or problems. Fortunately some people reject this teaching. But unfortunately many replicate it not only in their intimate relations but in all relations—including international ones.

In short, if relations based on chronic violations of human rights are considered normal and desirable in these formative intimate relations, they provide mental models for condoning such violations in other relations.

A global campaign against violence and abuse in childhood relations is needed, which has a number of core elements:

- The first is education: raising awareness of the consequences—personal and global—of either dominator or partnership childhood relations, as well as education providing both women and men the knowledge and skills necessary for empathic, sensitive, nonviolent, authoritative rather than authoritarian childrearing.
- The second component is legal: the enactment and enforcement of laws criminalizing child abuse as well as legislation funding education for nonviolent, empathic and equitable childrearing.
- The third component relates to changing the mass media: raising consciousness of the constant representation of violence as a means of resolving conflicts and of the presentation in so-called comedies of situations in which family members abuse and humiliate each other.
- The fourth component is engaging spiritual and religious leaders to take a moral stand on this pivotal issue of intimate violence—the violence that every year blights, and all too often takes, the lives of millions of children and women and perpetuates cycles of violence in all relations.

This is the mission of the Spiritual Alliance to Stop Intimate Violence (SAIV) that I cofounded. Please see www.saiv.net for resources and information.

THE SECOND CORNERSTONE: GENDER RELATIONS

How a society constructs the roles and relations of the two halves of humanity—women and men—is central to the construction of every social institution, from the family and religion to politics and economics as well as to the society's guiding systems of values. It is even central to a nation's general quality of life. For example, "Women, Men, and the Global Quality of Life," a study based on statistics from 89 nations by the Center for Partnership Studies (www.partnershipway.org), found that the status of women can be a better predictor of general quality of life than even GDP or GNP, the conventional measures of a nation's economic health.

One reason for this is of course that women are half the population. Equally important is that, despite myriads of philosophical and religious pronouncements that values such as caring, compassion and nonviolence should govern human relations, in practice these values remain subordinate and excluded from social governance as long as the half of humanity with which they are primarily associated—the female half—remains subordinate and excluded from social governance.

This is not a matter of women against men or of something inherent in women rather than men. Stereotypically feminine traits, such as caring and nonviolence, can be found in both women and men. Stereotypical women's work, such as taking care of children and maintaining a clean and healthy home environment, can also be performed by both women and men. However, in societies adhering closely to the domination system, these traits and activities are considered appropriate only for women and inappropriate for "real men."

A sign of hope is that there is today strong movement toward real partnership in all spheres of life between women and men, along with a blurring of rigid gender stereotypes. Men are nurturing babies and women are entering positions of economic and political leadership. But this movement is still slow and localized and is in some cultures and subcultures fiercely opposed, for example, by so-called religious fundamentalist leaders.

What is needed is for the world's progressive leaders to give policy and fiscal priority to a global campaign for equitable and nonviolent gender relations. Giving priority to such so-called "women's" issues" has enormous implications for the environment, peace, population, economic equity and political democracy.

We cannot really talk of representative democracy as long as women still hold a small minority of political positions. We cannot realistically expect to end the arms build-ups that are today bankrupting our world and the terrorism and aggressive warfare that in our age of nuclear and chemical warfare threaten our species' survival as long as boys and men continue to be socialized to equate "real masculinity" with violence and control—whether through "heroic" epics or war toys or violent and brutal television shows. Nor can we realistically expect an end to racism, anti-Semitism and other ugly isms as long as people learn early on to equate difference—beginning with the fundamental difference between female and male—with superiority or inferiority, with dominating or being dominated.

THE THIRD CORNERSTONE: ECONOMIC RELATIONS

Under present economic systems, both free market and centrally planned, the problems of underemployment, polarization of wealth, hardship and suffering stemming from "structural adjustments" and other so-called globalization economic policies, are escalating. The gap between haves and have-nots is growing both between and within nations. Poverty is an intractable problem. And current economic policies are endangering our natural life-support systems. As is developed in my book, *The Real Wealth of Nations*, we need a new way of visualizing and structuring economics.

The real wealth of nations is not financial; it consists of the contributions of people and nature. We therefore need what we have not had: economic indicators, policies and practices that give visibility and value to the most important human work: the work of caring for people, beginning in childhood, and for nature. We need a caring economics.

To create the "high quality human capital" needed for the postindustrial information/knowledge age, we must recognize what both psychology and neuroscience tell us: that this capital largely depends on the kind of care children receive. We need strong social support for the caregiving work performed in the household economy.

There are important trends in this direction. For example, most West European nations offer monetary assistance and increasingly also education for parenting, along with paid parental leave, health care and high quality early childhood education. Satellite economic indicators are beginning to count the economic value of this work. For example, the Swiss government found that if it were included it would constitute 70 percent of the reported Swiss GDP.

But the general failure to give real value to this work in large part accounts for the fact that poverty and hunger have proven intractable. Indeed, it makes no sense to talk of hunger and poverty in generalities when the mass of the world's poor and the poorest of the poor are women and children. Even in the rich United States, women over the age of 65 are, according to U.S. statistics, twice as likely to be poor as men over 65. Most of these women are, or were, caregivers. We need economic inventions such as caregiver tax credits, Social Security credit for childcare, and a more accurate system of economic indicators that give visibility and value to this essential "women's work"—whether it is performed by women or men.

Development policies also need to shift their focus to women. Many studies show that in most regions of the developing world women allocate far more of their resources to their families than men do. We must include the work of caring and caregiving still performed primarily by women worldwide into national and international systems of economic measurement and accounting.

We should encourage and reward economic and social inventions that give value to caring and caregiving work in both the market and nonmarket economic sectors. For example, we have national programs to train soldiers to effectively take life—and we have pensions for them. By contrast, we have no national programs for training women and men to effectively care for children—even though we have solid scientific knowledge about what is and is not effective and humane childcare.

People need meaningful work. The negative income tax or guaranteed income for doing nothing is no solution. Clearly the most important and meaningful work is that of caring for other humans, particularly our children and our growing elderly population, and for our natural environment.

Redefining productive work also imbues work with what it lacks in a domination system—where it is primarily motivated by fear and the artificial creation of scarcities through wars and misallocation and misdistribution of resources. Giving value to caring and caregiving imbues work with meaning. It gives work a spiritual dimension, since at the core of all spiritual traditions is the valuing of compassion and love.

THE FOURTH CORNERSTONE: STORIES, BELIEFS AND SPIRITUALITY

We humans live by stories. Unfortunately many of the stories we inherited from earlier times teach that dominating or being dominated are the only alternatives. That there are today stories offering a partnership alternative of relations built on mutual benefit, mutual respect and mutual accountability is a sign of a major revolution in consciousness.

But for this revolution in consciousness to succeed, we need more than the emergence in bits and pieces of new stories. We need a concerted effort through the arts, music, and literature, as well as through science, to show that a partnership way of structuring human society is a viable possibility. We need to show that the struggle for our future is not between religion and secularism, right and left, East and West, or capitalism and socialism, but between traditions of domination and a partnership way of life. In short, we need the new language for describing societies offered by the partnership system and domination system.

These changes in language and in stories have enormous implications for both spirituality and morality. Spirituality becomes not so much an escape to otherworldly realms from the suffering inherent in a dominator world, but an active engagement in creating a better world right here on Earth. And rather than being used to coerce and dominate, morality is imbued with caring and love.

CONCLUSION

To spread the consciousness that we can, and must, change traditions of domination requires courage. It takes courage to challenge domination and violence in both international relations and intimate relations. It takes courage to actively oppose injustice and cruelty in all spheres of life: not only in the so-called public sphere of politics and business but in the so-called private sphere of parent-child, gender, and sexual relations.

It may not be popular, and may even be dangerous to do so, since domination and violence in intimate and intergroup relations are encoded in some religious and ethnic traditions that are our heritage from a more rigid dominator past. But it must be done.

We are at a time when the mix of high technology and the domination system can take us to an evolutionary dead end. High technology in service of conquest and domination—whether of people or of nature—is not sustainable.

We urgently need to shift from domination to partnership worldwide—and every one of us can play a role in this cultural transformation. Only if we consciously and concertedly build these four foundations for a partnership way of living can we move from a violent dominator culture to a more equitable, joyful, sustainable future for ourselves, our children, and generations still to come.

Different versions of this article have been previously published.

R E A D I N G **75**

Plaza de Mayo

Dacia Maraini

Every Thursday, every Thursday
Mr. General
I curl my hair
put on lipstick
to meet friendship and pain
at the Plaza de Mayo.

Every Thursday, every Thursday
Mr. General
I put on my party dress
to meet torture and hatred
at the Plaza de Mayo.

My son was young
black-haired and happy
Mr. General
But now long-eyed fish
deep in the River Plate
eat his body
bite by bite.

My hair, my hair
Mr. General
however much I tie it up
comes loose like snakes
and stands on end to the sky.

My shoes, my shoes
Mr. General

walk by themselves
in the dark street of terror.

My daughter was tall, blond, inquisitive
Mr. General
she raised her thin arm against you
they seized her, beat her, raped her
now I don't know whether she is alive or dead
but I hear her calling
with a cold and aqueous voice.

Every Thursday, every Thursday
Mr. General
I put on a belt of love
to meet death
in the circle of women-mothers
at the Plaza de Mayo.

I ate salt poison powerlessness
Mr. General
I drank hatred terror and loss
my son was beautiful and happy
Mr. General
my daughter tall and sincere.

I don't wish you death
Mr. General
death is such a little thing
something sweet and gentle

I don't want revenge
Mr. General
revenge saturates and weakens
it only satisfies the sick sex.

I don't wish you pain
Mr. General
pain purifies the heart
it makes it fly through the window
like my son's heart did.

I want the kind of love that creates love
I want desire that incites desires
I want life that creates life

I don't want mothers to give birth
to innocent and peaceful children
that later turn into tyrants, torturers,
and Generals like you
Mr. General.

R E A D I N G **76**

Do Muslim Women Really Need Saving?

Lila Abu Lughod (2002)

I was led to pose the question of my title in part because of the way I personally experienced the response to the U.S. war in Afghanistan. Like many colleagues whose work has focused on women and gender in the Middle East, I was deluged with invitations to speak—not just on news programs but also to various departments at colleges and universities, especially women's studies programs. Why did this not please me, a scholar who has devoted more than 20 years of her life to this subject and who has some complicated personal connection to this identity? Here was an opportunity to spread the word, disseminate my knowledge, and correct misunderstandings. The urgent search for knowledge about our sister "women of cover" (as President George Bush so marvelously called them) is laudable and when it comes from women's studies programs where "transnational feminism" is now being taken seriously, it has a certain integrity (see Safire 2001).

My discomfort led me to reflect on why, as feminists in or from the West, or simply as people who have concerns about women's lives, we need to be wary of this response to the events and aftermath of September 11, 2001. I want to point out the minefields—a metaphor that is sadly too apt for a country like Afghanistan, with the world's highest number of mines per capita—of this obsession with the plight of Muslim women. I hope to show some way through them using insights from anthropology, the discipline whose charge has been to understand and manage cultural difference. At the same time, I want to remain critical of anthropology's complicity in the reification of cultural difference.

CULTURAL EXPLANATIONS AND THE MOBILIZATION OF WOMEN

It is easier to see why one should be skeptical about the focus on the "Muslim woman" if one begins with the U.S. public response. I will analyze two manifestations of this response: some conversations I had with a reporter from the PBS *NewsHour with Jim Lehrer* and First Lady Laura Bush's radio address to the nation on November 17, 2001. The presenter from the *NewsHour* show first contacted me in October to see if I was willing to give some background for a segment on Women and Islam. I mischievously asked whether she had done segments on the women of Guatemala, Ireland, Palestine, or Bosnia when the show covered wars in those regions; but I finally agreed to look at the questions she was going to pose to panelists. The questions were hopelessly general. Do Muslim women believe "x"? Are Muslim women "y"? Does Islam allow "z" for women? I asked her: If you were to substitute Christian or Jewish wherever you have Muslim, would these questions make sense? I did not imagine she would call me back. But she did, twice, once with an idea for a segment on the meaning of Ramadan and another time on Muslim women in politics. One was in response to the bombing and the other to the speeches by Laura Bush and Cherie Blair, wife of the British Prime Minister.

What is striking about these three ideas for news programs is that there was a consistent resort to the cultural, as if knowing something about women and Islam or the meaning of a religious ritual would help one understand the tragic attack on New York's World Trade Center and the U.S. Pentagon, or how Afghanistan had come to be ruled by the Taliban, or what interests might have fueled U.S. and other interventions in the region over the past 25 years, or what the history of American support for conservative groups funded to undermine the Soviets might have been, or why the caves and bunkers out of which Bin Laden was to be smoked "dead or alive," as President Bush announced on television, were paid for and built by the CIA.

In other words, the question is why knowing about the "culture" of the region, and particularly its religious beliefs and treatment of women, was more urgent than exploring the history of the development or repressive regimes in the region and the U.S. role in this history. Such cultural framing, it seemed to me, prevented the serious exploration of the roots and nature of human suffering in this part of the world. Instead of political and historical explanations, experts were being asked to give religio-cultural ones. Instead of questions that might lead to the exploration of global interconnections, we were offered ones that worked to artificially divide the world into separate spheres—recreating an imaginative geography of West versus East, us versus Muslims, cultures in which First Ladies give speeches versus others where women shuffle around silently in burqas.

Most pressing for me was why the Muslim woman in general, and the Afghan woman in particular, were so crucial to this cultural mode of explanation, which ignored the complex entanglements in which we are all implicated, in sometimes surprising alignments. Why were these female symbols being mobilized in this "War against Terrorism" in a way they were not in other conflicts? Laura Bush's radio address on November 17 reveals the political work such mobilization accomplishes. On the one hand, her address collapsed important distinctions that should have been maintained. There was a constant slippage between the Taliban and the terrorists, so that they became almost one word—a kind of hyphenated monster identity: the Taliban-and-the-terrorists. Then there was the blurring of the very separate causes in Afghanistan of women's continuing malnutrition, poverty, and ill health, and their more recent exclusion under the Taliban from employment, schooling, and the joys of wearing nail polish. On the other hand, her speech reinforced chasmic divides, primarily between the "civilized people throughout the world" whose hearts break for the women and children of Afghanistan and the Taliban-and-the-terrorists, the cultural monsters who want to, as she put it, "impose their world on the rest of us."

Most revealingly, the speech enlisted women to justify American bombing and intervention in Afghanistan and to make a case for the "War on Terrorism" of which it was allegedly a part. As Laura Bush said, "Because of our recent military gains in much of Afghanistan, women are no longer imprisoned in their homes. They can listen to music and teach their daughters without fear of punishment. The fight against terrorism is also a fight for the rights and dignity of women" (U.S. Government 2002).

These words have haunting resonances for anyone who has studied colonial history. Many who have worked on British colonialism in South Asia have noted the use of the woman question in colonial policies where intervention into sati (the practice of widows immolating themselves on their husbands' funeral pyres), child marriage, and other practices was used to justify rule. As Gayatri Chakravorty Spivak (1988) has cynically put it: white men saving brown women from brown men. The historical record is full of similar cases, including in the Middle East. In Turn of the Century Egypt, what Leila Ahmed (1992) has called "colonial feminism" was hard at work. This was a selective concern about the plight of Egyptian women that focused on the veil as a sign of oppression but gave no support to women's education and was professed loudly by the same Englishman, Lord Cromer, who opposed women's suffrage back home.

Sociologist Marnia Lazreg (1994) has offered some vivid examples of how French colonialism enlisted women to its cause in Algeria. She writes:

> Perhaps the most spectacular example of the colonial appropriation of women's voices, and the silencing of those among them who had begun to take women revolutionaries . . . as role models by not donning the veil, was the event of May 16, 1958 [Just four years before Algeria finally gained its Independence from France after a long bloody struggle and 130 years of French control—L.A.]. On that day a demonstration was organized by rebellious French generals in Algiers to show their determination to keep Algeria French. To give the government of France evidence that Algerians were in agreement with them, the generals had a few thousand native men bused in from nearby villages, along with a few women who were solemnly unveiled by French women. . . . Rounding up Algerians and bringing them to demonstrations of loyalty to France was not in itself an unusual act during the colonial era. But to unveil women at a well-choreographed ceremony added to the event a symbolic dimension that dramatized the one constant feature of the Algerian occupation by France: its obsession with women. [Lazreg 1994:135]

Lazreg (1994) also gives memorable examples of the way in which the French had earlier sought to transform Arab women and girls. She describes skits at awards ceremonies at the Muslim Girls' School in Algiers in 1851 and 1852. In the first skit, written by "a French lady from Algiers," two Algerian Arab girls reminisced about their trip to France with words including the following:

> Oh! Protective France: Oh! Hospitable France! . . .
> Noble land, where I felt free
> Under Christian skies to pray to our God: . . .
> God bless you for the happiness you bring us!
> And you, adoptive mother, who taught us
> That we have a share of this world,
> We will cherish you forever! [Lazreg 1994:68—69]

These girls are made to invoke the gift of a share of this world, a world where freedom reigns under Christian skies. This is not the world the Taliban-and-the-terrorists would "like to impose on the rest of us."

Just as I argued above that we need to be suspicious when neat cultural icons are plastered over messier historical and political narratives, so we need to be wary when Lord Cromer in British-ruled Egypt, French ladies in Algeria, and Laura Bush, all with military troops behind them, claim to be saving or liberating Muslim women.

POLITICS OF THE VEIL

I want now to look more closely at those Afghan women Laura Bush claimed were "rejoicing" at their liberation by the Americans. This necessitates a discussion of the veil, or the burqa, because it is so central to contemporary concerns about Muslim women. This will set the stage for a discussion of how anthropologists, feminist anthropologists in particular, contend with the problem of difference in a global world. In the conclusion, I will return to the rhetoric of saving Muslim women and offer an alternative.

It is common popular knowledge that the ultimate sign of the oppression of Afghan women under the Taliban-and-the-terrorists is that they were forced to wear the burqa. Liberals sometimes confess their surprise that even though Afghanistan has been liberated from the Taliban, women do not seem to be throwing off their burqas. Someone who has worked in Muslim regions must ask why this is so surprising. Did we expect that once "free" from the Taliban they would go "back" to belly shirts and blue leans, or dust off their Chanel suits? We need to be more sensible about the clothing of "women of cover, and so there is perhaps a need to make some basic points about veiling.

First, it should be recalled that the Taliban did not invent the burqa. It was the local form of covering that Pashtun women in one region wore when they went out. The Pashtun are one of several ethnic groups in Afghanistan and the burqa was one of many forms of covering in the subcontinent and

Southwest Asia that has developed as a convention for symbolizing women's modesty or respectability. The burqa, like some other forms of "cover" has, in many settings, marked the symbolic separation of men's and women's spheres, as part of the general association of women with family and home, not with public space where strangers mingled.

Twenty years ago the anthropologist Hanna Papanek (1982), who worked in Pakistan, described the burqa as "portable seclusion." She noted that many saw it as a liberating invention because it enabled women to move out of segregated living spaces while still observing the basic moral requirements of separating and protecting women from unrelated men. Ever since I came across her phrase "portable seclusion," I have thought of these enveloping robes as "mobile homes." Everywhere, such veiling signifies belonging to a particular community and participating in a moral way of life in which families are paramount in the organization of communities and the home is associated with the sanctity of women.

The obvious question that follows is this: If this were the case, why would women suddenly become immodest? Why would they suddenly throw off the markers of their respectability, markers, whether burqas or other forms of cover, which were supposed to assure their protection in the public sphere from the harassment of strange men by symbolically signaling to all that they were still in the inviolable space of their homes, even though moving in the public realm? Especially when these are forms of dress that had become so conventional that most women gave little thought to their meaning.

To draw some analogies, none of them perfect, why are we surprised that Afghan women do not throw off their burqas when we know perfectly well that it would not be appropriate to wear shorts to the opera? At the time these discussions of Afghan women's burqas were raging, a friend of mine was chided by her husband for suggesting she wanted to wear a pantsuit to a fancy wedding: "You know you don't wear pants to a WASP wedding," he reminded her. New Yorkers know that the beautifully coiffed Hasidic women, who look so fashionable next to their dour husbands in black coats and hats, are wearing wigs. This is because religious belief

and community standards of propriety require the covering of the hair. They also alter boutique fashions to include high necks and long sleeves. As anthropologists know perfectly well, people wear the appropriate form of dress for their social communities and are guided by socially shared standards, religious beliefs, and moral ideals, unless they deliberately transgress to make a point or are unable to afford proper cover. If we think that U.S. women live in a world of choice regarding clothing, all we need to do is remind ourselves of the expression, "the tyranny of fashion."

What had happened in Afghanistan under the Taliban is that one regional style of covering or veiling, associated with a certain respectable but not elite class, was imposed on everyone as "religiously" appropriate, even though previously there had been many different styles, popular or traditional with different groups and classes—different ways to mark women's propriety, or, in more recent times, religious piety. Although I am not an expert on Afghanistan, I imagine that the majority of women left in Afghanistan by the time the Taliban took control were the rural or less educated, from non elite families, since they were the only ones who could not emigrate to escape the hardship and violence that has marked Afghanistan's recent history. If liberated from the enforced wearing of burqas, most of these women would choose some other form of modest headcovering, like all those living nearby who were not under the Taliban—their rural Hindu counterparts in the North of India (who cover their heads and veil their faces from affines) or their Muslim sisters in Pakistan.

Even *The New York Times* carried an article about Afghan women refugees in Pakistan that attempted to educate readers about this local variety (Fremson 2001). The article describes and pictures everything from the now-iconic burqa with the embroidered eyeholes, which a Pashtun woman explains is the proper dress for her community, to large scarves they call chadors, to the new Islamic modest dress that wearers refer to as *hijab*. Those in the new Islamic dress are characteristically students heading for professional careers, especially in medicine, just like their counterparts from Egypt to Malaysia. One wearing the large scarf was a school principal; the other was a poor street vendor. The telling quote from the young street vendor is, "If I did [wear the burqa] the refugees would tease me because the burqa is for 'good women' who stay inside the home" (Fremson 2001:14). Here you can see the local status associated with the burqa—it is for good respectable women from strong families who are not forced to make a living selling on the street.

The British newspaper *The Guardian* published an interview in January 2002 with Dr. Suheila Siddiqi, a respected surgeon in Afghanistan who holds the rank of lieutenant general in the Afghan medical corps (Goldenberg 2002). A woman in her sixties, she comes from an elite family and, like her sisters, was educated. Unlike most women of her class, she chose not to go into exile. She is presented in the article as "the woman who stood up to the Taliban" because she refused to wear the burqa. She had made it a condition of returning to her post as head of a major hospital when the Taliban came begging in 1996, just eight months after firing her along with other women. Siddiqi is described as thin, glamorous, and confident. But further into the article it is noted that her graying bouffant hair is covered in a gauzy veil. This is a reminder that though she refused the burqa, she had no question about wearing the chador or scarf.

Finally, I need to make a crucial point about veiling. Not only are there many forms of covering, which themselves have different meanings in the communities in which they are used, but also veiling itself must not be confused with, or made to stand for, lack of agency. As I have argued in my ethnography of a Bedouin community in Egypt in the late 1970s and 1980s (1986), pulling the black head cloth over the face in front of older respected men is considered a voluntary act by women who are deeply committed to being moral and have a sense of honor tied to family. One of the ways they show their standing is by covering their faces in certain contexts. They decide for whom they feel it is appropriate to veil.

To take a very different case, the modern Islamic modest dress that many educated women across the Muslim world have taken on since the mid-1970s now both publicly marks piety and can be read as a sign of educated urban sophistication, a sort of modernity (e.g., Abu Lughod 1995, 1998; Brenner 1996; El Guindi 1999; MacLeod 1991; Ong 1990). As Saba Mahmood (2001) has so brilliantly shown in her ethnography of women in the mosque movement in Egypt, this new form of dress is also perceived by many of the women who adopt it as part of a bodily means to cultivate virtue, the outcome of their professed desire to be close to God.

Two points emerge from this fairly basic discussion of the meanings of veiling in the contemporary Muslim world. First, we need to work against the reductive interpretation of veiling as the quintessential sign of women's unfreedom, even if we object to state imposition of this form, as in Iran or with the Taliban. (It must be recalled that the modernizing states of Turkey and Iran had earlier in the century banned veiling and required men, except religious clerics, to adopt Western dress.) What does freedom mean if we accept the fundamental premise that humans are social beings, always raised in certain social and historical contexts and belonging to particular communities that shape their desires and understandings of the world? Is it not a gross violation of women's own understandings of what they are doing to simply denounce the burqa as a medieval imposition? Second, we must take care not to reduce the diverse situations and attitudes of millions of Muslim women to a single item of clothing. Perhaps it is time to give up the Western obsession with the veil and focus on some serious issues with which feminists and others should indeed be concerned.

Ultimately, the significant political–ethical problem the burqa raises is how to deal with cultural "others." How are we to deal with difference without accepting the passivity implied by the cultural relativism for which anthropologists are justly famous— a relativism that says it's their culture and it's not my business to judge or interfere, only to try to understand. Cultural relativism is certainly an improvement on ethnocentrism and the racism, cultural imperialism, and imperiousness that underlie it; the problem is that it is too late not to interfere. The forms of lives we find around the world are already products of long histories of interactions.

I want to explore the issues of women, cultural relativism, and the problems of "difference" from

three angles. First, I want to consider what feminist anthropologists (those stuck in that awkward
relationship, as Strathern [1987] has claimed) are
to do with strange political bedfellows. I used to
feel torn when I received the e-mail petitions cir-
culating for the last few years in defense of Afghan
women under the Taliban. I was not sympathetic to
the dogmatism of the Taliban; I do not support the
oppression of women. But the provenance of the
campaign worried me, I do not usually find myself
in political company with the likes of Hollywood
celebrities (see Hirschkind and Mahmood 2002).
I had never received a petition from such women
defending the right of Palestinian women to safety
from Israeli bombing or daily harassment at check-
points, asking the United States to reconsider its
support for a government that had dispossessed
them, closed them out from work and citizenship
rights, refused them the most basic freedoms. Maybe
some of these same people might be signing petitions to save African women from genital cutting,
or Indian women from dowry deaths. However, I
do not think that it would be as easy to mobilize so
many of these American and European women if it
were not a case of Muslim men oppressing Muslim
women—women of cover for whom they can feel
sorry and in relation to whom they can feel smugly
superior. Would television diva Oprah Winfrey
host the Women in Black, the women's peace group
from Israel, as she did RAWA, the Revolutionary
Association of Women of Afghanistan, who were
also granted the *Glamour Magazine* Women of the
Year Award? What are we to make of post-Taliban
"Reality Tours" such as the one advertised on the
internet by Global Exchange for March 2002 under
the title "Courage and Tenacity: A Women's Delegation to Afghanistan"? The rationale for the $1,400
tour is that "with the removal of the Taliban government, Afghan women, for the first time in the
past decade, have the opportunity to reclaim their
basic human rights and establish their role as equal
citizens by participating in the rebuilding of their
nation." The tour's objective, to celebrate International Women's Week, is "to develop awareness of
the concerns and issues the Afghan women are facing as well as to witness the changing political, economic, and social conditions which have created

new opportunities for the women of Afghanistan"
(Global Exchange 2002).

To be critical of this celebration of women's
rights in Afghanistan is not to pass judgment on any
local women's organizations, such as RAWA, whose
members have courageously worked since 1977 for
a democratic secular Afghanistan in which women's
human rights are respected, against Soviet-backed
regimes or U.S.-, Saudi-, and Pakistani-supported
conservatives. Their documentation of abuse and
their work through clinics and schools have been
enormously important.

It is also not to fault the campaigns that exposed
the dreadful conditions under which the Taliban
placed women. The Feminist Majority campaign
helped put a stop to a secret oil pipeline deal
between the Taliban and the U.S. multinational
Unocal that was going forward with U.S. administration support. Western feminist campaigns must
not be confused with the hypocrisies of the new
colonial feminism of a Republican president who
was not elected for his progressive stance on feminist issues or of administrations that played down
the terrible record of violations of women by the
United State's allies in the Northern Alliance, as
documented by Human Rights Watch and Amnesty
International, among others. Rapes and assaults
were widespread in the period of infighting that
devastated Afghanistan before the Taliban came in
to restore order.

It is, however, to suggest that we need to look
closely at what we are supporting (and what we are
not) and to think carefully about why. How should
we manage the complicated politics and ethics
of finding ourselves in agreement with those with
whom we normally disagree? I do not know how
many feminists who felt good about saving Afghan
women from the Taliban are also asking for a global
redistribution of wealth or contemplating sacrificing their own consumption radically so that African
or Afghan women could have some chance of having what I do believe should be a universal human
right—the right to freedom from the structural
violence of global inequality and from the rav-
ages of war, the everyday rights of having enough
to eat, having homes for their families in which to
live and thrive, having ways to make decent livings

so their children can grow, and having the strength and security to work out, within their communities and with whatever alliances they want, how to live a good life, which might very well include changing the ways those communities are organized.

Suspicion about bedfellows is only a first step; it will not give us a way to think more positively about what to do or where to stand. For that, we need to confront two more big issues. First is the acceptance of the possibility of difference. Can we only free Afghan women to be like us or might we have to recognize that even after "liberation" from the Taliban, they might want different things than we would want for them? What do we do about that? Second, we need to be vigilant about the rhetoric of saving people because of what it implies about our attitudes.

Again, when I talk about accepting difference, I am not implying that we should resign ourselves to being cultural relativists who respect whatever goes on elsewhere as "just their culture." I have already discussed the dangers of "cultural" explanations; "their" cultures are just as much part of history and an interconnected world as ours are. What I am advocating is the hard work involved in recognizing and respecting differences—precisely as products of different histories, as expressions of different circumstances, and as manifestations of differently structured desires. We may want justice for women, but can we accept that there might be different ideas about justice and that different women might want, or choose, different futures from what we envision as best (see Ong 1988)? We must consider that they might be called to personhood, so to speak, in a different language.

One of the things we have to be most careful about in thinking about Third World feminisms, and feminism in different parts of the Muslim world, is how not to fall into polarizations that place feminism on the side of the West. I have written about the dilemmas faced by Arab feminists when Western feminists initiate campaigns that make them vulnerable to local denunciations by conservatives of various sorts, whether Islamist or nationalist, of being traitors (Abu Lughod 2001). As some like Afsaneh Najmabadi are now arguing, not only is it wrong to see history simplistically in terms of

a putative opposition between Islam and the West (as is happening in the United States now and has happened in parallel in the Muslim world), but it is also strategically dangerous to accept this cultural opposition between Islam and the West, between fundamentalism and feminism, because those many people within Muslim countries who are trying to find alternatives to present injustices, those who might want to refuse the divide and take from different histories and cultures, who do not accept that being feminist means being Western, will be under pressure to choose, just as we are: Are you with us or against us?

My point is to remind us to be aware of differences, respectful of other paths toward social change that might give women better lives. Can there be a liberation that is Islamic? And, beyond this, is liberation even a goal for which all women or people strive? Are emancipation, equality, and rights part of a universal language we must use? To quote Saba Mahmood, writing about the women in Egypt who are seeking to become pious Muslims, "The desire for freedom and liberation is a historically situated desire whose motivational force cannot be assumed a priori, but needs to be reconsidered in light of other desires, aspirations, and capacities that inhere in a culturally and historically located subject" (2001:223). In other words, might other desires be more meaningful for different groups of people? Living in close families? Living in a godly way? Living without war? I have done fieldwork in Egypt over more than 20 years and I cannot think of a single woman I know, from the poorest rural to the most educated cosmopolitan, who has ever expressed envy of U.S. women, women they tend to perceive as bereft of community, vulnerable to sexual violence and social anomie, driven by individual success rather than morality, or strangely disrespectful of God.

BEYOND THE RHETORIC OF SALVATION

Let us return, finally, to my title, "Do Muslim Women Need Saving?" The discussion of culture, veiling, and how one can navigate the shoals of cultural difference should put Laura Bush's self-congratulation about the rejoicing of Afghan women liberated by American troops in a different light. It is deeply problematic to construct the Afghan woman as someone in need of saving. When you save someone, you imply that you are saving her from something. You are also saving her *to* something. What violences are entailed in this transformation, and what presumptions are being made about the superiority of that to which you are saving her? Projects of saving other women depend on and reinforce a sense of superiority by Westerners, a form of arrogance that deserves to be challenged. All one needs to do to appreciate the patronizing quality of the rhetoric of saving women is to imagine using it today in the United States about disadvantaged groups such as African American women or working-class women. We now understand them as suffering from structural violence. We have become politicized about race and class, but not culture.

As anthropologists, feminists, or concerned citizens, we should be wary of taking on the mantles of those 19th-century Christian missionary women who devoted their lives to saving their Muslim sisters. One of my favorite documents from that period is a collection called *Our Moslem Sisters*, the proceedings of a conference of women missionaries held in Cairo in 1906 (Van Sommer and Zwemmer 1907). The subtitle of the book is *A Cry of Need from the Lands of Darkness Interpreted by Those Who Heard It*. Speaking of the ignorance, seclusion, polygamy, and veiling that blighted women's lives across the Muslim world, the missionary women spoke of their responsibility to make these women's voices heard. As the introduction states, "They will never cry for themselves, for they are down under the yoke of centuries of oppression" (Van Sommer and Zwemer 1907:15). "This book," it begins, "with its sad, reiterated story of wrong and oppression is an indictment and an appeal. It is an appeal to Christian womanhood to right these wrongs and enlighten this darkness by sacrifice and service" (Van Sommer and Zwemer 1907:5).

One can hear uncanny echoes of their virtuous goals today, even though the language is secular, the appeals not to Jesus but to human rights or the liberal West. The continuing currency of such imagery and sentiments can be seen in their deployment for perfectly good humanitarian causes. In February 2002, I received an invitation to a reception honoring an international medical humanitarian network called Médecins du Monde/Doctors of the World (MdM). Under the sponsorship of the French Ambassador to the United States, the Head of the delegation of the European Commission to the United Nations, and a member of the European Parliament, the cocktail reception was to feature an exhibition of photographs under the clichéd title "Afghan Women: Behind the Veil."

The invitation was remarkable not just for the colorful photograph of women in flowing burqas walking across the barren mountains of Afghanistan but also for the text, a portion of which I quote:

> For 20 years MdM has been ceaselessly struggling to help those who are most vulnerable. But increasingly, thick veils cover the victims of the war. When the Taliban came to power in 1996, Afghan Women became faceless. To unveil one's face while receiving medical care was to achieve a sort of intimacy, find a brief space for secret freedom and recover a little of one's dignity. In a country where women had no access to basic medical care because they did not have the right to appear in public, where women had no right to practice medicine, MdM's program stood as a stubborn reminder of human rights. . . . Please join us in helping to lift the veil.

Although I cannot take up here the fantasies of intimacy associated with unveiling, fantasies reminiscent of the French colonial obsessions so brilliantly unmasked by Alloula in *The Colonial Harem* (1986), I can ask why humanitarian projects and human rights discourse in the 21st century need rely on such constructions of Muslim women.

Could we not leave veils and vocations of saving others behind and instead train our sights on ways to make the world a more just place? The reason respect for difference should not be confused with cultural relativism is that it does not preclude asking how we, living in this privileged and powerful part of the world, might examine our own responsibilities for the situations in which others in distant places have found themselves. We do not stand outside the world, looking out over this sea of poor benighted people, living under the shadow—or veil—of oppressive cultures; we are part of that world. Islamic movements themselves have arisen in a world shaped by the intense engagements of Western powers in Middle Eastern lives.

A more productive approach, it seems to me, is to ask how we might contribute to making the world a more just place. A world not organized around strategic military and economic demands; a place where certain kinds of forces and values that we may still consider important could have an appeal and where there is the peace necessary for discussions, debates, and transformations to occur within communities. We need to ask ourselves what kinds of world conditions we could contribute to making such that popular desires will not be overdetermined by an overwhelming sense of helplessness in the face of forms of global injustice. Where we seek to be active in the affairs of distant places, can we do so in the spirit of support for those within those communities whose goals are to make women's (and men's) lives better? Can we use a more egalitarian language of alliances, coalitions, and solidarity, instead of salvation?

Even RAWA, the now celebrated Revolutionary Association of the Women of Afghanistan, which was so instrumental in bringing to U.S. women's attention the excesses of the Taliban, has opposed the U.S. bombing from the beginning. They do not see in it Afghan women's salvation but increased hardship and loss. They have long called for disarmament and for peacekeeping forces. Spokespersons point out the dangers of confusing governments with people, the Taliban with innocent Afghans who will be most harmed. They consistently remind audiences to take a close look at the ways policies are being organized around oil interests, the arms industry, and the international drug trade. They are not obsessed with the veil, even though they are the most radical feminists working for a secular democratic Afghanistan. Unfortunately, only their messages about the excesses of the Taliban have been heard, even though their criticisms of those in power in Afghanistan have included previous regimes. A first step in hearing their wider message is to break with the language of alien cultures, whether to understand or eliminate them. Missionary work and colonial feminism belong in the past. Our task is to critically explore what we might do to help create a world in which those poor Afghan women, for whom "the hearts of those in the civilized world break," can have safety and decent lives.

REFERENCES CITED

Abu Lughod, Lila
    1986 Veiled Sentiments: Honor and Poetry in a Bedouin Society. Berkeley: University of California Press.
    1995 Movie Stars and Islamic Moralism in Egypt. Social Text 42:53–67.
    1998 Remaking Women: Feminism and Modernity in the Middle East. Princeton: Princeton University Press.
    2001 Orientalism and Middle East Feminist Studies. Feminist Studies 27(I):101–113.
Ahmed, Leila
    1992 Women and Gender in Islam. New Haven, CT: Yale University Press.
Alloula, Malek
    1986 The Colonial Harem. Minneapolis: University of Minnesota Press.
Brenner, Suzanne
    1996 Reconstructing Self and Society: Javanese Muslim Women and "the Veil." American Ethnologist 23(4):673–697.
El Guindi, Fadwa
    1999 Veil: Modesty, Privacy and Resistance. Oxford: Berg.
Fremson, Ruth
    2001 Allure Must Be Covered. Individuality Peeks Through. New York Times, November 4: 14.
Global Exchange
    2002 Courage and Tenacity: A Women's Delegation to Afghanistan. Electronic document, http://www.globalexchange.org/tours/auto/2002-03-05_CourageandTenacityAWomensDele.html. Accessed February 11.
Goldenberg, Suzanne
    2002 The Woman Who Stood Up to the Taliban. The Guardian, January 24, Electronic document, http://222.guardian.co.uk/afghanistan/story/0,1284,63840.
Hirschkind, Charles, and Saba Mahmood
    2002 Feminism, the Taliban, and the Politics of Counter-Insurgency. Anthropological Quarterly, Volume 75(2):107–122.
Lazreg, Marnia
    1994 The Eloquence of Silence: Algerian Women in Question. New York: Routledge.

MacLeod, Arlene
    1991 Accommodating Protest. New York: Columbia University Press.
Mahmood, Saba
    2001 Feminist Theory, Embodiment, and the Docile Agent: Some Reflections on the Egyptian Islamic Revival. Cultural Anthropology 16(2):202–235.
Mir-Hosseini, Ziba
    1999 Islam and Gender: The Religious Debate in Contemporary Iran. Princeton: Princeton University Press.
Moghissi, Haideh
    1999 Feminism and Islamic Fundamentalism. London: Zed Books.
Najmabadi, Afsaneh.
    1998 Feminism in an Islamic Republic. *In* Islam, Gender and Social Change. Yvonne Haddad and John Esposito, eds. Pp. 59–84. New York: Oxford University Press.
    2000 (Un)Veiling Feminism. Social Text 64: 29–45.
Ong, Aihwa
    1988 Colonialism and Modernity: Feminist Re-Presentations of Women in Non-Western Societies. Inscriptions 3–4:79–93.
    1990 State Versus Islam: Malay Families, Women's Bodies, and the Body Politic in Malaysia. American Ethnologist 17(2):258–276.

Papanek, Hanna
    1982 Purdah in Pakistan: Seclusion and Modern Occupations for Women. *In* Separate Worlds. Hanna Papanek and Gail Minault, eds. Pp. 190–216. Columbus, MO: South Asia Books.
Safire, William
    2001 "On Language." New York Times Magazine, October 28: 22.
Spivak, Gayatri Chakravorty
    1988 Can the Subaltern Speak? *In* Marxism and the Interpretation of Culture, Cary Nelson and Lawrence Grossberg, eds. Pp. 271–313. Urbana: University of Illinois Press.
Strathern, Marilyn
    1987 An Awkward Relationship: The Case of Feminism and Anthropology. Signs 12:276–292.
U.S. Government
    1907 Our Moslem Sisters: A Cry of Need from Lands of Darkness Interpreted by Those Who Heard It. New York: Fleming H. Revell Co.
    2002 Electronic document, http://www.whitehouse.gov/news/releases/2001/11/20011117. Accessed January 10.
Walley, Christine
    1997 Searching for "Voices": Feminism, Anthropology, and the Global Debate over Female Genital Operations. Cultural Anthropology 12(3):405–438.

Integrating the Themes: HIV/AIDS in Women's Lives

Sonia M. Kandathil and *Janet Lee*

Sonia M. Kandathil works as a public policy consultant and focuses on women's health research and legislation, in particular HIV/AIDS. She served nationally at the U.S. federal level, educating policymakers about current HIV/AIDS issues and has also worked in the office of Rep. Lois Capps (D–CA) where she served as a legislative assistant, helping to craft key HIV/AIDS legislation. Ms. Kandathil earned her MPH from Oregon State University, USA, and is currently finishing her doctoral dissertation on the influences of relationship dynamics on the use of HIV prevention technologies for women. She recently coauthored the article, "An Overview of Effective and Promising Interventions to Prevent HIV Infection," published as part of the World Health Organization's compendium entitled, "Preventing HIV/AIDS in Young People: A Systematic Review of the Evidence from Developing Countries."

We close *Women Worldwide* with a focus on HIV/AIDS in women's lives because this phenomenon illustrates the nexus of issues covered in all chapters and represents the intersectionality of such themes as poverty, education, sexuality and bodies, reproductive health, families, and sex work. At the core of this disease is a crisis of gender inequality that ultimately impedes women from making decisions about their bodies and lives. This conclusion seeks to provide a sharpened understanding of the confluence of chapter themes by introducing the AIDS epidemic as a case study and providing examples in the form of personal narratives about women living with HIV/AIDS worldwide. We hope to apply knowledge already gleaned throughout *Women Worldwide* to the practical example of HIV/AIDS. This application begins with a brief overview of the pandemic and is followed by two sections that discuss interconnected explanations for the feminization of the disease and suggest individual and social structural-level strategies for addressing the problem. Following this essay are personal narratives by women that provide real-life examples of struggles with the disease. These stories illustrate despair, courage, and hope, as well as provide reflections on the themes of the preceding chapters.

More than 25 years have passed since the discovery of HIV, the virus that causes AIDS. Although at first the epidemic in the U.S. was most pronounced among men who have sex with men (who may consider themselves gay or not), as the epidemic progressed and the dynamics of the disease changed, what was once considered a disease that primarily affects this group is today a disease that affects all people, and especially heterosexual women. Indeed, global trends indicate that women represent the new face of HIV/AIDS. At the

A global view of HIV infection

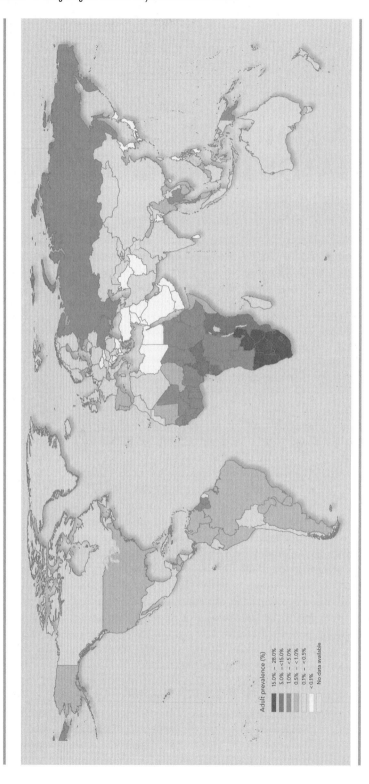

Adult prevalence (%)

15.0% – 28.0%
5.0% – <15.0%
1.0% – <5.0%
0.5% – <1.0%
0.1% – <0.5%
<0.1%

No data available

end of 2007, almost 40 million adults were living with HIV/AIDS and approximately half of these infections occurred among women (UNAIDS, 2007). This is now characterized as pandemic since it is an epidemic of infectious disease that has spread through populations and across continents worldwide. This "globalization" of the disease reflects the forces of cultural and economic globalization that have increased the vulnerability of many women, especially in the Global South.

The problem is felt most profoundly in sub-Saharan Africa where women are disproportionately affected by HIV/AIDS, making up 61 percent of adults living with HIV. In addition, young women in sub-Saharan Africa aged 15–24 years are three times more likely to be infected than young men of the same age (UNAIDS, 2004, 2005; UNAIDS/UNFPA/UNIFEM, 2004). Of all women living with HIV worldwide, 89 percent of them live in this region (UNAIDS, 2007). Similar trends exist in other parts of the world, where the epidemic is steadily growing among women in southern and southeastern Asia, eastern Europe and central Asia, Latin America, and the Caribbean. Data from the United States show women comprising almost one-quarter of all HIV/AIDS cases there with most women acquiring the disease through heterosexual sex. Further analysis indicates the racial and ethnic inequities among HIV-positive women in the United States as Black women comprised over half of all new infections in 2006, followed by Hispanic and then White women (Centers for Disease Control and Prevention, 2008a, 2008b). The first story about Janice, Marvelyn, and Michelle, three African-American women whose lives changed when they were diagnosed HIV positive, illustrates the special burden of the disease for Black women who account for almost two-thirds of all women living with HIV/AIDS in the United States.

A serious consequence of HIV/AIDS infections among women is its effect on children. Hundreds of thousands of children across the world become infected with HIV every year, with most acquiring the disease from mothers during pregnancy, birth, or breastfeeding. As of 2007, approximately 2 million children under 15 years worldwide are infected, with 9 out of 10 children living in sub-Saharan Africa (UNICEF, 2008). In addition, millions more children who are not infected with HIV are indirectly affected by the epidemic as a result of death and suffering associated with AIDS in their families and communities. It can be argued that every child growing up in an area with high HIV prevalence is affected by the epidemic, regardless of whether they, or a close family member, are infected. Approximately 15 million children worldwide have lost one or both parents to AIDS, putting them at risk for poverty, homelessness, school drop-out, discrimination, and loss of life opportunities (UNICEF, 2008). Resisting these realities is 12-year-old Honduran Keren Dunaway featured in Story 2. Keren is HIV positive, open about her status, and optimistic about her future since she has both medical and emotional support. Her parents are founders of *Llaves,* an AIDS advocacy group, and Keren herself travels the world speaking out on AIDS. She has started *Llavecitas,* a children's magazine associated with *Llaves.*

THE FEMINIZATION OF HIV/AIDS

Rapidly rising rates of HIV infection among women have led scientists to coin the term "feminization of AIDS" to describe perceived and real gender inequalities that exist within the constructs of this social phenomenon. Specifically, the term implies an increase in the very real difference in the incidence and prevalence of HIV/AIDS between women and men, the importance of the role that gender inequities play as contributing factors in the rising rates of HIV/AIDS among women, and the particular ways in which HIV/AIDS affects women in their everyday lives. This definition allows an exploration of the nuances and factors associated with the pandemic among women and children. Indeed, HIV/AIDS is one of the most intriguing diseases to study because no single risk factor has been attributable to increases in incidence and prevalence, especially among women. Instead it is the confluence (or coming together and blending) of biological, behavioral, and sociocultural factors associated with the many themes of *Women Worldwide* that has led to the feminization of AIDS. This is a particularly profound revelation because it means that a variety of strategies are needed to curtail the problem.

In terms of biological factors, the human body is a complex organ of thousands of different cells and systems. While both the male and female bodies are equally sophisticated and during most instances equally susceptible to disease, women appear to be more physiologically vulnerable to getting HIV than men due to the specific biology of the female genital tract with its larger surface across which the virus may pass. This means that the chances of male-to-female transmission are greater than female-to-male. In addition, the presence of certain sexually transmitted infections (STIs) (such as herpes, chancroid, and primary syphilis) that cause genital ulcers and lesions also help facilitate the acquisition of HIV among women.

Despite these biological factors, most scholars argue that the primary driver of HIV/AIDS is sociocultural factors that structure the lives of women and men differently and shape their behaviors. In societies where cultural norms about female sexuality fuel stigma and discrimination, and misogynous values devalue the lives of girls and women, gendered behaviors make women more vulnerable to AIDS as well as other health problems: a key theme of chapter 5 on women and health. Indeed, scientists isolated several behaviors that increase HIV risk among women. The first factor is lack of power in families and sexual relationships. As discussed throughout *Women Worldwide*, when women are socialized to be submissive on issues related to the body and sexuality and are therefore unable to negotiate condom use successfully, demand comprehensive sexuality education, and fight for reproductive rights, they are not only at higher risk of contracting the disease but also less likely to be able to access critical services. As Penny Van Esterik explains in chapter 3, the ability to have control over the body is central for women's autonomy and power. There is a strong relationship between gender-power imbalances and a woman's HIV/AIDS status, as women's subordination not only increases risk factors contributing to HIV, but effectively limits women's ability to negotiate and control their sexuality. And as Meg Wilkes Karraker and Patti Duncan emphasize in chapters 7 and 8 on family and violence against women, the case of girls in child marriages is a case in point. The risk for HIV infection is especially increased among adolescent women who engage in relationships or sex acts with men who are significantly older. Older men may prefer girls and young women as sexual partners because they are perceived to be HIV free. This commonly held perception, plus the economic need of many young women, makes for a dangerous and potentially fatal combination. Several studies show that the greater the age differences between men and women, the higher the risk for HIV infection (Gregson et al., 2002; Kelly et al., 2003). Differences in age represent power inequalities between men and women or girls and therefore are determinants of such unsafe behaviors as lack of condom use and inadequate communication around safer sex.

Power inequalities in relationships are also, of course, implicated in interpersonal violence, a focus of chapter 8, that underscores the importance of acknowledging how gender-based violence and relationship control contribute to women's vulnerability to HIV/AIDS. Story 3 features Jacqueline from Uganda who was brutally beaten and raped by her husband prior to his death by AIDS. She was unable to ask him to wear a condom because she feared his violence. This story also features Isata from Sierra Leone who was gang-raped by rebels during the conflict in her country. As Mary Hawkesworth explains in chapter 12 on war and peace, women are especially vulnerable in conflict situations, during military occupations, and when they are forced to relocate or become refugees.

The second factor associated with gendered power imbalances that puts women at increased risk of exposure to HIV/AIDS is the issue of multiple sexual partnerships. Women who are in relationships with men who have sex with other women (including sex workers) are at an especially high risk. As emphasized by Charmaine Pereira and Priya Kandaswamy in their focus on sexuality in chapter 4, women tend not to be in a position to address sexual behaviors of husbands and partners because they are economically dependent upon them and/or cultural norms forbid such communication. Juanita Elias discusses economic dependency in chapter 9 on work and employment, emphasizing the vulnerabilities encountered by women who are not economically self-sufficient. In addition, women who themselves have multiple partners are also at a high risk. When women's economic security is threatened and where opportunities for income generation are limited or not available, women are often forced into situations that put them at increased risk for HIV. One of these situations is sex work: perhaps the only option for women who need to support children and families.

Some women engage in "formal" sex work which takes place in establishments like brothels, nightclubs, drinking houses, and massage parlors (Tawil et al., 2002). Other women, however, engage in informal sex work as streetwalkers or self-employed call girls. These women may also occasionally participate in what is often termed "survival sex," a form of sex that generates income or leads to access and privileges necessary for everyday survival, including food, housing, healthcare, etc. (Otto, 2007). Other women may hold jobs that generate very little income and resort to sex work as a way to supplement their wages to support themselves and their families (Tawil et al., 2002). Ana Isla and Trina Filan discuss such situations in chapter 10 when focusing on environmental politics. As women lose traditional relationships to the land and are forced into cities where they are vulnerable to exploitation, they may seek sex work in order to provide for themselves and their families. Becoming environmental refugees as a result of the consequences of global climate change is one situation that leads women into "survival sex." Story 4 features Srey from Cambodia who was forced to become a prostitute when she was 14 years old and who subsequently was infected by HIV. Although her story is poignant, she survives to help similarly trafficked girls.

Finally, studies show that use of alcohol and drugs doubles women's risk of contracting HIV/AIDS, and women who frequently use are at a higher risk for contracting HIV than those who do not (Rasch et al., 2000; Zule, Flannery, Wechsberg, and Lam, 2002). Alcohol and especially drug use can push women into such risky behaviors as commercial sex work where money and drugs are easily traded for sex, and women may experience further risk for contracting HIV. Drug use also decreases inhibitions, helping to facilitate multiple partners and the lack of consistent condom use. While these behaviors have been associated with increased risk of getting HIV/AIDS, it is important to note that they occur within certain sociocultural contexts that also confer increased vulnerability on women. What this means is that women who use drugs, engage in multiple partnerships, and fail to use condoms consistently are not necessarily freely "choosing" these behaviors. Rather, they tend to be influenced by forces outside of their control. As emphasized in the chapters 4 and 8 on sexuality and gendered violence, there is a complex interplay of behavioral and sociocultural factors which work together to intensify risk among women.

These three behavioral factors discussed above (lack of power in families and relationships; multiple sexual partnerships; and alcohol and drug use) are linked in their relationship to women's economic and political status in societies. Indeed, this focus on poverty and citizenship are central themes running through all chapters of *Women Worldwide*, especially the focus on political and socioeconomic consequences of economic globalization. In this way, as discussed by Juanita Elias in chapter 9 on work and economics and by Melanie Hughes and Pamela Paxton in chapter 11 on women and politics, poverty and lack of political rights are key factors in understanding the feminization of HIV/AIDS. As discussed, across the globe women depend on husbands, male partners, or male family members for economic security. In situations where money and resources are limited and both men and women of the same household are HIV positive, it is often the male whose treatment needs are served first. Just as in patriarchal societies when food is scarce and men and boys eat first, when resources are scarce, males are the ones who get treatment. Property and inheritance rights have also been cited as a reason for supporting treatment for men versus women. If a woman's husband dies, the property may be inherited by his family of origin, thus providing no means of financial support for wives and children. And finally, of course, poverty has been implicated in lack of access to treatment where women with limited income generating power cannot afford costly medication. Poverty in families and communities, especially in sub-Saharan Africa, is a central aspect of the stories featured here.

Associated with poverty, lack of education can also lead to increased risk of HIV for women. As already discussed in other chapters of *Women Worldwide*, many young women around the world receive little or no education or are forced to drop out of school to help support their families. As a consequence, women and girls are not only less educated, but know less about HIV/AIDS than do boys and men. Sometimes this lack of information is associated with norms of female modesty and chastity. Studies indicate that the more education and training young women have, the less likely they are to engage in risky behaviors. Where access to education between men and women has been equal, HIV infection rates are found to be significantly lower (Over, 1998). The way illiteracy and lack of education limit women's access to health outcomes constitute an important point made by Mehra Shirazi in chapter 5 on women's health.

Poverty can also be a consequence of HIV/AIDS in terms of the way the disease impacts households and leaves women to bear the economic burden of the disease. This is the case for South African Mantombi Nyawo featured in Story 5. She cares for a host of children that include her own youngest offspring as well as grandchildren. She struggles on a small income made more precarious by a husband who spends money on nonessential items and by the loss of income associated with the deaths of the parents of her grandchildren. Indeed, according to recent data, AIDS-related losses can reduce household income by nearly 80 percent. This significant loss in income not only leads women into risky behaviors but exacerbates the overall household vulnerability to HIV/AIDS. Household vulnerability means that a woman's property and inheritance rights may not be secure. In economic terms, property and land are chief assets and are not only considered places to live and sources of income but are often used as collateral for credit and other needed services. Story 6 features Parvati and Fatima, both from India. Parvati lives in hardship and poverty with few resources to deal with her failing health and dependent children. Fatima is more fortunate in having resources and a supportive family. She has been able to turn her tragedy into work with UNIFEM to advocate for ending violence against women.

A DAY IN THE LIFE **Dutiful Daughter** by *Amber Wilburn*

Kagiso ("peace") lives in a small rural village in southeastern Botswana called Tsholofelo ("hope"). The village was founded in 1965, two years after the borders between Botswana and South Africa were established, requiring that all Botswana-born people had to return to Botswana. Kagiso's grandparents and her parents as infants were among the first settlers of the village, which her grandparents helped to name.

Each day Kagiso arises at 3 a.m. in order to prepare for her day, which normally consists of keeping house, caring for her mother, and harvesting corn. Often, as is the case today, she will travel to the neighboring village, Tebogo, to purchase food and supplies. Thankfully, it is July—the coolest month of the year—which means the June harvest has come to an end and hunting season begins. When the June harvest is good, and the ancestors smile upon the village by bringing rain, the men return within a week; however, when the ancestors are unhappy—as seemed to be the case this year—the men will be gone longer.

Today, Kagiso will travel to the river to do laundry and then to Tebogo. Her cousins, Kefilwe and Sethunya, will join her. They will start their journey early since they want to return before nightfall at 6 p.m.; they never know who (or what) they will run into on the way.

But first . . . .

"O tsogile jang?" ("How did you wake?"), Kagiso asks her mother as she places a dish of maize porridge and a cup of *kgadi*[1] on the dirt floor next to her mother's bedside. The two women live in a small, one-room house with circular clay walls and a pointed thatch roof. This house is the same style as those found in the village Tsholofelo's first inhabitants lived in.

"Ke tsogile sentle, ngwana," ("I'm well, child"), her mother responds, attempting to pick up the bowl. *"Sitwa,"* ("Feeling cold"), she adds breathlessly before Kagiso can gather her own breakfast. Kagiso finds a piece of cloth to cover her mother who is too weak to feed herself. Like a dutiful daughter, Kagiso feeds her. They share few words, mostly about the weather and the June harvest.

After her mother finishes, Kagiso eats and dresses. She prepares her mother's lunch and leaves it by the door. In any other village, because she and her mother gave birth to no male children, they would be despised; however, since they are descendents from Tsholofelo's founders and her mother is an elder, they receive much respect. This means that instead of her mother having to fend for herself in her daughter's absence, female neighbors will come and care for her until Kagiso returns.

Kagiso is wearing a traditional bright orange, yellow, and brown handmade skirt with a nontraditional bright yellow T-shirt she was given after she visited Tebogo. Her mother told her the yellow shirt complemented her dark skin beautifully. If she knew Kagiso received it from a woman working at the Tebogo clinic, she would have had a fit. In fact, Kagiso's mother may disown her if she discovers Kagiso and Sethunya both visit the clinic once a month while doing laundry, for doing so would imply they had the sickness.

At about 5 a.m., Kagiso, Kefilwe, and Sethunya gather and set off for the river. While on their walk, they speak of the lengthy time their men will be away hunting and the latest village gossip. This journey to and fro takes them a good portion of the day; Tebogo is nearly three and one-half hours away, and the river another hour.

They arrive at the river around 9:30 a.m. and begin their wash. About an hour later, two women from the Tebogo clinic arrive and give them their "supplies"; Kagiso and Sethunya both receive a month's supply of antiretroviral drugs for themselves and their mothers, while Kefilwe receives a month's supply for herself and her three sons. The women converse with the clinic workers in broken English and with each other in their native language, *Tswana*. Kagiso learns that her and her mother's regimens have been increased: instead of taking two pills each day, they will now take three in six-hour sequences starting at 7 a.m.

Once the *baeng* (visitors) leave, the women talk about learning of the sickness (HIV). Kagiso shares how as a young girl she heard her mother and other women speak of their husband's working in the diamond mines. In later years, she would join these discussions and note the hushed conversations about a new sickness the men were bringing back. When she asked her mother what the sickness was, she was severely reprimanded.

"No one speaks of it," her mother told her, "and neither will you."

Upon returning one year, Kagiso's father became ill and died two years later of an unknown cause. Soon after his death, her mother began suffering from *boswagadi*, or the widow's disease. Though a ritual purification was performed as is customary to rid *boswagadi*, her mother had not recovered. That same year Kagiso's own husband died while returning to the village.

They talk about the day, five years ago, when Kagiso convinced them to stop at the Tebogo clinic where they were told of a disease called HIV/AIDS that was increasing in their country. Remembering her chastisement as a child, Kagiso refused to be tested—for like many Batswana, she did not want to know if she had it. The clinician's description of HIV transmission sounded very much like *meila*[2]. Listening to the symptoms, Kagiso determined that her father and husband died of the sickness and that her mother did not have *boswagadi*, but HIV/AIDS. They took the medications offered. Since neither of them could read the English label, they were told when and how to take the medications. They planned to meet secretively each month by the river; news travels fast between villages, even those four hours apart.

Though Botswana has one of Africa's most progressive programs for HIV/AIDS treatment, which includes free or cheap generic antiretroviral drugs, Kagiso sees little evidence of these programs in her rural village. Tebogo, though relatively poor by rural standards, at least has a clinic where medications are offered and received. She, on the other hand, travels eight hours a month, crushes four (now six) pills per day and places them in her and her mother's food, a small price to pay for life.

After the laundry is complete, the women hide the medications in their folded laundry and head for Tebogo to purchase the onions and potatoes. They do not return to Tsholofelo until nearly 5:30 p.m.

Instead of joining the other village members, Kagiso returns to her home to wash and feed her mother. Around 9, her mother is given swill with crushed medication and then put to bed.

Exhausted, Kagiso will follow soon, after she washes the dishes, tidies the house, and washes herself. Thankfully, crushing the medicine does not take very long, nor does mixing it with the next day's meal. After this she is ready to sleep, only to begin another day.

[1] A drink made from distilled brown sugar
[2] A pollution caused by violation of sexual taboos transmitted through blood and semen

Across the globe, but particularly in developing nations, many women cannot control or inherit property as written by statutory and customary law. As Meg Wilkes Karraker explains in her discussion of practices of inheritance and descent in chapter 7, if a marriage ends through dissolution or death (from AIDS), surviving wives may lose control of property and resources to the husband's family. Sadly, this weakens women's ability to mitigate the harsh consequences of HIV infection by impeding their opportunities to draw on their property's capital for economic stability. HIV-positive women are most affected by these laws through ensuing stigma and discrimination. Very often when family and community members find out about their HIV status they are rebuffed, turned away from their homes, disinherited, and left to other risky means to support themselves and their children.

STRATEGIES FOR CHANGE

Comprehensive Prevention Services

Comprehensive prevention services generally include combinations of the following strategies: (1) behavior change programs that attempt to decrease risky behaviors; (2) harm reduction programs for injection drug users; (3) voluntary counseling and testing for HIV infection; (4) treatment programs integrating reproductive health services, including a focus on reducing sexually transmitted infections; and finally, (5) prevention of HIV transmission from mother to child. While there is no single "magic bullet" to ultimately end HIV, many of these prevention efforts complement one another to significantly reduce infection among women.

First, behavior change interventions have been used globally with targeted and general populations to increase the likelihood of risk-reduction behaviors and moderate the chances of risky behavior. Successful programs employ individual and small group cognitive behavioral interventions, community-level strategies, educational approaches, face-to-face counseling, and skills building techniques. These interventions have worked to successfully delay the initiation of sexual contact, promote the correct and consistent use of condoms during sexual activity, reduce the numbers of sexual partners for those engaging in sex, and improve communication and negotiation skills among sexual partners. One good example of an effective behavioral change intervention is the highly successful South African loveLife program. The program consists of a media campaign, a peer facilitated loveLife-style school program, youth-friendly clinic activities, out-of-school sessions, and community dialogues. Youth who are exposed to loveLife are more likely to report increased condom use the last time they had intercourse and to report consistent condom use overall (loveLife, 2007). The loveLife program is featured in Story 7 that shares an interview with AIDS activist Thembi Ngubane at the 2008 XVII International AIDS conference in Mexico City. The story discusses how Thembi dealt with her HIV status as a mother with AIDS. She hopes to inspire others through advocacy for others with the disease.

Second, harm reduction programs for injection drug users that include syringe exchange and substitution or methadone maintenance therapy (MMT) have been found to reduce the risk of contracting and spreading HIV among this population. Advocates have argued that harm reduction services need to be more fully integrated and extended by making programs available to mothers, incorporating sexual and reproductive health into harm reduction programs, providing gender-sensitive drug treatment, providing tailored services for drug-using sex workers, and connecting with domestic violence and rape prevention services. Such programs assume that women can be best served by acknowledging their life circumstances and formulating programs and policies to address these circumstances (Pinkham and Malinowska-Sempruch, 2008). For example, the Cape Town

Women's Health CoOP program was successful in significantly reducing substance use and decreasing sex risk behaviors among black and mixed-race women in South Africa.

Third, over the years, voluntary counseling and testing strategies have been featured as complementary parts of a comprehensive HIV-prevention strategy. The primary purpose of these programs is to help people safely learn about their status, give key advice on how to reduce risk behaviors to prevent HIV, and refer people to appropriate psychological and medical services. Voluntary testing and counseling are problematic in societies with stigma and discrimination about HIV and where treatment therapy is either alien or unaffordable. Work in this area seeks to address and change community norms in order to encourage voluntary testing and access to appropriate services. As Katharine Sarikakis and Leslie Regan Shade explain in chapter 2 on world media, mobile (cell)phones can be used for education to encourage such testing. A recent example of this is the Text to Change project in Uganda that uses SMS technology to spread information about HIV/AIDS to mobile phone users in order to improve attitudes, knowledge, and behavior (Net Squared, 2008). This innovative project, funded by the United States Agency for International Development (USAID), hopes to address stigma, prevent discrimination, and provide information about where to go for help.

Fourth, As Patti Lou Watkins, Alicia Bublitz, and Hoa Nguyen emphasize in chapter 6 on reproductive freedom, treatment programs integrating reproductive health services are imperative since they are most effective at preventing transmission. In sub-Saharan Africa, HIV-infected women want to prevent pregnancy for two primary reasons: first, if they have children, they are afraid that they will leave their children behind as orphans; and second, they are afraid of transmitting the virus to newborns who have a 50 percent chance of getting HIV. This latter reason works as HIV-prevention since in Sub-Saharan Africa alone, the number of HIV positive births would be 31 percent higher if contraception was absent (LePard, 2008). Although contraception can augment programs aimed at preventing the transmission of infection from mothers to babies (see below), contraceptive services thwart more HIV-positive births than the detection of HIV positive women during pregnancy and the administration of drugs to prevent maternal to child transmission (LePard, 2008). This is why advocates strongly argue for the integration of reproductive health and HIV programs. Alongside contraceptive services are treatment programs for sexually transmitted infections (STIs) that can decrease the risk for acquiring HIV/AIDS in the first place. Scientists and advocates also argue that early detection and subsequent, but timely, treatment of STIs must be part of a comprehensive prevention package to successfully combat HIV/AIDS. For example, a randomized controlled trial providing STI treatment in Mwanza, Tanzania, showed a nearly 40 percent reduction in HIV incidence (Grosskurth et al., 1995). Other studies, however, reveal contradictory results where STI treatment had little effect on HIV incidence. This may be due to the difference in study settings, such as the maturity of the HIV epidemic in various regions (Sangani, Rutherford, and Wilkinson, 2004).

Finally, prevention of mother to child transmission (PMTCT) of HIV/AIDS is a cornerstone of HIV prevention, employing the use of HIV antiretroviral drugs to pregnant women and their newborns to drastically reduce the chance of HIV being passed from mother to child before, during, or after labor. PMTCT services have been the primary point of access to HIV services for women, yet globally, less than one-half receive these services. As discussed in chapter 5 on women's health, access is a key theme underscoring multiple health issues. Access is important because a full range of services that include PMTCT as well as voluntary counseling and testing, and education on breast-feeding alternatives, can reduce the risk of HIV transmission from mother to child by about 50 percent (Guay et al., 1999). A good example of a comprehensive PMTCT program is one offered in Thailand where policymakers, clinicians, and the women themselves were involved in a study to assess its uptake and subsequent efficacy. The intervention consisted of voluntary counseling and testing, a short course of *zidovudine* (the antiretroviral used to prevent mother-to-child transmission), and formula feeding. In addition to reducing the number of HIV infections transmitted to babies, the intervention was successful in improving communication and providing counseling services as part of a comprehensive PMTCT program (Kanshana and Simonds, 2002).

The aforementioned strategies have been used successfully to mitigate risk and improve HIV/AIDS outcomes for women. Despite their success, however, results are still lacking and point to the need for more structural interventions that go beyond programs aimed at individual behaviors and instead address the wider social practices and institutions or the context in which wellness and illness occur. As already discussed in previous chapters, social structure implies embedded institutions (like family or media, medicine, and religion) and norms (agreed upon ideas and values) that shape the actions of individuals. As Mehra Shirazi emphasizes in chapter 5, health is not just a medical concept but must be understood in the context of social forces, especially those associated with cultural and economic globalization. It is within this new wave of interventions that scientists and advocates are focusing their energy to combat HIV/AIDS. While the strategies associated with comprehensive prevention services are combined with each other in order to be most beneficial, so these services are also combined with structural-level interventions in order to help shape HIV outcomes.

Structural Interventions: Gender Empowerment and Women's Activism

Because the HIV crisis among women is fundamentally viewed as one of gender disempowerment, many contend that the key to most effectively addressing HIV/AIDS among women is to provide structural interventions beyond individual-level behaviors with the goal of empowering women. In 2003, United Nations Secretary-General Kofi Annan convened a task force on women, girls, and HIV/AIDS to highlight many of the additional structural approaches needed to reduce prevalence rates among women and girls. These approaches include the empowerment of women and girls through activism and advocacy in five key areas. The first area involves empowering women through economic sustainability; the second, through education and access to knowledge and information; the third, through challenges to misogyny, or cultural norms that devalue women and denigrate the feminine; the fourth, through women's control of HIV-prevention methods; and finally, fifth, through policy at the international level.

First, since poverty is both a cause and a consequence of HIV/AIDS, advocates argue for strategies to *empower women economically*. Most of the stories featured in this conclusion to *Women Worldwide* illustrate the negative consequences of poverty for women and their children. When women are economically self-sufficient, they are able to take control of their lives, support children and families, and avoid risky behaviors like sex work. Strategies for economic empowerment include increased access to credit and business opportunities, livelihood training, attempts to protect women's food and income security, and securing access to property (Kim, Pronyk, Barnett, and Watts, 2008). Providing women with micro-credit loans has substantial impact on women by improving livelihood and self-esteem, broadening social networks, and increasing decision-making power in families. All these factors work to encourage contraceptive use and lower birth rates. However, only one study in South Africa, the Intervention with Microfinance and Gender Equity (IMAGE), has been conducted on micro-credit programs and their relationship to HIV incidence. Although these programs did not significantly reduce the incidence of HIV among participants, they were successful in reducing the rates of physical and sexual violence. They helped shift gendered cultural norms by providing gender training to both female and male participants and successfully reduced the levels of intimate partner violence among women (Kim et al., 2007). Nonetheless, scientists and advocates are encouraged by the results and are eager to support further research on the effects of microfinance initiatives on HIV incidence (Laver, 2008).

Beyond these strategies for poverty reduction, however, is the need to address the forces of economic globalization that continue to provide wealth to much of the Global North at the expense of many of those living in the Global South. As discussed throughout *Women Worldwide*, the processes of globalization that include economic restructuring, structural adjustment policies (SAPs), as well as increased militarism and conflict, "cheapen" women's labor and their bodies, making their lives more expendable and putting then into risky situations as a result of loss of livelihood, migration, and/or refugee status. Economic systems that devalue women and cheapen their labor also increase women's vulnerability and put them at risk not only for contracting HIV, but for being in a situation that constrains their ability to seek help and treatment for the disease.

Second, it is important to *empower girls and women through access to education*. The more educated and skilled young women are, the more likely they are to protect themselves and not participate in risky sexual behaviors. Studies reveal that women with post-primary education were five times more likely to know the facts about HIV than women who did not have that education, thus reducing their risk for HIV infection. Increasing educational possibilities for women also has a strong impact on reducing the risk of poverty, thus reducing overall risk for HIV infection.

In response, scientists and advocates have called for integrated education that not only promotes the literacy of young girls but provides them with valuable life skills that can help mitigate the impact of HIV/AIDS. As illustrated in Story 8 featuring "Mama's Club," a group in Uganda, when women come together to share their stories, they provide important medical and legal advice for each other at the same time that they build solidarity in a community of friends and advocates. Life-skills education often uses creative methods such as role or game playing to teach and instruct about different issues. Some of the skills that are taught in these classes are negotiation, managing of peer pressure, self-esteem, tolerance and compassion, and assertiveness skills. Classes can also teach other subjects such as personal hygiene and vocational skills like horticulture, sewing, or typing. These life-skills training classes often take place within the context of HIV/AIDS education in schools. Advocates agree that the education offered should be age-appropriate and start in primary school or before children become sexually active. The U.S.-based nonprofit organization CARE has education projects in several countries and partners with local, grass-roots organizations who are culturally attuned to the needs of the community. For example, Project YIELD (Youth Initiatives to Enhance Out-of-School Learning for Development) in Rwanda works with youth and women's associations and over 150 local officials to provide education to over 8,000 youth. At the center of this grassroots initiative is the development of Community Knowledge Centers, which build upon existing literacy centers. The purpose of this education initiative is not only to improve literacy among youth (and especially among young women), but also to improve gender equity and facilitate dialogue on key development issues such as HIV/AIDS (CARE, 2009).

Third, addressing the pandemic in women's lives means *empowering women through challenges to cultural norms that subordinate women to men.* Such norms may place women in inequitable positions that lower their social status and make their lives less valuable than those of their brothers. Misogynous practices make women vulnerable to gender-based violence that increases their risk for HIV. However, as Patti Duncan emphasizes in chapter 8 on violence against women, it is important to avoid a cultural relativism that suggests "culture" explains women's plight in their relationship to HIV/AIDS. This approach tends to create or maintain stereotypes, especially in the Global North, that these problems are a result of cultural forces elsewhere, thus "exoticizing" the problem and avoiding serious exploration of its causes and consequences. Instead we must examine the intersections of gender with race, ethnicity, nationality, class, sexuality, religion, and so forth, to specifically understand the historical, economic, and sociopolitical contexts that shape women's lives. It is therefore important to move from a focus on "culture" or "tradition" to a more critical examination of the effects of institutional structures. As a result, effective strategies for change reference specific local contexts, institutions, and, increasingly, global practices, that contribute to the multiple causes of this pandemic.

With this in mind, some scholars and policymakers argue for zero tolerance vis-à-vis gendered violence and advocate a fourfold strategy involving the following steps: (1) Begin a dialogue with prominent community members about the ill effects of violence on women, families, and the entire community. This involves encouraging women into leadership

Used with permission of Signe Wilkinson and the Washington Post Writers Group in conjunction with the Cartoonist Group. All rights reserved.

positions and providing the context for their success. However, as discussed in chapter 11 on women and politics, this is a complex and often difficult process that does not necessarily ensure women's interests are being served. Still, with education and knowledge about HIV and with political clout to enact policy, women leaders are in a position to help enforce strategies for change; (2) Promote media campaigns to address violence against women and promote dignity for all human beings. As chapter 2 on world media underscores, new changes in information and communication technologies (ICTs) provide opportunities for the sharing of knowledge on this issue; (3) Focus directly on men to help them reframe their ideas about acceptable gendered practices; and (4) Provide adequate treatment and counseling services for women who have been the victims of sexual abuse.

The fourth example of structural interventions is the need to recognize the relationship between reproductive rights and HIV/AIDS and *empower women through women's control of HIV-prevention methods*. This means that the ability of women to decide if, when, and how they will participate in sexual relations is central to HIV prevention. As discussed in chapters 4 and 6 on sexuality and reproductive freedoms, when women have control of the conditions of their everyday lives, they can willingly make decisions in their best interest. A central issue here is their ability to negotiate condom use with partners since women who do not insist on condom use are more likely to participate in unprotected sexual activity that puts them at risk of both pregnancy and HIV infection. Several studies have indicated that many women find negotiating condom use difficult: insisting on condoms may compromise expectations for feminine modesty, for example, or men may retaliate with violence. As a result, researchers and advocates have called for a concerted effort to improve female-initiated HIV prevention options such as the female condom (see sidebar on next page).

Finally, it is important to *empower women through international advocacy and policy*. Across the globe there are transnational feminist organizations and coalitions working at this level to address the HIV/AIDS pandemic. As explained by Valentine Moghadam in chapter 1 on transnational feminisms, transnational feminist networks (TFNs) address the policies of neoliberal economic globalization that are a cause of much of the world's poverty and, as such, are implicated in the HIV/AIDS pandemic. TFNs also provide humanitarian aid, and it is these feminist efforts that support women and children affected by the disease. Many transnational feminist organizations like the International Women's Health Coalition and the Global Coalition on Women and AIDS believe the root cause of HIV/AIDS among women is gender inequity and to that end have lent their voices to creating and shifting policy that deals directly with this problem. Story 9 discusses Tatiana and Dina, celebrities in Russia and Ukraine, whose portraits are exhibited in a campaign to increase awareness of, and education about, the disease in women's lives. Eastern Europe and central Asia have faced significant increases in the numbers of new HIV infections in recent years. Nearly 90 percent of newly reported HIV diagnoses in 2006 were from two countries: the Russian Federation (66 percent) and Ukraine (21 percent).

At the level of international policy, initiatives have been implemented to address HIV/AIDS among women. The United States Congress passed the President's Emergency Plan for AIDS Relief (PEPFAR) and reauthorized it in 2008 to the cost of US$50 billion. This commitment is the single largest pledge by any government in the world to end HIV/AIDS. The funding provided by this bill has provided lifesaving drugs, expanded care efforts, and promoted comprehensive HIV prevention. Although the first version of the bill failed to address the critical need of gender integration in HIV prevention programs, its reauthorized

The Female Condom

The female condom is a thin sheath or pouch worn by a woman during sex. It entirely lines the vagina and helps to prevent pregnancy and sexually transmitted diseases (STDs), including HIV. Two types of female condom are available.

THE FC/FC2 FEMALE CONDOM

The FC female condom has been available in Europe since 1992 and was approved by the US Food and Drug Administration (FDA) in 1993. It is available in many countries, at least in limited quantities, throughout the world. This female condom carries various brand names in different countries, including *Reality, Femidom, Dominique, Femy, Myfemy, Protectiv'* and *Care.*

The FC female condom is a polyurethane sheath or pouch about 17 cm (6.5 inches) in length. At each end there is a flexible ring. At the closed end of the sheath, the flexible ring is inserted into the vagina to hold the female condom in place. At the other open end of the sheath, the ring stays outside the vulva at the entrance to the vagina. This ring acts as a guide during penetration and it also stops the sheath bunching up inside the vagina.

There is silicone-based lubricant on the inside of the condom, but additional lubrication can be used. The condom does not contain spermicide.

In 2005 the makers of the FC female condom announced a new product called FC2. This has the same design as the original version but is made of nitrile, which may make it cheaper to produce. The FC2 began large-scale production in 2007. The United Nations Population Fund (UNFPA) is already procuring the FC2. The FDA approved the FC2 in December 2008 and the World Health Organization has stated that the product is acceptable for bulk procurement by UN agencies.[1]

THE VA W.O.W. CONDOM FEMININE

The VA w.o.w. Condom Feminine (or VA for short) has been distributed as part of HIV prevention efforts in South Africa since 2004. More recently it has become available in Brazil, Indonesia, and through government clinics in Portugal. Having gained the "CE mark" for European marketing, its manufacturer plans to expand its availability in European shops and clinics. One more trial is needed before the product can gain FDA approval for sale in the USA.

Like most male condoms, the VA is made of latex. When not stretched it is much shorter than the FC—around 9 cm (3.5 inches)—though it is highly elastic. It has a rounded triangular frame at the open end and a sponge inside the closed end, which helps to anchor it inside the vagina.

The VA is lubricated and does not contain spermicide. Oil-based lubricants should not be used with this female condom as they can damage latex.

HOW DO YOU USE THE FEMALE CONDOM?

Open the package carefully. Choose a position that is comfortable for insertion—squat, raise one leg, sit or lie down. Make sure the condom is lubricated enough.

If you are using the FC or FC2 female condom, make sure the inner ring is at the closed end of the sheath, and hold the sheath with the open end hanging down. Squeeze the inner ring with thumb and middle finger (so it becomes long and narrow), and then insert the inner ring and sheath into the vaginal opening. Gently insert the inner ring into the vagina and feel it go up. Place the index finger inside the condom and push the inner ring as far as it will go. Make sure the condom is inserted straight, and is not twisted inside the vagina. The outer ring should remain on the outside of the vagina.

To begin inserting the VA, hold the sponge and frame close together and place the closed end in front of the vagina. Use two fingers to push the closed end containing the sponge inside the vagina as far as it will go. Make sure the sponge is opened up flat once it has been inserted. The frame should remain on the outside of the vagina.

The penis should be guided into the condom in order to ensure that the penis does not slip into the vagina outside the condom. Use enough lubricant so that the condom stays in place during sex. The female condom should not be used at the same time as a male condom because the friction between the two condoms may cause the condoms to break.

If the condoms slips during intercourse, or if it enters the vagina, then you should stop immediately and take the female condom out. Then insert a new one and add extra lubricant to the opening of the sheath or on the penis.

To remove the condom, twist the outer ring or frame gently and then pull the condom out keeping the sperm inside. Wrap the condom in the package or in tissue and throw it away. Do not put it into the toilet. It is generally recommended that the female condom should not be reused.

The female condom may feel unfamiliar at first. The female condom may feel different and some people find it difficult to insert. Some women find that with time and practice using the female condom becomes easier and easier.

WHAT ARE THE BENEFITS?

- Opportunity for women to share the responsibility for condoms with their partners.
- A woman may be able to use the female condom if her partner refuses to use the male condom.
- The female condom will protect against most STDs and pregnancy if used correctly.
- The FC or FC2 female condom can be inserted up to 8 hours before intercourse so as not to interfere with the moment.
- The FC and FC2 female condoms are made of polyurethane and nitrile, which are less likely to cause an allergic reaction than latex. These materials can be used with oil-based as well as water-based lubricants. No special storage requirements are needed because polyurethane and nitrile are not affected by changes in temperature and dampness. In addition, these materials are thin and conduct heat well, so sensation is preserved.

WHAT ARE THE DISADVANTAGES?

- The outer ring or frame is visible outside the vagina, which can make some women feel self-conscious.
- The FC and FC2 female condoms can make noises during intercourse (adding more lubricant can lessen this problem).
- Some women find the female condom hard to insert and to remove.

- It has a higher failure rate in preventing pregnancy than nonbarrier methods such as the pill.
- It is relatively expensive and relatively limited in availability in some countries.
- It is recommended that the female condom be used only once.

WORLDWIDE USE AND AVAILABILITY

The female condom is used in public health programs in more than 90 countries and is commercially marketed directly to consumers in 10 countries.[2] It is quite widely used in some places where it is actively promoted, such as South Africa, Zimbabwe, and Brazil. However, in many parts of the world it is hardly available at all.

In fiscal year 2008, the makers of the FC female condom sold 34.7 million units worldwide, up from 25.9 million in 2006 and 14 million in 2005.[3] Many of these condoms were purchased by donor agencies such as USAID and UNFPA. The VA currently sells in much smaller quantities. Altogether, female condoms account for only around 0.2% of global condom use.

In 2005, nearly two thirds of all female condoms were used in Africa, while the next largest shares went to North America and Europe. Asia accounted for less than 1% of the global total in 2005, though figures for later years may be higher due to growth in India.[4]

References:

1. FDA (2008), "Obstetrics and Gynecological Devices Panel–December 11, 2008"
2. The Female Health Company (2007, May) "Female Health Company Quarterly Report of Financial Condition"
3. The Female Health Company (2008, December 1), "The Female Health Company Reports Record Results for Fiscal Year 2008, at High End of Guidance"
4. UNFPA (2005), "Donor Support for Contraceptives and Condoms for STI/HIV Prevention 2005"

Source: www.avert.org

version contains new language that provides clear guidance on integrating gender across all prevention, treatment, and care programs. Despite this, the bill contains some provisions that undermine prevention efforts for women.

First, the bill stipulates a focus on "abstinence-until-marriage" and "be faithful" activities rather than condom promotion. This provision ignores the reality that young women may have little choice to abstain and instead are coerced into sex. It also ignores the double standard of sexual conduct and the fact that marriage itself has not been proven to be an effective strategy for HIV prevention. In fact, the opposite holds true: studies indicate that married monogamous women are most at risk for getting HIV from their husbands, who may engage in multiple sexual partnerships. Second, the legislation also includes a problematic "conscience clause," which not only allows groups receiving PEPFAR dollars to exclude people from critical prevention services on the basis of religious and moral grounds but also allows them to withhold care for people whose behavior may be "objectionable," such as sex workers and injection drug users. Advocates insist that this provision promotes discrimination and will perpetuate stigma among marginalized groups most in need of services.

Addressing gender equities in the HIV/AIDS world is both a complex and an optimistic proposition since the problem itself is multifaceted. As we have learned, we cannot simply focus on HIV/AIDS alone and must address the intersection of behavioral, social, and political issues. Each chapter of this book—from a focus on the politics of the body, to women's status in families, to economic vulnerabilities resulting from economic globalization, to their political status as citizens—confers knowledge that can help us understand and address the pandemic. Although on the one hand the task can seem daunting, on the other hand it is a task women worldwide are ready to undertake. For years, advocates were haunted by lack of any gender parity in HIV programming until, through hard work and dedication to feminist goals, we are beginning to see an integration of approaches that are having real and beneficial consequences for women and children all over the globe. There is widespread agreement that alongside comprehensive treatment strategies that focus on behavioral changes, structural changes associated with gender empowerment are key to ending the HIV/AIDS pandemic. Coalitions, organizations, and networks at both local, grassroots, and transnational levels are providing advocacy and activism aimed at eliminating poverty and gendered violence; promoting girls' education, literacy, and improved status in families and communities; as well as destigmatizing HIV/AIDS and its impact on women's lives. To address HIV/AIDS is to address the disempowerment of women worldwide. To prevent HIV/AIDS and improve the quality of lives of those infected is to empower women to live with dignity and hope.

We began the book with good news and bad news to highlight the contemporary situation of women worldwide. Now, after exploring the myriad themes of women's lives and emphasizing the ways these themes are connected, we close the book with similar warnings and hope. Warnings reflect the problems of poverty, lack of social and political rights, gender-based violence, and threats associated with economic globalization, militarism, and global climate change. Hope encompasses knowledge that women are strong and resilient and will fight for their own rights, and those of other women, in this rapidly changing world. Central in this work is that of women and other marginalized groups learning to be allies with and for each other: coming together with conscious understandings of privilege and with knowledge of the differences that divide us. It is important for us to recognize the ways global power imbalances (such as those between the Global North and South or between "developed" and "developing" countries) situate us differently in the struggle according to our specific local histories and contexts as women and men in the world. Figuring ways to create meaningful and politically viable connections across these differences remains a challenge. Importantly, our goals for social justice cannot be achieved in isolation, but require individuals coming together in organizations and coalitions with the political will for change. Equality and social justice are important principles shaping this political will, as well as strategies for women's participation and empowerment. Together we can change the world!

REFERENCES

CARE. (2009). *Youth initiatives to enhance out-of-school learning for development (YIELD) project.* Retrieved February 5, 2009, from http://www.care.org/careswork/projects/ RWA073.asp.

Centers for Disease Control and Prevention. (2008a). *HIV/AIDS among women.* Retrieved January 25, 2009, from http://www.cdc.gov/hiv/topics/women/resources/factsheets/women.htm.

Centers for Disease Control and Prevention. (2008b, September). *MMWR analysis provides new details on HIV incidence in U.S. populations.* Retrieved January 25, 2009, from http://www.cdc.gov/hiv/topics/women/resources/factsheets/pdf/wsw.pdf.

Gregson, S., Nyamukapa, C. A., Garnett, G. P., Mason, P. R., Zhuwau, T., Caraël, M., et al. (2002). Sexual mixing patterns and sex-differentials in teenage exposure to HIV infection in rural Zimbabwe. *Lancet, 359*(9321), 1896–1903.

Grosskurth, H., Mosha, F., Todd, J., Senkoro, K., Newell, J., Klokke, A., et al. (1995). A community trial of the impact of improved sexually transmitted disease treatment on the HIV epidemic in rural Tanzania: 2. Baseline survey results. *AIDS, 9*(8), 927–934.

Guay, L. A., Musoke, P., Fleming, T., Bagenda, D., Allen, M., Nakabiito, C., et al. (1999). Intrapartum and neonatal single-dose nevirapine compared with zidovudine for prevention of mother-to-child transmission of HIV–1 in Kampala, Uganda: HIVNET 012 randomised trial. *Lancet, 354*(9181), 795–802.

Kanshana, S., and Simonds, R. J. (2002). National program for preventing mother–child HIV transmission in Thailand: Successful implementation and lessons learned. *AIDS, 16*(7), 953–959.

Kelly, R. J., Gray, R. H., Sewankambo, N. K., Serwadda, D., Wabwire-Mangen, F., Lutalo, T., et al. (2003). Age differences in sexual partners and risk of HIV–1 infection in rural Uganda. *Journal of Acquired Deficiency Syndrome, 32*(4), 446–451.

Kim, J., Pronyk, P., Barnett, T., and Watts, C. (2008). Exploring the role of economic empowerment in HIV prevention. *AIDS, 22* (Suppl *4*), S57–71.

Kim, J. C., Watts, C. H., Hargreaves, J. R., Ndhlovu, L. X., Phetla, G., Morison, L. A., et al. (2007). Understanding the impact of a microfinance-based intervention on women's empowerment and the reduction of intimate partner violence in South Africa. *American Journal of Public Health, 97*(10), 1794–1802.

Laver, M. S. (2008). SHAZ! Shaping the health of adolescents in Zimbabwe, *XVII International AIDS Conference.* Mexico City.

LePard, T. (2008). Senate passage of landmark HIV/AIDS bill; Failure to maximize prevention efforts [Press Release].

LoveLife. (2007). *HIV in the Melmoth Area, Kwazulu-Natal: An assessment of effects associated with loveLife's intervention.* Retrieved Feb 1, 2009, from http://www.lovelife.org.za/corporate/research/MELMOTH_FEB.PDF.

Net Squared. (2008). *Expanding HIV prevention and uptake of HIV voluntary counseling and testing through interactive short message services in Uganda.* Retrieved Feb. 3, 2009, 2009, from http://www.netsquared.org/projects/expanding-hiv-prevention-and-uptake-hiv-voluntary-counseling-and-testing-through-interactive-short-message-services-uga.

Otto, D. (2007). Making sense of zero tolerance policies in peacekeeping sexual economies. In V. E. Munro and C. F. Stychin (Eds.), *Sexuality and the law—Feminist engagements* (p. 2). London: Routledge.

Over, M. (1998). The effects of societal variables on urban rates of HIV infection in developing countries: An exploratory analysis. In F. L. Ainsworth, and M. Over (Eds.), *Confronting AIDS: Evidence from the developing world* (Chapter 12A, pp. 241–253). Brussels: European Commission and World Bank.

Pinkham, S., and Malinowska-Sempruch, K. (2008). Women, harm reduction and HIV. *Reprod Health Matters, 16*(31), 168–181.

Rasch, R. F., Weisen, C. A., MacDonald, B., Wechsberg, W. M., Perritt, R., and Dennis, M. L. (2000). Patterns of HIV risk and alcohol use among African-American crack abusers. *Drug and Alcohol Dependence, 58*(3), 259–266.

Sangani, P., Rutherford, G., and Wilkinson, D. (2004). Population-based interventions for reducing sexually transmitted infections, including HIV infection. *Cochrane Database Syst Rev*(2), CD001220.

Tawil, O., Carael, M., Mendoza, A., Munz, M., Stanton, J., and Jenkins, C. (2002). *Sex work and HIV/AIDS: Technical update.* Geneva: UNAIDS.

UNAIDS. (2004). *AIDS epidemic update.* Geneva: Joint United Nations Programme on HIV/AIDS and World Health Organization.

UNAIDS. (2005). *AIDS epidemic update.* Geneva: Joint United Nations Programme on HIV/AIDS and World Health Organization.

UNAIDS. (2007). *AIDS epidemic update.* Geneva: Joint United Nations Programme on HIV/AIDS and World Health Organization.

UNAIDS/UNFPA/UNIFEM. (2004). *Women and HIV/AIDS: Confronting the crisis.*

UNICEF (2008). *Children and HIV/AIDS.* Retrieved Oct. 9, 2009, from http://www.unicef.org/aids/index_introduction.php.

Zule, W. A., Flannery, B. A., Wechsberg, W. M., and Lam, W. K. (2002). Alcohol use among out-of-treatment crack using African-American women. *American Journal of Drug and Alcohol Abuse, 28*(3), 525–544.

SUGGESTIONS FOR FURTHER READING

Boler, T. and Archer, D. (2008). *The politics of prevention: A global crisis in AIDS and education.* Melbourne, Australia: Pluto Press.

Izumi, K. (2007). *Reclaiming our lives: HIV and AIDS, women's land and property rights and livelihoods in Southern and East Africa, narratives and responses.* Pretoria, South Africa: Human Sciences Research Council.

Kalipeni, E. ed. (2009). *Strong women, dangerous times: Gender and HIV/AIDS in Africa.* Hauppauge, NY: Nova Science Publication.

Roberts, D., Reddock, R., Douglas, D., and Reed, S. (2008). *Sex, power and taboo: Gender and HIV in the Caribbean and beyond.* Miami, FL: Ian Randle Publishers.

Susser, I. (2009). *AIDS, sex and culture: Global politics and survival in Southern Africa.* Hoboken, NJ: Wiley-Blackwell.

Williamson, J., Foster, G., and Levine, C. (Eds.). (2006). *A generation at risk: The global impact of HIV/AIDS on orphans and vulnerable children.* New York: Cambridge University Press.

Janice, Marvelyn, and Michelle: USA

January W. Payne (2008)

Janice was 27 years old and eight weeks pregnant with her son when she was diagnosed with HIV in 1991. The Queens, N.Y., resident believes that the father of her older child—a daughter, now 24—gave her the infection. She's far from alone in acquiring the virus from a man she thought she could trust. "Some people have the attitude that it can't happen to them," says Janice, who asked that her real name not be used. "If you're not practicing safe sex, you're at risk, because you don't know if your partner is monogamous or not."

With her diagnosis, Janice joined the ranks of thousands of black women in the United States who are living with HIV/AIDS. Those ranks have swelled in the years since her son's birth, and black women continue to be struck particularly hard by the virus, new research shows. As of 2005, that group accounted for 64 percent of the more than 126,000 women who were living with HIV/AIDS in the United States, according to the Centers for Disease Control and Prevention. The rate in 2006 of new infections in black women, moreover, was nearly 15 times that in white women—55.7 infections versus 3.8 infections per 100,000 women, respectively—according to the latest data, which appear in the September 12 issue of the CDC's *Morbidity and Mortality Weekly Report.*

That study comes on the heels of a dramatic upward revision of the agency's assessment of how rapidly HIV is spreading. In August, the CDC estimated that about 56,300 new infections occurred nationwide in 2006, up from earlier estimates of about 40,000. This week's report breaks down the new infections by race, gender, age, and other demographic measures.

Many assume that HIV primarily affects homosexual men, who are, in fact, heavily afflicted. Nevertheless, high-risk heterosexual contact was the source of 80 percent of newly diagnosed infections

in women in 2006, the CDC reports. Yet many black women may not realize when they're having sex with a high-risk partner. In black communities, discussion of homosexuality is largely taboo, and some women report being infected with HIV/AIDS by boy friends or husbands who they later find out were sleeping with men. The so-called down-low phenomenon first garnered widespread attention in 2004 when J. L. King wrote the book *On the Down Low: A Journey Into the Lives of "Straight" Black Men Who Sleep With Men*, about his own experiences as a married man who slept with other men but considered himself to be heterosexual.

Unprotected sex between infected men may play a role in the increasing number of black women being infected, says C. Virginia Fields, president and CEO of the National Black Leadership Commission on AIDS. Black men had an HIV incidence rate that was six times that of white men in 2006, according to the new CDC report. Gay and bisexual men accounted for about 63 percent of all infections in black men that year.

Another concern, Fields says, is the number of black men who return home from prison or jail and have sex with wives or girlfriends without first getting tested for sexually transmitted diseases. The CDC estimates that HIV prevalence among those who are incarcerated is nearly five times higher than that of the general U.S. population. About 9 percent of those infections were found to occur during incarceration in an April 2006 CDC study of inmates in the Georgia Department of Corrections' system. One in 15 black men age 18 and older is incarcerated, compared with 1 in 106 white men, according to a Pew Center on the States analysis of U.S. Department of Justice statistics.

Neither the down-low theory nor incarceration theory has been linked by scientific research to HIV/AIDS infections in black women, but "because of how this [disease] is spreading through heterosexual black women, both of those discussions are plausible," Fields says.

That's why, experts say, it's important not to assume that your partner or past partners are not infected. "AIDS does not discriminate. Unsafe sexual practices and unsafe drug behaviors with someone who is infected can and will lead to HIV infection," says SharenDuke, executive director of the New York City–based AIDS Service Center, a community organization that provides HIV testing, mental health services, medical care, support groups, and other services. "It has crossed all racial, cultural, and class backgrounds."

Yet many women make the mistake of having unprotected sex with an unsafe partner. Some, like 24-year-old Marvelyn Brown, a Tennessee native who now lives in New York City, say they didn't ask their sexual partners to wear condoms because it made them feel special that the men involved trusted them enough to forgo protection. In her recent autobiography, *The Naked Truth: Young, Beautiful, and (HIV) Positive*, Brown says that when she contracted HIV at age 19, she didn't care enough about herself to require that her boyfriend consistently use condoms. "If you love yourself, you can protect yourself," she says, "and that eliminates HIV from the beginning." Yvonne Gooden also believes she contracted HIV through unprotected heterosexual sex. The Yonkers, N.Y., mother of two was diagnosed with HIV in 1993 and AIDS in 1995. And like many others, she thinks that low self-esteem played a role in her not protecting herself during sex.

Women should feel "empowered to make sure that their partner uses a condom," says Raymond Martins, medical director of the Whitman-Walker Clinic in Washington, D.C., a nonprofit organization focused on HIV/AIDS treatment. "Especially in the black community, that doesn't seem to always be the case."

Gooden's disease has left her feeling fatigued much of the time. Although medical strides have been made in making HIV/AIDS manageable, black women like Gooden still bear a tremendous burden of associated death and disability. In recent years, HIV/AIDS has been among the top three causes of death for African-American females ages 25 to 34. Some of those deaths might be preventable if

HIV-positive people were consistently diagnosed early in the course of their infections, before AIDS arises. To improve HIV detection, the CDC recommended in 2006 that everyone aged 13 to 64 get tested at least once. For years, experts have been advocating routine HIV testing in people who seek treatment for other sexually transmitted diseases. Michelle, 44, a busy New York City mother of three who once refereed basketball games in her spare time, was diagnosed with HIV at age 33 when she sought treatment for chlamydia. She'd contracted both infections from her fiancé. "I was infected because of love," says Michelle, who asked that her real name be omitted to protect her children's privacy.

While the CDC recently upped its estimate of new HIV infections occurring annually nationwide, Washington and New York City have been dealing with the issue for years—with minority groups and men who have sex with men especially hard hit. African-Americans comprise 57 percent of Washington's population but account for 81 percent of new HIV infections. And 90 percent of new HIV infections in women occur in black women, according to the District of Columbia Department of Health.

In New York City, residents are contracting HIV at three times the national rate, according to a recently released estimate from the New York City Department of Health and Mental Hygiene. The new figures suggest that 72 of every 100,000 Big Apple residents was newly infected with HIV during 2006, compared with a national rate of 23 per 100,000 residents. Blacks comprised nearly half of the city's new HIV infections that year.

A woman's background can also affect her HIV risk, experts say. "Many of the women that we work with have a history of childhood sexual abuse and trauma," Duke says. This type of history can impact a woman's decisions—including whether or not she chooses to have safe sex. In some cases, women may be forced to have unprotected sex by an abusive partner, Fields says.

Michelle and Janice are both in committed relationships now: Each has a man in her life who is HIV negative, and both say they practice safe sex to help keep their partners from becoming infected. Gooden says that her HIV-negative boyfriend of 12 years gets routine HIV tests. "I chose not to have sex [after being diagnosed with HIV] until I met someone who understood that putting on a condom was important to me," she says.

Both Janice and her 16-year-old son, who was born with HIV, are in good health. She takes three medications daily, exercises three times a week, eats healthily, and sees a therapist to discuss any issues that bother her.

Brown, who takes seven pills per day, is also doing well. The diagnosis has even helped her in dating, she says. "You can tell a lot about a man's character when you tell him that you have HIV," Brown says. "I used to date a guy for years before I found out that he was no good. Now I find out in the first 10 minutes."

S T O R Y   **2**

Keren: Honduras

The Associated Press (2008)

Keren Dunaway was 5 when her parents used drawings to explain to her that they both had the HIV virus—and so did she. Now the 12-year-old is one of the most prominent AIDS activists in Latin America and a rarity in a region where few children are willing to break the silence and tell their classmates they have HIV for fear of rejection. She edits a children's magazine on the virus.

One Sunday evening, in 2008, Keren shares the stage with the Mexican president and U.N. Secretary-General Ban Ki-moon as they open an international AIDS conference. She flashes a dimpled smile, exposing a row of braces, and settles comfortably into her chair before expertly fastening on a microphone. She talks matter-of-factly about the virus she has had since birth.

"It's like a little ball that has little dots, and is inside me, sort of swimming inside me," she said in an interview with The Associated Press, curling her fist as she recalls what her parents explained to her with drawings long ago.

Keren's openness about her HIV status comes as the virus's victims grow increasingly younger. Worldwide, people ages 15–24 accounted for 45% of people infected with HIV in 2007, according to the 2008 U.N. AIDS report. In Latin America, 55,000 of the nearly 2 million people with the virus were under 15 years old, the vast majority of them infected by their mothers. Only 36% of pregnant women in the region receive medicine to prevent transmission, although that is an increase of 26% since 2004. And while more than 60% of the adults with HIV receive antiretroviral drugs in Latin America, only about one-third of children do. Experts say less research and funding have been dedicated to medicine for HIV-positive children, who require smaller doses and additional medication to offset the aggressiveness of antiretrovirals. Even so, children born with HIV are increasingly looking forward to long lives.

"There's a whole new generation of young people that were born with HIV that are reaching adulthood. It presents very interesting challenges," said Nils Katsberg, UNICEF'S director of Latin America and the Caribbean.

It won't be easy encouraging HIV-positive children to speak out in Latin America, where talking openly about sexuality is often taboo. When she first started school, Keren's classmates refused to play with her. Speaking out about HIV made all the difference. At 9, she began accompanying her parents—founders of the AIDS advocacy group "Llaves"—on talks to schools. She has visited half-a-dozen countries to share her story.

Last year, she started up "Llavecitas," a children's version of a magazine her parents publish. The Llaves foundation distributes 10,000 copies every two months across Honduras.

But too often, children with HIV "live in a culture of secrecy," said Maria Villanueva Medina, a psychologist with Casa de la Sal, a group that runs an orphanage for children with HIV in Mexico City. "They can't talk about their diagnosis in the school because they can be kicked out. They can't talk about it in their communities with their neighbors."

At Casa de la Sal, children are told about the virus around the same age as Keren was, but few dare to tell their schoolmates even where they live. Casa de la Sal is adapting to a new reality. When it first opened 22 years ago, many of the children died by the time they reached their teens. Today, the orphanage has not had a death in eight years. The government provides antiretrovirals. Faced with the challenge of preparing the children for adulthood, the orphanage eventually began sending them to regular schools instead of giving classes within the institution. The hope is that someday, many will be outspoken advocates for their own cause.

"We need to start getting young people involved in leadership again in HIV and AIDS because it's easy to get kind of complacent," said Joe Cristina, whose Los Angeles–based Children Affected by AIDS Foundation helps fund the orphanage.

Keren writes an upbeat editorial each week. ("I want to congratulate all the boys and girls who have graduated and got good grades. Keep it up!!") She is now popular among her classmates.

She takes singing and acting lessons, dreams of going to Hollywood and breathlessly notes that she shares the same Zodiac sign—Sagittarius—and favorite color—purple—with her teen idol, Miley Cyrus.

"Sometimes I have so much fun that I forget I have this virus," she said.

But she often gets e-mails from other children with HIV worried about telling the truth to their friends. "I tell them to first explain about the disease, how it's transmitted, how it can't be transmitted, what it is," she said. "And then they should tell them with confidence that they have it—if they want."

STORY 3

Jacqueline, Isata, and Adele: Uganda, Sierra Leone, and Rwanda

Phyllida Brown (2004)

After Jacqueline Nakitende's husband died in 1999, the Ugandan widow sorted through his possessions. Inside his briefcase, she found what may turn out to be her own death sentence: test results confirming that her husband was HIV-positive. He had often forced her to have sex, and once he raped her so violently that she miscarried. Nakitende had wanted to use condoms, not because she suspected her husband's infection but to space her pregnancies. But she dared not ask. "He wouldn't use condoms. He would have beaten me," she told Human Rights Watch. Now in her early thirties, she and four of her five children are living with HIV.

Across the world, women like Nakitende are facing a disproportionate risk of HIV infection, mainly because men control them at home and use them as pawns of war.

Inside the home, lacking money, property, and information about their rights, many women are dependent on partners and other male relatives who reinforce control through violence, often sexual. "In a patriarchal society, your body doesn't necessarily belong to you," says Bella Matambanadzo, a Zimbabwean journalist and AIDS activist.

Outside the home, the dangers are more dramatic. In conflict zones around the world, rape is a systematic weapon of war, a prize for soldiers, a technique of ethnic cleansing, and even a means to deliberately spread HIV.

The women of sub-Saharan Africa—home to 26 million of the world's 40 million people now living with HIV—are particularly hard hit. In April, a decade after the genocide in Rwanda, Amnesty International and the Kigali-based widows' organization AVEGA reported unprecedented rates of HIV infection among more than 1,100 rape survivors surveyed. Only a small minority of those who are infected are receiving life-prolonging antiretroviral drugs. In eastern Congo, gangs of soldiers have raped women and girls unchecked during the war and its aftermath. Although Congo reports relatively low HIV rates nationally, up to a quarter of women raped in these attacks may be infected, according to press reports. And in Darfur, western Sudan, government-backed militias are systematically raping women and girls from rival ethnic groups.

Isata was 15 when rebels in Sierra Leone abducted and gang-raped her. "I was a virgin before. They ruined me," she told Physicians for Human Rights (PHR). "I was at home when they came and kidnapped me. . . . They demanded [$83.00]. My family has no money. . . . They said to my parents, 'Come and see how we use your children.' They undressed five of us, laid us down, used us in front of my family and took us away with them [to the bush]. . . . I can't remember how long I was held. . . . I don't like to talk because of the memories. . . . When I escaped, I couldn't walk—the pain. I was bleeding from my vagina. That night, God gave me strength to walk. When I made it back, my mother couldn't believe it. Since I got back I have been so sick. . . . I never used to get sick like this. . . . I would like to go back to school, but I can't concentrate anymore, I can't do anything."

Isata's household is among the one in eight in Sierra Leone that experienced at least one incident of war-related sexual violence during the 1991–2002 civil war, according to a survey by PHR. Among women reporting such incidents, 89 percent said they had been raped and 33 percent reported being gang-raped.

Against realities like these, the official "ABC" prevention advice pumped out by many governments in the past two decades—"Abstain, Be Faithful, Use Condoms"—is bitterly irrelevant to most women. What can abstinence mean if, as the United Nations Joint Program on HIV/AIDS (UNAIDS) estimates, one-fifth to one-half of all girls and young women worldwide are forced into their first sexual encounter? How will being faithful protect you if your partner is not? What hope is there of safer sex when you have no control over the terms of the act? "Most of the time, the woman is dependent on the man, and therefore she has no voice to negotiate condom use," says AIDS activist Ludfine Anyango, of ActionAid in Nairobi, Kenya, who is herself living with HIV.

While mass rapes in armed conflict have captured media attention, the ancient problem of violence in the family is still the most pervasive form of violence against women worldwide. While reports vary widely between and within countries, surveys of women across the world find that 10 to 60 percent report at least one episode of physical violence, including sexual violence, by their partner, according to Claudia Garcia-Moreno, a public health physician at the World Health Organization (WHO). In most countries where high percentages are HIV infected, married women are at great risk from husbands who sleep around but still insist on frequent marital sex. And when husbands are violent, wives may fear asking them to use condoms.

"We used to think that women who were married were in the safe group," says Matambanadzo. But, as the Zimbabwean journalist points out, in many societies marriage might as well be prison. Kenyan AIDS activist Anyango agrees: A women who asks her husband if he is sleeping around will be beaten and thrown out of the house. "But she cannot go back [to her parents'] home, because that is not culturally acceptable." Nor can she leave if she has children who need her. Traditional practices in which widows are "inherited" by their deceased husband's brothers, or the husband's property reverts to his family, force women into yet more economic dependence on men and still greater vulnerability to HIV.

Violence and increased vulnerability to HIV infection are not confined to poor countries or poor communities. Various studies have found that in the U.S. 28 percent of women report at least one episode of physical abuse by a partner; between one in five and one in seven college-educated women can expect to be raped during her lifetime; and 42 percent of college-educated women report forced sexual contact or attempted rape. So far, because of design problems, most studies have only hinted at a link between violence and HIV infection. But in May *The Lancet* reported clear evidence that South African women whose male partners are violent or controlling face a 50 percent higher risk of becoming infected with HIV than other women.

Good data on the relationship between war-related violence and HIV infection are even harder to come by. In failed states and conflict zones, anonymous HIV surveillance is rarely reliably maintained. Nor does it take a rocket scientist to figure out why women are reluctant to have HIV tests when a positive result means stigma, abandonment, destitution, and zero prospect of treatment. Adele, who was gang-raped during Rwanda's genocide, described her hopelessness in an April report by the London-based group African Rights: "I haven't gone for a medical examination. But I'm very unwell with a cough that won't go away. I am getting thinner from one day to the next. I've had enough of life. It means nothing to me."

Despite the paucity of rigorous studies, there is little doubt that war-related rape has infected large numbers of women with HIV. Brutal rapes leave women bleeding and bruised, and many suffer serious physical damage such as fistulae—ruptures of the walls that separate the vagina from the bladder and bowels. The virus spreads easily in blood, and it also replicates in certain immune-system cells that proliferate where tissue is damaged.

No matter how they are infected—by a loved one or a vicious rapist—women in many societies bear a disproportionate share of the burden of AIDS. Some face new threats of violence if they disclose their status to their male relatives. Others turn to selling sex for survival and cannot return to their homes, or they are turned out of their homes because they are sick and then survive by selling sex. Many—even when they themselves are sick—must care for family members with AIDS. "The women of Zimbabwe are cleaning up and mopping up after the epidemic," says Matambanadzo. In some rural areas, she says,

caregivers may have to collect as many as 24 buckets of water, walking up to eight miles a day, just to wash laundry soiled by the diarrhea and vomit of the sick person. "But when the women themselves become sick, there is no one to care for them. . . . They are often labeled as the ones who gave their husbands a disease. They are called witches."

Even if a woman escapes HIV infection after rape, she is likely to suffer other sexually transmitted diseases, unwanted pregnancy, mental trauma, and rejection by her relatives. Indirectly, any and all of these can increase her physical, social, and economic vulnerability to HIV.

While many national policy-makers are fatalistic or complacent, grassroots activists, some NGOs, and a few governments are demanding and taking action. In some of the richer countries, women and girls who have been raped are immediately given a short course of antiretroviral drugs—the same treatment provIded to health workers who sustain needlestick injuries. Some experts argue that even though this post-exposure prophylaxis (PEP) has not yet been proven to block HIV transmission, it should be offered to all raped women. In South Africa, where 40 percent of rapes involve girls under 18, the South African government bowed to activists' pressure and introduced PEP for all rape victims. Amnesty International and Human Rights Watch have called for stronger training and awareness of the program among health workers, police, and courts, and for such specific reforms as making PEP available to girls under 14 without relatives' consent.

Other advocates are pushing governments to adequately fund the development and testing of HIV-killing gels or foams that women could insert into the vagina without their partner's knowledge.

Key to long-term change is exposing and documenting the role of violence in increasing women's vulnerability to HIV—an issue marked by medical, academic, and political neglect. Recently, NGOs have emphasized violence against women as a health problem in its own right, and are now trying to secure concrete changes in law, policy and practice that will reduce women's risk of infection and increase their access to treatment.

"We are trying to get civil society to draw more attention to the links between violence against women and their vulnerability to HIV," says Kathleen Cravero, deputy executive director of UNAIDS and a member of the newly formed Coalition on Women and AIDS, which is working to make concrete changes to women's lives. Amnesty's call for all governments to shoulder their responsibilities to protect women, by ratifying without reservation the UN Convention on the Elimination of All Forms of Discrimination against Women, is a key example of how to achieve this, says Cravero.

So are the actions of women around the world. Take for example Grace, a professional woman in Nairobi who tested positive for HIV in 2000. She took her husband and his family to court when they tried to evict her from the home she had paid for

herself. She won, and her husband has been ordered to give back her home. She was lucky to have a supportive family, a lawyer, and—crucially—money. But her case has drawn attention to the plight of less independent women. There are now proposals to change Kenya's constitution to broaden women's property rights. For Kenyan AIDS activist Anyango, the key to progress is to educate women about their rights, to support each other, and to persuade lawyers and other professionals to give their time to fight their cases. "I have gone through it and know what is right and wrong," she says. "I am able to stand up for myself. We in the HIV/AIDS community believe that everyone must get involved in the fight."

S T O R Y   4

Srey: Cambodia

Wong Kim Hoh (2008)

She was not much older than the 450 Singapore teenagers gathered to hear her speak.

But her life could not be more different from theirs.

Srey Mom is from Cambodia. She started working at the age of seven, was abandoned at 10, was tortured into becoming a child prostitute at 14, and contracted HIV when she was 16.

Now 20, she is an activist, determined to help other Cambodian girls avoid her fate.

For many of the Singapore students who attended World Vision's 30-hour Famine Camp at the Anglo-Chinese School in Barker Road recently, she put a human face to the problems of human trafficking and child prostitution which plague Cambodia and other South-east Asian countries.

The relief and advocacy agency has run the camp annually since 1985 to educate and motivate Singapore youths to act on global issues such as hunger, poverty, HIV/AIDS and the environment.

International agencies estimate that there are two million children enslaved in the sex trade in the region. In Cambodia, up to 30,000 sex workers are estimated to be below 16 years old, and about a fifth of the country's female sex workers are infected with HIV.

Poverty is one of the biggest reasons why the trade thrives, with even parents known to sell their daughters.

"Girls as young as 10 have been sold at prices ranging from US$50 to US$200 (S$68 to S$270)," says Chammap Nay, 24, an aid worker with World Vision in Cambodia.

While heartbreaking, Srey Mom's story is an all too familiar one in her country.

Born the only daughter and the last of seven children to a village baker and his wife, she left school after just one month to hawk bread. Her father died when she was 10. Her mother remarried and took only the boys with her to Phnom Penh.

"She left me behind," Srey Mom recalled. "She said I was too young and that I should look after my 70-year-old grandmother. I just helped villagers harvest rice and wash clothes for tins of rice and salted fish."

When she was 13, she accompanied a neighbor to Phnom Penh after he told her he knew where her mother and siblings lived. But the man abandoned her in the city. To survive, she slept on the streets and begged before becoming a helper at a fruit stall.

"One well-dressed woman often came to buy from me. She was kind and sometimes paid me more. One day, she told me she could get me a job as a prawn peeler, which would pay one million riel (S$340) a month. I was so happy."

But the woman sold her to a couple who ran a brothel near the Thai border.

"There were about 50 young girls in the house, and they were wearing nice clothes and make-up," she recalled. "The woman told me to wait while she went out to buy me clothes. She never came back."

Srey Mom was shocked when the couple told her that she would have to have sex with men to pay them back.

When she refused, she was locked in a tiny dark room, and denied food for a week. She was also beaten and tortured with electric wires until she submitted.

"Every day I was forced to have sex with between 3 and 10 men. On weekends, I sometimes had 20 clients," she said quietly.

The men were Cambodian, Thai and foreigners, and the couple kept all the money she earned. Within two years, she was infected with HIV.

One day she fled the brothel, with three of its henchmen in pursuit. She ended up in a village and hid herself in a rubbish bin until she felt hot water poured on her.

A crowd brandishing sticks and knives had gathered, thinking she was a thief. After she explained her predicament, they raised money for her bus fare back to Kampong Cham.

She was reunited with her mother but, without medication, she soon started suffering from tuberculosis and fungal and other infections.

Word spread that she had AIDS and it affected her mother's drink stall business.

"She screamed at me to get out of the house and told me to go somewhere and die," she recalled.

Desperate, she became a sex worker again.

"I always told my customers to use condoms but many didn't and I couldn't tell them I had AIDS. Some of them were young students," she said, her head hanging down.

One day she fainted outside a hospital while trying to seek treatment. A World Vision Trauma Recovery Centre (TRC) volunteer came to her aid, and turned her life around.

The center takes in sexually exploited or trafficked children, helps them recover and learn skills to earn a living. Since it was started in Phnom Penh in 1997, it has taken in about 700 children, helping them to reconnect with their families and communities, or fostering them to healthy homes. Srey Mom was given free medication, reconciled with her mother, and given a sugar cane presser to start a business. Unfortunately word of her illness leaked and it hit her business.

TRC officials convinced her to become a campaigner for the center in Phnom Penh, a role she now relishes.

"I work with trafficked girls. I encourage them to share their experience, raise awareness so that we can prosecute brothel owners and traffickers and put a stop to this problem," she said. She has also become a speaker at international conferences, including a child-trafficking forum in Hanoi last year. Today, her earnings help to support her mother and brothers.

St Andrews Junior College student Rachel Cheong, 18, who attended the camp, came away moved by the activist's story. "A group of us went up to her after her talk to hug her and we told her she was strong and inspiring and to keep on fighting," she said.

Mantombi Nyawo: South Africa

Nicole Itano (2005)

There was an unusual chill in the air the day they set Nozipho Mathenjwa's spirit free. A cold wind whipped through the Mathenjwa homestead and dark clouds threatened rain. Mathenjwa had passed from this world three months before and the family gathered to cleanse the homestead, so her spirit could join the ancestors. Mantombi Nyawo shed no tears that day as she prepared a special meal to honor her dead grandchild, though inside she grieved that she and her grandchild had fought during their last days together.

Just three months before, Mathenjwa, 25, had been laid to rest next to her mother, Lungile Mathenjwa, who died in her mid-40s, under rocks and dirt in the yard of the home where three of the remaining Mathenjwa children still lived. Both women were taken by AIDS, the illness Nyawo calls "umbulalazwe": the disease that is killing the whole world.

MOTHER DIES FIRST

Lungile died first, in February 2003, leaving her five children in the care of Nozipho. But less than a year later, the daughter followed her mother, and Nyawo was left to care for the remaining five children, although the youngest lived in another village with other relatives and one of the oldest girls had run away to stay with her boyfriend.

"I didn't understand what was happening, why my children were dying," says Nyawo, a heavy, dark-skinned woman with drooping breasts, who guesses that she is in her late 60s.

It was only after Lungile died, when Nozipho fell seriously ill, that Nyawo learned about AIDS and how it was spread. At the nearby hospital in the small town of Ingwavuma, they taught her how to take care of someone who was sick and gave her gloves to protect herself as she cared for her ailing granddaughter.

But Nyawo fears that she may have caught HIV before she learned these things, as she tended her daughter and granddaughter through their illnesses. Following traditional healing practices, she used her finger to clean the excrement from their anuses, believing that if they bled during the process the blood would wash away the disease.

Now she knows how risky such actions were. Once, after Nozipho died, Nyawo even went to the local hospital for an HIV test. She never went back for the results.

"I was afraid that someone would recognize me there and say 'this woman, she has AIDS,'" Nyawo said.

EACH DAY A STRUGGLE

Each day is a struggle to feed her large family, which includes the Mathenjwa children as well as half a dozen of her youngest children and several grandchildren whose parents live elsewhere, all of whom stay in Nyawo's kraal. Their only income is the about $250 they receive from the state each month for Nyawo's pension and the disability grant her husband receives for his weak lungs, the lasting legacy of years working in a Johannesburg gold mine.

But her husband Obert, a thin lanky man, often spends his money on frivolous things like new jeans or a cell phone, while she puts hers toward food, school fees and clothes for the children. Each month, she buys the Mathenjwa children a large bag of white corn meal, South Africa's staple food. During the month, she tries to give them a bit of meat or some vegetables to put on top of the pap, a thick corn gruel, but often the children must fend for themselves.

Often, though, the children claim she is stingy, that she is fat because she keeps the best bits for herself. Once, they say, grandfather asked the eldest boy, Phumlani, to help slaughter a pig. The only meat the Mathenjwa family got in return for his help was the snout. Nyawo says this is not true, that there is simply not enough to go around.

Once, Nyawo says, she could grow enough corn and vegetables to feed her whole family. Her husband kept cattle and occasionally hunted for antelope and baboons. But the game is all gone and four years of drought have yielded withered harvests.

Nyawo is also getting old and has no energy to plow so large a field. It is an effort to haul her large body and she limps from a bad knee. In her compound, as in many others here, there are children and old people but few able-bodied laborers. The young people in any case do not want work in the fields. They dream of modern clothes and life in the city.

CHILDREN CHANGE

These days, Nyawo is often baffled by the behavior of her orphaned grandchildren. After Nozipho died, 12-year-old Mfundo began picking fights with neighboring children. He stabbed his sister Sbuka and arrived scraped and bloody on the day of Nozipho's cleansing ceremony after a fight over a wire car.

"He wants to hit everyone," said Obert, shaking his head the day of the ceremony. "He doesn't respect his elders."

Sbuka, aged 16, became sullen. Often she would respond to Nyawo only in monosyllables: yes, no.

Just before Christmas, one of Sbuka's teachers asked if she would like to go live with her mother in a township several hundred miles away. The teacher's siblings had all left home and her mother wanted a girl to help her around the house. In return, the family would pay her school fees, buy her clothes and feed her. Sbuka saw the offer as a chance to escape from the hunger and poverty of Machobeni, but Nyawo wouldn't agree.

"Her mother gave me this child and told me that I must look after her," says Nyawo, lying on a mat in her kraal, her waist wrapped in the pink towel she often uses as a skirt. "I cannot let her go so far away. How will I know what is happening to her? If she goes, it is without my permission and I am no longer responsible for her."

She was angry that the teacher had never come to speak to her, to ask her permission. She was also worried that the police might come to arrest her if Sbuka was no longer staying with her, since she had applied for a foster care grant from the government for her, although the grant had not yet come.

"This woman must come to speak to me to tell me why she wants to take away my child."

Sbuka did not argue. She simply grew silent, refusing to speak to her grandmother for months.

"She won't talk to me about it," she said sulking. "She won't listen to me."

Now Nyawo is worried that Sbuka is misbehaving, running around with boys. But does not know what to do or how to control her.

"These children today, they have no respect," Nyawo says sadly. "That is why there is this disease that is killing us."

Parvati and Fatima: India

Aasha Kapur Mehta and Sreoshi Gupta (2005)

ON A FOOTPATH OF DESPAIR

Parvati and her family live in abject poverty. Her home is a 6-foot by 6-foot space, on a footpath in Kurla, Mumbai. A plastic sheet with holes in it is a makeshift roof. A few planks thrown on the pavement serve as flooring. The family's prized possessions are a few plastic buckets and broken cans of water, a few clothes, a stove and some utensils.

Both Parvati and her husband are migrants from Bihar. Parvati's parents married her off at the age of 12. A few years later, she came to Mumbai and stayed in Kurla with her husband's sister, while her husband worked as a plumber earning Rs 3,000 per month (US$67). As long as her husband was working she did not need to work and they ate well. About four years ago, however, her husband fell ill, testing positive for HIV. The little money they had was spent on doctors and medicines. Once her husband's HIV status became known, they were soon thrown out of her sister-in-law's home and forced to live on the footpath with their 6 children, all under the age of 12.

With her husband unwell and unable to work, six children to feed and no income, they contemplated suicide. Committed Communities Development Trust (CCDT), a local organization heard of their plight and was able to provide some help with basic rations, advice about nutrition and medication, and support for education of the children. Parvati was able to start working as a part time cleaner, cleaning floors and washing utensils and clothes, in three houses to earn about Rs 1,500.

Besides working from 9am–4pm everyday to bring in her meagre income, Parvati also has to look after her children and her ailing husband, who suffers from coughs, vomiting, diarrhea and severe fatigue. There are days when her husband cannot get up, even to take medicine on his own. On these days, she has to take leave from work to care for him. Although he is on anti-retroviral (ARV) treatment, this does not stop the fever, vomiting and diarrhea. To get water, Parvati and her children have to go to the chaul tap that is a 15-minute walk from their makeshift shelter. They must make 10 trips each day to get the water they need. In addition, her husband needs to be helped to the toilet which is about half a kilometer away.

Parvati and her husband went to the hospital for medication several times each month when he was first diagnosed. Each visit was expensive, even though they went to the public Baba Hospital in Kurla instead of a private hospital. Money was needed for X-rays and CD-4 tests, so Parvati had to borrow money from the people whose houses she cleaned. She sold her jewelry for Rs 10,000 four years ago, when her husband first fell ill. The doctor prescribed medicines for six months, at Rs 800 per month. But they could not afford to pay for medication beyond 4 months, so it was discontinued. No other help was available in Mumbai.

In recent times, Parvati's health has begun to suffer. Her young children look after her when she's sick. She has had to cut back her cleaning work to just two houses now, earning only Rs 1,200 per month. With no other family or government support available (except for ARV medication from the public hospital), Parvati's sole hope of survival for herself and her family is the CCDT.

FAMILY SUPPORT SHINES A LIGHT AT THE END OF THE TUNNEL

In 1994, when she was just 17 and not yet finished with her studies, Fatima was married off by her family. Despite being fairly assertive in her conservative family and expressing her desire to complete her studies and graduate instead of getting married, family pressure proved too much.

A few years later, her husband began to look ill, and her family asked him to get tested for tuberculosis. He felt insulted and refused to seek any medical attention. Two years after this, her father-in-law had to be operated on for cancer and was in need of blood. As the only son, her husband was asked to give blood but he refused. Under pressure from her family members he eventually agreed, whereupon he learned that he was HIV-positive. He chose not to inform anyone, including Fatima and both their families, and took no steps, such as using condoms, to protect his wife from infection. Instead, he tried to self-medicate, buying "medicine" from TA Majid, a famous quack in Kerala.

In 1998, Fatima's husband was tested again, and this time, the doctor told her brother-in-law that her husband had AIDS and that both she and her husband would die within two months, and indeed he did die two months later. Her father took her to get tested. She was tested twice within three weeks, the test positive both times. Incredibly, all this time, Fatima still had not been told that her husband had AIDS and had just died from it. She also had no clue that she was HIV-positive. Her husband had chosen not to disclose his status to anyone for fear that Fatima's parents would take her away. Instead, he allowed his family to blame her for his illness. After his death, her mother-in-law, deciding that Fatima was at fault and that she too would soon die, said that no share of the property would be given to her.

Fortunately, Fatima's father welcomed her back to his house. One day, she found her test report in her father's bag, and that was how she finally discovered that she was HIV-positive. Her initial reaction was outrage at her husband for knowingly exposing and infecting her with the virus, followed by a deep sense of despair about her future.

But Fatima's brother's wife had a friend at the Bombay Municipal Corporation, and she felt that since science had progressed so much, there had to be hope. So she persuaded Fatima to go to the BMC where she was counselled and told that with treatment she would be able to live out her life, instead of dying in a few months. She met many other HIV-positive people, one of whom was setting up a support group and asked if she would work with them. She was hesitant at first but realized that the only

difference between her and the person forming the support group was their gender. "If he can live, why not me—I have to die some day. But let me try and do something constructive with my life." Earlier, the doctor had given her just a few months to live but now, with treatment it could be a few years she thought to herself.

So she asked her father if she could work with the support group. Girls typically didn't work in her home, but in view of her circumstances, her father felt that if she worked, it might help her. Less than a year after she was diagnosed, and only two months since knowing she was HIV-positive, Fatima joined the positive network. She was the only girl, and she was only twenty years old. Slowly, the network helped her to take charge of her life, by arming her with the information, counseling and peer support she needed to deal with her situation.

At home, her condition prompted some challenges, but her family has remained supportive throughout. At first, she was not allowed to work in the kitchen because her family was afraid she might cut her hand while working with a knife. But her father's elder brother or "tayaji" said she had to be allowed to do some work—at least knead flour or something else useful in the kitchen. Now, Fatima cooks at home and everyone in her family eats what she cooks. She also looks after her niece—no one in her family has ever said that the child should not go near her for fear of infection. The only discrimination she has suffered is from her husband's relatives. Children who had grown up with her were kept away from her after her status was known.

Today, Fatima is a confident and healthy 27-year-old woman who is a senior representative of the Positive Women's Network in Maharashtra, a grantee of UNIFEM's Trust Fund to End Violence against Women. She was encouraged to resume her studies and is now in her final year of college and learning to work with computers. The only opportunistic infection she has had is herpes. She takes good care of her nutrition, has a very positive outlook on life and rarely falls ill. She saw the worst side of life while caring for her husband after his diagnosis. He suffered through several opportunistic infections—tuberculosis, diarrhea, fever, weight loss and even memory loss. He had no access to anti-retroviral treatment. While he was bed-ridden she would care for him all day and all night, bathing, shaving and dressing him, and all without knowing why he was even ill in the first place. But her story has turned out well; she is one of the fortunate few. Because of her family's support, she is pursuing her education, and working through the positive network to improve the HIV/AIDS information and care services of government hospitals in her area. She can negotiate and demand facilities at government hospitals, and many of the suggestions given in the context of care needs draw on her suggestions.

S T O R Y **7**

Thembi: South Africa

Erika Nelson (2008)

When she tested HIV positive in 2002 at the age of 16, Thembi Ngubane of South Africa scarcely had an idea what HIV meant. Now 23, she is one of the foremost HIV activists on the planet. She received worldwide recognition in 2006, when National Public Radio featured a stunning audio diary she kept in 2004 and 2005. Here at the XVII International AIDS Conference, she has been a near-ubiquitous presence, giving speeches and even co-chairing a major session on the state of the HIV pandemic. And did we mention that she has a 3-year-old, HIV-negative daughter? We were fortunate enough to have the opportunity to sit down with Thembi and hear her incredible story.

Can we start by hearing the story of how you found out that you were positive?

I tested HIV positive in 2002. I was 16. The reason why I went for an HIV test was because my ex-boyfriend at that time had gotten sick in the past few months, and then he died. No one would tell me why he died. No one would tell me what he had. I felt it was my responsibility to actually find out for myself if he did have HIV or AIDS. The only thing to do, was for me to go for an HIV test.

You didn't know for sure that he died of an AIDS-related illness?

I didn't know for sure, but when I saw him when he was sick I could see the symptoms. At school they used to tell us that if a person is sick, if he has HIV, you could see the symptoms when the immune system is very weak. The person would lose hair; the person would get so thin. He had some of the symptoms, but I was not sure because I was not very well-informed about HIV.

What happened when you went to get tested?

It was scary, because of my being healthy and looking healthy, yet suspecting that I might be HIV positive. It didn't seem real. Also, because I wanted to prevent so many things: I didn't want to die, I didn't want to get sick, and I didn't want people to know. It was a matter of going and finding out for myself and keeping it to myself.

When I was told that I was HIV positive, I could not believe them. I kept on asking them, "Why do I have HIV? Why do I still look healthy? Why am I not thin? Why am I not sick? Why am I not feeling sick? I feel normal and I look normal. Why do I have HIV?"

It was very hard for me to accept, but the reality was there. It was either accept it and take responsibility, or ignore the fact that I had HIV.

When you went to get tested, did you go all alone?

Yes. I went alone. It was not planned. I didn't plan it. I was just curious, because at that time in Khayelitsha it was 2002 and they just opened a loveLife youth center. I wanted a reason to go inside, but I didn't want people to see me. Because if people saw me go into loveLife, they would think that I'm having sex.

It was very hard for me to go there. Since I was alone, I thought, "Why don't I just sneak into loveLife?" So, I was sneaking around in there and just taking a tour. It was too much for me, because I could see condoms. I was like, "Oh man, condoms — in front of these people? There are old people here."

I felt like maybe people here understand. I thought, "Let me ask if they can do an HIV test." Lucky for me, I met someone that I knew who has HIV and he was a counselor.

I asked him if I could have an HIV test. He asked, "Why do you want to have an HIV test?" I said, "At school they tell us that if you ever, ever, ever have sex, you must have an HIV test. So I thought, why not?" [Laughs.] But I was covering the whole thing up!

LoveLife is a clinic or a center? What is it like?

LoveLife is a youth center. It does many different things: you go for birth control; you go for checkups for STDs [sexually transmitted diseases]; you go for HIV tests and they then refer you to the nearest clinic; you go there for counseling; and you go there for sex education.

What happened when you got the news? Who told you and what happened?

The counselor told me. He first explained the procedure and everything. I was just sitting there, just rolling my eyes and thinking, "Well, you can say whatever. I don't look sick, so I'm not."

So poof! The news was "You are HIV positive." I argued with him for 10 minutes. I argued with that guy. I mean, I argued with that guy. I really wanted an explanation. I ended up believing, no, I'm not sick. These people are just trying to scare me. What the hell? I don't look sick. These people are just trying to scare me.

But as soon as I got out of the center, I was starting to hit reality. I was facing people, and I felt like everyone could see that I was HIV positive. I felt like I was losing weight at that moment. I felt like I was going to die tomorrow. Everything just came so quickly. It was like an earthquake!

I panicked. In my panic, I felt I had to tell someone. [Laughs.] Sometimes I think back and I'm like, I did a stupid thing: I have just gotten tested and I'm confused, and then, poof, I go and tell my boyfriend. But I thought he was in danger. I thought, "If I really am HIV positive and my ex-boyfriend didn't tell me he had HIV, and now I have HIV, what about Melikhaya? I owe it to him. I have to go and warn him. I have to go and tell him. He must go for an HIV test to see what's going on."

There I was. I went to him. Lucky for me, we met on the way. I said, "I'm coming from loveLife."

He was like, "loveLife? What are you doing in loveLife?" Because people who go to loveLife are people who have STDs and who go for birth control.

I said, "No, I just went for an HIV test."

"And?" he asked me.

"They say I'm positive."

Then he laughed it off. He said, "Come on. You don't look sick. You know what a person who has HIV looks like. You are not that sick, I mean come on. They are wrong, you know? They're just trying to scare you!"

That was it. I felt like it's not a big deal. Why should I make it a big deal? I just went home. I must put it behind me. I must forget about it. I went home and I didn't tell anyone up until I returned to Melikhaya's place to find out that he had told everyone in the house. He just turned over and was like, "Did she just tell me that she has HIV? I mean, HIV causes AIDS. Oh my God! She's going to die and I'm going to die!"

There he was telling his mother that both of us are going to die because I tested HIV positive. It was a drama of the year! It was a drama. They all wanted to kill me, if I can say so, because at that time no one understood. I also didn't understand. I wasn't even sure if I was going to make it. I was just defending myself. I'm not going to die. I'm going to go to the clinic. I'm going to get something. There must be something that can be done. But I was only saying those words just to stop them from saying all those things about me.

Did Melikhaya go and get tested at that point?

After this drama with me being HIV positive, his family actually called me and they separated us. They said we must break up. We broke off, but I said to him, "I don't mind our relationship ending, because I also have a choice. If I wanted to date someone that has AIDS and I don't have AIDS, I would also think twice. But you don't even know whether you are HIV positive. The only thing that you can do for yourself, and for me as a favor, is to go and have an HIV test."

I don't care about our relationship. We can break up because HIV is not going away from me. We broke off and he went for an HIV test. Luckily, he tested HIV negative. He later came to the support group and I was so pissed because the support group is for people that have HIV. He was coming from school and he came with all these pamphlets. I didn't know what he was doing there, because he probably didn't have HIV and yet there he was. I thought that maybe he had come here to rub it in.

He comes, and he's like, "Thembi, I just went for an HIV test and I tested HIV negative. I'm sorry I didn't understand at first. I panicked. I've read about HIV. I went to counseling and I understand that you are not going to die."

I had all this information that he was picking up the whole week at the libraries and putting one and one together. He asked for me back and I was like, okay. But I said, "You know, you're negative and I'm positive. It's not going to work, but let's try." [Laughs.] So we tried. But he told me that he was in the window period. They say that he's HIV negative, but he must go back again to see because the virus sometimes gets into your blood and hides.

He went again after three months and he was HIV positive. His family said, "You were HIV negative and went back to her! You went back to her to take the virus! You come back, and now look at you, you are sick!" No one understood. But we understood because we know how HIV works. We understood that he had HIV maybe before I even met him.

You can never tell, you know. You never know who has it and who hasn't. You never even know how long you have had it up until you go for an HIV test. It was a matter of, "I don't blame you, Thembi. I don't blame myself, because I was in a relationship before you. It's not like just because you tested HIV positive before me that I'm going to blame you. It's not like that."

Ever since then, we tried to convince our families and educate them. My family didn't have a problem at all. My mother is Christian. It's interesting, because my mother is Christian and my grandmother is a traditional healer. I come from a really interesting family. I'm strictly science, yet my background is half religious and half pseudo science.

My family was very supportive. My grandmother didn't try anything, she just said, "You know what? HIV/AIDS doesn't have a cure, but you can take your treatment. I'm not going to do any remedies for you because you must not take them. The only thing that you have to do is to go to the clinic."

My grandmother also said, "You have to pray to God. That's the only thing you have to do. You have to pray to God that everything will be all right."

I had support from my family and I took Melikhaya under my wing. We tried to convince his family, tried to educate his mother. At the end of the day, we couldn't fight [about this anymore] and now we are one big, strong family. We have Onwabo and everyone is happy. [Onwabo is Thembi's 3-year-old daughter.]

That's right! You got pregnant after you tested positive.

Yes.

Can you tell me a little bit about that?

[Laughs.]. That is also one of the decisions that sometimes you think, "Maybe I shouldn't have done it. But anyway, it happened."

Just before I tested HIV positive, just like any young woman, I always wanted to have a family. There was a break point where I first [said,] "This HIV has taken everything from me. I won't be able to get married. Who would marry me?"

All these questions were popping up until Melikhaya and I got through some talking and were like, I want to have a kid, because everyone was screaming this stupid stuff in my head, like, "The kid is going to get sick. The kid is going to get infected. You're going to die and the kid is going to be an orphan. Maybe the kid will be a strange kid because you won't be there and the father won't be there. Maybe the family won't treat the kid when you are not there."

All of these things were coming to me, and they made me feel like I'm useless. This HIV thing really does kill you, kills your love, or kills your dreams. The only thing I have to do now is sit like this and wait to die. Just wait until I die.

There was a moment when I felt like, you know what, since I was going to a support group the support really helped me. I realized no one can be me. I'm only me. I can only make decisions for myself. If I choose that this HIV is going to an obstacle in my life, that's what it's going to be. But if I choose, I'm going to fight it. I'm going to live my life the way I wanted to live it before I had HIV. It's just going to get along with that. That's how it's going to happen.

I was like, okay, I'm going to push it. I'm still young. I don't want to die. I don't want to just be forgotten: "Thembi died of AIDS." That's all I had. Nothing behind, you know.

I didn't do it for a selfish reason, to have a baby to love me, or something like a legacy to leave behind. I did it because I wanted someone to love for myself. I wanted to love him [Melikhaya]. I wanted to give him everything. I wanted her to love me back. I don't know how to put it. That's all I wanted to do.

There was a chance, I was told, that the baby [my daughter] might be HIV-positive. I prayed to God that the baby—I know I didn't do anything wrong. The baby won't be HIV-positive. God will not punish me like that. I had to believe. I said, Melikhaya, I believe. Even if the baby is HIV-positive, there is hope out there. The baby might be HIV-positive, but who knows? The cure can come out anyway, anytime. It's not like it's the end of the world and we have to wait and say, "I'm going to have a baby when the cure comes." That's not going to happen. This is life. This is reality. This is about me. It's not about HIV. It's all about me, what I want in life, and what I believe in.

We talked to my doctor. Lucky for my daughter, he was very understanding. He took me through the procedure and explained to me what exactly is going to happen when I get pregnant. He should check my CD4 count, check my viral load, check my CD4 count, check my viral load.

Everything just meshed there and then. It meshed. Everything just meshed. I was put on nevirapine (Viramune); I was taken off efavirenz (Sustiva, Stocrin). I was put on another medication. [inaudible] CD4 count was [inaudible] too high. It was perfectly in health and I was also perfectly in health.

I said I'm not going to breastfeed. There are likely chances—I got on nevirapine and my baby got AZT. I knew when I give birth, on that day, before they could even come back with the results, I already told my family, no, Onwabo is going to come out negative. I knew it.

The second test, everyone was like, "Oh my God, Thembi, we hope that you didn't breastfeed the baby. We hope that you were not careless with it." I said, no, don't worry.

Onwabo was HIV-negative, and now she's crazy! [Laughs.]

She's three, right? So—

Yes. She is so crazy now! She's crazy. But I'm happy. I wouldn't say that I wish—of course I wish I didn't have HIV, but I love my life now. I wish I didn't have it. If they would say, what's the one thing that you want? I would say, you know what? I want to live a positive, normal life as long as I can.

I wouldn't say I want to be negative, because I know that's not going to happen. But if I would still have a chance to go back and change, I would change everything.

I feel lucky. I know that everything happens for a reason. God put me in this situation. I'm in this situation for a reason, but a lot of people died just in front of me. I'm still here. Why? I ask myself. Yes, I'm taking medication. A lot of people die while taking medication. But I'm still here. Why? I'm here for a reason.

What is that reason?

I'm here to inspire people. I feel like I'm here to inspire people because with me being here, with me struggling, getting sick, going through some of the crises, going through a relationship, having a baby, and still coming out and talking to people and say, "I'm here, I'm a woman, I'm HIV positive, and I'm living my life normally." It can happen! It can happen. But I always say that prevention is better than a cure. Prevention is better than a cure.

What do you think gives you the courage to speak out when so many people don't?

I think it's because it helps me. I think I saw the impact it has on me. That's why I think it's like this every time I talk. I get healed. Because every time I talk about it, it feels like a new wound. I speak about it all the time, so I'm used to it. It's like every time I start to talk about it, it feels like it's a new wound. I'm opening up old sores. To talk, it heals me again. Every time I talk it heals me again and again. That's the courage.

What's it like being a positive Mom? Are you able to talk to your daughter at this point? She's still very young, but—

She's still very young, but I know that God is going to give me much more time, up until she gets a little bit bigger, so that I can explain everything. At this point, she's young but she knows that I go and talk, but she actually doesn't know what I'm talking about. But I have everything fixed up for her. I have the [inaudible] copies. I have all the work that I have done. I have pictures. I put them in a box.

When she's old enough to understand and ready enough to see, whether I'm here or not, I know she's going to be part of me. Everything is going to be fine.

What's it like being out in your community? You're sort of out to the whole universe. Do you experience stigma at all in the township where you live?

Yes. Stigma in every community is going to take a long time before we actually break the stigma, especially in Khayelitsha, because of how people's minds act. People are still stereotyped. There are a lot of cultural beliefs and there are a lot of myths going around.

Sometimes there's too much stigma and sometimes some people say I'm doing the right thing, and you get those people who are like, "What's up with you going around talking about your status? It's something confidential. You should hide it. You don't have to tell the world about it." Some people think I'm exploiting myself, something like that.

Other people are too jealous. I help people. I've had comments like, "You know what, even if you can go and tell the world, the fact is you're going to die anyway." It's not going to go away just because you go and tell it, so you can enjoy it while it lasts.

You get comments like that, but who cares? It's not like everyone's going to be here up until the universe explodes. We're all going to die!

I can say I'm bulletproof. People say whatever they feel like saying. All I'm doing is focusing on what I'm doing. I don't care about all the comments, whether they are good or whether they are bad. I do what I feel is right for me and now I have a responsibility. I have Onwabo.

How do you think HIV has changed you?

It has changed me for the better, because I think if I really didn't have the test, I wouldn't be who I am today. I would still be the ignorant whoever I was, whatever I was then. I would still think low of people that have HIV. I wouldn't be involved in any HIV work. Imagine! Imagine not knowing your status and being involved in HIV work, that's crazy! [inaudible] I would be one of those people who say, "Oh, well, it can never happen to me. It's not like I'm sleeping around." I use a condom once, sometimes, it's not like, you know, you know what I mean, I would be one of those people, I wouldn't take anything seriously. It has transformed me into this place, and that is actual. I'm taking things more seriously and it has made me grow so quickly.

Thembi, thank you so much for talking with me. Is there anything else you want to share with our readers?

I think that, as people, we should actually acknowledge that HIV is here and we need to do something about it. We should stop blaming people and blaming each other. We should work around it. Work around the stigma and discrimination, work around everything that's surrounding it. Because at the end of the day, the children are going to suffer and we are also going to suffer. Since I'm a mother, I really don't want Onwabo to grow up in a world like this. I really don't want her, in the future, sitting like this and thinking, "Oh my God, I tested HIV-positive." I mean, come on! As if we didn't have the courage to do anything about it. We do have it! It's just that we don't want to or we don't see it, I don't know. But it's up to an individual. You have to push yourself.

Mama's Club: Uganda

Rachel Scheier (2006)

A group of HIV-positive mothers in Uganda have banded together to form the "Mama's Club." Twice a month they share medical and legal information, but perhaps most important, they remember they are not alone.

Grace Tumuhirwe was infected with the AIDS virus when her uncle raped her at the age of 12. A few years later, when she began to show symptoms, her family threw her out, and she rented a room in a Kampala slum. She found a boyfriend, who helped her with money, and soon she found herself pregnant. Now she has a year-old HIV-positive son.

Robinah Kaimbombo was married off as a teen to a much older man. He died of AIDS a decade later, leaving her with four children and infected with the virus herself. She was relieved when another man came along and offered to help with the bills. She insisted they use condoms, but one night, he came home drunk and raped her and she became pregnant again. When her daughter was born HIV-positive, her husband disappeared.

Fatumah Namata was infected with the virus by her husband. When she confronted him, he said it had nothing to do with him and left her with five children to support. Two of them are HIV-positive.

These women are all members of the Mama's Club, a group that offers psychosocial support to HIV-positive mothers and pregnant women in Uganda.

Twice a month, the women gather in a room at TASO—The AIDS Support Organization—the country's oldest and largest HIV-AIDS support group, in Kampala. They drink milky tea and brainstorm ways to make money, like raising poultry and selling crafts. They learn about how to care for HIV-positive infants. Those who are pregnant learn about their need to receive antiretroviral drugs during pregnancy and delivery and to not breastfeed past the first three months to prevent passing on the virus to their babies. They share stories of stigma and discrimination. But mostly, they sit and chat. They remind each other that they are not alone.

"PATHETIC SITUATION" FORUM

"Most of these women are single, widowed or have been chased away from their homes because of their HIV status," said Lydia Mungherera, a doctor who was working in the clinic at TASO in the late 1990s when she realized that a whole host of issues that were not strictly medical faced HIV-positive mothers and pregnant women. "The whole idea was to start a forum for all these pathetic situations."

In 2004, with a few small private donations, Mungherera gathered a handful of TASO clients who were also mothers to start the group. Two years later, it has 50 members and a waiting list. Mama's Club accepts infected women who are expecting or have infants up to the age of 3. During these early years, she said, infants are most vulnerable to developing health problems and mothers are just learning how to cope with the dual challenges of having a new infant and being HIV-positive.

With antiretroviral drugs and proper care, the risk of mother-to-child transmission of HIV can be as low as 1 percent. But in developing countries, the number of infants who are born HIV-positive is still unacceptably high, according to a March 2006 World Health Organization report.

According to the report, less than 10 percent of HIV-positive women in developing countries received the drugs that prevent mother-to-child transmission of the virus between 2003 and 2005. As a result, about 1,800 children a day are born with HIV. Each year, over 570,000 children under the age of 15 die of AIDS, most having acquired the virus from their mothers, the report said. It blamed frail health systems in poor countries and inadequate drug supplies, among other factors.

IGNORANCE AND STIGMA

Mungherera and members of the Mama's Club said that ignorance and stigma are also to blame. In Uganda and elsewhere, many women learn they are infected when they are pregnant. That's when they will go to a clinic and be encouraged to take a test. Women who test positive under any circumstances are counseled not to have more children and not to engage in unprotected sex. But women say that's easier said than done.

"In our country, the woman doesn't have the right to say no to sex or to having children," said Pross Kevin, a 48-year-old member of the Mama's Club. "The man is the one. If he wants to have sex—protected or not—it is his decision."

In Uganda, as in many African countries, women face huge cultural expectations to bear children. A romantic relationship is traditionally not considered legitimate unless it produces a baby.

Another problem, say club members, is discrimination against HIV-positive pregnant women by health workers. Members of the Mama's Club went to a local human rights group with testimonies documenting the problems in order to bring them to the attention of the public. They described how nurses and midwives in the delivery ward at Mulago Hospital, Kampala's major public health facility, had neglected and insulted patients upon learning that they were HIV-positive.

SHUNNED BY DELIVERY NURSE

One woman said she believed her baby was infected with the virus because nurses refused to attend to her during delivery. Another woman said a nurse asked her "why she had gotten pregnant in the first place." Stories about the issue appeared in the local press. Though they have no hard statistics, Mama's Club members believe that such instances of discrimination have become rarer since the issue was brought to light.

Recently, representatives from a local women lawyers' group have visited meetings to educate the women on their legal rights on such issues as marital property and medical treatment in public hospitals. Also, the executive director of TASO, Alex Coutinho, gave a speech about the need for HIV-positive men to be more supportive of their partners and called for a "Tata's Club."

The Mama's Club survives on scattered private donations and the proceeds from a charity walk it held last year. Mama Club member Kevin said with or without money, the mothers will keep meeting twice a month.

"At least, if we are together then maybe we can help each other," she said.

S T O R Y   **9**

Tatiana and Dina: Russia and Ukraine

UNAIDS (2008)

"If in my country I have fans that listen to me, I am ready to endlessly tell them about HIV prevention and how it is wrong to discriminate against people living with HIV," said Tatiana Lazareva, TV Presenter and one of the 25 women from Russia and Ukraine who are participating in the "Stars against AIDS" campaign organized by UNAIDS. This is an unprecedented project to tackle stigma and discrimination in the Eastern Europe region. UNAIDS has brought together a group of successful women from Russia and Ukraine to help dispel the taboos and prejudice that often surround AIDS and to reduce discrimination against people living with HIV. Female celebrities from the artistic, media and sports communities have joined their talents and voices to ensure a proactive response to the AIDS epidemic.

Twenty-five famous women agreed to be photographed by the well-known photographer Serge Golovach who offered his services to the campaign for free. Through an exhibition of these portraits, the project aims to raise awareness about AIDS, increase the dissemination of HIV information and reduce stigma and discrimination toward people living with HIV.

"At first I was reluctant to participate in this project as I hardly knew anything about the scale of the HIV epidemic in my country and had never come across HIV in my daily life," said actress Dina Korzun. "I thought that closing my eyes to it would be the simplest thing to do. However, I found it was far more important to make an effort and search for information. I then realized that the major challenge of this disease is ignorance, and hence, intolerance," she added.

The exhibition opened in May, 2008, at the Stella Art Foundation in Moscow. The opening was attended by Elena Khanga and Maria Arbatova—two of the celebrities that have participated in the project—along with representatives from the Russian Ministry of Health and Social Development, the UNAIDS Programme Coordinator in Russia and the heads of UN agencies in the country. The exhibition is expected to tour Russia and Ukraine throughout 2008. A selection of the portraits will also be published as a 2009 calendar which will be launched at this year's World AIDS Day.

Eastern Europe and Central Asia have faced significant increases in the numbers of new HIV infections in recent years. An estimated 150,000 people were newly infected with HIV in 2007 bringing the number of people living with HIV in Eastern Europe and Central Asia to 1.6 million compared to 630,000 in 2001, an increase of 150%. Nearly 90% of newly reported HIV diagnoses in 2006 were from two countries: the Russian Federation (66%) and Ukraine (21%). Furthermore, up to 40% of all new infections throughout the region were women.

This project is important because it encourages greater public discussion around AIDS. We have seen in many other countries that when there is more public awareness of AIDS, HIV prevention programs work more effectively and there is greater support for people living with HIV. The 25 women who are part of this project are helping make this kind of public discussion possible. We are very grateful for their engagement and support," said Lisa Carty, UNAIDS Programme Coordinator of the Russian Federation.

Credits

CHAPTER 1

Epigraph:

Excerpt from "Mountain Moving Day" by Yosano Akiko from *River of Stars: Selected Poems of Yosano Akiko* by Sam Hamill and Keiko Matsui Gibson. Copyright © 1997 by Sam Hamill. Reprinted by arrangement with Shambhala Publications Inc., Boston, M.A. www.shambhala.com.

Sidebars:

"World Conferences on Women" is excerpted with permission from *Outcomes on Gender and Equality.* Copyright © United Nations.

"Tools for a Populist Uprising: Ready to Collaborate Across Red and Blue? Here are Some Ways to Get Started" by Noah Grant and Layla Aslani and "10 Policies for a Better America: A *Yes!* Take On What Americans Want" by Sarah van Gelder and Noah Grant. Reprinted with permission from "Purple America" in the Fall 2008 issue of *Yes!* magazine. *Yes!* is a non-profit, ad-free national publication that offers positive solutions for creating a just and sustainable world. To subscribe, visit www.yesmagazine.org/subscribe or call (800) 937-4451.

Readings:

Reading 1, "Women Still Have a Long Way to Go" was originally published as "Progress Report on Discrimination Against Women: Women Still Have A Long Way to Go, a UN Committee Reports" by Cynthia G. Wagner in *The Futurist*, Vol. 42, No. 3, May–June 2008, p. 9. Used with permission from the World Future Society, 7910 Woodmont Avenue, Suite 450, Bethesda, Maryland 20814 USA. Tel: 301-656-8274, www.wfs.org.

Reading 2, "Are Women Human?" is reprinted by permission from *Are Women Human? And Other International Dialogues* by Catharine A. MacKinnon. Cambridge, Mass.: The Belknap Press of Harvard University Press. Copyright © 2006 by Catharine A. MacKinnon.

Reading 3, "The Messy Relationship Between Feminisms and Globalizations" by Manisha Desai in *Gender & Society,* Vol. 21, No. 6, December 2007, pp. 797–803. Copyright © 2007 Sociologists for Women in Society. Reprinted with permission of Sage Publications, Inc., via Copyright Clearance Center.

Reading 4, "Under Western Eyes: Feminist Scholarship and Colonial Discourse" by Chandra Talpade Mohanty is reprinted by permission of the publisher from *boundary 2,* Vol. 12, No. 3, pp. 333–358. Copyright © 1984, Duke University Press. All rights reserved.

Reading 5, "Comrades" from *Jump and Other Stories* by Nadine Gordimer. Copyright © 1991 by Felix Licensing, B.V. Reprinted by permission of Farrar, Straus & Giroux, LLC; A.P. Watt Ltd on behalf of Felix Licensing BV; and Penguin Group Canada, a Division of Pearson Canada Inc.

Reading 6, "Edge of the Earth" by Hafsat Abiola from *Imagining Ourselves,* edited by Paula Goldman. Copyright © 2006 by The International Museum of Women. Reprinted with permission of New World Library, Novato, CA. www.newworldlibrary.com.

CHAPTER 2

Epigraph:

Excerpt from "Ladies First" by Queen Latifah. Words and Music by Shane Faber, Queen Latifah and Mark James © Warner-Tamerlane Publishing Corp., Now & Then Music, WB Music Corp., Queen Latifah Music Inc., Forty Five King Music, Forked Tongue Music and Simone Johnson Pub. Designee. All rights on behalf of itself and Now & Then Music. Administered by Warner-Tamerlane Publishing Corp. All rights on behalf of itself, Queen Latifah Music Inc., Forty Five King Music, Forked Tongue Music and Simone Johnson Pub. Designee. Administered by WB Music Corp. All rights reserved. Used by permission.

Sidebars:

"Social Networking Goes Global" a comScore press release is reprinted by permission of comScore, Inc.

"I'll Never Return" by Meena is reprinted by permission of RAWA.

Readings:

Reading 7, "Glamour and Honor: Going Online and Reading in West African Culture" by Wendy Griswold, Erin Metz McDonnell, and Terence Emmett McDonnell in *Information Technologies and International Development,* Vol. 3, No. 4, Summer 2006, pp. 37–52. Reprinted by permission of Annenberg Press, University of Southern California, and the authors.

Reading 8, "Women Enter the World of Media" by Manal Ismail and Maysam Ali is reprinted with permission from Gulfnews.com, March 15, 2008.

Reading 9, "Beautiful Betty: An 'Ugly' New TV Character Brings Gender, Class, Ethnic and Body Issues to the Screen" by Yeidy M. Rivero in *Ms,* Winter 2007, pp. 65–66. Reprinted by permission of *Ms.* magazine, © 2007.

Reading 10, "Mirror, Mirror on the Wall" by Tiya Miles in *Testimony: Young African-Americans on Self-Discovery and Black Identity,* edited by Natasha Tarpley. Copyright © 1995 by Natasha

Tarpley. Reprinted with permission of Beacon Press, via Copyright Clearance Center.

Reading 11, "Grover Goes Global: Exporting Sesame Street with Sensitivity" by Anthony Kaufman is reprinted by permission of the author from *Utne*, March–April 2007, pp. 32–33.

Reading 12, "'Telling Our Own Stories': African Women Blogging for Social Change" by Oreoluwa Somolu is reprinted with permission from *Gender & Development*, Vol. 15, No. 3, November 2007. pp. 477–489. Copyright © 2007 Routledge.

CHAPTER 3

Epigraph:

Excerpt from "At the Party" by Ursula K. Le Guin. Copyright © 1986 by Ursula K. Le Guin. First appeared in *CALYX*. Used by permission of the author and the author's agents, the Virginia Kidd Agency, Inc.

Sidebars:

"At 50, Barbie's Stylin; with New Tats" by Tiffany Hsu and Don Lee is reprinted with permission from *Los Angeles Times*, March 6, 2009.

"Intersexuality Is a Human Rights Issue" by Mauro Cabral, International Gay and Lesbian Human Rights Commission.

Readings:

Reading 13, "Transgender Identity in Japan" was originally published as "Sexual Minorities Enjoy Limited Rights Today" by Hiroko Tabuchi—The Associated Press from DallasVoice.com, May 12, 2006. Used with permission of The Associated Press. Copyright © 2006. All rights reserved.

Reading 14, "Premenstrual Syndrome as Scientific and Cultural Artifact" by Anne E. Figert from *Integrative Physiological & Behavioral Science*, May 2005, Vol. 40, No. 2, pp. 102–113. Reprinted with kind permission from Springer Science and Business Media, and the author.

Reading 15, "Perfectly Normal" by Lesléa Newman. Copyright © 1990 by Lesléa Newman. First appeared in *Secrets: Short Stories* by Lesléa Newman, published by New Victoria Publishers. Reprinted by permission of Curtis Brown, Ltd.

Reading 16, "Spain Bans Skinny Sizes on Mannequins" by The Associated Press, March 13, 2007. Used with permission of The Associated Press. Copyright © 2007. All rights reserved.

Reading 17, "Changing Faces" by Lisa Takeuchi Cullen is reprinted with permission from *Time*, July 29, 2002. Copyright © 2002 Time Inc.

Reading 18, "Mi Estomago (My Belly)" by Marjorie Agosin is reprinted with permission from *Women and Aging: An Anthology by Women*, edited by Jo Alexander, Debi Berrow, Lisa Domitrovich, Margarita Donnelly, and Cheryl McLean. Copyright © 1986 by CALYX, Inc.

Reading 19, "Unveiled Sentiments: Gendered Islamophobia and Experiences of Veiling Among Muslim Girls in a Canadian Islamic

School" by Jasmin Zine is reprinted with permission from *Equity & Excellence in Education*, 39(3): 239–252, 2006. Copyright © 2006 University of Massachusetts Amherst School of Education.

CHAPTER 4

Epigraph:

Excerpt from "Love Poem" by Audre Lorde. Copyright © 1975 by Audre Lorde from *The Collected Poems of Audre Lorde* by Audre Lorde. Used by permission of W. W. Norton & Company, Inc.

Sidebars:

Bar graph illustrating the prevalence of FGM/C among younger and older women from p. 3 of *Female Genital Mutilation/Cutting: Data and Trends,* 2008. Reprinted with permission from Population Reference Bureau.

"UNICEF Fact Sheet: Female Genital Mutilation/Cutting." Copyright © The United Nations Children's Fund (UNICEF), May 2006. Reprinted with permission.

"Radical Feminism in Political Action: The Minneapolis Pornography Ordinance" by Emily Warren. Reprinted with permission of the author and The Humphrey Institute of Public Affairs, University of Minnesota.

"Sex Trafficking—The Facts" is reprinted with permission from *New Internationalist*, September 2007, pp. 12–13.

"Child Sex Tourism FAQs." Copyright © 2009 World Visions Inc. Reprinted with permission.

Readings:

Reading 20, "Toward a Vision of Sexual and Economic Justice" was originally published as "On Sexual-economic Relations" by Kamala Kempadoo. This paper was first prepared for and presented at the Barnard Center for Research on Women Colloquium, "Toward a Vision of Economic and Sexual Justice," Barnard College, New York, November 20, 2007. Reprinted with permission of the author.

Reading 21, "Distant View of a Minaret" in *Distant View of a Minaret and Other Stories* by Alifa Rifaat, selected and translated from the Arabic by Denys Johnson-Davies. Copyright © in translation Denys Johnson-Davies 1983. Reprinted with permission from Quartet Books, Ltd.

Reading 22, "Cambodian Sex Workers" originally published as "Cambodian Centre Steers Trafficked Women from Sex Trade" by Karoline Kemp is reprinted with permission from *Herizons*, Winter 2007, pp. 8–9. Copyright © 2007 Karoline Kemp.

Reading 23, "Sex Tourism Booming on the Caribbean Coast" is reprinted with permission from *PlusNews*, November 18, 2008. Copyright © IRIN 2008. All rights reserved.

Reading 24, "Lesbian, Gay, Bisexual, and Transgender Rights and the Religious Relativism of Human Rights" by D.Ø. Endsjø is reprinted with permission from *Human Rights Review*, Vol. 6, No. 2, June 2005, pp. 102–110. Copyright © 2005 Springer Netherlands.

Readings:

Reading 36, "In the Family" by Maria Elena Llano, translated by Beatriz Teleki from *Short Stories by Latin American Women: The Magic and the Real,* edited by Celia Correas de Zapata. Reprinted with permission from the publisher. Copyright © 1990 Arte Publico Press, University of Houston.

Reading 37, "Mothers, Fathers, or Parents: Same-Gendered Families in South Africa" by Carien Lubbe is reprinted with permission from *South African Journal of Psychology,* 37(2), 2007, pp. 260–283. Copyright © Psychological Society of South Africa.

Reading 38, "Female Headship and the 'Feminization of Poverty'" by Sylvia Chant, International Poverty Centre, *In Focus,* May 2004. Reprinted with permission of the United Nations Development Programme.

Reading 39, "Old Maid" by Vivian N. Limpin from *Imagining Ourselves,* edited by Paula Goldman. Copyright © 2006 by The International Museum of Women. Reprinted with permission of New World Library, Novato, CA. www.newworldlibrary.com.

Reading 40, "Indonesian Feminists Confront Polygyny" was originally published as "Feminist Polygamy? Indonesian Activists Confront a Strange New Excuse for the Practice" by Yenni Kwok in *Ms.,* Fall, 2007. Reprinted by permission of *Ms.* magazine, © 2007.

Reading 41, "Too Young to Marry: Child Brides are Stripped of Their Rights, Their Health, Their Lives" by Allison Ford in *Ms.,* Winter 2009, pp. 30–31. Reprinted by permission of *Ms.* magazine, © 2009.

Reading 42, "The Bride's Voice: Religious Women Challenge the Wedding Ritual" by Irit Koren in *NASHIM: A Journal of Jewish Women's Studies and Gender Issues.* Copyright © 2005. Reprinted by permission of Indiana University Press.

CHAPTER 8

Epigraph:

Excerpt from "With No Immediate Cause" from *Nappy Edges* by Ntozake Shange. Copyright © 1978, 1983 by Ntozake Shange. Reprinted by permission of St. Martin's Press, LLC; and Russell & Volkening as agents for the author.

Sidebars:

"Ending Violence Against Women: From Words to Action. Study of the Secretary-General," October 9, 2006. Reprinted with permission from the United Nations.

"Power Surge: Rural Women in South Africa Are Doing It for Themselves" by Heidi Bachram is reprinted with permission from *New Internationalist,* May 2007, p. 9.

Readings:

Reading 43, "The Conservation of Energy" from *Mrs. Dumpty* by Chana Bloch. Copyright © 1998 by the Board of Regents of the University of Wisconsin System. Reprinted by permission of The University of Wisconsin Press.

Reading 44, "Prevalence of and Risk Factors for Sexual Victimization in College Women in Chile" by Jocelyn A. Lehrer, Vivian L. Lehrer, Evelyn L. Lehrer and Pamela B. Oyarzún in *International Family Planning Perspectives,* Vol. 33, No. 4, December 2007, pp. 160–175. Reprinted with permission of the Guttmacher Institute.

Reading 45, "Killed in the Name of Honor" was originally published as "Culture of Discrimination: A Fact Sheet on 'Honor' Killings," Amnesty International. Posted July 20, 2005. Reprinted with permission.

Reading 46, "No Longer Silent: Sexual Harassment Finally Gets a Hearing for China's 330 Million Women Workers" by Megan Shank in *Ms.,* Winter 2009, pp. 24–25. Reprinted by permission of *Ms.* magazine, © 2009.

Reading 47, "War Against Women: Congo and Kosovo." Originally published as "War Against Women: The Use of Rape as a Weapon in Congo's Civil War" is reprinted with permission from *60 Minutes,* CBS News. August 17, 2008. "Signs of Rape Scar Kosovo" by Peter Finn, Washington Post Foreign Service, Sunday, June 27, 1999, page A1. Copyright © 1999 The Washington Post Company. Reprinted with permission.

Reading 48, "Domestic Violence in Afghanistan" originally published as "Long Viewed as Chattel, Afghan Women Slowly Gain Protection" by Kirk Semple is reprinted with permission from *The New York Times,* March 3, 2009. Copyright © 2009 The New York Times. All rights reserved.

Reading 49, "Finding Dignity in Exile" by Ingrid Drake is reprinted with permission from *Yes!* magazine, Spring, 2004. *Yes!* is a non-profit, ad-free national publication that offers positive solutions for creating a just and sustainable world. To subscribe, visit www.yesmagazine.org/subscribe or call (800) 937-4451.

CHAPTER 9

Epigraph:

Excerpt from "Artist's Statement" by Mariko Kadidiatou from *Imagining Ourselves,* edited by Paula Goldman. Copyright © 2006 by The International Museum of Women. Reprinted with permission of New World Library, Novato, CA. www.newworldlibrary.com.

Sidebars:

"The World's Top 25 Non-financial TNCs, Ranked by Foreign Assets, 2006" is adapted from Table A.I.15 in *World Investment Report 2008: Transnational Corporations and the Infrastructure Challenge.* Published by the United Nations Conference on Trade and Development.

"Occupational Hazards for Women" is excerpted from the Occupational Hazards section of the *Anthology on Women, Health, and Environment.* Reprinted by permission of the World Health Organization.

Readings:

Reading 50, "Women Farmers Toil to Expand Africa's Food Supply" by Megan Rowling in Reuters India, December 26, 2008. Copyright © 2008 Reuters. Reprinted with permission.

Reading 51, "Women and Tourism" originally published as "Opening Doors for Women" by Shaker Hussain is reprinted by permission of the author from *The Daily Star,* Saturday, September 25, 2007.

Reading 52, "Assembly Line" by Shu Ting, translated from the Chinese by Carolyn Kizer from *A Splintered Mirror: Chinese Poetry from the Democracy Movement,* translated by Donald Finkel. Translation copyright © 1991 by Donald Finkel. Reprinted by permission of North Point Press, a division of Farrar, Straus & Giroux, LLC.

Reading 53, "Oil, Islam, and Women" by Michael L. Ross in *American Political Science Review,* Vol. 102, No. 1, February 2008, pp. 107–123. Reprinted with the permission of Cambridge University Press.

Reading 54, "Girl" from *At the Bottom of the River* by Jamaica Kincaid. Copyright © 1983 by Jamaica Kincaid. Reprinted by permission of Farrar, Straus & Giroux, LLC. Reprinted outside of the US and electronically with permission of The Wylie Agency LLC.

Reading 55, "Banking on Women" originally published as "Banking on Women: Microcredit in Northern Ghana" by Sean Kelly is reprinted by permission of the author from *Natural Life Magazine,* 2007, pp. 34–35. "An Empire for Poor Working Women, Guided by a Gandhian Approach" by Somini Sengupta is reprinted with permission from *The New York Times International,* March 7, 2009, p. A6. Copyright © 2009 The New York Times. All rights reserved.

Reading 56, "The 40-Percent Rule: Norway Forces Corporations to Put Women on Boards; Can the U.S. Do the Same?" by Martha Burk in *Ms.,* Summer, 2006, pp. 57–58. Reprinted by permission of *Ms.* magazine, © 2006.

CHAPTER 10

Epigraph:

Excerpt from "Tsunami You Hit My Island Home" by Thrishana Pothupitiya, Sri Lanka, 2005.

Sidebars:

"Climate Change" is reprinted with permission from WEDO.

"Top 10 Surprising Results of Global Warming" from LiveScience.

"Talking Trash" by Martin Medina is reprinted with permission from *Foreign Policy,* September/October 2008, pp. 40–41.

"Sisters on the Planet" is reprinted with permission from WEDO.

"10 Community Conservation Ideas: Build Stronger Communities and Protect the Environment Together" by Sandra Williams, April 16, 2008. Copyright © Sandra Williams. Reprinted with permission of the author, Sandra Williams, Self-Help Books Feature Writer for Suite101.com.

Readings:

Reading 57, "Temperatures Rising: Four Essays on a Theme: Women and Climate Change." Originally published as an excerpt from "A Huge Challenge and a Narrow Discourse: Ain't No Space for Gender in Climate Change Policy?" by Minu Hemmati and Ulrike Röhr and reprinted by permission of *Women & Environments International Magazine,* Vol. 76/77 Women & Climate Change issue, Spring/Summer 2007. Copyright © 2007 Hemmati & Röhr; all rights reserved. An excerpt from "Temperatures Rising" by Myralyn O.A. Nartey is reprinted by permission of *Women & Environments International Magazine,* Vol. 76/77 Women & Climate Change issue, Spring/Summer 2007. Copyright © 2007 Nartey; all rights reserved. An excerpt from "Japanese Women's Roles in Climate Change Mitigation: An Industrialized Country's Perspective" by Sabrina Regmi is reprinted by permission of *Women & Environments International Magazine,* Vol. 76/77 Women & Climate Change issue, Spring/Summer 2007. Copyright © 2007 Regmi; all rights reserved. "Gendered Struggles for the Commons: Food Sovereignty, Tree-Planting and Climate Change" by Leigh Brownhill in *Women & Environments International Magazine,* Spring/Summer 2007, pp. 34–37. Reprinted by permission of the author.

Reading 58, "Waikiki" is reprinted by permission of the publisher (Calyx Books) from *Light in the Crevice Never Seen* by Haunani-Kay Trask. Copyright © 1994 Haunani-Kay Trask.

Reading 59, "The Exposure of Bedouin Women to Waste Related Hazards" by Ilana Meallem and Yaakov Garb is reprinted by permission of the authors from *Women & Environments International Magazine,* Fall/Winter 2008, pp. 44–48.

Reading 60, "An Ugly Picture for Flower Workers and Their Children" by David A. Taylor in *Environmental Health Perspectives,* Vol. 114, No. 8, August 2006, p. A463.

Reading 61, "Poverty, Pests and Pesticides Sold on South Africa's Streets" by Dr. Hanna-Andrea Rother is reprinted by permission of the author from *Women & Environments International Magazine,* Fall/Winter 2008, pp. 36–40.

Reading 62, "The World of the Gift Economy" by Genevieve Vaughan is reprinted by permission of the author from *Off Our Backs,* Vol. 38, No. 1, July 1, 2008, pp. 62–65.

CHAPTER 11

Sidebars:

"The History of American Women in Politics" is reprinted with permission from *Campaigns & Elections,* January 2007, p. 12.

"Rwanda Votes for Women" from *New Internationalist,* November 2008, p. 27.

"Women's Suffrage: A Timeline" is reprinted with permission of the International Women's Democracy Center.

"Transgender Mayor" was originally published as "Oregon Town Elects Nation's First Transgender Mayor" by The Associated Press. Used with permission of The Associated Press. Copyright © 2008. All rights reserved.

"Illegal Homosexuality Around the Globe" from LGBTI Rights Global Overview, International Lesbian and Gay Association.

Readings:

Reading 63, "Revenge" by Kim Rogers is reprinted by permission of the author.

Reading 64, "Please Mind the Gap" by Alyssa McDonald is reprinted by permission from *New Statesman,* November 26, 2007, p. 21. © New Statesman Ltd. All rights reserved.

Reading 65, "Women Taking the Lead" by Emira Woods is reprinted by permission of the author from *The Crisis,* May/June 2006, Vol. 133, No. 3, p. 50.

Reading 66, "Women's Words: A Moroccan Scholar-Activist Links Language and Power" by Aimee Dowl in *Ms.,* Summer 2007, p. 30. Reprinted by permission of *Ms.* magazine, © 2006.

Reading 67, "*Dal Dy Dir*/Stand Your Ground: International Lessons on Women's Equality From a Small Nation" by Laura McAllister in *Hecate,* pp. 107–122, 2006. Reprinted with permission from the author and *Hecate.*

Reading 68, "The Public and Private Domain of the Everyday Politics of Water: The Constructions of Gender and Water Power in the Andes of Peru" by Juana Vera Delgado and Margreet Zwarteveen is reprinted with permission from *International Feminist Journal of Politics,* Vol. 9, No. 4, December 2007, pp. 503–511. Copyright © 2007 Routledge.

Reading 69, "The Post-Katrina, Semiseparate World of Gender Politics" by Pamela Tyler in *The Journal of American History,* December 2007, pp. 780–788. Copyright © 2007 by Organization of American Historians. Reproduced with permission of Organization of American Historians via the Copyright Clearance Center.

CHAPTER 12

Epigraph:

Excerpt from "Gone Are Those We Love" by Fadwa Tuqan from *Women of the Fertile Crescent: Modern Poetry by Arab Women,* edited and copyright © 1981 by Kamal Boullata.

Sidebars:

"Adolescent Girls Affected by Violent Conflict: Why Should We Care?" by the Gender and Peacebuilding Working Group of the Canadian Peacebuilding Coordinating Committee.

"Taking Strategic Action: What Can Women Peacebuilders Do?" from pp. 12–13 in *Inclusive Security, Sustainable Peace: A Toolkit for Advocacy and Action.* Copyright © Hunt Alternatives Fund and International Alert 2004. All rights reserved.

Readings:

Reading 70, "The City in the Desert" in *The Forbidden Zone* by Mary Borden. William Heineman, Ltd., 1929.

Reading 71, "Children of War" by Wray Herbert is reprinted with permission from *U.S. News & World Report,* December 20, 2004, Vol. 137, Issue 22. Copyright © 2004 U.S. News & World Report, L.P.

Reading 72, "Abuse of Power: Sexual Exploitation of Refugee Women and Girls" by Elizabeth G. Ferris is reprinted with permission from *Signs: Journal of Women in Culture and Society,* Spring 2007, Vol. 32, No. 3, pp. 584–590. Copyright © 2007 by The University of Chicago.

Reading 73, "Rape in Darfur" originally published as "War Against Women" by Femke van Zeijl is reprinted with permission from *New Internationalist,* June 2007, pp. 10–12.

Reading 74, "Building Cultures of Peace: Four Cornerstones" by Riane Eisler was first published in *Off Our Backs,* Vol. 38, No. 1, pp. 44–48. Copyright © 2008 by Riane Eisler. Reprinted by permission of Riane Eisler.

Reading 75, "Plaza de Mayo" by Dacia Maraini is reprinted by permission of the translator, Gail Wronsky.

Reading 76, "Do Muslim Women Really Need Saving? Anthropological Reflections on Cultural Relativism and Its Others" by Lila Abu-Lughod is reprinted with permission of the American Anthropological Association from *American Anthropologist* 104 (3): pp. 783–790. September 2002. Copyright © 2002 American Anthropological Association. Not for sale or further reproduction.

CONCLUSION

Sidebars:

"A Global View of HIV Infection." Figure 2.2 from p. 33 in *2008 Report on the Global AIDS Epidemic* by UNAIDS. Copyright © Joint United Nations Programme on HIV/AIDS (UNAIDS) 2008. Reprinted with permission from UNAIDS.

"The Female Condom" is reprinted by permission of AVERT

Stories:

Story 1, "Janice, Marvelyn, and Michelle: USA." originally published as "Black Women's Burden: An Epidemic of HIV" by January W. Payne is reprinted with permission from *US News & World Report,* September 12, 2008. Copyright © 2008 U.S. News & World Report, L.P.

Story 2, "Keren: Honduras" was originally published as "Keren: Thriving as a Child Activist" by The Associated Press. Copyright © 2008 The Associated Press. Used with permission. All rights reserved.

Story 3, "Jacqueline, Isata, and Adele: Uganda, Sierra Leone, and Rwanda" originally published as "Violence and the Virus: Infecting Women with AIDS" by Phyllida Brown is reprinted by permission of the author from *Amnesty International Magazine,* Amnesty International USA. Summer 2004.

Story 4, "Srey: Cambodia" was originally published as "A Child Prostitute at 14, an AIDS Activist Today" by Wong Kim Hoh is reprinted with permission from *Asiaone,* June 23, 2008.

Story 5, "Mantombi Nywao: South Africa" was originally published as "Mantombi: Raising Her Grandchildren Alone" by Nicole Itano in *Womens News,* August 23, 2005. Copyright © 2005 by Fund for the City of New York/Women's eNews. Reprinted with permission, via the Copyright Clearance Center.

Story 6, "Parvati and Fatima: India" was originally published as "The Impact of HIV/AIDS on Women and Their Families—Stories from South Asia" by Aasha Kapur Mehta and Sreoshi Gupta, November 17, 2005. Reprinted with permission of UNIFEM.

Story 7, "Thembi: South Africa" was originally published as "Thembi Ngubane: Mother, Activist, South African . . . and Proof That You Can Thrive with HIV" by Erika Nelson from www.TheBody.com, August 3, 2008. This article is reprinted with permission of www.TheBody.com, the internet's largest HIV/AIDS resource.

Story 8, "Mama's Club: Uganda" was originally published as "HIV Positive Women Talk It Over in Mama's Club" by Rachel Scheier in *Women's eNews,* July 23, 2006. Copyright © 2006 by Fund for the City of New York/Women's eNews. Reprinted with permission, via Copyright Clearance Center.

Story 9, "Tatiana and Dina: Russia and Ukraine" was originally published as "Stars Against AIDS: Tackling the HIV/AIDS Problem in Eastern Europe and Central Asia" in *UNAIDS,* May 19, 2008. Reprinted with permission of UNAIDS, www.unaids.org.

PHOTO CREDITS

Index